1989

CHANGE IN

Rural America

causes, consequences, and alternatives

CHANGE IN

Rural America

causes, consequences, and alternatives

Edited by

RICHARD D. RODEFELD, Ph.D.

Department of Agricultural Economics and Rural Sociology,
Pennsylvania State University,
University Park, Pennsylvania

JAN FLORA, Ph.D.

Department of Sociology and Anthropology,
Kansas State University,
Manhattan, Kansas

DONALD VOTH, Ph.D.

Department of Agricultural Economics and Rural Sociology,
University of Arkansas,
Fayetteville, Arkansas

ISAO FUJIMOTO, M.A.

Department of Applied Behavioral Sciences,
University of California, Davis,
Davis, California

JIM CONVERSE, Ph.D.

Department of Sociology and Anthropology,
Kansas State University,
Manhattan, Kansas

THE C. V. MOSBY COMPANY

SAINT LOUIS   1978

Cover illustration courtesy of John Deere.

The C. V. Mosby Company
11830 Westline Industrial Drive, St. Louis, Missouri 63141

Library of Congress Cataloging in Publication Data

Main entry under title:

Change in rural America.

    Bibliography: p.
    Includes index.
    1. United States—Rural conditions—Addresses,
essays, lectures. 2. Agriculture—Economic aspects—
United States—Addresses, essays, lectures. 3. Sociology,
Rural—Addresses, essays, lectures. I. Rodefeld,
Richard D., 1943-
HN57.C47   301.35′0973   78-4644
ISBN 0-8016-4145-4

GW/M/M 9 8 7 6 5 4 3 2 1

The red ball of the sun in an evening mist
Or the slow fall of rain on planted fields
Or the pink sheath of a newborn child
Or the structural weave of the universe
Witnessed in a moving frame of winter stars—
These hold affidavits of struggle.

Carl Sandburg, *The People, Yes*

This volume is dedicated to our grandparents, whose lives as agriculturalists were affidavits of struggle for a better life for themselves and their descendents:

Henry C. Rodefeld (1895-1964)	Dairy Farmers and livestock trucker,
Hannah (Halvorson) Rodefeld (1901-)	Blooming Grove Township, Wis.
William Redepenning (1894-)	Livestock farmer, London, Wis.
Hazel (Eaton) Engelman (1905-1977)	Housewife, Long Beach, Calif.
Henry M. Flora (1895-1976)	Wheat and cattle farmers,
Etta (Wigington) Flora (1897-1975)	Quinter, Kan.
W. O. "Bill" Leighton (1900-)	Wheat and cattle farmers, quarter
Edna (Gregg) Leighton (1901-)	horse breeders, Quinter, Kan.
Gerhard J. Voth (1878-1944)	Diversified farmers,
Anna (Richert) Voth (1879-1967)	Mayes County, Okla.
Peter Johann Rempel (1877-1935)	Diversified farmers,
Helena (Schmidt) Rempel (1882-1973)	Inola, Okla.
Walter Converse (1878-1955)	Purebred livestock breeders,
Zella (Beck) Converse (1885-1957)	dairy farmers, and plant breeders
	Plain City, Franklin County, Ohio
Ernest Kimsey Bell (1881-1963)	Dairy farmers and sawmill operator,
Blanche (Galbraith) Bell (1882-1967)	Fairfield Township, Ohio
Komakichi Fujimoto (1868-1926)	Shipwright, housewife,
Toyo (Ogura) Fujimoto (1874-1935)	Wakayama, Japan
Yasumatsu Tanaka (1882-1964)	Small farmers, small business
Okuno (Kakimoto) Tanaka (1896-1940)	operators, and workers,
	Seattle, Wash.

Preface

The major objective in this volume is to provide the reader with a better understanding of twentieth century changes in the rural sector of the United States. This is done by focusing on initial changes that occurred in six areas: agricultural technology, farm organizational and occupational structure, transportation, communication, urban population distribution, and rural economic base. We do not argue that all social and economic changes in the rural sector can be explained by changes in these areas. We do assert, however, that many rural changes cannot be adequately understood without knowledge of the nature, magnitude, causes, and consequences of changes in these six focal areas.

The volume is divided into five sections and twelve chapters. Each of the sections begins with an introductory essay whose primary purpose is to briefly review the organization and content of the section and the chapters in it. The topic addressed or function served by articles in each chapter is indicated. Relevant relationships with other sections and their chapters are noted, and relevant articles in other chapters are also identified. References are included to articles that discuss the topics in more detail, argue positions divergent to those represented, or discuss relevant topics not addressed in this volume. Generally, references that can be easily and inexpensively obtained are not included in the text. However, many of these have been included as references.

In Section one, the focus is on agricultural technology, beginning with a discussion of the nature and magnitude of changes in agricultural technology (Chapter 1). Next, the consequences of these changes on the number and characteristics of farm people and farms (Chapter 2), on rural neighborhoods and communities (Chapter 3), and on the urban sector and society as a whole (Chapter 4) are reviewed.

Farm organizational, occupational, and class structures are the focal topics in Section two. The nature and magnitude of changes in these areas (Chapter 5) and the consequences for all sectors of society (Chapter 6) are addressed.

The first two sections establish that changes have occurred in farm technology and organizational structure (type) with major consequences for all sectors of society. Section three (Chapter 7) addresses the question of what major causal forces and initial conditions brought about these changes. Forces emanating from both the farm and nonfarm sectors are identified and discussed.

Section four focuses on rural areas and communities. In Chapter 8 historical overviews and distinguishing characteristics of rural neighborhoods, places, and communities are discussed. The impact of changes in transportation and communications on rural communities is reviewed in Chapter 9. Changes in urban population distribution (urban to rural migration, suburbanization) and the rural economic base (industrialization) and their impact on rural communities are addressed in Chapter 10.

Section five is devoted to alternatives for the future, including solutions to problems created by changes in the six focal areas. Chapter 11 contains articles reviewing alternative responses to changes in farm technology and farm size and organizational structure. Chapter 12 reviews alternative responses to rural community decline and change.

This volume makes important contributions in a number of areas. First, it is concerned explicitly with the dynamics of change processes; that is, the nature and magnitude of initial changes in six areas, the consequences of these changes for various sectors of society, the causal forces and conditions bringing about these initial changes, and alternatives for the future.

Second, the readings reflect the diversity existing within the rural sector. The contemporary characteristics, dominant changes, and problems of people, communities, and institutions vary considerably within the rural sector. More specifically, major differences in these phenomena are observed between rural areas differing in types of agricultural production; farm types (organizational structure); economic bases; occupational and racial composition of the populations; proximity to larger communities; and population numbers and changes (growth-decline). As an example, rural areas and communities that are growing rather than declining in size differ considerably in the causes and consequences of these changes and in the contemporary characteristics of their institutions.

Large portions of the material in Chapters 2, 3, 6, 8, and 9 deal with declining rural areas and communities. On the other hand, most of the material in Chapter 10 (consequences of urban sprawl and rural industrialization) deals with rural areas experiencing rapid rates of growth. Chapters 5 and 6 (trends and consequences of changes in farm organizational structure) include information on regional differences between family- and nonfamily-type farm areas. About half of the articles focus on specific regions or states. All regions are represented in the readings. The greatest number deal with the Midwest, followed by the South, West, and East. Remaining articles deal with the entire rural sector or larger society, often with regional comparisons.

Third, the readings create a knowledge base from which the future of the rural sector can be assessed and suggest a wide range of alternative responses to likely changes and resultant problems. Since a considerable amount of material has been included on changes occurring in the rural sector and their causes, a solid base exists from which to predict likely changes in the future. Knowledge of past consequences of changes allows discussion on the desirability or undesirability of likely future changes for the rural and urban sectors, and society as a whole. Chapters 11 and 12 present a range of future responses that include allowing the changes to continue, accelerating rates of change, or completely reversing the direction of change. Most of the material in these chapters provides suggestions for either stopping or reversing changes that are occurring and ways in which the problems from these changes can be eliminated or reduced. These alternatives or solutions cover the entire political-ideological spectrum.

Fourth, a major emphasis is on rural-urban interrelationships between social, economic, technological, and environmental phenomena. The text is explicitly concerned with causal relationships. Generally, the material shows how causal forces and conditions emanating from a variety of locations (rural, urban, different institutional areas) within society have resulted in major farm changes. These farm changes have had major consequences (direct and indirect) for all levels (individual, family, farm, neighborhood, community) and segments (institutional areas, population, class structure) of the rural sector and have had major consequences for the urban sector as well.

Another aspect of this concerns the interdependencies existing between the rural and urban sectors. It is pointed out that many of the major causal forces bringing about changes in farm characteristics have come from the urban sector. Examples are governmental policy and programs, economic structure, activities of land-grant colleges, and capital flow. In addition, many of the changes that have occurred in transportation and communication originated in the urban sector. Urban-to-rural migration, suburbanization, urban sprawl, and the relocation or expansion of urban industries to rural areas emanated from the urban sector. The preceding changes have had major consequences for all levels and segments of the rural sector. Readings are also included that discuss the consequences for the urban sector of changes occurring in the rural sector (rural migrants, food prices and quality). This should be of particular interest to urban students of rural change.

Fifth, extensive coverage is provided of major social and economic problems for both the rural and urban sectors resulting from the focal changes. While both negative and positive consequences are discussed, a major portion deals with the former. Examples from the rural sector are the decline of rural communities, the decline of the family farm, and the rapid growth of some rural communities.

Sixth, materials also have been included that either directly address major rural controversies, conflicts, and critical issues or provide a knowledge base from which these issues can be discussed. For example, has the development and adoption of new agricultural technology been the major cause of rural community decline, reduced food quality, increased health risks to workers and consumers, and environmental degradation and led us in the direction of a food disaster? Is the family-type farm being replaced by corporate-industrial–type farms? Is the rural sector now part and parcel of the "mass society"? Does the movement of urban people to rural areas create more problems than it solves? In general, have these changes resulted in largely negative or positive consequences for the various sectors of society?

Seventh, the organization of the materials in the text allows instructors considerable flexibility in developing the structure and content of their courses. While the text focuses on the causes and consequences of changes in six focal areas, the content can easily be restructured to focus on: the rural community, rural social and economic problems, rural-urban interdependencies, consequences of technological change, or critical issues. Since all of the first four sections are relatively self-contained, they can be covered in whatever order is desired. The amount of emphasis given to the various sections, chapters, and topics is varied easily. Individual readings, chapters, or sections can be omitted to reduce or alter the emphasis in a particular area. On the other hand, emphasis can be increased either through lecture material or supplementary readings. Once the logic and framework of longitudinal change processes has been developed, it is easy to integrate material focusing on the contemporary characteristics of the rural sector. In addition, no overarching ideology, conceptual framework, or interpretation is imposed on the material other than that of longitudinal change. Instructors are free to adopt whatever perspective (structural-functionalism, conflict theory, internal colonialism, dependency theory, political-economy) they find most useful or reflective of reality.

Finally, the volume contains relatively inaccessible or previously unpublished articles from a wide variety of sources. These articles were selected for their high readability; a little less than half of them were written by academicians. Areas represented include rural sociology, agricultural economics, geography, biology, business, English, history, sociology, anthropology, and economics. The articles by nonacademic authors are as equally diverse; most were written by journalists, but some also come from public interest groups, voluntary organizations, and governmental bodies. The major sources from which the articles were drawn are periodicals, newspapers, books, and professional journals. A number of the selections have not previously appeared in print. Almost all of the remaining selections are from relatively inaccessible or nontraditional sources. Because the selections have such a wide variety of authors and sources, they vary considerably in length, complexity, and writing style. Even though readability varies, all of the selections have been reviewed and ranked by the editors both for importance and readability. The selections included are those receiving high and consistent rankings from all reviewers. Consequently, we think both instructors and students will derive a good deal of satisfaction from the approach and materials.

We would like to thank the numerous individuals who assisted us in the development of this text. This includes the North Central Regional Center for Rural Development at The Iowa State University, which provided a grant allowing the editors to meet and lay the groundwork for this volume. Special thanks are extended to those highly skilled professionals who typed the bibliographies, prospectus material, table of contents, and introductory essays and papers: Olivia Mejarado, Department of Sociology, Michigan State University; Cheryl Blaisel, Joyce Kling, and Rochelle Bush, Department of Agricultural Economics and Rural Sociology, Pennsylvania State University; and Cosette Rodefeld, Department of Chemistry, Pennsylvania State University, friend and wife of the senior editor.

Appreciation is also extended to colleagues who have reviewed many of the introductory essays and original papers: Robert Bealer, Kenneth Wilkinson, Kevin Goss, and Mark Lancelle, Department of Agricultural Economics and Rural Sociology, Pennsylvania State University; Frederick Schmidt, Department of Sociology, University of Vermont; and Frederick Buttel, Department of Rural Sociology, Cornell University.

We would also like to thank the numerous authors and copyright holders for allowing the inclusion of their materials. Without their excellent work, this volume would not have been possible.

RICHARD D. RODEFELD

Contents

SECTION TWO

The nature, magnitude, and consequences of change in farm organizational, occupational, and class structure, 121
RICHARD D. RODEFELD

The nature, magnitude, and consequences of changes in agricultural technology

Jan Flora and Richard D. Rodefeld

The agrarian transformation, which began with the Industrial Revolution in the early nineteenth century and snowballed from World War I to the present, is more than anything else a technological transformation. Thus, this book begins with an examination of the consequences of technological change in agriculture. However, that transformation did not occur of its own volition. It occurred because of certain social, political, and economic characteristics of the American system of capitalism.

The agrarian transformation was and is integrally related to dynamics of change in the entire system. Thus, although technological change may have acquired a dynamic of its own at certain times and places, our framework is not one of technological determinism. This should be kept in mind as the nature and consequences of agricultural technology are examined.

1 The nature and magnitude of changes in agricultural technology

Hambidge illustrates the historic impact of the larger society on technological change in agriculture. He identifies urbanization-industrialization and war as the two principal catalysts for the development of mechanized commercialized agriculture. (Major causes of technological change in agriculture are examined in Section three.) Table 1 shows that the 10-year period including World War II represented the largest absolute increase in fertilizer usage until the late 1960's and that the largest growth in number of farm tractors, although beginning in the second half of the 1930's, was accelerated by World War II and only began to level off in the middle of the 1950's.

Wars and urbanization-industrialization are closely linked. America's twentieth century wars have been fought on foreign soil. Hence, their domestic economic impact has been to drastically increase industrial output. This has increased demand for labor in the industrial sector; and, especially during World War II, has meant a sucking up of rural workers from the countryside (Table 2, Chapter 2). The rural labor shortage has triggered mechanization of agriculture. Wars and resultant labor shortages develop within the context of the dialectic between decentralized decision-making in most of the farm sector and the tendency toward concentration, which arises out of that decentralization. Thus, the period following war has been characterized by overproduction in agriculture, wild swings in the agricultural business cycle, and an acceleration of the tendency toward concentration as farm laborers, share croppers, and farmers with the least capital to back them up are the first to "bite the dust" and seek urban employment.

Durost and Bailey separate technical change into two parts[1]: (1) mechanical and (2) technological (changes in fertilization; improvement of varieties and breeds; and consequent changes in cultural practices, including monoculture and irrigation).

---

[1]They also mention the managerial revolution. The most important aspects of managerial change are encompassed by shifts in farm type, discussed in Section two.

Loftsgard and Voelker (Chapter 3) speak of labor-saving techniques (mechanization) and land-saving techniques (investment in irrigation, fertilizer, high-yielding varieties). Although mechanization is labor displacing, it does not have to result in increased sizes of farms, as evidenced by the growth of mechanization in Japan and Taiwan. It may free labor for increased use of land-saving techniques, such as double and triple cropping, interplanting, and reclamation, as in China. In the United States, the much higher price of labor vis-à-vis capital inputs that can be substituted for labor precludes adoption of land-saving techniques as a means of labor absorption in agriculture, if one takes as given the declining terms of trade for the farm sector as opposed to the urban industrial sector from which farmers buy their inputs. (The secular decline of the farm parity ratio[2] shows that farmers' terms of trade are declining.) Thus, as long as agriculture is principally a competitive sector, and the industrial sector remains an administered price sector, the number of persons employed in agriculture will continue to decline.

Although "technological" or land-saving innovations can be utilized regardless of the size of farms, social structure acts as an intervening variable and causes them to be somewhat scale specific in certain capitalist third-world countries. There, small farmers do not have the wherewithal to purchase modern inputs, since credit agencies are oriented toward middle-sized and large farms as are extension services. The political structure is dominated by large-farm interests in alliance with urban interests. Section three shows that similar tendencies exist in the United States but in more muted form.

Improvement in varieties and breeds, fertilization, and irrigation are all oriented toward increasing production per acre. As Durost and Bailey's article and Table 4 (Chapter 2) illustrate, the advances in crop yields in the past 30 years in the United States have been spectacular, and some advances have been made in efficiency of feed conversion in meat animals.

The American system has demonstrated a tremendous capacity to produce food, but that capacity has resulted largely from improvement of cultural practices rather than growth in the size and versatility of agricultural machinery. The chief advantage of mechanization for the farm operator is reduction of labor costs or expansion without increased labor costs. The dominant view with respect to farm mechanization has been that there is a harmony of interests between the farmers' desire for profit via substitution of capital for labor and the interests of society as a whole. For instance, Kelly (1967) argues that displacement of labor from agriculture is an unmitigated good as long as it is profitable, since it frees people for urban industrial jobs. He argues that this is especially important in the developing countries of the world (where, in fact, capital-intensive development in both rural and urban areas has created a huge surplus labor supply). Kelly's argument carried to its extreme is described tongue in cheek by Logsdon.

Carleton is more realistic in speaking of "underemployment for many seasonal agricultural workers at least during the transition period to mechanization." He is equally concerned that mechanization in certain specialty crops may create a labor shortage in others because mechanization of one crop may shorten the work season for migrant workers in a particular area, and the migrant stream may dwindle as workers shift to more lucrative regions. This situation provides impetus for mechanization in the labor-deficit crops.

The precise way in which decisions to mechanize are made is illustrated by the economic impact of the tobacco harvester, discussed by the USDA-ERS article. The harvester was economical to operate if wage rates exceeded $1.35 (1969 prices) and if the machine was operated at capacity (40 acres). The average size of a tobacco farm was less than 10 acres in 1969, and it was estimated that as many as 350,000

---

[2] Parity ratio equals returns per costs.

farm people would be displaced. No additional information is needed to know whether the harvester was adopted.

With the increase of wage rates people have begun to be displaced by the mechanical harvester. Still, as McElroy pointed out, a series of social costs arise from the displacement of large numbers of tobacco farmers and laborers. Not only are such costs not figured into the decision of whether to adopt the harvester, but no one has ever bothered to estimate what those costs might be. Although all Agricultural Experiment Stations in the tobacco area have research programs for development of labor-saving technology in tobacco, none "has a program of concerted effort conducive to facilitating the adjustment of people displaced from agricultural employment." The small group in the U.S. Department of Agriculture of which McElroy was a part was the only federal entity considering the question.

2 The consequences of changes in agricultural technology for the numbers and characteristics of farm people and farms

The most immediate and dramatic consequence of the technological revolution in agriculture has been a precipitous decline in numbers of farm people and a large increase in average farm size. This has had a major impact on other farm characteristics: increased productivity, greater sales and income per farm, increased value of land per farm (Table 3), increased use of fossil fuels and other capital-intensive inputs, and shifts in managerial and ownership patterns (the latter is discussed in Section two). Finally, there have been tertiary impacts of technology: differentiation of agricultural class structure and growth in inequality of distribution of income, wealth, and power.

Impact on numbers of farm people. The agricultural mechanization process described by McElroy (Chapter 1) has occurred in similar—although possibly less dramatic—fashion throughout the United States during the past half century. Hamburger ("Thousands Forced to Leave Land") illustrates the incessant need for farmers to capitalize and increase their scale of operations, with no assurance even then that they can survive. Hamburger ("Dramatic Population Reduction Inspires Technological Changes") also gives a glimpse of the dramatic changes in labor requirements that occurred in the cotton South with the introduction of the mechanical cotton picker. He suggests that mechanization of cotton harvesting resulted from labor shortages. Vandiver (Chapter 7) suggests a more complicated interrelationship, which also includes acreage limitations in the 1930's and 1950's as a cause of the exodus from the cotton South. Bagdikian (Chapter 2) gives a glimpse of the structure of plantation agriculture, showing the power the boss has over the black sharecropper and why, when circumstances seem right, rural southern blacks give up a life-style they love for an uncertain future in the urban north.

Table 2 shows shifts in farm population since 1910. The beginning of decline in farm employment was World War I, although that decline was temporarily arrested by the Depression. The 5-year period with greatest "out-migration" of farm population was 1940 to 1945—World War II, although the rate of out-migration remained at a high level through the 1960's. Consistent with Hambidge's view (Chapter 1), World Wars I and II soaked up the work force and provided an impetus for agricultural mechanization. Table 1 (Chapter 1) shows that the increase in number of tractors began leveling off after 1954 and actually declined after 1964. This does not necessarily indicate a slowing of the process of mechanization, but rather the continued growth in the size of tractors. There is a remarkable correspondence between the growth of agricultural mechanization and the shrinkage of the farm population (compare Tables 1 and 2).

Substitution of energy-intensive inputs for human labor. The agrarian transformation has resulted in enhanced incomes and in much less drudgery for those remaining on farms (Tables 4 and 5). Few persons would want to return to the "good old days." But agricultural development as it has occurred in the United States has been heavily dependent on inputs of cheap nonrenewable energy. Agriculture was once an endeavor that created usable energy from a renewable solar source with a liberal amount of renewable human energy. It has now become a system of transforming nonconsumable, nonrenewable energy into food and fiber, which can be consumed. Perelman argues that when one combines the energy contained in farm fuels, fertilizer, and the making of agricultural machinery, these energy inputs exceed the food energy produced by a factor of at least five. This negates the misleading but often mentioned statement that the American farmer produces enough food for himself and fifty-two others as a meaningful indicator of productivity of efficiency.

Fossil fuels have been viewed as relatively cheap, and in agriculture human labor has been considered a factor on which to economize. Obviously, we cannot swing the pendulum so far in the opposite direction as to view human labor as cheap and nonrenewable energy inputs as the only important costs. Can the market system be relied on to sort out relative prices of input? (It hasn't done a very good job so far.) Could a system of energy equivalents inputs subsidies be devised to bring the pricing system in line with optimum energy conservation? Do we need to look toward changing social structure rather than manipulating the economic system? Is the present system realistically the best?

Effects on class structure and life quality. The growth of mechanization and technology in agriculture has resulted in a more complex class structure in agriculture. While incomes and levels of living of farm families have risen substantially (Table 5), income inequality within the agricultural sector has also increased (Table 6). Rural farm income is much more unequally distributed than is income in central cities of metropolitan areas and for urban and rural nonfarm people in nonmetropolitan areas. Rural farm and nonfarm inhabitants have much higher rates of poverty than all other groups (nearly 18%).

Inequality of income among the farm population arises ultimately from the fact that the farm sector is the largest competitive price sector, in an economy dominated by an administered price system. This argument has been elaborated by Keyserling (1977). An integral part of competitive capitalism is cutthroat competition, and the emergence of inequalities as some firms expand and others subsist or go out of business. Farming is a competitive sector in another sense—farm labor is largely unorganized and has income levels ranking with the lowest occupational groups, as indicated by Shaffer.

Associated with low income levels is a powerlessness that is manifested, among other ways, in the inability to combat unsafe working conditions arising from technological agriculture (Wellford). Mechanization and technology contribute to increasing income and wealth inequalities within the agricultural sector because they allow for greater variation in farm size and capitalization than was true when farming was a simpler endeavor.

3 The consequences of changes in agricultural technology for rural neighborhoods and communities

Loss of functions and autonomy of rural communities and neighborhoods. Loftsgard and Voelker, much like Durost and Bailey (Chapter 1), attribute major changes in rural life to substitution of capital for land, technological revolution, and substitution of capital for labor (mechanization). This has resulted in farm consolidation, higher levels of living for those who remain, more limited opportunities for getting started in farming, and a high rate of out-migration. Smaller communities and neighborhoods have declined in population, while those with more than 1000 inhabitants have generally remained stable or have increased in size. Social institutions such as schools have consolidated, with a presumed increase in quality of instruction. Lively (Chapter 8) illustrates that community decline is not a new phenomenon. He indicates that small trade centers in Ohio and Minnesota in the early 1930's were declining in number and losing functions.

Not all services decline uniformly. Paulson and Carlson point out that farm consolidation and the loss of farm population result in decline of general retail trade, but farm input firms continue to flourish. Jordan looks at small-community life more impressionistically and finds that young people leave not only because there are few jobs in the small community but also because there is little "action" and because the close-knit community has its bad side (censure of deviance) as well as its good side (neighborliness).

Other problems arising in small communities that have experienced high out-migration are related to the age structure that comes to look like an hour glass rather than a pyramid. A high proportion of older people and children places a strain on medical, educational, recreational and other services, since there are few people in the productive age groups to generate tax dollars to cover such services. Since elderly people are on fixed incomes and since the principal local tax—the property tax—is based on real property, tax levies that would support needed services are often voted down.

From another perspective, the urban-to-rural shift that began recently is in part based on a positive view of small-town life—freedom from pollution, noise, and traffic; lower crime rate; and the very neighborliness some youthful out-migrants want to escape (Fuguitt and Zuiches, Hanson, and Beale, Chapter 12).

Growth of nonagricultural activities in rural areas. Until the beginning of the 1960's, the rural population as a whole followed the pattern of the farm population. However, in many sections of the country, rural out-migration diminished and in many instances actually reversed, as a smaller proportion of rural people depended directly on agriculture. Beale found that for the nation as a whole in the 1960's, predominantly rural counties showed a higher rate of growth in private nonagricultural jobs than did predominantly urban counties. In the 1960's half the growth in jobs in nonmetropolitan areas were in the manufacturing sector. From 1969 to 1973 manufacturing jobs comprised only 18% of new nonmetropolitan jobs.

Counties characterized by recreation and retirement activities have shown the greatest growth among nonmetropolitan counties in the 1970's, with those having senior state colleges ranking next. There has been a shift from manufacturing to service-related activities as the principal source of new employment in nonmetropolitan areas. Moreover, population growth in the early 1970's has been greater for nonmetropolitan counties than for metropolitan counties, and such growth has not been confined to nonmetropolitan counties adjacent to metropolitan areas or to those containing large places. However, predominantly agricultural counties have continued to decline, although at a much reduced rate (Beale, Chapter 12). Still, more sparsely settled regions, such as the Great Plains, have continued to experience net rural out-migration with its attendant problems (Beale, Chapter 3).

Whether particular rural communities are continuing to decline, are turning around, or are actually booming from the influx of urban migrants, all share the characteristic that agricultural employment represents a declining portion of their economies; and what agriculture remains is transformed. That such a drastic transformation was necessary is questionable. Few question the assumption that the transformed agriculture is superior in many regards to more traditional farming and to farm communities of a generation or more ago. Berry does raise the question of whether the right path was taken, suggesting that both practically and philosophically it would have been better if a diversified agriculture with a simpler, if less streamlined, marketing system that allowed for a mystical relationship among the farmer, the land, and the community had been adhered to. He raises the question of the morality of uprooting millions of Americans from such an environment against their wills.

4 The consequences of changes in agricultural technology for the urban sector and society as a whole

The rural-urban migrant—better or worse off? It is generally agreed that migration has in general benefitted—at least economically—those who have moved from rural to urban areas. White southern migrants had the greatest difficulty assimilating in northern cities; white migrants from the north, the least. Chicanos and blacks adjusted by insulating themselves (or being forced to insulate themselves) from the dominant culture by living in ghettos or colonies (Bagdikian, Chapter 2). Age and education seem to be more powerful predictors of job quality than is migrancy itself. The one group of migrants (although not strictly rural-to-urban migrants) for whom assimilation has been a failure, are migrant farm laborers who seek to settle out of the migrant stream. Fuller points out that little has been done to facilitate their adjustment.

Morrison (1972) also compares rural-to-urban migrants with their counterparts who have always lived in urban areas. He finds that among whites rural-to-urban migrants have somewhat lower incomes than urban nonmigrants, but that as length of residence in urban areas increases, poverty and income differences decline. For blacks, there is little or no difference between incomes of migrants and urban nonmigrants and no relationship between poverty and length of urban residence for the migrants. This suggests that discrimination against blacks is sufficient that they are viewed as an undifferentiated mass by employers.

Effects of rural-to-urban migration on the urban sector. McNamara summarizes the effects of rural migration on urban areas. The rural-to-urban shift has resulted in persons in the productive age groups, especially young women, making up a much higher proportion of the population in urban than rural areas. The total urban population is thus much more productive, reflecting the fact that the urban sector is the leading economic sector.

McNamara cites a Rockefeller Brothers report that there were as many as 1.2 million surplus farm families in spite of rural-to-urban migration. This surplus was exacerbating urban tensions, creating serious problems of adjustment for rural-to-urban migrants, creating higher crime rates,[3] contributing to class and ethnic segregation, and increasing pressure on central city services. This "excess" of population in both urban and rural areas has been partially resolved by the decentralization trends that began in the 1960's and have accelerated in the 1970's. Still, the contradiction remains that there are surplus workers in both rural areas and metropolitan central cities. McNamara indicates this has sometimes caused a cheapening of labor in urban areas as well as rural areas. While he views this cheapening as a "maladjustment of the economic situation," it may be seen more fruitfully as an integral feature of our economic system, which thrives on having a certain amount of surplus labor.

Effects on food costs and quality. It is often stated by farmers and representatives of agribusiness that since Americans spend a smaller percentage of income for food, the American food system is the most efficient in the world. That percentage has both a numerator and a denominator, however. High mean family income contributes to the low percentage as much as the low per unit cost of food. In addition, lower-income families spend much higher percentages of their income on food than high-income families (Table 7). It is true that technology has reduced food costs substantially. This has been accomplished in part through overproduction, which results in a rural-to-urban transfer of wealth as farmers subsidize nonfarmers through their lower farm incomes.

Mechanization (labor-saving methods) has contributed to a reduction in cost of

[3] The idea that rural migrants were disproportionately involved in the riots of the 1960's has been discredited. McNamara's argument that rural migrants disproportionately engage in criminal activity is open to serious question. It can still be argued that the rural exodus has been a significant factor in increasing urban unrest and decreasing the livability of the cities as a result of its contribution to larger metropolitan agglomerations.

production, but the role of future mechanization in cost reduction is unclear (Raup, Chapter 5). Further mechanization of specialty crop production (especially harvesting) is likely to reduce production costs. Growth in the size of tractors and implements in grain production may increase per unit costs as large farmers trade machines for leisure and machinery is utilized fewer and fewer hours per year.

The effects of investment in land-saving techniques on the cost of producing a unit of food are also unclear. Future advances in crop yields that would compare with those of the past several decades are impossible without significant genetic breakthroughs, which will depend on heavy research expenditures. Whether the costs of those investments are reflected in food prices depends on who pays for the research.

Similar circumstances exist with regard to pest control. The costs of chemical pest control will continue to mount as known chemicals become less effective. Biological pest control will entail increased research costs or agricultural labor expenditures if there is to be a return to diversified agriculture as a means of eliminating pest problems resulting from monoculture. Irrigation has always been expensive and will continue to be so. Its cost has not been recognized because most surface-water irrigation systems have been paid for through taxes rather than higher food costs. Fertilizer costs will continue to mount if chemical fertilizers are adhered to. Organic farming as an alternative to chemical agriculture has distinct possibilities (Chapter 11) but requires higher labor inputs.

Cost of food cannot be separated from quality. Rodale points out known and potential dangers of pesticides and feed additives, all of which were designed for more "efficient" food production. As the dangers of these chemicals become clearer, Americans may be more willing to pay for organically produced food. Likewise, with growing affluence consumers may choose more savory and expensive foods picked by hand rather than those picked by machine *(Consumer Reports)*.

The most important determinant of food cost (and quality) is not the on-the-farm technical revolution, but the structure of the food system as a whole. Parker (1975), in summarizing a Federal Trade Commission study, concludes that three-fourths of our food is processed or handled by firms that are oligopolistic. While the supermarket revolution initially caused a decline in gross margins—from the 1930's to the 1950's—these margins have climbed back to the 1930's level. In 1967, the four largest grocery chains averaged 51% of all grocery sales in metropolitan areas—up from 46% in 1954. The more concentrated the industry, the higher are advertising expenditures as a percentage of sales and the higher are profits. The *Consumer Reports* article shows how corporate tomato growers in Florida were able to diminish the quality of tomatoes by pressuring the U.S. Department of Agriculture to establish smaller minimum-size requirements for gas ripened tomatoes than for vine ripened ones grown chiefly in Mexico. McCarthy (1975) discusses the role of profit in the food industry's push for synthetic foods that are less nutritious than natural or unprocessed foods. Political power has a greater effect on food costs than do changes in technical efficiency.

Effects on the environment. Clark summarizes the environmental case against chemical and for organic farming. He emphasizes the following results of technology in agriculture: the growth in the energy input-output ratio; the decline of soil quality; the vulnerability to disease for crops that are not rotated and of which there are few varieties and of livestock fed in assembly-line fashion. He recommends a return to crop rotation and manure application, biological control of pests, and increased use of renewable energy sources, which includes more human power. Wellford (Chapter 2) explains the magnitude of the risk in using organophosphate pesticides that are highly toxic but rapidly biodegradable. They replaced persistent chlorinated hydrocarbons such as DDT, which had carcinogenic tendencies. He estimates that there are 50,000 to 75,000 acute pesticide poisonings per year, disproportionately affecting children and farm workers. Commoner points out the possibly disastrous consequences of heavy chemical fertilization for the ecosystem and for human health in

California. Todd emphasizes the decline in agricultural diversity of crop varieties, of microbes in the soil, and of the social base itself. He claims this decline results in a much more precarious existence for plants, animals, and humans.

Research necessary to determine the validity of these predictions of ecological catastrophe is in its infancy.

Conclusion

Two broad alternatives are available to American agriculture, with respect to how farm technology is used. One is to continue in the same general direction as in the last several decades, using the market mechanism and the political power of the dominant forces in agriculture as the chief criteria for allocation of resources. This would involve a continued, though perhaps slower, decline in farm numbers; the replacement of human labor with machines; continued dominance of chemical agriculture, with some cutback in fertilizer usage as the marginal return for a given level of application declines with price increases; and steady growth in vertical integration and in the market power of larger growers. The latter and other possibilities have been reviewed by Breimyer and Barr (1972).

Milk (Chapter 4), taking into account evidence such as that appearing in this section, outlines one alternative: movement toward more labor-intensive agriculture. He argues, "unprecedented substitution of capital for labor [in U.S. agriculture] has already transcended 'optimum' societal returns." Negative results include massive population shifts to congested cities, increased unemployment, declining rural communities, extreme inequalities within agriculture, a more precarious agriculture dependent on increasingly scarce inputs, and food that is not as nutritious or safe as it should be. Most agricultural economists and other experts have failed to recognize these costs because they have used profitability of the firm as the criterion for evaluating economic success. They also believe that elimination of labor in agriculture is *ipso facto* a good thing and that rural poverty is best solved by out-migration of "excess" labor. Milk disagrees. He argues that out-migration merely contributes to the problems of urban areas.

Capital's share in agriculture has become disproportionately large (investment per worker in agriculture is four and a half times that of the economy as a whole). Milk proposes a number of policies (alternatives) that would slow or reverse the labor exodus from agriculture: limiting agricultural subsidy payments to $5000 per person per year; limiting agricultural cooperative membership to workers and resident farmers; enacting a minimum family income for all Americans; prohibiting vertical integration (processors as farmers); enforcing strict antipollution measures in agriculture; unionizing farm workers; and enacting homestead property tax exemptions for small farmers. Other alternatives to a continuation of past changes in agricultural technology and their consequences are found in Chapter 11.

REFERENCES

Breimyer, Harold F., Barr, Wallace: Issues in concentration versus dispersion. In Guither, Harold D., editor: Who will control U.S. agriculture? Cooperative Extension Service, Special Publication 27, Urbana, Ill., Aug. 1972, University of Illinois Press.

Kelly, Clarence F.: Mechanical harvesting, Scientific American **217**(2):50-59, Aug. 1967.

Keyserling, Leon: Farmworkers in rural America, 1971-72, Statement to U.S. Senate Committee on Labor and Public Welfare, Hearings before the Subcommittee on Migrant Labor, Part 1, Washington, D.C., 1972, U.S. Government Printing Office, pp. 27-36.

McCarthy, C.: Bon chemical apetit. In Lerza, Catherine, and Jacobson, Michael, editors: Food for people, not for profit, New York, 1975, Ballantine Books, Inc., pp. 57-64.

Morrison, Peter A.: The impact of rural-urban migration in the United States, Publication No. P-4752, Santa Monica, Calif., 1972, The Rand Corporation.

Parker, Russell C.: Concentration in the food industry. In Lerza, Catherine, and Jacobson, Michael, editors: Food for people, not for profit, New York, 1975, Ballantine Books, Inc., pp. 115-122.

1

The nature and magnitude of changes in agricultural technology

---

American agriculture—the first 300 years

GOVE HAMBIDGE

In writing a history of agriculture in this country from the colonial period to the World War, Edwards traces the changing conditions and policies that most affected farmers.

The colonial period, he notes, covered almost two centuries, and its influence lasted much longer. It strongly stamped American habits and institutions. Two characteristics of this period were especially notable. (1) The colonies were predominantly agricultural, and the attitudes of the small farmer characterized the people as a whole. (2) Life was fluid because it was continually beginning over again on the frontier. Frontier isolation tended to make people narrow, but primitive conditions made them resourceful, self-reliant, practical, hard-working. These have been typical American traits.

Englishmen predominated in the 13 Colonies. They came mostly from a rural background where agriculture was not yet highly developed. Their farming methods were not suited to the wilderness, and at first they almost starved in spite of an abundance of wilderness food. Not until they had learned new ways from the Indians did they make a success of the new life. Agriculture in this country became a blend of European and Indian practices and has remained so ever since.

Since landownership was the key to individual success in England, it became equally important in the Colonies. Three ways of acquiring land were especially significant. (1) Under the manorial system, large tracts were granted to individuals, who were practically feudal overlords and collected quitrents from settlers. With such an abundance of land in America, this system was hard to enforce. Eventually manors became plantations and the owners made a profit from slave labor rather than land. (2) Under the New England system, a trading company took title to the land. Settlers were granted rights—usually to an area the size of a township—as a group, not as individuals. Through town meetings, the group acted as a corporation in dividing the land fairly among individuals, and some of it was held in common. This system, designed to be like the Biblical commonwealth, developed group action, compact social communities, democratic institutions. (3) Under the headright system of Virginia and other southern Colonies, any settler had a right to 50 acres of land—equivalent to a dividend on a share of company stock. This system became highly corrupt and was eventually replaced by "treasury rights"—the sale of 50-acre tracts to individuals by the Commonwealth.

Agricultural tools and implements in the Colonies were extremely crude. Labor was scarce, since four freemen out of five were independent farmers. This led to various systems of unfree labor. Many people sold themselves as voluntary indentured servants for 5 to 7 years in order to get to America. Others were involuntary indentured servants for 7 to 10 years —paupers, vagrants, debtors, petty criminals "condemned" to the Colonies, or innocent persons shanghaied by professional kidnappers. Many of these "redemptioners," though poor, came of good stock, accumulated a stake for themselves, became independent and often prosperous. The trade in indentured servants was checked about 1700, and the importation of slaves from Africa then began in earnest. By 1760, slaves made up two-fifths of the population of the southern Colonies; in South Carolina they outnumbered the whites 2 to 1.

At first the colonists grew their crops in the clearings they found; then they began making clearings,

□ Excerpt from Farmers in a changing world—a summary. In Hambidge, G., editor: Yearbook of agriculture, 1940, Washington, D.C., 1940, U.S. Government Printing Office, pp. 10-19.

using the Indian method of girdling and burning trees. Indian corn became the major crop because of its many advantages, but the European grains were also grown—wheat, rye, barley, oats, buckwheat, peas. Livestock was scarce; all animals had to be imported, and none but the better-financed settlements could afford an adequate supply. As the number of livestock increased, native annual grasses in the clearings proved inadequate for forage, and this led to the importation of timothy, bluegrass, clover.

Almost from the beginning, Edwards points out, there were laws regulating production and marketing, passed either in England or by the Colonies themselves. Some were successful, some visionary. Tobacco production was restricted again and again to prevent glutting the market and to insure the growing of food crops. There were price-fixing agreements for tobacco, official grading, destruction of surpluses. Rice growing was encouraged, and there were laws to fix the exchange value of the product, standardize quality, prevent deceitful packing. The growing of indigo was stimulated by premiums. Bounties were paid for hemp and flax, and growers were subsidized by various Colonies. There were likewise bounties for the production of naval stores, as well as official standardization. Extraordinary efforts, never very successful, were made to encourage silk production, including not only bounties but compulsory planting of mulberry trees. Cotton, sugar, spices, wine, and subtropical fruits were also subject to stimulative or regulative legislation.

Most of the colonial trade was overseas, but a sizable amount developed between the Colonies. New England quickly became a commercial and shipping center, trading especially with the West Indies and along the coast. The middle Colonies became a fur-trading and grain-exporting region. The South contributed more than any other region to overseas trade, the chief product being tobacco. Several factors interfered seriously with the trade of the Colonies, including a long series of navigation acts, designed to assist in creating a self-sufficient economic empire, which prohibited the shipping of most products anywhere except to England, in English or colonial ships.

Small farmers, backwoodsmen, city laborers, mechanics were the driving force back of the Revolutionary War. In effect they were revolting against the large landed and commercial interests that represented England in the government of the Colonies. They wanted more liberal land policies; paper money to pay off their debts; an end of absentee landlordism, property qualifications for voting, taxation without representation, expensive justice.

After the war the last vestiges of feudalism were abolished by "frontier 'radicals' like Jefferson."

Thereafter land could be held in fee simple. Probably the most important development relating to land was the formation of policies for disposing of the vast western area won from England. Fortunately the States with claims to western land ceded them to the Confederation and this enabled the country to develop as a federation of equal States instead of a system of provinces dependent on the older States. In 1785 and 1787 ordinances were passed that laid down the principles and procedure later followed in the disposition of public land. There were two divergent views from the beginning, one group favoring a cautious and the other a liberal land policy. Gradually the second viewpoint won.

Land policy came to center around three specific issues. (1) Graduation. The best land was settled first, leaving islands of poor land unsold. In 1854 prices were graduated downward on the unsold land. (2) Preemption. At first efforts were made to drive off squatters. Frontier farmers banded together, finally forced enactment of the preemption law in 1841. Settlers could then take up (preempt) land before it was surveyed and placed on sale. (3) Homestead. Conservative leaders as well as eastern landowners and manufacturers opposed a too liberal land policy. Pioneer farmers and land speculators joined forces with labor to have land distributed free to actual settlers; one of their slogans was "Vote yourself a farm." Underneath the political struggle, says Edwards, "lay the conviction that equality of economic power was essential if genuine freedom and democracy were to thrive in America." The bill for free homesteads was passed by the House in 1852, but it became part of the slavery issue and was not finally enacted until 1862.

The opening of new lands and the westward expansion between 1790 and 1850 was marked by one of the greatest migrations in the history of the world. In 1790 there were 4,000,000 people in the United States, of whom 94 percent were in the 13 original States; within 60 years there were 23,000,000 people and 32 States. "Land was the great magnet . . . available almost for the asking . . . an irresistible temptation." The first great trek was into the Old Northwest (bounded by the Ohio, the Great Lakes, and the Mississippi) opened up by the Ordinances of 1785 and 1787. Settlers rushed in even before the surveys were completed. The same wave of migration settled western New York. After 1815, the migration increased, stimulated by depression in Europe and our own Eastern States, the increasingly liberal land policies of the Federal Government, victories over the Indians, the use of steamboats on western rivers, the Louisiana and East Florida purchases. Ohio, Indiana, Illinois, Michigan were soon admitted to the Union.

The immense demand for cotton following the invention of the cotton gin in 1793 pushed planters westward into the Old Southwest, where a plantation aristocracy developed. In 1834 Alabama for the first time took the lead in cotton production away from Georgia, and in 1839 Mississippi led for the first time. The acquisition of the Louisiana Territory in 1803 increased the area of the United States by 140 percent. The westward tide moved into Texas in 1830, bringing annexation and war with Mexico. Before 1850 the Oregon Territory was acquired from England, and Mexico ceded California. Then came the gold rush to the Pacific coast.

The opening of fertile western lands caused a depression in eastern agriculture, made possible the development of industries and cities, had a liberalizing influence on American politics, and above all affected American psychology because of the feeling that the individual always had a chance to start life over again by taking up new land.

The virgin soil of the Old Northwest grew wheat well, and during the 1850's wheat production shifted westward to Illinois, Indiana, and Wisconsin. Corn, marketed in the form of whiskey and hogs, also did well in the new country.

Eastern agriculture went through two major changes by 1860. (1) Prior to 1810, methods were backward except in a few progressive areas, and production for home use was the rule—perhaps mainly because there was no large urban market. Then the growth of cities stimulated production for sale. As a result, better tools and more scientific methods were used, production became more specialized, land values rose, farmers began buying instead of making home and farm equipment. At the same time, young people began leaving the farm for the city. (2) Western competition also forced eastern farmers to specialize. By 1850 there were 7,000 miles of railroads, and shortly thereafter Western States were pouring wool, wheat, pork, beef into eastern markets. Eastern farmers perforce turned to the production of potatoes and other vegetables, orchard fruits, fluid milk, cheese, butter, hay.

Meanwhile, southern agriculture also underwent changes. The application of power to textile manufacturing in England and later in New England resulted in an enormous demand for cotton, and the invention of the cotton gin enabled American producers to meet this demand. More and more the South specialized in cotton, which became the largest export crop of the United States. This expansion revived slavery, which had been on the wane. As soil resources were used up in the eastern areas, growers moved westward, finally reaching the prairie regions of Texas. The Southeast had little to compensate for

this loss, and its story, Edwards notes, would have been different had western migration been better regulated.

Of vital importance to farmers was the development of the transportation system, prior to 1860. The Colonies were tardy in road and bridge building. The completion of the Philadelphia-Lancaster Turnpike in 1792 started a boom in turnpike building by private companies, which charged heavy tolls—$12 a ton per hundred miles, on the average. Even with some State aid, however, this did not provide an adequate road system, and in 1808 Jefferson's Secretary of the Treasury, Albert Gallatin, advocated public expenditure for a Nation-wide system of canals, turnpikes, and river improvements. The Cumberland Road (834 miles—$7,000,000) was the major result.

In 1815 a steamboat ascended the Mississippi and Ohio Rivers from New Orleans to Louisville in 25 days. This inaugurated a tremendous expansion. The Northeast and Southwest were bound together by river trade, and the favored cities—particularly New Orleans—grew rapidly. For a long time steamboats were the chief means of travel in settling the West. Coastwise traffic, however, became more important in the long run; by 1860 the value of commodities carried by coastwise vessels was six times that of exports abroad.

Canal building was begun partly to bring inland products to seaports for the steamship traffic. The first big project was the Erie Canal, completed in 1825. Before the canal, it had cost $100 to ship a ton of farm products from Buffalo to New York in 20 days; now it cost $15 and the trip was completed in 8 days. Farm prices and land values went up; new cities were born; New York became the biggest American seaport. Other States began canal building, and a series of feeder canals was constructed in the Old Northwest. The whole development greatly stimulated western agriculture, but the cost of the internal improvements was enormous, more than the States could bear. After the panic of 1837, "it became part of the American credo that a public utility could not be built and operated successfully except by private enterprise."

Then came railroads, to challenge the supremacy of canals and eventually win. Western railroad building did not get a good start until 1850, but by 1860 Illinois was the greatest corn State as a result of the opening of the prairies by railroads, and the flour-milling and stock-raising centers inevitably moved westward.

Edwards argues that after 1862, when the Homestead Act was signed, there were many major mistakes in United States land policy. In the first place, the act itself did not and could not do what its supporters had in mind. It offered 160 acres of land free to the settler. This was enough for a farm in the East and Middle West, including even eastern Kansas, Nebraska, and the Dakotas. But by 1862 these areas were largely settled. Homestead lands lay mostly west of the 100th meridian, in areas of low rainfall, where eastern farming methods did not apply; it was obvious to anyone who knew the West that 160 acres was too little for dry-farming or grazing, too much for irrigation. Moreover, there were two competing systems of land disposal in effect. The better lands often were purchased in huge blocks by speculative syndicates, which gouged the farmer. The administration of the land laws was also full of abuses, and fraud and graft were common.

Some of the subsequent land laws also had the effect of encouraging overexploitation of resources by large corporations and other interests. A movement toward conservation began in 1891, when the Timber Cutting Act and the Preemption Act were repealed, the policy of selling the public domain (except special lands) was abandoned, and forest reserves were authorized. The old Forestry Office became a bureau of the Department of Agriculture in 1897. The Carey Act of 1894 provided for irrigation under State auspices; the Reclamation Act of 1902 put the Federal Government into irrigation. Laws passed between 1906 and 1920 reserved all mineral rights for the Government, permitted only carefully regulated leasing. Meanwhile 148,000,000 acres was added to the timberland reservation and Gifford Pinchot inaugurated an active forest conservation policy. Between 1904 and 1916 efforts were made to improve the Homestead Act by granting larger tracts on the inferior western lands that remained undistributed.

If settlement had been better managed as a public policy, says Edwards, there might now be more farm owners, fewer tenants, and far better conservation of national resources. But most people were not then thinking in those terms. The object, natural enough at the time, was to settle and develop the wilderness as rapidly as possible.

Edwards traces the main developments in farm machinery as a major influence shaping the history of American agriculture. Many machines, developed between 1830 and 1860, were being used by farmers before the Civil War—the mechanical reaper (most significant single invention), mechanical raker and binder attachments, the steel plow, the grain drill, the corn drill, the threshing machine. The Civil War was a turning point in mechanization. A million farmers were withdrawn from production to fill the biggest army the world had ever seen, and machinery had to be used on a large scale if those left on the farms were to do their job effectively. Thus between

1860 and 1910 there was a general displacement of man labor by horse labor, and additional machines were invented to be run by horses.

After 1910 another great period began, marked by the substitution of mechanical power for horses. In this development too, war (the World War) was a turning point because it demanded greater production by fewer hands (though the farm depression of the 1920's perhaps stimulated mechanization even more through the need to cut production costs to the bone).

By no means all of the increased efficiency of agriculture is due to machines, but they have been a major force in bringing more land under cultivation, making it possible to produce up to and beyond the market demand, enlarging farms, shifting production to level lands, reducing labor requirements, lightening farm toil.

Developments in transportation after 1860 were as important to farmers as those in machinery. When settlement on a large scale was to be undertaken the Federal Government was called on to further it; the same thing happened in the case of railroad expansion. By 1914 "the railroad mileage of the United States . . . exceeded that of all Europe and represented more than a third of the world's total"; it increased eight times while the population was increasing three times. This expansion would not have been possible without Government aid. After 1850 the Government gave more than 159,000,000 acres of land to the railroads and granted two railroads $16,000-$48,000 for each mile of line they constructed. State and local subsidies were extensive and varied. Altogether, perhaps three-fourths of the cost of railway construction was borne by public authorities.

Farmers favored this aid and in addition mortgaged their land to buy railroad bonds, because the railroads promised to bring them unbelievable prosperity. When the extravagant hopes were not realized, the failure was attributed to grasping railroad barons. In fact, many serious charges could rightfully be made against the railroads. To correct the evils, farmers banded together, started the Grange, organized State and local tickets, forced railroad reforms and rate regulation by States and later by the Federal Government. In 1887 the Interstate Commerce Act was passed, in 1903 the Elkins Act, in 1906 the Hepburn Act, in 1910 the Mann-Elkins Act.

From the 1870's to the World War there was a progressive decline in rates. Competition doubtless was more of a factor in the east-west traffic rate reduction. The result was a rapid development of the West. Colonization was actively promoted by the railways. The Northwest and North Central States became the grain kingdom; meat packing was stimulated by the invention of the refrigerator car, which also spread dairy and poultry production westward.

After the Civil War, agriculture went through a long period of revolutionary change and growth, stimulated by mechanical improvements, transportation, the homestead policy, but above all by the expansion of domestic and foreign markets, which in turn resulted from industrialization and the growth of great cities whose workers had to be fed and whose factories demanded raw materials. Cereals were by far the most important commercial crop, making up half the total value of all crops in 1899. Corn production rose from 800,000,000 bushels in 1859 to a peak of over 3,000,000,000 in 1906, wheat from 200,000,000 to over 1,000,000,000 in 1915. Great milling and shipping centers developed near the heart of the grain country. Livestock production was stimulated likewise, and this brought the big livestock trading and packing centers. Butter and cheese making shifted from the farm to the factory to supply the immense demand as the dairy industry moved westward. Incubators and cold storage enabled farmers to meet the urban need for poultry products. The cotton regions, which were in a desperate plight after the Civil War, soon caught up with their 1860 production of 3,841,000 bales, and by 1910 were producing 11,609,000. By 1899 a third of the cotton crop was being used in domestic mills, and in 1909 more cotton was consumed in southern mills than in the northern. Wool production for the domestic market increased in importance. The first eastward shipment of fruit from California was made in 1867; by 1899 the total was 193,000,000 pounds of fresh deciduous fruit a year. The Southern States began sending fruits and vegetables north. Tobacco production grew.

Foreign as well as domestic trade in farm products rose sharply after the Civil War. Though city workers here and abroad benefited from the cheap food supply, many European farmers were ruined by American competition and immense numbers migrated to this country.

The peak of food exports came about 1900; after that there was a rapid decline caused by more effective competition in Europe, the development of new agricultural regions, and tariff and other policies of foreign governments. But the domestic market in the United States was then expanding and the American farmer was able to adjust his production by a gradual shift toward an increased output of sugar, dairy products, fruits, and vegetables. Cotton and tobacco exports also increased. The period 1900-1914 was relatively prosperous for agriculture, since production was fairly well balanced with demand.

The vast expansion in agriculture after the Civil War was entirely in the direction of commercial farm-ing, and this brought a train of new and complex problems. Farmers were thrown into competition with one another; they had to produce at the lowest possible cost; they had to have money for machines and other needs; they found commodity prices set by the new cotton and grain exchanges and the speculators in futures; they were squeezed by high freight rates, by monopolies, by loan sharks, by commission men. The only way they could fight their battles was by organization. So they organized, first in the Granger movement. One major outcome was a rapid growth of cooperative buying, selling, and even manufacturing. These early efforts of the farmer "to perform the function of middleman, manufacturer, capitalist, and banker through cooperative enterprise met with only short-lived success," because of lack of capital, inexperience, fair and unfair competition; but it paved the way for the cooperative movement of later years. In the 1880's came the Northwestern and the Southern Alliances, which started many cooperative enterprises; in 1895 another expansion in cooperative activity began; in 1902 the Farmers' Union was formed, and it developed plans that forecast certain aspects of present-day agricultural thinking. In 1914 the Clayton Act recognized the need for farmer cooperatives, and they have had legal protection ever since.

The post–Civil War period of rapid agricultural expansion also saw the development of a Federal Department of Agriculture. Founded in 1862, it was actually the result of almost a hundred years of preliminary steps. In 1776 there was a tentative proposal for Congress to set up a standing committee to assist agricultural societies. Two decades later Washington proposed a board of agriculture, and a similar proposal was made in 1817. Meanwhile consuls and naval officers aboard were sending back seeds and improved breeds of livestock. In 1836 Henry L. Ellsworth, Commissioner of Patents, undertook to distribute these seeds to farmers. In 1839 Congress appropriated $1,000 for the work, as well as for statistical and other investigations. An Agricultural Division was inaugurated in the Patent Office, and regular appropriations were made after 1847. In 1854 a chemist, a botanist, and an entomologist were employed.

When an independent Department was established in 1862, Isaac Newton, who headed the agricultural work in the Patent Office, became Commissioner and laid the foundations for a broad policy of research and education. Almost from the beginning, therefore, "the Department made notable contributions to the field of scientific agriculture," partly because "men of outstanding ability served as division chiefs and research workers." The Department gradually added divisions, beginning with chemistry, statistics, entomology, in response to need and demand. In 1884 it took on regulatory work in addition to fact-finding and education when the Bureau of Animal Industry was organized to clean up cattle diseases.

The year 1862 also saw the founding of the land-grant colleges under the Morrill Act, and in 1887, under the Hatch Act, Congress authorized a national system of State agricultural experiment stations—several had been started by the States, beginning with Connecticut in 1875—which served as a link between the colleges and the Federal Department. Finally in 1889 the Department was given Cabinet status, and its appropriations were increased, its functions widened. Highly trained explorers went to far countries and brought back valuable crop plants; extensive breeding work got under way; protection of the national forests was undertaken; enforcement of the Food and Drugs Act was given to the Department. After 1900 county demonstration work began, and in 1914, under the Smith-Lever Act, Congress gave financial aid to extension divisions in the State colleges, which were to cooperate with the Federal agency. Meanwhile marketing problems were receiving increased emphasis, and an Office of Markets was created in 1913. Weather reporting and road construction had also become Department functions.

Meanwhile agricultural education also went through a period of early growth until the Land Grant College Act of 1862 granted large amounts of land to the States to be sold for funds to create and maintain agricultural and mechanical colleges. A system of direct Federal subsidies was created by legislation in 1890 and 1907. The colleges had a difficult time at first because of lack of funds, lack of qualified teachers, lack of a sufficient body of agricultural knowledge, and political interference, but they gradually proved their economic and scientific value. They in turn sponsored agricultural courses in the grade schools, beginning with Wisconsin in 1905. Meanwhile agricultural high schools had been started, and eventually (1917) this led to the Smith-Hughes Act, granting Federal funds to the States for agricultural education in the secondary schools.

The development of specialized schools and colleges has had profound effects on agriculture, scientifically, economically, and socially. It is significant, Edwards notes, that at critical points in this development there was always a demand for Federal aid and cooperation.

At the end of his article Edwards sums up the influence of agriculture on governmental policy in the United States.

The Civil War may be considered as a dividing line. Until that time agricultural production was dominant in this country. Events that showed the powerful influence of farmers before the war included the formation of the Democratic-Republican Party in opposition to traders, bankers, speculators; purchase of the Louisiana Territory; the War of 1812, "begun and carried through by ardent expansionists"; abandonment of property qualifications for voting and office holding; public education; destruction of the National Bank, greatest monopoly of its day; the policy of moving Indians beyond the Mississippi; the preemption, graduation, and homestead acts.

After the Civil War, agriculture was on the defensive and business enterprise in the ascendancy. Industrialization got under way in earnest. By 1889, for the first time, the income derived from manufacturing was greater than that from agriculture; since 1910, the income from manufacturing has exceeded that from agriculture in every year, and the United States has ranked first among industrial countries. Agriculture expanded also and controlled the European market, but farmers never did reap the benefits to anything like the same extent as businessmen. Farmers could not combine to fix prices or control output. As prices fell, their fixed charges rose. Mortgages and tenancy steadily increased. Credit facilities for farmers were lacking, and they suffered from contracted currency. As a result of these and other conditions, frequent farm revolts have characterized the entire period since shortly after the Civil War.

Railroad reform and regulation, won by the Grange, was the first great post-war victory of organized farmers. Even though many of the Granger laws were not enforced and were soon repealed, the battle taught farmers much, brought them into united action, started a far-reaching cooperative movement. An outstanding result of Granger activity, says Edwards, "was the firm establishment of the principle that a State government has power to regulate businesses clothed with a public interest." The Interstate Commerce Act also "marked the entrance of the Federal Government into the sphere of business regulation."

Currency reform—"the same money for the bondholder as for the plowholder"—was another great objective of farmers resulting from the monetary situation after the war. In 1874 a farm group united with labor to form the Independent National Party, which became the Greenback Labor Party in 1878, when it polled a million votes, and in 1888 was absorbed into the Union Labor Party. Meanwhile State Alliances organized in the South in the 1870's eventually united (1888) as the National Farmers' Alliance and Industrial Union. A similar organization, the Northwestern Alliance, was formed in 1880. Both advocated free silver, paper money, tax reform. In 1892 a combination of the Western Alliance and Knights of Labor became the Populist Party, which in 1894 elected seven Congressmen and six Senators. Though the party fought for a considerable list of agrarian measures, it concentrated on free silver in the campaign of 1896 and supported Bryan, who polled 6,500,000 votes. Bryan's defeat marked the end of the Populists as an effective organization.

Though farmers had a measure of prosperity in the early 1900's the agrarian reform movement did not die out but broadened and deepened. Several organizations were formed and two headquarters were established in Washington. The Nonpartisan League eventually became "a force to be reckoned with in the national political arena." Achievements between 1912 and 1920 that resulted from long-standing farm demands included the Federal Reserve Act, the county agent extension system, a Federal Farm Loan Board and 12 regional banks for long-term credit, and subsidies by the Federal Government for vocational agriculture in the public schools.

What's happened to farming

DONALD D. DUROST and WARREN R. BAILEY*

A hundred years ago most of the Nation's population were farmers. Anyone could go west, claim his 160 acres, and become a farmer. With farming predominant it naturally was largely subsistent—the family consumed much of what it produced, and sold or bartered a small surplus to fill out other living needs.

Farming was also largely self-sufficient. Tools were simple—a plow, a cultivator, a reaper, a scythe, and a hoe. Farmers built houses, barns, and fences out of trees felled in clearing the land for crops . . . Raised work animals for power and grew the "fuel" to feed them . . . Saved as seed stock the biggest corn ears and the best calves . . . Raised sons to till the fields, daughters to cook and weave.

Farming was truly a "way of life."

As the frontier marched westward, farming continued to expand in number of farms, acres in cultivation, and workers employed until about the period 1920-1930. Since then, the number of farms and workers has declined except briefly during the economic depression of the 1930's. Acres of cropland continued constant from the 1920's until the 1950's before declining. We now harvest crops from about the same acreage as at the beginning of this century—roughly 60 million fewer acres than at the peak.

Up to about 1920 the nature of farming had not really changed very much in 100 years. Most farmers were still largely self-sufficient with respect to what they needed for production. Horses and mules were

☐ From Hayes, J., editor: Yearbook of agriculture, 1970, Washington, D.C., 1970, U.S. Government Printing Office, pp. 2-10.
*Donald D. Durost and Warren R. Bailey are economists with the Farm Production Economics Division, Economic Research Service.

the chief source of power except for the threshing, which was done with the aid of steam engines. Soil fertility was supplied by rotating row crops with close-grown crops, grasses, and legumes.

Crop yields were about the same—corn, 26 bushels; wheat, 14 bushels; and cotton, 170 pounds—as the early 19th century. Production technology had changed hardly at all. Farming practices represented family skills, and consisted chiefly of conventional wisdom handed down from father to son.

Some folks imagine farming is still like that. They do not realize that since the mid-1920's we have seen three fullscale revolutions in U.S. agriculture—mechanical, technological, and business management—which together are changing the nature of farming.

The real beginning of the mechanical revolution in farming was marked by the advent in the late 1920's of the general purpose type tractor—soon to be mounted on rubber-tired wheels. Horse-drawn farm machines were quickly adapted to its use.

With this tractor you could plow, disk, harrow, cultivate the rows of corn and cotton, mow and bale hay, stack the bales, pull a grain harvester or a corn picker, haul trailer loads, and dozens of other jobs. This tractor essentially emancipated farming from its dependency upon animal power.

In 1930, we had over 19 million horses and mules on farms, and less than a million tractors. Today we have so few farm horses and mules that we stopped counting them in the 1959 Census of Agriculture. But we now have nearly 6 million farm tractors and their size and adaptability continually amaze.

After the general purpose type tractor, in quick succession came the self-propelled grain combine, the rice harvester, the corn picker, and the cotton picker.

We now have mechanical harvesters for almost every crop . . . Field forage harvesters and powered silo fillers . . . Machines that dig and load potatoes, pick canning tomatoes (not the fresh), strip tobacco leaves, shake the nuts from walnut and almond trees . . . And we have a seemingly endless list of materials handling machines—bale loaders, hydraulic scoops, and so on. Imagine, we have self-propelled ladders on which the fruit picker or pruner can stand and move himself from tree to tree.

The mechanical revolution is continuing—tractors with power steering and power brakes, automatic transmissions and other automative adaptations, plus hydraulic lifts.

With all of these new tractors and machines, total manhours required in farming have declined from 23 billion in 1930, to 15 billion in 1950, 7 billion in 1968. Consequently, output per manhour doubled in the two decades between 1930 and 1950, and almost tripled in the 20 years since 1950.

The mechanical revolution has permitted each worker to grow more acres of corn or cotton and to perform each task more precisely and more timely.

The second revolution—the technological—had its real beginning with the advent of corn hybrids soon after 1930. Up to that time crop improvement had consisted largely of plant and seed selection rather than plant breeding as such.

Hybridization combines "hybrid vigor" with the heavier yielding habit of one parent variety and the sturdier plant structure of another. Associated with other practices of that era, hybridization increased the expected yields of corn by 20 to 25 percent. Eventually, the impact was even greater because of the potential it gave for combining other technologies such as fertilizer, increased plant populations, narrow row spacing, and chemical herbicides.

Up to World War II, corn typically was grown in a 3-year rotation of corn-oats-clover, without fertilizer, in 40-inch rows, planted 10,000 seeds to the acre, and the Corn Belt yield was about 38 bushels an acre.

Today, corn seldom is rotated. Leading growers typically fertilize with 150 pounds of nitrogen, plant 25,000 seeds to the acre in 20-inch rows, control weeds with herbicides, and get yields of 130 to 150 bushels an acre. The average Corn Belt yield is now 90 to 100 bushels.

The impact is two dimensional on total corn production—where we once planted 33 acres of each 100 and got 1,250 bushels, we now plant the whole 100 and get 9,000 to 10,000 bushels.

We converted our grain sorghum to hybrids in a span of 4 years, about 10 years ago. The direct impact was a 25 percent increase in yield.

The U.S. acre yield of wheat has doubled since 1930 —from 14 to 28 bushels—without assistance from hybridization. The gain resulted from improved natural varieties, better and more timely tillage, more effective pest control, and heavier soil fertilization. The technical problem of wheat hybridization is now solved. Hybrids are appearing in parts of the wheat region. Again, they too promise 25 percent higher yields.

Cotton lint yields have increased threefold since 1930, now average 515 pounds an acre. Part of the increase is due to a shift of acreage out of the lower-yielding southern Piedmont to the Mississippi Delta and the irrigated Southwest, where yields average 650 pounds and 1,000 pounds respectively. Again, the gain was due to improved technology—varieties, pesticides, herbicides, soil fertilization, and so on.

Other crop yield increases per acre since 1930: rice, 2,100 to 4,500 pounds; tobacco, 775 to 2,000 pounds; peanuts, 700 to 1,750 pounds; soybeans, 13 to 26 bushels; potatoes, 65 to 215 hundredweight.

Nothing equalling the spectacular new technologies in crop production has occurred in livestock—except the feed conversion ratios in broilers and turkeys.

By 1950 we were producing broilers commercially with a feed efficiency of about 3 pounds of grain ration per 1 pound of broiler live weight, and that was a gain of 40 percent over conventional farm performance. Now the ratio has been reduced to 1.8 pounds of ration per pound live weight, and it will go still lower.

Nothing like that gain in feed-conversion efficiency has occurred with hogs or beef cattle. The ratio for hogs is 3.5 to 4 pounds of grain (feed concentrates) per pound of live weight gain. But in cattle feeding the ratio is 6 to 9 pounds of grain per pound of live weight gain. These differences in feed-conversion ratios largely explain why chicken is priced so much lower than pork and beef in the supermarket.

The substantial increases in pork and beef output have resulted directly from the huge increase in feed output plus a corresponding increase in number of animals.

The mechanical and scientific revolutions have both directly and indirectly changed the nature of farming.

Understandably, farming today is highly commercial, thoroughly market oriented. From production largely for home use, it has shifted to production for sale. Today, nearly all farm output—except some feed and crop seed—goes through commercial channels.

It is true for part-time as well as full-time farms. Even in low income areas farmers supply only a part of their meat, chicken, eggs, and milk needs, and not much else. Most farm families buy their food from the supermarket because it saves work in preparation, is handier, and more sanitary.

In fact the term "commercial farmer" no longer serves to distinguish a group who are market oriented because all are thus oriented.

The greater degree of market orientation means that farmers are now highly conscious of their commodity prices, whereas formerly they were more concerned about their production costs.

Today's farming is also market oriented in another way, that of product specification and quality. Each farmer once produced the type, size, and quality of product he individually thought best, only to find that when he got there the market wanted something different. Actually, farmers often had little control of the quality they produced.

Today's farmer knows what is wanted, produces commodities according to specification—formula-fed broilers of a specified age and weight, hennery eggs, cattle fed to an exact weight and finish, wheat with a minimum protein. Product specification often is part of a production contract between the farmer and the buyer-processor.

Farmers no longer need rely on their conventional wisdom, as to what the market wants. And, today's farmer has far more control over the quality and specifications of what he produces. He uses a known, specified technique and process. Much of the guesswork on quality is gone.

It follows that the new farm production technologies are now more standardized, more widely known and accepted. Thus, we know the amount of fertilizer (element by element), the row spacing, and the plant population for top yields of corn; the feed ration for a meaty broiler; and how to produce fine head lettuce. Our producers do not skimp or take chances on the production mix—they simply cannot afford to.

Just as today's farming is more market oriented, so is much of the food processing migrating off the farm.

Remember when a farmer sold and delivered fresh, raw milk to the final household consumers? Now his milk is picked up daily at the farm, taken to a plant for pasteurization, homogenization, vitamin D irradiation, and bottling for delivery to food store or home. Likewise, the separation of cream from milk is now done almost entirely off the farm.

Cattle feeding (grain fattening) formerly was done entirely by farmers on farms, particularly those in the Corn Belt. Now much of the cattle feeding is done in huge specialized lots where fattening rations are carefully formulated, feed ingredients mixed and metered out to each feeding pen. Animals are fattened to the exact degree of finish desired.

Broilers, eggs, and turkeys were once predominantly farm enterprises, often a sideline managed by the farmer's wife. Now these products are produced mainly in specialized facilities, not associated with a "farm," where feed rations are carefully formulated, and environment is carefully controlled. Only in some local areas are "farm" or "ranch" eggs, chickens, and turkeys still available directly to consumers.

Many other products were sold directly to consumers from a roadside stand or an open air "farmer's market"—an area with individual sales booths. Farmers brought their apples, pumpkins, potatoes, fresh apple cider, eggs, live chickens, hams, and dressed beef and pork.

The traditional "farmer's market" has all but disappeared. Fruit and vegetables are now harvested, sold, and delivered in truckload lots directly to wholesalers. Poultry and meat animals are sold alive, directly to slaughtering plants, country auctions, country buyers, or are consigned to commission selling houses.

Thus many functions formerly done by farmers on their farms have moved to off-farm processing plants. The employment and wages have migrated too, although often both farm and nonfarm people work in the off-farm plants.

Farmers themselves now chiefly produce just the primary ingredients of food and fiber. Thus, the term "farming" does not embrace all that it once did 100 or even 50 years ago.

Product specialization has taken a regional dimension, and in some instances is shifting between regions.

Corn production continues to be concentrated in the Corn Belt, where climate and soils are suited to the corn plant. In the Southeast corn, traditionally used as human food and feed for work animals, has always been secondary to cotton, peanuts, and tobacco.

Milo (grain sorghum) production is concentrated in the Great Plains where it has replaced some of the corn acreage in recent decades. In fact, milo has entered the western Corn Belt. To a lesser extent milo is grown in the irrigated valleys of the Southwest. In 10 years the crop has expanded from 550 million to 750 million bushels, due mainly to the higher yielding hybrids and to more acres irrigated.

Soybeans—traditionally a Corn Belt crop—have recently entered the Mississippi Delta. In 10 years the crop has expanded from 500 million to a billion bushels.

Cotton acreage and production have declined in the lower yielding area, the Southeast, and have increased in the better adapted, higher yielding areas of the Mississippi Delta and the irrigated Southern Plains and Southwest (including California).

Both fresh and processing type vegetable production has increased in the Southwest, in Texas, and in Florida. Winter crop head lettuce is grown in southern California. Fall and spring crop lettuce is produced in Texas and Florida.

Staked vine-ripened and green-picked tomatoes are available to consumers throughout the country all seasons of the year. The green-picked are shipped to warehouses near population centers for ripening in controlled temperature holding rooms until they are red ripe.

Cattle feeding (grain fattening) originated in the Corn Belt, where range steers were brought to be fattened by the farmer on corn he grew himself. That activity has continued to expand along with the expansion of corn grain supplies, U.S. population, and consumer demand.

More recently, beef fattening has moved into the Southern Plains, the Southwest, the Central Valley of California, and the Pacific Northwest, where milo grain or barley are indigenous or accessible, and where consumer markets are expanding. In these new areas, the fattening is done in huge specialized feedlots of up to 100,000 head capacity, quite unlike the on-farm feeding which still predominates in the Corn Belt.

Traditionally, we associate cattle raising with the range country of the Plains and the West. That is where the calves and steers came from to be fattened on Corn Belt farms.

In recent decades cattle "ranching" has expanded in the Southeast on land no longer used for cotton; to be more accurate, it has "come back," For it was in the Coastal Plains of the Carolinas that cattle ranching—in the American tradition of cowboys, branding, and roundups—got its start, long before the Civil War. Carolinians carried the art and folklore West.

Some surplus cattle from the Southeast is now finding its way to Corn Belt feedlots.

We now have about 900,000 fewer operating farms than in 1960! But essentially all the land is still in production, because of farm consolidation.

All the net decrease in number of farms has come in the smaller farm operations, those whose product sales are under $10,000 a year. In fact, we now have 184,000 more farms whose product sales are above $10,000. And the percentage increase is greatest among those farms whose sales are above $40,000. We had 194,000 such farms in 1968, their annual product sales averaging above $100,000.

More than 4 out of each 5 dollars worth of farm products are produced on farms with sales over $10,000.

Large farms are feasible today because modern machines permit each man to till more land. Greater output per farm unit means a larger volume of business, larger gross, and larger net income.

Contrary to common belief, the larger farms do not have much lower unit costs of production than fully mechanized one-man or two-man farms. The reason is that technical economies pertain to size of plant rather than size of business. And in farming, the "plant" is the man and his complement of machines.

We will continue to have small and part-time farms for various reasons. The income supplements the earnings from a nonfarm job of the operator, his wife, a son, or a daughter.

Many continue to farm because they own the land, and they can custom-hire the more exacting production operations like harvesting. Modern technology is available to them.

Often the small or part-time farm has been inherited and is being operated "on the side." Small farms have great staying power. At worst, the small farmer with a nonfarm job may field rent his cropland to a neighbor.

Though fewer and larger, most of our farms are still the family type. They differ not in number of workers or in business organization, but only in acres, resources used, and total output.

The dwindling number of small farms raises a fear that huge corporations may take over the business of farming, as they have in automaking, retail food sales, and so on. Such fears are greatly magnified.

Interestingly, we have always had some corporation farms—the XIT ranch in Texas, the Dalrymple Farms in North Dakota, the Campbell wheat ranch in Montana, and so on. These have operated side by side with conventional ranches and farms for decades.

A recent nationwide survey shows a rising number of corporations farming. But most are family type corporations—a form of business organization that is useful under some circumstances.

Farms today are more specialized.

Years ago farms were highly diversified, with many individual enterprises. Feed crops were carefully balanced against livestock enterprises, and a high degree of complementarity existed between enterprises and in the use of land and labor.

Today, farmers are concentrating on fewer but much larger crop or livestock enterprises. For example, we now see many one-enterprise and two-enterprise farms where formerly there were three to five enterprises. Specialization is aided, of course, by the availability of purchased production needs and custom services. Consequently there is less reason to diversify, and fewer problems of resource use within the farm business.

Farmers are now purchasing way more production goods and services, as they must if they are to have today's modern technology.

Even 40 years ago they were still providing most of their production needs—horsepower (and its feed), soil fertility (clover rotations), livestock feeds, crop seeds, and workers. Each farmer owned the machines to perform almost every farming operation.

Today's farmer buys prodigious amounts of production needs—fertilizer, formula feed, hybrid seeds, insecticides, herbicides, tractor fuel—and employs a myriad of custom services such as machine harvesting, fertilizing, pesticide spraying, and airplane crop dusting. Almost any production operation or harvesting can be custom hired.

This availability of custom services means that anyone can engage in farming. Anyone who owns or rents land can become an "instant" farmer and achieve essentially the same unit-cost efficiencies as other farmers. Likewise, a person can continue in farming beyond the usual retirement age.

Purchasable inputs and services also permit the small or part-time producer of commercial crops to use most of the same production techniques and technology as the "commercial" farmer, because the technology in the form of material and custom services is broadly available to anyone.

Farming is also changing in its life style.

Once it was easy to define and clear to see the distinction between farm and nonfarm, between rural and urban. Those who lived in the open country could surely be farmers; those who lived in town were nonfarmers. Today, many farmers live in town and many urban workers live in the country. When either group engages in both farming and another occupation, are they farmers or nonfarmers?

Many farmers are combining a farm enterprise—such as corn production—with a nonfarm "enterprise" such as working in a country bank, whereas formerly they combined only farm enterprises. This is "diversification" of a different sort.

Raising broilers or producing table eggs is a "moonlighting" activity of many otherwise full-time nonfarm workers. Thus, off-farm income is increasingly important to farm people everywhere.

For example, when in 1968 the average income of farm-operator families was $9,627, about $4,841 of it was net income from farming and $4,786 came from nonfarm sources—wages, rent, dividends, business earnings.

During the 1950's and 1960's a third revolution has appeared in U.S. farming, the revolution in business methods and financial management. With it, the farmer has now taken his place with other businessmen as a user of production credit, a contractor of production services, an employer of workers, and a user of systematic accounts and records.

Table 1. Change in number of tractors, value of machinery, and amount of commercial fertilizer used, United States

Year	Number of tractors (thousands)[1]	Value of machinery and equipment (in dollars)[4]		Commercial fertilizer consumed (in short tons)[5] (thousands)
		Total (millions)	Per farm	
1910	1[2]			5547
1920	246			7176
1930	920	3302	597	8171
1935	1048[2]			6275
1945	2354	5147	1094	15,128
1954	4345			22,773
1964	4786			30,681
1969	4619[3]	25,343	9770	38,948
1974	4467[3]	48,403	22,302	
Percentage change				
1935-1974	+326	+1366	+3636	+521

Source: Data from Historical Statistics of the United States, 1975, pp. 455, 469; 1945 Census of Agriculture, Vol. 2, p. 311; 1969 Census of Agriculture, Vol. 2, p. 19; 1974 Census of Agriculture, Vol. 1, Part 51, p. 4; Washington, D.C., U.S. Government Printing Office.
[1]Census of Agriculture data; excludes Hawaii and Alaska; excludes steam- and garden-type tractors.
[2]Estimates only.
[3]Includes Hawaii and Alaska.
[4]No data collected between 1945 and 1969.
[5]U.S. Department of Agriculture survey data; includes Hawaii, Alaska, and Puerto Rico for all years except 1920 to 1944. Prior to 1944, the data were for calendar years, and after 1944, for years ending June 30.

The last farmer

GENE LOGSDON

Hardly anyone believed the shocking report that the USDA leaked to the press back in 1976. "A source close to the Secretary of Agriculture revealed yesterday the existence of a hitherto suppressed study," said the *Times* earnestly. "The study proves with mathematical certainty that by the year 2053, there will be only one farmer left in the U.S."

Politicians denounced. Bureaucrats disclaimed. Economists scoffed. "Ridiculous," they said as of one voice. "Farm numbers will stabilize about the turn of the century."

But the year 2000 came and went with no let up in the attrition of farmers from farming. To agribusinessmen, the question was no longer *if* only one farmer would remain, but far more interesting, whose customer would he be???

Not many would have bet that Marvin Grabacre of Illinois would end up being the sole survivor.

"Marvelous Marv," as the folks came to call him, was only four years old in 1976. In hindsight, there were signs from the very beginning that Grabacre was a cut above even the select group that would become 21st Century farmers. At the tender age of 11, given the job of mowing the extensive family lawn, Marv talked a local repair shop into selling him four worn-out riding mowers for $10 each. He repaired the mowers, hooked them in tandem, and mowed the whole two-acre lawn in 15 minutes.

His crowning achievement was in talking old Mrs. Lacey into letting him cut down two trees and tear out a fence around her lawn so he could mow faster.

That project established the pattern that would carry Grabacre to the top. Reduced to simplest terms, his winning philosophy was: "If you have a problem, your machinery's not big enough." As a result, he bought the biggest equipment made, and if that wasn't big enough (which it never was), he'd make his own. He was the only person ever to try to build a corn combine that could be used in the off season to cut and shred fencerows—trees, brush, fence, posts and all—at 5 mph. He was also the first to pipe a navigable stream underground so he could farm over the top in longer rows, and fly on wheat with a four-engine bomber.

You could always tell a Grabacre operation. Short-

□ Reprinted from Farm Journal Magazine, Copyright 1975, Farm Journal Inc.

ly after he moved in on some newly purchased ground, all trees, fencerows, buildings, woodlots, steep hills and even streams vanished, leaving only an unbroken expanse of dirt.

Grabacre's idea of happiness was to start out in the morning on one of his big tilling and planting rigs and not have to turn around until sometime next week.

His holdings grew rapidly from the original 10,000 acres, which he inherited from his father, until by 2000 he was farming 500,000 acres of his own and renting that much more. It was just as easy to double 500,000 as it was to double 50, he found.

Absurd as it may sound, Grabacre woke up one morning to find that he owned, or at least operated, all the farm land east of the Mississippi. He no longer figured his cost per acre, but cost per county, or cost per state, or sometimes, as with Maryland and Delaware, cost per region.

But of course, for tax purposes, he still just barely broke even. When Ohio showed a good profit, sure as hell Alabama showed a bad loss.

His project to pipe the Ohio River underground so he could plow the whole valley unimpeded was costing him more money than SCS and the Army Engineers had estimated—even though the government was cost-sharing 85% of the bill to rid the Ohio Valley once and for all from the danger of floods.

"You've got to get more efficient," said Grabacre's attorney, who was making $285,000 a year and spending winters on the Riviera—exactly what Grabacre intended to do once he got ahead of the game.

"I must be doing something wrong," he decided. He went to Washington to check with USDA.

Strangely enough, USDA was bigger than ever, doing what it had been trying to do for 100 years: "helping keep small farmers in business."

"Well, it was necessary to increase staff and budgets when the number of farmers dropped from a million to a half a million," explained the Secretary of Agriculture to the General Accounting Office in 2051. "Obviously we must continue to expand when the number drops from half a million to one."

Everybody in Washington understood that kind of logic. But it was little consolation to Grabacre.

So he used his farm magazines to see what his neighbors were doing.

There was only one neighbor left—the guy who

owned everything west of the Mississippi. A little column in the back of one of the journals caught his eye. The gist of the piece was that regardless of what a few old-fogey economists thought, the eastern half of the United States just was *not* a viable economic farm unit anymore.

"While we believe firmly in the family farm," the article stated, "there's no reason at all why such a farm should remain as small as only half of our nation. The farmer must eventually get big or get out."

So Grabacre flew out over the Mississippi looking for states where broken-down fences and shabby barns might indicate a chance to buy land cheap. The drouth was still putting a squeeze on the Great Plains; cattle were still losing money, the labor unions were still on strike in California, and the Inland Empire was still running out of water. Grabacre shook his head sadly. That other farmer wasn't keeping up with the times. He'd be better off in some other line of work.

By then Grabacre had consolidated all the bankers of the Farm Credit System, under his own name. But when he asked them for another loan, they informed him that he had already borrowed all the money they had available.

So he talked a consortium of Middle East oil barons into lending him the money, and he bought his last neighbor out. Actually it was just business as usual for Grabacre. He sold most of Arizona, Utah and New Mexico to developers at an outrageous price to get the downpayment.

And so in 2051, two years ahead of the computer projection, agriculture was at last united and could speak with one voice—Grabacre's.

But Grabacre was too busy to speak with one voice or any voice at all. Unable to find a man equal to the task of taking over his empire, he was installing a computer in Kansas City to do the job so he could retire.

It was no big deal actually, because the programming was so simple. All the computer needed to know was: If you have a problem, your machinery isn't big enough.

The first move the new computer made was to buy China. "I know I can swing the deal by selling half of Manchuria to Russia and half to Japan," the computer told Grabacre. "We can level the mountains on the rest of it, pipe the Yangtze and Yellow rivers underground and make a clean 15% profit putting the whole works into soybeans."

Grabacre grinned. The future of agriculture was in good hands.

HAND LABOR VERSUS THE MACHINE . . .

Trends in fruit and vegetable harvesting

WALTER M. CARLETON*

Even with recent technological advances, mechanization of fruit and vegetable crops is not keeping pace with that of the major farm crops or even with that in livestock farming. Although cotton farmers are by far the chief users of seasonal farm hands, beans, tomatoes, and potatoes require the largest numbers of seasonal workers among vegetable crops. Among the fruit crops, apples, strawberries, and citrus fruit require the most seasonal workers. Other crops with significant seasonal demands include asparagus, peaches, cucumbers, surgarcane and tobacco.

Although labor requirements for crops vary widely, some fruit and vegetable crops require more than 100 man-hours per acre. Here are figures showing harvest-

Crop	Time of principal harvest	Man-hours per acre
Strawberries, fresh	May	505
Snap beans	Sept., Oct.	102
Tomatoes, fresh	June, July, Aug.	67
Cabbage, fresh	May, June	64

ing labor requirements for a Virginia farm. These are samples from one location and under one set of conditions; however, they do serve to emphasize the magnitude of the problem.

A great deal of progress has been made during the past few years with tomato harvesters, although mechanical harvesting is not yet a reality on a large com-

☐ From Agricultural Engineering **44**(3):139, Mar. 1963.
*Member ASAE.

mercial scale. The switch to mechanization will not, however, be an immediate transition, because plant breeders must develop suitable varieties for mechanical harvesting. At present, tomatoes for processing are more suitable for mechanical harvesting than other fruits and vegetables because the first ones to ripen can remain on the vines for several days before spoiling, making it practical to use a once over method of harvesting. Harvesting fresh tomatoes for consumer use is difficult as these must be picked while at a definite pre-ripe state.

Although specific performance figures on machines for harvesting tomatoes are elusive, preliminary tests indicate that one machine with its operator and sorters, plus the crew to operate tractors and fork lifts, will reduce the labor force to approximately one-fifth of that previously required. As the machines are improved, this probably will be further reduced. It is conceivable that a crew operating one machine could harvest as much as 100 tons per 10-hr day. With such labor savings, the grower could afford to invest in machines for mechanizing the crop.

Widespread mechanization of fruit and vegetable harvesting will result in underemployment for many seasonal agricultural workers, at least during the transition period to mechanization. The average skill level of workers must be increased as the complexity of machines increases. This will in turn raise the wages of those workers who do remain in agriculture. As the shift toward machines continues, with resulting labor displacement, foreign and interstate workers are likely to be the first to be affected because of the difficulties of movement for short-time employment.

The displacement of workers in one crop by mechanization will cause labor shortages in other crops For example, in southwestrn Idaho, migrant workers were offered a long employment season including the harvest of crops such as onions, fruit, lima beans, seed corn, and potatoes. As mechanization proceeds in the potato harvest, the area has become less attractive to migrant crews, since the harvest season is considerably shortened.

Increased difficulties in recruiting labor for a given area may accelerate mechanization in other crops. For example, potato harvest mechanization in Minnesota was accelerated when a labor shortage occurred because of mechanization in the sugar beet harvest.

Without doubt, the longtime effect of the labor problem will be to accelerate mechanization of many fruit and vegetable crops which are now the least mechanized. Farmers will be faced with the choice either of mechanizing these crops or of switching to other crops which can be handled by available machines.

Potential mechanization in the flue-cured tobacco industry with emphasis on human resource adjustment

SUMMARY

Large numbers of people are still employed in the production, marketing, and processing of flue-cured tobacco in the Southeastern United States. Mechanization and new technology in this industry, and the resulting displacement of workers, could constitute a problem of substantial social and economic proportions unless new employment opportunities are developed. Full mechanization of the tobacco industry, however, is tending to be inhibited by certain environmental forces. Uncertainty about future demand for tobacco products surely influences investment decisions of farmers. Government tobacco programs, which limit acreage and production and restrict leasing and rental arrangements, are largely barriers to the adoption of full-scale mechanization. Also, extensive program changes and rapid mechanization would have important implications for the people involved.

□ Excerpts from USDA-ERS Agricultural Economic Report No. 169, Washington, D.C., Sept. 1969.
Note: Although "Negro" is used in this text, the figures upon which the analysis is based may include a very small percentage of American Indians, Spanish Americans, and other minority groups because of the rapidly changing composition of this highly mobile work force.

Mechanization of the tobacco industry

During 1967, about 295 million man-hours of labor were required to produce the Nation's flue-cured tobacco crop. Current technology if adopted without restriction by Government programs, could reduce labor input in tobacco production by about half.

Production mechanization, however, is costly. A mechanical harvesting system requires a capital outlay of $52,000 ($40,000 for bulk-curing barns and

$12,000 for the harvester and support equipment). Operated at capacity (about 40 acres), the mechanical harvester is the least costly form of harvesting when wage rates exceed a level of about $1.35 per hour; this wage level will probably be reached soon.

In addition to equipment cost, the small size of production units, resulting largely from restrictive Government programs, has served as an effective deterrent to extensive mechanization of production, particularly in harvesting.

To acquire production units of 40 acres would require substantial combining of fragmented allotments. In the Coastal Plain of North Carolina—the area with largest units—the average production unit was only 8.9 acres in 1968. Multiple-unit farms (farms having one or more sharecroppers) averaged 19 acres of tobacco, compared with 7 acres for single units. The Piedmont area had even smaller production units, estimated at about 5.8 acres of tobacco per unit.

Mechanical harvesting increases the need for skilled harvester operators, tractor drivers, and hoist operators. Employment of more skilled workers, primarily males, would reduce the traditional, seasonal opportunities for females and children to work the harvest; thus, family income would be expected to decline in many cases if mechanization occurs rather fully.

Mechanization of auction sales and processing plants is occurring rapidly. This mechanization reduces the need for heavy manual labor. Mechanized handling of loose leaf tobacco increases the proportion of jobs that can be done by women. Overall, employment in the marketing and processing industries can be expected to decline substantially in the future.

Though complete mechanization of production would probably have minimal effects on the processing industry, marketing (auction) facilities would probably be relocated near the tobacco production centers; for example, they would shift from the Piedmont area to the Coastal Plain.

Demand for tobacco

Uncertainty about future demand further deters producers from investing large sums in new technology that may have limited alternative uses. Demand for tobacco in 1975 is currently projected to be about the same as in 1968. However, concern over the relationship between cigarette smoking and health is increasingly causing various public and private agencies to try to reduce demand. The future effect of the health issue on demand is not known. Changing technology in cigarette manufacturing has, however, reduced and is expected to further reduce the amount of domestically produced tobacco used per 1,000 cigarettes manufactured.

People affected

About 84,000 commercial tobacco farms in the study area . . . and over 350,000 persons in these farm households could be directly affected by mechanization and other changes in the flue-cured industry. If mechanization occurs rather fully, many workers would have to find alternative sources of income, though even now, a number have income from other sources. In 1964, about 46 percent of these farms were operated by tenants, and over half the people in commercial farm households were tenant families. Compared with whites, a much higher proportion of Negro farmers are tenant operators; however, the total number of each is similar. Average age of tobacco farmers is 47, compared with about 37 for the total U.S. work force. This higher average age is coupled with an educational attainment substantially below that of all U.S. workers—7.6 years of school, compared with 12.2

Hired workers on flue-cured tobacco farms have highly seasonal employment. In the Coastal Plain area of North Carolina, the seasonal job of longest duration is priming—averaging 16.6 days during the 1967 harvest. Croppers averaged 3.6 months of employment in tobacco in the same year. These croppers, with an average educational attainment of 4.3 years, would face especially severe problems in obtaining new employment.

Economic activity in the study area

About 4.1 million residents resided in the flue-cured area under study in 1966. Population in the area had increased 8 percent from 1960. Yet net outmigration from 1960 to 1966 amounted to 69,500 persons. The 1967 unemployment rate in the study area was only 4 percent, and nonmetropolitan areas within the area averaged 4.6 percent. These rates do not, however, indicate the extent of hidden unemployment and underemployment, especially on the smaller farms.

In the study area, the number of children born per woman—particularly to Negro women—is appreciably above the U.S. average. Thus, substantial expansion in local jobs is needed to maintain a satisfactory employment level and to decrease outmigration to other areas where the outmigrants would be at a relative disadvantage in the labor force.

As mechanization of agriculture releases workers, compensating growth in nonfarm employment will be required for satisfactory economic and human resource adjustment. Without such growth, economic recession and increased outmigration will occur, which could create problems of serious proportion. Fortunately, nonfarm employment in the study area grew at a rate of 24 percent between 1962 and 1967, compared with 14 percent for the Nation. Industries likely to use low-skill workers displaced from the tobacco industry are manufacturing, trades, and services. However, specific future job requirement of these growing industries are not known.

POLICY IMPLICATIONS

Government program restrictions hinder amalgamation of producion units into a size of operation that would effectively use available production technology. Of the 194,374 farms receiving flue-cured tobacco allotments in 1968, less than 1 percent had allotments exceeding 20 acres per farm. Eighty-nine percent had allotments of less than 6 acres each. Average allotment per farm was 3.13 acres. Major program restrictions curtailing amalgamation are discussed below.

Lease and transfer of allotments are restricted to within-county boundaries; tobacco acreage on the producing farm after transfer cannot exceed 50 percent of the recipient farm's cropland; and lease and transfer of allotment is for a single year only. New leases must be negotiated annually.

Production through renting allotment and poundage quotas from others is limited to production of rented allotment and quotas on the farm from which they were rented. Thus, tobacco fields are often miles apart.

Purchases of acreage and poundage quotas must include purchase of the whole farm to which they are allocated; thus the cost of such purchases is substantial.

However, if extensive program changes were authorized, removing the restrictions discussed above, important employment and income implications would result. Some of the more important are outlined below.

(1) Permitting transfer of allotment across county boundaries would remove tobacco production from hilly areas with small, irregular fields and concentrate it in areas where large, level fields could be effectively mechanized. In the process, the hilly areas would lose employment, related economic activities, and tax base.

(2) Amalgamation of operating units into units of approximately 40 acres and fully mechanizing production would mean that a large number of people now deriving income from tobacco production would be deprived of this source of income.

(3) Under a mechanized production system, many hired workers now employed in tobacco would lose this opportunity for work. Moreover, such workers tend to have skills that are less than competitive in other labor markets.

(4) Welfare programs would have to be expanded for some older and less educated farmers and workers displaced from employment.

(5) Retraining of displaced workers would need to be accelerated, as would the rate of growth in economic sectors other than agriculture, if widespread unemployment or high outmigration rates or both are to be avoided in the study area.

Effects of alternative policies on production, mechanization, and possible displacement of workers can be defined to a substantial degree. It can also be generally shown that the workers likely to be affected are highly disadvantaged, compared with the total U.S. work force. Specific data on the impact of displacement of both hired and family workers, however, are less readily defined because of the dearth of information relative to these workers. Information is lacking on such worker characteristics as age, sex, mobility, and the extent of dependence on income from tobacco. In addition, little is known of alternative employment opportunities and specific skills and educational requirements of them. Such data are needed for more complete evaluation of the potential social and economic consequences of changes in the tobacco industry.

Manpower implications of trends in the tobacco industry

ROBERT C. McELROY*

PROBLEMS AND NEEDS

The total absence of data on hired workers and a limited amount on others employed in tobacco in combination with the lack of information on job requirements of growing industries offering potential employment prohibits the kind of evaluation this matter demands. Data are required for determining such points as:

- How many potential displacees will not be retrainable and therefore potential welfare recipients?
- Cost of this potential welfare caseload?
- Estimated job growth (and decline) by industry and area.
- Job requirements of expanding industries.
- Number requiring further education and/or training or retraining?
- Cost of this education and training?
- Potential social returns on education and training.

The fact that such information is not available, especially in view of the magnitude of innovation and displacement in agriculture during the past several decades, poses a serious question about the balance of social direction. <u>On the one hand</u>, the development of technology has been and is being financed by fed-

□ Excerpts from a talk given at the Association for Public Program Analysis Conference, U.S. Civil Service Commission, Washington, D.C., June 16, 1969. Reprinted in Farm workers in rural America, 1971-1972, Part 4a, U.S. Senate Committee on Labor and Public Welfare, 92nd Congress, Washington, D.C., 1972, U.S. Government Printing Office, pp. 2185-2186. Prepared at the request of the Bureau of Training, U.S. Civil Service Commission, this paper draws freely on the work of an ERS task group on this subject. All use of data and ideas in the form presented is the sole responsibility of the author, however, and does not necessarily represent the views of the ERS Task Group or the Department of Agriculture.
*Economics Development Division, ERS, U.S. Department of Agriculture.

eral funds. It is by no means limited to the development of mechanical harvesters. Other developments in labor-reducing technology in tobacco, for example, include the following:

- disease resistant and uniform ripening varieties
- seedling production (chemical sterilization of plant beds in lieu of burning to prevent disease and reduce weeding labor requirements)
- transplanting (mechanical transplanters and direct field seeding)
- chemical growth regulators ("Suckers") and weed control
- improvements in on farm curing (electronic temperature control and bulk curing)
- handling methods (mechanization in the marketing sector—lifts, conveyors, etc.)

The USDA and every Experiment Station (Federally supported) in the tobacco States has now and has had for years a research program for the development of tobacco labor-saving technology and for other crops. There are comparable efforts in the Land Grant system in all other States for the important crops grown.

<u>On the other hand,</u> I do not know of one Experiment Station which has a program of concerted effort conducive to facilitating the adjustment of people displaced from agricultural employment. For that matter, aside from the small ERS group surveying the situation, I know of no such effort at the Federal level. This is not a criticism of efforts devoted to the development of labor-saving technology; the benefits are sufficiently well-known that they require no enumeration here. In view of the foregoing enumeration of the paucity of information on those displaced and the consequent and as yet non-quantifiable social cost, however, I do question the balance in direction of national social efforts.

2

The consequences of changes in agricultural technology for the numbers and characteristics of farm people and farms

Dramatic population reduction inspires technological changes

TOM HAMBURGER*

WILSON—The technological changes in the last 30 years at the 33,000-acre Wilson family farm are astonishing. Even more amazing is the fact that they are continuing.

For example, the Wilson fields average about 50 acres each, limited by the drainage ditches that surround them, but Robert E. Lee Wilson III, Board chairman of the Lee Wilson Co., sat in his office recently discussing future expansion of the fields until they are a mile long and a mile wide.

The six-row cultivators now in use handle the 50-acre fields nicely, but tractors capable of cultivating 18 rows at a time now are available and a 70-foot disc capable of discing 48 rows just has been introduced by one implement company.

The new equipment is more efficient and expensive and Wilson knows that to meet the expense the farm will have to become more efficient.

"We'll have to figure out a way to drain the land without ditches," he said in his office. "We'll have fields that are a mile long and a mile wide. They're doing it now in the Imperial Valley [California] and there must be some way we could get underground drainage in the big fields here."

The dramatic loss of population from Wilson and other towns in the South after World War II inspired one of the most dramatic technological revolutions in history. The population has dropped from more than 10,000 before the war to 1,048 today.

The Wilsons, for example, employed as many as 3,000 workers before World War II. Today, they have 200 employes.

In searching for answers to the problem of farming

□ From Arkansas Gazette, Little Rock, Ark., May 19, 1977.
*Reporter of the Gazette staff.

without cheap labor, the Wilsons were daring. Sometimes they made mistakes.

In the 1960s, for example, when the Mexican labor needed to weed cotton fields was no longer available, the Wilsons invested in geese.

That's right, geese. The company paid $16,000 a year for the birds because it was known that, while they don't care for cotton shoots, they thrive on Johnson grass, a weed that plagues cotton fields. The geese were set loose on thousands of acres of fenced cotton fields and Robert E. Lee Wilson III liked them because they "work from dawn to sundown, seven days a week." But the noise they made, the fences that were needed and their inefficient methods doomed the project.

HERBICIDE EXPERIMENT

The Wilsons concentrated their efforts in an area they had pioneered a few years earlier. In the 1950s, in co-operation with a national chemical company, the Wilson plantation became the first farm in the United States to experiment with aerial application of herbicides. Company officials came down to witness the results. They were pleased and a workable answer to the labor shortage in chopping weeds was born. Chemical farming spread across the country in a very few years.

The change in the number of Wilson employes reflects the effect mechanization has had on agriculture in Arkansas in the last three decades. Farm methods at Wilson have changed from that of a Southern plantation to "agribusiness."

A new position at the company, "marketing manager," has become about the most important. Robert E. Lee (Bob) Wilson V, 24, is the Lee Wilson Co.'s marketing manager and his primary responsibility is

26

watching the company's trading on the Chicago Board of Trade futures market.

In the last decade, the futures market has become a crucial part of American farming. The reduction of federal price supports and the instability of the market caused by speculators following the recent boom in international trade has caused the market to fluctuate wildly. To protect themselves farmers have had to become market experts. In the last five years, trading volume has more than doubled from 18.3 million contracts in 1972.

"Due to these fluctuations," Bob Wilson says, "profitability today depends as much on careful marketing as it does on your ability to farm well."

Hudson Wren, recently retired general manager of the Wilson holdings and the company's historian, joined the company in January 1945, when much of the Wilson land was farmed with mules. The property then was still divided into 40-acre tracts, he said.

Today the Wilson's 33,000 acres is farmed from two company "headquarters" and three or four men are responsible for every 1,000 acres. When Wren joined the Wilsons, the company had purchased 40 35-horsepower John Deere tractors, Wren said, for $1,600 each. The tractors were replacing mules and, in addition to increasing efficiency, the change was opening up new land for growing cash crops. For each 40-acre unit, eight to 10 acres had to be set aside to grow feed for the mules. As the mules were replaced, acreage for cash crops thus increased 25 per cent.

BLACKS LEAVE AREA

The war and its economic prosperity raised the hopes and expectations of many of the blacks who lived at Wilson, as it did elsewhere in the South, and blacks left the area in record numbers. More tractors were needed to take up the slack caused by the sudden outmigration.

Wren remembers the coming of the tractor and other devices to save labor as "kind of a happy marriage" because the labor was leaving for better opportunities just as mechanization was coming in.

The change at Wilson, and the rest of the country after the initial breakthrough of mechanization, was swift. When steel became plentiful again after World War II, the Wilson Co. ordered more tractors, Wilson farm manager Jim Germany recalled. The efficiency of the tractors pulling two-row cultivation equipment was considered spectacular.

In those early days, a 35-horsepower tractor with a two-row cultivator attached could farm about 30 acres a day. Today's tractors work 120 acres a day pulling six-row equipment. The 85 to 185-hp tractors also pull herbicide and fungicide as they drive, thus making the operation even more efficient. "It has

practically eliminated hand labor," Mike Wilson said.

As fast as tenant farmers would leave the land, Germany recalled, "we would combine land. . . . As fast as the land was available we took it."

HOUSES DISAPPEAR

By 1950, all the 40-, 80- and even 120-acre farm units were gone. The green, red-roofed farmworker houses began to disappear and the company began to reorganize the farm.

In 1950, Robert E. Lee Wilson III took over management of the farm from his father. He changed the organization of the plantation, dividing it into 20 farms averaging about 1,500 acres. These became the responsibility of individual farm managers, each of whom was put in charge of 10 tractor drivers, 15 pieces of heavy farm equipment and as much itinerant hand labor as was necessary during peak seasons. The managers reported to Wilson through a general farm manager. Records and books were kept for each farm and the managers paid the parent company rent for use of the land. Each 1,500-acre plot was worked with 12 to 14 persons working on it year round and hundreds employed during chopping and harvest season.

FARM IN 2 UNITS

Today the 33,000-acre Wilson farm is divided into just two units. Much of the land is farmed by tenant farmers who rent the land from the company, work closely with company officials and share in the profits. An average of three or four men work each 1,500 acres now.

Steve Wilson, the second son is manager, along with Germany, of one of the units. He starts his day at 6 a.m., supervising the fields from his Ford LTD, equipped with a two-way radio. He is consulted by radio about all major decisions concerning the farms in his unit and, when necessary, he drives to the farms to supervise in person.

Also in the 1950s, the company began a policy of land leveling to better use the increasingly expensive equipment. The Wilsons used earth moving machinery to level out the knolls, fill in the low spots and give the acreage a slight, 1½ foot a 1,000 feet tilt to assure proper drainage. In the last 25 years, the Wilsons have graded about 1,000 acres annually at a cost of $75 to $150 an acre and have leveled most of the land.

The Wilsons hope to be able to lessen the odds of danger from drouth. This year they started a $1.5 million project to irrigate 10,000 acres of farmland.

During peak season, the company still employs itinerant hand labor, mostly from Memphis. In 1950, when Robert I. Lee Wilson III took over operation of the company from his father, 3,000 itinerant laborers were brought in to help in peak seasons. In 1964, the company used only about 500 extra hands and in 1976 hired only a few busloads of choppers from Memphis. In the future they may discontinue hiring outside labor altogether. "When the minimum wage goes to $3 an hour, we may not be able to afford to do any chopping at all," Mike Wilson says.

Most of the reduction in hand labor was the result of the introduction in the early 1960s of mechanical cotton pickers.

During planting season, a reduction of labor was made possible in the last decade with the development of a technique that permits herbicide and fungicide to be applied from a tractor at the same time as seeds are planted. Formerly, Steve Wilson said, the herbicide and fungicide were added on separate trips.

A veteran Wilson farm hand, in his 70s, retired five years ago in part because he was unable to handle the new, more complicated tractors that require tractor drivers to mix the chemical herbicides and fungicides for their tractor before they work each field.

But a farmworker's retirement is different at Wilson from what it was in years past. The Wilson Co., at its expense, instituted a pension plan for its employes in 1967. The plan provides, when combined with Social Security, approximately three-quarters of a farm worker's wage at retirement.

Thousands forced to leave land

TOM HAMBURGER*

Above the portals of Washington's Union Station are engraved the words: *"The farm. Best home of the family. Main source of national wealth. Foundation of civilized society. The natural providence."*

REYNO—Herbert Cox, 43, sighed as he gazed from his work at a service station here toward the tractor visible in one of the fields surrounding this Randolph County community. This is the first spring in 26 years that Cox hasn't been farming.

Cox's problems and his dreams give human shape to the recent history of farming in Arkansas. Like hundreds of other farmers across the state, Cox left his life's work after the 1976 harvest, forced out by an economic situation that since 1940 has reduced the number of farm workers in Arkansas by 247,813, or 82.3 per cent, and the number of farms by 72 per cent.

The force that moved Cox off the land is changing the social and economic fabric of Arkansas. Cox is a victim of a 20th Century agricultural revolution.

Rural population in Arkansas dropped 26 per cent between 1950 and 1970 while cities across the state grew rapidly. The growth problem of cities like Little Rock and Pine Bluff (both grew 20 to 30 per cent in the 1960s alone) can be attributed in part to the changing agricultural scene.

Since 1952, farm prices have increased by only 6 per cent, while overhead has risen by 122 per cent.

□ From Arkansas Gazette, Little Rock, Ark., May 16, 1977.
*Reporter of the Gazette staff.

Changes in Arkansas farming 1940-1969

	1969	Per cent change	
		Since '59	Since '40
Total number of farms	60,433	−36.4	−72.1
Average acres per farm	260	+49.9	+211.8
No. of 500 acres	7,517	+21.4	+211.8
Pct. acres owned by blacks	2	−36.1	−50.5
No. farmers, farmhands	146,000	−34.2	−50.9
Total net income per farm	$ 5,499	+42.6	unavbl
Products value (1,000s)	972,837	+20	+132

Figures from *Southern Exposure*, fall, 1974.

The declining profit margins have caused farm operators to increase the size of their operations or go out of business.

When Cox, the son of a farmer, started out 26 years ago he was in good shape. With his father-in-law, he farmed 250 acres, a large tract in those days. He and his wife and two children had a good life. Three other families also earned their livelihood from the farm.

Cox was able to keep up with innovations during his first two decades on the land.

Cox started his farming career with a $2,250 tractor and a two-row cultivator. He had two employes then and "had to work a lot of hours." In 1957, just after Cox lost one of his employes, he bought a more powerful tractor and a new, four-row cultivator for $5,600.

Even with one less man, the new tractor made his farm work easier. He worked with one full-time hand and "had a good life," he recalled.

In 1967, with expensive chemical technology replacing hand labor to control weeds and with generally increased costs of production, Cox had to improve efficiency. So he invested $6,700 in a new six-row cultivator, and his last field hand left to become a truck driver.

Cox's last field hand had company. During the 1960s, according to state census data, agricultural employment in Arkansas declined almost 45 per cent, a decrease of 44,125 workers. The decline was greatest in Delta counties.

Fortunately, there was an increase of 134,218 in nonagricultural employment during the same period.

Census figures show that black farm workers have been displaced at a much faster rate than whites. Of those displaced, 85.5 per cent were nonwhite.

WORKED ALONE

In the 1970s, Cox worked the land alone and did well at first. His landlord raised the rent from a fourth of his crop to a third, but his new six-row cultivator and chemical farming were, if lonely, efficient.

Six years ago, Cox and his family managed to scrape up the capital to buy a combine for about $15,000.

Costs, however, continued to rise. In five years a combine similar to the one Cox bought would sell for about $32,000. Land prices were soaring and diesel fuel went up from 12.5 cents in 1972 to 44 cents last fall. Cox's fellow farmers were selling to larger interests.

Finally the spiral caught up with Herbert Cox. "I had to get out," he says with a shrug. "I wasn't making any money.

"All the farmers were trying to get more land to justify the high equipment. They had to have volume to stay in business.

"I was born and raised on the farm and stayed here my entire life except for two or three years," Cox said.

Cox's post-farming career was relatively easy. He knew auto mechanics and found a job at a local garage.

LACKED SKILL

There are hundreds of other farmworkers who had no such skill and who, like Cox, stayed in hometowns that offered little employment. The displacement of farmers has created a challenge for social service agencies throughout Arkansas.

In Randolph and other agricultural counties, training and placement programs were developed through the Community Service Administration, formerly the Office of Economic Opportunity.

Mrs. Frances Moore, community program director for the Black River Area Development Corporation, works with farm families in a three-county region of northeast Arkansas.

"So many of them are out of jobs and have no other skill and are reluctant to move to cities," she said. There are no estimates on the number of unskilled farm workers in the state, but BRAD has a caseload of hundreds in Randolph county alone.

A nonprofit agency to work with migrant and unemployed farm workers was established with Labor Department funds last year. Known as the Arkansas Council of Farmworkers, the agency handles the cases of 444 farmworkers, providing counseling, job placement and housing assistance.

GROWTH PROBLEMS

Mechanization has created growth problems for cities in farm areas. Such cities have mushroomed, providing jobs for the former farm workers. Walnut Ridge (population 3,800), for example, has about nine factories.

To house displaced farm workers, Walnut Ridge has a crowded row of trailers that rent for about $15 a week. The trailers have a high turnover rate and a high crime rate.

A frequent problem with many of the farm workers is their unwillingness to work through the spring. "Then they leave to find farm work," Mrs. Moore said.

"Its a cycle," she noted. "Grandpa did it so they are going to farm. Even when there isn't work, they would rather stay and get farm work when they can."

Herbert Cox will stay at the service station but he would prefer to be in the fields. "Naturally I would, because I always have been used to farming. No one will ever completely get that out of his system."

Table 2. Frequency and change in farm work force and farm population numbers, United States

Year	Number of farm operators (millions)[1]	Number of hired farm workers (millions)[3]	Total farm employment (millions)[4]	Total farm population (millions)[5]	Net change in farm population through migration (thousands)[7]
1910	6.36[2]	3.38	13.56	32.08	
1935	6.81[2]	2.88	12.73	32.16	−288
1945	5.86[2]	2.12	10.00	24.42	−8008
1954	4.78[2]	2.08	8.65	19.02	−6903
1964	3.16	1.60	6.11	12.95[6]	−4407[6]
1969	2.73	1.18	4.60	10.31[6]	−3033[6]
1974	2.31				
Percentage change					
1935-1969	−60	−59	−64	−68	

Source: Data from Historical statistics of the United States, Washington, D.C., 1975, U.S. Government Printing Office, pp. 88, 96, 449-453, 457, 465, 467-468.
[1]Census of Agriculture data.
[2]Excludes Hawaii and Alaska.
[3]These are simple averages of last of month employment estimates; from composite sources, including the Census of Agriculture and Census of Population; excludes Hawaii and Alaska.
[4]Estimated in the same way as "Number of hired farm workers" but also includes family workers—farm operators and members of their families doing farm work without wages.
[5]Estimates from composite sources.
[6]Includes Hawaii and Alaska.
[7]Census of Population figures, including net change through reclassification of residence (even though occupants have not moved); figures are for 5-year periods.

The black immigrants

BEN H. BAGDIKIAN

At 6:40 on the evening of March 4, 1967, Walter Austin, who had lived for almost half a century within 60 miles of the Mississippi, actually saw the river for the first time. Still wearing his four-dollar overalls, he was sitting in the back seat of an automobile, jammed in with four other members of his family, crossing a high bridge. His eyes were red with the fatigue of the last 38 sleepless hours. But he stared down through the dusk at the aluminum reflection of the greatest body of water he had ever seen, and he said the same thing that rose out of him earlier when someone told him that in New York City there is a building 102 stories high: a low, slow, "Good gracious!" The car moved across the bridge, its occupants turning to keep in

□ From Saturday Evening Post, July 15, 1967, pp. 25-29, 64-68.

sight the massive river that had been the source of life and of suffering for five generations of Austin families. And then the river was gone, and they turned forward again to look uncertainly into the darkness ahead.

It was the most momentous crossing of their lives. From that time on their experiences would be like nothing they or their ancestors had ever known. That morning they had been just another impoverished Negro family working the fields on a remote Mississippi plantation. But at noon, with hardly a backward glance, they had slammed the doors of the two cars driven by a relative and a friend and headed north for a new life in the city. They carried all they could from the last hog they would ever butcher—the salted jaw, a slab of salt pork, two hams, 100 pounds of lard—

stashed in the car like sacred objects. Riding with them as well was a new and confusing collection of hopes and fears.

That day the Austins—father, mother, five children aged 17 to 6, and one grandchild—added their eight lives to a flow of Americans that is one of the great un-sung sagas of human history. It is an uprooting of more people in a shorter period of time than almost any peacetime migration known to man, a vast trans-fer that is changing America.

In a wicked moment Franklin Roosevelt once put a chill on a convention of the Daughters of the American Revolution by greeting them, "My fellow immi-grants," and it is true enough that one thing all Ameri-cans share is a background of migration. The Ameri-can Indians were immigrants, probably from Asia; the forebears of most white Americans came from Eu-rope in the largest intercontinental human movement in history; the ancestors of most American Negroes were the 400,000 Africans brought into the South as slaves between 1619 and 1808. Now the descendants of these Negro immigrants are making another mass move, this time within the United States.

In this generation, some four million Negroes have left the South, most of them for six states: California, Illinois, Michigan, New York, Ohio and Pennsylvania. Where 50 years ago three quarters of Negro Americans were in rural areas, today three quarters are in cities. And the tide still runs strong. In 1960 there were four American cities that were 40 percent Negro; by 1970 there will be 14, and practically every city of any size will have a core of migrant Negroes, piling up, des-perate. Like previous migrants, they are truly aliens, used to different customs, a different climate, essen-tially a different language, different everything. Their ghettos are countries within countries, in which nearly every inhabitant feels foreign to what sur-rounds him. But what surrounds the city Negroes is more hostile than anything any white alien has ever encountered. For them the ghetto perimeters are closed as tightly as foreign borders.

This exodus of southern Negroes is one of the most dramatic demographic events of the midcentury, yet it is a clandestine operation. When the Negro goes, he goes suddenly and secretly, because he is afraid of the white man. Generally, the Negro is a share-cropper, living in a feudal, noncash economy—his plantation owner provides him land and credit. When the harvest is over, the plantation owner announces that, after deducting the cost of food, fuel, seed, fer-tilizer and other things the sharecropper has obtained on credit, the sharecropper's profit is such and such. Or, much more likely, the owner tells him he owes the plantation as much as $100 or $500.

To the Negro this kind of debt is so astronomical

that no one, laborer or landlord, expects that it will ever be paid off in cash. Only by working off the debt can the Negro family be clear. As manual farm work gives way to huge machines, the means of paying back the debt disappears. When that happens, most plan-tation owners are resigned to seeing their tenants leave.

Even so, there is often a question of who gets the paid-for television or kitchen range, in light of the debt, the landlord or the departing family's friends and relatives? And the rural Negro has been taught in the harshest way never to make an important de-cision without the approval of his landlord. So when he moves North, the Negro usually goes unannounced, a final gesture of rebellion and fear.

The families themselves seldom know when they will go until the moment comes. Moving vans are un-known to the dirt roads of the rural South, and de-parture frequently depends on the car of a visiting relative. Thus the times of greatest population loss in the South are the holidays—Christmas, New Year's, Memorial Day, July 4, Labor Day, any long weekend when city relatives can make the long trip down from the North. And at funerals. The South loses more than the dead at funerals. A brother from Chicago who comes down for the ceremony, having driven the 12 hours since work let out on Friday, arrives Saturday morning before dawn, and suddenly some of the youngsters, or the whole family, decide to go back with him.

Sometimes the mail arrives with the awaited pass-port: bus tickets sent by older children in the city. The next day the younger children drop out of school, and after dark that night the family heads for the station, carrying in their hands everything with which they will start their new life.

Or a mother takes the youngest child to "visit my sick aunty in the city," where she gets a job and sends the tickets back for her husband and the older chil-dren, and the next Saturday night the husband pays a neighbor $1.50 to drive him and his children and their suitcases to the station. Morning on the plantation finds the shack abandoned, and another rural family has entered the central mass of an American metrop-olis.

The decision to abandon a way of life, even one you love, can seem very simple.

"Christmas morning, last Christmas morning," Walter Austin said in his deep and vibrant voice, "I got up and I cried." Weeping did not seem to go with the dark, weather-beaten face. Austin is 48, has black hair without gray and a black moustache, and wears rugged-looking overalls and rubber boots clotted with mud. "I cried, and then I thanked the Lord to be living, because I could have been gone, and I was glad to be here, and all my children well. And the children had food. It put me in debt, but they had food, special Christmas food. For Christmas I saw to it that they had fresh apples and oranges."

Over and over he returned to the subject of moving to the city where, he knew, it takes even more money than in the country.

"Yes, yes, but you need *some* money here. You need *some* money here. I can't sit here with eight children" —he kept referring to eight children, though his two oldest sons had left for the city within the last two months—"I can't have my children around me and nothing to give them to eat. I feel bad in the morning. I feel *bad* in the morning, hearing the kids get up crying because they want something to eat and I can't find enough for them to eat. Then I feel bad. Then I feel like crying."

So the easy decision is really whether to eat or not. But there is a harder question for older people who know only their rural life and who love it. Walter Austin and his wife, Bessie, who is also 48, were born in Holmes County, Miss., but 10 years ago moved the 50 miles to Merigold, Miss., in Bolivar County.

"I don't want to leave Mississippi," Austin said. "I never been out of Mississippi except one time in my whole life, and that was only one week. Tell you the truth, up to the sixteenth day of March, 19 and 57, I never been out of Holmes County. I never been in no kind of trouble, never paid a fine, never been to court. I'll peck on wood"—he reached over the torn leatherette arm of the chair in his living room and rapped the bare wood floor of the shack with his knuckles— "I've been just plain Walter all my life."

We had spent hours talking country-versus-city, and there wasn't much doubt where he stood, given a free choice and enough food.

"I likes to farm. I loves it. I can raise my chickens, raise my hog, I have my garden with peas and beans and potatoes and squash and cucumbers and onions and greens. You can't do that in town. You can't raise a hog in town. I'm just a home child. I just don't want to leave home unless I have to. I'll be frank with you, I like the country."

He lifted his leather cap and scratched his hair.

"I know in the city you's supposed to have an education. If you got me a job in the morning and I was supposed to separate the salt from the sugar, I couldn't do it, not if they was in the same kind of bag. I couldn't do it, Cap'n, because I can't read."

His wife, with a soft face drawn with worry, and a blurry right eye blinded by a stroke seven years ago, told about a visit she made once to Chicago.

"I stayed with my husband's brother. I didn't even walk on the outside. That's all I know, what I saw from his place. I just couldn't stand that noise.

"I'd be satisfied working right here. If we had work. If I had enough to live on and be comfortable, oh, I'd stay. I'd stay."

What did she mean, "comfortable"?

"Nothing extra. You come into this world with nothing, and when you leave you can't carry anything away. I need some covers—quilts, you know—comfortable mattresses, some beds don't need to be propped up. I would like some clothes."

She thought for a moment and then worried that I might misunderstand her desire for clothes. She didn't mean for herself (she bought her last dress in 1956, her husband had never bought a suit and limited his new clothes to a four-dollar pair of overalls each year).

"I mean for the children. And nothing fancy, just not all sewed up. Not half-priced or leftovers but good common clothes, you know? Not eight-dollar dresses, just good three-dollar dresses. What I need most is extra underclothes and socks. We have enough outerclothes so the kids can wear clean things to school, but the children have to wash their underwear and socks every night so they'll be clean in the morning. If they had extra sets they wouldn't have to wash them every night."

Walter Austin looked in mock severity at the apple of his eye, his 10-year-old daughter, Bessie.

"I gets up at four o'clock every morning. At four o'clock I'm up, Sunday, Saturday, rain, sleet or snow. I put on my clothes, wash my face, go out and feed my hog, feed my chickens, and then I come back in and see if the kids has washed their clothes before they went to bed, and if they didn't, then I gets them up early so they can do it before schooltime and give their underclothes and socks a chance to dry in time. Ain't that so, Bessie?"

Bessie obviously was the most recent transgressor, and she smiled sheepishly and said to her father, "Suh?" By "early," Austin explained, he meant the backsliding child rose at 5 A.M. instead of the usual 6.

To Mrs. Austin the prospect of the city held out the deadly danger that children would learn to drink. Walter Austin would miss his farming and would no longer experience the pride of running and repairing a large combine. But the children had different thoughts. Frances, 17, whose formal, bland expression masked a quick and taunting wit, was fatalistic—"I think things would be just the same whether I go or stay"—but she looked excited when she described how well-dressed her girl friends and relatives were when they returned from the city. David, 14, also wore an outer mask of solemnity, but his black-cloth visor cap worn at a rakish angle hinted at the adolescent itch. "I just don't want to farm. No, suh, I just don't want to be a farmer." Hearing about the city, Bessie simply glowed wordlessly. Her younger sister, Zettie

Mae, 8, and brother, Wendell, 6, looked bewildered and polite.

But their parents kept reminding themselves how much better off they are now than they were in their youth. Neither of them had ever lived in so good a house as this one. It had a tight roof, the five rooms were lined with wallboard. There was a cold-water faucet in the kitchen and a privy out back (some plantation shacks lack even a privy). Three open gas grates heated the place in winter, and they had some chairs, bedsteads, and from a few good years in the early 1960's a television set and a freezer, all paid for.

"My mother's house back in Holmes County," Walter Austin said, "you could see the chickens through the floor and the blue sky through the roof. And when I was a kid, what I had to eat for the whole day was one slice of hog jaw and corn bread with flour gravy, sometimes not even that.

"Now here's David here, fourteen years old and he's in—what grade is it? Eight—yes, the eighth grade. When I was seven years old I was trying to go to school but, Lordy, I just had to work. When I was seven years old I had to walk three miles before sunup, get a mule and feed it and then work that mule in the fields until dark, all of that for only eight dollars a month.

"I married Bessie, here, the only wife I've ever known, when we were both seventeen, and the day we got married we ate corn bread and flour gravy. We started with an old wood stove, a bed, a pig and a calf my mother-in-law give me."

The family worked for 20 years on a plantation in Holmes County. At the end of that time, Austin was driving a tractor for $4.50 a day, during the season and when weather was good. Mrs. Austin and the children did sharecropping for the same plantation, planting, chopping (weeding) and picking a cotton crop. They provided the labor and the landlord provided the land and their rent-free house. The landlord also gave them credit for their share of the cost of their seed and fertilizer and lent them $40 a month for food until the crop was harvested and sold.

"The four kids and I," Mrs. Austin said, "that last year, did twenty-six bales. We had to keep the kids out of school to do it. But I got tired, just tired going with the crops, weighing my own cotton, tromping it, putting it on the trailer. I got so tired. As a woman, I couldn't farm no more." At that time she had seven living children, ages 19 to 4, the older ones working in the field, the younger ones brought out in boxes to play all day near the cotton rows. Two infants died early, and a daughter later died of leukemia at the age of 16. "And all we got for that year and twenty-six bales of cotton was a hundred and fifty dollars. The four kids and I, from May to October. When I told the boss man I just couldn't sharecrop with the four kids

no more, he told us we'd have to move. That's when we come down here."

(The average price farmers received for cotton in 1956 was $152 a bale, so the Austins' half share apparently was $1,976, minus $480 lent for food and their share of seed and fertilizer; neither they nor anyone they knew ever saw an accounting.)

Walter's brother heard of an empty house in Bolivar County, and they moved, and though they loved Holmes County better than anyplace else on earth, they considered themselves much improved. People had a little bit more. In Holmes, median income for the rural Negro family was $895 a year; in Bolivar it was $1,198. The Austins didn't know that, but they sensed it, and they sensed that their new plantation owner and agent were more benign. And the house was better.

Life was not easy, of course. They had more children. Their daughter, Jean, had leukemia and spent the last six weeks of her life in University Hospital in Jackson, 100 miles away, where her father lived, penniless, in a chair in her room, fed by compassionate nurses. After she died, he returned home to find that his daughter, Bessie, had been born, and his wife was back in another hospital with the stroke that blinded her right eye. But, then, life had never been easy, and their family kept its strong bonds and Walter Austin his mastery within the family.

The world of the Austins in Mississippi was simultaneously enormous and tiny. Their little home was a dot in the Mississippi delta, a flat ocean of land made from the silt of centuries of flooding, land as rich as any on earth. Square mile after square mile of cotton fields stretch out, in the winter a rusty sea with here and there a scrap of windblown paper snagged on a dry stalk like a whitecap. The huge landscape is punctuated by an occasional small town, a cotton gin, a stand of oaks, and the clusters of Negro shacks in the fields. Like most southern rural Negroes, the Austins lived on a dirt road without a name, in a house without a number. But though the view seems endless, their neighbors were few, their life concentrated around their own family.

"Watch for a burned-out house on the highway," a relative instructed me, "turn left and go in three miles and look for a brown house with a tan 1959 Chevy that's broke down."

I was lucky to have met the Austins before they decided to move and to be with them when they changed their minds, for their experience told much about the thoughts and emotions of families facing the great migration. Before he knew he would go, Walter Austin had uppermost in his mind the improvements he had seen since his youth and all the things he liked in the country and feared in the city. He was genuinely undecided. The plantation owner had told him there would be no guaranteed work the next year because their cotton acreage was being rented to a big agricultural operator. But the owner held out the possibility of a job in a machine shop in a nearby town, or, at least, some days of casual labor in the fields.

The pressure increased, especially during the winter, when work ceases in the delta fields. Merchants knew at once that Austin had been put in the doubtful category. Where credit for food, bottled gas and doctors had once been immediate, everyone wanted cash. Families around them were going away. Ten years earlier 50 families worked and lived on that plantation. Now there were six. Within the last year the two houses on either side of the Austins had been vacated and torn down, and the skies of the delta now were regularly streaked with smoke from empty shanties being burned down to clear the ground for growing. The smoke got thicker after a one-dollar-an-hour wages-and-hours law for agricultural workers began last winter. When motorists stopped one day to watch a spectacular fire consuming a plantation shack, the agent in charged called out, "Wages and hours got that one."

Yet the Austins hung on. He was a good worker. His plantation agent, within the limits of feudalistic white supremacy, was a decent man. Each day Austin rose at 4, went to the plantation headquarters at 7. If there was work, he returned after dark, $10-minus-debts the richer. If there was no work, as was most often the case, he went home and worked in his yard and garden.

Mrs. Austin rose at 5:30 to start breakfast of sausage and corn bread, if they had it. The children rose at 6 and got ready for the 7:20 school bus, if they all had shoes. After school they played with the children of the few remaining neighbors, did homework, had supper of greens and salt pork, and were in bed around 8.

The end of the week was different. On a typical Saturday, David lighted a fire in the backyard under an ancient iron pot and heated water for the washing. Frances did the wash in a round, wringer-style washing machine on the back stoop and hung it on the "clothesline"—two strands, one old electrical cable, the other old barbed wire. David helped his father clean up the backyard. The hog grunted, and Walter Austin rubbed its head with his glove—"Baby, you want your breakfast?"—and told David to fetch the slops. Instantly at the trough were the pig, three puppies, two cats, four kittens and two roosters.

The three younger children, bundled in bright donated clothes, played hopscotch on packed earth at the end of some cotton rows, tiny scarlet figures under a huge sky, chased by their puppies, Frisco, Fuzzy and Alaska.

In the evening they look at television. "I can't read,"

Walter Austin explained. "so I have to get the news and weather on the TV."

And they sang, Bessie leading and her mother and the others following. They coaxed David to do his imitation of a local preacher. His father called gaily to his children in the living room, using the private names he dreams up at their birth, and he alone uses: "Preacher" for Wendell, "Chicken" for Zettie Mae, "Barbie" for Bessie, "Ben" for David, and "Root" for Frances.

"Ben," he said, "Let's hear the one, 'Your God and My Love.'"

During the singing, the three youngest children played school with the most magnificent Christmas gift any Austin ever got, a plastic-and-chrome children's table-and-chair set from two years ago. As always, Bessie was the teacher, sitting at the table, facing Zettie Mae and Wendell in chairs.

"Wendell," she said imperiously, "spell . . ." and she said what sounded like, "gown."

Wendell, puzzled: "Gown?"

Bessie, impatiently, "Yes, 'gown.'"

Wendell, timidly, "Like, 'machine gown'?"

Bessie, outraged, "No, Wendell, no! Like, 'Yesterday they went. Now they is gown.'"

Everyone laughed, though teachers know that this kind of misunderstanding is significant in explaining the difficulties in reading and learning among children whose natural tongue is not standard English.

Later there were baths, in a galvanized washtub put in Frances's room, the most private one, with a heater.

During the evenings the Austins constantly churned over their view of the future. "I wants to stay, I wants to stay," Walter Austin said. "If I could just get that machine-shop job or work in the boss man's pig farm where they works rain or shine. But how in the world am I going to feed eight kids on fifteen dollars a week?"

Periodically he'd resign himself to moving. "But after the snow is off up there. I is naked here, and up north I'm going to freeze."

None of us was prepared for what happened. One Sunday, photographer Matt Herron and I decided to visit the Austins' small church in the fields. Eight years ago 70 people would attend but now, with the migration, only 20. As we drove we were surprised to see Walter Austin and David out on the road, flagging us down. Walter Austin looked grave, his face gray with tension.

"They don't want you to go to the church because they's afraid it'll get burned down. The deacons, they ask would you please not go."

He explained that the day before, the plantation agent announced that Austin would have to move, telling him angrily, "Those white men kept coming and coming and coming to your place, and that's more than I can take. I know what they're doing. They're down here organizing a union. The state's full of them. So you better leave." Austin could take some time, the agent said, but he had to go.

The concern in Walter Austin's face was justified: To fall out of favor, angrily and castastrophically, with the boss man, especially for unauthorized dealings with outsiders, implied peril to life and limb.

The nearest public phone was six miles away. We drove to it and Austin called a married daughter in Springfield, Ill. She was alarmed. She urged her father to come that night "before something happens, please, Daddy." But Austin's voice was calm as he spoke on the phone. "No, baby, I need a week to sell my freezer and my hog and take care of things."

We drove Walter and David Austin back to their home and went to see the plantation agent, a round-faced man in his 60's. He and his wife, the plantation bookkeeper, were civil though they were often angry. They recited our movements in the state for the last week; it is not difficult for plantation operators in Mississippi to keep track of suspicious strangers. They told us they knew we were stirring up "our people" and forming a union. Furthermore, we had violated common rules of courtesy. "You can drive down that road," he said, "and you can maybe stop at a house once. But to keep coming and coming and coming and staying after dark—that's too much."

After about an hour we persuaded him we were not organizers, and we parted in a friendly way. In a sense, this was unusual, but what the agent did was even more so. The next day he went to Walter Austin and apologized for falsely accusing him and said he could stay. Austin says he thanked the agent, but he had decided to move, and so he told the agent that he was going through with it. "Boss Man, you was dissatisfied with Walter, so Walter's going to move."

The agent told him he didn't have to sneak off like all the others. And Walter Austin didn't.

The next Saturday morning the Austin place looked like the center of a carnival. A total of 23 neighbors and friends were in and out of the house, up on the roof dismantling the motorized television antenna (bought for $149 four years ago and now sold for $5), carrying out the freezer (bought for $400 and now sold for $50). There was gaiety and almost no sentimentality.

Walter Austin, quietly, calmly, and with humor, left no doubt who was in charge. At 7 he had gone to the agent's house, returned a ladder, a set of wrenches, and paid back $7 the agent had lent him last fall so David could have shoes for school. Neither one said anything, but they both knew Walter Austin was leaving that day.

Austin quietly directed his son-in-law and his oldest son, who had driven down in the night from Springfield. Wandering through the yard was Walter's 29-year-old brother, who worked on the same plantation, and toward the end he said almost to himself, "I'm the only one left." When the time came, Walter and his brother looked at each other briefly, and Walter said, "Goody-bye, son."

Frances and her boyfriend talked constantly, arms linked. An old parlor chair, the one with the torn leatherette covering, couldn't be taken, and they gave it to Frances's boyfriend, who carried it out. Walter said, "You get to keep the chair, Robert, but you'd like to keep Frances."

A recent plantation acquaintance tried too often to engage Walter's attention, and finally in exasperation Walter said to him politely, "Well, good-bye and come see me."

"How will I know where you'll be?" the acquaintance said too eagerly. "I don't even know where you're going."

Austin: "I'm going yonder."

Acquaintance: "Where's yonder?"

Austin, nodding northward: "Up."

Finally, Walter Austin walked through his stripped house. Gone from the living-room walls were the photographs of his children and some of his 15 grandchildren; the shadowbox of Jesus with the burned-out electric bulb; the pink plastic cross with the chrome crucifix; the small window frame containing postcards of Cherokee Indians and a table of decimal equivalents; and the too-bright picture of a romantic thatched-roof cottage surrounded by seed-catalogue flowers with the legend. GOD SHALL SUPPLY ALL YOUR NEEDS.

Walter Austin looked around and saw one remaining artifact on the faded blue wall—a calendar of the "Delta Burial Corporation. Seldom Equaled, Never Excelled," the society to which they paid $3.75 a month to guarantee them a decent Mississippi funeral. He hesitated a moment, then lifted the calendar off its nail and handed it to Bessie. "Barbie, in the green car."

In the kitchen he looked at the stove he had just bought on time but not made any payments on, at two lamps he had long paid for, the wringer washing machine for which he paid $200 and owed only $95 more, all left behind to be picked up by the dealer in town. Asked why he was leaving behind the lamps and the half-paid-for machine, he said, "I'm not looking for trouble. I'm just looking for a little peace and a little love."

And then he left, and when the car engines were started, Walter Austin never looked back.

As the cars moved rapidly northward, one could

almost feel the arguments for staying sinking out of sight and the ones for going coming to the top. Before, the need for food and money had dominated conversation. Now, deeper things, long repressed, came to the surface. I asked if he had any fear of facing the strange life in the city at his age.

"Well, I guess so. But it had to come. It had to come. Back in Mississippi I was forty-eight years old, but I was still like a child. I needed the white man for protection. If the colored man had that he could keep out of lots of trouble. He could get credit. He could do lots of things, lots of things. But he just had to have that protection. If you didn't have that protection all kinds of things could happen, all *kinds* of things, just like could happen to a child without a daddy."

His eyes were red and tired, but he talked on.

"You'd get up every morning, and you'd ask the boss man what to do, and every morning he'd tell you, just like you was a child. When you got your pay, he'd take out of it what he wanted for what you owed. He didn't ask you. Now I had a good boss man, for Mississippi, and if I had something special now and then, I could ask him to let me have all my pay, and he'd let me have it. But usual thing, he'd take out what he wanted. He handled most of your bills.

"Now I figure in the North one man pays you, and then you got to take care of your bills yourself. I know a man can get into a mess of trouble handling his own bills, but I reckon that ought to be up to him, to learn and decide himself. But not on a Mississippi plantation. They figured I was a child."

He described the tensions and treacheries on a plantation where all are struggling for approval and survival, and helped explain the too-eager acquaintance that morning. "You always had to watch those other boys on the plantation and be careful who you trusted and who you didn't."

You knew Walter Austin had not been caught up in the civil-rights movement because he still referred to Negroes in the white supremacists' term, "boys," and called all white men "boss man" or "captain."

"If the boss man was always giving the easy jobs to a boy, and he and The Man always had their heads together, then you better be careful with that boy, 'cause he's probably telling the boss everything he knows about you. So on the plantation you learn to be careful what you say, what you do, and who you speaks to. And if the boss man asks you about somebody else, and you don't want to be telling him no lies, you got to tell him you just don't know nothing."

The cars were still in Mississippi, but in Walter Austin's mind already "here" was North.

"Here you can be with who you wants and ride with who you wants."

The Sunday before, while we rode to the phone booth, we had to stop for gas. It was what is known in Mississippi as an "integrated car," and the white gas-station proprietor had a common reaction: He fixed a menacing, unblinking stare at Walter Austin and kept it on him as he deliberately and slowly wiped every window of the car. To a Negro this stare, whether in an integrated car or behind a voting table, is a serious threat.

As the landscape streamed by, it caught different eyes at different times. Walter Austin would turn whenever we passed a small farm on its own plot of land. When we began to pass large used-car lots, a small smile leaked onto David's solemn face. Frances watched the increasingly large neighborhoods of ranch houses with their lawns, the largest number of middle-class houses she had ever seen, and the first not associated with the plantation hierarchy. "I'd like a house like that," she said once, "with one of those checkerboard tiles on the floor." Did she think she'd ever live in one? She thought about it seriously and then said, "Yes, I think I will."

Walter Austin and I joked a little over his calling me "Captain," which I had asked him not to do. At the time, two weeks earlier, he had said, "I know, but it's hard to stop. Up north you say, 'yas suh,' and they looks at you like you was crazy. But when you're brought up from the time you can talk, and your mammy makes you go back and say it every time you forgets to say 'yas suh,' then it's hard to stop all of a sudden."

Periodically, he would lapse into "captain" or "boss man" when we talked. But after we crossed the Mississippi River, he never did it again.

The cars went into the foggy night toward Springfield, Ill., with a homing instinct that affects almost every migrant. It was common during the foreign immigrations to have whole villages—from Sicily, Russia, Poland, Germany, Ireland—be transplanted to some particular American city. The same thing now happens within the country. There are counties in West Virginia from which most departing people go to Cincinnati, others from which they go to Cleveland. In Chicago there are two blocks made up largely of Holmes County Mississippians. The compass of the migrating poor is seldom fixed by a job already arranged and waiting, but by the presence of close relatives and friends.

In his youth, Walter Austin cut wood with a friend in Holmes County. During World War II the friend got a job on the Illinois Central Railroad, and took a room in Springfield. Later he bought a couple of rooming houses there and retired. From time to time the railroad man would return to Holmes County. Once he came to attend a wedding of his cousin with Walter Austin's cousin. When the cousins were evicted from their plantation, they moved to Springfield into a flat owned by the railroad man. In 1956 Austin's sister was told by her plantation owner that her family had to move, so the sister went to Springfield where she stayed with her cousin and got a job in Kennedy's Laundry. Four years later Austin's oldest daughter, Etoyre, decided there was no future in Mississippi, so when her aunt came from Springfield for a funeral, the daughter took her older children and rode back to Springfield. She also got a job in Kennedy's Laundry and found a flat, saved some money and sent bus tickets to her husband. They both saved some more money and sent tickets for their remaining small children and a full-fare ticket for the next oldest daughter, Mae Jessie, to accompany them. So Mae Jessie did this, taking her own daughter, an infant (no fare), and leaving her other children behind with her mother. She, too, got a job in Kennedy's Laundry, found a flat, and sent down tickets for her children and one for her mother to accompany them and visit.

Last winter Mae Jessie drove down for a New Year's visit, and the oldest Austin son, Walter Jr., decided to ride back with her. Walter Jr., unmarried, got a job sorting hides. A month later, Etoyre, the other married daughter in Springfield, drove down for a vist with her parents. Walter Austin's second oldest son, Jimmie Lee, who was married and had three children, was telling his parent he just didn't see how he could get enough work to support his family in Mississippi when the sister's car unexpectedly drew up in front. Jimmy Lee rushed to the window, saw who it was and said, "Daddy, I'm gone." He drove back to Springfield and got a job washing dishes, staying with his sister. A week later he drove down with his brother-in-law and fetched his wife and children. His wife got a job in Kennedy's Laundry.

Like an endless chain, whole tribes go link by link to some city where a base has been established. When the crisis came to Walter Austin, there was never any doubt where he would go, and when he got there, there were suddenly a total of 36 Austins within a scant half mile.

It was a scene of joy and relief, at 2 o'clock of a Sunday morning, when the two cars finally arrived at their destination, and the Austins of Merigold, Miss., became the Austins of Springfield, Ill., share-croppers no longer but city dwellers now. Standing wearily on the sidewalk, they looked up with awe at Jimmy Lee's house, a neat, white clapboard with five spacious rooms and its own bathtub and toilet. Waiting inside were the older daughters who had come North earlier, and they helped sort the newcomers and send them to nearby homes to sleep the remaining hours of the night.

That day Walter Austin's family made the rounds of the relatives' homes. At Walter's sister's there were guitars, singing and joshing. The older women put on their wigs and urged Frances to try one. Bashfully, she put one on and imitated the modeling she had seen on television. Suddenly she was changed. One moment she was the shy country girl, the next a poised young women. She lifted off the wig and said quietly, "I'm going to get one."

The next morning Jimmy Lee's wife took Frances with her to Kennedy's Laundry and introduced her to the boss, George Bochmer. He said, "I like to hire Mississippi people. They're good workers." So 29 hours after her arrival in the city, Frances Austin, working beside white women, was feeding flatwork into a presser and earning more than her father ever did in his 41 years of labor.

That same morning Mrs. Austin and her older daughter went out looking for a flat. In Jimmy Lee's house there were seven preschool children, crying, running, fighting, all tended by a new baby sitter, Walter Austin. He was no longer in overalls. Someone had lent him a white shirt, a pair of slacks and a too-large suit jacket. He stood in the middle of the kitchen with an open carton of milk. He cried out, "Hush, child," to one girl, and tried to restrain another one who was pounding a nail file into the linoleum with a hairbrush. "Soon as they find a place for us to stay, I'm hoping to find a job. Some kind of a job." Then, milk carton still in hand, he looked with bewilderment at the children. "This is one job I do not like."

The Austins had a small start. Four days later they found a pinched five-room flat for $65, where the whole family sleeps in just three beds and the beds are the only furniture in the place. The day after that, Walter Austin got a job that his son Jimmy Lee first had when he moved—mopping floors and washing dishes in a restaurant at $40 a week. His 17-year-old daughter earns $5 more than he does.

The Austins are in real need. They require medical attention, furniture, city clothes, and Walter Austin needs a job that will buy these things. But in some ways they are luckier than many migrants. For one thing, almost by chance, they followed the newer, less hopeless migratory routes from the rural South—more and more to the West and more and more to the medium-size cities. In the smaller cities the rate of growth is often better than in the huge ones, the Negro districts are distinct but lack the oppressiveness of square miles of squalor, and in a smaller community it is easier to match available men with available jobs.

Walter Austin had just left Merigold, Miss., which has a population of 602. When he heard that his new home, Springfield, and 86,000 people, of whom 5,000 are Negroes, he opened his eyes wide and said, "Good gracious!"

In Chicago there are a million Negroes.

II

The fact that migrants move means they hope for something better. The hope lasts remarkably long, so long that it seems a miracle in such places as the ghettos of cities like Chicago. Alice Perkins has been there almost two years now; she is wiser to the struggle than the Austins, harder to the squalor, but she still hopes for something better, hopes in the diminishing optimism that time and the ghetto steadily wear away.

She is a statuesue woman of 27 with a husky voice and a sardonic expression, and she lives in a second-floor flat on Van Buren Street in the middle of Chicago's West Side ghetto. Official statistics show that in 1960, eighty percent of all dwellings in her block were substandard and 30 percent lacked normal plumbing, but you don't need statistics to get the message: rubble and garbage is spread in vacant lots, the stairways are dark and dirty. Her door is untypically painted a fresh green, and on it her husband has used gay, red Christmas tape to letter out most of his name: HARRY PERKI—. But the door, typically, is locked several different ways and shows wounds from having been forced open several different ways. Inside there are rats the size of cats, and the children sleep crossways, usually four to a bed. The younger ones are normally barefoot and half bare-bodied so that the three older children can be properly dressed for school. Yet Alice Perkins and her husband have no doubt about the decision she made in the middle of a cotton field two years ago.

That day in August, 1965, she had, as usual, got up at 5:30 in their three-room shack, washed her face in a pail in the kitchen and, without breakfast, gone out to get on the back of a truck. In the field a mile away she dragged a bag nine feet long, putting in cotton balls, the ones a machine left behind. Early in the day the plantation agent started yelling that the cotton she and the others had picked was full of burrs and sticks. At noon she walked a half mile to a store and ate 10 Saltines, five pieces of baloney and a soda pop. Back in the field, The Man kept after them. "You-all are pullin' this goddamn cotton. I'm paying you to pick it, and you're just pullin' the goddamn stuff."

Toward the end of the afternoon he was still at it, and Alice Perkins said, "I don't have to take this no more. I'm going." She said it to herself.

She got back home that night at 6 o'clock. She had picked 84 pounds and made $2.10 minus lunch, for 11 hours. She cooked turnip greens and a pound of salt pork for her five children and her husband, who came home after dark from driving a tractor at $6 a day. The children went to bed, the oldest one, Beatrice, then 7, in a cot in their front room, the infant in the double bed she and her husband used, also in the front room. Her husband and two neighbors played a game of cards, pit-a-pat, also in the front room.

Without telling Harry about it, she found two pieces of lined paper and a short pencil, and she wrote a letter to her aunt in Chicago. "I can't stand it no more," she wrote, "please, Aunty, send me a ticket." She walked in the dark across the dirt road to a neighbor's house where she got an envelope and put the letter and a nickel in her rural mailbox. This was a Wednesday. Tuesday the tickets arrived. Then she told her husband she wanted to take their three youngest children and go. If she found no job in two weeks she would return. He listened quietly and said, "OK, baby."

So Alice Perkins joined the silent tide that goes by car, by bus, and still by that old reliable carrier of the cotton Negro, the Illinois Central Railroad.

On the platforms of the South they are there every day. The toothless old Negro woman in men's trousers, rubbers over slippers, a ragged coat, scarf over her head, a cardboard box tied with twine, the last tenacious root of a family gone earlier.

The neatly dressed woman in her 30's comforting her weeping teen-age daughter, "Don't cry, baby. Take care of Daddy and the kids and I'll be back when I find a place."

The young woman in her 20's, so like Alice Perkins, with three wide-eyed preschool children, hugging older people on the platform and then, as the locomotive sounds its mournful southern cry, mounting the steps with her children, her eyes moist.

The old Negro porter watches the flat countryside stream monotonously by, as he has for 32 years on this run.

"It started in 1947. This train went through the delta, and there was nothing but black faces, for years and years and years. I used to wonder, "Where are they coming from? How can there be anybody left? My God, they must be coming right out of the ground. They got to stop sometime.'

"Well, couple of years ago it seemed to slack off. You begin to see some whites now. Used to be twenty-thirty Negroes for every white on this train. Now it's more like three-to-one."

But there are still Negroes. At Durant, the station stop nearest the heart of the delta, more country people get on with boxes and old suitcases. As the train pulls out, it leaves others behind. Through the rain-splattered window you see the lonely Negro shack with three tiny children frozen in place, one boy hanging clothes on a line, his hand stopped in the act as he stares, another boy with a water pail in his hand, and at the pump a skinny-legged girl, her arm high on the motionless pump handle as the water shrivels to a trickle—all watching the speeding persimmon-and-brown cars with the big picture windows bearing dry, warm people holding passports.

The passport is a yellow ticket one-and-a-half-inches long that reads, "Illinois Central R.R. Co., coach, ticket, Durant, Miss. to CHICAGO, ILL. Good in coaches only, for one passage. . . ." It costs $23.65 for adults, $11.83 for young children, and for the people who got on in Durant with a typical family, if they earned average Negro wages, it took every cent they earned for six weeks. To collect that much money, when food is scarce, and to decide to migrate is a decision that has torn millions of families in this generation.

Alice Perkins took that other mode of the Underground Railroad—the bus. On a Wednesday before the Christmas holidays, Harry Perkins got a letter from Alice in Chicago. He had to quit school in the fifth grade and can't read (Alice went through ninth grade), so he paid a neighbor 50 cents to drive him the two miles to his mother-in-law's house where she read the letter. Tickets for him and the two older children were inside. The next day the children turned in their school books. Saturday morning Harry went to work as usual. That night he got his week's pay, $36 minus $10 taken out toward his debts. By now it was dark. He walked home, pulled out a footlocker he had quietly bought in Clarksdale for $7.95 two weeks ago, put in two bedspreads, one quilt, two sheets, three pairs of pants, two shirts and three hats for the children. He paid the neighbor 50 cents again to drive him and the children to his mother-in-law's, where her son drove them to the 9:30 night bus from Clarksdale.

The children had never been to Clarksdale (population, 21,000), and when they saw it Harry Jr., 6, said, "Daddy, is this Chicago?"

On the bus was a man named Willie, brother of a friend, returning after a visit. Willie lived in Chicago and worked in a barrel factory where he thought there was an opening. Three days later Harry Perkins was stacking steel rings for $1.55 an hour, and three days after that he was running an automatic welder. He now makes $2.00 an hour with six or seven hours' overtime for about $100 a week.

Harry Perkins is a boyish, handsome, open-faced man who can't read but knows letters and remembers street signs and bus routes. At Christmas time he used the holiday tape to make letters on the wall over the double bed where he and his wife and their new infant sleep: ALICE.

Both of them insist on an unrelieved list of advantages Chicago has over their old life: Now they eat together at the same table because they have enough dinner plates; they have milk and fresh fruits and meats they never ate before; instead of a cold-water tub and washboard she gets the week's laundry delivered for $9; the school doctor and dentist examine their children regularly; instead of paying a neighbor $1 to take them shopping she can walk to a local market or take the rapid transit for 30 cents downtown; there the children often stayed out of school for lack of clothes but never here; down there Christmas meant at best a piece of simple clothing for each child, but here they have turkey and fur-lined jackets and guitars for the children.

"Look," Harry Perkins said as he sat in his tiny blue-and-pink kitchen, "for the first time in my life I own an innerspring mattress, three of them, a gas oven, a dinette, a TV, a stereo set. They treat me like a grown man. Down there the police killed colored men, two I knew just in the last couple of years we were there."

Alice Perkins shook her head slowly. "There ain't nothing I miss down there."

He nodded. "That goes for me."

Did that mean they would be happy to continue just as they are?

Alice Perkins looked surprised and said, "No, of course not."

And then she and her husband began a new recital that told the story of why families who move hopefully into the big cities then turn bitter and apathetic. Compared to the desperate poverty and endemic violence of the rural South, the city is obviously better in pay, in food, in material goods. But as the years go by, it becomes plain that the city makes demands the family never before had to meet: more education to get ahead, better clothes to enter the better world, participation in the vague and remote territory outside the ghetto in order to succeed. Food and a tight roof are no longer the focus of life. Simple survival is no longer enough; they must meet the requirements of high-speed urban life. Typically, the families enter eager and striving and then in three or four years get stalled. The Perkinses were still ambitious.

Now the children want a bicycle, a piano, some new clothes like the ones they see on TV in *American Bandstand*. Harry Perkins would like to get a car. Mrs. Perkins has fallen in love with sectional couches. But she then described what they want more than anything else. With her husband's solemn nod of approval, she said softly, "A better house with no rats, in a better neighborhood, you know, some space for the kids to play in their own yard, with some grass in the back and in the front."

A nice house in a nice neighborhood is the conventional American family dream, but it has a special meaning in the ghetto, where most families are enclosed in a triple prison. The first is their own home. Slum-tenement doors are locked. The knock is answered, if at all, by a voice, "Who's there? What you want?" Unless the voice is familiar and the message safe, that may be the last communication from the other side. Young children are forbidden to go out alone, and hundreds of thousands of them spend all their time, except for a few hours a week, locked inside their rooms, often with the harshest discipline to quell their restlessness. Only when they go to school is there freedom. When the three Perkins schoolchildren go, they run like rabbits released from cages. The fear is real, for outside there is the second prison: the neighborhood.

The range of movement of most slum dwellers is measured in yards and, at most, a few blocks. The density is enormous, the possibilities for play and relaxation almost nil. A 50-by-100-foot playground operated by the Marilac settlement house near the Perkinses' flat is the only one available to 4,000 children. One result of this merciless compaction is the teen-age gang, which follows a territorial imperative that includes murder of teen-agers who intrude from other neighborhoods. For all of them are trapped in the larger prison, the ghetto itself.

In Chicago the ghetto is divided in two territories, the West Side, with more than 300,000 Negroes, and the South Side, with more than 600,000. Each is a vast black island surrounded by whites. In 1950 there were only 500,000 Negroes in the city, in about five smaller islands interspersed among white neighborhoods. But now the spaces between the islands have been abandoned by whites who moved to the suburbs. So now the West Side is almost 9 square miles of black territory, the South Side, 30 square miles. On the South Side there remain a few white ethnic neighborhoods, resentful and belligerent, and some middle- and even upper-income blocks. But the mass is black and poor, the former rows of white homes partitioned and bringing in as much as 200 per cent of their old rents. In 1950 it was possible in any given ghetto to walk five blocks to a white neighborhood; now on the South Side a man can walk ten miles almost in a straight line, and never pass a home occupied by whites.

Inside the ghetto the schools are wretched, the unemployment rate three times the outside rate, the municipal services minimal, the landscape demoralizing. The uneducated parents get stalled in their climb up the work ladder, trapped in their ghetto. They produce new generations of the defeated.

So Alice Perkins, her large brown eyes longing, says,

"I want a house of my own. Out in the suburbs. Like Maywood. A friend of mine drove me out there once and, oh, I want to move to a place like Maywood."

Maywood is about nine miles out on the expressway that goes by the Perkinses' flat, an "industrial suburb" in the metropolitan sprawl. It has its own character, a pleasant place of 27,000 working-class people with small one-family houses with small lawns front and back, children on swings in the yard or skipping rope on the sidewalks. There are 5,000 Negroes in Maywood, and they average $1,500 a year more than Negroes in the central city.

What are the odds of the Perkinses, or any ghetto family, making it out to a Maywood? About 1-in-11. In 1960 Chicago had 813,000 Negroes in its central city, the ghetto, and only 77,000 in the suburbs. In 1950 the ratio was about the same.

III

Elijah is a child of migrants, a child of the ghetto. He is Negro, thin, 126 pounds, five-foot-four, narrow-headed with slicked-down black hair, and he walks slightly stooped. If you didn't look closely you wouldn't pay attention to him in a group of six. But he is now 18, and has shot a few people. He has been involved in more burglaries and robberies than is wise to recall, and has had two personal friends murdered and countless others badly wounded. He has recently emerged from jail, where he was sent for shooting another boy in the stomach.

Elijah isn't his real name, though he insisted that his real name be used.

"Listen, I want people to understand, I want people to believe that these things happen, really, man, not to just a few oddballs but every kid I knew, every kid I grew up with on the South Side of Chicago. I don't mean they all went to jail. Two kids I knew well got killed. But some never went to jail, even. But this is what they grew up with. I want to help my people, and I want other people to know what's going on."

But it would be unfair to him, to his family and to his pregnant girlfriend to use real names. They are all struggling to repair their lives.

His parents came from Mississippi in 1952, but his mother came briefly to Chicago in 1949 for Elijah to be born. So since the age of three he has been in the ghetto. His training ground has been the tenement and the massive public-housing project.

The tenements are typified by one building in the ghetto, a grimy red-brick three-story place with three carved granite archways that tell you this was once a respectable neighborhood. Today there are 18 families in the building, and except for one that arrived last year from Texas, all have been in Chicago seven years or more. There are large signs all over the outside of the building, ordering trash to be thrown in barrels. Under the signs are glaciers and foothills of garbage that harbor huge rats. The children play among them with easy familiarity. (Landlords, by law, are required to provide private trash collections, but few of them ever bother; if an intense campaign by tenants and the settlement houses puts pressure on them, some will bribe city trash crews to collect the accumulation.) The tenement hallways are uriniferous, the walls covered with badly spelled obscenities ("thomas muther is a hoe"). In one corridor there is loose garbage, some feces in a corner and a raw egg broken on the floor. Out of one flat come two children less than four years old, one wearing only a dirty diaper, the other only a tiny T-shirt. Behind them comes a very old woman flailing at them with a leather strap. The children laugh and run down the corridor, one stepping in the egg, the other in the feces.

Ten of the 18 families are on welfare. Only five of the 18 families have a man as head of the household. There are 123 human beings who live in the old wreck of a building, of whom 98 are dependent children, 73 of them without a father at home. Eight of the households, despite great poverty, illness and other difficulties, have a tidy flat and a complete family. The landlord is considered better than average; the building has a market value of $25,000, and his gross rents are $24,000 a year.

Elijah spent the first part of his life growing up in such a building, and the rest in the other kind of ghetto dwelling, the large public-housing project. For most tenement residents, the project is a highly desired escape from what they have. Rents are lower— in Chicago they run from $40 to $90 a month for modern, well-equipped flats, with space enough to avoid having children of different sexes sleeping in the same beds and the same rooms. There are no rats. So just as the old tenements are better than the leaky three-room shacks of the South, "the projects" are deliverance from the chaos and squalor of the tenements. But after a few years in the projects their tenants begin to suffer their drawbacks, and many pray harder than ever for deliverance to the suburbs, or any place that is clean and airy and not packed with an incredible density of human beings.

Cities like Chicago turned to high-rise projects to house as many families as cheaply as possible as quickly as possible and, in many cases, to keep Negroes within the bounds of the ghetto. On a strip of land two blocks wide and less than four miles long, the Chicago Public Housing Authority built 65 buildings, 38 of them 16 stories or higher. In these buildings, in less than half a square mile, live 42,800 people. Little was done in surrounding areas to provide for

the cliff-dwellers when they came out of the project. Boredom and noise are constant. In the summer the young who are still innocent wait for the event of the night—the turning on of the outside lights of the stairwells, and as each building does it a great soft wind seems to blow through the projects as thousands of watching children go, "Ah."

It is not surprising that territorial warfare and delinquency grow in such places. One wonders what would happen if a place of the same population, like Rapid City, S. Dak., instead of having its slightly more than 42,000 citizens spread over its present 16 square miles, had them all—including the sturdy, hard-working, middle-class folk—jammed into one quarter of a square mile. The people of Rapid City live 2,701 to the square mile; the project dwellers in Chicago's South Side live 170,000 to the square mile.

Elijah is the unhappy product, first of the horizontal and then of the vertical ghetto.

He is the oldest of 10 children, and he remembers that when his family came from Mississippi his father worked in the stockyards. The children kept coming, but work at the stockyards got scarcer. First there was no more lunch money, then no breakfasts. His father spent more days at home, then began to drink. When Elijah was 7, his father disappeared.

At the age of 11, Elijah joined the Cobras, a street gang that dominated his neighborhood. They fought rival gangs who intruded in their territory, or tried to date their girls, or uttered real or imagined insults. Avenging honor and protecting territory were the motivations for gang fights, the justifications for maiming and murder. Looking back and explaining it, Elijah often uses the word, "recognition."

"The poor people were the dumbest people because they didn't have any backing, they didn't push, nobody gave them any recognition. So most of us started gang fighting because of that. With the knowledge I've acquired since then it seems like I would never dream of going back to a life like that. But before I got the knowledge, it seemed fine, it seemed right, it was an art. The things you did you didn't mind telling about because you were trying to get more recognition with the bunch. You would meet girls, girls you never could have otherwise, the ones who dressed nice and looked nice. When your name was mentioned, everyone's eyes and ears opened."

After he joined the gang he began skipping school, attending parties in empty flats, drinking wine, having girls, smoking marijuana. He thinks his father's absence made a difference. "When your father is there, there are things you wouldn't dare bring into the house because your father would give you a whipping. I could do lots of things I could get by with, things my father would know about because he's a man and I'm a man, stealing, drinking, girls, smoking reefers."

As he moved into his teens, Elijah became more violent. "I could see I wasn't going to become anybody. All this was hitting me at the same time as the gang fighting, and it made me even harder because I knew this, I knew I wasn't going to become anybody, and I hated the whole world then.

"I began to use the gun more frequently, and in a gang fight I'd be the first to swing, the first to shoot. I hated conditions. I hated everything. I hated people around me because they had more than I had. I hated it when the kids were supposed to go to school and only had torn or dirty pants, and after you get to school there wasn't any lunch money, and you stood outside and got laughed at, and when you got home there was hardly anything to eat there, either."

Three things made a difference in Elijah's life. He went to jail for shooting a boy and read a book whose dust jacket in the prison library caught his eye: "I Dare You to Explore the Powers of Your Mind." With the help of a prison worker he began to read and to look into his own emotions.

He got five years' probation and came out to discover that his father had returned home, dried out, and was working at a good job in construction.

And he met Jim Taylor, a Y.M.C.A. street-gang worker who lives and works with teen-agers in the tougher neighborhoods, a schoolteacher who realized he wasn't reaching his students and quit to go where they lived. With Taylor's help Elijah signed up for a Y.M.C.A. study program where he works half a day and goes to school, combing the last years of high school and the first two years of college.

This will take until 1971. His work during that time will be with street gangs. "You've got to have something for these kids to do." Elijah said. "You've got to have someone who cares about them. Not just spending a few hours like most schoolteachers and then, zip, out of the neighborhood. But really caring, man.

"And you need new prizes, new rewards. Now it's the kid who fights the hardest, drinks the most, has the most girls, kills best. I'd like to make the big man, the one who's top of his class, and give him a special prize, a real good prize that would make people open up their eyes and ears. It would help, I know it would."

Elijah speaks with a combination of the soft Mississippi accent of his parents and the hip talk of the ghetto. He has studied and thought a great deal lately about the Negro American in the ghetto.

"When the Negro is born in the South, he grows up with hatred for the white man, but in the South they kill him if he shows it. So he comes to Chicago, and he lives here on the South Side and he takes out his hatred on other Negroes. You get born with hatred because you see the white man in his Cadillac, and you see your father walking. The hate is in you, and when someone attacks you, the hate is going to come out, no matter if it comes out against your own people."

Elijah and his fellow migrants are mysteries. In the face of endless defeat, first on the farms and now in the ghetto, they have recurring hope. It is often expressed in riots and demonstrations but it is there. The newest arrivals continue to work hard at the lowest pay in the expectation that it will lead to something better. The history books claim that the American genius has been to collect ethnic minorities at the bottom and then let them disperse up through the surrounding society. But the American Negro continues to be more densely packed, more hemmed in, and more confined to the bottom than any other migrant minority. And yet he continues to hope.

Elijah had been standing at a window through which I could hear the level roar of boisterous children, their sounds echoing between the 16-story buildings. He turned around, his brow wrinkled with concentration, and said with passion:

"The thing is that you grow up and, you *know*, you *know*, man . . ." He paused and said slowly and quietly, "*No-body cares!* Mothers are screaming at babies, there's no father, teachers are screaming at the students, and when the bell rings they leave the building before the kids do. And when you're dropping out of school, you know very well that they're really glad to see you go. You're glad to go, too, but you remember afterward that they were glad to see you go."

Elijah sat down, and after a time he spoke again.

"Nobody cares. Nobody. That's what you grow up with. The people on the outside, they have their own immediate problems, so they got no time for our problems. The ones here who get anywhere, they don't care about anybody else once they get up on their pedestal. They look down on their own people, and they say, 'They're fools' and then go on about their business."

And then the incredible hope and resilience:

"My kids, someday, are going to finish school—a *good* school. They're going to have a set of goals, to think ahead, to make sense. But most of all, they got to have environment."

Environment?

"Live in a good house in a nice neighborhood with a real school. Out of . . ." and he pointed out the window to the tenements, the projects, the street with the squeal of the police siren receding. "Out of here. Period."

Table 3. Change in farm numbers, land, size, value, and sales, United States

Year	Number of farms (millions)[1]	Land in farms[1] (millions of acres)	Average acreage per farm[1]	Value of farm land and buildings (in dollars)[1]		Market value of farm products sold[1]	
				Total (millions)	Per farm[3]	Total (millions)	Per farm
1910	6.37	881	139	34,885	5480		
1935	6.81[2]	1055[2]	155[2]	32,859	4823	9821[4]	1442[5]
1945	5.86[2]	1142[2]	195[2]	46,389	7918	16,231	2770
1954	4.78[2]	1158[2]	242[2]	97,583	20,405	24,645	5156
1964	3.16	1110	352	159,932	50,646	35,292	11,176
1969	2.73	1063	390	206,717	75,714	45,563	16,689
1974	2.31	1017	440	342,098	147,838	81,531	35,234
Percentage change							
1935-1974	−66	−3.6	+184	+941	+2965	+730	+2343

Source: Data from Historical Statistics of the United States, Washington, D.C., 1975, U.S. Government Printing Office, pp. 450-451, 457, 464.
[1]Census of Agriculture data.
[2]Excludes Hawaii and Alaska.
[3]Computed for 1935 to 1964.
[4]U.S. Department of Agriculture survey data.
[5]Computed.

Table 4. Change in yields and hours of labor for selected crops and livestock, United States[1]

Year	Wheat		Corn		Cotton		Milk cows		Egg chickens		Hay	
	bu/ acre	hrs/ 100 bu	bu/ acre	hrs/ 100 bu	lb/ acre	hrs/ bale	lb/ cow	hrs/ cwt	eggs/ yr	hrs/ 100	ton/ acre	hrs/ ton
1915-1919	13.9	98	25.9	132	168	299	3790	3.7			1.25	10.4
1925-1929	14.1	74	26.3	115	171	268	4437	3.3	117	1.9	1.22	9.8
1935-1939	13.2	67	26.1	108	226	209	4401	3.4	129	1.7	1.24	9.1
1945-1949	16.9	34	36.1	53	273	146	4992	2.6	161	1.5	1.35	6.2
1955-1959	22.3	17	48.7	20	428	74	6307	1.7	200	.9	1.61	3.7
1965-1969	27.5	11	77.4	7	485	30	8733	.9	219	.4	1.94	1.9
Percentage change												
1935-1939 to 1965-1969	+106	−84	+197	−94	+115	−86	+98	−74	+70	−76	+56	−79

Source: Data from Historical Statistics of the United States, Washington D.C., 1975 U.S. Government Printing Office, pp. 500-501.
[1]U.S. Department of Agriculture survey data.

Farming with petroleum

MICHAEL J. PERELMAN*

Agriculture in this country has changed greatly since the second World War. Farm machinery and chemicals have greatly increased the quantity of food and fiber a farmer can produce, but because farm products are not in short supply, the result has been a decline in the number of workers engaged in farming, while the total product has changed very little. This agricultural revolution, therefore, has had substantial consequences for society as a whole; as many previous articles in this magazine have pointed out, modern farming has also had substantial and adverse effects on the environment. The increased economic efficiency of our farms must therefore be weighed against the social and environmental costs of mechanized agriculture.

Since 1940 the number of operating farms has been reduced from 6.3 million to 2.8 million, with one million of those disappearing since 1961. At the same time farm population has been reduced from 31.9 million (23.2 percent of the population in 1940) to 9.4 million (4.8 percent of the population in 1970). While these reductions have been taking place there has been little change in the numbers of acres tilled. In 1940 there were approximately 1.01 billion acres devoted to the production of farm products, while today there are about 1.1 billion. The number has fluctuated somewhat, with a high of 1.2 billion in the early 1950s, but the trend since that time has been steadily downward.[1]

The result is that there has been a marked increase in average farm size. In 1940 the average farm size was about 167 acres; by 1960 the average size had jumped to 297, and in the last ten years another 92 acres has been added, making the average farm close to 400 acres.[1]

These changes have been, in part, a response to great increases in the overall efficiency in farm production in recent years. Former Secretary of Agriculture Clifford Hardin describes this trend when he writes:

"Using a modern feeding system for broilers, one

□ From Environment **14**(8):8-13, Oct. 1972. Reprinted by permission of Scientists Institute for Public Information. Copyright © 1972, Committee for Environmental Information.

*Michael J. Perelman is assistant professor of economics at California State University at Chico.

man can take care of 60,000 to 75,000 chickens. One man in a modern feedlot can now take care of 5,000 head of cattle. One man with a mechanized system can operate a dairy enterprise of 50 to 60 milk cows.

"Agriculture, in short, does an amazingly efficient job of producing food."[2]

The technological revolution in agriculture has not, however, taken place without having a considerable impact on other sectors of society and on the environment in which it has occurred. To assess this impact, the framework which has set the conditions for change must be examined.

If we measure efficiency by output per farm worker, then we must agree with Secretary Hardin's analysis. On the other hand, should we measure efficiency by output per manhour? After all, no man alive can really feed 75,000 chickens by himself. In reality he is aided by many other men who make equipment and other necessities for raising chickens, even though some of them might have never set foot on a farm. Yet without their production of the capital and other inputs, the modern farm would wither away. For instance, estimates by the Department of Agriculture indicate that in 1947 five million persons were engaged in work directly supplying farmers. By 1954 their numbers had increased to six million. Assuming a 40-hour week, these "workers spent from 10 to 11 billion hours in producing goods and services purchased and used by farmers in 1947 to 1954."[3]

Table 1 gives us some idea of the importance of non-farm inputs to agriculture. The table lists total farm production expenses between 1954 and 1969. These expenses are broken down into different categories, and the total value of farm marketings is also given for comparison. Notice that the cost of capital represents between one-third and one-fourth of all expenses. More than 10 percent of the total costs fall into the category labeled "miscellaneous" expenditures, which include pesticide use, cotton ginning, and many similar items. These miscellaneous expenditures, as well as the capital on the farm, have diminished the farm labor force; as a result, hired labor represents less than 10 percent of total farm costs. The question we must ask is: Does society benefit from the replacement of farm labor by capital?

Table 1. Farm production expenses, United States, 1955-1969, in millions of dollars*

Year	Feed livestock and seed** purchased	Ferti- lizer and lime	Capital equipment: re- pairs, operation‡, de- preciation, and other capital consumption††	Hired la- bor†††	Taxes on farm property†	Interest on farm mortgage debt‡‡	Net rent to nonfarm landlords	Miscella- neous‡‡‡	Total production expenses
1955	5,995	1,185	7,300	2,615	1,141	402	1,057	2,204	21,889
1960	7,935	1,315	8,210	2,923	1,502	628	1,010	2,829	26,352
1965	9,299	1,754	9,055	2,849	1,943	1,077	1,328	3,628	30,933
1966	10,448	1,952	9,508	2,889	2,108	1,205	1,442	3,854	33,406
1967	10,541	2,124	10,241	2,878	2,275	1,343	1,305	4,068	34,775
1968	10,338	2,125	10,851	3,045	2,526	1,477	1,308	4,342	36,012
1969	11,505	2,013	11,500	3,192	2,753	1,602	1,303	4,576	38,444

*Includes Alaska and Hawaii, beginning 1960.

**Includes bulbs, plants, and trees.

†Includes expenditures for repairs and maintenance of farm buildings and other land improvements, petroleum fuel and oil, other motor vehicle operation, and repairs on other machinery.

††Estimated outlay necessary at current prices, for the replacement of capital equipment that has been used up during the year.

†††Includes cash wages, perquisites, and Social Security taxes paid by employers.

‡Includes taxes levied against farm real estate and farm personal property.

‡‡Interest charges payable during the calendar year on outstanding farm mortgage debt.

‡‡‡Includes interest on non-real-estate debt, pesticides, ginning, electricity and telephone (business share), livestock marketing charges (ex- cluding feed and transportation), containers, milk hauling, irrigation, grazing, binding materials, tools for sirup, horses and mules, harness and saddlery, blacksmithing, and hardware, veterinary services and medicines, net insurance premiums (crop, fire, wind, and hail), and mis- cellaneous dairy, nursery, greenhouse, apiary, and other supplies.

Source: Agricultural Statistics, 1970, U.S. Dept. of Agriculture, Washington, D.C., 1970.

MECHANIZATION

Probably the most impelling cause of the increase of efficiency has been the development of various kinds of machinery for planting, spraying, cultivat- ing, harvesting, or any other farm activity that once required a large labor force. Without the modern ma- chinery now available large farms would be unwork- able. Many farm operations must be accomplished in relatively short periods of time during the year, and the reliability of the machinery used to perform these chores on time and over large acreages is far greater than that of human labor. Most importantly, the use of machinery is far more economical than the use of labor. The number of acres in production in the U.S. has remained roughly constant since 1950, but in the same period the total value of farm machinery tripled from 12.1 billion dollars to 34.2 billion dollars.[1]

As a result of this mechanization, agriculture has taken on more and more of the aspects of industriali- zation. Fields are larger; rows are straighter; ditch- banks and fencerows are cleaner, and altogether there is less diversity. All acreage is treated in a uniform, assembly-line way. The application of these tech- niques, that is, the forcing of biological systems into a man-made form, has caused numerous problems which have in turn been temporarily solved with more sophisticated technology. Lack of diversity in the fields exacerbates pest problems, for instance, by removing natural controls, while the regularity of

plantings provides economic incentives for increased mechanization of fertilizer and herbicide application. These in turn require greater expenditures of energy resources and at the same time make easier the ap- plication of larger and larger amounts of polluting farm chemicals.

This is illustrated by the increase in power-driven pesticide application equipment between 1951 and 1964. In 1951 farmers owned 517,000 power-driven sprayers and dusters. In 1964 the number had in- creased to 1,128,000, and it is even greater now.[4] Still, crop pests continue to cause economic losses and con- trol costs increase. The small farmer is at an economic disadvantage because of the kind of machinery avail- able. The Department of Agriculture describes spray- ing and dusting equipment as "lumpy"—that is, it cannot be divided into smaller units of use as oth- er inputs such as feed and fertilizer. A small farmer, treating only a few acres, may be required to purchase the same piece of equipment that a large farmer could use, without modification, to treat hundreds of acres. This observation is borne out by the fact that for every $100,000 worth of products grown a large farm opera- tion used a single sprayer while several small farms needed six individual sprayers to do the same job.[4] While the larger pieces of farm equipment are often rented rather than purchased by small farmers, a sub- stantial economic advantage is held by the farms

Table 2. Mechanical power replaces human power on the farm

Year	Tractor horsepower (millions)	Man hours (millions)	Cost of operating and maintaining farm capital (millions of dollars)
1920	5	13,406	(not available)
1950	93	6,922	5,640
1960	154	4,590	8,310
1969	203	3,431	11,500

Source: Changes in Farm Production and Efficiency, A Summary Report, 1970, U.S. Dept. of Agriculture, Statistical Bulletin No. 233, Washington, D.C., June 1970.

large enough to own their own harvesters, combines, and so forth.

The best-known form of agricultural mechanization is the tractor. As late as 1920, more than 20 million horsepower was provided by horses and mules.[5] These animals had to be fed from the land. With the adoption of the tractor, this land was freed to produce food animals for humans. Not only was land freed by the tractor; labor was also freed, because one man plowing with a tractor could do the work of several men plowing with a mule. The net effect of mechanization on farm labor requirements is shown in Table 2.

AGRICULTURAL FUEL CONSUMPTION

The displaced workers left the farms to go to the cities where they needed agricultural, as well as other, goods and services. But as we produced more goods, we consumed more and more of our stored energy.

In the United States farmers use the average tractor 400 hours per year.[6] Since the average tractor is about 40 horsepower, we can estimate that each tractor represents about 16,000 horsepower hours of use.[7] Assuming that the average tractor consumes about one-tenth of a gallon of fuel per horsepower hour, then its use represents 1,600 gallons of fuel per year.[8] Since we have five million tractors in the U.S.,[9] we can estimate that tractors alone consume about eight billion gallons of fuel.

These eight billion gallons represent about 1,000 trillion BTU of heat value. The average American consumes about 12,000 BTU daily, or an annual rate of consumption of about 4,380,000 BTU, the equivalent of about 30 gallons of gasoline. Since our population is about 200 million, we consume as food about 876 trillion BTU; the energy value of the food crops we consume in the U.S. is therefore about equal to the energy we burn in our tractors alone.

Electricity also contributes a great deal to farm production. Electricity use by farmers accounts for about 2.5 percent of all electricity used.[10] In 1968 U.S. electricity generating plants consumed the equivalent of a little more than 14,000 trillion BTU of fossil fuel.[11] Thus, agriculture consumes the equivalent of 350 trillion BTU of fuel, or an equivalent of almost 2 million BTU for each inhabitant of the United States. The heat value of 2 million BTU is approximately equal to that of 14 gallons of gasoline.

Total energy use is much higher. Delwiche estimates we use more than 10 million BTU of energy for each acre of land we cultivate.[12] In 1964, at the time of the last Census of Agriculture, we devoted about 319 million acres to the production of food crops. This much land (which does not include acreage in cotton, tobacco, and grazing land) would therefore require the equivalent of about 150 gallons of gasoline for each American we feed or about five times as much energy as we consume in food. Even here we have not taken into account the energy required to produce the farm equipment, nor the energy used to store and distribute the food. For instance, farmers purchase products containing 360 million pounds of rubber, about 7 percent of the total U.S. rubber production, and 6.5 million tons of steel in the form of trucks, farm machinery, and fences. Farms consume about one-third as much steel as the automotive industry.[13]

Our fertilizer industry also consumes enormous amounts of energy. Our current technology requires about 10 million calories for each kilogram of nitrogen fertilizer we produce commercially.[14] In 1969 U.S. farms consumed about 7.5 million tons of nitrogen fertilizer which required[14] the equivalent in heat value of more than 1.5 billion gallons of gasoline, or about eight gallons for each American we feed.[15] But then our nitrogen fertilizer makes up only one-fifth of our total commercial fertilizer supply.[15]

The implication is not that agriculture is the main user of energy in our society. In 1970, the U.S. consumed about 64,000 trillion BTU of energy. Thus, the average American consumes the equivalent of about 5,000 gallons of gasoline per year. For instance, a typical American consumes the energy equivalent of about 10 gallons of gasoline annually just to watch a black and white television set.[15] By that standard, agriculture's consumption of 150 gallons of gasoline to feed and clothe one person does not seem extravagant. Besides, we use more than 20 percent of our acreage for exports which feed citizens of other nations, and we use some of our crops for industrial purposes. But agriculture could be an energy *producing* sector of the economy. The crops we harvest capture the energy of the sun and store it in a useful form so that we can use it to nourish our bodies or to perform some other service for us. And yet our agriculture has become a major consumer of our stores of energy. In fact, agriculture uses more petroleum than any other single industry.[16]

If we are facing an energy crisis, then we might do well to measure efficiency in terms of output per unit of energy instead of output per unit of labor, not only in agriculture but elsewhere in our economy.

If we should decide to measure efficiency in terms of the conservation of energy, then American agriculture comes out very poorly. Harris estimated that Chinese wet rice agriculture could produce 53.5 BTU of energy for each BTU of human energy expended in farming it.[17] For each unit of energy the wet rice farmer expends he gets more than 50 in return; for each unit of fossil fuel energy we expend we get about one-fifth in return. On the basis of these two ratios, Chinese wet rice agriculture is far more efficient than our own system.

Let us take a moment to look at the type of technology we will need in the future. Population is growing, and more people will be competing for a fixed or diminishing supply of natural resources. All other things being equal, the "excess" of people should lower the values of labor relative to the value of raw materials. But our technology is based on a historical pattern of rising prices and falling raw materials costs. Take the price of gasoline, for example. We saw earlier that 30 gallons of gasoline had a heat value almost sufficient to supply a human with enough calories to keep him alive for a whole year. We pay about ten dollars for this much fuel. Even at these low costs, about one-half to one-third of the cost of owning and operating a tractor is the cost of fuel.[18] If we paid as much for a calorie of gasoline as we paid for a calorie of corn, the cost of operating farm machines would be prohibitive. (Food, of course, has other nutritional values than energy, and this comparison with gasoline is meant only to be suggestive.)

Furthermore, with population growth we need to discover ecologically sound means of employing our population. Agriculture and the conservation of natural resources seem a good place to start.

One example might help to explain how the Chinese, for instance, have been able to maintain their resources. In the part of the U.S. where I live we clear our lands of rice stubble by burning the fields; in China, rice stubble was used for all sorts of purposes, but it was also burnt as a cooking fuel. The heat from the stove was drawn off through pipes and led to large black blocks of subsoil which absorbed the heat. These blocks made nice, warm beds for the Chinese. Sooner or later, the beds began to crumble; the heat and the nutrients from the smoke had opened the blocks to microbial life. So the crumbling beds were returned to the fields where they made excellent fertilizer. Everything was used and nothing was wasted. According to some, Chairman Mao is maintaining this ethic in China today.[19] As the *Peking Review* wrote last year, "There is nothing in the world which is absolute waste. 'Waste' under one condition may be valuable under different ones."[20]

HYBRID CORN

However, we have no such ethic, and because we do not appreciate the worth of our natural resources, neither our yields nor the quality of our food is very high. The history of our corn crop is instructive here.

American soils have been almost legendary for their fertility. One commentator was only slightly exaggerating when he said that our soils are so rich that "if you tickle them with a hoe, they laugh with a harvest."[20] We were so mindless about preserving this fertility that we have been forced to spend a lot of time studying our depleted farm soils. Part of our carelessness was understandable; we seemed to have a boundless supply of land, and as long as there was new land to put under cultivation, the effects of soil depletion were not considered. For instance, between 1870 and 1920 corn yields remained constant while acreage increased, but about two-thirds of the increased acreage was located in eight cornbelt states where the mean yield was 20 percent higher than the U.S. average. Then, between 1920 and 1925, yields increased slightly, but this increase in yield was made possible because less fertile land, like that found in Texas and Oklahoma, was taken out of production. Soon after the beginning of the 1920s yields began to fall, and, although acreage remained constant until the early 1930s, production began a downward trend. From the 1937 low, yields rose to 74 percent above the 90-year mean for the period 1870 to 1960. One part of the explanation is that production was discontinued on more than 17 percent of the 1937 acreage in the relatively low yielding southern states. This land was probably taken out of production because the soil was too depleted to continue further cultivation of the corn. Another reason for the rising yields of the late 1930s was the introduction of high-yield hybrid corn.[21] The pattern of corn yields is shown in Figure 1. The more extensive root systems and aggressive feeding characteristics of the hybrids enabled them, when first introduced, to extract fertility which was inaccessible to open pollinated varieties. That is, hybrid corn sped up the rate of soil depletion. But there was another reason why the hybrid corn produced more. The increased yields were bought at the cost of lower protein content.[22] The agronomists refer to what

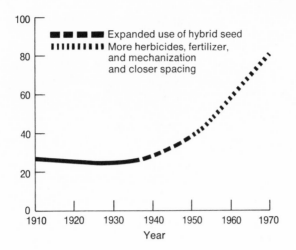

Fig. 1. Corn yields in the United States. (Source: Witwer, S. H. In Aldrich, Daniel G., editor: Research and technology on the U.S. food supply, Publication No. 92, Research for the world food crisis, A symposium presented at the Dallas meeting of the American Association for the Advancement of Science, Dec. 1968, Washington, D.C., 1970, pp. 77-124.)

they call the inverse nitrogen law, which says that the more nitrogen we find in a crop the less we can expect its yield to be. Similarly, the higher the yield the less nitrogen we can expect to find. Nigrogen is found in all proteins and may be taken as a rough indication of the protein level of the corn. For example, low-yield Indian corn has shown a protein content of from 12 to 15 percent. Over the years we selected those seeds which produced more, while the protein content fell substantially.

"In 1911, before hybridization . . . the mean concentration in this feed grain was reported as 10.30 percent for a single grade. By 1950 the top grade among 5 then listed contained 8.8 percent while the lowest had 7.9 percent. By 1956, among 50 tested corn grains from the outlying experiment fields of the Missouri Experiment Station, one sample of these hybrids reached a low of 5.15 percent of 'crude' protein, or a value just half of what it had been 45 years ago."[23]

At first, livestock men complained about the value of hybrid corn as a feed,[24] but this complaint is rarely heard now, because feed today is supplemented with heavy doses of fish protein. Most of this comes from fish caught off the shore of Peru where the people suffer from protein deprivation. The U.S. imports enough fish protein to eliminate one-half of the protein deficiency in the entire continent of South America.[25] That is, our corn crop uses foreign protein subsidies to produce a sufficiently nutritious animal feed, and in so doing diminishes the amount of fish protein

available for human needs elsewhere in the world. Moreover, when we produce larger yields through heavy fertilizer applications, we upset the balance of nutrients in the soil and induce deficiences in our foods.[26]

Commercial fertilizers have aggravated another problem which our farming methods have caused, namely, soil depletion. A committee of the National Academy of Sciences estimates that we have lost about one-third of our topsoil.[27] According to Barry Commoner, the organic content of our Midwest soils has declined in the last 100 years by about 50 percent. (It is not the fertilizer itself, of course, but the intensive cultivation it makes possible, that leads to soil depletion.)

Perhaps the most important property of hybrid corn is its regularity; because all the hydrid corn plants are just about the same height on the stalk, mechanical harvesting becomes a simple matter. Thus hybrid corn helped to speed up the mechanization of agriculture. More than anything, hybrid corn demonstrated the productivity of "efficient" agriculture.

However, our technology weakens our crops and makes them more susceptible to disease; witness the recent southern corn leaf blight epidemic. The chemicals we use to aid in farming are dangerous to many different life forms: birds, pets, and even humans. Yet all this is considered efficient. In fact, economists have not paid much attention to the drawbacks of our technology while they try carefully to assess its benefits solely in terms of dollar profits.

What we need is a complete redefinition of efficiency. We need to think of efficiency in such a way that when someone says a farm or a factory is efficient we mean that it makes our lives better than any other kind of farm or factory.

NOTES

1. *Statistical Abstracts of the United States*, 1971, U.S. Dept. of Commerce, Washington, D.C.
2. Hardin, Clifford M., "Foreword," *Contours of Change, U.S.D.A. Yearbook of Agriculture*, Washington, D.C., 1970, p. xxxiii.
3. Cited by Reuban W. Hecht and Eugene W. McKibbon, *Power to Produce, Yearbook of Agriculture, 1960*, U.S. Dept. of Agriculture, USGPO, Washington, D.C., 1960, pp. 317-331.
4. "Use of Pesticide Application Equipment," U.S. Dept. of Agriculture, Economic Research Service Bulletin, Washington, D.C., 1964.
5. Fox, Austin, *Demand for Farm Tractors in the United States*, U.S. Dept. of Agriculture, Economic Research Service, Agricultural Economic Report No. 103, Washington, D.C., Nov. 1966, p. 1.
6. In 1956 tractors were used an average of 605 hours annually. See *Farm Tractors, Trends in Type, Size, Age and Use*, U.S. Dept of Agriculture, Agricultural Research Service. Agricultural Information Bulletin, Aug. 1960. However, Paul Strickler, an agricultural economist with the Farm Production Economics Division

of the U.S.D.A., wrote to me to say that unpublished data show that the average usage has fallen to about 400 hours.

7. *Changes in Farm Production and Efficiency, 1970*, U.S. Dept. of Agriculture, Economic Research Service, Statistical Bulletin No. 233, Washington, D.C., June 1970.
8. Professor Robert Wallace, coordinator of the division of agriculture, Chico State College, personal communication.
9. *Farm Tractors, Trends in Type, Size, Age, and Use*, ibid.
10. *Food Costs-Farm Prices: A compilation of Information Relating to Agriculture*, Committee on Agriculture, House of Representatives, 92nd Congress, 1st Session, USGPO, Washington, D.C., July 1, 1971, p. 20.
11. *Statistical Abstract*, U.S. Dept. of Commerce, US GPO, Washington, D.C., 1970, p. 506.
12. Delwiche, C., "Nitrogen and Future Food Requirements," *Research for the World Food Crisis*, A Symposium Presented at the Dallas Meeting of the American Association for the Advancement of Science, Dec. 1968, Daniel G. Aldrich, Jr., ed., Publication 92, American Association for the Advancement of Science, Washington, D.C., p. 204.
13. *Agricultural Statistics*, U.S. Dept. of Agriculture, Washington, D.C., 1971, p. 494.
14. Rappaport, Roy A., *Pigs for the Ancestors*. Yale University Press, New Haven, 1967, p. 262, referring to Marvin Harris, "Cultural Energy," unpublished.
15. McColly, Howard F., "The Place of Petroleum," *Power to Produce, Yearbook of Agriculture*, 1960, USCPO, Washington, D.C., 1960, pp. 61-69.
16. Orleans, Leo A., and Richard P. Suttmeir, "The Mao Ethic and Environmental Quality," *Science*, 170:1173-76, Dec. 11, 1970.
17. *The Peking Review*, Feb. 5, 1971.
18. The history of U.S. corn yields is summarized from James O. Bray and Patricia Watkins, "Technical Change in Corn Production in the United States, 1890-1960." *Journal of Farm Economics*, 46(4):741-765, Nov. 1964.
19. Nicol, Hugh, *The Limits of Man, An Inquiry into the Scientific Bases of Human Population*, Constable, London, 1967, p. 88: "In 1900 Lawes and Gilbert published a voluminous paper in which they pointed out *inter alia* that in non-leguminous crops such as cereals and turnips, in the state in which they are usually harvested, a characteristic effect of nitrogenous fertilizers is to increase yields per acre of starch, sugar, and fat—the non-nitrogenous constituents . . . (t)his magisterial statement has not been mentioned in any textbook as far as I know." (J. B. Lawes and J. H. Gilbert, *Phil. Trans. Roy. Soc.*, B, 1900, 192:139-210.) One exception, though it is not a textbook, is William Albert Albrecht, *Soil Fertility and Animal Health*, Fred Hahne Printing Co., Webster City, Iowa, 1958.
20. Albrecht, William A., "Diagnoses or Post-Mortems?" *Natural Food and Farming*, Sept. 1959, pp. 6-32.
21. *Feedstuffs*, June 14, 1947.
22. Lappe, Francis Moore, *Diet for a Small Planet*, Ballatine, New York, N.Y., 1971, p. 12.
23. For instance, the application of nitrogen fertilizer in Alberta has aggravated the problem of sulphur deficiency in alfalfa and clovers. See M. Nyborg and C. F. Bentley, "Sulphur Deficiency in Rapeseed and Cereal Grains," *Sulphur Institute Journal*, 7(3):16-17, Fall 1971, and see also Michael Blake, *Concentrated Incomplete Fertilizers*, Crosby Lockwood, London, 1967, p. 14 ff.
24. *The Life Sciences*, National Academy of Sciences, Washington, D.C., 1970, p. 1, 961.
25. Commoner, Barry, "Nature Under Attack," *Columbia Forum*, 11(1), Spring 1968.
26. Albrecht, William A., "The 'Half-Lives' of Our Soils," *Natural Food and Farming*, Sept. 1966, pp. 7-11.
27. Revelle, Roger, and Hans E. Suess, *Tellus*, 9(1): 18-27.

Table 5. Change in farm operator and family incomes and levels of living, United States

Year	Net income of operators from farming, per farm (in dollars)[1]	Median farm-family income, all sources[3]	Percent of all farms receiving services	
			Electricity	Telephone
1910	652			
1935	775		10.9	
1940	706		30.4	
1945	2063		47.9	
1950	2421		84.0	
1955	2606[2]		94.2	
1960	2795[2]	2875	96.5	67
1965	3564[2]	4119	98.2	77
1970	5674[2]	6773	98.4	84
1975		10,845	98.6	90

Source: Data from Agricultural Statistics: 1951, p. 647; 1956, p. 569; 1961, p. 580; 1966, p. 591; 1971, p. 533; 1976, pp. 466, 500, 505; Historical Statistics of the United States, 1975, pp. 473, 483; Washington, D.C., U.S. Government Printing Office.
[1]U.S. Department of Agriculture survey data.
[2]These figures are for the preceding year.
[3]U.S. Bureau of the Census data.

Table 6. Median income, poverty status, and inequality of U.S. families by metropolitan and nonmetropolitan (urban, rural-farm, and rural-nonfarm) residence, 1969

Residence	Families		
	Median income (in dollars)	Percent below poverty	Index of income concentration[1]
Metropolitan			
Total	10,474	8.5	.351
Central cities	9507	11.0	.365
Nonmetropolitan			
Total	7832	15.4	.374
Urban	8573	12.1	.360
Rural nonfarm	7477	17.8	.369
Rural farm	6811	17.5	.413

Source: Data from U.S. Bureau of the Census: Census of population: 1970, General social and economic characteristics, Final Report PC(1)-C1 United States Summary, Washington, D.C., 1972, U.S. Government Printing Office.
[1]Gini index—the larger the number, the more unequal the distribution.

LEFT BEHIND

For a plantation hand, progress of blacks seems far removed

Sugar work make a man old, Mr. Adams says; last year's pay: $3,420
It's better than it was

RICHARD A. SHAFFER*

THIBODAUX, La.—It is early morning on Leighton Plantation, and the acres of lush, green sugarcane are waving in a breeze from across Bayou Lafourche. It is cool. But already Webster Adams is sweating. Since before dawn, he has been swinging a machete, cutting grass in the cane fields. It is hot work, and every few minutes he pauses to mop his face with the sleeve of his ragged shirt.

"Sugar work make a man old before his time, that's for sure," he says with a sigh. "Every year I make a little more money at it, but I never seems to get my head above water."

Webster Adams, a quiet, gentle man of 49, is a field hand and tractor driver on this 2,400-acre sugar plantation just outside Thibodaux on the rich delta of the Mississippi River. Like most of the state's 16,600 cane workers, he is black. And like most, he is struggling to

get by in a world where progress is often difficult to discern. For despite substantial economic and social strides by many blacks in recent years, Mr. Adams and 7.4 million other black Americans remain trapped in the poverty they have endured for generations.

His annual income has more than doubled in the last decade, climbing from $1,338 in 1963 to $3,420 last year. But the rising cost of living has wiped out much of that gain.

Last year the typical Louisiana cane worker supported a family of six on a paltry $3,116. That was up from $1,560 about 10 years ago but was still $2,028 below the federal government's official poverty level for farm families of that size.

By some measures, Mr. Adams and his fellow workers have actually lost ground. During the last decade, while the median income of the nation's black families was inching upward from 53% to 58% of the median white-family income, earnings of the Louisiana sugarcane worker held steady at a fourth of the national white level.

"Every time the sugar worker climbs a few rungs, the whole ladder moves up, so he's always at the lowest level," says Sister Anne Catherine Bizalion, a French nun and executive director of the Southern Mutual Help Association, an Abbeville, La., group that seeks to improve the lot of cane workers.

Ironically, cane-worker poverty persists in a day when the sugar industry itself seems sweeter than ever. Because of a world-wide scarcity of sugar and increasing demand, American consumers are paying $2.17 for a five-pound bag of sugar, nearly three times the price of a year ago and the highest level in history. As a result, growers are expected to harvest a record profit. Despite Hurricane Carmen, which flattened 20% of the Louisiana crop last month, the state's cane this year is expected to bring a gross price of $383.6 million, or 149% more than last year's crop.

In the past, little of the industry profits, however, have filtered down to the workers. Witness the shoddy condition of the plantation housing, known as "quarters," in which most workers live. White Louisiana growers lately have spent considerable sums to improve the quarters—the number with indoor toilets, for example, has risen to 83% from 18% five years ago—deplorable housing still abounds in the state's 17-parish sugar belt.

The Adams family, for example, lives in a weathered, four-room shack about a half-mile from the plantation owner's spacious brick home, which is set in a grove of massive, ancient live-oak trees gracefully draped with Spanish moss.

Although the Adams home, which dates from Reconstruction, is the shabbiest place on Leighton Plantation, it is far from the worst in the area.

The Adams home, which the family lives in rent-free, has a front wall of unpainted cypress that is rotten in places and shakes in the wind. The only plumbing is one cold-water spigot in the kitchen. "At night, if you get up and turn on a light," Mr. Adams says, "you find the kitchen table be black with roaches."

To keep out summer mosquitoes and winter winds, the inside walls are prepared with pages of the Thibodaux Daily Comet, the local newspaper. There aren't any closets: clothes are hung on the bedroom walls and covered with sheets of plastic to protect them from the water that drips through the cardboard ceiling when it rains.

"So much rain fall inside this house, you might as well be standing outside," says Mr. Adams' wife, Laura Victor.

For his part, the plantation owner, Fernand Price, says the Adams house is "simply not worth fixing." It is one of five located on land he sold to a housing developer, and it will be razed within a year. When

that happens, the Adams family will be moved into another plantation house, perhaps one of the 10 in which toilets and paneling recently were installed.

"I try to do the best I can by these people," Mr. Price says.

Earlier this year, the prospect of record sugar profits prompted efforts to improve the lot of plantation workers through amendments to the 40-year-old Sugar Act. The act sets quotas and subsidies for sugar production and authorizes the Department of Agriculture to establish fair wages and reasonable working conditions. But in a surprise move, the House voted to let the entire act expire, and even if the legislation is resurrected after the November elections, observers see little chance that the worker amendments will be part of it.

As it happens, Mr. Adams already receives some of the benefits proposed by labor advocates. He is covered by workmen's-compensation insurance, for example, and for the last four years has been given a week's paid vacation annually. Otherwise, however, his job has few rewards.

Occasionally, the work is hazardous. He spent one recent day in the fields holding a flag to guide crop dusters and repeatedly was sprayed with a chemical designed to kill insects in the cane. "You got to wash that stuff right off soon as you get home," he says.

Some days he cuts grass with a hook-bladed machete, known locally as a "cane knife," or helps repair machinery at the equipment shed. Usually, however, his work consists of guiding a tractor back and forth across a field. During the late spring and summer, the season when the cane is planted and cultivated, his tractor pulls a drag-chopper, a machine that breaks and turns the earth. From mid-October through December, during the hectic harvest season, known as "grinding time," he hauls cane from the harvesting machines in the field to the raw-sugar mill about 100 yards from his front door.

He says the secret of his job, especially in the summer, is "to work as fast as you can early in the morning so you can fool around later in the day when the sun be beating down on you. That way the man can't say you ain't done nothing." he explains with a grin that reveals a half-mouthful of teeth, all decaying at the gum line. "You got to keep cool."

Following that admonition, he has cut vents in his battered, sweat-stained hats and doesn't always insist that Laura patch the holes in his faded shirts. "You get to let things breathe," he says.

"IT'S BETTER THAN IT WAS"

A wiry man (he is five-feet, six-inches tall and weighs 142 pounds) whose hair is just beginning to turn gray, Mr. Adams has worked in the cane fields since he was 10 years old and is fairly content with his lot despite its hardships. "Farm work ain't good, but it's better than it was, that's for sure. My daddy plowed with mules; I got a tractor," he says.

"Unless the mill is running, life is quiet here. I got a garden to raise me some okras and beans. If I went to town, I'd always be looking for work. And anyway, I'd just be driving a tractor for the Highway Department or something because all I can do is drive a tractor. Lord, I be driving a tractor the day I die."

Every weekday before dawn, Mr. Adams strolls a few yards down the gravel road to the equipment shed near the sugar mill, followed by a pack of scruffy cats that live under his porch. As he refuels his tractor, he chats with the other hands about the weather, their families and last night's television programs.

"Look like we in for another hot day," says Welmon Pharagood, a fellow tractor driver and father of 10.

"Yep," Mr. Adams says. "It do, it do. A hot one. That's for sure."

He swings his cooler of ice water onto the tractor, then climbs aboard and drives to the fields, drag-chopper in tow. Partly obscured by a cloud of dust, his tractor lumbers and bounces across the fields until 8 a.m., when he stops for breakfast—a bologna sandwich he has brought in a paper sack.

NO TIME TO THINK

"Out in them cane fields, you ain't got time to think," he says, sitting in the shade of the tractor and sipping on ice water. "You just be turning them rows or chopping that ground, and you be looking to 4:30, when you be knocking off. You be half-hoping it rain and cool off and half-hoping it don't so you can get in them hours."

Mr. Adams is paid by the hour; if he doesn't work, he doesn't get paid. When it rains there is little work to be done on all but the largest sugar plantations, and Mr. Adams is idle much of the year, especially January through March, when the harvested fields are a swamp of brown cane stubble. During this period, the family gets by on food stamps and earnings from the harvest time. However, the harvest income isn't saved in cash: it is used to buy such staples as rice and beans in 25-pound sacks and canned goods, which are stored to feed the family during the lean months of late winter.

During this year's harvest, which began on Leighton Plantation this week, Mr. Adams will be paid $2.50 an hour—the new wage set by the Agriculture Department and up from $2. "That money will help out a little bit, but food and everything has gone up so much, it still won't be enough," he says.

Each working day at noon, Mr. Adams returns home for his main meal of the day. When he arrives his wife is in the kitchen stewing okra and frying homemade flour cakes. She is 47 but looks much older. She suffers from a chronic circulatory condition that requires frequent trips to the closest charity hospital, in New Orleans, 60 miles away.

In the living room, which doubles as a bedroom, daughters Daisy Mae and Louise, who are both in their 20s, are arguing whether a young doctor on "As the World Turns" should confess that he is the hit-and-run driver everyone is looking for. Except during cane-planting time, neither daughter works outside the home; both spend most of their days watching television. Louise is unmarried and lives with her parents. Daisy lives two houses away. She is separated from her husband, Willie, who was also a tractor driver on Leighton until he recently moved to another plantation. In a corner sits grandson Mickey, who is three years old but has just begun to talk.

Mr. Adams thumbs a little tobacco into his pipe and settles into a broken-down chair to watch television until his food is on the table. Although he fishes occasionally, television is his principal pastime. "Mostly, I like Westerns," he says, "but I sometimes does watch the news."

It is television news that has provided almost all his contact with recent black history. He remembers the civil-rights movement, for instance, as a series of film clips of sit-ins, marches and riots.

Still, the movement did make important changes in the lives of his children. When he was a boy, he recalls, he had to walk several miles, barefoot, over gravel roads to a one-room, all-black school. His daughters were taken to integrated schools by buses that stopped at their door. One of 14 children, Mr. Adams had to quit school after the first grade to go to work in the sugar fields to help support his family. Consequently, he can neither read nor write. Louise, however, completed the ninth grade; Daisy Mae, the eighth.

"I DOESN'T VOTE"

For Mr. Adams himself, however, the benefits of the civil-rights movement are less apparent.

Since the Voting Rights Act of 1965, for example, the proportion of registered black voters in Lafourche parish has increased 40%. But Mr. Adams has never bothered to register. "I doesn't vote because sometimes you votes for the right man and sometimes you votes for the wrong one. And whoever gets in isn't going to care about me anyway, so what difference does it make?"

Legally, he now can live wherever he wishes. But,

like almost all cane workers, he feels bound for economic reasons to the plantation housing supplied free by the grower. "I don't make enough wages to pay rent in town," he explains.

Today he can eat and drink in formerly all-white restaurants and taverns. But his family is too poor to dine out, and when he does go for an occasional beer, he prefers to sip it in what he calls "colored bars."

"I tell you the truth," he says, "I think what that Martin Luther King did was good. That's for sure. But it never made much difference to me."

Agribusiness: overkill on the farm

HARRISON WELLFORD

In July, 1970, a 16-year-old boy in North Carolina collapsed and died after walking bare armed and barefooted through his father's tobacco field. The cause of death was acute pesticide poisoning. The boy's arms and legs had brushed against tobacco leaves which had been sprayed one day before with "Big Bad John," the trade name for an insecticide containing the poison, parathion. A few weeks later at another farm in North Carolina's tobacco country, a boy fell into convulsions and died after playing barefoot on his front lawn. The cause of death was puzzling at first; then his parents remembered that *five weeks earlier,* a container of parathion had overturned on their way home from a farm supply store. They had washed out the trunk of the car near the spot where the boy died. While the cause of death has not been definitely confirmed, the dead boy displayed the classic symptoms of massive organophosphate poisoning. Before the summer of 1970, tobacco farmers controlled their pests with DDT and other chlorinated hydrocarbons, pesticides which are relatively safe to the touch. Now these pesticides are being phased out because of their long-term hazards to the environment. As a result, ironically, the use of other pesticides has suddenly created higher levels of immediate danger. In North Carolina and in other cotton and tobacco regions of the nation, new substances hundreds of times more toxic than DDT are coming into general use. Parathion, the most popular substitute for DDT on cotton and tobacco, is an organophosphate insecticide. Unlike DDT it does not persist in the environment and does not accumulate in human tissue. It does have one drawback: when absorbed through the skin or in-

gested, it poisons rapidly by a devastating assault on the nervous system. A few drops of parathion concentrate on the skin will sicken a man and a few more will kill him.

Organophosphates belong to a class of chemicals developed as by-products of nerve gas research during World War II. They attack the nervous system by suppressing blood enzymes known as cholinesterases which help regulate the body's nerve impulses. Organophosphates like parathion and Phosdrin are the biggest pesticide killers in this country. Low-level exposures create chronic eye irritations, nausea, cramps, depression, and chronic fatigue. If exposure is stopped, the patient usually recovers. The long-term effects of chronic exposure to organophosphate poisoning remain unknown.

In the spring of 1970, over 20 children became violently ill with nausea and stomach cramps when their elementary school in Phoenix, Arizona, was doused by the spray of a lethal agriculture chemical drifting from a nearby sugarbeet field. The spray contained the organophosphate Thimet, the second most toxic of all pesticides in common use. When the crop duster made his run, the wind was blowing about 10 miles per hour from the direction of the field toward the school. The stench from the spray lingered in its hallways for several days. At first, Robert Rayburn, administrator of the state pest control applicators board, a regulatory body responsible for pesticide safety, maintained that none of the chemical had drifted from the sugarbeet field to the school. When he was confronted with the sick children, he remained unconcerned: "This is one of the hazards of living next to a field which must be sprayed to save crops. People should learn not to build houses next to fields in these areas."

What is remarkable about this incident is not only

the insensitivity of the state pest control official, but that a farmer can spray his field with a pesticide as toxic as Thimet on a windy day a few hundred yards from an elementary school and *break no law.* "There was no violation of law here," said Rayburn. All the law requires is a one-fourth-mile corridor between the area sprayed and the school. In this case the intervening distance was precisely that. The lesson is that methods of application, such as aerial spraying, can be as important as basic toxicity in predicting the hazards of a pesticide.

Paraquat is a nitrogen compound which is used as an herbicide; it is different from Thimet and parathion in that it has a delayed effect. The Chevron Chemical Company, using billboards and radio spots, has heavily promoted the use of Paraquat on cotton and soybeans in the South. Finding themselves deluged with requests for Paraquat from farmers, professional crop dusters wrote to the Civil Aeronautics Board for guidance in its use. CAB responded in 1969 with an unprecedented warning: Paraquat in small quantities can have "a delayed and irreversible effect on the lungs. There is no known antidote at this time." The pulmonary fibrosis develops gradually. By the time the victim realizes that his lungs are damaged it is usually too late.

Presently Paraquat is being sprayed promiscuously over the cotton and soybean fields of the South. Chevron's hard-sell ad campaign and the Paraquat label fail to mention that this chemical, when ingested, has no antidote. According to an official at the National Communicable Disease Center, Chevron's claim that one has to drink Paraquat to get a toxic dose is not true. Both the Center and the Pesticide Regulation Division (recently transferred from the Department of Agriculture to the Environmental Protection Agency) warn that inhalation may be a hazard and have recommended that it be used only with masks, goggles, and protective clothing. The cautions are rarely followed in practice.

In August, 1970, a pesticide aerial applicator in Napoleonville, Louisiana, wrote to the CAB complaining about pressure from growers to apply Paraquat. He stated that many soybean fields are surrounded by tenant shacks, that some of these homes rely on open rain barrels and wells for water, and that often people are working in the fields while they are being sprayed. He questioned the discrepancy between the elaborate precautions the CAB suggests for aerial applicators for their own protection and the lack of concern by any federal agency for the people on the ground who may breathe Paraquat vapors or ingest it through their water supply.

On a large California ranch in 1965, a four-year-old boy and his three-year-old sister were playing around a spray rig while their mother worked in the field. The boy took the cap off a gallon can of tetraethylpyrophosphate (TEPP) left on the rig. The three-year-old put her finger in the can and licked it. She vomited immediately, became unconscious, and was dead on arrival at the nearby hospital. TEPP is the most deadly of all pesticides in common use. The estimated fatal dose for TEPP concentrate for an adult is one drop orally or one drop on the skin, a toxicity which puts it in a class with nerve gas.

The Federal Commission on Pesticides and Their Relationship to Environmental Health (Mrak Commission) reported a case of a woman who ate the tip and several leaves of a mint plant growing near a plot being treated with an experimental pesticide. She developed a nearly fatal case of "fulminating intoxication." The mint she had eaten grew adjacent to rose plants whose roots had been treated with Temik, Union Carbide's trade name for the insecticide aldicarb.

Temik is one of the most poisonous chemicals ever developed for general use in the United States. It is a carbamate insecticide and, like the organophosphate parathion, it inhibits the cholinesterase enzymes vital to nerve transmission. The only other insecticide of acute toxicity comparable to Temik in its technical form is the organophosphate TEPP. Temik is one of the few pesticides more toxic to mammals than to insects. It is at least five times as toxic to the laboratory rat as to houseflies. Union Carbide envisions a potential market for Temik equivalent to that of the carbamate Sevin, which has sales approximating $80 million. Temik was sold commercially for the first time in 1970 to treat cotton in the Mississippi Delta. Union Carbide is preparing to launch a major advertising campaign this year to promote Temik and hopes to extend its use to potatoes, citrus fruits, and other crops.

Union Carbide has worked hard to insure that Temik can be used safely and has invested nearly $10 million in its development. The company bases its safety claims on the fact that Temik is formulated as granules covered with a chemical coating which permits the poison to be gradually released. The granules are planted two inches under the soil so that in normal use exposure to wildlife is eliminated. The aldicarb poison in Temik is absorbed by the roots of the cotton and gives the cotton plant a built-in systemic insecticide for up to 10 weeks or more.

Union Carbide has organized the most elaborate safety program ever developed for a pesticide, including a 24-hour emergency telephone number for medical assistance and safety instruction, instruction of physicians, poison control centers in areas where Temik is used, and special courses in safe handling and emergency procedures for all regional distributors, warehousemen, and field personnel.

Despite these precautions, lingering doubt about Temik's safety under field conditions caused the Pesticide Regulation Division to hold up its registration for over three years. Some leading scientists doubt whether it should ever have been registered. The carbowax coating on the Temik granules can be dissolved by moisture. Farm workers will be handling Temik in humid climates where sweat and rain may remove the coating.

When Temik is used on thousands of farms instead of a few carefully monitored experimental acres, Union Carbide will almost certainly find it too expensive to enforce its present safety procedures. There are bound to be accidents.

THE NUT BEHIND THE SPRAY CAN

Pesticides such as these are used by thousands of farmers every day. A recent survey of small farmers in Hawaii revealed that 46 per cent regularly use Paraquat, 33 per cent use parathion, and 18 per cent use TEPP. The hazards—both short-term in the form of acute toxicity to users and long-term in the form of potential impact on birth defects, cancer, or mutations in man—provide a standard for measuring responsiveness to the public interest in industry, the executive agencies, and Congress.

The pesticide makers and the federal government claim that even these deadly poisons are safe for general use if the label on the container prescribes a safe use. The motto "Stop: Read the Label," usually with the credit "Courtesy of the National Agricultural Chemicals Association," can be found in most farm and gardening publications.

This motto projects the pesticide lobby's image of social responsibility. Its basic theme is that pesticide problems, if they exist, arise only through consumer misuse. For those who followed the struggle for automobile safety legislation, the motto has a familiar ring. As scapegoat for consumer injuries, the nut behind the wheel has now been joined by the nut behind the spray can.

As protection against pesticide hazards, the label hardly satisfies the industry's obligation to public safety. First, four out of five pesticide accidents occur where the nut behind the spray can is less than five years old. Second, many studies have shown that few farmers or homeowners read the label before using pesticides. Even if the user tries to read the label, he may have little chance of understanding it. A two-year study by the University of Illinois completed in 1971 found that "the average pesticide label is suitable only for those with at least 10 to 12.9 years of formal education."

Some labels are so contradictory that they provoke laughter rather than outrage, as this excerpt from congressional hearings in 1969 shows:

Mr. Naughton [committee counsel]: Mr. Chairman, this is a labeling for concentrated insecticide, fly and roach spray, manufactured by the Hysan products Co. of Chicago:
The cautions include the following statements:
Use in well-ventilated rooms or areas only. Always spray away from you. Do not stay in room that has been heavily treated. Avoid inhalation.
On the other side, the directions for use start out in this manner:
Close all doors, windows, and transoms. Spray with a fine mist sprayer freely upwards in all directions so the room is filled with the vapor. If insects have not dropped to the floor in three minutes, repeat spraying, as quantity sprayed was insufficient. After 10 minutes, doors and windows may be opened.
Rep. Rosenthal: If there is anybody around to open them. [Laughter].
Rep. Fountain: Any comment on that particular label?
Dr. Hays [Pesticide Regulation Division Director]: I have no comment. I would have to study the label carefully.

This helps explain why labels have been ineffective in preventing the 75,000 acute pesticide poisonings which the National Product Safety Commission estimates occur each year. This is only a rough estimate. Until very recently there has been no nationwide attempt to compile records on pesticide poisonings. The Mrak Commission lamented in 1969 that no federal agency has a clear picture of pesticide hazards in America and predicted that the actual number of accidents far exceeds those reported. Some local studies support the Mrak estimate. Of 1,000 deaths subjected to medico-legal investigation over a 10-year period in Florida, pesticides caused nearly 10 per cent of all deaths and were the leading cause of death for the under-five-year age group. Pesticides are also the leading cause of fatal poisonings in Puerto Rico.

None of these estimates take into account the long-term hazards which may result from chronic exposure. These effects may be far more subtle than direct poisoning upon ingestion. Researchers who compared two groups of homeowners, one spraying pesticides once a week or more, the other spraying less often, found that the heavy use group had significantly reduced lung capacity, more asthma and chronic sinus inflammation, and twice as much chronic hayfever. The long-term effects of chronic exposure to pesticides on the incidence of cancer, birth defects, and mutations remain unknown.

Until very recently, the Agriculture Department's Pesticide Regulation Division was egregiously nonchalant about investigating the accident records of the pesticides it regulates. This attitude was revealed in hearings before a House subcommittee in 1969:

Rep. Fountain: Approximately how many reports do you receive annually on pesticide poisoning?

Mr. Dellavechia [PRD staff]: Last year we investigated 151 accidents.

Mr. Naughton: You think the 150 poisoning reports or 175 that you receive annually is a fair share of the total number of pesticide poisonings?

Dr. Hays [PRD director]: I think it is a reasonable estimate. . . .

Mr. Naughton: The poison control centers [set up by the Public Health Service] . . . receive . . . 5,000 reports of poisonings by pesticides annually, of which approximately 4,000 involved children under five. The poison control people advise us that in their opinion the number of poisonings is actually eight to 10 times greater . . . the number of pesticide poisonings is somewhere in the area of 50,000 annually.

Rep. Fountain: It is obvious you weren't aware they receive about 5,000 reports a year.

Dr. Hays: That is correct.

Rep. Fountain: How many of the 150 or so reports . . . you receive . . . involve human beings?

Dr. Hays: Of the 151, 52 of these involved humans [the other victims were cows, horses, and other farm animals].

The risk from the new generation of pesticides is greatest for the farm workers who pick vegetables and fruits sprayed by organophosphates and carbamates. This is a very defenseless population. Many suffer from malnutrition, a condition which increases their vulnerability to pesticide poisoning. Most have no union to bargain for their safety. These workers and the land owners who hire them are alarmingly ignorant about pesticide hazards. But this ignorance is often compounded by the land owner's refusal to comply with the few safety regulations which do exist.

The list of violations is tedious to relate. Farm workers in contact with pesticides have no place to wash their hands, recently sprayed fields are not posted, waiting periods after spraying are not observed, medical care is not available. But while violations of these standards threaten the health of farm workers, the Department of Agriculture (USDA) continues to deliver huge agricultural subsidies to growers who regularly ignore health laws. On July 27, 1970, California Rural Legal Assistance unsuccessfully petitioned USDA to cut off payments to 30 agricultural growers who received subsidies of $7.1 million in 1969, while allegedly violating these laws.

In 1966, California reported 1,347 cases of occupational disease attributed to pesticides and agricultural chemicals. Farm laborers accounted for more than half (704) of the 1,347 reports, and part of the agricultural work force is excluded from these statistics. Even based on these figures, the farming industry has the highest rate of occupational disease in California, more than two and one half times that for all other industries.

PAX ARSENICA

There comes a time in the study of any regulatory agency when one stumbles across the paradigm case of an enforcement fiasco. This is a case where life seems to imitate art—where all the nuances of failure are so apparent that they assume the proportions of caricature rather than truth. The Pesticide Regulation Division's treatment of pesticides containing arsenic is such a case.

In the summer of 1969, an Iowan removed weeds from his yard with an arsenic crabgrass killer. The herbicide was in granular form and was sprinkled on the lawn. Three weeks later he mowed the lawn. Just to be neighborly, he tossed the grass clippings into the next yard for some horses grazing there. Four horses died in 48 hours and two more died later. One month later investigators found that the granules were still on the grass.

Because of cases like this, public health officials have long objected to the use of arsenicals around the home. In order to be effective against rodents inside and weeds outside, arsenic is often placed in corners, cupboards, or basements in the home or scattered on the lawn outside. Both uses make them available to children and pets. The four classes of arsenicals—lead arsenate, sodium arsenate, sodium arsenite, and arsenic trioxide—have accounted for an estimated 3,000 accidental poisonings, most of them of children under five, every year for the last 10 years. In 1965, the Department of Health, Education, and Welfare officially requested PRD not to permit use of arsenicals around the home. HEW was influenced by the President's Science Advisory Committee in its 1963 report, "The Uses of Pesticides," which stated: "As a corollary to cautious registration of new pesticides, more hazardous compounds might well be removed from the market when equally effective and less hazardous substitutes are found." The arsenicals have several more benign substitutes.

Despite their alarming accident record and the presence of safer substitutes on the market, the arsenicals became the beneficiaries of PRD's extraordinary reluctance to take enforcement action against an established product. Unlike DDT, where the hazards to man are long-term and almost impossible to link to concrete victims, the arsenicals are acutely toxic—there are documented cases of multiple human victims, most of them children. Yet even here, the burden of proof which PRD requires before it will suspend a product led to years of delay and unnecessary poisonings.

In August, 1967, two years after HEW had filed its objection, the Department of Agriculture (USDA) issued a "notice to manufacturers" informing the makers of sodium arsenite and arsenic trioxide that their products were soon to be cancelled for home use.

This notice greatly alarmed the Pax Company, a small Utah corporation which had suffered net operating losses for three straight years. Its only profitable products were herbicides containing arsenic trioxide. Pax anxiously awaited the cancellation order which usually quickly follows a notice. Four months went by and no order arrived. PRD then sent another note to Pax saying that it was contemplating the issuance of a cancellation order and would give the company 30 days to submit its views. Another eight months went by with no further word from Washington. Then on July 25, 1968, PRD published in the Federal Register a notice that the registration of Pax's products was to be cancelled within 90 days (a 60-day bonus over the normal 30-day deadline). But just before cancellation was to go into effect, PRD once again backed off and granted Pax more time to compile data on the toxicity of its products. It informed Pax that action would be delayed "until further notice." Pax was now in its 15th month since the original notice from USDA *and still counting.*

In March, 1969, USDA informed the company that it intended to implement cancellation in "the near future" and asked for more information. Then suddenly the logjam broke. USDA announced on July 18, 1969, that the registration of Pax's arsenical herbicides would be cancelled in 30 days. The stalemate was ended, not by new information about the hazards of arsenic around the home, but by what a federal judge was later to call "psychological pressure" applied to Department of Agriculture officials by a congressional subcommittee. He was referring to the Fountain (Rep. L.H., of North Carolina) hearings, in which USDA representatives were thoroughly embarrassed by the Pesticide Regulation Division's lack of action on arsenicals. In fact, Dr. George Irving, head of the Agricultural Research Service, admitted that he personally had concluded long ago that arsenicals were too dangerous for home use. Yet they were still being marketed. After extracting this information, subcommittee counsel James Naughton sharply questioned Irving's subordinate, PRD director Hays:

Mr. Naughton: You don't have doubts about arsenicals. You have an accident history. You may have a lingering doubt that maybe an exception could be made for this product. It's been two years.

When did they submit this information that caused you to have some doubts that maybe it's not as dangerous as some of the others?

Dr. Hays: About July of 1968.

Mr. Naughton: All right. That's a year ago.

Dr. Bayley [Dr. Hays' superior in USDA]: They submitted some more this spring.

Dr. Hays: Following this there were. . . .

Mr. Naughton: And I'm sure they will be happy to keep on submitting information indefinitely as long as it will keep their product on the market. Hasn't that occurred to you?

Dr. Hays: I'm sure there will come a point. . . .

Mr. Naughton: How many more poisonings of children will it take?

Dr. Hays: We would hope none.

Mr. Naughton: Yet you are willing to take the chance.

The Fountain subcommittee succeeded where HEW and hundreds of victims had failed, for USDA cancelled the Pax products soon after the hearings. Pax, still undaunted, promptly requested appointment of a science advisory panel, an action which delayed implementation of cancellation once again. Then with the Fountain committee off its back, USDA delayed appointment of the committee for nine months, until April, 1970. Pax's products had enjoyed 32 months of reprieve *and were still counting.*

The panel's first meeting was not scheduled until August, 1970, but there were signs that Pax's time was running out. On June 26, 1970, USDA refused to renew the registration of Pax's Three-Year Crabgrass Control (one of Pax's several arsenical registrations) "pending the outcome of administrative proceedings" in Pax's case. Dr. Thomas Harris, chief of pesticide registration at HEW, urged prohibition of the Pax product because of its acute toxicity and the possibility that it may cause skin and lung cancer. In an affidavit supporting PRD's action, he cited a survey of 8,000 smelter workers exposed to arsenic trioxide. The incidence of respiratory cancer among workers of 15 years or more experience was eight times that of workers not exposed to arsenic.

In August, 1970, in the 36th month since USDA's original notice and over five years since HEW's objection to home arsenicals, Pax launched a new strategy of delay. It went into federal court to seek an injunction against the convening of the science advisory panel which *it* had requested. It also asked the court to order the Department of Agriculture to approve the registration of its crabgrass killer and it won. Willis W. Ritter, chief judge of the United States District Court in Utah, found that USDA, despite three years of deliberations, had acted "arbitrarily, capriciously, and beyond its authority under the Insecticide Act, and *in violation of the due process* clause of the Administrative Procedure Act. . . ." Judge Ritter apparently was taking pity on a small, nearly bankrupt Utah company which must compete with corporate giants like Chevron and Dow Chemical. He was also impressed by PRD's reluctance to take action in the Pax case until embarrassed by a congressional committee and by its failure to cancel or suspend even more hazardous products.

The effect of USDA's delays and Judge Ritter's decision is that Pax now has a monopoly in home herbicides containing arsenic. The six other companies which also proposed these herbicides but which dropped out of the market in compliance with USDA's initial notice in 1967 must marvel at the price they have paid for believing PRD meant what it said. The Department of Agriculture has now appealed the case to a higher court.

As the Pax and DDT cases clearly show, federal procedures for cancellation of dangerous pesticides seriously need streamlining. These drawn-out procedures make a mockery of the legal requirement that the burden of establishing safety remains with the maker of a pesticide after it is registered. In the Pax case, the hazards are very concrete and there are no overriding public benefits, given the substitute herbicides and rodenticides available. Yet cancellation procedures offered Pax an almost endless opportunity for delay.

3

The consequences of changes in agricultural technology for rural neighborhoods and communities

Changing rural life in the Great Plains

LAUREL D. LOFTSGARD and STANLEY W. VOELKER*

Economic forces stemming from changes in agricultural technology have encouraged declining farm numbers, increasing farm size, more leisure and greater mobility of rural people. Documentary statistics concerning many of these factors have become part of the economist's vocabulary, so there seems little need to repeat all of them here. The effects of technological changes vary somewhat from area to area, depending upon local situations. The purpose of this paper is to associate these and other changes with their effects on rural living in the Great Plains. In so doing, we will use North Dakota as an example because the experiences here are representative of at least a large part of the northern Plains area.

UNDERLYING CAUSATIVE FACTORS

The technological advances most basic to changes in rural life are those which increase the physical productivity of land (substitution of capital for land) and mechanization (substitution of capital for labor). From these two phenomena, the first round effect is largely shrinking farm numbers and fewer people employed on farms. But from this situation, one can extend a wide network of cause and effect relationships that encompass outmigration of people, changes in per capita income, structure of businesses, personal leisure, school organization, education levels, churches, and the goals and values of individuals. Each of these items is a facet or partial explanation of changing rural life in the Plains.

The increase in average farm size and the resulting decrease in farm numbers have come mainly from at-

tempts of thousands of farmers to adjust the acreage operated to production abilities of family labor and mechanization. Although some operators are going broke and are being "forced" out of farming, a major share of farm consolidation has come from death and retirement of older operators. As these units are merged with other farms, farm income tends to increase and a more desirable living is possible for remaining farmers. Concurrently, however, the opportunities to get started in farming diminish, which in turn augments the exceedingly high rate of outmigration from the Plains.[1]

Other factors, equally or more importantly, responsible for outmigration are a lack of industrial development, birthrates which have been among the highest in the whole country[2] and a decline in number of retail firms that supply goods and services to farm families.[3] The inherent effects from these factors on the supply and demand for human employment necessitate the outmigration process.

CHANGES IN LEVELS OF LIVING

Many goods and services, considered luxuries a decade ago, are fast becoming necessities—running

□ Published with the approval of the Director as North Dakota Agricultural Experiment Station Journal No. 36. From Journal of Farm Economics **45**:1110-1117, 1963.
*North Dakota State University and Economic Research Service, U.S. Department of Agriculture.

[1]U.S. Bureau of the Census, "Current Population Reports: Population Estimates," Series P-25, No. 72, May 1953, and No. 247, April 1962.
[2]The two Dakotas consistently have been among the top five states in the various statistical ratios used to compare birthrates of various segments of the population, such as fertility ratios, number of children ever born per 1,000 women, and net reproduction rates. See T. Lynn Smith, "Fundamentals of Population Study," J. B. Lippincott Co., 1960, pp. 297-307; and U.S. Bureau of the Census, "United States Census of Population, 1960," Series PC(1)-B and Series PC (1)-C.
[3]According to data compiled from the Annual Statistical Reports of the Sales Tax Division, North Dakota Tax Commission, the number of retail firms in villages and farm service centers of less than 3,000 inhabitants decreased 8 percent between 1954 and 1962.

water, "clean" heat and various home appliances. The proportion of rural farm dwellings with electric lighting increased from about 15 percent in 1940 to 97 percent at the present time.

Heating and cooking fuels in farm homes were almost exclusively coal and wood in 1940. By 1960, more than half the farm dwellings were heated with fuel oil or gas and 94 percent were using either gas or electricity for cooking (Table 1). By 1960, more than two-thirds of the dwellings had home food freezers and running water; more than half had flush toilets and either bathtubs or showers. The proportion with telephones increased from 28 to nearly 70 percent.

Television has been the spectacular change. It has supplemented radio as a communications medium for farmers (weather and market reports, agricultural extension programs, local announcements and news), but more importantly it has provided a means of entertainment and relaxation, overshadowing that formerly provided by radio or phonograph. The first television station in North Dakota made its initial broadcast in the spring of 1953. Seven years later, 88 percent of the rural farm dwellings had television sets. At present, 90 to 95 percent of the farms are within range of at least one of the 11 television stations in the state.

Table 1. Percentage of North Dakota rural farm dwellings using various household and amenity items in 1940, 1950 and 1960

Item	Year		
	1940	**1950**	**1960**
	Percent	*Percent*	*Percent*
Electric lighting	15.5	67.7	97.0[a]
Radio	87.2	97.2	97.1
Television	0	0.8	87.7
Telephone	27.9	41.6	69.6
Heating fuel:			
Coal, coke, or wood	98.5	69.3	42.3
Fuel oil, utility gas, or bottled gas	1.4	28.5	57.2
Cooking fuel:			
Coal, coke, or wood	93.1	41.4	5.2
Utility gas or bottled gas	0.6	38.8	36.5
Electricity	0.2	11.8	57.2
Running water inside structure	6.0	26.3	68.4
Flush toilet inside structure	2.9	15.3	56.3
Bathtub or shower in structure	3.3	18.3	57.8
Home food freezer	—[b]	—[b]	71.4
Clothes dryer	—[b]	—[b]	40.1

Source: Compiled from U.S. Census of Housing.
[a]Estimate made by Ulteig Engineering Corporation.
[b]Data not available.

The proportion of farmers with automobiles increased from 83 percent in 1940 to 94 percent in 1959. Almost all farm families now have either an automobile or a pickup truck and over a third of them have two or more automobiles. Accompanying this increased number of vehicles in rural areas has been a steady improvement of roads and highways. In 1959, 78 percent of the farms were located on all-weather roads, compared with only 32 percent in 1940.[4]

Extended vacation trips are becoming more common and farm families increasingly are participating in bowling, curling, water sports, golf, riding clubs and various social activities that previously were enjoyed mainly by townsfolk.

COMMUNITY ADJUSTMENTS

During the settlement period (1880-1915), townsite companies laid out many more cities and villages in North Dakota than were actually needed for the then prevailing horse-and-wagon type of agriculture. The advent of the automobile and tractor, the subsequent improvement of roads and highways, the combination of farms, and the declining rural population all have accentuated the continuing struggle for survival among the villages.

The total population of the 12 cities, which had 5,000 or more inhabitants in 1950, increased 31 percent during the 1950's. Population changes for villages of less than 3,000 are shown in Table 2.[5]

Sales-tax collections show the changes in retail trade of cities and villages of various sizes. During the last five years, the volume of retail trade in the 12 largest cities increased 3 percent. Villages in the 2,000 to 3,000 size range showed little or no change, while

[4]U.S. Bureau of the Census, "United States Census of Agriculture 1959."
[5]Compiled from U.S. Bureau of the Census, "United States Census of Population 1960," Series PC(1)-A. None of the cities and villages in North Dakota is in the 3,000 to 4,999 population range.

Table 2. Population changes for villages of less than 3,000 inhabitants

Size of village (number of inhabitants 1950)	Number of villages in group	Percentage of villages with		
		Population decrease of 10 percent or more	Less than 10 percent change (+ or −)	Population increase of 10 percent or more
2,000-2,999	6	0	66.7	33.3
1,000-1,999	42	7.1	69.1	23.8
500-999	44	22.7	52.3	25.0
100-499	215	55.3	37.2	7.5
Less than 100	26	73.1	26.9	0

those in the 1,000 to 2,000 size range lost an average of 8 percent of their retail trade. Some of the villages with 500 to 1,000 inhabitants lost much of their retail trade, while others made substantial gains. Considerable change in farm trade patterns is occurring among villages of this size. Of the villages in the 100 to 500 size range, only a few held their own or gained, the average for this group being a decline of 14 percent.

A detailed examination of changes in population and retail trade of individual villages indicates a fairly regular pattern concerning their future. Between 50 to 60 of the 345 villages in North Dakota are emerging as the "primary farm service centers." These are—and for the next few years probably will continue to be—the most important shopping and marketing centers for farmers in all parts of the state, except those within 20 to 30 miles of the 12 urban centers. These primary farm service centers are not dying or decadent villages. On the contrary, they have considerable vitality. Most of them have experienced substantial population gains since 1940 and now have between 1,000 to 3,000 inhabitants. Apparently, it takes a farm center of at least 1,000 population to provide a minimum of medical and dental services and the wide variety of goods and services required by present day farm families. Correspondingly, villages now having less than 1,000 inhabitants likely will continue to decline, unless some type of economic activity can be found to offset the decrease in farm business.

The shifts in population from the farms and smaller villages to the larger villages and cities intensifies the need for changes in various organizations and institutions. School systems and rural churches are two types of institutions which are adversely affected by population decreases.

SCHOOL REORGANIZATION

North Dakota consistently has been one of the top states in the percentage of personal income absorbed by public school revenues. At the same time, it has ranked very low among states in academic training and average salary of its teachers.[6] One reason for the relatively high costs per pupil and low quality of instruction in many rural areas of North Dakota has been the operation of an excessive number of small schools, which in turn has been encouraged by the small-district type of organization.

This situation, however, is changing. The number of school districts has declined from 2,871 to 829 since 1945, with most of the reorganizations being accomplished since 1957. During this same period, the number of one-teacher elementary schools decreased from 3,043 to 652, resulting partly from reorganizations and partly from decreasing school population in rural areas. The number of high schools decreased from 443 to 302.

Because of anticipated population decreases in the open country and smaller villages, school reorganization probably will continue as a burning issue in many communities. The disposition of smaller high schools is a particularly difficult problem. Sixty percent of the high schools now have fewer than 100 pupils each and only 14 percent have more than 200 pupils. Oddly enough, extremely small high schools are not characteristic of the more sparsely-settled areas. The vast majority of those with less than 100 pupils are in the eastern third of the state, where the settlement pattern is relatively dense. With few exceptions, they are located within 15 miles of other high schools via all-weather highways, so transportation is not a limiting factor.

Costs per pupil in the small high schools are unavoidably high, despite comparatively low teacher salaries and elimination of some science and modern language courses. Nearly all of the schools with less than 50 pupils have failed to meet accreditation standards. Some schools with 50 to 99 pupils are doing a fairly good job—71 percent are accredited—but if they attempt to provide the same quality of instruction and as rich a curriculum as that offered by larger high schools, their costs per pupil are very high. To cite an example, an accredited high school in a small village in the Red River Valley had a teaching staff of four for its 31 pupils in 1962. Its instruction cost per pupil was $1,055, compared with the state average of $589 and per pupil costs of $709 and $692 in two nearby high schools that had 153 and 108 pupils, respectively.[7]

School reorganization in North Dakota has resulted in an increasing proportion of farm children attending graded elementary and high schools in the villages, where presumably they benefit from a higher quality of instruction and a richer curriculum than would be possible in the open country. These changes have been accompanied by an increasing proportion of pupils completing the 8th grade and an increasing proportion of 8th grade graduates who graduate from high school. During the late 1940's, the number of 8th grade graduates in North Dakota, expressed as a percentage of the number of first graders eight years prior, varied from 57 to 64 percent. This percentage

[6]Research Division, National Education Association, "Rankings of the States 1962," Research Report No. 1962-R1, 1201 16th St. NW, Washington 6, D.C., January 1962.

[7]Compiled from data contained in Biennial Reports and mimeographed releases of the North Dakota State Superintendent of Public Instruction, Bismarck, N. Dak.

has increased fairly steadily since 1950 and reached 78 percent in 1962. Similarly, since the late 1940's, the number of high school graduates, expressed as a percentage of 8th grade graduates four years prior, has increased from about 48 percent to 79 percent.[7]

PARISH REORGANIZATION

For many years, North Dakota has had a large number of churches relative to population. Reasons for this include (1) the high proportion of foreign-born among the homesteaders, who established foreign-language churches which tended to continue as separate denominations after their members became English speaking; and (2) rivalry among denominational missionaries during the settlement period. The result of these factors has been an excessive number of small, struggling churches in rural areas. This is not a true characterization of all rural congregations and communities. Many strong, vigorous rural churches, effectively serving their respective communities, are ample testimony of what the rural church can and should be.

The number of rural churches in North Dakota has been declining for various reasons. Some simply died a lingering death as the young people moved away and older members died. Some denominations have closed their open-country churches and consolidated their members in a few centrally located village churches. Some parish reorganization has been achieved through interdenominational cooperation. Outright mergers of local churches of different denominations have been somewhat more successful than formation of federated churches.

Parish reorganization to date has amounted to only a small part of what needs to be done, in view of the population shifts that have occurred and that seem likely in the future. As time goes on, parish reorganization will become increasingly dependent on interdenominational cooperation.

CHANGES IN ATTITUDES

The changes just discussed indicate that the goals and values of rural people are changing. For North Dakota, these changes in attitudes are especially significant, because it is a relatively new state in terms of agricultural settlement, with a very high proportion of the original settlers emigrating from Europe.[8] This state has been a rural "melting pot" that apparently is entering the final stages of an acculturation process that began a half century ago.

The foreign-born settlers came from almost every part of Europe, bringing with them their particular

types of peasant culture. These subcultures were highly diverse—about the only characteristics they had in common were the peasants' passionate desire for landownership and the high place given to frugality and hard physical labor in the scale of values. Some groups had a rich heritage of folk music, dances and festivals, while others eschewed sports, movies, dancing and other forms of social entertainment. Some groups placed a high value on education and willingly made sacrifices so that their children could take advantage of whatever schooling was provided by the community. Others were decidedly anti-intellectual and regarded schooling beyond rudimentary knowledge of the "three R's" as unnecessary extravagance.

About one-fourth of the immigrant stock came out of highly paternalistic cultures, in which the husband-father ruled the family clan with iron discipline, made most of the important decisions for his sons long after they reached adulthood, selected their wives, and held the family bank account in his own name. The housewife had a subservient status. At the other extreme, nearly half of the foreign stock came from cultures in which the status of men and of women was about the same as in the American culture.

Some of the culture groups assimilated quite rapidly into the American way of life, while others, especially those that were highly paternalistic, clung tenaciously to their European customs, values and language (at least in the home) through four or five generations. For this latter group, acculturation has been an exceedingly painful process, accompanied by intra-family tensions because of the threatened status of the husband-father and the breakdown of long-held traditions of filial obedience.

The rural culture that is emerging on the northern Plains from this varied background is the result of many changes in rural attitudes. The wants and desires of farm people are becoming more like those of their city cousins, possibly because they are now reached by the same mass media of communication. The neatly landscaped farmstead, surrounded by a carefully tended shelterbelt, is replacing the big red barn of former years as the rural status symbol.

The rising levels of living on farms (which incidentally denote a distinct break with past traditions of frugality), plus changes in agricultural technology, mean that farmers are placing more and more reliance on purchased goods and services for both family consumption and farm production. Farmers and village businessmen thus are becoming more dependent on each other. This mutuality between farm and village is augmented by school and church reorganization, the Rural Areas Development Program, and community projects in general.

[8]In 1920, for example, 40 percent of the rural adults in North Dakota were foreign-born and another 38 percent were of foreign parentage.

Discussion: changing rural life in the Great Plains

FRANKLIN L. PARSONS*

The intent of this paper by Loftsgard and Voelker was to *emphasize* the human side of "The Changing Rural Life in the Great Plains." This the authors have done in their report on (1) causative factors of change, (2) levels of living, (3) community adjustments, (4) school reorganization, (5) parish reorganization and (6) changes in attitudes.

The authors point out that almost all farmers now have clean heat, electricity, telephone, television and at least a third have two automobiles. I am surprised that the authors didn't mention the long winter vacations in Florida, Arizona, or California that the "rich" wheat farmers of the Great Plains states are reported to be enjoying. Or, about those farmers who fly into Minneapolis to see a baseball game.

The authors might have analyzed the relative economic position of rural people to nonfarm people. They might also have indicated the wide range in relative economic well-being among farm families. This would have given a sharper image of human values.

Our studies at the Federal Reserve Bank of Minneapolis indicate that most farmers in this upper Midwest region desperately need to solve two basic problems—relatively low incomes and underutilization of labor in order to enjoy a better life.

Our studies indicate that more than two-thirds of all upper Midwest farms averaged net incomes of $3,000 or less during a recent five-year period. This does not consider the imputed costs of interest on capital or operators' labor. Furthermore, labor on upper Midwest farms was only 63 percent utilized.

It occurs to me that these data for over two-thirds of upper Midwest farmers indicate a considerable amount of human discomfort from the viewpoint of inadequate incomes and underemployment.

While it's true that most farmers do have a car, a television set and occasionally an outboard motor, these items frequently are of ancient vintage—fre-

quently secondhand from their more prosperous city cousins; and I doubt if most farmers spend much on vacations if they take one at all.

Why is it that so many low-income farmers continue to remain on the farm? I suspect that are several reasons; there really is no place to go—many couldn't find a job; they like farming—it is an independent way of life and a farmer may prefer to wear patches on his pants and to go fishing when he wants to, to fighting the traffic in the city and punching a time clock. These are the human values of farm living. Perhaps many are able to work a few days a year for the county or city or on some other off-farm job, or perhaps a pension or "nest egg" permits them to hang on even though the figures suggest they should have "adjusted" long ago. *Capacity, ambition, age* and *health are considerations* which influence what might be done to help these people to a better way of life.

Of the young people between 10 and 19 years of age on farms, only 10 percent to 15 percent are likely to have the opportunity to become *class I* operators. It is significant that around 40 percent of the people on farms today are under 21 years of age. It is easier for the young to adjust. Loftsgard and Voelker might have commented on this aspect of human problems on Great Plains farms.

In the comments on community adjustments, I could wish they might have said something about the desirability for consolidation of small villages and governmental units to meet the new and changing conditions. Someone needs to spell out or outline how this can be accomplished with the least amount of human economic misery in the Great Plains.

In the discussion of school reorganization in the rural areas, I wish the authors had put in a plug for some reorganization of curriculum which would give more of our rural young people more nonagricultural vocational training. The more skills that can be developed in carpentry, plumbing, electricity, mechanics, etc., the better off will be our farm young people who can't stay on the farm.

☐ From Journal of Farm Economics **45**:1117-1118, 1963.
*Federal Reserve Bank of Minneapolis.

Is rural main street disappearing?

ARNOLD PAULSEN and JERRY CARLSON*

People in small towns are asking: "Will one big farmer out here be as good a customer for main street as two small farmers used to be?" To some stores on main street the answer is "yes,"—to others it's "no."

A 1956 Iowa State University study in southwest Iowa gives us some information on what happens when farms consolidate. It tells what happens to the volume of output and the demand for inputs. It helps explain what's going on in rural towns.

Suppose Tom sells his 160 acres and leaves for greener pastures. Joe, a neighbor farming 240 acres across the road, buys the land and begins farming all 400 acres.

Although total land area in farms doesn't change with consolidation, spending to operate it—and production from it—does change. It's likely that Tom's former land is now part of a more efficient operation. Some costs per acre will be up, but the land will likely be yielding more, so costs per bushel of output will drop. Local grain dealers or livestock shippers might handle more volume, thus, make more money.

Joe will probably need less machinery investment per acre, since he can use his tractor, plow, baler, combine, etc., on more land. Tom's old machinery will be sold to other neighbors. But if it's old, beat up, or small, the large farmer will not buy it. Joe will likely turn to bigger and more specialized equipment. Farm consolidation pressures used machinery prices downward.

MUST BE OF SERVICE

The local machinery dealer will be by-passed for whatever new machinery Joe might buy if the dealer can't repair heavy and complicated machinery and doesn't stock all kinds and sizes of hydraulic cylinders, electrical parts, roller chains, and so on. Consolidation and improved equipment means dealers will be called upon for a wider array of specialized services. It's not only machinery dealers that are hit with the effects of consolidation and modern farming. Fertilizer sales will climb, since Joe can afford it and

knows how to make it pay. Tom didn't. In the southwest Iowa study, the average farmer who left the farm had spent only $30 for fertilizer; farmers who took over had been spending $308 and planned to spend $401 when they got the extra land. Joe will probably buy more fertilizer per acre and a more specific fertilizer mix with more additives than did Tom.

With consolidation, consumer-goods stores on "main street" can expect changes in the blend of farm-family spending. There are fewer farmers in the community to buy groceries and other necessities. But if remaining farmers gain larger net incomes through bigger operations, they'll spend more on their families. They'll call for a higher standard of living. They won't spend much more for groceries but will spend more for housing, furniture, appliances and recreation.

As consolidation continues, the third grocery store in town might become a bowling alley, the second clothing shop a fine furniture store and the only hardware store will find more demand for gadgets and quality household appliances.

Remember, these changes are happening because of the technical revolution in agriculture and throughout the country. They'll continue regardless of government farm programs.

Now let us superimpose a land retirement program over these "normal" changes.

In Rosland, South Dakota, the local implement dealer said a third of the farmers had left, and on the way out they sold their machinery to the remaining two-thirds. This had clearly "cut business by two-thirds."

In other communities, some firms report business as usual even though 25 percent of the local land is retired. Can such diverging reports both be true? Yes, we think so.

SIDE EFFECTS OF CONTROLS

Farm production was trimmed, only slightly overall, by past conservation reserve, but the effect was much more in some areas or in some crops. Under production control, farmers buy less fuel and machinery, sell less grain and livestock. Businesses feeling the impact would be grain elevators, feed mills, livestock buying points, machinery sales outlets, repair shops, fuel distributors, fertilizer dealers.

☐ From Better Farming Methods **33**:12, Dec. 1961.
*Dr. Arnold Paulsen is a staff member of the Center for Agricultural and Economic Adjustment at Iowa State University. Jerry Carlson is a former Graduate Assistant in Information Services at the same University.

Consumer-goods business like clothing and appliance stores would (1) only gradually feel some tightening in sales as people in machinery, grain and other local "agribusiness" firms slowed spending, and (2) might eventually see some people move off the farm and perhaps out of the community as a result of land retirement. Retailers would chalk up the lost business to land retirement.

If small, poor farmers are the main participants, the high-class restaurants, the fine furniture store and the Buick-Cadillac-Olds dealer may see little impact because the participants never could afford to trade there anyway.

The administrators of the soil bank have long known that land retirement may effect townspeople. As a result, heavy land retirement in the conservation reserve was on a "local option" basis. In 1960, 59 communities in 14 states asked state Agricultural Stabilization and Conservation Committees to allow local farmers to break through the 25 percent ceiling on land retirement within communities. Thirty-nine requests were approved because they appeared to have overwhelming support of local businessmen.

About 28 million acres are in the conservation reserve now. This does not retire the excess capacity to produce grain. At one dollar corn we have regularly added to stocks. If land retirement were used to manage the excess capacity, much more land would have to be idled. If we don't use this excess capacity to produce for storage, we cut down on the need for the services of rural communities. Any production control program would have an adverse effect on rural towns.

Part-time land retirement would affect local communities less than a whole-farm plan, at least in the first few years. Since more people would stay, at least for a while, it would not reduce spending for consumer goods so much. A soil-bank pattern sprinkling land retirement over many regions would spread the impact over more communities. It would not, however, reduce the total effect on "main street," rural U.S.A.

Farm-related businesses can be classed three ways depending upon their relationship to agriculture. Each class is affected differently by price and volume changes in agriculture.

1. Consumer-goods businesses are related to agriculture through net farm income. Net corresponds to a salary check and comes to town for things like clothing, food, furniture, automobiles and recreation. As a city grows in size, farmers become relatively less important customers. These businesses are financially indifferent as to whether farmers' net incomes are from good crops, good prices or government payments.

2. Production-goods businesses are related to agriculture through farm business expenditures. Gross production expenditures are more important to rural towns than farmers' net income. Modern farmers continue to spend large sums even though profits are down. Fifty percent of gross farm income goes back to town for fuel, tractors, machinery, buildings, labor, taxes, interest and other business expenses. Another 20 percent of gross is spent for feed and livestock purchases. Much of this business expense money is spent locally. Across the United States, a trade chain of 6 million people work in industries supplying 4 million farmers with tools and supplies to keep agriculture rolling. Farmers buy production goods as they need them and can pay for them. Production-goods businesses benefit from agriculture with a large volume and prices satisfactory enough to keep it buying inputs in large quantity.

3. Handlers, haulers, and processors depend on the physical out-flow of farm products. The stream of products flowing from agriculture creates jobs for 10 million people. Their number and prosperity depend to a large extent on how large this volume is. Processing firms' profits sag if volume is low.

Prices of farm products, within a range, are of little concern to the handlers, haulers, and processors. They're paid for handling pounds of volume, not dollars of value.

Firms making and delivering goods coming to and flowing from the farm business depend upon volume and markup. These last two categories of "main street" firms are concerned about farm output and business spending. Farmers could take severe net income cuts and this group of firms could prosper as long as agriculture makes enough to keep producing in volume and paying business bills.

In contrast, grocery stores, clothing shops, furniture stores and other consumer-goods retailers on "main street" are concerned about farmers' net. They're also interested in having farmers around to spend it.

Retailers keep an eye on farm-business production volume, too. Why? Because a cut in production volume would trim sales, services, and profits of local businessmen linked with agriculture as a business operation. These people also patronize local consumer-goods retailers, and an output cut would find its way into retail consumer stores through them.

It's important for "main street" merchants to think of farm people and the farm business separately. Agriculture's main economic weight swings up and down with the volume of farm business and not so much with farm-family consumption. Agriculture is a growing industry even though there are fewer farmers. It buys more goods from industry and sends more raw material to processors every year.

Kansas out-migration: focus on Centralia

DAVID JORDAN*

The Centralia train depot has gray shingles around the top of the outside walls and white boards around the bottom. The chimney on the roof appears to be looking for an excuse to fall on somebody's head. I gingerly squeeze my car in next to an aging green pickup truck and a battered early-'60s Chevy with a University of Kansas sticker across the back window.

I climb out into the muck of what I guess is the parking lot. It's between two sets of railroad tracks.

The depot looks deserted. The door to the waiting room sticks. I shove and it grudgingly swings open. The waiting room is empty, except for a pile of lumber stacked against the east wall. There's a bulletin board with a notice of nondiscrimination of employment on it, but the notice doesn't say who the employer is. High up on the World War II–military-green wall is a round metal plate over the hole where a heater pipe once fit.

It is very cold in the waiting room. I can hear the wind outside. Even it seems to echo in the empty room.

Beyond the west wall of the room, in the depot agent's office, Gene Riggins is talking on the phone to his son, John.

"Well, I thought you boys were comin' on up tonight," he says. A pause. "No, no. That's all right. I was just expecting you up tonight."

The conversation goes on. I re-read the notice of nondiscrimation in employment. The employer must be the Missouri Pacific Railroad, since this is a MoPac depot.

The railroad—then the Atchison & Pike's Peak—was laid through this area in 1867, eight years after the establishment of Centralia. The town was a mile north of where it now stands until the railroad came through. The community relocated to trackside. In the late 1800s, the Missouri Pacific absorbed the Atchison & Pike's Peak.

"Come on in, come on in," calls Mr. Riggins from beyond the wall. The agent's office looks like the waiting room, with a few sticks of ancient furniture added.

Mr. Riggins has a weight-lifter's build: thick body atop stumpy legs. A friendly, good-old-boy sort with a gravelly voice, he is the father of Centralia's three celebrities—Junior, John and Billy Riggins.

Junior and John started as running backs for KU

against Penn State in the Orange Bowl game after the 1968 football season. Billy was a red-shirt sophomore on the Jayhawk squad last fall. They became, as one local girl wryly put it, "a legend in their own time" while playing for the Centralia High Panthers.

Gene says Junior, who will be 26 this week, is now working for a sporting goods firm in Kansas City. John, 24, was a first-team running back last year with Broadway Joe Namath and the New York Jets, but during the off-season he is back at KU working toward his degree in broadcast journalism. Billy is in his third year studying public relations and journalism at KU.

Gene settles himself on the edge of a table and squints through his black-rimmed glasses at the ticking oil stove.

"My boys'll never come back here," he says. "There's nothing here for 'em."

John created a minor uproar in Centralia last fall when he told a New York sports writer that the most exciting thing to do in his home town on the prairie was to "go next door and watch the sows have baby pigs." Why, said the local residents when the story got to Kansas, there aren't any HOGS inside the city limits.

"If you're going to have progress in a small town, you have to keep your people," Gene observes.

He thinks the main problem is jobs: "If you get a job around here, you'll be lucky to get $3 an hour in wages. And you can't live on that—raise a family, buy a home, pay insurance."

Gene has had his job as depot agent since 1946. Back then, trains came through eight times a day. And the town had passenger service.

Now, trains come through twice a day. Passenger service ended at least 15 years ago. A freight will stop if there is a full carload to be picked up. Usually the trains only stop to pick up wheat, milo or corn from C-G-F Grain, which is across Main Street from the depot. Nemaha County led the state in 1972 wheat yield per harvested acre.

Gene stretches his legs out in front of him and crosses his pointy-toed cowboy boots. He is concerned about his boy Billy, he says. Billy didn't get to play much on KU's football team last fall. Gene wishes the boy had gone to K-State.

• • •

The temperature hovers around 40. The wind slices down Main Street. The clouds remain catatonic gray.

☐ From The New Newspaper, Vol. 2, No. 4, Apr. 20, 1973.
*Professor of Journalism, Kansas State University.

I feel very conspicuous walking around town with people LOOKING at me. Right now I'm studying an advertising poster in the window of the City Clerk's office. It says *Boothill* is playing at the Seneca Theater March 14-17. *The New Centurions* will play March 18-19-20.

I start down the street and—what? A familiar face!

"Mr. Jordan, what are you doin' here?" says Allan Flentie, smiling as he strides briskly up the sidewalk.

"Working on a story, believe it or not."

"In CENTRALIA?" An amazed grin.

"Certainly. Would you like to be an interview victim?"

Arrangements are made to meet in a few minutes at the Centralia Cafe. Flentie moves quickly away. He is a journalism student at Kansas State University, and he is out of school for spring break. He returned today from skiing in Colorado, and he has to see about getting his car fixed (he tore the muffler off on an icy mountain road) so he can go to Omaha tonight to see his girl.

The cafe is the communal gathering spot for Centralia. Just about any time from 7 a.m. to 9 p.m. you can find five or six farmers sitting at one table or three or four shopkeepers at another table or even as many as six or seven women sitting at another table. The cafe-sitters drink coffee and talk about the townspeople who aren't sitting there with them.

Flentie enters the cafe. He is a muscular young man of 20 with rugged movie star looks. He is a junior at K-State.

"Until I got to college, I didn't think you could beat Centralia," Flentie says, fingering his coffee cup and gazing around the cafe.

He played linebacker and offensive guard on the high school football team, and his father—Rex Flentie, owner of Flentie's Hardware on Main Street—was president of the school board.

"Things weren't too REVEALING, really. You didn't get exposed to much. During the week you wouldn't do anything. Dad had the store, so I helped out there. You watch a lot of television. Channel 27 and Channel 13 out of Topeka.

"On Friday nights there'd be, oh, a basketball game. Saturday night everybody'd go to Seneca. Go up there and drink beer. There's a place up there where everybody congregates. Called the Pizza Hut.

"It's kind of a 'bad' place now. It used to be real nice, kind of a high class place. But lately a lot of Nebraska guys have started to come down there because this is an 18-year-old state and they can get beer. There's been a lot of trouble up there any more, a lot of fights and stuff.

"And then Sunday you'd come back, get together, and drag main. Get in your car and drive around town. It doesn't take long before you get pretty bored.

Sometimes you'd go up to the park by the high school and play football or basketball or sit around."

Maybe being bored didn't bother Allan in high school, but it does now. He says his folks are at him for not sticking around town during spring break.

"There isn't anything to do up here. There isn't anybody my age to hang around with. I feel kinda out of place. It's pretty lonely," he says.

After living at home previous summers, he hopes to get a vacation job elsewhere this year. He looked for work in Colorado, and plans to try Manhattan and Wichita.

"Do you have any ideas about coming back to Centralia when you finish school?" I ask.

"None whatsoever," Flentie says, staring into his coffee cup. "My field is public relations." He looks up and laughs. "There's not many openings here in Centralia for that."

• • •

Why do the youth leave small towns and rural areas?

Economic thinkers lean heavily on the changing structure of farming and the lack of industry in rural areas as parts of the answer.

A century or more ago, when Willa Cather's iron-willed men started doing battle with the harsh prairie, they farmed 80 or 160 acres with horses and sweat. Then came the machines and another vicious socio-economic spiral began to spin.

With a tractor and a combine, Fred Farmer could do more work. He could farm more land. And he needed less help to do it. So Joe Hand was out of a job. Eventually Fred Farmer NEEDED to farm more land if he was going to make enough money to pay for the machines, because tractors and combines are expensive.

He bought out Ed Neighbor, who was not quite so iron-willed. And then he needed more machinery and more stock and more seed so he could work his newly-acquired land efficiently. So the size of farms grew and the number of farms dropped. Cost of farming went up.

Now some kid is right out of high school or at college and he wants to stay in Nemaha County and farm. But unless he is the favorite son or nephew or son-in-law of Fred Farmer, he CAN'T.

A small tractor costs $5,000 to $7,500. A small combine costs about $13,000. And then there is land and livestock and materials. Wilton Thomas, an agricultural economist with the K-State extension service, estimates that the moderately successful farmer who operates a family farm is managing an investment of $100,000 to $250,000.

So the new kid is probably out of luck. Thomas estimates that, because the costs of farming are rising and the sizes of farms are climbing, only one farm youth out of two who want to stay in agriculture can do so.

This puts the new kid in the same situation as Joe Hand and Ed Neighbor. They can't work in agriculture. Since rural areas have no labor pool, there is very little industry.

Only 8% of Nemaha County's people work in industry, compared with a statewide percentage—which itself is not too spiffy—of 17.3%.

The jobs that are available don't pay well. The median income for Nemaha County families in 1970 was $6,428 a year, compared with the state's median family income of $8,693. Also, 19.3% of the county's families live in what the government classifies as poverty. The state percentage of 9.7%.

So the farmless farmers take their families to Topeka or Wichita, or to Omaha or Denver, and job hunt. And the mass movement continues.

Community and regional planning types, furthermore, tend to emphasize the lack of facilities and services as causes of out-migration.

Centralia has no doctor, no dentist, no drug store. The nearest hospital is in Seneca, 11 miles away. If you come down with beriberi or tear your arm half off in a threshing machine, you have to wait for an ambulance to come from Seneca, get you and take you back.

Centralia's water, pumped in from wells west of town, is so hard some residents swear their faces pucker up when they wash.

The city has no sewer system. Everyone in town has a septic tank, and when there is a hard rain, weird things begin to happen in the drainage ditches around town—like the one north of the high school. There's this odor, see. . . .

Centralia has no taxis for getting around town. It has no bus service or train service or plane service for getting OUT of town.

There are no houses to rent in Centralia. There are no houses to buy. There are no apartments available, and there are no facilities for the elderly.

As for shopping, start with Main Street. There's Hightower's IGA grocery. When Emet's dad took over a building that had housed a restaurant and a barber shop and opened the store in 1925, there were five other groceries in town. Now the IGA has one competitor.

Emet took over the store in 1935, borrowing $500 to reopen it after the Depression put his dad out of business. After 38 years, Emet just sold out to Remi Haverkamp.

On the corner is Horalek & Myers. Or Myers. Depends on what you want to call it. The clothing store was started as a partnership in 1921, and Art Myers bought his Partner out in 1923. But the sign out front still says "Horalek and Myers."

Then there's a place called Marx's Clothing. It just closed. Mildred and Roy Marx came to Centralia to teach school in 1928, but a year later they opened a clothing store. They decided to retire, so a few weeks ago they closed up the store.

On another corner is Hy Klas Food Store. Orlo Drinkwater's been running it since 1953, when he converted his feed store into a grocery. He's getting on, and he'd like to find somebody to buy him out.

Up on the next block, there's a building which was built to be a theater. Then it was a garage. Then a roller skating rink. Now it's Flentie's Hardware. Allan Flentie's dad, Rex, has run the store since 1948. Rex, who works in cowboy boots, Wrangler jeans and a baseball-type cap, got the Pioneer Seed Corn dealership five years ago. The hardware is stacked around—and hung over—big piles of seed bags that run down the middle of the floor.

Catty-cornered, across the street, the fancy building is the First National Bank of Centralia. With its blonde brick and big plate glass windows, it is the most attractive—and apparently newest—building in town. Craig Bachman is vice president of the bank and pretty much runs the show. He is also the mayor of Centralia and the son-in-law of Burton Lohmuller, who owns the bank.

Backtracking down to the street next to the railroad tracks is the avenue Centralians call Bourbon Street. The Retail Liquor Store sits by itself—a small white building—in the middle of the block, opposite the train depot. The youngbloods like to drift in there of an afternoon and buy a little something they can carry in a small brown bag to a service station where there is a handy pop machine and some friendly faces.

And there's Durland's Auto Parts, and McBratney's Hardware and the Case distributorship and a few other places, but . . .

Recreational and cultural activities?

• • •

During the week, you go to school all day. After school you work on the farm if you live in the country and you work around your family's store or as a 50-cent-an-hour waitress if you live in town. At night you watch TV or listen to the radio. MEDIA BOMBARDMENT! Urban visions superimposed on rural life styles. Channel 27 out of Topeka: Dennis Weaver stalks the streets of New York City, playing a hick cowboy in cowboy boots wooing and winning in the big town. McCloud! WLS and WHB: wild urban rock sliding down the cold night wind from Chicago and Kansas. Friday night you go to a ballgame. If you play, you may be a local hero of sorts. Saturday night you hop in the car and hustle off to Seneca, where the theater plays **The New Centurions** *a year late and the bartenders at the Pizza Hut don't check your i.d. Or to Frankfort, for the dance at the VFW Hall. Or* *to Corning for the dance at the Catholic Church. On Sunday you get in the car and drag town: Number Nine to Main to Number Nine and back to Main. And all the while you keep hoping that somebody doesn't put the word out on what you've been up to lately, because if they do, it will be all over town and sooner or later it will get back to your folks and then. . . .*

Confining!

Boring!

This place is so . . . OUT OF IT!

As to that gossip: it results from the fact that Centralia and other small towns like it have for years constituted what sociologists call a *Gemeinschaft* community. And, as your basic sociology textbook will tell you, a *Gemeinschaft* community is a society characterized by (1) an assignment of status to the whole person, so that his job and the rest of his life form a unity; (2) a high degree of cohesion based on the widespread sharing of common attitudes and aims; and (3) a sense of unlimited commitment to the community, which is conceived as an enlarged kinship group, the source of one's personal identity.

Gemeinschaft communities compare with *Gesellschaft* ones. Urban communities are *Gesellschaft* societies, in which the people tend to relate to each other only according to specialized roles—often occupational in nature.

If you've got a store in financial trouble and you go to a banker in an urban community, he's liable to reject you because your business is a poor credit risk. You relate to the banker as a man who can loan you money. He relates to you as a businessman who wants a loan. Personally, you don't know each other from Adam Walinsky.

But, if you live in a town like Centralia and you want a loan to prop up your failing business, maybe

the banker relates to you as the guy who played tight end to his quarterback on the Panther football team in 1951, or the guy who ran a pretty nice little store until your wife ran off with a vacuum cleaner salesman and you started hitting the bottle. He knows you, likes you, feels sorry for you. He's liable to help you out with that loan.

What it amounts to is that a small town resident trades his privacy for understanding and sympathy. And for gossip. Maybe it's sympathetic gossip—and maybe it's not so sympathetic—but it's still gossip.

A case in point involves another one of Centralia's services—its one-man police force. He got the boot a few days back after some kids swiped the cherry bubble off the top of his squad car. Gossip is zipping back and forth all over town about that little incident. The kids say the cop was asleep in the car when the bubble was lifted.

Okay, so the cop got canned. But, says one of the local citizens, "He had a lot of problems. He drank some. But then he only got paid somethin' like $299 a month, and he had to take a terrible lot of abuse and insults around here. It was an unfortunate thing."

A lot of the kids aren't too hot about that *Gemeinschaft* stuff. They don't *want* people in town to know all about them. They watch TV and they pick up some non–small-town attitudes—pink maxi dresses, e.g.— and they don't want to be told they can't adopt these attitudes. And they don't have unlimited commitment to the community.

Perhaps loss of commitment to the community is contagious. Or maybe years of communal downward spiraling produce psychological and physical immobility in people. For whatever reason, the residents who have remained in many small Kansas towns have reacted to their impending demise with apathy.

If the disease is terminal, why fight it?

Quantitative dimensions of decline and stability among rural communities

CALVIN L. BEALE*

Our country is dotted with the remains of towns that reached their zenith generations ago—some be-

☐ From Whiting, L. R., editor: Communities left behind: alternatives for development, Ames, Iowa, 1974, Iowa State University Press, pp. 3-21.
*Calvin L. Beale is Leader, Population Studies Group, Economic Research Service, U.S. Department of Agriculture, Washington, D.C.

fore the Revolutionary War. This is not to imply that the phenomenon of the declining community has gone unnoticed. It has been 100 years since historian Charles Jones wrote a book-length study called "The Dead Towns of Georgia." But only the present problems of the Great Plains and western Corn Belt have caused sufficient concern to produce a rational consideration of the extent and consequences of the trend and approaches to its resolution.

Communities may decline for various reasons: natural disasters, exhaustion of natural resources, loss of transportation advantages, and loss of political status, for example. But community decline, as measured by population loss, has been at a maximum only since declining manpower needs in agriculture occurred simultaneously with forces that acted to relocate and centralize many business and community functions into larger units. Since World War I we have had the paradoxical situation that the faster our national population has grown, the faster and more extensively our small communities have declined.

About 31 percent of all counties in the country declined in population during the 1930s, when national population growth was low because of low birth rates and lack of immigration. As national population growth revived in the 1940s and went even higher in the 1950s, the number of declining counties actually rose. Despite the much higher potential for growth as a result of the high birth rate of the period, 49 percent of all counties decreased in population in the 1950s as a widespread exodus to the cities occurred. Furthermore, the rate of loss among the losing counties rose. In the 1930s less than a third of the losing counties declined by as much as 10 percent in the decade, but in the 1950s, over half the losers had losses of 10 percent or more. Thus, although losses occurred in many counties earlier in the century, both the extent and depth of the losses increased after the Great Depression. It is only natural that awareness and concern about the matter should emerge.

I am not suggesting that perpetual population growth is necessarily good. Our traditional romance with the growth concept has cooled. The recent Commission on Population Growth and the American Future[1] recommended that our national population growth be slowed and eventually ended and offered persuasive arguments that as a nation we would benefit from such a result. But cessation of growth is different from active decline generated by rapid and highly selective out-migration. Further, it must be recognized that every county in the entire North Central region (Illinois, Iowa, Indiana, North Dakota, South Dakota, Nebraska, Missouri, Minnesota, Wisconsin, Michigan, Ohio, Kansas) has had levels of childbirth more than sufficient to replace the parental population. The rural people of the region who are now reaching the end of the childbearing period have had

[1]The Commission on Population Growth and the American Future was created by Congress at the request of the President and functioned from 1970 to 1972. The commission's final report was *Population and the American Future*. 186 pp. Government Printing Office, 1972.

65 percent more children than are needed for parental replacement. In other words, the North Central rural population would increase by 65 percent in every quarter century under the family size levels that people chose for themselves in the 20 years after World War II. Thus, if the rural areas do not develop economic conditions that permit retention of this potential population growth, the only alternative is further migration to the cities.

In discussing population trends, both towns and counties will be considered, with focus on the North Central states, the West North Central ones in particular. Although it is fair to say that rural communities everywhere have had difficulty with population retention in modern times, different regions have by no means had identical trends.

In any review of the population commentary on the subject, one quickly and often encounters the cliché, "the dying small town." I think comprehension of the problem by professional research workers, concerned public officials, and the public in general has been hampered by the extent to which this phrase, with its sense of hopeless finality, has permeated our consciousness. Certainly there has been considerable misunderstanding in Washington over the years about the actual trends in small communities. Part of the problem is that the term "small town" has no precise meaning. One person may use it who has in mind the grain elevator, creamery, and railroad siding hamlet of his Corn Belt youth, and his listener may be a big city native to whom any place of less than 50,000 people is a small town. The distinction is critical, because small towns of different sizes have fared differently, and variations of even several hundred in average population are associated with differences in retention of population. These variations in turn are almost certainly related to the increased variety of services and employment available in communities as population exceeds typical threshold levels at which the support of particular services and businesses becomes feasible.

Of course, the stereotype of "the dying small town" has its kernel of truth—as most stereotypes have—but when used indiscriminately as a description of all or even most small places it becomes badly misleading.

POPULATION CHANGE IN TOWNS AND COUNTIES

In a cooperative project with the Economic Research Service, Glenn Fuguitt of the University of Wisconsin has compiled data on the population changes of nonmetropolitan towns. The North Central region has nearly 5,600 incorporated towns of less than 2,500 population located in nonmetropolitan counties. This

Table 1.1. Population change in nonmetropolitan rural towns, North Central Region, 1960-70*

Size of town, 1960	Number of places with population loss, 1960-70			Total population		
	Total 1960	Number	Percentage of total	1970	1960	Percentage change, 1960-70
			(%)	(thou)	(thou)	(%)
All towns under 2,500 persons	5,566	2,803	50.4	3,498.4	3,339.3	4.8
1,000-2,499	1,063	383	36.0	1,750.5	1,640.1	6.7
900-999	150	50	33.3	148.8	142.5	4.4
800-899	217	91	41.9	190.5	183.7	3.7
700-799	261	101	38.7	205.6	195.5	5.2
600-699	289	118	40.8	203.7	186.9	9.0
500-599	334	146	43.7	188.9	182.3	3.6
400-499	505	241	47.7	233.6	227.0	2.9
300-399	605	324	53.6	212.9	210.6	1.1
200-299	828	493	59.5	205.8	204.4	0.7
100-199	933	599	64.2	134.2	140.4	-4.4
Under 100	381	257	67.5	23.9	25.9	-7.7

Source: U.S. Census data by Department of Rural Sociology, University of Wisconsin, and Economic Research Service, U.S. Department of Agriculture.

*Nonmetropolitan status as of 1963. Incorporated places only. Excludes places that were incorporated or disincorporated during the decade.

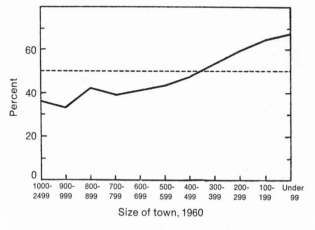

Fig. 1.1. Percentage of nonmetro rural towns with population loss, 1960-70, North Central region. (Source: Unpublished data from USDA-Univ. of Wis., project on population change in nonmetro towns.)

is 30 percent of all incorporated places of all sizes in the entire country. Of these rural North Central towns, 49.6 percent increased in population in 1960-70 and 50.4 percent decreased. But despite a small majority of losers, the overall population in the towns increased by 4.8 percent because the gaining towns tended to grow by larger amounts than the declining towns lost (Table 1.1). Some 3.5 million people lived in rural towns of the region in 1970, and contrary to a general impression, the number had grown by about 160,000 in the previous 10 years. But an inspection of the data by size of rural place shows considerable contrast between the largest places—those of 1,000 to 2,499 population—and the smallest—those of less than 500 population. About 64 percent of the largest places had population increases, compared with just 41 percent of the group with less than 500 people.

A further look at the data for towns of less than 1,000 people, grouped by size intervals of only 100 population each, shows that the likelihood of population retention or loss is sensitive to very small differences in population size (Figure 1.1). From less than 100 people up to 800 people, each increment of 100

population reduces the probability of a town losing population. Sixty-seven percent of the incorporated towns of less than 100 population declined. With each additional 100 people, 3 or 4 percent fewer places declined. Only among places of less than 400 people were losses more common than gains. In the 400-500 size group, 48 percent lost; from 700-800 just 39 percent lost; above that point, places of just 800-1,000 people were only a little more likely to lose population than cities of 10,000 or 25,000 people.

Places of less than 1,000 in the West North Central states had a higher probability of loss than those in the East North Central group. And among West North Central towns, declines were more numerous than gains in places with less than 500 population.

There was no increase in the 1960s in the percentage of rural-sized towns in the North Central states that lost population. The portion losing, 50.4 percent, was remarkably similar to that in the 1950s, 50.6 percent. And places of less than 500 people actually showed some reduction in incidence of loss in the 1960s. East of the Mississippi River a decentralizing trend into the nonmetropolitan countryside was evident, as open country areas shifted from a 4 percent loss of population to an 8 percent gain. Such a gain means that many of the rural towns of the East North Central division have more populous trading zone hinterlands than before. In major contrast, the open country population of the West North Central states declined by 10 percent; nearly as large a decrease as that of the 1950s (12 percent). Although there is a sense of decline in many of the West North Central towns, the more substantial loss of population has been occurring in the open country. There has been a relative drawing-in of the West North Central rural population into the towns.

Quite aside from the reality of decline in many of the small towns of the North Central region is the fact that the decline is more visible because those states have had a much greater propensity to incorporate their rural towns that have most other states. This is particularly true in the seven North Central states west of the Mississippi River (Minnesota, Iowa, Missouri, North Dakota, South Dakota, Kansas, Nebraska). In that area in 1960 were was a ratio of only 1,647 total rural people for each incorporated rural town. By contrast, the ratio of rural people to rural towns was 3,739 to 1 in the East North Central states, and 6,720 to 1 in the 12 Southern states east of the Mississippi River. In California, the extreme case, there were more than 37,000 rural people for every incorporated rural town.

Many states simply have not incorporated small towns. In such cases there is no measurement of population change available from the census and no formalized structure of local municipal government to experience decline and discouragement. The comparative lack of incorporated towns elsewhere is particularly true of places with less than 500 people. The 12 Southern states referred to have three times as many rural people as the West North Central states but less than half as many incorporated places of un-

der 500 population. The Middle West, especially in the Plains and Western Corn Belt, has a much larger inventory of communities accustomed to an organized corporate life and therefore more sensitive to decline and more observable when they do decline.

There appear to be 14 counties (6 in Missouri, 5 in Kansas, and 1 each in Indiana, Nebraska, and Ohio) that have had consecutive population decline in every census since 1890, showing how long and unremitting an adjustment of population to changed circumstances can be. But the more important losses that continue to shape everyday life are probably those that have occurred since 1940. In general, they are the heaviest declines and have taken place since the end of the rather atypical period of the Great Depression.

A comparison of county population changes from 1940 to 1970—without regard to intermediate changes—shows the concentration of the heaviest losses in the West North Central division (Table 1.2 and Figure 1.2). A handful of counties have declined by more than half in 30 years. About 97 of the 619 counties in the West North Central region have lost 35 percent or more of their 1940 population, but they are not closely grouped. They include most of the Flint Hills grazing area in Kansas, the southern Sand Hills in Nebraska, the Corn Belt margin counties along the Nebraska-Kansas border and the Missouri-Iowa border, and many counties in Western North Dakota.

Table 1.2. Population change of counties, 1940-70, and average initial population, North Central Region

| Population change 1940-70 | North Central Region | | | | | |
| | Number of counties | | | Average 1940 population | | |
	Total	ENC[a]	WNC[b]	Total	ENC	WNC
						(thou)
Total	1,056	437	619	38.0	60.9	21.8
Loss	547	120	427	17.0	22.4	15.5
−35.0 or more %	104	7	97	10.2	12.3	10.1
−20.0−−34.9%	190	29	161	16.9	19.2	16.4
−10.0−−19.9%	136	41	95	18.7	23.6	16.5
0.0−−9.9%	117	43	74	21.3	25.2	19.1
Gain	509	317	192	60.5	75.5	35.9
0.0-9.9%	101	49	52	22.9	22.4	23.3
10.0-19.9%	78	41	37	26.1	30.4	21.4
20.0-29.9%	65	42	23	35.4	40.0	27.1
30.0-49.9%	96	71	25	129.4	157.1	50.7
50.0 or more %	169	114	55	69.5	76.7	54.5

[a]East North Central Division.
[b]West North Central Division.

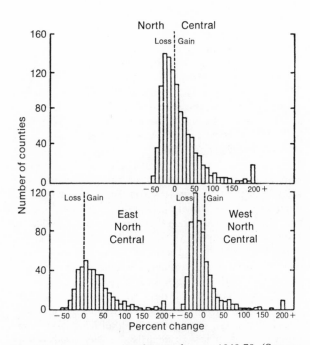

Fig. 1.2. Counties by population change, 1940-70. (Source: 1970 and 1940 Census of Population.)

Very few of the counties with heaviest losses are east of the Mississippi River.

In general, the higher the rate of loss, the smaller the initial average county size. Those decreasing by 35 percent or more had a 1940 average population of 10,200, those with up to 10 percent loss averaged 21,300 people initially, and those that gained by more than 50 percent averaged 69,500.

In the course of a decade, out-migration rates are highest for persons reaching age 20 during the period. In counties of most severe population loss—say where it has dropped by 20 percent in just 10 years—the net out-migration rates are often 50 percent or more for young adults. However, they are much lower for persons over 30. In less extreme cases of loss, the out-movement of young adults will be 35 to 40 percent and that of persons over 30 will be less than 10 percent. With some exceptions, the rural communities of the North Central region are not suffering from rapid out-movement of established families but from continued loss of young adults. And this loss extended over several decades leads to progressively smaller numbers of established families and children.

The pattern of out-migration by age is illustrated in Figure 1.3. Part of the data relates to all counties in South Dakota that did not have a city of 10,000 or more people in 1960. These counties experienced an overall decline of 6.6 percent in population from 1960-70. For contrast, the chart also shows migration rates for a block of 15 counties in the Nebraska Sand Hills that averaged 15.2 percent population decline in the same decade.

In the rural and small town counties of South Dakota, out-migration was nearly 15 percent for the 1960 population surviving to 1970. It was 43 percent for those who reached age 20-24 during the decade but less than 10 percent for all groups aged 35-39 or older.

In the Sand Hills counties, overall net out-movement was nearly 20 percent. The rate reached majority proportions among youth attaining age 20-24, where 60 percent left during the 10 years, and remained above 10 percent for all age groups up through persons reaching age 50-54. In this area, it is the minority of youths who remain behind who are probably most selective in character, rather than those who leave. Active displacement of population extends to people well up into middle age, where considerable personal strain may attend a move made that late in life.

FACTORS INDUCING POPULATION LOSS

The most important factor behind the decline of population in rural areas of the North Central region has been dependence on industries with declining manpower needs—farming in particular and mining to a lesser extent. One farmer can handle a great in-

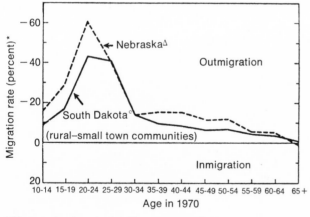

*Change due to net migration expressed as a percentage of persons expected to survive to 1970.

Δ15 contiguous Sand Hills counties.

°Counties with no town of 10,000 or more people in 1960.

Fig. 1.3. Net migration rates by age, for selected Nebraska and South Dakota counties, 1960-70. (Source: Unpublished data from USDA-Univ. of Ga., net migration project.)

Table 1.3. Population change, 1960-70, of counties by percent of workers employed in agriculture and mining 1960, North Central Region

| Percentage of workers employed in agriculture and mining, 1960 | Number of counties with | | Population | | |
	Population increase 1960-70	Population decrease 1960-70	1970	1960	Percentage change 1960-70[a]
			(thou)	*(thou)*	*(%)*
Total	526	530	56,575.0	51,617.5	9.6
50% and over	6	88	466.8	536.1	−12.9
40-49	15	144	1,578.1	1,733.4	−9.0
30-39	64	138	2,827.2	2,870.5	−1.5
20-29	105	97	4,062.8	3,953.1	2.8
Less than 20%	336	63	47,640.2	42,524.5	12.0

[a]The relationship between percentage change in population 1960-70 and percentage employed in agriculture and mining 1960 is $Y = 17.36 − .56X$ with a coefficient of determination (r^2) of .37. On the average there was a .56 percentage point decline in population change for every percentage point increment in employment in agriculture and mining.

Table 1.4. Change in private nonfarm wage and salary employment, 1959-69, and population, 1969-70, by rurality of counties[a]

	Employment		Population		Percentage change	
					Employment	Population
Area and rurality of counties	1969	1959	1970	1960	1959-69	1960-70
	(thou)				*(%)*	
United States	55,862.9	41,293.0	203,156.4	179,323.2	35.3	13.3
0-29.9% rural	39,712.0	29,897.8	122,899.6	106,699.2	32.8	15.2
30.0-49.9	7,194.6	5,115.2	30,221.3	26,139.0	40.7	15.6
Predominantly rural	8,956.4	6,280.0	50,035.5	46,485.0	42.6	7.6
50.0-69.9	5,586.8	3,926.4	27,193.8	24,547.3	42.3	10.8
70.0-99.9	2,391.9	1,681.6	14,649.5	13,752.1	42.2	6.5
Entirely rural	977.7	672.0	8,192.3	8,185.6	45.5	0.1
East North Central Division	12,108.3	9,251.9	40,252.5	36,225.0	30.9	11.1
0-29.9% rural	8,700.8	6,815.4	25,129.4	22,549.8	27.7	11.4
30.0-49.9	1,768.1	1,277.0	6,390.8	5,680.6	38.5	12.5
Predominantly rural	1,639.4	1,159.6	8,732.2	7,994.6	41.4	9.2
50.0-69.9	1,139.1	809.9	5,381.9	4,914.8	40.6	9.5
70.0-99.9	410.5	288.8	2,649.6	2,420.1	42.1	9.5
Entirely rural	89.9	60.9	700.7	659.7	47.7	6.2
West North Central Division, 1st tier[b]	3,049.3	2,252.6	11,317.2	10,491.2	35.4	7.9
0-29.9% rural	2,167.7	1,612.3	5,828.2	5,269.7	34.5	10.6
30.0-49.9	286.1	198.1	1,332.3	1,140.1	44.4	16.9
Predominantly rural	595.4	442.2	4,156.7	4,081.4	34.6	1.8
50.0-69.9	312.7	232.8	1,847.8	1,784.2	34.3	3.6
70.0-99.9	176.7	131.1	1,326.2	1,303.3	34.7	1.8
Entirely rural	106.1	78.3	982.7	994.0	35.5	−1.1
West North Central Division, 2nd tier[c]	1,055.7	796.2	5,013.3	4,929.9	32.6	1.7
0-29.9% rural	621.2	466.3	2,127.6	1,953.0	33.2	8.9
30.0-49.9	227.5	164.4	1,104.7	1,066.7	38.3	3.6
Predominantly rural	207.0	165.5	1,781.0	1,910.2	25.1	−6.8
50.0-69.9	91.7	73.4	658.3	655.7	24.9	0.4
70.0-99.9	22.1	17.1	183.1	198.2	29.0	−7.6
Entirely rural	93.2	74.9	939.6	1,056.3	24.4	−11.0
South Region	15,410.3	10,519.6	62,795.2	54,973.1	46.5	14.2
0-29.9% rural	8,718.3	6,032.3	29,029.1	24,206.8	44.5	19.9
30.0-49.9	2,380.2	1,623.2	9,740.5	8,429.3	46.6	15.6
Predominantly rural	4,311.8	2,864.2	24,025.6	22,337.0	50.5	7.6
50.0-69.9	2,412.8	1,583.5	11,246.8	10,080.6	52.4	11.6
70.0-99.9	1,358.6	917.0	8,202.2	7,737.7	48.1	6.0
Entirely rural	540.4	363.6	4,576.6	4,518.7	48.6	1.3

Source: U.S. censuses of population and county business patterns.
[a]Counties grouped by percentage of population classified as rural in 1960.
[b]Iowa, Minnesota, and Missouri.
[c]Kansas, Nebraska, North Dakota, and South Dakota.

crease in acreage with modern technology, and farmers need high volume to counteract eroding profit margins, so a major reduction in the number of farms has resulted from these forces. Mining activity has experienced the same reductions in manpower from mechanization as has farming, and in addition has had employment losses from exhaustion of deposits.

If the counties of the North Central region are grouped by degree of dependence on farm and mine employment in 1960, the association between such dependence and population retention is very clear (Table 1.3). In the region as a whole, there were 94 counties in which more than 50 percent of employed workers were in agriculture (farm production work) or mining. All but six of them decreased in population during 1960-70. There were 159 counties where 40-49 percent of all workers were in agriculture and mining, and all but 15 decreased in population. Only where farm and mine work dependence was less than 30 percent did half of the counties avoid population loss, and only where such work was less than 20 percent of all work did growth occur in the great majority of counties. The bivariate correlation between percentage in farm and mine work and rate of population growth was $r = -.61; r^2 = .37$.

The nature of this relationship creates very different patterns of population change between the West North Central states and the East North Central states. Nearly all counties where agricultural and mining dependence was over 40 percent were in the western half of the region. Such levels of dependence make any population growth very unlikely. New jobs in other industries can rarely be developed fast enough under such conditions to offset decline in the traditional work.

In the United States in general, the more rural counties did succeed in obtaining the highest growth rate of private nonagricultural wage and salary jobs during the 1960s. For example, the entirely or predominantly rural counties of the United States as a whole had a 43 percent increase in such jobs, compared to a growth of 34 percent in the predominantly urban counties (Table 1.4). Rural nonagricultural job growth was especially high in the South where the rural counties averaged better than 50 percent growth in these jobs in just 10 years. Nonagricultural job growth levels in the East North Central states resembled those of the United States as a whole, with the more rural areas having rapid growth. West of the Mississippi River, the average nonagricultural growth rates were lower, and the comparative advantage of higher growth in the more rural counties was absent. As a result, a county with a given level of agricultural or mining dependence was less likely to decline in the East North Central states than in the western group.

The Plains tier of states in the West North Central division has suffered not only from the heaviest dependency on extractive industries but also from the least relative success in obtaining alternative employment. These states (the Dakotas, Nebraska, and Kansas) had higher nonagricultural job growth in the predominantly urban counties rather than in the rural ones, contrary to the national pattern; and the growth rate of the rural counties was only 25 percent, compared with 41 percent east of the Mississippi River and 51 percent in the South. The Plains tier of the West North Central states has not been able to obtain significant rural job development, despite the very modest absolute increase that would be needed to produce rapid percentage gains from a small base.

Note from Table 1.4 that a 45 percent increase in private nonagricultural wage and salary jobs in the entirely rural counties of the nation resulted in only a 0.1 percent increase in population, whereas a 33 percent job gain in the most urban counties was accompanied by a 15 percent increase in population. Growth in a job sector that has one job for every twelve people—as was the case in the entirely rural counties at the beginning of the decade—simply does not have the same power to hold population as does growth in a job sector that has less than four people for each job (such as in the most urban counties).

Unlike large areas of the South, the out-movement from the small communities of the North Central region is not generally associated with poverty or race. Except for Indian communities and parts of southern Missouri, the out-movement generally comes from areas of high educational standards, good median incomes, and reasonable housing conditions. In effect, the rural areas of the Midwest have avoided poverty by exporting their youths.

However, the pressures on the supply of jobs within the region have not been equal. There are substantial differences in childbearing patterns that in turn produce different potential rates of labor force increase. In some areas, such as northern Missouri, southern Iowa, or southeastern Kansas, people have had comparatively small families. In such areas only a moderate rate of job growth is needed to cope with the oncoming labor force. But some other areas of different cultural and religious background have childbirth rates sufficient to double the population each generation. In these counties, the labor force would grow by more than 25 percent in the 1970s if none of the young people left. Even a partial slowdown of the out-migration rate would soon result in local population gain.

EFFECTS OF DECLINE

Data that measure the effects of decline on rural communities are not regularly reported and therefore are not easy to quantify. But several things can be said. As noted earlier, the typical process of decline is for young adults to leave the community in large proportions as they finish high school and not return. As successive classes of young people leave, the average age of the community rises and the age structure becomes rather distorted so that after awhile, the number of people in their 50s or 60s may come to exceed the number in their 20s or 30s. The birth rate begins to fall because of the shortage of young adults, and the population then ages even faster. If the median age of the population passes 35 years, deaths are likely to begin to exceed births, and a condition occurs in which the community declines in population both from migration and because there are more deaths than births.

The average age in hundreds of midwestern rural towns is now over 40 years, and in many it is over 50 years.[2] Where the latter figure applies, towns are usually small hamlets of just several hundred people, but median ages of over 40 occur in many larger places and in some entire counties. The median age of the entire U.S. population, by contrast, is 28 years. Where the median age is up into the mid-40s, the proportion of people who are 65 years old and over is a fourth or more of the total population. This is a far higher proportion of older people than is normal, and it has far-reaching effects on the context of life in such communities—for both the old and the young.

With the relative absence of families of childbearing age, the average number of people per household (or per occupied housing unit) is somewhat low. For example, the nonmetro towns of less than 1,000 population in Wisconsin, Minnesota, and South Dakota have an average household size of 2.87 persons, compared with 3.21 persons in those states as a whole. But more significant than this is the fact that average household size is declining generally, even in towns without population loss. People live longer, so we have more older, husband-wife families where the children have grown up and left. People are more financially independent in old age now and are less likely to move in with their children after retirement or widowhood than in the past. And in the younger age groups, people are less likely to remain in the parental household until marriage. The result of these factors is that small average household size requires more occupied housing units to accommodate a given population than formerly. Nationally, households are increasing at a more rapid rate than total population, so a community that is decreasing in population is not necessarily decreasing in households.

It might come as a surprise to many to learn that although the towns of less than 1,000 population in Wisconsin, Minnesota, and South Dakota had an overall decline of 0.7 percent in population during 1960-70, they had an increase of 5.3 percent in the number of occupied housing units. And whereas 62 percent of them had population declines, only 42 percent had household declines. Even among towns as small as 300-399 people, the average trends of population and household change were in opposite directions. These differences are not extreme, but they do have significance. The housing function—and the goods and services that it supports—has held up better in the small communities than total population changes would indicate.

I have not attempted to estimate information on characteristics other than age of migrants from the rural communities of the North Central region. I think it safe to say that it is widely assumed by locals and outsiders alike that many of the brightest young people leave. It is certainly true that the bulk of those leave who seek a college education or specialized occupations. Some return after college; many do not. Many of the careers open to college graduates are disproportionately located in urban areas. Throughout the Midwest, the major current educational difference between urban and rural adults of less than 50 years of age is the proportion who have gone to college, not the proportion who have completed high school. High school enrollment rates for 16- and 17-year-olds are generally higher in rural areas than in urban.

But the out-movement is not limited to the more ambitious. It has taken so large a proportion of young people, especially west of the Mississippi River, that

[2]In the three North Central states for which age data of small towns are published—Wisconsin, Minnesota, and South Dakota—90 places had populations with a median age of 50 years or more in 1970. Nine of these had populations with a median age of over 60 years. All the latter were places of less than 200 population.

Table 1.5. Median income of counties in West North Central States, 1960 and 1970, by population change, 1960-70

Population change, 1960-70	Counties	Median family income		
		1970	1960	Percent change
	(number)	*($)*	*($)*	
Total[a]	619	8,985	5,154	74.3
10% gain or more	77	10,696	6,239	71.4
0-9.9% gain	127	8,835	5,237	68.7
0-9.9% loss	209	7,652	4,278	78.9
10-14.9% loss	108	6,877	3,766	82.6
15% loss or more	98	6,531	3,760	73.7

[a]Total includes St. Louis city. Values for counties with 15 percent loss or more partly estimated.

all economic and ability classes are represented. In addition, it is clear that the educational attainment of rural populations has risen rapidly, regardless of the effects of out-migration. As an example, in Iowa the median education of the rural population in 1960 was 1.5 years less than that of the urban; by 1970 both medians had risen, but the difference had been reduced to 0.1 year by the more rapid rural rise.

Further, it cannot be said that decline of population has prevented income increases. Grouping counties in the West North Central states by population change shows that those losing population had lower average family incomes than those gaining population (Table 1.5). This accords with the typical heavy dependence on agriculture of losing counties, and shows an income rationality in the population movement. But as a class, the declining counties experienced more rapid rates of income growth from 1959-69 than did those where population was increasing. The reasons for this are not clear from the information available. The comparative returns from the 1959 and 1969 crop and livestock years could be a factor, so could the increase in employment of women in rural areas, or the shifting of the adult population in declining counties toward middle-age where income is typically at its peak. Whatever the factors, counties with decreasing population typically have an income disadvantage relative to those with increasing population in the same region. But the demographic decrease has apparently

not prevented progress in attaining higher incomes and narrowing the relative income gap.

THE FUTURE

In one sense, the 1970-80 decade is the last chance that many small communities will have in the immediate future to stabilize their populations. I refer to the fact that despite the overall population loss, most small communities presently have fairly large numbers of youth 10-19 years old as a result of the high birth rates of the 1950s. In both the East and West North Central divisions, there are more rural youths of this age than there were in either 1960 or 1950 (Table 1.6).

However, the out-migration of rural adults who would now have children under 10 years old, coupled with the decline in the birth rate of the 1960s, has greatly undercut the number of very young children. In 1970, there were only 76 percent as many rural children under 5 years old in the East North Central states as there were in the 10-14 age group, and only 67 percent as many in the Plains tier of the West North Central states. The rapid decrease in the birth rate since 1970 is further reducing these proportions. Thus, once the present cohorts of rural youths now 10 years and older are out of school, the subsequent groups leaving school will be successively smaller for many years to come. If those youths reaching adulthood in the 1970s do not feel any greater attraction to remain-

Table 1.6. Rural population under 25 years old for subdivisions of the North Central Region, 1970, 1960, and 1950

Age	East North Central Division			West North Central Division—1st tier[a]			West North Central Division—2nd tier[b]		
	1970	1960	1950	1970	1960	1950	1970	1960	1950
	(thou)								
Population by age									
Under 5 years	893.2	1,152.7	1,034.7	318.4	445.9	467.6	153.9	256.4	275.9
5-9 years	1,114.6	1,112.0	905.9	409.6	440.0	418.6	204.0	254.1	287.5
10-14 years	1,176.9	1,010.6	792.3	440.3	410.7	376.6	230.2	231.6	214.1
15-19 years	966.2	754.1	674.2	355.5	312.7	318.2	194.7	174.6	196.2
20-24 years	628.7	514.2	597.7	204.0	194.3	252.3	104.7	113.9	164.7
	(%)								
Indexes of population by age[c]									
Under 5 years	75.9	97.9	87.9	72.3	101.3	106.2	66.9	111.4	119.9
5-9 years	94.7	94.5	77.0	93.0	99.9	95.1	88.6	110.4	108.2
10-14 years	100.0	85.9	67.3	100.0	93.3	85.5	100.0	100.6	98.0
15-19 years	82.1	64.1	57.3	80.8	71.0	72.3	84.6	75.8	85.2
20-24 years	53.4	43.7	50.8	46.3	44.1	57.3	45.5	49.5	71.6

Source: U.S. censuses of population.
[a]Iowa, Minnesota, Missouri.
[b]Kansas, Nebraska, North Dakota, South Dakota.
[c]Index, age group 10-14 years =100.0

ing in the rural and small town environment than did those in the 1960s, population declines in the Midwest—especially in the western half—could become more widespread, because there will be fewer births to offset the out-migration.

In the West North Central states, the proportion of jobs that are agricultural (plus mining) continues to be high in many counties. Even after the farm consolidations of the 1960s, more than half of the West North Central counties still have more than 30 percent of their workers in farm production work. Under the pattern of economic development in recent years, such a proportion is usually too high to permit any population increase. Although I would expect somewhat faster nonextractive industry and business growth in the 1970s in these counties, it is unlikely to occur at a pace sufficient to avoid further population declines in many counties or towns that are already low in population. If the statistical relationship between extractive industry employment and population change observed in the region in the 1960s were to persist in the 1970s, about 280 West North Central counties might expect to decrease in population in the 1970s. This would be less than the 415 that decreased in the 1960s. The interplay of nonextractive development trends and the birth rate will determine whether the actual number proves to be larger or smaller than this projection.

The East North Central states no longer have high exposure to population decline from lowered agricultural and mining manpower needs. Only 7 percent of the counties in this division now have even a fifth of their workers in farm or mine work. Some areas in this division will be susceptible to population decrease, but it is just as likely to be from problems with their manufacturing mix or movement out of central city counties as from agricultural or mining trends.

Many rural areas of the North Central region that have extensive districts unsuited to agriculture and well suited to recreation or retirement have been attracting population rapidly. This is especially true in the Missouri Ozarks and the lower peninsula of Michigan, and it is partly true in northern Wisconsin and Minnesota. This trend has reversed longstanding population declines in many counties and small towns. Given the increasing prevalence of steady retirement incomes among growing numbers of older people, plus the increased emphasis on recreation activity, this trend will almost certainly spread to additional areas, particularly where there are lakes—natural or otherwise—and cheap land. It is a force that is bringing many urban natives and former rural people back into rural areas, but it cannot be expected to affect all rural areas equally or materially.

The smaller the community setting examined, the

more extreme its characteristics can be. For example, counties do not show as high median ages, as small average household sizes, or as extreme trends of growth or decline as some towns do. We must expect many places to continue to experience major declines, even if the larger county community of which they are a part shows increased retention of people. Data from the Fuguitt study (1963) show that size of place does not have as much association with population retention where the place is within 50 miles of a metropolitan city. The forces of population spread and redistribution that characterize most Midwestern metro cities affect villages of less than 500 people to some extent, just as they do places of several thousand. Such places may become attractive for cheap housing or as a commuting refuge from urban congestion. But away from the metro perimeters, I expect a continuation of the existing pattern of predominant population loss among very small places. Even as early as 1951, Chittick found that half of the towns in South Dakota with 250-500 population did not have drug stores, fuel dealers, or household appliance stores; two-fifths lacked banks; and a third had no eating places.[3] Such communities may be incorporated and have a sense of identity and a desire for perpetuation, but they are not generally centers with an adequate minimal range of urban services. Their origin was often the product of a limited span of years in between the railroad and automotive eras. They typically have little to attract industry. Their prospects for active survival may be dim except to serve as satellite residential and retail nodes, dependent economically on larger towns.

But by the same token, I am impressed with the ability of a majority of places of more than 500 people to retain their population. The forces that impelled metropolitan concentration of industry have been weakened, especially for manufacturing. There are many factors persuading firms to seek nonmetropolitan locations, if not for their headquarters then at least for branch plants. And the results show up clearly in employment data for the United States as a whole. The cities have lost some of their urbanity, and the rural areas have lost much rusticity. Especially among people who have finished the wandering and questing period of post-high school youth, there is an increasing willingness—if I interpret both polls and events correctly—to live in smaller-scale communities. This may be most difficult to translate into economic feasibility in the West North Central states. But the potential for demographic stability after the present inevitable period of transition to lower population levels is evident in many areas.

[3]Douglas Chittick, *Growth and Decline of South Dakota Trade Centers, 1901-51*, Agricultural Experiment Station, Bulletin 448 (Brookings: South Dakota State College, 1955), p. 44.

The agricultural crisis as a crisis of culture

WENDELL BERRY

In my boyhood, Henry County, Kentucky, was not just a rural county, as it still is—it was a *farming* county. The farms were generally small. They were farmed by families who lived not only upon them, but within and *from* them. These families grew gardens. They produced their own meat, milk, and eggs. The farms were highly diversified. The main money crop was tobacco. But the farmers also grew corn, wheat, barley, oats, hay, and sorghum. Cattle, hogs, and sheep were all characteristically raised on the same farms. There were small dairies, the milking more often than not done by hand. Those were the farm products that might have been considered major. But there were also minor products, and one of the most important characteristics of that old economy was the existence of markets for minor products. In those days a farm family could easily market its surplus cream, eggs, old hens, and frying chickens. The power for field work was still furnished mainly by horses and mules. There was still a prevalent pride in workmanship, and thrift was still a forceful social ideal. The pride of most people was still in their homes, and their homes looked like it.

This was by no means a perfect society. Its people had often been violent and wasteful in their use of the land and of each other. Its present ills had already taken root in it. But I have spoken of its agricultural economy of a generation ago to suggest that there were also good qualities indigenous to it that might have been cultivated and built upon.

That they were not cultivated and built upon—that they were repudiated as the stuff of a hopelessly outmoded, unscientific way of life—is a tragic error on the part of the people themselves; and it is a work of monstrous ignorance and irresponsibility on the part of the experts and politicians, who have prescribed, encouraged, and applauded the disintegration of such farming communities all over the country.

In the decades since World War II the farms of Henry County have become increasingly mechanized. Though they are still comparatively diversified, they are less diversified than they used to be. The holdings are larger, the owners are fewer. The land is falling more and more into the hands of speculators and pro-

fessional people from the cities, who—in spite of all the scientific agricultural miracles—still have much more money than farmers. Because of big technology and big economics, there is more abandoned land in the county than ever before. Many of the better farms are visibly deteriorating, for want of manpower and time and money to maintain them properly. The number of part-time farmers and ex-farmers increases every year. Our harvests depend more and more on the labor of old people and young children. The farm people live less and less from their own produce, more and more from what they buy. The best of them are more worried about money and more overworked than ever before. Among the people as a whole, the focus of interest has largely shifted from the household to the automobile; the ideals of workmanship and thrift have been replaced by the goals of leisure, comfort, and entertainment. For Henry County plays its full part in what Maurice Telleen calls "the world's first broad-based hedonism." The young people expect to leave as soon as they finish high school, and so they are without permanent interest; they are generally not interested in anything that cannot be reached by automobile on a good road. Few of the farmers' children will be able to afford to stay on the farm—perhaps even fewer will wish to do so, for it will cost too much, require too much work and worry, and it is hardly a fashionable ambition.

And nowhere now is there a market for minor produce: a bucket of cream, a hen, a few dozen eggs. One cannot sell milk from a few cows anymore; the law-required equipment is too expensive. Those markets were done away with in the name of sanitation—but, of course, to the enrichment of the large producers. We have always had to have "a good reason" for doing away with small operators, and in modern times the good reason has often been sanitation, for which there is apparently no small or cheap technology. Future historians will no doubt remark upon the inevitable association, with us, between sanitation and filthy lucre. And it is one of the miracles of science and hygiene that the germs that used to be in our food have been replaced by poisons.

In all this, few people whose testimony would have mattered have seen the connection between the "modernization" of agricultural techniques and the disintegration of the culture and the communities of farming—and the consequent disintegration of the structures of urban life. What we have called agricultural progress has, in fact, involved the forcible displacement of millions of people.

I remember, during the fifties, the outrage with which our political leaders spoke of the forced removal of the populations of villages in communist countries. I also remember that at the same time, in Washington, the word on farming was "Get big or get out"—a policy which is still in effect and which has taken an enormous toll. The only difference is that of method: the force used by the communists was military; with us, it has been economic—a "free market" in which the freest were the richest. The attitudes are equally cruel, and I believe that the results will prove equally damaging, not just to the concerns and values of the human spirit, but to the practicalities of survival.

And so those who could not get big have got out—not just in my community, but in farm communities all over the country. But as a social or economic goal, bigness is totalitarian; it establishes an inevitable tendency toward the *one* that will be the biggest of all. Many who got big to stay in are now being driven out by those who got bigger. The aim of bigness implies not one aim that is not socially and culturally destructive.

And this community-killing agriculture, with its monomania of bigness, is not primarily the work of farmers, though it has burgeoned on their weaknesses. It is the work of the institutions of agriculture: the university experts, the bureaucrats, and the "agribusinessmen," who have promoted so-called efficiency at the expense of community (and of real efficiency), and the quantity at the expense of quality.

In 1973, 1000 Kentucky dairies went out of business. They were the victims of policies by which we imported dairy products to compete with our own and exported so much grain as to cause a drastic rise in the price of feed. And, typically, an agriculture expert at the University of Kentucky, Dr. John Nicolai, was optimistic about this failure of 1000 dairymen, whose cause he is supposedly being paid—partly with *their* tax money—to serve. They were inefficient producers, he said, and they needed to be eliminated.

He did not say—indeed, there was no indication that he had ever considered—what might be the limits of his criterion or his logic. Did he propose to applaud this process year after year until "biggest" and "most efficient" become synonymous with "only"? Did these dairymen have any value not subsumed under the heading of "efficiency"? And who benefited by their failure? Assuming that the benefit reached beyond the more "efficient" (that is, the bigger) producers to lower the cost of milk to consumers, do we

than have a formula by which to determine how many consumer dollars are equal to the livelihood of one dairyman? Or is *any* degree of "efficiency" worth *any* cost? I do not think that this expert knows the answers. I do not think that he is under any pressure—scholarly, professional, moral, or otherwise—to ask the questions. This sort of regardlessness is invariably justified by pointing to the enormous productivity of American agriculture. But any abundance, in any amount, is illusory if it does not safeguard its producers, and in American agriculture it is now virtually the accepted rule that abundance will destroy its producers.

And along with the rest of society, the established agriculture has shifted its emphasis, and its interest, from quality to quantity, having failed to see that in the long run the two ideas are inseparable. To pursue quantity alone is to destroy those disciplines in the producer that are the only assurance of quantity. What is the effect on quantity of persuading a producer to produce an inferior product? What, in other words, is the relation of pride or craftsmanship to abundance? That is another question the "agribusinessmen" and their academic collaborators do not ask. They do not ask it because they are afraid of the answer: The preserver of abundance is excellence.

My point is that food is a cultural product; it cannot be produced by technology alone. Those agriculturists who think of the problems of food production solely in terms of technological innovation are oversimplifying both the practicalities of production and the network of meanings and values necessary to define, nurture, and preserve the practical motivations. That the discipline of agriculture should have been so divorced from other disciplines has its immediate cause in the compartmental structure of the universities, in which complementary, mutually sustaining and enriching disciplines are divided, according to "professions," into fragmented, one-eyed specialties. It is suggested, both by the organization of the universities and by the kind of thinking they foster, that farming shall be the responsibility only of the college of agriculture, that law shall be in the sole charge of the professors of law, that morality shall be taken care of by the philosophy department, reading by the English department, and so on. The same, of course, is true of government, which has become another way of institutionalizing the same fragmentation.

However, if we conceive of a culture as one body, which it is, we see that all of its disciplines are everybody's business, and that the proper university product is therefore not the whittled-down, isolated mentality of expertise, but a mind competent in all its concerns. To such a mind it would be clear that there are agricultural disciplines that have nothing to do with crop production, just as there are agricultural obligations that belong to people who are not farmers.

A culture is not a collection of relics or ornaments, but a practical necessity, and its corruption invokes calamity. A healthy culture is a communal order of memory, insight, value, work, conviviality, reverence, aspiration. It reveals the human necessities and the human limits. It clarifies our inescapable bonds to the earth and to each other. It assures that the necessary restraints are observed, that the necessary work is done, and that it is done well. A healthy *farm* culture can be based only upon familiarity and can grow only among a people soundly established upon the land; it nourishes and safeguards a human intelligence of the earth that no amount of technology can satisfactorily replace. The growth of such a culture was once a strong possibility in the farm communities of this country. We now have only the sad remnants of those communities. If we allow another generation to pass without doing what is necessary to enhance and embolden the possibility now perishing with them, we will lose it altogether. And then we will not only invoke calamity—we will deserve it.

Several years ago I argued with a friend of mine that we might make money by marketing some inferior lambs. My friend thought for a minute and then he said, "I'm in the business of producing *good* lambs, and I'm not going to sell any other kind." He also said that he kept the weeds out of his crops for the same reason that he washed his face. The human race has survived by that attitude. It can survive *only* by that attitude—though the farmers who have it have not been much acknowledged or much rewarded.

Such an attitude does not come from technique or technology. It does not come from education; in more than two decades in universities I have rarely seen it. It does not come even from principle. It comes from a passion that is culturally prepared—a passion for excellence and order that is handed down to young people by older people whom they respect and love. When we destroy the possibility of that succession, we will have gone far toward destroying ourselves.

4

The consequences of changes in agricultural technology for the urban sector and society as a whole

Attributes and influences in assimilation

VARDEN FULLER

Does the rural migrant make out successfully? How well does he fare? Has the family adjusted to urban life? Although these questions seem simple and reasonable they become elusively complex when one attempts to make them operational and meaningful for research purposes.

From whose point of view should the rural migrant be examined? One can ask the migrant or members of his family what he or they believe and thereby try to obtain a *self-assessment*. One can try to obtain objective data on occupation and employment, level of living, community participation, and similar criteria and thereby make an *external assessment*.

With whom should the rural migrant be compared? Rural migrant versus urban migrant and urban nonmigrant in the relocation area? Rural migrant versus ex-peer nonmigrants in the exodus area? Rural migrant before and after? All of these comparisons have been made, but nobody seems to be very certain of what the results mean. The most usual comparison is rural migrant (variously farm-born, farm-reared, rural-born, or rural-reared) versus urban (sometimes divided into urban migrant and urban nonmigrant). The crucial question, it would seem, is whether or not rural-reared persons have bettered themselves by moving to the city.[1]

To whom and to what should the migration be considered crucial? The comparison posed as crucial is presumably less so for those who have already made the decision and the move than for those who are trying to make the decision. It is less crucial to program administrators and policymakers than the compari-

son of rural migrants with others within the relocation scene. For the public interest, it should not be enough to know only whether rural migrants bettered themselves or believed they had. Rather, if their capacity and performance were found to be inferior in some respects—education, health, training, etc—the need of corrective action to enhance capacity and improve level of performance would be suggested.

Some early studies of migrants found the amount of education to be not important to success in relocation; later ones say otherwise. In their first to third years of relocation, rural migrants can and often do present a near hopeless prospect of integration; after five to ten years, few traces of their rural beginning are to be found. Theorems about kinship influences that appear to hold for the time being in the Ozarks cannot be verified in Pennsylvania or Michigan. Residential migrancy and occupational mobility are no longer coidentifiable to the extent they formerly were, i.e., decentralization of industry and commutable transportation systems make job mobility more feasible without the need of migration; consequently, a great deal of unseen occupational and social assimilation can and does occur.

Leaving aside the specific environmental context of rural-urban migration and otherwise simplifying by omitting important variables, a streamlined two-dimensional research grid for the farm population only might be as in the table on the following page.

This highly generalized and oversimplified scheme fails to consider time from two points of view: (1) the specific time surveyed and (2) the amount of elapsed time that the subjects had for assimilation. Further, "exotic" situations—particular areas, ethnic groups, race—if recognized even minimally would greatly compound the design.

□ From Rural worker adjustment to urban life: an assessment of the research, Ann Arbor, Mich., 1970, Institute of Labor and Industrial Relations, University of Michigan and Wayne State University, pp. 61-75.

Forms of assimilation and source of evidence	Type of migrant			
	Youth	Part-time farmers	Termi-nating farmers	Wage laborers
(1) Occupation and employment				
(a) Exterior assessments				
(i) Macroevidence*				
(ii) Microevidence**				
(b) Self-assessments (micro)				
(2) Community and social life				
(a) Exterior assessments				
(i) Macroevidence				
(ii) Microevidence				
(b) Self-assessments (micro)				
(3) Gains and losses: economic, social, and personal				
(a) Exterior assessments				
(i) Macroevidence				
(ii) Microevidence				
(b) Self-assessments (micro)				

*National or regional impersonal data.
**Personal and local data.

The foregoing exercise does not describe either what has been or exhort as to what should have been. It does lay out some of the possibilities that would have entered into comprehensive development of knowledge. Since individual pieces of research have only dealt with fragments of the columns and with either a collapsed category or a selected category of the rows, one recognizes immediately their limited power of generalization. Very little of what is known is (or should be) claimed as being other than a finding of that particular survey.

OCCUPATIONS AND EMPLOYMENT

There have been two national (sample) surveys of farm-reared people in nonfarm environments. The first, in 1952, was a by-product of political behavior research which was done at the Survey Research Center, University of Michigan.[2] The second (to which reference has already been made) was done in 1958 by the Economic Research Service, U.S. Department of Agriculture.[3] It was a by-product of research on lung cancer risks done for the Public Health Service.

The earlier (Freedman) study offers only quite general and cautious generalizations, which were restricted principally to occupational and social status. The farm-reared were found to be disproportionate in low-status positions, but the writers viewed this as not inherent in rural people. As newcomers to the urban social system, a marginal position was to be expected and was "likely to disappear in succeeding generations," they said. The Freedmans claimed their findings were "consistent with the hypothesis that farm to urban migration has provided a base for the upward social mobility of other elements in the population."[4]

The USDA survey is considerably more instructive. Its comparisons are between the farm- and nonfarm-born population, 18 years and older. Of 25.8 million native farm-born adults, only 9.5 million were living on farms in 1958 (sample: 35,000 households). As reported from other surveys, disproportions were found in blue- as against white-collar occupations. The nonfarm-born had approximately half in each; the farm-born was 35.5 percent white-collar, 60.5 percent blue-collar, and 4 percent farm workers. These relative proportions tended to remain fairly stable through all age groups, except for smaller portions of farm-born in farm work after 24 and until 55 years and over.

The ERS authors had a less esoteric explanation of the large blue-collar proportions than had the Freedmans:

Logically, it is not surprising that farm people go principally into so-called blue-collar jobs when they leave the farm. The types of job skills that farm-reared people acquire, such as competence in construction work, or in operation and repair of machinery, plus the fact that they are accustomed to manual labor, suits them for work as truck drivers, factory operatives, craftsmen, or laborers. Furthermore their average level of formal education is often too low to make them readily suitable for many types of white-collar work without further training.[5]

Ex-farm people were found by ERS to be broadly distributed by industry classification. They were not significantly differentiated as to proportions of self-employment. They were unemployed at the same rate as others even though their labor force participation was a bit higher in the age 18-24 category.

These results on occupational achievement and employment from the national surveys will not be compared with those derived from some of the different kinds of the microlocality studies.

In Des Moines, Iowa, comparisons were made on the above-mentioned and other aspects of assimilation between farm migrants, rural nonfarm migrants, urban migrants, and natives.[6] As usual, farm migrants were disproportionally in the lower status occupations. Classified as "manual" and "nonmanual" instead of by color of collar, the comparative percentages ran as follows:[7]

	Manual	Nonmanual
Farm migrants	57.7	42.3
Rural nonfarm migrants	49.8	50.2
Urban migrants	37.1	62.9
Des Moines natives	54.3	45.7

Variance analysis was employed to identify relationships underlying these gross differences. Individual occupational ratings (North-Hatt scores) were found to be closely related to years of schooling in all four samples, especially after high school. When schooling, age, and migrant-residence category were trichotomized against occupational ratings, migrancy was found to have no significant relation to occupational achievement. Schooling was the dominantly associated variable.

Median family income was lowest for farm migrants ($6,220) and highest for urban migrants ($7,360). Since the differences were the greatest in the older age categories, the authors believe this was due to the greater education of the urban migrant which made him eligible for continued advancement into higher paid job classifications.

Some employment-related aspects of migration and assimilation were considered in a Wilmington, Delaware study.[8] "Urban migrants more often came in response to a specific job offer than rural migrants did, while almost a third of the blue-collar workers from rural backgrounds stated 'other' reasons, essentially marking their dissatisfaction with their previous residence. Otherwise, rural-urban differences were not of any great importance. Work mattered to all categories of migrants, but specific job opportunities more often played a part in the coming of white-collar workers, and perhaps of the urban migrants as well."[9]

This unplanned looking for work characterized blue-collar versus white-collar migrants of all origins but was usually more pronounced for the rural blue-collar segment. Two-thirds of the blue-collar group had made no premigration trip to Wilmington or had come to visit friends or relatives as against two-fifths of the white-collar segment. Coming to Wilmington prior to migration in "preparation for the move" and "in connection with work" was characteristic of half the white-collar categories versus one-fifth of blue-collar urban origin and one-fourth of blue-collar rural origin. All migrants into Wilmington had depended heavily upon relatives, friends, and neighbors as against institutional sources for "aid or information." The outstanding category was blue-collar rural origin, of whom 86 percent listed this course of information and aid. The smallest dependence on friends, relatives, and neighbors was by the white-collar rural origin—50 percent.[10]

The author summarized his findings on this point as follows:

Formal structures, especially those built around work, do in any case seem to play a very large part in the initial contact of high-ranking migrants with the city, while less formal structures, especially ascriptive solidarities, do seem to be more important in the migration of low-ranking groups. Correspondingly, the high-ranking migrants take more extensive preparation for migration, accumulate more general information about their destinations, and get assistance from a wider variety of specialists. Such differences in the form of the migrant's initial relationship to the city surely affect his subsequent involvement in the city's life.[11]

A self-assessment approach was used in Racine, Wisconsin "for a test of 12 general hypotheses derived from a theory of value assimilation." The comparison was migrant Mexican-Americans versus an Anglo residence group.[12] It appears that more than half of the Mexican-Americans believed that the changes in their life after settling in Racine were "good"; the proportion was a little higher for the few Anglos who had migrated. Since a large majority of the Mexican-Americans had come to Racine for "work-oriented reasons" (like looking for a job?) and half the Anglos who migrated to Racine stated "family oriented, other" reasons, one assumes that the Mexicans had found satisfactory jobs and the Anglos were happy with their relatives.

In general, the Mexican migrants seemed to be assimilating well into the industrial structure of Racine. Occupational mobility from first job was equal for those starting in agriculture and those starting in the operative category. At higher levels of occupational mobility, Mexicans fell behind the Anglos. The Mexicans had less favorable perceptions of change than were held by Anglos with agricultural antecedents.

Very little questioning on abilities and performance of off-farm migrants as industrial workers has been done of employers. Similarly, it has not seemed to be fashionable to ask the worker directly and unambiguously about his nonfarm work experience—his adjustment to a group work situation, to highly specialized job divisions, to the foreman, to the union (if one), etc. Scarcely any of those researching the field have tried to find out about the process—how many changes of job, what on-job training, what outside basic education or skill training—that led to whatever occupational "status" the migrant had acquired.

The results obtained from a few of the inquiries made are worth noting. A Kingsport, Tennessee, study[13] in 1955 attempted

> to find out who made the better workers—men with farm or nonfarm backgrounds—we used three indexes: (1) length of time a worker served, (2) whether or not he ever attained a semiskilled position, and (3) in the case of farmer employees, whether or not his separation left him in good standing with the company for re-employment.[14]

Kingsport was then fairly recently industrialized within a predominantly agricultural area. The two companies involved had grown rapidly since the 1920's and had used workers from farms as one of their principal sources of manpower—approximately one-fourth of the total in 1925-34, over one-third in 1935-44, and under one-fifth in 1945-55.

The author summarized his findings in this paragraph:

> In only two cases was a significant difference observed between farm and nonfarm workers. (1) Of those hired between 1943 and 1946, 25 percent of the nonfarmers but only 13 percent of the farmers were promoted. (2) In the period up to 1937, there was a low but significant correlation (0.21) between those with farm backgrounds and those who stayed with the company ten years or more. About 79 percent of the farmers and 64 percent of the nonfarmers were in the long-service group. At no time was there a significant difference in standing between farmers and nonfarmers when they left the company. For the period as a whole, 81 percent left in good standing, the percentage being insignificantly higher for those of farm origin.[14a]

A more recent (1962) study in Michigan also found differences in capacity and performance as between farm and nonfarm workers to be negligible.[15] Twenty firms in Muskegon and Kalamazoo counties, with employment of 1,000 or more, were the base for a study of production workers, one-third of whom were women. All firms had some employees with farm backgrounds, but only six percent of all employees were currently part-time farmers.

The objectives of this study were:

(1) To determine if industrial employers discriminated, positively or negatively, with respect to employing farmers simply because of their general attitude towards farmers.

(2) To learn how the nonfarm on-the-job experience of farmers differs importantly from the experience of employees not associated with farming.

(3) To determine the impact, if any, of labor unions on the employment practices of industrial employers in hiring farmers.

(4) To gain insights into how to educate and train farmers to gain industrial employment.[15a]

It was found that employers tended not to be conscious that workers with a farm background might be different. Self-recruitment was dominant among production workers, whatever their background. Selection for employment involved no criteria unfavorable to farmers; part-time farmers were only told that they must accept and agree that the job came first. The majority of the firms had observed no difference in on-the-job progress, but 15 percent said that farm people had progressed more rapidly (on-the-job training generally prevailed). Some firms noted superior mechanical abilities and a more affirmative attitude toward work by farm people, but "there was no evidence that managers view farmers as a unique group."

JOB VS. SOCIAL AND CULTURAL ASSIMILATION

Looking at the job assimilation in its simplest and least attenuated form can give one an exaggerated impression of how easily total assimilation occurs. In the Michigan and Kentucky situations reviewed above, very little geographic or cultural adjustment was involved. The Mexican-Americans coming to Racine had mainly moved from Texas and, hence, had made a considerable geographic change. But, as is generally their characteristic, Mexican-origin people are self-assimilating into particular types of work in which they have developed good working reputations and into their own preestablished *colonias* which appear to be what they did in Racine. In this sort of pattern, the culture is transported and consequently social assimilation within the *colonia* comes quite readily. Neither the distance of migration nor the social composition of the main city are of immediate relevance.

Negroes also have their own general pattern; for most, it is the long jump from the rural South to a major city ghetto in the North. Within the ghetto, as within the *colonia*, a restricted form of social assimilation can occur quite readily and with it a fair prospect of limited job assimilation. Temporarily at least, the Negro ghetto and Mexican-American *colonia* forms of job and social assimilation have a degree of stability. Less can be said for the southern Anglo, the off-reservation Indian, and the migratory farm worker—the latter comprising shifting elements of several ethnic origins. These several segments in their differing unfortunate situations, have not enjoyed even a temporary and limited form of job and social assimilation. In the short and the long run, they are largely uncohesive and peripheral peoples.

The foregoing observations imply that some elements of rural and off-farm migrants face a relatively uncomplicated assimilation centering mainly on the occupational adjustment of the family's principal breadwinner; in contrast, for others this adjustment is bound up in a complex of social and ethnic problems from which they cannot be readily insulated and which affect other family members as well as the breadwinner. As will be noted subsequently, the rural southern Anglo has had a quite singular set of adjustment difficulties deriving from particular cultural-ethnic attributes. In a parallel way, but for somewhat different reasons, job assimilation by ethnic-regional minorities and migratory farm workers has to take attenuating circumstances into account. In these two instances, perverse government policy has further intensified assimilation difficulties.[16] For reasons too well-known to warrant further comment, job assimilation by Negroes does not exist in isolation from a vast complex of attentuating factors, both current and historical.

Nevertheless, rural sociologists have believed there was something inherently particular or peculiar about people who have been rural. Consequently, they have spent countless hours attempting to find out whether rural-urban migrants were concentrated in particular parts of towns, whether they "neighbored" more or less, their church attendance, the organizations they belonged to, their voting habits, how many periodicals they received, whether they had a phone, how they made friends and who they were, whether they believed the results of their move had been good, in what social class they placed themselves and was it better than their parents', were their children having trouble in school, what educational and career ambitions did they hold for their children, and so on.

If the population sampled had a fair proportion of recent arrivals or had population elements culturally or ethnically exotic to the relocation area, there was a fair likelihood of finding some differences—even some statistically significant ones. Some authors have been candid enough to acknowledge that their discovered differences were not likely to prevail very long as the subjects in the sample had more time to adjust to urban life. Rarely has an author presented findings that seem to have any policy or program implications other than that the people should have been better educated. Otherwise, practical recommendations have been virtually nonexistent.[17]

Aside from the particular groups already noted —Mexican-Americans, Negroes, Indians, southern whites, and migratory farm workers—it can be said that, given their level of education, job training and experience, and age, the assimilation of rural-urban migrants has evolved about as one would expect in the open, fluid society of the United States.

At this advanced stage of the off-farm exodus, this reviewer does not see that a useful purpose is served in presenting a detailed account of the research literature on social assimilation. Moreover, since the problems of assimilation of ethnic-regional minorities are comprehensive and not particularly related to off-farm or rural-urban migration, the relevant and useful research comes in other contexts. Accordingly, it is mainly the southern white farmer and the migratory farm worker whose adverse situations fall more clearly within the rural-urban rubric and, therefore, warrant further discussion.

The work of Eldon D. Smith was noted previously.[18] He found that, of the rural relocatees in Indianapolis, Mississippi Negro migrants adjusted much better than did southern whites (from southern Kentucky and Tennessee). Moreover, some important differences showed up between northern whites and southern whites. This author's reasoning and findings on these latter differences are well put under the heading, "Satisfaction with Urban Opportunities Related to Social Adaptability to Urban Life," as follows:

Obviously the difference in day-to-day demands of urban existence and rural existence have resulted in differences in the customs and habits of rural and urban communities. The more individualistic habits of farm people, and their greater emphasis on hunting, fishing, and other non-commercial forms of recreation are familiar. Within the more heavily industrialized areas of the North, considerable interpenetration of rural and urban cultures has occurred through improved transportation and commercial and recreational activities. This has resulted in a great deal of similarity of customs and mores in country and city. Because of a much lesser degree of such industrial development in the South, this interpenetration is probably less complete, and, in addition, the cultural differences between the rural areas of the South and the urban areas of the North are magnified by the interregional (North-South) cultural distinction.

In view of this, one might expect that the change to life in a Northern urban community would require somewhat fewer adaptations for the Northern white migrant than for the Southern white. The Southern white migrant must not only adjust to a new job and a new set of housing accommodations; he must adapt himself to a new set of customs, a markedly different "kind of people."

The South, unlike the Midwest, was settled early by people of essentially homogeneous Anglo-Saxon culture. The waves of settlers of Dutch, German, Scandinavian, French and various other nationality origins that swept across the Midwest bypassed the states south of the Ohio River almost completely. The rural areas as well as the urban areas of the North are to this day a mosaic of nationality groups. Thus, the experience of associating with people of dissimilar background, religion, habits, etc., is simply part of the process of growing up in rural areas of the Midwest and Northeast. On the other hand, in the South, particularly in its rural areas, there has been little opportunity for such experiences simply because the later immigration from continental Europe did not penetrate the region. The necessity of adapting to cultural heterogeneity and a changing cultural complex may have developed more highly in the Midwestern than in the Southern farmer the capacity for adapting to unfamiliar social situations.

Summarizing, as a result of experiences of the past that have been built into his culture, and over which he has no control, the Midwestern farmer migrating to a Northern urban center might be expected (1) to have a smaller adjustment to make and (2) to have a more highly developed capacity to make the necessary adjustment than does the Southern farmer. It must be emphasized, however, that if this hypothesis is valid, it constitutes no indictment of the character of Southern farm people. It merely means that these people who migrate from Southern farms to Northern urban areas face somewhat more difficult problems of preparation and assistance in addition to employment information.

In general the hypothesis is substantiated by the study of Indianapolis migrants. Northern whites appear to be rapidly assimilated into the urban culture and soon lose their identity as migrants. Distinctive speech habits and other cultural factors identifying them as migrants are generally lacking. They make new friends more rapidly than do Southern whites and their capacity for making new friends among urban people and people from other regions also appears to be somewhat superior. Northern white migrants were not found grouped together in identifiable communities as were the Southern whites. Reports of employers indicate that they (Northern whites) are stable workers with no unusual rate of turnover, suggesting that return migration is not very important and that they have been able to adjust satisfactorily. They are reportedly quite easily trained to new skills, particularly mechanical skills. The fact that they are favorably regarded as workers is evidenced by the fact that the beginning wages of Northern whites in Indianapolis are significantly higher than those of Southern whites even after allowing the differences in educational preparation.[19]

Smith further noted that because southern white migrants had a propensity to return home after a brief period, "employers often regard them as poor employment risks for jobs requiring any substantial training period and consider them inferior workers for even unskilled jobs."[20]

Working with a less formal research design and contemporary with Smith, J. S. Slotkin also observed that southern whites had a great complex of difficulties in becoming socially and industrially integrated in a locality near Chicago and that there was much returning back "home."[21]

Why the outstanding lack of success in southern white migration has not been more challenging to researchers is difficult to understand. Those who tried to move and returned plus the much larger number remaining in place now constitute a large proportion of the white Americans in rural poverty.[22] They present a research gap, not seriously attenuated by issues of race and prejudice, in which something worthwhile could still be done. But at this juncture, considering the unresolved state of the "urban crisis," the relevant research frame would not be rural-urban mobility alone.

As regards migratory farm labor, the question of assimilation has been blocked by a pervasive fundamentalism to the effect that migratory workers had to exist because seasonal crop production needed them.[23] This sort of fundamentalism has afflicted researchers to the extent that most of their interests have centered on how to ameliorate the ordeals of migratory life rather than on how to eliminate the conditions that forced people into continued migrancy.

Migratory workers do not follow the sun with joy nor do they relish their poverty; when they have the opportunity to settle down, the evidence is they do so. They do not voluntarily become migratory workers because farmers have need of seasonal labor.

This heterogeneous population can realistically be looked upon as direct evidence of an assimilation failure in the American labor economy. A substantial proportion of migratory workers started out being off-farm migrants seeking relocation. Changes in the organization and technology of the plantation system which forced out tenants, sharecroppers, and wage laborers were the principal factors which promoted migrancy. Failing to find employment asssimilation in place, they have had to subsist on peripheral quasiassimilation in a system of semiemployment.

California is the scene of continuous efforts to settle down and become stabilized in a regular job and place of residence. Although we have virtually no formal knowledge of this process, the Okie-Arkie migrants of the 1930's have done well, thanks, to a large extent, to the tight labor market of the Second World War. Others of the contemporary migratory labor population are still trying to achieve some sort of stabilization. They face great obstacles, at the center of which are poverty and an elusive work base, which William Metzler has documented in a study made in Kern County, California.[24]

In this chapter we have been concerned with attributes and influences bearing upon success or failure in achieving assimilation. We have found that, by group and by area, widely differing results have been experienced. Can any general conclusion be drawn? The President's National Advisory Commission on Rural Poverty undertook to state one;

The total number of rural poor would be even larger than 14 million had not so many of them moved to the city. They made the move because they wanted a job and a decent place to live. Some have found them. Many have not. Many merely exchanged life in a rural slum for life in an urban slum, at exorbitant cost to themselves, to the cities, and to rural America as well. Even so, few migrants have returned to the rural areas they left. They have apparently concluded that bad as conditions are in an urban slum, they are worse in the rural slum they fled from. . . ."[25]

NOTES

1. Lyle W. Shannon, "Occupational and Residential Adjustment of Rural Migrants," *Labor Mobility and Population in Agriculture*, Iowa State University, Center for Agricultural and Economic Adjustment (Ames, 1961), p. 126.
2. Ronald Freedman and Deborah Freedman, "Farm-Reared Elements in the Nonfarm Population," *Rural Sociology*, Vol. XXI, No. 1 (March 1956), pp. 50-61.
3. Calvin L. Beale, John C. Hudson, and Vera J. Banks, *Characteristics of the U.S. Population by Farm and Nonfarm Origin*, U.S. Department of Agriculture, Agricultural Economic Report No. 66, 1964.
4. As a matter of fact, there is apparently a shade of truth underlying the proposition that the Freedmans call a "hypothesis" and which they speak of as though it were a highly shared and normalized one. Farm migrants are, to a limited extent, the successors of foreign immigrants with respect to providing a manpower base for the sustained growth of the industrial economy. But that comes by "the turn of the screw" and not by deliberate arrangements or destiny as the Freedman's impassive statement of their hypothesis implies. Apparently, this is not a generally accepted proposition, for other sociologists finding disproportionate numbers of rural migrants in lower status occupations seem to regard it as abnormal and implicitly unfair.
5. Beale, Hudson, and Banks, *op. cit.*, p. 12.
   In Kansas, two investigators had the extraordinary idea of asking in Employment Service offices about what farmers applied for when they wanted nonfarm work. The results, in order: construction, factory, truck driving, mechanical, retail trade, and machine shop. See John A. Schnittker and Gerald P. Owens, *Farm-to-City Migration; Perspective and Problems*, Kansas Agricultural Experiment Station, Agricultural Economic Report No. 84 (Manhattan, 1959).
6. Ward W. Bauder and Lee G. Burchinal, *Farm Migrants to the City: A Comparison of the Status, Achievement, Community, and Family Relations of Farm Migrants with Urban Migrants and Urban Natives in Des Moines, Iowa*, Iowa Agricultural Experiment Station Research Bulletin 534 (Ames, 1956).
7. *Ibid.*, p. 366.
8. Charles Tilly, *Migration to an American City*, University of Delaware, Agricultural Experiment Station and Division of Urban Affairs (Newark, 1965).
9. *Ibid.*, pp. 19-20.
10. This was not exclusive dependence (some had had multiple sources), but the dominant source over all was relatives, friends, and neighbors.
11. Tilly, *op cit.*
12. Shannon, *op. cit.*
13. Clopper Almon, Jr., "Origins and Relation to Agriculture of Industrial Workers in Kingsport, Tennessee," *Journal of Farm Economics*, Vol. XXXVIII, No. 3 (August 1956).
14. *Ibid.*, p. 835.
14a. *Ibid.*
15. Ralph A. Loomis, *Farmers in the Nonfarm Labor Market*, Michigan State University, Agricultural Experiment Station Research Report 24 (East Lansing, 1964).
15a. Loomis, *op. cit.*
16. Reference is made especially to the role of the Bureau of Indian Affairs which serves as a catch-basin for that vast collection of ambiguities and venalities which ultimately denies the American Indian the possibility of being either an American or an Indian and to the role of the Farm Labor Service which, to guarantee the labor supply for seasonal crop harvests, has endeavored to keep migratory farm workers on the move.
17. For more ample (and sympathetic) discussions of the literature on sociologic aspects of assimilation, see George M. Beal and Wallace E. Ogg, "Secondary Adjustments from Adaptations of Agriculture," *Problems and Policies of American Agriculture* (Ames: Iowa State University Press, 1959) and Shannon, *op cit.*
18. Eldon D. Smith, "Nonfarm Employment Information for Rural People," *Journal of Farm Economics*, Vol. XXXVIII, No. 3 (August 1956).
19. *Ibid.*, pp. 821-22.
20. *Ibid.*, p. 823.
21. James Sydney Slotkin, *From Field to Factory* (Glencoe, Illinois: The Free Press, 1960).
22. Alan R. Bird and John L. McCoy, *White Americans in Rural Poverty*, U.S. Economic Research Service, Agricultural Economic Report No. 124, 1967.
23. Varden Fuller, "Economics of Migrant Labor," *Social Order*, Vol. 10, No. 1 (January 1960).
24. William H. Metzler, *Farm Mechanization and Labor Stabilization*, University of California, Giannini Foundation Research Report No. 280 (Berkeley, 1965).
25. *The People Left Behind*, A report of the President's National Advisory Commission on Rural Poverty (Washington, D.C., 1967), p. ix.

Impact of rural migration on the city

R. L. McNAMARA*

The paths of migration are many; within localities, from farm to city, regional, city to country—all have had great significance in the development of this na-

☐ From *Labor mobility and population in agriculture*, Assembled and published under the sponsorship of the Iowa State University Center for Agricultural and Economic Adjustment, Ames, Iowa, 1961, Iowa State University Press, pp. 151-157.
*University of Missouri.

tion. The concern here is primarily with the meaning of migration from rural areas to cities. At the outset, I believe we should recognize the traditional relationship of country and city with respect to population replacement or maintenance of numbers. Cities were not able to maintain their numbers through their own replacement power, and so, many of the earlier students of the field were correct in their observation that the country was the seedbed of replacement. The upsurge of the birth rate generally has somewhat changed this relationship, but the great growth of urban industry with its demands for manpower has sustained the need for recruits to supply labor in urban industry.

Likewise, large numbers of persons employed in agriculture found themselves in a disadvantaged position as the agricultural economy was making needed adjustment to modern conditions. This together with the continued high fertility of rural areas, particularly those areas remote and less productive of opportunity, has resulted in high out-migration rates from rural areas to cities and industrialized areas generally.

Migration has had momentous effects on society both at the point of origin and the point of destination. The result is one of general observation: many of the established social structures of the home society have been disrupted. In this connection rural sociologists have very properly pointed out the distressing effects on homes, neighborhoods, and on many of the processes for maintenance of satisfying social living. In the city, migration, though not forgetting its benefits, has resulted in conflict with competing ethnic groupings; has brought about maladjustment of the economic situation including sometimes the cheapening of labor; and serious congestion in certain urban areas.

Rural migrants have contributed to the relative surplus of persons in the economically productive ages of the urban population. In 1950, persons aged 20 to 49 in the urban population of the United States constituted 46 percent of the total, but the proportion in those ages in the rural-farm category was only 31 percent. Also, the ratio of dependents to gainful workers is relatively low in urban areas.

But apparently we must deal with the fact that we are an urbanized nation. As Gulick puts it, "It may well be a generation before we have a satisfactory description and analysis of what is happening to us in and around the great cities as America becomes urbanized and a new metropolitan culture comes to dominate our life. From now on most Americans will be born, grow up, live, work and die in great metropolitan complexes; some in cities, some in expanding suburbs, but mostly in urban surroundings. From now on we are an urbanized civilization."[1]

Now whether the city we think of is St. Louis, Detroit, Leopoldville, Bombay, or Bangkok the headlines concerning growth and problems of adjustment are essentially the same. Migrants entering a world of strangeness from one of easy familiarity produce what one writer has called the "waking sickness," not just a physical, emotional, or social illness, though it has aspects of all three, but a disorder of rapid social change.[2] The following comment, though its setting is a continent away, could very well be one we might hear in urban field studies here. "The house was different; the food was different; the people were different; suddenly the world was full of strangers, behaving strangely. The family was different too. There was no supporting network of relatives, no grandmother to give advice, no grandfather to make decisions. The problems were different; there was talk of police and passes, job and jails. The roles were different; mothers worked away from home, and children —if lucky—went to school."[3]

From a world of readily recognized norms for social and personal conduct, the migrant is literally in a world he never made—for him an atmosphere of normlessness, where his reference points are vague or unknown, and where his usual behavior which has long given him identity and satisfaction is termed deviancy.

The pessimistic tone of this chapter thus far could be taken to mean that there is an unfailing regularity of maladjustment of recent rural migrants in the city. This is far from true, for many migrants, probably most of them, are adjusting to their new environment, supporting themselves, and staying out of trouble. Nevertheless, the difficulties of a considerable minority confront city people, their public and private agencies, with trying social and economic problems. Focusing in the central city and particularly in specific areas, distressing reports and judgments are brought to public attention. For example, in a major midwestern city receiving large numbers of migrants from the rural South, law enforcement officials and social agency workers estimate that: (1) 50 percent of the major criminal activity involves southern migrants; (2) 50 percent of the juvenile delinquency involves children of southern migrants; (3) 30 percent of the help given by relief agencies is received by southern migrants; and (4) 20 percent of the southern migrants are unemployed. All this in an urban center in which a small segment of probably not more than 10 percent are southern migrants of recent origin.

One should hasten to observe, however, that what is perceived to be proper conduct in the city may not "square" with habits of the newcomer and that the migrant in the city is a vulnerable, highly visible person because of, among other reasons, his manner of speech, of dress, his understanding of courtesy and cleanliness. None of these marked him unusual or de-

[2]H. Jack Geiger, "When Africans Go To Town," *Saturday Review*, Sept. 3, 1960, pp. 43-46.
[3]*Op. cit.*, p. 44.

[1]Quoted from Population Bulletin, Sept., 1960, p. 128.

viant in his place of origin but may result in his being a central participant in conflict situations in the city. Hesitancy to accept the newcomer and conflict with the strangers are not new in this country. At an earlier time, complaints were made against German immigrants in the city because "they drank beer and sang songs on Sunday" and against the Italians because they "frolicked in the streets" on festival days. The descendants of these ethnic groups, now quite urbanized, may in their turn now be calling attention to the "improper" behavior of rural migrants and their repeated violation of rules of the game.

It would appear that the recency of migration is an important consideration. Learning the ways of the city is not accomplished quickly. It must be remembered that newly arrived migrants are not culturally deprived persons but rather that they bring with them, from a different setting, a full load of custom and tradition with knowledge of "what works" in interpersonal and inter-group relations. To state their relationship as a hypothesis: (1) as diversity between the migrants' culture of orientation and urban culture increases, maladjustment also increases; (2) as isolation prior to migration increases, maladjustment also increases; (3) as education increases, maladjustment decreases. Adjustment as used here is a very general term. An individual is personally adjusted if he is relatively satisfied with life as he experiences it. An individual is socially adjusted if he manages to avoid violating the mores and laws of the society in which he lives and if he manages to avoid serious conflict in his relationships with others. Of course, conflict with others includes interpersonal conflict, strife between the person and members of groups to which he belongs, and inter-group conflict or strife between the individual and members of groups to which he does not belong.[4] Carefully planned research is badly needed on adjustment of rural migrants in the city, and these need to be focused so that action programs of private and public agencies are clearly indicated and can be most promising of success.

However engrossing the situation of the individual migrant and his family may be, it should be seen as a part of the general phenomenon of population redistribution. The statements made earlier in this chapter on this point may be made more specific by referring to a preliminary statement by Clarence Senior writing for the American Society of Planning Officials.

BACKGROUND

Internal migration involves about one person in every five of the total population: approximately 30 to 33 million persons have moved their homes annually each year since World War II. Almost all move into new neighborhoods; over 5,000,000 have moved from one state to another each year.

Much of this movement represents a continuation of the long-time trend of our population from country to city. Metropolitan areas contained about 30 percent of all our people in 1900 and about 60 percent by 1956. Most estimates for 1975 reach at least 66 percent.

Many of the new urban dwellers come relatively short distances geographically, but if they come from farms, they are likely not to know as much about the complexities of city living as would be desirable. Studies have found that it takes 5 to 10 years for newcomers from the farm to equal the voting participation rates of the older urban residents, for example.

Large numbers of the migrants must bridge both long geographical distances *and* great cultural differences, since much of the movement is between regions of the country. Many come from those sections of the country where large numbers of persons are disadvantaged when judged by any of the usual indices such as high death rates, high birth rates, widespread illiteracy, low per capita income, high proportions in agricultural, forestry, and extractive occupations, etc.

PREMISES

A. Internal migration will continue and probably increase if the speed of economic development is maintained or improved.

B. It is essential to the health of the entire national economy that migration continue and even increase, in the interests of efficient allocation of human and other natural resources. (There are at least 1,200,000 "surplus" farm families, according to the recent Rockefeller Brothers report on the United States economy, for example. A forthcoming report from *Resources for the Future* advocates *speeding up* internal migration.)

C. The migration is often wasteful in time, money, and energy. It penalizes many of those who pull up their stakes to travel in search of a job, or a better job, or better life chances for their children. Often tiny life savings are gambled on the move to the city. The move may well turn out to be relatively successful economically; often it is harmful to family life and to the personal development of individuals involved.

D. The migration also often helps contribute to the further complication of life in large urban areas. Probably most city dwellers do not understand the dynamics of urban change; that the "emptying out of the central city" and the "flight to the suburbs" have a natural history of many decades is not widely realized. The entry of conspicuously different ethnic groups into areas which have been declining steadily

---

[4]Adapted from "Migration and adjustment," a design for research on urban adjustment of the rural migrant in St. Louis, Robert L. Hamblin, pp. 2-3 (unpublished).

for years dramatizes the deterioration, may well cause further "flight," and may lead to deterioration in human relations. The stranger becomes both the symbol of the end of an era and the "cause" of urban blight.

E. Successful urban living involves a variety of patterns of learned behavior:

1. The newcomer must learn, and learn rapidly, how to cope with new and strange problems. Habits learned in different, and usually simpler, surroundings do not make for satisfactory results in the new environment. Customary ways of making a living, keeping house, raising children, visiting friends and neighbors, playing, and worshipping, may all, and all at one time, be called into question. Matters treated casually in the old environment may, in the new, suddenly become invested with high emotional content (e.g., disposal of refuse). Added to all these puzzling changes often goes the reduction in self-esteem which comes from being labelled as a "problem," from being treated as a member of a conspicuous "minority," instead of as a person.

2. The "host" people also must learn to cope with new situations, to understand what is happening and how to help speed up the adjustment process. Neighborhood and city transitions can be brought about peaceably and without major personal, social, economic, and political disruption. However, citizens must be aware of the factors involved and organize to guide the process.

The task would be far too extensive to document the impact of these changes on the city, but some general statements may be made. The development of suburban areas along with loss or little change of population in the central city has meant often the moving out of middle-class families and their replacement (or partial replacement) by lower-income families. The net result may mean a considerable reduction of tax revenue simultaneously with a greatly increased need for schools and other public services.

It may be well to consider the school as an example of the impact of migration on urban centers. The school is always a key factor in the adjustment of the migrant whether one considers rural schools where our potential migrants receive their formal training or city schools where children of migrants are in attendance. Limited training of many rural migrants from south Missouri who are in St. Louis may mean simply that these people had not advanced far enough in

school to receive the kind of training (vocational and otherwise) for which they were best suited. Or it may mean the school was not offering the choices of training most useful in an area where at least half the young people will not remain but will live their adult lives in the city. In any event, the reality of the situation is that few job opportunities exist for those of limited skills. In response to this type of problem among rural migrants, the Ford Foundation in St. Louis and several other cities, as a part of its "Great Cities" project, is financing "on the job" training administered and conducted by the city school system. This program is being well received by both employers and employees. Following a well-established American pattern, private support will continue until it is demonstrated that such training programs should become the responsibility of the public school system. Then we must face such logical questions as—who should pay the bill, and should training in urban trades and industries be a primary concern of the rural areas that are characterized by high out-migration?

Another project in St. Louis financed by the Ford Foundation is that of arranging for special classes in English composition and remedial reading for children of migrants. In part, this has been developed because of the high "drop-out" rate of migrant children. It is intended to develop comprehension of written material and to stimulate interest in communication by writing. Professor Corey in a half jesting, half serious piece has called attention to making the school a meaningful life experience as well as a highly disciplined formal learning situation.[5] Actually, school people do recognize this need, but acting on the need involves greater school expenditures and undoubtedly a re-orientation of the role of the school in our society.

To conclude, it would appear that redistribution of our population will continue, a major part of which will be movement of rural people to urban residence; that the "stranger" will continue to confront urban people with difficult problems of personal and community adjustment; that adjustment is a two-way street; that new services in the school and in social agencies, for example, are needed to smooth the way for newcomers; and that carefully designed studies can provide the knowledge to speed assimilation and thus reduce personal tension and social and economic loss.

[5]Stephen M. Corey, "The poor scholar's soliloquy," Illinois Education, Dec., 1958.

Table 7. Percentages of median family incomes of thirds of population ranked by size of income that are spent on three food-cost plans for four-person families, and percentages of U.S. disposable income spent on food, United States

	Income group					Percent of U.S. disposable income for food
	Lowest third	Middle third		Highest third		
	Food cost plans					
Year	Low-cost	Low-cost	Moderate-cost	Liberal-cost	Liberal cost	
1957	54.7	24.0	32.4	36.3	20.6	20.7
1961	50.8	21.7	29.2	33.1	19.3	19.8
1965	42.8	18.9	25.3	29.4	16.4	18.1
1969	35.4	16.4	21.0	25.7	14.6	16.4
1973	35.2	15.8	20.4	24.9	13.5	15.8

Source: Data from Blakley, Leo V.: Domestic food costs, American Journal of Agricultural Economics **56**(5):1105, Dec. 1974. Computed from the U.S. Bureau of the Census' Current Population Reports and the U.S. Department of Agriculture's Family Economics Review.

Down on the farm

ROBERT RODALE

The city slicker was always the butt of jokes when farmers got together in days of old to swap stories. They laughed about their city cousins' inability to milk cows, swing a scythe properly, harness a horse, or do any of the other jobs the farmer was adept at. Farmers may not be laughing quite the same today, because they are using machines for most of their work just like city factory workers. But ignorance in the cities of what goes on down on the farm is just as deep as it ever was, if not deeper. Now, however, the ignorance is of what the farmer is doing to the food he produces.

The whole subject of food production methods is a loaded one, just waiting for the hot spark of public attention to touch off an explosion. Rachel Carson ignited the spark on insecticides in the environment, and Ralph Nader did it on the safety stance of the auto industry. Sooner or later someone will give the same treatment to the methods used to make animals gain weight more cheaply. All the elements of tragedy are

present, just as in the insecticide and auto safety issues. A period of rapid technological "improvement" took place at a time when regulation was lax and scientists failed to comprehend all the facets of their new developments. The "improved" practices are now entrenched in the farm economy.

Almost every steer, pig and chicken gets drugs in its food daily, not to cure or even prevent disease, but to control the bacterial flora of its intestinal tract so the animal can gain more weight on less food. They accomplish that job efficiently. The question is, what effect does the practice have on people eating the meat? Use of some of the chemicals is supposed to be discontinued several days before slaughter of the animals, but farmers don't always bother. Thus, small residues are present in meats people eat day after day. There is evidence that some people have become allergic to certain antibiotics through long-term contact with them through the meats they eat. Taken ill, these people are denied antibiotic treatment because of their allergy. Worse yet, the allergy may show up only after antibiotic therapy has started.

Some medical scientists have openly objected to routine use of synthetic chemicals in animal feeds, but their words have fallen on deaf ears. The subject keeps popping up, however. The Ontario Medical Association has voiced its concern over human consumption of antibiotics-laden meat and is cooperating with the Ontario Veterinary Association in investigating the matter. In the U.S. we rely on government clearance of antibiotic feeds as a guarantee of the safety of meat. But serious questions have been raised as to just how valid that guarantee is.

Most disturbing of all, however, is that farmers often use drugs to substitute for proper sanitation or higher-quality feed ingredients. Chickens kept in clean pens show no benefit from antibiotics. Yet feeding antibiotics is cheaper than keeping pens clean, so almost all farmers do it. The demand for leaner meat stirred farm scientists to reach for more drugs. Lean-

ness can be promoted by use of high-protein feeds, which are expensive. California farm scientists found, however, that feeding the anti-inflammatory drug cortisone to animals produced the same effect at less cost. Why use high quality feed when drugs would do the job cheaper, they reasoned.

The fact that antibiotics and other synthetic chemicals in feed earn untold millions for American farmers, food processors and drug and chemical manufacturers gives them a certain amount of protection. The profitability of a practice is over-emphasized when evaluating its safety, unfortunately. Sooner or later, someone is going to kindle the spark. Then Pandora's Box of trouble will open for all who have exploited drugs at the expense of the purity of the meat we eat.

Why tomatoes you buy this winter may be tough, tasteless and costly

The United States Department of Agriculture, at the behest of a small number of Florida tomato growers, is once again preparing to limit the number of vine-ripened tomatoes that can be marketed in the United States during this winter and spring. In addition to raising the price of tomatoes, the USDA's policy, if enacted, will promote the sale of inferior-grade, gas-ripened tomatoes.

Tomatoes are an important food. An estimated one per cent of the average family's winter food budget is spent on tomatoes. A medium-sized tomato provides an adult with half of his daily requirement for Vitamin C and contains only about 35 calories.

Over 95 per cent of the fresh tomatoes sold to consumers in this country during the winter and spring are produced in Florida and Mexico. Although the same varieties of tomatoes are grown in Mexico and Florida, growing practices in the regions differ markedly.

About 80 per cent of the Florida tomatoes are picked while still green and reddened artificially by treating them in chambers containing ethylene gas. Unlike Florida tomatoes, most Mexican tomatoes are not picked until they have begun to ripen on the vine. Once picked, a partially ripened tomato will continue to ripen on its own.

The scientific literature suggests that a vine-ripened tomato is superior in both taste and nutrition to

a gas-ripened tomato. Although the USDA has questioned those findings, it has failed to commission new studies to settle the matter unequivocally. Tomato experts do agree, however, that a mature tomato is superior to an immature tomato in terms of taste and texture.

Maturity in a tomato, however, is not to be confused with color. A tomato reaches maturity several days before showing any outward sign of color. A tomato can thus be fully mature while still green. If picked immature, however, a green tomato can be made to redden, but it will never be good to eat. Such a tomato is likely to be tough and relatively tasteless. A pink tomato on the vine is a mature tomato by definition. Vine-ripe tomatoes are generally picked at the first sign of color to prevent spoiling in transit.

There is no way to judge from the outside appearance whether a green tomato has reached maturity. A Florida farmer who picks his tomatoes while still green and colors them artificially by exposing them to ethylene gas will invariably send a large number of red but immature tomatoes to market. Before sending a harvest crew into his fields a green-tomato grower will typically open a number of tomatoes and examine their seeds. If the seeds of a tomato are white and if they can be readily cut with a knife, that tomato is not yet mature. The trouble with that technique is that tomatoes (even those on the same cluster) don't mature simultaneously. Thus, no matter how many tomatoes he cuts into and examines, a farmer cannot be

☐ From Consumer Reports **38**(1):68-69, Jan. 1973.

certain about the next tomato unless it, too, is opened, examined and discarded.

In a recent random survey conducted by two University of Florida scientists, 40 per cent of one shipment, and 78 per cent of a second shipment of so-called mature green Florida tomatoes were cut open and found to be immature. Indeed, Jack Peters, manager of the growers' Florida Tomato Committee, told a meeting of growers that the study "very definitely confirms the experiments you and I have been observing for many years; and that is, much of the time we are shipping these green tomatoes . . . [which] are not really as mature as would be required to supply the consumers with a quality product".

FOOLING MOTHER NATURE

The move from vine-ripened to gas-reddened tomatoes in Florida, with the accompanying reduction in quality, is in keeping with recent trends in agriculture whereby the nutrition and taste of many foods is often sacrificed for the sake of efficiency. A farmer who picks his tomatoes while still green will generally send a crew into a field only two or three times to harvest his tomatoes. A vine-ripe grower, on the other hand, may have to send a crew into the same field some twenty times to collect the tomatoes as they ripen on different dates. By picking his tomatoes green, moreover, when they are still relatively tough, the green-tomato grower reduces the number of bruised tomatoes that have to be discarded.

MARKETING ORDERS

If, as is anticipated, the USDA should some time this winter or spring limit the supply of vine-ripened tomatoes, the result will be an increased supply of gas-reddened Florida tomatoes on the market— only half of which are U.S. Grade No. 1 tomatoes. Tomatoes are graded according to their outside appearance. No. 3 U.S. grade, and to a lesser degree No. 2 grade tomatoes, are characterized by growth cracks, discoloration or puffiness. Such tomatoes are more likely to have internal defects and provide smaller usable portions than an unblemished U.S. Grade No. 1 tomato. Unlike tomatoes shipped from Florida, 80 to 85 per cent of the Mexican tomatoes exported to the United States are U.S. Grade No. 1 tomatoes.

The Agricultural Marketing Agreement Act of 1937 permits a certain proportion of the growers in a given region to recommend that the Secretary of Agriculture impose market restrictions on all the farmers in that area in order to boost farm prices. Orders may simply limit the quantity each farmer may market or they may restrict the sale of inferior-grade products.

Currently there are some 49 marketing orders in effect on various fruits and vegetables in 37 states.

Products affected by those orders have a total farm value of $2.3 billion a year. According to the USDA, those orders are designed to enable growers "to build stable, orderly markets for their crops and improve their returns."

In the late 1960's the Florida growers became concerned over the increased sale of Mexican tomatoes in the United States. Representatives of the Florida growers sought without success to get the State and Commerce Departments to restrict the import of Mexican tomatoes by means of a tariff or a quota. Following that rebuff, the growers sought relief by means of a marketing order. The trick in this case, however, was to devise a marketing order, which, while limiting imports, would have minimum impact in Florida. As one grower explained, "We are trying to limit Mexico; we are not trying to limit ourselves . . . Let's face it . . . We're trying to eliminate our competition." Since half of the Florida tomatoes are No. 2 and No. 3 U.S. Grade tomatoes, compared with only 15 to 20 per cent of the tomatoes imported from Mexico, the Florida growers understandably wanted no part of a marketing order that limited supply on the basis of quality.

THE QUARTER-INCH BARRIER

The ingenious strategem hit upon by the Florida growers, therefore, and adopted by the USDA, established one minimum-sized requirement for vine-ripened tomatoes and another for gas-reddened tomatoes. Under the standards recommended by the Florida growers, in order to be marketed, vine-rippened tomatoes had to measure at least $2^{17}/_{32}$ inches in diameter, a full quarter of an inch more than gas-reddened tomatoes. The order thus worked to eliminate from the market a disproportionate number of vine-ripened tomatoes, the bulk of which had previously been imported from Mexico. In addition to raising the price that the American consumer pays for tomatoes by restricting supply, such an order works to promote the sale of inferior Florida gas-reddened tomatoes at the expense of Mexican and Florida vine-ripened tomatoes. Just how much such an order will cost the American consumer this winter remains to be seen. But a special study group commissioned by President Nixon has predicted that the cost will be "significant."

That the Florida growers would propose such a scheme is not surprising. That the USDA should go along with their plan is a sharp reminder of the extent to which government agencies often end up serving the special interest groups that they are supposed to be regulating.

The Florida tomato industry does not consist, moreover, of a large number of small family-run farms that face ruin at the hands of the Mexican growers. That industry, rather, is limited to some 165 farms, some of which run 5000 acres or more. The author of this report visited a 12000-acre tomato farm in Palm Beach County that was recently purchased by Ogden Corp., a huge conglomerate, and the 124th largest industrial corporation in America. In 1971 Ogden reported sales in excess of $1 billion. A few miles from Ogden's farm in Palm Beach County, Gulf and Western Industries, the nation's 65th largest industrial giant with annual sales of $1.5 billion, has a larger winter tomato farm. It and other Gulf & Western tomato farms located throughout the state account for one-eighth of the tomatoes grown in Florida.

Early in 1971, two years after the USDA first adopted the discriminatory dual size requirement recommended by the Florida growers, the U.S. Court of Appeals in Washington, D.C., taking particular note of the closed-door manner in which the USDA fell in step behind the Florida growers, suspended that order and required the USDA to conduct a public hearing. The Court, in ruling on a suit filed by a group of Arizona importers, criticized the USDA for reaching its decision without considering testimony and evidence offered by consumer groups and others affected by the

proposed order. Such a practice, the Court said, creates "a seed bed for the weed of industrial domination." Pursuant to the Court's ruling, the USDA held a public hearing in Orlando, Florida, in the fall of 1971. At a five-week hearing, conducted at the headquarters of the Florida tomato growers association, various consumer groups, including CU, importers and chain store officials, argued against the readoption of a marketing order that discriminated against vine-ripened tomatoes. The USDA's decision to hold the hearing at the grower's meeting place was indicative of the bias that permeated the entire proceeding, as was the decision to exclude from evidence studies suggesting that vine-ripened tomatoes are nutritionally superior to gas-reddened tomatoes. Scientific literature, moreover, pertaining to the size of tomatoes was overlooked while the testimony of a grower who had measured the size of tomatoes from one week to the next with his fingers was accepted.

Upon completion of the hearings, the USDA, to no one's real surprise, announced that it was again prepared to maintain a dual size minimum requirement for vine-ripened and gas-reddened tomatoes. CU is challenging the USDA's decision in the courts.

U.S. agriculture is growing trouble as well as crops

WILSON CLARK

Until recently, most Americans have taken an adequate supply of food for granted. The great productivity of agriculture in this country is still seen as the best available hope for assuaging the international food crisis. But the American system of agriculture is beginning to show signs of wear.

The key to U.S. food production—and what some also see as its weakest link—is that our farms have become dependent on fossil fuels, rather than on human or animal labor. In a study made for the Office of Civil Defense by the Stanford Research Institute, the dimensions of the energy dependence of agriculture become clear. "We can state immediately," said the authors, "that without petroleum, field crop production is virtually impossible in the United States [agricultural] system."

A basic use of energy on the farm is for powering

machines—for planting, spraying, fertilizing and harvesting crops. Economist Michael Perelman of California State University at Chico points out that powering the more than five million tractors in the United States requires eight billion gallons of fuel—the equivalent of the energy content in the food produced. In a very real way, the food products on our tables today are produced as much by dead plants (the fossil fuels) as by living ones. (Recently, several oil companies have begun experimental programs to produce single-cell protein *directly* from fossil fuels, bypassing the fields altogether and linking the human food chain directly to nonrenewable resources.)

The production of fertilizers and farm chemicals such as pesticides and herbicides requires extensive use of fossil fuel energy. Studies made by Barry Commoner and his associates at Washington University in St. Louis indicate that, between 1946 and 1968, nitrogen fertilizer and pesticide use in farming increased

534 percent and 217 percent, respectively. According to Commoner, in 1949 about 11,000 tons of nitrogen fertilizer were required to produce the equivalent crop yield per acre in Illinois that 57,000 tons produced in 1968.

Even though more corn was produced per acre in 1968 than in the 1940s, the efficiency with which crops used available fertilizer actually declined fivefold. Fertilizer's overuse has led to serious environmental problems, such as the addition of nitrates to water supplies. Nonetheless, synthetic fertilizers have made our agricultural productivity legendary.

Since the recent escalation of international petroleum prices, however, the cost of making fertilizer has increased 40 percent, and even at such high prices a fertilizer shortage of 500,000 tons existed here in 1974. The shortage may become even worse.

Modern agriculture has also become dependent on synthetic chemicals—mostly derived from fossil fuels—for pest and weed control. In primitive agriculture, and in diversified farming, pest control consists largely of planting multiple crops which will not be completely destroyed by pest infestations. Such methods are not practical in large-scale, or monoculture, cropping, where one variety of wheat or corn may be planted in fields stretching many square miles. While the use of pesticides and herbicides has contributed greatly to the volume of production by minimizing losses, the environmental effects have been serious and much publicized. Ultimately, the oil crisis may force a return to less energy-intensive methods of pest control, even if environmental precautions don't.

Another high energy user in modern, mechanized agriculture is irrigation. A complex of dams and canals designed to bring water from northern California to the farmlands of the southern part of the state will cost $12 billion when completed—nearly $500 for each man, woman and child in California. The pumping requirements of the water project have been estimated at 13 billion kilowatt-hours of electricity per year. Since the net generation of electricity from the hydroelectric dams will amount to only five billion kilowatt-hours per year, the project will suffer an energy deficit of eight billion kilowatt-hours per year, a substantial part of the state's overall energy bill. Energy-intensive irrigation systems are being installed on a mammoth scale in other areas, including the Pacific Northwest.

All of this intensive use of mechanization and farm chemicals has transformed the substance and the look of the entire food system, as a trip to a mechanized farm graphically illustrates. In the lush Salinas Valley south of San Francisco, agriculture has become a major industry, replete with an army not of people but of field machines which plant seeds, fertilize the soil, apply pesticides and mechanically harvest such crops as lettuce. Whereas ten years ago nitrogen fertilizer application of 300 pounds per acre to a crop would have seemed quite high, it is now common practice in the Salinas Valley to apply more than 1,000 pounds to each of two crops planted on each acre of land per year, or up to 2,500 pounds yearly. Mechanical harvesting enables many crops to be boxed in the field, trucked to a nearby depot, and then shipped—by truck or train—to various points across the United States.

Eric Hirst, of the Federal Energy Administration, found that the food system in 1963 consumed an average of 6.4 units of primary energy (mostly from fossil fuels) to deliver each unit of food energy to the consumer. In some cases, such as with processed fruits and vegetables, more than 15 units of fossil fuel energy were used to deliver each unit of food energy to the consumer. Today the ratio is even greater.

One of the basic ways that the American diet contributes to high energy use is the extensive consumption of animal protein, particularly beef. Frances Moore Lappé, in her book, *Diet for a Small Planet*, points out that an acre of cereal can produce five times as much protein as an acre devoted to meat production; legume crops (peas, beans) can produce ten times as much as meat; and leafy vegetables 20 times as much as meat. As food expert Dr. Georg Borgstrom of Michigan State University says: "The livestock of the rich world is in direct competition with the humans of the poor world." Dr. Borgstrom calculates that the difference in food calorie consumption between the rich nations and poor nations is much greater than is generally recognized. In the United States, the average daily calorie (kilocalorie, or large calorie) consumption of an adult is 3,300 food calories, but in India consumption is 1,990 calories. However, since meat consumption is so much lower in India, the grain fed to animals (which are then consumed by humans) represents only 763 additional calories, compared to a whopping 10,017 additional calories of grain fed to animals in the United States. Says Borgstrom: "The difference in calorie intake per capita per day between the United States and India is not, as generally assumed, 1,310, but rather 9,182 calories. This in itself reflects an awesome discrepancy which illuminates a much overlooked aspect of the food-and-people issue."

According to Dr. Herman Koenig, the director of Michigan State University's Ecosystem Design and Management Program, the production of beef cattle in the United States is too mechanized to be really efficient. Some feedlots in America are designed to feed tens of thousands of cattle at a time. The Monfort of Colorado, Inc., feedlots near Greeley process more than 100,000 cattle yearly in a highly automated, computer-controlled operation. Cattle arrive at the lots when they weigh from 700 to 800 pounds, are then fed in pens, and slaughtered five months later when they reach 1,100 to 1,200 pounds. Corn shipped to the Monfort operation from company-owned elevators in the Midwest arrives in yellow torrents. The daily flaking and cooking of corn for Monfort cattle at the company's mills yields more cornflakes than the Kellogg corporation makes each day for human consumers.

Such gargantuan operations are wasteful to energy, according to Koenig, who says that cattle feedlots which have 200 to 300 head of cattle are the optimum size for efficient energy and resource use. On a regional and national scale we may have to think smaller to improve the economy and save energy. "One alternative we should begin to think of is the possibility of limiting the scale of mechanization to provide job opportunities. This carries with it the potential of generating an increased spatial distribution of people and processes to put us in better harmony with the natural environment. It might also relieve some social stresses."

Even the Department of Agriculture, which has done much to promote large-scale farming, has published several technical studies which confirm that small farms can be quite efficient. The department's Economic Research Service says that "the fully mechanized one-man farm, producing the maximum acreage of crops of which the man and his machines are capable, is generally a technically efficient farm. From the standpoint of costs per unit of production, this size farm captures most of the economies associated with size."

Nevertheless, small farms are disappearing daily from the American landscape while corporate farms have become the rule. The Tenneco corporation, for example, which has enormous assets in oil production, chemicals and shipbuilding, has moved into corporate farming in California and other western states under the motto: "Our goal in agriculture is integration from the seedling to the supermarket."

As American agriculture shifts noticeably from small farms using modest amounts of resources to factory farms and distribution systems gobbling limited energy resources, University of Wisconsin researchers John and Carol Steinhart say that "there has been no reduction in [agriculture and food labor] at all—only a change in what workers do. Yesterday's farmer is today's canner, tractor mechanic and fast food carhop." Bruce Hannon, of the University of Illinois Computation Center in Urbana, recently illustrated the energy use entailed in the packaging of food. The McDonald's restaurant chain used the equivalent of 12.7 million tons of coal in 1971 to feed its patrons. For each

customer, that was the equivalent of 2.1 pounds of coal. Hannon points out that his objective was not to single out McDonald's for criticism, but to point out the waste inherent in the convenience-food life-style of contemporary America.

As much of the world faces famine today and in years to come, the waste of America's food and agriculture system stands out as a particularly sore thumb of affluence. The choices open to the food-rich nations (Canada, New Zealand, Australia and the United States) are either to export technology or export food.

"None of these [countries] is in a position to give grain away," say the Steinharts, "because each of them needs the foreign trade to avert ruinous balance of payments deficits. Can we then export energy-intensive agricultural methods instead?"

The historic answer to this question lies in the green revolution. Under the scientific direction of agronomists such as Dr. Norman Borlaug, yields of many strains of wheat, corn and rice were improved by the development of hybrids, and improved seeds were distributed widely in poor nations. To get high yields, however, the new seeds often require high rates of fertilization, pesticide use and mechanical irrigation. Thus, the green revolution has a dependency on fossil fuel—a resource in critically short supply, and available only at a high cost.

Dr. David Pimental, an agriculture specialist at Cornell University, is pessimistic over the future of the green revolution. "Modern, intensive agricultural practices of the western world and those proposed by 'green revolution' agriculture will not offer a solution for the world food problem. . . . To feed a world population of 4 billion while employing modern intensive agriculture would require an energy equivalent of 1.2 billion gallons of fuel per day. If petroleum were the only source of fossil energy and if all petroleum reserves were used to feed the world population using intensive agriculture, known petroleum reserves would last a mere 29 years."

Another tragic by-product of the rise of energy-intensive agriculture is the fate of natural seed stocks, which were widely used only a few decades ago. Since the advent of "miracle" hybrid seeds, the older seeds have, in many cases, been lost through neglect—ending a genetic continuity of many millennia. Agricultural researchers are experiencing great difficulty in acquiring stocks of native seeds for preservation programs. According to a recent United Nations report on genetic resources, "the older diverse [crop] varieties . . . are sown no more; many of the wild relatives with which they maintained genetic interchange have been swept away."

The problem of genetic diversity is equally challenging—and frightening—in the advanced nations. The National Academy of Sciences published a major work on the genetic vulnerability of major crops which concluded that such vulnerability stems from genetic uniformity, and that some crops were highly susceptible. In 1970, a blight wiped out 15 percent of the corn, and the situation was corrected only when seed growers developed new seed which was not vulnerable to blight. But seed development is dependent on genetic "banks" which store thousands of varieties of native seed: If the seed is not available, then new varieties can't be developed.

There is a national seed storage facility in Fort Collins, Colorado, but funds are limited and the director of the facility, Dr. Louis Bass, fears that without sufficient funding the seed storage program will not be adequate to meet the challenge of genetic erosion. The consequences of the loss of native seed germplasm are staggering, when one thinks that within one short generation, human beings could throw away key evolutionary links in the food system—all in the name of progress.

The alternatives to continuing the present system, which delivers each calorie of food to the consumer at the expense of 10 to 20 calories of fossil energy, include searching for better ways to use natural fertilizer, instead of depending on synthetic fertilizers. And, in fact, interest in the use of organic materials for fertilization is picking up—not just among home gardeners—but in major cities such as Chicago, which has undertaken a study of the potential use of sewage in conjunction with farming in nearby Illinois and northwestern Indiana.

Other ways to decrease energy use are to encourage the development of smaller, less energy-intensive farms; to use farming methods based on diversity and to plant legumes such as soybeans, which add nitrogen to the soil and minimize the need for nitrogen fertilizers; and to use biological pest-control methods as substitutes for the intensive use of chemicals. In addition, hand spraying of pesticides and herbicides, rather than application by large machines and airplanes, can save energy in large doses. Diversity of this sort could be the starting point for the development of a sound, efficient agricultural system.

Such a system would also make better use of natural energy sources such as solar power. Solar crop-drying techniques are under development in many states, including Indiana, where 60 million gallons of liquid petroleum fuel and 1.5 billion cubic feet of natural gas are now used yearly to dry the corn crop. Windmills can be used to pump water for agricultural irrigation, rather than fossil-powered electrical pumps. Methane gas can be made on the farm from various organic substances, including animal wastes.

To create such an agricultural system, with the concomitant result of better land use and a more widespread population, will not take place overnight, but it will be necessary in the energy- and resource-short years to come. As the English economist Ernst Friedrich Schumacher, has written: "The challenge presented by the energy problem is one of developing a new life-style—a development which logically and inevitably must begin with a change of man's relation to the soil, of which he is a product and which alone sustains his life."

Can we survive?

BARRY COMMONER*

No one can escape the enormous fact that California has changed. What was once desert has become the most productive land in the world. The once-lonely mountain tops are crisscrossed with humming power lines. Powerful industries, from old ones like steel to the most modern aerospace and electronic operations,

□ Reprinted with permission from The Washington Monthly. Copyright 1969 by The Washington Monthly Co., 1028 Connecticut Ave., N.W., Washington, D.C. 20036.
*Barry Commoner is Director of the Center for the Biology of Natural Systems at Washington University, St. Louis, Missouri.

have been built. California has become one of the most fruitful, one of the richest places on the surface of the earth. This is all change, and it is good.

But there are other changes in California. Its vigorous growth has been achieved by many men and women who came to give their children a healthy place to live. Now, however, when school children in Los Angeles run out to the playing fields, they are confronted by the warning: "Do not exercise strenuously or breathe too deeply during heavy smog conditions." For the sunshine that once bathed the land in golden light has been blotted out by deadly smog. In a number of California towns the water supplies now contain levels of nitrate above the limit recommended by the U.S. Public Health Service; given to infants, nitrate can cause a fatal disorder, methemoglobenemia, and pediatricians have recommended the use of bottled water for infant formulas. The natural resources of California, once a magnet that attracted thousands who sought a good life, now harbor threats to health. Beaches that once sparkled in the sun are polluted with oil and foul-smelling deposits. Rivers that once teemed with fish run sluggishly to the sea. The once famous crabs in San Francisco Bay are dying. Redwoods are toppling from the banks of eroding streams. All this, too, is change, and it is bad.

Thus, much of the good that has been produced in California, through the intelligence and hard work of its people, has been won at a terrible cost. That cost is the possible destruction of the very capital which has been invested to create the wealth of the state—its environment.

The environment makes up a huge, enormously complex living machine—an ecosystem—and every human activity depends on the integrity and proper functioning of that machine. Without the ecosystem's green plants, there would be no oxygen for smelters and furnaces, let alone to support human and animal life. Without the action of plants and animals in aquatic systems, there would be no pure water to supply agriculture, industry, and the cities. Without the biological processes that have gone on in the soil for thousands of years, there would be neither food crops, oil, nor coal. This machine is our biological capital, the basic apparatus on which our total productivity depends. If it is destroyed, agriculture and industry will come to a naught; yet the greatest threats to the environmental system are due to agricultural and industrial activities. If the ecosystem is destroyed, man will go down with it; yet it is man who is destroying it. For in the eager search for the benefits of modern science and technology, we have become enticed into a nearly fatal illusion: that we have at last escaped from the dependence of man on the rest of nature. The truth is tragically different. We have become not less dependent on the balance of nature, but more dependent on it. Modern technology has so stressed the web of processes in the living environment at its most vulnerable points that there is little leeway left in the system. We are approaching the point of no return; our survival is at stake.

These are grim, alarming conclusions; but they are forced on us, I am convinced, by the evidence. Let us look at some of that evidence.

A good place to begin is the farm—on which so much of California's prosperity is based. The wealth created by agriculture is derived from the soil. In it we grow crops which convert inorganic materials— nitrogen, phosphorus, carbon, oxygen, and the other elements required by life—into organic materials— proteins, carbohydrates, fats, and vitamins—which comprise our food.

The soil, the plants that grow in it, the livestock raised on the land, and we ourselves are parts of a huge web of natural processes—endless, self-perpetuating cycles. Consider, for example, the behavior of nitrogen, an element of enormous nutritional importance, forming as it does the basis of proteins and other vital life substances. Most of the earth's available nitrogen is in the air, as nitrogen gas. This can enter the soil through nitrogen fixation, a process carried out by various bacteria, some of them living free in the soil and others associated with the roots of legumes such as clover. In nature, nitrogen also enters the soil from the wastes produced by animals. In both cases the nitrogen becomes incorporated into a complex organic material in the soil—humus. The humus slowly releases nitrogen through the action of soil microorganisms which finally convert it into nitrate. In turn, the nitrate is taken up by the roots of plants and is made into protein and other vital parts of the crop. In a natural situation the plant becomes food for animals, their wastes are returned to the soil, and the cycle is complete.

This cycle is an example of the biological capital that sustains us. How has this capital been used in California?

The huge success of agriculture in California is a matter of record; it forms the largest single element in the state's economy. To achieve this wealth a vast area in the center of the state has been transformed from a bare desert into the richest agricultural land in the nation. How has this been done? How has this transformation affected the continued usefulness of the soil system, especially the nitrogen cycle?

When the first farmers came to the San Joaquin Valley, they found fertile soil and sunshine; only water was needed to make the valley bloom. This was obtained first from local streams and later, increasingly, from wells which tapped the huge store of water that lay beneath the entire Central Valley. As the bountiful crops were taken, the soil, originally rich in nitrogen, became impoverished. To sustain crop productivity, inorganic nitrogen fertilizers were added to the soil. But with the loss of natural soil nitrogen, humus was depleted; as a result the soil became less porous, and less oxygen reached the roots, which were then less efficient in taking up the needed nutrients from the soil. The answer: more nitrogen fertilizer, for even if a smaller proportion is taken up by the crop, this can be overcome by using more fertilizer to begin with. California now uses more nitrogen fertilizer than any other state—an average of about 450 pounds per acre in 1959.

One of the rules of environmental biology is: "Everything has to go somewhere," and we may ask: Where did the extra nitrate added to the soil, but not taken up by the crops, go? The answer is clear: The unused nitrate was carried down into the soil, accumulating at greater and greater depths as the water table fell due to the continual pumping of irrigation water.

With the water table falling, agriculture in the Central Valley was headed for disaster; recognizing this fact, the state constructed the Friant-Kern Canal, which began to supply the valley with above-ground irrigation water beginning in 1951. Irrigation water must always be supplied to soil in amounts greater than that which is lost by evaporation; otherwise salts accumulate in the soil and the plants are killed. So, following the opening of the new canal, the valley water table began to rise toward its original level— carrying with it the long-accumulated nitrates in the soil.

Now there is another simple rule of environmental biology that is appropriate here: "Everything is connected to everything else." The valley towns soon learned this truth, as their drinking water supplies— which were taken from wells that tapped the rising level of underground water—began to show increasing concentrations of nitrate. In the 1950's, the Bureau of Sanitary Engineering of the California Department of Public Health began to analyze the nitrate content of city water supplies in the area. They had good reason for this action, for in July, 1950, an article in the *Journal of the American Water Works Association* had described 139 cases of infant methemoglobenemia in the United States identified since 1947; 14 cases were fatal; all were attributed to farm well water contaminated with more than 45 ppm of nitrate.

At first, only a few scattered instances of high nitrate levels were found in valley water supplies. However, a study of 800 wells in southern California counties in 1960 showed that 88 of them exceeded the 45 ppm limit; 188 wells had reached half that level. In that year, the U.S. Public Health Service recommended that a nitrate level of 45 ppm should not be exceeded, warning:

Cases of infantile nitrate poisoning have been reported to arise from concentrations ranging from 66 to 1100 ppm. . . . Nitrate poisoning appears to be confined to infants during their first few months of life; adults drinking the same water are not affected, but breast-fed infants of mothers drinking such water may be poisoned. Cows drinking water containing nitrate may produce milk sufficiently high in nitrate to result in infant poisoning.

In Delano, a 1952 analysis showed only traces of nitrate in the city water supply; in 1966, analyses of three town wells obtained by the Delano Junior Chamber of Commerce showed nitrate levels of 70-78 ppm. In 1968, a study by the Water Resources Board, made in reply to a request by State Senator Walter W. Stiern, showed:

Nitrate concentrations in ground-water underlying the vicinity of Delano are currently in excess of the limit . . . recommended by the U.S. Public Health Service . . . similar geologic and hydrologic conditions occur in other areas of the San Joaquin Valley and the state generally.

So agricultural wealth of the Central Valley has been gained, but at a cost that does not appear in the farmers' balance sheets—the general pollution of the state's huge underground water reserves with nitrate. Fortunately, there appear to be no reports of widespread acute infant methemoglobenemia in the area as yet. However, the effects of chronic exposure to nitrates are poorly understood. We do know that in animals nitrate may interfere with thyroid metabolism, reduce the availability of vitamin A, and cause abortions. Moreover, there is evidence that even small reductions in the oxygen available to a developing human fetus—which might occur when the mother is exposed to subcritical levels of nitrate—result in permanent damage to the brain. In sum, the success of agriculture in the Central Valley has been won at a cost which risks the health of the people.

Nor does the nitrogen problem end there. Much of the nitrogen fertilizer applied to the soil of the Central Valley finds its way into the San Joaquin River, which drains the irrigated fields. As a result, the river carries a huge load of nitrate into the San Francisco Bay-Delta area. Here the added nitrate intrudes on another environmental cycle—the self-purifying biological processes of natural waters—bringing in its wake a new round of environmental destruction. The excess nitrate—along with excess phosphate from agricultural drainage and municipal wastes—stimulates the growth of algae in the waters of the Bay, causing the massive green scums that have become so common in the area. Such heavy overgrowths of algae soon die off, releasing organic matter which overwhelms the biological purification processes that normally remove it. As a result, the natural balance is destroyed; the water loses its oxygen; fish die; the water becomes foul with putrefying material. In the cooler words of the Department of Interior report on the San Joaquin Master Drain, "Problems resulting from nutrient enrichment and associated periodic dissolved oxygen depression are numerous in the Bay-Delta areas."

So the agricultural practices of the great Central

Valley have overwhelmed the natural nitrogen cycle of the soil with massive amounts of fertilizer; once this cycle was broken, the rivers were contaminated with nitrate. Reaching the Bay-Delta area, the excess nitrate has destroyed the natural balance of the self-purifying processes in these waters, with the foul results that are only too well known to those who live in that once-sparkling natural area.

This much is known fact. But once the natural cycles of the Bay-Delta waters are disrupted, other biological disasters may soon follow. At the present time, in a number of regions of the Bay-Delta waters, the bacterial count exceeds the limit recommended by the California Department of Public Health for water contact sports. This may be due to the entry of too much untreated sewage. But experience with the waters of New York harbor suggests another, more ominous, possibility which connects this problem, too, to the drainage of nutrients from agricultural areas, as well as from treated sewage. In New York harbor, in the period 1948-1968, there has been a 10-20-fold increase in the bacterial count despite a marked *improvement* in the sewage treatment facilities that drain into the bay. Here too there has been an increase in nitrate and phosphate nutrients, in this case largely from treated sewage effluent. The possibility exists that bacteria, entering the water from sewage or the soil, are now able to *grow* in the enriched waters of the bay. If this should prove to be the case, changes in water quality such as those which have occurred in the Bay-Delta area may lead to new, quite unexpected, health hazards. The soil contains many microorganisms which cause disease in human beings when they are first allowed to grow in a nutrient medium. There is a danger, then, that as the Bay-Delta waters become laden with organic matter released by dying algae (resulting from overgrowths stimulated by agricultural and municipal wastes), disease-producing microorganisms may find conditions suitable for growth, resulting in outbreaks of hitherto unknown types of water-borne disease.

Nor does the nitrogen story quite end here. We now know that a good deal of the excess nitrogen added to the soil by intensive fertilization practices may be released to the air in the form of ammonia or nitrogen oxides. In the air, these materials are gradually converted to nitrate and carried back to the ground by rain. In 1957, a national study of the nitrate content of rainfall showed excessively high levels in three heavily fertilized regions: the Corn Belt, Texas, and the Central Valley of California. There is increasing evidence that nitrate dissolved in rain can carry enough nutrient into even remote mountain lakes to cause algal overgrowths and so pollute waters still largely free of the effects of human wastes. Recent pollution problems in Lake Tahoe may originate in this way.

I cite these details in order to make clear a profound and inescapable fact of life: that the environment is a vast system of interlocking connections—among the soil, the water, the air, plants, animals, and ourselves —which forms an endless, dynamically interacting web. This network is the product of millions of years of evolution; each of its connections has been tested against the trial of time to achieve a balance which is stable and long-lasting. But the balance, the fine fabric of physical, chemical, and biological interconnections in the environment, is a delicate one; it hangs together only as a whole. Tear into it in one place— such as the soil of the Central Valley—and the fabric begins to unravel, spreading chaos from the soil to the rivers, to the Bay, to remote mountain lakes, to the mother and her infant child. The great Central Valley has become rich with the fruits of the land, but at a cost which has already been felt across the breadth of the state and which is yet to be fully paid.

Nor do we yet know how the destructive process can be halted, or if indeed it can be. In Lake Erie, where the natural balance of the water system has already been largely overwhelmed by excessive nutrients, no one has yet been able to devise a scheme to restore its original condition. The Bay-Delta waters may suffer the same fate. The recently released Kaiser Engineers' report on the San Francisco Bay-Delta Water Quality Control Program predicts that the drainage of agricultural nutrients (nitrogen and phosphorus) from the San Joaquin will continue unabated for at least the next 50 years if present agricultural practices persist. The report proposes a system which, to control only the deleterious effects of the drainage in the Bay-Delta area, will cost about $5 billion in that period. And even at that cost the plan will only transfer the problem to the ocean—where the waste nutrients are to be discharged—which can only bring disaster to this last remaining natural resource, on which so many of our future hopes must rest.

The root of the problem remains in the soil, for if the disrupted balance is not restored there, its destructive effects will only spread into further reaches of the environment. Tragically, each year of continued over-fertilization of the soil may make recovery increasingly difficult. For example, we know that inorganic nitrogen nutrients stop the nitrogen-fixing activity of microorganisms and may eventually kill them off or at least encourage them to mutate into non-fixing forms. If the natural fertility of the soil is ever to be restored, we may have to rely heavily on these microbial agents; but this becomes less and less possible as we continue to use massive amounts of fertilizer. In effect, like a drug addict, we may become "hooked" on continued heavy nitrogen fertilization and so become inescapably locked into a self-destructive course.

This same tragic tale of environmental disaster can be told of another prominent feature of California agriculture—insecticides. One important aspect of the biological capital on which agricultural productivity depends is the network of ecological relationships that relate insect pests to the plants on which they feed, and to the other insects that, in turn, prey on the pests. These natural relations serve to keep pest populations in check. Pests which require a particular plant as food are kept in check by their inability to spread onto other plants; the other insects which parasitize and prey upon them exert important biological control over the pest population.

What has happened in attempts to control cotton pests—where the great bulk of synthetic insecticide is used in the United States—shows how we have destroyed these natural relations and have allowed the natural pest-regulating machinery to break down. The massive use of the new insecticides has controlled some of the pests that once attacked cotton. But now the cotton plants are being attacked instead by new insects that were never previously known as pests of cotton. Moreover, the new pests are becoming increasingly resistant to insecticide, through the natural biological process of selection, in the course of inheritance, of resistant types. In Texas cotton fields, for example, in 1963 it took 50 times as much DDT to control insect pests as it did in 1961. The tobacco budworm, which now attacks cotton, has been found to be nearly immune to methylparathion, the most powerful of the widely used modern insecticides.

California, too, has begun to experience environmental disaster from the intensive use of insecticides. Consider only a single recent example. In 1965 the rich cotton fields of the Imperial Valley were invaded by the Pink Bollworm from Arizona. The Department of Agriculture began an "eradication" program based on a fixed schedule of repeated, heavy, insecticide sprays. The Pink Bollworm was controlled (but by no means "eradicated"); however, the cotton plants were then attacked by other insects which had previously caused no appreciable damage—the beet army worm and the cotton leaf perforator. The insecticide had killed off insects that were natural enemies of the army worms and perforators, which had in the meantime become resistant to the sprays. Catastrophic losses resulted. The problem is now so serious that Imperial Valley farmers have proposed the elimination of cotton plantings for a year in order to kill off the new pests, which cannot survive a year without food.

California is beginning to experience the kind of insecticide-induced disaster already common in Latin American experience. In the Cañete Valley of Peru, for example, DDT was used for the first time in 1949 to control cotton pests. Yields increased—temporarily. For soon the number of insects attacking the cotton grew from 7 to 13 and several of them had become resistant to the insecticides. By 1965, the cotton yields had dropped to half their previous value, and despite 15-25 insecticide applications, pest control was impossible. Productivity was restored only when massive insecticide application was halted and biological control was reestablished by importing insects to attack the pests.

These instances are, again, a warning that agricultural practices may be destroying the biological capital which is essential to agricultural productivity—in this case, the natural population of insects that attack insect pests and keep them under the control of a natural balance. Again, if the ecologically blind practice of massive insecticide treatment is allowed to continue, there is a danger of permanently losing the natural protective insects—and agriculture may become "hooked" on insecticides.

And here too we see disaster spreading through the environmental network. In 1969, the Food and Drug Administration seized two shipments of canned jack mackerel, an ocean fish originating from Terminal Island, Los Angeles, because of excessive residues of DDT and related insecticides. Insecticides draining off agricultural lands into the Bay-Delta area have caused levels of DDT which exceed the amount allowed by the FDA to appear in the bodies of striped bass and sturgeon. It is possible that the recent decline in San Francisco Bay crabs may be due to the same cause. Spreading through the food chain, DDT has begun to cause disastrous declines in the population of birds of prey, and there is some evidence that gulls are being affected as well. The latter would extend the web of disaster even further, for the gulls are vital in controlling waste in shoreline waters.

Now let me follow the track of environmental disaster from the farm to the cities of California. Again, nitrogen is a valuable guide, this time, surprisingly enough, to the smog problem. This problem originates with the production of nitrogen oxides by gasoline engines. Released to the air, these oxides, upon absorption of sunlight, react with waste hydrocarbon fuel to produce the noxious constituents of smog. This problem is the direct outcome of the technological improvement of gasoline engines: the development of the modern high-compression engine. Such engines operate at higher temperatures than older ones; at these elevated temperatures the oxygen and nitrogen of the air taken into the engine tend to combine rapidly, with the resultant production of nitrogen oxides. Once released into the air, nitrogen oxides are activated by sunlight. They then react with waste hydrocarbon fuel, forming eventually the notorious PAN—the toxic agent of the smog made famous by Los Angeles.

The present smog-control technique—reduction of waste fuel emission—by diminishing the interaction of nitrogen oxides with hydrocarbon wastes, enhances the level of airborne nitrogen oxides, which are themselves toxic substances. In the air, nitrogen oxides are readily converted to nitrates, which are then brought down by rain and snow to the land and surface waters. There they add to the growing burden of nitrogen fertilizer, which, as I have already indicated, is an important aspect of water pollution. What is surprising is the amount of nitrogen oxides that are generated by automotive traffic: more than one-third of the nitrogen contained in the fertilizer currently employed on U.S. farms. One calculation shows that farms in New Jersey receive about 25 pounds of nitrogen fertilizer per year (a significant amount in agricultural practice) from the trucks and cars that travel the New Jersey highways. Another recent study shows that in the heavily populated eastern section of the country, the nitrate content of local rainfall is proportional to the local rate of gasoline consumption.

Thus, the emergence of a new technology—the modern gasoline engine—is itself responsible for most of the smog problem and for an appreciable part of the pollution of surface waters with nitrate. And no one needs to be reminded that smog is a serious hazard to health. Again we see the endless web of environmental processes at work. Get the engines too hot—for the sake of generating the power needed to drive a huge car at destructive speeds—and you set off a chain of events that keeps kids off the playground, sends older people to a premature death, and, in passing, adds to the already excessive burden of water pollutants.

This is some of the tragic destruction that lies hidden in the great panorama of the changing California environment—costs to the people of the state that do not appear as entries in the balance sheets of industry and agriculture. These are some of the great debts which must be paid if the state's environment is to be saved from ultimate destruction. The debts are so embedded in every feature of the state's economy that it is almost impossible to calculate them. Their scale, at least, can be secured from the figure produced for the water quality-control system which will transfer the pollution problem of the Bay-Delta area to the ocean: $5 billion over 50 years, and continuing at $100 million a year.

At what cost can the smog that envelops Los Angeles be cleared up—as it surely must if the city is to survive? Start with the price of rolling back air pollution that risks the health and well-being of the citizens of the Bay area, the Peninsula, and San Diego. And do not neglect the damage already done by smog to the pine forests in the area of Lake Arrowhead. Nitrogen oxides have just been detected in Yosemite Park; what will it cost if the state's magnificent forests begin to die, unleashing enormous flood problems? How shall we reckon the cost of the huge redwoods on the North Coast, which need for their secure footing the soil built up around their roots during annual floods, when these floods are stopped by the new dams and the trees begin to topple? How shall we determine the cost of the urban spread which has covered the richest soil in the state? What will it cost to restore this soil to agriculture when the state is forced to limit intensive, pollution-generating fertilization, and new lands have to be used to sustain food production? What is the price of those massive walls of concrete, those freeways, which slice across the land, disrupting drainage patterns and upsetting the delicate balance of forces that keeps the land from sliding into ravines? Against the value of the new real-estate developments on landfills in San Francisco Bay, calculate the cost of the resulting changes in tidal movements, which have decreased the dilution of the polluting nutrients by fresh water from the sea and have worsened the algal overgrowths. Or balance against the value of the offshore oil the cost of a constant risk of beach and ocean pollution until the offending wells are pumped dry. Finally, figure, if possible, what it will cost to restore the natural fertility of the soil in central California, to keep the nitrogen in the soil, where it belongs, and to develop a new, more mixed form of agriculture that will make it possible to get rid of most insecticides and make better use of the natural biological controls.

If the magnitude of the state's environmental problems is staggering, perhaps there is some consolation in the fact that California is not alone. Most of Lake Erie has been lost to pollution. In Illinois, every major river has been overburdened with fertilizer drainage and has lost its powers of self-purification. Automobile smog hangs like a pall over even Denver and Phoenix. Every major city is experiencing worsening air pollution. The entire nation is in the grip of the environmental crisis.

What is to be done? What can be done? Although we are, I believe, on a path which can only lead to self-destruction, I am also convinced that we have not yet passed the point of no return. We have time—perhaps a generation—in which to save the environment from the final effects of the violence we have already done to it, and to save ourselves from our own suicidal folly. But this is a very short time to achieve the massive environmental repair that is needed. We will need to start, now, on a new path. And the first action is to recognize how badly we have gone wrong in the use of the environment and to mobilize every available resource for the huge task of saving it.

Yet all the marvelous knowledge in our universities and laboratories seems now to stand helpless, while the air becomes fouler every day, beaches covered with oil, and precious water and soil more heavily laden with pollutants.

But there is another crisis—one that has struck the nation's entire scientific community. This crisis, like the environmental one, is also man-made and disastrously short-sighted; it is the drastic curtailment of the funds for research and education.

What a tragedy! At the very moment that the nation has begun to sense the urgency of the environmental crisis, when the first steps in the large and urgent task must be taken in the laboratories and classrooms of our universities, the tools are denied the men who would use them.

The huge undertakings listed here cannot even be begun unless we drastically reorganize our priorities. We cannot continue to devote the talent of our engineers and the competence of our workers to the production of overpowered, pollution-generating cars that do violence on the road and in the ecosystem. We cannot burden our productive resources with a monstrous device like the SST—which, if used in the U.S., will bring the violence of airport noise to 60 million Americans. We cannot continue to waste manpower and resources on weapons that become obsolete before they are produced—and which, if ever used, will destroy this planet as a place for human life. In a crisis of survival, business as usual is suicide.

The environmental crisis has brought us to a great turning point in this nation's history. We have become a nation that wields the greatest power in the history of man: power in the form of food, industrial plants, vehicles, and the weapons of war. We have also become a nation beset by violence: on the battlefield, on the highways, in personal encounters, and, more

fundamentally, in the destruction of the natural, harmonious fabric of the environmental system which supports us. It is this fundamental violence to the world in which we live which divides us, as we compete among ourselves for the earth's goods, unaware that each of us, in our own way is thereby contributing to the destruction of the whole that supports us all.

The time has come to forge a great alliance in this nation: All of us now know that if we are to survive, the environment must be maintained as a balanced, harmonious whole. We must all work together to preserve it. If we fail, we shall abandon the place where we must live—the thin skin of air, water, soil, and living things on the planet Earth—to destruction. The obligation which our technological society forces upon all of us, young and old, black and white, right and left, scientist and citizen alike, is to discover how humanity can survive the new power which science has given it. Every major advance in the technological competence of man has enforced new obligations on human society. The present age of technology is no exception to this rule of history. We already know the enormous benefits it can bestow, and we have begun to perceive its frightful threats. The crisis generated by this knowledge is upon us.

We are enormously fortunate that our young people—the first generation to carry strontium 90 in their bones and DDT in their fat—have become particularly sensitive to this ominous paradox of the modern world. For it is they who face the frightful task of seeking humane knowledge in a world which has, with cunning perversity, transformed the power that knowledge generates into an instrument of catastrophe.

The environmental crisis is a grim challenge. It also is a great opportunity. From it we may yet learn that the proper use of science is not to conquer nature, but to live in it. We may yet learn that to save ourselves we must save the world that is our habitat. We may yet discover how to devote the wisdom of science and the power of technology to the welfare, the survival of man.

A modest proposal: science for the people

JOHN TODD*

I HAVE been assured by a very knowing *American* of my Acquaintance in *London;* that a young healthy Child, well nursed, is, at a Year old, a most delicious, nourishing, and wholesome Food. . . . I GRANT this Food will be somewhat dear, and therefore very *proper for landlords;* who, as they have already devoured most of the Parents, seem to have the best Title to the Children.

JONATHAN SWIFT, 1729
A Modest Proposal

A single overview is increasingly dominating human affairs while diversity and indigenous approaches are being set aside with the flourishing of modern science and technology. If the present trend continues, the world community will be shaped into a series of highly planned megalopolises that are regulated by an advanced technology and fed by a mechanized and chemically sanitized agriculture.[1] This future course is countered largely by the tenacity of many peoples throughout the world, including many indigenous peoples, marginal and peasant farmers, traditional craftsmen, and new generations seeking alternatives to the modern industrial state. However, national and international agencies and business enterprises are vigorously attempting to "raise the standard of living" of most of these peoples and to incorporate them into the framework of the dominant societies. The rapid influx of populations into urban areas indicates that these attempts are successful in at least one respect—namely, that the numbers and impact of those who live apart from the mainstream of society are constantly being reduced. The world is rapidly becoming more homogeneous, and therein may lie one of the most serious problems confronting modern societies.

Most current solutions to the immense problems facing us utilize the latest techniques of systems engineering and involve resource and social management on a previously unattainable scale.[2] Increasingly, governments and international agencies are coping with the future by planning and acting on a world-wide basis. FAO's (Food and Agricultural Organization of United Nations) ambitious plan known as the Indica-

tive World Plan for Agricultural Development exemplifies this approach and will strongly influence, if not dictate, agricultural development in many of the poorer nations over the next quarter century.[3] There are a number of dangers built into top-down management at national or supranational levels as progressively fewer people are going to be making more and more of the recommendations. This could lead to a lessening of the representation of people and points of view involved in shaping society, particularly if systems-specialists take it upon themselves to select the inputs and come up with the answers to future planning. Unfortunately, there is no guarantee that the methods currently in vogue will do any more than identify the crises which are piling up, and if important social or environmental variables are omitted, then these plans may actually aggravate our problems.

It is my contention that we are in danger of losing an important amount of social variability in the human community at the same time that we are losing the required amount of biological variability in our life-support bases. If we continue on our present path, at the present rate, then our chances of maintaining healthy communities and environments will be reduced dramatically before the year 2000, perhaps beyond a point where society as we know it will be capable of functioning.

A few years ago a group of scientists and humanists began a search for ways in which science and the individual could come to the aid of people and the stressed planet. We all shared the uneasy feeling that modern science and technology have created a false confidence in our techniques and abilities to solve problems. We were also disturbed that most futurology seemed to jeopardize the continued survival of man by displaying a real ignorance of biology. It was clear from the outset that social and biological diversity needed to be protected and, if at all possible, extended.

We felt that a plan for the future should create alternatives and help counter the trend toward uniformity. It should provide immediately applicable solutions for small farmers, homesteaders, native peoples everywhere, and those seeking ecologically sane lives, enabling them to extend their uniqueness and vitality. Our ideas could also have a beneficial impact

*John Todd is a director and cofounder of the New Alchemy Institute, Woods Hole, Mass.

on a wider scale if some of the concepts were incorporated into society at large. This modest and very tentative proposal suggests a direction that society might well consider.

At the foundation of the proposal is the creation of a biotechnology which by its very nature would

1. function most effectively at the lowest levels of society;
2. be comprehensible to and utilizable by the poorest of peoples;
3. be based upon ecological as well as economic realities, leading to the development of local economies;
4. permit the evolution of small decentralist communities which in turn might act as beacons for a wiser future for much of the world's population; and
5. be created at local levels and require relatively small amounts of financial support. This would enable poorer regions or nations to embark upon the creation of indigenous biotechnologies.

UNNATURAL SELECTION: LOSS OF DIVERSITY

It is necessary, before describing a way of reviving diversity at all levels, to evaluate how its loss threatens the future of man. Suppose some wise alien from another planet were commissioned to investigate earth. He would no doubt be dismayed at the outset by the tendency of the dominant societies, whether "communist" or "capitalist," to be constantly selecting the most efficient or profitable ways of doing things. Our visitor would ascertain clearly that our narrow approaches are reducing our options and that people are being conditioned and habituated to the options that remain. To him it would represent an evolutionary trap, and after his survey of energy use and agriculture was completed, he would confidently predict a major catastrophe. There would be no need to go on to industry, the university, or government, despite the fact that much ecological insanity resides in them also.

Examples of unnatural selection are everywhere.

For hundreds of years prior to the industrial revolution a wide variety of energy resources were used by man. Besides animal power and human toil there was a subtle integration of resources such as wind and water power, and a variety of fuels including peat, wood, coal, dung, vegetable starches, and animal fats.[4] This approach of integration through diversity in providing the energy for society has been replaced by an almost exclusive reliance on fossil fuels and nuclear power. Energy sources are often linked together into huge transmission grids which provide electric power over large sections of the country. The industrial revolution took place only where there was a large-scale shift to fossil fuels as an energy source. The costs resulting may yet overshadow its benefits. The production of air pollutants and highly dangerous radioactive wastes continues to increase rapidly, and no downward trend is immediately in sight, despite an increased environmental awareness. Modern society, by reducing the variety of its basic energy sources while increasing its per capita energy needs, is now vulnerable to disruption on an unprecedented scale. It would be fool-hardy to disregard the very real possibility of a small group of people destroying our power transmission systems. Tragically, there are no widely disseminated backup sources of power available to help the majority of people in a nation hooked on massive amounts of electricity. Our society was not as precariously based as this in 1776, or even 1929.

On this country's farmlands changes have taken place over the last fifty years that have not yet had their full impact on the nation. The majority of the population has been displaced from relatively self-sufficient farms by large monoculture farm industries. That many of the displaced farm people are on welfare or adding to the ghetto's problems is not usually considered by agricultural planners. Unfortunately, the trend is world-wide as former colonial regimes and the present economic involvement by powerful industrial nations have created a climate of uncontrolled urbanization in Third World countries. There is a contemporary theory that contends that the industrial powers have contributed directly to the conditions that led to their dangerously high population levels.[5]

Proselytizers on behalf of modern agribusiness rarely consider the key role of numerous and diverse small farms as a social buffer during periods of emergency or social breakdown. This oversight could well be the result of a lack of civilian research into the needs of a major industrial nation under the stress of severe crises, despite the fact that a disaster could occur.[6] A depression like that which befell the country in 1929 could well take place; but if one should happen in the 1970s the social consequences would be much more severe. In 1929, a large percentage of Americans had friends or relatives on farms that could operate a self-sufficient basis during lean periods. Today the situation is alarmingly different, as the rural buffer is largely gone and far fewer people have access to the land. The problem is compounded by the fact that today's farms have little resemblance to those of forty years ago; the modern farm is in no way independent, and like other businesses requires large amounts of capital, machinery, and chemicals to maintain its operations.

The replacement of rural populations and cultures by agribusiness operated primarily on the basis of short-term incentives rather than as legacies for future generations, is resulting in a tremendous loss of biological and social diversity in the countryside. When the land and landscapes become just another commodity, society as a whole suffers. It would not be so serious if the loss of a viable countryside were all that was threatened by modern agriculture, but a closer look at present agricultural methods suggests that many of them are causing a severe loss of biological variability, so vital to any sound and lasting agriculture.

THE GREEN REVOLUTION: UNNATURAL SELECTION

Over the past several decades the agricultural sciences have created a number of major advances in food raising, and the widely acclaimed green revolution has come to symbolize the power of applied science and technology working on behalf of all people. Our confidence has been renewed that mushrooming populations can be fed if only Western agriculture can be spread rapidly enough throughout the world.[7] But the green revolution has not been shaped by an ecological ethic, and its keenest enthusiasts are usually manufacturers of chemicals and agricultural implements backed by government officials, rather than farmers and agricultural researchers who are generally aware of the immense complexity of stable agricultural systems. A brief examination of the ads in a wide variety of American journals and magazines would lead one to believe that the agricultural revolution is actually a chemical revolution, and perhaps it basically is.

A number of biologists and agricultural authorities are cautious about the future, as they foresee environmental decimation which will offset the agricultural gains before the turn of the century.[8] Among some of them, there is a disquieting feeling that we are witnessing the agricultural equivalent of the launching of the *Titanic*, only this time there are several billion passengers.

The modernization of agriculture has resulted in the large-scale use of chemical fertilizers upon which many of the new high-yielding strains of grains depend. Coupled with this is a basic emphasis on single cash crops which are grown on increasingly larger tracts of land. The dependency on fertilizers for successful crops has created depressed soil faunas and an alarming increase in nitrates in the ground waters of some areas. The nitrate levels are often above the safety limits set by the U.S. Public Health Service for infants' drinking water.[9]

Accompanying the widespread use of chemical fertilizers has been the rapid increase of biocides to control pests and weeds. These, in turn, have reduced the number of species of soil animals in many farm fields, with subsequent reductions in the quality of humus, which is essential to the sustained health of soils.[10] Unfortunately, these changes are occurring just as we are beginning to discover how much the soil fauna, particularly the earthworms, contribute to plant growth and health.[11] The use of biocides has triggered a vicious cycle: soils decline in quality, which in turn makes crops more vulnerable to attack by pests or disease organisms. This creates a need for increasingly large amounts of pesticides and fungicides for agricultural production to be sustained.

The full impact of biocides has yet to come. It is as if ecology and agriculture represent a modern Janus in their antithetic stances. While a team of ecologists has recently announced that the full impact of DDT often does not show up in long-lived birds, predatory animals, and humans for twenty-five years after application,[12] agricultural planners confidently predict a 600-percent increase in the use of pesticides in Third World countries over the next few years.[13] By the year 2000 the developing nations, as the beneficiaries of an uncontrolled experiment, will have reason to resent the blessings of modern technology.

The most notable achievement of the green revolution has been the creation of new high-yield strains of rice, wheat, and corn.[14] World agriculture has in the space of a few years been made more efficient, and in the short run, more productive because of these supergrains, particularly the Mexican semidwarf varieties of wheat. They represent a triumph of the modern plant breeder's art, but are in no way a panacea to the world food shortage. The grain revolution has an Achilles' heel; the new varieties, grown on increasingly vast acreages, are causing the rapid extinction of older varieties and a decline in diversity of the germ plasm in nature. The genetic variability which initially enabled the new types to be created is threatened, and the very foundation of the new agriculture is being eroded. In Turkey and Ethiopia thousands of local wheats have become extinct over the last several decades, and the phenomenon is widespread.[15] It is possible that the genetic variability of wheats could be irreplaceably lost. Erna Bennett of FAO has stated that "the world is beleaguered as far as its genetic resources are concerned."[16] Some of the most influential agricultural experts are deeply aware of the problem and are attempting to create the necessary "gene banks" before it is too late. It has been suggested that the race to save our genetic resources may be hampered by another biological fact of life, namely that seed storage may not be enough since "reserves" of the original microclimates and ecosystems may also be required if the viability of the local strains is to be maintained.[17]

The trend away from cultivating local varieties to a few higher-yielding forms is placing much of the world's population out on a limb. If the new varieties are attacked by pathogens the consequences could be world-wide rather than local, and plant breeders may not be able to create new strains before it is too late. Such events are not without precedent. An earlier counterpart of the green revolution occurred in Ireland in the eighteenth century, with the introduction of the Irish potato from the western hemisphere.[18] Production of food dramatically increased, and by 1835 a population explosion had taken place as a result of the land's increased carrying capacity. During the 1840s a new fungal plant disease appeared, destroying several potato crops, and one-quarter of the Irish people died of starvation.[19] The recent devastation of coffee plants in Brazil is partly the result of their narrow genetic base and their consequent vulnerability to leaf rust disease.[20] The 1970 corn leaf blight in the U.S. was caused by a fungus which attacks plants that carry the T gene for male sterility, and 70-90 percent of the corn hybrids carry this gene.[21] Despite heavy applications of fungicides, corn blight spread with heavy crop losses.

Clearly, a modern agriculture frantically struggling to right the wrongs of its single vision is not ecologically sane, no matter how productive, efficient, or economically sound it may seem.

There are other hidden perils associated with the modernization of agriculture,[22] but the loss of genetic diversity is perhaps the most obvious example of general changes taking place at every level of society. Since a scientific or technological advance on one level (e.g., the supergrains) may be pushing us closer to disaster, on another, it is time to look carefully at the roots of the alternatives before these avenues have disappeared behind us.

PSYCHIC DIVERSITY AND THE HUMAN EXPERIENCE: A NARROWING PATH?

The environmental dilemma is mirrored by comparable changes in people themselves. Unnatural selection is causing a loss of diversity in the human sphere, and this loss may lead toward social instability. The roles of most individuals are becoming ever more reduced as they relinquish the various tasks of living and governing to myriads of machines and specialists. Unlike our ancestors we have little direct control over the creation of our power and energy, food, clothing, or shelter. Claude Lévi-Strauss has shown how far this narrowing of roles has progressed, particularly with regard to our direct experience of the world around us. People fly faster, travel farther, and partake of more of the world, and yet in doing so, the world, sampled widely but without depth, becomes more elusive and farther from their grasp.[23]

It is highly probable, although difficult to prove, that the simplification and impoverishment of the lives of most of us lie close to the roots of much of the chaos threatening modern society. Erich Fromm has suggested that violence particularly is related to boredom:[24] It seems highly likely that boredom is one result of impoverishment or retreat from function.

Retreat from function is a negative trend since it removes the individual from the totality of his world. Restoring and extending genuine interaction with the life processes is the only lasting way to reverse this course, and this should begin at the basic functional levels of society, within the life-spaces of the individual or the small group. Fraser Darling, in his perceptive studies of remote Scottish peoples, showed how self-sufficiency was a positive force in their lives.[25] The most independent communities were far more diverse and socially vital than single-industry towns heavily dependent on a lifeline to the outside. He also came to realize that they coped far better in their dealings with the world at large. Equally important, the independent communities cared for their environment and were less prone to despoil it for short-term monetary gain. Another study of two California farm communities (Arvin—Denuba) revealed a comparable story.[26]

Modern science and its technologies have shaped industrially based societies that dominate the world today. These societies have an almost unlimited capacity to manipulate and destroy nature and men. In the long run they will not prove adaptive: as our options narrow, the specter of a future which is unhumane and in violation of nature looms larger. To reverse this trend, a moral, intellectual, and scientific renaissance will be required. Fortunately the basis for an adaptive view of society in nature is beginning to emerge and an attendant science and philosophy exists in embryonic form today.

NEW ALCHEMY AND A RECONSTRUCTIVE SCIENCE: AN ALTERNATIVE FUTURE

The direction of contemporary science is powerfully influenced by its patrons: the military and large corporations with their governmental cohorts. If a major scientific project or discipline does not hold out some promise of profit or military supremacy, it is not usually supported. The driving wheel of science in industrial societies is not a dispassionate seeking of knowledge. Science rarely addresses itself to the needs of human beings at the level of the individual or small group. With a sprinkling of notable exceptions, particularly in medicine, modern science and its technologies affect the majority of mankind in a negative or oppressive way, if at all. Science ignores, rather than addresses itself to, the richness and range of human potential. Knowledge is being replaced by hardware, not so much because hardware is superior to knowledge, but because it is more profitable. Unfortunately, technology as we know it cannot be expected to correct its own ills. These must be replaced with wisdom and practices that are fundamentally restorative rather than destructive.

An alternative science must seek to act on behalf of all people by searching for techniques and options that will restore the earth and create a new sense of community along ecological lines. Many talented people are working in the cities on urban problems, trying to make the cities livable and human, but very few are interested in making the countryside and farmlands livable by providing viable alternatives to the present rural destruction. Tools and techniques for individuals or small groups, however poor, must be sought to enable rural dwellers to work toward recapturing and extending their biological and social diversity. This new science must also link social and scientific purpose with the aim of creating a reconstructive knowledge that will function at the basic levels of society. If it did address itself to social and environmental microcosms, any group of people would be able to create its own indigenous biotechnic systems, gain more control over its own lives, and become more self-sufficient.

The ideal is to find ways of living that will help alleviate oppression at all levels, against the earth as well as against people. Ecology and personal liberation together have the potential to create environments within which people can gain increasing control over the processes which sustain them. This philosophy, call it "New Alchemy," in seeking modes of stewardship, attempts to fuse ethics with a scientific commitment to microcosms, because in caring for the immediate, a dynamic may be born that will ultimately lead to a saner tomorrow.

CENTERS FOR NEW WORLD RESEARCH

The New Alchemy Institute has established a few small independent centers in a variety of climates and environments, including the tropics. In this way we hope to induce a high degree of diversity into research and approaches to land stewardship. However, there does run within the organization a common thread, namely a holistic view of the task ahead. No research is undertaken in a vacuum. Energy is linked to food production, food production to the larger questions of environment and communitas. Where possible, wastes, power, gardens, aquaculture, housing, and surrounding ecosystems are studied simultane-

ously. In the foreseeable future all elements of the systems will be linked in a variety of ways so that the most viable living environment can evolve. Thus a holistic view becomes possible at the level of the social microcosm.

The New Alchemy farm on Cape Cod in Massachusetts typifies our research approach to the rural problems of tomorrow. The fundamental strategy has been to integrate an array of low-cost yet sophisticated and efficient biological and solar energy systems. This has created a productive and self-contained microcosm—stewardship responsive to local conditions.

With respect to our *preliminary* model at Cape Cod, windmills, solar heaters, intensive vegetable gardens, field crops, and fish cultures are linked together in mutually beneficial ways. Brief descriptions follow.

The wind generator. A wind generator is a streamlined windmill that generates enough power to run an electric generator. It was once popular in rural areas during the 20s and 30s, before the advent of rural electrification. Our wind generator, which cost very little, was assembled primarily from scrap auto parts.[27] However, it is by no means perfected, and a great deal still needs to be learned about producing electricity inexpensively from the wind. Recent designs and new gearing systems, discoveries of solid-state power converters, and efficient storage batteries and air-foil blade designs, coupled with a dwindling supply and increased cost of fossil and nuclear fuels are making wind generators increasingly practical as an alternative energy source.

Fish ponds. Below the windmills, at the entrance to the gardens, are two small solar-heated aquaculture minifarms. One is covered with a dome having a clear plastic skin and curved surface to trap the sun's heat and store it in a "tropical" pond fashion.[28] The other covered pond of more conventional design uses a solar heater for additional warming of the water. Both ponds are maintained around 80° F throughout the late spring and summer months. Within the 25-foot-diameter pools, *Tilapia*, a tropical fish of high food value, is raised. These fish derive their feed primarily from massive algae blooms whose growth is stimulated in waters warmed by the sun and enriched by small amounts of animal manure. Edible-size fish have been cultured in as brief a time as ten weeks. . . .

Other food sources will come from research involving the production of high-protein insect-food in polluted waters. In order to accomplish this, insects with an aquatic larval stage are being reared in large numbers in the tiny ponds. These provide an ecological food source for *Tilapia* and other fish.[29] The insects currrently being cultured are midges or Chironomids, tiny nonbiting mosquitolike insects which commonly swarm on summer evenings. The larval stage, normally found in the bottom muck in ponds, is cultured on burlap mats suspended in the fertilized ponds. The problems of food production and water purification are interconnected at the point of fertilization. At present, in order to obtain high yields, animal manures are used as fertilizer. The ponds are, in fact, polluted to increase production. While growing, the larval midges help to purify the ponds. They accomplish this by feeding on microscopic organisms whose populations are increased by the manure, and perhaps also by direct assimilation of nutrients in the enriched waters. At this stage the insect-rearing ponds use only manure, but there are plans to shift some of the culture over to human sewage, thereby linking sewage purification with the rearing of insects for fish culture.

The sun and the wind are coupled in the backyard fish system to optimize productivity. It is a self-sufficient approach to the rearing of aquatic foods and there is little in the way of capital involved. It requires only labor and a large array of ecologically derived ideas, many of which have yet to be completely elucidated.

Household purification system. Human sewage is being partially purified in one practical experiment. A small glass-sided A-frame structure is used to elevate temperatures over a series of pools that purify household sewage and wastes, through the culture of aquatic plants, live-bearing fishes, and insects of a variety of species. The produce from the household waste purification system is fed in turn to a flock of chickens. The wastes, partially purified by the living organisms, are subsequently used for irrigating the lawn and tree crops. Sewage, ordinarily an expensive and awkward problem for society, becomes a beneficial source of energy when dealt with on a small scale. New animal feeds are found and local soils enriched.

Intensive vegetable gardens. The birthplace of much of our agricultural research is in the gardens below the ponds. Several experiments intended to help find ways of culturing plants and animals without using expensive and harmful biocides have been initiated. One large project, is a systematic search for varieties of vegetables that may have some built-in genetic resistance to insect pests. Most modern plant breeders have assumed that pesticides are an inevitable tool in agriculture; consequently, knowledge is scant concerning vegetable varieties with an intrinsic ability to resist pest attacks. In another research project the efficacy of interplanting vegetables with herbs and flowers that have a suspected ability to trap or repel pests is being tested, along with techniques for performing reliable yet simple experiments in highly productive vegetable gardens.[30] Each of the experi-

mental gardens, regardless of the research taking place, is treated as a miniature ecosystem, and many of the biological processes are monitored to determine aspects of diversity and "stability" in each of the systems.

Integrating gardens–fish ponds. Ideas for future research projects are being tested in the gardens. For example, one experimental plot is being used to look into the value of using nutrient-laden water from the small fish ponds for irrigating crops. Some fish species, when cultured in high densities, apparently secrete a fatty substance that tends to reduce evaporation. Consequently, pond water containing moisture-conserving substances as well as nutrients may be highly useful for irrigating crops, especially under arid conditions. Early laboratory trials with lettuce and parsley indicated that the water from tanks containing fish has a "hermetic" quality that conserves moisture around the roots of the plants. Field trials conducted in 1973 demonstrated the agricultural value of using aquaculture wastes. Lettuce yields were increased up to 112 percent over controls.

Already we can begin to envisage closely linked aquatic and terrestrial food systems suited to regions where water is seasonal and limited. Vegetation for food and for shelter from the sun could be nurtured from water stored and enriched in aquaculture ponds. Many of the earth's arid regions may one day sustain small communities within microenvironments that are biologically complete without the need to import large amounts of food, energy, and capital.

Ecologically derived structures. The investigations of a small group of people at a single New Alchemy center are coming together most completely in a project initiated in 1973. A direct involvement in process has drawn us toward the idea of creating living structures that are ecologically derived and reflect all that we have learned. Our initial approach to such housing is to have the structures evolve directly out of the ongoing aquaculture, waste, greenhouse, and solar and wind energy research. On a microscopic scale such a strategy seems to make good sense, as the threads of each person's investigations are spun together to create a structure that mimics nature and perhaps will enable us to live in, rather than apart from, her. These structures will be self-regulating and eventually will provide inhabitants with shelter and a wide variety of aquatic plant and animal feeds as well as vegetables and fruits.[31] Such systems have the potential to provide the majority of food needs as well as housing for their inhabitants. Only the essential grains would need to come from outside.

The ark. Our first structure, just started, is called the "ark." It is a solar-heated greenhouse and aquaculture complex adapted to the rigorous climates of the northeast. If suitable internal climates can be maintained, we will eventually attach living quarters to the structure. The prototype will include a sunken greenhouse, an attached aquaculture pond, and a diversity of light and heat conservation and distribution components. . . . It will be an integrated self-regulating system requiring the sun, power for water circulation, waste materials, and labor to sustain its productivity. The electricity to drive the circulation pump will be provided by a windmill. The heat storage-climate regulation component will be a 13,500-gallon aquaculture pond. Solar heat will be trapped directly by the covered pond and by water circulating through the solar heater. The attached greenhouse will be built below the frost line and will derive its heat from the earth, direct sunlight, and from the warmed pond water passing through pipes in the growing beds within the structure.

The intensive fish-farming component will be comparable to those already pioneered by New Alchemists. Several crops of *Tilapia* fish will be cultured through the warm months and a single crop of perch and trout during the cooler seasons. The aquaculture system may prove productive enough to underwrite the construction and maintenance costs of similar food-growing complexes in the future.

The greenhouse will be used to raise high-value vegetables and greens fertilized by wastes from the aquaculture pond. If our solar-heated ark should prove successful, then ecologically derived low-energy agricultures may thrive in northern climates.

So far, while building our models, we have learned that incredibly little is known about devising and caring for small-scale systems for communities that are both ecologically complete and restorative of environments. The contemporary colossal sense of scale, combined with the fragmentation of knowledge by the scientific establishment, has effectively blocked the development of an alternative for the future that is humble and yet ecologically wise. There are as many mysteries to be explored in the workings of the wind, the sun, and the soil on a tiny plot of ground as exist in the grandiose schemes of modern science. The totality of the human experience becomes available to each of us as we begin to learn to function at the level of the microcosm.

BEYOND OURSELVES: A PEOPLE'S SCIENCE

A few people working at a handful of centers cannot alone affect the course of human events. The elitism underlying contemporary science must be eliminated and a reconstructive science created. Knowledge should become the province of many, including all those struggling to become pioneers for the twenty-first century. If responsibility and diversity are to be established at the level of the individual, then individuals with a wide array of backgrounds and experiences should take part in the discovery of the knowledge and techniques required for the transformation ahead. A lay science, addressing itself to problems at basic levels of society, could restore diversity to the human sphere and establish an involvement for many in the subtle workings of the world around them.

Already a number of lay scientists are working with us investigating the backyard fish farm concept, experimenting with the raising of *Tilapia* under intensive culture conditions.

Other lay researchers are involved in experiments to determine the value of ecologically designed food gardens. One of the experiments is a systematic search for varieties of vegetables that may have some genetic resistance to insect pests. Another is a search to determine the techniques of interplanting vegetables with herbs and flowers with a suspected ability to trap or repel pests and to nurture natural control agents of those pests.

Only with the help of hundreds of earth scientists could this kind of information be acquired on a country-wide scale, in a relatively short period of time. The research on resistance and ecological design must take into account soils, environments, and climates from a diversity of regions in order to comprehend the forces underlying a balanced and restorative agriculture. Such a study has not been attempted by orthodox research organizations, nor is it likely to be attempted.

It is too soon for us to have developed much experience in guiding a lay science that will create its own independent dynamic. If we are at all successful, individuals and groups will within a few years branch out and explore the questions that seem most relevant to them and their own lives. Indigenous centers for learning through direct involvement in the process of reconstruction will spring up, providing an alternative to the colonization and fragmentation of knowledge by the universities.

Our initial approach was to compile two working manuals covering the research that is now part of the peoples' research program.[32] One of the manuals deals with agricultural research and the other is a guide to the fish farm project. The agricultural manual attempts to show the garden as an experimental system and leads the potential investigator through problems often faced by ecologists. After working with the manual in an experimental garden the problems and concepts gradually become comprehensible. The aquaculture investigator's manual uses a somewhat different method, following more of a "cook book" approach, with a step-by-step guide through the fish culture experiment.

There is a strong tendency in the academic world

of modern science to publish more and more (usually about less and less) to be considered a successful scientist. To peruse most research publications is an almost absurd experience. The contents are dreary, fragmented, and usually border on irrelevancy. What a far cry from the scientific writings of men like Charles Darwin, who would not publish his theory of evolution without years of intensive labor. Today, a Darwin would probably be sacked from even the most progressive college. Despite almost a lifetime of illness, his intense intellectual activity ultimately resulted in the publication of books on evolution and natural selection, earthworms, the formation of coral reefs, and the behavior of humans and animals which remain of real value to this day.

Although the criticism of scientific publishing is usually valid, it still seems clear that publishing will have to remain a corner need for publications that are readily understandable, relevant, and directly applicable to the needs of the new pioneers. They should reflect education in the broadest sense, in which individuals, society, and the biosphere are seen in holistic and meaningful terms.

Already it is apparent that an alternative science is evolving on a world-wide scale, and will continue to grow. There are common threads weaving the tapestry that underlies the lives of the new pioneers and scientists; among these are a strong sense of the human scale, a desire to comprehend the forces of communitas, and a passion for ecology and its teachings, which imply ethics and awakened sensibility and morality. These are forces in their own right, and though pitted against the shadow of technological man destroying man and nature, and a science operating in a moral vacuum, they may still represent the beginning of a hopeful path along which we may one day travel.

NOTES

1. R. B. Fuller, *Operating Manual for Spaceship Earth* (New York: Pocket Books, 1970). See also J. B. Billard, "The Revolution in American Agriculture," *National Geographic* 137, no. 2 (February 1970). Both works represent the prevailing views in global engineering, city design, and agriculture.
2. J. Platt, "What We Must Do," *Science* 162 (1969): 1115.
3. A. H. Boerman, "World Agricultural Plan," *Scientific American* 223, no. 2 (1970).
4. Murray Bookchin, "Ecology and Revolutionary Thought," *Anarchos* 1(1968). This essay is also in "Post-Scarcity Anarchism"—a much more accessible source.
5. Barry Commoner, *The Humanist*, November-December 1970.
6. Platt, "What We Must Do."
7. Boerman, "World Agricultural Plan"; L. R. Brown, *Seeds of Change* (New York: Praeger, 1970).
8. Barry Commoner, "Soil and Fresh Water: Damaged Global Fabric," *Environment* 12, no. 3 (1970); W. C. Paddock, "How Green Is the Green Revolution?" *BioScience* 20, no. 16 (1970); John H. Todd, Editorial, The New Alchemy Institute Bulletin 1 (1970), Box 432, Woods Hole, Mass. 02543.
9. Commoner, "Soil and Fresh Water."
10. C. R. Malone, A. G. Winnett, and K. Helrich, "Insecticide-Induced Responses in an Old Field Ecosystem," *Bulletin Environ. Contam. Toxicol.* 2, no. 2 (1967).
11. R. Rodale, ed., *The Challenge of Earthworm Research* (Emmaus, Pa.: Soil and Health Foundation, 1961).
12. H. L. Harnson et al., "Systems of DDT Transport," *Science* 170 (1970): 503.
13. Paddock, "How Green Is the Green Revolution?"; President's Science Advisory Committee, *The World Food Problem* 1(1967). See also *Chem. Eng. News* 49, no. 2 (1971).
14. L. P. Reitz, "New Wheats and Social Progress," *Science* 169 (1970): 952.
15. G. Chedd, "Hidden Perils of the Green Revolution," *New Scientist* 48(1970): 724.
16. Ibid.
17. John E. Bardach, personal communication.
18. *World Food Problem.*
19. Redcliffe N. Salaman, *The Influence of the Potato on the Course of Irish History*, Tenth Findlay Memorial Lecture, University College, Dublin, 27 October 1943 (Dublin: Brown & Nolan).
20. Chedd, "Hidden Perils."
21. N. Gruchow, "Corn Blight Threatens Crop," *Science* 169(1970): 961.
22. N. Pilpel, "Crumb Formation in the Soil," *New Scientist* 48 (1970): 732.
23. Claude Lévi-Strauss, *The Savage Mind* (Chicago: Univ. of Chicago Press, 1966).
24. Erich Fromm, *The Revolution of Hope: Toward a Humanized Technology* (New York: Harper & Row, 1968).
25. F. F. Darling, "The Ecological Approach to the Social Sciences," *Amer. Sci.* 39, no. 2 (1951).
26. W. Goldschmidt, *As You Sow* (Glencoe, Ill.: Free Press, 1947).
27. E. Barnhart, "A Windmill for Generating Electricity," *The Journal of the New Alchemists* 1(1973): 12-15.
28. W. McLarney, "An Introduction to Aquaculture on the Organic Farm and Homestead," *Organic Gardening and Farming*, August 1971, pp. 71-76; J. H. Todd and W. O. McLarney, "The Backyard Fish Farm" *Organic Gardening and Farming*, January 1972, pp. 99-109. W. McLarney, *The Backyard Fish Farm Working Manual*, Readers Research Project No. 1, New Alchemy Institute (Emmaus, Pa.: Rodale Press, 1973). See also *Journal of the New Alchemists* 2(1974) New Alchemy Institute, Woods Hole, for more recent work with endemic aquaculture systems in cool-temperate climates.
29. W. McLarney, S. Henderson, and M. Sherman, "The Culture of Chironomids," *Journal of the New Alchemists* 2(September 1974).
30. J. Todd and R. Merrill, "Insect Resistance in Vegetable Crops," *Organic Gardening and Farming*, March 1972; R. Merrill, "Companion Planting and Ecological Design in the Organic Garden," *Organic Gardening and Farming*, April 1972; R. Merrill, *Designing Experiments for the Organic Garden: A Research Manual*, Readers Research Project, New Alchemy Institute, Woods Hole, Mass. 1973.
31. J. Todd, R. Angevine, and E. Barnhart, *The Ark: An Autonomous Fish Culture—Greenhouse Complex Powered by the Wind and the Sun and Suited to Northern Climates* (Woods Hole, Mass.: New Alchemy Institute, 1973).
32. McLarney, *Backyard Fish Farm Working Manual*; Merrill, *Designing Experiments for the Organic Garden.*

The new agriculture in the United States: a dissenter's view

RICHARD G. MILK*

INTRODUCTION

Competent observers of the world economic panorama call attention to this point: with very few exceptions, low income countries have a large proportion of the labor force in agriculture and high income countries have a small proportion in agriculture.[1]

Our United States economy increased the proportion of workers in non-farm occupations from 27 per cent in 1800 to 41 per cent in 1860.[2] The proportion of the labor force in farming dropped from 55 per cent in 1860 to 27 per cent in 1920.[3] A recent Federal Reserve Bulletin shows an average farm employment of 3,462,000 persons in agriculture in 1970 out of a total civilian labor force of 82,715,000. This was a mere 4.0 per cent of the labor force.[4] This change, over two centuries of our history, was accomplished by the substitution of capital for labor. The capital input per unit of labor input increased from $0.87 in 1910 to almost $4.00 per unit in 1960.[5] This Iowa State University Center study showed a projected decrease in labor inputs of 2 per cent a year over the 1960-1980 period.[6] The authors calculate that employment in agriculture would be less than 2 million workers out of a total work force of approximately 97 million workers in 1980.[7] This would imply a two per cent employment rate in agriculture with astronomical capital investments per worker. Another economist asserted that the United States "actually required fewer than 300,000 farms," in 1970.[8]

Many economists question the validity of extrapolating trend lines of past decades indefinitely into the future. Is it possible for this "capital for labor" substitution to go on "forever"? At what point do society's concerns and problems become aggravated by this economic phenomenon? Could perhaps we in the United States economy already have passed a cost-benefit equilibrium point where "societal costs" now exceed the so-called "economic gains" of this factor substitution?

Hypothesis. Strong evidence now exists that this unprecedented substitution of capital for labor has already transcended "optimum" societal returns. Perhaps continued stress upon this substitution by economists, the governmental agencies and the general public, will prevent full employment potentialities of the United States, slow down economic growth and excessively interfere with non-economic national goals. A third segment of this hypothesis is: appropriate measures must be presented to the American public for achieving some more satisfactory equilibrium point where the total societal "costs" and "benefits" are maximized by some (as yet unformulated) equation of society's optimum capital-labor combination in American agriculture.

Criterion for evaluating the hypothesis. Traditionally, agricultural economists have concentrated their attention upon "maximization of profits of agricultural firms." Volumes of books, bulletins and articles have been published "justifying" the "inevitable" substitution of capital for labor in American agriculture.

□ From Land Economics **48**(3): 228-235, Aug. 1972. Copyright © by the Board of Regents of the University of Wisconsin System.

The research on which this article is based was originally prepared for an economics faculty seminar at South Dakota State University at Brookings, 1968. The author wishes to express appreciation for helpful suggestions by John Thompson, Loyd Glover, H. A. Gilbert, Allyn Lockner, Robert Antonides, Russell Berry and Max Myers—all of the South Dakota State University faculty. He acknowledges deep indebtedness to reviewers of the editorial staff of *Land Economics* for constructive criticisms of the original essay. Gratitude is here expressed also to Dr. Eugene Fox, Department Head of Economics and to Dr. Lyndon Dawson, Chairman of the Research Committee at Northeast Louisiana University for their encouragement to re-write the manuscript.

*Assistant Professor of Economics, College of Business Administration, Northeast Louisiana University at Monroe, Louisiana.

[1]Jagdish Bhagwati, *The Economics of Underdeveloped Countries* (New York and Toronto: McGraw-Hill Book Company, 1966), pp. 44-49.
[2]John M. Peterson and Ralph Gray, *Economic Development of the United States* (Homewood Illinois: Richard D. Irwin, Inc., 1969). These authors point out that, on the world scene in 1950 about 60 per cent of the population was engaged in agriculture whereas in the more advanced industrial nations the proportion of workers has fallen below ten per cent, p. 18.
[3]*Ibid.*, p. 150.
[4]*The Federal Reserve Bulletin*, Washington, D.C., August 1971, Table A-66.
[5]Earl O. Heady, Edwin O. Haroldsen, Leo V. Mayer, Luther G. Tweeten, *Roots of the Farm Problem* (Ames, Iowa: Iowa State University Press, 1965), p. 19.
[6]*Ibid.*, p. 204.
[7]Based upon an estimated addition of 14.5 million to the labor force from 1970 until 1980. Projected in, Thomas J. Hailstone and Michael J. Brennan, *Economics: An Analysis of Principles and Policies* (Cincinnati, Ohio: South-Western Publishing Company, 1970).
[8]Willard W. Cochrane, *The City Man's Guide to the Farm Problem* (Minneapolis: University of Minnesota Press, 1965), p. 212.

But . . . the winds of change are sweeping across the United States. On university campuses; in the urban slums; among "taxpayer revolt" associations; among conservationists and ecologists; among individuals concerned about our nation as part of a planetary population; in the legislative chambers of the respective states and of the national Congress; among consumers of farm products; among the increasingly oppressed and exploited "short period" employees of big farm operators—there are strong voices lifted in protest against "profit maximization" as a unitary goal for governmental programs and economic research related to farm problems. Consequently, it is necessary to evaluate this essay's hypothesis on national goals and not on some criterion that can no longer be accepted as an exclusive one. What are our national goals? The vast majority of the citizens of the United States still subscribe to those goals officially stated in the preamble of our constitution: *life, liberty and the pursuit of happiness.*[9]

"National goals" are not proclaimed in any specific legislative or executive actions. Perhaps the closest we have to official documents on this score are: the Employment Act of 1946; the pronouncements of the President of the United States in his annual economic report to Congress as required by that law; and the opinions expressed by the Council of Economic Advisors. The 1946 law contains a phrase that the federal government shall use all practicable means "to promote free competitive enterprise and the general welfare, conditions under which there will be useful employment opportunities, including self-employment—and to promote maximum employment, production, and purchasing power."

Most of the 16,000 economists in the United States have a "general consensus" that the nation's goals (in economic affairs) can be centered largely on these six objectives: *economic growth, full employment, price stability, economic freedom, equitable distribution of income, and economic security.*[10]

Evidence to substantiate the hypothesis. One indication of the validity of the hypothesis is the excessively distorted returns to capital in agriculture as compared to the return to labor.

In a recent issue of the *American Journal of Agricultural Economics*, Theodore Lianos made a study of the relative share of income going to labor in agriculture. In his conclusion, he shows that in 1968 labor obtained (from Cobb Douglas production function formulas) only 19.99 per cent of the income in agricul-

ture; as contrasted with over 80 per cent of the income for capital. This is a complete reversal of relative shares of national income to labor and to capital for the economy as a whole. The process of distortion seems to be proceeding at an accelerated rate. In 1949 labor was receiving almost 43 per cent of the income in agriculture.[11]

Planning within the American national economy for the future United States agriculture should contain sober and compassionate reflections upon the problems of farm laborers. Padfield and Martin have carried out perceptive studies in this area. As a summary they say:

There is no "farm labor problem"—there is a general problem of people who end up doing farm labor because of their culture or their circumstances. There is a general problem of people who end up unemployed after being displaced in their primary occupation.

These human problems are the problems of society rather than simply of the farm sector or of the mining sector in particular. This is not just for humanitarian reasons, but because the permanent displacement of workers on a wholesale basis adversely affects the whole economy.[12]

Our agricultural laborers have the least security, least social benefits, least political influence, and the least public interest of any group in the United States. Dr. Theodore Schultz has commented that the study of the problems of farm labor is considered to be the "least glamorous" of any area in agricultural economics.[13]

Unfortunately, what few studies have been made have had a bias in the consideration of labor as an "inferior input." Waldo has verbalized this assumption: "the only way to increase income to farm laborers would be to accelerate the outmigration of labor from agriculture.[14]

Bonnen notes that 40 per cent of all poverty found in the United States is located in rural areas—much of this among farm laborers. As long as these "pockets of poverty" survive, there will be a steady flow into urban slums. This can only, in the aggregate, increase our national social problems.[15]

[9]Irwin Edman, *Fountainheads of Freedom* (New York: Reynal and Hitchcock, 1971), p. 407.

[10]Campbell R. McConnell, *Economics, Principles, Problems and Policies*, 4th ed. (New York: McGraw-Hill Book Company, 1969), p. 11.

[11]Theodore P. Lianos, "The Relative Share of Labor in United States Agriculture, 1949-1968," *American Journal of Agricultural Economics*, August 1971, p. 420.

[12]Harland Padfield and William E. Martin, *Farmers, Workers and Machines: Technological and Social Change in Farm Industries of Arizona* (Tucson: University of Arizona Press, 1965).

[13]Theodore W. Schultz, *Farm Labor in the United States*, C. E. Bishop, ed. (New York: Columbia University Press, 1967).

[14]Anley D. Waldo, "The Impact of Outmigration and Multiple Job-holding Upon Income Distribution in Agriculture," *Journal of Farm Economics*, December 1965, p. 1243.

[15]James T. Bonnen, "Present and Prospective Policy Problems of United States Agriculture: as Viewed by an Economist," *Journal of Farm Economics*, December 1965, pp. 1225-1234.

The only answer agricultural economists have had in the past about "excess labor on American farms" has been: "have them go somewhere else." But many economists re-emphasize Bonnen's point of view. Dr. Knight has said that agriculture can no longer treat the big cities as the huge "dump heap" for excess labor. He emphasizes that we must tackle the socio-economic disorders in the city and country simultaneously as one problem.[16]

There is mounting evidence that the amount of capital being utilized by American agriculture is disproportionately large, in comparison with the rest of the national economy. Most of our "Principles of Economics" textbooks give the estimate of the average capital invested per worker in the United States as approximately $20,000 per worker in 1970 (Hailstones and Brennan estimated the average to be $18,000 in 1967).[17] According to *Statistical Abstract*, the total assets in agriculture in 1970 were estimated to be 307 billions of dollars.[18] Utilizing the size of the agricultural labor force previously referred to, this would indicate an investment of over $88,000 per worker, about 4½ times the national average.

With the awesome shortage of capital which our nation faces to meet the crises of pollution, urban decay, revitalization of urban rapid transit, etc.—why should our public and our governmental policies permit such a flagrant discrepancy of capital allocation? Perhaps valid arguments could be made if the high investment raised the living standards of the workers; but on the contrary this capital for labor substitution is a force of impoverishment of the already impoverished! A few economists challenge the assumption that the substitution of capital for labor is the *only* answer for agriculture. Breimyer believes that there has been an *over-application of non-farm capital*, and that this *over-investment* has lowered the realized marginal returns for farm labor![19]

The types of "farm programs" which have been enacted over the past 40 years have become deflected from their original objectives and are now powerful instruments for doing the opposite of what they were originally intended to achieve. The public mood for initiating and supporting the various successions of laws and programs was basically, to help alleviate the problems of low income farm families and sec-

ondly, to prevent large numbers of agricultural firms from collapsing (a condition that could increase the price of food over the long run). To a great extent, the distortions and manipulations of farm programs occur because they have been based upon price supports for farm products.

Swerling has concluded that price supports have amounted to a regressive redistribution of income. He says that the statistical justification for such commodity programs has been derived from low per-capita estimates of farm income; these low estimates are due to large numbers of low-income farm people (who themselves receive little from these programs); and concludes that such commodity programs are very ill suited to relieving rural poverty.[20]

Neale states that agriculture has been vainly searching for some method of shifting the risks of employment and of income in agriculture on to society. He observes that commodity support programs were woefully inept attempts to spread the costs of declining employment opportunities.[21] Instead of benefiting "poor farm families," in the past forty years governmental programs have resulted in substantial federal gifts to property owners.

More and more economists are questioning the use of the Federal Treasury to transfer wealth to a few fortunate landowners. Floyd summarized the feeling of many in saying bluntly: "From the viewpoint of equity, it is questionable as to whether society, faced with poverty in many areas, should give large subsidies to owners of fixed assets in agriculture."[22]

There are conflicting theories on this rather sensitive question as to whether or not the large expenditures by the federal government on farm programs have influenced the great expansion of capital investments in agriculture to displace labor. Those who defend the entry of huge agricultural business firms into commercial agriculture say that this direct application of new advanced technology has reduced food prices. Other economists say that there are no positive indications of "great economies of scale," and the question is unanswerable because an indeterminate number of farms are owned by wealthy men who purposely (for income tax deduction reasons) want to lose money on the farm operations.

However, one of the most careful studies of the

[16]Wyllis R. Knight, *The Structure of American Industry*, Walter Adams, ed., 4th ed. (New York, New York: and London, England: The MacMillan Company, 1971), pp. 28-29.

[17]Hailstone and Brennan, *op. cit.*, p. 35.

[18]United States Department of Commerce, *Statistical Abstract* (Washington, D.C.: United States Government Printing Office, 1970), Table 927, p. 592.

[19]Harold F. Breimyer, "Why Do Farmers Over-Invest?" *Journal of Farm Economics*, May 1966, pp. 475-477.

[20]Boris Swerling, *Toward Positive Policies for American Agriculture*, Vol. I (Palo Alto, California: Stanford University Food Research Institute Series, November, 1960), p. 329.

[21]Walter C. Neale, "The Risks and Costs of Economic Development," Vol. II, *Problems of United States Economic Development* (New York: Committee for Economic Development, 1958), p. 263.

[22]John E. Floyd, "The Effects of Farm Support Prices on the Returns to Land and Labor in Agriculture," *Journal of Political Economy*, April 1965, p. 158.

problem seems to indicate that the commodity-price support programs have raised prices to consumers by at least 10 and probably closer to 20 per cent.[23] In view of the world trade crisis in which our country is now involved, this evaluation comes as a particularly severe shock. Nor can there be any glib answer that, if a price decline should occur, it would be the "little farmer"that would be most hurt.

The so-called evidences of the "inevitability" of farms becoming larger and larger can be placed into serious question. This theory may be based upon a dominating conclusion of Marx: that only by forming large-scale farm units would it be possible to achieve greater efficiency. Schultz has called this assumption (held by many agricultural economists around the world) into question and cites as refutation the extraordinary productivity of Japanese farms (which average only 2.1 acres in size).[24]

Suppose price supports were discontinued—who would be most hurt—the consumers, the big operators or the smaller farms? The answer would depend upon political pressures to "heal the damage" of such a rude shock to planning.

Tweeten discovered that large commercial farms would be hardest hit by price declines in the short-run—although he postulates they might perhaps withstand price declines over a long run better than small farms.[25]

He reported that in 1963 the proportion of farms reporting a profit were estimated as follows: 68 per cent of farms reporting less than $5,000 of sales; only 22 per cent of farms having $15,000 to $25,000 of sales; only 22 per cent of farms having gross sales of $100,000. Years ago my major professor at Cornell, George F. Warren, emphasized that extremely large, highly capitalized farm units would be much more vulnerable to price declines than the more modest farm enterprises. If only 22 per cent of these big commercialized farms make profits *with* price supports, the losses under price declines would be unbearable. Except, of course, for those owners using such properties as income tax dodging fronts—a practice which may not always be possible.

There is no reason, however, to think that even if a 20 per cent reduction in food costs should occur, that it necessarily would be the small farm operators or even the larger farm operators (divorced from food processing enterprises) who would "suffer." Why can such a statement be categorically printed? Because, in the United States as well as in other parts of the world: more money is made *from* the farmers than is made *by* the farmers!

In 1969, the food processing industries reported as "value added by manufacturing" 30 billion dollars.[26] When we compare this segment of the financial structure of only one of the various component parts of the other United States industrial firms related to agriculture (agricultural machinery; chemical fertilizers; feed manufacturing firms; tobacco manufacturing; textiles from cotton and wool; and food retailing) we are confronted with a total economic volume far out of proportion to the total cash receipts from farms of 42.5 billion dollars (in 1967).[27] In 1971 the food processing industry reported an estimated profit return, after taxes, of 12.9 per cent, based upon the first nine months' calculations.[28] It would be difficult to "calculate backwards" as to the total sum of profits based on the total value of sales, on the basis of the value added data, but a profit margin in excess of two billion dollars does not seem unlikely. Considering all of the other firms involved in supplying agriculture with inputs and the firms using farm products as raw materials, it does not seem unlikely that the total profits made "from the farmer's needs and products" exceeded 10 billion dollars. If the American consumers and the American farmers could each share in even one fourth of those profits, the total goals of greater economic justice and greater equality of distribution of incomes might be better served.

Strong evidence is now mounting that the substitution of capital for labor (in terms of annual cost inputs) is causing grave ecological problems. Forty years ago, crop rotations were generally prescribed for sound farm management. The great advantages were: to utilize leguminous plants to take nitrogen from the air and reduce the need for purchasing nitrogenous fertilizers; the utilization of ground cover to prevent soil and water erosion; the combination of livestock operations with other farm activities to utilize the forage for the animals and the manure from the animals for the fields; to break the cycle of reproduction and spread of weeds, crop insect enemies and crop diseases; and to provide for a more even distribution of available labor supply throughout the farm year. But the name of the game today is specialization

[23]Kenneth L. Robinson, "The Impact of Government Price and Income Programs on Income Distribution in Agriculture," *Journal of Farm Economics*, December 1965, pp. 1225-1234.

[24]Theodore W. Schultz, *Economic Crises in World Agriculture* (Ann Arbor: University of Michigan Press, 1965), p. 12.

[25]Luther G. Tweeten, "The Income Structure of United States Farms by Economic Class," *Journal of Farm Economics*, May 1965, pp. 207-221.

[26]*Statistical Abstract, op. cit.*, Table 1141, p. 691.

[27]John R. Brake and Peter J. Barry, "Flow-of-funds Social Accounts for the Farm Sector: Coment," *American Journal of Agricultural Economics*, November 1971, p. 667.

[28]Special Report, "Survey of Corporate Performance," Third quarter of 1971, *Business Week*, November 13, 1971, p. 78.

using chemical fertilizers in place of natural nitrogen-producing plants; using herbicides and insecticides instead of crop rotations; flushing manure into the nearby creeks or rivers from cemented feed lots or milking barns; and using migratory labor for peak periods of labor demand. Are the ecological and sociological consequences of these substitutions of capital for labor going to be so costly to society as to demand a re-evaluation of these short-cut procedures?

Ever since the Employment Act of 1946, our nation has sought to devise programs that will help to alleviate unemployment. The net effect of our farm programs over the past 25 years has been to reduce employment opportunities within agriculture. In 1949 there were ten million persons employed on farms in the United States as contrasted to the 3.4 million in 1970.[29]

Have our programs, directly and indirectly financed by our federal government resulting in a destruction of 6.5 million job opportunities, been a wise allocation of scarce resources? Many economists feel that in almost any society—if there is a serious choice between policies which will promote maximum employment and those which will promote maximum output—the decision for maximum employment becomes more crucial when unemployment is destroying morale and undermining the society.[30] For a sector like American agriculture, where maximum output is no longer a desired objective, this has special validity. This generalization is usually more applicable among the so-called under-developed nations, as Gunnar Myrdal pointed out to the recent International Conference of Agricultural Economists held in Minsk, Russia.[31] But where labor is under-utilized—is there not some logic in assuming some validity of the preceding comments, even among the industrialized countries? If economists and statesmen can shift gears away from the myopian look at each individual national economy they might see that on a planetary basis we face a great paucity of capital and a superabundance of labor.

We have, at least partially, ignored in the United States that an intangible social relationship exists between man and the land.[32] Four illustrations of our awareness of this inter-relatedness are: (a) the Homestead Act provisions which provided for putting people on the land—to care for and develop it; (b) the wholesale "escape" to the suburbs (the fastest growing area of our population growth); (c) the desire for conserving some of our nation's forests, rivers and scenic areas where man can feel surrounded by the environment instead of by fellow humans; (d) the multiplicity of problems that huge masses of people encounter in the megalopolis of today. (Professor Baumol has suggested there may be geometric progressions of economic and social costs involved with urban growth.[33]) Instead of programs that force people into the cities, our economy may need programs that will keep them more evenly dispersed over the countryside.

The social function of land is aptly illustrated in Mexico. There, the 23,000 collective farms (known as ejidos and originating in the revolution of 1911-1919; not in any way similar to Russian-style collectives) where nearly two thirds of the rural people live, do not provide very much food for sale to the urban sector. These ejidos provide an enormous "social function" for over a fourth of the total Mexican population by providing a way by which they support themselves (at a low level of living, it is true) and are not public welfare charges; they have a sense of belonging, a feeling vastly different from the condition of virtual slaves which their grandparents had on the pre-revolutionary haciendas; and they have not been dumped into the growing urban slums. Mexican economists conclude that some miraculous, immediate modernization of all agriculture in Latin America would be an almost unimaginable catastrophe.[34]

What are the alternatives? What kinds of changes might the American public demand of our national and state legislators to bring about a higher degree of achievement of our national goals for all people related to agriculture, and not just the owners of farm property? The following are some of the more interesting possibilities.

Several recent food products scares and the inadequacy of the state meat inspection laws have led some crusaders to suggest that all food processing firms be chartered (or legally incorporated) by either the Food and Drug Administration or the United States Department of Agriculture. There could be stronger enforcement of laws already in existence; such as the 160 acre limitation on lands irrigated, partially supported (in the construction or operation) by public

[29]The United States Department of Agriculture, *Agricultural Statistics* (Washington, D.C.: United States Printing Office, 1966), Table 648.
[30]Charles P. Kindleberger, *Economic Development*, 2nd ed. (New York: McGraw-Hill Book Company, 1965), p. 260.
[31]Gunnar Myrdal, *Agricultural Development and Planning in the Underdeveloped Countries Outside the Socialist Sphere* in the Papers and Reports of the International Conference of Agricultural Economists, Fourteenth Conference, 1970 (Oxford, England: Institute of Agrarian Affairs, 1971).
[32]Ernest Feder, "La Función Social de la Tierra y la Pobreza Rural en América Latina," Mexico City: *El Trimestre Enconómico*, enero-marzo, 1970, p. 26.

[33]W. J. Baumol, "Macroeconomics of Unbalanced Growth," *American Economic Review*, June 1967, pp. 415-426.
[34]Feder, *op. cit.*, p. 33.

funds.[35] Limitations on payments to individual farm operators for cooperation with specific farm programs might be lowered to $5,000 per person per year. Income tax laws could be tightened to prohibit losses on farm operations to be deducted from income tax returns by either individual or corporate enterprises.

Dr. Heady, one of the leaders in the agricultural economics profession in many respects, has suggested that farm operators pay "taxes in kind." This would produce several results in addition to a partial solution of the supply problem; it could reduce annual capital expenditures by farm operators.[36]

Tighter laws could be made and enforced in the operation and functioning of agricultural cooperatives. At the present time some of these are fronts for huge wealthy landowners who do not live or work on their farms. A tighter law might provide that membership in the cooperative would be limited exclusively to (a) those farmers who lived on and worked on their farms and (b) to the employees of the packing shed, cannery or whatever processing is involved in that cooperative.

If the nation does enact legislation that will provide a minimum income for a family of four, with incentives for the recipients to earn additional income without being penalized, there could be long-run advantages if the minimum so established were greater for rural area (but not suburban) than for metropolitan areas. This falls in line with the thinking of Professor Cochrane who said that the most humane and economical assistance for the 2.7 million poor rural families headed by an elderly or poorly educated individual would be to help them where they are.[37]

The intention of the original Agricultural Adjustment Act was that the services of farm income adjustment programs would be financed out of the profits of these processing firms (the "processing tax"). This designation was declared unconstitutional (although the processing tax itself was not specifically declared unconstitutional). It does not seem impossible for another legislative attempt to be made in that direction; a tax on both the profits of the producers of inputs to agriculture and the processors and sellers of agricultural products (making exception only to those products shipped abroad for export); such taxation to finance the entire program of the United States Department of Agriculture and various farm family support programs devised from time to time by Congress.

Congress could pass a law prohibiting a firm from being both a farmer and a processor of farm products or a supplier of the inputs of agriculture (exempting small milk distributors, etc., whose gross income is less than $50,000 a year). Reasons already exist for this possibility—but acceptance of the tax proposal in the preceding paragraph would make this a necessity. The economic profit-motivated incentives to diversify vertically have reached fantastic proportions; with one firm boasting in its brochures of owning seven million acres of valuable farm land; and with hatchery, feed mill, broiler raising, poultry processing plant and distribution center combinatons handling several million birds each.[38]

Perhaps, instead of incentive payments to farmers for reducing farm acreage, we should have incentive payments to encourage farmers to build comfortable housing (fully equal in every respect to the standards of low cost housing in urban centers) for permanent farm employees; and give economic incentives for granting *annual* farm employment.

Perhaps much stricter anti-pollution law enforcement will assist in a return to crop rotations and other labor-consuming activities instead of high fertilizer run-off; flushing manure into streams; and dangerous pesticide and herbicide residues.

The nation may now be ready to permit some form of licensing of farm operators,[39] farm owners, suppliers of farm inputs, and purchases of farm prod-

[35]In 1965, for example, in the Imperial District (of the great Imperial Valley of California) there were 400,000 acres of irrigated land, but fewer than 800 landowners, some of them irrigating several thousand acres each. Source: Roscoe Fleming, "Ruling on Acreage Shake California," *The Christian Science Monitor,* January 25, 1965. Recently the "Consumer Crusader," Ralph Nader has released an intensive study by one of his research teams dealing with this complex distortion of "the public's original intent, through Congress" and the pressure policy of bureaucracy with the passage of years, apathy of the general public and "power-less" leverage of the small farm workers.

[36]Earl O. Heady, "Tax in Kind to Reduce Supply and Increase Income Without Government Payments and Marketing Quotas," *American Journal of Agricultural Economics,* August 1971, pp. 441-447.

[37]Cochrane, *op. cit.,* p. 224.

[38]If this proposal sounds over-drastic, it should be looked at in a broader perspective. The author is not suggesting there is any evil exploitation by farmers of the agro-business complex. On the contrary, the author is well aware of the enormous contributions these business firms have made to the total American picture of agricultural efficiency. Nor is he suggesting that agro-business is greedy or immoral. The stock share corporation is an essential part of our free market-economy; but the search for maximization of profits is amoral—the scope and range of activities (parameters) are determined by society, as well as by profit considerations. The company-owned store and the company-owned town are historic examples of where overriding social concerns in the long run, forced discontinuance of such practices even though, from the profit-maximization standpoint, they seemed wise investments.

[39]J. R. Bellerby, *Agriculture and Industry-Relative Income* (London, England: MacMillan Co., Ltd., 1956). (Other writers have tossed this idea about but not to the extent of nearly a full chapter, as Bellerby has.)

ucts.[40] If such a program were to be initiated, it might well be patterned after the land use planning committees of the late 1930's. With our democratic traditions it is more probable that our populace will prefer a locally centered program (such as on a county basis) over a program of state or federal regulation. In such a county-committee licensing, it would seem important (from Japanese, British, and French experiences) that the following elements be equally represented: the farm owner-operator, the farm tenant, the farm laborer, the farm owner (who is not an operator), and the general consumer. Concurrently, the following elements might well be diligently excluded: suppliers of farm "inputs" and purchasers of farm products. We cannot escape one fundamental reality of our democracy: public policy has to take into consideration, and into the planning, those people who are going to be primarily affected by possible changes.[41] Concurrently it can also be said that persistent exploiters of a group should not be given leverage positions from which they can continue their exploitations.

The nation may have overly subsidized farm capital, even though our large federal land banks, for example, no longer have any government ownership involved in them: They do not have to pay any corporate income taxes; they are exempt from the various states' usury laws; and they can raise capital in in the nation's money markets because the public assumes that Uncle Sam will make good on their securities if the system ever got into trouble.[42]

In view of the great amount of capital now required to own and operate a typical American farm, it may be desirable to re-study the English landlord-tenant system under which there is no stigma attached to being a farm tenant. In England, there are instances of many farm operators' families remaining on the same farm for many generations.[43]

The time may have arrived when capital may be under used in other segments of our society, that special tax concessions on motor fuel, and special pricing privileges for electricity and water used on farms be re-studied. We are going to encounter grave shortages:

in water, in electricity, and in all sources of energy for power within our nation within the next two decades.

Somehow, rational and yet equitable arrangements must be made to raise the average income of the farm worker in the United States. The seasonal nature of farm production has made strike-threats (of the possibility of losing an entire year's production) so apparent that, until recently, farm areas have been virtually "exempted" from labor union activities. But this "excuse" of the perishability of farm products has been horribly abused. In 1968, the average median income of farm laborers (including foremen) in the United States was $1,696 a year.[44] In the same year the average farm operator (and farm manager) made $3,439 a year. In England labor laws give farm laborers 70 per cent of industrial earnings.[45] In Sweden the system of governmental support for agriculture since World War II has been so constructed that it is in the farm operator's interests to pay farm wages generously. As a result, farm income has been raised essentially to the same level as non-farm income in Sweden.[46]

One extremely timely option open to state legislative control would be a broader extension of the homestead exemption clauses in the administration of property taxes. Many fiscal authorities are suggesting that the property tax be completely eliminated. This may happen gradually but is not likely to happen immediately. A homestead exemption could be drafted that would be broad enough to cover: (1) a small (measured by all four criteria of size: acreage, total investment, self-employment and volume of sales) farm when and if no member of the family received outside employment, and (2) a rural home owned by a family which had a year around employment on a farm within a certain radius—such as five miles (as an arbitrarily set example, and not as a specific recommendation). Concurrently, the property tax could be extended to *all* of the farm assets of the larger farms, and not limited to land and buildings.

It could fall within this range of possibilities to suggest that farm operators be required to fulfill all of their labor employment needs within their own county. A phasing out of the use of migratory labor might result in some shifts of locale of agricultural production—but could certainly contribute to long-

[40]Department of Research, AFL-CIO, "The Crisis in Land Use," Robert B. Carson, ed., *The American Economy in Conflict* (Lexington, Massachusetts: D. C. Heath and Company, 1971). This article reveals the growing concern of the general public on land usage—even usage on private lands.

[41]Lynn M. Daft, "Public Policies for Rural America: Legacies or Leading Edges," *American Journal of Agricultural Economics*, May 1971, p. 255.

[42]John A. Prestbo, "The Ever-Growing Farm Credit System," *Wall Street Journal*, November 3, 1970 (editorial page).

[43]D. R. Denman, "Land Ownership and the Attraction of Capital Agriculture, A British Overview," *Land Economics*, August 1965, pp. 209-216.

[44]*Statistical Abstract, op. cit.*, 1969, p. 327.

[45]W. J. Thomas, "The Changing Structure of Agriculture's Labor Force," Proceedings of the 12th International Conference of Agricultural Economists (London: Oxford University Press, 1966), p. 307.

[46]Lars G. Sandberg, "Income and Price Policy in Swedish Agriculture since World War II," *Journal of Farm Economics*, November 1965, p. 1012.

range economic benefits to many families and to even greater social advantages to the children of these gravely disadvantaged persons involved in our total farm picture.[47]

Until our farm supply situation and our economic returns to *all* persons involved in agricultural production are considerably higher than they are at the present time, Congress should demand immediate cessation of the "dam building craze" of the Bureau of Reclamation. The Nader research team is particularly anxious to stop the 1.4 billion dollar "central Arizona project." The report issued by these investigators points out that these enormous projects of the Bureau of Reclamation (they have built 153 major dams and irrigation projects in the 17 Western States) not only have required billions of dollars to build and operate but have driven thousands of farmers out of their jobs and greatly increased the amount of money which the United States Department of Agriculture must spend to curtail surplus crop production and to support agricultural prices. These huge conflicting programs have "hit the general taxpayer—both coming and going."[48]

A foreign observer might be tempted to suggest that the United States needs some kind of land reform. The author believes that rural people do have some common interests everywhere in the world. But there is a vast difference between a nation where the major stream of income is derived from the land—which is worked by 75 to 80 per cent of the people and owned by only 2 to 10 per cent of the people—and a nation where less than 10 per cent of either the income stream or the agricultural employment is involved.

Our readjustments towards securing a better distribution of income have been to deal with incomes and not with the sources from which those incomes arise. If, at some future date, pressures build up for a more equal opportunity of obtaining shares of wealth for rural people, it will have to be part of a more comprehensive and orderly transfer from generation to generation for all citizens and not just for farm families.

SUMMARY AND CONCLUSIONS

Simplistic extension of trend lines that are indicated by projections into the future of the vastly increased application of capital in American agriculture, with a continuing large reduction in the labor force utilized in American agriculture, seems too out of line with the realities of a world shortage of capital, excessive unemployment within the United States and the now-becoming-exhausted patience of the American taxpayer to continue to directly or indirectly subsidize the fulfillment of such projections.

Strong evidences are cited as to the possibility that the trends have already been pushed too far. The resulting disequilibriums now require entirely new kinds of research by agricultural economists and general economists.[49] Entirely new approaches are needed for our national farm problem, centering on the human beings involved and not on the maximization of profits of fewer and fewer firms. The exact nature of those changes will be determined by legislators, organizations of farm workers, ecologists, conservationists, and the general public of consumers and taxpayers. But it is quite possible that these changes will fall in line with the general philosophy of a previous article by this writer: "In stark simplicity (this general rule) states that control of (and profits from) the major 'factors' of farm production: (technological advances of inputs and processing; land ownership; labor utilization, mechanization; capital, management, marketing, and governmental programs of 'assistance to rural people') ought to be allocated exclusively to the 'farm population' (owners who live on the land—and not in the big cities, tenants, laborers and supervisors) and not be permitted to 'escape' to the non-farm sector."[50]

[47]Sir Winston Churchill made an especially appropriate comment relevant to this suggestion. He was, of course, speaking of the entry of part-time workers into England from other commonwealth nations; but to this writer it applies with equal force to our local, county-level and community-level industrial and agricultural firms: "I lay down this principle in this democratic Parliament, that no man should be imported into a country as a laborer unless you also accept him as a human being." Herbert V. Prochnow, *The New Speaker's Treasury of Wit and Wisdom* (New York: Evanston: and London: Harper and Row, 1958), p. 243; over one-fourth of all the 400,000 farm workers in California are under sixteen years of age. In Skagit, Whatom and Yakima counties of Washington, over 99 per cent of migrant family children (ages 6-14) worked; Robert Coles, a child psychiatrist who has recorded interviews with migrant families and their children, points out the life of terror, of estrangement, "of being hemmed in by a hostile world—a life long memory of long painful forced marches." Excerpts from: Elain Magalis, "Child Laborers in the Fields," *The New World Outlook*, New York, November 1971, pp. 14-19.

[48]UPI Press Release "Dam Building Agency Should Halt Senseless Projects, Probers Say," *The Arkansas Gazette*, Little Rock, November 7, 1971.

[49]In particular, general economists, such as the author, who are leaving the field of "specialty of agricultural economics" because that specialty is now dominated by a fanatical "capital for labor substitution fundamentalism!"

[50]Richard G. Milk, "A General Theory of Agricultural Income for Rural People," *Indian Journal of Economics*, Allahabad, India, July 1966, pp. 13-31.

SECTION TWO

The nature, magnitude, and consequences of change in farm organizational, occupational, and class structure

Richard D. Rodefeld

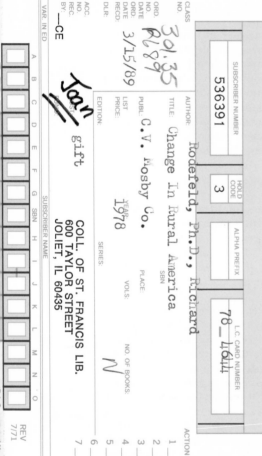

one, mechanization and other technological changes in ... a profound effect on the characteristics of farms in the ... rk force numbers have declined; while the size, value, ... e of the remaining farms have risen substantially. This ... er these changes have contributed to changes in farm ... l thus the relative positions of the major farm types. ... tructure" can embrace a variety of farm characteristics, ... t of farmland ownership, nonland resource ownership, ... dividuals and families managing farms on a daily basis. ... identified, based on the *simultaneous* levels of ownership ... nanagers: family, tenant, larger-than-family, and indus-

... rs, production, and sales have been dominated by rel-... levels of land ownership, capital ownership, and labor ... Most commonly, farms with these characteristics have ... or "family-type" farms. Family-type farms have domi-... reas, and production and sales in most. The socioeco-... orted the historical dominance of this farm type are ... oter 1) and by Raup and Rodefeld (Chapter 5).

... nt exceptions to the overall dominance of family-type ... rical period, region, and type of production. The second ... umerically is the "tenant-type." These farms are man-... ies who do most of the farm work and ordinarily own ... es. They are the same as family-type farms in these ... , since the managers own none or little of the farmland. ... her individual or family, a small group of individuals, or ... may or may not reside in the same community as the ... per) farms largely replaced Southern plantations after ... wing importance in other regions through the economic ... r reasons for the rise and decline of this farm type in the twentieth century are reviewed by Rodefeld and Hamburger (Chapter 5) and Kolb and Brunner (Chapter 6).

In contrast to the two preceding farm types, both of which are relatively small (family-sized), large-scale farms, employing large numbers of hired workers—either seasonal or full-time—have been important in both the South and West and in vegetable, fruit, cotton, and cattle-ranching areas. Hambidge (Chapter 1) and Barnes (Chapter 5) review regional differences in farm sizes and types and the major causes of these differences, including why many programs and policies intended to support family-sized farms failed in certain areas. Taylor and associates (1955), Slocum

121

(1962), and Mangus (1940) provide more detailed discussions of regional differences in farm sizes, types, and other farm characteristics.

Two types of large-scale farms can be identified. Both are "larger-than-family–sized," since hired personnel do most of the physical work. The managers of "larger-than-family–type" farms, however, own all or most of the farmland and usually own all or most of the nonland resources as well. The managers of "industrial-type" farms on the other hand own little or none of the farm land. The managers of these farms may (minority owners, renters) or may not (hired managers) own major portions of the nonland resources.

The question of whether or not major changes are occurring in the relative importance of the major farm types is important because such shifts may have consequences for other farm characteristics, farm people, rural communities, and the urban sector. A good deal of additional research is necessary, but present knowledge suggests that the consequences of farm-type change may be considerable, with implications for all sectors (Rodefeld, Chapter 5). While Chapter 6 is devoted to this subject, some of the major implications are reviewed here.

Generally, rural community change can be expected since small, family-type farms and the population they support have dominated most farm areas since initial settlement. These farms and people provided a major portion of the base from which the social and economic structure of most communities evolved. If this farm type and its work force are being replaced by different farm types and work forces, the structure and functioning of rural communities may experience major changes as well.

More specifically, changes in farm types are likely to result in farm-size changes as well. Farm type is highly related to size (acreage, sales, or both). In 1964, family-type farms had average sales of $7,000; tenant, $10,300; larger-than-family, $73,000; and industrial, $109,600. Assuming a strong relatinship between value of sales and acres operated, it is quite clear that if family-type farms are being replaced by any of the other types, the rates of farm numerical decline and rates of size expansion will be greater than if these changes were not occurring. The magnitude of the change will be greatest when either of the family-sized types (family, tenant) is replaced by larger-than-family–sized types (larger-than-family or industrial). As farm numbers decline and size increases, levels of concentration in land ownership and operation, capital ownership, production, and sales also will increase. These changes will be greater than if no changes had occurred in farm types.

Farm type is also related to the density of the farm population; that is, the number of people per square mile or acre. Generally, areas dominated by family-sized farms have much greater population densities than areas dominated by larger-than-family–sized farms. If the latter are replacing the former, the size of the farm work force and its density will decline at a more rapid rate than if changes in farm types were not occurring. If these declines are not offset by other processes, the population numbers of rural neighborhoods and communities will be reduced, and the size or number of social and economic institutions and organizations in these places will decline.

The possible magnitude of such changes can be illustrated with the results of a Wisconsin study. In 1968 the size of and farm work-force (laborer year equivalents) densities of state farms (mostly family-type farms) and a sample of industrial-type farms were determined. State farms operated an average of 101 crop acres, and each work-force member operated 60.5 crop acres. Industrial-type farms averaged 1734 crop acres, and each work-force member operated 111 crop acres. It was estimated that if all current state farms were replaced by industrial-type farms, the number of farms would be reduced by 94%, crop acres operated per farm would increase 1700%, and the size of the work force (laborer-year equivalents) would decline by 46% (Rodefeld, 1974). These are conservative estimates since industrial-type farms were disproportionately engaged in more labor-intensive types of production.

Changes in farm types will also bring about changes in farm work-force occupational composition and class structure. The work force of family-type farms is dominated by individuals and families who simultaneously occupy the positions of landowner, capital owner, manager, and laborer. On the average Wisconsin farm in 1968, hired workers accounted for only 10% of the work force. The other 90% consisted of owning managers (operators) and their families.

If family-type farms are replaced by tenant-type farms, resident owning managers and their families will be replaced by two groups: nonresident owners (of capital, land, or both) and nonlandowning managers (tenants) and their families. If family-type farms are replaced by larger-than-family–type farms, their work forces will be replaced by a relatively small number of resident owning managers and a large number of hired workers, either seasonal or full-time, depending on the type of production. If family-type farms are replaced by industrial-type farms, their work forces will be replaced by three groups: nonresident (possibly absentee) owners (capital, land, or both), a small number of hired managers, and a large number of hired workers. To illustrate the magnitude of the changes involved in either of the last two farm type changes, in 1968 a Wisconsin sample of larger-than-family–and industrial–type farms had work forces consisting of 11% managers (owning or hired) and 89% hired workers.

Changes in the occupational composition and class structure of the farm work force are significant because past research has found strong relationships between the farm positions occupied by individuals and families and their background, socioeconomic status, family structure characteristics, and degree of involvement in community institutions and organizations. For instance, in the past when landowning managers have been compared to nonowning managers (renters, tenants), the former generally have been found to have: higher residential and occupational stability, incomes, levels of living and wealth, ages, and levels of involvement in all community institutions and organizations. Similar differences generally have been reported between farm managers (owning and nonowning) and hired workers. In addition, farm managers usually had higher levels of education and smaller family sizes than hired workers.

These differences suggest that changes in farm type and the occupational composition of the farm work force will also result in changes in community compositional characteristics (such as levels of education, income, and stability), population structure and functioning (such as age distributions, fertility rates, dependency ratios, and rates of outmigration), and the structure and functioning of community institutions and organizations (such as numbers, sizes, and types of businesses, schools, churches, formal organizations, and informal groups and levels of voting and political activity).

Finally, it also has been suggested that changes in farm type may have implications extending far beyond the rural sector. If these changes result in the loss of jobs for rural farm and nonfarm people (as seems likely), rates of rural out-migration to urban areas will increase unless employment opportunities are expanded in rural areas. As in the past, this movement is likely to increase the social and economic costs for both the sending and receiving areas. If the large number of relatively small, family-type farms that presently exist are replaced by a much smaller number of large, nonfamily types, the likelihood of monopoly and collusion in the marketplace will increase. If such practices occur, food prices may be higher than if the farm type changes had not occurred. On the other hand, it is commonly assumed that larger farms would have higher levels of productivity and efficiency, which if passed on to the consumer would result in lower food prices than with smaller farms. However, the assumption of greater efficiency on these larger farms has not been observed in most areas of agricultural production. Some evidence suggests that the workers on these larger farms may have less work satisfaction and greater alienation, which might result in lower productivity and efficiency and higher food prices. It has been suggested that concentration in land ownership may result in reduced accessibility for nonfarm people to land for ownership or recreation. It has also been charged that large, absentee-owned farms may be more ecologically destructive than smaller "family" farms.

5 The nature and magnitude of changes in farm organizational, occupational, and class structures

The major concern in recent debate over change in farm types is whether the family-type farm is declining relative to other farm types, in particular to industrial-type farms owned by large, nonfarm corporations. The latter have commonly been referred to as "corporate" farms.

Two markedly different positions have emerged in this debate. The first is that while farm numbers have declined and average farm sizes have increased greatly in recent decades, the relative position of "family" farms has not changed. Individuals and families managing farms on a daily basis continue to own most of the land and capital associated with farm production and still provide the majority of farm labor. These levels have not declined. Farm numbers and sales continue to be dominated by owner-managed and/or family-sized farms, and no changes have occurred in their relative positions. Differences exist between regions, but these are of long standing. It is pointed out that corporate farms, particularly those owned by large nonfarm corporations (one type of industrial farm) account for very small percentages of U.S. farm numbers, land, and sales and may have declined in recent years (Rodefeld). This has been the dominant position in policy-making circles, at least at the federal level, to date. The diversity of support for this position is indicated in the reading entitled "Selected Quotations—Family Farms are Dominant. . . ." In another article Cordtz reviews the widespread failure of large corporate farms in recent years and the major reasons for their failure.

The second assessment is that while family farms have dominated U.S. farm numbers and sales historically, they are rapidly being replaced by corporate farms. The major evidence given for this position is the continuing decline in farm numbers, the increased size of those remaining, and the widely reported entrance of large nonfarm corporations into agricultural production. Numerous opinion polls show that most farmers and many nonfarmers believe corporate farms are replacing family farms (Rodefeld). While this position has not dominated to date, it has received support from a variety of sources, including most of the major farm organizations ("Selected Quotations—Family Farms Are Declining . . ."). A number of articles are included that are consistent with this position. Robbins describes the development of an immense 380,000-acre industrial-type farm in North Carolina. Hamburger reports a large increase in the purchase of Arkansas farmland by non–U.S. citizens and reviews some of the reasons for this movement. The growing involvement of corporations in agriculture through vertical integration, and production and market control are described by Hightower.

Rodefeld points out that there are numerous reasons for predicting that family-type farms will decline relative to other farm types (tenant, larger-than-family, and industrial). A conceptual basis for this argument is presented. The general argument is that major changes have occurred in the historical conditions that have supported the dominance of family-type farms. Evidence is reported supporting the predicted changes in almost all respects. Levels of land ownership, capital ownership, and labor provision by farm managers have declined. Farms with high levels of land ownership by their managers, capital ownership by their managers, and labor provided by their managers have declined in each instance relative to farms with low levels of each of these dimensions. Small-scale farms have declined relative to large-scale farms. Both family- and tenant-type farms have declined relative to larger-than-family–and industrial-type farms.

In a more abstract sense, levels of structural differentiation between land ownership, capital ownership, management, and labor have increased. Farms with low levels of differentiation on all these structural dimensions are declining relative to those with high levels on one or more of these dimensions.

6 The significance of farm organizational structure and the consequences of its change

There seems to be little doubt that major structural changes, including the decline of the family-type farm, have occurred. The conditions responsible for these changes (Rodefeld, Chapter 5, and Section three) seem likely to persist. The status of the family-type farm will decline further as the provision of land and capital, management, and labor functions become more highly differentiated within the organizational structure of agriculture. This raises the question of what the consequences of these changes will be for other farm characteristics, farm people, rural communities, and the urban sector. While this question has already been addressed in a general sense, it is discussed in greater detail by readings included in Chapters 5, 6, and 11.

Both Raup and Barnes (Chapter 5) discuss the significance of farm types and sizes and the implications of their changes. While Raup expresses uncertainty about whether major farm-type changes are occurring, he discusses the implications of such changes for the farm, rural, and urban sectors. Barnes states a number of reasons why urban residents should be concerned with farm landholding patterns and reviews some of the major consequences of large landholdings.

Stinchcombe reports the results of a cross-cultural review of the relationships between types of agricultural enterprises and property systems (farm types and occupational structure) and the patterns of class relations and class characteristics in rural social life. Five major types of farms or systems are identified: manorial or hacienda, family-sized tenancy, family small-holding, plantation, and capital-extensive–wage-labor ranch. The legal privileges, life-style, technical knowledge, and political and organizational characteristics of individuals occupying ownership, managerial, and laboring positions on these farms are described.

While the manorial system is not highly relevant, all of the remaining types have structural counterparts in the United States; that is family-sized tenancy is equivalent to tenant-type farms; family small-holding farms to family-type; plantation and ranch to larger-than-family–and industrial-type. Major differences are observed between each of the types or systems. These differences provide one basis for predicting the consequences that would result from the replacement of family-type farms with other types.

Three articles have been included dealing specifically with tenant-type farms and tenancy in the United States. In a 1936 article, Kennedy compares the income, diet, clothes, housing, and privileges of a plantation owner's family with that of tenants (sharecroppers) on the farm. Whether this was an actual case study or consisted of fictional characters is not known. Kolb and Brunner review the major reasons for the increase in tenant-type farms up to the 1930's, major differences between tenants and owning managers, the consequences of these differences for rural communities, the characteristics of farmland ownership in 1946, and measures to strengthen family-type farms. The Hamburger articles, here and in Chapter 2, describe the transformation of one of the largest family-owned plantations in the South from a large number of small tenant-type (sharecropper) farms to a reconsolidated, extremely large, family-owned, industrial-type farm. Efforts of the landowning family to improve the quality of life for those remaining in the community are described.

The articles on tenant-type farms were included for three reasons: first, to gain a better understanding of an earlier time, when farms of this type were more important, and, second, to provide one example of how this pattern has been transformed in the South in recent years. The third reason is because some of the major structural changes occurring presently are a decline in land ownership by farm managers, a decline in farms with high levels of land ownership by their managers, and a rise in the status of farms with low levels of land ownership by their managers. Even though the specific types of tenant farms increasing in recent decades (majority rented, all rented) are not the same as those that dominated in the past (crop-share, livestock-share, cash-share) and have much larger sizes than previously, the general characteristics of tenant-type farms and those who manage them may still be similar. At the very least, earlier research provides a set of hypotheses for the major consequences of replacing family-type with tenant-type farms in the future. Two of the best comparative studies of family- and tenant-type farms and their work forces were carried out by Schuler (1938a,b) and Charlton (1947). A recent review and summary of research in this area was done by Rodefeld (1974).

The remaining articles in this chapter address the questions of what the consequences might be if larger-than-family–sized (larger-than-family–or industrial-type) farms replace family-type farms in the future. Two articles have been included that speak in defense of the trend toward larger-than-family–sized farms. The Chamber of Commerce has opposed legislation that would exclude large, non-farm corporations from farming. Their opposition is based partly on the belief that such farms are more efficient than smaller-sized farms. It should be kept in mind while reading this article that it is second-hand and from a supporter of restrictive legislation *(NFO Reporter)*. Seckler argues that large, industrial-type farms can achieve significant economies of scale, are not likely to ever be pervasive in number or total significance, and are likely to have a number of major, positive consequences for the farm work force and rural communities. It is a brief, but thought-provoking article.

McDonald summarizes a U.S. Department of Agriculture review of economies of scale in farming (Madden, 1967). Frequently alluded to in the literature, this study showed that in most areas of production well-managed one-and two-operator farms had levels of efficiency comparable to larger-sized farms.

The article from the *Cooperative Builder* reports on work by Philip Raup that indicates a replacement of family-type farms by larger-than-family–sized types will have a number of undesirable consequences for rural communities. These include the possibility of higher relative food prives, nationally, resulting from increased concentration in the food industry. In addition they may drive up the costs of using land for purposes other than food production.

The article by Goldschmidt summarizes a classic study in rural sociology. In 1944, Goldschmidt studied two Califorña, rural communities, located in the same general area and similar in sizes and economies. The farm sector of one community, however, was dominated by larger-than-family–sized farms, many of which were owned by nonresidents (industrial-type). In the other community, smaller, family-sized farms dominated the farm sector, most having resident owning managers (family-type). The two communities were compared on a wide variety of population, economic, social, institutional and organizational characteristics. The major results from this study, showing dramatic differences between the two communities, are reported in this brief article. The reader should note, however, the study was carried out 30 years ago and may not apply to other regions and types of production, particularly those requiring full-time, year-round workers. However, the study does suggest a series of concrete hypotheses on differences between rural communities dominated by family-type or larger-than-family–sized farm types and what changes might be expected in changing from the former to the latter.

Bible's article is a summary of testimony presented at hearings held in by the U.S. Senate Select Committee on Small Business. The possible consequences of family-type farm decline and industrial-type farm growth for soil and water resources, local services and businesses, land prices and availability, social and moral structure, and market structure are discussed. The role of federal programs and policies in bringing about farm-type changes is reviewed, and suggested remedies are listed. One of the major problems identified is the lack of strong, empirical data on the kinds and magnitude of consequences that would result from family-type farm decline and "corporate" or industrial-type farm growth.

Very little information exists on the consequences of decreased capital ownership by farm managers, including whether this occurs as a result of farmer involvement in production, marketing contracts with agribusiness corporations (vertical integration), or both.

Conclusion

In summary, it appears major changes are occurring in the organizational structure of farms. In addition to decreased farm numbers and increased farm sizes, levels of land ownership, capital ownership, and labor provided by farm managers have declined. Family-type farms are declining relative to other types, particularly larger-than-family and industrial. From current knowledge a continuation of these changes suggests major consequences for other farm characteristics, the composition and characteristics of the farm work force, rural communities, the urban sector, and society as a whole. As pointed out earlier, however, little contemporary research has been carried out relevant to the question of farm-type change and its consequences. Two exceptions are those studies reported by Heffernan (1972) and Rodefeld (1974). Research in this area should have a high priority for social scientists.

The major forces and conditions bringing about these changes in farm organizational structure and type are addressed primarily in Chapter 7 and Section three. Alternatives to changes occurring in farm types are discussed primarily in Section five, Chapter 11.

Additional articles relevant to the question of farm-type change and its consequences have been included in Chapters 5, 7, and 11. Chapter 11, for instance, contains articles dealing with small farms, subsistence farms, organic farms, tenant-type and/or minority operated farms, and hired farm workers. A number of other excellent articles or books have not been included in this text because they are readily and inexpensively obtained. These include Barnes and Casalino (undated, approximately 1972), Barnes (1973), Ray (1969), Lerza and Jacobson (1975), Guither (1972), and Guither (1973). The two publications edited by Guither are entitled "Who Will Control U.S. Agriculture?" The first (1972) reviews trends underway, the major causes and likely consequences of their continuation. The second (1973) is a series of six articles which examine four major alternatives to family-type farms (referred to as a dispersed, open market agriculture). These alternatives are: a corporate agriculture, a cooperative agriculture, a government-administered agriculture, and a combination. The major implications of a change toward each of these alternatives is reviewed.

While no separate section has been included on the characteristics of different occupational or status groups in farming, a number of articles in the volume address this topic. Included are articles dealing with tenants, sharecroppers, black farmers, Chicano farmers, hired farm laborers, subsistence farmers, low-resource or small-scale farmers, and part-time farmers. Other readings available in this area include Rushing (1972) and Marshall and Thompson (1976). For more detailed discussions of farm occupational groups and class structure the reader is referred to Gross (1958), Smith (1969), and Rodefeld (1974).

Not all elements of farm organizational, occupational, and class structure nor major changes occurring in the farm sector have been addressed in this volume. The magnitude of consequences associated with various changes for all sectors of society, the availability of material or appropriate material, and the values of the editors all played a role in these decisions. Examples of topics that merit a good deal more attention and discussion are the trends, causes, consequences, and/or problems of: declining managerial independence (Harris, 1969); increasing levels of specialization between regions and states and within states; an apparent trend toward more extended family operations; the changing statuses and roles of men, women, and children in farming (Joyce, 1976); regional shifts and changes in types of production; large scale irrigation and reclamation projects; loss of water for irrigation; increased part-time farms and farmers; and the problems of small-scale and minority farms and farmers.

REFERENCES

Barnes, P.: The sharing of land and resources in America, Harrison-Blaine of New Jersey, Inc., 1973.

Barnes, Peter, and Casalino, Larry: Who owns the land? A primer on land reform in the U.S.A., Berkeley, 1972, Center for Rural Studies.

Charlton, J. L.: Social aspects of farm ownership and tenancy in the Arkansas Coastal Plain, Agricultural Experiment Station Bulletin 545, Fayetteville, Ark. June 1954, University of Arkansas.

Gross, E.: Work and society, New York, 1958, Thomas Y. Crowell Co.

Guither, H. D.: Who will control U.S. agriculture? In North Central Regional Extension Publication 32, Cooperative Extension, Urbana, Ill., 1972, University of Illinois.

Guither, H. D.: Who will control U.S. agriculture? A series of six leaflets, In North Central Regional Extension Publication 32-1, Urbana, Ill., 1973, University of Illinois.

Harris, Marshall: Intergeneration transfer of farm wealth. In Brake, J. R., editor: Emerging and projected trends likely to influence the structure of midwest agriculture, 1970-1985, Monograph No. 11, Iowa City, Iowa, June 1970, University of Iowa Agricultural Law Center.

Heffernan, W.: Sociological dimensions of agricultural structures in the United States, Sociologia Ruralis **12**(3/4):481-499, 1972.

Joyce, L.: Annotated bibliography of women in rural America, AE-RS 125, University Park, Pa., 1976, Pennsylvania State University.

Lerza, C., and Jacobson M., editors: Food for people not for profit, New York, 1975, Ballatine Books, Inc.

Madden, J. Patrick: Economies of size in farming, USDA-ERS Agricultural Economic Report No. 107, Washington, D.C., 1967.

Mangus, A. R.: Rural regions of the United States, Washington, D.C., 1940, Work Projects Administration.

Marshall, R., and Thompson, A.: Status and prospects of small farmers in the South, Atlanta, 1976, Southern Regional Council, Inc.

Ray, V. K.: The corporate invasion of American agriculture, Denver, 1968, National Farmers Union.

Rodefeld, R. D.: The changing occupational and organizational structure of farming and the implications for farm work force individuals, families and communities, Unpublished Ph.D. dissertation, Madison, Wisconsin, May 1974, University of Wisconsin.

Rushing, William A.: Class, culture and alienation: a study of farmers and farm workers, Lexington, Mass., 1972, D. C. Heath & Co.

Schuler, E. A.: Social status and farm tenure—attitudes and social conditions of corn belt and cotton belt farmers, Social Research Report No. 4, Washington, D.C., Apr. 1938a, U.S. Department of Agriculture.

Schuler, E. A.: The present social status of American farm tenants, Rural Sociology **3**:20-33, Mar. 1938b.

Slocum, Walter L.: Agricultural sociology, New York, 1962, Harper & Row, Publishers.

Smith, T. Lynn: A study of social stratification in the agricultural sections of the United States: nature, data, procedures and preliminary results, Rural Sociology **34**:496-509, 1969.

Taylor, Carl C., and others: Rural life in the United States, New York, 1949, Alfred A. Knopf, Inc., pp. 239-494.

Wellford, Harrison: Poultry peonage, Sowing the wind, New York, 1972, Grossman Publishers.

5

The nature and magnitude of changes in farm organizational, occupational, and class structures

Societal goals in farm size

PHILIP M. RAUP*

To the anthropologist how land is held, the size units, and the control structures that generate decisions over land use are major definitional characteristics of a social or economic group [14, 16, 18]. We accept this without question in the study of primitive societies. Questions of land tenure and farm size are central to the study of developing economies in intermediate stages of evolution from agrarian to industrial societies. There is less agreement on the significance of these questions for advanced industrial societies.

History is rich with examples of industrial nations that have constructed major policies around an implicit or explicit model of what was believed to be a desirable structure of farm sizes. The massive creation of large collective and state farms in the Soviet Union after 1928 both altered and defined the nature of the Soviet interpretation of socialism. The collective farm became the single most important symbol of the Soviet system. This is no less true of the kibbutz in Israel. In Western Europe after 1956, negotiations creating the European Economic Community revolved around agricultural policies that were dominated by a concern for their impact on the structure of farm sizes and types [1]. The farm size question, in short, does not disappear with the decline of agriculture and the dominance of industrial society. The purpose of this chapter is to explore the evolution and current dimensions of this question in the United States and to attempt some projections of probable future trends.

☐ From Ball, A. G., and Heady, E. O., editors: Size, Structure, and Future of Farms, Ames, Iowa, 1972 Iowa State University Press, pp. 31-38.

*Philip M. Raup is Professor of Agricultural Economics, Department of Agricultural and Applied Economics, University of Minnesota.

HISTORICAL ROOTS OF AMERICAN POLICY SUPPORTING SMALL FARMS

The roots of conflict over the appropriate structure of farm sizes go deep into the colonial history of North America. Settlement companies of "gentlemen adventurers" sought and received the assurance of large-scale grants from the British Crown. Puritan colonists carved out individual clearings and tenaciously insisted on a structure of small private plots, matching their convictions regarding the proper forms for civil and religious governance. To the squatters who pushed westward ahead of settlement, it was abundantly clear that title to land in this wild continent had to be earned and defended, in the most fundamental senses of the terms, by the sacrifices and hazards of pioneering. These conflicting attitudes toward the proper mode of settlement were distilled in the constitutional debates that preceded 1789. By the time the new constitution was sent to the several states for ratification, the die was cast. The new country was to be a nation of small farms.

The decisive steps were taken with the adoption in 1784 and 1785 of two ordinances by the Continental Congress. The Ordinance of 1784 (later replaced and expanded by the Northwest Ordinance of 1787) provided for the creation of new states in the territories lying west of New York, Pennsylvania, and Virginia. The Ordinance of 1785, for which a committee chaired by Thomas Jefferson had prepared the first draft, established a procedure for the survey of these lands ahead of settlement into square-mile lots and six-mile-square townships. The land was to be sold in alternate lots of whole townships and square-mile sections. A subsequent land act of 1800 ordered that lots of 320 acres should be surveyed and offered for sale; in

1805 this was altered to provide for the sale of 160-acre tracts; 80-acre tracts were authorized by a land act in 1820; and in 1832 the federal surveyor was authorized to lay out quarter-quarter sections, or 40-acre tracts, preparatory to sale. At the then prevailing price of $1.25 per acre, the public lands were thus brought within the price range of virtually all prospective settlers. [23].

Although debate over farm-size policy was continuous from the creation of the Union until enactment of the Homestead Act in 1862, it is clear in retrospect that a serious question never existed about the outcome. The pace of westward expansion was too rapid, government on the frontier was too weak, and the endowment of desirable land too great to permit its enclosure and concentration in large units and few hands. Inexorable though these forces may have been, they were given direction and institutional form by men who had clear ideas of what they wanted and had specific goals in view. While many men could claim roles as architects of U.S. land policy, the name of Thomas Jefferson dominates this policy field decisively. No account of the evolution of American policy toward farm size is complete without an examination of the goals he set.

For Jefferson and the men of the eighteenth century who championed small farms the reasons were largely political and (as we would recognize today) sociological: freedom, independence, self-reliance, ability to resist oppressors—these were the qualities of the small property-owning farmers and husbandmen that most impressed Jefferson [17]. And the right to own property, especially land, was central to the argument. To Jefferson, John Adams, and many others the key issue was the right to occupy and thus acquire vacant land, without thereby acknowledging any claims of superior tenure by the British Crown [10]. The right to land, in that day, was the right to a job. Freedom to enter upon land was crucial to an exercise of occupational choice. From the beginning those architects of American land policy who supported small farms rested their support on two beliefs: they were the seedbed of independence and democracy and they defined the relevant full-employment policy of the day.

The second argument was not stated in those terms. Jefferson was many things, but he was not an economist. Although well acquainted with the physiocrats from his residence in France from 1784 to 1789, he was largely untouched by their economic arguments. He explicitly rejected their faith in large-scale estate farming. "Agriculture, to him, was not primarily a source of wealth but of human virtues and traits most congenial to popular self-government. It had a sociological rather than an economic value. This

is the dominant note in all his writings on the subject" [17]. Yet in spite of his preoccupation with political and social dimensions of land policy, employment policy clearly was a key part of his concern. His letter to James Madison from Paris in 1785 is explicit: "The earth is given as a common stock for man to labour and live on. If for the encouragement of industry we allow it to be appropriated, we must take care that other employment be provided to those excluded from the appropriation. If we do not the fundamental right to labour the earth returns to the unemployed" [19]. Freedom of entry to land and thus to employment was therefore a cornerstone of historic American policy toward the small or family farm.

It remained for the liberal economists of the nineteenth century to add a third argument in support of numerous small farms: they guaranteed the competitive structure of the economy. In the classical tradition reaching from Adam Smith through David Ricardo to John Stuart Mill, this argument gained steadily in strength. Belief in an open, competitive economy guided by market forces called for a model that in reality could be subjected to empirical test. Agriculture provided this, and nineteenth century American agriculture provided it best of all. Industry could be plagued with monopoly, cartels, tariffs, and concentration. If agriculture remained open, competitive, and characterized by numerous small firms, this was a sufficient reference base to give reality to the myth of a competitive economy.

In the nineteenth century it was no myth. The Preemption Act of 1841 validated what had become a standard frontier practice. The settler was given the right to choose his tract of land ahead of sale and even before survey and was given a preclusive right to buy 160 acres at $1.25 per acre when the lands were subsequently offered for sale. The final step was taken with the Homestead Act of 1862, which gave him 160 acres outright if he would settle on it for five years and improve it. Earlier land laws had been preoccupied with the establishment of the minimum size of units in which lands would be surveyed and offered for sale. The Preemption and Homestead acts in effect set upper limits to the transaction unit in land, favoring the farmer and discouraging the speculator [13].

A policy in support of small farms has thus been central to three of the functional beliefs on which American society has been erected: self-governing democracy, freedom of occupational choice, and competitive markets as guides to economic behavior. It is clear why a threat to the structure of comparatively small, family-sized farms evokes concerns that reach far beyond agriculture. A society can function as democratic, open, and competitive if its members believe that it is all these things. When belief is shaken, functional reality is put to a severe test. It is not true that American society is undemocratic, closed, and noncompetitive. But trends in the structure of agriculture are making it imperative that traditional beliefs find new reenforcement. Lacking this, any growth of concentration in agriculture, decline in family-type farms, or increasing restrictions on freedom of entry have symbolic impacts far greater than can be measured by food bills, export accounts, or fractions of the gross national product.

A concern with increasing size and declining numbers of farms is one dimension of society's interest in the agricultural structure. A second dimension relates to the nature of arm landowners. Who owns the land is in some situations a more important question than in what size of units it is held. This has been dramatized by the growth of corporation farming. The chapters to follow will explore this question in more detail. Here it is important to note one of the major reasons why the expansion of farming corporations gives rise to a concern that is much more than agricultural.

A major feature of early American land policy was abolition of primogeniture and entail. Jefferson had this goal firmly in mind in early drafts of what became the Ordinance of 1787, which provided that newly settled lands in the Northwest Territories would be held in fee simple tenure; could be leased, sold, and bequeathed by will; and would pass "in equal parts" to the heirs of an owner leaving no will. A decade earlier he had succeeded in writing a repeal of primogeniture and entail into the Virginia constitution in words that were to serve as models for drafters of constitutions for other states. Article 15 of the constitution of the state of Minnesota, for example, reads as follows: "Sec. 15—All lands within the state are declared to be allodial, and feudal tenures of every description, with all their incidents, are prohibited. Leases and grants of agricultural lands for a longer period than twenty-one years hereafter made, in which shall be reserved any rent or service of any kind, shall be void."

The significance of the corporation farm in this context is that it threatens a reversal of the abolition of entail. A corporation has no mortal life. Its life-span is indeterminate. Conditions attaching to its possession of land are not necessarily terminated by death of any of the owners or officers. A corporate farm could remain intact through generation after generation. Although its ownership structure may increase in complexity and diffuseness, its operating structure need not. This is not the case with ownership of land by individuals. Death of the owner precipitates a change in management, terminating any restrictions on the use or disposition of land that were internal to the

firm. Death of corporate owners does not have this result.

In the expansion of corporation farming, the most important long-run consequences concern management. As the *London Economist* has pointed out, in the modern corporate world "the only way to get rid of bad managers which is currently accepted is to take them over. A board of directors is almost never, in this country at least [England], sacked by its shareholders. Why not? Because the institutional investors, the only people who could change the current system, take the view that they cannot show more than passive disapproval by selling a company's shares (and there are often limits on doing this)" [8].

The indefinite life of a corporation, in other words, can become one of its handicaps. Death does not force a change of management, as it does in a proprietary firm. As long as corporate firms are small and numerous enough to preserve a realistic element of competition, this serves to keep management vital; and the possibility of failure provides a device for the elimination of incompetence. If firms are able to avoid competition or are big enough to smother it, there are few ways to remove incompetent or moribund management. When concentration reaches a certain level, the threat of take-over by a conglomerate thus becomes almost the only device that can insure managerial vitality. But this insurance can only be purchased by the threat of still further concentration.

The structure of American agriculture has not yet reached a point where these potentials become reality. In spite of drastic changes in crops and livestock products produced, markets served, and geographic location of production, there has been a remarkable constancy in the pattern of size distribution of American farms over the past century. The concept of a "large farm" has changed, and 40-acre commercial farms have virtually disappeared, but the proportion of farms smaller than one-half average size or larger than twice average size has changed very little [5].

This constancy has also characterized the fractions of total value of farm products sold that have been contributed by family-type farms since World War II. Family farms were 95 percent of all farms in 1949, 1959, and 1964 and accounted for 63, 69, and 64 percent of the value of farm products sold in each of those years [22]. This pattern may not be repeated when the data from the 1969 Census of Agriculture become available. Massive changes in the 1960s have altered the distribution of farm sizes in Florida, California, Arizona, and some of the southern and mountain states. Approximately one-third of the agriculturally used land in Florida in 1968 was in corporation farms [27]. The comparable figure for Utah was 28 percent and 22 percent for Nevada, and the range was from 12 to 17 percent for the Mountain states and California. Corporate farms in California in 1968 accounted for 83 percent of the acreage in melons, 60 percent of lettuce acreage, 34 percent of the cotton, and 27 percent of the acres in citrus. Over 41 percent of the fed cattle sold were from corporate feedlots [21].

These levels of concentration are not always associated with farming corporations. Many of the largest farms are operated as partnerships, limited partnerships, or sole proprietorships. But the degree of concentration is great enough and the trend strong enough to raise doubts about the continuing competitive structure of American agriculture.

In its extreme version the small-farm ethos of agricultural society was unrealistic even in Jefferson's day, and he was political realist enough to sense this. But it retained elements of both symbolic and functional vitality throughout the nineteenth and early twentieth centuries and until after World War II. The symbolic dimension has been severely shaken in the past 25 years, and that accounts for one element of societal interest in the structure and size of farms.

EFFICIENCY IN RESOURCE ALLOCATION AS A SOCIETAL GOAL FOR FARM SIZE

If societal goals for farm size structure are defined in explicit economic terms, a most important criterion in the past has been to ensure optimum efficiency in the use of resources in food and fiber production. It is increasingly apparent that, in the spectrum of societal goals, efficiency in resource use is diminishing in discriminating power as a guide to a desirable structure of agriculture.

An instructive parallel can be drawn from the field of forestry. As long as timber (or fiber) was the desired product of forest management, the goal of the forest manager was clear and single valued: maximize the cubic feet of new growth per acre per year, subject to relevant cost constraints and estimates of demand elasticities. Given the increasing importance of forest management for recreational purposes, for watershed protection in conjunction with game management programs, and for visual consumption as greenbelts or landscapes, the success criteria for managers become much more complex. Maximum growth of new wood per acre per year may be a poor guide to success or may even defeat the new purposes of forest management. The optimum size of a forest management unit may thus be quite different when forest valuations rest increasingly on recreational and related uses.

A similar trend is emerging in agriculture. The values of rural sites for nonfarm use and of well-tended open space are increasing faster than our ability to devise changes in our institutions to enable a proper evaluation of benefits and a proper assignment of costs. The optimum size of farm is thus a decreasing function of efficiency measured in terms of costs, returns, and resource allocation within the farm firm. Optimum size, of course, never was exclusively a function of allocative efficiency, narrowly defined. But when food costs absorbed one-half to one-third of total consumption efforts or expenditure (a situation that prevailed in the United States from the mid-nineteenth century to World War I), any increase in allocative efficiency within the food-producing firm was a relevant goal and led to significant increases in real income.

The situation in 1970 was fundamentally changed. Food expenditures were estimated at only 16.5 percent of disposable personal income and expenditures on foods produced on U.S. farms at less than 15 percent [33]. The farmers' share of consumer expenditures on food in 1968-69 was approximately 40 percent, or less than 6 percent of disposable personal income [32]. A decrease in farm receipts from the sale of food products in the United States of approximately 18 percent would be required to make one percentage point difference in the amount of disposable personal income spent on food in 1970. Between 1947 and 1958 the value added in on-farm production of crop and livestock products dropped from 29 percent of total civilian expenditures on food to 18 percent [12]. Measured as a percentage of the gross national product, value added on farms in the production of food is currently estimated at less than 1 percent. These are among the reasons why society's interest in the size-of-farm question has less to do with costs of production or allocative efficiency and more to do with intangible values, including distributive equity, community structure, population distribution, and rural amenities.

These are the considerations that led Dovring to conclude: "Precisely because the choices no longer hinge on compelling economic reasons, there is an increasing risk that they may be made for apparent ones. For instance, those who go on advocating 'factories in the fields' might carry the day not because they are right but because they are believed. The leeway for propaganda is in fact widening with the options" [6].

FARM SIZE AND THE INFORMATION REVOLUTION

One of the critical requirements of modern society is valid and timely data, and it weighs heavily on small businesses, including farming. In the same way that complex export and import regulations discourage small firms from entering foreign trade, the growing complexity of taxation, data collection, and welfare systems have an inhibiting effect on family businesses. The requirement that forms must be filled out, specified records kept, or data supplied is an added fixed cost to the small firm. If the volume of business is too low to permit labor specialization in accounting and record keeping, the burden of this type of fixed cost can be heavy. The increasing importance of credit in farming has also required more complex farm records. Up to a point these record-keeping requirements can be beneficial to the small firm. There is little doubt that the gradual inclusion of the farming population in the ranks of income tax payers from the thirties to the seventies has improved the quality of farm record keeping. But this is not an unconstrained benefit. The growing significance of tax policy in guiding management decisions has undoubtedly had a differentially heavy impact on businesses large enough to have significant tax obligations but too small to justify the employment of top quality professional advice in this field.

The basic problem arises from the fact that information is not equally available. The firm or individual with a volume of business large enough to justify the employment of a full-time tax consultant or the hiring of expensive part-time services has a differential advantage. Rural banks, the Farm Credit Administration, the Cooperative Agricultural Extension Service, and some input suppliers or marketing firms have attempted to supply these services. The effort is only partially successful, and the services are available primarily to the larger farmers. Smaller farms are typically at a disadvantage in accommodating to the data and information revolution.

The significance of the impact of this data revolution on size and structure of business firms is not fully appreciated. Berle[2], Drucker[7], Warner[34], Shonfield[29], Galbraith[11], Servan-Schreiber[28], and others have stressed the fact that power in the modern business firm rests with the managers. Galbraith's argument is perhaps the most inclusive because he sets it squarely in a social focus and looks beyond immediate economic consequences. Over the past two centuries, he points out, the locus of power has always rested with those who could control the scarcest critical resources. This has shifted successively from land to capital to people. Capacity to generate talent gives power to universities and to technical training institutions. Capacity to organize this talent gives power to the state in socialist systems, to the military in dictatorships, and to what Galbraith has labeled the "Technostructure" in capitalist economies. This provides a new orthodoxy in analyzing the consequences of firm size for society. A "good" size of firm is big enough to make effective use, not of land, not of

capital, but of a critical mass of highly skilled people.

But this argument needs to be carried a step further. The capacity of managers to manage, and of the technostructure to mobilize talent rests on ability to command data. Information becomes the critical resource, and ability to yield or withhold data defines the locus of power. This provides an additional criterion for appraising societal interests in the size of farm. Does the farm size structure interfere with data flows? Are firms achieving a size and command of markets that enable them to avoid or ignore the interests of the state in publicly available statistics?

Two corporations, Purex and United Fruit, controlled 34 percent of the production of green leafy vegetables in the United States in 1970 [15]. Expansion plans are expected to raise this to 40 percent by 1974. Concentration on this scale dramatizes the warning voiced by the administrator of the Statistical Reporting Service of the U.S. Department of Agriculture in 1968 when he asked "who can or will furnish reliable data on integrated farming operations, what can be reported as a valid price received by a 'farmer' enveloped in an integrated enterprise . . ." [31]?

The public interest in data may be one of the ultimate tests of the performance of farms of various size. They may produce cheaply, they may market efficiently, they may meet all tests imposed upon socially responsible employers; but if they monopolize data, they defeat the public interest. And the structure that insures a flow of valid data is clearly to be preferred.

NONFARM RURAL LAND USERS AND THE STRUCTURE OF FARM SIZES

Some uses of rural land by nonfarm people are a by-product of the gradual dismantling of the agricultural structure and are almost surely transitional. Rural residences, second homes, hobby farms, and vacation cabins have been established in many areas where agriculture is on the way out but where there is still an available residual population generated by previous agricultural activities. This labor supply provides household service personnel, handymen, winter caretakers for summer homes, herdsmen for livestock, caretakers for riding horses, local farmers who will "field-rent" crop or pastureland, woodcutters who will deliver a supply of firewood, and a host of others. Types of rural land use by nonfarm people have been constructed on this labor base in New England, the Lake states, Appalachia (especially in the weekend commuting areas of New York, Washington, Baltimore, and Philadelphia), the Ozarks, and in less geographically defined areas around almost all our major urban centers. Many of these nonfarm rural land users are the unacknowledged beneficiaries of what once were communities of small family-type farms. Their patterns of use are built, as it were, out of the wreckage of once viable rural institutional and demographic structures.

In the "second home" trade a common observation is that the city man who buys a charming old farm is probably buying decades of deferred maintenance. This applies to more than the physical structures. These communities are in decay, although they may still provide a residual labor supply and levels of services that would be intolerable in cities but add quaintness and color to the rural scene.

Many nonfarm people have thus developed a dependency on a disappearing structure of farm sizes. The costs of their second homes, hobby farms, or cabins on the lake are understated. Any farming that survives in these areas will almost surely not reproduce the labor supply, the wage rates, or the community structures that now prevail. It remains to be seen whether or not urban-based users of these lands will be willing to pay the full costs of their present use patterns. Farmers who remain in recreational areas become in effect unpaid landscape gardeners for the tourist trade. They are unlikely to continue this role. The precipitate decline of agriculture in many areas has created transitional patterns of land use and capital values that rest on infirm foundations. In this sense, nonfarm users of rural lands become residual legatees of the agricultural estate. If they have an interest in maintaining a balance in these communities that will preserve the rural values they thought they were buying, it will require more effort and more money than they have been willing to invest in the past.

This too is the sense in which nonfarm people can be said to have an interest in the structure of farm sizes that is not measured by their food bill. A food and fiber supply is still the basic product of our agricultural plant. But in terms of relative income elasticities of demand, it is clear that the role of agricultural communities as a support base for recreational and rural residential land uses is one of the most active growth sectors. And a corollary is that the concern of the larger society with the structure of farm sizes is progressively less dependent on variations in the cost of food and increasingly focused on the consequences for community structure.

CHANGING FARM SIZE AND THE QUALITY OF LIFE IN SMALLER CITIES AND TOWNS

Why are people concerned about big farms, business concentration, or more recently, conglomerates? One reason is that loss of business headquarters may impair the quality of life and variety of available services (both public and private) in cities and towns. Over the years 1935-70 there has been a migration of business headquarters from Main Street to Wall Street that can be detected at many levels: from small town to county seat, from county seat to regional center to metropolitan area, and from metropolitan area to major financial center.

The transfer of business or corporate headquarters generates the greatest concern when metropolitan area centers lose headquarters to major financial capitals; i.e., when the "big boys" begin to fear the "giants" [25]. Although loss of business headquarters is a serious problem for large cities, it may be fatal for small towns. This process is well advanced in rural America. An increasing number of rural towns find themselves left with few decision makers who have power to affect the life of the community in significant ways. The local bank (if there is one) is affiliated with a county seat or regional center bank. Key credit decisions are made at "headquarters." The local merchant is increasingly a franchise holder with a sharply restricted area of managerial decision making. Local suppliers of farm inputs are typically plant managers for regional chains. Even in communities where farm commodity marketing is handled through local cooperatives, these are typically linked in a federated structure that must of necessity concentrate key decisions "up the line." As a result, those rural communities that have not emerged as growth poles in the process of business concentration are progressively being stripped of risk takers, of local opportunities for the development of entrepreneurial talent, and of leaders whose interest in the community is rooted not only in a job but in a commitment of personal capital and prestige.

This process is generating a fundamental change in rural community structure and function. And it is yielding a structure of "have" and "have not" communities, even in productive rural areas. As Ruttan [26] has noted, "a prosperous agriculture no longer implies a prosperous rural community." The statement can be made even more emphatic. Some of the areas where the greatest technical progress has been made are dotted with declining and decaying rural communities. The juxtaposition of rural progress with poverty has been given a new definition in our time.

This economic bifurcation in rural areas is measured in two dimensions: income and wealth. In the past, farmers and small-town residents shared in both. They typically were underrewarded through the income stream but could compensate through the wealth flow. It is this reward system that is breaking down in many rural communities [24].

Sharing in both income and wealth has been sustained in most farm sectors because land ownership has been relatively dispersed and land values have continued to rise. But many small-town residents and village tradesmen and merchants have not shared in these capital gains. There are in the South, in the Middle West, and in the Great Plains and Mountain states thousands of small towns in which urban real estate values have gone up very little since 1960 or have actually declined. At the same time, farm real estate values have gone up rapidly in surrounding areas. This is the sense in which it can be said that many residents of rural communities have been denied a share in rising affluence. They have not shared adequately in income flows and have scarcely shared at all in increases in wealth.

In Minnesota in 1960 there were 423 small towns of under 500 population and another 212 places with 501–1,500 population. Two surveys in 1963 and 1965 have shown clearly that residential real estate values in towns under 1,500 population experienced a marked relative decline after 1960. Houses and lots of approximately equivalent size and quality in towns of under 500 population were worth in 1965 only about two-thirds to three-fourths as much as similar residential properties in towns of 2,001 to 5,000 population[9]. In terms of regional distribution the lowest values for small-town residential properties were reported in southwestern counties of Minnesota where farmland values per acre are the highest in the state. Real estate values in the smallest towns in this area showed actual declines after 1960[30]. The deprivation of small-town residential property owners could not be more sharply underlined. Their shares in recent changes in wealth have been the lowest in the state, and those of their farming neighbors have been among the highest.

The rural failure to share in rising wealth has its counterpart in urban neighborhoods and core city areas, providing the raw material for a "revolution of falling expectations" in both rural and urban America. Small-town residents, blue-collar workers, and men and women who regard themselves as "middle class" in this generation for the first time in their family history provide the explosive content of this revolution. They see values being destroyed, in both figurative and literal senses of the term, and their sense of injustice is keen and rising.

A major dimension of society's interest in size and number of farms is thus not related directly to the farm economy in a narrow sense. It concerns the future of settlement policy, the configuration of urban places, and the generation of an economic base that can make life rewarding in smaller towns. Whether or not these are desirable goals is a key question for public policy in an industrial society. If a decentralized pattern of smaller urban settlements is desired, its achievement will be closely interrelated with the structure and size of farms. And if current trends in

farm size continue, the most lasting consequences will be those that result in fundamental changes in our structure of urban places.

SOCIETAL GOALS FOR FARM SIZE IN THE FUTURE

Writing from Europe in the midst of the depression years of the 1930s, one of the ablest students of trends in farm size structure pointed out that large-scale agriculture had made great strides throughout the eighteenth century and up to the middle of the nineteenth. The turning point was about 1850.

Until that period the operators of large holdings were generally able to carry out more rapidly and more successfully than the small farmers the changes involved in the scrapping of the old three-field system. In a comparatively short span of time, however, the operators of small holdings have succeeded in eliminating this disadvantage. Since 1850 they have challenged the large landowners in almost all regions and have made permanent gains, even when they have derived no particular support from the agricultural policy of the government[4].

How had this judgment changed by 1970? Can we still say that small holdings (or family-type farms) are successfully challenging large-scale agriculture in the second half of the twentieth century? Some of von Dietze's judgments have not been supported. Throughout the first 65 years of the twentieth century it seemed clear that mechanization was to be the determinant of farm size. Von Dietze's evaluation falls squarely in the middle of that period. He felt that small holdings could not take advantage of mechanization. We know now that this is not necessarily true. The size of a small holding has increased, but the feasible size of a mechanized farm unit has proved to be smaller than thought possible in the 1930s.

Since about 1965 it has been increasingly clear that those aspects of technology that enable man to control or modify the environment are of growing importance. Irrigation, disease control, pollution control, and weather modification appear to be key technologies in the latter part of the twentieth century. What are their implications for size of farm? Do they promise a decisive advantage for large-scale farms?

The answers to these questions are still unclear. We do know that pollution problems are a function of concentration and intensification. We do know that the market price system is defective as it affects waste disposal and pollution control. As Dales[3] has emphasized, "The price signals that the government gets from the market are 'false,' in the sense that they are largely echoes of its own arbitrary decisions about the supply of rights." Tax policy, programs for the subsidization of water supply for irrigation, the criteria by which we allocate rights to plant and market crops that are in surplus, controls (or the absence of controls) over farmland use in urbanizing areas, and our structure of local government that guarantees a suboptimization of the public interest in land use planning are examples of the arbitrary allocation of rights of which Dales speaks. And all these policy parameters exert powerful influences over the emerging structure of farm sizes.

Some of the most advanced applications of farm technology, for example, can be found in the great valley farms of California. Driving north from Los Angeles to Bakersfield in the spring of 1970, the student of inconsistent land policies could have observed water being used in the southern San Joaquin Valley to irrigate wheat and cotton within 150 miles of the water-starved industries and residents of the Los Angeles area. These are the leading crops for which billions of dollars have been spent in the past decade in an effort to reduce output. The criteria by which these farm program payments have been distributed have favored larger farms, in that entitlement has been a constant function of historical crop acres, while production costs show a declining trend over the range of farm sizes characteristic of family farms.

The extent to which these programs have violated the criteria of allocative efficiency and distributive equity has removed the question of limitations on farm program payments from the restricted field of agricultural policy. Urban voters in the 1970s seem likely to provide decisive political support for what could be the most prominent expression of public policy toward size of farm since the Homestead Act of 1862 and the Reclamation Act of 1902, i.e., a decision to put an upper limit on government farm program payments.

The principal opposition to a limitation of this kind comes from farmers [20]. Many of them read into any program limit a potential threat to their opportunity to expand, even though the majority may not in fact be affected by any of the limits likely to be adopted. A Montana study, for example, determined that in 1968 a limit of $20,000 on government farm program payments per producer would have affected only 89 Montana wheat farmers. Of these, only five would probably have found the limitation onerous enough to lead them to choose not to participate in the acreage reduction features of the wheat program. At the upper end of the farm size scale, the farmer opposition is typified by the statement attributed in the spring of 1970 to a representative of large-scale producers, whose response to the criticism that the cotton program was jeopardizing all government farm programs was, "We seem to have a ticket on the Titanic. In that case, we may as well go first class."

These are the considerations that make it clear that

an optimum farm size structure is a cultural variable in the final analysis. Given the levels of efficiency that can be achieved on moderate-sized farms in American agriculture, the question of farm size expansion is largely irrelevant on agrotechnical grounds. It is highly relevant on social, political, and, in the broadest sense, cultural grounds. These seem clearly to be the foundations on which decisions as to farm size should increasingly be made in urban-industrial societies.

REFERENCES

1. Beck, Robert, et al. The Changing Structure of Europe, chap. 5. Univ. Minn. Press, Minneapolis, 1970.
2. Berle, A. A. Power without Property, pp. 69-76. Harcourt, Brace. New York, 1959.
3. Dales, J. H. Land, Water and Ownership. Can. J. Econ. 1(4): 804.
4. Dietze, C. von. Small Holdings. Encyclopaedia of the Social Sciences, vol. 14, p. 102. Macmillan, New York, 1934.
5. Dovring, Folke. Income and Wealth Distributions: The Exponential Functions, p. 20. Univ. Ill. AE 4212, June 1969.
6. ———. Variants and Invariants in Comparative Agricultural Systems. Am. J. Agr. Econ. 51 (5): 1272.
7. Drucker, Peter. The Practice of Management. Harper, New York, 1954.
8. Economist. Oct. 12, 1968, p. 67.
9. English, John C., and Raup, Philip M. The Minnesota Rural Real Estate Market in 1965. Univ. Minn. Dept. Agr. Econ. Rept. 529, March 1966.
10. Freund, Rudolf. John Adams and Thomas Jefferson on the Nature of Landholding in America. Land Econ. 24 (2): 119, 1948.
11. Galbraith, J. K. The New Industrial State, chap. 6. Houghton Mifflin, Boston, 1967.
12. Gale, Hazen F. Industry Output, Labor Input, Value Added and Productivity Associated with Food Expenditures. Agr. Econ. Res. 20 (4): 123.
13. Gates, Paul W. The Homestead Law in an Incongruous Land System. Am. Hist. Rev. (1936): 652-81.
14. Gluckman, Max. The Ideas in Barotse Jurisprudence, chap. 3. Yale Univ. Press, New Haven, 1965.
15. Goetsch, Forest L. New Names Enter Corporate Farming. Doane's Agr. Rept. (May 1970): 27.
16. Goody, Jack. Death, Property and the Ancestors, chap. 13. Stanford Univ. Press, Stanford, 1962.
17. Griswold, A. Whitney. Farming and Democracy, pp. 26-31. Harcourt, Brace, New York, 1948.
18. Haar, B. Ter. Adat Law in Indonesia, chap. 2. Inst. Pacific Relations, New York, 1948.
19. Jefferson, Thomas. Letter to Rev. James Madison. Works, vol. 8, p. 196. 1904.
20. Mitchell, Donald. Limiting Government Payments: Effect on Montana Wheat Producers. Mont. State Univ. Dept. Agr. Econ. (mimeo), 1969.
21. Moore, C. V., and Snyder, J. H. California's Corporate Farms. Calif. Agr. Exp. Sta. (mimeo), May 1970.
22. Nikolitch, Radoje. Family-Operated Farms: Their Compatibility with Technological Advance. Am. J. Agr. Econ. 51 (3): 534.
23. Pattison, William D. Beginnings of the American Rectangular Land Survey System, 1784-1800, pp. 95, 205. Univ. Chicago Dept. Geog. Res. Paper 50, 1957.
24. Raup, Philip M. The Impact of Trends in the Farm Firm on Community and Human Welfare. Univ. Minn. Dept. Agr. Econ. Staff Paper P 70-4, March 1970.
25. Reid, Samuel Richardson. Conglomerate Growth: Consistency

with Economic Theory of Growth. In Economics of Conglomerate Growth, pp. 53-54. Oregon State Univ. Press, 1969.

26. Ruttan, Vernon W. Agricultural Policy in an Affluent Society. J. Farm Econ. 48 (5): 146.

27. Scofield, William H., and Coffmar., George W. Corporations Having Agricultural Operations. USDA Agr. Econ. Rept. 142, August 1968.

28. Servan-Schreiber, Jean-Jacques. The American Challenge, chap. 24. Hamish Hamilton, London, 1968.

29. Shonfield, Andrew. Modern Capitalism, pp. 380-82. Oxford Univ. Press, London, 1965.

30. Solum, Dale O., and Raup, Philip M. The Minnesota Rural Real Estate Market in 1963. Univ. Minn. Dept. Agr. Econ. Rept. 526, June 1964.

31. Trelogan, Harry C. Cybernetics and Agriculture. Agr. Econ. Res. 20 (3): 81.

32. U.S. Department of Agriculture. Marketing and Transportation Situation, MTS 176, p. 6, 1970.

33. ———. National Food Situation. NFS 122, p. 5, 1967; NFS 132, p. 6, 1970.

34. Warner, W. Lloyd. The Corporation in the Emergent American Society, pp. 4-12. Harper, New York, 1962.

The great American land grab

PETER BARNES*

With three out of four Americans now jammed into cities, no one pays much attention to landholding patterns in the countryside. How things have changed. A hundred years ago, land for the landless was a battlecry. People sailed the oceans, traversed the continent and fought the Indians, all for a piece of territory they might call their own. America envisioned itself—not entirely accurately—as a nation of independent farmers, hardy, self-reliant, democratic. Others saw us this way too. Tocqueville noted the "great equality" that existed among the immigrants who settled New England, the absence of rich landed proprietors except in the South, and the emergence in the western settlements of "democracy arrived at its utmost limits."

Along with industrialization, however, came urbanization and the decline of the Arcadian dream. Immigrants forgot about land and thought about jobs instead; the sons and grandsons of the original pioneers began to leave the farms and join the immigrants in the cities. Radical agitation shifted from farm to factory. Frontiersmen's demands for free land and easy credit were supplanted by workers' demands for a fair wage, decent conditions and union recognition. In due course a kind of permanent prosperity was achieved, and America directed its energies outwards, not inwards. Consumers bought their food in neatly wrapped packages, at prices most of them could afford, and forgot about the land.

Why, then, in 1971, should we turn back to look at

□ From The New Republic **164**(23): 19-23, June 5, 1971.
*Peter Barnes, author of *Pawns: The Plight of the Citizen-Soldier*, (Knopf), is the West Coast Editor of *The New Republic*.

our landholding patterns? One reason is that the land is still the cradle of great poverty and injustice. Another is that the beauty of the land is fast disappearing. Canyons are being dammed, redwoods felled, hills strip-mined and plateaus smogged. Wilderness and croplands are giving way to suburban sprawl and second-home developments. And the balance of nature itself is threatened by excessive use of pesticides.

The deterioration of our cities should also cause us to look back at the land; population dispersal in some form is a necessity. At the same time, there is a growing recognition that nagging social problems—burgeoning welfare rolls, racial tensions, the alienation of workers from their work—have not responded to treatment. Many of these problems have their roots in the land, or more precisely, in the lack of access to productive land ownership by groups who today make up much of the urban poor. Mexican-Americans, Indians and even some blacks are beginning to raise the point that more of America's land ought to belong to them. Given the dead-end nature of most antipoverty programs today, it is an argument worth listening to.

The schizoid character of American landholding patterns was first implanted during colonial days. In New England the land was divided fairly evenly among the many; in the South, mostly because of large royal grants, it was concentrated in the hands of the few. As a consequence, New England politics revolved around such institutions as the town meeting and the popular militia, while Southern society and politics were dominated in all aspects by the landed gentry. Jefferson warned that perpetuation of the large plantations would lead to the ensconcement of an "aristocracy of wealth" instead of an "aristocracy of virtue and talent," and even talked of freeing the slaves; but the plantation owners were hardly inclined to abdicate their privileged positions voluntarily.

With the winning of independence and the establishment of a national government, America had an opportunity to create a nation unfettered by the proclivities of European nobility. Men like Jefferson looked forward to a vigorous agrarian democracy, fostered by public education and a judicious distribution of the government's western domains. Then as now, however, politicians were less interested in promoting agrarain democracy than in making a quick buck. The history of the giveaway of America's public lands—hundreds of millions of acres over a century and a half—constitues one of the longest ongoing scandals in the annals of modern man. Fraud, chicanery, corruption and theft there were aplenty, but more scandalous was the lack of concern for the social consequences of uneven land distribution. Congress at times did enact such farsighted measures as the Homestead Act of 1862, but far more often it authorized the wholesale disposal of public lands to speculators rather than to settlers. And what Congress didn't surrender to the land hoarders, the state legislatures, the Land Office and the Interior Department usually did.

In the early nineteenth century, the typical speculator's gambit was to form a "company" which would bid for massive grants from Congress or the state legislatures, generally on the pretext of promoting colonization. Once a grant was obtained—and it never hurt to be generous with bribes—the land would be divided and resold to settlers, or, more likely, to other speculators. The enormous Yazoo land frauds—in which 30 million acres, consisting of nearly the entirety of the present states of Alabama and Mississippi, were sold by the Georgia legislature for less than two cents an acre, and then resold in the form of scrip to thousands of gullible investors—was perhaps the most famous of these profit-making schemes. Huge fortunes were made in such swindles, often by some of the most respected names in government. The social consequences were not limited to the quick enrichment of a fortunate few. The issuance of vast tracts of land to speculators also had the effect of driving up land prices, thereby impeding settlement by poor Americans. And, since grants were not always completely broken up, they had the additional effect of implanting in the new territories of the South and West the pattern of large landholdings that persists to this day.

Texas landholding patterns, for example, date from this early period, though grants to the original American *empresarios* were made by Mexico rather than Washington. At first there was a rush to purchase and occupy Texas lands granted to Stephen M. Austin and others. After the initial "Texas fever" subsided, many immense and valuable estates remained intact, and could be acquired for a relative pittance. Today many of these enormous tracts are cotton plantations, cattle ranges or oil fields owned by wealthy individuals and corporations.

The concentration of land ownership in California, now the most productive agricultural region in the world, is perhaps most extraordinary of all. According to a 1970 study by the University of California Agricultural Extension Service, 3.7 million acres of California farmland are owned by 45 corporate farms. Thus, nearly half of the agricultural land in the state, and probably three-quarters of the prime irrigated land, is owned by a tiny fraction of the population. This monopolization didn't just happen; it was and still is abetted by federal and state policies.

Land in California originally acquired its monopoly character from the prodigious and vaguely defined grants issued by first the Spanish and then the Mexican governments. Upon California's accession to the union, the United States government could have incorporated these *latifundia*—still almost totally unpopulated—into the public domain, or ordered them divided into small farms for settlers. It chose, probably without much thought, to swallow them whole and to allow them to remain private. Almost immediately they fell prey to wily speculators and defrauders, who either bought out the heirs of the grantees or forged phony title papers and bluffed their way through the courts. Several of the original Spanish grants are embodied in giant holdings today: the Irvine Ranch (88,000 acres in Orange County), the Tejón Ranch (268,000 acres in the hills and valleys northeast of Los Angeles, 40 percent owned by the Chandler family, which publishes the Los Angeles *Times*), Rancho California (97,000 acres to the northeast of San Diego, jointly owned by Kaiser and Aetna Life), and the Newhall Ranch (43,000 acres north of Los Angeles).

The struggle for acquisition of the Mexican land grants was only the beginning of the empire-building period in California. For some reason American history books are filled with tales about the robber barons of finance and industry—the Rockefellers, Morgans, Carnegies and Harriamns—but almost always neglect to mention the great cattle barons of the West. At the top of any listing of the latter must certainly be the names of Henry Miller, James Ben Ali Haggin and Lloyd Tevis.

Miller was a German immigrant who arrived in San Franciso in 1850 with six dollars in his pocket, and amassed an empire of 14 million acres—about three times the size of Belgium—before he died. Starting out as a butcher, he soon realized that the big money lay in owning cattle, not chopping them into pieces for a handful of customers. He also recognized, in advance of other Californians, that water was far more valuable in the arid West than gold.

Miller's strategy was to buy up land along the rivers of California's central valleys, thereby acquiring riparian rights to the water. Then he would irrigate the river banks with ditches, providing his cattle with natural grasses on which to graze. Homesteaders further back from the river would lose their water and be forced to sell to Miller at dirt-cheap prices.

Miller had other tricks as well. According to Carey McWilliams' *Factories in the Field*, a large portion of Miller's empire "was acquired through the purchase of land scrip which he bought from land speculators who, a few years previously, had obtained the scrip when they, while in the employ of the United States as government surveyors, had carved out vast estates for themselves." At one point in his career Miller set out to acquire some dry grasslands in the San Joaquin valley under the terms, ironically, of the Swamp Lands Act of 1850. This was a law under which the government offered alleged swamp lands to individuals free of charge if they would agree to drain them. The law provided that the land had to be underwater and traversable only by boat. Miller loaded a rowboat onto the back end of a wagon and had a team of horses pull him and his dingy across his desired grassland. Eventually the government received a map of the territory from Miller, together with a sworn statement that he had crossed in a boat. Thousands of acres thus became his.*

On a par with Miller in deviousness and ambition was the team of Haggin and Tevis, a pair of San Francisco tycoons who, among other things, had interests in the Southern Pacific Railroad and Senator George Hearst's far-flung mining ventures. By the 1870s, Haggin and Tevis had accumulated several hundred thousand acres in the San Joaquin valley from former Mexican grantees, homesteaders, the Southern Pacific Railroad and assorted "swamps." They fought bitterly for water rights to the valley's rivers, and, as Margaret Cooper has recounted in an unpublished University of California master's thesis, they were no strangers to fraud. Their empire-building was capped in 1877 by a masterfully engineered land-grab that must rank among the classics of the genre. Under the impetus of California's Senator Sargent, who was acting on be-

half of Haggin and Tevis, Congress hurriedly approved the Desert Land Act, and the bill was signed by President Grant in the last days of his administration. The law had the effect of removing several hundred thousand acres from settlement under the Homestead Act. These lands, which were said to be worthless desert, were to be sold in 640 acre sections to any individual—whether or not he resided on the land—who would promise to provide irrigation. The price was to be 25 cents per acre down, with an additional $1 per acre to be paid after reclamation.

Needless to say, much of the land in question was far from worthless. The chunk of it eyed by Haggin and Tevis was located close to the Kern River, and was partially settled. A San Francisco *Chronicle* story of 1877 describes what happened next:

> The President's signature was not dry on the cunningly devised enactment before Boss Carr [Haggin and Tevis' agent in the valley] and his confederates were advised from Washington that the breach was open. It was Saturday, the 31st of March. The applications were in readiness, sworn and subscribed by proxies. . . . All that Saturday night and the following Sunday, the clerks in the Land Office were busy recording and filing the bundles of applications dumped upon them by Boss Carr, although it was not until several days after that the office was formally notified of the approval of the Desert Land Act.

Thus, by hiring scores of vagabonds to enter phony claims for 640 acres, and then by transferring those claims to themselves, Haggin and Tevis were able to acquire title to approximately 150 square miles of valley land before anybody else in California had even heard of the Desert Land Act. In the process, they dislodged settlers who had not yet perfected their titles under old laws and who were caught unawares by the new one. The *Chronicle* called the whole maneuver an "atrocious villainy" and demanded return of the stolen lands. A federal investigation followed, but Haggin and Tevis, as usual, emerged triumphant.

All this skullduggery would be of little contemporary interest were it not for the fact that the empires accumulated by the likes of Miller, Haggin and Tevis are still with us in only slightly different form; they have become the vast, highly mechanized corporate farms that monopolize California's best farmland and produce most of the fruit and vegetables and much of the sugar and cotton that America consumes. The fate of Haggin and Tevis' holdings is particularly interesting. In 1890, in order to perpetuate their empire beyond their deaths, the two entrepreneurs incorporated under the name of Kern County Land Company. Until the 1930s most of the company's vast acreage was still used for cattle grazing. In 1936 a copious deposit of oil was discovered beneath the company's lands, producing a colossal windfall for the heirs of Haggin

---

*Horace Greeley, who voted for the Swamp Lands Act, confessed later that he had been "completely duped. . . . The consequence was a reckless and fraudulent transfer of . . . millions of choice public lands, whole sections of which had not enough muck on their surface to accommodate a single fair-sized frog."

and Tevis. Rather than pay taxes on the full amount of its oil earnings, the company began sinking them into irrigation pipes and sprinklers, thereby upgrading rangeland worth $25 an acre into prime cropland worth $1000 an acre, and later into orchards worth up to $4000 an acre. By 1965 a share of Kern County Land Company stock that sold for $33 in 1933 was worth (after splits totaling 40 for 1) $2680—and had paid $1883 in dividends. Finally, in 1967, Kern County Land Company was bought by Tenneco (of whom more in my next article).

Meanwhile, the Civil War had led to the abolition of slavery, but not to the end of the plantation system. Thaddeus Stevens, leader of the Radical Republicans, proposed dividing the large Southern estates and giving to freed Negroes and landless whites forty acres and some cash. "Homesteads to them [Negroes]," he argued, "are far more valuable than the immediate rights of suffrage, though both are their due." This was too venturesome a proposal, however, even for the Radicals, and it did not get far in Congress. As a result, Negroes and poor whites in the South remained landless, and a century later a large Southern grower would tell a CBS newsman making a documentary on farm workers, "We no longer own our slaves, we rent them."

In other parts of the country Congress continued to squander the national patrimony with abandon. The railroads were granted 134 million acres, plus another 49 million by the states. Often the railroads would allow settlers to stay and improve the land, then evict them later and sell the upgraded property at a considerable profit. Congress did nothing to remedy such abuses. It was busy enacting—in addition to the Swamp Lands Act and Desert Land Act—such giveaways as the General Mining Law of 1872 and the Timber and Stone Act of 1878. Under the latter, lumbermen and quarry operators acquired millions of acres at $2.50 an acre, largely by using the same "dummy entryman" technique that Haggin and Tevis had so advantageously employed. Under the former, landgrabbers were able to acquire large tracts of public land for purposes that had nothing to do with mining or even settlement.

Congress was not entirely blind to what was happening, and it did strike some blows for agrarian democracy, but these were to a considerable extent diluted or subverted by subsequent legislation and administrative betrayals. Under pressure from landless frontiersmen, Congress passed the Pre-emption Act of 1841, allowing families to settle on 160 acres of unsurveyed public land, with first right to purchase when the land was ultimately placed on sale. This was as far as Congress was willing to go at the time, since the South feared homesteading would undermine slavery.

In 1862, however, with no Southerners sitting, Congress adopted the Homestead Act, partially as a reward for Union soldiers. The law stands as a milestone in the history of American land policy. For the first time, full title to public land was to be granted free of charge to actual settlers. A family could acquire up to 160 acres—one quarter of a square mile—if it occupied and improved the land for five years. It was a fine law in theory, but by the time it was enacted a substantial portion of the best land in America was already accounted for. Congress made things worse as historian Paul Wallace Gates has noted, by removing additional valuable acreage from homestead settlement—usually by giving it to the railroads, or, as under the Morrill Land Grant Act, to the states, who in turn sold it to speculators. Shoddy administration by the Land Office did not help matters either. Cattlemen and speculators, both large and small, made widespread use of the "dummy entryman" trick and other ruses to acquire holdings far in excess of 160 acres, and the Land Office lacked either the will or the ability to stop them.

By the turn of the century almost all the available land in America had been staked out by one interest or another, and many Populists and reformers were displeased with the result. The Great Plains states were, by and large, democratically settled, but the same could not be said for the South and West. Henry George described California as "a country not of farms but . . . of plantations and estates," and thought a single tax on land was the remedy. The social effects of maldistributed land were most readily seen in the impoverishment of tenant farmers and sharecroppers in the South, and the exploitation of Chinese and Japanese laborers in the West.

Almost providentially, however, an opportunity to correct the mistakes of the past and to open up new lands for homesteading presented itself. Thanks to modern civil engineering, the arid expanses of the West, once useful only for grazing, could be irrigated and turned into cropland. Much of the land beyond the Rockies could thereby be transformed into a kind of New Midwest, characterized by family owned and operated farms. The instrument of this transformation would be a massive federal reclamation program; the Reclamation Act of 1902 was its charter.

F. H. Hewell, first director of the federal Reclamation Service, explained the purpose of the Reclamation Act as "not so much to irrigate the land, as it is to make homes. . . . It is not to irrigate the land which now belongs to large corporations, or even to small ones; it is not to make these men wealthy, but it is to bring about a condition whereby that land shall be put into the hands of the small owner, whereby the man with a family can get enough good land to support that family, to become a good citizen, and to have all the comforts and necessities which rightfully belong to an American citizen." Theodore Roosevelt was more succinct: "Every [reclamation] dollar is spent to build up the small man of the West and prevent the big man, East or West, coming in and monopolizing the water and land."

Federal reclamation would bring about this democratic renaissance by using both a carrot and a stick. The carrot would be subsidized water; the stick was lodged in two crucial provisions of the 1902 Act—the 160-acre limitation, and the so-called residency requirement. The first provided that no person could receive federal water for use on more than a homestead farm of 160 acres; the second provided that water would be delivered only to "an actual bona fide resident on such land, or occupant thereof residing in the neighborhood." By attaching these twin limitations to its delivery of subsidized water, federal reclamation would, in the words of one of its sponsors, "not only . . . prevent the monopoly of public land, but . . . break up existing monopolies throughout the arid region."

It sounded confiscatory—indeed, almost revolutionary—but the large Western landowners could hardly complain. They had, in the first place, acquired their empires at prices that were scandalously low and through stratagems that were at best unethical and at worst illegal. Moreover, it was not as if Congress was about to drive them into unwilling bankruptcy. The law did not require them to accept federal water; it merely provided that, if they chose to sip at the public trough, they would, in due course, have to sell their lands in excess of 160 acres. Subsequent regulations established that they could receive subsidized water for ten years before parting with their excess holdings —a time span which allowed for enough farming profit to satisfy all but the greediest.

Nevertheless, the intended transformation of the West did not occur. Great dams were built, rivaling the pyramids of Egypt in their wondrousness; reservoirs were formed, and aqueducts constructed. By 1970 the Bureau of Reclamation spent almost $10 billion and irrigated nearly seven million acres. Yet land monopoly is more firmly entrenched in the West than ever; federal water has flowed and continues to flow in great quantity to the huge, absentee-owned corporate estates that should, under the law, have been broken up and sold to small resident farmers. In the words of former Senator Wayne Morse, the wholesale, continuing violations of the 1902 Act constitute "a water steal reminiscent of the scandals" of Teapot Dome and the "great land frauds."

Nearly a century ago the San Francisco *Chronicle* warned: "The land . . . taken by two or three men is

sufficient to afford homes and independence to hundreds of intelligent, industrious and honest settlers. It is this class that makes, as it is the other [land monopolists] that ruins a country. The confirmation of title to the monopolists means the transfer of ownership of the soil to a nonresident aristocracy, and its continued cultivation by a race of aliens and coolies. Let it be awarded to the settlers, and schools, roads, churches and general prosperity will ensue."

This and similar warnings went unheeded; the South and West developed as the *Chronicle* feared. Ownership of particular estates shifted hands over the course of several depressions, panics and booms, and in recent years the trend has been toward ownership by large corporations—often oil companies or conglomerates. But though the names have changed, the pattern of large landholdings has held steady throughout. A nonresident landed aristocracy—today composed of such diverse persons as Sen. Eastland and the directors of Tenneco—enjoys vast power.

Along with absentee ownership, racial exploitation became a way of life in the West, as it previously had in the South but as it never did in the Midwest. Chinese and Japanese field hands were succeeded by Hindus, Filipinos and Mexicans. The treatment of Japanese farmworkers is particularly instructive. For many years they were enthusiastically praised by California growers; they performed the most menial tasks with great skill and without asking favors (such as transportation and boarding) of their employers. Soon, however, the Japanese began leasing land for themselves—usually "useless" marsh or desert which they would reclaim and plant with rice or other crops. Through thrift and hard work, they even began achieving their ambition to own land. This was too much for the land monopolists, who succeeded in passing the Alien Land Act of 1913, designed to force the Japanese to sell their improved lands to them.

Other effects of concentrated land ownership were as the *Chronicle* foresaw. Schools, shops and civic institutions never blossomed in those parts of the South and West dominated by giant landholdings. Enormous disparity of wealth and power is rarely conducive to widespread involvement in public affairs, and is even less so when large portions of the population are migrants, or are barred by one means or another from voting. Why, after all, should an absentee landlord spend his taxes on good public schools, when his own children go to private school and an educated work force is the last thing he wants?

What was not foreseen was the impact that land monopoly would eventually have on American cities. If the Southern plantations and Mexican land grants had been broken up, if Western land had been distributed in limited-size parcels to actual settlers as generously as it was handed out in prodigious chunks to speculators, if the reclamation law had been vigorously enforced, it is doubtful that the cities would be as overcrowded and as beset as they are today. Blacks and landless whites would, in smaller numbers, have migrated to the cities, but they would not have been so ill-prepared had they descended from landowning farmers. They would have had dignity, schooling, some experience in public affairs, and perhaps savings enough to establish a foothold.

The question now is whether we are going to compound the errors and injustices of the past, or remedy them.

Sharecroppers, once backbone of state, now almost extinct

TOM HAMBURGER*

In 1950, farm economists say, the sharecropper was the backbone of the Arkansas economy. Now, there are almost no sharecroppers left in Arkansas.

"They were here one day and gone the next," Clay Moore, an agricultural economist with the state Cooperative Extension Service, says.

Black and white sharecroppers in Arkansas provided their labor in Arkansas fields in exchange for a share of the crop they produced using the landowner's equipment.

"The only thing the croppers provided was labor," Moore noted. "Now, when chemicals do the chopping and a picker does the picking, there is very little labor in producing cotton so the whole basis of sharecropping has disappeared."

In 1950, the last year that census officials counted the number of sharecroppers in Arkansas, Crittenden County had 5,900 farms and 44,503 sharecroppers.

By 1959, the number of farms had shrunk to less than 2,000 and "there were no more sharecroppers to speak of," Moore said.

"In St. Francis County, they suffered such a drop in the number of tenant and sharecroppers," Moore said, "that census officials refused to believe it."

The Scott community, a settlement of 350 families located a half hour from Little Rock, lost most of its sharecroppers in the mid-1960s, a little later than the rest of the state. Mrs. Mary Harper, a Scott resident whose family sharecropped, recalled the change.

"It was a shock," Mrs. Harper, who now works with a self-help organization called the Scott Area Action Council, recalled. "We didn't know if we were going to make it. The bossman came and told us there would

☐ From Arkansas Gazette, Little Rock, Ark., May 20, 1977.
*Reporter of the Gazette staff.

be no more sharecrop and people would have to find a job. This hit them bad because they didn't know how to get a job."

She estimates that 500 persons have left Scott since that day in 1966, leaving about 350 black families at Scott and with "more leaving every day."

Most residents at Scott will tell you that the changes since the mid-1960s, while difficult at first, probably resulted in higher standards of living for those who left. For those who stayed, the Scott Area Action Council and other agencies have made improvements (they built 11 modern houses recently with plans for nine more), but the residents feel left behind and a bit forgotten.

"It used to be nothing but houses all through here," Mrs. Lee Anna Smith, who lives in a sharecropper shack with her two children, recalled. "I lost all of my friends. Some went up north and some went to Little Rock. It's really sad. I'm here all alone with the kids and no one to visit with."

Mrs. Smith's house has no running water, poor lighting and walls lined with newspaper. There are 11 similar plank houses, some without front doors, left in the community, according to Mrs. Brenda Givens, a member of the Action Council. She estimates that almost all of the black housing at Scott is substandard.

Mrs. Harper said that nearly all houses occupied by blacks at Scott are former sharecropper houses provided by plantation owners. Today, they still are owned by the plantations and most of the residents stay rent free.

John Barnes, 61, of Scott is saddened by the sudden changes, but says that "no one has starved since they had to quit farming. In a way it really helped the people. People who worked here never thought about owning a car or a home, but after they went out and got a job they got those things."

At Walnut Ridge, Community Service Administration personnel deal with hundreds of impoverished white former sharecroppers and farmworkers.

Mr. and Mrs. Lloyd Vaughn have five children and live in a dilapidated house outside of Walnut Ridge. Mrs. Vaughn says her husband loves to farm and finds work for a few months in the spring of each year.

The Vaughns depend on food stamps and other social services, but they prefer their life to moving to the city where jobs are more available.

The family lived at Chicago for three years while her husband worked as a welder, but they returned to Arkansas. "We left because we were tired of the gangs on our front steps," she said. "We wouldn't go back to Chicago."

Selected quotations

Family farms are dominant and not declining. Corporate farms are insignificant, are not increasing, and are possibly declining.

• • •

Radoje Nikolitch, agricultural economist, U.S. Department of Agriculture: "Changes—radical changes—are the order of the day in agriculture; and their study, in all aspects, should be the main task of our professional endeavors. However, despite all these changes, many characteristics of the organization of the farming industry remain basically unaltered. May I suggest that one of these, the coexistence of family farms and larger-than-family farms in their traditional regional locations, is likely to stay with us for a long time." (Family operated farms: their compatibility with technological advance, American Journal of Agricultural Economics **51**[3]:545, 1969.)

• • •

William H. Scofield, agricultural economist, U.S. Department of Agriculture: "Considering all the evidence we have to date, I believe we must conclude that 'outside' corporations have not as yet taken over any significant proportion of farm production." (Corporate farming and the family farm, Ames, Iowa, 1970, Iowa State University Press, p. 17.)

• • •

Seth S. King, journalist, New York Times: "The great debate over the health of the family farm and the threat of an agriculture dominated by huge corporations has induced extensive study by the Department of Agriculture. Its findings unequivocally refute the assertion that the family farm is moribund." (The family farm is not dead, Saturday Review **15**[31]: 14-16, July 29, 1972.)

• • •

Emanuel Celler, Chairman, Antitrust Subcommittee, U.S. House of Representatives: Suppose some company comes along and with its tremendous power assumes, say, 300 or 400 farms with a value of $150 million. Would you suggest any kind of action or would you just look at it with your arms folded?

J. Phil Campbell, Under Secretary, U.S. Department of Agriculture: As long as they were not endangering the family farm, we would not be perturbed by this. Now if this development went to the point that it endangered the family farm, we would be perturbed, but nothing of this type has occurred. . . .

Chairman Celler: Well, there have been some very large entities that have done just that, have there not?

Mr. Campbell: They have not adversely affected the family farm across the United States, Mr. Chairman.

Chairman Celler: The Ralston Purina people have gone pretty far, haven't they?

Mr. Campbell: Yes, sir, they have.

Chairman Celler: What would you have done with reference to that company?

Mr. Campbell: Mr. Chairman, the free enterprise competitive system took care of Ralston Purina, and the competition was so tough from the independent operators that Ralston Purina sold out and got out. Ralston Purina got out of the broiler business in the last 90 days, because they could not stand the competition from the independent operators. . . .

Chairman Celler: Purex recently cut back on their lettuce planting by about 20 percent. Did you encourage that?

Mr. Campbell: No, sir, we had nothing to do with that. Their competition, I am certain, forced that.

Chairman Celler: Tenneco recently sold 30,000 of its 130,000 acres of California farmland. Did you encourage that, or had you admonished them in any way?

Mr. Campbell: We had nothing to do with that, Mr. Chairman.

Chairman Celler: Why wouldn't you have something to do with that? Or more accurately, what was your interest?

Mr. Campbell: Under the free enterprise competitive system, it took care of itself, and we had no law to do anything in the first place, and we would not be suggesting that we be given any authority because our family farmers are doing so well for themselves that these people can't compete with them.

Chairman Celler: Would you want the Congress to give you some authority in that regard?

Mr. Campbell: Not at the present time, because our family farmers are taking care of the problems themselves.

Chairman Celler: You would not want any authority after the cow gets out of the stable, but as a prevention would you want some authority?

Mr. Campbell: Not at the present time, because we see no danger to the family farm at all, Mr. Chairman.

Chairman Celler: The Gates Rubber Co., which is not a farming operation, recently liquidated a subsidiary established to grow sugar beets in Colorado. Sugar beets have no relation, of course, to rubber. Before liquidation, were you interested in their operations in any way?

Mr. Campbell: We were an interested bystander and observer but we were not officially interested in any respect whatsoever. . . .

Chairman Celler: I can see that there is probably nothing in any statute that requires you to keep an eye on it, but I wonder whether or not you should be watchful of a situation of that sort.

Mr. Campbell: Mr. Chairman, I think we should, and I think the testimony that I have just given illustrates that we are watching very carefully, because I provided all of the information in my testimony with regard to the total situation of production in agriculture, and we are concerned, and we are watching it. We feel as though we need no authority because the family farmer has been doing quite well in competition with these people that you have just listed in your question. . . .

William L. Hungate, U.S. Congressman, Missouri: Thank you, Mr. Chairman. Mr. Secretary, I want to be sure I understood this. Was it actually your statement, as I understood it, that the family farm is in no jeopardy?

Mr. Campbell: That is correct. The figures that I have given show that the family farmer produces 95 percent of everything that is produced today.

(Verbal testimony, regarding a proposed family farm antitrust act, before the Antitrust Subcommittee of the Committee on the Judiciary, U.S. House of Representatives, March 22 and 23, 1972; Family Farm Act, Serial No. 28, Washington, D.C., 1972, U.S. Government Printing Office, pp. 29-30.)

• • •

William J. Kuhfuss, President, American Farm Bureau Federation: "On the basis of present available data relative to corporate farming in the United States, the Board [of Directors, A.F.B.F.] took action opposing the principles of this legislation (proposed Family Farm Act). . . . The entry of huge conglomerate corporations into agriculture in recent years has attracted a great deal of attention; however, there is little solid evidence that this is a serious problem." (Letter to the Antitrust Subcommittee of the Committee on the Judiciary, U.S. House of Representatives; Family Farm Act, Serial No. 28, Washington, D.C., 1972, U.S. Government Printing Office, p. 138.)

Corporate farming: a tough row to hoe

DAN CORDTZ*

An old, emotion-laden controversy is once again stirring up the nation's farmers and their political friends. The rallying cry, as in the past, is that the family farmer—that fiercely independent yeoman idealized since Thomas Jefferson's day as the backbone of a free society—is being driven off the land. This time the villains are said to be a few dozen big corporations that have recently started growing and harvesting their own crops. And the most feared culprits of all are a handful of conglomerates aiming, as one publicly proclaimed, to integrate food production "from seedling to supermarket."

National farm organizations, congressional sub-

committees, and a number of Nader-style research organizations are bitterly protesting this "corporate invasion." Many are calling for state and federal legislation to revise long-standing farm policies that they claim have favored large-scale agriculture. Some even espouse national land reform to redistribute large holdings among independent owner-farmers. It's not clear what will come of all this agitation, but in an election year it cannot be dismissed. An Agriculture Department official concedes that the furor "raises the specter of legislation against vertical integration."

There is a good deal of irony in the farmers' alarm. For it is being registered at a time when the corporate farms in question are turning out to be no menace at all—except, perhaps, to their parent companies' profits. With the rarest of exceptions, their performance

☐ From Fortune **86**(2):134-139, Aug. 1972.
*Article by Dan Cordtz with research associate Sharon Sabin.

has ranged from disappointing to disastrous; not one has been a conspicuous success. Several have gone broke or staged a hasty withdrawal after heavy losses. Most of the others are reducing their operations and drastically altering their basic strategies. The biggest and most determined are quietly shifting their emphasis from growing to the sprawling, often chaotic, processing and distribution system that represents two-thirds of the nation's $105-billion annual food costs.

No public agency formally keeps track of the financial records of big corporate farms. But Agriculture Department officials can rattle off the names of more than a dozen spectacular failures. Among them:

Gates Rubber Co. tried for three years to grow sugar beets, corn, and vegetables on 10,000 acres in eastern Colorado before selling off its land and fleet of expensive equipment in early 1971.

In 1967, CBK Agronomics, Inc., began acquiring what was to have been 80,000 acres in Missouri, Texas, and California, planning to grow diversified crops and feed cattle, but gave up last year and went into coal mining.

Multiponics, Inc. (originally Ivanhoe Associates, Inc.), drained or cleared 35,000 acres in Florida, Arkansas, Mississippi, and Louisiana in 1969 and produced two crops of soybeans, cotton, and grain. But it ran into financial problems, failed in an effort to sell a public stock offering, and is now in bankruptcy proceedings.

Great Western Ranches, Inc., assembled a four-million-acre complex of operating orchards and ranches in the West, along with timber and recreational land, paying the owners with stock. It went bankrupt last year.

An analysis by the *Farm Journal* of these and other flops cited a number of reasons why corporate newcomers have done so badly as farmers. In most cases, it said, "financially oriented brass didn't really understand farming. And the front-line manager farmed strictly first class, figuring he had plenty of money to spend because the outfit was big." Gates Rubber, for example, bought a fleet of expensive new tractors in 1968 to work its Colorado farmland. They later went for bargain prices. The *Farm Journal* also noted that the companies tried to grow too fast, "so they didn't have a chance to make little mistakes before they made big ones," and they incurred heavy expenses for specialized advisers and for travel between scattered locations.

THE GREAT CORPORATE LAND RUSH

There is nothing unprecedented, of course, about large corporations in farming—even corporations that are also involved in other activities. Until recently, however, most of them were enterprises whose main business had something to do with supplying farmers or processing their output. Del Monte Corp., the big canner, has always grown a portion of its raw material. Currently it raises about one-fourth of its needs. Similarly, Florida's giant Minute Maid produces a substantial share of the lemons, oranges, and grapefruit that it converts into frozen juices—sometimes as much as half.

But what *was* new was a land rush starting in the late 1960's by companies that previously had no connection with agriculture. It was touched off in great part by a 1964 Agriculture Department report predicting that enormous increases in food production would be needed to take care of population growth by the end of this century. As recently as three years ago, Arthur D. Little, Inc., turned out a report on "Corporate Opportunities in Production Agriculture," and a number of investment advisers were touting food production as an important new growth industry. Alert companies quickly started buying land or farms, and many well-known corporate names showed up among the ranks of the investors. The list includes Uniroyal, Boeing, Kaiser Industries, American Cyanamid, Getty Oil, and such insurance companies as Connecticut General, Aetna, and John Hancock Mutual.

Some of these companies never saw farming as a major part of their business. They were attracted more by the potential appreciation in the value of their landholdings than by the prospects of making money from crop production. A few are simply cultivating their acreage until they are ready to develop it for residential or recreational purposes. Land development, in fact, has become an important activity for a number of firms that have traditionally been large-scale farmers, such as the giant Irvine, Newhall, and Tejon ranches in California.

Nevertheless, most of the companies that went into farming were very serious indeed about making money. But the profits have been sparse at best. For one thing, forecasts of food shortages now appear erroneous. The trend line of American population growth is flattening out. Moreover, growing concern about obesity and good health has slowed the rate of increase in per capita food consumption.

Most of the corporate newcomers, it now seems clear, made still another fundamental mistake. They assumed that, with modern managers and the economies of scale, they could grow crops much more efficiently than smaller, independent farmers. On the surface, that idea appears to make sense. In practice, it simply hasn't worked out.

An old adage holds that the essential factor in profitable farming is "the shadow of the owner on his land." In the early days of large-scale industry, a similar argument was made about manufacturing plants. But personal, day-to-day supervision by a man with a substantial stake in the enterprise *does* appear to be more important in agriculture. The modern assembly line is based on the control of variables, on the establishment of repetitive procedures that eliminate the need for workers to make choices. "Farming," as Professor Sidney S. Hoos of the University of California (Berkeley) points out, "is saturated with uncertainties: weather, soil, seed, yields." Such uncertainties call for countless important decisions that must be made out in the field, not behind a distant desk.

For many of the problems, moreover, there are no standard answers that can be listed in an operating manual. The response must often be intuitive, sometimes an outright gamble. The typical independent grower is better equipped than a hired manager to accept the responsibility of taking these chances. He is so familiar with his land that its problems and capabilities are second nature to him. He is usually very knowledgeable about his crops. He is acutely conscious of risks, and philosophically willing to accept frequent setbacks as part of the game.

WHY BIGGER IS NOT BETTER

The critical importance of close personal involvement helps to explain why independent farmers, agricultural economists, and even many corporate farm managers agree that the most efficient producing unit is a farm that can be run by its owner. Studies by the U.S.D.A. and agricultural schools across the country have concluded that economies of scale in farming end rather quickly. While optimum acreage obviously varies with the crop and can never be established with great precision, the figures sugegsted by most research are surprisingly low. A 1967 Agriculture Department report, for example, said that for California cling-peach growers average costs were minimized in orchards of 90 to 110 acres. Even for field crops such as cotton, alfalfa, and barley, which lend themselves to almost total mechanization, producers in the San Joaquin Valley were found to achieve lowest average cost at about 640 acres.

Most of the economies of scale in farming are achieved by such practices as buying supplies in discount quantities, keeping hired workers busy all of the time, and fully utilizing expensive mechanical equipment. A well-managed farm of moderate size can readily accomplish all of these things. But as soon as the operation grows beyond the ability of its owner to stay on top of his field operations, where critical decisions must be made daily, costs begin to mount. Overhead, in particular, can soar as extra layers of management are needed. An experienced supervisors, with

no direct personal stake in the enterprise, will not only demand higher salaries than an owner might pay himself, but will almost certainly be less conscientious or willing to work long hours under unpleasant conditions.

Some understanding of what attracted so many corporations to farming, and of the problems they have encountered, can be gained by contemplating the corporate record in the broad, lush valleys of California. Not surprisingly, the Golden State has attracted more companies than any other. It is the nation's leading agricultural state, and it is far out in front in production of fruits and vegetables with more than 35 percent of U.S. output. William H. Scofield, who is responsible for corporate farm research in the U.S.D.A., explains why so many companies invested in growing these particular commodities. Field crops, such as corn, grain, or cotton, require large investments in huge tracts of land with below-normal prospects for appreciation. They have long been highly mechanized, which reduces the opportunities for improving efficiency by eliminating undependable and costly hand labor. Most of the output is sold on a contract basis to a few large, established buyers. Field crops have relatively low value, and profit margins are small. Finally, there is little or no opportunity for product differentiation. "With vegetables and certain fruits," Scofield says, "there is more to be gained by maintaining high standards of quality and uniformity in order to differentiate a grower's products."

A look at the experience of four large companies is revealing. One of them, S. S. Pierce Co., has abandoned farming except for a minority interest in a much smaller company that survived the bankruptcy of Pierce's farming subsidiary. The others—Purex Corp. and United Brands Co.—are still operating after major setbacks, but with their ambitions as well as their operations sharply scaled down. And the fourth, giant Tenneco, has sold off 70,000 acres. Its main objective now is to establish its Sun Giant brand as a nationally known label on prepackaged fresh produce—80 percent of it grown by other farmers.

The first three companies entered farming in a way that later caused serious difficulties. They acquired and merged several operations that were widely scattered geographically and kept on most of the former owners as managers. In each case these once-independent operators chafed under the constraints of taking orders from, and reporting to, corporate executives who were not familiar with farming. Coordination proved difficult, particularly in the scheduling of harvesting so that trained crews and expensive equipment could be used efficiently.

THE SHADOW OF CESAR CHAVEZ

And in California, at least, corporate farming turned out to have a rather special labor problem. All four of the companies turned out to be highly vulnerable to the organizing drive of Cesar Chavez' United Farm Workers Organizing Committee. Since the National Labor Relations Act does not apply to farm workers, Chavez has relied on boycotts of farm products, and the support of militant sympathizers among consumers, to force producers to sign labor contracts. In the case of a small grower, whose output is sold along with that of many others and cannot be differentiated, this tactic has not been particularly effective. But corporations whose main business depends on the sale of other, readily identifiable products can quickly be hurt by a nationwide buyers' strike.

The threat of a boycott, of course, is even more devastating to companies whose farming operations constitute a relatively small part of total operations. As a consequence, all four firms were among the first to capitulate and sign contracts with the United Farm Workers. The result was an important increase in labor costs (between 25 and 30 percent, by most estimates) that their smaller nonunion competitors did not have to pay. Moreover, although company executives are reluctant to talk about it on the record, most complain that signing a contract has led to more—rather than fewer—problems with workers. The United Farm Workers, they claim, is critically short of leadership at the shop-steward level. In many cases only Chavez himself can persuade workers to live up to the terms of the contract on grievances. In at least one instance, militant workers actually picketed union headquarters to protest an order to return to work.

By far the saddest record is that of S. S. Pierce, the venerable Boston distributor of premium-price food products. In 1969 and 1970 it acquired Pic 'n Pac Foods, Inc., a California company specializing in freezing strawberries, and five major independent strawberry growers or processors. All of the companies, Pierce declared proudly in its annual report, were profitable operations. The merged subsidiary didn't stay that way long.

Robert F. Gammons, president of S. S. Pierce, refuses to discuss the embarrassing venture. And Dave Walsh, head of the reorganized company that now bears his name, will not be specific about what he calls "poor management" that led to the debacle. But competitors in the Salinas Valley suggest a number of things that went wrong. To begin with, Pierce management failed to recognize that strawberries do not lend themselves to cultivation on a large scale. They are an extremely valuable, and equally delicate, crop.

In a good year a farmer in a cooperative can earn $9,000 on just three acres. Strawberries also require constant, careful attention. Walsh says they should be grown in blocks no larger than 100 acres. But Pierce had some 2,000 acres planted, in units as large as 500 acres.

This not only put a strain on management, but made the company heavily dependent on hired field labor. As the only major strawberry grower with a union contract, Pic 'n Pac's wage costs were higher than those of its rivals. New work rules also hampered its ability to exercise tight control over the labor force, and in spite of the labor agreement it was faced with work slowdowns and stoppages over grievances. With expenses soaring, Pic 'n Pac discovered that even its big volume gave it no real influence on prices. As they dipped in 1970, the company found itself deep in red ink. In two years Pierce replaced the management of Pic 'n Pac three times, but this March the subsidiary went into receivership—$3 million in debt to some 100 creditors. In its last year of operations it actually lost $4,500,000 on sales of $10 million.

CHIQUITA WHAT?

United Brands entered California farming with decades of agricultural experience. The company from which it grew, United Fruit, had long operated banana plantations in Central and South America. It had succeeded remarkably in achieving widespread acceptance of its Chiquita label—so much so that 42 percent of all bananas sold in the U.S. bear its brand and command premium prices. It also had close contacts with major purchasers of produce and long experience in dealing with a fresh and perishable product. With this background, United Brands thought it saw a golden opportunity in the fragmented lettuce business. But the lettuce business turned out to be much harder to control than the oligopolistic banana trade.

In a nine-month period starting in late 1968, United Brands acquired eight major independent grower-shippers. It planned to sell its lettuce directly to supermarket chains through its own thirty-three district sales offices. The company also counted on prepackaging the lettuce and branding it with the Chiquita label.

None of the company's plans really worked out. Banana jobbers could not take on the task of selling lettuce, a much more perishable product that requires entirely different storage and handling facilities. Lettuce buyers for the chains, with established relationships with produce brokers, had no more interest in buying from the banana distributors. The brokers themselves were furious at the attempt to go around them and did their best to undercut United Brands. With so many lettuce growers around, this was easy to do. The extent of United Brands' failure to stabilize the price is revealed by the fact that last year the f.o.b. price of California lettuce ranged from 90 cents to $7 for a twenty-four-head carton.

But the greatest disappointment of all was the dismal flop of the branding effort. United Brands, partly because of management problems and partly because its contract with Chavez reduced its authority over the harvesting crews, was unable to maintain a premium level of quality in enough of its lettuce. Even when the lettuce packed in the field was superior, the company could not control the speed and care with which it was moved into the stores and onto the produce stands. Company officials admit that much of the branded lettuce did not measure up to customers' expectations. And, to United Brands' consternation, unhappy buyers tended to take out their grievances on Chiquita bananas as well. After a few months, the branding project was abandoned and corporate executives now say that they don't believe anyone can do it successfully with a highly perishable product that is in abundant supply from many sources.

United Brands' western growing subsidiary, Inter Harvest, Inc., is still in the lettuce business, but is has cut its output by about 12 percent from 1970 and has increased its crop diversification to reduce its risks somewhat. More important, it is putting greater emphasis on its packing and shipping business, where potential profits are greater.

Purex, the big manufacturer of bleaches and detergents, also went into farming in 1968, believing that its experience in selling to the food chains would prove a significant advantage in selling produce. Like United Brands, Purex was mesmerized by the notion of collecting a premium on branded produce. But it had no more luck in achieving public acceptance of its label and also encountered high costs because of its contract with Chavez (two top managers resigned to protest the agreement).

For two years the company made modest profits in farming. But with lettuce prices falling below production costs and celery prices "a disaster," the company's other major crops were hit in early 1971 by a freeze in Arizona and the Imperial Valley of California. The total loss amounted to $550,000. Last year a hailstorm in Colorado and another freeze in California brought an additional $1-million loss. For the fiscal year ending June 30, 1971, Purex reported $800,000 in red ink from its farming operations, and will show a smaller deficit for the year that recently ended.

THE STOCKHOLDERS WERE UNHAPPY

The reaction of Purex stockholders illuminated another pitfall not usually foreseen by corporations tempted to go into agriculture. Commercial growers are accustomed to not only the risk but the probability that more years will be bad than good. "We count on one really good year out of seven," a large lettuce grower in Salinas acknowledges philosophically. In that good year, when both weather and prices are favorable, the previous losses will be more than wiped out. But few corporate shareholders are so tolerant. Purex management spent some unhappy minutes at last fall's annual meeting explaining why agriculture—alone of the company's many business activities—had sustained losses in an otherwise excellent year.

Purex has taken a number of drastic steps in an effort to make its farming operations profitable again. It has given up 11,000 acres of leased land and has sold 1,200 acres of its own holdings. It has leased out its entire Colorado operation and converted much of its remaining acreage to low-risk, low-profit crops. It has eliminated more than 2,000 acres of lettuce, cut its lettuce-growing areas to three, and has combined the management of its Yuma and Phoenix properties.

TALL TALES ABOUT TENNECO

The company that, more than any other, has come to symbolize conglomerate farming is Tenneco. Many of the company's top executives would be happy to eschew the distinction. For Tenneco is the favorite target of the vocal opponents of big agriculture and is constantly being attacked—often unfairly. A recurrent public charge, for example, is that Tenneco's totally integrated operation gives it an enormous advantage as a grower. According to this assertion, the company gets all its machinery from J. I Case, one of its subsidiaries, buys its fuel and lubricants from another subsidiary, grows crops on its vast landholdings, packs them in its own plant in containers made by still another subsidiary, and markets its produce through its own distribution firm.

The fact is, however, that Tenneco's agricultural subsidiary, Heggblade-Marguleas-Tenneco Inc., is primarily a packing-marketing company that grows a relatively small portion of its produce. Although it does use some Case equipment (by no means all) in its growing operations, it buys none of Tenneco's petroleum products and no containers from Packaging Corp. of America, another subsidiary. Tenneco's refineries are 2,000 miles away, and Packaging Corp's California plant does not make the small trays H-M-T needs.

Tenneco has also been accused of growing crops at

a loss in order to put pressure on the 500 independent growers whose fresh fruits and vegetables it packs and markets. But this charge is based on the incorrect assumption that H-M-T somehow benefits from keeping prices low. The opposite is the case. Although the company handles some commodities on a flat per-carton fee, most of its service is performed for a commission based on the f.o.b. price. The higher that price, the more money it makes.

Finally, the claim has been made that Tenneco doesn't care about losing money farming, because it simply charges the losses off against swollen profits earned by other units of its conglomerate empire. It is conceivable, although officials deny it, that the company is losing money—or at best making very little—from actual farming. But far from being attracted to growing crops as a potential tax loss, Tenneco is quite clearly cutting down on it.

Tenneco moved into farming with its acquisition in 1967 of Kern County Land Co., owner of almost two million acres of oil, grazing, and farm land in California, Arizona, and New Mexico. Attracted by the apparent undervaluation of these assets, Tenneco took over the company in the wake of an unsuccessful attempt by Occidental Petroleum Corp. Kern County Land, in spite of its vast holdings, has been a farm operator only on a very minor scale. Nearly all of its agricultural land had been leased to others who actually grew crops on it. When Tenneco took command, this traditional policy was significantly altered. Although most of the acreage is still farmed by tenants, Tenneco brought 35,000 acres under cultivation by its own management.

Unlike many of the other big corporations seeking a foothold in food production, however, Tenneco did not overlook the all-important question of assuring a market for its crops. In January, 1970, it acquired Heggblade & Marguleas Co., one of California's largest packers and marketers of fresh fruits and vegetables. The newly created Heggblade-Marguleas-Tenneco has been identified by its president, Howard P. Marguleas, as "a marketing-dominated production company." Even that probably overstates the importance of *growing* food in H-M-T's plans.

Within the past two years the company has sold 70,000 acres of farmland and now operates only 20,000 acres. Marguleas says that he has no desire to produce more than about one-fifth of the fruits and vegetables that H-M-T sells. These, Marguleas says, will generally be crops designed to fill out H-M-T's product line or to take advantage of what the company sees as an opportunity now going begging.

For example, Marguleas says, H-M-T is currently planting table grapes. "Everyone else is planting wine grapes," he acknowledges. "But we've always been believers in *not* following the pack."

Similarly, Marguleas explains, "we feel that there is a place for very early peaches, plums, and nectarines, and that they can be grown successfully in the southern part of Kern County and in Arizona, but most people seem to think it's too speculative, so we are planting them ourselves. We think that we can produce good, high-quality early tomatoes and other vegetables in Kern County, but very few others seem to be willing to experiment with them. We know that there is a market for summer grapefruit and more lemons. It is in these areas of experimentation and high risk that we are planting our own crops. We're growing the crops that other growers can't grow or don't choose to grow." Although he does not mention it, such a strategy also takes H-M-T out of head-to-head competition with hungry, low-margin independent farmers and concentrates on crops whose anticipated premium price can cover any higher costs.

H-M-T is unwilling to reveal its farming costs, of course, but Marguleas insists that its efficiency as a grower is equal to that of its independent large-scale competitors. Clearly, though, there is a good deal of overhead involved in its operations, and its investment in equipment is probably greater than that of most growers in the area. In any event, H-M-T has obviously concluded that there is more money to be made as a packer and marketer than as a farmer. And so it is in distribution that Marguleas' imagination and expertise are principally being brought to bear.

WHERE THE REAL MONEY IS

Marguleas declares that H-M-T's ambition is to achieve public acceptance—ultimately at premium prices—of pre-packaged produce branded with its own Sun Giant label. The problems are enormous, however. In a sense, Marguleas is attempting to swim upstream. Over the past decade, fresh produce has steadily lost ground to processed fruits and vegetables—canned, frozen, and used in convenience foods such as TV dinners or partially prepared dishes. And while more fresh produce is prepackaged in plastic-covered trays before being placed on grocery shelves, Agriculture Department researchers say that prepackaging encounters considerable resistance from buyers, who prefer to be able to pick and choose among fruits and vegetables displayed in bulk.

Marguleas concedes that probably 60 percent of housewives fall in this category, but he insists that retailers are going to be forced to prepackage because of the difficulty and prohibitive cost of staffing stores with qualified people to care for bulk fruits and vegetables. And once consumers accept prepackaged produce, he is confident, H-M-T will be able to establish the superiority of its Sun Giant brand.

"IT WILL EAT A LOT BETTER"

Marguleas is counting on quality control and, even more, on quick and costly packaging and shipping to give Sun Giant produce a competitive edge. Some tree fruit, for example, will be picked five or six days later than it normally is, then rapidly cooled and prepackaged in H-M-T's new $6-million plant before being rushed to market. "Our fruit won't look that much better," Marguleas admits, "but is will eat a lot better. And when a housewife discovers how good it is, we think she'll look for the Sun Giant brand after that."

The company has already engaged in tests of the program in three markets—Montreal, Cincinnati, and San Diego. While Marguleas won't reveal the results in detail, he insists that they were satisfactory. In San Diego last year Sun Giant peaches were sold for six weeks in several stores of the Lucky chain. For the first two weeks they were sold at the same price as bulk peaches, 29 cents a pound. Then the Sun Giant price was raised to 39 cents a pound, but sales continued to increase.

Marguleas does not deny that there are difficulties to be overcome. The company is still learning, he says, and "we're at least two or three years away from a national surge in prepackaged fruits and vegetables." Two problems still facing him are assuring a continuous supply of produce of sufficiently high quality to merit premium prices, and retraining growers and harvesters in the more demanding new techniques required. Test marketing will also continue for some time. This summer H-M-T is selling Sun Giant peaches, plums, nectarines, tomatoes, green onions, cauliflower, and zucchini through markets in half a dozen cities.

The stakes are high, not only for Tenneco but for consumers, other shippers, and for farmers. If Marguleas is successful, he will undoubtedly be followed by a rush of imitators. The emphasis on branded, advertised, premium-quality produce will almost surely result in an increase in the average price of fresh fruits and vegetables as consumers are persuaded to upgrade their purchases. And the costs of carrying out such marketing programs could also accelerate the trend to concentration in produce wholesaling that has already taken place at the retail level. But it could be a lifesaver for some of the companies that are casting about for a way to salvage their disappointing agricultural ventures. *Growing* food can probably be better left to real farmers, but the big corporate investors may yet find in distribution the profits that they have been pursuing in agriculture.

Photo captions

"Some of the most expensive lettuce in California" is grown in well-kept fields near Salinas by Inter Harvest, the western growing and packing subsidiary of United Brands. According to the rueful company official who so described the lettuce, the main problem is that overhead costs seem to grow faster than the company's volume. Six managers and supervisors, for example, spend much of their time traveling between four growing areas in California and two in Arizona. In addition, because the company is one of only four lettuce growers to have signed a contract with Cesar Chavez' United Farm Workers Organizing Committee, its labor costs are significantly higher than those of its nonunion competitors. Inter Harvest, nevertheless, has done better than many another corporate investor in farming. An S.S. Pierce subsidiary dropped $4,500,000 on sales of $10 million in an effort to grow strawberries on a grand scale in the fields below. In fact, farming has turned out to be so profitless and trouble-filled that many of the corporations that invaded agriculture in the late 1960's are now in full retreat.

• • •

Sun Giant oranges move along a grading line in Heggblade-Marguleas-Tenneco's new $6,300,000 packing plant near Bakersfield, California. The eight-acre facility includes an ice-water bath for rapid cooling of fruit, nine giant cold-storage rooms, grading lines for seven different commodities, and special equipment for packaging fruits and vegetables in individual trays with a stretch-film overwrap. The plant, with a capacity of ninety carloads of produce a day, is a central component in Tenneco's plan to cut back farming operations, where large corporations have trouble turning a profit, and concentrate on marketing a full line of prepackaged fruits and vegetables under a nationally known brand name.

• • •

The complexity and inefficiency of the country's distribution system for fresh foods is nowhere more evident than in the ceaseless activity at the New York City Terminal Market at Hunts Point in the Bronx. Four thousand motor vehicles and as many as 400 railroad cars pass through the 111-acre market each day. The 105 wholesalers who do business there handle more than $1,500,000 of produce daily, supplying 2,300 jobbers, who in turn sell to retail stores.

In extreme cases, as many as a dozen middlemen can be involved in the trek from field to family table. The case of last year's carrot crop is a typical example of what happens to most fruits and vegetables. Farmers in fourteen states grew almost 1.9 billion pounds. Close to 317 million pounds were sold directly to processors for freezing and canning. A billion pounds were packed fresh by 1,100 packer-shippers and sent on to 5,200 merchant-wholesalers, who then resold the carrots to 204,900 retail stores and to the rapidly growing number of institutional consumers, such as hospitals, schools, and restaurants. Nearly 539 million pounds were sold by the packer-shippers directly to 25,400 supermarkets. Helping to match up buyers and sellers was an army of 1,000 agents and brokers. The price grew from 9½ cents per pound in the field to 13½ cents at Hunts Point to 22 cents at the checkout counter. Corporations like Tenneco hope to profit by streamlining the system.

Boxed insert

The continuing decline in farms in the U.S. is an indisputable fact. In three decades the number has fallen from over six million to 2,900,000. But the gross statistics are misleading. Practically all of the drop took place in farms with gross cash sales of less than $10,000 a year—most of it among farms with sales below $5,000. The nostalgic proponents of small-scale family farming regard this as a major tragedy. They assert that thousands of self-supporting families are thus being expelled from a wholesome way of life and forced into crowded cities. This population loss, they add, spells doom for many small towns and cities whose economic base rests on farmers in the surrounding countryside.

But a farm with sales of less than $5,000 a year cannot realistically be described as a family farm—if such a farm is defined as one that will furnish a decent living for a family. The net income of farms with sales below $5,000 averages only about $1,300 a year. Even farms with sales between $5,000 and $10,000 a year average only about $3,400 in gross profits. Families operating such farms can hardly aspire to a rising living standard, college education for their children, or the material comforts that most Americans regard as essential. It is significant that the nonfarm income of these farmers far outweighs their farm profits—by more than six times in the case of farms with sales below $5,000.

The more relevant question is what is happening to farmers who operate on a scale that *does* earn them a living equal to that of the average industrial worker. The answer is reassuring. While some such farmers undoubtedly do go out of business, the Agriculture Department estimates that the number of farms with annual sales above $10,000 (in current dollars) has tripled since 1939 to more than one million. Over three-fourths of them have sales between $10,000 and $40,000. Such farms typically net about 35 percent on sales, and can be operated by the members of a family and at most a hired hand or two. Moreover, farms of this size still account for 30 percent of all cash receipts by growers.

The dimensions and impact of corporate farming may also be exaggerated. Only 1.2 percent of commercial farms in the U.S. are incorporated, and nine-tenths of them are merely family-owned farm businesses that have grown to a size that makes a corporate structure desirable for tax or inheritance purposes. Just 1,800 farms—less than 0.1 percent of the total—are operated by corporations with more than ten shareholders. They cultivate about 15 million acres (1.6 percent of all land in commercial farms) and account for less than 3 percent of total farm sales.

Small-scale farmers do face an important challenge, however. The same concentration that took place long ago at the retail level is now apparently under way among packers, shippers, and wholesale brokers. If the plans of companies like Tenneco are successful, the trend could accelerate rapidly. This confronts growers with the prospect of an even greater imbalance in the relative bargaining power of many sellers and few buyers. Recognizing the danger, many farmers are showing revived interest in the old cooperative movement and in trying to get a piece of the more profitable business of processing and marketing their crops.

Selected quotations

Family farms are declining, while large nonfamily farms and corporate farms are increasing.

• • •

Tony T. Dechant, President, National Farmers Union: "We in the National Farmers Union believe 'the corporate invasion of American agriculture' by non-farm interests is real. It is leaving behind 'wasted towns, deserted communities, depleted resources, empty institutions, and people without hope and without a future.' The invasion is still in the beginning stage. Some people see this trend as inevitable—that is, cannot be stopped. Not only can it be stopped, it must be stopped." (In Ray, Victor: The corporate invasion of American agriculture, Denver, 1968, National Farmers Union, p. v.)

• • •

Alan Bible, Chairman, Select Committee on Small Business, U.S. Senate: "The investigation [hearings before the Subcommittee on Monopoly on the effects of corporation farming on small business] also has turned up a large number of corporations buying and operating large tracts of agricultural land, particularly in the Great Plains States. These are farming companies that displace independent farmers and ranchers in a community." (Report to the U.S. Senate, December 20, 1969; Impact of corporation farming on small business, Senate Report No. 91-628, Washington, D.C., 1969, U.S. Government Printing Office, p. 1.)

• • •

Minneapolis Tribune: "Family farmers received an overwhelming vote of confidence from farm and city people alike in a statewide survey completed by a highly-regarded polling organization in Minnesota.

The results, published in the Minneapolis Tribune and later inserted in the Congressional Record, showed 95% of those interviewed felt it was important that the family farm survive, 76% considered it an efficient method of producing food, and 57% thought corporate farming was a bad development. The only disturbing response came to a question asking whether family farmers or corporation farms would be likely to be the major source of food by the year 2000.

Only 20% of those interviewed felt that the family farm would still be producing most of the food by the end of the century. Those saying corporate farms probably will have the upper hand by then ranged from 51% of the people on farms to 75% of those living in Minneapolis, St. Paul, and Duluth." (Newspaper poll discloses corporate farm opposition, NFO Reporter, Nov. 1972.)

* * *

Leonard R. Kyle, agricultural economist, Michigan State University: "This group of fairly conservative agricultural economists (more than a dozen agricultural economists teaching at Midwestern universities) expects a continued increase in the concentration of production on fewer and fewer farms. In 25 years, this could result in a nearly complete demise of typical family farms in the units classified as commercial full-time farms." (The State Journal, Apr. 15, 1972.)

* * *

Joe Belden, Exploratory Project for Economic Alternatives: "Nearly everyone agrees that family farmers are the most efficient producers of food and fiber, and that their predominance results in social and economic benefits to rural society and to the nation as a whole. Yet the best evidence indicates that the family producer is in decline. A new direction for agricultural policy must seek to reverse this trend." (In Beldon, J., and Forte, G.: Toward a national food policy, Washington, D.C., 1976, Exploratory Project for Economic Alternatives, p. 119.)

380,000-Acre plantation is being started in the wilderness

North Carolina area is being cleared for cattle and crops

WILLIAM ROBBINS*

ROPER, N.C.—A wealthy New York investor is carving what is believed to be the country's largest private plantation out of an eastern North Carolina wilderness of swamps and forested lowlands. Experts say the development holds both great agricultural potential and environmental hazards.

Cleared land stretches away in fertile plains, and bulldozers continue to thrust at the bogs beyond the tree-fringed horizon, toppling pines and sweetgums and tearing away undergrowth to bare the soft, dark earth.

The domain, called First Colony Farms, was created a year ago by Malcolm P. McLean, who gained his wealth in the trucking industry. It totals 380,000 acres, nearly 600 square miles.

The clearings, swamps, and forests occupy most of Dare and Tyrrell Counties and parts of two others in a broad swath stretching 55 miles from a point just east of here to Croatan Sound, which separates Roanoke Island, where Sir Walter Raleigh established his own first colony, from the mainland.

On this vast expanse, Mr. McLean plans to raise thousands of cattle and develop the nation's largest

*In a special report to the New York Times.

hog-growing operation, planned ultimately to produce a million head a year, and to raise the thousands of acres of corn and soybeans needed to sustain the livestock, as well as winter wheat to precede the soybeans in a double-cropping sequence.

At some future date, aides say, may come the final stage of such an integrated complex. The say it may attract a slaughtering plant, though they expect that to be under separate ownership.

The concerns of environmentalists focus mainly on the possible effects land clearing has on wildlife in the area, principally black bear, and the effects of animal waste and pesticides on aquatic life resulting from the run off of drainage water into the area's many estuaries.

There also are fears about the effects of intensive cropping and grazing on the land itself which is a soil of unusual facility.

THOUSANDS OF ACRES CLEARED

"When I started here a few years ago this was all woods," said Earl Spruill, the clearing and drainage manager. About 25,000 acres have been prepared for planting this year, and vegetation has been bulldozed from additional thousands of acres that await further preparation for planting.

"There are big problems ahead of them," said Dr. Harvey Bumgardner, a soil specialist who is part of a group at North Carolina State University that will study First Colony for Mr. McLean. "But properly managed, this can be the most fertile soil in the world," he said.

First Colony Farms is committed to following the group's environmental recommendations, according to Simon Rich Jr., the 29-year-old general manager of the development. A preliminary report from the university is due this fall, with a final report scheduled a year later.

Meanwhile, corn is sprouting in the new ground and wheat stands nearly knee high. After those crops are harvested in June, soybeans will be planted. Eventually, if all goes according to plan, the grains will feed thousands of cattle and a million hogs a year.

Pastures for the cattle are being planted and construction has started on the first of many units that will house the hogs.

MILLION HOGS A YEAR

Five such units are scheduled for completion this year and five more next year. Each would cost $1-million to build and would handle 10,000 hogs a year, from breeding through slaughter. The goal is a million hogs annually.

Much of the agricultural potential and part of the environmental risk are evident in the black and rich soil. It is a peat composition laid down over the ages as trees and foliage have fallen and decayed. On such soil, farmers here have been able to get extremely high yields of corn. But first the land must be drained and cleared, a process that costs about $300 an acre.

Once cleared, the soil is extremely acid, requiring heavy applications of lime and, in the first two or three years, nitrogen.

Dr. B. J. Copeland, an environmentalist on the study team, explained some of the environmental problems in a telephone interview.

One is in the nature of the land, which tends to sink under cultivation and during use as pasture.

"Subsidence has been serious in places like this," he said. There is a danger that some of the land could sink back into swamp, "without the ability to bring back the sort of vegetation it had," he said.

The problem could be alleviated, he said, through the development of a system that would keep enough water in the drainage ditches to retain ground moisture up to the crop level.

In addition, the ground itself is a fire hazard. When dry, peat soil will burn, as about 2,000 acres did recently at First Colony Farms.

That problem also can be alleviated by "proper water management," Dr. Bumgardner, the soil specialist, said in another telephone interview.

Other problems are related to the drainage.

"No one knows the impact of the drainage into the estuaries," Dr. Copeland said. "Nitrogen from either fertilizer or animal waste that gets into the water could cause eutrophication [a condition caused when streams or lakes are choked with weeds that decay and deplete the oxygen]."

EFFECT ON WILDLIFE

"We wonder also what development on such a scale will do to wildlife," and what effect farm pesticide would have on aquatic life, Dr. Copeland said.

State officials have made "no major investigation" of conditions at the development, according to Arthur W. Cooper, Assistant Secretary of the North Carolina Department of Natural and Economic Resources. His agency is "interested," however, he said, because the project's "magnitude puts them in a different category" from surrounding farms.

Aides at First Colony say that it is the largest holding of its kind under individual ownership in the country. The claim is difficult to prove because of the nature of land records, which often shield owners behind dummy corporations and names, but it is probably true.

Holdings of California's Kern County Land Company, which has merged into Tenneco, Inc., were larger than Mr. McLean's, but that is a stock company.

The owner of this vast acreage is the man who built the McLean Trucking Company into a big corporation and Sea-Land Services into an associated containership operation with a large fleet. Those interests merged into R. J. Reynolds Industries in 1969 and Mr. McLean became a director in the corporation.

Mr. McLean, a 60-year-old native of North Carolina who now lives in New York City, said in a telephone interview that the land represented a $50-million cash investment, with no mortgage involved.

However, to farmers in this area, Mr. McLean is little more than a name, and the vast size of his acquisitions has stirred little controversy. There has been some concern that operations as big as First Colony's ultimate goal for hog production might swamp local markets. But most farmers in the region appear to agree with Malvin Respess of nearby Pinetown. "If he can farm more efficiently than I can, let him go to it," Mr. Respess said.

They appear to doubt that he can, and they show more concern over two other, much smaller enterprises, one by a Japanese and one by an Italian company.

The Japanese operation involves 7,500 acres just

north of First Colony, purchased recently by Shima-American Inc., a Japanese trading firm based in Osaka.

Simon Rich's brother Robert, a real estate broker, is supervising the company's clearing and drainage, using methods like those employed at First Colony.

The Italian purchase, made in January, involved 45,000 acres about 70 miles south of here, near Morehead City. The operation has been incorporated under the name of Open Grounds Farm, with a New Orleans man named Giovanni Rametta as its president, but those involved have declined to name the Italian parent company.

Little work has been done thus far on the site of that venture.

Some farmers express fear that the purchases indicate a trend to foreign development of United States agriculture; that could threaten their booming export trade.

But those foreign ventures would fit into small corners of First Colony Farms. And the pace of activity and depth of investment indicate that it is here to stay.

New type of owner may speed land boom, push some out

TOM HAMBURGER*

There's a new breed of farm owner coming to Arkansas.

One of the new breed just concluded last week what is said to be one of the largest land sales in Jefferson County, buying 4,460 acres for an undisclosed price. The buyer is Lehndorff Farms, Ltd., a subsidiary of a Hamburg, Germany, investment corporation.

The current Jefferson County land sales record of $7.3 million was paid by Prudential Insurance Company last year. Prudential also owns large farms in Chicot, Mississippi and Prairie Counties.

Another foreign farm owner, Crown Prince Frans Josef II of Lichtenstein, operates a 9,000-acre farm near Texarkana.

The presence of these new owners may cause land prices, which have more than doubled in farming areas in recent years, to rise even higher and may continue to force small farmers from the land, according to investment counselors.

Although the number of foreign or out-of-state investors in Arkansas is small, the number soon will increase dramatically, according to Steve Weber, foreign investments chief for Oppenheimer Industries of Kansas City, the country's largest land investment company. The firm handles no account of less than $1 million.

Weber now is directing his foreign clients to Arkansas. He says the rise in farmland prices in the Arkansas Delta, where prime land now costs between $1,000 and $1,300 an acre, an increase of $300 over last year,

□ From the Arkansas Gazette, Little Rock, Ark., May 15, 1977.
*Reporter of the Gazette staff.

has only just begun. He believes Arkansas now provides a better buy for his clients than land in the cornbelt states, where a land boom that has pushed the price of prime land up to $5,000 an acre "is getting out of hand."

The recent rise in Arkansas land prices is part of a national trend that already has hit the cornbelt states of Iowa, Kansas and Illinois, where prices jumped an average of 35 per cent last year, Weber said.

Land prices first went up sharply about nine years ago, according to Little Rock land appraiser Wesley Adams. Adams says the land has increased 129 per cent between 1967 and 1976, but the real boom has occurred within the last five years.

Adams recalled that in 1975, rich farmland in Poinsett County was selling for about $750 an acre. Late last year, he said, similar land sold for $1,304 an acre.

The current boom, market experts say, means more than just a new crop of big landowners, like corporations and foreign investors. The boom also accelerates the trend toward fewer and larger farms and makes it harder for young farmers to get started. Farmers who rent farmland (in 1969, 12.6 per cent of Arkansas's farmers were tenant farmers, down from 24.3 per cent in 1959) are finding that increased land values raise their rent.

"The high price of land makes it impossible for a young man to go into farming any more," Brinkley banker Albert Rusher said last month, "and it makes it hard for the old farmer with small acreage to stay in business." Rusher has watched land prices double in his area in the last five years.

The rise in land prices, Rusher noted, is expected to speed this trend by forcing less-profitable farmers to sell out. The price rise also makes it difficult for farmers who need to expand their farms to spread high equipment costs over more acres.

COST-PRICE GAP WIDENS

USDA statistics indicate that in 1952, 1,659 bushels of corn would pay for a 30-horsepower tractor, but in 1971 it took 3,291 bushels. As prices go up, more land is absorbed into existing farms.

The number of farms in the country has declined from 4 million in 1960 to 2.8 million last year, according to the Agriculture Department. A 1969 study showed that 5.5 per cent of the country's farmers controlled more than 54 per cent of the farmland, and nine per cent of the land was owned by corporations.

There is general agreement that the land boom started with the international demand for American crops. In 1972, worldwide weather problems hurt crops, the American dollar was devalued, and the Soviet Union began buying grain. In 1974, more than 40 per cent of the domestic rice, wheat, cotton and soybean production was exported.

That doesn't explain why land prices increased sharply over the last two years while farm income was dropping from the peak of $33 billion in 1975 to last year's $22 billion.

One reason for the present surge is that big farmers have plenty of money and credit. The small farmer, whose capital is limited, is tempted to sell out as the larger farms grow bigger.

Weber, who owns a farm, said that because the large farmer's "present land has increased so much in value, they can easily borrow to buy more land, and they don't mind paying $100 or $50 more an acre than they think it is worth, because they know from experience that inflation will pay for that in a year or less."

FOREIGN COMPETITION

Another reason for the current and predicted surge in Arkansas land values is the presence of foreign interests.

"Western Europeans are interested in investing in farmland," Weber said, "because they are concerned about security. Five years ago they were more secure. Now they are worried about increasing socialism, kidnapers, Communists and terrorists. There is a lot of old wealth in Europe, and they know from experience that after wars and conflicts are all over, it's the land that enabled them to retain their positions. They are looking to American farmland because they feel it is the last place in the world where land will be confiscated."

Weber said his company would begin taking European investors to Arkansas in "the next two to six weeks" to look at property. Arab and Asian investors have shown little interest in American farmland, he said. There are not very many foreign investors, he continued, but they are "a strong psychological force on the market."

The presence of any number of foreign investors "helps prop up the price of the land," he said. Most of his clients "are investors, but some are speculators." Weber said it is relatively easy for foreigners to buy Arkansas land. Iowa, for example, restricts the number of acres nonresident aliens may own to 640. He anticipates a 15 to 30 per cent jump in the price of Arkansas land next year.

ABSENTEE OWNERS

Lehndorff and Prudential employ local farmers to manage their farms, and the Northern Trust Company of Chicago operates a farm management firm at Memphis to oversee land purchased by the company. Northern Trust currently farms about 5,000 acres in Arkansas and plans to expand in the future.

Shortly before he became Labor secretary, F. Ray Marshall studied small farmers in Arkansas and concluded that they "can be at least as efficient and often more efficient in some crops than their larger competitors."

Some experts are concerned about the effects of such absentee ownership.

In 1974, Eric Thor, a former administrator of USDA's Farmer Co-operative Service, said in an interview with *The New York Times* that "the real risk in a hired manager is that he can't make decisions very well. He knows that if he makes a bad decision, he might get fired, so he waits for someone higher up to approve it. Sometimes it's too late to save a crop."

Everett Tucker III, farm loan officer for the Commercial National Bank at Little Rock, is worried about out-of-state ownership for different reasons. He is hopeful that the land investment boom that has hit the cornbelt won't find its way to Arkansas.

"Farm ownership at the local level is advantageous," he says. "It hurts the local community when an outside owner comes in. It helps our economy to have the land stay under local ownership."

THREAT DOUBLED

Clay Moore of Little Rock, an economist with the Agriculture Extension Service, disagrees.

"It isn't necessarily bad for foreign investment to come in because local farmers will rent the land...," he said. "I don't know how much loose money there is running around, but these isolated cases, in my judgment, do not fortell a sizable moving in of foreign capital. . . . It takes more than a few swallows to make a sign of spring."

Vincent Foster Sr., a Hope realtor specializing in farm sales, says the number of swallows is increasing.

"We've had Spaniards, Italians looking at land through here and a lot of investors are coming down here because of the cornbelt prices and the California drouth."

Land in Southwest Arkansas is selling for $700 an acre, Foster said, "a 100 per cent increase in five years. We have the cheapest land in the United States in relation to productivity. If the bean market doesn't break, I think we'll see a reasonable increase in prices."

Foster also worries about the effect of a land boom.

"The prices continuing to inflate way out of proportion to the yield [of farm land] causes a hardship on the local farmer."

Corporate power in rural America

JIM HIGHTOWER*

Boeing Aircraft . . . Purex . . . Goodyear Tire & Rubber . . . Royal Crown Cola . . . Tenneco . . . American Brands . . . Dow Chemical . . . Alico . . . Bank of America . . . Prudential Insurance. These are not exactly names to conjure up images of the old homestead or of the yeoman farmer, but these are a few of the major corporations that have moved into farming in this country and that are radically changing rural America.

Food and fiber today are big business. In fact, they are the biggest business—bigger than automobiles, bigger than electronics, bigger than defense hardware. In 1970, Americans paid a grocery bill of $91 *billion*. Adding in their restaurant tab, food totalled $114 billion.

It is a myth that the small family farmer still is bringing that bounty to market. While they total more than half (56.5%) of all farms, the last reported Census of Agriculture shows that these small independent farmers made only 7.8% of all farm sales.

On the other hand, a mere 9/10 of 1% of this country's farms made off with 24.3% of the farm sales. These are the giant producers, averaging sales of $272,000 in a year. These few also accounted for:

29% of all feed bought
39% of all livestock and poultry bought
24% of all machinery hired
11% of all fuel bought
17% of all seed bought
16% of all fertilizer bought
41% of all farm labor hired.

□ From WIN **8**(12):8-10, July 1972.
*Agribusiness Accountability Project.

These are 1964 figures. The 1969 Census of Agriculture will show sizeable increases in each of these categories. For example, the U.S. Department of Agriculture (USDA) admitted that by 1969 these giant farms "accounted for at least 1/3 of total sales by all farms." USDA projects that they will account for more than half of the farm marketings by 1980.

No longer does the farm exist as a way of life. It is a business. As farmers in North Carolina say, "Get big or get out." Food today is the product of a factory, running on an assembly line that extends from the field through the checkout counter of your supermarket. Increasingly, that factory is vertically integrated—that is, one company is involved in two or more of the phases of producing, processing, distributing, advertising and retailing.

Consider Tenneco, Inc., the nation's 34th largest corporation. Over the years, this conglomerate, based on gas pipelines, has grown by leaps and bounds, recently plowing much of its huge profit into agribusiness enterprises. They own one of the biggest farms in the country, the giant Kern County Land Company in California, controlling more than 1.7 million acres of land. The J.I. Case Farm Machinery Company is a direct subsidiary of Tenneco and one of the biggest in the business. Tenneco Chemicals is deeply involved in agricultural herbicides and pesticides. Packaging Corporation of America is a Tenneco subsidiary that makes food containers. Heggblade-Margoleas is a Tenneco subsidiary and the largest marketer of fresh fruits and vegetables in the nation, pushing Tenneco's own "Sun Giant" label. Now, Tenneco even has begun to retail food directly, through quick-service grocery stores in its chain of Tenneco Oil Company filling stations.

So we have one huge corporation, integrating practically every phase of the food system. Tenneco plants seed on its own land, hires its own labor, applies its own chemicals, operates its own tractors on its own gasoline and oil, processes its own crops in its own plants, packages its produce in its own containers, markets its own brand through its own marketing subsidiary and retails that brand in its own grocery stores. It even has its own agricultural lobbyist in Washington.

Tenneco is not alone in this concentration. There even are vertically-integrated corporate families in agriculture—the Bentsen family in south Texas, for example, grows citrus on 25,000 acres of their own land; they own Tide Products, Inc., a processor and distributor of agricultural chemicals and now a subsidiary of Union Carbide Corporation; they own or effectively control five banks in Hidalgo County and are involved in the ownership and management of others throughout the Rio Grande Valley; and now they have their own man in Washington, United States Senator Lloyd Bentsen.

Then there are the massive canners, which do much more than can. Del Monte Corporation, for example, grows much of its own produce on more than 100,000 acres of land that it controls; it owns processing plants throughout the United States and in nine other countries; it owns 14 can manufacturing companies and a label printing concern; it owns five trucking operations and an ocean terminal; and it owns 24 public restaurants.

USDA attempts to minimize the importance of corporate agriculture by pointing out that corporations account for only 1% of all farms and operate only 7% of the land in farms. But in the area where it counts—domination of the marketing process—it is clear that corporations are in charge of rural America. Increasingly, a handful of corporate enterprises control entire commodities. Iceburg lettuce is pretty much in the hands of three California producers—United Brands, Purex and Bud Antle (substantially owned by Dow Chemical Company). Minute Maid, a subsidiary of Coca Cola Company, processes 20% of the frozen orange juice in the country. H.J. Heinz sells 37.8% of the country's ketchup.

In addition to these, there are banks, railroad companies, seed and feed suppliers, supermarkets and many other corporate entities that are moving beyond their traditional roles and achieving domination within the food industry. In the face of this kind of economic power, small farmers and farm workers are powerless. In Russia, they have developed a system of state farming; here, we have developed a system of corporate farming. From the viewpoint of the people who actually till the soil and produce the crops, there is not much difference, for in both systems control flows from the top down.

Incredibly, this concentration and integration receives the full blessing and support of the Department of Agriculture, which has abandoned the farmer, the farm worker and the majority of rural Americans and has made its bed with the processors, marketers and other business interests surrounding agriculture. Former Secretary of Agriculture Clifford Hardin benignly observed recently that "1/5 of the total farm output in 1970 was produced under contract or some other form of coordination or integration." The Secretary went on to say that "many observers believe the trend toward contract marketing will accelerate."

That is a self-fulfilling prophecy, for governmental intervention is the only way to prevent an acceleration of the trend toward corporate control of agriculture and rural America. While the USDA looks on, apparently un-moved and certainly un-moving, the family farmers and the farm workers of the country increasingly are falling under the control of the agribusiness giants that have integrated and concentrated the agricultural economy.

Despite the much-heralded independence of the farmer, the day is gone when he was in charge in rural America. Today, the food processors and other corporate enterprises dominate production and are the power brokers in rural America. Increasingly, it is these forces that tell the farmer what he will produce, how much of it, when and for what price. There is more than chicken feed to Ralston-Purina Company, which holds contracts with small, southern chicken producers and completely dominates their economic lives. This corporate invasion of poultry has thousands of these small farmers, reducing them from hearty free-enterprisers to assembly-line cogs in this vertically-integrated industry.

The National Farmers Organization, an aggressive outfit trying to gain bargaining power for small farmers, knows about the impact of the processor. When NFO dairy farmers began to gain bargaining strength in the sale of raw milk, Beatrice Foods Company and Boswell Dairy Company simply refused to purchase milk from any producer aligned with NFO. The processors could get their raw milk elsewhere, while the NFO dairy farmers were left to drink what they could and pour out the rest.

The plight of farm workers, with their scandalously low wages and their miserable living conditions, is too well known to have to document again here. By our best estimate, 75-85% of the farm workers in this country are employed by these major food and industrial corporations, so it is they who are accountable for farm worker misery and degradation. Consider Del Monte again. This processing giant hired up to 39,000 farm workers at one time in 1969. It had 1970 sales of $681,492,000 and profits of more than $14 million. Yet, this industrial "leader" took the official action in 1970 of opposing congressional extension of unemployment compensation to farm workers. Del Monte has also opposed an increase in the $1.30 minimum wage for farm workers.

But more is involved here than nostalgia for the small homesteader and hand-wringing for the plight of farm workers. The answer is not to give everybody 160 acres and a mule. But neither is the answer to continue stumbling along blindly, allowing private economic interests to re-make rural America in their own peculiar image. It is one thing to buy food from a corporation rather than from a family farmer, but it is quite another thing to have to add on the staggering social costs that come with that shift in the make-up of agriculture.

In the last thirty years, 100,000 farms a year have succumbed to the "agricultural revolution," and USDA predicts that another million farms will disappear by 1980. In that same period, 30 million Americans have been forced to leave their homes in the countryside and to seek refuge in the cities. The 1970 Census shows that farm population declined 38% since 1960 and that it fell below 10 million people for the first time since the nation was settled.

The cities, the rural areas and the people all have been hit hard by this migration. We know what has happened in the cities, choked by rural refugees and in turn choking them. Things have not been better back home. A presidential commission found 14 million people left behind rural poverty in 1967. Whole towns are being boarded-up and abandoned—for every six farmers that fold, one small-town businessman closes his doors. The countryside is scarred by deserted farms, empty stores and padlocked schools.

There has been a violent revolution in rural America, and it has had no nobler objective than profits.

Incredibly, our government has failed either to impede that revolution or to comfrot its victims. A walk into any urban ghetto or a drive along the backroads of rural poverty is testimony enough that there has been a massive failure of national leadership. Something is leaving our national life and our national character, yet no public official is standing up to say "no" or even to question whether it is desirable.

There is nothing inevitable about agribusiness domination of rural America—it is not the unalterable workings of some economic dialectic. Agribusiness has taken over because government officials have made deliberate decisions to promote it and because there has been no national policy to regulate its growth.

What kind of government leaves millions of its citizens to the whim of corporate power? Is rural America to be more than a food factory, and will we deal with independent family farmers, farm workers, small-town residents and the majority of rural Americans as more than the waste products of agribusiness?

If we determine as a nation that rural America should be a place for people to live and work, rather than just a vast resource to be strip-mined by corporate agribusiness, then we can begin to develop a national rural policy that will focus first on people and that will not be based on agribusiness profits or trickle-down schemes of rural development.

The first step in developing a national rural policy is to understand what exists in rural America today. The second step is to understand that what exists is not immutable.

Trends in U.S. farm organizational structure and type

RICHARD D. RODEFELD*

Compared to most other elements of the economy, the farm sector has been unique historically in a num-

□ Revised version of "Evidence, Issues, and Conclusions on the Current Status and Trends in U.S. Farm Types," Unpublished paper presented at the Rural Sociological Society Meeting, San Francisco, Calif., Aug. 1975.
*Assistant Professor, Department of Agricultural Economics and Rural Sociology, The Pennsylvania State University, University Park, Pa.

ber of ways. Almost all farms have been managed on a daily basis by one individual or a family. Moreover, such managers have owned most of the farmland and nonland resources (capital) and, with other family members, have provided most of the farm labor. As recently as 1964, farm managers owned 54% of all land in farms (Table 1). Along with other family members, they did about 75% of all farm work in 1969

(Nikolitch, 1972:18). While the ownership of farm capital (machinery, livestock, feed, crops) has never been determined, it can be inferred that farm managers have owned a high percentage of the total. There has been little rental or leasing of farm capital. Two types of farm managers have had low levels of ownership—hired managers and those involved in crop-share arrangements. While such farms have been important in some areas, they have never accounted for a high percentage of total U.S. farm numbers or sales.

When classified according to their levels (high or low) of land ownership by their managers, capital ownership by their managers, or labor provision by their managers (and other family members), farms with high levels have accounted for the majority of farm numbers in all areas and acreage, sales, or both in most areas. In 1910, farms managed by individuals who owned all the land in the farm accounted for 53% of all farm numbers and 53% of all farmland. An additional 9% of all farms, containing 15% of all land, were managed by individuals who owned some of the land in these farms and rented the remainder (Table 2). Farms have not been classified according to the level of capital ownership by farm managers. Farm managers, however, have owned a high percentage of the capital on their farms. This suggests farms with high levels of capital ownership by their managers have dominated farm numbers, acreage, and sales. As recently as 1969, an estimated 94% of all farms, accounting for 62% of all farm sales, had more than half of their labor provided by their managers and other family members (Table 5).

A sense of the patterning in American agriculture is possible through considering structural types of farms that emerge when they are classified by *simultaneously* invoking levels of land ownership, capital ownership, and labor provision by their managers. Since farms may have high levels on all three dimensions; high levels on two, low on one; a high level on one, low levels on two; or low levels on all three—a total of eight structural types can be identified.[1] At this point, only the farm types generated by simultaneously viewing levels (high or low) of land ownership and labor provision by farm managers (Fig. 1) will be considered.

On the average, farms of type A have the smallest size of all four types and have high levels of *both* land ownership and labor provision by their managers. The managers of these farms normally own all or most of the farm capital; hence, these farms have low levels of differentiation (separation) between all the factors of production. While a variety of terms have been used to refer to farms with these structural characteristics (Rodefeld, 1974:21), most commonly they have been called *family* or *family-type* farms; an appropriate technical term is "landowner managed: family-sized."

The exact number, acreage, and sales of family-type farms have never been determined. It seems likely, however, that they have accounted for a majority of total farm numbers in all areas and a majority of acres operated and sales in most. This conclusion is based on the historically high levels of land and capital ownership and labor provision by farm managers and by the dominance of landowner managed, capital-owner managed, and family-sized farms. Farms with characteristics approximating those of farms in this category accounted for 76% of all farms in 1959 and 50% of all sales (Table 8).

Farms of type D are the polar opposite, structurally, of family-type farms. These farms have low levels of both land ownership and labor provision by their managers. They may be managed by hired managers

[1] If a determination is also made of who owns most of the capital—when not owned by the manager (i.e., the land owner, hired laborer[s] or neither)—15 unique structural types can be identified. For a more detailed discussion of this classification system and characteristics of the unique structural types, see Rodefeld (1974: Chapter 3).

Level of land ownership by farm manager[1]	Level of labor provision by farm manager[1]	
	High Family-sized	Low Larger-than-family–sized
High: land owner managed	A Family-type	C Larger-than-family–type
Low: Non (land) owner managed	B Tenant-type	D Industrial-type

Fig. 1. Types of farms considered by levels of land ownership and labor provision by the farm manager. High = more than 50%; low = 50% or less.

by renters (all or most land rented), or through share arrangements. Landowners and/or employers may be retired farmers, nonfarm individuals or families, small groups of unrelated individuals, or family- or nonfamily-owned corporations. Hired managers normally do not own any capital; renters ordinarily own all or most. The majority of work on farms in this category is provided by hired workers, either seasonal or full-time, depending on the type of production. Levels of differentiation are high between land ownership, management, and labor and may or may not be high between capital ownership and management. The technical label for farms in this category is "non–landowner-managed: larger-than-family–sized." While a variety of popular and classificatory terms have been used in referring to farms in this category (Rodefeld, 1974:21-22), they will be called *industrial-type* in this paper. While the number of industrial-type farms has never been great, they have the largest average size (acreage, sales, or both) of all farm types. They have been economically significant in the South and West and in vegetable, fruit, cotton, and cattle-ranching areas. Farms with characteristics approximating those of this farm type accounted for 1% (26,000) of all farms in 1959 and 6.7% of total sales (Table 8).

Farms classified in category B have low levels of land ownership and high levels of labor provision by their managers. As with industrial-type farms, they may be managed by hired managers, renters (all or most of land rented), or share-managers. The land may be owned by a variety of individuals or corporations. Levels of capital ownership may be high (renters) or low (hired managers). An appropriate technical label for farms in this category is "non–landowner-managed: family-sized." In this paper they will be referred to as *tenant-type* farms.

On the average, these farms have been larger in size than family-type farms. A high percentage of all tenant-type farms have been located in the South. Most of these have been crop-share (sharecropper) types of operations on former plantations. In other regions tenant-type farms operated by renters or those using a livestock-share basis have dominated. Farms classified by the Census of Agriculture as tenant operated (all land rented—either for cash or on shares) accounted for 26% of all land in farms in 1910 and 31% in 1930 (Rodefeld, 1974:155). In 1959, farms with characteristics approximating those of tenant-type farms accounted for 19% of all farms and 19% of all farm sales (Table 8).

Farms in category C are the same as family-type units in that they have high levels of both land and capital ownership by their managers. They are different since they have much larger sizes on the average.

Like industrial-type farms, those in category C have low levels of labor provision by the farm manager, and the majority of farm work is performed by hired workers, either seasonal or full-time. An appropriate technical label for farms in this category is "landowner managed: larger-than-family–sized." It will be referred to here as *larger-than-family–type*.

While larger-than-family–type farms can be found in all modes of production, they have been concentrated in the same regions and types of production as the industrial-type forms. In 1959, farms with characteristics approximating those of the larger-than-family–type accounted for 3.8% (139,000) of all farms and 23.7% of all sales (Table 8).

CONDITIONS AND FORCES THAT HAVE RESULTED IN FAMILY-TYPE FARM DOMINATION

To explain the predominance of *family-type* farms in American agriculture, it is necessary to see why farm managers historically have owned most of the farmland and capital and have performed most of the farm labor. Explanations are also necessary for the historical dominance of landowner-managed farms, capital-owner–managed farms, and family-sized farms. These will be summarized in this section (Rodefeld, 1974: 110-210).

High levels of land ownership by farm managers and the dominance of landowner-managed farms before 1900 can be explained largely by five general factors. First, this was a result of conscious policy decisions and explicit programs by the federal government to sell and distribute land in small units, preferably to farm operators (managers). Pertinent examples are the ordinances of 1784, 1785, and 1787; the Preemption Act of 1841, and the Homestead Act of 1862. These policies and programs were advocated and enacted for a variety of reasons both ideological and pragmatic. Second, there was a lot of extremely cheap land available. Small farm sizes and low per-acre costs resulted in relatively low purchase prices. As recently as 1940, the average value of real estate per farm in the United States was only $4650 (Evans, and others, 1973). Third, high wages could be obtained throughout America's settlement period for both farm and nonfarm work. This allowed an individual or family to acquire the financial resources necessary to purchase a farm, or at least make a down payment, in a relatively short time. Fourth, both native and foreign settlers often placed a high value on owning their own land. Many foreign settlers came from societies where most farmers were denied access to land ownership. Also, ownership was necessary to benefit from appreciations in land values. Fifth, incentives for farmland ownership by nonfarmers have not been great. Rental rates have been low and the risks associated with farming great. Rates of return for invested capital have usually been higher and more certain in the nonfarm sector.

From the end of settlement (1880 to 1900) up to 1935, the ownership of farmland by farm managers and the relative status of landowner-managed farms declined substantially. From 1910 to 1935 the amount of farmland owned by farm managers declined from approximately 60% to 50% (Table 2). Farms managed by individuals who owned all the land in the farm declined from 53% of all farms in 1910 to 47% in 1935. Their percentages of total land declined from 53% to 37% in the same period (Table 2). Farms managed by individuals who owned none of the land increased in percentage of total numbers from 38% to 43% in this period and in share of acreage from 32% to 38% (Moyer and others, 1969: Tables A5 and A6).

The shifts toward non–landowner-farms occurred for a number of reasons. First, the size of the farm population and demand for land continued to expand, while the supply of free or cheap land declined. This resulted in larger purchase prices for land and farms. Also, the development of advanced horse-drawn and (later) mechanized equipment increased farming costs. Rising land and capital costs lengthened the amount of time necessary for beginning farmers to save enough money for land down payments, and subsequently their number of years in nonlandowning positions. Second, an increasing number of retired farmers, farm widows, and nonfarm heirs chose to retain their farms by renting them out, operating through share-tenants, or employing hired managers. Some of the major reasons for retention were lack of buyers, desire for rental or operating income, sentiment, and appreciation in land values. Third, the economic crash of the 1930's resulted in the foreclosure and loss of many farms by their indebted owners. Until purchasers could be found for these farms, they were either rented out or were operated by share-tenants or hired managers.

The high prices received by farmers in World War II allowed many farmers to purchase farms and pay off mortgages in short time periods and provided the resources for the purchase of additional acreage. As a result, levels of land ownership by farm managers and the status of landowner-managed farms reversed itself and rose once again.

The ownership of farm capital by farm managers has been high and capital-owner–managed farms have dominated in American agriculture for two general reasons. First, the costs of nonland resources have been low and well within the reach of most farm managers. In the middle of the 1800's, for example, the average value of these resources per farm was less

than $500. This value had risen considerably by 1940 but even then was estimated at only $1600 (Evans and others, 1973). Second, there have been few incentives for the ownership of nonland farm resources by nonfarmers.

The major conditions contributing to high levels of labor provision by farm managers and other family members and the dominance of family-sized farms are as follows. First was the decision by the federal government to sell land in small-sized units. This was more successful in the East and Midwest than in the South and West. Second, in most areas and types of production, size and labor requirements were small enough so that the farm manager and other family members were able to perform most of the needed work. Third, increased mechanization allowed farm managers and family members to do even more of the total work than previously. Fourth, periodic shortages of farm labor and high labor costs have discouraged the employment of hired personnel and the establishment of larger-than-family–sized farms.

Other factors have discouraged the establishment of larger-than-family–sized farms as well. The dominant ownership pattern of large numbers of small farms has made it difficult and costly to assemble large tracts of land for extensive farming operations. Most farm work is nonroutine, changing with the seasons and the impact of natural phenomena like rain, frost, or insects. Resultant changes in tasks and schedules reduce work-force efficiency. It also has been suggested that hired workers have high levels of alienation and are difficult to motivate, which reduces efficiency further. Biological, climatic, and economic uncertainty made agricultural production risky. These forces are important for very large farms with high ratios of fixed costs and possibly narrower profit margins. On large, highly differentiated farms prices have to be high and stable enough to yield rates of return to the owners competitive with those obtainable in the nonfarm sector. Historically, however, low prices have been the rule in agriculture. The managers of smaller farms have been forced, or were willing to accept rates of return lower than in the nonfarm sector.

HAS THE FAMILY FARM DECLINED RELATIVE TO "CORPORATE" FARMS?

In recent years, there has been considerable debate on the present and changing status of family farms and one type of industrial farm—those owned and operated by large, nonfarm corporations; that is, "corporate" farms. Two divergent conclusions have been asserted in this debate. The first is that the historical dominance of U.S. farm numbers and sales by "family" farms is rapidly being replaced by that of corporate farms. The major evidences given for this position are: (1) the continuing decline in farm numbers and the increased size of those remaining and (2) the widely reported entrance of large nonfarm corporations (for example, Boeing, Greyhound, Tenneco, Coca-Cola, Gates Rubber, Purex, CBK) into agricultural production (Barnes and Casalina, 1972; Kotz, 1971; Hightower, 1971; Halverson, 1972; U.S. Senate, 1968). Numerous opinion polls show that most farmers and many nonfarmers believe corporate farms are replacing family farms (Rodefeld, 1974:19).

The second assessment is that, while farm numbers have declined and average farm sizes have increased greatly in recent decades, the relative position of family farms has not changed. It is argued that the individuals and families managing farms on a daily basis continue to own most of the land and capital associated with farm production and still provide the majority of farm labor; levels of ownership and labor have not declined. A further claim is that farm numbers and sales continue to be dominated by owner-managed and/or family-sized farms, as they have historically. No changes have occurred in the relative positions of farms with these characteristics. Differences exist between regions and types of production, but these are matters of long standing. It is also pointed out that corporate farms, particularly those owned by large nonfarm corporations, account for very small percentages of U.S. farm numbers, land, and sales and even may have declined in recent years (King, 1972; Soth, 1971; Brewster, 1958; Stewart, 1960; Nikolitch, 1969, 1972; Harl, 1970; Campbell, 1972).

There is some truth in both views. Notwithstanding the strong and persuasive evidence that family farms have not declined, there are good reasons to predict family-type farms should be declining relative to other types and that industrial-type farms should be experiencing rapid growth. Major changes have occurred in the historical conditions responsible for the high levels of land ownership, capital ownership, and labor provision by farm managers and in the dominance of landowner-managed, capital-owner–managed, and family-sized farms (Rodefeld, 1974:110-210).

REASONS THAT SUGGEST FAMILY-TYPE FARMS HAVE DECLINED RELATIVE TO OTHER TYPES

As new mechanical devices became available in the twentieth century (particularly after the Depression), a variety of forces functioned as incentives for their adoption. The continual development of larger machines and their adoption by farmers resulted in greatly reduced farm numbers and increased farm sizes. The number of farms reached its peak in approximately 1935 at 6.8 million farms. By 1970 farm numbers had been reduced to 2.7 million (a 60% reduction). In the same time period, average farm size increased 146% or from 157 to 387 acres (Moyer and others, 1969; Ball and Heady, 1972). Increased farm size, rising land prices, and the increased values of farm buildings and building-related equipment have increased the average value and cost of U.S. farms considerably. From 1940 to 1972 the average value of farm real estate (land and buildings) increased from $4650 to $77,520. Average values per farm doubled from 1963 to 1972 (Evans and others, 1973). While past and present average farm values vary from one region to another, all regions have experienced large increases in farm sizes and values.

As farm sizes and values have increased, it has become increasingly difficult for young, financially unaided individuals to purchase farms and for families to transfer farms intact from one generation to the next. The managers of small farms are hard put to expand the size of their operations through the purchase of additional land; the general problem is acquiring enough capital to make a down payment. The bidding up of land prices beyond justifiable levels in some areas (primarily by nonfarmers) and the rising percentage of net farm income required to pay escalating property taxes have intensified the difficulties of land acquisition. If additional land is desired or required and financial resources are inadequate for land purchase, the only other alternative is land rental.

At the same time, incentives for land ownership by nonfarmers (both individuals and corporations) have risen. Because of the rapid and continuing rise in the value of farmland, investment in it is attractive as an inflation hedge or for speculation on long-term appreciation. Changes in urban values and life-styles suggest that nonfarm investments may increase because of persons hoping to obtain amenities associated with farm ownership. A number of tax benefits can be obtained from farmland ownership. These benefits increase as the amount of nonfarm income and one's tax bracket increase. Also, major reductions have occurred in the uncertainties associated with agricultural production, prices, and income. Production risks have been reduced in various ways through the development of more productive and disease-resistant varieties of crops, plus new herbicides and pesticides; by more accurate weather forecasting; via increased yields and gains from genetic engineering in livestock and the control of livestock diseases; and by the development of new machinery and equipment that reduce the exposure of crops to the risk of bad weather. Price and income fluctuations and the risk of low prices have been reduced as a result of numerous governmental programs; such as cropland diversion, acreage allotments, commodity storage programs, marketing orders, price supports, and commodity payments.

The existence of incentives for farmland ownership suggest that if capital is available for investment, purchases of farmland by nonfarmers should rise. It also suggests an increasing number of retired farmers, farm widows, and nonfarm heirs may be retaining their farmland. The increasing difficulties of farmland purchase by farm managers (or prospective managers), in conjunction with increased incentives for ownership by nonfarmers, suggest levels of land ownership by farm managers should be declining and ownership by nonmanagers should be increasing. They also suggest that farms with high levels of land ownership by their managers should be declining relative to those with low (or lower) levels of ownership.

A situation similar to land ownership exists regarding the nonland resources (capital). The average value of such farm capital rose from $1600 in 1940 to $24,200 in 1972 (Evans and others, 1973), a fifteenfold increase. Most of the 1972 value was accounted for by the value of machinery (48%) and livestock (40%). The reasons for the increased value of these resources are many: (1) the continued substitution of capital for labor, (2) the increased use of purchased versus homegrown imputs, (3) adoption of larger-capacity machines, (4) inflation, (5) increased machinery and livestock prices, and (6) increased numbers of livestock per farm.

As the costs of these resources increase, it should become more difficult for beginning, financially unaided farmers to acquire them through purchase, for families to transfer them intact intergenerationally, and for farmers to purchase them for expansion purposes. As these costs increase and pressures for farm-size expansion continue, it is likely farm managers will increase their use of nonland resource rental, leasing, and custom hiring.

As the difficulty of capital ownership has increased for farm managers, the incentives for their ownership by nonfarm individuals and corporations have increased. Some nonland resources provide inflationary hedges; can appreciate dramatically in value; and may be appealing for the honor, prestige, or status conveyed by them. A good example is investment in premium breeding stock or race horses. As with land ownership, numerous tax benefits can be gained from farm capital ownership. Nonfarm income can be converted to farm assets, which are taxed at capital gains rates when sold. This rate is considerably lower than that paid normally by individuals with high incomes. The depreciation of nonland resources, interest payments for the purchase of these resources, and farm operating losses may be deducted from taxable income. Both absolute and relative benefits from these tax provisions appear to increase as the amount of taxable income increases.

The levels of production, price, and income risk associated with the ownership and production of crops and livestock have been reduced for previously enumerated reasons. Ownership of nonland resources by nonfarmers may increase for speculative reasons. If world food demands exceed supply, dramatic increases can occur in the prices received for U.S. agricultural goods. Given the incentives associated with the ownership of nonland farm resources, increased levels of ownership by nonfarmers is suggested.

Decreased levels of capital ownership by farm managers may also occur through an expansion of vertical integration, production contracts, or both, where nonfarm integrators own farm capital. Incentives for such arrangements exist. They provide assured markets and the acquisition of necessary inputs for farm managers and reduce their capital needs and expenditures. For integrators producing farm input supplies (such as feed, seed, fertilizer, petroleum) such arrangements result in increased market control and ensure a more stable demand for their products. For integrators processing farm products, such arrangements ensure a steady flow of quality-controlled products while allowing a prescheduling of production, handling, and processing of products for greater efficiency. They also ensure farm product availability in the desired quantities and qualities. A quest for market power and control may be another incentive.

If it is becoming more difficult for farm managers to purchase their nonland resources, while incentives for ownership by nonfarmers are increasing; then levels of capital ownership by farm managers should decline. If this occurs, then farms with high levels of capital ownership by their managers will likely decline relative to those with lower levels of ownership.

Increased importance of large farms with low levels of labor provided by their managers (larger-than-family–sized) should be observed for three general reasons. First, many of the historical restraints associated with such farms have either been eliminated or greatly reduced. The difficulties of land aggregation have declined as farm sizes and consolidation have increased. Improvements in transportation (such as roads, pick-up trucks, airplanes) and communication (such as two-way radios, closed-circuit television) have reduced the time costs, management risks, and uncertainties associated with the operation of large or dispersed units. As mentioned previously, the uncertainties associated with agricultural production, prices, and income have been greatly reduced. With increased levels of specialization and mechanization, the amounts of nonroutine farm work have been reduced with resultant increased levels of work-force efficiency. It also appears that large farms can now compete successfully with the nonfarm sector for labor. Some research suggests levels of work satisfaction may not be as low nor levels of alienation as high among hired workers as has been commonly assumed.

Second, it has been argued that as size increases, certain costs are reduced, and certain benefits are increased. These "economies of scale" continue beyond the range of family-sized farms, thus serving as incentives for the establishment and operation of larger units. As size increases, it appears that other things happen: (1) awareness and adoption of new technologies by managers occurs sooner; (2) access to credit sources becomes easier, and costs decrease; (3) economies of buying and selling increase; (4) fixed costs are reduced; (5) economies of work role and product specialization increase; (6) access to contractual relationships (vertical integration) and favorableness of their terms increase. Low labor costs relative to the nonfarm sector encourage larger-than-family–sized farms. The operation of multiple units, widely dispersed geographically, spreads weather risks and allows for year-round production. If different products are grown, the risk of price fluctuations is reduced. It also has been suggested that the costs, labor requirements, and technical complexities associated with some new automated production and irrigation systems exceed the resources and capabilities of personnel on family-sized farms.

Third, another set of forces, less directly related to internal economies of scale has served as incentives for the establishment and operation of larger-than-family–sized farms. Government price supports and commodity payments have been tied to farm size—as size increases, the returns on invested capital and the magnitude and certainty of profit margins provided by government programs increase. As farm size grows, the many tax benefits increase, especially to nonfarmers with high incomes. Other incentives are attempts to achieve power equalization with input suppliers and output processors by increasing size and the willingness of communities and society to absorb certain costs resulting from the operation of extremely large operations (for example, pollution by large feed lots, community decline).

Incentives also exist for the increased ownership and operation of large farms by nonfarm corporations. This change will enhance increased levels of differentiation for all dimensions of farm organizational structure. All of the incentives for nonfarm ownership of land and capital and for the operation of larger-than-family–sized farms apply to nonfarm corporations as well. Moreover, there are additional incentives relatively unique to nonfarm corporations. Agribusiness corporations can realize all of the advantages coming from vertical integration with farmers by producing the goods themselves. They can also increase returns by eliminating some intermediaries and can reduce costs by buying internally. Generally, nonfarm corporations can benefit from increased diversification and risk spreading across product lines, crop types, and geographical areas. They may also be able to achieve greater internal economies or profits, or both, in agricultural production by: (1) increasing the retention rate of skilled agricultural workers through providing them with off-season jobs in other corporate divisions, (2) employing underused corporate staff in the agricultural activities, (3) applying large-scale advertising and merchandising techniques to agricultural goods, (4) taking advantage of unique financing and tax benefits, (5) providing their own research and development departments, and (6) hiring a higher quality farm work force.

PREDICTED CHANGES IN FARM ORGANIZATIONAL STRUCTURE AND TYPE

As discussed in the preceding section, the ownership of farmland and farm capital has become more difficult for individuals and families managing farms on a daily basis. The difficulty will increase in the future if the pressures for expansion of farm size continue. At the same time, numerous incentives exist for the ownership of farmland and capital by nonfarm individuals and corporations. These conditions suggest that levels of farmland ownership by farm managers and the status of farms with high levels of land ownership by their managers should be declining. Similarly, levels of farm capital ownership by farm managers and the status of farms with high levels of capital ownership by their managers should be declining.

Many of the historical restraints to the establishment and operation of large-sized farms employing hired laborers (larger-than-family–sized) have been eliminated or reduced. In addition, numerous incentives exist for the establishment and operation of such farms. This suggests that levels of labor provided by farm managers and the status of farms with high levels of labor provided by their managers should be declining. Units with low levels of labor provided by their managers, large-scale farms, or both should be increasing in either absolute or relative terms.

Changes should also be observed in the ownership arrangement (sole proprietorships, partnerships, corporations) of farm businesses and in the status of farms with high levels of business ownership by their managers. As implied in much of the foregoing discussion, incentives exist for nonfarm individuals and corporations to both own and operate farm businesses, the latter achieved by hiring individuals to manage and work the farms on a daily basis. Ownership of farm businesses by farm managers and the status of farms with high levels of business ownership by their managers should be declining.

If all of the preceding changes are occurring simultaneously, then farms characterized by high levels of land ownership, capital ownership, *and* labor provision by their managers (that is, family-type farms) should be declining relative to farms with low levels on one or more of these dimensions (that is, tenant, larger-than-family, and industrial-type farms).

In the following sections empirical evidence relevant to the predicted changes is presented and discussed.

Changes in the level of land ownership by farm managers and the status of farms with high levels of land ownership (landowner-managed) by their managers

A substantial amount of evidence supports the predicted decline in farmland ownership by farm managers and increased ownership by nonmanagers. Barlowe and Libby (1972:25-26) report rental payments to nonfarm landlords increased from $491 million in 1940 to $1.5 billion in 1970, a three-fold increase. Harris (1969:518) reports that mortgaged indebtedness and farm tenancy (none of land owned by manager) is increasing, especially in rich land areas of high capital requirements per farm. Hopkins (1970) maintains land leasing is becoming the dominant tenure pattern in the Midwest, particularly for higher income farms.

A number of authors have reported the increased ownership of farmland by nonfarmers (Parsons and Owens, 1951; Van Vliet, 1958; Moore and Dean, 1972). Barlowe and Libby (1972:25-26) aver, "It is common knowledge that doctors, lawyers, bankers, and other urban investors have acquired considerable tracts of valuable and productive farmland around urban areas and in prime agricultural and ranching areas." The same authors point out that while acquisitions by nonfarmers accounted for 33% of all farm acquisitions from 1959 to 1967, they accounted for 38% from 1968 to 1970. In Iowa, Berry (1964) found the percentage of farm landlords engaged in business and professional occupations was growing, while a decreasing percentage were farmers. Reports in the press of large-scale land purchases by wealthy individuals (Robbins, 1974), large nonfarm corporations (Hightower, 1972), and non–U.S. citizens (Hamburger, 1977) are also consistent with the predicted changes.

The most definitive data, however, are provided by the Census of Agriculture. Prior to 1969 the individuals managing farms on a daily basis (operators) were asked how many of the acres operated were owned and rented. If all the land was rented, the specific rental arrangement was determined (for example, cash, cash-share, crop-share, livestock-share). Farms operated by hired managers, who owned none of the land, were also identified. Table 1 reports the total numbers of acres owned and not owned by farm managers in the period 1935 to 1964. Because of a change in the definition of a farm operator in 1969, comparable figures do not exist for 1969 and 1974 (Rodefeld, 1976).

From 1935 to 1954, the number and percentage of

Table 1. Change in farm numbers, acres owned and not owned by individuals and families managing farms on a daily basis, and total acres, United States

| Year | Farms (in millions) | Acreage[2] | | | | | |
		Owned (in millions)	Percent	Not owned (in millions)	Percent	Total (in millions)	Percent
1910[1]	6.4					879	100
1935	6.8	523	49.6	531	50.4	1054	100
1950	5.4	669	57.7	492	42.3	1161	100
1954	4.8	675	58.2	485	41.8	1160	100
1959	3.7	628	56.4	496	43.6	1123	100
1964	3.2	603	54.3	507	45.7	1110	100
1969[1]	2.7						
1974[1]	2.4						
Percent change							
1954-1964	−33.3	−10.7		4.5		−4.3	

[1]Comparable data were not available because the definition of a farm operator in 1969 and 1974 was different from that in 1964 and earlier years.
[2]Data from Moyer, D., and others: Land tenure in the United States: development and status, USDA-ERS Agricultural Information Bulletin No. 338, Washington, D.C., 1969, Tables A5 and A6.

total acres owned by farm managers increased. After reaching a peak of 675 million acres (58.2% of total acres) in 1954, however, the number of acres owned by farm managers declined to 603 million acres in 1964 (54.3% of total). This is a 10.7% reduction in 10 years. The number of acres not owned by farm managers increased by 22 million acres from 1954 to 1964, a 4.5% increase. The percentage of total acres not owned increased from 41.8% to 45.7% in the same period.

In summary, individuals and families managing farms on a daily basis owned a majority (54.3%) of all farmland in 1964. However, the number and percentage of total acres owned declined substantially from 1954 to 1964. While comparable data does not yet exist for more recent years, farm managers would not own a majority of all farmland presently if the downward trend between 1954 and 1964 were continued. The reduced levels of land ownership by farm managers suggest that the status of farms with high levels of land ownership by their managers has declined relative to those with lower levels. Data presented in Table 2 address this issue.

All farms from 1910 to 1964 have been classified into one of three categories based on the portion of acres owned by the individual or family managing the farm on a daily basis. Farms with the highest levels of land ownership by their managers (100%) declined in

Table 2. Distribution and change[1] in U.S. farms and acres of land (in millions) in farms by the portion of land operated that was owned by the farm manager

| | Portion of land operated owned by farm manager | | | | | | | | | |
| | Full-owner (100%) operated | | Part-owner (1-99%) operated | | | | Hired manager-tenant (0%) operated | | Total | |
Year	Number of farms	Acres	Number of farms	Acres owned	Acres not owned	Total acres	Number of farms	Acres	Number of farms	Acres
1910	3.4	465	.59	—[2]	—[2]	134	2.46	280	6.4	879
1935	3.2	391	.69	132	134	266	2.95	397	6.8	1054
1950	3.1	419	.83	250	173	423	1.42	319	5.4	1161
1954	2.7	397	.87	278	195	473	1.12	290	4.8	1160
1959	2.1	349	.83	279	219	498	.75	277	3.7	1123
1964	1.8	319	.79	284	249	533	.56	258	3.2	1110
1969[3]									2.7	
1974[3]									2.4	
Percent change										
1910-1964	−47	−31	34	—[2]	—[2]	298	−77	−8	−50	26
1950-1964	−42	−24	−5	14	44	26	−61	−19	−41	−4
1959-1964	−14	−8	−5	2	13	7	−25	−7	−13	−1
Percent of total										
1910	52.7	52.9	9.3	—[2]	—[2]	15.2	37.9	31.9	100	100
1935	47.1	37.1	10.1	12.5	12.7	25.2	42.8	37.7	100	100
1950	57.4	36.2	15.3	21.6	14.9	36.5	27.2	27.4	100	100
1954	57.4	34.2	18.2	23.9	16.8	41.7	24.4	25.0	100	100
1959	57.1	30.9	22.5	25.4	19.5	44.9	20.4	24.1	100	100
1964	57.6	28.7	24.8	25.6	22.4	48.0	17.6	23.3	100	100
1969[3]										
1974[3]										

[1]Data from Moyer, D., and others: Land tenure in the United States: development and status, Agricultural Information Bulletin No. 338, Washington, D.C., 1969, Tables A5 and A6.
[2]Figures not available.
[3]Because of a change in the definition of a farm "operator" and the resultant elimination of the hired manager classification category, Census of Agriculture data on the number of farms and acres of land in farms by type of manager (operator) for these years are not comparable with pre-1969 data.

almost all respects to farms with lower levels of land ownership (99-0%). The number of "full-owner" farms declined from 3.1 million in 1950 to 1.8 million in 1964, a 42% reduction. Farms with some or none of the land owned (nonfull owner) declined from 2.25 to 1.35 million, a 40% reduction. Because of the similar percentage rates of decline, full- and nonfull-owner farms accounted for 57% and 43% of all farms in both 1950 and 1964.

From 1950 to 1964, the number of acres operated by full-owner farms slipped from 419 to 319 million acres, a decline of 100 million acres and 24%. The acreage of nonfull-owner farms rose from 742 to 791 million acres, an increase of 49 million acres and 6.6%. The percentage of total acres accounted for by full-owner farms declined from 36.2% in 1950 to 28.7% in 1964.

Farms with none of the land owned by their managers have also experienced major reductions in both numbers and acreages. From 1950 to 1964, their numbers declined by 61% and the acreage operated by 19%. While these farms accounted for 27% of all farms and 27% of all acreage in 1950, they accounted for only 18% and 23%, respectively, in 1964.

While the reductions in farms with the lowest levels of land ownership (0%) is not as predicted, not all of the more specific types included in this category have declined. Table 2 hides the fact, for instance, that farms operated by hired managers increased their total farm acres operated from 100 million (8.6%) in 1954 to 113.4 million (10.2%) in 1964. The number of hired-manager farms declined by 14% from 1954 to 1964, while their acres operated increased by 13% (Moyer and others, 1969). While the figures are not fully comparable, the number of commercial-sized (sales of $2500 or more) tenant-operated farms (cash rent, cash-share, crop-share, livestock-share, and other) declined from 391,929 in 1964 to 271,291 in 1969, a 31% reduction. Their percentage of total acres operated declined by less than 8%. The number of farms with all of their acres rented only declined by 12% (59,000 to 52,000) however, and they increased their acres operated from less than 34.5 million acres to 44.3 million acres, a 28% increase.* Most of the decline in the number of tenant-operated farms and all of the decline in acres operated have resulted from the decline in tenant farms operated on a share basis (crop, livestock, or combinations). A high percentage of these were probably located in the South. Moyer and associates (1969:15) estimates that more than

*From U.S. Bureau of the Census, Census of Agriculture **2:**763, 764, 1964; **2:**43, 67, 1969.

70% of the numerical decline in tenant farms since 1930 occurred in the South.

While farms with the highest levels of land ownership by their managers and most of the types with the lowest levels of ownership have declined, farms with intermediate levels (Table 2) have increased greatly. From 1950 to 1964, while total farm numbers were declining by 41%, part-owner farms declined by only 5%. As a result, their percentage of total farm numbers increased from 15.3% to 24.8%. Land operated advanced from 423 to 533 million acres in the same period, a 26% increase. Part-owner farms increased in percentage of total acres operated from 36.5% in 1950 to 48% in 1964.

The increasing percentages of total farm numbers and acreage in this category are consistent with the predictions. Unfortunately, these cannot be evaluated fully since it was impossible to divide part-owner farms into those with more than and less than half of their land owned by the manager. Farms with more than half the land owned by their managers should be declining relative to its opposite. There are some indications that they may be true. Contrary to earlier time periods, part-owner farms are now being expanded in acreage primarily through renting rather than through land purchases. From 1935 to 1950, 75% of the increased acreage in part-owner farms occurred through increases in owned acreage. From 1950 to 1954, 56% of the increased acreage was owned. In more recent time periods, however, most of the increased acreage has occured through rental. Total acreage in part-owner farms increased by 60 million acres from 1954 to 1964. Of this increase, 6 million acres were owned (10%), while 54 million were rented (90%). As a result of the preceding, the percentage of land in farms partly owned by the managers declined consistently from 59% in 1950 to 53% in 1964. If it is assumed that half of all part-owner farms in 1950 and 1964 had managers who owned more than half the land in their farms and these farms accounted for half the total acres owned and rented by part owners, then the following would be observed. Landowner-managed farms (more than half of land owned by the manager) would have accounted for 65% of all farms in 1950 and 70% in 1964. Their percentages of total acres operated would have declined from 54.4% to 52.7%. The acreage owned by the managers of these farms would have declined from 47% of acres in farms in 1950 to 41.5% in 1964. At a minimum, a high and increasing percentage of land in part-owner–operated farms is not owned by the farm manager. This suggests that a high and increasing percentage of part-owner farms have less than half their land owned by their managers.

Changes in the level of nonland resource (capital) ownership by farm managers and the status of farms with high levels of capital ownership (capital-owner managed) by their managers

Data on the ownership of farm capital are inadequate. No information exists on either the amount of total capital owned by farm managers and nonmanagers or the ownership of more specific capital items (such as machinery, livestock, crops). While the percentage of total capital owned by farm managers historically cannot be specified, the conclusion that it has been high clearly can be inferred. For instance, the leasing of farm machinery, livestock, and buildings and the custom growing of livestock and crops have never been widespread. Custom harvesting has achieved significance in only a few crop areas, particularly wheat. Involvement of farms in vertically integrated relationships where the integrator provides (owns) major portions of the capital has been very limited. The only farm managers who have not had high levels of capital ownership are hired managers and the managers of tenant farms, particularly those involved in share arrangements. Hired managers normally would not own any capital; tenant managers usually owned at least some capital although the variability has been considerable.

A good deal of evidence exists, however, that the high level of capital ownership by farm managers has declined in recent decades. Moyer and associates (1969:9) point out that, generally, vertical coordination contracts, custom farming, and the rental of equipment, machines, and buildings are among those tenure forms experiencing rapid growth. Harris (1974) has made a similar observation, also pointing out that the leasing of buildings and related equipment is in a "trial" stage. Expenditures by farm managers for machine hire (rental and leasing) and custom and contract work increased from $612 million in 1949 to $1.8 billion in 1974 (Nikolitch, 1972:21; U.S. Bureau of the Census, 1974 Census of Agriculture Preliminary Report, Dec. 1976). About 53% of all farms throughout this time period reported these types of expenditures.

Some cross-sectional evidence suggests that custom work and leasing are likely to increase as farm size expands. In a study of large grain farms in the Great Plains, Krenz and associates (1974) found that 54% of the farms studied reported the hiring of custom combining (including trucking) and 50% reported hiring custom spraying. As the size of these large operations increased, the percentage of acres custom combined and sprayed also increased (87% and 64% of the acres, respectively, in the largest size category). About one-fourth of the sample farms reported they had leased machinery, though mostly it was for short periods of time and small numbers of items.

Decreased ownership may also occur if the custom feeding of livestock or custom growing of crops is increasing. In these arrangements, nonfarmers own the livestock or crops and cover the costs of production and marketing. In the area of beef feeding, Meisner and Rhodes (1974) state:

The practice of custom feeding greatly facilitated the rapid structural evolution of cattle feeding. Custom feeding enabled feedlots to pass much of the burden of capital provision and risk-bearing to their customers. . . . Large size feedlots have tended to depend upon custom feeding for outside investors as a method to spread risks and utilize the feedlot's heavy investment in fixed plant and equipment. As feedlots increased in size, a higher percentage of the cattle were generally custom fed.

Texas studies of the state's major commercial feeding area found that two-thirds of the cattle on feed in 1966-67 were owned by customers rather than the feedlots, and that by 1969-70, nine-tenths were customer-owned.

Studies during the 1960's generally found a relatively close correlation between feedlot size and the percentage of its cattle being custom-fed for individuals not associated with the ownership of the feedlot.

. . . In total, outside investors were estimated to be financing one-fourth of our nation's fed beef in mid-1973.

Although their numbers and relative importance are unknown, Raup (1972b) reports the existence of many operations where nonfarm investors own breeding stock or fruit trees but do not own the farmland on which these resources are located.

Decreased ownership by farm managers also occurs under many types of production contracts and vertical integration. In the broiler industry, for instance, major feed companies supply the feed, chicks, medicine, markets and often the equipment. The farm manager (usually a landowner) provides the land and buildings, daily management, and labor. The relative importance of production contracts and vertical integration has increased in the last decade. From 1960 to 1970 the percentage of the total value of agricultural production handled under these arrangements increased from 19% to 22%. In some commodities, almost all production was handled through these arrangements in 1970: sugar cane and beets, 100%; broilers, 97%; processing vegetables, 95%; citrus fruit, 85%; potatoes, 70%. In other commodities, large increases occurred from 1960 to 1970: feeder cattle, 13% to 22%; eggs, 15% to 40%; turkeys, 34% to 56%; processed vegetables, 75% to 95% (Sundquist and Guither, 1973). The problem in interpreting these figures is that while levels of capital ownership by farm managers are known to be low in some areas (like poultry production), the extent of ownership in the other areas varies considerably, and the value of such ownership is unknown.

Decreased capital ownership by managers has also occurred as a result of the increased acreages in farms with hired, nonowning managers. These farms increased in acreage operated between 1954 and 1964 from 100 to 113.4 million acres (Moyer and others, 1969). There is reason to believe farms with hired, nonowning managers have increased since 1964 (numbers, acreage, or both) although this cannot be confirmed since this type was eliminated from the Census of Agriculture tenure classification in 1969.

In summary, it is clear that the individuals and families managing farms on a daily basis still own a high percentage of all farm capital. Given these high levels of capital ownership by farm managers historically, however, there appears little doubt that this level has declined considerably in the last decade. Certainly the expenditures for and values of capital not owned by farm managers has risen. Certainly, also, the numbers and percentages of farms with some or all of the capital not owned have increased and the amounts, and percentages of capital owned by the farm manager have decreased. What the magnitude of these changes has been, however, cannot be determined.

Decreased ownership of farm capital by farm managers suggests that farms with high levels of capital ownership by their managers have declined relative to those with lower levels of ownership. At a minimum, the status of farms where all of the capital is owned by the manager has declined. In areas and types of production with high and/or increasing levels of machinery rental, custom work, custom feeding, and vertical integration (contractual production), the status of farms with a majority of capital owned by the manager has likely declined. Given the very high levels of capital ownership by farm managers, however, total farm numbers, acres, production, and sales are still undoubtedly dominated by capital-owner–managed farms.

Changes in the provision of farm labor by farm managers and the status of farms (family-sized) with high levels of labor provided by their managers

Farm managers and family members continue to provide a high percentage of total farm labor. As Nikolitch (1972:18) points out, "the proportion of family labor employed on farms has remained about the same since 1930. In the country as a whole, family labor accounted for 76% of total farm employment during 1930-39 and 75% in 1969." At the same time, however, other evidence shows the increasing importance of hired workers, provides important qualifications to this apparent lack of change, and indicates the predicted decline in the proportion of labor by farm managers has occurred in more recent time periods.

The increased importance and usage of hired labor is indicated by a number of facts. Expenditures for hired labor have increased greatly. In 1959, total expenditures by commercial farms were $2.5 billion. This figure increased to $3.3 billion in 1969 and to $4.5 billion in 1974. As discussed earlier, expenditures have also increased for custom and contract work. Again, the percentages of total and commercial farms reporting expenditures for hired labor have increased. From 1959 to 1964, the percentage of total farms reporting the use of hired workers increased from 48% to 50% (Nikolitch, 1972:17). The percentage of commercial farms reporting expenditures increased from 74% to 80% in the period 1959 to 1969. The percentage reporting the presence of relatively full-time workers (that is, those employed 150 or more days) increased from 12.5% to 14.3% over the same period. The number of hired workers reported on farms has increased. From 1959 to 1964, the average number of hired workers on commercial farms increased from 2.4 to 2.6. Average numbers rose for farms in all tenure categories—the range was 9% for part-owner–operated to 41% for hired-manager–operated (Moyer and others, 1969:19).

Major changes have also occurred in the composition of the hired work force. In particular, those workers employed for short periods of time have declined at rapid rates, while workers employed for longer periods of time have increased in absolute numbers and in percentage of the total hired work force they represent. From 1963 to 1968 the number of hired farm wageworkers declined by 19%. All categories of wageworkers, regardless of number of days employed, declined. From 1968 to 1973, however, the total number of wageworkers declined by only 8.5%. Workers employed 1 to 24 and 25 to 149 days declined by 16% and 11%, respectively. Workers employed 150 to 249 and 250 or more days, however, experienced −3.5% and +23.0% changes (Rodefeld, 1975:49). Tables 3 and 4 provide even stronger evidence supporting a confirmation of the predicted changes.

Table 3 reports an increase of 1% in total worker numbers over the two most recent 3-year periods. The only worker category declining in absolute numbers was that with fewer than 75 days worked. Workers employed 150 days or more had the highest percentage increase in numbers, and their percentage of total worker numbers increased from 20% to 22%. Since the numbers of farm managers and family workers declined in this period, even while the numbers of hired workers, particularly full-time workers, increased, it is highly likely the percentage of total farm work done by hired workers increased.

Table 4 shows that in the 1968 to 1973 time period the worker days of wage work done by hired workers

Table 3. Frequency and change in the incidence of persons (in thousands) who did any farm wagework during the year, by duration of farm wagework (in days), United States*

Time period	Total workers	Duration of farm wagework in year (in days)			
		Less than 75	75-149	150-249	250 or more
1968-1970	2659	1857(69%)	286(11%)	206(8%)	310(12%)
1971-1973	2677	1761(66%)	308(12%)	249(9%)	358(13%)
Percent change	1	−5.2	7.7	20.9	15.5

*From McElroy, R. C.: The hired farm working force of 1973: a statistical report, USDA-ERS Agricultural Economic Report No. 265, Washington, D.C., 1974, p. 10.

Table 4. Frequency and change in the worker-days of farm wagework (in millions) by duration of farm wagework, United States*

Time period	Total worker-days of wagework	Duration of farm wagework in year (in days)			
		Less than 75	75-149	150-249	250 or more
1968-1970	212	42(20%)	30(14%)	41(19%)	98(47%)
1971-1973	232	38(16%)	32(14%)	50(22%)	111(48%)
Percent change	9.4	−9.5	6.7	22	13.3

*From McElroy, R. C.: The hired farm working force of 1973: a statistical report, USDA-ERS Agricultural Economic Report No. 265, Washington, D.C., 1974, p. 10.

Table 5. Change in farm numbers and sales by levels of labor provided by farm managers,[1] United States[2]

Level of labor provided by manager	Farm numbers (in thousands)			Percent change 1959-1969	Farm sales (in millions of dollars)			Percent change 1959-1969
	1959	1964	1969[3]		1959	1964	1969	
Family-sized	3530 (95.5%)	2996 (95.1%)	2580 (94.4%)	−26.9	21,136 (70%)	22,648 (65%)	27,296 (62%)	29.1
Larger-than-family-sized	165 (4.5%)	154 (4.9%)	146 (5.6%)	−11.5	9226 (30%)	12,427 (35%)	16,730 (38%)	81.3
Total	3695 (100%)	3150 (100%)	2726 (100%)	−26.2	30,362 (100%)	35,075 (100%)	44,026 (100%)	45.0

[1]Level of labor provided by the farm manager is defined operationally as the percentage of total farmwork done by the farm manager and the manager's family. A low level indicates 50% or less of the total work was done by the manager. A high level indicates more than 50% of the total work was done by the manager.
[2]The figures in this table were computed by Nikolitch (1972:4). Institutional farms and farms in Alaska and Hawaii were excluded. Estimates for 1949 were not included since the definition of family- and larger-than-family–sized farms were not the same as those used in 1959 and 1964. See Rodefeld (1974; 1975) for a more complete discussion.
[3]All 1969 figures were estimated by the author of the original report.

increased 9.4%, also indicating a likely increase in the percentage of total farm work done by hired workers. Days worked declined only for the category of less than 75 days and increased slightly for those working 75 to 149 days. The percentage increases were largest for those working 150 days or more. These two categories increased their percentage of farm wage work done from 66% to 70% of the total from 1968 to 1973.

The preceding data indicate the growing importance of hired workers in the farm labor force. They also suggest that the earlier stability in the percentage of total work by hired workers may be explained by the fact that the numbers of seasonal workers declined at high rates, while those of full-time workers decreased at lower rates or increased. There is a strong likelihood that the percentage of total farm work by farm managers and family members declined for the most recent time periods assessed.

The question of whether farms with high levels of labor provided by their managers and other family members (family-sized) have declined relative to farms with lower levels (larger-than-family–sized) is assessed in Table 5.

In special tabulations, the Census of Agriculture classified all farms in 1959 and in 1964 according to whether they employed more or less than 1.5 worker-years of hired labor. The available labor supply of the average farm family has been estimated (Nikolitch, 1972) to be 1.5 worker years. Using this figure as a cut-off point, the results in Table 5 are consistent with the prediction. While the absolute numbers of both farm types declined from 1959 to 1969, the rate of decline was much higher for family-sized (27%) than for larger-than-family–sized farms (11%). As a result, their percentage of total farm numbers declined from 95.5% to 94.4%. While the absolute value of sales increased for both farm types from 1959 to 1969, the rate of increase was much lower for family-sized farms (29% versus 81%). As a result the percentage of total sales by family-sized farms declined from 70% in 1959 to 62% in 1969.

While 1969 figures were not available for geographical areas, from 1959 to 1964 larger-than-family–sized farms increased in percentages of total sales in every geographical region. The increased percentages ranged from 1% (middle Atlantic) to 13% (New England) (Nikolitch, 1972:9). They increased in percentages of total land in farms, cropland harvested, and value of land and buildings in almost all of the eleven regions assessed. They decreased in percentages of total land in pastures in six of eleven regions and in the United States as a whole (Nikolitch, 1972:12). The increases in larger-than-family–sized farms from 1959 to 1964 were not restricted to their traditional geographical locations of importance.

Changes in the status of large- and small-scale farms

Even though acres operated and value of sales do not directly measure any of the structural dimensions being assessed in this paper, they are included because of their strong relationships with levels of land ownership and with labor provision by farm managers and family members. As both number of acres operated and value of sales increase, the percentage of farms renting land and the percentage of land not owned by the operator increase (Johnson, 1974:19, 22, 31, 43). Moyer and associates (1969:18-19) noted:

The percentage of commercial farms reporting hired labor and the average number of hired laborers reported seems to be related to size of farm and tenure of operator. As size of farm increased, the proportion of farms reporting hired labor and the average number of laborers reported increased.

In 1964, only 14.5% of the farms with sales exceeding $100,000 were family-sized, and they accounted for only 8.4% of this grouping's sales (Nikolitch, 1969:39).

If, as predicted, large farms with low levels of land ownership, labor provision by farm managers, or both are replacing smaller farms with higher levels of ownership, labor provision, or both; it is also reasonable to predict that extremely large-sized farms in terms of both acreage and sales should be increasing. Table 6 shows changes that occurred from 1930 to 1974 in the numbers of farms and acres operated with more than 1000 acres.

The results are as predicted. Increases have occurred in both the absolute numbers and total acres operated by these farms from 1930 to 1974. Farms with less than 1000 acres, on the other hand, decreased in both regards. While farms exceeding 1000 acres accounted for 28% of the land in 1930, the figure rose to 58% in 1974. From 1930 to 1969 these percentages increased for all four major regions of the country, suggesting growth of these farms has not been restricted geographically. From 1964 to 1974, farms exceeding 1000 acres increased from 24.4% to 33.7% of total U.S. cropland, and from 43.7% to 53.7% of irrigated land.

Table 7 reports changes in the numbers and sales of farms with sales of more and less than $100,000. Again, the results are consistent with the predictions. The number of the largest farms has been increasing in absolute terms, while the number of smaller-sized farms has been declining. The value of sales increased for all farms from 1959 through 1974, but the rate of increase was considerably greater for the largest farms, 774% versus 47%. The percentage of all farm numbers accounted for by these largest farms increased from 0.5% in 1959 to 6.6% in 1974. Their per-

Table 6. Change in farms operating less and more than 1000 acres[1]

Year	Numbers (in thousands)			Acres in farms (in millions)			Percent of total acres by farms with more than 1000				
	Less than 1000	More than 1000	Total	Less than 1000	More than 1000	Total	North-east	North Central	South	West	Total
1930	6214(98.7%)	81(1.3%)	6295	713	277	990	2.5	12.3	24.9	64.8	27.9
1940	6001(98.4%)	101(1.6%)	6102	699	336	1065	3.0	16.4	29.5	73.7	34.3
1950	5267(97.7%)	121(2.3%)	5388	668	495	1163	3.3	20.6	36.1	82.3	42.6
1959	3569(96.4%)	136(3.7%)	3705	568	555	1123	5.3	25.5	43.4	86.8	49.4
1969	2579(94.5%)	151(5.5%)	2730	485	578	1063	6.6	33.0	47.4	89.3	54.4
1974	2159(93.3%)	155(6.7%)	2314	427	590	1017	—[2]	—[2]	—[2]	—[2]	58.0
Percent change											
1959-1974	−39	11	−37	−25	6	−9					

[1]Data from U.S. Bureau of the Census, Census of Agriculture.
[2]Figures not available.

Table 7. Changes in the numbers and sales of farms with sales of less and more than $100,000

	Year					Percent change 1959-1974
	1929	1959	1964[2]	1969[3]	1974	
Farm characteristics by sales class						
Number (in thousands)						
Less than $100,000 sales	6293.0	3685	3125	2678	2159	−41
More than $100,000 sales	2.4	20	31.4	52	153	665
Total	6295.4	3705	3156.4	2730	2312	−38
Sales (in billions of dollars)						
Less than $100,000 sales	—[1]	25.6	26.8	30.3	37.6	47
More than $100,000 sales		5.0	8.5	15.3	43.7	774
Total		30.6	35.3	45.6	81.3	166
Percent of total by farms with more than $100,000 sales						
Number	.04	.5	1.0	1.9	6.6	
Sales		16.3	24.2	33.6	53.8	
Type of sales						
Crops		17.6	24.4	28.1	50.0	
Livestock and poultry		15.1	24.0	41.2	56.3	
Region of sales						
Lake states		3.5	7.6	13.1	—[4]	
Appalachia		5.0	9.1	15.8		
Corn belt		5.4	9.4	18.9		
Southeast		23.8	35.7	33.4		
Mountain		28.4	39.5	54.0		
Pacific		44.7	59.3	66.3		

[1]This figure and those following were not available for 1929.
[2]The 1929 to 1964 figures were obtained from Nikolitch (1970).
[3]The 1969 and 1974 figures were obtained from the U.S. Bureau of the Census, Census of Agriculture.
[4]This figure and those following had not yet been obtained at the time this paper was written.

centage of total sales increased from 16.3% in 1959 to 53.8% in 1974. The growing significance of these large farms has not been restricted to any one type of production or region. From 1959 to 1974, their percentages of both total crop and livestock and poultry sales increased. From 1959 to 1969 percentages of total sales in the three regions within which they were least significant in 1959 increased in the following decade, as they did in two of the three regions within which they were most important in 1959. Incomplete data for 1974 suggest an acceleration in the trend. Farms with sales over $100,000 increased 194% from 1969 to 1974 compared to an increase of 67% from 1964 to 1969.

Changes in the beef-feeding industry are also consistent with the predicted increases in large-scale farms and the increased significance of large farms with high levels of differentiation. From 1962 to 1973, the number of commercial feedlots with a handling capacity of more than 1000 head, increased their absolute numbers from 1517 to 2040 while smaller feedlots were declining in number. These large feedlots increased their percentage of total cattle fed from approximately one-third to two-thirds in the period from 1962 to 1973. Furthermore, the level of concentration is apparently greater than indicated because some operations have more than one lot (Meisner and Rhodes, 1974).

Trends toward concentration of sales in larger-scale operations are likely to continue. Forty-nine percent of a sample of large-scale (income of $50,000 or more) grain producers in the Great Plains indicated plans to expand in the future (Krenz and others, 1974:8). A 1974 survey of the largest hog operations in the United States (those with 4000 or more head) found that about half planned to expand in the next 5 years (Rhodes and others, 1974).

Changes in the ownership of farm businesses (sole proprietorships, partnerships, and corporations) by individuals and families managing farms on a daily basis and the status of farms with high levels of business ownership by their managers

As business entities, almost all farms have been organized as either sole proprietorships, partnerships, or corporations. The type of organization involved has both legal and tax implications for the business owners. Sole proprietorships are owned by one individual or family (usually nuclear); partnerships by two or more individuals or families. Corporations can be owned by either small or large numbers of individuals and families.

Historically, a high percentage of all farm businesses has been organized as sole proprietorships or as partnerships. In 1969 for instance, 85.4% of all

commercial farms were sole proprietorships and 12.8% were partnerships. Together they accounted for 98.2% of all farm businesses in 1969 and 90.3% of the land in farms. Only 1.2% (21,513) of the commercial farms in 1969 were organized as corporations. They accounted for 8.8% of the land in farms. While no information exists on how many were owned or controlled by single individuals or families, only 1797 (.1%) had more than 10 shareholders. These farms accounted for 1.6% of commercial farmland (U.S. Bureau of the Census, Census of Agriculture, 1969).

Clearly, individuals or families own almost all farm businesses, and these businesses contain most of the land in farms. In 1969, sole proprietorships, partnerships, and corporations with 10 or fewer shareholders accounted for 99.3% of all farm businesses and 97.5% of all commercial farm acreage (U.S. Bureau of the Census, 1969). From 1969 to 1974, no change occurred in the percentage of commercial farms organized as either sole proprietorships or partnerships. Corporations increased from 21,513 (1.2%) to 28,656 (1.7%) (U.S. Bureau of the Census, Census of Agriculture, 1976).

So far there has been no answer to the questions of how many of the businesses are owned by individuals or families managing farms on a daily basis or what changes have occurred in their levels of ownership. Farm business owners may or may not manage the farms on a daily basis. Other individuals or families may be employed for this purpose. While definitive data are lacking, it appears that a high percentage of all farm businesses has been organized and owned by farm managers. The major exceptions are businesses employing hired managers and possibly some of the farms managed by tenants, particuarly those involved in share-type arrangements (cash, crop, livestock). The latter number of farms is unknown, but in 1964 only 18,000 farms (less than 1%), operating 10% of the land in farms, employed hired managers.

While far from definitive, evidence exists that the ownership of farm businesses by farm managers has declined in recent years. Farms employing hired managers, for instance, increased in percentage of total numbers from 1950 to 1964, the last year this assessment was made by the Census of Agriculture (Rodefeld, 1974:155). Also, the number of corporations increased by 7143 between 1969 and 1974. It is likely that a portion of these corporations were not owned or controlled by one individual or family and that an even larger portion were not managed on a daily basis by the owners.

In 1969, 457,700 farm-business owners (18.8% of the total) did not reside on their farms. This does not include the owners of corporations, who were not assessed in this respect by the Census of Agriculture.

The major questions are how many owners managed their farms on a daily basis while the farms were in production and what changes have occurred in these numbers. While this information has not been reported by the Census of Agriculture, a reasonable estimate is possible.

In 1959, 267,000 individuals (7.6% of the total) managed farms on a daily basis while not residing on them. This number increased to 291,000 (9.5% of the total) in 1964. Assuming the direction and rate of change in the number of such managers was the same from 1964 to 1969 as from 1959 to 1964 (an increase of 9%) there would have been 317,190 (an increase of 26,190) in 1969. Thus, an estimated 140,510 (457,700 minus 317,190) farm business owners did not manage their farms on a daily basis in 1969 (U.S. Bureau of the Census, Census of Agriculture, 1969:174).

While the number of business owners not managing their farms is unknown for 1964, the lower limit would be 18,000—the number of farms with hired managers. The change from this lower limit in 1964 to the estimated 1969 level was from 18,000 (1% of commercial farms) to 140,510 (8.1% of commercial farms). The percentage increase in the number of such farms from 1964 to 1969 was 677%. The total number of farms declined in the same period by 15.6%.

The major conclusions in this section are as follows. First, individuals and families managing farms on a daily basis continue to own a high percentage of farm businesses. Second, ownership of farm businesses by farm managers declined substantially from 1964 to 1969. Finally, this suggests farms with high levels of business ownership by their managers have declined relative to those with low levels from at least 1964 to 1969.

Change in the status of farms with high levels of land ownership and labor provision by their managers

As predicted initially, levels of land ownership, capital ownership, and labor provision by the individuals and families managing farms on a daily basis have declined. The statuses of farms with high levels of land ownership, capital ownership, labor provision, and business ownership by their managers have also declined. Small-scale farms have declined relative to large-scale farms. These various changes imply that a decline also has occurred in the relative status of farms with simultaneously high levels of land ownership, capital ownership, and labor provision by their managers; that is, the historically dominant family-type farm.

Unfortunately, decline in the family-type farm cannot be empirically verified since farms have never been classified in this manner. Farms have been classified, however, according to their simultaneous levels of land ownership and labor provision (Table 8).

Tenant-type farms experienced the greatest rates of decline from 1959 to 1964. Farms classified in this category experienced a 28% reduction in numbers and were the only farms experiencing an absolute decline in value of sales (9.1%). Their percentage of total farm numbers declined from 19.5% to 16.5% and of sales from 19.5% to 15.3% of total.

Family-type farms declined in numbers at about the same rate as did larger-than-family–type farms, 11.9% and 12.2%, respectively. While the absolute value of the former's sales increased from 1959 to 1964, their percentage change in sales was the third lowest of the four farm types (11.9%). Even though family-type farms accounted for a higher percentage of all farm numbers in 1964 (78.6%) than in 1959

Table 8. Change in farm numbers and sales by structural types,[1] United States[2]

Farm type	Farms (in thousands)		Percent change	Sales (in millions of dollars)		Percent change
	1959	1964		1959	1964	
Family	2808 (76%)	2475 (78.6%)	−11.9	15,224 (50.1%)	17,276 (49.3%)	11.9
Tenant	721 (19.5%)	521 (16.5%)	−27.7	5912 (19.5%)	5372 (15.3%)	−9.1
Larger-than-family	139 (3.8%)	122 (3.9%)	−12.2	7202 (23.7%)	8915 (25.4%)	23.8
Industrial	26 (.7%)	32 (1%)	23.1	2024 (6.7%)	3512 (10%)	73.5
Total	3695(100%)	3150(100%)	−14.7	30,362(100%)	35,075(100%)	15.5

[1]Landowner-managed farms (family and larger-than-family types) have high levels of land ownership by their managers, and operationally in this table consist of all full- and part-owner operated farms (1% to 100% of land owned by managers). Nonlandowner-managed farms (tenant and industrial) have low levels of land ownership by their managers, and in this table consist of hired-managers–and tenant-operated farms (0% of land owned). Family-sized (family and tenant) and larger-than-family–sized (larger-than-family and industrial) farms are defined operationally as before (Table 5).

[2]See Rodefeld (1974; 1975) for the procedures followed in the computation of these figures.

(76%), their percentage of total sales declined from 50.1% in 1959 to 49.3% in 1964. While the larger-than-family–type farms experienced a 12.2% reduction in numbers from 1959 to 1964, they had the second highest percentage increase in sales (23.8%). Their percentage of total farm numbers increased from 3.8% to 3.9%, and their percentage of total sales from 23.7% to 25.4% in the same period.

Industrial-type farms were the only ones that grew in absolute numbers from 26,000 in 1959 to 32,000 in 1964. They also experienced the largest percentage increase in value of sales (73.5%) and increased in percentage of total farm numbers (0.7% to 1%) and total sales (6.7% to 10%) from 1959 to 1964.

The declining significance of family-sized farms, regardless of land ownership level, is clearly indicated in Table 8. Family-sized farms declined by 534,000 farms in the period assessed. Larger-than-family–sized farms declined by only 11,000, however. The rapid decline of tenant-type farms can be explained largely by the rapid rates of mechanization throughout the South in this time period and the consolidation of these farms into larger units.

The results in Table 8 should be qualified in a number of respects. First, this is not an ideal classification since it was impossible to divide the part-owner–operated farms into those with more and with less than half the land owned by the manager. Farms with either all or some of the land owned were combined in this classification and constituted the land-owner–managed farm types. As a result, the numbers, sales, and percentages of total numbers and sales of both the family- and larger-than-family–type farms are overestimated. Conversely the numbers and sales of the tenant and industrial-type farms have been underestimated. If part-owner farms had been properly classified, the percentage reductions in family-and larger-than-family–type farms would have been greater, and their percentage increases in sales less than reported. Tenant-type farm numbers and sales would not have declined as much, and the increases in industrial-type farms would have been greater.

Second, no comparable information exists for the most recent time period. Increases in larger-than-family–sized farms and large-scale farms since 1964, however, suggest that family and tenant-type farms continued to decline relative to larger-than-family–and industrial-type farms. Third, no information exists on either the current or changing status of these farm types in different states, regions, or types of production.

SUMMARY AND CONCLUSION

A variety of conditions have resulted in high levels of farmland and capital ownership and of labor provision by the individuals and families managing farms on a daily basis. One consequence of this has been the numerical domination in all geographical areas, and the economic domination in most, of farms with high levels of land ownership, capital ownership, and labor provision by the farm managers and other family members. Another consequence has been the numerical dominance in all geographical areas, and economic dominance in most, of farms with high, *simultaneous*, levels of land and capital ownership and labor provision by their managers. Most commonly, farms possessing these structural characteristics have been called "family" or family-type farms.

Almost all past studies of farm change have shown no declines in levels of land and capital ownership and of labor provision by farm managers and no decline in the status of farms with family-type characteristics. However, numerous inferential reasons suggest declines should be occurring. A review of existent evidence confirmed these and other expectations.

Levels of farmland ownership, capital ownership, labor provision, and business ownership by farm managers have declined. In each instance, farms with high levels of land ownership, capital ownership, labor provision, and business ownership have declined relative to farms with lower levels. Small-scale farms have declined substantially, relative to large-scale farms. Both family- and tenant-type farms have declined relative to larger-than-family– and industrial-type farms. From 1959 to 1964, industrial-type farms experienced the greatest increases of all farm types in numbers and sales.

While family-type farms still account for a majority of farm numbers, they do not account for a majority of either production or sales at the present time. By one estimate, family-type farms accounted for 78.6% of all farms in 1964 and 49.3% of all sales. If part owners owing less than half the land in their farms had been removed from the family-type category, however, both of these percentages would have been lower. In addition, 13 years have passed since these estimates were taken. The dramatic increases in the numbers and sales of very large farms (1,000 or more acres, $100,000 or more in sales) since 1964 suggest substantial declines in both family-and tenant-type farms from 1964 to the present.

Have family-type farms declined as a result of "corporate" farm growth? If a "corporate" farm is defined as a farm owned and operated by a large, nonfarm, nonfamily corporation, then there is little evidence to date that this has been the case. In 1969, the Census of Agriculture reported only 1797 corporations with ten or more shareholders engaged in farming. These corporations (0.1% of all farms) accounted for only 1.5% of the land and 2% of the sales. While there is some evidence that the Census of Agriculture underenumerated farming corporations, it is not clear how many of these were non-family corporations. Even if all were, however, the general conclusion would not be altered. However, family-type farms have been replaced in part by industrial-type farms. While all or most farms owned by nonfarm, nonfamily corporations would be classified in this category, they would be a minority of the farm numbers in this category and would account for a minority of industrial-type farm sales. While all or most large, nonfarm corporations in farming may be industrial-type farms, not all industrial-type farms are legally incorporated. Large, nonfarm corporations may be declining in agricultural production even while industrial-type farms are rapidly increasing.

At the same time, it need be said that to accurately assess trends in farm types and changes in the levels and types of structural differentiation, more detailed information is required in a number of areas. We need to know more about who owns farmland and farm capital (the farm manager, laborers, nonfarmers—what type of nonfarmers), who is managing farms on a daily basis, who is doing the farm work (managers, laborers—what type of laborers) and how much of the farm work are they doing. Once this information is obtained, then farms could be classified (at the very least) by their levels of differentiation between land ownership, capital ownership, management, and labor.

Given the demonstrated trends toward larger farms with higher levels of differentiation (lower levels of ownership and labor provision by managers) on all dimensions of organizational structure, much more empirical and conceptual work is needed to explore the causal forces bringing these changes about and the consequences of these changes for other farm characteristics, farm people, rural communities, and the urban sector.

REFERENCES

Ball, A. G., and E. O. Heady: Trends in farm and enterprise size and scale In Ball, A. G., and Heady, E. O., editors: Size, structure and future of farms, Ames, Iowa, 1972, The Iowa State University Press.

Barlowe, R., and Libby, L.: Policy choices affecting access to farmland. In Guither, H. A., Who will control U.S. Agriculture? North Central Regional Extension Publication 32, Urbana, Ill., 1972, University of Illinois.

Barnes, P., and Casalino, L.: Who owns the land? A primer on land reform in the U.S.A., Berkeley, Calif., 1972, Center for Rural Studies.

Berry, R. T.: Share rents as an obstacle to farm improvement and soil conservation, Journal of Land Economics **40**:346-352, 1964.

Bowles, G., and Sellers, W. E., Jr.: The hired farm working force of 1963: with supplementary data for 1962, USDA-ERS Agricultural Economic Report No. 76, Washington, D.C., May 1965.

Brewster, J. M.: Technological advance and the future of the family farm, Journal of Farm Economics **40**:1596-1608, 1958.

Campbell, J. P.: Family Farm Act, Testimony before the U.S. House of Representatives, Committee on the Judiciary, Hearings Before the Anti-trust Subcommittee (No. 5), 92nd Congress, on H.R. 11654 and similar bills, Mar. 22-23, 1972, Serial No. 28, Washington, D.C., 1972, U.S. Government Printing Office.

Evans, C. D., and others: The balance sheet of the farming sector, 1973, USDA-ERS, Washington, D.C., Oct. 1973.

Halverson, G.: U.S. farmers: what road ahead? Christian Science Monitor, Aug. 28-Sept. 1, 1972.

Hamburger, T.: New type of owner may speed land boom, push some out, Arkansas Gazette, Little Rock, Ark., May 15, 1977.

Harl, N. E.: Agricultural structure and corporations—economics and emotions, In The National Farm Institute: Corporate farming and the family farm, 1970, The Iowa State University Press.

Harris, M.: Shifts in enterpreneurial functions in agriculture, Am. Journal of Agricultural Economics **51** Aug. 1969.

Harris, M.: Enterpreneurial Control in Farming, USDA-ERS Agricultural Economics Report No. 542, Washington, D.C., Feb. 1974.

Hightower, J.: Corporate power in rural America, Paper presented at the New Democratic Coalition Hearing, Washington, D.C., Oct. 12, 1971.

Hightower, J.: Corporate power in rural America, WIN **8**(12):8-10, July 1972.

Hopkin, J. A.: Financing farm growth-requirements and alternatives, In National Farm Institute, Corporate farming and the family farm, Ames, Iowa, 1970, The Iowa State University Press.

Johnson, B. B.: Farmland tenure patterns in the United States, USDA-ERS Agricultural Economic Report No. 249, Washington, D.C., Feb. 1974.

Kendall, D.: Half of country's food, fiber grown on super farms, Capital Times, Madison, Wis., Aug. 5, 1974.

King, S.: The family farm is not dead, Saturday Review **15**(31):14-16, July 29, 1972.

Kotz, N.: Conglomerates reshape food supply, Washington Post, Washington, D.C. Oct. 3, 1971.

Kotz, N.: U.S. policy handcuffs small farmer, Washington Post, Washington D.C., Oct. 5, 1971.

Krenz, R. D., Heid, W. G., Jr., and Sitler, H.: Economics of large wheat farms in the Great Plains, USDA-ERS Agricultural Economic Report No. 264, Washington, D.C., July 1974.

McElroy, R. C.: The hired farm working force of 1968: a statistical report, USDA-ERS Agricultural Economic Report No. 164, Washington, D.C., June 1969.

McElroy, R.C.: The hired farm working force of 1973: a statistical report, USDA-ERS Agricultural Economic Report No. 265, Washington, D.C., July 1974.

Meisner, J. C., and Rhodes, V. J.: The changing structure of U.S. cattle feeding, Special Report 167, Columbia, Mo., Nov. 1974, University of Missouri.

Moore, C. V., and Dean, C. W.: Industrialized farming, In Ball, A. G., and Heady, E. O.: Size, structure and future of farms, Ames, Iowa, 1972, The Iowa State University Press.

Moyer, D., and others: Land tenure in the United States: development and status, USDA-ERS Agricultural Information Bulletin No. 338, Washington, D.C., June 1969.

Nikolitch, R.: Family operated farms: their compatibility with technological advance, American Journal of Farm Economics **51**(3): 1969.

Nikolitch, R.: Our 31,000 largest farms, USDA-ERS Agricultural Economics Report No. 175, Washington, D.C., Mar. 1970.

Nikolitch, R.: Family-size farms in U.S. agriculture, USDA-ERS Agricultural Economics Report No. 499, Washington, D.C., Feb. 1972.

Parson, K. H., and Owen, W. F.: Implications of trends in farm size and organization, Journal of Farm Economics **33**:893-903, 1951.

Raup, P. M.: Corporate farming in the United States, staff paper

P72-32, St. Paul, Minn., Dec. 1972, University of Minnesota.

Rhodes, V. J., Finley, R. M., and Grimes, G.: A 1974 survey of large-scale hog production in the U.S., Special Report 165, Columbia, Mo., Aug. 1974, University of Missouri.

Robbins, W.: 380,000 acres plantation is being started in the wilderness, New York Times, New York, May 8, 1974.

Rodefeld, R. D.: The changing occupational and organizational structure of farming and the implications for farm work force individuals, families and communities, Unpublished doctoral dissertation, Madison, Wis., May 1974, University of Wisconsin.

Rodefeld, R. D.: Evidence, issues and conclusion on the current status and trends in U.S. farm types, Unpublished paper presented at the Rural Sociological Society Meeting, San Francisco, Calif., Aug. 1975.

Rodefeld, R. D.: The assessment of farm (operating-unit) and farm operator characteristics by the U.S. Census of Agriculture: shortcomings and procedures for their alleviation, Agricultural Census, Hearings before the Subcommittee on Census and Population, House of Representatives, 94th Congress, Serial No. 94-76, June 22-23, 1976, Washington, D.C., 1976, U.S. Government Printing Office.

Soth, L.: Corporate farm invasion mostly myth, Des Moines Sunday Register, Des Moines, Iowa, Nov. 28, 1971.

Stewart, H. L.: The organization and structure of some representative farms in 1975, Journal of Farm Economics **42**(2):1367-1379, 1960.

Sundquist, W. B., and Guither, H. D.: The current situation and the issues. In Guither, H. D., editor: Who will control U.S. agriculture? A series of six leaflets, North Central Regional Extension Publication 32-1, Urbana, Ill., 1973, University of Illinois.

Timmons, J. F.: Tenure and size. In Ball, A. G., and Heady, E. O.: Size, structure and future of farms, The Iowa State University Press.

U.S. Bureau of the Census, Census of Agriculture, Washington, D.C., 1930-1974, Government Printing Office.

U.S. Bureau of the Census, 1974 Census of Agriculture: preliminary report, United States, Washington, D.C., Dec. 1976, U.S. Government Printing Office.

U.S. Senate, Committee on Small Business, Corporate farming, Hearings before the Subcommittee on Monopoly, 90th Congress, on the Effects of Corporate Farming on Small Businesses in the Great Plains and Upper Midwest, Washington, D.C., 1968, U.S. Government Printing Office.

VanVliet, H.: Increased capital requirements and the problem of getting started in farming, Journal of Farm Economics **40**:1613-1621, 1958.

6

The significance of farm organizational structure and the consequences of its change

Agricultural enterprise and rural class relations[1]

ARTHUR L. STINCHCOMBE*

ABSTRACT

Property is far more important in rural stratification than in urban stratification, where occupational position predominates. There is less similarity of the property systems in commercialized agriculture than there is in urban occupational structure. In agricultural production for markets, the main types of property systems are commercialized manorial systems, plantation systems, and ranching systems. Each of these produces a distinctive pattern of class relations, determining the sharpness of differences of legal privileges and style of life, and shaping the distribution of technical culture and political activity.

Marx's fundamental innovation in stratification theory was to base a theory of formation of classes and political development on a theory of the bourgeois enterprise.[2] Even though some of his conceptualization of the enterprise is faulty, and though some of his propositions about the development of capitalist enterprise were in error, the idea was sound: One of the main determinants of class relations in different parts of the American economy is, indeed, the economic and administrative character of the enterprise.[3]

But Marx's primary focus was on class relations in cities. In order to extend his mode of analysis to rural settings, we need an analysis of rural enterprises. The purpose of this paper is to provide such an analysis and to suggest the typical patterns of rural class relations produced in societies where a type of rural enterprise predominates.

PROPERTY AND ENTERPRISE IN AGRICULTURE

Agriculture everywhere is much more organized around the institutions of property than around those of occupation. Unfortunately, our current theory and research on stratification is built to fit an urban environment, being conceptually organized around the idea of occupation. For instance, an important recent monograph on social mobility classifies all farmers together and regards them as an unstratified source of urban workers.[4]

The theory of property systems is very much underdeveloped. Property may be defined as a legally defensible vested right to affect decisions on the use of economically valuable goods. Different decisions (for instance, technical decisions versus decisions on distributions of benefits) typically are affected by different sets of rights held by different sets of people. These legally defensible rights are, of course, important de-

☐ From Am. J. Sociol. **67**:165-176, 1961. Reprinted by permission of The University of Chicago Press.

*Johns Hopkins University.

[1]James S. Coleman, Jan Hajda, and Amitai Etzioni have done me the great service of being intensely unhappy with a previous version of this paper. I have not let them see this version.

[2]This formulation derives from Talcott Parsons' brief treatment in *The Structure of Social Action* (Glencoe, Ill.: Free Press, 1949), pp. 488-95.

[3]Cf. especially Robert Blauner, "Industrial Differences in Work Attitudes and Work Institutions," paper delivered at the 1960 meeting of the American Sociological Association, in which he compares class relations and the alienation of the working class in continuous-process manufacturing with that in mechanical mass-production industries.

[4]S. M. Lipset and R. Bendix, *Social Mobility in Industrial Society* (Berkeley, Calif.: University of California Press, 1959). The exceedingly high rate of property mobility which characterized American rural social structures when the national ideology was being formed apparently escapes their attention. Yet Lipset discusses the kind of mobility characteristic of frontiers and small farm systems very well in his *Agrarian Socialism* (Berkeley, Calif.: University of California Press, 1950), p. 33. In 1825 occupational mobility only concerned a small part of the population of the United States. The orientation of most nineteenth-century Americans to worldly success was that of Tennyson's "Northern Farmer, New Style": "But proputty, proputty sticks, an' proputty, proputty graws."

terminants of the actual decision-making structure of any social unit which acts with respect to goods.

But a property system must be conceived as the typical interpenetration of legally vested rights to affect decisions and the factual situation which determines who actually makes what decisions on what grounds. For example, any description of the property system of modern business which ignores the fact that it is economically impossible for a single individual to gain majority stock holdings in a large enterprise, and politically impossible to organize an integrated faction of dispersed stockholders except under unusual conditions, would give a grossly distorted view. A description of a property system, then, has to take into account the internal politics of typical enterprises, the economic forces that typically shape decisions, the political situation in the society at large which is taken into account in economic decisions, the reliability and cost of the judiciary, and so forth. The same property law means different things for economic life if decisions on the distribution of income from agricultural enterprise are strongly affected by urban *rentiers'* interests rather than a smallholding peasantry.

It is obviously impossible to give a complete typology of the legal, economic, and political situations which determine the decision-making structure within agricultural organizations for all societies and for all important decisions. Instead, one must pick certain frequent constellations of economic, technical, legal, and labor recruitment conditions that tend to give rise to a distinct structure of decision-making within agricultural enterprises.

By an "enterprise" I mean a social unit which has and exercises the power to commit a given parcel of land to one or another productive purpose, to achieve which it decides the allocation of chattels and labor on the land.[5] The rights to affect decisions on who shall get the benefit from that production may not be, and quite often are not, confined within the enterprise, as defined here. The relation between the enterprise and power over the distribution of benefit is one of the central variables in the analysis to follow, for instance, distinguishing tenancy systems from smallholding systems.

Besides the relation between productive decisions and decisions on benefits, some of the special economic, political, and technical characteristics which seem most important in factual decision-making structure will be mentioned, such as the value of land, whether the "owner" has police power over or kinship relations with labor, the part of production destined for market, the amount of capital required besides the land, or the degree of technical rationalization. These are, of course, some of the considerations Marx dealt with when describing the capitalist enterprise, particularly in its factory form. Plantations, manors, family-size tenancies, ranches, or family farms tend to occur only in certain congenial economic, technical and political environments and to be affected in their internal structure by those environments.

A description and analysis of empirical constellations of decision-making structures cannot, by its untheoretical nature, claim to be complete. Moreover, I have deliberately eliminated from consideration all precommercial agriculture, not producing for markets, because economic forces do not operate in the same ways in precommercial societies and because describing the enterprise would involve providing a typology of extended families and peasant communities, which would lead us far afield. I have also not considered the "community-as-enterprise" systems of the Soviet sphere and of Israel because these are as much organizational manifestations of a social movement as they are economic institutions.[6]

Systems of commercialized manors, family-sized tenancies, family smallholdings, plantations, and ranches cover most of the property systems found in commercialized agriculture outside eastern Europe and Israel. And each of these property systems tends to give rise to a distinctive class system, differing in important respects from that which develops with any of the other systems. Presenting argument and evidence for this proposition is the central purpose of this paper.

VARIATIONS IN RURAL CLASS RELATIONS

Rural class structure in commercialized agriculture varies in two main ways: the criteria which differentiate the upper and lower classes and the quality and quantity of intraclass cultural, political, and organizational life. In turn, the two main criteria which may differentiate classes are legal privileges and style of life. And two main qualities of class culture and organization are the degree of familiarity with technical culture of husbandry and the degree of political activation and organization. This gives four characteristics of rural class structures which vary with the structure of enterprises.

First, rural class systems vary in the extent to which

---

[5]Occasionally, the decisions to commit land to a given crop and to commit labor and chattels to cultivation are made separately, e.g., in cotton plantations in the post bellum American South. The land is committed to cotton by the landowner, but labor and chattels are committed to cultivation by the sharecropper.

[6]However, the origin of the *kolkhoz* or collective farm does seem to depend partly on the form of prerevolutionary agriculture. Collectivization seems to occur most rapidly when a revolutionary government deals with an agriculture which was previously organized into large-scale capitalist farms.

classes are differentiated by legal privileges. Slaves and masters, peons and *hacendados*, serfs and lords, colonial planters and native labor, citizen farmers employing aliens as labor—all are differentiated by legal privileges. In each case the subordinate group is disenfranchised, often bound to the land or to the master, denied the right to organize, denied access to the courts on an equal basis, denied state-supported education, and so on.

Second, rural stratification systems vary in the sharpness of differentiation of style of life among the classes. Chinese gentry used to live in cities, go to school, compete for civil service posts, never work with their hands, and maintain extended families as household units. On each criterion, the peasantry differed radically. In contrast, in the northern United States, rich and poor farmers live in the country, attend public schools, consume the same general kinds of goods, work with their hands, at least during the busy seasons, and live in conjugal family units. There were two radically different ways of life in rural China; in the northern United States the main difference between rich and poor farmers is wealth.

Third, rural class systems vary in the distribution of the technical culture of husbandry. In some systems the upper classes would be completely incapable of making the decisions of the agricultural enterprise: they depend on the technical lore of the peasantry. At the other extreme, the Spanish-speaking labor force of the central valley in California would be bewildered by the marketing, horticultural, engineering, and transportation problems of a large-scale irrigated vegetable farm.

Fourth, rural classes vary in their degree of political activity and organization, in their sensitivity or apathy to political issues, in their degree of intraclass communication and organization, and in their degree of political education and competence.

Our problem, then, is to relate types of agricultural enterprises and property systems to the patterns of class relations in rural social life. We restrict our attention to enterprises producing for markets, and of these we exclude the community-as-enterprise systems of eastern Europe and Israel.

CLASS RELATIONS IN TYPES OF AGRICULTURAL ENTERPRISE
1. The manorial or hacienda system

The first type of enterprise to be considered here is actually one form of precommercial agriculture, divided into two parts: cultivation of small plots for subsistence by a peasantry, combined with cultivation by customary labor dues of domain land under the lord's supervision. It fairly often happens that the domain land comes to be used for commercial crops,

while the peasant land continues to be used for subsistence agriculture. There is no rural labor market but, rather, labor dues or labor rents to the lord, based on customary law or force. There is a very poorly developed market in land; there may be, however, an active market in estates, where the estates include as part of their value the labor due to the lord. But land as such, separate from estates and from manors as going concerns, is very little an article of commerce. Estates also tend to pass as units in inheritance, by various devices of entailment, rather than being divided among heirs.[7]

The manorial system is characterized by the exclusive access of the manor lord (or *hacendado* in Latin America) to legal process in the national courts. A more or less unfree population holding small bits of land in villein or precarious tenure is bound to work on the domain land of the lord, by the conditions of tenure or by personal peonage. Unfree tenures or debts tend to be inheritable, so that in case of need the legal system of the nation will subject villeins or peons to work discipline on the manor.

Some examples of this system are the hacienda system of Mexico up to at least 1920,[8] some areas in the Peruvian highlands at present,[9] medieval England,[10] East Germany before the reconstruction of agriculture into large-scale plantation and ranch agriculture,[11] the Austro-Hungarian Empire, in the main, up to at least 1848,[12] and many other European and South American systems at various times.

The manorial system rests on the assumptions that neither the value of land nor the value of labor is great and that calculation of productive efficiency by the managers of agricultural enterprise is not well developed. When landowners start making cost studies of the efficiency of forced versus wage labor, as they did, for instance, in Austria-Hungary in the first part of the nineteenth century, they find that wage labor is from two to four times as efficient.[13] When landowners' tra-

[7]In some cases, as in what was perhaps the world's most highly developed manorial system, in Chile, an estate often remains undivided as an enterprise but is held "together in the family as an undivided inheritance for some years, and not infrequently for a generation. This multiplies the number of actual owners [but not of haciendas], of rural properties in particular" (George M. McBride, *Chile: Land and Society* [New York: American Geographical Society, 1936], p. 139).
[8]Frank Tannenbaum, *The Mexican Agrarian Revolution* (New York: Macmillan Co., 1929), pp. 91-133.
[9]Thomas R. Ford, *Man and Land in Peru* (Gainesville: University of Florida Press, 1955), pp. 93-95.
[10]Paul Vinogradoff, *The Growth of the Manor* (London: Swan Sonnenschein, 1905), pp. 212-35, 291-365.
[11]Max Weber, *Gesammelte Aufsätze zur Sozialund Wirtschaftsgeschichte* (Tübingen: J. C. B. Mohr, 1924), pp. 471-74.
[12]Jerome Blum, *Noble Landowners and Agriculture in Austria, 1815-1848* (Baltimore: Johns Hopkins Press, 1948), pp. 23, 68-87.
[13]*Ibid.*, pp. 192-202.

ditional level of income becomes insufficient to compete for prestige with the bourgeoisie, and they set about trying to raise incomes by increasing productivity, as they did in eastern Germany, the developmental tendency is toward capitalistic plantation or ranch agriculture.[14] When the waste and common become important for cattle- or sheep-raising and labor becomes relatively less important in production, enclosure movements drive precarious tenants off the land. When land becomes an article of commerce and the price and productivity of land goes up, tenancy by family farmers provides the lord with a comfortable income that can be spent in the capital city, without much worry about the management of crops. The farther the market penetrates agriculture, first creating a market for commodities, then for labor and land, the more economically unstable does the manorial economy become, and the more likely is the manor to go over to one of the other types of agricultural enterprise.

In summary, the manorial system combines in the lord and his agents authority over the enterprise and rulership or *Herrschaft* over dependent tenants. Classes are distinct in legal status. In style of life the manor lord moves on the national scene, often little concerned with detailed administration of his estate. He often keeps city residence and generally monopolizes education. Fairly often he even speaks a different language, for example, Latin among Magyar nobility, French in the Russian aristocracy, Spanish, instead of Indian dialects, in parts of Latin America.

The pattern of life of the subject population is very little dependent on market prices of goods. Consequently, they have little interest in political issues. Even less does the peasantry have the tools of political organization, such as education, experienced leadership, freedom of association, or voting power. Quite often, as, for example, in the Magyar areas of the Hapsburg monarchy or among the Indian tribes of Latin America, intraclass communication is hindered by language barriers. A politically active and competent upper class confronts a politically apathetic, backward, and disenfranchised peasantry.

2. Family-size tenancy

In family-size tenancy the operative unit of agriculture is the family enterprise, but property rights in the enterprise rest with *rentier* capitalists. The return from the enterprise is divided according to some rental scheme, either in money or in kind. The rent may be fixed, fixed with modification in years of bad har-

vest, or share.[15] The formal title to the land may not be held by the noncultivator—it is quite common for the "rent" on the land to be, in a legal sense, the interest on a loan secured by the land.

This type of arrangement seems to occur most frequently when the following five conditions are met: *(a)* land has very high productivity and high market price; *(b)* the crop is highly labor-intensive, and mechanization of agriculture is little developed; *(c)* labor is cheap; *(d)* there are no appreciable economies of scale in factors other than labor; and *(e)* the period of production of the crop is one year or less. These conditions are perhaps most fully met with the crops of rice and cotton, especially on irrigated land; yet such a system of tenancy is quite often found where the crops are potatoes or wheat and maize, even though the conditions are not fulfilled. A historical, rather than an economic, explanation is appropriate to these cases.

The correlation of tenancy arrangements with high valuation of land is established by a number of pieces of evidence. In Japan in 1944, most paddy (rice) land was in tenancy, and most upland fields were owner-operated.[16] The same was true in Korea in 1937.[17] South China, where land values were higher and irrigated culture more practiced,[18] had considerably higher rates of tenancy than did North China.[19] In Thailand tenancy is concentrated in the commercialized farming of the river valleys in central Siam.[20] In Japan, up to World War II, except for the last period (1935-40), every time the price of land went up, the proportion of land held in tenancy went up.[21]

The pattern of family-size tenancy was apparently found in the potato culture of Ireland before the revolution, in the wheat culture of pre–World War I Rumania[22] and also that of Bosnia-Herzegovina (now part of Yugoslavia) at the same period.[23] The sugar-

---

[14]Weber, *op. cit.*, pp. 474-77.

[15]But share rents in commercialized agriculture are often indicators of the splitting of the enterprise, as discussed above: it most frequently reflects a situation in which land is committed to certain crops by the landlord and the landlord markets the crops, while the scheduling of work is done by the tenant and part of the risks are borne by him.
[16]Sidney Klein, *The Pattern of Land Tenure Reform in East Asia* (New York: Bookman Associates, 1958), p. 227.
[17]*Ibid.*, p. 246.
[18]See Chan Han-Seng, *Landlord and Peasant in China* (New York: International Publishers, 1936), pp. 100-103.
[19]*Ibid.*, pp. 3-4; and Klein, *op. cit.*, p. 253.
[20]Erich H. Jacoby, *Agrarian Unrest in Southeast Asia* (New York: Columbia University Press, 1949), pp. 232-35.
[21]Ronald P. Dore, *Land Reform in Japan* (London: Oxford University Press, 1959), p. 21.
[22]Henry L. Roberts, *Rumania: The Political Problems of an Agrarian State* (New Haven, Conn.: Yale University Press, 1951), pp. 14-17; Tables IX, X, p. 363.
[23]Jozo Tomasevich, *Peasants, Politics, and Economic Change in Yugoslavia* (Stanford, Calif.: Stanford University Press, 1955), pp. 96-101, 355.

cane regions of central Luzon are also farmed in family-size tenancies, though this is so uneconomical that, without privileged access to the American market, cane culture would disappear.[24] It also characterizes the cotton culture of the highly productive Nile Valley in Egypt[25] and the cotton culture of the Peruvian coast.[26] This pattern of small peasant farms with rents to landlords was also characteristic of prerevolutionary France[27] and southwest England during the Middle Ages.[28] In lowland Burma a large share of the rice land is owned by the Indian banking house of Chettyar,[29] and much of the rest of it is in tenancy to other landlords. The land-tenure system of Taiwan before the recent land reform was typical family-size tenancy.[30]

Perhaps the most remarkable aspect of this list is the degree to which this system has been ended by reform or revolution, becoming transformed, except in a few Communist states, into a system of smallholding farms. And even in Communist states the first transformation after the revolution is ordinarily to give the land to the tiller: only afterward are the peasants gathered into collective farms, generally in the face of vigorous resistance.

The system of *rentier* capitalists owning land let out in family farms (or *rentier* capitalists owning debts whose service requires a large part of farm income) seems extremely politically unstable. The French Revolution, according to De Tocqueville, was most enthusiastically received in areas in which there were small farms paying feudal dues (commuted to rent in money or in kind).[31] The eastern European systems of Rumania and parts of Yugoslavia were swept away after World War I in land reforms. Land reforms were also carried through in northern Greece, the Baltic states, and many of the succession states of the Hapsburg monarchy (the reform was specious in Hungary). A vigorous and long-lasting civil war raged in Ireland up to the time of independence, and its social base was heavily rural. The high-tenancy areas in central Luzon were the social base of the revolutionary Hukbalahaps during and after World War II. The Communist revolution in China had its first successes in the high-tenancy areas of the south. The number of peasant

riots in Japan during the interwar period was closely correlated with the proportion of land held in tenancy.[32] Peasant rebellions were concentrated in Kent and southeast England during the Middle Ages.[33] In short, such systems rarely last through a war or other major political disturbance and constantly produce political tensions.

There are several causes of the political instability of such systems. In the first place, the issue in the conflict is relatively clear: the lower the rent of the *rentier* capitalists, the higher the income of the peasantry. The division of the product at harvest time or at the time of sale is a clear measure of the relative prerogatives of the farmer and the *rentier*.

Second, there is a severe conflict over the distribution of the risks of the enterprise. Agriculture is always the kind of enterprise with which God has a lot to do. With the commercialization of agriculture, the enterprise is further subject to great fluctuation in the gross income from its produce. *Rentiers*, especially if they are capitalists investing in land rather than aristocrats receiving incomes from feudal patrimony, shift as much of the risk of failure as possible to the tenant. Whether the rent is share or cash, the variability of income of the peasantry is almost never less, and is often more, than the variability of *rentiers'* income. This makes the income of the peasantry highly variable, contributing to their political sensitization.[34]

Third, there tends to be little social contact between the *rentier* capitalists living in the cities and the rural population. The *rentiers* and the farmers develop distinct styles of life, out of touch with each other. The *rentier* is not brought into contact with the rural population by having to take care of administrative duties on the farm; nor is he drawn into local government as a leading member of the community or as a generous sharer in the charitable enterprises of the village. The urban *rentier*, with his educated and often foreign speech, his cosmopolitan interests, his arrogant rejection of rustic life is a logical target of the rural community, whose only contact with him is through sending him money or goods.

Fourth, the leaders of the rural community, the rich

[24]Jacoby, *op. cit.*, pp. 181-91, 203-9.

[25]Doreen Warriner, *Land Reform and Development in the Middle East* (London: Royal Institute of International Affairs, 1957), pp. 25-26.

[26]Ford, *op. cit.*, pp. 84-85.

[27]Alexis de Tocqueville, *The Old Regime and the French Revolution* ("Anchor Books" [Garden City, N.Y.: Doubleday & Co., 1955]), pp. 23-25, 30-32.

[28]George Homans, *English Villagers of the Thirteenth Century* (Cambridge, Mass.: Harvard University Press, 1941), p. 21.

[29]Jacoby, *op. cit.*, pp. 73, 78-88.

[30]Klein, *op. cit.*, pp. 52-54, 235.

[31]De Tocqueville, *op. cit.*, p. 25.

[32]Dore, *op. cit.*, p. 72 (cf. this data on tenancy disputes with the ? on tenancy, p. 21).

[33]Homans, *op. cit.*, p. 119.

[34]Though they deal with smallholding systems, the connection between economic instability and political activism is argued by Lipset (*op. cit.*, pp. 26-29, 36) and by Rudolf Heberle (*Social Movements* [New York: Appleton-Century-Crofts Inc., 1951], pp. 240-48; see also Jacoby, *op. cit.*, p. 246; and Daniel Lerner, *The Passing of Traditional Society* [Glencoe, Ill.: Free Press, 1958], p. 227). Aristotle noted the same thing: "it is a bad thing that many from being rich should become poor; for men of ruined fortunes are sure to stir up revolutions" (*Politics* 1266[b]).

peasants, are not vulnerable to expulsion by the land-owners, as they would be were the landowners also the local government. The rich peasant shares at least some of the hardships and is opposed in his class interests to many of the same people as are the tenants. In fact, in some areas where the population pressure on the land is very great, the rich peasants themselves hold additional land in tenancy, beyond their basic holdings. In this case the leadership of the local community is not only not opposed to the interests of the tenants but has largely identical interests with the poor peasants.

Finally, the landowners do not have the protection of the peasants' ignorance about the enterprise to defend their positions, as do large-scale capitalist farmers. It is perfectly clear to the tenant farmer that he could raise and sell his crops just as well with the landlord gone as with him there. There is no complicated co-operative tillage that seems beyond the view of all but the landlord and his managers, as there may be in manorial, and generally is in large-scale capitalist, agriculture. The farmer knows as well or better than the landlord where seed and fertilizer is to be bought and where the crop can be sold. He can often see strategic investments unknown to his landlord that would alleviate his work or increase his yield.

At least in its extreme development, then, the land-owning class in systems of family-size tenancy appears as alien, superfluous, grasping, and exploitative. Their rights in agricultural enterprise appear as an unjustifiable burden on the rustic classes, both to the peasantry and to urban intellectuals. No marked decrease in agricultural productivity is to be expected when they are dispossessed, because they are not the class that carries the most advanced technical culture of agriculture. Quite often, upon land reform the productivity of agriculture increases.[35]

So family-size tenancy tends to yield a class system with an enfranchised, formally free lower class which has a monopoly of technical culture. The style of life of the upper class is radically different from that of the lower class. The lower class tends to develop a relatively skilled and relatively invulnerable leadership in the richer peasantry and a relatively high degree of political sensitivity in the poorer peasantry. It is of such stuff that many radical populist and nationalist movements are made.

3. Family smallholding

Family smallholding has the same sort of enterprises as does family tenancy, but rights to the returns from the enterprise are more heavily concentrated in the class of farmers. The "normal" property holding

is about the size requiring the work of two adults or less. Probably the most frequent historical source of such systems is out of family-tenancy systems by way of land reform or revolution. However, they also arise through colonization of farmlands carried out under governments in which large landlords do not have predominant political power, for instance, in the United States and Norway. Finally, it seems that such systems tend to be produced by market forces at an advanced stage of industrialization. There is some evidence that farms either larger or smaller than those requiring about two adult laborers tend to disappear in the industrial states of western Europe.[36]

Examples of such systems having a relatively long history are the United States outside the "Black Belt" in the South, the ranch areas of the West, and the central valleys of California, Serbia after some time in the early 19th century,[37] France after the great revolution, most of Scandinavia,[38] much of Canada, Bulgaria since 1878,[39] and southern Greece since sometime in the nineteenth century. Other such systems which have lasted long enough to give some idea of their long-term development are those created in eastern Europe after World War I; good studies of at least Rumania[40] and Yugoslavia[41] exist. Finally, the system of family smallholding created in Japan by the American-induced land reform of 1946 has been carefully studied.[42]

Perhaps the best way to begin analysis of this type of agricultural enterprise is to note that virtually all the costs of production are fixed. Labor in the family holding is, in some sense, "free": family members have to be supported whether they work or not, so they might as well work. Likewise, the land does not cost rent, and there is no advantage to the enterprise in leaving it out of cultivation. This predominance of fixed costs means that production does not fall with a decrease in prices, as it does in most urban enterprises where labor is a variable cost.[43] Consequently, the income of smallholders varies directly with the market price of the commodities they produce and with variability in production produced by natural

---

[35]See, e.g., Dore, *op. cit.*, pp. 213-19.

[36]Folke Dovring, *Land and Labor in Europe, 1900-1950* (The Hague: Martinus Nijhoff, 1956), pp. 115-18. The median size of the farm unit, taking into consideration the type of crops grown on different sized farms, ranges from that requiring one man-year in Norway to two man-years in France, among the nations on the Continent.
[37]Tomasevich, *op. cit.*, pp. 38-47.
[38]Dovring, *op. cit.*, p. 143.
[39]Royal Institute of International Affairs, *Nationalism* (London: Oxford University Press, 1939), p. 106.
[40]Roberts, *op. cit.*
[41]Tomasevich, *op. cit.*
[42]Dore, *op. cit.*
[43]Wilfried Kahler, *Das Agrarproblem in den Industrieländern* (Göttingen: Vandenhoeck & Ruprecht, 1958), p. 17.

catastrophe. Thus, the political movements of small-holders tend to be directed primarily at maintenance of the price of agricultural commodities rather than at unemployment compensation or other "social security" measures.

Second, the variability of return from agricultural enterprise tends to make credit expensive and, at any rate, makes debts highly burdensome in bad years. Smallholders' political movements, therefore, tend to be opposed to creditors, to identify finance capital as a class enemy: Jews, the traditional symbol of finance capital, often come in for an ideological beating. Populist movements are often directed against "the bankers." Further, since cheap money generally aids debtors, and since small farmers are generally debtors, agrarian movements tend to support various kinds of inflationary schemes. Small farmers do not want to be crucified on a cross of gold.

Third, agrarian movements, except in highly advanced societies, tend to enjoy limited intraclass communication, to be poor in politically talented leaders, relatively unable to put together a coherent, disciplined class movement controlled from below.[44] Contributions to the party treasury tend to be small and irregular, like the incomes of the small farmers. Peasant movements are, therefore, especially prone to penetration by relatively disciplined political interests, sometimes Communist and sometimes industrial capital.[45] Further, such movements tend to be especially liable to corruption,[46] since they are relatively unable to provide satisfactory careers for political leaders out of their own resources.

Moreover, at an early stage of industrial and commercial development in a country without large landowners, the only sources of large amounts of money available to politicians are a few urban industrial and commercial enterprises. Making a policy on the marketing and production of iron and steel is quite often making a policy on the marketing and production of a single firm. Naturally, it pays that firm to try to get legislation and administration tailored to its needs.

Fourth, small-farmer and peasant movements tend to be nationalistic and xenophobic. The explanation of this phenomenon is not clear.

Finally, small-farmer and peasant movements tend to be opposed to middlemen and retailers, who are likely to use their monopolistic or monopsonistic position to milk the farm population. The cooperative movement is, of course, directed at eliminating middlemen as well as at provision of credit without usury.

Under normal conditions (that is, in the absence of totalitarian government, major racial cleavage, and major war) this complex of political forces tends to produce a rural community with a proliferation of associations and with the voting power and political interest to institute and defend certain elements of democracy, especially universal suffrage and universal education. This tends to produce a political regime loose enough to allow business and labor interest groups to form freely without allowing them to dominate the government completely. Such a system of landholding is a common precursor and support of modern liberal democratic government.

In smallholding systems, then, the upper classes of the rural community are not distinct in legal status and relatively not in style of life. Social mobility in such a system entails mainly a change in the amount of property held, or in the profitability of the farm, but not a change in legal status or a radical change in style of life.[47]

A politically enfranchised rural community is characterized by a high degree of political affect and organization, generally in opposition to urban interests rather than against rural upper classes. But, compared with the complexity of their political goals and the level of political involvement, their competence tends to be low until the "urbanization of the countryside" is virtually complete.

4. Plantation agriculture

Labor-intensive crops requiring several years for maturation, such as rubber, tree fruit, or coffee, tend to be grown on large-scale capitalistic farms employing either wage labor, or, occasionally, slave labor. Particularly when capital investment is also required for processing equipment to turn the crop into a form in which it can be shipped, as for example in the culture of sugar cane and, at least in earlier times, sugar beets, large-scale capitalist agriculture predominates.

---

[44]I.e., as compared with political movements of the urban proletariat or bourgeoisie. They are more coherent and disciplined than are the lower-class movements in other agricultural systems.

[45]An excellent example of the penetration of industrial capital into a peasant party is shown by the development of the party platforms on industry in Rumania, 1921-26 (Roberts, *op. cit.*, pp. 154-56). The penetration of American populists by the "silver interests" is another example.

[46]Cf. *ibid.*, pp. 337-39; and Tomasevich, *op. cit.*, pp. 246-47. The Jacksonian era in the United States, and the persistent irregularities in political finance of agrarian leaders in the South of the United States, are further examples.

[47]The best description that I know of the meaning of "property mobility" in such a system is the novel of Knut Hamsun, *Growth of the Soil* (New York: Modern Library, 1921), set in the Norwegian frontier.

The key economic factor that seems to produce large-scale capitalist culture is the requirement of long-term capital investment in the crop or in machinery, combined with relatively low cost of land. When the crop is also labor-intensive, particularly when labor is highly seasonal, a rather typical plantation system tends to emerge. In some cases it also emerges in the culture of cotton (as in the ante bellum American South and some places in Egypt), wheat (as in Hungary, eastern Germany,[48] and Poland[49]), or rice (as on the Carolina and Georgia coasts in the ante bellum American South).[50]

The enterprise typically combines a small highly skilled and privileged group which administers the capital investment, the labor force, and the marketing of the crops with a large group of unskilled, poorly paid, and legally unprivileged workers. Quite generally, the workers are ethnically distinct from the skilled core of administrators, often being imported from economically more backward areas or recruited from an economically backward native population in colonial and semicolonial areas. This means that ordinarily they are ineligible for the urban labor market of the nation in which they work, if it has an urban labor market.

Examples of plantation systems are most of the sugar areas in the Caribbean and on the coast of Peru,[51] the rubber culture of the former Federated Malay States in Malaya[52] and on Java,[53] the fruit-growing areas of Central America, the central valleys of California, where the labor force is heavily Latin American, eastern Germany during the early part of this century, where Poles formed an increasing part of the labor force,[54] Hungary up to World War II, the pineapple-growing of the Hawaiian Islands,[55] and, of course, the ante bellum American South. The system tends to induce in the agricultural labor force a poverty of associational life, low participation in local government, lack of education for the labor force, and high vulnerability of labor-union and political leadership to oppression by landlords and landlord-dominated governments. The domination of the government by landlords tends to prevent the colonization of new land by smallholders, and even to wipe out the holdings of such small peasantry as do exist.

In short, the system tends to maintain the culture, legal and political position, and life chances of the agricultural labor force distinct both from the urban labor force and from the planter aristocracy. The bearers of the technical and commercial knowledge are not the agricultural laborers, and, consequently, redistribution of land tends to introduce inefficiency into agriculture. The plantation system, as Edgar T. Thompson has put it, is a "race-making situation"[56] which produces a highly privileged aristocracy, technically and culturally educated, and a legally, culturally, and economically underprivileged labor force. If the latter is politically mobilized, as it may be occasionally by revolutionary governments, it tends to be extremist.

5. Capitalist extensive agriculture with wage labor: the ranch

An extensive culture of wool and beef, employing wage labor, grew up in the American West, Australia, England and Scotland during and after the industrial revolution, Patagonia and some other parts of South America, and northern Mexico. In these cases the relative proportion of labor in the cost of production is smaller than it is in plantation agriculture. Such a structure is also characteristic of the wheat culture in northern Syria. In no case was there pressure to recruit and keep down an oppressed labor force. In England a surplus labor force was pushed off the land. A fairly reliable economic indicator of the difference between ranch and plantation systems is that in ranch systems the least valuable land is owned by the largest enterprises. In plantation systems the most valuable land is owned by the largest enterprises, with less valuable land generally used by marginal smallholders. The explanation of this is not clear.

The characteristic social feature of these enterprises is a free-floating, mobile labor force, often with few family ties, living in barracks, and fed in some sort of "company mess hall." They tend to make up a socially undisciplined element, hard-drinking and brawling. Sometimes their alienation from society

---

[48]Weber, *loc. cit.*

[49]Victor Lesniewski and Waclaw Ponikowski, "Polish Agriculture," in Ora S. Morgan (ed.), *Agricultural Systems of Middle Europe* (New York: Macmillan Co., 1933), pp. 260-63. Capitalist development was greatest in the western regions of Poznan and Pomerania (cf. *ibid.*, p. 264). There seem to have been many remains of a manorial system (*ibid.*, p. 277).

[50]Albert V. House, *Planter Management and Capitalism in Ante-bellum Georgia* (New York: Columbia University Press, 1954), esp. pp. 18-37.

[51]Ford, *op. cit.*, pp. 57-60.

[52]Jacoby, *op. cit.*, pp. 106-8, 113.

[53]*Ibid.*, pp. 43, 45, 56-61.

[54]Weber shows that, in the eastern parts of Germany during the latter part of the nineteenth century, the proportionate decrease of the German population (being replaced by Poles) was greater in areas of large-scale cultivation (*op. cit.*, pp. 452-53).

[55]Edward Norbeck, *Pineapple Town: Hawaii* (Berkeley: University of California Press, 1959).

[56]Cf. Edgar T. Thompson, "The Plantation as a Race-making Situation," in Leonard Broom and Philip Selznick, *Sociology* (Evanston, Ill.: Row, Peterson & Co., 1958), pp. 506-7.

takes on the form of political radicalism, but rarely of an indigenous disciplined radical movement.

• • •

The types of agricultural enterprise outlined here are hardly exhaustive, but perhaps they include most of the agricultural systems which help determine the political dynamics of those countries which act on the world scene today. Nor does this typology pretend to outline all the important differences in the dynamics of agricultural systems. Obviously, the system of family-sized farms run by smallholders in Serbia in the 1840's is very different from the institutionally similar Danish and American systems of the 1950's.[57] And capitalistic sheep-raisers supported and made up the House of Lords in England but supported populistic currents in the United States.

[57]E.g., in the average size of agricultural villages, in the proportion of the crop marketed, in the level of living, in education, in birth rate, in the size of the household unit, in the intensity of ethnic antagonism, in degree of political organization and participation, in exposure to damage by military action—these are only some of the gross differences.

However, some of the differences among systems outlined here seem to hold in widely varying historical circumstances. The production and maintenance of ethnic differences by plantations, the political fragility of family-size tenancy, the richer associational life, populist ideology, corrupt politics of smallholders, and the political apathy and technical traditionalism of the manor or the old hacienda—these seem to be fairly reliable. Characteristics of rural enterprises and the class relations they typically produce are summarized in Table 1.

This, if it is true, shows the typology to be useful. The question that remains is: Is it capable of being used? Is it possible to find indexes which will reliably differentiate a plantation from a manor or a manor from a large holding farmed by family tenancy?

The answer is that most of these systems have been accurately identified in particular cases. The most elusive is the manor or traditional hacienda; governments based on this sort of agricultural enterprise rarely take accurate censuses, partly because they rarely have an agricultural policy worthy of the name. Often even the boundaries of landholdings are not of-

Table 1. Characteristics of rural enterprises and resulting class relations

Type of enterprise	Characteristics of enterprise	Characteristics of class structure
Manorial	Division of land into domain land and labor subsistence land, with domain land devoted to production for market. Lord has police power over labor. Technically traditional; low cost of land and little market in land	Classes differ greatly in legal privileges and style of life. Technical culture borne largely by the peasantry. Low political activation and competence of peasantry; high politicalization of the upper classes
Family-size tenancy	Small parcels of highly valuable land worked by families who do not own the land, with a large share of the production for market. Highly labor- and land-intensive culture, of yearly or more frequent crops	Classes differ little in legal privileges but greatly in style of life. Technical culture generally borne by the lower classes. High political affect and political organization of the lower classes, often producing revolutionary populist movements
Family smallholding	Same as family tenancy, except benefits remain within the enterprise. Not distinctive of areas with high valuation of land; may become capital-intensive at a late stage of industrialization	Classes differ neither in legal privileges nor in style of life. Technical culture borne by both rich and poor. Generally unified and highly organized political opposition to urban interests, often corrupt and undisciplined
Plantation	Large-scale enterprises with either slavery or wage labor, producing labor-intensive crops requiring capital investment on relatively cheap land (though generally the best land within the plantation area). No or little subsistence production	Classes differ in both style of life and legal privileges. Technical culture monopolized by upper classes. Politically apathetic and incompetent lower classes, mobilized only in time of revolution by urban radicals
Ranch	Large-scale production of labor-extensive crops, on land of low value (lowest in large units within ranch areas), with wage labor partly paid in kind in company barracks and mess	Classes may not differ in legal status, as there is no need to recruit and keep down a large labor force. Style of life differentiation unknown. Technical culture generally relatively evenly distributed. Dispersed and unorganized radicalism of lower classes

ficially recorded. Further, the internal economy of the manor or hacienda provides few natural statistical indexes—there is little bookkeeping use of labor, of land, of payment in kind or in customary rights. The statistical description of manorial economies is a largely unsolved problem.

Except for this, systematic comparative studies of the structure and dynamics of land tenure systems are

technically feasible. But it has been all too often the case that descriptions of agricultural systems do not permit them to be classified by the type of enterprise.[58] Perhaps calling attention to widespread typical patterns of institutionalizing agricultural production will encourage those who write monographs to provide the information necessary for comparative study.

[58]E.g., the most common measure used for comparative study is the concentration of landholdings. A highly unequal distribution of land may indicate family-tenancy, manorial, plantation, or ranch systems. Similarly, data on size of farm units confuse family smallholding with family tenancy, and lumps together all three kinds of large-scale enterprise. A high ratio of landless peasantry may be involved in family-tenancy, plantation, or manorial systems. Ambiguous ref-

erences to "tenancy" may mean the labor rents of a hacienda system, or the cash or share rents of family-size tenancy, or even tenancy of sons before fathers' death in smallholding systems. "Capitalistic agriculture" sometimes refers to ranches, sometimes to plantations, and sometimes to smallholdings. "Feudalism," though most often applied to manorial systems, is also used to describe family-size tenancy and plantation economies. "Absentee landlordism" describes both certain manorial and family-size–tenancy systems.

Mr. McClintock and his tenants

RENWICK C. KENNEDY

"The Lord never made a 'possum without makin' a persimmon tree," said Mr. Yance McClintock.

"Meaning what?" asked his bookkeeper.

"Meanin' we always get along somehow."

"You got along well enough this year. You done fine. We cleared about $6,000. It's the best year we've had since 1928."

"Yes, it's been a good year, and I picked up more than that in cotton futures."

"You might say the Lord done well by you," the bookkeeper said, grinning.

"He helps them that help themselves. If all the niggers had paid out we'd have done better."

"You haven't lost anything. Take off the profit and the interest on the advances and you haven't lost a penny on a single nigger."

"Yes, but that profit and interest belong on there. I gave them credit and put out the goods to them."

"You did, and we charged them 25 per cent profit and 12 per cent interest. A bit steep I said to myself, though it's none of my business. But all I'm saying' is that you didn't actually lose any money you put out in advances. It all come back."

"I know. I know. But keep those balances on the books. Maybe we'll get it next year."

• • •

Mr. William Lowndes Yancey McClintock, known to his friends as Yance, is the wealthiest man in the Alabama village of Yaupon. His property and investments are worth more than $100,000. He owns 3,000 acres of land, part of which is in cultivation, part in pasture and part idle or in forest. Thirty-five tenant families, most of them Negroes, live on his land and produce cotton and other crops. The tenant population of his plantations is about 200 men, women and children.

Mr. McClintock owns 400 head of cattle. He sells the calves and the culls every fall.

In the village McClintock's Bargain Store handles general merchandise and carries a large stock of goods. It sells to the general public at one set of prices and to the McClintock tenants at another that is much higher. The store also issues advances to other tenants beside those on the McClintock land, taking crop liens as security.

The McClintock home in Yaupon is the show place of the village. It is a modern house, not in the best of taste, revealing a combination of Sears-Roebuck, Spanish and Colonial influences. There are authentic pre-Confederate houses in the best southern tradition to be found in the community, but the McClintock house is invariably pointed out to the visitor as the triumph of architecture in Yaupon.

Mr. McClintock's wife is named Luella. She is a well-kept woman. She and Mr. McClintock are in the late forties. They have three children. The eldest, a daughter, is married. The two sons are attending a first-class country-club university. They are costing their father a great deal of money.

* * *

The McClintock family has always been well fed. In fact its relish of food is almost pathological. But there has always been an abundance of food for them to eat. The two boys are fat young men. Mr. McClintock weighs 205 pounds and is only 5 feet 8 inches in height. The one great tragedy of Mrs. McClintock's life is that she weighs 175 pounds. The family taste runs to meats and rich pastries. There are usually two meats on the table and sometimes more. With a bountiful pantry and a full refrigerator and an excellent cook the McClintock meals are perfectly ravishing to every gourmet who is fortunate enough to sit down at the family table. Even so, the provision is so generous that more is left than is eaten. It is not to be wondered at that the two boys are stout, pudgy fellows, that Mrs. McClintock is as slender as a sack of mule-feed, and that Mr. McClintock looks like a swollen frog.

Excellent as is the fare at home, nothing delights Mr. McClintock so much as the opportunity to eat at a hotel or restaurant. His usual order at a restaurant is a $1.50 steak, which he likes half rare.

Eph is a tenant on Mr. McClintock's farm. He has a wife and eight children. Eph made his crop on an allowance of $3.50 a week during the working season. Part of this he spent for food and part for other things. Eph is not fat. His family is not fat. Everyone of them is lean and thin and hard. They are hard as bones. You would feel their bones if you put your hand on them. In the late winter there comes a time when you can almost see their bones.

Eph and his family are undernourished. They are too weak to be efficient workers in the early spring. Later on in the summer when the blackberries and plums and gardens and field crops have come in they fatten up a bit. For the major portion of the year Eph and his family live on the pellagra diet of corn bread, sorghum molasses and sweet potatoes. These are excellent foods but a faulty diet when one has nothing else. Even these are never very plentiful at Eph's house except just after harvest.

Eph has two small pigs that he and his family will eat in two weeks' time this winter. He also has a scrub cow. The cow is usually dry and a poor milker when fresh.

The boys trap a few rabbits in the winter and catch a few fish out of the creek. On most days of the year no meat is eaten at Eph's house.

Eph has never eaten a $1.50 steak in his life.

* * *

Mr. McClintock is the best dressed man in Yaupon. He dresses as if he were an important business man in Birmingham, or a prominent politician in Montgomery. His sons dress well. His wife is the most extravagant dresser of the whole family. In her struggle to disguise her hopelessly fat body she spends enough money to clothe a whole plantation of tenants.

On those Sunday mornings when Mr. McClintock goes to church he is a fashion plate in the flesh. His dark gray overcoat with fur collar cost $70. His rather flashy checked suit cost $40. His shoes are Florsheims for which he paid $10. His Stetson hat cost $10. An Arrow shirt, pale brown with a stripe $2.50, tie $1.50, imitation silk underwear $2.50, hose $1, eyeglasses $25, fountain pen $10, trick pencil $5, watch and chain $65, silk handkerchief $1. Total outfit $243.50. This estimate does not include hair cut, shave, shine and dry cleaning, nor the $30 which reposes in his wallet.

Mr. McClintock has three overcoats, six suits of clothes for winter wear and a dozen summer suits. He also has hunting and golfing clothes of the very best style and quality.

Sam Campbell is one of Mr. McClintock's tenants. Sam lives down on the river plantation where it does not matter how a man's clothes look. In the winter Sam wears all the clothes he has. Next to his skin is a ragged cotton union suit. Over this Sam wears two old cotton shirts, a new part woolen shirt, cotton overalls and overall jacket. When new Sam's clothing cost: union suit $1, cotton shirts 69 cents each, woolen shirt $1.39, overalls and jacket $1.95, hat $1.50, shoes $1.48. Total $8.70. But only Sam's woolen shirt is new.

Sam's children have to stay close by the fire during the winter. The two small children wear only cotton dresses and nothing more above or beneath. Sam's wife saves the infrequent flour and meal sacks to make clothes for the children.

Some of the McClintock tenants have better clothes than Sam, but a good many of them do not. Even the white clerks in Mr. McClintock's store who make $50 a month are not able to dress with elegance.

* * *

Mr. and Mrs. McClintock are very proud of their house. It cost $20,000. There are fourteen rooms in the house. Some of the rooms are furnished completely with antique pieces. Mrs. McClintock always enjoys showing her old furniture to visitors. She is not able to name its period and style but this detracts nothing from her pleasure. In 1925 she went to New Orleans and bought outright from an antique store enough furniture for four rooms. Since then she has picked up a few other pieces.

The house is provided with the usual modern equipment. There are telephones, radios, a piano, electric refrigeration, a heating system and a miscellaneous collection of electrical devices. No wonder Yaupon is proud of the McClintock house!

Even more than her old furniture Mrs. McClintock enjoys her rugs. The rugs, she says, cost $2,500, which is a very large amount for rugs in Yaupon.

Willie Gilmer is a tenant on Mr. McClintock's upland plantation. Willie and his family are not proud of their house though they like it well enough if only it did not leak. It is a two-room cabin with a dog-run between the rooms. There is a stick-and-mud chimney for each room. A door opens from the dog-run into each room and each has two wooden shutters for windows.

Willie has no cook-stove. His wife cooks on the open fire. There is an old iron bed in one room. The children sleep on a mattress on the floor. The mattress is made of feed sacks sewed together and stuffed with moss. Willie has three chairs with cowhide seats, two home-made tables and a few boxes with shelves nailed in them for his furniture. His cabin has never been painted. It is old. And it leaks.

Willie made four bales of cotton for Mr. McClintock the past year, besides other crops.

● ● ●

Mr. McClintock keeps two automobiles and trades them in for new ones every year. He sees football games every Saturday in the fall, sometimes driving his car several hundred miles to a game. He bets on the games and often loses. He plays golf regularly and always uses a $1 ball. Sometimes he loses several balls in an afternoon. He smokes $1 worth of good cigars daily.

Mr. McClintock is a leading member of the First Baptist church, attends frequently and pays $150 a year to the support of the church.

His tenants, too, are all members of the Baptist church.

Man and his land

J. H. KOLB and E. de S. BRUNNER

LAND TENURE

Thus far the discussion has proceeded without mention of the arrangements by which farms of a given size, value, and productive power are operated. Land is valuable, of course, only because on it men find shelter and employment and from it food and fiber can be raised and minerals extracted. It is the foundation of life. But land has value only in its relation to people. Land is, of course, owned. To be useful it must be operated, which means labor. Because it is wealth, it can be taxed for certain purposes. For the same reason, it is a capital resource which can be used as security for borrowing money. This very recital indicates the importance of both social uses of land and social policies with respect to land. Men have evolved two major relationships by which they are associated with

□ From a study of rural society, Boston, 1952, Houghton Mifflin Co. Excerpt.

specific plots of land from which they can produce needed agricultural commodities. The *owner* possesses his acres, controls them, and is the sole beneficiary of their productivity after his expenses are met. The *tenant* lives upon and cultivates land that belongs to another individual, with whom he shares both the proceeds of his toil and usually the responsibility of management.

The hunger for land. There are few races that do not display a desire for land, and the more rural races are the stronger this desire usually is. To the peasant, land represents ultimate security. Agrarian unrest has often developed where a growth of commercialization caused the tillers of the land to lose their complete control of it, as will be shown in a later chapter.

Causes for rise of farm tenancy. The American tradition has always been one of landownership, largely because, for nearly three centuries after the first settlements on the Atlantic seaboard, so much land was available for so little money. Even yet there is no pressure of population on the land such as one observes in the Orient. The so-called tenancy problem did not present itself in this country until after the Civil War, and when it came it was directly associated with the declining quantity of good land available for homesteading under federal grant.

But there was at least one other cause for the rise in farm tenancy in the United States. Young men desiring to be farmers and not possessing sufficient capital to buy a farm sought one they could work on shares. Conversely, elderly farmers desiring to retire sought to rent their farms, often to their own sons or nephews. The blood tie, therefore, was prominent in early tenant arrangements, and though its importance decreased, even as late as 1930 one fifth of the farm tenants were related to their landlords. This national average was brought down by the South, where the proportion is less than one tenth. In the Middle West, Middle Atlantic, and New England states it was nearly one third. There are no subsequent national data on this point, though some surveys show that kinship is still important in these three regions.

It was the prevalence of the kinship factor in the early development of farm tenancy, along with a few other factors such as the tenant's desire to be free to climb the agricultural ladder from tenancy to ownership when possible, that is responsible for the short lease, usually one year, which prevails in many sections. Such short leases facilitated speedy adjustments within the family when necessary, but they are frequently considered socially disadvantageous when the tenant is not related to the landlord, since the necessity for an annual renewal of the lease makes for insecurity and removes some of the incentive to conserve soil and property.

The agricultural ladder. In the United States the rise of a young farmer to full ownership of his land has been likened to climbing a ladder. The usual pattern is that he begins as a helper for his father or a hired hand on a neighbor's farm, saves enough to become a tenant, and finally buys his own farm. In time two additional rungs were added. One was that of a mortgaged owner, the other that of part-owner or part-tenant. Actually thousands never go beyond the first rung, many leaving farming entirely. During the depressions of the 1890's and 1920's some owners had to step down a rung or two. In the last decade the high cost of land and equipment has made the ladder more like a mountain for some, and new devices have been tried to keep the farm in the family, of which more later.

In this matter of farm tenancy three rural sciences meet. To the soil scientist, tenancy has become almost synonymous with "mining" rather than cultivating the land. To the economist, tenancy means the problem of having a farm support more than one family. The sociologist is interested in the effect of tenancy and its arrangements on the tenant and the social life and institutions of his community.

Growth and decline of farm tenancy. The growth of farm tenancy in the United States has been uneven. When first measured by the census in 1880, it was found that 25.6 per cent of the farms were tenant-operated. Ten years later the proportion had risen to 28.4 per cent.

During the closing decade of the nineteenth century began the rapid rise in the price of farm land which lasted for thirty years. Tenancy also rose apace, among many other reasons because it then took longer for a prospective owner to accumulate sufficient capital to purchase a farm. The proportion of tenant-operated farms increased by more than one fourth, and stood in 1900 at 35.3 per cent of the total.

Many felt that this was an alarming portent in American life. By the end of the first quarter of the twentieth century, 38.6 per cent of American farms were tenant-operated, according to the 1925 agricultural census. The next five years saw a more rapid increase than any previous decade, to 42.4 per cent of the farms in 1930 and more than half the farm land. This was one result of the agricultural depression of the 1920's. From then on, however, the proportion of farms operated by tenants declined, very slowly at first, to 39.7 per cent in 1940, then more rapidly, to 31.7 per cent in 1945 and 26.7 per cent in 1950. This decline to practically the levels of 1880 is a reflection of the high prices for farm products during the 1940's, which enabled many tenants to buy their farms.

These national data conceal a number of important differences. Tenancy has always been relatively higher in the southern region than elsewhere because of the concentration of Negroes and share-croppers. In 1930 this region had one half the nation's farms but three fifths the tenants. The dramatic decline in the rate of tenant operation of southern farms from 55.5 per cent in 1930 to 40.4 per cent in 1945 and 34.0 per cent in 1950 is associated with the decline in the number of share-croppers and the increase in wage labor and mechanization. This decline was in turn accelerated by the reduction in cotton acreage under the Agricultural Adjustment program, and the attendant increase in diversification and new patterns of farm management. The middle western states have also had high ratios of tenant operation. Here one cause was the higher cost of farms, and another was the relatively large number of business and professional people in small cities and towns who purchased farms as investments and hence desired tenant operators. Such farms were not available for sale to tenants desiring to climb the agricultural ladder. The proportions were 34.0 in 1930, in 1945 29.2 and 23.1 in 1950. The other census divisions have always had relatively few tenants, but their proportions increased slightly between 1930 and 1940, and then declined.

In considering these data, reference to Professor Wayland's study of the *Social Patterns of Farming*,[1] discussed at some length in the previous chapter, makes it clear that tenancy has decreased least in those patterns which best represent the traditional family farm in the United States. The family farm, owner operated, represents one of the values held by rural people, and every national farm organization has repeatedly endorsed this ideal. Yet it is evident that farms in this social pattern have lagged behind others in improving the owner-tenant ratio of the last years. Even the agrarian prosperity of the 1940's has not solved this problem, though the situation shows improvement.

Trend in tenure studies. A long-time look at the situation confirms this conclusion. From 1880 to 1940 for the United States as a whole and for every census division, the number of owners in each thousand males gainfully employed in agriculture has declined. In the same period the number of tenants has increased for the United States as a whole and for all but the New England, Middle Atlantic, and Pacific divisions; the number of laborers has gained except for the South. These data are summarized below.

Year	Owners	Tenants	Laborers
1880	547	187	266
1900	474	256	270
1920	451	283	266
1940	414	273	313

Source: Carl C. Taylor, Louis J. Ducoff, and Margaret J. Hagood, *Trends in Tenure Statistics of Farm Workers in the United States since 1880* (Washington, D.C.: Bureau of Agricultural Economics, United States Department of Agriculture, 1948), p. 1.

Social effects of tenancy. If, as appears, the ratio of tenant-operated farms among the family-commercial patterns of farming has been slow to decline, it is important to examine the social effects of tenancy. If tenancy is a function of industrialism, it is an inevitable phenomenon of the present state of development in the Western world, yet there are many who maintain that landownership is one of the strongest bulwarks of national safety. However, the United States has in the past placed powerful assistance at the disposal of those who crave their own stake in the land

[1]Sloan R. Wayland, *Social Patterns of Farming* (New York: Columbia University Seminar on Rural Life, 1951).

and it may do so again, not only by advancing credit, but possibly by carrying out some of its developing policies for land utilization.

Whether an unavoidable accompaniment of industrialism or not, areas of high tenancy differ from areas of high ownership in certain respects. The social scientist is interested in these differences, and the conditions they create are frequently problems for the rural educator, social worker, and clergyman.

There have been numerous studies of this point. As the chapter on standards of living shows, tenants are likely to have a somewhat lower standard of living than farm owners, at least as measured by the proportion possessing telephones, automobiles, musical instruments, bathtubs, electric lights, furnaces, and other conveniences. In these respects the tenant who is related to the owner of the farm makes a better record than the tenant who has no such tie.

These facts do not necessarily discredit either tenants or tenancy. The tenant is usually younger than the owner. He has not had an opportunity to acquire all the conveniences of life. He is perhaps trying to save for a first payment on his future farm. Moreover, he is more likely than the owner to have young children.

Effects on community usually adverse. When all allowances are made, however, it is clear that the social consequences of a high proportion of tenant-operated farms in a community are unhappy. Studies made by the Institute of Social and Religious Research seem to show that such effects begin to appear when the ratio of tenant- to owner-operated farms exceeds one in five.

Up to this point, for instance, the proportion of tenants belonging to church and social organizations is approximately the same as that of owners. Beyond this point, the differences become more pronounced. For example, in middle western counties where 50 per cent or more of the farms are tenant-operated, only one third as many tenants as owners are listed as active church members. Although these figures may vary with the type of organization, the trend is the same for lodges, farm bureaus, and all important types of social organizations.

An obvious corollary follows: In tenant-dominated communities all types of social organizations tend to be weaker and less progressive than in localities in which owners preponderate. One obvious reason for this lies in the insecurity of the renter's tenure. If he operates under a short-term lease he is not sure how long he will remain in the community. He hesitates to form ties until he feels more certain of permanence. Eventually, perhaps, he habituates himself to living more apart from organized social life than does the owner who, because of his capital investment, is likely to be more securely anchored to the locality and therefore more interested in its social life.

Another reason for the less satisfactory condition of social organizations where tenants form a considerable fraction of the population frequently lies in the phenomenon of absentee landlordism. Inevitably absentee landlords become interested chiefly, if not exclusively, in the return from the farm. Community betterment, especially if it raises taxes, is unwelcome and hence opposed. When taxes consume a large part of the landlord's income, such an attitude is understandable.

The unfortunate social consequences of farm tenancy are especially noticeable in the South, where the problem is also complicated by the large number of share-croppers. But even elsewhere class distinctions between tenants and owners occur, since the two groups often belong to different churches, lodges, and other social organizations.

Who owns the land?[2] The discussion thus far leads to the question who owns the farm land of the United States. In 1946 over 85 per cent of it belonged to individuals. Two thirds of the owners were farmers, and they held seven tenths of the individually owned acreage. One in twelve was a retired farmer. This group in the aggregate had one tenth of the land. Three per cent of the owners were housewives. Of the remaining fourth of the owners, two in five were business or professional persons who held one seventh of the acreage; three in five were clerical workers or laborers, whose holdings accounted for only one acre out of 20, frequently averaging less than 30 acres. Less than half of the clerical workers and more than two thirds of the laborers lived permanently on their land. Presumably, these farms were near towns or cities which had disproportionate numbers of residential and part-time farmers. Probably also many of the holdings of these two occupational categories would not be classified as farms under the new 1950 definition of farm.

Eighteen per cent of all of the above landowning individuals were landlords only, while another 15 per cent farmed some of their land and rented the rest. Over half of the first group and about two fifths of the second were dependent upon rent from this land for the principal source of their income.

Farm land not owned by individuals was divided among corporations, public authorities, and all other types. As [Table 1] shows, there were wide regional fluctuations. It is probably that some of the corporation land was held by incorporated family farms. It

[2]Data in the following three paragraphs taken from B. T. Inman and W. H. Fippin, *Farm Land Ownership in the United States* (Washington, D.C.: Bureau of Agricultural Economics, United States Department of Agriculture, 1949), p. 51.

[**Table 1.**] Percentage of land in farms by major types of owners, United States and regions, 1945

Region	Type of ownership			
	Individual	Corporate	Public	Other*
United States	85.4	5.6	4.9	4.1
North East	96.3	2.9	0.3	0.5
North Central	94.0	2.1	2.7	1.2
South	88.5	7.4	2.3	1.8
West	69.1	8.1	11.7	11.1

*Three fourths of this is Indian land.
Source: B. T. Inman and W. H. Fippin, *Farm Land Ownership in the United States* (Washington: Bureau of Agricultural Economics, United States Department of Agriculture, 1949), p. 51.

is significant that despite the large number of farms acquired by insurance companies and banks by foreclosure during the long depression of the 1920's and 1930's, less than 6 per cent of the farm land of the United States was corporation owned in 1946. Many of these were operating corporations. On the other hand, 3 per cent of the persons having title to farm land owned 41 per cent of the acreage in the hands of individuals. Much of this was western grazing land, but every region showed some tendency toward concentration of ownership. The slow but steady increase in the number of farms of one thousand acres and over shown by the censuses of the last half century indicates that this concentration is increasing.

This fact illustrates a contradiction in the values held by Americans. On the one hand, there is the belief that farm land should be owned by those who till the soil in family-sized units. On the other hand, under our philosophy of free enterprise we believe that any individual may acquire as much land as he wants and can pay for. Only in the Territory of Puerto Rico is there a limitation on the maximum number of acres (five hundred) any individual or corporation may own. This is a matter of national land policy. It raises the question as to whether measures are needed to strengthen or facilitate family farm ownership.

Strengthening the family farm. The announced objective of a number of laws dealing with agriculture enacted by Congress in the last two decades has been to strengthen the family farm. The Under Secretary of Agriculture, Clarence J. McCormick, speaking before the assembly of the Food and Agriculture Organization in June, 1951, declared this to be our national policy and urged land reform as a major activity of the organization and its member governments. How far has this policy been implemented?

One early effort in this direction was that of the Homestead Act to enable settlers to acquire farms on generous terms. While the purposes of this act were frequently abused, it was measurably effective so long as large areas of public land remained unsettled. At present, despite continued agitation for its repeal, there is a 160-acre limitation on farm land acquired from the Federal Government. A few states have laws exempting homesteads from seizure for debt. Farm credit legislation and the Agricultural Adjustment Act of 1933, discussed elsewhere, as well as other legislation of the 1930's, was aimed to help family farms.

In 1937 Congress set up the Farm Security, now the Farmers' Home, Administration. It was charged, among other things, with helping selected tenants to purchase farms through loans. Low interest rates and repayment of principal in from twenty to forty years were provided, together with some guidance in farm management. This tenant-purchase program is akin to comparable programs in several other countries, notably in Ireland, where over a period of some decades the proportion of owner-operators among the total farm population was increased from 3 to 97 per cent.[3]

The program of the Farmer's Home Administration and its predecessor for aiding selected tenants to become owners is in the nature of a demonstration rather than an ambitious program to eliminate tenancy among American farmers. Thus far it has reached only about sixty thousand farm families and is financially assisting over four thousand additional tenants each year. To date, over 98 per cent of the payments have been made when due, and only six of the first ten thousand purchase loans have been defaulted. This compares favorably with the general farm credit situation discussed in a later chapter.

Several organizations, notably several insurance companies, have adopted the same plan in financing the large number of farms it was necessary for them to acquire by foreclosure during the agricultural depression.

Broader aspects of the problem were attacked by a presidential tenancy committee, which reported in 1937. It planned in some detail for a Farm Security Corporation to help tenants toward ownership and made suggestions as to rehabilitation work. Other recommendations were designed to discourage land speculation, to improve lease contracts and landlord-tenant relations, to relieve small homesteads of taxation, and to safeguard civil liberties. The need for improved education and health services was also stressed. Several state commissions appointed by governors have made reports agreeing in the main with the proposals just noted. One state report went so far as to propose higher tax rates where several farms

are under one ownership. One state, South Carolina, has conducted a highly significant demonstration in one county in improving landlord-tenant relations. This has been accomplished by joint meetings under Extension Service auspices, at which problems and difficulties were discussed frankly. As a result tenant houses have been improved, home gardens started, and production has improved.

These proposals have not been translated into effective operation; in fact, they have been ignored by Congress save for the important exception of the tenant-purchase program of the Farmers' Home Administration. But the fundamental fact is that no long-time national policies for agriculture can wholly succeed, whether they relate to prices, soil conservation, or production adjustment, unless some of the basic problems of tenancy are solved. Such policies would be handicapped by a pattern of land tenure that promises little security, and therefore little incentive, for millions of farm families. Such conditions make migration from the land inevitable. Certainly some of these youth should migrate, but if the present situation continues, the more able children of tenants will be forced to seek opportunity elsewhere, away from the farm land which needs their vitality.

There is no possibility of expanding the tenant-purchase program to enable eligible tenants to become farm owners. The cost to the Government would run into billions. The answer appears to be not only in the proposals of the Presidential Committee on Farm Tenancy, but also in new legislation that would protect tenants. Such legislation might provide for longer terms for leases, compensate the tenant for making improvements to land and buildings, and protect him from undue control in his farm-management program. Such provisions are written into law in a number of countries, notably England, which for over sixty years has had agricultural legislation far in advance of that which exists at present in any of the United States. On the basis of the experience of these other countries, it is safe to claim that such legislation, adjusted to the American situation, would prove a powerful incentive for the tenant to conserve rather than to mine the soil, induce more farmers' sons to remain in agriculture, result in a more careful selection of tenants by landlords, and improve the level of the community itself by giving security and therefore stability to the tenant and his family.

Our future farmers. The foregoing proposals relate largely to present tenants and their situation. Of late increasing attention has been given to the problem of maintaining the family on the farm over generations.

About a third of the individual owners of farm land in 1946 had acquired their acres through gift or inheritance or by a combination of these with some pur-

[3]Cf. Elizabeth Hooker, *Readjustments of Agricultural Tenure in Ireland* (Chapel Hill: University of North Carolina Press, 1938).

chase money. One in ten had bought all their land from relatives. Except for a few who had homesteaded, the rest, more than half, had had to purchase all their land from persons unrelated to them.[4]

There are two phases of one problem here. It is difficult for a young man wishing to farm to acquire sufficient capital to purchase a farm unless he is assisted by his family. The great increase in the price of land and equipment and necessary restrictions on the proportion of farm value that can be borrowed, create the danger that the prospective farmer will be content with too small an acreage and find himself underemployed. One alternative is for farms on the market to be added to the holdings of a contiguous farmer, accelerating the trend toward larger units.

The prospective farmer who has his family's farm available is in a better position. However, if there are other heirs, he usually has to buy them out and hence meets the same basic problem. Nevertheless, an Iowa study shows such a person gains some advantage in the family situation, though his advancement to ownership status is often delayed.[5]

A new agricultural ladder? The state colleges of agriculture have begun to study the problem of keeping the farm in the family. Coöperating committees have been set up in several regions. Some devices tried by farm families in order to keep the farm in the family have been explored. Among these are family farm-operating agreements and father-son farm agreements.

As some agricultural economists see it, the new ladder begins with project agreements such as those involving 4-H Club or Future Farmers of America projects. The next step would be a formalized apprenticeship, often with a monthly wage allowance to the son, from which he meets his own expenses. The third rung would be a partnership, which would begin the necessary transfer arrangements. Finally would come the assumption of full ownership.

Where more than one son desires to continue in farming the problem is more difficult unless the enterprise is large enough to warrant a partnership. In some cases the family farm has been incorporated.[6]

There has not been enough experience to date to determine which of a number of methods is best in each of various situations which might arise when a family farm must change hands. The amount of research and the general interest in the problem is evidence that a social need has been recognized. The various experiments under way indicate that rural society is feeling its way toward new devices that will satisfy the high value placed on land ownership by the operator's family and in keeping the farm in the family over the generations.

There are situations, of course, in which keeping the farm in the family may work counter to other values and desires, for instance, education for a son or daughter, or the entrance of a son into an occupation which greatly interests him and for which he has more aptitude than he has for agriculture. Any arrangements worked out to meet the general problems must obviously be only for those who desire to use them.

[4]B. T. Inman and W. H. Fippin, *op. cit.*, pp. 33-42.
[5]Robert A. Rohwer, *Family Factors in Tenure Experience* (Ames: Iowa State College, Agricultural Experiment Station, 1950), Bulletin 375.

[6]Edmund deS. Brunner, *Case Studies of Family Farms* (New York: Columbia University Seminar on Rural Life, 1949).

Technology, delta town co-exist

TOM HAMBURGER*

WILSON—There is an English Tudor village in the middle of the Arkansas Delta.

The town of Wilson comes upon you with little warning before you get there on Highway 61, you're shooting across the Delta passing through rather forlorn farm communities. The impression changes suddenly when you hit Wilson.

☐ From the Arkansas Gazette, Little Rock, Ark., May 18, 1977.
* Reporter of the Gazette staff.

The streets of Wilson are lined with stately cottonwoods, and the houses, unlike those in some Arkansas farm communities, are well-kept.

While many small farm communities look deserted, with stores boarded up and town centers extinguished, Wilson (population, 1,048) is thriving.

Its town center has been remodeled in English Tudor style. Moss is growing on the old-style roofs now, and the wood has aged. Wilson looks like an English village.

At noon time, the town square is busy as town folk and farmers head to the Wilson Tavern (the menu features quail, steak and shrimp daily) and its adjacent club, Ye Olde Pub.

Around the square, all the businesses at Wilson have Wilson in their name: Wilson Tavern, Wilson Insurance Agency, Wilson Motor and Implement Company, Bank of Wilson, Wilson Drug Store, Wilson Construction Company, Wilson Service Station.

It isn't that the businessmen at Wilson lack imagination or desire consistency. All the Wilson businesses are named for their owners, the Robert E. Lee Wilson family.

BARONIAL TRADITION

The third, fourth and fifth generations of Robert E. Lee Wilsons are living at Wilson and are carrying on a baronial tradition. The town was founded in the 1880s by "Boss Lee" Wilson (Robert E. Lee Wilson Sr.), a lumberman, who wrested what later became the world's largest cotton plantation from the swamp and virgin forest.

Today, Robert E. Lee Wilson III, 63, and three of his four sons, Robert, 24 (called Bob), Steve, 29, and Mike, 34, operate the Wilson holdings (1976 sales: $12 million), which, besides the companies mentioned above include a 33,000-acre farm (the largest family farm in Arkansas), two Mississippi County towns (Wilson and Marie) and a good portion of a third (Keiser), two planting seed plants, most of the stock of a seed oil mill, a railroad, a petroleum company and a 13,000-acre ranch in Nevada.

In the late 1950s, Robert E. Lee Wilson III, the chairman of the Board of the Lee Wilson Co., changed what was a company-owned town into an incorporated city with an elected mayor and five aldermen.

Robert E. Lee Wilson III was elected mayor, and he has been re-elected ever since. His middle son, Steve, is assistant mayor. The director of the railroad, Mack Davison, is director of the Wilson Housing Authority.

At the time the city was incorporated, Wilson gave the city its four parks, a fish-stocked lake and eight-hole golf course.

Believing that ownership provided "a sense of pride," the Wilsons have begun selling the company-owned houses to the residents, most of whom are former employes, at giveaway prices. (A large, handsome 3,300-square foot home near the town center sold two years ago for $10,000.)

LIBRARY, CLINIC

The family also established a library and put up $65,000 in 1969 for a dental-medical clinic. In the last five years, the town has been without a doctor or dentist, a victim of a doctor shortage in eastern Arkansas.

Mike Wilson continues to interview candidates to fill the vacancy "but they want us to guarantee too much money," he said.

The Wilsons are concerned with other social needs as well. The Wilsons made it their goal in the early 1960s to provide housing for the town's poor, some of whom are former company employes.

"This has become kind of a retirement center," Mike Wilson said, "because we have such active housing and social service programs."

In 1940, there were at least two families living in red-roofed Wilson Co. plank houses on every 40 acres of land at the Wilson plantation. There are few plank houses left. Now, three people work every 1,000 acres.

SHACKS DISAPPEARING

The red-roofed houses, once landmarks in the 50 square miles of Mississippi County owned by the Wilsons, are disappearing fast.

"Our goal is to get rid of those shacks," Mike Wilson says. "We plan to have a big party when we burn the last shack, and I hope it will be soon."

In 1962, the Wilsons decided to seek federal aid to develop low-income housing at Wilson. In 1969, they rented their first 28 units. The apartments are small, neat, desegregated and look more attractive than most government projects. Average rent is $51 a month.

Since 1969, the Wilsons have built 40 more housing units at Wilson, several at Keiser and Marie. The company is currently building 40 duplex homes using an energy-saving design, the first in the Southwest built with Housing and Urban Development funds.

The Wilson Housing Authority apartments are all built by the Wilson Construction Company and the sites are purchased from the family firm.

A nonprofit corporation was formed by the Wilsons to lease low-income rental units to the housing authority at the two nearby towns of Keiser (population 900) and Marie (72).

'NOT FOR PROFIT'

"They [the Wilson] are not into it for profit," Davison says. "They are just interested in housing for the people that work for them." Out of the 68 units, Mike Wilson estimates two dozen are present or former company employees.

The school at Wilson was one of the first in the state to have an indoor swimming pool and all-weather track. Inside the main door of the modern, air conditioned Wilson Elementary School is a large portrait of Robert E. Lee (Boss Lee) Wilson Sr.

Boss Lee traded his 160 acres of cleared farm land in the 1880s for 2,100 acres of swamp timber land to get wood for the mill at Golden Lake. As he made money on the timber, he bought more swampland, cleared it of timber and reinvested.

Unlike most timber interests in the area, Boss Lee held on to the cleared land.

RICH, BLACK LOAM

It was a good decision. For thousands of years the flooding Mississippi had laid down layer upon layer of rich black loam carried from its northern drainage basin. The land that Wilson cleared is among the richest in Arkansas. Hudson Wren, former executive vice president of Lee Wilson Co., says that no one knows how deep the rich loam soil is. Some authorities say it may be hundreds of feet deep. A lot of farmers elsewhere make do with less than one foot.

In the late 1890s, to drain the swamps, Boss Lee organized the Land Clearance of Mississippi County. In doing so, he incurred the wrath of other lumbermen who wanted the flooding to float logs to the river.

The plantation grew to 65,000 acres, plus cotton gins, stores, a bank and all the houses and other real estate at Wilson and five nearby communities. These properties were gathered in Lee Wilson Co. When Boss Lee died, he left the estate to his son, Robert E. Lee Jr. (called Roy), and a trusted employe, James H. Crain.

During the next 15 years, the two made the first moves toward mechanized farming, and ventures into new businesses. In the mid-1930s when timber supplies diminished, they turned over big chunks of acreage to soybeans and established the Wilson Soya Company to process the beans into oil and meal. To make fuller use of their cotton crop they helped put together Delta Products Company, a co-operative cottonseed oil mill near Wilson.

LEGACY SPLIT

In 1948, the family legacy was split. Roy Wilson's two sisters persuaded him to put the plantation into partial liquidation so they could take out their share of the estate. After the split-up Lee Wilson Company was left with 22,500 acres and the neighboring towns of Keiser and Marie. Roy's sisters got the remaining acreage. A few years later, Crain resigned, and Bob Wilson III took over management of the company.

Under Wilson III's leadership, the Wilsons began diversifying into several areas. The company began growing alfalfa and established an alfalfa dehydrating facility at Wilson. The soya mill was closed in the early 1970s, but the company's seed operation was expanded. Today the company's seed division handles 4,000 tons of cotton seed annually and processes more than 1,000,000 bushels of registered and certified soybean and wheat seed. The company's international sales have expanded recently.

POLO PLAYERS

Robert Wilson III went to Yale, was captain of the polo team, and until recently kept a stable of race horses. Wilson III and his sons were active polo players and until two or three years ago, Steve played occasionally at Memphis.

Mike attended the Citadel. Steve the University of Arkansas and Bob the University of Virginia.

Why do they return to Wilson?

Mike: "It's an inheritance."

Steve: "I love farming."

Bob: "I thought of law school but decided to come home."

Bob Wilson, son of Robert E. Lee Wilson III, is legally named Robert E. Lee Wilson V because his eldest brother, Robert E. Lee Wilson IV, died of leukemia at age 7. Robert E. Lee Wilson III, strongly wanted to perpetuate the family name and so gave his next born, Bob, the name of his deceased brother.

Judging by the English Tudor architecture and the old south manners, this Mississippi County city might appear to be a vestige of two lost cultures.

The appearances are deceiving. The Wilson company has kept close watch on changing agricultural conditions and has been in the forefront of major developments in agriculture during the revolution of the last three decades.

Chamber of Commerce says family farm must go*

WASHINGTON—The Chamber of Commerce of the United States has invited its small town affiliates to commit suicide by supporting concentration of agriculture into large units which can by-pass smaller town merchants and marketing firms.

In a new study which gives special acknowledgment to Dr. Leonard R. Kyle of Michigan State University "for his personal guidance in the preparation of this report," the Chamber of Commerce comes out stoutly against NFO's Family Farm Act which would forbid non-farm businessmen and corporations with $3 million in assets from getting into agricultural production.

"It is quite possible that the current wave of state and federal legislation to prohibit farming by major corporations will be counter-productive in an industrialized food system where consumers interests are paramount," the C of C report says. "The enactment of such legislation may impose any restrictions on large corporations which would impair the availability of credit and prohibit large corporations from contracting directly with producers to insure orderly supply of quality products for processing and marketing.

"New laws may create roadblocks, but it is doubtful that they will stay the forces that are pushing for larger sized production units."

Big agriculture is the most efficient, the C of C paper contends, pointing out how the big operators can go around small town merchants and marketers.

"Older studies on the economics of size . . . have generally shown that costs decrease with increasing output but level off and remain constant for the largest farms sampled or simulated. Many of these studies, particularly in the Corn Belt, of cattle feeding, hog, corn and soybean production units have generally found that most economies of size have been reached with units requiring the labor and management of only two or three men. . . .

"More recently various researchers have questioned the current validity of older research and have demonstrated that some very large farms operate at a profit even in the Midwest. Usually these successful firms have been able to buy many of their inputs, excepting labor and management, for from 15 to 25 per cent less than the price paid by most small units.

"Also the larger units are thought to have the ability to sell at an advantage through the control of a larger quantity and because they can by-pass the first steps in the usual marketing chain and handle this function for a lower unit cost."

The Chamber of Commerce brochure carefully avoids another "efficiency" claimed for the large farm units in the studies to which it refers: the ability to avoid taxes by charging farm earnings off against non-farm losses and vice versa, and similar tax dodges.

Although the national C of C "study" has been out for about three months, only one smaller town Chamber of Commerce is known to have raised any questions about what "Big Brother" is advocating. That occurred in Missouri, where one local Chamber of Commerce called a special meeting on the implications of the report which relates "efficiency" to going around small town businesses.

The C of C report contends that the trend toward bigness is irreversible, pointing out that "in nearly every type of firm involved in marketing food, the number of firms are decreasing and the firms are becoming larger in size. These large firms in the processing and marketing field will want to assure themselves of the one thing essential to their continued successful operations: supply of the commodities they are processing and marketing.

Benefits of large agribusiness operations in the farming field would accrue to commercial farmers who can survive the competition, to consumers, to stockholders and employees of the big firms, and to the nation through expanding exports, the C of C contends.

The problems which consolidating farms into industrialized operations confront include the Family Farm Act pressed by NFO in both national and state legislatures, the displacement of farmers and farm workers which more mechanization will bring, the problems of the rural communities as employment declines in commercial agriculture, and probable unionization of farm workers.

The report suggests that the big agribusiness concerns "might be well advised to exert a more positive concern and influence toward solution of the problems of rural people."

It also suggests that "the government may . . . need to consider laws which keep workers on the job while mediating the problems causing work interruptions. . .

"The real danger is to the integrity of the food supply. Major interruptions of farm work or operations

□ From NFO Reporter, Corning, Iowa, Jan. 1975.
*Special from the Reporter, Washington Correspondent.

in processing plants at crucial times cannot be offset by overtime work in the following months. All crop planting and harvesting has some very critical timing aspects which are not as favorable again for several months. All animals require daily care or drastic losses will occur. Thus, any major threat to the basic food supply, because of interruptions due to strikes or substantial delay of farm work or processing, would probably not be tolerated by the consuming public."

The report concludes:

"We must now focus on more intensive use of existing resources for increased production. We must streamline the sequence of operations beginning with purchased farm inputs and carrying on through to the consumer . . .

"The above changes mean more structural adjustments in agribusiness—both on and off the farm. . . .

"American agribusiness is coming 'of age' in an industrialized economy and in a world of international interdependence. This must be recognized as such on the farm, in industry, and throughout our Federal Government."

Why corporate farming

DAVID WILLIAM SECKLER*

I find myself at this meeting in a rather unusual position: as an academic economist not overly enamoured either of big business or of our ceaseless, and at times senseless, pursuit of an ever-expanding GNP in this country, I come in defense of corporate farming.

First, let me give some of the background of the company with which I am familiar. The Ceres Land Company of Sterling, Colorado, is a fairly large agricultural corporation engaged in all phases of the cattle industry in eastern Colorado. It began strictly as a cattle feeding company and expanded into part ownership of a slaughtering facility for its cattle. It has recently acquired several thousand acres of land in eastern Colorado for purposes of development under sprinkler irrigation and for growing cattle on irrigated pasture. Two years ago the company formed a joint partnership with an eastern investment firm. The company, therefore, appears to qualify as a "corporate farm" both in terms of scale of operation and with respect to participation by nonagricultural interests.

The keystone of this company is vertical integration through the cattle industry. We may as well begin by explaining why vertical integration affords attractive opportunities in the livestock industry. The cattle cycle is somewhat as follows: A cow has a calf; this calf is raised up to a 500-pound animal on range or wheat land and then enters a feedlot for fattening, after which it goes to a slaughtering facility. With each of these stages are associated costs of transportation, buying and selling commissions, and shrinkage. Of course, these costs for any given animal will vary widely, depending upon how far it is transported and how often it changes hands through each of these cycles; but in our experience where the typical feeder animal is raised in Texas, perhaps fattened on Kansas wheat pasture, then transported to Colorado for finishing, and finally retransported to Denver for slaughtering, these costs add up to a minimum of $10 per head and may range as high as $35 per head. Vertical integration substantially reduces these costs and thus creates a powerful inducement to that form of organization in the livestock industry.

The Ceres Land Company has become interested in large-scale farming operations only within the past two years. This interest was generated by the attractive opportunities offered by the utilization of new techniques of sprinkler irrigation in the development of the lands overlying the Ogallala Basin in eastern Colorado and western Nebraska.

Let us pause briefly to note a potentially serious problem in the development of this Basin. The Basin, for all practical purposes, is a closed aquifer with comparatively little recharge; thus, using this water supply in irrigation is essentially a mining operation which depletes the resource. A report of the U.S. Geological Survey states that in 25 years, given current rates of pumping, the Basin will contain 40 percent less water than it now has. The depth of the water

☐ Proceedings of North Central Workshop, Chicago, Apr. 1969. Agricultural Economics Report No. 53, Lincoln, 1969, University of Nebraska.
*Acting Associate Professor of Agricultural Economics, University of California, Berkeley.

table in the Ogallala Basin varies considerably; some wells will dry up before other wells. The lands acquired by the Ceres Land Company overlay some of the deepest water tables in this Basin and should be good, we estimate, for a hundred years. But certainly, some of the shallower wells will dry up before then. Thus, there is a very real danger of a dust bowl arising again in these Plains unless conservation practices are instituted. In order to avert this possibility, it has been proposed that it be made a condition of the issuance of water well permits (retroactive, if possible) that the holder of the permit be required to replant his acreage in native grasses to the satisfaction of the Soil Conservation Service if the well is no longer used at any future time.

Let us now return to the opportunities offered by sprinkler technology. There are two basic systems which are of interest here. The "rotary" system is basically a large metal pipe mounted on wheels which rotates around the field. The "stationary" system consists of PVC plastic pipes buried under the ground from which risers with sprinklerheads extend above ground. The rotary system costs about $200 per acre to install, including the well and wellhead equipment, and the stationary system about $300 per acre. But the stationary system has several advantages. It may be installed on rougher terrain and in irregular shapes; thus, a greater proportion of any given area may be developed into irrigated agriculture. It lasts longer and provides some temperature control of the field. Both systems may be regulated by clocks or moisture sensing devices to provide virtually completely automated control of irrigation.

With these systems, land in eastern Colorado previously capable of supporting only one 500-pound heifer per nine acres of rangeland can be converted in the space of a few months into land yielding 150 bushels of corn per acre, or land capable of supporting three 500-pound heifers per acre of irrigated pasture. Since these systems are installed on light, sandy soil, the costs of plowing, disking, and other land tillage operations are reduced on the order of two-thirds over furrow irrigation. One may equipped with these systems can conveniently irrigate some 1,200 acres of land.

Equally important is the fact that, by concentrating the control of large acreages in the hands of a few highly trained personnel, sprinkler technology liberates significant economies of scale latent in the agricultural firm. We list these economies in order of importance:

1. The division of managerial talent among specialized personnel and extending the influence of highly talented personnel over a large amount of business. The Ceres Land Company, for example, has a Ph.D. in Nutrition and a Ph.D. in Agronomy on its staff. It also has two full-time veterinarians and a highly trained comptroller. Perhaps even more important is utilization of these complex skills described as managerial talent. If one has a supply of this highly scarce resource, it pays to use it over the largest feasible volume of business.

2. In agriculture generally and particularly in the livestock sector of agriculture, large efficiencies can be achieved through capital-intensive means of production. But capital-intensive means of production are by their very nature rather "lumpy"—they cannot be easily subdivided in small units. Lumpy investments require large operations in order to lower average costs. But, if an efficient size can be attained, the advantages of capital intensity are significant. For example, the Ceres Land Company uses only an average of one full-time employee per 1,000 head of cattle in its feedlot operations.

3. Market selling power. By slaughtering one's own cattle which are fed one's own crops in one's own feed yards, these crops are, as it were, "condensed" into a high-valued, easily transportable commodity sold on national and even international markets. By this means, more competitive and stable prices are available to the seller.

4. Lastly, of course, there are certain advantages of buying power. Volume purchases of equipment and fertilizer give the large-scale operator certain advantages. However, the economies stemming from this source have perhaps been overemphasized in the literature, and it is very easy to make too much of them.

We have attempted to indicate above that there are sound economic reasons for corporations to engage in agriculture. If efficiently managed, large-scale farming can be a very profitable enterprise, fully comparable in terms of returns on investment to virtually any other sector of the economy. It is quite likely that, given these profit opportunities and the failure of the stock market to provide an adequate hedge against inflation, we shall see a great deal of corporate farming in the future.

Let us now turn to two other considerations—the question of tax advantages to corporate farming and the social impacts of corporate farming on rural communities.

In reading the agenda for this meeting, I noticed with some relief that Professor Levi has undertaken the task of examining tax advantages in corporate farming. I in no way wish to deny that agriculture offers some attractive tax advantages to outside interests. I do, however, wish to point out one fact: If one is to attempt to explain outside investment in agriculture by "tax advantages," it is not enough to simply show that there are tax advantages in agriculture. One must show that there are *more* tax advantages in agriculture than in other sectors of the economy. We must not fall for the easy trap of thinking that one man's legitimate deduction is another man's evasion. When one contemplates the tax advantages in real estate speculation, in the stock market, in mining and oil development, and in other sectors of the economy, it is hard to believe that agriculture is especially privileged.

I am personally convinced that this country stands in dire need of a general tax reform. Our tax structure is systematically designed to allow wealthy individuals to escape the progressive income tax while providing no refuge to working people. On this question of general reform, I am wholeheartedly in agreement. I believe, however, that the proposed restrictive legislation against corporations in agriculture is a step in the opposite direction. It is a discriminatory movement designed to keep tax advantages for certain vested interests in agriculture to the exclusion of other people. This movement must be recognized for what it is—simply another case of special pleading, a device for reducing competition, and another stratagem for subsidizing agriculture at the expense of the rest of the nation.

Let us now consider the possible effect of corporate farming on rural America. This question has two aspects: first, the extent of the development of corporate farming as compared to family farming and, second, potential social costs and benefits of corporate farming per se.

It is a natural tendency of human thought to extrapolate a present trend to infinity. Such an extrapolation has occurred over the present issue, and images are evoked of vast corporate farms dominating agriculture. I think this image is very far fetched. It is far fetched if for no other reason than that large-scale corporate farming has historically entered only those areas of agriculture (with the possible exception of ranching) which have been characterized by rapid, capital-intensive technological change. This is certainly true of the livestock industry, and we see it happening again with respect to the development of new lands under sprinkler irrigation. I can think of no reason why corporations would wish to "gobble up" the typical midwestern family farm. If any corporation were foolish enough to do so, it would soon find itself with a highly indigestible lump producing acute pain and nausea from which relief could be obtained only by the corporate equivalent of a strong purgative.

Thus, while one may expect family farms in the traditional agricultural regions to increase substantially in size over time, and while corporate farming as we have come to think of it may dominate new land developments in the agricultural sector, it is very doubtful if corporate farming will ever constitute over one-third of the farming of the United States.

With that in mind, let us look at some of the possible social consequences of corporate farming. Insofar as it involves the development of previously undeveloped lands, employment and incomes of the communities in the developing areas grow. This has certainly been the case in eastern Colorado. Towns in that area are undergoing a virtual "boom" under the stimulus of land development. But there is another, and perhaps in the long run, even more important impact of corporate farming on rural communities. This is the different social order it entails.

The peculiar nature of agriculture differentiates its management problems from the management of most other sectors of the economy. We cannot here go into the reasons for this differentiation; we shall only mention its consequences. First, almost without exception, only people with a long experience in agriculture—farm boys—can manage farms efficiently. The state of the art has not sufficiently progressed to the state of science to allow easy transference of managerial talent from other sectors of the economy to agriculture (excepting, of course, in such specialized functions as accounting). Secondly, partly because of the background of the managers, partly because of the diverse, diffuse, and complex nature of farming operations, strictly salaried managers are not generally efficient. They must have a "piece of the action" through partnerships, stock options, or similar incentive devices.

The consequence of these two factors is that the new class of agricultural managers become propertied men in their own right, influential in their communities, but essentially of different origin than the traditional power structure of the rural communities. They are, generally speaking, the sons of agricultural "hired men" or former tenants or sons of tenants of the landowning classes. They are parvenus in the rural community and, as Pirenne has observed, in such people reside the seeds of profound social change.[1] This change in the social order of rural America is one of the most promising consequences of corporate farming. While it is too early to see its ultimate effects, one consequence has already appeared. The recent agitation against corporate farming by affluent family farmers at least partly stems

[1]Henri Pirenne, *Economic and Social History of Medieval Europe* (New York: Harcourt, Brace, & World, Inc., 1937), Chapter 2.

from a fear of losing the social and political control of rural America.

Many a tear has dropped over the passing of the family farm. Having been born and raised on a family farm myself, this sentiment is not wholly unfamiliar to me. I submit, however, that we have a curiously distorted image of family farming in America. The image properly includes the peaceful life, the fine home, and the stimulating environment for children on the family farm; but it should also include the ramshackle, unsanitary buildings of the itinerant laborer and the tenant farmer upon which American agriculture has been erected. It is common knowledge that of the 3 million farmers in the United States today, only 1 million produce around 90 percent of the value of agricultural output. It is this 1 million to which we habitually refer when we speak of family farming. But the other 2 million are also family farmers; and this class of people, together with the class of agricultural labor, has not figured highly in our sentiments. The impact of corporate farming on agricultural wage rates and the opportunities provided to landless persons to obtain a good living in agriculture strikes me as one of the most promising social consequences of corporate farming.

In rereading Pirenne the other day, I came across the following passage wherein he describes the rise of the commercial and merchant classes out of the stagnant agriculture of medieval feudalism.[2]

First, it is incontestable that commerce and industry were originally recruited from among landless men who lived, so to speak, on the margin of society where land alone was the basis of existence. Now these men were very numerous. Apart altogether from those who in times of famine or war would leave their native soil to seek a livelihood elsewhere and returned no more, we have to remember all the individuals whom the manorial organization itself was unable to support. The peasants' holdings were of such size as to secure the regular payment of the dues assessed upon them. Thus the younger sons of a man overburdened with children were often forced to leave their father in order to enable him to make his payments to the Lord. Thenceforth they swelled the crowd of vagabonds who roamed through the country, going from abbey to abbey taking their share of alms reserved for the poor, hiring themselves out to the peasants at harvest time, or at the vintage, and enlisting as mercenaries in the feudal troops in times of war.

I need not belabor the analogy; I shall simply close.

[2]*Ibid.*

The family farm is the most efficient unit of production

ANGUS McDONALD

Even the USDA will sometimes admit that the family-run operation is equally as efficient or more efficient at production than the large corporate farm, and that the advantages of the corporate farm lie in the tax laws, easier access to credit and vertical integration. In 1967, a USDA economist, J. Patrick Madden, reviewed 138 studies on the production costs of different size farms and found mechanized 1- and 2-man farms to be consistently the most efficient. The results of Madden's survey were published by the USDA's Economic Research Service as a technical report, *Economies of Size In Farming*. Here, Angus McDonald, former Washington representative for the National Farmers Union, summarizes the Madden report.

PETER BARNES

Over the years there has been a vast propaganda campaign designed to convince the American people that the family farm is inefficient and that super-

☐ In Barnes, P., editor: The people's land, Emmaus, Pa., 1975, Rodale Press, pp. 86-88.

farms, owned and operated by millionaires and conglomerate corporations, represent the wave of the future.

Swept under the rug, ignored and suppressed are many studies which prove without any reasonable doubt that the small or medium-sized unit is more efficient than the large corporate unit.

These studies, based on solid facts, are not wishful thinking. They are the result of hundreds of analyses of the costs and gross profits of many types of farming, including fruit, grain, livestock, cotton, vegetables, alfalfa and dairy. Here are a few examples:

Fruit farms in California

On non-mechanical peach farms in the Marysville area of California, average production cost per ton declined up to a productive unit of about 60 acres. Beyond that size, slight reductions in harvesting costs and machinery investment per acre were realized, but these were offset by higher costs of hired supervision.

On mechanized peach farms the average cost declined up to a farm size of between 90 and 110 acres. After that point there was no reduction in cost on larger units.

Iowa cash grain and crop-livestock farms

Hilly farms in southern Iowa showed lowest costs for units of about 320 to 360 acres. This represented a two-man operation and a three-plow tractor. In northeast Iowa, there was little difference in costs between 400- and 800-acre units.

Irrigated cotton farms

A study of Texas high plains farms concluded that a one-man farm with adequate capital could be as efficient as any of the larger farms. A one-man farm of 440 acres, with 102 acres of cotton and six-row machinery resulted in an expenditure of 71 cents for every dollar of gross income. None of the larger farms could go below this.

On heavy soil in Fresno County, California, costs of producing cotton proved to be lowest on a four-man farm of 1,134 acres. On light soils a 710, four-man farm proved to be most efficient. A one-man, 193-acre farm had a cost-revenue ratio of 0.83, the four-man farm had a cost-revenue ratio of 0.76. There was no increase in efficiency after this point.

Imperial Valley vegetable farms

This particular study concluded that with contract services, long-run costs are constant from the very small farms up to 2,400 acres. Another conclusion was that the Imperial Valley farmer achieves no advantage in owning equipment and actually has advantages over larger farms which own equipment used at less than full capacity. This assumes that contract facilities are available for the small and medium-sized farms. The general conclusion is that there are no significant economies based on size.

Kern County cash crop farms

In this area of California the 640-acre unit was most efficient. After that point costs per revenue dollar began to climb.

Oregon wheat farms

One-man wheat farms achieved lower average costs than two- or three-man farms. On farms smaller than 1,000 acres the costs were slightly higher. Increases in size beyond 1,000 acres resulted in increased costs.

Dairy farms

The most efficient unit in New England was a two-man operation with 70 cows and costs estimated at $2,000 a year for labor and management. However, if no charge is made for labor, the one-man farm with 35 cows achieved lower costs.

In Iowa there was only a slight reduction in costs as herds were expanded from 34 to 58 cows. In Arizona, average costs declined sharply up to a herd of 150-head, but management difficulties typically occurred when the herd reached 150 to 175 cows.

In Minnesota the two-man dairy with 87 cows and 490 acres was just a shade more efficient than the one-man, 48 cow, 290-acre operation.

Feedlots

A USDA study concludes that economies of size are attainable in a size range of 1500 to 5000 head. Beyond this point the cost curve declines slightly, but the savings are insignificant. Other studies indicate that gigantic feedlots are apt to be much less efficient because they are not operated at full capacity. Consequently the percentage of fixed costs are greater than in the small feedlot.

Economist takes issue with corporate farming

Academic papers prepared by an agricultural economist at the University of Minnesota are surfacing in Washington, says the Cooperative League of the USA (CLUSA), and they promise to add fuel to the controversy over corporate vs. family farming.

Purpose of the articles, in the words of the author, Prof. Phillip M. Raup, is "... to set forth some of the key questions raised by the appearance of firms large enough to pose a threat of monopoly power in rural America."

Raup observes that the corporate farm by its very nature and because of its large size will impose certain of its costs upon others—namely, the people of the community where it is located.

In practice, he says, "the economic and political power that accompanies large size provides a constant

☐ From *Cooperative Builder*, Vol. 48, No. 44, Nov. 1, 1973.

temptation to the large firm to take the benefits and pass on the costs.

"In many cases the rural community declines. Per capita costs of public services go up or the quality of service deteriorates, or both; and the youth of the community are forced to go elsewhere if they are to obtain adequate training and employment. Poor schools, poor roads, deficient housing and limited cultural opportunities tend to be associated with rural communities dominated by large firms. Examples can be found in California, Colorado, Florida, Texas, the Mississippi Delta states and elsewhere."

How does the efficiency of the large-scale farm compare with the smaller family operation? Raup says, "Virtually all current studies of economies of size in agriculture yield the same conclusion. In all but a few types of farming, well managed one- and two-man farms can obtain most of the gains to be had from increased size, as measured by decreases in cost per unit of output."

How about the argument that incorporation is necessary in agriculture to achieve the same advantages in farming that industry realizes through wholesalers, marketing and research firms, and other insti-

tutions in the commercial chain from producer to consumer?

Raup says agriculture already has as highly developed a chain of institutions. "Among these institutions are the agricultural cooperatives, farm political organizations, and a complex structure of informational and governmental organizations, including universities, experiment stations, extension services, the Soil Conservation Service, the Farm Credit Administration, crop and livestock statistical reporting . . ."

A stronger argument to consider, says Raup, is the market power the large firm can exercise in both purchasing and marketing, especially in cases where a producing firm also owns a processing or marketing outlet.

"The effects of concentration in agriculture are quite likely to drive up the relative price of food, in the long run," says Raup. "They are sure to drive up the costs of nonfood producing uses of rural land. It is this consequence of a trend toward large-scale firms in agriculture that should be of greatest concern . . .

"The research that is called for is an inventory of who owns rural America, and not simply its agricultural land."

A tale of two towns

WALTER GOLDSCHMIDT*

It is difficult to prove causation in history, for each society is unique and the forces are complex, but there are few who doubt that the nature of rural land tenure is intimately related to the character of the social order. By and large, where democratic conditions prevail, the man who tilled the soil was a free-holder and in control of his enterprise. Where, on the other hand, farming lands are owned and controlled in urban centers and the men engaged in production are merely peasants, serf or hired laborers, democratic institutions do not prevail. . . .

It is a remarkable fact that in this scientific era, so little empirical research has been done on this vital relationship. Indeed, I know of none other than the one I conducted in 1944, which was published by the

□ Testimony at hearings on land monopoly in California, 1972.
*Walter Goldschmidt is a Professor of Anthropology at the University of California, Los Angeles. The study Goldschmidt refers to was prepared for the Senate Small Business Committee in 1946 and is entitled *Small Business and the Community*.

US Senate in 1946. This study on the California towns of Arvin and Dinuba was one of "controlled comparison." We selected two towns which, as nearly as was possible, were alike in basic economic factors except that they differed in farm size. In scientific terms we treated farm size as the "independent variable," and examined the character of social life and organization in the two communities as the "dependent variable."

We found that the two towns varied remarkably—variances that were consistent, statistically significant, and all in support of the principle that independent family farms create a healthier rural community. Though the total dollar volume of agricultural production was the same, the communities differed in the following important ways:

• The small farms community (Dinuba) had twice as many business establishments as the large-farm town (Arvin) and did 61 percent more retail business, especially in household goods and building equipment.

• The small farms supported about 20 percent more people and at a measurably higher level of living.

• The majority of the small farm community population were independent entrepreneurs, as against less than 20 percent in the large farm community, where nearly two-thirds were agricultural wage laborers.

• The small farm community in all instances had better community facilities: more schools, more parks, more newspapers, more civic organizations and more churches.

• Physical facilities for community living—paved streets, sidewalks, garbage disposal, sewage disposal and other public services—were far greater in the small-farm community; indeed, in the industrial-farm community some of these facilities were entirely wanting.

• The small farm community had more institutions for democratic decision-making and a much broader participation in such activities by its citizenry.

It is reasonable to ask whether in fact the size of farms was the essential determinant of these differences—and needless to say, this question was raised. Research under natural conditions cannot produce those perfect controls that a laboratory will provide, and we examined with great care the alternate hypotheses that were put forward by critics of this study. The alternate explanation most frequently argued was that Arvin was much younger than Dinuba. When we plotted the growth of the towns, we found that Arvin was between 20 and 25 years younger, but that the facilities that differentiated the two communities were, in all instances, much older than this differential in age. We also made some comparisons with neighboring towns of Arvin's age where the farms were smaller and these, too, showed a richer local social life than the larger-farm community.

It was part of the original design to engage in a second phase of the study, in which we would investigate all the rural communities in the San Joaquin Valley. Had we been able to do this, and had it supported the comparison between Arvin and Dinuba—as I am confident it would have done—there would have been no question of the cause of the differences between Arvin and Dinuba.

But a powerful pressure against the study developed, spearheaded by the Associated Farmers and picked up by the national press. Pressure was brought to bear on the Bureau of Agricultural Economics, so that its director ordered me to discontinue the investigation after I had completed work on Arvin and Dinuba.

In the quarter century since the publication of that study, corporate farming has spread to other parts of the country, particularly to the American agricultural heartland which has always been the scene of family-sized commercial farmers. This development has, like so many other events of the period, been assumed to be natural, inevitable and progressive, and little attention has been paid to the costs that have been incurred. I do not mean the costs in money; I mean the costs in the traditions of our society and its rural institutions . . .

In California we had created a new kind of agriculture, based upon extensive holdings, heavy mechanization and capitalization, and above all on the existence of a large class of laborers. Thus the essentials of industrial production, which have characterized urban economic activities since the industrial revolution, were introduced into the rural landscape, and with them went the elements of urban social life.

With these theoretical considerations in mind, we can return to the comparison between Arvin and Dinuba. Clearly the study revealed precisely those differences that are expressed in the theory of urbanization: increased differentials in social status and class distinctions, impoverishment, the absence of social ties based upon sentiment and the substitution of wages instead, a general lack of participation in the social system by the majority of the people, and a sense of alienation among them.

American society was built on the assumption that the population would consist largely of independent entrepreneurs, artisans, self-employed professionals and, above all, independent farmers. Industrialization has effectively eroded this concept for urban populations. The independent family farmer has been an important leaven, preserving that quintessential independence of spirit that has characterized American culture. The study of Arvin and Dinuba has shown what effect corporate and large-scale control can have on rural community life. The vision of the future under increased corporate control of the land is the vision of Arvins rather than Dinubas—indeed of super-Arvins.

Is this an inevitable development? Is it possible that there is no stemming the tide of an evolution toward corporate control of agriculture? There is no real evidence that this is the case. Government policies with respect to tax laws, agricultural subsidies and farm labor have been potent forces affecting the growth of large-scale and corporate farming. This growth cannot therefore be said to be natural; it is the result of force-feeding, of the injection of fiscal hormones, if you will. If the growth of corporate farming can be force-fed, so too can the time-honored traditions of American life.

Impact of corporation farming on small business

ALAN BIBLE

I. INTRODUCTION

This is a preliminary report on the subcommittee's findings in a continuing investigation of the impact of corporation farming on small business and the economic and social structure of rural America.

The subcommittee is vitally interested in public policy implications of rapid movement of large corporations,[1] including conglomerates, and other non-farm interests into farming. The evidence indicates direct business involvement in agriculture is relatively new, becoming important in the 1950's and a significant trend in the last 5 years or so.

Preliminary study shows increasing corporate control by companies, many in the food and feed fields, of poultry, egg, and livestock production. This normally involves some degree of vertical integration with little or no actual ownership of land or direct operation of the agricultural enterprises involved.

The investigation also has turned up a large number of corporations buying and operating large tracts of agricultural land, particularly in the Great Plains States. These are farming companies that displace independent farmers and ranchers in a community.

A 1967 survey, completed with assistance from both county assessors and Federal officials, showed 452 corporations owned 1,633,529 acres of South Dakota farm land.[2] The number of corporations involved in farming in Nebraska was estimated at 500.[3] A preliminary study in Minnesota shows at least 230 corporations engaged in farming in that State.[4]

An Internal Revenue Service report showed 17,578

farming companies filed Federal income tax returns in 1965.[5]

A. Scope of investigation

The investigation is designed to determine the effect of corporation farming on small business in rural communities, the impact on the sociological and moral environment of existing independent family farms and ranches, and likely patterns of use of water and other natural resources by corporate farm operators.

Incorporation by partners or families, usually done to take advantage of special tax provisions or facilities transfer of farm and ranch units from generation to generation, is not at issue in this investigation. It is estimated these farming corporations make up 20 to 30 percent of the total.

Several other important areas, related to corporation farming and raised repeatedly in the testimony, also are not dealt with directly. One is the impact of corporation farming on consumer price levels. Another is the efficiency of different types of agricultural systems and the question of whether the family farm system deserves protection and support.

The subcommittee began the investigation after receiving reports, mainly from farm-oriented organizations, of widespread concern over the growth of corporation farming. Farm-rural spokesmen express concern that corporation farming is being accepted, and occasionally given Government support, without public discussion or questioning of its benefits or its consequences.

Several witnesses urged the subcommittee to push corporation farming controls to give policymakers time to consider its impact before it becomes an irreversible trend. To permit farm incorporation to proceed without control, one farm economist testified,[6] appears to be an unjustified gamble. He said the evidence points to the need for a policy of cautious experimentation that includes explicit provisions for slowing farm incorporation until probable long-run consequences have been fully analyzed.

The investigation deals with the important policy

☐ From Farm workers in rural America, 1971-1972, part 3, U.S. Committee on Labor and Public Welfare, Hearings before the Subcommittee on Migratory Labor, 92nd Congress, Washington, D.C., 1972, U.S. Government Printing Office.

[1] These large corporations, including conglomerates, were cited by various witnesses (during the hearings or in material submitted for the record) as being engaged in farming: American Cyanamid, Bunge Inc., CBK Inc., Del Monte, Gates Rubber Co., Goodyear Rubber Co., Gulf & Western, H. J. Heinz Co., International Systems & Controls Co., Jewel Tea Co., Libby, McNeill & Libby, Massey-Ferguson, Minute Maid Groves, Oppenheimer Industries, Pacific-Gamble-Robinson Co., Pillsbury Co., Ralston Purina, Swift & Co., Tenneco, and Textron Inc.

[2] "Corporation Farming," hearings before Subcommittee on Monopoly, Select Committee on Small Business, U.S. Senate, 90th Cong., second sess., Ben H. Radcliffe, p. 23.

[3] Hearings, Elton Berck, p. 44.

[4] Ibid., Arnold Onstad, p. 264.

[5] Ibid., Ben H. Radcliffe, p. 24.

[6] Ibid., Prof. Philip M. Raup, p. 249.

question of whether this nation wants an agriculture made up of independent farmers and ranchers or whether it is willing to shift to an industrialized agriculture.

There is considerable opposition to the latter course. One farm leader termed growth of corporation farming one of agriculture's most urgent problems. A sociologist said this trend, if allowed to continue, will erode the social and economic strength of rural communities. Still another witness predicted stepped-up farm-to-city migration, slowed economic activity in small towns and cities, more rural poverty, and monopoly control of food production if company farms become dominant.

The subcommittee, in opening the investigation, returned to a problem area last considered more than 20 years ago by the Senate Small Business Committee. That study, entitled "Small Business and the Community—A Study in Central Valley of California on Effects of Scale of Farm Operations," was completed in 1946.[7]

The committee carefully compared the economic and social life of the Central Valley communities of Arvin and Dinuba, one surrounded by independently owned and operated family farms and the other by large corporation farms. Except for the difference in size and makeup of farming enterprises, these agricultural communities were nearly identical.

Despite these basic similarities, the study disclosed some striking economic and social differences.[8] The family farm community supported 20 percent more people at a better standard of living than the corporation farm community. It had nearly twice as many individual establishments with 61 percent more retail trade. In addition the family farm community had more and better schools, churches, recreation facilities, civic organizations, and public services.

B. Field hearings held

The subcommittee has held public hearings in two cities thus far. At initial hearings May 20-21 in Omaha, testimony was taken from 15 witnesses from nine States in the Great Plains. The subcommittee heard 19 witnesses from three Upper Midwest States at the second hearing July 22 in Eau Claire, Wis.

Witnesses included representatives of Farmers Union, the Grange, Independent Bankers Association, National Farmers Organization, and National Catholic Rural Life Conference. Farm economists and

sociologists, farm cooperative and poultry producer representatives, church leaders, and other experts also appeared.

Most of the testimony centered on (1) exploitation of underground water; (2) federal tax favoritism; (3) corporate buying patterns for farm production items; (4) inflationary land acquisition practices; (5) government sales of large-acreage surplus installations; (6) corporate production of poultry, eggs and livestock; (7) erosion of the public livestock marketing system; (8) breakdown of rural institutions; (9) migration of farm and rural people to the cities, and (10) threat to banks, dealers and retailers in towns and cities in agricultural trade areas.

All of these issues are dealt with in detail in succeeding sections of this report.

C. Lack of data

Preliminary subcommittee study indicated there has been no recent indepth, comprehensive investigation of either corporation farming or its implications. Questioning of witnesses about current research, whether by organizations or universities or individuals, clearly showed this to be the case. A few state or regional studies are underway but none deal on a national basis with the overall problem.[9]

This issue has not had the attention its importance would seem to indicate, either in or out of Government. Howard Bertsch, administrator of the Farmers Home Administration, expressed dismay in his testimony at lack of public discussion of social implications of this basic change in agriculture's structure.[10]

The whole dialog of the social virtues and social values of family farming in this country had died. And I believe the most important product, perhaps of these hearings which this committee is conducting, will be the renewal of this dialog because if we ever get the American people talking about this issue and understanding this issue, I have the greatest faith in the ultimate outcome. But when we let dialogs like this subside, then we encourage evils like corporate farming to grow.

Although the economic and social ramifications of this issue are important to farm and city people alike, the subcommittee found that it has had little attention and consideration in agriculture and almost none elsewhere. The Department of Agriculture has recognized, through public statements, that the issue needs attention. But there is no evidence the agency has done

---

[7]Report, "Small Business and the Community—A Study in Central Valley of California on Effects of Scale of Farm Operations," prepared by the Special Committee to Congress, December 23, 1946.
[8]See Appendix A for a summary of the Arvin-Dinuba study. [Not reproduced here.]

[9]Examples are the Minnesota Task Force on Corporation Farming, a citizens study group, with work described on pp. 263-269 of the hearing record; and a legislative council study, South Dakota Legislature, p. 20 of the same period.
[10]Ibid., Howard Bertsch, p. 99.

more than conduct some cursory surveys through field offices.

The record indicates this policy area needs much more attention from university researchers, too. Even the publicly-supported land grant institutions, which traditionally are looked to for farm-rural policy direction, have done little to build public awareness or understanding of this issue. As one university witness put it:[11]

We need some research, we need it now, not next year, we need it tomorrow. We don't really know what the social impact is of this change that is going on. We can talk all we want to today but I am embarrassed, we have very few answers.

II. IMPACT ON SOIL AND WATER RESOURCES

A good deal of testimony at the hearings dealt with the impact of corporation farming on soil and water resources. The possibility that companies would "mine" both land and water to obtain rapid profits, then move on to new areas, was repeatedly suggested.

Heavy and unregulated pumping of underground water for irrigating large-scale company projects was singled out as a relatively new and critical problem area. The subcommittee concludes the fear of exploitation is based on sufficient experience with older corporate farming operations in California and elsewhere to be seriously considered.

Most of the water problems cited in the testimony dealt with the Ogallala Basin, a vast underground reservoir underlying parts of Nebraska, Colorado, Kansas, Oklahoma and Texas. This water resource has been built up over centuries.

Farm-rural witnesses emphasized that they oppose heavy withdrawal from the Ogallala because it is a closed basin that could be pumped dry in a generation or less. It is not fed by surface streams or lakes. Its recharge rate is severely limited, coming solely from rain water seeping through the soil.

It is obvious to the subcommittee that both Federal and State agencies know too little about this basin or what is happening to it. The U.S. Geological Survey has sufficient data to estimate the basin's capacity at 80 million acre-feet of water. It has calculated that about 30 million acre-feet is recoverable through surface pumping.

The serious and long-term consequences of heavy pumping from the basin were suggested in this exchange:[12]

Question. (You say) the resource is replenished at the rate of less than one inch per year. How much is that in terms of this?

Witness. Well, the average annual rate of recharge is estimated at 430,000 acre-feet. But the recharge rate is not a sufficient factor in the development of the reservoir for beneficial use since the recharge is balanced by outflow. This balance in the reservoir has been established over many centuries. Consequently any withdrawal from the reservoir is, in effect, "mining" of the water. It begins to throw that reservoir out of balance as it is tapped . . .

There is considerable concern over public policy implications if, through heavy pumping for irrigation, an underground water resource is exhausted. The long-term outlook appears grim for dryland areas now drawing on Ogallala Basin water.

That specific problem was described this way by a witness who has studied soil and water conditions in northeast Colorado for many years:[13]

Many wells have been developed on sagebrush covered sand dunes, generally considered to be unsuited to crop production. By the heavy application of fertilizer, high yields of feed grains are being obtained. However, these soils under row-crop production will sift during the winter months without fall cover crops. If the water resource is exhausted, these fields will have to be abandoned and they will become barren, blowing desert.

Another witness told the subcommittee that heavy pumping for a new 40,000-acre corporation farm in northwestern Florida already has stopped the flow of artesian wells in the area.[14]

The subcommittee concludes that the critical policy question revolves around whether the water use will be regulated, how rapidly it will be exhausted, and who will benefit. It is clear that the entire Nation— not merely the farmers, ranchers and businessmen in these areas—has a stake in proper use of water from the Ogallala and similar underground sources.

It was suggested repeatedly in the testimony that farming companies and other absentee investors lack the permanence, and thus a strong commitment, to long-term soil and water conservation. There is evidence this concern is well founded.

One witness contended soil conservation is often ignored by corporate operators, who remove waterways, contour strips and terraces to accommodate big machinery. He described one specific example:[15]

Soil stewardship is something that the average farmer is dedicated to, but is not held in very high esteem by corporation operations. I know of instances in my community where a large operator removed the fences, ignored the waterways, and planted the whole farm with one crop. A heavy rain

---

[11]Ibid., Douglas G. Marshall, p. 228.
[12]Ibid., Amer Lehman, pp. 102-103.

[13]Ibid., Amer Lehman, p. 105.
[14]Ibid., Howard Bertsch, p. 98.
[15]Ibid., Edwin Sommers, p. 219.

struck and took enough topsoil from the field to fill the road culvert and then buried the road with so much mud that the road grader got stuck in an attempt to remove it. These things are serious, they affect generations to come.

A similar report came in testimony on developments in Central Wisconsin's sandy soil area, where a good supply of underground water is attracting investors. Specifically criticized was bulldozing of shelter belts, wide strips of trees up to 20-feet tall planted under government programs in the drought years of the 1930's. The belts, which have served for 30 years or more as permanent windbreaks, are uprooted to clear the way for irrigation equipment and longer rows for big machinery.

Wind erosion of the sandy soil involved was described this way by a witness who illustrated his critical remarks with photographs:[16]

It has progressively built up a fence row until it is 6- to 15-feet high. When the old fence is built up in the sand you build another. In these two pictures overdrift is gradually sifting into the next field, it already has destroyed a large part of an alfalfa crop. It must be remembered that these drifting-like particles make up part of the area's topsoil.

We can go through this area and we find where the shelter belt has been bulldozed out, we see pictures of what happens when winds come along. Some day that impersonal decision-making process will decide if it is no more economically feasible to produce on this land, and then the people left in that community will have to live with whatever is there, and our Government again perhaps will have to go on a planting program to preserve what is still left there.

One farm leader contended corporation managers are so pressed with demands for profits that they should not be trusted with either soil or water resources. His testimony was interrupted at that point by this exchange dealing with underground water exploitation, temporary status of the corporate farm operator, and public costs of restoring an exhausted water resource:[17]

Question. Now, if a corporation gets into corporate farming and starts, for example, vast irrigation projects and is only concerned about the immediate profit for the next 5 or 10 years . . . may they not simply destroy the soil and deplete the water table and then walk off and leave it?
Witness. I think that is true. It has already happened in many areas and this seems to be the pattern.
Question. I conducted some hearings . . . on the Central Valley, Calif., project where we now have a Federal reclamation project costing $500 million. There were vast corporate landholders. One of the railroads is holding 55,000 acres, who have punched wells down 600 feet and drained the water table down to what's called the corcoran clay. They soon were out of water, so they punched through

the corcoran clay some 300 feet and drained the water table down there. It is down 1,200 feet and they're beginning to get brackish water in all parts of the Central Valley. So now we're engaged in a reclamation project, part of the objective of which is to spend some taxpayers' money to restore the water table and bring it above the corcoran clay again. Now, isn't this the kind of problem that we could run into with uncontrolled exploitation and use of the land by irrigation and otherwise?
Witness. I certainly think so . . .

It also was suggested that huge poultry and livestock feeding operations, which are concentrated in limited areas and produce odors and a high volume of manure, will create serious air and water pollution problems. Scientists calculate that a 10,000-head beef feedlot creates as much waste matter as a city of 160,000 persons.[18]

Public tension over waste disposal methods is sure to accompany development of these company operations, creating serious environmental quality problems for State and local governments.

The subcommittee concludes that serious resource policy questions have been raised regarding the likely impact of corporate farming on soil and water conservation. It is clear that too little is known about the problem. It also is clear that time is a critical factor in dealing with exploitation of resources that can be depleted in a generation or less. This policy area needs immediate attention.

III. IMPACT ON LOCAL SERVICES AND BUSINESS

Several months ago the daily newspaper in a small agricultural community in Kansas (pop. 8,483) published an editorial alerting its readers to the dangers of corporation farming. The Wellington Daily News, itself a small business with a farm-rural trade area readership, summed up its concern this way:[19]

The thought of one giant corporation controlling all of the agricultural wealth of Sumner County would provide a lifetime of nightmares for our merchants. Small town insurance firms wouldn't have anyone to insure. Realtors wouldn't have anything to sell to anyone. Implement dealers could forget it. Petroleum dealers would go out of business or out of town, or like most of us, both.

There was considerable evidence submitted at the hearings to show that this is the likely impact of widespread company farming in the trade area of any small town or city directly tied to agriculture.

The large company farms, as a general practice, buy equipment and production supplies discounted and direct from either wholesalers or the factory, by-

---

[16]Ibid., Gilbert Rohde, p. 202.
[17]Ibid., Tony T. Dechant, p. 11.

[18]Ibid., Arnold Onstad, p. 263.
[19]Ibid., Tony T. Dechant, p. 69.

passing retail and dealer establishments in nearby towns and cities.

One example of direct buying was provided in the report of purchase of $250,000 in farm equipment by Shinrone Inc., which operates a large farm in Sac County, Iowa.[20] The equipment was purchased from manufacturing plants in Brantford, Canada, and in Detroit, Mich., and Algoma, Wis. The same witness reported corporation farming companies also play off local dealers against each other so low bids, if they are made locally, provide little or no profit.

Also obtained direct are credit, insurance, legal assistance, and other business services obtained locally by independent farm and ranch operators.

One witness[21] pointed out that many company farms are directly affiliated with large oil, tire and other makers of farm production supplies and thus find it doubly profitable to buy direct.

These company farm practices result in a competitive production cost advantage over independent operators and lost volume sufficient to drive small retailers, dealers and service establishments out of business. Especially hard hit are local implement dealers, farm supply stores, and feed and seed outlets.

Service establishments, highly important in small towns and cities, would be hit hard, too. A substantial drop in local demand will eventually force banks, law offices and similar service institutions to cut back or close entirely. The outlook was described this way by one rural banker witness:[22]

> The rural community lives from the gross income of the family farm or the small, closely held family farm corporation. Because towns and banks are in the business of serving people, the banker sees that the disappearance of these families would cause his town and his bank to disappear . . . The fact remains that the small town can not exist without people on the land, no matter how productive a vast corporation farm may be.

Buying and financing practices of company farms also work against attempts by banks and other local institutions to keep money circulating in the community's trade area. A banker from Chippewa Falls, Wis., (pop. 11,708) told the subcommittee:[23]

> . . . it hurts our communities because they (company farms) have a tendency to purchase supplies, feed, fertilizer outside the service area of the community. They hurt us in our business of banking particularly in that financing automatically comes from the bank at their head office and, in turn, any excess deposits eventually will drift back into the

home office and circulate in that monetary system rather than in the system in which its original origin was.

A study[24] of 190,000 farm families using supervised credit of the Farmers Home Administration in 1967 showed they grossed $3.2 billion and spent all of it locally. The breakdown showed $736 million spent for clothing, food and other consumer items; $1.7 billion for goods and services to produce crops and livestock, and $704 million to retire debts and buy new farm machinery.

Commenting on the close relationship the study showed between farm families and local business firms, the agency's administrator told the subcommittee:

> The managers of large-scale corporation farms deal directly with the wholesalers or even the manufacturers of the products they need . . . In an area where corporation farms dominate there is no place for the village farm supply dealer, the co-op grain elevator, the small banker. You simply can not have corporation farms and small business enterprises cheek and jowl. On the other hand, where family farms thrive, small businesses flourish, too.

The economic health of many small businesses in farm-rural communities already is substantially weakened by population attrition. Business volume provided by farm families has been dropping steadily in America's agricultural midsection, where roughly every third farmstead now is vacant.[25]

Although the subcommittee did not receive any testimony on the subject, it also is interested in the impact of corporation farming on franchise businesses, both independently-owned and otherwise. These small businesses are an important element in small towns and cities dependent on the agricultural economy. These include outlets of such companies as J. C. Penney, Western Auto, Gamble's, Woolworth's and Ben Franklin.

The long-term outlook for corporation farm purchase patterns was described recently by John A. Hopkin, finance at the University of Illinois.[26] He said corporate farms in the future will either be closely linked with certain suppliers or will set up their own supply subsidiaries.

A limited amount of research has been completed in an attempt to show the consequences to small business of sharp declines in the number of farm customers. It appears that a measurable farmer-customer relationship with businessmen exists.

The Department of Commerce, in a survey involving South Dakota,[27] showed the State had a net loss of

[20]Ibid., Tony T. Dechant, p. 68.
[21]Ibid., Edwin Sommers, p. 219.
[22]Ibid., Pat DuBois, p. 71.
[23]Ibid., William Pickerign, p. 277.

[24]Ibid., Howard Bertsch, p. 96.
[25]Ibid., Keith C. Davison, p. 192.
[26]Ibid., Tony T. Dechant, p. 68.
[27]Ibid., Ben H. Radcliffe, p. 23.

6,027 farm families in a five-year period ending in 1963. In the same period 1,101 businesses closed their doors in that State.

Farm-rural observers told the subcommittee this shows that one small business, on the average, is forced to close its doors every time six farm families leave a trading area. This rule of thumb, it was indicated, could be applied to most agricultural trade areas.

IV. IMPACT ON LAND PRICES AND AVAILABILITY

The land resource base has long been recognized as one of this country's most precious endowments. It has been developed through policy decisions designed both to conserve it and to accomplish social and economic objectives.

Congress since the 1850's has adopted policies to encourage families to settle on the land and to develop its agricultural potential. Family farming has been developed and protected since through such legislation as the Homestead Act, the Morrill Act, the Farm Credit Act and the Capper-Volstead Act.

Ownership and control of the land remain a most important consideration. The subcommittee, therefore, is attempting to determine the impact of corporation farming on both land prices and availability.

The issues involved include the effect of outside investment capital on land prices, the availability of land for expanding independent farm and ranch operations, and the question of whether the public interest is served when large land tracts are acquired by farming companies.

Evidence submitted at the hearings deals with land prices, corporate land acquisition practices, and the availability of good farm land. Little research has been done on land policy changes that appear to be taking shape. It is difficult, therefore, for the subcommittee to come to any significant conclusion.

Prices of good farmland have been going up steadily since World War II. But there is evidence that competition for good land in areas where large corporate farming operations have been started, or are being set up, is forcing prices up to unusually high levels.

Prices well above what appears justified by normal returns on investment are paid in assembling large holdings, some totaling 10,000 acres or more. Nonfarm investors appear able to pay $25 to $100 an acre more over the going price to acquire desired land parcels.

This makes it difficult for independent owners and operators to buy or rent additional land, either to get bigger or to put together economically viable units. This is especially true of younger operators with limited borrowing ability. It raises the possibility that high bids by outside interests are pricing land out of the market for most independent farmers and ranchers.

The former director of the Farmers Home Administration in Colorado testified that nonfarm capital has been a major factor in the "inflationary competition" for land. The competition for productive agricultural land, this farm-rural expert said, has driven present market values well above the present capacity to earn a reasonable return on investment.[28]

Recent data on this problem was submitted to the subcommittee by the chairman of a task force investigating corporation farming in Minnesota.[29] The task force found that more than half the acquisitions of farmland by business interests had taken place in the last 3 years. Purchases by 41 nonfarm investors during that period totaled more than 100,000 acres.

The researchers also found, in analyzing questionnaire returns, that 27 real estate dealers know of standing offers by outside companies or investors to buy large tracts of Minnesota farm land.

The standing offers are likely to result in purchases because they include a sizable premium over going market prices. Eleven real estate dealers reported a $25-an-acre premium offered for land in large tracts. Three reported a premium of $50 an acre. Five said the standing offer was $100 or more an acre over the going market price.

Land acquisition practices of one large corporation in northeast Colorado were described by one witness to show the likely impact on land prices.[30] Purchases involved were arranged by a real estate firm for Gates Farms Inc., a subsidiary of the Gates Rubber Co.

The unusual pattern, which involved water rights as well as cropland, was described this way:

The expansion of underground water development by individual farmers and small corporations between 1960 and 1966, as a result of the introduction of new cash crops and mechanical irrigation methods, was very rapid.

Then in 1967, a real estate broker began optioning land for an undisclosed principal. The option required the seller to establish the availability of ground water in a minimum amount of 1,000 gallons per minute under pumpage and to obtain a well permit from the State ground water commission. . . .

When the options were exercised, the undisclosed principal was identified as Gates Farms, a subsidiary of the Gates Rubber Co., a substantial conglomerate corporation. The already disordered development at this point began showing signs of panic. Some farmers obtained permits, drilled wells and capped them in order to protect their potential development rights.

[28]Ibid., Amer Lehman, p. 106.
[29]Ibid., Arnold Onstad, p. 263.
[30]Ibid., Amer Lehman, p. 105.

At the same time the Ground Water Commission, influenced to a considerable degree by local pressure, tightened its policies for granting permits. As a result a good many farmers can not now obtain permits, including some who had sold part of their land to the Gates Farms.

Studies by the Department of Agricultural Economics at the University of Minnesota show that 14 percent of land sales in that State in 1967 were to investor buyers, midway in the 11- to 17-percent range of the last 10 years. The possibility that this could sharply reduce the amount of land available to individual farm operators, however, is suggested in this comment from an expert witness:[31]

Although still a relatively low figure, sales to investor buyers at the rate of 14 percent of all sales in each year could bring about a major change in the landownership pattern in the course of a relatively few years, if investors buy land but do not sell.

Concern over land availability in the future also involves the fact that farming companies are permanent entities, unbroken by death, retirement or other personal considerations. This comment by a witness makes the point:[32]

. . . once the land is permitted to get into corporate hands it is going to be difficult to reverse the process and restore family ownership. A corporation is a "legal person" which may have a hundred year life or a perpetual life. In family farming there is a turnover in ownership, once in a lifetime. On the average there is a change of ownership at least once in each generation, either from the members of a family to a relative or from one private owner to another. But, since a corporation never dies, the land tends to remain in the corporate hands even though some of the stockholders may change from time to time. And I think this is a key point because how are the family farmers going to have access to land once that has gotten into corporate hands? Land which is swallowed up by the corporations is likely to be gone for good as far as family-type operators are concerned.

It seems clear, based on information submitted to the subcommittee, that corporation farming has considerable impact on land prices and availability.

The upward pressure on land prices, the insistence of acquiring the best land, and permanence of corporate ownership would seem to work against the traditional policy of supporting and protecting the independent farmer and rancher. There is no doubt that continuing this trend will erode, and eventually undermine, the position of the independent operator in the agricultural economy.

V. SOCIAL AND MORAL IMPLICATIONS

One of the most significant results of the study comparing Arvin and Dinuba was the conclusion that the family farm community had more and better schools, churches, recreational facilities, civic organizations and public services.

The hearings reflected a fear that these same things would be undermined in any community where company farming becomes dominant. The concern also involves prospects for a "company town" atmosphere in these communities with local government and public services eroded by the influence of absentee owners.

The problem deals, too, with such intangibles as community spirit and the need for good neighbors. One witness, a Kansas wheat farmer, put it this way:[33]

In closing I wonder how many farm people realize what it would be like to have a 40,000-acre corporation farm for a neighbor. Do you think it would cast a vote for a school bond issue? Or support good roads down every section line? Or help you combine wheat if you were laid up and unable to work? Or support the church building fund drive?

The threat of an eroded tax base was mentioned repeatedly. This drop in the amount of taxable property is expected to result from removal of family farm buildings from large tracts acquired by company farms and small business closeouts resulting when company farms take their business outside the community. One witness described the likely impact:[34]

. . . declines in the tax base will make it more difficult to provide good education, police protection and other locally-controlled public services. If the towns industrialize, they may not feel these effects. But the open country residents will be especially vulnerable.

The same witness told the subcommittee that the change in the characteristics of the farm-rural population that would accompany corporation farming—hired managers and migrant workers becoming predominant—would erode the quality of local government. Here is his statement:[35]

There could be strong tendencies toward local political apathy on the part of new farm population. Resident farm-owners have a sense of responsibility to hold offices and to participate in financing public services. The new farm employes may not see that they have much of a stake in local political participation. Moreover they will be few in number and are likely to be pressured by companies that employ them. Local political participation of the farm population may very likely decrease.

In addition to eroding the tax base, there are indications company farms also would be able, and anxious,

[31]Ibid., Philip M. Raup, p. 243.
[32]Ibid., Edwin Christianson, p. 206.

[33]Ibid., Philip Doyle, p. 112.
[34]Ibid., Douglas G. Marshall, p. 232.
[35]Marshall, *op. cit.*

to cut tax rates as well. The prospects for this reduction in support for locally-controlled public services are explored in this comment:[36]

> With only a small population to contend with, many of whom will be employed by them, the farming companies will see little need to assume fiscal and other responsibilities for the local areas. This will be especially pronounced if nonfarm population does not increase. If it does, the townspeople might succeed in getting the companies to carry their share of the taxes. But even then, local politicians could be influenced by the farming companies.

The churches, which exert considerable influence in most farm-rural communities, also would be hard hit by the changes that company farming would bring. The same expert witness explores this possibility:[37]

> The local churches, especially those few that remain in small hamlets and in the open country, might close up. There will be fewer farm families to support them. Besides, many of these are tied to ethnic groups and extended families. Out-migrating members of the old ethnic groups of families may well be replaced with personnel with other (or perhaps no) ethnic ties and who will not be members of the local family groups. Churches depending on such groups are more apt to fail.

The evidence clearly shows that one of the social consequences of a shift to corporate farming is continued, and probably accelerated, farm-to-city migration. The cost of this upheaval has not been adequately measured. There is no doubt, however, that the price is substantial both in terms of human hardship and of public dollars to underwrite solutions to already critical urban problems.

Also involved are the human characteristics that many sociologists and religious leaders feel are most fully developed in a farm-rural setting. One witness, for example, said working on the land is desirable because it demands a capacity for orientation and adaptation, patient waiting, a sense of responsibility, and a spirit of perseverance and enterprise.[38]

These intangibles usually are dismissed, however, by social scientists and other researchers who contend they are difficult to quantify through empirical research. Admittedly it is difficult to reduce them to the statistics needed for charts and graphs. These factors should be among those considered, however, in making policy judgments about corporation farming and other farm-rural policy choices.

The larger question of the kind of "citizen" a farming company becomes in a community is a critical consideration. One expert witness suggests that most corporations entering agriculture are likely to foil this important social test:[39]

> I see corporations appearing in agriculture that are not large enough to be socially responsible but are large enough to ignore the wishes of their communities. And I am afraid that we may emerge from this period of change having gotten the worst of both possible worlds, having traded effective and efficient small units of production which were not growing rapidly enough to keep pace with technological change for larger corporate units of production which were not large enough and well financed enough to be socially responsible and financially flexible.

It is clear to the subcommittee that these considerations are highly important in assessing the impact of corporation farming on the social and moral strength of farm-rural communities. Although much more research is needed, it appears a compelling case is made that the impact would be both considerable and highly undesirable from a public policy standpoint.

VI. IMPACT ON MARKET STRUCTURE

There is evidence that much of this country's corporation farming is a nearly invisible type operation aimed at control of farm commodities at the producer level and bypassing of traditional markets rather than direct operation of farms and ranches.

This is achieved through contracts with producers, plus some actual ownership and operation of feedlots and similar facilities. One common characteristic is that little or no corporation-owned land is involved.

The objective may be vertical integration of production and processing of a product within a single firm. It may be building a captive market for manufactured feed or some similar product. Or it may be having fat cattle or other meat animals directly available for slaughter when markets are strong.

Large nonfarm corporations using this approach can control sizeable volumes of farm products without acquiring large land tracts, investing in farm machinery, or establishing farming subsidiaries.

Most companies involved are either processors (packers, freezers, canners, etc.) or suppliers (mainly feed manufacturers). Heavy applications of technology also are usually programed in these operations (prepared feeds, growth stimulants, automatic feeders, etc.).

It is estimated that nonfarm corporations, including some of the largest feed companies, now control 98 percent of U.S. boiler production.[40] Companies also are involved in production of feed cattle, hogs, lambs, turkeys, eggs and vegetables.

[36] Marshall, *op. cit.*
[37] Marshall, *op. cit.*
[38] Ibid., Msgr. John G. Weber, p. 113.
[39] Ibid., Philip M. Raup, p. 241.
[40] Ibid., Albert Ebers, p. 165.

This corporation-controlled production bypasses the regular market system, thus upsetting supply-demand factors that set prices. The result is a breakdown of markets for products where buyers and sellers no longer are numerous enough to impose competitive checks on each other. Markets in some instances are totally destroyed.

A witness with first hand experience as a contract grower explained to the subcommittee how nonfarm corporations destroyed the market by gaining control of virtually all broiler production:[41]

Question. Are these mostly feed firms?

Witness. There are quite a few . . . a producer or grower cannot grow broilers without first having a contract with a processor. There is no market at the grower level . . . it is reasonable to project that it will not be very many years when a half dozen firms will produce all of the broilers . . . through contracts with growers; these farmer producers or growers being no more than glorified hired men, deprived of management and financial risks.

Question. How are they deprived of financial risks? A good percentage of them have gone bankrupt in my part of the country . . .

Witness. Their feed company or the integrated firm furnishes the broiler to the farmer. All the farmer furnishes is the building and equipment. The firm furnishes the broilers and they furnish the feed and it's their chickens. When they want you to bring it in, you sell it.

Question. But they set the price of the feed and they set the price they'll pay for the broiler?

Witness. They set the price of the feed but I don't know where the market price of a broiler is set. It's their chicken and they just take it away. I can't sell it to anybody else.

Question. They set the price that you're going to get for it; isn't that correct?

Witness. Yes. These farmers will probably never receive the just wages and hours deserved, without becoming a labor union . . . the egg and turkey industries are fast following the route of broilers. I think you know that last year the turkey industry has really gone through the wringer, you might say, and the egg business the same. In the South they . . . call it a burnout. The firms that can stand the financial strain, will end up owning or controlling the egg and turkey industries.

One expert witness told the subcommittee that these attempts by corporations to control the product will, as they expand, gradually dry up open markets with prices set in these markets becoming less and less representative of supply-demand conditions. He also explained other expansion consequences:[42]

Management will likely continue to gravitate from the hands of farmers to those of processors and suppliers and the farmer's role reduced further toward that of a laborer. Integrating companies may not completely take over the production of food and fiber by owning the land and capital and hiring the labor so long as they can earn more with their resources in other uses. Also, by using contract, integrating companies may be able to avoid some employee costs, such as social security, workmen's compensation, and possibly union wages, which would likely come with complete ownership of land and other production resources.

One farm leader[43] contended integrators and others contracting for production frequently are large enough to be a key factor in establishing local market prices. One of the most serious aspects of the entry of the corporation into farming, he stated, is its ability to "interfere with and manipulate" the market.

A critical statement also was submitted by a leading dairy economist[44] who contended there is more cause for concern as a result of contract farming than with outright corporate farmownership. He explained its market impact:

When this approach is taken, the corporation offers a select group of farmers a modest income with reduced risk, but takes away from the farmer his managerial freedom and the possibility of a higher income in a competitive market. The production of those farms under contract to the corporation may be used in turn to force down prices to the remainder of agriculture.

It is clear from the testimony that contract farming and other approaches used by nonfarm corporations has an impact on the market system, ranging from total destruction in the broiler industry to lesser degrees in other areas. The extent to which it undermines the open market is not well documented. Much more public discussion and research is needed on this issue so obvious abuses can be curbed and the public interest protected.

VII. IMPACT OF FEDERAL TAX POLICIES

A number of witnesses criticized "tax loss farming" and other Federal tax advantages and contended they are the most important factor attracting corporation and other nonfarm investors into agriculture.

The subcommittee concludes from the limited evidence available that Federal tax policy is one of the main determining factors, if not the most important. It is clear that substantial capital gains, favorable depreciation rates on machinery and equipment, and tax losses written off against nonfarm income are returning sizable tax savings to absentee investors.

Independent operators earning a living entirely from farming or ranching make some use, of course, of capital gains and depreciation provisions. But they

[41]Albert Ebers, *op. cit.*
[42]Ibid., Paul L. Farris, p. 177

[43]Ibid., Tony T. Dechant, p. 66
[44]Ibid., Arthur Miller, p. 273

normally have little or no taxable nonfarm income against which to offset farming losses. The tax loss advantage, therefore, accrues almost entirely to outside investors.

The independent farmer normally is not as concerned with tax brackets as he is in managing his farm to maximize current income. The very wealthy operator, on the other hand, normally seeks to maximize capital gain in an attempt to cut his tax bite from 50 percent or more down to a maximum of 25 percent.

Widespread incidence of "tax loss farming" was clearly shown in the hearings, both for wealthy individuals using farm investments as a tax haven and for corporations whose principal business is farming.

Recent Internal Revenue Service figures[45] show a large proportion of the wealthy taxpayers involved in some phase of farming write off sizable losses against nonfarm income. They show, for example, that 119 individuals reporting incomes of $1 million or more in 1965 were involved in some phase of farming. Of this total, 103 wrote off farm losses against other income.

It is clear that this tax writeoff provision is widely used.[46] The IRS figures show that 680,000 of the 3 million farm income tax return filed in 1965 had farm losses offsetting nonfarm income.

It was estimated this represented a loss of up to $400 million in Federal revenue. The subcommittee was told that much of this "loss" would appear later on returns as capital gains taxed at a much lower rate.

The Government also had data on the 17,578 corporations reporting farming as their principal business in 1965. The figures showed these corporations had $4.3 billion in gross receipts in the most recent tax year—roughly 10 percent of total farm gross income. Yet only 9,244 reported a profit for tax purposes. And the taxable income involved totaled a mere $199 million.

Favorable capital gains treatment also is a most important factor in the tax favoritism hit by farm-oriented witnesses. One expert witness,[47] singling out for criticism the 25-percent ceiling on the tax on long-term capital gains, called it a "graduated and progressive subsidy" to wealthy nonfarm investors

moving into agriculture. He added these critical comments:

There is nothing sacred about the 25-percent ceiling on the tax on long-term capital gains. As it stands now, this relatively low ceiling is an open invitation to speculation in land. It is difficult to avoid the conclusion that much of the recent interest in farm investments by nonfarm investors would fall away if the capital gains tax ceiling were raised, say, to 40 or 50 percent. This 25 percent limit on capital gains taxes is inconsistent with the principle of the progressive income tax and is distorting capital flows, with no clear benefit to the public interest.

One witness[48] submitted a copy of a magazine article that spells out how off-farm investors use Federal tax provisions to build tax-free wealth. A section of the article, carried under the subhead "How to 'Grow' Tax-Sheltered Fortunes in Cattle," spells out which tax provisions are used to write off investment expenses against personal income, "time" the income, and convert regular income to capital gains:

1. Depreciation on farm machinery and buildings, farm supply expenses, and all labor and management costs are deductible.
2. Expenditures for soil and water conservation and land clearing are deductible (in every other business costs of a similar character must be characterized).
3. Income from Commodity Credit Corporation loans is controllable, making it possible to choose the most convenient tax year in which to report the income.
4. Timber, farm buildings, livestock and unharvested crops sold with the land get capital gains treatment.

The article sums up ways investors write off expenses against personal income, use the investment credit, take profits taxable at capital gains rates, and accumulate a cattle operation sheltered indefinitely from the bite of Federal income taxes:

. . . all expenses (except the cost of land) are deductible from ordinary income either as business expenses or by way of depreciation. So, while the herd is building up, you can use these deductions to offset other highly taxed income.

. . . many of the expenses you will incur qualify for the 7-percent investment credit—producing an immediate dollar-for-dollar slash in your personal tax bill. These would include, for example, the cost of fences to contain the cattle, drain tiles to improve pasturage, paved barnyards and water wells, but not the cost of purchasing the cattle.

. . . the herd builds up tax free . . . Simply trade off the calves produced by your herd for additional heifers, which will produce more calves . . . trade off for more heifers, and so on.

. . . much of the income produced by the herd will be tax-

[45]Ibid., Ben H. Radcliffe, pp. 24-25.
[46]The Internal Revenue Service figures show this 1965 breakdown: Individuals with $1 million or more income—119 engaged in farming with 103 writing off farm losses; $500,000 to $1 million—202 in farming with 170 reporting farm losses; $100,000 to $500,000—3,914 in farming with 2,874 reporting farm losses; $50,000 to $100,000—12,398 in farming with 7,424 reporting farm losses; $20,000 to $50,000—69,132 in farming with 30,380 reporting farm losses; $15,000 to $20,000—66,003 in farming with 23,843 reporting farm losses.
[47]Ibid., Philip M. Raup, p. 249.

[48]Ibid., Elton Berck, p. 49.

sheltered, long-term capital gain. For example, you get long-term gain if you sell out the whole herd. Furthermore, if you've held them at least 12 months, you get a long-term gain on the sale of cattle culled from the breeding herd, even if they've been fully depreciated.

The beef cattle operation was called the classic illustration by one expert witness.[49] With most of the investment in land and a breeding herd, he pointed out, opportunities are maximized for appreciation in capital value and subsequent taxation of gain at not more than 25 percent. This advantage is progressively attractive to investors with annual incomes exceeding $25,000.

The same witness contended any attempt to help agriculture by income tax concessions contains an automatic bonus for bigness.[50] He added:

Completely apart from any question of concessions to farmers, or favored tax treatment, the nature of the farm business creates certain attractions for the wealthy investor. To him, the primary advantage lies in the high ratio of durable assets to total assets in an agricultural investment. Assets that can be treated as capital, and taxed under capital gains provisions, are an invitation to the man of wealth to acquire them and seek ways to convert the largest possible amount of current income into an appreciation in his asset values.

Thus, the subcommittee finds, it is both capital gains and "tax loss farming" that attracts industrial corporations and other nonfarm interests into agriculture. Both must be dealt with if this trend is to be slowed or reversed.

VIII. SURPLUS LAND SALES AS A FACTOR

There is some evidence that Government surplus disposal policies have resulted in transfer of large-acreage surplus defense establishments to corporations and other nonfarm interests for farming, livestock feeding, and other agricultural purposes.

These abandoned installations are attractive to these nonfarm interests because they provide an easy way to obtain large land tracts, clear in most instances of farm buildings, hedgerows, terraces, and other deterrents to large-scale farming. They also have appeal because they no longer contain public roads or other right-of-way rights.

These military installations, usually dating from the 1940's, are normally sold as a unit after being declared surplus. It is impossible to sell this land to previous owners, who long ago obtained other farming units or moved to the city, or to find a way to break them up into units that could be purchased by individual farm operators.

Evidence was presented to the subcommittee on only one example.[51] It was the recent transaction involving the 27-year-old Hastings (Nebr.) Naval Ammunition Depot. A sizable portion was purchased by the city of Hastings under provisions of the State's Industrial Development Act. The city, according to the testimony, immediately entered into a lease-purchase agreement that turned it over to a corporation for a huge hog feeding operation.

Several members of the Nebraska Legislature tried unsuccessfully to amend the State's Development Act in time to stop revenue bond financing to the city that made the purchase possible. The amendment specifically would have barred issuance of bonds under the act for livestock production purposes.

Opponents of the Hastings transaction contended attempts by Government, both State and Federal, to provide new jobs by returning installations to the public fall short when corporations are allowed to take them over for agricultural purposes.

Although the Hastings situation involves the Defense Department, it is suggested that the Atomic Energy Commission and other Federal agencies also have been involved in transfers of large-acreage surplus installations to corporate interests. The subcommittee feels this is a policy area that should be explored further.

IX. SUMMARY OF REMEDIAL PROPOSALS

Many of the witnesses urged the subcommittee to consider specific proposals to meet the challenge posed by industrial corporations and other nonfarm interests moving into agriculture.

Several of the proposals have been before Congress in one form or another in recent years or considered by the Food and Fiber Commission, the Food Marketing Commission, or other studies authorized by Congress.

The changes proposed generally involve one of two approaches. One is strengthening the farmer and rancher, through such things as bargaining power and credit and better prices, so competition from nonfarm interests can be overcome. The other involves removing tax and other incentives encouraging nonfarm investors and adopting land use restrictions and other roadblocks to corporate entry into agriculture.

Also included are requests for various kinds of investigations into corporation farming and related issues.

Congress clearly has authority to act on many of the proposals (Federal tax policy, disposal of surplus military installations, etc.). Others involve policy decisions reserved to the States (land use regulations,

---

[49]Ibid., Philip M. Raup, p. 246
[50]Raup, *op cit.*

[51]Ibid., Elton Berck, pp. 46-47.

irrigation well permits, etc.). Still others fall into undefined areas or those involving joint government action (soil conservation, air and water pollution, reporting procedures for publicly owned corporations, etc.).

These are the main proposals submitted:

1. Limit use of underground water for irrigation to quantities normally restored to these acquifers by natural recharge.
2. Control Government sales of large-acreage surplus defense establishments to prevent them from coming under control of corporations for farming, livestock feeding, or other agricultural purposes.
3. Tighten antitrust laws to assure competition, specifically making it illegal for a single corporation to produce, process, and retail farm products.
4. Enforce existing laws limiting use of public irrigation water to a specified number of acres per user and includes a similar limitation on all future Government water development projects.
5. Use the Government's subpena powers to determine (1) the names of stockholders of corporation farms; (2) whether company farms are involved in an effort to monopolize food processing, distribution and production, and (3) whether company farms violate antitrust laws in buying equipment, fertilizer, feed, and other production items direct and discounted.
6. Restrict farm size by limiting either the number of acres or volume of sales.
7. Increase the State homestead exemption on agricultural real estate where a farm family makes its home.
8. Require farm and ranch ownership registration (owner's name and address, property size and location, acquisition date and type of ownership) with farm companies required, in addition, to list stockholders with more than a 5-percent interest and report any ties to farm supply, processing or marketing firms.
9. Prohibit obstruction, boycott or intimidation of farmers organizing cooperatives or other collective efforts to increase bargaining power.
10. Provide authority and funds for continuing economic studies of the food and fiber industry structure by Government regulatory agencies, Federal economic research groups, and educational and private research institutions.
11. Enact legislation to assure parity prices and income protection, through Government payments and other assistance, to a family farm level of production with the Department of Agriculture defining family farm units on a county-by-county basis.
12. Enact Federal tax legislation to prohibit persons who are not bona fide farmers from using losses incurred in their farming operations as an offset to income from other sources.
13. Prohibit chain grocery stores and others engaged in food processing and distribution from operating feedlots and other agricultural facilities.
14. Enact a graduated land tax to discourage large land holdings by either individuals or corporations.
15. Enact a law prohibiting purchase of farm land by corporations with stockholders exceeding a certain number.
16. Empower county boards to set up farm land resources commissions directed to (1) regulate farm land transfers; (2) prohibit undesirable forms of agricultural enterprises that represent poor land use or are out of character with those existing in the county; (3) regulate public nuisances resulting from air and water pollution arising from feedlots, egg factories, and confinement types of dairy and livestock operations, and (4) licensing and regulating water use for irrigation.
17. Refine, expand, and adequately fund the farm credit system.
18. Extend and improve restraint of trade, monopoly and unfair trade practices laws that limit capacity and thrust of corporate growth and made at the expense of smaller independent enterprises.

The causes of change in farm technology, size, and organizational structure

Richard D. Rodefeld

The development of new technology and its adoption by farmers has had major consequences for all sectors of U.S. society (Section one). Major changes also are occurring in the organizational structure of farms. Present knowledge suggests such alterations also have had, or will have, major importance for all sectors of society (Section two).

Knowledge of the conditions bringing about changes in farm size and structure is critical. It is necessary to better understand changes that already have occurred and to predict more accurately the directions and rates of future changes. Knowledge also is required if alterations are to be made in either the direction or rates of farm size and structural change by altering the causal forces responsible.

Some of the major causal forces responsible for changes in farm technology, size, and structure have been identified or alluded to in other chapters. This essay reviews, expands, and reorganizes what appear to be the major forces and conditions responsible for structural change in American agriculture. It begins with a review of the major factors influencing the adoption of new technology and how this technology has been used to expand the size of farm operations. In the remainder of this essay, causal forces emanating from eight general areas are identified, and their significance for farm size and structural change are discussed. Readings included in Chapter 7 and relevant readings in other chapters are discussed in this context. Other references, either easily obtained or of major importance, also are noted.

The adoption of new technology and increased farm size

Two major dimensions of farm size have changed markedly in the last 30 to 40 years: the quantity of production per acre or livestock unit and the physical size of acreage and number of livestock. By increasing the amount of production per acre or livestock unit, a farm's output may increase even though its physical size remains constant. As pointed out in Chapters 1 and 2, great increases have occurred in this dimension since the Depression. Increases in the quantity of crop production per acre have resulted from many developments: higher-yielding and more disease-resistant varieties of seeds; soil testing; commercial fertilizers, including custom blends; herbicides; pesticides; new cultural practices in seedbed preparation and planting; and irrigation systems. Likewise, increases in the quantity of production per livestock unit have been made possible through various means: genetic engineering, artificial insemination and the resultant diffusion of better bloodlines, antibiotics, improved feed concentrates, rationally based feed rations, carcass evaluations and carcass-yield pricing, milk testing, and improved production records. Colleges of agriculture, extension systems, the United States Department of Agriculture (USDA), and private industry have played major roles in the development of this knowledge and its diffusion to the farm population. All of the foregoing improvements can be viewed as necessary conditions for increasing production per acre and livestock unit, per worker and farm.

The second major dimension of farm size is the number of acres or livestock units associated with a farm operation or work-force member. This dimension also has increased greatly since the Depression. In fact, the average farm size has increased dramatically even though the farm work force has been substantially reduced. In 1880, the average U.S. farm size was 134 acres. By 1935, the year in which the number of farms in this country (6.8 million) was at its peak, the average size had increased to 155 acres. By 1970, the average farm size had escalated to 387 acres and the number of farms had declined to 2.7 million (Moyer and others, 1969:35-36; Ball and Heady, 1972:43-44). While average farm size increased only 16% from 1880 to 1935, it expanded 150% between 1935 and 1970. In this latter period, the number of farms declined by 60%.

The development of powerful energy sources and complementary equipment systems was the major condition necessary for these changes to occur. It was met with the development of tractors with internal combustion engines, using inanimate energy sources. While there were 27 million horses being used on U.S. farms in 1917, only 3 million remained in 1960. In the same time period, the number of tractors increased from 51,000 to 5 million (Higbee, 1963:10). This development created a potential for each work force member to account for a greater quantity of crop or livestock production while working a constant or reduced number of hours. Thus, in 1910, it took 147 hours of labor with horse-drawn equipment to produce 100 bushels of corn; in 1960, some corn belt farmers required only 4 hours of labor with mechanized equipment (Higbee, 1963:9) to produce the same quantity.

The advance of mechanical technology was a necessary, but not a sufficient, condition for increasing farm size and production per worker. This is quite clear since farm size and production per worker could have remained constant while the mechanical advances were used to reduce the number of work hours. Such did not happen. It appears that farmers purchased or rented additional land and continued to work at least as many hours after the introduction of tractors as they had when using horses. This resulted in expanding farm sizes, increased production per worker, and declining farm numbers. The reasons why farmers chose to expand their farm sizes rather than reducing their work hours provide a more sufficient explanation for changes in farm size and production per worker.

There were many incentives for farmers to adopt new technology and tractors and to use this technology to expand the sizes of their operations. The adoption of new mechanical devices reduced the physical demands and harshness of farm work. It allowed farmers to reduce the length of their workweek, if they chose. Many of these factors are mentioned in the Reeder article. Mechanization also occurred as a result of labor shortages. Hambidge (Chapter 1) points out the recurrent nature of this problem. Vandiver and Hamburger (Chapter 2) identify labor shortages as one of the major causes of mechanization in the South. Vandiver and Carlton (Chapter 1) also point out that mechanization, once underway, can create labor shortages, which in turn bring about greater mechanization.

While the difficulty of farm work and labor shortages help to explain why farmers adopted mechanical devices, they do not explain why farmers used this technology to expand the size of their operations. Economic factors have played a major role in this process. Except for periods of war, overproduction and low prices for farm production have been the rule. At the same time, however, farm production costs (such as machinery, fertilizer, labor, petroleum products) have constantly risen. This "cost-price squeeze" has resulted in very narrow profit margins, low farm incomes, and low levels of living. This long-standing problem is discussed by Hambidge (Chapter 1), Hamburger (Chapter 2), Reeder and Taylor (Chapter 11). Farmers have responded to this problem with collective action (such as farm organizations, cooperatives, revolts), by leaving farms, or by acquiring supplemental jobs (full-time or part-time). They have also responded by adopting mechanical devices to reduce labor costs and, along with other technology, to expand the size of their operations. Rodale points out that the economic insecurity of farmers and their desire for higher incomes have made them highly vulnerable to sales pitches from chemical companies and salesmen.

The preceding is not a complete explanation for increased farm size, however. A number of other factors have encouraged this change as well. They are discussed not only because they bear on farm size, but also because they help explain the declining levels of farmland and nonland resource ownership by farm managers, the growing importance of very large-scale farms employing large numbers of hired labor, and the decline of family-type farms.*

Government programs and policies

A wide variety of governmental programs and policies have had the effect of encouraging expanded farm size and increased differentiation of farm organizational structure.

Federal and private crop insurance programs have reduced the risks of crop losses (Rudd and MacFarlane, 1942; Dorow, 1972). The federal cropland diversion, acreage allotments, and commodity storage programs have adjusted farm output to stabilize prices. Federal marketing orders, price support loans, and commodity payments have stabilized both prices and income. The stabilization of feed-grain prices and agriculture as a whole, has had the indirect effect of stabilizing livestock prices (Rudd and MacFarlane, 1942; Parsons and Owens, 1951; Dorow, 1972; Kyle and others, 1972; Madden and Partenheimer, 1972; Quance and Tweeten, 1972).

Reduced price risks and uncertainties encourage the establishment of larger-than-family–sized farms and the ownership of farmland, nonland resources, or both by nonfarmers. As pointed out earlier (Rodefeld, Chapter 5), one of the major hurdles to extremely large farms in the past was the high level of risk and various uncertainties (production, prices, management) associated with farming. As farms increase in size, their ability to withstand income variability—especially losses—decreases. Dorow (1972:44) explains that:

As farms become larger and more commercialized, they use a higher proportion of capital to labor and of variable capital to fixed capital. They also use more purchased inputs and a lower proportion of farm-produced inputs such as operator labor and equity. Therefore, they operate on a lower margin of return over direct costs per unit of sale.

High risk and uncertainty also impede large farms by reducing credit accessibility. Kyle and associates (1972) note and Dorow (1972:44) explicates further: "As a firm expands by using credit, the possibility of losing its equity becomes greater. Added uncertainty increases the probability of loss. This concept restricts borrowing by the expanding farmer and also lending by the credit agency."

It should be noted that low levels of risk and uncertainty, while approaching the state of a necessary condition for very large farms, clearly are not sufficient conditions. Many factors—such as price and profit levels, labor and land availability, and quality and availability of capital—also influence the viability of large farms.

Another effect of decreased income variability, particularly the certainty of government support and diversion payments has been the encouragement of nonfarm investments in farm land (Dorow, 1972). Kyle and associates (1972:11) suggest that wealthy investors, farm and nonfarm, are highly responsive to protected income. Raup (1972b) and Timmons (1972) both point out that by the early 1950's, it became clear there would be no repetition of the 1920 to 1921 price disasters and the associated destruction of capital values in land. Low land prices, cushioned farm prices, and a storehouse of new technology created a climate for a reappraisal of farm investment possibilities by nonfarmers.

Government crop diversion, price supports, and commodity payments have been

*The following review has been extracted largely from another source (Rodefeld, 1974:110-210).

sources of expansion for other reasons as well. Crop-diversion programs removed 20% of all cropland from production in the period from 1962 to 1966. If a farm was optimally organized before the diversions, this acreage would have to be replaced through acquisition or lease to once again achieve the previous optimum (Quance and Tweeten, 1972). This was often done, resulting in increased farm size. Dorow (1972:45) also points out that

> Price supports and commodity payments have been based almost entirely on acres and output. The larger the farm and its output, the greater are the benefits of the income support programs in terms of dollars received. The present program with payments based on commodity output and high limits per farm, tends to encourage the trend toward larger farms.

In a recent year, 28% of the farmers participating in income support programs and receiving more than $1000 got 79% of all payments (Dorow, 1972:48-49). In 1970, farms with sales exceeding $20,000 (20.4% of all farms) received 56% of all direct government payments (Kyle and others, 1972:10). Both absolute and relative benefits from past farm programs have risen with increases in farm size. The larger the farm size, the greater the return on invested capital and the greater the magnitude and certainty of the profit margin (Waldo, 1970; Ball and Heady, 1972; Kyle and others, 1972; Quance and Tweeten, 1972). With the capital, security, and credit accessibility derived from federal programs, the larger farmer was able to expand beyond that amount needed to compensate for diverted land (Kyle and others, 1972; Quance and Tweeten, 1972). It also appears that the programs provided the capital to cover the cash operating costs and returns to equity and operator labor on many of the larger farms. The existence of these farms would have been threatened greatly with a discontinuation of the federal programs (Quance and Tweeten, 1972).

Some government policies have contributed also to low labor costs. In this vein are low minimum wages; disqualification of agricultural workers for unemployment compensation; failure to grant labor organizing rights for farm workers; lax farm-safety laws and regulations; and limited health, welfare, and legal assistance programs. "Low cost labor gives benefits to large operations. When costs are forced up on large-scale operations, those farms that use mainly family labor become more competitive" (Guither and others, 1972:34). The inequity in this is perhaps magnified presently. Pickler (1970) has suggested that "the necessity of cheap labor" in order to have large-scale farms may no longer be true. He points out that it has been proved quite conclusively in poultry and beef production that large farms can pay parity wages and thereby compete with industry for labor.

Another force bringing about increased size and manager-laborer differentiation is the increasing technical complexity of agriculture caused, in part, by governmental rules and regulations. Raup (1972a) points out that the growing complexity of taxation regulations and data submission requirements generally result in added fixed costs, which are difficult for many small firms to handle because of their low volumes. As size and volume increase, the possibility of hiring specialists for these responsibilities occurs. Apart from this, the growing quantity and complexity of relevant information places ever-increasing time demands on managers who wish to keep abreast of market conditions and production advances (Hoffman, 1970; Brake, 1972; Breimyer and Barr, 1972). The two ideas can be joined to see the same effect, especially with new federal regulations. Thus, Barlowe and Libby (1972:24) argue that "by introducing new elements of cost and uncertainty into production, environmental concern would seem to encourage further concentration in units large enough to permit required investment in environmental quality. . . ." Most likely, such firms would exceed family size.

Government programs and policies may influence the level of manager-landowner differentiation by influencing access to capital and credit. "If public policies do not sufficiently limit inflation so that long-term loans are feasible, then a shift in the methods of financing risk capital will take place" (Guither and others, 1972:33). Most of the suggested methods (joint ventures, partnerships with lenders, public stock) result in increased manager/landowner differentiation. The same outcome is suggested for any policies limiting the availability of credit for land purchases.

In addition to the effects already mentioned, the unwillingness of the federal government to enforce the 1902 Land Reclamation Act has allowed extremely large, and in many cases absentee-owned, farms to be established in areas reserved for small (160-acre), family–owned and managed farms. Also, water subsidies have contributed to the establishment of huge farms. A number of articles have been included in Chapter 7 (Vandiver, McGinnis, Merrill, Hightower) and Chapter 11 (*St. Paul Pioneer Press*, Belden and Forte, Bulbulian) that explore in greater detail the impact of governmental programs and policies on farms. Gates (1936) provides a good discussion of the Homestead Act and land grants.

Hightower (Chapter 7) argues that a symbiotic relationship between the federal government and agribusiness has been one of the major reasons for the decline of small, family-type farms and the growth of larger nonfamily types, particularly the industrial type. Federal programs, tax laws, farm labor legislation, research, and a host of related things have consistently favored large, nonfamily-type farms and agribusiness as a result of this relationship.

The development of new technology

While the development and adoption of new technology have allowed farmers to expand the sizes of their operations, they have had other less obvious consequences as well. For instance, the risk and uncertainty associated with the production of crops and livestock has been reduced by scientific and mechanical-technical advancements. In crop production, genetic engineering has produced varieties with more disease resistance, greater compatibility to specific climatic and geographical regions, plus greater consistencies of shape and maturation dates. The last change is a necessary condition for mechanizing the harvesting of crops that in the past have required labor-intensive harvesting. The development of the MH-1 tomato variety of *Hard Tomatoes, Hard Times* fame (Hightower, 1972), for instance, made the mechanization of tomato harvesting possible. New herbicides and pesticides have reduced the threats of weeds and insects to crop production. More accurate and longer-range weather forecasting has increased the farmer's ability to coordinate planting and harvesting activities with nature's circumstances. Genetic engineering and artificial insemination have brought about less variance in rates of gain, feed-conversion ratios, and carcass yields for livestock and less variance in udder characteristics and milking time for milk cows. Progress has also been made in the ability to prevent or control animal diseases, decreasing the risks associated with large concentrations of livestock.

Mechanical advancements have had a major effect on the risks associated with crop production. Large tractors and associated equipment—such as planters, harvesters, hay crimpers, and crushers—have reduced risk by allowing the farmer to plow, plant, and harvest crops rapidly; thus reducing the length of time crops are exposed to the risks of bad weather. Glass-lined silos, grain dryers, and irrigation systems allow the farmer a certain freedom from some aspects of weather vagaries. Soil testing and bulk application of fertilizer assure that appropriate quantities of uniformly distributed fertilizer are applied.

The combined effects of both scientific and mechanical advancements are summed up by Raup (1970:106) who states:

Where major modifications of the environment are possible and disease can be controlled, we find agriculture producing firms that are increasingly similar to industrial firms. Much of the work can be reduced to routine repetitive tasks that do not require selection from a wide range of possible decisions before each task is performed.

Areas of agricultural production already meeting these criteria are poultry, much of vegetable production, and cattle feeding. Hog production may also be ready to enter this stage. *The Wall Street Journal* (Meyer, 1974:32) reported a consortium of nonfarm investors were planning a 6000-acre hog–growing and processing operation in Missouri that would produce, process, and market in excess of 2 million head a year.

Management risks, uncertainties, and errors associated with large units have been reduced by the foregoing as well as by the construction of all-weather roads, modern trucks, aircraft, telephones, two-way radios, and closed-circuit television. Improvements in transportation and communication have allowed closer supervision and coordination of activities on large and dispersed farms and increased the managerial effectiveness of these farms as a result (Dorow, 1972; Madden and Partenheimer, 1972). These developments also have made it physically and economically possible to construct large operating units from widely dispersed, smaller farms. Dispersed operation spreads and reduces the risks of weather and insects in crop production.

Another source of benefits that have disproportionately favored large farms and contributed to increased differentiation is the early acquisition of new knowledge and adoption of technology generated by the public and private sectors. The larger a farm is, the more likely its manager will be among the first to hear about new advancements and the more likely capital necessary for adoption will be available (Heady and Ball, 1972). Because time lags of varying dimensions exist between the earliest adopters and the majority of farmers, any production and income gains associated with the adoption are reaped first by the largest farms. The greater the benefits and the longer the adoption time lag, the greater the advantages accruing to the larger farms.

There are two general reasons why the operators or managers of large farms tend to hear about new developments earlier. First, they seek out such information more frequently than do smaller farmers. They subscribe to greater numbers of farm magazines and journals and have more contacts with extension agents and university personnel. More trips are made within and outside the state to view new developments; some of the largest farm operations even have their own research staffs (Moore and Dean, 1972; Wilkening and Rodefeld, 1973). Why these differences exist is not entirely clear. The larger farm operators usually have higher levels of both education and income, which have some significance. Heady and Ball (1972:392) suggest, "capital and knowledge are to an extent complimentary resources, and the farmer without the capital to utilize knowledge has less incentive to attend meetings or read books and pamphlets to acquire information." Secondly, those creating the new knowledge— primarily agricultural experiment stations, universities, and private industry—have concentrated and directed their diffusion efforts toward the largest farms (Hightower, 1971; Heady and Ball, 1972; Rhodes, 1972; Thompson, 1973).

Some parties would contest the second point. Indeed a major debate in recent years has concerned the impact of land-grant university research and extension service activities in bringing about increased farm size and structural change—including the decline of family-type farms and their replacement by much larger, nonfamily types. Merrill, Friedland, Hightower, and Demarco (Chapter 7) and Belden and Forte (Chapter 11) argue that the benefits of research and extension activities have accrued disproportionately to larger, nonfamily-type farms. By contrast, Caldwell and York (Chapter 7) defend the activities of the land-grant complex and argue that the results of these efforts have been widespread and available to *all* farm types and sizes. Guither, Krause, and Bottum (1972) provide a good review of extension-service activities in this regard.

Less debatable is the fact that development of new, expensive, large-scale equipment systems has encouraged larger, more highly differentiated production units (Carver, 1911; Moyer and others, 1969). The best examples are egg-laying operations and beef feedlots. Hundreds of thousands of hens may now be fed and watered and their waste disposed of and eggs collected, washed, sorted, and graded with low inputs of physical labor per bird. Some beef feedlots grind, mix, and feed grain auto-

matically, by computer. One such feedlot in Colorado handles more beef per year*
than all the farms in Wisconsin. While these operations decrease the amount of physical labor per unit of output, they require huge capital investments and, usually, large
quantities of hired labor to handle the volume of production. Hoffman (1970) believes this new technology is the single most important factor in bringing about large,
highly differentiated farms.

Economies of scale

Another major force increasing the average size of farm operations and reducing
farm numbers is the increased number and growing importance of farms employing
hired, nonowning workers. After family-sized farms have adopted all available labor-
saving technology, a necessary condition for increased size is expansion of the work
force. While increases in larger-than-family–sized farms have not been a major source
of average farm-size expansion in the past, they may be the major source of future
expansion. The increasing importance and trend toward large farms, using hired
labor, documented previously (Chapter 5) suggests that either some or all of the historical restraints to large size have been overcome or are being overcome or that other
forces have entered the scene resulting in benefits that exceed past costs. All of these
seem to be operating; Krause and Kyle (1970:752) note:

A relatively new set of technical, financial, tax and other institutional variables apparently provide increased incentives for units with over $250,000 of farm output. It is now relatively easy to
find very large farms operating on a scale not thought practical ten years ago. Perhaps this is
part of the gradual industrialization of agricultural production. No longer is the belief tenable
that weather, biological processes, and superior incentives of unpaid family members provide
impossible barriers to a large-scale industrialized agriculture.

Two general sets of antecedent factors have played a major role in the establishment of increasingly large farms. One series of changes has removed or reduced many
of the past hurdles to very large farms. The foremost of these changes has been a major reduction in the risks and uncertainties associated with farm income. These have
already been discussed. The second general category of forces is the benefits derived
from increased farm size and manager-laborer differentiation: cost reduction and income expansion. Both appear first as consequences of increased size and differentiation and then as causes of further movement in the same direction.

Preston (1971:14) captures this notion in discussing the significance of cost conditions for changes in firm size:

The impact of cost conditions on industry structure is of special importance. If economies of
scale are very substantial within an industry—that is, if average unit costs decline by substantial amounts as plants and/or firms increase in size—then smaller enterprises will be at a competitive disadvantage as compared to larger ones. The competitive process will then lead eventually to the survival of a relatively smaller number of relatively larger firms, and hence to a
higher level of concentration, than would be the case if economies of scale were absent or negligible.

Four areas in which scale economies exist have already been discussed: benefits
from government subsidy and support programs; tax benefits; adoption of new technology; and the development of extremely expensive, large-scale equipment systems.
Scale economies can be suggested in eight additional areas. Each will be considered
briefly.

Economies of volume buying and selling. Among the most frequently mentioned
benefits associated with large farm size are the decreased cost of inputs and increased prices obtained through large-volume buying and selling (Carver, 1911;

*Based on 1974 figures.

Raup, 1969, 1972b; Krause and Kyle, 1970; Aines, 1972; Breimyer and Barr, 1972; Guither and others, 1972; Ottoson and Vollmar, 1972; Sundquist, 1972). Breimyer and Barr (1972:17) explan this relationship as follows: "If net unit margins may be widened through volume, discount buying of inputs or volume selling, the incentive to expand volume is very strong. The pressure to increase total net income in this way is widely felt." In other words, while increased farm size results in greater benefits derived from volume buying and selling, equally important is the fact that knowledge of, or belief about, this relationship may itself serve as a major reason for decisions to expand farm size. All of the factors to be discussed below reflect this same phenomenon.

Access to risk-reduction sources. A second benefit positively related to increased farm size is access to risk-reduction sources and the economic benefits derived from income stabilization. "Large commercial or industrialized farms may have more ability to utilize various methods of reducing risk including the various private sources. These include easier access to capital sources, contractual arrangements, price stabilization, specialized insurance, and other approaches" (Dorow, 1972:45). Thus, decreased risk and uncertainty not only allow for increased farm size, but also encourage expansion by the fact that as farm size increases even greater reductions in uncertainty are brought about.

Benefits from greater credit accessibility and lower costs. Accessibility to and cost of credit have served as incentives for increased farm size by their interrelationship. Public capital sources, such as the Farm Credit Administration, have proved most beneficial to larger operators. "Larger scale farmers with the greatest initial capital have always been the major beneficiaries of publicly supplied agricultural credit" (Heady and Ball, 1972:386). Historically, larger farmers have also been able to obtain lower interest rates and have had greater access to major capital sources such as large city banks and equity markets (Krause and Kyle, 1970; and Brake, 1972). Loans from these sources have been based on present equity; thus qualification for loans and the amount obtainable have been direct functions of the farmer's capital position. Again, medium- and larger-size operators probably take greatest advantage of the futures market—another source of financing (Guither and others, 1972).

Economies of specialization of function. A fourth incentive for larger, more highly differentiated farm units is the belief that major efficiencies can be gained from separating manager and laborer status-roles (Carver, 1911; VanVliet, 1958; Aines, 1972; Ottoson and Vollmar, 1972). Pickler (1970:761) states, "Industry has known for decades that more efficient production results when management and labor are supplied by different people." The greater the extent to which this is true, or believed to be true, the greater the trend toward units with high levels of manager-laborer differentiation. All other things being equal, the greater the differentiation, the larger the necessary farm size.

Reduced fixed costs. Larger units are also encouraged to obtain the maximum spread of fixed costs over units of production (Krause and Kyle, 1970). Thus, for any given machinery inventory, the larger the number of acres on which the machinery is used, the lower the per-acre machinery costs.

Multiple unit operations. Increased farm size is also encouraged by the reduced uncertainty and possibility of higher prices associated with the operation of dispersed operating units. Farms located in different climatic zones may have the ability to deliver a uniform product on a year-round basis (Krause and Kyle, 1970). Furthermore, if different products are produced, the risks associated with price fluctuations can be diversified (Rhodes, 1970; Aines, 1972).

Marketplace concentration and integration. Forces emanating from input suppliers and output processors also encourage increased farm size. These sectors of the economy are becoming increasingly concentrated. Firms operating here attempt to minimize costs and inconveniences by buying and assembling farm products in the large volumes and quality they require (Kyle and others, 1972:9). This suggests that larger farms may be differentially rewarded for their larger quantities of production. The already high and growing concentration among supplier and processor firms is also creating a condition of power disequilibrium within the agricultural sector. Basically, farmers are losing whatever power they may have once had in influencing the prices they pay for inputs and receive for outputs. A reestablishment of equilibrium can be brought about in a variety of ways. The only major option for an individual farmer acting unilaterally, however, is to increase bargaining power by increasing business size. To be effective in this sense certainly necessitates operations with high levels of structural differentiation (Krause and Kyle, 1970; Wilkening, 1970; Guither and others, 1972; Kyle and others, 1972).

Externalization of costs. Historically, many communities have been willing (or forced) to absorb certain costs generated by economic firms in their vicinity. The magnitude of these often increase with farm size (Raup, 1969). Society's willingness to absorb these costs, instead of charging them to the generating firms, has artificially inflated the levels of economic efficiency and profit margins for large farms and contributed to their establishment. Raup (1973:3963-3965) articulates this point best when he states:

> Only in the past decade has serious attention been given to the fact that the large agricultural firm is also able to achieve benefits by externalizing certain costs. The disadvantages of large scale operation fall largely outside the decision-making framework of the large farm firm. Problems of waste disposal, pollution control, added burdens on public services, deterioration of rural social structures, impairment of the tax base, and the political consequences of a concentration of economic power have typically not been considered as costs of large scale by the firm. They are unquestionably costs to the larger community.
>
> The effect of firm size on the environment is closely related to effects on people. What has appeared to be an example of economies of scale in agribusiness production often turns out on close examination to be an example of successful transfer of pollution control or waste disposal costs and consequences to the neighboring community. Examples include packing plant and feedlot wastes in livestock feeding areas, water pollution through heavy use of agricultural chemicals in irrigated areas, watershed and water table deterioration where large-scale drainage has been attempted, and the disturbance of ecological balance associated with heavy use of insecticide and related agricultural chemicals.

Seckler (Chapter 6) and Henkes (Chapter 11) both discuss the preceding types of factors, and Krause and Kyle (1970) give an excellent review of them.

Tax policy

A number of federal income tax provisions have created incentives for the ownership of farmland and resources by nonfarmers (Parsons and Owen, 1951; VanVliet, 1958; Hoffman, 1970; Krause and Kyle, 1970; Waldo, 1970; Aines, 1972; Barlowe and Libby, 1972; Brake, 1972; Dorow, 1972; Raup, 1972b). Money invested in farmland and nonland resources is taxed at maximum capital gains rates of 25% (pre-1968) or 35% (1969 or later) upon sale of those resources. The greater the extent to which personal income tax rates exceed those figures, the more benefits are derived by investing in farm assets taxed as capital gains.

Some building-related equipment and many nonland resource assets (machinery, breeding stock) are depreciable. Their ownership is attractive since depreciation is deductible from ordinary income. Interest payments on nonland-resource indebtedness also can be deducted for tax purposes. The ability to follow a cash versus accrual accounting system permits increases in inventory not subject to income tax until sold. If beef cows are held until the death of the owner, no income taxes are paid on the sale of these assets (VanVliet, 1958; Hoffman, 1970; Waldo, 1970; Aines, 1972; Barlowe and Libby, 1972; Breimyer and Barr, 1972; Dorow, 1972; Raup, 1972b; Sundquist, 1972).

Farm operating losses may be deducted from taxable income (Parsons and Owen, 1951; Sundquist, 1972). The ownership of production assets (crops, livestock, machinery) would appear necessary to experience such losses. The extent to which this provision has been used is evident from 1966 Internal Revenue Service data on returns reporting farm income. All returns were classified into five categories on the basis of amount of taxable income and magnitude of farm profits or losses. The highest grouping reported more than $25,000 taxable income and either more than $10,000 of farm profits or more than $10,000 farm losses. Of the 90,000 individuals in this grouping (average gross income $41,500, average farm receipts $44,950), 61% reported farm losses. On the other hand, only 13% of the 673,000 individuals in the lowest grouping (average gross income $1260, average farm receipts $5460) reported farm losses. It appears that a high percentage of individuals in the highest grouping had nonfarm occupations since 50% of them reported off-farm wage income, 56% reported dividend income, and the group averaged $42,242 nonfarm taxable income (Kyle and others, 1972:7).

While tax benefits have been available to all persons, the greatest relative benefit has been obtained by high-income individuals, many of whom are nonfarmers. Both absolute and relative benefits appear to advance as the amount of taxable income increases. Tax concessions are not significant for most ordinary farmers (Parsons and Owen, 1951; Dorow, 1972; Raup, 1972b, 1973).

Tax policies concerned with depreciation allowances have particularly provided benefits to large farms located in smaller farm communities. Since good markets for second-hand machinery exist in such communities, large farms have been able to depreciate their machinery quickly, sell it for high prices, and purchase new items (Raup, 1973). Similarly, tax benefits associated with land clearing and conservation improvements have accrued disproportionately to larger farms (Waldo, 1970) as have benefits from following "cash" versus "accrual" accounting procedures (Dorow, 1972; Raup, 1972b).

State and local taxes are important influences as well. It is pointed out later that inheritance taxes are making it increasingly difficult to transfer farms intact from one generation to the next. In addition, farm property taxes as a percentage of operator's net income have risen from 5.1% in 1945 to 17.6% in 1970 (Barlowe and Libby, 1972: 26). This reduces the family's disposable income, lowers its attainable level of living (Bradford, 1954), and increases the difficulty of farm and land ownership.

Articles by Raup (Chapter 5), Bible (Chapter 6), Bulbulian (Chapter 11), and Henkes (Chapter 11) further discuss the significance of tax laws and policy.

The interrelationships of changes in farm type, size, and capital requirements

A very strong relationship exists between certain farm structural characteristics and farm size. As pointed out in Chapter 5 (Rodefeld), farms with high levels of differentiation on one or more dimensions of structure (low levels of land ownership, capital ownership, labor by the farm manager) tend to be considerably larger than farms with low levels of differentiation on these dimensions. If family-type farms are being replaced by one or more of the nonfamily types, farm size will increase at a more rapid rate than if changes in farm type were not occurring. One of the major conclusions in Chapter 5 was that farm-type changes are occurring. Conversely, increasing farm size is one of the major causes for the decline of family-type farms. As farm sizes have increased, the value of both land and nonland resources and the amount of capital necessary to secure these resources have increased as well. As this has occurred, the difficulties experienced by beginning and existent farmers to acquire farms, to expand through additional purchases and to transfer them intergenerationally have increased.

These three problems are discussed in Chapter 7 in the article from the *Wisconsin Farmers Union News* and in Chapter 11 articles by Perry, Limivere, Bulbulian, and Belden and Forte; but they need review and emphasis here.

Increased farm capital requirements. In 1940 the average value of production assets per farm in the United States was $6200. By 1972 this value experienced an almost unbelievable jump to $102,100. The 1972 figure was 16.5 times higher than that in 1940. The average value per farm doubled from 1963 to 1972. In both 1940 and 1973, farm real estate (land and buildings) was the largest single component of total farm value. In the same years, real estate accounted for 74.2% and 76.3%, respectively, of the total farm value (Evans and others, 1973:26). Of course, these figures are national averages. A good deal of variability exists from one region and type of production to another. For example, the total value of an average dairy farm in southeastern Wisconsin increased from a 1960 to 1964 average of $81,050 to $113,200 in 1969 (a 40% increase). The total value of an average hog-beef–fattening farm in the corn belt went from $113,300 to $187,980 (a 56% increase) in the same period (Orazem, 1972: 66).

These increased values reflect changes in the worth of both real estate and nonland resources (livestock, machinery, crop inventories). From 1940 to 1972, 76.4% of the $95,900 increase in the average farm value was accounted for by real estate appreciation. The remaining 23.6% was comprised by the increased value of nonland resources (Evans and others, 1973:26).

Average farm size increased from 151 acres in 1930 to 387 acres in 1970 (Ball and Heady, 1972:44). With all other things equal, that alone would push up the average value of farm real estate. Concomitantly, however, the index of U.S. farmland prices—per-acre costs—increased every year from 1939 to 1972, with the exception of 1950 and 1954 (Raup, 1972b:7). The major reasons for the increased value of farmland are a general upward price trend, the increased productivity of land, reduced risks, and a fixed quantity of fertile land balanced against increased demand by farmers wishing to expand (Murray, 1970:41) and by nonfarmers wanting land for a variety of reasons (Timmons, 1948; Brake, 1970, 1972; Breimyer and Barr, 1972; Dorow, 1972). Increased contractual relationships may have the same effect in the future (Miller, 1960).

Real estate values have been increased also through gains in the worth of farm buildings and building-related equipment. Labor has increasingly been replaced by capital, as seen in such things as barn cleaners, silage unloaders, pipelines, and automated feeding systems. The prices of buildings and equipment have increased for a variety of reasons (Brake, 1970, 1972). A similar story obtains with nonland production assets. Thus, in 1940, the average value per farm of these was $1600; in 1972 their value was $24,200. This is approximately a 15-fold increase. Machinery costs account for 48% of it, while 40% can be attributed to the increased value of livestock (Evans and others, 1973:26). Among the major reasons for the increased value per farm of nonland production assets are: substitution of capital for labor; increased use of purchased versus homegrown inputs; adoption of larger-capacity machines; inflation; increased machinery, equipment, and livestock prices; and larger numbers of livestock per farm (Brake, 1970, 1972; Ball and Heady, 1972).

The increased difficulty of farm acquisition by young, financially unaided individuals. Increased farm size and value have made it increasingly difficult over time for financially unassisted individuals to attain farm ownership. Traditional credit arrangements require down payments ranging from 35% to 40% of a farm's real estate value. Since many units now have a real estate worth ranging from $100,000 to $150,000, this would require a down payment between $35,000 and $60,000. Brake (1972:133) notes, "Obtaining this much is simply out of the question for many prospective young farmers unless they have access to substantial family help." If the profitability of operations remains low and interest rates are high or rising, the length of repayment will take longer and, therefore, will be more costly (Brake, 1970). Additional capital would be required for the purchase of necessary nonland resources. A number of other authors have also discussed this topic, reaching the same conclusion as Brake (Taylor, 1926; Kelso, 1934; Schickele, 1937; Timmons, 1948; Moore and Dean, 1972; Paarlberg, 1973).

Unsupported farmers have continued to gain access to farming in recent years, but it has required a good deal of sacrifice and extraordinary personal effort. The number gaining such access has been greatly reduced, and those who do have less security and certainty of final success than was the case previously (VanVliet, 1958). In the future, young persons may still be able to enter agriculture as small operators, part-time farmers, or tenants, but they are likely to have even greater difficulty than presently in acquiring control of large commercial farms (Kyle and others, 1972).

The increased difficulty of farm expansion through the purchase of land. Where farmers presently own some land, rising real estate prices make it increasingly difficult to expand operations by purchasing additional land. If pressures exist for expansion but farmers are either unwilling or unable to buy additional land, they will most likely rent, lease, or work additional land on shares. As the proportion of all land operated that is rented increases, the level of manager-landowner differentiation increases. We must be concerned with the forces making expansion through purchase more difficult.

In terms of a general principle, it appears that (ceterus paribus) the lower the amount of equity held by a farmer in the operation, the less likely any additional land purchases will be and the smaller the number of acres that can be purchased. The smaller the equity, the more an existent owner is like a beginning farmer with little or no equity. Both face the same problem—the inability, without help, to generate the necessary down payment for the purchase.

As equity increases, borrowing power increases. This suggests that as farm size and equity increase, the difficulty associated with purchasing any given quantity of additional land will decrease. Moore and Dean (1972:222) have noted one condition, however, that results in the separation of manager and landowner status roles even for larger farms. They state:

> Technical and monetary economies of size provide continued incentives and economic pressure to expand production or size. However, rapid firm growth from retained earnings alone is very difficult. This leads management to seek sources of equity financing outside the firm and even more important from outside agriculture. Risk or equity capital from outside the industry has led to a separation of resource ownership and the management input.

Another phenomena affecting both the ability of initial acquisitions and expansion through purchase is the escalation of land prices beyond levels justifiable in terms of agricultural production earning capacity. The greater this disparity, the more hazardous the assumption becomes that such land can be paid for out of future earnings (Timmons, 1948). This is neither a new problem nor one restricted to urban expansion. In 1936, Sanders (1936:16) pointed out, "In the past, land prices that were above values justified by earning power of the land have probably been the greatest force fostering tenancy's growth." Parsons and Owen (1951) report that farmers are unable to compete successfully with city money for the purchase of farms within driving distance of Chicago. Other authors point out that the same thing is happening in better land areas elsewhere in the country because of purchases by nonfarm investors (Bradford, 1954; VanVliet, 1958).

The increased difficulty of transferring farms from one generation to another. In 1953, a North Central Research Committee estimated that as many as 80% of all beginning farmers received substantial assistance in entering farming (Bradford, 1954:1013). Wisconsin research, studying a sample of the largest owner-managed farms in the state, found that over 50% of these units had been owned by the fathers of the present owner-managers, and about 75% of the managers' fathers had themselves been farm owners. Higher percentages of the surveyed owner-managers reported receiving financial assistance from their parents than did a sample of hired, nonowning farm workers and a random sample of all state farmers (Wilkening and Rodefeld, 1973:4927-4929). These figures suggest that beginning farmers may yet attain ownership status if financial assistance, from the family or elsewhere, is provided. However, increasing capital requirements, under certain conditions, are creating hazards to mobility.

The major problem is that of intergenerational transfer. Traditionally, and at the present time, farm families have been relatively large, averaging from three to four children. Often there is a strong feeling held by both parents and their children that all siblings should be treated equally on inheritance matters. Sometimes this sentiment has been codified into state laws. Whatever the case, a problem is created because most parents only have one farm. This means that if any of the children want to retain the farm, they must buy out the remaining inherited shares from their siblings. The smaller the number of purchasers, the greater the number of brothers and sisters inheriting and the higher the price of the farm, the greater the difficulty of purchase and retention within the family (Schickele, 1937; Timmons, 1948; Brake, 1970). Though inheritance is an important route to farm ownership, it is a problematical route.

Incentives for the ownership of farmland and nonland resources by nonfarmers

The growing difficulty of farm managers in attaining high levels of land and nonland resource ownership need not necessarily result in growing acquisitions by nonfarmers. For this to occur, nonfarmers must have capital available to invest, there must be opportunities and incentives to invest. Unless all three conditions are met, investments (ownership) by nonfarmers will not occur and other changes might be observed. Government or cooperative ownership might increase. The prices of farm products might be raised high enough to allow ownership by farm managers. If no buyers were available for the resources, their values might decline to affordable levels.

Ownership of farmland and nonland resources by nonfarmers has increased, of course. Capital has been available for investment (Hoffman, 1970; Krause and Kyle, 1970; Aines, 1972). Investment opportunities have been created by farmers soliciting capital for expansion purposes (Brake, 1972) and through the purchase of land and nonland resources in the marketplace. In addition, numerous incentives exist for ownership by nonfarmers.

Some of these incentives have already been mentioned. Government programs and new technology have reduced farm risks and uncertainties. Substantial tax incentives exist for the ownership of farmland and nonland resources by wealthy nonfarm individuals and corporations. Numerous incentives exist for the ownership, operation, or control of farm resources by large, nonfarm corporations.

At least four other incentives can be identified. First, some nonfarmers have purchased farmland, speculating its value would increase with time. One group of investors is interested in land primarily as a long-range investment and expects its value to increase at a rate similar to the past. The second group of investors is interested in more spectacular gains. These investors speculate or gamble on land conversion to higher value uses such as housing, business, and industry (VanVliet, 1958; Krause and Kyle, 1970; Aines, 1972; Barlowe and Libby, 1972; Breimyer and Barr, 1972). Speculation may be involved in livestock ownership, especially premium breeding stock. The winning of a grand championship at a prestigious fair or breed show appreciates the animal's value. The increase may be dramatic. The ability to consistently win high prizes in these shows increases the value of all livestock from the farm. The proven ability of a sire to produce offspring with highly desirable characteristics results in higher stud fees and, in some cases, its sale to an artificial breeding company for a large sum. A few years ago, a Canadian bull was purchased by a

Wisconsin artificial breeding company for a million dollars. The speculative aspect of livestock ownership is best exemplified by the ownership of race horses.

A second motive for investment, is the fact that the ownership of farmland is an attractive hedge against inflationary impacts on income and capital (Parsons and Owen, 1951; Hoffman, 1970; Rhodes, 1970; Barlowe and Libby, 1972; Briemyer and Barr, 1972; Raup, 1972b). The ownership of some livestock, especially premium breeding stock, in most cases is a good inflation hedge. While no index figures are known, a review of dispersal sales and advertisements indicate large increases have occurred in the prices of purebred livestock over the last two decades.

Third, farm resources may be purchased to obtain various amenities. Recent changes in urban values and life-styles have increased the demand for farm and recreational land by urban people (VanVliet, 1958; Barlowe and Libby, 1972). A high percentage of present urban residents would prefer to live in rural areas. This is particularly true if the residence is within commuting distance of a large place (Fuguitt and Zuiches, 1973). Better highways, faster cars, and relatively cheap gasoline have allowed urbanites to acquire farms and large lots for residential, recreational, and esthetic purposes, while retaining their urban jobs. Urban problems, the "return to the land" movement, the increased popularity of organic and natural foods, the extension of many urban services to rural areas, and other similar factors have undoubtedly contributed to urban out-migration.

Nonfarmers may purchase premium livestock for the prestige, status, honor, and publicity derived. Purebred bloodlines carry the breeder's name or a name selected by the breeder. With artificial insemination, a bloodline can be diffused throughout the United States in a matter of years. The "Pabst" and "Carnation" bloodlines are known to dairy farmers nationally. The winners of championships in major livestock shows receive statewide and regionwide publicity, and winners of the Chicago International Livestock Show receive nationwide attention.

Fourth, certain assumptions about the future also have contributed to the conclusion that acceptable profits from the ownership and operation of farms can be expected. Increasing population numbers, a fixed amount of land in the world, the declining quantity of prime agricultural land, deterioration, rising consumer incomes, and rising demand for livestock products have resulted in "the creation of a climate of opinion in which food production emerged as a safe long-run growth industry" (Raup, 1972b:14).

Incentives for the ownership and control by large corporations

Increases in farm size and structural differentiation and the decline of family-type farms have been brought about, in part, by the increased ownership and operation of farms by large corporations. By "large corporation" is meant a legally incorporated firm with numerous shareholders and a highly differentiated organizational structure. Most are likely to have publicly traded stock. Farms owned or operated by such corporations tend to be very large (acreage and sales) with high levels of differentiation in all dimensions of organizational structure except, perhaps, land and capital ownership.

A number of conditions and forces have already been identified that serve as incentives for large corporations to engage in farming. While some of these may be applicable to any potential operator, they have particular appeal for the large corporation as just defined. Moreover, certain other factors apply mainly to agribusiness corporations or large corporations generally and can be profitably reviewed.

Corporations in agriculturally related industries have incentives to engage directly in farm production. Processors require a steady flow of quality-controlled products or produce. Input suppliers seek market control and a stable demand for their output. While these objectives can be attained in the open market or through vertical integration with farmers, the same results can be accomplished—with some advantage—if corporations own or rent land and produce the goods themselves.

Production costs can be reduced by eliminating marketing steps and their costs; middlemen margins can be reduced or eliminated by buying internally (Krause and Kyle, 1970). Higher prices may be obtained for one's agricultural production through supermarket merchandising techniques such as large-scale advertising and the sale of differentiated products. It may be possible to reach special or higher priced markets (Krause and Kyle, 1970; Aines, 1972; Moore and Dean, 1972). Aines (1972: 177) predicts farm-related, rather than nonfarm, industry will be the major corporate force establishing linkages with farm production. "Linkage will continue to grow as long as and to the extent that there are significant synergistic business relationships between farming and farm related industry."

Incentives also exist for both farm managers and agribusiness corporations to engage in vertically-integrated relationships. The provision of nonland resources by the integrator alleviates the necessity of the manager to purchase them. It also frees up manager financial resources for land and nonland resource purchases. Theoretically, the acquisition of necessary inputs and a market for the output (at a predetermined price) is assured. Contract production and integration with input suppliers and output processors makes the procurement of some inputs and the disposal of output more secure (Krause and Kyle, 1970; Sundquist, 1972). Miller (1960) has suggested, however, that farmers may only be replacing one type of uncertainty in these arrangements (inputs and prices) with another (contract renewal and terms).

On the other side, vertical integration allows input suppliers to increase market control and ensures a more stable demand for a portion of their output. Processors require a steady flow of quality-controlled products. Integration allows for prescheduling of production, handling, and processing of products for greater efficiency and ensures availability of farm products in the desired quantities and quality (Krause and Kyle, 1970; Aines, 1972; Moore and Dean, 1972; Sundquist, 1972). Breimyer and Barr (1972) suggest the quest for power and control may be another incentive for integration from the integrator's perspective.

A number of incentives and supportive conditions exist for the ownership and operation of farms by large corporations, regardless of their major activities. Some of these factors are also applicable to the establishment of large, highly differentiated farm operations, regardless of who owns them. The following breakdown reemphasizes these conditions.

Diversification and risk spreading. The acquisition of farming operations by large corporations can result in reduced investment and economic risks for them. This is brought about by engaging in activities located in different sectors of the economy. Risks also can be reduced within the agricultural sector by carrying out production activities in different geographical regions and for various commodities (Krause and Kyle, 1970; Rhodes, 1970; Aines, 1972; Moore and Dean, 1972).

Cost reduction and profit-increasing factors. Agricultural production costs may be reduced and profits increased in a variety of ways when the farm is a part of a large corporation. It may be possible to employ hired workers in other divisions in off-seasons. As these opportunities increase, work-force stability and the ability to recruit and retain high-quality workers should increase. Costs of labor recruitment and training thereby can decline (Krause and Kyle, 1970).

Economies may be gained if the efforts of well-trained but underused specialists already on the corporation's payroll can be employed in the operation of an acquired farm (Aines, 1972). Raup (1969:1277) also points out that large firms have a greater capacity and flexibility in the purchase of management services. "A scale large enough to justify employment of a resident nutritionist, entomologist, veterinarian, accountant, or tax consultant may be a measure of optimum size in some types of production." Large corporations are able to recruit and retain a higher-quality work force by paying higher wages and salaries (Krause and Kyle, 1970b; Pickler, 1970). They also may be large enough to have their own research and development division. The presence of specialized managers and technicians can result in early detection of new innovations.

Large corporations enjoy some unique tax advantages (Krause and Kyle, 1970; Raup, 1972b). If one unit in an integrated operation receives favorable tax treatment, as many types of farming do, then profits from other segments of the corporation can be steered into the favored segment. Similarly, credit and capital for the corporate farming operation may be obtained at a lower cost by tapping other divisions of the corporation possessing a surplus. Stocks and bonds can be sold, and the stock market may be accessible. Large loans are normally negotiable at relatively lower rates than those open to smaller farmers. The interest rates may be as much as 0.9% lower (Aines, 1972; Ottoson and Vollmar, 1972). Unused corporate borrowing capacity can be used to generate income flows, realizing attractive rates of return on limited investment capital (Aines, 1972).

Mergers. In some cases, large corporations have become engaged in agricultural production through their acquisition of other corporations that, while primarily non-agricultural, may have had a farming operation as a subsidiary unit (Moore and Dean, 1972).

Manager availability. One of the factors that hindered the establishment of large, highly differentiated farming operations in the past was a shortage of highly qualified farm managers and the difficulty of hiring them when they were available. In the past, salaries were low and most managers preferred owning their own farms. These are no longer major problems. Farm managers of high quality are available for hire (Parsons and Owen, 1951; Raup, 1969a), and owners of large farm operations are able to pay high salaries (Pickler, 1970).

Supportive attitudes. The alteration of conditions that previously hindered the establishment of large farms, the existence of incentives for the ownership and operation of these units, and, possibly, the successful development of giant firms in the nonagricultural sector have all contributed to the establishment of attitudes among corporate personnel that satisfactory returns can be obtained from agricultural production (Krause and Kyle, 1970; Aines, 1972). Such attitudes and beliefs are likely to be strengthened, and corporate involvement increased, the greater the success of large corporations now in farming (Hoffman, 1970; Guither and others, 1972).

Evolutionary determinism. Replacement of the numerous small farms that have characterized America's past by a smaller number of larger, highly differentiated corporate or industrial-type firms is taken as inevitable by many persons. This outcome is expected because of past changes in the nonagricultural sector. Its occurrence in agriculture is viewed as the logical conclusion of inexorable, irreversible, and, often, unspecified change processes.

This view is reflected in the statements of numerous authors. Sinclair (1958) points out that 80% of the total population falls in the employee class and that this shift to "industrial feudalism" can be attributed to the technological developments that have taken place since the Industrial Revolution. "It seems logical, therefore, to argue that the same changes will occur in agriculture." Higbee (1963:34) notes considerable concentration has taken place in the food-processing industries. "Consolidation at the farm level is only following a pattern which has been set farther up the line. As the two segments of production and processing are linked to the big distributing chains, the integration will be complete." Pickler (1970:761) states:

Looking to the future, I expect large-scale farming to become as matter-of-fact as chain retailing is now—the only question is how soon. The economic forces are weighted so heavily in favor of increasing sizes of agricultural production and marketing that any social pressures and traditions to the contrary are not likely to stand.

The views of the U.S. Chamber of Commerce (in the *NFO Reporter* article in Chapter 6) seem to fall in this section as well.

This position receives further credence from an impressive base of sociological theorizing. In varying degrees, the inevitability of structural differentiation and increased scale has been articulated by Marx, Durkheim, Weber, and numerous contemporaries such as Becker, Toennies, and Redfield. While Durkheim deals most directly with the differentiation process, his work is also among the least satisfying in terms of identifying the major, *specific* conditions bringing this change about. With the possible exception of Marx, the same charge applies to all the mentioned theorists.

My own belief is that observable—but little understood—change processes are frequently conceptualized in "evolutionary" terms because this is the path of least resistance. This largely avoids the difficult and complex questions of causality and is suspect by that fact. By contrast, Raup (1972b) has argued that differentiation and concentration in agriculture may not proceed exactly as they did in the industrial sector and may be less inevitable because of some major differences in developmental sequences. In this volume, Seckler (Chapter 6) and Henkes (Chapter 11) review some of the reasons for the involvement of large corporations in farming. Hamburger (Chapter 5, May 15) and Hightower (Chapter 5), Bible (Chapter 6), and Merrill and McGinnis (Chapter 7) argue that one of the major causes of small, family-type farms declining has been the growth of ownership or operation by large nonfarm corporations.

Lack of knowledge and research on changes occurring in farm size, structural differentiation, and farm type or the consequences of these changes and those in technology

As pointed out in Chapter 5, the recognition that major changes have been occurring in levels of farm structural differentiation and the status of family-type farms is a recent phenomena. The belief that these changes were not occurring has had a number of consequences. First, there has been a lack of support for or opposition to federal and state legislation to discourage non–family-type farms or strengthen the status of family-type farms. Second, legitimacy and support have been lacking for the development of more definitive information on changes occurring in farm organizational structure and types and the causes and consequences of these changes. As a result, deficiencies exist in all these latter areas.

With the recognition, however, that major changes either have occurred or are occurring, empirically based information on the consequences of changes in farm technology, size, or structure is imperative. Both citizens and their representative officials require such knowledge in their attempts to decide whether a continuation of agriculturally relevant changes in the future is desirable or not. Ideally, this information should exist for each sector of society: farm people and farms, rural nonfarm people and rural communities, urban people and cities. But, as McElroy (Chapter 1), Rodefeld (Chapter 5), and Friedland (Chapter 7) point out, little research has been carried out in recent decades on any of these topics. These authors suggest, rather strongly, that with more complete knowledge of both the positive and negative consequences of changes before they occurred, substantially different public decisions may have transpired.

Conclusion

Achieving an adequate understanding of the causal forces that have resulted in adoption of new technology, increased farm size, increased differentiation of farm organizational structure, and decline of family-type farms is no easy task. This difficulty is a result of the limited resources that have been devoted to these questions in the past, the resultant lack of knowledge, and the complexity of these change processes.

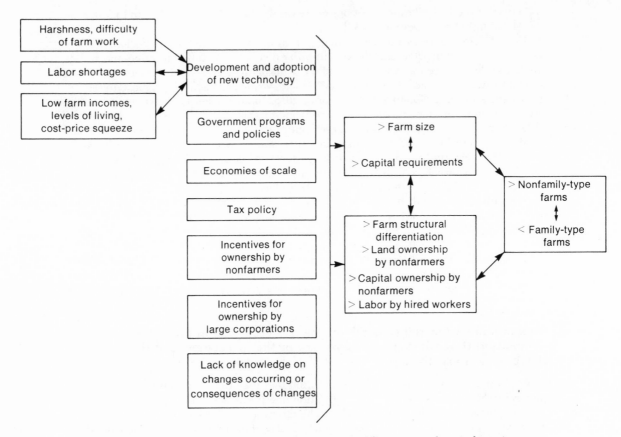

Fig. 1. Causal forces and conditions resulting in increased farm size and capital requirements, increased farm structural differentiation, and increased status of nonfamily-type farms (decline of family-type farms).

Complexity results from the facts that: explanations are sought for changes in four discrete areas, the causal forces emanate from a number of general areas and a much larger number of more specific phenomena, and the changes we seek to explain are themselves interrelated.

The focal concerns that have been discussed and their major interrelationships are portrayed in Figure 1 in an attempt to provide a measure of simplification.

The harshness and difficulty of farm work and farm labor shortages have been two of the more important reasons for the initial adoption of mechanical devices. These devices were used to expand farm size, and other production-expanding technology was adopted in an attempt by farm operators to raise their low incomes and levels of living and lessen their economically precarious positions (cost-price squeeze). Paradoxically, the adoption of new mechanical devices has itself created labor shortages, and the adoption of production-expanding technology has been one of the major causes of overproduction and resultant low prices for farm production. The result of the preceding has been a vicious circle of causality, the major initial consequences of which have been the continual expansion of farm size and a declining farm population.

In addition, new technology and a variety of government programs and policies have encouraged expansion of farms beyond the family-size range and the increased ownership of farm resources by nonfarmers; this has been done by reducing levels of price, production, and management risks. Technological and government program benefits have often been tied to farm size, hence, have provided additional incentives for size expansion. It has also been observed that a variety of costs can be reduced, profits increased, or both by expanding farm size. These "economies of scale" continue beyond the range of family-sized farms, thus encouraging expanded farm size generally and larger-than-family–sized farms as well.

As farm size has increased, the capital requirements for the ownership of both farmland and nonland resources have increased as well. As a result, ownership by farm managers has become increasingly difficult. At the same time, increased ownership by nonfarmers has been encouraged by the numerous tax benefits derived from this ownership and a variety of other incentives applicable to both nonfarm individuals and nonfarm corporations. No widely supported reservations have been voiced to these ongoing changes, in part because definitive information has been lacking on their directions, rates, causes, and consequences.

The major outcomes of the preceding have been the continued adoption of new technology—used primarily to expand farm size—increased farm capital requirements, increased ownership of farmland and nonland recources by nonfarm individuals and corporations, and increased provision of farm labor by hired workers. As these changes have proceeded, the status of farms with high levels of land ownership, capital ownership, and labor provision by their managers has declined relative to farms with low levels on these dimensions. As a result, the status of family-type farms has declined relative to nonfamily types (tenant, larger-than-family, and industrial).

One implication of the preceding is that if a decision is reached by policy-makers to preserve relatively small, family-type farms, alterations will be necessary in many areas. Alterations in any one area, or a few areas, are likely to have little or no effect on the dominant trends. Rather, programs and policies encompassing all of the major causal forces are indicated.

REFERENCES

Aines, R. O.: Linkages in control and management with agribusiness. In Ball, A. G., and Heady, E. O., editors: Size, structure and future of farms, Ames, Iowa, 1972, The Iowa State University Press.

Ball, A. G., and Heady, E. O.: Trends in farm and enterprise size and scale. In Ball, A. G., and Heady, E. O., editors: Size, structure and future of farms, Ames, Iowa, 1972, The Iowa State University Press.

Barlowe, R., and Libby, L.: Policy choices affecting access to farmland. In Guither, H. A., editor: Who will control U.S. agriculture? North Central Regional Extension Publication 32, Urbana, Ill., 1972, University of Illinois.

Bradford, Lawrence A.: Critical problems of young families in getting established in farming, Journal of Farm Economics **36:**1011-1020, 1954.

Brake, J. R., editor: Emerging and projected trends likely to influence the structure of Midwest agriculture, 1970-1985, Monograph No. 11, Iowa City, Iowa, June 1970, University of Iowa Agricultural Law Center.

Brake, J. R.: Capitalizing agriculture in coming years. In Brake, J. R., editor: Emerging and projected trends likely to influence the structure of Midwest agriculture, 1970-1985, Monograph No. 11, Iowa City, Iowa, June 1970, University of Iowa Agricultural Law Center.

Brake, J. R.: Capital and credit. In Ball, A. G., and Heady, E. O., editors: Size, structure and future of farms, Ames, Iowa, 1972, The Iowa State University Press.

Breimyer, H. F., and Barr, W.: Issues in concentration versus dispersion. In Guither, H. D., editor: Who will control U.S. agriculture? North Central Regional Extension Publication 32, Urbana, Ill., 1972, University of Illinois.

Carver, Thomas N.: Principles of rural economics, Lexington, Mass., 1911, Ginn and Co.

Dorow, N. A.: Policies affecting capital accumulation and organizational structure. In Guither, H. D., editor: Who will control U.S. agriculture? North Central Regional Extension Publication 32, Urbana, Ill., 1972, University of Illinois.

Evans, C. D., Warren, F. G., and Reinsel, R. D.: The balance sheet of the farming sector, 1972, USDA-ERS Agricultural Information Bulletin No. 359, Jan. 1973.

Fuguitt, G., and Zuiches, J.: Residential preferences and population distribution: results of a national survey, Paper given at the Annual Meeting of the Rural Society, College Park, Md., Aug. 24, 1973.

Gates, P. W.: The Homestead Law in an incongruous land system, American Historical Review **41**(1):4, July 1936.

Guither, H. D., Krause, K. R., and Bottum, J. C.: Effects of access to technical knowledge and commercial inputs. In Guither, H. D., editor: Who will control U.S. agriculture? North Central Regional Extension Publication 32, Urbana, Ill., 1972, University of Illinois.

Heady, E. O., and Ball, A. G.: Public policy means and alternatives. In Ball, A. G., and Heady, E. O., editor: Size, structure, and future of farms, Ames, Iowa, 1972, The Iowa State University Press.

Higbee, E.: Farms and farmers in an urban age, New York, 1963, Twentieth Century Fund.

Hightower, Jim: Hard tomatoes, hard times: failure of the land-grant college complex, Society **10**:10-22, Nov.-Dec. 1972.

Hoffman, A. C.: Trends in the food industries and their relationship to agriculture. In Brake, J. R., editor: Emerging and projected trends likely to influence the structure of Midwest agriculture, 1970-1985, Monograph No. 11, Iowa City, Iowa, June 1970, University of Iowa Agricultural Law Center.

Hopkin, J. A.: Financing farm growth-requirements and alternatives. In The National Farm Institute: Corporate farming and the family farm, Ames, Iowa, 1970, The Iowa State University Press.

Kelso, M. M.: A critique of land tenure research, Journal of Land and Public Utility Economics **10**(4):391-402, Nov. 1934.

Krause, K. R., and Kyle, L.: Economic factors underlying the incidence of large farming units, the current situation and probable trends, American Journal of Agricultural Economics **52**: 748-760, Dec. 1970.

Kyle, L., Sundquist, W. B., and Guither, H. D.: Who controls agriculture now?—The trends underway. In Guither, H. D., editor: Who will control U.S. agriculture? North Central Regional Extension Publication 32, Urbana, Ill., 1972, University of Illinois.

Madden, J. P., and Partenheimer, E. J.: Evidence of economies and diseconomies of farm size. In Ball, A. G., and Heady, E. O., editors: Size, structure and future of farms, Ames, Iowa, 1972, The Iowa State University Press.

Meyer, Gene: If proposed corporate farm succeeds, future of small producer may be in doubt, The Wall Street Journal, New York, Feb. 19, 1974.

Miller, Walter G.: Farm tenure perspective of vertical integration, Journal of Farm Economics **42**(2):307-316, 1960.

Moore, C. V., and Dean, G. W.: Industrialized farming. In Ball, A. G., and Heady, E. O., editors: Size, structure and future of farms, Ames, Iowa, 1972, The Iowa State University Press.

Moyer, D., Harris, M., and Harmon, M.: Land tenure in the United States: development and status, USDA-ERS Argicultural Information Bulletin No. 338, June 1969.

Murray, W. G.: Farm size and land values. In The National Farm Institute: Corporate farming and the family farm, Ames, Iowa, 1970, The Iowa State University Press.

Nikolitch, Radoje: Family-size farms in U.S. agriculture, USDA-ERS Agricultural Economics Report No. 499, Feb. 1972.

Orazem, Frank: Economic status of income groups by farm size. In Ball, A. G., and Heady, E. O., editors: Size, structure and future of farms, Ames, Iowa, 1972, The Iowa State University Press.

Ottoson, H. W., and Vollmar, G. J.: The nonfamily corporation in farming. In Ball, A. G., and Heady, E. O., editors: Size, structure and future of farms, Ames, Iowa, 1972, The Iowa State University Press.

Paarlberg, Don: Future of the family farm, Role of giant corporations, Part 3B-Appendixes, U.S. Senate, Committee on Small Business, Hearings before the Subcommittee on Monopoly, 92nd Congress, Washington, D.C., 1973, U.S. Government Printing Office.

Parsons, K. H., and Owen, W. F.: Implications of trends in farm size and organization, Journal of Farm Economics **33**:893-903, 1951.

Pickler, E. B.: Discussion—the incidence of large farming units, American Journal of Agricultural Economics **52**:761, Dec. 1970.

Preston, Lee E.: The industry and enterprise structure of the U.S. economy, Morristown, N.J., 1971, General Learning Corporation.

Quance, L., and Tweeten, L. G.: Policies, 1930-1970. In Ball, A. G., and Heady, E. O., editors: Size, structure and future of farms, Ames, Iowa, 1972, The Iowa State University Press.

Raup, P. M.: Economies and diseconomies of large-scale agriculture, American Journal of Agricultural Economics **51:**1274-1282, Dec. 1969.

Raup, P. M.: The impact of trends in the farm firm on community and human welfare. In Brake, J. R., editor: Emerging and projected trends likely to influence the structure of Midwest agriculture, 1970-1985, Monograph No. 11, Iowa City, Iowa, June 1970, University of Iowa Agricultural Law Center.

Raup, P. M.: Societal goals in farm size. In Ball, A. G., and Heady, E. O., editors: Size, structure and future of farms, Ames, Iowa, 1972a, The Iowa State University Press.

Raup, P. M.: Corporate farming in the United States, Staff paper P72-32, Minneapolis, Minn., Dec. 1972b, University of Minnesota.

Raup, P. M.: Needed research into the effects of large scale farm and business firms on rural America, Role of giant corporations, U.S. Senate, Committee on Small Business, Hearings before the Subcommittee on Monopoly, 92nd Congress, Washington, D.C., 1973, U.S. Government Printing Office.

Rhodes, V. James: The role of farming in agricultural production, marketing and processing, Agricultural Economics Paper No. 1970-26, Columbia, Mo., 1970, University of Missouri.

Rhodes, V. James: Policies affecting access to markets. In Guither, H. D., editor: Who will control U.S. agriculture? North Central Regional Extension Publication 32, Urbana, Ill., 1972, University of Illinois.

Rodefeld, R. D.: The changing occupational and organizational structure of farming and the implications for farm work force individuals, families and communities, Unpublished Ph.D. dissertation, Madison, Wis., May 1974, University of Wisconsin.

Rudd, Robert W., and MacFarlane, David L.: The scale of operations in agriculture, Journal of Farm Economics **24**(2):420-433, 1942.

Sanders, J. T.: An effective homestead exemption will reduce farm tenancy, Oklahoma Agricultural Experiment Station Current Farm Economics **9:**1, 1936.

Schickele, Ranier: Tenure problems and research needs in the Middlewest, Journal of Farm Economics **19**(1):112-127, 1937.

Sinclair, Sol: Discussion—technological advance, Journal of Farm Economics **40**(1):1609-1612, 1958.

Sundquist, W. Burt: Scale economies and management requirements. In Ball, A. G., and Heady, E. O., editors: Size, structure and future of farms, Ames, Iowa, 1972, The Iowa State University Press.

Taylor, C. C.: Rural sociology: a study of rural problems, New York, 1926, Harper & Row, Publishers.

Thompson, Ron: Problems of limited resource farmers, Paper given in Department of Agricultural Economics, Michigan State University, Oct. 30, 1973.

Timmons, J. F.: Farm ownership in the U.S.: an appraisal of the present situation and emerging problems, Journal of Farm Economics **30**(1):78-100, 1948.

VanVliet, H.: Increased capital requirements and the problem of getting started in farming, Journal of Farm Economics **40**(1):1613-1621, 1958.

Waldo, A. D.: Discussion—the incidence of large farming units, American Journal of Agricultural Economics **52**(5):762-763, Dec. 1970.

Wilkening, E. A.: An approach to the study of agricultural systems, Paper read at the annual meeting of the Rural Sociological Society, Washington, D.C., 1970.

Wilkening, E. A., and Rodefeld, R. D.: Wisconsin incorporated farms II: characteristics of resident owners, hired managers and hired workers, Role of Giant Corporations, Part 3B-Appendixes, U.S. Senate, Committee on Small Business, Hearings before the Subcommittee on Monopoly, 92nd Congress, Washington, D.C., 1973, U.S. Government Printing Office.

7

Causal forces resulting in farm technology, size, and organizational structure changes

Why farm equipment gets bigger and bigger

NORMAN REEDER

How many farmers really need a 5-plow tractor, let alone one of the new 100-horsepower models now on the market?

Even those on the manufacturing side seem hesitant when faced with this question. Nobody knows how many of these jumbo tractors will be bought, a branch manager told me. But the trend is clear: Today the big dollar volume in tractor sales is in the 4-plow and 5-plow sizes—the largest generally available up to last year.

Don't think the dealer is pushing the big stuff, said the branch manager. By and large dealers are trying to sell equipment the farmer no longer wants. Later I heard the same opinion from a farmer. Farmers would get better service and save time and money if the manufacturer would put one factory branch in each state and deal directly with the customer, said this man who in the past three years has invested nearly $50,000 in new and bigger tillage and harvesting machines which the nearest dealer is totally unequipped to service.

Neither are college ag engineers and farm management specialists urging farmers on principle to buy bigger and bigger. Some earnestly question whether a $13,000 or $14,000 tractor-plow rig or combine can be a wise investment for many family farm operations outside of the Great Plains wheat belt. At the University of Illinois, scientists are trying to work out reliable guides to the size equipment which would prove the most economical under any given set of conditions. But so far they have not much more to offer than educated guesses.

Only the farmers who are buying these 7-plow tractors and combines with 4-row corn heads seem to be sure that these are tools of the size they need.

☐ From Nation's Agriculture **39**(3):10-13, Mar. 1964.

"The 121-horsepower 5010 that pulls seven 16's cost us only a little more than the latest model 5-plow tractor, which is just slightly more powerful than the ones we have," said the Burns brothers, Bill and Jim, who farm something over 1,000 acres along the Wabash in Lawrence county, Illinois. "By keeping the 5010 going two shifts a day we count on it to do all our plowing and to step up the pace of spring work so we can finish corn planting a good two weeks sooner. We believe it will plow as much ground as we turned with the two 5-plow rigs, each requiring a man, working regular hours last year."

The Burns brothers reached their decision to buy the big tractor and plow with the aid of Floyd Fuller, fieldman for the Lincoln Farm Bureau Management Association of which they are members. After a close look at the entire farm operation, Fuller advised them to go ahead.

The big tractor is scheduled to turn 60 acres each 24 hours when soil moisture conditions are good. One of the brothers or their regular hired man will run it during the day. For the night shift they will entrust the rig to part time hired help.

"We have a good man lined up," said Bill Burns. "So we aren't going to worry. Especially knowing this big equipment can take a lot of punishment and abuse. If a man hits a fence with this rig all that happens is to mash down the fence. The tractor and plow can keep right on going."

The brothers grow 800 acres of corn, 100 acres of beans, 90 acres of wheat and put up 120 acres of hay. They start planting corn the last of April, weather permitting, and this year they hope to have the last of it in the ground well before the end of May. Illinois research shows a consistent advantage in yield from early planting. On a corn crop of 800 acres early planting can easily make a difference counted in thousands of dollars.

Some of the corn is planted on land from which they first take a cutting of hay. With the big tractor and one extra man they hope this year to keep right on plowing, fitting and planting corn while the haying crew hustles to keep ahead

The brothers operate in partnership with their mother, Mrs. Pearl Burns, and two other landowners. They feed out 300 head of cattle and 2,500 head of hogs a year, and run a herd of 80 registered Angus cows. They have two 24 by 65 silos to fill which together hold 1,800 tons. In silo filling the big tractor will give them a lift where they need it. In the demonstration last fall the 5010 tractor ran their 2-row field chopper both faster and smoother than their 5-plow tractors did.

Since they bought the tractor and plow the Burns brothers had bought a new 2-ton truck with 18-foot body, hoist equipped. Their previous truck, with 16-foot body on hoist, is staying on the job to work alongside the new one.

"That extra two feet of length makes room for 6 to 8 extra hogs every load," said Jim Burns. "Last year the hog market dropped $2 a hundred while we were getting a bunch to market with our one truck. We can't afford to let that happen again. It is just as important to get to market on time with what you raise as it is to get crops planted on time."

In addition to hogs and cattle, the Burns brothers use trucks to haul grain, fertilizer and cobs for bedding. An auger which fits on the back of the new truck will be used to fill their corn planter with bulk fertilizer.

William Good, Calhoun county, Michigan, is another farmer who has confidently stepped up to the biggest tractor in the line. He will go into his fields this spring with a 119-horsepower Allis-Chalmers D-21 and seven 16-inch plows. He counts on it to plow 40 acres in a 10-hour day in most of the soils he works. His 5-plow tractor will follow up with a 15-foot disk and right behind it will be the 4-plow tractor with 4-row corn planter.

Last year Good plowed a day with the 4-plow and 5-plow rigs, then disked with the 5-plow and planted with the 4-plow tractor. The 1964 operation should go 50 percent faster, he said. He needs the extra capacity. Last year he worked 750 acres; this year he has taken on approximately 1,000 acres of cropland. It is nearly all rented. He owns only 120 acres. Good will grow 500 acres of corn, 200 acres of soybeans and 50 acres of oats. He has 250 acres of winter wheat to harvest this year.

All crops are harvested by Good's two Gleaner C combines, the largest model, with 4-row corn heads for both. One of these crowds the capacity of his neighbor's 550-bushel portable dryer working around the clock at the rate of three batches a day.

Good says big equipment is a snap to handle. His wife runs a 4-row combine and likes the job. "The cab is air conditioned, so it is comfortable in hot or cold weather," she says. "And the big machine is really easy to run." Her husband says: "The D-21 is the easiest handling tractor I ever drove. To steer it you move nothing but a valve. Even on the roughest ground this big baby doesn't fight you."

A self-propelled combine may help more than a bigger tractor. Burl Branz, Ford county Illinois, says if he had to make a choice he would choose the John Deere 45 self-propelled combine he bought a year ago over the 5-plow 4010 tractor he got at the same time. But he is well satisfied with his whole investment in $14,000 worth of bigger equipment. With the trade-ins he had, his cash outlay was just about $8000.

"Bill Janssen (fieldman for the Pioneer Farm Bureau Farm Management Association of which Branz is a director) said he could find only 2 bushels per acre field loss behind the combine in corn last fall," said Branz. "This compares with all the way from 8 to 20 bushels per acre lost with the picker and sheller attachment I used up to this year. The combine picks up down corn better, and by simply snapping the ear off with no husking action, it just about eliminates shelling at the snapping rolls."

Branz says his new combine cut the time required to harvest his 105-acre soybean crop to between 4 to 5 days last fall compared with 8 to 9 days it had required with his pull-type combine.

One of his problems when harvesting with the mounted two-row picker-sheller was that it tied up his best tractor for the season. With a low-rate drying system he wasn't able to get on with fall plowing during his waiting time. So he got behind with the whole cropping operation. "I had one of the lowest machinery investments per tillable acre in this farm management association for a while after going up from 235 to 470 acres, but I was at a disadvantage," said Branz. "I was definitely under-equipped."

Branz didn't get a bigger plow when he bought the 4010 tractor. Instead he used the same 4-bottom plow he had pulled (sometimes with difficulty) behind his 3-4 plow 70 Diesel tractor. "I plow a third faster with the 4010 and the same plow," he said. "And it makes the job a lot easier on me. The bigger tractor has better power steering and seating."

This young farmer has found that stepping up to 5-plow power and combine corn harvesting puts him in a position where he could probably handle his 470 acres without hired help.

Dr. A. G. Mueller, farm management specialist at the University of Illinois, says a number of farmers are finding they can handle between 400 and 500 acres with just their own labor plus some seasonal help when they equip with the big new tractors and harvesters.

Farmers who buy the big new equipment aren't kicking on the price they have to pay. At least none of those interviewed by this writer are. On the other hand, every last one of them said he would like to see the manufacturers beef up the equipment in step with the power these big new tractors deliver.

"I would be willing to pay a 50 percent higher price if the manufacturer would go all the way–build farm equipment up to the standards of industrial machinery," says Paul Dehring, a Macomb county, Michigan, farmer, commenting on the two-row self-propelled field chopper he owns. "Power is up, the engines are rugged, but the crop gathering mechanism is little if any improved over its original design for half this power," was Dehring's complaint. "This stuff has got to be beefed up," he says. "We can't afford breakdown after breakdown in the field."

Ivan and Allen Wiseman, Edwards county, Illinois, put the problem this way: "When a farmer buys a new and bigger harvesting machine he might just as well figure on losing the best part of the first week having it rebuilt to do the job. They just don't test these new machines under severe enough conditions. Crops get heavier year by year. Manufacturers need to get their sights up and design all machinery for today's bigger job—and tomorrow's still bigger one."

The chemicals keep coming

ROBERT RODALE

Pesticide is now a dirty word in most of American society. The message of persistent poison hazard has gotten through to millions of homeowners, gardeners, conservationists, bird-watchers and anti-pollutionists.

Note that the farmers are missing from that list. With the exception of organic farmers, our agriculturists are doing business as usual. The spray rig is still used; DDT and some other poisons are being phased out for certain uses, but other chemicals are being phased in. Tremendous promotional muscle has been used by the chemical industry to defend the multi-billion dollar farm market for insect killers, and the chemical salesmen have enjoyed widespread success.

Commercial farmers represent an entirely different type of customer from gardeners to the chemical salesman. Farmers are in business and listen closely to stories that crops will be destroyed unless this or that pesticide is used. Often tremendous sales pressure induces farmers to buy and use certain pesticides despite contrary advice by county agents or state agricultural experts.

Such a story was told in the book, *Chemical Fallout.* R. van den Bosch, an insect ecologist working on biological controls at the University of California at Berkeley, attacked the myth that the agricultural extension service with its county agents, farm advisors and extension entomologists largely control the type of pest-control methods used on farms. "Greater influence is exercised by the chemical and agro-service company salesmen and field representatives," van den Bosch said. Citing a 1966 study by Iowa State University, he showed that "farmers in that state place greater reliance on the chemical dealer than on the agricultural extension service for information on agricultural chemicals." What makes that revelation especially sad is that the agricultural extension service is far from being a voice of ecological awareness. The county agents are educated by agricultural colleges, which are greatly influenced by chemical farming ideas. The college professors get grants from chemical companies and often mouth the chemical line. Thus county agents are often just as likely to recommend pesticides as are the chemical salesmen, but perhaps without the shameless promises of bumper yields and rich profits. Salesmen make those promises, however, and farmers listen carefully.

The mistakes that such pressure can generate is illustrated by van den Bosch's article "The Azodrin Story in California." Azodrin, a product of Shell Chemical Company, was created to control cotton insects. Government tests of Azodrin began in 1964 and soon showed that while it killed bollworms, it was "one of the most highly destructive materials of entomophagous anthropods (predators and parasites) of any that we have ever tested," van den Bosch said. Treatment of a cotton field with Azodrin would kill the first crop of bollworms, but succeeding waves of the insects would find the fields clean of their usual insect enemies. In only one Agricultural Experiment Station test did Azodrin substantially increase cotton yield. Other tests were inconclusive. The experiment station therefore warned cotton farmers that using Azodrin could be an ecologic and economic hazard.

Despite the warnings, Shell Chemical went ahead with a major advertising and promotion campaign of Azodrin in 1967. Farmers were "desperately in need of a replacement for the largely outlawed organochlorine insecticides," said van den Bosch, and were receptive to promises made for this new insecticide. But Shell made a suggestion which, according to van den Bosch, was unprecedented in the U.S. The company advocated Azodrin spraying before the bollworms came to keep the field clean of insects. "Prophylactic use of insecticides in cotton has long been recognized as bad practice by California's research and extension personnel," said van den Bosch. He pointed out that prophylactic treatment puts chemicals where there is no infestation, hastens insect resistance, costs extra money and causes more environmental pollution. Prophylactic treatment of cotton has been a disaster in Peru, Colombia and Nicaragua; yet that history and the warnings of the experiment station did not deter the California farmers. The chemical company won out.

What happened? The yield of cotton in the San Joaquin Valley in 1967 "was one of the lowest of the last decade," van den Bosch said. Because of the complicating factors, it is difficult to put the blame directly on Azodrin, but it's clear there were no outstanding benefits from use of the chemical. There was, however, widespread damage to wildlife. Because the effect of Azodrin on humans was not then known, inspectors would not go into fields immediately after application. But four days later they found enough dead animals and birds to suspect that the chemical kill "may well have been massive." Crop dusters reported seeing sick pheasants shortly after they sprayed. There were even body counts. In Arizona, 365 dead birds of 17 species were picked up along 12 miles of field edge, and the California Fish and Game Department reported a "lack of living birds in treated areas where bird life had formerly been abundant."

Far more damaging to the integrity of American agriculture than one pesticide mistake is the frustration felt by an expert in applied insect ecology when the sound and scientific recommendations of his government department are overridden effectively by chemical company advertising campaigns. Sale of chemical pesticides is extremely profitable, and commercial farmers represent a market hungry for such products. The public seems to believe the pesticide problem has been solved by Rachel Carson's *Silent Spring* and subsequent publicity and ecological awareness. DDT has been banned, and experts have made so many statements about the harm of pesticides that we tend to think progress is being made toward a more natural agriculture. That, in fact, is not the case.

For many years the National Agricultural Chemicals Association published a report listing the official Food and Drug Administration tolerances for pesticide residues on all commercial crops. The same format and type size was used year after year. In 1964, the listing of permitted chemicals on foods and fiber crops was accommodated in 23 pages. By 1968 the listing had grown to 31 pages. The 1969 book had 33 pages. You would think that with all the anti-pesticide publicity in recent years, the book would at least stay the same size, but not so. Recently, publication of the annual tolerance report was suspended by NACA.

There has been a steady growth in the number of insecticides that may be applied to our foods. In 1964, farmers were allowed to apply 56 different pesticides on apples. By 1968, the number had increased to 67. In 1970, there were 72 permitted. The same kind of growth has been allowed on all foods. Furthermore, an apple grower in 1964 could theoretically sell an apple containing 350.45 parts per million of pesticide chemicals. By 1968, the tolerance had risen to 461.55 parts per million. In 1970, it was 379.70 parts per million, lower than 1968 but still higher than 1964.

Aggressive chemical sales activity has produced the dramatic and extensive mixing of chemical pesticides into our food supply. But the chemical producers could not have achieved the heights of pollution they now occupy without the willingness of American farmers to use their products. The farmers' dreams of affluence haven't been realized, though, for chemicals are expensive and neither yields nor prices have been consistently high enough to justify their added cost. But because farmers keep hoping, the public keeps suffering.

The changing realm of King Cotton

JOSEPH S. VANDIVER*

"What would happen if no cotton was furnished for three years? England would topple headlong and carry the whole civilized world with her save the South. No, you dare not make war on cotton. No power on earth dares make war on cotton. Cotton is king!" thundered James H. Hammond of South Carolina in the United States Senate.

The year was 1858, and King Cotton was riding high. The South produced nearly four million bales of cotton that year. Since the invention of the cotton gin in 1793, the sleepy tempo of the Southern economy had quickened to a boom, and the moribund institution of slavery had revived to meet the vastly increased labor needs of the expanding plantations.

The planter himself lived in a state of luxury without prior parallel in American life. Stephen Duncan, a Mississippi planter of the 1850's, owned eight plantations, 1,018 field slaves, and 23 house slaves, and produced 4,000 bales of cotton. His beautiful Greek Revival mansion near Natchez exemplified the legendary "Big House," its white pillars and porticos rising above the rolling green lawns and gardens that stretched for miles across the Mississippi countryside. Another planter, Greenwood Leflore, reputedly spent $10,000 to furnish one room of his mansion with imported Louis XIV chairs and sofas covered with gold leaf and crimson brocade.

"Great times in the Big House," recalled Isaiah Turner, a former Virginia slave. "Folks had plenty of money, and what they didn't buy, we raised for them. I remember the big parlor. Company come all the time, and the folks had big dinners. Fine ladies! Beautiful and they dressed like princesses. . . ."

The Civil War destroyed the institution of slavery which was so central to the entire plantation system. Many have chronicled the death of the Confederacy. However, what is not as well recorded is that, despite the devastation of the war, the plantations in the domain of King Cotton survived.

The green and white cotton fields of 1966 look much

*Joseph S. Vandiver is professor of sociology and chairman of the department at the University of Florida. He was born in the Mississippi Delta, and his research concerned Southern plantation areas. His other specialized interests include demographic research on fertility, minority problems, and the processes of sociocultural change in emerging societies, especially in Africa.

the same as those of 1859, but things have changed at the Big House. Morton Rubin, in his book, *Plantation County*, describes the living room of a contemporary Alabama plantation home:

None of the furniture in the room is older than twenty years. . . . The other rooms of the house—the dining room, electric kitchen, and bedroom upstairs—are too much like other American homes in the ten to twenty thousand dollar income class to warrant detailed description. . . . The house, like the plantation, is as modern as its owners can make it.

Despite the physical comfort, today's planter has little time to sit on the veranda sipping mint juleps. He is up at dawn, visiting the fields in his pickup truck or Land Rover and spending countless hours seeing that his tractors and mechanical harvesters are in good running order. He is a hard-working businessman managing an increasingly mechanized business. Cotton acreage had never risen much above the 10 million mark before the Civil War, but in 1930 the Southern soil was covered with 42 million acres of cotton. Today, improved agricultural methods have allowed Southern and Western cotton planters to reduce this acreage so that on one-third as much land they still produce about 15 million bales a year—nearly three times the amount produced in 1859, the peak year in pre-Civil War cotton production.

The plantation remains, but the system by which it operates, and the social corollaries of that system, have changed radically in the century since the end of the Civil War. How has King Cotton managed to survive? How has the transformation in his kingdom come about? And what effect has it had on the lives of his subjects—landowners and field hands alike?

FROM SLAVE TO SHARECROPPER

After the Civil War, laborless planters and jobless Negroes came together to form a new system that was, in many respects, very like the old. The freed slave, now a "sharecropper," continued to live in a rent-free house on the planter's land and was paid for his labor not in regular wages, but by a share of the crop produced on the acreage designated as "his." The cropper was in theory free to leave at any time if he did not care to continue working for a particular planter, and the high rate of interplantation mobility indicates that many did move. But the fact remained that the sharecropper's freedom consisted almost entirely of freedom to move from place to place *within* the plantation network. Few were equipped by training or habit—or lured by the prospect of better opportunities elsewhere—to abandon the cotton fields altogether.

The sharecropping system had obvious advantages for the planter. First and foremost, it supplied cheap labor. In addition, it anchored the laborer and his family until "settlement time" following the harvest; the cropper was not likely to leave the plantation before receiving his share of the year's profits. This assured the planter a guaranteed labor force and reduced the threat of interplantation competition for workers during "picking time" and other periods of peak demand. The cropper's interest in producing as much as possible on "his" acreage presumably motivated him to work hard. In bad years, the sharing system transferred some of the losses from the planter to the cropper.

The system also provided the planter with the opportunity to cheat his workers if he wanted to. The planter kept all the books concerning the operation, and the sharecropper had neither the education nor the legal protection to take issue with the planter's calculation of his share.

A side benefit for the planter was his operation of the plantation store. The sharecroppers could buy there on extended credit—but often at interest rates as high as 10 to 25 percent. Planters have defended this system on the grounds that their customers were very poor credit risks, but it is certain that the plantation commissaries were in business to make money as well as to provide a service for the Negro tenants of the plantation.

The sharecropping system also had advantages, though less obvious ones, for the newly emancipated Negro. The foremost was probably security. The system provided him a house, enough land to raise his own food, and enough credit at the plantation store to buy what he could not raise. It provided him the security of being retained throughout the season. And it allowed him to continue doing the kind of field work with which he was familiar.

At the same time, it gave him a sense of independence to have a certain acreage set aside as "his," which he could work as he pleased without the direct supervision of a white overseer. The freed Negro's reluctance to work as a laborer in a gang, so reminiscent of slavery, appears to have survived even today in plantation areas of the Deep South. Harold A. Pedersen, in an article on attitudes toward modernization in the Delta, relates a story told to him by a planter who was having trouble getting Negro men to work as tractor drivers on his newly mechanized plantation, despite the lure of higher pay.

As the story goes, a planter who planned to go fishing asked a small Negro boy how much he would charge to row the boat. The boy replied, "Two dollars," and the planter agreed. After they were out in the boat, however, the planter began to think that the price was unusually high, and asked the boy how much he was paid for his regular work at the local bait store. "One dollar," was the reply. Realizing that the planter expected some further explanation, the boy went on: "Well, you see, Mr. Joe (the owner) is in and out, but when you and me are out in that boat you're there looking at me all the time." The Negro tractor driver too works under the unblinking gaze of a white supervisor who is "there looking at him all the time," and he too dislikes it.

In addition to freedom from constant supervision, sharecropping had other advantages in the eyes of plantation Negroes. Most important were the eternal hope of a really good year and the certain and defined access to "furnish" from the landlord. Under the "furnish" system, the planter provided the cropper with the farm tools and implements necessary for his work plus a restricted credit for some food during the cold season and occasional extras such as tobacco and work clothes. One observer noted that the very fact that the planter provided each cropper with a mule was a lure; the animal was used for work, to be sure, but it also provided transportation to church, to town, and to the fishing stream. This "furnish" supplied by the landlord was considered an advance against the proceeds of that cropper's share, and the opportunity for dishonest bookkeeping thus provided the planter with yet another chance to cheat the cropper.

Thus the sharecropping system assured the planter his traditional supply of black field labor and assured the former slave his traditional access to food and shelter provided by the white man. The paternal role of the planter and the dependent role of the Negro field hand were basically unaltered. The sharecropping arrangement set the mold of stratified plantation society more firmly than ever, until the tradition-shattering days of the Great Depression.

By 1930, 25 percent of all farm operators and 44 percent of all tenant farmers in the South were sharecroppers. Most of these—particularly in cotton plantation areas—worked under some such arrangement as the "standard" sharecropping pattern described above. Certain variations on the theme emerged in some parts of the South, however.

In the 1920's, a quasi-sharecropping system had developed in the Corpus Christi area of Texas. It later spread to the Mississippi Delta and throughout the cotton country of the Southeast. Under this system, the worker became part laborer and part cropper—usually more the former than the latter, though he was likely to be statistically classified as a sharecropper. A small acreage which he and his family worked on shares immobilized him through the season, but much of the time he worked as a day hand on acreage unassigned to shares. Various modifications emerged; some plantations assigned workers exclusive rather than shared benefits from very small tracts, a system reminiscent of the *minifundia* arrangements of Colombia and other parts of Latin America. Or, as plantations become increasingly mechanized, tractor drivers, who were needed constantly during the season, might be anchored by shares assigned to their families.

THE SHARECROPPER'S REVOLT

In 1930, however, mechanization still seemed far away, and the traditional system of sharecropper field labor was the accepted arrangement on most plantations. Then came the depression. Planters had to cut back on the number of workers they could maintain, and many sharecroppers were turned off the land they had come to regard as their own. Unemployment spiralled, and labor agitation was in the air. The first sharecroppers' union sprang up in Tallapoosa County, Alabama, in 1931. It was organized by industrial workers who stressed the hardships of the depression to kindle grievances among the Negro croppers who had been or faced the threat of being displaced from the land.

In 1934, the Southern Tenant Farmers Union was organized in Arkansas. It challenged cotton country tradition not only by the mere fact of its existence, but by being bi-racial—an alliance of the Negro and the poor white. Retribution was swift and merciless, making the brief career of the STFU one of the bloodiest episodes in the history of American unionism. Howard Kester, one of the leading organizers of the STFU, described the situation in his 1936 book, *Revolt Among the Sharecroppers:*

While violence of one type or another has been continually poured out upon the membership of the union . . . it was in March 1935 that a "reign of terror" ripped into the country like a hurricane. For two-and-a-half months, violence raged through northeastern Arkansas and in neighboring states. . . . Meetings were banned and broken up; members were falsely accused, arrested and jailed, convicted on trumped-up charges and thrown into prison; relief was shut off; union members were evicted from the land by the hundreds; homes were riddled with bullets from machine guns; churches were burned and schoolhouses stuffed with hay and floors removed; highways were patrolled night and day by armed vigilantes looking for the leaders; organizers were beaten, mobbed and murdered until the entire country was terrorized.

Kester describes the famous STFU strike of 1936:

On a given night the strike bills were distributed throughout the territory. So effectively were they distributed that many people thought an airplane had dropped them down on the cabins. On the following day, a strange emptiness hung over the cotton fields. Most of the workers did not go to the fields, and those who did soon returned to their cabins. . . . A labor official from Little Rock made a trip through the cotton country to see how effective the strike was. He reported that he saw two workers picking cotton. The strike was effective, and the cotton hung in the bolls until the union told the men to go back to work.

The STFU eventually foundered, but the Delta would never be the same again. The mold had begun to crack. In the decades that followed, three forces—acreage restriction, Negro emigration from the South, and mechanization—were to revolutionize the cotton kingdom.

SUBSIDIES FOR THE RICH, PENALTIES FOR THE POOR

When, starting in 1933, the Agricultural Adjustment Administration (AAA) restricted cotton acreage, plantation labor demands were further reduced. Some planters retained their croppers even though there was little work for them to do. Others, feeling the pinch, cut their labor force again and turned more croppers off the land. Shrewd croppers often used their persuasive powers to obtain enough "furnish" to end the season in debt, assuming that the planter would retain those croppers who owed him money.

Acreage restrictions not only reduced the total labor needs of the plantation, but also encouraged a shift from sharecropping to wage labor. Government payments for acreage restrictions, soil conservation, and the soil bank required division of receipts between owner and tenant. The sharecropper, defined as tenant, was thus eligible for such payments, but landowners operating the entire establishment as a unit employing wage labor had the right to unshared retention of the government money.

By transferring their laborers from a sharecropping to a wage basis, and by other legal maneuvers, many planters were able to cheat their tenants out of AAA payments. A government research team found, in 1936, that landlords had received an average of $822 per plantation, compared with $108 per plantation for *all* the tenants put together. As observers Fred S. Frey and T. Lynn Smith accurately remarked at the time, the AAA program had turned out to be no more than "a mere subsidy to planters."

The reduced rate of Negro migration from the South during the 1930's, combined with the reduced need for plantation labor under the acreage restriction program, led to a labor surplus. This situation further aided the planters in monopolizing AAA payments, since they did not have to offer a crop share in order to get workers. But in forsaking the customary share-cropping arrangement for the express purpose of profiting at the tenant's expense, the landlord was contributing to a breakdown of a way of life. Not only did his action alter the external economic relationship between the Big House and the field workers, but it contributed to the growth of mistrust and hatred among the already destitute black laborers of the cotton country. No longer could the planter be counted upon to provide for "his people."

THE GREAT MIGRATION

Many planters retained workers they did not need during the depression and gave their sharecroppers a fair share of the AAA payments. But when World War II broke out, even these sharecroppers left the land by the thousands to join the armed forces or to take well-paid jobs in the urban war-industry centers.

During the decade between 1940 and 1950, well over one million Negroes left the South. The state of Mississippi alone lost an estimated 258,000—many of them sharecroppers and their families. They headed for the big industrial centers of the North and the West—for New York, Chicago, Detroit, and Los Angeles. Between 1940 and 1950, state-by-state estimates show that the Negro population increased by 243,000 in New York; by 193,000 in Michigan; by 180,000 in Illinois; and by 259,000 in California.

Once started, the pattern of migration seemed self-perpetuating. The Negro exodus from the South not only continued, but, according to most estimates, increased during the period from 1950 to 1960. During this time, the state of Mississippi lost some 264,000 Negroes—several thousand more than in the preceding decade. Again, it is evident that a large proportion of these people were plantation field laborers and their families.

Part of the reason for this continuing migration may have been the government's re-imposition of cotton acreage restrictions during the 1950's. Employment opportunities for unskilled labor were shrinking in the North after the war ended, but they were shrinking even more rapidly in the plantation areas of the South. An additional 243,000 Negroes poured into New York state (mostly into the ghettos of Harlem and Bedford-Stuyvesant in New York City); 159,000 into Illinois; 110,000 into Michigan; and 220,000 into California.

MAN AND MACHINE

Plantation mechanization in the cotton country, even more than renewed acreage restriction, reduced work opportunities and spurred continuing Negro migration during the 1950's. Many planters had mechanized during the war to escape dependence on an unsure labor force. Others expressed bitterness over having been left short of hands during the 1940's after they had retained extra workers during the depression out of a sense of paternalistic responsibility. Now they no longer felt compunctions about replacing men with machines.

A circular situation developed; departing workers encouraged mechanization, and mechanization encouraged workers to leave. To the extent that laborers viewed mechanization as inevitable, decisions about migration may have been influenced in advance of actual mechanization on their own plantations. Planters sometimes purchased machines to use if needed, leaving them idle as long as workers were still there; an unused mechanical picker in the machine shed could in itself be a powerful factor inducing the remaining workers to accept whatever terms were available.

By the 1950's, it was evident that weed control, rather than harvesting, was the final challenge to be overcome for full mechanization of cotton production in the humid Southeastern climate. Most planters felt that checkerboard planting, the rotary plow, and the flamethrower, while useful, could not be depended on in wet years to control the growth of weeds. Thus a certain labor reservoir of weed choppers was needed. With these people on hand, there was a tendency to use them for a variety of operations, so many planters ran a less mechanized business than existing skill and equipment made possible.

By the end of the 1950's, such partial mechanization reached into all portions of the cotton belt. The process started earlier and advanced more rapidly in the Delta areas of Arkansas, Mississippi, and Louisiana than elsewhere. In every area, it advanced unevenly. Harold A. Pedersen and Arthur F. Raper tell the story of "Tractor Plantation" where the entire operation was mechanized except for two tenant tracts, still farmed with mules in the old way; the occupants had been on the plantation a long time and were permitted to remain, undisturbed by the transformation under way around them.

Under the impact of partial mechanization, share-cropping receded rapidly in the latter part of the 1950's. Bolivar County, Mississippi, which had 10,643 sharecropping units in 1930, reported only 975 in the 1959 Census of Agriculture. Plantations have always used casual labor from nearby towns and cities during periods of peak demand, but, with the reduced working force on the land, such labor has become relatively more important. These day workers are sometimes recruited by "truckers" who haul them to the plantations; the wise planter seeks the cooperation of a dependable trucker to maintain an adequate labor supply.

Very recently, the last barriers to full mechanization have been giving way. In 1962, about 75 percent of the cotton in the Delta areas of Mississippi and Louisiana was harvested mechanically. More important, the chemical breakthrough in weed control by the use of herbicides promises to be effective enough and inexpensive enough to clear the remaining bottleneck to complete mechanization. Widespread adoption of herbicides is now occurring, particularly in the Delta.

As plantations come to rely upon mechanization and wage labor for their operations, they are evolving a new institutional structure and new occupational roles. The modern plantation is a small bureaucracy, with laborers working under a labor supervisor and with machine operations under the "manager." The fact that the title of "manager" goes to the man with responsibility for the machines suggests where the greatest importance is placed. Workers with a problem go to their supervisor; on the traditional plantation, the owner was personally accessible to the workers and handled their requests directly.

All indications suggest that the mechanization process is now accelerating in plantation areas, particularly in the Mississippi Delta. There is no indication that the final stages of mechanization are required because of lack of labor. Rather the impetus and the irreversibility of the process itself seem to be involved. There is little basis to assume, optimistically, that its completion will be painless to those Negroes who are providing the field labor still utilized.

In early June of 1965, the ghost of the depression-spawned STFU stirred, and the first plantation strike in three decades hit the Mississippi Delta. The STFU's successor was the Mississippi Freedom Labor Union, organized in close alliance with the cotton-belt civil rights movement.

A GHOST WALKS THE DELTA

Challenging the white overlords of the Delta's quarter-of-a-billion-dollar-a-year cotton industry, Negro plantation workers struck for higher wages. The tractor drivers were only receiving $6 for a 14-hour day, and $3 for a 10-hour day was the going rate for weed choppers (mostly the wives and children of the tractor men). The workers demanded $1.25 per hour for both drivers and choppers.

The planters were adamant in their refusal to give in to the union demands. "Wages are really too high now," said one planter, "because we don't really need hand labor. We could do the job better, quicker, and cheaper with machinery and chemicals." The implication was clear; the weed choppers, by striking, were only hastening their own replacement by angering the planters into full and immediate mechanization.

Current labor agitation in the Delta, like that of the 1930's, reflects the existence of a labor surplus combined with diminishing opportunities for employment. Contrary to the trend from 1930 to 1960, recent population estimates in the Delta and "brown loam" plantation counties of Mississippi indicate that, since 1960, the number of nonwhites in this area has remained stationary or has actually increased. Other figures, which are not broken down by race, show that the state lost a total of only 12,000 people in the period 1960-1963; even if we assume that all of these 12,000 were Negro, this figure is well below the three-year average for Negro migration out of Mississippi for any period since 1940. More complete data are lacking, but it appears that, if Negro migration from the cotton country has indeed slowed down to this degree—presumably as a result of the current weakness of the "pull" of Northern metropolitan areas for nonwhites of low skill—then a marked piling up of young adults must be occurring at the very time that agricultural wage labor is being replaced by herbicides and mechanical picking.

This labor situation will undoubtedly exercise a powerful effect on the nature of the civil rights movement in the plantation areas of the South. These areas are already islands of poverty in the Southern countryside. In 10 typical cotton counties of Alabama, Arkansas, Louisiana, Mississippi, North Carolina, and South Carolina, 61 percent of the residents in 1959 were nonwhites; of these, 44 percent received a family income of less than $1,000 for the year, and fully 90 percent received less than $3,000. What will happen as the current wave of social protest penetrates this group, whose already precarious livelihood is now in danger of being cut off altogether by the advent of tractors and weed killers in the cotton fields?

The 1965 protests of the Mississippi Freedom Labor Union and the responsiveness of many Negroes in the area to the theme of "black power" in 1966 offer hints of what may come. The under-employed Negroes in the poverty areas of the cotton belt find migration unpromising, have plenty of time to demonstrate, and have little to risk by doing so. As one young MFLU striker was quoted in *Newsweek:* "We ain't got nothin', so we ain't got nothin' to lose."

This much is certain—fewer and fewer young Negroes will wind up spending their lives as plantation field hands, picking cotton and chopping weeds. The plantation of Southern legend is gone for good. Whether or not the large tracts of machine and chemical cultivated acreage that are now emerging will still be called "plantations," and whether or not their operators invest themselves with the sentimental trappings of the old order, the transition will likely be a painful one.

FURTHER READING SUGGESTED BY THE AUTHOR

Southern Tradition and Regional Progress, by William H. Nicholls. Chapel Hill, N.C.: University of North Carolina Press, 1960.

Mississippi: The Closed Society, by James Wesley Silver. New York: Harcourt, Brace and World, 1966.

The New Revolution in the Cotton Economy, by James Harry Street. Chapel Hill, N.C.: University of North Carolina Press, 1957.

Family farm problems

There was a joke, not so very long ago, that the only way a person could get into farming was through marriage or inheritance. Then land prices shot upward to the point where the joke became reality. Now, it seems, one can't even afford to inherit a farm.

We are indebted to Prof. Philip Raup of the University of Minnesota for supplying the figures that support such statements. With the cost of an "average farm" starting at around $250,000—that's a quarter of a million bucks—the chances of any young family going into farming are practically nil.

Prof. Raup removed the "practically." He said: "With average ability and luck it is out of the question for a beginning farm family to accumulate a sufficient down payment to buy into an agriculture enterprise on this scale, even if we assume the most generous credit terms available."

Now, farmers grow old and think of retirement, just like the rest of us, so farms come up for grabs; valued at a quarter-million or half a million or more dollars. A nice inheritance for the children? Well, sure, if the children are interested (and there's no guarantee that

farm children have any more desire to follow in the Old Man's footsteps than any other children), and as Raup pointed out, if they can handle the taxes involved in the transfer.

The taxes were set up in the days before runaway land valuations, Raup said, and they are big enough to make it impossible for families in good farm areas to pass their holdings on to their children without selling some land to pay the tax costs of transfer.

The situation is made to order for delivering Minnesota farms into the hands of Colossal Conglomerates, Inc., for only big operators have the cast or credit to deal.

We can see no gain to the world in turning the land of independent farmers over to corporate boards of directors—whether in New York or Tokyo. We prefer to take our food chances with the man with calloused hands, the private citizen and taxpayer.

Prof. Raup suggested legislative action to reduce inheritance taxes on farmland. This certainly should be looked into. But a 70 percent increase in land values in three years can't be changed by any legislature. Perhaps time will alter the figures. Right now it appears there are an awful lot of Future Farmers of America with no farms in their future.

□ From *Wisconsin Farmers Union News*, Chippewa Falls, Wis., February 14, 1975.

Big ones eat the little ones in machine-made farm crisis

H. C. McGINNIS

An estimated one and one-half million people left the nation's farms during each of the three years prior to 1940—the last year for which figures are available—and over 40,000 of the families involved were farm owners. Many of these unfortunates come from

very productive farming States with no unusual climatic features. Most of such dispossessed people become migrants, others settle on submarginal land to eke out bare existences, still others crowd into city slums where they live in unbelievable squalor. These disasters come mostly through the rapidly increasing trend in American agriculture toward mass produc-

□ From *America* **61**(14):374-376, July 11, 1942.

tion. In farming, as in industrial life, the big ones are eating the little ones.

If the present trend remains unchecked, that dependable anchor of civilization—the family unit farm—will soon by a thing of the past. While there are still thousands of productive, family-size farms which afford a healthful and satisfactory living for large families and then a sufficient income for the parents upon their old age, they are becoming strikingly fewer with each generation. This trend, largely due to agricultural inequalities, has been greatly accentuated during the past decade or so. This is due to several proved reasons.

Of the reasons, two are most important. One, easily corrected by a change in Government regulations, is a development in the Agricultural Adjustment Administration's workings which the Government never expected. The other is the rapidly growing system of "farm management" which invites the consolidation of scores of family-size farms into huge tracts which are farmed mechanically for absentee landlords, usually corporations or big business men. There are also two reasons why the general public must become conversant with these farm trends. First, the time is at hand when the nation's political democracy must be translated into economic democracy. Second, any matter which affects adversely thirty-three million people constitutes a social problem which cannot be safely ignored.

The AAA program, which was intended to help small farmers, has caused—through its $10,000 limit on benefits—the large owner who formerly rented most of his ground to take over this land for personal operation. In other cases, the "haves" have dispossessed tenant farmers by overbidding them when their leases came up for renewal. On the surface, it would appear that this affects only tenant farmers but it also affects the family-size farm as we shall later see.

In one sparsely populated North Dakota county, thirty families were put off their farms in this way and the Tolan investigating committee found that most of them went on relief, since other work was not locally available. In another Dakota community, one farmer farms 8,000 acres and when his AAA payments reached the maximum limit, he deeded land to his son who became the possible receiver of another $10,000. Another Dakotan, owning land in two counties, asked twenty of his renters to move so he could become eligible for maximum AAA benefits. In Iowa, one farmer, originally farming 200 home acres, leased 40 acres 3 miles away, 440 acres 6 miles away, and 320 located 75 miles from home. Motorized, rubber-tired equipment, plus trucks for carrying smaller pieces, make such farming possible.

In communities where productive land and excellent highways make such farming possible, the impact of dispossessed tenants is not immediately felt. Families dispossessed from northern Iowa's rich farms, for example, may crowd out those on southern Iowa's poorer lands by outbidding. These southern Iowans may later dispossess people on still poorer Ozark land. The Ozarkians, not being able to find cheaper land, either hitch up Old Dobbin or crank up the jalopy and, with their meager belongings, swell the migratory hordes who flood the West and Southwest.

Continuing this illustration, we see that while the dispossessed tenant is usually forced to leave the district, the family-size farmer also suffers, either through bankruptcy or a greatly reduced standard of living. When large-scale, mass-production farming invades a district, its operators, well heeled, use only the latest equipment which reduces unit cost considerably. In the Corn Belt, mechanical pickers, by eliminating much hand labor and many other costs, enable their owners to sell corn at a price which drives the smaller man out of business. Machines are being developed which not only pick corn mechanically, but also shell and bag it in the same operation, delivering it ready for market without the cost of further handling and storing.

Such developments eliminate the 80 to 160-acre farmer, for only large-scale operators can afford such equipment and, say what you will, the man with the hoe is not competition for tractor-powered, mechanized equipment. Incidentally, there can be no just complaint against the increased use of mechanized equipment which increases production and lowers food costs to the consumer. The problem is to use machines to produce more wealth and create better living standards for the many, not a very few. In today's farming, as in industry, machines can be a boon to everyone, eliminating drudgery and bettering living standards, or else a means of further stripping the "have-nots" by the "haves."

Since it is evident that the present economic system is not based upon a sufficiently high morality to cause those who are driving America's farm homes into oblivion to cease their selfishness, nor is there sufficient morality in those farm bloc legislators, who are supported by those who are hogging Government benefits, to give any great hope for corrective legislation in the near future, obviously the family-size farm and its occupants are in for continued rough sledding. Community-owned mechanized equipment of the latest type, which will permit the small independent farmer to compete successfully with the low production cost of the large operators, seems a logical answer.

But the dispossessing of the settled tenant farmer

by those who find the AAA's offerings too tempting to ignore need only be temporary, for an adjustment in the benefit scale, favoring the small farmer either by decreasing the $10,000 maximum or else by spreading payments rather thin as they reach the top, would end much of this evil. Some such changes are badly needed, for, although temporarily lessened by the war, the migrancy of farm families has reached crisis proportions. Some say that most of these migrants are of the habitually ne'er-do-well type, but the Tolan committee found otherwise. In one group of 1,343 migrant families examined, only 11 were habitual roamers, 10 were subject to unknown causes, and the balance were victims of injustices in our agricultural system. The families examined ranged from 3 to 11 persons each and the ages of the family heads ranged between 25 and 45, the greatest productive period in farming.

However, the correction of back-firing Government regulations is not the complete solution. Mammoth-scale farming under farm management systems for absentee landlords threatens to create a class of farm barons who will rival the princes of industry. Comparatively few people who are not directly connected with or interested in agriculture realize the growth of this trend which threatens the security of twenty-five per cent of the nation. When one talks about large scale farms, he means those with a minimum income of $30,000 annually.

The Tolan committee, investigating why over 4,000,000 people wander over the country homeless and jobless, uncovered some startling facts. In Ohio, long known for the prosperity of its family-size farms, a 9,000-acre farm was one brought to its attention. This one farm meant the end of many small farms and the closing of many happy homes. One expects 9,000-acre farms in the wheat country, but certainly not in States like Ohio where diversified crops have been the rule. Several other Ohio farms approached this one in size. Similar conditions were found in other States where, a few years ago, 300 acres were a large holding.

In one Arizona district, there are 35,000 acres of cotton owned by absentee landlords, virtually all living in other States. A reputable committee witness reported that he saw not a single first-rate dwelling in the district and, in fact, very few of any kind. The exceptions were houses for foremen and shacks for irrigation tenders. During the growing season, however, the land is dotted with tents and shacks of migrant workers. The tract is under the control of professional farm managers whose sole interest is to make profit for themselves and the owners. Obviously there is no place here for the family-raising, independent grower, who cannot hope to compete with his mammoth neighbor.

A reliable survey made in 1938 in California showed 38 farming corporations holding 991,009 acres. $72,825,295 was reported by 18 corporations as the value of the land and improvements tied up in 428,131 acres. Another corporation reported a book value of $25,152,660 for its farms. How can a farmer feed a family when he has to buck competition like that? The answer is, he does not. When the family becomes too hungry, he either moves into the hinterland to do subsistence farming or else becomes another migratory worker.

Most of the large-scale operations are under the management of management concerns which style themselves "master farmers." Staffed by men who study the latest scientific methods and then devote themselves to mass production and increased profits through mechanization, these organizations encourage absentee landlordism by making it profitable. In order to operate economically, the management concerns must unite large acreages, which are usually owned by wealthy industrialists and by corporations which seek to escape taxes. One management company operates 190 such acreages, including a 2,000-acre one owned by a railroad.

The increasing number of wealthy industrialists who have become absentee farm owners is significant. In some wealthy circles, it has become all the rage. Such practice can scarcely be called a fad, for farms operated by professional management offer a safe place for surplus funds. Perhaps a deeper lying reason is that mass production tends to lower the price of farm products—for obviously the small producer must match the selling prices of his big competitors—and cheaper food means less demand for higher wages.

So the absentee landlord, when an industrialist, plays both ends toward the middle. He not only makes farm profits; he also depresses food prices so that industrial workers will increase his profits by not demanding wage increases. Not satisfied with that, he often further increases his profits by buying his farm equipment from its manufacturers, thus eliminating the local implement dealer who is now wondering how long he can last. With his territory denuded of inhabitants and with absentee owners buying direct, this time-honored community service is preparing to fold its tents and silently steal away.

In sections where professional-managed, absentee-owned farms exist, conditions become steadily worse for small farmers. While those few who are hired by management companies to handle mechanized equipment are much better off than farm laborers, the less fortunate are reduced to seasonal laborers or, stubbornly continuing farming, compete against ruinous prices. Their sons, who formerly acquired farms by first working as farm hands, then renting and finally buying, now seek either industrial employment or migratory labor. Their daughters also must seek elsewhere for husbands and homes of their own.

The more one goes into the ramifications of this problem, the less inviting it becomes; for it affects not only the nation's farm population but will ultimately dangerously lower the national social standard. The entire situation is only another aspect of laissez-faire policies, and since a higher morality in the nation's economic life does not appear imminent, cooperative production by small farmers seems the best practical answer immediately available.

Agribusiness and the decaying rural environment

RICHARD MERRILL

. . . rapid movement of large conglomerate corporations and other non-farm interests into agriculture . . . is a matter of serious concern to thousands of rural people across America. We are rapidly approaching the time . . . when this nation must decide whether the family farm . . . defined in terms of both size and degree of managerial independence, is forced to vanish from the American scene. This is the same family farm which year after year has proven itself to be the most efficient and effective producer of food and fiber in the world.

SEN. GAYLORD NELSON, 1968

We have come to realize in the union that the issue of pesticide poisoning is more important today than even wages, although wages are very low, working conditions are unbelievable, and bargaining power is nil. . . . Our people who are poisoned are not permitted to have coverage under the workman's compensation program . . . we are not going to be part of the systematic poisoning of hundreds of our people in the fields.

CESAR CHAVEZ, 1969

THE FARMER AS EXPATRIOT

Sometime around the beginning of the 20th century, the number of farms in the United States reached a total of six million. The total was still around six million in 1940. During this time a few changes in the rural countryside took place: the average size of the farm increased slightly, more land was "reclaimed" and tractors began to fill the horse's niche in the fields. But throughout the whole period the number of farms remained fairly constant. "Six million American farms" served for 40 years as a basic concept in agricultural economics.

But following World War II, the number of farms began to decline rapidly. War-time economy had relocated many people from agriculture, forcing the remaining farmers to mechanize or cease to be farmers.

Since the war, while the United States has grown by 55 million people, 3 million farms have disappeared in the technological revolution that is still sweeping agriculture. More than 30 million people have abandoned rural lands and towns for the cities so that 75% of our people are now crowded onto less than 2% of the land.

In many ways, the relocation of our rural society and the emergence of large landholders in farming areas have created the national crisis of the environment and society which lies at the heart of all the talk about ecology. Indeed, the problem of the changing relationship between the people and the land and the deprivation of many of opportunity on the land has set off a chain of further reactions culminating in a vast unplanned and uncontrolled migration of rural America into the large urban centers of the North and West and in an upheaval in the life of rural society itself. We point with pride to the fact that now only a small percentage of the total population produces our food needs. But we tend to forget that for many people the transition was involuntary and without adequate compensation: that many people have been forced from their land only into an economic and social limbo in rural towns and urban ghettos, and that the "efficient" operations of modern agricultural technology have produced vast ecological disruptions in America's rural environment.

"DUN AND BRADSTREET SODBUSTERS"

In terms of levels of productivity, there have been three agricultural revolutions. The first came when man began substituting animal power for human muscles. The second brought machine energy to replace animal energy, and put the findings of scientific research onto the farm. The third, the farmers' adoption of business management techniques, to capitalize

□ From Modern agriculture and the quality of life, pp. 6-12.

Some agricultural statistics—U.S.A.

Year	% pop. on farm	Aver. acre/farm	Total no. farms	Commer. fert. used	Total val. farm mach.	Thous. lbs. DDT prod.
1920	30.1	147	6518			
1930	24.9	151	6546			
1940	23.2	167	6350	8556 tons		
1948						20,240
1950	15.3	213	5648	20,345 tons	12,166 mil. $	
1953						84,366
1958						145,328
1960	8.7	297	3962	24,374 tons	22,344 mil. $	
1968				37,383 tons	31,136 mil. $	
1969	5.1	378	2971			

on farm technology, has been most responsible for the above trends in rural emigration and land tenure patterns.

There are several examples to show that big business now rules the agrarian scene, especially in the South and West and particularly in Florida, California, Texas, Arizona and Hawaii. In 1969 the largest 40,000 farms . . . less than 2% of the total . . . accounted for more than one third of all American farm sales. Big canners like Minute Maid, a subsidiary of Coca Cola, and Libby-McNeill and Libby, own about 20% of Florida's citrus groves, compared with less than 1% in 1960. In California, corporate farms account for 90% of the melon crop, 46% of the cattle sold, 38% of the cotton produced and 30% of the citrus fruits. In addition, forty five corporations now own 3.7 million acres or nearly half of the farm land in the state. On a national scale, two conglomerates, Purex and Unified Brands, now control one third of the green leafy vegetable production in the United States. Other blue chips getting into farming, according to the Agribusiness Accountability Project, include Gulf and Western, Penn Central, Del Monte, Getty Oil, Goodyear, Monsanto, Union Carbide, Kaiser Aluminum, Aetna Life, Boeing and Dow Chemical. (1)

Why have major non-farm corporations suddenly become interested in farming? Why is agriculture moving from a large-scale mechanized operation into a corporate enterprise? There are several reasons. For one, we can quote Simon Askin, Tenneco's Executive Vice-President for Agriculture and Land Development. "We consider land as an inventory, but we are all for growing things on it while we wait for a price appreciation for development. Agriculture pays the taxes plus a little."

By investing tax-free monies in farm land and thus increasing its real estate value, a company can sell the land to other speculators with earnings in the form of capital gains (taxes at 25% rather than 43%). As a short term investment then, farm land can be quite lucrative.

The rate at which land is being "developed" in this way is staggering and it is not inaccurate to say that agricultural land today is urban land tomorrow. Consider California, which leads the nation in value of farm produce, and where the current rate of conversion of agricultural land to other uses is over 300 acres per day! An examination of the trends in irrigated farmlands for counties at the periphery of urban sprawls shows that during the period 1954-1964 nearly 200,000 acres of such land was urbanized and lost to food production. (2) That amounts to nearly 800 acres per week of *prime agricultural land!* Moreover, the trend is accelerating. According to the Soil Conservation Service between 1967 and 1980 another two million acres, or nearly 20% of all farm land will have "gone under" to urban development.

Besides land speculation, many corporations may also use farming as one part of conglomerates that control every stage of the food production and distribution process from "seedling to supermarket." For capital, these corporations have their own chemicals and machinery, processing and packaging plants. With this level of competition the small farmer is forced off of his land and into the cities. Even Orville Freeman, when he was Secretary of Agriculture, noted that "there could be real trouble if (the conglomerates) move into agriculture . . . They already have contributed to the building up of land values. They can go into a farm and write off their losses as a tax deduction on a very profitable operation elsewhere. When this happens, dangerously unfair competition takes place."

Examples of the incorporation of agriculture and its effects can best be seen in California where agriculture remains the biggest state's biggest business.

THE SECOND GREAT GOLD RUSH

Speeding along highway 99 in central California it is hard to imagine the nature of the farming operations that are taking place in the hinterlands of one of the richest agricultural areas in the world. For many years California has been the leading farm state. The value of its farm products exceeds $4 billion a year. Besides growing 24% of the table food in the country, California supplies the nation with 40% of its vegetables, fruits and nuts, 90-100% of 15 food crops and leads the nation in another 25. This production generates at least $12 billion in related businesses such as canning, processing, shipping, distribution and banking.

For the most part, however, farmers in California are not the industrious, earth-bound individuals that America has so long revered. Rather, they are the same corporate giants and large landholders who have controlled the political, social and ecological destinies of California for over a century (2,3): Bank of America, Southern Pacific, Wells Fargo Bank, DiGiorgio Corp., Kern County Land Co. (now called Tenneco), etc. Outfits like these from the beginning of statehood history have seized ownership of California's prime agricultural land through Mexican land grants, federal railroad grants and land speculation subsidies. Today with most farm land in the hands of a few large corporate farms (18% of the farms control over 80% of the agricultural economy in the state), land monopoly in California remains little more than a carry over from the Spanish Ranchos and speculation of the gold rush days.

These corporate farms differ from the family-type farm inasmuch as the direct sale of farm products is not their only source of income, nor is farming their only . . . or even primary interest. Usually the farming operations are tied in with packing houses, canneries, shipping concerns, wineries, distilleries, cotton gins, etc., while others are controlled by retail outlets such as Safeway or Del Monte. Most of the owners act as directors of other food-related industries. Also, since most corporate farms are only part of a larger business complex, they are usually bound by interlocking directorates with other economically powerful kinds of corporations . . . utilities, railroads and manufacturing industries. Their combined influence is generally recognized as being one of the most influential lobbies in Washington.

At the financial head of the vast California agricultural industry is the Bank of America, which finances half of all agriculture in the state. Says Rudolph Peterson, past president of the Bank: "Bank of America has a deep stake in agriculture. We are the world's largest agricultural lender with lines of credit for agricultural production running at about a billion dollars a year. Our total agricultural commitment is probably around $3 billion. In a very real sense, then, agriculture is our business."

Peterson is also on the boards of Dillingham Corp. (which controls much of Hawaii's sugar crop), Kaiser Industries, Consolidated Food Corp., the State Chamber of Commerce and the DiGiorgio Corp.

DiGiorgio, in turn, is one of the largest growers in California. Today DiGiorgio Corp. has become an international complex of consumer goods, forest products, recreational vehicles and land development. The corporation has four directors in common with Bank of America, including Robert DiGiorgio who is also on the boards of directors for Pacific Vegetable Oil Corp., Philadelphia Fruit Exchange, Inc., and Pacific Telephone and Telegraph Co.

Other sorts of inter-corporate structures in agribusiness enterprises could be described at length for Kern Co. Land Co. (Tenneco), Tejon Ranch (owned partly by the L.A. Times whose editor Norman Chandler is a director of Safeway Stores, Santa Fe Railway, Pan American Airways etc.), California Packing Corp. (Del Monte), Hunts Foods and Industries (owner of Wesson Oil, Snowdrift Co., United Can and Glass Co., Fuller Paint Co., Ohio Match Co., etc.) and others. And these are only a few of the many tie-ups between agriculture and the centers of economic power which spread into every major bank and large corporation in the state. The result: one of the tightest corporate monopolies in the country. The situation is well summed up by Anne Draper in a recent pamphlet *The Dirt on California: Agribusiness and the University:* "It would be an exaggeration to say that agribusiness is the master of the social order in California, but it would be an exaggeration only because agribusiness shades into the financial power structure so neatly and it is that combination which is the master."

Against such mega-farming activities the small farmer is forced to sell the products of his toil on the so-called open market, while at the same time he must buy machinery, fuel, chemicals etc. at administered prices . . . fixed by the giant monopolies that control most of the farm land! Obviously the idea of free enterprise in the agricultural market place becomes little more than a platitude when farms are no longer operated by farmers but by the same people who run the utilities, railroads, banks, canneries and retain chains.

AGRIBUSINESS ON THE WELFARE ROLES

Agribusiness is given other competitive advantages by the Federal Farm Subsidy Program. For many years these programs of giving monies to agriculture have been concerned with production and not with the problems of the small farmer. The subsidies help redistribute income from workers to growers and from small growers to big growers. They are designed to benefit primarily the narrow interests of large landowners and farmers, making them some of the largest welfare recipients in the country. (4,5)

Basically there are four kinds of subsidies which the federal and state governments dole out:

Income maintenance subsidies are given in the form of payments or special legislation to increase farm income and to deal with the income problems of overproduction and fluctuating prices (overproduction in the sense of producing more than peoply will buy at prices allowing farmers a profit, not in the sense of producing more than people would eat if they could afford it). These are the payments that the government gives to farmers for *not* growing a crop that may be flooding the market. According to Congressman V. Conte from Mass., the list of farm subsidy recipients amounts to "an incredible scandal sheet, clearly demonstrating the bankruptcy of our farm program." (*Cong. Rec.* 3/27/71, H3029). Conte notes that in 1969 five payments of income subsidies were made of over $1 million, 15 of between $500,000 and $1 million, 388 of between $100,000 and $500,000 and 1290 of between $50,000 and $100,000 simply for agreeing *Not to cultivate land!* In California alone, 3751 farmers received a total of $93.6 million for limiting their production of cotton and other price supported crops. Attempts to legislate a limit to the amount of income subsidy have been consistently defeated by Congress, notably by such staunch liberals as Brooke, Church, Cooper, Fulbright, Hatfield, Javits, Kennedy, etc.

While farm workers go without adequate housing, food and decent wages, and California's small and marginal farmers continue to decline to 5000 a year, men like J. G. Boswell (also a director of Safeway), draw huge cash subsidies for *not* growing crops. Besides owning over 100,000 acres of land in Kings, Tulare and Fresno Cos., the Boswell Co., in 1969, received over $4.4 million from Government subsidies.

At the same time a subsidiary of Boswell, Ascott Ltd. received over $500,000 from the Australian Government for growing cotton on 10,000 acres of land northwest of Sydney. Thus while Boswell was being paid by one country to contribute its crop to a bountiful world cotton market, the U.S., in an effort to protect its own prices, was obliged to pay Boswell over $4 million *not to grow* cotton in this country! (With a sense of subtle justice, it's interesting to note that Japan buys Australian cotton to produce low-priced textiles . . . some of which are exported to the U.S. at prices low enough to affect the market for American mills.)

Labor subsidies. Neither the federal nor state governments give farm workers the same legal rights to unionization, minimum wages and other conditions that they give to other workers in other industries. Furthermore, both levels of government have special programs actually supplying growers with extra-cheap labor. For decades, economic powers in agriculture have also been instrumental in keeping wages of farm workers at a minimum, usually below subsistence level, breaking strikes and preventing farm workers from organizing their labor forces into viable union organizations. (3,6) The result is that farm workers have been suppressed to the bottom of the labor force in our society with respect to income, bargaining power and working conditions. The efforts of Cesar Chavez and the United Farm Workers Organizing Committee (UFWOC) in California to negotiate contracts with growers and improve the life of those living in rural poverty is only the beginning of a struggle that should have been resolved decades ago. But, as Carey McWilliams notes in his book *Factories in the Field*, "It is impossible to attempt a solution of the farm labor problem without considering the basic issue of land ownership."

Research subsidies. The federal government and to an even greater extent, the California government, supply funds to the Universities for research on *growers'* problems. Other industries must pay for their own research. It is worth emphasizing here that the displacement of farm laborers by machines is unique in two respects from that which takes place in other industries. First, agriculture is the only industry where the government actually finances the development of technologies that displace labor. Second, most American businesses are unionized . . . and one of the prime functions of a union is to extract compensation from employers for new labor-saving devices. Farm workers, and to a lesser extent, tenants and small farmers receive no such compensation.

Water subsidies. The federal government, through the Bureau of Reclamation, state governments, and local water agencies supply large growers with cheap water at the expense of taxpayers. The case of the California Water Plan and the illegal avoidance of the 1902 Reclamation Law (the 160 acre limitation) by large landholders have been described in detail elsewhere. (2,7) Suffice it to say that these landowners are getting billions of tax dollars in subsidies from construction of federal and state water projects while at the same time the value of their land is enhanced because of these projects.

It is clear that the government subsidy programs simply add to the basic farm problems of low income to small farmers and workers, overproduction and unstable prices. The privileged few seem to get these huge government handouts as a matter of course. In fact, it is not an exaggeration to say that government policy not only supports big business in agriculture, but actually rewards it to the exclusion of small growers and with little regard for the effects that it brings on the distribution of land in this country.

Speculations, monopolies and labor exploitation are not the only cause for alarm with the operations of corporate farming. Equally disturbing is what the corporations do to the land once they have it. Anxious to maximize profits, land is regarded as simply another replaceable input to be "mined" for immediate profit. And with short-sighted ends of economic efficiency, ecologically backward farming practices have become a matter of policy for agribusiness: the planting of monocultures, the unrestrained use of chemicals and crops with a narrow genetic base, the relocation of livestock from farms to "feeding areas" etc., all enhance the increasing degree of biological problems facing agriculture today. For example, Antle Corporation in the San Joaquin Valley of California is the largest lettuce producer in the nation . . . supplying over 11% of all lettuce in the country. In 1967 Antle leased 300 acres of prime farm land from Dow Chemical Corporation. In exchange, Dow obtained minority stock in the Antle firm. As of 1970 Antle sprayed its lettuce fields with 2, 4-D herbicide manufactured at Dow which even the Army admits can cause serious birth defects in humans. There are numerous other examples, but the result is the same: treatment of land for future use is usually of marginal consideration since profits are a relatively short-termed event. With economic obligations as a singular priority, little attention is given to the long-range conservation of cultivated lands. Efficiency rules.

"EFFICIENCY" ON THE FARM

It's easy to defend the activities of agribusiness as being necessary for efficiency and inevitable to progress, a logical extension of growth in other industries. But there is a good deal of ambiguity about "efficiency" in agriculture; the notion needs perspective before it can be swallowed whole by a growing economy.

The experience with industry would naturally lead one to assume that greater size brings greater economic efficiency, that is, that agriculture is subject to an economy of scale. But a strict analogy with industry is not possible for agriculture since we are dealing with very different kinds of resources. Land is not indefinitely extensible like a factory. Rivers, swamps, mountains or towns get in the way. What can be arranged within the compact limits of a factory must be arranged over an expanse of country. Where a factory can acquire needed capital within the limits of its own fiscal resources, the more unpredictable natural conditions of water, weather and top-soil cannot be easily manipulated to an economy of scale. It follows that the advantages of large scale production are far more limited in agriculture than in industry. In most cases it can be shown that the smaller farm is more efficient from a strictly economic viewpoint. (8)

In fact it is things having little to do with size which affect the small farmer more than the scale of his operation. Most significant is the relationship of the farmer with distributors and processors and the fact that the small grower is highly vulnerable to price resistance from these middle men. He must negotiate in advance. He cannot, as tradition would have it, simply harvest a crop and take it to market where he can be reasonably sure that it will sell. He must produce, in advance of a set price, for a constructed market. The corporate farm, on the other hand, with its own processing and distributing plants, or at least with the economic power to control such operations, has a tremendous competitive advantage in marketing its produce. Even in situations where there is no substantial difference in "efficiency" between a small and large farm, but where the farmer's survival depends on a contract with a distributor, the small farmer is at a grave disadvantage by virtue of his meager resources.

There is also the idea that large-scale mechanized farming operations produce more food per acre of land. Now, that machines save labor goes without saying. That the American public tends to ascribe most of the good things in life to machines also goes without saying. But how much machines raise the productivity of land is another matter. In most cases, machine tillage actually extracts lower yields (pounds of food per acre) than labor-intensive agriculture. Essentially the use of machines saves (displaces) labor and is otherwise irrelevant to yield.

There are also problems with measuring agricultural efficiency in terms of the labor saved. For example, we hear that in 1930 it took one farmer to feed ten Americans, while today one farmer can supply himself and 42 other Americans with food and fiber. However, today's farmer is aided by many other people who never set foot on the farm: petrochemical technicians and salespeople, tractor assemblymen, irrigation firms, utility companies, oil corporations that supply tractors with the estimated 0.8 billion gallons of fuel used annually in this country, (9) and many others who provide outside capital and resources for the operations of agriculture.

To show the high levels of energy consumption in modern agriculture, Fred Cottrell compared the energy budgets of Japanese and American farming. (10) Using data from two comparable rice farms, one in Japan and the other in Arkansas, he found that in Japan an acre could be cultivated and harvested with about 90 man-days (about 90 horsepower hours). On the Arkansas farm, more than 1,000 horsepower hours of energy were used just to power the tractor and trucks. Moreover, the consumption of electrical energy exceeded 600 hp-hours. These data do not even include the energy required to produce the tractors and other equipment, nor the energy in the fossil fuels used to make the fertilizers and pesticides. Some people believe that the "efficient" American grain farmer consumes more than one calorie of fossil fuel energy for each calorie of food produced. (11) For perspective, we can compare this with data from tropical forest subsistence agriculture. Using only human energy, the Tsembaga in the central highlands of New Guinea obtain 16 kilocalories of food energy for every one kilocalorie invested in clearing, planting, cultivation and harvest. (12) If we are facing an energy crisis, then farming operations based increasingly on "labor-saving" fossil fuel energy are absolutely irrational, and efficiency measured in terms of *total* energy inputs is depressingly low.

If we measure efficiency by profitability, then large corporate farms are certainly more efficient than small farms . . . otherwise major corporations would not be making the investment. But this kind of efficiency has other kinds of "costs" which are rarely included in the profit margin. First, since profit is directly related to yield, then an economically profitable agriculture must seek, develop and use those technologies and cropping systems which give maximum food in the minimum amount of time: mechanization, monocultures and chemicals. However, if we have made our point, these things tend to be socially and ecologically disruptive, and the net cost of this disruption is probably much higher than we think.

Also much of the profits of large farmers are due to federal and state tax policies which are one of the main factors encouraging large corporations to go into farming. Capital gains, favorable depreciation rates on equipment, and tax losses written off against nonfarm income are major benefits that return sizeable tax savings to absentee investors and thereby permit them to operate with cost structures entirely different from those of the small farmer. Also, the independent small farmer is far less likely to have taxable nonfarm income against which to offset loss. Finally, as noted above, much of agribusiness' profits are due to federal subsidies. In fact, without the price supports from government (the people's taxes), expenses on the average would exceed receipts for farms with over $40,000 sales. (13) If farming is becoming a tax-supported write-off for corporations, then profit would seem to be a poor guide to efficiency on the farm.

In a real sense, misconceptions about efficiency in agriculture parallel those held about production in other industries; the gross is routinely mistaken for the net, consumption is treated as if it were production, and capital is spent to reduce income. What is needed is a new interpretation of an efficient farm operation, one that involves something other than minimum labor and maximum yield and profit. Somehow it must include on the balance sheet those social and ecological problems brought on by big farm technologies, and reflect the stability and independence of the food producers in our society. The point here is to question seriously whether we can continue to operate our agriculture like a factor in the field . . . where the sole criterion is economy of scale . . . and to point to the fact that a modern agriculture racing one step ahead of ecological and social disruption is illogical and biologically self-defeating no matter how productive or economically sound it may be.

Next time we will try to show that concern for the revitalization of small independent farming operations is based on a good deal more than sentiment or nostalgia. We will examine some alternative approaches to agriculture based on up-to-date, more ecologically sound methods of food production made possible by regeneration of the small farm, an increase in the living complexity of the agricultural landscape and a drastic change in the role of the farm worker in our society.

REFERENCES

1. Barnes, P. Land Reform in America. New Republic. June 5, 12, 19, 1971.
2. Power and land in California. 1971. Ralph Nader Task Force Report on Land Use in the State of California. vol. 1. Center for the Study of Responsive Law. Wash., D.C.
3. Hosmer, Helen. 1938. Who are the Associated Farmers? The Rural Observer, vol. 1, no. 8, Simon J. Lubin Society of California, Inc., San Francisco.
4. Schultze, C. 1971. The distribution of farm subsidies: who gets the benefits? Brookings Institute (L.A. Times, 15 May 71).
5. Clawson, M. 1970. A new policy direction of American agriculture. Journal Soil and Water Conservation, Jan.-Feb., 1970.
6. Committee on Labor and Public Welfare. 1970. Hearings Before the Subcommittee on Migratory Labor, Parts 3-A,B, Efforts to Organize. U.S. Government Printing Office, Wash., D.C.
7. Taylor, Paul S. 1970. The fight for water. AFL-CIO American Federationist, Dec. 1970. Also, for a 13 page bibliography on anti-monopoly water laws in California write: Charles Smith, 1 San Mateo Road, Berkeley, Ca. 94707.
8. Sasuly, Richard. 1964. The family farm in California. California Farm Research and Legislative Committee. 740 Hilmar St., Santa Clara, California.
9. Perelman, M. 1971. Efficiency in Agriculture. Dept. Economics, Chico State College, offprint.
10. Cottrell, F. 1955. Energy and Society. McGraw-Hill, New York.
11. Odum, E. P. 1971. Fundamentals of Ecology. 3rd. ed. W. B. Saunders, Philadelphia.
12. Rappaport, R. A. 1971. The flow of energy in agricultural society. Scientific American, Sept. 1971, pp. 117-132.
13. Legislative Reference Service. 1965. Farm Programs and dynamic forces in agriculture. U.S. Senate Committee on Agriculture and Forestry. U.S. Government Printing Office, Wash., D.C.

The social impact of technology

WILLIAM H. FRIEDLAND*

Over the past century, millions of dollars have been expended on the development and dispersal of agricultural technology through the complex network of the "agricultural establishment": the United States Department of Agriculture, the land-grant complex of universities, the agricultural experiment stations, and agricultural extension programs. The social† effects of technological change have been studied accidentally, however, rather than systematically. This paper shall argue:

1. Research has been geared overwhelmingly to technology, overlooking and ignoring social consequences.
2. The social consequences of this technological research has been to exacerbate and accelerate the shift of population from rural to urban *and* to produce an antisocial pattern of income distribution.
3. When social research has taken place and threatened powerful interests in agriculture, such tendencies have been cut off.
4. California's support for research in agriculture has been even more disproportionately loaded toward the technological than have been the efforts of other states.
5. It is no accident that social researchers on rural society know far more about land reform and related issues of political and social control of rural society outside the United States than they do inside.

While the central burden of this paper will not deal with which strata in rural society have benefited from these developments, it is clear that these tendencies have continually created a push out of agriculture and rural society of those farmers who have become defined as "marginal" at any given period of time. Few established sectors within agriculture have been concerned about the push out of agriculture since the period of the New Deal; prior to that time, the continued existence of the family farm was a major political question in this country. After the New Deal, the issue was raised only fragmentarily

□ Paper prepared for the First National Land Reform Conference, San Francisco, Calif., Apr. 25-28, 1973.
*Professor, University of California, Santa Cruz.
†"Social" is used here in its broadest sense to connote sociological, economic, and political effects.

and rarely by groups within the agricultural establishment. Today, the issue is rising once again but in a context in which the continuance of the family farm and the encouragement of developments other than the continuing trend toward corporate agribusiness appear to be almost insuperable. This paper will address itself to the research issues involved in the current movement toward larger and larger corporate entities within agriculture.

RESEARCH GEARED TO TECHNOLOGY

The degree to which research is geared to technological rather than social research is evident in a walk through any college of agriculture in the United States or a perusal of the research being supported by any agricultural experiment station in any of the states. Although I am not able to report at the present time the dollar value of research geared to technology as against social effects, the differences in emphasis are clear as one examines the sheer size of faculties in any land-grant university. The overwhelming bulk of the faculty is involved in entomology, genetics, engineering, plant pathology, and similar kinds of research. In California, specialized work is carried on in pomology, enology, and in many other technical subjects. In contrast, the numbers of agricultural economists is small, and the rural sociologists are insignificant.

The net results are that we know very little, in fact, about the social consequences of such research except in the most general way. While some studies were conducted years ago on the dramatic effects of mechanization—the cotton harvester, the tractor, other similar mechanization processes—little research has been done on mechanization effects more recently. Perhaps even more importantly, few if any attempts have been undertaken to assess the social consequences of research not involving mechanization. Thus, the many researchers that have produced new strains of crops, new systems of water dispersal, insect control procedures, and so on all have had social consequences; but there exists no knowledge about what these consequences have been.

Three distinct sets of social consequences have been produced by the patterns of research in agriculture.

First, the increased complexity of agriculture, a

product of scientific and technological research, has contributed to the shift of population from rural to urban society. Lest my point be misunderstood, let me make perfectly clear my recognition that rural-to-urban population shift is a long-standing tendency whose effects have been seen in every industrializing society. What is at issue, however, is the *degree* to which population shift occurs. Not all industrializing and industrialized societies have made the shift with the dramatic vehemence of the United States. Indeed, the questions must inevitably be asked: Was the amount of shift that we experienced in the United States necessary?

The second major consequence has been to produce a pattern of income distribution that I would characterize as antisocial. In those parts of the United States where agriculture is at its most advanced stage—advanced being defined in terms of the complexity of the division of labor, most highly capitalized, and soon—a pattern has emerged in which a tiny segment of the population is extremely wealthy while the overwhelming majority are extremely poor. Thus, in a study of agricultural sections of the United States, Smith (1969) found that in Imperial County, California, and Palm Beach County, Florida, only 4.4% and 2.3% of farm personnel were "upper class," while 87.3% and 90% were "lower class" respectively. While the patern in other agricultural areas is not as heavily split, with a larger segment of "middle class" personnel, the tendency to move toward a small number of ever-richer growers and a large number of poorer rural classes is definitely pronounced. Indeed, the relative smallness of poor rural strata has been a product of the continual mobility of this group into the urban sector of American society.

The third consequence of research has been to exacerbate the process of growth of large agricultural production units to the point that the significant entry into agribusiness by large nonagricultural corporations has become the phenomenon of the past decade. Thus, we have not only seen small farmers being pushed out of agriculture but large corporations—some with no previous connections to any agriculture—being attracted to the economic potential of agribusiness. While I cannot provide a detailed examination of how this process has operated (this will be the subject of future work on my part), the point should be made that scientific and technological research has increased the amount of capitalization required to remain economically viable in agriculture. Current economies of scale have produced a continuing process of land aggregation which, taken together with credit arrangements and the way in which information dispersal operates through the agricultural extension network, have made it increasingly

difficult for small growers to remain in agriculture.

That agricultural research should be geared more toward the scientific-technological than to social effects is not entirely surprising: if apples are infested by a mosaic or nematodes are destroying potatoes, one would hardly call on an economist or a sociologist for assistance. Thus, the issue is not that the bulk of funds are devoted to technological work but that such work goes forward *without* consideration of what the consequences will be of any given piece of research.

Consider, for example, the case of the tomato harvester, which was introduced in California after 1964. While Schmitz and Seckler (1970) have argued that the net effect of its introduction was economically beneficial, no information is systematically available as to *who* benefited; for example, which segments of society are enjoying the economic savings produced through this equipment. The tomato harvester, it should be remembered, was not the product of a single set of agricultural engineers but of a complex group concerned with problems such as genetics (the need for a tougher skin and a differently shaped tomato), water research, and other technical specialties. By 1964, when the bracero program ended, all of this research was ready to go into effect. The results are seen by comparing Tables 1 and 2 on page seven; Table 1 shows the rate of acceptance of the tomato harvester, while Table 2 shows the tonnages produced during the crucial years. Until 1964, in California, it is estimated that the number of workers involved in the tomato harvest approximated 50,000; these numbers have dropped by an estimated 40% (Harper, 1967), while tomato acreages have increased.

What were the social effects of the introduction of the tomato harvester? No systematic study of this matter has been undertaken, but some information is available from a preliminary study conducted by the writer in 1968. First, it is clear that the sex ratio of tomato harvesters has changed from an overwhelming representation of men to a predominance of wom-

Table 1. Number of tomato harvesters used in California, by year

Year	Number of harvesters
1959	1 (Prototype)
1961	34
1962	30
1964	90
1965	262
1967	485 (Blackweiders)

Source: California Tomato Grower, Sept. 1960; July-Aug. 1961; Dec. 1961; Oct. 1962; Nov. 1964; Nov. 1965; Nov. 1967.

Table 2. California tomatoes for processing—1959-1967 (estimates)

Year	Acres harvested	Production (in tons)	Total value (in dollars)
1959	129,000	1,997,400	43,543,000
1960	130,000	2,249,000	52,627,000
1961	146,800	2,319,000	69,802,000
1962	177,760	3,218,000	88,817,000
1963	129,000	2,463,900	62,583,000
1964	143,000	3,003,000	75,976,000
1965	122,800	2,468,300	87,378,000
1966	162,500	3,136,200	94,086,000
1967	186,700	3,192,600	123,554,000

Source: California Tomato Grower, Oct. 1963; Mar. 1968.

en. Second, workers now probably come almost entirely from the United States, even if some make their base of operations in Mexico; for example, there are no braceros involved in the harvest. Third, there are indications that acreages are increasing in production units. Particularly with the development of water-sorting processes and the separation of sorting from harvesting, larger acreages are probably economically beneficial for production. Finally, accompanied by the greater availability of water through the California Water Project on the west side of the San Joaquin Valley, a shift in production is probably developing to that area from the San Joaquin delta area. If these effects are held up by research presently underway,* it would indicate that a distinct contribution has been made to increasing size in California agriculture by the land-grant complex (in this case, the Davis campus of the University of California).

There have been other effects that are indicated that have not yet been studied in detail. One has been an introduction of a new division of labor, since the harvesters require operators, mechanics, and others. Another effect appears to be the drawing out of the household and into the labor force for the flash peak harvest of many women who might not otherwise be gainfully employed. While both these effects may appear to be socially desirable, the fact is that we have little or no knowledge about what their consequences have been for family structure and geographical mobility.

The fact that so little is known about the social consequences of technological innovation in agriculture is not accidental. The shape of knowledge about such social effects is a deliberate product of the way in

*EDITOR'S NOTE: The research referred to by the author has since been completed. The results have been reported in: Friedland, William H., and Barton, Amy: Destalking the Wily Tomato, Monograph No. 15, Davis, Calif., University of California Press; and in Friedland, William H., and Barton, Amy: Tomato technology, Society 13(6):35-42, Sept.-Oct. 1976.

which investment policies have been made in the generation of knowledge. While I cannot yet present data on how research has been shaped in the state of California, this state is well known and unusual for its relative lack of knowledge in the social realm, particularly when compared to other states, such as New York, Iowa, and Wisconsin. In many states with prominent land-grant universities, it is common to find departments of rural sociology. This has not been the case either at Davis or Riverside, the two predominant agricultural colleges within the University of California system. What accounts for this fact? Again, I cannot as yet provide detailed data, but the crucial experience of one social scientist in the 1940's provides an indication as to what occurred. This was the experience of Walter Goldschmidt (1946, 1947), an anthropologist who studied Wosco, Arvin, and Dinuba to determine the effects of patterns of land ownership. The basic findings, that social life was more satisfying in Dinuba with its smaller landholding patterns, was anathema to powerful landed interests in this state. The melancholy chronicle of how Goldschmidt was hounded and the way in which his professional work was impeded at the early stages of his career have been documented elsewhere by Kirkendall (1964). Goldschmidt found it easier to conduct his social science work in Africa, becoming a prominent Africanist, rather than be harassed by powerful forces in American society. In this respect, the fact that so many rural sociologists shifted their interests from the denudation of American rural society to countries other than the United States can hardly be regarded as accidental. The harassment of Goldschmidt and other similar incidents probably helped shape the situation in which so many rural sociologists know far more about land tenure and land reform in Peru, Malaya, and India than in New Jersey, California, or (God forbid!) Mississippi.

If California has been relatively backward compared to Wisconsin, New York, or Iowa, those states have experienced their own forms of direction of knowledge about rural society. Thus, the University of Wisconsin hosts the Land Tenure Center, an organization that apparently knows far more about land tenure outside the United States than inside.* Similarly, an enormous amount of research has been conducted at the University of Iowa on the way in which innovations are diffused and adopted by farmers (Rogers, 1962) but relatively little has been done on the increasing corporate structure of agriculture in that state.

Among former colleagues in the Department of Rural Sociology and the Department of Agricultural Economics at Cornell University, I found both greater knowledge and interest in foreign countries than I did about the condition of rural society and the continuous denudation of the rural population.†

WHAT IS TO BE DONE? APPROACHES TO CHANGE IN AGRICULTURAL RESEARCH

It should be clear that any proposal for change in agricultural research confronts an establishment of staggering size spread through the fifty states. This institutional network not only encompasses the land-grant colleges and their colleges of agriculture, but the agricultural experiment stations and the agricultural extension networks. Linked to it is a host of other institutions ranging from the centers of establishment power as embodied in the Secretary of Agriculture, the lesser individuals and bodies within the USDA, and the complex of farm organizations with informal affiliations to this government-education network. There are other bodies too; we need not list them lest we frighten outselves into inaction.

Moving such a network will not be easy. While states such as California are beginning to feel some

pressures and a tiny number of projects are being funded that represent a new tendency toward critical social research in agriculture and rural society, "two swallows do not a summer make." Even if the amount of projects or dollars are increased a hundred-fold, the effects will still be negligible. In addition, all such projects remain terribly vulnerable to internal political pressures within the land-grant complex— pressures in which establishment agriculture has long been shown its predominance.

If a significant shift is to be made, not only toward increasing social research with its (hopefully) important social consequences, a more powerful lever is needed. In proposing the particular proposals set out below, I want to emphasize their limited capability for producing change: these proposals will not, in and of themselves, produce any significant change in the character of rural society. What they should do is to permit the beginning of an open discussion of the effects of public policy on public life. I am limiting myself to proposals concerning the organization of research in agriculture because it is in this area that I have the greatest knowledge and because proposals concerning other aspects of agricultural and rural reform will be forthcoming from other panels of this conference.

In brief what I propose for reform of agricultural research priorities is the following:

1. Require every proposal funded by an Agricultural Experiment Station (AES) to contain a social impact statement. The social impact statement would be a delineation by the proposer as to what the anticipated social effects would be of the particular piece of research. The researcher should also be required to delineate which social groups would be affected by the research and how. The researcher should also be required to state the methods by which the prognostication as to social effects has been developed.

2. Require each AES to create and fund an evaluative unit. This unit, which should be administratively separate from the AES itself to permit organizational autonomy (such as the ability to call the shots without being worried about the pressures of the AES directors), should conduct continuing evaluative research on all AES-funded projects. Such research should seek:

   a. To determine the extent to which social predictions made by researchers are fulfilled
   b. To develop accurate data on the actual social consequences of specific research projects
   c. To improve evaluative methodology and make it more accessible to scientists, so that they may make improved predictions as to the effects of their research
   d. To open, as a result of the accumulation of such

---

*The Land Tenure Center is supported largely by the Agency for International Development, which is interested, of course, in land tenure questions outside of the United States. Two points perhaps might be made: first, the U.S. government continues to be more concerned with land tenure issues *outside* of the country than inside; second, the University of Wisconsin apparently has few resources itself to conduct studies about land tenure issues within Wisconsin and the United States.

†In 1969, just prior to my departure from Cornell, the University's administration became worried about a migrant labor camp on an orchard run by the College of Agriculture. At the request of the administration, I prepared a proposal that the College of Agriculture use the camp for research and demonstration as to what might be done by migrant workers with an enlightened management. The College of Agriculture found itself unable to fund a budget of only $10,432 to initiate the project. Subsequently, when the issue arose again, the College's administration bulldozed the camp out of existence. This way of "solving" social problems went largely unprotested by social scientists in the College. Other attempts were undertaken to work with low-income rural residents by junior faculty, but these were continually harassed and made ineffectual. See Watson (1972).

data, to public discussion what the directions of research *ought* to be

The proposal put here is not intended to turn scientists into social scientists. It is intended to lay the basis for a more effective evaluative methodology, making scientists more sensitive to issues of the social consequences of their research, and opening to public discussion the way in which research in agriculture ought to go.

REFERENCES

Goldschmidt, Walter R.: Small business and the community: study in the Central Valley on effects of scale of operations, Report of the Special Committee to study problems of American small business, United States Senate, 79th Congress, Washington, D.C., 1946, U.S. Government Printing Office.

Goldschmidt, Walter R.: As You Sow. New York, 1947, Free Press.
Harper, Robert G.: Mechanization and the seasonal farmworker, Farm Labor Development Apr. 1967.
Kirkendall, Richard S.: Social science in the Central Valley of California: an episode, California Historical Society Quarterly, Sept. 1964, pp. 195-218.
Rogers, Everett M.: Diffusion of innovations, New York, 1962, Free Press.
Schmitz, Andrew, and Seckler, David: Mechanized agriculture and social welfare: the case of the tomato harvester, American Journal of Agricultural Economics **52**(4): 569-577, 1970.
Smith, T. Lynn.: A study of social stratification in the agricultural sections of the U.S.: nature, data, procedures, and preliminary results, Rural Sociology **34**(4): 496-509, 1969.
Watson, Lark, Gatehouse, Michael, and Dorsey, Elanor: Failing the people: a special report on the New York State College of agriculture, Washington, D.C., 1972, Agricultural Policy Accountability Project.

The land grant college complex

JIM HIGHTOWER and SUSAN DeMARCO

The land grant colleges were created by Congress to be a kind of people's university, reaching out to serve the needs of rural communities. Instead, they became a handmaiden to corporate agribusiness and are in large part responsible for the sad state of rural America today.

In 1972, the Agribusiness Accountability Project organized a task force to investigate the land grant college complex. The task force conducted an exhaustive study which led to the publication of *Hard Tomatoes, Hard Times*, a thoroughly documented critique of the land grant college complex that has stimulated much debate and even some small reforms. Here, Jim Hightower and Susan DeMarco summarize the basic findings of the task force.

PETER BARNES

The land grant college complex consists of three interrelated units: the colleges of agriculture, created in 1862 and 1890 by two separate Morrill Acts; the state agricultural experiment stations, created in 1887 by the Hatch Act; and the Extension Service, created in 1914 by the Smith-Lever Act to disseminate research to the people.

Reaching into all 50 states, the complex is huge, intricate and expensive. The public's total investment in this complex, including assets, comes to several billion dollars in any given year, paying for everything from test tubes to experimental farms, from chalk to carpeting in the dean's office.

☐ From Barnes, P., editor: The people's land, Emmaus, Pa., 1975, Rodale Press, Inc.

There is no doubt that American agriculture is enormously productive and that this is largely the result of mechanical, chemical, genetical and managerial research conducted by the land grant college complex. But the question is whether the achievements outweigh the failures, whether benefits are overwhelmed by costs.

The focus of agricultural research is warped by the land grant community's fascination with technology, integrated food processes and the like. The distorted research priorities are striking:

- 1,129 scientific man-years (smy) on improving the biological efficiency of crops, and only 18 smy on improving rural income.
- 842 smy on control of insects, diseases and weeds in crops, and 95 smy to insure food products are free from toxic residues from agricultural sources.
- 200 smy on ornamentals, turf and trees for natural beauty, and a sad 7 smy on rural housing.
- 88 smy on improving management systems for livestock and poultry production, and 45 smy for improving rural institutions.
- 68 smy on marketing firms and system efficiency, and 17 smy on causes and remedies of poverty among rural people.

In fiscal year 1969, a total of nearly 6,000 scientific man-years were spent doing research on all projects at all state-agricultural experiment stations. Based on

USDA's research classifications, only 289 of those scientific man-years were expended specifically on "people-oriented" research. That is an allocation to rural people of less than five percent of the total research effort.

An analysis of these latter research projects reveals that the commitment to the needs of people in rural America is even less than appears on the surface. In rural housing, the major share of research has been directed not to those who live in them, but to those who profit from the construction and maintenance of houses—architects, builders, lumber companies and service industries.

Other "people-oriented" projects tend to be irrelevant studies of characteristics stemming more from curiosity than a desire to change conditions. At Cornell, for example, a study found that "employed homemakers have less time for housekeeping tasks than non-employed homemakers." Other projects are just as irrelevant:

- Mississippi State University researchers discovered "that families in poverty are not of a single, homogeneous type."
- The University of Nebraska is at work on a study of "factors affecting age at marriage."
- A regional research study unveiled the fact that "the rural population is dichotomous in racial composition" and "pre-retirement family incomes have a direct bearing upon economic expectations for retirement."
- University of Nebraska researchers surveyed football coaches in the state and got 60 percent agreement "that introduction of a federally-sponsored school breakfast program would benefit the nutritional health of teenage athletes."

The primary beneficiaries of land grant research are agribusiness corporations. These companies envision rural America solely as a factory that will produce food, fiber and profits on a corporate assembly line extending from the fields through the supermarket checkout counters. It is through mechanization research that the land grant colleges are approaching this agribusiness ideal.

Mechanization means more than machinery for planting, thinning, weeding and harvesting. It also means improving on nature's design, *i.e.*, breeding new food varieties that are better adapted to mechanical harvesting. Having built machines, the land grant research teams found it necessary to build a tomato that is hard enough to survive the grip of mechanical "fingers"; redesign the grape so that all the fruit has the good sense to ripen at the same time; and restructure the apple tree so that it grows shorter, leaving the apples less distance to fall to their mechanical catchers. Michigan State University, in a

proud report on "tailor-made" vegetables, notes that their scientists are at work on broccoli, tomatoes, cauliflower, cucumbers, snapbeans, lima beans, carrots and asparagus.

If it cannot be done by manipulating genes, land grant scientists reach into their chemical cabinet. Louisiana State University has experimented with the chemical Ethrel to cause hot peppers to ripen at the same time for "once-over" mechanical harvesting. Scientists at Michigan State University are using chemicals to reduce the cherry's resistance to the tug of mechanical pickers. And a combination of ferric ammonia citrate and erythorbic acid is being used at Texas A&M to loosen fruit before machine harvesting.

Once harvested, food products must be sorted for size and ripeness. Again, land grant college engineers have produced a mechanical answer. North Carolina State University, for example, has designed and developed an automatic machine "which dynamically examines blueberries according to maturity." The University of California and other colleges have scientists at work on machinery that will sort tomatoes.

Who is helped and who is hurt by this research?

It is the largest-scale growers, the farm machinery and chemicals input companies and the processors who are the primary beneficiaries. Machinery companies such as John Deere, International Harvester, Massey-Ferguson, Allis-Chalmer and J. I. Case almost continually engage in cooperative research efforts at land grant colleges. These corporations contribute money and some of their own research personnel to help land grant scientists develop machinery. In return, they are able to incorporate technological advances in their own products. In some cases they actually receive exclusive licenses to manufacture and sell the products of tax-paid research.

If mechanization research has been a boon to agribusiness, it has been a bane to millions of rural Americans. Farmworkers have been the earliest victims. There were 4.3 million hired farmworkers in 1950. Twenty years later that number had fallen to 3.5 million. As a group, those laborers averaged $1,083 for doing farm work in 1970, making them among the very poorest of America's employed poor.

Farmworkers have not been compensated for jobs lost to mechanization research. They were not consulted when that research was designed, and their needs were not a part of the research that resulted. They simply were left to fend on their own—no retraining, no effort to find new jobs for them, no unemployment compensation, no research to help them adjust to the changes that came out of the land grant colleges.

Independent family farmers also have been largely

ignored by the land grant colleges. Mechanization research by land grant colleges is either irrelevant or only incidentally adaptable to the needs of some 87 to 99 percent of America's farmers. The public subsidy for mechanization actually has weakened the competitive position of the family farmer. Taxpayers, through the land grant college complex, have given corporate producers a technological arsenal specifically suited to their scale of operation and designed to increase their efficiency and profits. The independent family farmer is left to strain his private resources to the breaking point in a desperate effort to clamber aboard the technological treadmill.

Like the farmworker, the average farmer is not invited into the land grant laboratories to design research. If he were, the research package would include machines useful on smaller acreages, assistance to cooperative ownership systems, and a heavy emphasis on new credit schemes. In short, there would be a deliberate effort to extend mechanization benefits to all, with an emphasis on at least maintaining the competitive position of the family farm in relation to agribusiness corporations. These efforts do not exist, or exist only in a token way.

Mechanization also has a serious impact on the consumer. Land grant researchers are not eager to confront the question of food quality, choosing instead to dwell on the benefits that food engineering offers agribusiness. The University of Florida, for example, recently developed a new fresh market tomato (the MH-1) for machine harvesting. In describing the characteristics that make this tomato so desirable for machine harvest, the University pointed to "the thick walls, firm flesh, and freedom from cracks." It may be a little tough for the consumer, but agricultural research can't please everyone. The MH-1, which will eliminate the jobs of thousands of Florida farm workers who now hand-pick tomatoes for the fresh market, is designed to be harvested green and to be "ripened" in storage by application of ethylene gas.

Convenience to the processor often outweighs taste for the consumer. For example, University of Wisconsin researchers developed a process for making mozzarella cheese in five and a half minutes, compared to the usual time of four hours. The flavor of the final product is reported to be "mild, but satisfactory for the normal uses."

The colleges also are engaged in "selling" the consumer on products he neither wants nor needs, and they are using tax money for food research and development that should be privately financed. At Virginia Polytechnic Institute, for example, eight separate studies have been conducted to determine if people would buy apple and grapefruit juice blended. Other projects involve surveys to determine what in-

fluences the shopper's decision-making. If this research is useful to anyone, it is food marketers and advertisers, and reports on this research make clear that those firms are the primary recipients of the results. The corporations who benefit from this research should pay for it and conduct it themselves.

The consumer is not just studied and "sold" by land grant research; he is also fooled. Chickens have been fed the plant compound Xanthophyll to give their skin "a pleasing yellow tinge," and several projects have been undertaken to develop spray-on coatings to enhance the appearance of apples, peaches, citrus and tomatoes. Other cosmetic research projects that are underway at land grant colleges include:

- Iowa State University is conducting packaging studies which indicate that color stays bright longer when bacon is vacuum-packed or sealed in a package containing carbon dioxide in place of air, thus contributing to "more consumer appeal."
- Scientists at South Carolina's agricultural experiment station have shown that fluorescent light treatment can increase the red color in machine-picked tomatoes and cause their texture and taste to be "similar to vine-ripened tomatoes."
- Kansas State University Extension Service, noting that apples sell on the basis of appearance rather than nutrition, urged growers to have a beautiful product. To make the produce more appealing, mirrors and lights in supermarket produce cases were cited as effective selling techniques.

Service to agribusiness is not by coincidence. In dozens of ways, corporate agribusiness gets into the land-grant complex. It is welcomed there by administrators, academics, scientists and researchers who share the agribusinessman's vision of integrated, automated agriculture.

Corporate executives sit on college boards of trustees, purchase research from experiment stations, hire land-grant academics as private consultants, advise and are advised by land grant officials, go to Washington and state capitols to urge more public money for land-grant research, publish and distribute the writings of academics, provide scholarships and other educational support, invite land-grant participation in their industrial conferences and sponsor foundations that extend both grants and recognition to the land grant community.

Money is the web of the tight relationship between agribusiness and the land-grant complex. It is not that a huge sum of money is given—industry gave $12 million directly to state experiment stations for research in 1969. Rather it is that enough money is given to influence research done with public funds.

At least 23 land-grant colleges have established private, tax-exempt foundations to handle grants and contracts coming into their institutions for research. Through these curious mechanisms, corporations funnel money to public universities to conduct research. By this shell game, private research can be undertaken without obligation to report publicly the names of the corporations that are making research grants, the amounts of those grants, the purpose of those grants or the terms under which the grants are made.

These foundations also handle patents for the colleges. When a corporation invests in research through a foundation, it is done normally with the understanding that the corporation will have first shot at a license on any patented process or product that results.

On research patents that do not result from corporate grants, the procedure for licensing is just as cozy. At Purdue University, for example, a list is drawn of responsible companies that might have an interest in the process or product, and the corporations are approaches one by one until there is a taker.

There is nothing inevitable about agribusiness domination of agriculture. Had the land-grant community chosen to put its time, money, expertise, and technology into rural people, rather than into corporate pockets, rural America today might have been a place where millions could live and work in dignity. It is time to re-orient the colleges so that they begin to act in the public interest.

Statement before the Senate Subcommittee on Migratory Labor

JOHN T. CALDWELL

Dr. Caldwell: Thank you very much, Mr. Chairman.

I am Dr. John T. Caldwell, chancellor of the North Carolina State University, and I am former president of the University of Arkansas, a land-grant university, and a graduate of Michigan State, and I was president of the association a few years ago.

I am not an agriculturalist. I have spent the last 25 years as a university administrator.

I am accompanied at this hearing by people who are agriculturalists in a professional way, and who are also engaged in administration, those whom you have already named, Mr. Chairman.

Mr. Chairman, you have been very generous in your time this morning, and I have the feeling you will want us to make this short.

Senator Stevenson: I have a feeling I have been a little too generous with the time of the other witnesses, and I apologize to you for that. Take as much time as you would like.

If you do feel that you could conserve time, we will place your entire statement in the record, and you may summarize it if you wish.

Dr. Caldwell: Mr. Chairman, we have this longer

□ Statement of the national association of state universities and land-grant colleges represented by Dr. John T. Caldwell, Chancellor, North Carolina State University; Dr. Alvin I. Thomas, President, Prairie View A. & M. College in Texas; Dr. Orville Bentley, Dean, College of Agriculture, University of Illinois; and Dr. George McIntyre, Assistant Dean, College of Agriculture, and Director, Extension Service, Michigan State University.

statement, which runs to 20 pages or so, which we will have inserted in the record, and I wrote a shorter summary statement that I think I will read.

Senator Stevenson: Fine. Without objection, the longer statement will be inserted at the end of your testimony.

Dr. Caldwell: Mr. Chairman, I will now read my summary of the longer statement.

Mr. Chairman, my name is John Caldwell. I am Chancellor of North Carolina State University at Raleigh, North Carolina, a Land-Grant State University. I have been Chancellor of N.C. State for 13 years and prior to that was President of the University of Arkansas, also a Land-Grant State University. I received my bachelor's degree from Mississippi State University, also a land-grant institution.

Mr. Chairman, I am accompanied to this hearing on your invitation by the following persons: President Alvin I. Thomas, Prairie View A & M College; Dean Orville Bentley, College of Agriculture, University of Illinois; Assistant Dean George McIntyre, College of Agriculture, Michigan State University; Ralph K. Huitt, Executive Director, National Association of State Universities and Land-Grant Colleges.

In response to your specific questions we have prepared a rather extensive statement which we are filing with your secretary. I shall make a summary statement at this time, and then I shall ask President Alvin Thomas to make a statement to the Committee with particular reference to your Question 3 on the Land-Grant Colleges of 1890, the so-called "black land-grant colleges." I shall be pleased to respond to any questions during or following my statement and will refer to my colleagues when appropriate.

Mr. Chairman, you presented our Association with five questions. All of them bear directly or indirectly upon a basic question of the validity of the work of the land-grant colleges in serving American agriculture. The questions indicate a particular concern for the "family farmers" and farm workers and the responsiveness of the land-grant colleges to the people who live and work on farms or who have been displaced from farming.

I am confident that you and your colleagues are earnestly interested in getting at the facts which will help you in your deliberations on behalf of American farmers and farm workers. We, too, are interested in the facts. We want you to have them; we want you to have them without prejudice; and we want you to have them in the total perspective of American agriculture and the American society.

The land-grant colleges have been a vital part of American life in all its dimensions for over a century. The Agricultural Experiment Stations since 1887 and the Cooperative Extension Services since 1914 are integral to the spirit and accomplishments of these more than one hundred institutions. Because they are "human institutions" they require constant revitalization. They never have been perfect and they never will be. I would be hard put to it, however, to identify any American institutions which have built into themselves as many devices and mechanisms for keeping themselves vital and responsive. Even so, we welcome any informed criticism or questions from the Congress or any other source that cause us to sharpen our self-appraisal and keep us responsive to the needs of people. So, Mr. Chairman, we welcome your questions and we appreciate this opportunity to speak.

The American farm economy is the envy of the rest of the world, and for good reason. The American enterprise system of which agriculture is a fundamental part, plus the enlightened public policies which have encouraged it, plus the indispensable research and educational activities of the land-grant colleges, all combined, have brought this success. We cannot escape feeling some pride in this achievement of abundant food and fiber for our Nation, of a higher standard of living for our farmers, and of the enrichment of American life made possible by an efficient agriculture.

Now to your questions.

Question 1: To what extent has the land-grant college system assumed responsibility and developed programs to assist farm workers and farmers and others in rural America who have been displaced or affected by the development of new agricultural technology?

Answer: In our view the Nation has not done enough to assist displaced farm workers or others adversely affected by changing farm economy, either in rural areas or urban areas. Land-grant researchers and extension workers have always had as a goal improvement in the quality of community and family life in rural America. A basic approach has been the raising of income to the farm family, but along with it other efforts by home demonstration agents and in recent decades community development specialists. Where supplemental jobs and income were needed, our researchers and extension workers have promoted cooperatively new industry. We have, however, never been given the funds to pursue an individual counseling-guidance-retraining program for the rural dweller, either displaced or on the way to being dis-

placed from farming. We cannot be all things to all people. We cannot, therefore, undertake the responsibilities of the public school system at either state or county levels; we cannot undertake the responsibilities of state and county departments of public health and the medical profession; we cannot take on the responsibilities of public welfare departments. Nor are we bankers and chambers of commerce. We are, however, concerned, aware, sometimes prodders, and thorough cooperators with every public and private agency charged with responsibilities for retraining, for family welfare, for medical care, for industrial development, and the like. The record is replete. Recent legislation and enlarged funding are permitting our institutions to become more heavily engaged in readjustment activities.

Question 2: What are the land-grant colleges doing to assist the family farmer and farm worker adjust to changing conditions in rural America and maintain their economic viability? Are you satisfied that existing steps are adequate? If not, what additional steps to assure that land-grant colleges are responding to all people of rural America are you proposing?

Answer: This question seems to assume that the land-grant colleges neglect the family farmer. And then it asks whether we are satisfied with what we are doing.

The family farm has been and is the characteristic farm enterprise of America. The central purpose of our land-grant research and extension has been to improve the efficiency of human effort in the farming enterprise. These efforts have been and are primarily devoted to the family-owned and operated farm.

There seems to be some notion abroad that the family farmer is neglected. This is not true. Every improved strain of wheat is just as available to the family farm as it is to some absentee-owned corporate farm. Every cultivation practice that is improved helps every farm.

Mr. Chairman, there is a great deal of ignorance today, a great deal of innocence, and a considerable amount of romantic idealizing about farming. Because of this ignorance and innocence and romanticizing, there exists a fertile field for demagoguery. Family farms can be either self-subsistence farms or commercial farms, or a combination. In primitive agriculture all farms were self-subsistence farms and supported a primitive existence. Practically all family farms today are commercial farms. To be a happy human experience or even a tolerable human experience, the farm has to be profitable. Our research and extension efforts have been aimed at making farming happy and profitable for those who farm. Only a sound economic unit can pay a decent wage to a farm worker and provide a decent return to the owner and his family for their investment and labor. Our objective has been to make the farm unit a viable, economic human enterprise.

Family farms come in all sizes. Corn-hog farms of great size can be managed efficiently by a farm family with only occasional supplemental labor. A rice farm of 640 acres in Arkansas can be operated by a family. A small tomato patch in a mountain county in North Carolina combined with supplemental wages from other work becomes a family farm. A beef cattle farm can be managed in very large acreage by a family. But in all cases the products of research and extension advice are needed: for disease control, pest control, resistant varieties, improved yield varieties, tillage and fertilization practices, economic advice on land utilization, and so on.

Mr. Chairman, we glory in the service we have rendered the American farm family in freeing it from drudgery and poverty. Only the innocent or the ignorant or the romanticist would argue against efficiency in the use of human labor on the farm, represented by modern technology. The logic of arguing against machinery and fertilizer would take mankind back to primitive practices and to doomsday.

Are we satisfied with our effort? No. We never have been satisfied with it. We keep pressing. The Congress of the United States, the State Legislatures, the County Boards of Commissioners are more and more help in our efforts to improve American agriculture. If the planned programs of Experiment Stations and Extension Services all could be supported, we would indeed be responding more adequately to the needs of rural America.

Question 3: What do you see as the appropriate future role of the Colleges of 1890, the so-called "Black Land-Grant Colleges"?

Answer: Dr. Alvin I. Thomas will speak to that question when I am done.

Question 4: Who are the current beneficiaries of the research and other efforts of the land-grant colleges, and does your organization consider the current allocation of institutional resources and distribution of benefits equitable?

Answer: Unequivocally, every man, woman and child in America is the beneficiary of the research and educational efforts of the land-grant colleges. America has lots of problems which are documented daily. But a shortage of food and fiber is not one of them. This is not to say that every American has equal access in his purchasing power to this abundant supply. But that is a problem of distribution of income and is quite beyond the Experiment Stations, Extension Services and colleges of agriculture to solve.

On the second part of that question I would have to respond in this fashion. We do not believe that any of our present efforts should be diminished in providing an efficient and prosperous agricultural enterprise for the country. We do believe additional resources can be put into rural development efforts and family support efforts such as the nutritional aide programs of recent years. What needs to be done in rural America, however, goes far beyond the jurisdiction and responsibility of the colleges of agriculture.

Question 5: What mechanisms are needed, if any, to make the land-grant college system accountable to the public interest? Are changes needed in the composition of advisory committees at either the national level or on individual campuses? Is it necessary to have more public disclosure regarding research projects, administrative operations, foundation activities, fiscal policies, patent and licensing practices, industry contributions, and potential faculty conflicts, of interest?

Answer: Mr. Chairman, the phrasing of this question I regard as unfortunate in its implications. The land-grant college system is thoroughly and completely accountable to the American people, to this Congress, to the State Legislatures, to County Boards of Commissioners, to women's

organizations, to commodity groups, to farmers. In every conceivable way we try to report to our many constituencies, to hear them, and to serve them. I know of no calculated effort anywhere to conceal anything we do or to avoid responsiveness to the people who support us and to the people we serve. Furthermore, the integrity of our scientists and our teachers and our extension workers is not for sale. If in the vast organization and far reaches of what we call the land-grant college enterprise for agriculture there is some abuse, some malfunction, there are ample means for correcting them when they become known to us.

We are not a self-serving institutional system. We are in no position to be other than accountable, open, candid, and amenable to correction. I am not aware of any specific measures that devolve upon us to make public our relationships and involvement and activities than we already do. Whenever any citizen suspects a fault, I know no barrier in this free society to his calling it to our attention and getting a decent answer.

Finally, Mr. Chairman, may I add another comment and then my conclusion. I have first-handed knowledge of efforts to assist undeveloped and underdeveloped agricultural economies of other nations to improve their efficiency and their output in the interest of their people. In these circumstances much of what we in the United States take for granted stands out starkly as a gaunt need. Research is a need: on soils, on pests, on seeds.

An array of services is needed, what we call the agri-business complex. Who is going to furnish the viable and reliable seed? Who the fertilizers? Who the insecticides? And when the crop is ready, who is going to buy it and store it and transport it and get it to market at a time and in a condition that makes it saleable? Who is going to furnish the credit for either the little operator or the large operator that will help him improve his efficiency, improve his income and raise the level of life for his family.

Mr. Chairman, a peculiar and amazing thing in recent years, in recent months, and even in recent weeks has been surfacing in the public media, in politicians' speeches, and in youthful rhetoric. What I am referring to is not only peculiar and amazing; it is also pitiful. An overwhelmingly urban population can easily take for granted an efficient agriculture. And then those few who become concerned about it may bring with their concern an ignorance, an innocence, and a romanticism that misses the point entirely. For thousands of years men have used their intelligence to try to free humanity from drudgery and burdens that sustained only poverty for all but a few. Man has sought to release himself, his body and his time and his mind for a higher quality of life. The goal of the land-grant colleges has been to further man's accomplishments on behalf of the human spirit. Nowhere has this success been more apparent and brought more blessings than in the agricultural enterprise and the homes of rural America. We join wholeheartedly with any public or private endeavors to mitigate and overcome the hardships of those who for one reason or another find themselves left behind or not accommodated in the changing prosperity of rural America. At the same time we reassert our clear commitment to an efficient and prosperous American farmer.

Statement before the Senate Subcommittee on Migratory Labor

E. T. YORK, Jr.

Mr. Chairman, Members of the Committee:

I appreciate this opportunity to appear before your Committee to comment on the publication, "Hard Tomatoes, Hard Times" by the Agri-business Accountability Project.

We in Florida have a very special interest in this report because the term "hard tomatoes" in the title refers to a variety of tomatoes developed by the Institute of Food and Agricultural Sciences (IFAS) of the University of Florida.

No one could have suspected that this poor little innocent looking vegetable could have gained such national attention and notoriety by being a part of the title of the report under consideration here. In addition to the initial publicity surrounding the publication of the report, Nicholas Von Hoffman last week saw fit to comment editorially on CBS Morning News about this tomato—in a very unfavorable light.

In view of all of this publicity, I would like for you, Mr. Chairman, and the Members of this Committee to have some firsthand knowledge of this tomato. Indeed, I would like for you to take it home with you. And if I could parrot a very common TV commercial today, I would say "Try it—you will like it!"

I have also brought some of these tomatoes to Mr. Hightower and his staff for them to try also. I do this because it is obvious from this report that those responsible for its preparation have never had previous exposure to this tomato.

The report and many of the related newspaper articles referred to the development of "bell shaped" tomatoes which would lend themselves to mechanical harvesting. I would call your attention to the fact that these are not "bell shaped" tomatoes, they are nice and round as nature, according to Mr. Hightower, must have intended tomatoes to be. The reference to the "bell shape" undoubtedly came from much publicity given some 10 years ago to the development of such a tomato in California suitable for mechanical harvesting. The Florida tomato has little or no kinship with the California variety—despite the assumptions by the writers who apparently had not seen the Florida product.

Throughout the report the writers emphasize that

□ Statement by Dr. E. T. York, Jr., Vice President for Agricultural Affairs, University of Florida, June 20, 1972.

the Land-Grant colleges assume a consumer be-damned attitude—being concerned only with helping agri-business. They cite the development of the MH-1 tomato as evidence of this and imply that while it may be great for mechanical harvesting, it is too hard and tough to be a quality product for the consumer.

Actually nothing could be further from the truth. Many consider the MH-1 tomato to have the best eating quality of any tomato produced in Florida.

Attached to my statement is a letter (Attachment 1) from Mr. J. S. Peters, Manager of the Florida Tomato Committee—an organization of Florida tomato growers. I am also attaching a statement (Attachment 2) prepared by Dr. Pat Crill, who is concerned with the tomato breeding program of the University. These two documents provide some interesting commentary on the MH-1.

First it is emphasized that this is, indeed, a very high quality tomato—in fact, taste panels and consumer preference tests have indicated it to be the highest quality Florida tomato available today. In one supermarket evaluation of consumer preference, the MH-1 was selected three to one over other tomato varieties available in the market. Although this is the first year of any volume production of MH-1, wholesale buyers have been willing to pay premiums for this variety because of its high quality and acceptance by the consumer. The very idea that producers would choose to grow a product unacceptable to the consumer is grossly irrational.

Because of its firmness and thick walls, the MH-1 is more adapted to high speed handling procedures used to move fruit from the farm to the consumer. This results in considerably less waste with more of the fruit being marketable which again reduces consumer costs and results in a higher quality product on the supermarket shelf.

Although the MH-1 has a potential for mechanical harvesting, 100% of the commercial tomato acreage in Florida is at the present time hand picked. Consequently, the variety is well suited to hand harvest, as well as having a potential for machine harvest. The MH-1 is preferred by farm laborers over conventional varieties as it is much easier and more profitable to pick by hand. The laborer can pick more than twice as many fruit as with conventional varieties.

The special harvesting techniques which have been

developed by the University are designed to utilize present labor under much more improved working conditions. The semi-harvester is dependent on labor to be feasible and when used with MH-1 has yielded a superior product that reduces cost to the consumer.

The report implies that there is something undesirable in the use of ethylene gas to hasten the ripening of tomatoes which may have been picked mature-green.

As a matter of fact, ethylene gas is a natural product, released in the ripening process of many fruits and vegetables and has been used under controlled conditions for the purpose of speeding up the natural ripening process of numerous fruits and vegetables. There is absolutely nothing harmful about the use of ethylene gas. Actually the MH-1 requires the use of less ethylene gas than most other varieties which are picked green because the firmness of the MH-1 enables the tomato to be picked at later maturity dates. In fact, many MH-1 tomatoes are being marketed without the use of any ethylene gas in the ripening process. Indeed, this variety, because of its superior shipping and keeping qualities, may be the first major market tomato which can be harvested and sold by the producer in a red ripe condition.

It is also pointed out that MH-1 variety is adaptable to mechanical harvesting not just because it is a firm tomato but because being jointless, it separates from the vine without an attached stem. Stems of other varieties cause damage to tomatoes with which they come in contact during the trip from the vine to the consumer.

Certainly all of this provides a much different picture of the MH-1 than Mr. Hightower and his report have presented to the American people. The MH-1 has, in fact, many quality characteristics which make it a much improved tomato for the consumer.

This erroneous image of the MH-1 tomato is very characteristic of many aspects of this report. It indicates very clearly that Mr. Hightower and his staff did not do their homework well.

The report indicates that "research" was conducted in Washington and on several Land-Grant college campuses, including the University of Florida. I don't know the nature of the "research" at my institution—but I have yet been unable to find any member of our University community who has ever talked with this group—or, in fact, who have ever heard of them until this report was issued.

They refer to themselves as a research organization. Yet their product doesn't come close to deserving such a label.

The writers have taken material out of context—they have been masterful at times in the use of half truths—they have completely misrepresented many

facts. The results of all of this is the most biased, distorted, and generally irresponsible piece of writing I have ever seen. Furthermore the language of the report insults and belittles the people of the Land-Grant colleges by referring to them as "soft headed" and "the most rested group you will ever meet." In many instances the writers use unnecessarily crude and offensive language. For example, they refer to some of the work of the Land-Grant colleges as "sociological bullshit."

I am not suggesting that there is no basis for criticizing the programs of the Land-Grant agricultural colleges. No public institution is immune and all organizations and institutions can benefit by fair, reasonable, and meaningful criticism. However, to be helpful, such criticism should reflect some degree of objectivity—should have some relationship to factual situations and need not be crude and offensive.

But aside from the abusive rhetoric, one must conclude that this report could have been written only by people who were both extremely naive and wantonly careless and irresponsible in making broad, generalized conclusions on the basis of a few carefully selected observations.

This report is so irresponsible, it does not deserve to be dignified by a detailed response. Mr. Hightower and his colleagues have gone to such extremes in their distortion of facts and biased analyses, the task of putting this report in perspective would be relatively simple; however, we do not have time to do that here today.

We have brought together in a separate document some material collected very hurriedly over the past three or four days to illustrate some of the programs and activities of one Land-Grant university—the University of Florida—in serving all of the people of Florida—not just agri-business as the report alleges. This brief summary refers to specific activities with individual farmers or with rural families or homemakers. The report also includes a few statements supplied by farmers or their families, indicating something of what these programs of research and extension have meant to them. I should emphasize that these statements do not represent a complete cross section or any sort of statistical random sampling. However, I would invite this Committee, or any other group interested in getting the facts surrounding the attitudes of farm and rural people, to conduct such a survey to determine what the people who are the users and beneficiaries of these programs think about them.

We emphasize this point to call attention to one very major deficiency in this report. The writers point out that the report was based upon research done in Washington and on the campuses of several Land-Grant colleges. There is essentially no reference in the report of the attitudes of farmers and rural people concerning the programs of the Land-Grant universities. Obviously no one is going to measure the impact of these programs by "research" in Washington, or even on university campuses. One has to get out and see what is happening and sample the attitudes of those who are being served by these programs. Obviously this was not done.

I would suggest, Mr. Chairman, that one of the best ways to measure the effectiveness of these Land-Grant college efforts—one of the best ways to evaluate the judgments made by Mr. Hightower and his group—would be to get reactions from the very people who Mr. Hightower charges are not being served by these colleges—to see if they agree with his conclusions. I am confident that if this were done, you would find that this small sampling of attitudes which we have included in this summary would be reflective of the general feeling of most farm and rural people. We would be extremely happy to have such a survey made in Florida if you would care to do so.

I wish we had time to respond specifically to each charge made in this report. This is not possible. However, I would like to take one situation in my home state which I think answers in a very meaningful way, many of the erroneous allegations made by Mr. Hightower and his colleagues.

Following are statements made in the report:

The Land-Grant community has done approximately nothing to extend the benefits of technology and management techniques to the vast majority of farmers and other rural Americans. (Page 245).

Had the Land-Grant community chosen to put its time, its money, its expertise and its technology into the family farm rather than in corporate pockets, then rural America today would be a place where millions could live and work in dignity. (Page 247).

Today the (Land-Grant) complex serves only one constituency: corporate agri-business. (Page 248).

It is not that Land-Grant colleges are tied to agri-business, but that they are tied exclusively to it. (Page 191).

Throughout the report many references are made to the fact that Land-Grant colleges are concerned very little with improving rural income or with helping the consumer.

On Page 73 the writers say, "A great deal of agricultural research involves tampering with nature's plan, using the sciences of genetics and chemistry. In a large part this research stems from Land-Grant communities faith in technology and fascination with the gadgetry."

Let me demonstrate what "technology and genetic gadgetry" have meant to the peanut growers in Florida over the last 30 years. We chose peanuts to illustrate this for several reasons—first, this is an

Table 1. Frequency distribution of 1971 farm peanut allotments by size groups in Florida

Size groups	Number of farms	Percent of total
3.0 Acres and less	530	12.3
3.1-5.0	961	22.3
5.1-7.5	768	17.8
7.6-10.0	526	12.2
10.1-20.0	876	20.3
20.1-30.0	283	6.6
30.1-40.0	145	3.4
40.1-50.0	77	1.8
50.1-75.0	68	1.6
75.1-100.0	36	0.8
100.1-200.0	27	0.6
200.1-300.0	4	0.09
300.1-400.0		0.0
400.1-500.0	1	0.02
Over 500	1	0.02
Total	4,303	

allotted crop so that we have accurate records of the size of farm operations. It is a crop that is grown primarily by small farmers. Furthermore, it is grown in an area of the state that is experiencing some of the adjustment problems referred to in the report.

In 1971 there were some 4,303 farms having peanut allotments in the state. The attached table indicates a breakdown of these farms according to size. Approximately one-third of the farms had allotments of five acres or less; two-thirds had ten acres or less; 85% had 20 acres or less; 95% had less than 40 acres. Insofar as we can determine, only two of the 4,303 farms could be classified as corporate farms—and these from all indications are incorporated family farms.

Over these past 30 years there have been some very significant advances in the technology of producing peanuts. The most significant of these advances has been the development of improved varieties which have greatly increased the yields of Florida peanuts. The attached chart (Figure 1) gives some indication of how yields have changed as new varieties, developed by the University of Florida, have come on to the scene. This chart indicates that the yields per acre of peanuts have essentially quadrupled since the early 40's. The new Florunner peanut which was released a couple of years ago is now being grown on essentially all of the acreage within the state. Furthermore, about 80% of the acreage in Alabama was planted to this variety last year as well and very high acreages in many of the surrounding states. The increased returns to Florida peanut growers in 1971 alone was some $13 million over the previous year's level. It is estimated that the increase in farm income throughout the South as a whole resulting from these new

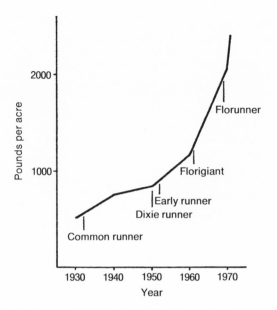

Fig. 1. Peanut yield; Florida statewide average, 1930-1971. The new varieties developed by University of Florida plant breeders have made possible a four-fold increase in peanut yields. This increase in 1971 alone was worth over $13 million to Florida peanut growers. The increase in farm income in the South, resulting from these new peanut varieties, amounted to $100 million in 1971.

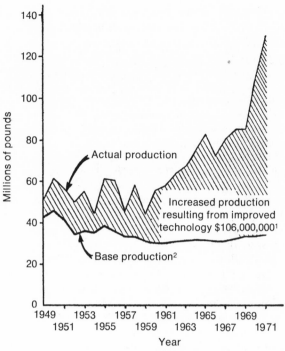

[1]Value of increased production at the average price for the 1971 year.

[2]Base production based on the average production per acre for the 5 years 1944-1948.

Fig. 2. Value of improved technology in Florida peanut production, 1949-1971.

peanut varieties amounted to some $100 million in 1971.

Figure 2 indicates what improved technology has meant in terms of increased production and income to peanut growers in Florida over the past several decades.

I would submit that this has been a very significant contribution to increasing the income levels of rural people. I would also contend that it has been aimed at helping all classes of farmers including the very smallest. The family farm has not been destroyed, but it has been modernized and much of the drudgery has been removed.

I would also remind you that while farmers have benefited by this—the ultimate beneficiary is the consumer in that through higher production it has been possible to provide the consuming public an ample supply of peanuts at reasonable costs.

If this is the results of "genetic gadgetry and other technology"—I would say lets have more, not less, of it.

Finally, to emphasize the fact that the consumer is the ultimate beneficiary of this work, I would like to give you some samples of this new peanut variety which has added millions of dollars to the pockets of peanut growers throughout the South and which is

providing millions of dollars worth of nutrition and eating pleasure to the consuming public.

These peanuts were processed by a grower cooperative near Williston, Florida which is doing a thriving business. Incidentally, we might point out that the University of Florida was instrumental in helping this cooperative get established and in operation—another indication of how a Land-Grant university has rendered assistance to farm and rural people.

We could use many other commodities to illustrate the same point—the extent to which the development and application of improved technology has helped farm and rural people. We could also talk at length of the manner in which such technology has helped the consumer. In fact, the Hightower report points to the claims by Land-Grant institutions concerning the "staggering achievement wrought by agricultural research." These claims cited in the report include the following:

• The farmer of today is able to produce food and fiber for himself and for 45 others; up from 11 others that he could provide for in 1940.

• Because of the farmer's increasing productivity millions of other Americans are freed from farming and are able to pursue other occupations.

• The consumer receives an abundant and steady supply of more food products than ever before.

• Because of the farmer's productivity the American consumer pays a mere 16% of his disposable income on food, the lowest rate in the world.

• As the producer of America's agricultural abundance the farmer is the major contributor towards a favorable balance of payments position for this country.

• American agricultural technology and know-how stands as a final bulwark against world-wide famine.

"Everyone of these points can be conceded" says Mr. Hightower. "The question is whether the achievements outweigh the failures—whether benefits are overwhelmed by costs."

We might wish Mr. Hightower had made a thorough and objective analysis of costs vs benefits of Land-Grant agricultural programs. It would be very interesting to speculate on just what our nation would be like today had the advances cited above not been made.

Throughout the report there are many suggestions that we would be better off without the technological developments than with them. The argument against developing MH-1 to aid in the mechanization of tomato production is a good example of this type of persuasion.

It is abundantly clear that if these arguments against the development and application of technology had been successfully applied over the past 100 years, our nation today would be one of the most undeveloped areas of the world. The development and use of improved technology has helped make the U.S. the most advanced agricultural nation on earth. Similarly, the development and application of improved technology in industry has made us the great industrial nation that we are today.

If what this nation has accomplished through its agricultural and industrial revolution is undesirable, someone had better get the word to most of the other nations on earth which are striving desperately to make the same type of progress in agricultural development as we have achieved in the United States. Indeed, throughout the world, the developing nations are attempting to create agricultural research and educational programs modeled after our own Land-Grant system—convinced that this is the best way to achieve their goals for stimulating economic development and improving the social and economic status of their citizens.

What are the returns to society from public investments in agricultural research and education? Studies conducted at the University of Chicago (which I would remind you is not a Land-Grant institution) have indicated that the annual returns to society on accumulated investment in research on hybrid corn to be about 700%. A parallel study in Minnesota on poultry innovations indicate annual returns of 89% on research in breeding and nutrition. Other studies have indicated that on the average the external rate of return to society on all investments in agricultural research and extension in this country is in excess of 100% annually.

We refer to hybrid corn research. Certainly this has been one of the most dramatic breakthroughs in agricultural technology within our country. I am sure, Mr. Chairman, that you are quite aware of the impact of this in your own state. In the five year period from 1928-1932, Illinois grew on the average 9,300,000 acres of corn with an average yield per acre of 36 bushels. This was before hybrid corn and associated technology came on the scene. In 1971, Illinois had an average corn yield of 102 bushels per acre.

This is a good example of how "genetic gadgetry" has enabled the state of Illinois to essentially treble its corn production with less than a 10% increase in acreage. Obviously to have produced the same amount of corn in 1971 with yield levels of the late 20's and early 30's would have required almost 30 million acres of land.

I would also emphasize the impact of corn blight on corn production in Illinois. In 1969, Illinois produced about 950,000,000 bushels of corn. In 1970, because of the corn blight situation, production dropped to 736,000,000 bushels. Primarily because of the Land-Grant's system of "genetic gadgetry" it was possible to overcome this corn blight situation to the point today that it no longer poses the serious threat so evident two years ago.

We have emphasized the contributions which improved technology has made to higher agricultural production. At times this works to the detriment of the farmer, since prices of farm products frequently drop sharply when supply exceeds the demand for these products. However, I would emphasize the other side of that coin—the interests of the consumer. When production of a given commodity drops, the price to the consumer is likely to increase sharply. For example, a recent study of egg prices show that a 5% increase in production may result in a 20% reduction in price. Similarly, a 5% drop in production may result in a substantial increase in price to the consumer.

The poultry industry is an example of how improved technology has been passed on to the consumer. The absolute prices per pound of eggs and broilers are lower today than in the 1930's. (Table 2) Also, the quality of the products is superior to the ones sold in

Table 2. Five year analysis prices received by Florida poultrymen for eggs & broilers

Year	Egg price (per dozen)	Broiler price (per pound)
1941-45	37.2	27.2
1946-50	54.2	37.1
1951-55	53.4	28.0
1956-60	44.2	18.2
1961-65	35.2	14.2
1966-70	32.2	13.6

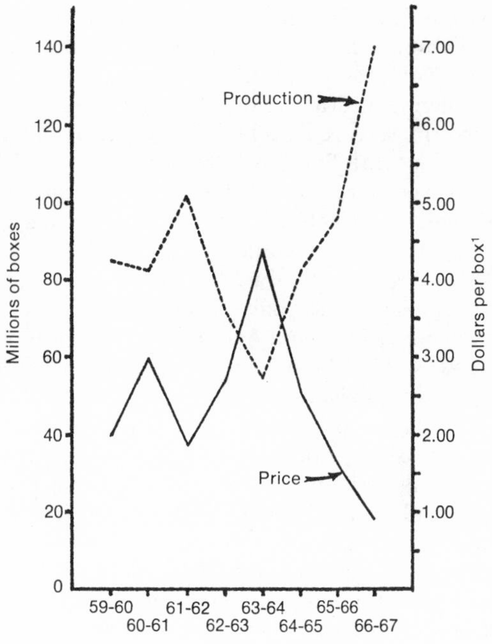

[1]Season average on-tree price per box.

Fig. 3. Relationship between orange production and orange on-tree price.

the 1930's. This is particularly significant considering the amount of general inflation the U.S. has had during this period.

Figure 3 illustrates the relationship between prices and production quite well in the citrus industry in Florida. These data show essentially an inverse relationship between production and prices. My point is that higher production may not always work to the advantage of the producer—but in most instances it certainly works to the advantage of the consumer. This fact illustrates again a point which has been so readily apparent over the years—that the *primary* beneficiary of improved agricultural technology has been the consumer. Hence, research aimed at developing such technology is in a very real sense "people oriented."

Similarly, for a more recent impact of technology on consumer price and quality, the price for a 6 ounce can of frozen orange concentrate has declined since the late 1950's. Solids equivalent to one additional orange have been added and processing technology now retains the orange essence to further improve quality.

A recent government report reveals that the U.S. consumers have benefited greatly from improved technology in agriculture. It shows that the food purchased by all consumers in 1968 (99.4 billion dollars) would have cost $16 billion more if it had been produced by the 1940 production and marketing practices. Of course, this means that low income people, who spend a higher percent of their income on food, would benefit more from this change than other consumers. Hence, if we were still producing food with 1940 technology, there would be considerably more people classified at poverty level than is currently the case.

Due to the nature and organization of U.S. agriculture most of the benefits of technology change is passed on to the consumer regardless of whether it is produced by small farmers, larger farmers, corporations or cooperatives.

One might take this statement and attempt to prove

the contention that such technology was not in the farmer's interests. However, I doubt if anyone can seriously contend that it is not in the consumers interest—or in the interest of the public generally.

What, then, is the alternative? To prohibit the use of such technology as Mr. Hightower's report suggests in the case of mechanization of tomatoes?—or continue to take advantage of such technology which can ultimately be in the consumer's interests. I think the answer is obvious.

The major thesis of the Hightower report is to the effect that the Land-Grant colleges are concerned primarily with serving big corporate farming interests and agri-business generally. In fact, there is this specific statement: "Today the complex serves only one constituency: corporate agri-business."

We have already partially addressed this assertion. I would also point out that in Florida corporate farms constitute less than 5% of the total farms in the state. Furthermore, many of these so-called corporate farms are nothing more than family farms that have been incorporated for business purposes. Many of the really large corporate operations don't look to or need the help of Land-Grant colleges because they may, in fact, have their own research organization.

The report makes quite an issue of financial support

received by Land-Grant colleges from agri-business firms. I think that this, too, needs to be put in perspective. For example, reference is made to the fact that "chemical drug and oil companies invested $227,158 in research at Florida's Institute of Food and Agricultural Sciences—accounting for 54% of research sponsored there for private industry in 1970." This implies that a very high percentage of our total research support comes from chemical drug and oil companies. Actually the $227,958 referred to by the report represents less than 1% of the total budget of the Institute of Food and Agricultural Sciences at the University of Florida. It represents less than 2% of the total research budget.

In Florida we do not do contractual research for agri-business firms or anyone else. We accept a research grant only when the funds can be used to enable us to do a job which we need to do anyhow and which is consistent with our basic mission.

Much of the support we receive is in the form of relatively small grants related to the testing or evaluation of chemicals or other products which we normally would be testing in order to advise farmers concerning the suitability of their use. Despite the Hightower allegations, any work we do is fully available to the public.

Many commercial grants are also related to scholarships or graduate assistantships. Normally no strings whatsoever are attached to these grants. They are made by industry in recognition of the fact that industry is, in fact, dependent in a large measure upon the Land-Grant colleges for the development of trained manpower. These grants are rather modest investments in the development of such trained manpower.

The report says that "Land-Grant colleges must get out of corporate board rooms and they must get corporate interests out of their labs." I cannot speak for all states, however, in my own state I would point out that we do not permit our personnel to serve as members of the Board of Directors of agri-business firms. In fact, we do not even permit our personnel to consult with agriculturally related organizations in our state. We recognize that there is always that possibility of being accused of conflicts of interest even though no such conflicts might exist.

I recognize that there may be instances of relationships between universities and agri-business firms which might give rise to the sorts of concerns expressed in the report. However, one of my serious concerns about the many phases of the report is that the writers make broad, sweeping indictments of the entire system without pointing out that the evidence which they use for making the system-wide indictments is very limited and may, in fact, apply only to a very small percentage of the total.

In closing, Mr. Chairman, let me say again that I think that this report represents one of the most biased, distorted, unfair and generally irresponsible pieces of writing I have ever seen.

There is an old story about the farmer who every morning before getting ready to start plowing would pick up a large pole and almost knock the mule down by hitting him in the head. When quizzed about his action the farmer said, "I'm just trying to get his attention."

I suppose the most charitable thing we can say about this report is that the intentions of the authors were merely to gain the attention of the Land-Grant complex. Perhaps the sort of excesses resorted to in the report can be justified by the writers—just as by the farmer. However, I would contend that there may well be better ways of getting ones attention and that the end result may be even more productive than to resort to the type of tactics which have been used in this case.

I would repeat to you what I said to a local newspaper reporter who asked me to comment on the report. About the only part of the report that I can agree with is the recommendation in the summary—calling for a "full-scale public inquiry into the Land-Grant college complex."

Although I don't think this report merits the attention it has received, in the light of the charges made, perhaps a full-scale inquiry could be appropriate at the state level as well as by Congress.

Such an inquiry should include a careful examination of the authority given Land-Grant colleges of agriculture by Congress and state legislatures along with the manner in which these institutions have carried out this authority.

You realize, I am sure Mr. Chairman, that the programs of the Land-Grant institutions are scrutinized annually by both Congress and state legislatures in the appropriation process. If these programs are as misdirected and ineffective as Mr. Hightower alleges, the report, "Hard Tomatoes, Hard Times," is just as much an indictment of Congress and state legislative leaders as of the Land-Grant system.

Agribusiness and agrigovernment: power, profits, and poverty

JIM HIGHTOWER

In 1970, the American grocery bill came to $91 *billion*. Add in the restaurant tab, and the total food bill for that year was $114 billion. The farm system that produces, processes, markets, and profits from that food is not what most Americans presume it to be. It is not the little family farmer bringing those goods to market. It is agribusiness. Like television sets and panty hose, food is the product of a massive industrialized system that Carey McWilliams has dubbed "factories in the field."

In fact, America's number-one-industry is food—not defense hardware, not transportation, not electronics, but food. Involved here are the big growers, bankers, seed companies, farm-machinery manufacturers, chemical producers, management consultants, packagers, processors, wholesalers, marketing specialists, supermarkets, and advertising companies. This complex is studded with well-known brand names. Many nonfarm industries, including some of the nation's biggest corporations and conglomerates, are playing an increasingly important role within the farm complex. From tilling soil to bagging your groceries, big business is in charge.

But these agribusinessmen are in charge of more than grocery profits; they, primarily, are accountable for the miserable plight of some 14 million rural Americans who live in poverty. More directly, they are accountable for the exploitation of millions of farm workers and their families. Agribusiness interests work hand in hand with government bureaucrats, land-grant-college academicians, well-placed congressmen, and Department of Agriculture appointees to assure a rural America in their own image, a rural America that is more aptly symbolized by the dollar sign than by the old farmhouse.

AGRIBUSINESS

The Jeffersonian ideal of the little family farmer survives today mostly as a carefully preserved myth. Because most people have a nostalgic faith in the goodness of the family farmer, and because politicians are reluctant to restrict the enterprise of the small farmer, it is profitable for agribusiness to keep that

myth alive. The United States Department of Agriculture (USDA) lines up on the side of agribusiness and helps the industry perpetuate this little deception. The reality of the farm economy is something else.

In the first place, the total number of farms has been declining radically while the average size of farms has been increasing. In 1945, there were some 6 million farms, averaging 167 acres each. In 1971, USDA reported that there were less than 3 million farms, averaging 389 acres. That is half as many farms, averaging twice as much acreage. In short, the farmland was not retired; it simply has been concentrated in fewer hands. Although the USDA and agribusiness try to soft-pedal it, the stark truth is that this rate of concentration will continue. *Barron's*, a magazine that caters to the corporate executive, enthusiastically reported in 1968 that

farming has become big business and the old homestead never will be the same again. USDA officials estimate that within the next two decades 500,000 large-scale corporate farms will do the work of today's three million enterprises.

But the proper measure of a small farmer and a big grower is not acreage; it is sales. USDA considers a small farmer to be one who has sales of under $5,000 a year. The medium-sized farm grosses between $5,000 and $20,000. A large farm is one that grosses over $20,000, while a "largest" category exists for the really big boys: $100,000 and up. USDA was happy to report in March of 1970 that over half (56.5 percent) of all farmers were in the small-farm category. Large farmers were a mere 11.7 percent, and USDA pointed out that the largest farmers were practically insignificant: 0.9 percent, to be exact.

USDA did not stress the fact that those small farmers came away with only 7.8 percent of all farm sales. The medium-sized farmer did better, pulling in 29.2 percent of sales. But the large farmers pulled off 38.7 percent of the sales, and the insignificant largest group managed 24.3 percent of the take. That is, less than 13 percent of all the farmers in this country are making away with two-thirds of all farm sales!

It is in that top 13 percent that agribusiness lurks. But consider only the upper crust of these big farms, those who had sales of over $100,000. These are the most industrialized operations. According to the 1969 Census of Agriculture, these agribusinessmen averaged sales of $272,000. Furthermore, this top 1 percent of growers accounted for 29 percent of all feed bought, 39 percent of all livestock and poultry bought, 24 percent of all machinery hired, 11 percent of all fuel bought, 17 percent of all seed bought, 16 percent of all fertilizer bought, and 41 percent of all labor hired. These few growers had 29 percent of all inputs purchased by farms in 1964, and that percentage is increasing each year. What we have here is a dramatic statistical presentation of the agribusiness complex: huge growers and their dependents in the feed, livestock, farm-equipment, fuel, seed, and fertilizer industries.

The most significant thing about the dominance of agriculture by these largest growers is that, steadily, it is becoming total. In the five years between the 1959 Census of Agriculture and the one taken in 1964, these growers increased their numbers by more than half (to 31,000), and they increased their share of total farm sales by a third (to 24 percent). Five years later, USDA reports that "In the general race toward larger business size, the number of farms with sales of $100,000 or more probably reached 40,000 in 1969, and their gross sales accounted for at least one-third of total sales by all farms."

Who are some of these profit reapers? What are some of the names that are painted up on the barns and that are making the decisions of today's agribusiness? Many family names remain prominent, corporate families like DiGiorgio and Antle in California, Wedgeworth and Duda in Florida, and Brand and Bentsen in Texas.

The processors are the very embodiment of agribusiness. Involved here are the giant brand names such as Stokely-Van Camp, H. J. Heinz Company, Libby McNeill and Libby, Coca Cola, Campbell Soup, Ocean Spray Cranberries, Ralston Purina, General Foods, Green Giant, and dozens of others. A good example of this category is Del Monte Corporation.

Del Monte Corporation claims to be the largest producer and distributor of canned fruits and vegetables in the world, marketing 250 different styles and packs of food. Del Monte is much more than that. The company owns 32,000 acres of farmland and leases an additional 77,600 acres throughout the United States. They operate processing plants in nine foreign countries, including South Africa. They own fourteen can-manufacturing companies, twenty-four public restaurants, five trucking operations, a tuna-freezing company, an ocean terminal, a label-printing concern, and dozens of other agribusiness enterprises. Del Monte is a major employer of seasonal farm workers, ranging in 1969 from a low of 6,000 to a peak of 39,000. Thousands more are hired indirectly by Del Monte, through crew leaders and by contractual arrange-

ments. To house those workers, the company owns several labor camps. In California, they have surrounded some of their camps with barbed wire. In 1970, when it looked like farm workers were about to be included in the national unemployment compensation program, this multimillion-dollar corporation took the time to oppose such coverage.

The giant supermarket chains are involved in more than simple marketing of farm produce. They have contracts and other corporations to literally every element of the food industry. Safeway offers a clear example of this involvement.

Safeway Stores, Incorporated, is the second largest retail food chain in the country; its 2,000-plus stores accounted for $3.7 billion in sales in 1968. Safeway does not employ farm workers, but it has made a major effort to keep them down. The corporation has been among the most recalcitrant of food stores in the United Farm Workers' Organizing Committee's (UFWOC) efforts to gain support for its consumer boycotts. A look at Safeway's board of directors tells why: They share directors with two railroads, three major California banks, the *Los Angeles Times*, Continental Can Company, Caterpillar Tractor Company, one of the largest land owners and growers in the country, and numerous other agribusiness corporations.

Agribusiness is a capital-intensive industry. Whether it is the First National Bank of McAllen, Texas, the Mercantile-Safe Deposit and Trust Company of Baltimore, Maryland, or the Prudential Insurance Company of America, financial institutions are major partners in the agribusiness industry. None is more involved than California's Bank of America.

Bank of America is the very embodiment of agribusiness. A former president of the bank noted in 1968 that they had $3 billion in agriculture. Al Krebs, a California journalist, reports that the bank finances over half of the agriculture in that state. What is more, the bank owns 5,000 acres of farmland in the San Joaquin Valley, which it leases to a subsidiary called Agri-business Investments, Inc. Five hundred farm workers are employed there, and the bank has refused a UFWOC request to negotiate about unionizing those workers.

Many nonagricultural corporations have moved into agribusiness, some for profits and some simply looking for a tax loss. In the last decade, nearly 7,000 corporations have come into farming and related activities. Among these new agribusinessmen are some of the corporate powers of America. Dow Chemical Corporation has important ties to California agribusiness; Penn Central railroad has agricultural interests in Florida; Union Carbide is involved in Texas; and the Goodyear Tire and Rubber Company is a grower in Arizona. Tenneco is a conglomerate that offers a striking insight into the depths of this corporate involvement in agribusiness.

Tenneco is a conglomerate that probably is best known for its oil and gas products. But this massive corporation is just as deeply immersed in agribusiness. For starters, it owns the Kern County Land Company, a million-acre spread in California that leases another 700,000 acres of farmland elsewhere. That giant company is a major employer of farm labor, and it includes subsidiary ownership of processing plants and a farm-management company. The J. I. Case Company is one of the largest manufacturers of farm machinery in the country, and it is a direct subsidiary of Tenneco. Another subsidiary, Tenneco Chemicals, is a major producer of pesticides, while Tenneco's Packaging Corporation of America also is deeply involved in the food industry. Of the six members of Tenneco's board of directors who are not directly tied to the company, two are bankers, one is president of the Southern Pacific Company, and another is president of Texas A and M.

This is only a sample of those who are involved in the industrialization of American agriculture. Without question, these agribusinessmen have proven a force for efficiency. Although the number of farmers has declined radically, and although the total amount of acreage being farmed is less than ever, the world has never known agriculture production to approach today's American bounty. Grocery shelves and bins are well stocked with something in the neighborhood of 8,000 edible items, and agribusiness has turned out a surplus of nearly all of them. Back in World War II, each farmer was able to produce enough food and fiber for himself and eleven others; now he has the money, the chemicals, the equipment, and the techniques to feed and clothe himself and forty-two others.

But, as Max Lerner wrote in his classic study *America as a Civilization:* "In looking at the splendid efficiency of the best American farming, it is easy to forget how much of it rides on the backs of humble, anonymous men."

FARM WORKERS IN AGRIBUSINESS

It can be stated bluntly: Agribusiness exploits farm workers. To the industry, these field laborers are a necessary evil, wanted when it is time to hoe a field or harvest a crop, but definitely not wanted once the task is done. What is important here is attitude: Somehow farm workers are just another cost of production, not human beings. As a USDA official put it way back in 1929: "Mass production has thus brought about what may be called the mechanization of the human element in the industry. The harvesting gangs are called in when wanted just as the tractor and the gang

plow are brought out of the shed when needed." Today, USDA statisticians give official sanction to this dehumanization by listing hired labor along with machines, gasoline, seed, and fertilizer as just another "purchased input."

When confronted with the situation of its farm workers, agribusiness ducks behind the myth of the family farmer, claiming that any tampering with the status quo simply would drive employers to the wall and leave workers without any employment. Nonsense. The farm-wage bill in 1964 came to $2.8 billion. More than $1 billion of that (37 percent) was paid by the large farmers, and another $1.1 billion (41 percent) was paid by that 1 percent of farmers in USDA's largest category. In short, agribusiness paid 78 percent of the total wage bill. Those 1.8 million small farmers, who are the focus of so much agribusiness concern, laid out only $144 million for wages (5.2 percent of the total). In terms of number of workers hired, the picture is the same. An overwhelming 92.7 percent of farms had no laborers or had what amounts to one hired hand for less than a full year.

Without question, farm workers are the responsibility of agribusiness, that 13 percent of growers who hire nearly all workers and who financially and structurally are best positioned to do right by their employees. That those businessmen do not do right is obvious to even a casual observer. Farm workers are the waste product of American agribusiness.

USDA reports that "about 2.6 million different persons did some work on farms for cash wages or salary in 1969." About 1.5 million of those did farm work only; on the average, they were able to find work for only 95 days of the year and were able to earn a pitiful $1,030. The remaining 1 million combined an average 109 days of other kinds of work with 50 days of farm work in an effort to make ends meet; they came away with $2,169 for their year's labor. Less than 12 percent of this country's farm workers were employed year-round; they were the highest paid, pulling down a whopping $3,485.

These wages are a scandal. On Edward R. Murrow's classic 1960 television documentary "Harvest of Shame," one Florida grower summed it up precisely when he said, "We used to own our slaves, now we just rent them." The federal minimum wage law was passed back in the New Deal. Farm workers specifically were excluded from that labor legislation, and it was not until 1966 that they finally were given partial inclusion. That inclusion requires only 0.6 percent of all farms to pay a minimum wage that today is 30 cents below the minimum that is paid all other workers.

At least that legislation covers some of the biggest agribusinessmen; 41 percent of the largest growers are required to pay their field workers $1.30 an hour. But even that token is too much for these agribusinessmen. On March 23, 1971, the U.S. Department of Labor (USDL) reported that "nearly three of every 10 farms visited by [USDL] investigators were found to be violating the minimum wage law." Some 8,000 farm workers had been underpaid by a total of $1 million. Speaking for the Department of Labor, Robert Moran reported that "untold thousands of farm workers are either unaware" of their right to the minimum wage or they "do not call violations to the attention of the Department of Labor for fear of losing their jobs."

USDL investigators found that many agribusinessmen had resorted to subterfuge: They would pay the minimum wage but would deduct excessive charges for housing, firewood, food, water, electricity, and harvest sacks or buckets. (Yes, many of these multi-million-dollar agribusinesses actually require their field workers to purchase the sacks that they must have for the harvest.) These subterfuges and outright violations simply reflect the fact that the growers resent having to pay even an inadequate minimum. As a grower in the area of Tampa, Florida, put it: "If a man wants to hire a worker for 50 cents a day, and that worker wants to do the work for 50 cents a day, why can't he do it?"

The condition of America's farm workers and their families is no secret. Since the early New Deal, not a year has passed without a congressional hearing, a presidential report, a White House conference, a major book, a television documentary, or some other high-intensity exposure of the misery of farm workers. That misery need not be detailed again here. Nothing has changed; farm workers and their families today live still in stiffling shelters that are without heat, plumbing, privacy, or hope for human happiness; their health continues to make a mockery of this nation's enormous wealth; their exploitative wages and inhuman working conditions persist in a day when all other laborers are ensconced in powerful, protective unions; and their economic and political powerlessness put the lie to this country's pretensions about freedom of opportunity.

John Steinbeck said all that needs to be said in this passage from *The Grapes of Wrath:* "There is a crime here that goes beyond denunciation. There is a sorrow here that weeping cannot symbolize. There is a failure here that topples all our success."

It might be expected that the government of a civilized society would respond to such obvious need. The American government has not. Because of the opposition of agribusiness, farm workers deliberately were excluded from practically every piece of New Deal labor legislation. Today, they are still denied the right

of collective bargaining, which was assured other workingmen by the Wagner Act of 1935. Whether a man is a government bureaucrat, a university professor, a carpenter, an aircraft engineer, or even a grower, he is entitled to unemployment compensation when he is out of work; the farm worker is not, even though his employment is among the most insecure. Farm work is the third most hazardous industry in this country, but only twenty-one states allow workmen's compensation for farm workers, and only fourteen of those give him the same protection afforded others. It is noted above that farm workers did not get minimum-wage protection until 1966, and even then the coverage was made dramatically less than that enjoyed by other workers. The child-labor standards are lower for farm workers, allowing an estimated 375,000 children of ten to thirteen years old to do farm work in 1969. Coverage of farm workers under the Social Security Act did not come until 1951, and today it remains less comprehensive than coverage for all other workers.

Of course, there have been some sops tossed. In the heyday of Kennedy's New Frontier and Johnson's Great Society, Congress was persuaded to grind out a few ameliorative programs for farm workers: a migrant health act, a migrant education act, a farm labor housing act, and a Migrant Division created in the Office of Economic Opportunity (OEO). From the beginning, these were Band-Aid operations, badly watered down in the legislative process and hopelessly underfunded in the appropriations process. What little promise they held was broken in the administration of the acts.

One of the best efforts to provide decent housing for migrants is the one that is tied to the recruitment of those workers through the Department of Labor's Farm Labor Service. Growers who use that service to get workers must meet housing standards set by the department. However, department regulations allow for variances from standard as long as they do not create a hazard. In 1969, the Chicago regional office of USDL decided against allowing variances. About 10,000 Michigan growers signed a petition demanding that variances be allowed, and other growers exerted political pressure in Washington. USDL quickly caved in, and variances were allowed. Many other growers simply decided not to use the recruitment service and, thus, not to have to answer to anyone about housing conditions.

The point is that farm workers are at the mercy of a grower's whim. Farm workers are powerless people; whenever their human needs conflict with an agribusinessman's perception of his own economic needs, it is the human need that will give way. That is because the agribusinessman is a full citizen in this society; he has an open channel of communication to decision makers.

The industrialization of American agriculture, along with its efficiency ethic, has produced more than agricultural abundance. On the one hand it has allowed a few men and a few corporations to amass great wealth and to hold enormous power; on the other hand, it has demanded that many men labor powerlessly in desperate poverty. That is no innocent paradox. Those men of wealth and power, eagerly assisted by their government, deliberately have designed and implemented an agricultural policy that further enriches the few while exploiting the many.

AGRIGOVERNMENT

It is not the inevitable workings of history that made agribusiness dominant and farm workers subsurvient in rural America; rather, it is the carefully managed impact of government policies. Farm workers are not the ones who have shaped those policies, nor have the great mass of small and medium-sized farmers been the ones to make the choices; those policies are the product of agribusiness. Just as farming has become concentrated in fewer and more powerful hands, so has rural political power, These men of wealth and power have set themselves up in Washington as an agrigovernment to assure socialism for agribusiness and free enterprise for farm workers. They have been wildly successful in both efforts.

The dimensions of agrigovernment

Wherever rural decisions are made in Washington, agribusiness has a presence. It permeates the city at all levels, from lobbyist to congressmen to secretary of agriculture.

In terms of sheer numbers, the agribusiness is most obvious as lobbyist. From such massive undertakings as the American Farm Bureau Federation and the United Fresh Fruit and Vegetable Association, to the more limited efforts of such outfits as the North Carolina Cotton Promotion Association, farm representatives abound in Washington. There likely is a lobbyist sitting in Washington for every product sitting on the grocery shelf. In addition, there are the agricultural-input representatives: the National Agricultural Chemicals Association, the National Association of Food Chains, the National Association of Frozen Food Packers, the National Canners Association, and countless others. The brand names have their own men, Libby McNeil and Libby, General Foods, and most others retain Washington lawyers to represent their special needs. There also are other lobby operations that have agribusiness sections or that can be counted on to support the interest of agribusiness, such as

the Liberty Lobby, the U.S. Chamber of Commerce, and the National Association of Manufacturers.

These lobbyists are effective. Day in and day out, they are in Washington, making daily rounds in the Congress and within the bureaucracy to make sure that things go their way. They have the resources to maintain Washington offices, to publish regular legislative newsletters, to take government officials to dinner, to buy tickets to political fund-raising functions, and otherwise to make their presence known and felt within the circles of power.

None of these lobbies has been a more active, more ardent, or more successful advocate of agribusiness than the American Farm Bureau Federation (Farm Bureau), which bills itself as "the voice of agriculture." This massive lobby was begun as a spin-off of the chamber of commerce movement in the 1920s and for many years actually had staff funded by the Department of Agriculture. Since the New Deal, the Farm Bureau has opposed literally every piece of progressive legislation to come along. Cesar Chavez, in the foreword to Samuel Berger's excellent book about the Farm Bureau, *Dollar Harvest*, has written:

> The Farm Bureau has been one of the most steadfast and consistent opponents of our efforts to unionize the country's farm workers. Arm and arm with other reactionary forces, it has resisted the attempt by farm workers to join together to bargain effectively and lift themselves from the bottom of the economic ladder. It has attempted to defame and discredit our Union and break its strikes. It has lead the battle in Washington to cripple unionization with restrictive legislation. It has fought every attempt to improve the conditions of farm workers by opposing legislation to give us such minimum protections as Social Security, unemployment insurance, and minimum wage and hour legislation.

In fact, the Farm Bureau's claim to be an organization of farmers is a fraud; the organization is a massive business conglomerate, with $4 billion in assets. As Samuel Berger has detailed, "the Farm Bureau business empire now spans the economy: from insurance to oil, from fertilizer to finance companies, from mutual funds to shopping centers. It has even acquired its own travel agency." The Farm Bureau is in league with agribusiness because it is an agribusiness. Far from being the farmer's spokesman, the Farm Bureau urges a government policy of farm elimination that would leave only agribusiness in rural America. What would happen to those farmers cast off the land? A former editor of *Farm Journal*, a close ally of the Farm Bureau, had an answer for that. He recently had taken up golf, and it had occurred to him while on the links that many of those expelled farmers could become golf caddies.

It is in the executive branch that agribusiness is supreme. Just as the military contractors have been found to control the Pentagon, agribusiness is in charge at the U.S. Department of Agriculture. Over the years, this department has become a massive bureaucracy that dedicates practically every effort to the service of the agribusiness complex.

The federal government made its first direct contribution to farmers in 1839, appropriating $1,000 to the agriculture division of the U.S. Patent Office. Part of that money was expended in the first agricultural program: the distribution of 30,000 packets of seed. Today, the department has nearly seventy programs and, according to the *National Journal*, "spends $1,000 about every 20 seconds." Like all bureaucracies, the department has mushroomed. In 1945, it had one employee for every seventy-three farms; now, that ratio has reached one employee for every twenty-four farms.

The important fact is that nearly all of those employees are equipped by education, by experience, and by temperament to serve agribusiness. Consider the top levels of the department, those presidential appointees who sit as decision makers:

Earl L. Butz is Secretary of Agriculture. He has spent his entire life shifting back and forth between the land-grant college campus, government, and corporate agribusiness. He has been dean of agriculture at Purdue University, an assistant secretary of agriculture under Ezra Taft Benson, and a director of the conservative Foundation of American Agriculture. At the time of his appointment by President Nixon, Butz was receiving salaries totalling $28,800 for service on the boards of directors of International Minerals and Chemical Corporation, Stokely Van-Camp, Ralston Purina and Standard Life Insurance Company.

Among his top assistants, Undersecretary of Agriculture J. Phil Campbell has been a grower, a member of the Farm Bureau, and Georgia's commissioner of agriculture. The Assistant Secretary of Agriculture Richard E. Lyng has been president of a seed corporation and served as California director of agriculture.

Don Paarlberg is director of agricultural economics. He has been a farmer and a member of the Farm Bureau. He is an agricultural academic, with a Ph.D. in agricultural economics from Cornell University. In the Eisenhower administration, Paarlberg rose within USDA to become assistant secretary of agriculture, where he is remembered best as the man who ordered the 1957 *Farm Population Estimates* to be destroyed because the publication contained some comments that were not favorable toward that administration's policy of deliberately discouraging the small farmer and enthusiastically supporting the agribusinessman.

The two major human programs of USDA are housing and food. James V. Smith is the administrator of the Farmers Home Administration, which makes loans and grants for rural housing and for farm operation. Smith is a lifetime farmer, a recipient of federal farm payments, a member of the Farm Bureau, and a former congressman. Edward J. Hekman is the director of the Food and Nutrition Service, which administers USDA's food programs. Hekman was president of the United Biscuit Company, a director of the Grocery Manufacturers of America, and vice-president of the National Association of Manufacturers. Hekman favors letting local officials determine who gets food stamps, and he has pushed a program "opening up the national school lunch program to private food management companies."

The heads of USDA's farm programs also are tied to agribusiness. Kenneth Frick is the administrator of the Agricultural Stabilization and Conservation Service, which handles disbursement of federal farm payments. Frick owns a 2,000-acre farm in California and has himself been the recipient of large farm payments. Odin Langen is the administrator of the Packers and Stockyards Administration. He is an active farmer, a member of the Farm Bureau, and a former member of Congress, where he served on both the House Agriculture and Appropriations committees.

In USDA's state offices, the situation is the same. President Nixon has named forty different men to serve as state directors of the Farmers Home Administration. Exactly half of those have been farmers; ten are members of the Farm Bureau, eleven have been involved in various agribusinesses, and fifteen have experience in banking, insurance, or real estate. This is the USDA agency that is supposed to do the most about reaching the small farmer and the rural poor. Similarly, Nixon has named a total of 167 men to serve on the state committees of the Agricultural Stabilization and Conservation Service; 113 of those are members of the Farm Bureau. These are Republican appointments, but it really does not make much difference which party is on top; agribusinessmen have the muscle to make sure that they will be comfortable with the men chosen to serve rural America.

Beneath the appointed policy makers is a wide-ranging bureaucracy, staffed increasingly with agricultural technocrats who have been educated at the land-grant colleges and whose careers have been a series of shifts from agribusiness to government. Nowhere has this incestuous relationship been more frankly stated than in a congressional exchange that took place on February 27, 1970, between Chairman Jamie Whitten, of the House Agricultural Appropriations Subcommittee, and Mr. Donald Campbell, who then was head of USDA's Packers and Stockyards Administration:

Mr. Whitten: How many resignations have you had?
Mr. Campbell: We have lost a number of men throughout the

years due to this salary structure. For example, the president of the American Stockyards Association used to be with us. The executive vice president of the Chicago stockyards used to be with us. One of our former employees is manager of the Tulsa, Okla., stockyard. One of our former men was president of the Baltimore stockyard before it went out of business.

Mr. Whitten: Now you are raising another question that is very serious here. You mean the Department is training people to run these various things that you are trying to regulate?

Mr. Campbell: No, sir, but industry has recognized the talent of our men and some of our men have gone out to industry.

Mr. Whitten: They recognized they were hiring somebody who knew how to get along on the inside?

Mr. Campbell: No, sir, I don't believe that is the case.

Mr. Whitten: They didn't know how to get along on the inside?

Mr. Campbell: They never asked for or succeeded in getting any favors.

Mr. Whitten: I said get along; I didn't say get favors.

Mr. Campbell: I don't really believe that is the case. They are good men.

The zenith of agrigovernment was reached in September of 1969, when President Nixon appointed a Task Force on Rural Development to recommend policies for his administration. The line-up on the Task Force was incredible. It was headed by Mrs. Haven Smith, who was serving at the time as the national chairman of the American Farm Bureau Women. The other eleven members read like the register of an agribusiness convention: Dr. Joseph Ackerman is the former managing director of the Farm Foundation; Dr. C. E. Bishop is an agricultural economist and a trustee of the Farm Foundation; Mr. William Erwin is a farm manager, a member of the Farm Bureau, and a former director of the Foundation for American Agriculture; Mr. Claude Gifford is director of the editorial page of the *Farm Journal*, an ultra-conservative apologist for agribusiness; Dr. Roy Kottman is dean of Ohio State University's College of Agriculture and Home Economics; Mr. Clifford McIntire is a former member of Congress, a former farmer, and now serves on the national staff of the American Farm Bureau Federation; Mr. True Morse has been a farm manager, a staff member of Doane Agricultural Service, Inc., undersecretary of agriculture in the Eisenhower administration, and a consultant to several agribusinesses; Dr. Emiel Owens is a professor of agricultural economics from Prairie View A and M; Mr. Al Schock is the president of Nordica Foods Company, Inc.; Mr. P. Kenneth Shoemaker is a vice-president of the H. J. Heinz Company; and Dr. Henry A. Wadsworth, Jr., is a professor of agricultural economics at Purdue University.

This one-sided task force held twelve meetings, all in Washington, D.C. There is no evidence that they went into rural America for testimony, facts, or even a breath of fresh air. Their report, "A New Life for the Country," was written by Claude Gifford, of the *Farm Journal*. That is like asking J. Edgar Hoover to write a report on civil liberties. Gifford does not disappoint us. The report reads like a chamber of commerce lunch talk. For example: "We should keep in the forefront of our thinking that jobs are created by the ingenuity and ambition of private enterprise"; "the antidote to 'big government' is more effective State and local government"; "private capital investment for rural development, where appropriate, is preferable to investment of government tax funds"; and "we commend the 4-H programs and Future Farmers of America Programs for their emphasis on private initiative through productive individual projects." In its nutrition and welfare chapter, the task force recommends more of the same old programs, but with stricter requirements:

The American people are filled with compassion for those who cannot work or who cannot perform up to normal standards. They also recognize that some who can work, don't. To protect the welfare assistance of those who are deserving, and to prevent any stigma from being directed at the deserving, safeguards should be built into assistance programs to sort out the few who do not merit the people's compassion.

This is the vision that agribusiness has for rural America. Its emphasis on private enterprise and self-reliance contrasts rather markedly with the corporate socialism that agrigovernment has achieved for agribusinessmen.

The agrigovernment harvest

Not only is agribusiness the largest American industry, but it also is the most heavily subsidized. The depth and range of those subsidies is far more than meets the public eye.

First, there are the blatant subsidy payments made directly to growers. These are of three types: (1) price supports paid to a grower of certain commodities if he will not plant certain amounts of those commodities, (2) land-retirement payments for removing acreage entirely from production, and (3) conservation payments made, ironically, to growers who undertake projects to improve their land. In the period from 1968 to 1970, the federal taxpayer has been handing out an average of $5 billion a year for these programs. It is unforgiveable naïveté to think that it is the small farmer who receives this welfare; as might be expected, agribusiness is the beneficiary. Charles Schultze, former director of the Bureau of the Budget, has reported that the large farms (those 7.1 percent of all farms having over $20,000 in sales) made away with almost two-thirds of the total farm-commodity payments in 1969. Small farmers (over half of the total) settled for a mere 8.9 percent of the subsidy benefits.

J. G. Boswell Company, a massive agribusiness in California, pulled down a $4.4-million subsidy in 1969; that one check was twice as much money as was available in USDA's grant program to build farm-labor housing. Some "farmers" were found to be getting subsidies on land being used for garbage dumps, gravel pits, and even a nudist camp. These kinds of distortions finally became too much for the public to bear. In 1970, Congress was persuaded to enact a $55,000 limit on the amount of subsidy that any one grower could collect. But the subsidy reapers are too sharp for that. The *Los Angeles Times* reported in January of 1971 that California's large cotton growers were keeping enough unplanted land to get their $55,000 limit, then renting the rest of their unplanted land "for 6 to 7 cents a pound of cotton, making up most of the money they were expected to lose in subsidies." Those who rented the excess acreage could also receive subsidies.

What the average American does not generally recognize is that he pays for that $5-billion subsidy twice. As a taxpayer, he lays out the money as a price support to keep farm prices up. As a consumer, he pays the supported prices. The real subsidy, then, is $10 billion.

Agribusiness reaches still deeper into the federal till. Consider the research subsidy. The land-grant college has provided the expertise and the resources that have allowed agribusiness to dominate rural America. Farm machinery, pesticides, hybrid plants, new feeds, processing methods, and even management techniques have been developed on these campuses at public expense, often at the specific request of agribusiness. In what can only be described as a paean to agribusiness, the *National Geographic* wrote in 1970 about "a $23,000 harvester that picks and bins 15 tons of tomatoes an hour, once the backbreaking work of 100 migrant laborers." Jules Billard, the wide-eyed author of the article, goes on to note that

the machine cuts plants underground, pulls them up with metal fingers, and gently shakes off the fruit. These tomatoes are miracles of plant genetics, bred to ripen all at once and having an easy-to-snap stem for bruiseless picking. As women cull, a conveyor feeds fruit into bins.

The tomatoes, untouched by human hands, plop into bins marked with the names of Heinz, Del Monte, Campbell, and other famous brands. The machine and its matching tomato were researched and developed at the University of California at Davis. It cost the taxpayer $1.3 million; it cost thousands of farm workers their jobs.

USDA does not always do the research for agribusi-

ness; there are times when the department gives the money directly to the business so that it can do its own research. In 1967, for example, General Mills, Incorporated, received $206,553 from USDA for the "evaluation and development of selected water-soluble graft polymers of starch." Every farmer needs that. In the same year, USDA awarded more than $40,000 to a subdivision of General American Transportation Corporation for "research to evaluate the air distribution and refrigeration systems and determine the thermal efficiency of a 40 foot long multipurpose van container." One is forced to wonder whether GATC might have built some of those 40-footlong multipurpose van containers once they had been researched and developed with tax dollars.

Then there is the labor subsidy. For years, growers have kept farm workers down by playing them off against an abundant supply of foreign workers. From 1951 to 1964, there was the Bracero program, as vicious a piece of legislation as ever appeared on the books. Under it, the federal government guaranteed and delivered Mexican workers to growers in areas where there was a "shortage" of domestic workers. Of course, a "shortage" was found wherever growers claimed one. It was so outrageous that Congress was spurred to act; they outlawed it in 1964.

The Bracero program is gone, but not the braceros. Through such bureaucratic devices as greencards and bluecards (both are types of temporary visas that effectively let Mexican workers in as freely as had the Bracero program), the border areas are flooded with docile and cheap labor. On top of these imports, there are the wetbacks, who cross without any sham of legality. It is a felony under federal law to "harbor" an illegal entrant into the United States. The growers demanded and their government granted an exception to that law: employment does not constitute harboring. These labor subsidies are not terribly hard on the taxpayer; it is the American farm worker who foots this bill for the grower. The price is his job, his income, and his power to make his employer treat him squarely.

There is much more. For example, there is a huge subsidy in water used by agribusiness. In a 1970 Brookings Institution publication, *Setting National Priorities*, Charles Schultze explains that

the price charged farmers for water from Federal irrigation projects is well below its economic cost. Part of the subsidy is paid by the taxpyaer, part by consumers of power from hydro-electric facilities whose rates are set high enough to cover some of the subsidy to irrigators. The resulting subsidies, however, do not accrue primarily to farmers who are struggling to make ends meet. They are directed predominantly toward larger farms. One study of Federal irrigation projects approved between 1964 and 1967 showed that the value of the water subsidy averaged $122,000 per farm served. This is equivalent to making a gift of $6,700 a year for fifty years to the average farmer concerned.

In addition, a whole range of services are provided free by USDA to agribusinessmen, from local conferences to marketing his produce abroad to educating his children at the land-grant college. There also is a major tax subsidy, called "the most important factor attracting corporation and other nonfarm investors into agriculture" by the U.S. Senate Subcommittee on Monopoly. Among the more attractive tax subsidies is a generous depreciation allowance for capital equipment; the government allows the grower to include such assets as cattle in the definition of "equipment." Thus, while the herd is growing fat, it also works to slim down the grower's tax payment.

Agribusinessmen seem always to be able to get a little help from their friends, even when it is not a scheduled subsidy. There was the sordid orange-juice affair of December, 1962. The Florida citrus industry had overproduced in oranges, and the orange-juice-concentrate market was glutted. Early in December, the industry appealed to USDA, which obligingly bought $1.5 million worth of juice, ostensibly for distribution in the school lunch program. But on December 12, there was a freeze in Florida, and orange juice skyrocketed in value. Supermarket prices were up by a third. The processors went running back to USDA and, incredibly, persuaded the department to terminate the earlier contract and return the juice. As Congressman Charles Vanik said at the time, the processors "now could make a 266 percent hot profit on the frozen juice deal with the Government because of the increased value of the orange juice." Among the folks to cash in on this little windfall were Libby McNeil and Libby, with 105,900 cases, and Stokely-Van Camp, with 80,000 cases.

In Hildalgo County, Texas, the home base of more migrant farm workers than any other area of the country, USDA expended $20 million for farm programs and research in fiscal year 1969. In that same year, all low-income programs from USDA, HEW, USDL, and OEO brought only $5 million to the people of that county. The latter money was condescendingly termed "welfare" by the recipients of the former.

MAKING THE DIFFERENCE IN RURAL AMERICA

Agribusiness produces a lot of food at a relatively cheap supermarket price. But a tomato costs more than the supermarket's listed price. That price, including huge federal subsidies and the agribusiness profits that are built into it, does not collect the huge social cost of exploited rural people. That added cost is too much.

Agribusiness and its partner agrigovernment never were inevitable. They exist today because big businessmen had the power and the resources to make them exist. There is no public mandate for agribusiness, there has never even been a public dialogue or full congressional debate on what rural America should be. In short, agribusiness has shaped rural America in its own image simply because the leadership of this country has utterly failed to create and articulate an alternate image, one that would include all rural people. Left to free enterprise, the countryside has fallen to the few strongest hands, and the rest have been forced to flee to the cities or to remain behind in bitter poverty.

Agribusiness need not always be the overlord of the countryside. The same deliberate policies that have made agribusiness dominant can be deliberately altered to make it responsive to the needs of all rural Americans. Farm workers, who have been excluded from the protective legislation that all other working people enjoy, including the right to organize and bargain collectively, could not be included. USDA, which now purchases from huge processors, could purchase from co-ops of small- and medium-sized farmers instead. The land-grant colleges, which have industrialized farming, could now turn their skills and resources to the needs of farm workers and rural communities. The tax laws of this country, which favor the rich corporation farmer, could be amended to encourage collective ownership of land by small farmers and farm workers.

This is a political battle, a part of the total struggle that includes the challenge to the military-industrial compex, the difficult effort against racism, the recent thrusts of the consumer movement, the fight against strip-mining companies, and the effort to deal with pollution. Agribusiness must become a major part of the battle to assert the superior morality of human values over the superior power of economic values. It is a total effort, as one radical thinker has phrased it, "to demand and create a society that would honor men."

A historical overview of U.S. rural communities and the consequences of changes in transportation and communication, urban population distribution, and rural economic base

Donald E. Voth and Richard D. Rodefeld

The readings in Section four deal primarily with the consequences for rural communities of changes in transportation and communications, of urban population decentralization, and of rural industrialization.[1] However, to present as complete a picture as possible of the rural community, materials dealing with the community in other parts of the book will also be discussed. Other materials that can be easily and inexpensively obtained and supplemental references will be identified in the discussion.

Community, as used here, refers to the population of a particular area which is inter-related through a set of institutions which provide most of the goods and services required on a day-to-day basis.[2] The community is identified by the existence of a population agglomeration, usually with some form of local government. Its boundaries are indistinct, however, as the community includes not only a central, densely settled region, but also the hinterland served by the center. Whether communities here are characterized by social or psychological bonds,[3] or both, among the residents is one of several crucial questions raised in the community research. Several of the readings in this section and in other sections address this question, with special attention given to local consequences of major societal changes.

Many studies have emphasized differences between two major types of communities: one characterized by intimacy and cohesion, the other by formality and complexity. The duality has been expressed with such terms as status and contract, mechanical and organic solidarity, Gemeinschaft and Gesellschaft, and folk and urban. All are attempts to incorporate in one composite measure, major differences between communities in their structures and functioning. Postulated and observed differences are largely attributed to differences in community size (population numbers) and levels of industrialization, modernization, or development. Classic statements of the opposite ends of the implied continuum are made by Louis Wirth, "Urbanism as a Way of Life," (1938) and Robert Redfield, "The Folk Society" (1946). Wirth, in describing the city, emphasizes the impact of size, density, and heterogeneity on the structuring of human activities and relationships. Redfield, in describing the small, preliterate community, finds that it is relatively homogenous and well-integrated and functions smoothly. He emphasizes the cooperative and communal spirit of the community.[4]

[1] References for more comprehensive treatments of community are identified at the end of this section introduction.
[2] This definition follows Schnore closely (1967:95). Hillery (1955) identified 94 different definitions.
[3] This concern is associated with the early work of Robert M. MacIver (1917) and the contemporary work of writers such as Robert Nisbet (1962).
[4] See also Redfield, 1930.

An unresolved issue in the literature is the argument that the small, rural community is more integrated, more solidary—more of a "community" in the psychological sense than is the large, urban community. The characterizations of Wirth and Redfield and of others treating "ideal" types have been criticized on several grounds.[5] It has been shown that not all urban communities are disorganized, nor are all folk communities idyllic. It is important to note that community size and level of modernization or development may vary independently and that the possibility for social solidarity or achievement of a psychological bond might vary independently with these two dimensions. Indeed, explicit consideration of independent variation among major community dimensions characterizes some of the more contemporary analyses (Warren, 1977).

While the impact of the focal changes on a variety of rural community characteristics is considered in this volume, particular attention is given to population numbers and economic base and their changes. Both have been found to be highly related to other community characteristics, such as population structure and functioning, compositional characteristics, and the structure and functioning of institutions and organizations of all kinds. For instance, generally, the larger the population numbers of a place or community, the greater the number, size and variety of all institutions and organizations. When changes occur in either population numbers or economic base, changes in other community characteristics are usually observed as well. Thus, in places experiencing declines in population numbers, the numbers or size, or both, and variety of social and economic institutions and organizations have also usually declined.

It need be said, however, that our knowledge in this area is far from complete. For instance, it is widely believed that communities of at least 50,000 and perhaps as many as 250,000 are required to obtain the maximum economies of scale in delivery of public services. On the other hand, there is evidence to suggest that the optimum size for the achievement of a sense of satisfaction with community services and for maximum participation in community affairs is much smaller, perhaps as small as two to five thousand.[6]

Because of the causal sequence of this book, important readings on the community are also located elsewhere. All will be discussed here. These materials can be classified into six broad subject matter areas. The first provides a historical and descriptive overview of American rural neighborhoods and communities. The second area deals with the direct and indirect consequences of changes in mechanization and agricultural technology for rural and urban communities. The third area examines the impact of farm organizational structure (type) and work-force composition and their changes on rural communities. The effects of changes in transportation and communication are addressed in the fourth area. The fifth topic is the impact of urbanization and industrialization on rural communities, and the final area deals with the alternative responses to rural community decline and change.

There is a clear transition in these materials from a focus on rural community decline as a result of changes in agriculture (Chapters 1 to 8) to rural community growth as a result of changes in transportation and communication technology, urban population decentralization, and decentralization of industry (Chapters 9 and 10). Obviously the characteristics and problems of declining and growing rural communities are markedly different, which suggests an important qualification when generalizing about "rural communities." Another useful point is that the solution to decline is not always growth—both decline and growth create peculiar problems for the quality of life in rural communities.

Several qualifications need to be made about these materials. First, the focus is

[5]See Kolb (1954) and Lewis (1951) for criticisms of this approach.
[6]See Voth and Patrick (1977), Dahl and Tufts (1974), Lustig and Reiner (1968), and Ostrom (1973). A review of this literature reveals an apparent unwillingness of some researchers to accept evidence of advantages of the small community in their own research.

on change in agricultural, transportation, and communication technology, urbanization, and rural industrialization. The consequences of changes in the other extractive industries (mining, forestry, and fishing)—although extremely important for the growth, decline, and change of many rural communities,—for the most part are not treated here. Second, the papers examining the impact of changes in agricultural technology tend to emphasize deleterious effects. Although this has been the predominant effect, some changes in agricultural technology have, in fact, strengthened rural communities. Land reclamation, the production of more labor-intensive crops, and the introduction of irrigation are possible examples. Finally, the effort to organize materials according to an analytic scheme has not been entirely successful, for the simple reason that research materials frequently defy simple classification. We attempt to overcome this by substantial cross-referencing.

8 Historical overviews and distinguishing characteristics of rural neighborhoods and communities

The historical overview of U.S. rural neighborhoods and communities begins with the first article in this volume. Hambidge (summarizing a lengthier discussion by Edwards) traces the settlement of America from its beginning to its end in the late 1800's. While little is said about the actual establishment of communities, there is considerable discussion of the structure within which settlement and community formation took place. Thus, forces influencing farm size and type, type of production, land acquisition, transportation networks, and the progression of settlement from the original thirteen colonies to the South and West are discussed. Hambidge also reviews many of the major changes that occurred in the rural sector of America up to the early 1900's.

The Ensminger article makes a number of important contributions. The concepts of rural "neighborhood" and "community" are defined, and the general processes resulting in their establishment are reviewed. Distinguishing characteristics of both entities are discussed, including significant regional differences and major changes from approximately 1900 to 1950.

Lively points out that the status of small rural trade centers (those with 25 to 100 people) and rural neighborhoods was declining in the North Central states as early as 1905 to 1929. Changes in capital and credit ratings, rural industries, transportation, and farm population numbers are identified as the major causal forces.

Field and Dimit review changes in the sizes and functions of South Dakota rural places from approximately 1900 to 1960. Changes in size—particularly decline—are attributed largely to changes in transportation facilities, commercialization of agriculture, loss of economic functions, and the availability of the jobs in urban industries.

Fuguitt reviews major changes occurring in the sizes of rural places from approximately 1920 to 1960. Empirical data on the size changes of incorporated rural places in Wisconsin from 1950 to 1960 are reported. Transportation changes, the initial size of the place, proximity and sizes of competing centers, and population change in the local area are identified as some of the major factors influencing the direction and rates of size changes. One of the major structural changes observed was the centralization of functions in larger rural places. Social action options available to rural communities that may prevent further decline are reviewed. Beale describes Midwestern population changes from 1960 to 1970 (Chapter 3) and for the entire United States more recently (Chapter 12).

A markedly different view of why rural communities are the way they are and what has determined their fate is articulated by Strasser. Her thesis, essentially, is

Cities dominate the American countryside economically, politically, and through insidious cultural controls. Decisions made on the topmost floors of towering marble slabs determine the fates of rural lands and the futures of country people. Urban values become national standards; mass media beam the message from the cities to every hollow and back-water town. Neither communications nor control often flows in the other direction. . . . This pattern of influence is common and long established in the United States.

This thesis is elaborated in the remainder of the article. The predominant historical relationships between the rural and urban sectors are identified as those of exploitation or domestic imperialism. This perspective has its counterpart in academic sociology under the more benign rubric of "metropolitan dominance," on the one hand, and in the analysis of colonialism in international relationships on the other (Casanova, 1965). A somewhat similar perspective is suggested by Heady (Chapter 12) and the influential community case study of Vidich and Bensman (1968).

Other articles of interest are those by: Davis (1955), who reviews the historical roots of world urbanization and trends in urbanization during the nineteenth and twentieth centuries; Fox (1967), who presents an overview of the development of American rural communities and policy guidelines based on the idea of nested heirarchies of communities; and, Raup (1961), who examines in detail the economic aspects of population decline in rural communities.

The consequences for rural and urban communities and people of changes in agricultural technology (Section one)

In Section one, the consequences of changes in agricultural technology for people and communities, both rural and urban were discussed. Major consequences of mechanical technology have been reduced employment opportunities, labor displacement, farm population out-migration, and decline (Carleton, USDA-ERS, McElroy, Hamburger, Table 2). Leaving the farm, has often been a difficult decision and process (Bagdikian). The out-migration of farm people and or failure to replace farm population numbers has resulted in the decline of rural open country neighborhoods, reduced employment opportunities in rural trade centers, and eventually population decline in most small centers and many larger ones. These changes have had additional consequences for all segments of community structure and functioning (Loftsgard and Voelker, Paulsen and Carlson, Jordan, Berry). Beale points out that while decline has been widespread, it has not been universal. Generally, the areas that have experienced the greatest rates of decline are those with economies dominated by extractive industries. The increased incomes and wealth of the remaining farmers (Tables 3 and 5) has undoubtedly moderated the effect of population loss. However, major "pockets of poverty" remain in rural areas (Table 6, Shaffer), and health problems persist (Wellford). Urban communities and people have been effected by: the movement of farm and rural nonfarm people to urban places (Fuller, McNamara); changes in food prices and quality; and the possible costs resulting from unwise environmental practices (Table 7, Rodale, *Consumer Reports*, Clark, Commoner, Todd, Milk).

The significance of farm organizational structure (type), work-force composition, and their change for rural communities (Section two)

As pointed out in Section two, the organizational structure and work-force composition of farms in a community hinterland and their changes have major implications for other community characteristics. Communities and areas dominated by relatively small, family-type farms differ markedly from those dominated by larger, nonfamily-types (Rodefeld, Raup, Barnes, Hamburger, Stinchcombe, Kennedy, Kolb and Brunner, Hamburger, Seckler, *Cooperative Builder*, Goldschmidt, Bible). The replacement of family-type farms by nonfamily types will likely result in increased farm sizes, reduced farm-population density and numbers, and major changes in the occupational composition of the farm work force. The latter is significant since major differences have been observed between family- and nonfamily-type farm work forces in background, socioeconomic status, family structure characteristics, and rates of involvement in community institutions and organizations of all kinds.

Unless offset by other processes, the decline of family-type farms will result in reduced community population numbers. Additional changes are also likely in community population structure and functioning, compositional characteristics, and the structure and functioning of all institutions and organizations as a result of changes in work-force occupational composition. The types and magnitudes of these changes will be determined in part by which farm type is declining and which type is increasing. A wide range of consequences also have been suggested for the urban sector.

9   The impact of transportation and communication changes on rural people and communities

Section four consists of two types of articles. The first type deals with changes in transportation and communication technology and their consequences for rural communities. The second type of article deals with the question of the homogenization of rural and urban society into a mass society as the consequence of mass communications, closer integration between rural and urban people, and so forth.

Changes in transportation. Banton compares the effects of the interstate highway system on two towns: one with high access and the other with low access. The Committee on Agriculture and Forestry of the U.S. Senate attempts to project the consequences of proposed rail reorganization on rural areas. Cottrell's article is a restudy of a Nevada town that he studied 20 years earlier and reported in "Death by Dieselization: A Case Study in the Reaction to Technological Change" (1951). Cottrell's study shows the remarkable transition of this small community from an economy almost entirely based on the railway to a more diversified and revitalized economy and community—belying some of the determinism evident in so much commentary about the "dying small town."

In addition to the original Cottrell study, which is easily obtained, the reader may wish to examine the Coates report (1974, 1975), which is a U.S. Department of Transportation study of the potential of transportation facilities to revitalize small communities.

Mass society and rural people. The second group of articles in this section deals with the consequences of mass society and mass communication on rural people. For many years, rural sociologists have concluded that rural people were becoming more similar to urban people in their cultural characteristics. Various reasons for this homogenization have been advanced. Others have challenged this hypothesis and have presented empirical evidence of persisting, and even increasing, differences between rural and urban populations.

The articles by Bealer, Willitts, and Kuvlesky and Fuguitt argue that rural and urban populations have become more similar because of increased modernization and increased interdependence between the city and the countryside. Changes in transportation and communication, trade, institutional and social relationships, occupational structure, and population played major roles in this process. The former article contains an excellent discussion of what historically has been meant by "rural" and how the preceding changes have made the historical definition less and less meaningful. Vidich and Bensman (1968) advance a similar argument, although they see the relationship as one of virtual domination of rural communities by the forces of mass society. The article by Glenn and Hill reviews recent empirical research and reports their analysis of rural-urban differences in attitudes and behavior. They demonstrate that, contrary to conventional wisdom, significant differences still exist.

Numerous other articles have been written on rural-urban differences and on the significance of this distinction. The reader who wants to pursue this issue might consider Dewey (1960) and Willits, Bealer, and Crider (1973, 1974), who report declining differences. Schnore (1966), Bealer and Ford (1966), Lowe and Peek (1974), Freedman and Freedman (1956), and Reiss (1959) argue that major differences persist. Another article of interest is by Nelson (1957), who examines the influence of mass industrial society on rural people.

10   The impact of changes in urban population distribution and rural economic base on rural people and communities

This topic is addressed through three types of articles.

Urban population decentralization. Improved systems of transportation have allowed people to live outside cities even while working in them. As a result, many—perhaps most—rural communities within commuting distances of cities have been transformed in recent decades. This has resulted in part from the fact that people born and raised in these communities increasingly have been able to work in the larger places and retain residences in their "home" community. More important, however, is the fact that urban residents increasingly have moved to the country while retaining their city jobs. The nature and consequences of these changes in rural community economic base and urban population decentralization are the first topics examined in this chapter.

Miller reviews changes in the size and economic base of small rural population centers (25 to 100) from 1800 to 1960 in a six-county region of West Central Pennsylvania. Until 1920 the economic base consisted mostly of extractive activities—lumber, mining, petroleum, and farming. Changes that occurred in these activities (rise and decline) and their impact on the sizes and densities of places is documented. Major declines occurred in all extractive industries in the twentieth century. The economic base of the region is now primarily residential. Improved means of transportation allowed people to reside in the smaller places or open country and commute to jobs in larger places. Major changes are reported in the characteristics of places as a result of this change in economic base.

Converse and Russell report the results of research on city workers who live in East Central Illinois agricultural villages. Among the questions they investigated were: why these workers lived in villages; how they liked village life; and how their place of employment affected their shopping habits.

The ability to commute to jobs in urban centers has also allowed farmers to acquire either full- or part-time, nonfarm jobs even while retaining their farm residences and operations. While definitive data are lacking, part-time farming appears to be increasing at a rapid rate. If major differences exist between full- and part-time farmers in their levels of integration in community institutions and organizations and other characteristics, this trend may have major implications for the communities experiencing such changes. Donahue investigated such questions by comparing the characteristics of full- and part-time farmers in the Twin-Cities area.

Relis reports problems created by urban-suburban sprawl in Santa Barbara, California. The articles by Branscome and Faux report the impact on rural communities and people in Appalachia and New England, respectively, and of urban residents moving into rural areas or purchasing land for second homes and recreation. Blobaum deals with the loss of agricultural land as a result of urbanization and conversion to other uses. The magnitude of the loss, its major causes, and the likely consequences of its continuation are reviewed. Other relevant and easily obtained articles are those by Martin (1957) and Barlowe and Libby (1972).

The impact of mining. The second type of article presented in this section deals with the history of mining, the impact of mining on rural areas and communities, and contemporary controversies concerning mining in rural areas. Included is the Miller article discussed earlier, Caudill's "Appalachia," *The Milwaukee Journal* articles, Recer's "Strip Mining Boom Jars Plains States," and the series by Mike

Dorgan (Chapter 12). An available publication, not reprinted here, is by Josephy (1973); it examines the potential consequences of large-scale mining for the Great Plains and the need for an impact analysis of such large-scale projects.

Rural industrialization. The third issue in this section concerns rural industrialization. This appears to be an attractive alternative for rural communities with declining populations and economies and appears to be occurring in many rural areas and communities that previously were losing population (Beale, Chapter 12). Summers and Lang report the results of reviewing a large number of studies that have investigated the impact of industrialization on small, rural towns. The focus is on the direct and indirect costs and benefits of such developments. They conclude

> In summary, industrial location in the rural community can bring employment, population growth and economic prosperity to the area; but as the studies have shown, these benefits do not come automatically nor do they apply in all cases. In some instances the structure of the community and the character of the particular industry merge to the benefit of both parties. More often the industry clearly gains while having a negligible or even negative effect on the host community over the long run.

A wealth of material has recently become available on rural industrialization and development and the effects. Some articles that may be of interest are those by Bealer (1972), Clemente and Summers (1972), Nolan and Heffernan (1974), Scott and Summers (1974), Fernstrom (1974), and Summers and others (1976). Of particular importance are Fernstrom (1974), which is an overview of issues and concepts related to rural industrialization intended for use by persons actively engaged in promoting it, and Summers and others (1976), which is a comparative analysis of 186 case studies dealing with rural industrialization.

12 Alternative responses to rural community decline and change

There are numerous alternatives to existing and projected changes in rural communities. In this discussion, it is useful to distinguish between those rural communities experiencing economic and population decline and those experiencing growth.

One alternative for declining rural communities, of course, is to allow a continuation of the existent trend or accelerate it. These alternatives are suggested by Carlyle and Clawson, respectively. The other major alternative is to slow, stop, or reverse the decline of rural communities. A number of possibilities exist for the achievement of this end. This might be achieved by increasing or reducing the rate of farm population decline. This would require a reversal of the trends toward increased mechanization, larger-sized farms and nonfamily-type farms. Possible ways of achieving these results are discussed in Chapter 11.

The other major option is to increase the size of the rural population, by reducing rates of out-migration and encouraging more urban people to change their residences. This also can be achieved through a variety of other means. Rural transportation and communication facilities could be improved, making commuting from rural residences to urban jobs easier and less costly in time. This would only benefit rural areas within commuting distances, however. In addition, increasing petroleum costs may discourage this alternative. Relis and Blobaum (Chapter 10) and Pfefferkorn suggest possible solutions to problems created by the urbanization of rural areas. Fuguitt and Zuiches report that a high percentage of present urban residents prefer living in rural areas within commuting distance of larger urban places. Many people also prefer living in more remote rural areas—given the opportunity. Whatever the reasons, migration to many rural areas has increased (Beale), and the migrants appear to be quite satisfied with their new lives (Hanson).

The other possibility, of course, is to create jobs in rural areas independent of their traditional economic bases. This may be achieved by developing available extractive resources, such as minerals (mining), or by recruiting new industries. These alternatives are discussed in Chapter 10. As indicated in the relevant readings, these are not without their difficulties, although some procedures and safeguards may reduce later problems (Dorgan).

Additional materials on population redistribution are by Hoover (1972), Morrison (1970), and Morrison and Wheeler (1976). The Morrison and Wheeler article is particularly useful in that it summarizes what was known about the new pattern of urban-to-rural migration as of 1976 and is readily available. Heady (Chapter 12) reviews some of the major issues in the area of rural industrialization and development.

Other resources on the community

This section does not purport to treat the entirety of community sociology. Those interested in pursuing this subject further should consider the following: Vidich and Bensman's case study (1968), which is particularly useful since it deals explicitly with the relationship between rural and urban society, and Schnore (1967), which presents an excellent discussion of the major issues in community sociology. Others that do the same and can be used as textbooks on the rural community are Bernard (1962; 1973), Mercer (1956), Nelson, and others (1960), Poplin (1972), Sanders (1975), and Warren (1972). Bell and Newby (1972), Stein (1960), and Vidich and others (1964) discuss and analyze community studies and the community-study approach. Several anthologies exist; Warren's (1977) is particularly useful although it, like most others, suffers from an excessive urban focus.

Three extremely useful bibliographical works are Smith (1970), Olson and others (1976), and Hawley and Svara (1972). Hawley and Svara deal with the issue of community power and decision-making, which has an extremely large literature not dealt with in this book. Their bibliographical essay, as well as parts of the Olson and others (1976) bibliography, provide at least a small window to this literature.

REFERENCES

Barlowe, R., and Libby, L.: Policy choices affecting access to farmland. In Guither, H. A., editor: Who will control U.S. agriculture? Cooperative Extension Service, Special Publication 27, Urbana, Ill., 1972, University of Illinois.

Bealer, Robert C.: Rural development: another go-around for interdisciplinary plunders, Paper prepared for the Training Seminar in Rural Development, College Station, 1971, Texas A & M University.

Bell, Colin, and Newby, Howard: Community studies: an introduction to the sociology of the local community, New York, 1972, Praeger Publishers, Inc.

Bernard, Jessie: American community behavior: an analysis of problems confronting American communities today, revised edition, New York, 1962, Holt, Rinehart and Winston, Inc.

Bernard, Jessie: The community, New York, 1973, McGraw-Hill Book Co.

Casanova, Pablo Gonzalez: Internal colonialism and national development, Studies in comparative international development, Vol. 1, No. 4, St. Louis, 1965, Washington University, pp. 27-37.

Clemente, Frank, and Summers, Gene F.: Industrial development and the elderly: a longitudinal analysis, The Journal of Gerontology **28:**479-483, 1973.

Coates, Vary: Revitalization of small communities: transportation options, first year report, Washington, D.C., 1974, U.S. Department of Transportation.

Coates, Vary, and Weiss, Ernest: Revitalization of small communities: transportation options, Vol. 1, Washington, D.C., 1975, U.S. Department of Transportation.

Cottrell, Leonard: Death by dieselization: a case study in the reaction to technological change, American Sociological Review **16:**358-365, 1951.

Dahl, Robert A., and Tufts, Edmund R.: Size and democracy, Stanford, Calif., 1973, Stanford University Press.

Davis, K.: The origin and growth of urbanization in the world, American Journal of Sociology **60:**429-437, 1955.

Dewey, Richard: The rural-urban continuum: real but relatively unimportant, American Journal of Sociology **66:**60-66, 1960.

Fernstrom, John R.: Bringing in the sheaves: effective community development programs, Corvallis, Ore., 1974, Oregon State University, Cooperative Extension Service.

Fox, Karl: Metamorphosis in America: a new synthesis of rural and urban society. In Gore, William J., and Hodapp, Leroy C., editors: Change in the small community: an interdisciplinary survey, New York, 1967, Friendship Press.

Freedman, Ronald, and Freedman, Deborah: Farm reared elements in the non-farm population, Rural Sociology **21**:50-61, 1956.

Hawley, Willis D., and Svara, James H.: The study of community power: a bibliographic review, Santa Barbara, Calif., 1972, ABC-CLIO, Inc.

Hillery, George A., Jr.: Definitions of community: areas of agreement, Rural Sociology **20**:119, 1955.

Hoover, Edgar M.: Policy objectives for population distribution. In Mazie, Sara Mills, editor: Commission on Population Growth and the American Future, research reports, Vol. 5, Washington, D.C., 1972, U.S. Government Printing Office, pp. 653-664.

Josephy, A. M., Jr.: Agony of the Northern Plains, Audubon **75**(4):68-101, 1973.

Kolb, William L.: The social structure and functions of cities, Economic Development and Cultural Change **3**:30-46, 1954.

Lewis, Oscar: Life in a Mexican village: Tepoztlan restudied, Urbana, Ill., 1951, University of Illinois Press.

Lowe, George D., and Peek, Charles W.: Location and lifestyle: the comparative explanatory ability of urbanism and rurality, Rural Sociology **39**:392-420, 1974.

Lustig, Fels, and Reiner, Janet S.: Local government and poverty in rural areas. In Rural Poverty in the United States, President's National Advisory Commission on Rural Poverty in the United States, Washington, D.C., 1968, U.S. Government Printing Office.

MacIver, Robert M.: Community, London, 1917, The Macmillan Co.

Martin, Walter T.: Ecological change in satellite rural areas, American Sociological Review **22**:173-182, 1957.

Mercer, Blaine E.: The American community, New York, 1956, Random House, Inc.

Morrison, Peter A.: The impact and significance of rural-urban migration in the United States, Santa Monica, Calif., 1972, Rand Corporation.

Morrison, Peter A., and Wheeler, Judith: Rural renaissance in America? The revival of population growth in remote areas, Population Bulletin **31**(3), Oct. 1976.

Nelson, Lowry: Rural life in a mass-industrial society, Rural Sociology **22**:20-30, 1957.

Nelson, Lowry, Ramsey, Charles, and Verner, Coolie: Community structure and change, New York, 1960, The Macmillan Co.

Nisbet, Robert A.: Community and power, London, 1962, Oxford University Press.

Nolan, Michael F., and Heffernan, William D.: The Rural Development Act of 1972: a critical analysis, Paper presented at the Annual Meeting of the Rural Sociological Society, Montreal, 1974.

Olson, Philip, Aucoin, Jackie, and Fort, Burke, editors: Community and urban community: a bibliography and course outline, Kansas City, 1976, University of Missouri–Kansas City, Department of Sociology.

Ostrom, Elinor, and Parks, Roger B.: Suburban police departments: too many and too small? Bloomington, Ind., 1973, Indiana University, Department of Political Science.

Poplin, Dennis E.: Communities: a survey of theories and methods of research, New York, 1972, The Macmillan Co.

Raup, Philip M.: Economic aspects of population decline in rural communities. In Heady, Earl O., editor: Labor mobility and population in agriculture, Ames, Iowa, 1961, Iowa State University, Center for Agricultural and Economic Development.

Redfield, Robert: Tepoztlan: a Mexican village, Chicago, 1930, University of Chicago Press.

Redfield, Robert: The folk society, American Journal of Sociology **52**:293-308, 1946.

Redfield, Robert: The little community: peasant society and culture, Chicago, 1963, University of Chicago Press.

Reiss, A. J., Jr.: Rural-urban and status differences in interpersonal contacts, American Journal of Sociology **65**:182-195, 1959.

Sanders, Irwin T.: The community: an introduction to a social system, New York, 1975, The Ronald Press Co.

Schnore, Leo F.: The rural-urban variable: an urbanite's perspective (including exchange with Bealer and Ford), Rural Sociology **31**:131-155, 1966.

Schnore, Leo F.: Community. In Smelser, Neil J., editor: Sociology: an introduction, New York, 1967, John Wiley & Sons, Inc., pp. 79-150.

Scott, J. T., Jr., and Summers, G. F.: Problems in rural communities after industry arrives. In

Whiting, Larry R., editor: Rural industrialization: problems and potentials, Ames, Iowa, 1974, Iowa State University Press, pp. 94-107.

Smith, Suzanne M.: An annotated bibliography of small town research, Madison, Wis., 1970, The University of Wisconsin, Department of Rural Sociology.

Stein, Maurice R.: The eclipse of community: an interpretation of American studies, Princeton, N.J., 1960, Princeton University Press.

Summers, Gene F., and others: Industrial invasion of nonmetropolitan America: a quarter century of experience, New York, 1976, Praeger Publishers, Inc.

Vidich, Arthur J., Bensman, Joseph, and Stein, Maurice R., editors: Reflections on community studies, New York, 1964, John Wiley & Sons, Inc.

Vidich, Arthur J., and Bensman, Joseph: Small town in mass society, Princeton, N.J., 1968, Princeton University Press.

Voth, Donald E., and Patrick, Mary S.: Research report: political participation and size of community, Small Town **8:**12-15, 1977.

Warren, Roland L.: The community in America, Skokie, Ill., 1972, Rand McNally & Co.

Warren, Roland L.: New perspectives on the American community: a book of readings, ed. 3, Skokie, Ill., 1977, Rand McNally & Co.

Willits, F. K., Bealer, R. C., and Crider, D. M.: The ecology of social traditionalism in a rural hinterland, Rural Sociology **39**(3):334-349, 1974.

Willits, F. K., Bealer, R. C., and Crider, D. M.: Leveling of attitudes in mass society: rurality and traditional morality in America, Rural Sociology **38:**36-45, 1973.

Wirth, Louis: Urbanism as a way of life, American Journal of Sociology **44:**1-24, 1938.

8

Historical overviews and distinguishing characteristics of rural neighborhoods and communities

Rural neighborhoods and communities

DOUGLAS ENSMINGER

THE PLACE OF LOCALITY GROUPS IN RURAL AMERICA

The rural community is the geographic area with which most of the community's members identify themselves. To ask a rural dweller his community in a given section of the country is almost certain to bring forth a fairly uniform response. A rural New Englander, for example, will most assuredly identify his place of residence with the name of his town or township. A Southern plantation owner will ordinarily identify himself with the larger trade center near his plantation, generally the county seat; while the sharecropper, tenant, or laborer is almost certain to name his local neighborhood. A Midwestern or Western farmer will most likely identify himself with his trade-center community or township, and if he is outside his county when you ask him where he lives, he may give his trade-center community first and then mention his county.

To the New Englander the town is his home and the socio-geographic unit that provides for the education of his children. The church is a town institution, while most formal organizations function within the town's boundaries. Moreover, meetings to discuss issues of importance to rural people are usually called by the individual towns, for town meetings are the traditional means by which the New Englander arrives at some consensus of opinion or of plan for action. Thus the town, or "community," in New England has become institutionalized, and is recognized by both townsmen and outsiders as a functional unit.

In the South the large landowner has few intimate social contacts with families in his immediate neighborhood. His social contacts are usually county-wide

☐ From Taylor, Carl C., and others: Rural life with United States, New York, 1949, Alfred Knopf, pp. 55-68, 72-77.

or span even greater areas, and the county-seat town is often the focal point for his trade, his recreation, and his church and school activities or requirements. On the other hand, the contacts of the Southern tenants and small landowners' are concentrated in the neighborhood and the near-by town. These tenants and small landowners seldom visit the larger towns and cities—and then only for highly specialized service—and they rarely attend public meetings outside their neighborhood or the near-by town. Among Southern sharecroppers and laborers, and especially among Negroes, social contacts are most intimate and meaningful within the neighborhood, for to these people the neighborhood is both home and community. Having few contacts with formal organizations and institutions other than the school and the church, which are largely neighborhood-centered, this group generally meets with the larger society only through visits to the county seat and an occasional trip to town on Saturday afternoon to visit friends on the streets and purchase supplies. Thus the neighborhood and the community, being about the only world their members know, are to them the most important geographic units.

Throughout the South historical, economic, and social considerations have inhibited the growth of socially significant trade-area communities. The county-seat town is often the only important trade center in the entire county, and more and more it functions as a community center. In contrast, the rural dweller in the North, Middle West, and West has a variety of social contacts, ranging from those in neighborhoods to those in larger towns and cities. His most frequent and meaningful contacts, however, are within the organizations and institutions of the trade center, and these trade-center communities, in addition to offering many organizations designed to meet interests and needs, are rapidly modernizing education through school consolidation. The church is gradually becoming a village-centered institution, and recreation, because of its present highly commercial character, is provided largely by the town.

Rural people in the United States, whatever their differences, share the common experience of living within rural communities, which are the most important groupings in the nation. To the rural family the rural community is "home" in the fullest possible sense, for it encompasses not only the household but the locality as well. Of the nation's nearly 14,000,000 rural families, more than half live in dispersed farm dwellings, while slightly less than half live in hamlets, towns, and villages that serve as social and economic service centers for rural people. Other features of the rural community are perhaps less important than its communal character, but they are not without real significance too. Among these features are the economic relations between the town and its surrounding farms, and the economic and social relations between the various "groups" of the rural community's population—all estimated in terms of wealth, occupation, and status.

Within most rural communities farm families form subgroupings around schools, churches, or general stores. Such social groups are even more localized than the communities, and "neighborliness" is one of their most important bonds. It is probably for this reason alone that these significant units have come to be known as "neighborhoods." Thus we can say that rural families, as well as living in the larger area of the rural community, live in a neighborhood that they readily identify, and that only the degree and the intensity of the common life determine the community and the neighborhood for any individual.

Sociologically defined, the rural *neighborhood* is that socio-geographic unit consisting of a small group of families to whom the area is a symbol of personal identity, and among whom intimate face-to-face contact contributes to a common life which signifies visiting, exchanging work, and providing education for the children or religious worship for the family. Geographically, these neighborhoods may be large or small, depending on the density of population and the topography. Because of the wide differences in the way rural people group themselves geographically, it is not possible to give a generalized definition of the rural community as is true in the case of the neighborhood. Research reveals that the locality group we call the "community" is similar to the neighborhood in that it, too, is a socio-geographic unit to which people express a feeling of belonging. It differs from the neighborhood in that it encompasses a larger area, frequently including several neighborhoods; it may be a single or multi-centered area, generally the former. Because it is a larger locality group with a larger population than the neighborhood, it is capable of providing a greater range of social and economic services. The range of services varies, however, from a few (like the neighborhood) to nearly complete services. The degree of identification people have with the community varies from weak to strong. Most of the residents claim identity with their community and are loyal to it, and because of their social and geographic relationships can act together in providing and supporting needed institutions, organizations, and services. Where neighborhoods prevail they usually cluster around a community center.

For both neighborhoods and communities social unity lies in the fact that the families within them express a feeling of belonging, while those outside recognize the members of the area as a group in and of themselves. The rural community usually has one major service center, with a population ranging from a few hundred to more than 2,500, which provides a variety of social and economic services for both the villagers and the farm people who live within a ten-to twelve-mile radius. This type of community is commonly referred to as a trade-center community, and the people within the area have a feeling of belonging to it and have a sense of community responsibility that can be counted upon when crises arise that call for concerted action. It is within this large trade-center area that schools are consolidated into one main community educational institution. And it is within such communities that farm and village people, having discovered their common interests, are more and more beginning to work together.

The essential differences between neighborhoods and communities are in size of area, population, in services provided, and in the degree of intimacy of relationships. The neighborhood is the smaller geographic group, which may range from 15 to 30 families in the South, and from 20 to 80 families in the Plains. Rural communities range in size from 80 to 500 open-country families, plus an approximately equal and not infrequently larger number in town. The neighborhood usually has a very limited range of services, while the community provides a variety of them. In some places these community services are adequate to meet most of the basic needs of farm and nonfarm residents. Neighborhood relations revolve around families and are very intimate; whereas in the community, which has a larger area than the neighborhood, relationships are more casual and therefore more impersonal, and they are increasingly concerned with individuals and special interests rather than with families.

These fundamental types of social structure—the

neighborhood and the community—vary from one part of the country to another, but one fact is common: it is within their confines that the rural dweller spends the greater part of every twenty-four hours, and it is into those confines that the science and culture of the larger society are usually brought to the rural family. In a chain of social contacts which stretches ultimately to the world's end, and in the infinite series of social relationships which derive from that chain, the neighborhood stands first and the community second as modes of intensive common life beyond the common life of the family itself.

An individual first makes contact with the larger society through his family; the neighborhood usually provides the first social experiences extending beyond the family; and the community is the focus of the varied associations that families enter into in order to satisfy their wants. The numerous associations—political, economic, religious, educational, recreative, literary, philanthropic, and professional—that have been created in the family's quest to meet its needs have enriched as well as complicated rural life. It is when family-to-family relationships become institutionalized through these associations existing within particular areas, so that definitely integrated systems of social interaction are formed, that we may define the family groups as neighborhoods and communities.

In the early development of neighborhoods and communities in the United States, one of the first patterns created by families living in a localized area was that formed by the grouping of twelve to forty families primarily for protection and mutual aid. These early groups were forerunners of today's neighborhoods, and they soon provided the nucleuses through which families organized for religious worship and for the education of their children. Organization within the neighborhood, although highly informal, served to help the families meet needs that, as individuals, they found beyond their reach to satisfy. This closely knit, highly informal neighborhood life has since developed into the complex pattern of organization that is characteristic of modern society. While today, as in the past, a farmer and his family may be part of the neighborhood life, his associations very often take him beyond the immediate area of family residence. And still, although the neighborhood as a simple locality group may be gradually disappearing, the neighborhood pattern continues among farmers. Indeed, among some groups, such as Southern sharecroppers and laborers, the common life is confined to the very limited geographic area of the neighborhood. The more common type of rural community life today, however, is a combination of intimate family-to-family association within the neighborhood and an in-creasing number of both personal and impersonal contacts spread over a much wider area. As for the future, farm people will undoubtedly continue to function as neighbors, but the wider vistas of social participation are bound to open up to them.

What are the origins of the rural community, the phases of its development? As America's population pushed westward, the ever-expanding agricultural economy and rapid industrialization rendered necessary wider areas of contact and communication than the simple neighborhood could afford, and this need was met by the rise of small-town service centers. Just where a town was to grow depended in part on the distances farmers were able and willing to travel, and on the expansion of family-to-family relationships, but in any event, the outer limits of the service area were determined primarily by whether or not a farmer could conveniently drive the distance to and from town by team in one day.

These new service centers soon became the mediums through which the farmer marketed his produce, laid plans for expanding school and recreational programs, and made contact with the still wider locality group. Moreover, the rural service center was the "show window" for the developing industries of the country. Thus, out of new needs a new social phenomenon, now widely known as the rural community, slowly began to emerge. At first these centers were thought of as little more than trade centers for most of the farm families. Psychologically a real difference existed between the villagers and the farmers; their economic interests seemed to conflict, and the villager, inclined to feel superior to the farmer, tended to dictate the pattern of social life in the community. But with the coming of the automobile and the consequent improvement of roads, all this began to change markedly, so that today farmers and villagers in many communities see their interests as reciprocal and mutual, and they therefore participate on an equal basis in organizations and share leadership in school and community programs.

In the United States there are today approximately 35,000 trade-centered rural communities and 240,000 rural neighborhoods. Since they are products of human association, they differ widely in the degree of self-consciousness and social integration they display. Some are in the process of becoming self-conscious groups, while others are disintegrating and disappearing. But in each neighborhood and community the customs and valued traditions of its people greatly influence it as a locality group. Geography, which largely determines the distribution of families, also plays an important role in the making of a neighborhood or a community.

What are some of the current trends in rural communities? In most of them, in accordance with an ever-widening and complex social horizon, individual-to-individual contacts are replacing family-to-family contacts. For just as neighborhood contacts were found inadequate as the frontier receded, so local communities are proving inadequate for the needs of rural families in this modern scientific age. And in much the same way that neighborhoods were linked with larger service centers, so communities today, through expanding human contacts, are forming new relationships that center around large and small cities. As the village center emerged to serve the adjacent neighborhoods, this new service-center pattern has emerged as a result of the increasing dependence of rural families on the outside community to satisfy the needs inspired by an increased standard of living. Since modern living in rural as well as urban America requires a wide range of social and economic services, new and ever-expanding patterns of human association have developed to meet the situation. Self-sufficient communities are in general the exception now rather than the rule. It is more realistic in discussing the pattern of rural life today to talk about a system of service areas, with the larger area usually including several communities, which it unifies through the maintenance of certain services and institutions that the smaller communities, as separate, individual units, cannot support.

Thus the rural family of today is simultaneously participating in many different groupings. The smallest of these groupings is the neighborhood, and next, with its organizations and institutions, is the community, which embraces the specialized areas for both organization and trade. Moreover, the family may participate in a number of different specialized areas. For example, the hospital may form the basis for one center, the purchase of clothing for another, highly specialized recreation for a third, while a fourth center may bring together the dairy, potato, or other commodity producers. As associations multiply, along with alternative choices between towns and cities for trade, school, and church facilities, community life is attaining a complexity that our grandparents never knew. The formation of organizations deliberately designed for the collective pursuit of some special interest does not encourage community feeling in the wider sense of participation. The feeling of community in this sense may eventually be forthcoming, but it depends on more than mere organization, as the instigators of consolidation in many rural school districts can testify. The point is that a community is integral, not partial; it is a whole circle of common life and arises spontaneously out of life itself.

THE SIGNIFICANCE OF NEIGHBORHOODS AND COMMUNITIES

Public and private agencies serving rural people are learning through experience that rural dwellers may be reached or motivated most effectively through their neighborhoods and communities. Therefore, when a given agency establishes a county advisory committee, it seeks local leaders who can speak for the people. Some go further and urge the formation of community committees that will bring together the leaders of the local organizations and of the neighborhood. The record to date shows that agencies have succeeded or failed depending upon the degree to which they have entered the culture of the people—that is, the degree to which they have become a part of the community. For to the rural dweller, the neighborhood and the community is a meaningful unit of society. It signifies a group of people who over the years have developed definite ways of thinking and behaving. The understanding of the neighborhood and the community thus presents a distinct challenge to all agencies serving rural people, for unless such agencies can find ways of integrating their programs into the culture of the community, they find it difficult to get the necessary response and co-operation from the residents.

Certain generalizations may be made about the types of services and activities that are most prevalent in neighborhoods and communities. A school, a church, and a store are the service institutions around which most neighborhoods center, while visiting or neighboring and kinship are characteristic features. For the community, a high school, churches, and economic and social services make up the circle of common life. It is true that many areas, having lost their schools, churches, and stores, continue to be neighborhoods, but neighborhoods and communities are more than geographic areas of people, since they have come into existence as such only because of the relationships that have developed between individuals living in a contiguous area.

Inasmuch as rural people have psychological and physical attachments to their neighborhoods and communities, the limits of such areas may be easily determined. This delineation is a preliminary step in understanding neighborhood and community relationships, and it also helps in visualizing how neighborhoods and communities work. Either of two methods—the individual or the group method—may be used in locating and determining the boundaries of neighborhoods and communities. In the individual method a schoolteacher, public health official, extension agent, or research worker may personally visit informed community leaders and secure their help in locating on a detailed highway map the last family to the north, to the south, to the east, and to the west that these informants consider as belonging to their neighborhood. The line connecting these points will be an approximate boundary line for the immediate neighborhood. Once the neighborhood is mapped, the next step is to determine the larger community center to which the neighborhood members have the strongest attachments, and in which they have most frequent associations. Where local neighborhoods are still a very important feature of the scene, the above technique will prove useful in the delineation of both neighborhoods and communities, for the neighborhoods will be found to "cluster" about given service centers. But where neighborhoods are not prevalent or strong, the leaders consulted should name the last families on the various roads leading from the main trade center who have the most frequent associations, and identify themselves most closely, with the community that is being mapped. If this procedure is followed for each major service center in distinct, well-integrated communities, the lines separating one community from others will jibe closely with the information supplied by the leaders in those adjacent communities. Any discrepancies can be adjusted by learning from the families in the dividing area the name of the community to which they profess the greater loyalty.

The group method of mapping may be used if several people are interested in the neighborhoods and communities. The people who are best informed about community matters should first be assembled for a two- to three-hour county meeting. The type of people who can usually make the greatest contribution to such a meeting are the representatives of each of the private and public agencies having county offices, and one or more leading citizens from the major community areas of the county. Each person present should understand that the focus is on communities—the places with major towns or centers—and not on the small neighborhoods that may have a one-room school or a crossroads store. The group can be aided by first locating the major centers, and then by concentrating on the area thought to be easiest to delineate. General lines of demarcation are not enough, and therefore details should be included by locating specific farms or landmarks considered as the outer bounds of the community that is being mapped. The group should agree on which families live on these outer limits of the community, and for this step such questions as the following may be helpful. If community meetings were called at two centers on the same night, and all families were equally interested, where would the line that separated the areas of attendance fall? If community-wide programs were planned, for recreation or education, for example, what is the farthest point at which one might expect family interest and response? On the map put an "X" at the point on each road leading from the community center that the group considers the farthest limit for families who feel attached to the community; then connect these points, and the community will be delineated. Having mapped one community area, continue by focusing on one community after another until all major areas have been outlined. Frequently the group can also go as far in the delineation of neighborhoods as to locate most of the recognized ones. Informants who know their areas intimately can locate approximate boundaries for most of them, although experience with the group method suggests that individuals in the group can be fairly precise in bounding communities, but tend to be less exact in locating and bounding neighborhoods. When this method is used, the lines bounding the neighborhoods and communities can be refined in one of the following ways. (1) Place the map in one of the most frequented county offices, and have rural dwellers assist in refining it as they stop in the office; (2) make systematic visits to each community to meet with representatives from each of the indicated neighborhoods; or (3) go into the neighborhoods and visit people who can advise and make needed refinements.

One will discover early in the process of mapping neighborhoods and communities that their boundaries seldom are related to political boundaries, that is, to minor civil divisions, school districts, or counties. The exception to this is the town in New England, which generally functions as a "community." In the Midwest, with the organization of many programs on a township basis, the township is taking on some of the characteristics of a community or neighborhood. In delineating biracial areas, both white and Negro communities and neighborhoods must be mapped, for their neighborhood areas are usually not coterminous, although white and Negro community boundaries will generally be identical.

It should be remembered, however, that neighborhood and community delineation is only a technique for fixing the boundaries of geographic areas in which there is a concentration of relatively fixed and institutionalized patterns of association. It is further examination of the relationships in each area that reveals the types of common experience the families share, and that make each neighborhood and community a significant social unit. And being the product of definite patterns of human association, neighborhoods and communities *are* significant social entities. Where the relationships are institutionalized, the neighborhoods and communities are, in a sense, already organized to do the things the people consider important. But the degree and method of organization will always vary, for the people, as self-conscious groups, have over the years evolved their own way of doing things. In some neighborhoods and communities they simply talk over their problems informally, decide that something should or should not be done, and, if necessary, choose a leader and support his action. Results are achieved just as definitely through these informal group relations as through the more formally organized associations. In fact, in reaching and motivating the common people, one may expect such institutionalized neighborhoods and community relationships to be the most effective channels, while a more formal method of organization may block interest and response if it goes counter to the accepted ways of doing things.

In crystallizing attitudes and in furnishing a focal point around which rural people may reach a consensus, neighborhoods and communities serve a very unique function. The history and development of school consolidation, for example, clearly shows that the people form their pro or con attitudes within the individual community or neighborhood. Some states (New York and Kansas in particular) have therefore passed legislation suggesting that the community be recognized in developing consolidated school programs. For another example, the Soil Conservation Service acknowledges that certain important human relationship factors must be considered when democratically controlled soil conservation districts are planned and operated. For while the soil conservation district is set up to conform with watershed areas, experience now indicates that neighborhoods and communities play an important part in crystallizing public opinion and in motivating farmers to practice conservation. To cite a specific instance, a recent study of the human relationship factors involved in establishing soil conservation in Stephenson County, Illinois, revealed that the spread of conservation practices depended upon giving successful demonstrations within the immediate neighborhood and preferably on the farm of a recognized neighborhood leader. It also showed that in obtaining acceptance of soil conservation programs, each community, being organized differently, should therefore be approached differently.

It is chiefly out of neighborhood and community group relationships that rural leaders have developed. Much discussion of leadership misses the mark because it fails to recognize that leadership is a group phenomenon—that to be a leader, a person must be a product of the group he represents. Moreover leadership does not exist unless the people indicate their acceptance of the leader through some form of group activity. Administrators of public programs repeatedly select individuals to aid them in carrying out their program. If they manage to select the person who is accepted by the neighborhood and community as a leader for the specific program, things go fairly well. Too frequently, however, the person selected is one who is best known to the agency personnel, but who is not considered a leader by the people. And many times programs that might make a real contribution to the community have failed to arouse interest simply because the real, effective leaders were not secured. Careful study of the community will reveal these natural leaders are present in all neighborhoods and communities, but time, patience, determination, and knowledge about leader-group relationships are required to find them. When they have been found, the agency may still have a prolonged educational job ahead in order to obtain their cooperation and effective participation. Yet the only safe and sound approach is through this leadership, for leadership taps the community nerve center. It can, however, work either for or against a program, and in the latter instance little will be accomplished until the influential leaders, having been recognized, are won over. While the real neighborhood and community leaders may or may not be the ones who stand out and provide leadership for organized groups, they will always be the ones who will be of most help in crystallizing neighborhood and community acceptance of new ideas and activities, especially when these are being brought in from the outside.

FORMAL ORGANIZATIONS AND INFORMAL GROUP RELATIONSHIPS

Although the number of formal and special-interest organizations is steadily increasing, rural areas still operate on a fairly informal basis in carrying on most of their group activities. As an illustration, if a neighbor dies in the middle of the harvest season, leaving his wife and family with a large field of corn to be husked, word is passed around at the school program that all the neighbors are to meet at sunup next morning to shuck the field of corn. Promptly at sunup, then, the farmers and their wives appear at the farmyard of the deceased and begin the day's work. The wives prepare the noonday meal while the men work in the field, and by dusk the job is completed. It is in such direct fashion that many rural communities meet emergency needs. The factors of kinship and of common locality of course contribute much to the personal and informal quality of rural life. But the trend today among rural people is toward patterns of formal organization, and this trend is one of the most significant in all of American rural life. It is important, therefore, to examine the nature of both formal and informal organizations as well as their relationship.

Formal organizations may be defined as associations of two or more persons who are co-operating in a common purpose, and whose association involves a formal structure of members and executive personnel. They may be broadly classified in accordance with the character of the purpose or objective into a few widely differing groups, such as, for example, farm organizations, fraternal bodies, churches, political parties, social clubs, cooperatives, rural youth organizations, economic organizations, civic clubs, and patriotic organizations. Taken together, these associations constitute the formal structure of organization for any community. But underlying and permeating this formal structure is the primary, tremendously intricate network of informal group relationships that may be classified as cliques, gangs, visiting groups, gossip groups, cracker-barrel groups, mutual-aid groups, and family relatives. These informal associations are the least tangible of group relationships, for while their presence and their numerous functions are very real, they do not involve the ritualistic procedures of the formally organized groups, and while they have leaders they do not have elected officers.

That these informal groupings have a profound influence on the functioning of rural community organization is generally recognized. The "whispering campaign" sometimes employed in elections is not idle gossip, and it is usually carried by the elusive "grapevine" that is the communication system of the informal community organization. And within almost every formal organization there is a circle of informal groups that may spell success or failure for any organized efforts made by the formal group. Too often in the analysis of community organization these informal, unofficial, transitory groupings of people are ignored. In one instance, for example, the decision as to whether a rural health association was to be allowed to function in a particular county hinged on the personality of an outstanding local physician, and on his ability to exert a favorable influence on the other physicians. He handled the situation successfully by holding a social dinner at his country home and broaching the question at the height of festivities. The desired decision was obtained, and the badly needed health program was given an opportunity to show what it could do. This sort of procedure may be thought of as a shapeless web of overlapping and often nebulous social relationships, with the web sometimes being thick and intertwined, and at the other times tenuous and flimsy. For these, as well as other, reasons scientific measurement is difficult. The importance of informal group relationships, however, transcends even that of the formal organizations, for it is

within these unconscious processes of society that customs, folklore, institutions, and social values have their inception. Moreover, it is inconceivable that any formal organization could arise or continue to function without the interplay of informal groups; the very acceptance of a common purpose and the will toward co-operation require some previous activity and communication of ideas, both of which are important functions of informal organization.

It would be false, therefore, to assume that formal and informal organizations are opposed or exclusive social entities. They are interdependent aspects of the same process of group formation. The formal organizations give society structure and continuity, but they are themselves developed and sustained by informal groups, which they in turn create. Thus any attempt to impose formal types of co-operative organization on rural people must take into consideration the informal organizations as a means of communication, cohesion, and the achievement of consensus. Communication is, as a matter of fact, one of the indispensable functions of informal organizations, for it gives rise to the "we" feeling, to the feeling of belonging which is so important for individual personality development and the maintenance of self-respect and independent choice. Many agencies, both governmental and private, have found out this fact the hard way, that is, through numerous failures in developing and maintaining co-operative organizations.

As for the vital factor of leadership, in informal organizations it depends largely upon direct word-of-mouth communication and upon sufficient opportunity to discuss problems and their social consequences. The leader is quite often some individual who, by combining intellectual and conversational ability, can crystallize opinions and beliefs toward some consensus on day-to-day problems. It may well be that the leader does not occupy any formal position of leadership, or is not consciously thought of as a "leader," but it is leadership that is indicated in such remarks as *"We'll* talk it over," or "Mr. Smith ought to know about that before we decide," or the more indirect *"We'll* get together and make up *our* minds." It is this type of leadership that imparts a sense of security, because a person feels that he and his neighbors, the individuals with whom he rubs shoulders day in and day out, understand each other and "what goes on." The leadership role under such conditions is highly personal and evanescent, and the leader is no longer an independent factor in the chain of social causation, but rather is regarded as a medium or product, as well as the source, of social influences.

Some individuals may find it difficult to realize that the informal, unofficial, transitory groupings of people are real social entities. It is necessary, therefore, to consider how these groupings can be objectively determined, and their structure and function demonstrated. In any community or neighborhood, or even in one's own club or profession, subtle alignments, cliques, and coteries are known to exist. Certainly it is an unwary observer who does not see the tendency of people to form intimacies and gossip groups, whether in the isolated rural neighborhood or in the urban apartment house. These are social realities to be ignored only at the individual's own risk.

If one were to go into a small rural neighborhood and ask each family to tell with whom it visits and how often, he would be getting at one of the important informal organizations, namely, the visiting group. In an intensive study of 44 white families in White Plains neighborhood in Charles County, Maryland, it was found that of 182 visiting relationships, 123, or 68 per cent, were with families inside the neighborhood. This study used verbal declarations of friendship and of visiting as bases for locating the informal groupings. Other studies that have been conducted have employed as bases the evidences of association implicit in such matters as the exchange of work, the borrowing and trading of material things, the seeking of advice in making important decisions or in times of trouble, and so on.

Rural families are commonly charted according to their geographic relations, that is, by delineation of neighborhoods and communities. The techniques just described chart a neighborhood according to the interpersonal relationships that bind it together, and that may in this sense be thought of as the fabric out of which a neighborhood is made. The importance of these informal channels lies in the fact that it is through them that people influence each other, for attitudes are developed, changed, and modified in informal give-and-take discussions. The real issues to be taken up in formal meetings generally get aired and partially resolved long before the formal meetings take place. These informal groups actually mold public opinion and provide much of the motivation for action.

THE CHANGING CHARACTER OF THE RURAL COMMUNITY

Rural America has recently shown an increasing number of public and private agencies engaged in sponsoring programs, and these programs have grown rather haphazardly, with each as a separate endeavor seeking the interest and co-operation of the rural people. This mushrooming of agencies and the establishment of independent county administrative offices began in the early thirties when many public programs were being designed to cope with the depression. Today most of the rural counties throughout the United States have such agencies as Agricultural Extension Service (which was, prior to the depression of the 1930's, the primary agency representing the Department of Agriculture and the land-grant colleges in the counties), Farmers Home Administration, Production and Marketing Administration, Soil Conservation Service, and Rural Electrification Administration. In addition to these agricultural agencies, counties often have organizations concerned with social security, public health, and public welfare, with each organization maintaining county offices. And apart from the governmental agencies, there are numerous county-wide organizations, such as the Farm Bureau, the Red Cross, and the county ministerial association. The agencies are being increasingly criticized, however, because they have not effectively utilized and worked through the established organizational and group channels that have been described in this chapter.

Most of the government agencies are legally responsible for establishing within the county, and sometimes within the community, sponsoring committees of local citizens. In administering their programs, however, the agencies are not legally tied to one another at the county and community levels. Most of them therefore operate separately from the federal to the state level, and thence to the county level. Because of the lack of integration among the various programs designed to reach the county, each agency tends to continue to operate independently in carrying its program from the county level to the community and thus to the rural people.

Moreover, since many agency people are specialists in various technical fields of agriculture, and have little or no training in sociology, they often ignore the established patterns of association prevailing among rural people. In line with this apparent dominance of agricultural technology, counties have been subdivided into areas that follow special-crop or livestock interests, soil types, and topographical or drainage features, while the neighborhood and community have not been universally recognized as a basis for subdividing a county into work areas.

It is not only the agricultural agencies that have divided the counties into subareas with little sense or recognition of community. The Department of Public Health often establishes clinics or holds meetings where interest is high, and then arbitrarily divides the county into sections so that few centers, bearing no relation to established communities, become the focal points of contact. And agencies such as the Production and Marketing Administration (formerly AAA) follow minor civil divisions or townships as subunits for administration. In fact, the Production and Marketing Administration generally elects community committeemen on a township basis.

If one were to ask observing persons from the different farming regions what changes are occurring in the community, the replies would in all likelihood be comments such as the following. People, and especially the youth, are leaving and must leave in increasing numbers because of decreasing opportunity in agriculture and rural employment. The village population is being dominated more and more by the older people, many of whom have retired from farming. The one-room schools are finding it difficult to survive because of declining enrollment combined with pressures from state and federal authorities to improve standards and services. In any event, the village-centered consolidated school is replacing the one- and two-room schools. Many of the open-country churches, which report decreases in membership and attendance, are closing, while a few are federating. Besides, the village-centered church is replacing the open-country church, and is displaying renewed leadership and interest in community affairs. Young people want a more vital recreational program than most rural communities will either sanction or provide, and as a result the youth are traveling to near-by towns and cities to participate in commercial recreational programs. As a closely knit, homogeneous group the neighborhood is disappearing, particularly in the older, more settled areas. Informal methods of organization, while still very much a part of rural life, are being increasingly supplemented by formal organizations. Social contacts and interests of rural people have expanded tremendously as, with the great advances in communication and transportation that form a chain linking neighborhood to community to county to district to state to nation. Farm and town people, becoming more aware of their interdependence, are participating jointly in activities whose aim is community betterment. There is increasing recognition of farm people as leaders both in and outside the community. Communities with limited social and economic resources are having to call more and more upon the county, state, and federal governments for aid in extending to rural people the essential services supplied by such modern facilities as schools, hospitals, and roads. Agencies and programs coming from the outside seldom recognize the "natural" community when they organize the county, and thus hinder the proper integration of community organizations through local leaders. The customary family participation in organized groups is giving away before a trend toward greater individual participation. In both interests and levels of living, communities are tending to become more heterogeneous, and the rural dweller, instead of participating in the affairs of only one community, frequently participates simultaneously in several. In summary, the general trend is

toward the development of larger village-centered communities with adequate population and resources to support consolidated schools, adequate recreational programs, and a wide range of economic service, with some of the larger communities evolving institutionalized patterns of behavior whereby they harness their resources and leadership through community councils and other democratic methods of organization.

Undoubtedly, these and other changes have taken place, or are now occurring in the rural communities of America. But change in such areas comes about largely as an orderly process and without much fanfare. The one linear trend observable for many years among communities throughout the country is the trend from locality or simple face-to-face neighborhood relations, to complex and impersonal relations, that is, to nonlocal contacts. A review of the history of settlement and of development of rural America reveals that this country, once predominantly rural, has changed so that it is now a country in which urban centers contain most of the population. This trend continues, along with the changes in the intensity and type of contacts among rural people and between rural and urban dwellers.

The neighborhood was formerly the only social unit or area that concerned its members. Today, except in a few relatively isolated sections, this condition no longer holds true. Farm families today may be part of a local neighborhood in that they "neighbor" with near-by farmers, but at the same time their interest encompasses the local grade school and the consolidated high school at the village center; the parent-teachers association and its sponsored school-lunch programs; the dairy-herd-improvement association; the soil conservation district that joins parts of three counties in one watershed; the church located in the community center; the Extension Service with its scientific help in farming, homemaking, and its sponsored 4-H and home demonstration groups; the Rural Electrification Administration cooperative that has headquarters in the adjacent county seat; and the farmers' organizations seeking to secure appropriate agricultural legislation. During the course of a year they may also, through meetings sponsored by the church, school, extension, or other organization, discuss such issues as world food and agriculture; the United Nations; prices and parity for agriculture and labor; economic outlook and food and crops needed for domestic and world markets; health and medical care; and the problems and needs of rural youth.

"Going to town" is no longer a great occasion, for members of the farm family commonly drive to town to see a movie, or to visit different trade or service centers for their specialized facilities, such as doctors, or hardware and clothing stores. The average farm family subscribes to a "weekly" or two, and if near a metropolitan area, a "daily" is delivered to the door. Radio programs of both local and world-wide interest are tuned in regularly. While still a part of the locality groupings, that is, of the neighborhood and community, the farm family is also now a member of, and a participant in, the world society. And these wider contacts and interests are made and fostered through a broad variety of special-purpose organizations that stem chiefly from the local community.

This trend from the simple to complex forms of associations has resulted in, or given impetus to, two other trends: (1) from family patterns of social participation to individual patterns, and (2) from community wholeness to community segmentation. While there are still many rural sections of the country in which informal methods of organization prevail as the dominant way of mobilizing groups, the trend is increasingly toward the more formal methods. Thus the individual, not the family, becomes the major participant. This trend has accelerated with the development of some of our agricultural programs: the Production and Marketing Administration makes it mandatory that farmers elect "community" committeemen; the Farmers Home Administration requires the appointment of county committeemen; the district organization for soil conservation demands that a governing board be elected; Extension, from its inception, has required local participation in program formation and direction. And without exception individuals, not families, are the participants.

It is not only the agency programs that have increased the formalization of participation; a host of formally organized groups have been "pushed" onto rural peoply by state and national organizations. Thus some rural communities today have from forty-five to seventy-five separate organized groups, and a farm family, through its various members, commonly participates in from four to ten individual groups.

The earlier definitions of the neighborhood and community emphasized the oneness of interest. Now, while the trade-center community has a certain common interest in such matters as education, religion, trade, and recreation, an increasing number of divergent values and conflicts are emerging. In the smaller group, which has greater homogeneity and fewer goals, the group interests are likely to be less numerous, and to be based on such factors as family descent, length of residence, age, and sex. But as society grows more complex, and the population's occupations, residences, mobility, incomes, and differences in religious beliefs increase, it becomes more differentiated, the number of groups is likely to grow, and the basis of organization assumes a corresponding intricacy.

In analyzing the rural organizations in Litchfield County, Connecticut, it is revealed that "the fractionization of rural Litchfield County society into voluntary contractual associations is explained partly by the diversity of the population and the variety of occupations and ways of life in the county. . . . Considering the wide variety of interests which people in different occupations, income classes, and so on have, it is not surprising that the society they compose is equally differentiated and compartmentalized." This is a vastly different rural society from the one that was developed by our forefathers in the settlement of this country, and that it will continue to change is certain. The challenge lies in understanding the significant group relationships and the basic trends in organization, and in continuing to interpret them in meaningful terms, so that those who seek to guide and give leadership to rural life programs may do so with knowledge and wisdom.

The decline of the small trade centers

C. E. LIVELY*

To those who know American rural life, the small economic center, consisting of one or two country stores, with perhaps a small manufacturing concern, an automobile service agency or a cream station and

☐ From Rural America **10:**5-7, Mar. 1932.
*Ohio State University.

25 to 100 people, is a familiar fact. In the past, such centers have not only been numerous, but they have played an exceedingly important part in the economic life of the farm population. The facts indicate, however, that in more recent years these centers have not only become less numerous, but their relative influences in farm life has been decreasing. For purposes

of this discussion, the small farm trade center is regarded as any rural center possessing from one to four business establishments.

THE DECLINE OF SMALL TRADE CENTERS

That the status of these small trade centers has been on the decline in the North Central States during the last twenty-five years, appears to be beyond doubt. In Minnesota,[1] between 1905 and 1929, the total number of such trade centers declined from 799 to 676, a decrease of 15.3 per cent. This decrease came in spite of the fact that much of northern Minnesota was settled after 1905. In Ohio where settlement had largely preceded our present transportation system, and where the density of population (and consequently of centers), was greater, the decline in number of these trade centers was even more pronounced. Here, during the same period of time, a decrease of 41 per cent occurred.

The number of small trade centers was obviously affected (1) by the number which grew in size until they passed beyond the limits of our definition (i.e., four business establishments), (2) by the number of new centers established, and (3) by the number which disappeared entirely as economic centers. That the general decline in numbers was not due primarily to growth in size, is evidenced by the fact that in Minnesota, 14 per cent and in Ohio 6 per cent of the centers existing in 1905 grew to possess five or more business establishments during the next twenty-five years. Due to the settlement of new territory after 1905, the number of new centers established in Minnesota was equal to 38 per cent of the total number existing in 1905; but in Ohio the corresponding percentage was but 20. Since in Minnesota 39, and in Ohio 43 out of every 100 such trade centers existing in 1905, had disappeared as economic centers by 1929, it is clear that the general decline in numbers of these centers was due mainly to actual disappearance of centers.

Certain changes in the capital and credit ratings of the business establishments of these small trade centers may be regarded as having some bearing upon their decline. Whether the chain establishments are included or not it appears that in Minnesota an increase in the average amount of capital per business establishment has occurred during the last 25 years. This increase approximates 40 per cent when the chain establishments are omitted. The proportion of business establishments which operated with $1,000 or less capital decreased from 42 per cent in 1905 to 33 per cent in 1929. Apparently, while these small trade centers have been decreasing in number, their

respective business establishments have been increasing in average size.

But while the average amount of capital employed by business establishments in these small centers has increased, their credit rating has decreased.[2] In Minnesota, in 1905, 72 per cent of the business establishments possessed a first-grade credit rating. By 1929 only 34 per cent possessed such a rating, the majority being given second-grade rating. The rate of change was approximately the same whether chain stores were included or omitted. Furthermore, there was a substantial increase in the proportion of business establishments with no credit rating. Such data suggest that business establishments generally, and the smaller ones in particular, are finding it increasingly difficult to survive in these small trade centers.

Important changes may also be noted in the economic composition of these small trade centers. Since 1905, the total number of business establishments in the Minnesota centers has declined 18 per cent and in the Ohio centers 38 per cent. These declines closely parallel the decline in total number of such centers. General stores and chain stores[3] declined at approximately the same rate in Ohio. In Minnesota the general store became relatively more important and the chain store relatively less important in numbers in these small centers. The former declined only 11 per cent as against 37 per cent for the latter.

Special retail stores decreased 42 per cent in Minnesota and 45 per cent in Ohio. The special grocery store held its own in Minnesota and nearly so in Ohio, but many other types of retail store declined rapidly. Hardware and implement stores declined 65 per cent; furniture and undertaking and lumber establishments decreased from 40 to 60 per cent; harness, drug and millinery stores practically disappeared.

The most pronounced changes have occurred in the rural industries group. As a class, these declined 45 per cent in Minnesota and 70 per cent in Ohio. This rate of decline was more than twice as great as for all business establishments. The blacksmith shop decreased 77 per cent. Creameries increased 22 per cent in Minnesota, but lost 93 per cent in Ohio. Feed and flour mills, cheese factories, shoemakers, wagon factories, and saw mills decreased from 75 to 100 per cent. Grain elevators gained a little in Ohio. Other industries which showed high rates of decline were such as cabinet making, basket factories, broom factories, cigar factories, etc. Throughout these industries and crafts, there was both a decrease in number of estab-

[1]The writer is indebted to the Minnesota Agricultural Experiment Station for materials gathered while a member of that station staff.

[2]According to Bradstreet's Commercial Ratings. Apparently there has been no change in credit rating policy which would account for the observed changes.

[3]The chain store is here defined as any system with two or more units located in two or more centers.

lishments and in the variety of those remaining. It appears that the rural craftsman who operated a small industry and took more pride in his craftsmanship than in his business ability is very rapidly disappearing from these small trade centers. He has been replaced by a machine operator in a larger trade or industrial center.

It is well known that the doctor has been rapidly deserting these small centers. The same may be said of the teacher and the preacher. But while these types of industry and person have been disappearing more rapidly than the trade centers themselves, it should be noted that such business establishments as confectioneries, lunch rooms, pool halls and automobile service stations have been increasing both relatively and absolutely.

CHARACTERISTICS OF DECLINE

A study of the history of these declining trade centers reveals some important facts. In the first place, the decline has been most pronounced in the old, established, long-settled areas and least in the more recently settled areas. Southeastern Minnesota and southeastern Ohio show the highest rates of decline and northern Minnesota and northwestern Ohio, least. The southeastern areas were well settled prior to the development of our present transportation system and consequently a large number of small centers were established. These areas were therefore, profoundly affected by the development of motor car transportation. The new areas grew up, so to speak, with the present system of transportation and the number of small trade centers established was more in harmony with present conditions. In some of these areas, where purely agricultural rather than semi-agricultural and industrial conditions have prevailed, a moderate increase in the number of small centers has occurred since 1905.

The decline of small trade centers has been associated also with decline of farm population, and commonly, though not invariably, with declining or stationary values of farm property. This is particularly evident where the older settled areas are hill areas with a relatively unprofitable agriculture. In these areas the farm population has decreased, the value of farm property has commonly declined and small trade centers show a high rate of decline.

The development of the rural free delivery resulted in the disappearance of numerous country post offices. This was followed by the disappearance of many country stores, many of which constituted the sole business establishment in a small trade center.

Shifts in mining, lumbering and other similar rural industries markedly affected the rate of change of small trade centers.

The growth of large industrial centers and the general urbanization of an area such as northeastern Ohio, has profoundly affected these small trade centers. In such an area, the chances of a small center increasing in size were above the average. The rate at which new centers were established was likely to be high also, though such centers were generally established to serve suburban rather than agricultural interests. Disappearance of such centers was more likely to occur as a result of absorption into larger units than as a result of lack of economic support.

The relation of small centers to the established avenues of transportation has been important. The small center located upon a railroad or upon a main highway was less likely to decline and disappear than one more remotely situated.

RELATION TO NEIGHBORHOOD ORGANIZATION

General observation plus a number of special studies[4] have established the importance of economic functions in rural neighborhood organization. These consist of not only mutual aid activities of value in carrying on the common occupation of farming, but also definite service relations with small neighborhood business establishments, such as the store, blacksmith shop and marketing or manufacturing agency. The location of these business establishments was commonly the location of school, church, grange or organization hall, post office and general sociability center. The development of more rapid means of communication and transportation and the consequent increase in the mobility of the farm population resulted in the severing of old ties, whether kinship, trading, or institutional in nature. Trading and service relations shifted more and more to the larger centers and the decline of the neighborhood economic agencies began. The growing economic relationships of the farm population with the towns resulted, inevitably, in increasing social relationships with townspeople, and a concomitant decline of neighborhood social activity. Decline of neighborhood institutions, school and church followed. These were superseded, in areas where the process has reached this stage; by consolidated schools, consolidated churches

[4]Kolb, J. H., Rural Primary Groups, Wisconsin Agricultural Experiment Station, Research Bulletin 51, pp. 19-20; see also his Service Relations of Town and Country, Research Bulletin 58, pp. 1-2; and Special Interest Groups in Rural Society, Research Bulletin 84, pp. 2-3. Morgan and Howells, Rural Population Groups, Missouri Agricultural Experiment Station, Research Bulletin 74, pp. 14, 30-33, 43. Taylor and Yoder, Rural Social Organization of Clark County, Washington Agricultural Experiment Station, Bulletin 225, pp. 35-36; also their Rural Social Organization in Whatcom County, Bulletin 215, pp. 24, 28. Zimmerman and Taylor, Rural Organization, North Carolina Agricultural Experiment Station, Bulletin 24, pp. 19-20, 25.

and village church connections, and the rise of special interest organizations on a township, larger village trade basin, or other similar territorial unit. Thus, it may be seen that the decline of the small trade center is but one aspect of rural neighborhood disorganization and realignment. Not all rural neighborhoods possess economic agencies such as the store or small creamery. Yet it appears likely that such economic agencies have been sufficiently widespread in the neighborhoods so that changes in these agencies may be regarded as one measure of neighborhood change. Thus, it appears likely that the decline in number of small trade centers during the last 25 years is paralleled by a somewhat similar decline in neighborhood organization. Two additional bits of evidence support this tentative conclusion. In the first place, the decline in number of small trade centers closely parallels, with some lag, the decline in number of all named centers as listed by the Rand McNally Atlas. Using Minnesota data it was found that new centers were likely to appear in the Rand McNally about five years before business establishments were founded, and that trade centers losing their business establishments were likely to disappear from the Rand McNal-

ly lists by the end of five years. Again, preliminary comparisons of the status of neighborhood organization with the rate of change of small trade centers during the last 25 years, in certain Ohio counties where the rate differential has been considerable, have indicated that in the areas where the decline of trade centers has been lowest, the rural neighborhood organization is most intact, and vice versa.

One additional generalization may be suggested. If small trade center trends are at all indicative of neighborhood organization trends, it appears to be a necessary conclusion, after a study of trade center trends, that rural areas, outwardly similar in many respects, have not experienced similar neighborhood changes. Areas with similar topography, type of agriculture, type of people and extent of transportation facilities appear to differ much in neighborhood solidarity. If this be true, it follows that local studies of neighborhood organization must be regarded as of only limited application. Efforts at organization involving neighborhood units should seek first to understand the neighborhood organization of the specific areas under consideration.

Population change in South Dakota small towns and cities, 1949-1960

DONALD R. FIELD and ROBERT M. DIMIT*

South Dakota communities have been undergoing many and relatively rapid changes for the past several years. Technological changes in agriculture have resulted in significant shifts in population, income distribution, and economic opportunities. Relatively low income, lack of job opportunities, outmigration of people, lack of industry, and an inadequate tax base in relation to public services demanded, constitute some of the problems which are greatly affecting the lives of the people in their local communities.

Settlement patterns developed in the 19th century were consistent with the transportation, communication, and social requirements of that time. However,

□ Excerpts from Agricultural Experiment Station Bulletin 571, Brookings, S. Dak., Mar. 1970, South Dakota State University, pp. 5, 7-13.
*Donald R. Field is a Professor in the Management and Social Science Division, College of Forest Resources, University of Washington, Seattle, Wash., and Robert M. Dimit is Professor of Rural Sociology, South Dakota State University, Brookings, S. Dak.

tremendous changes have taken place in technology, transportation, and communication which affect the lives of persons living in our contemporary society. It is becoming increasingly evident that the systems of community organization which have existed in the past are no longer adequate to meet present day needs.

Research projects by rural sociologists and others indicate people of South Dakota have experienced the effects of changes taking place in their local community. Knowing that communities are changing is not sufficient. We need to know why these changes are taking place, the result of these changes, and the kinds of adjustments needed to build communities which will be adequate in the future.

SOCIETAL CHANGE IN RELATION TO SOCIETAL FACTORS

The transformation of a rural trade center community from an isolated service center to a community interrelated with other communities in an urban society can be traced to numerous societal factors. Such factors are: the development of a transportation network, urbanization and industrialization, mechanization in agriculture, population redistribution, institutional reorganization, and diminishing local control.

These societal changes have worked to minimize the differences between "rural" and "urban" society in the United States. The countryside is no longer relatively isolated from the rest of society, but is an integral part of a total society which includes both urban and rural traits in its population, regardless of geographical residence. The society is increasingly interrelated; urban problems have their relevance for rural areas and, of course, the opposite is also true.

Transportation

Many articles have appeared throughout the years in which authors have discussed the factors associated with trade center growth or decline. One such article is by Carle Zimmerman.[1] In his bulletin, he describes the structure and facilities of small towns and examines the influences of modern transportation facilities upon these centers. At the time Zimmerman prepared his publication on small towns (1930), the question of the survival of that unit in reference to larger places was not of immediate concern. He assumed the trade center would be an important type of community for years to come. He was concerned instead, with the adjustment taking place in small towns as they began to compete with each other for village and farm business. In short, he was interested in the growth and decline of centers as they were or were not able to provide goods and services needed.

Commercialization in agriculture was emerging. Small towns which provided complete services or "multifunctions" would grow at the expense of the single function hamlets and neighborhoods. He states of towns that were growing:

All these communities have passed the minimum sizes in business organization necessary for supporting most of the services essential to a commercialized agriculture as it is organized at the present.[2]

The key variable in Zimmerman's analysis was the transportation system. He states,

Transportation made the present system of social organization possible. Merchandising and its satellites, such as advertising, services offered, prices offered, performed a good share of the active functions in the selection and development of the major trading centers.[3]

[1]Carle C. Zimmerman, *Farm Trade Centers in Minnesota, 1905-29*, Minnesota Agricultural Experiment Station Bulletin 269, St. Paul, 1930.
[2]*Ibid.*, p. 43.
[3]*Ibid.*, p. 37.

Change in transportation facilities was one of the first societal factors that affected the growth or decline of small towns. The impression one received from Zimmerman is that improved transportation facilities and a growing commercial attitude among farm operators occurred at about the same time. The construction of new and improved roads linking towns together had a profound effect on small town growth. As transportation improved, trade centers were able to exert an influence over a wider area. We might label this "rural trade center dominance." As one community became dominant, other rural communities in the immediate environs lost their function and declined.[4] As Zimmerman notes, farmers tended to trade predominantly at one center, usually the closest, by sheer necessity. But when better roads were constructed in the rural area, farmers often traded in several centers, depending upon goods desired and variety of goods available. The problem facing the trade center was apparent. It had to attract customers from a larger trade area. Zimmerman notes,

Families that once lived in the area of one or two centers were thrown into the area of several dozens of centers. An increase in the possibilities of travel to the trade center from 4 to 15 miles increased the area of the trade community from 50 square miles to 706 square miles.[5]

As one might expect, the communities to be affected first by an improved transportation system were those which were not located upon a transportation route. These towns were under 500 in population and included many neighborhoods.[6] Whereas physical and social isolation preserved these very small hamlets, a developing road and rail system reduced the need for their existence.

Several points can be made about the surviving trade centers. They were larger and fewer in number. The complexity of trade centers increased. The concentration of services in these centers allowed the addition of further specialized services.[7] The larger centers (primarily over 1,000) prospered as centralization of function occurred. According to Zimmerman:

Appearing trade centers are those that have developed to meet the needs of agriculture and of local community life

[4]Dominance of a small community over other small communities in an immediate area is contained in the assumptions and theory of urban dominance and central place theory. But little attempt has been made to apply these theories to the decline of small hamlets, neighborhoods, and small villages as transportation facilities began to develop in the rural area.
[5]Zimmerman, *op. cit.*, p. 37.
[6]C. E. Lively, *Growth and Decline of Farm Trade Centers in Minnesota 1905-1930*, Minnesota Agricultural Experiment Station Bulletin 287, St. Paul, 1932, p. 14.
[7]Zimmerman, *op. cit.*, p. 34.

and those that have developed as the population bases of certain new industries and needs.[8]

The growth and decline of agricultural trade centers in South Dakota parallels the trends identified by Lively and Zimmerman in Minnesota. Settlement of farm land in this section of the country took place as part of the western migration. The eastern half of the state was settled by homesteaders ahead of the western half partly because of soil and climate features. Chittick attributes rural settlement in this area in part to inadequate transportation.[9] According to the author:

Before the railroads, eastern South Dakota was settled almost entirely by rural farm population served by numerous hamlets and small villages. This scattered pattern of small trade centers was based largely on short distances, limited to ox or horse drawn conveyances, between towns.[10]

The rise of numerous trade centers can be attributed to the nature of farming. Chittick notes, "Agricultural methods and transportation facilities at the time required numerous small trade centers to service the unprecedented number of homesteaders."

Settlement in western South Dakota was encouraged by the construction of bridges across the Missouri River and the subsequent rise in amount of rail connections between sections of the state. Paul Landis, writing about South Dakota in 1933, acknowledged the importance of transportation as a means of settlement and then later as a means of adjustment.[11] Like Lively, Landis placed heavy emphasis upon transportation as a crucial factor in the early growth and decline of trade centers. Unlike the previous writers, however, he attempted to illustrate, in more detail, the impact of a combination of factors on trade centers. He also noted the importance of such additional factors as the realignment of rural post offices and population redistribution.

Transportation facilities had become well established in South Dakota by the 1930's. The movement of people from open country to larger trade centers and cities represents one important result of the development of transportation. The corresponding impact upon the smaller trade centers is obvious. One conclusion reached by Landis concerned the future of the local trade center. The author concluded that community survival is an economic and social problem

for the farmers to solve.[12] The loss of the merchandising and marketing function and a religious or educational function would, of course, be fatal to a small community.

It is interesting to note the compounding nature of the various factors upon trade center growth and decline. Competition and distance are key factors identified by Landis in trade center survival. Distance could here be defined in both a physical and a time dimension.

Trade centers could be affected by competition if the travel time between centers were reduced as well as by the actual physical distance between centers. Such may have been the case as transportation improved. Landis notes that prior to 1900 many trade centers were located in close proximity and a lack in the means of travel between centers insured survival.[13]

Competition was thus minimal for many items. The rise of rail transportation after 1900 increased the probability of competition from trade centers located on these routes. The period from 1900 to 1920 also witnessed the growing use of the automobile as a means of transporting products to markets and families to various trade centers for shopping purposes. Accordingly, Landis notes this same period as the one of greatest adjustments for the appearance and disappearance of trade center communities.[14]

He notes the similar time perspective of drastic change in his Washington study of small towns.[15] The decline of the hamlet and small trade center in Washington occurred between 1900 and 1910.[16] During this period, 210 places disappeared.[17] The importance of transportation on this change is also noted. The location of small towns near waterways or at the junction of two rivers greatly facilitated early trade center growth. Subsequent rail and road development had additional influences on growing and declining centers. According to the author, the relative influence of each means of travel in Washington corresponded to that found in his work in South Dakota (i.e., the growth of rail transportation 1900 to 1915, and the increased use of the automobile around 1915).

Lively, in his discussion, notes 1915 as an important time when many small trade centers declined and again according to Landis, 80% of growing trade centers had access to the railroad during this time.[18]

[8]Zimmerman, *op. cit.*, p. 32.

[9]Douglas Chittick, *Growth and Decline of South Dakota Trade Centers 1901-1951*, South Dakota State Agricultural Experiment Station Bulletin 448, Brookings, 1955.

[10]*Ibid.*, p. 14.

[11]Paul Landis, *The Growth and Decline of South Dakota Trade Centers 1901-1933*, South Dakota Agricultural Experiment Station Bulletin, 279, Brookings, 1933.

[12]*Ibid.*, p. 4.

[13]*Ibid.*, p. 20.

[14]*Ibid.*, p. 23.

[15]Paul H. Landis, *Washington Farm Trade Centers 1900-1935*, Washington Agricultural Experiment Station Bulletin 360, Pullman, 1938.

[16]*Ibid.*, p. 8.

[17]*Ibid.*, p. 22.

[18]Paul H. Landis, *op. cit.*, p. 27, *The Growth and Decline of South Dakota Trade Centers 1901-1933*. C. E. Lively, *op. cit.*, p. 27.

Maintaining this connection through 1930 helped stimulate growth. Only 10% of those trade centers which were located on a railroad declined during this period.[19] This is similar to the finding presented earlier.

Several factors operated simultaneously to affect the small town during the same period. About 1915, there were thousands of small post offices in rural settlements. But the number of post offices decreased accelerating decline in many communities which depended heavily upon this service. Likewise, rural outmigration and the processes of urbanization and industrialization began to influence patterns of growth and decline of trade centers in the rural area. As would be expected, small trade centers more distant from larger trade centers and cities declined first. The importance of a rural population to a trade center is noted by Landis:

South Dakota towns are for the most part trading points for a rural population surrounding them. Take away the rural population and the greater number of them will disappear; increase the rural population and they will prosper and perhaps even increase in numbers. Tributary population is probably the greatest single factor in the success or failure in the growth of a town.[20]

Commercialization in agriculture

With regard to commercialization in agriculture and the reorganization of trade centers, a similar point can be made. Improved transportation, as noted by Zimmerman and others, enhanced farm commercialization. Prior to the development of an adequate transportation system, farms were primarily small, were based upon subsistence, and were selfsupporting. The movement of products was limited to the local market and was directed toward providing a relatively few items which could not be produced on the farm.

Farm mechanization and commercialization represents not only a change from animal power to various forms of mechanical or electric power, but also a change in the attitudes toward farming by the individual operator. Mechanization began slowly during the 1920's and advanced tremendously prior to and during World War II.[21]

The impact of farm mechanization upon the growth and decline of the trade center community can best be described in terms of the impact upon the farm oper-

ation itself. The relationship between farm and trade center has previously been established. Therefore, we would expect that any change in the farm operation as it affects the farm population would have a corresponding effect upon the community.

As farmers turned more toward machinery for farm work, the additional costs required a large operation to compensate for the overall investment. Subsequently, farms became larger. For the community, this meant fewer farm families were living in a given trade area.

Mechanization reduced the need for extensive use of hired labor on the farm. Machines replaced men in many jobs.[22] No one has attempted to relate what effect the reduction of farm labor had upon the amount of trade in the local community. However, it is reasonable to suppose that it did have some effect on the volume of business for local retail merchants.

The capital outlay required for farm mechanization discouraged many farmers from continuing in farming, especially the operators of smaller land holdings. The number of tenant farmers decreased. In addition, the opportunities for farm youth to enter farming diminished, leading to the out-migration of many of the younger rural residents. The capital outlay for mechanization not only encouraged commercialization but helped transform the farmer from a "generalist" producing a little of everything to a "specialist" interested in producing a few commodities for market.

C. E. Lively supports the work of Zimmerman in his discussion of the small town.[23] He notes the change in small towns as a reflection of business involvement with commercial agriculture, competition among centers for such business, and the availability of an adequate transportation system. The importance of the relationship between the center and a growing commercialization of agriculture in the 1930's is a decisive factor in the growth and prosperity of not only the trade center, but the farm. According to the author:

The welfare of a commercial agriculture is dependent upon the size and quality of its markets, both immediate and ultimate; also upon the nature and quality of the local trading center. The facility with which farmers may reach a trading center that can easily and efficiently receive their products and, in turn, distribute to them supplies that they demand, is closely related to their prosperity and satisfaction.[24]

[19]*Ibid.*, p. 28.

[20]*Ibid.*, p. 30.

[21]Robert T. McMillan, *Social Aspects of Farm Mechanization in Oklahoma*, Oklahoma Agricultural Experiment Station Bulletin B-339, Stillwater, 1949. In this publication he indicates 1920-1945 as the period for the inception and advance of mechanization on the farm. The late 1930's prior to the war and during the war represent the greatest increase in production for a market economy.

[22]For a discussion of the influence of farm mechanization on changes in the farm operation and trade center, see Alvin Bertrand, *Agricultural Mechanization and Social Change in Rural Louisiana*, Louisiana Agricultural Experiment Station Bulletin 458, Baton Rouge, 1951.

[23]C. E. Lively, *op. cit.*

[24]C. E. Lively, *op. cit.*, p. 3.

Lively goes one step further than Zimmerman in his analysis when he notes the importance of population shifts, regional differences, and individual farm prosperity. In Minnesota, the growth and decline of trade centers corresponded to the economic base of a region. In an area of mining and lumbering, the growth of trade centers was slower than in areas of agriculture and high population density. In addition, the size of those places in mining areas (primarily northern Minnesota) was smaller and, as mentioned previously, a larger number of smaller places tended to decline initially. In sections of the state where cities and places over 2,500 appeared, the growth of smaller trade centers was more certain, although the number of such likewise declined.

However, in conjunction with the development of agriculture and the growth or decline of trade centers during this period, Lively notes the continued importance of transportation. He states:

The importance of transportation and communication in social organization is too well known to require elaboration here. Change in these facilities is a basic factor in the rise, decline, and realignment of groups.[25]

Improved roads and increasing use of the automobile for farm and family spelled trouble for many small centers. At the time the article was written (1931), the author indicates the importance of the car for trade center survival during the prior 18 years. Without the automobile, many small trade centers could maintain the trade function for which they were established. But with the increased use of the automobile, the communities failed to survive. According to Lively:

During this time many small trade centers have been thrown into competition with larger and more distant centers and, having no sound basis of existence except the monopoly of trade arising out of isolation, have been unable to survive the conflict and have declined or even disappeared entirely.[26]

The corresponding influence of the railroad on trade center prosperity is likewise noted.

Although the presence of a railroad route provided no complete assurances of growth for the trade center, 65.1% of those centers located along a railroad grew. Forty-seven percent of those trade centers which appeared from 1915 to 1930 had access to a railroad. On the other hand, of those that disappeared during the same period, only 21% were located near a railroad.[27] In connection with advantageous location near a railroad, Lively states:

The trade center that offers ready means of transportation of farm products out of the community and of farm supplies to the community is likely to obtain and hold the support of the farm population better than its competitor that offers less along this line.[28]

Although transportation is a key variable in the analysis of both Lively and Zimmerman, Lively attempts to introduce other factors associated with social and economic changes in the agriculture trade center.[29] We have mentioned briefly his reference to regional factors and population trends. He likewise notes the importance of the loss of a post office prior to the 1915 period for early trade center decline. The post office is associated with one function of the community. It provided income in salaries and attracted area residents to the trade center. But as roads were established linking smaller centers with larger centers, the smaller place usually lost the post office.

Changes in the farming enterprises were also noted by the author as having an influence upon the trade center. A general change from grain farming to dairy farming in Minnesota caused many farmers to bypass one trade center for another with a creamery and other milk marketing facilities. This, according to the author, stimulated growth in some of the more strategically located communities. In addition, specialization in the farm operation necessitated a complete service center to provide the range of services desired by the farmer.

Diminishing local control

The rural community was characterized by self-determination. Issues affecting the community were solved or determined at the local level. The farmer as well as the villager had an interest in community decisions. Town meetings with farmer involvement were an important arena of political control and influence in the community and county. Today, with increased federal and state intervention, community affairs no longer are determined completely at the local level.

Nowhere can this trend, with its concomitant effects upon community decision making, be more apparent than in the small rural community. State involvement in school consolidation, curriculum, and standards for teacher qualifications are examples in education. Federal controls over sanitation, political representation, incorporation, municipal laws, law

[25]C. E. Lively, *op. cit.*, p. 31.
[26]C. E. Lively, *op. cit.*, p. 32.
[27]C. E. Lively, *op. cit.*, p. 34.

[28]C. E. Lively, *op. cit.*, p. 34.
[29]Lively prepares a list of local factors associated with growing and declining centers. This list for appearing towns includes communication and transportation factors (i.e., grew up at a crossroads or began with a post office and a railroad). In addition, he notes industrial factors, convenience for rural trade, political center, etc. For disappearing towns, he notes decline of tributary population, industrial change, change in marketing patterns, and competition.

enforcement and debt ceilings represent areas of diminishing local control in government. The same may be said with regard to limitations of control in some local churches and certain branch businesses as a result of centralization of authority.

The importance of local control with respect to many rural institutions and corresponding development of the community is well documented.[30] Grass roots governments (i.e. local control) epitomize the rural tradition. Most communities possessed schools, rural post offices, municipal governments and churches. Today, the growing emphasis on consolidation, centralization and efficiency of scale, coupled with rural depopulation has meant a loss of local control. In many instances, a complete loss of the particular function has occurred. The decline in fourth class post offices during the 1920's is one example. When reorganization of post offices in rural areas was implemented, many communities declined.

School reorganization, during the 1940's and into the 1960's presented a similar picture. Schools, perhaps more than the post office, with their secondary and tertiary effects, at one time provided a major source of revenue for the community.[31] Thus, the loss of this institution would be greatly contested by community leaders. During the past 20 years, however, state and federal intervention has forced school consolidation. Subsequent educational policy has transferred many decision making powers to state and federal agencies.

Local governmental decision making powers have likewise been reduced as increased financial aid is provided from outside the community. Requirements as to how state and federal aid can be utilized, requirements on minimum health standards and minimum governmental responsibilities for communities impose financial burdens upon local government without the corresponding decision making powers to deal with the problems as the community leaders perceive them.

Specialization and centralization has not been restricted to the public sectors of the community. Individually owned business establishments in the community have been replaced by chain or branch operations. Grocery chain stores are active in small towns. In many cases, they are replacing individually owned stores where the local operator has failed to maintain a modern, efficient operation attractive to local residents. The trend in banking has been to larger operations. Small local banks have been taken over by larger, broader service banks. In each case, local leaders have mentioned the diminishing importance of a local unit in the total decision making structure.[32]

Rural migration

Migration from the farm and rural area has been a continuous process since before the turn of the century. Numerous articles have appeared discussing rural migration and the consequences of it for the farm and small town. Out-migration from rural areas has resulted from the industrialization and urbanization of the country as a whole. It has been a form of adjustment in response to labor shortages in the cities. Migration has been selective upon age, sex, and perhaps individual ability, although there is no documentation for the last quality. In some respects, migration has had positive consequences for the farm population and negative consequences for the small town. In this sense the reduction of the number of farmers in a particular area has allowed those remaining to expand their operations over a territory previously occupied. With the growing costs associated with farming and need for increased acreage, this would appear to be a positive side effect of farm migration. In terms of the community, the loss of residents is a negative consequence for reasons previously mentioned.

We have indicated the importance of a rural population for the growth and decline of trade centers in terms of potential customers, but perhaps more important is the long-range impact on the labor force population. In many instances, if a community aspires to attract an industrial firm or some other basis for diversified occupational opportunity, it must have an adequate labor force base to which the community can draw attention. Unfortunately for the small town, this has not been the case. The general trend in the rural area has been out-migration.

Gladys Bowles discusses rural migration in three periods.[33] During the 1920-1930 period, 6.1 million migrants were recorded leaving the rural area. Various reasons were given by the author for out-migration, but two of the most important were economic and educational. In the first case, transportation provided facilities or access for out-migration and in the second, the inability of the farmer to change his farming methods contributed to out-migration. On the other side of the ledger is the pulling force of industrialization. The combination of these factors provided the favorable conditions for rural out-migration. The transportation and communication facilities

[30]See for example, Roscoe C. Martin, *Grass Roots*, Harper and Row, New York, 1964.

[31]Arthur J. Vidich and Joseph Bensman, *Small Town in Mass Society*, Doubleday and Company, New York, 1958, p. 187.

[32]Gideon Sjoberg, "Urban Community Theory and Research: A Partial Evaluation," *American Journal of Economics and Sociology*, 14 (January 1955), pp. 196-206.

[33]Gladys Bowles, "Migration Patterns," *Rural Sociology*, 22 (March 1957), pp. 1-11.

served as a linking mechanism and the city provided the pulling force. In the 1920's, industrialization was labor intensive and the rural migrant could be absorbed.

Out-migration in the 1930-1940 period was somewhat less extensive than in the previous period. Only 3.5 million left the rural area. The depression reduced the number of employment opportunities previously available. In fact, during this period a considerable number of the population returned to the rural area. Not until the next decade, when our preparation and intervention into World War II occurred, did rural migration reach beyond 6 million. During this period, 8.5 million rural inhabitants migrated. Labor shortage in both defense and nondefense plants provided the pulling force and, as we indicated previously, agricultural mechanization reached a peak during the 1940-1950 period. This provided the necessary push. Beale indicates that during World War II (1940-1944) 4 million rural farm residents of labor force age migrated to the city.[34]

The impact of industrialization on rural migration over a 60-year period has had a differential effect depending upon the technological advances and emphasis on the firm. Changes in industrialization have likewise had varying consequences for the small town. Initially, industrialization was labor intensive and attracted people to the cities where jobs were abundant. Recently, however, industry has been moving to the countryside, which in many cases has stimulated small town growth. Industrialization of the rural area is not a guarantee of growth but in many cases has prospects for growth.

Industrialization in the United States proceeded rapidly as sources of power were harnessed for production purposes. If we confine our attention to the three factors of production—land, labor and capital—we can see what impact industrialization has upon the rural area. Although each factor of production is important to the entire process, one factor may comprise a disproportionate share of the total cost at a given time and thus greatly influence industrial decisions.

The greatest cost to the firm in the early days of industrialization was capital accumulation. Industrialization was restricted in production and growth by a lack of capital assets, while land and labor were relatively cheap and available commodities. Therefore, the growth of the firm depended upon the exploitation of labor and the land resource, while attempting to accumulate capital deposits. Furthermore, the lack of a labor supply in the emerging cities focused the attention of the firm on the rural area. Industry had little trouble attracting labor from the country. The attraction of the city, fewer work opportunities at home, and changes in agriculture stimulated rural migration.

Today the situation is reversed and in one respect the rural area and especially the small town finds itself in an enviable position. Sources of capital are abundant in and around metropolitan centers, where the majority of industrial firms are located, while land and labor costs have risen tremendously. On the other hand in rural America labor resources are relatively inexpensive. Subsequently we might anticipate, if firms are attempting to minimize costs of operation, they might consider moving to a region where lower land values and lower labor costs prevail. This in turn may reduce the necessity of the rural population to migrate and instead seek work in the immediate area.

Rural migration has generated other problems for the small community. Out-migration is selective. Many small communities have a high dependent population. In many rural areas, a high proportion of the people are in the age groups comprising children and adults over 65. The majority of those that migrate are working age adults. Beale reports in his study that 60% of those who migrate are under 20.[35] Writers have from time to time noted differences among rural out-migrants in education, personality type, and sex. Because of fewer occupational alternatives, out-migration of farm youth is extremely heavy.

Social change is a continuous process in society. As Everett Rogers has stated: "There is one main theme which runs like a red thread through the fabric of rural society today. It is social change."[36] The objective of this section was to explore social change in the context of the rural community. This was done from an individual community perspective from the viewpoint level of analysis. In the second case, social change was described in terms of the growth and decline of small towns.

Our approach was twofold. First, we described change in terms of those characteristics traditionally associated with a trade center as this type of community evolved in the settlement of the United States. Next, the focus was upon selected factors of societal change and their impact upon the growth and decline of small towns in general.

[34]C. L. Beale, "Rural Depopulation," *Demography*, Volume 1, 1964, p. 265.

[35]*Ibid.*, p. 269.
[36]Everett M. Rogers, *Social Change in Rural Society*, Appleton-Century-Crofts Inc., New York, 1960, p. 3.

The small town in rural America

GLENN V. FUGUITT*

Despite continuing urbanization, the small town is still an important part of the rural settlement fabric. These centers serve perhaps one-fourth of the nation's population living on over one-half of its land area. In 1960, incorporated centers under 2500 in size included about six per cent of the population of the United States. Perhaps more significant, however, is the fact that these make up fully three-fourths of all incorporated centers in the nation. This paper considers recent changes taking place in the small town, especially as they pertain to population size. Social and economic trends in the setting of the small town are related to these changes, and possible courses of action for individual small towns are explored.

For many years writers have predicted the doom of the small town. Yet small towns have persisted up to the present, and in most cases grown. This is particularly true of incorporated places over about 1000 in size. Table 1 shows recent trends for such places considered together. Places 1000 to 2500 in 1950 (all taken together) increased 27 per cent, while places 2500 to 10,000 increased 32 per cent. This compares favorably with the 29 per cent growth of the U.S. urban population over this decade. Places under 1000, however, are together growing at about one-half this rate.

Despite these aggregate increases, many individual small towns are declining, especially smaller ones in remote rural areas. Many others are facing a real challenge as a result of current changes in population

☐ From Journal of Cooperative Extension 8(1):19-25, Spring 1965. *Glenn V. Fuguitt is Professor of Rural Sociology, University of Wisconsin, Madison, Wisconsin. The research of the author presented in this paper was supported in part by Research Grant No. NSF G-S 444 from the Division of Social Services of the National Science Foundation, and by the Research Committee of the Graduate School from special funds voted by the State Legislature.

Table 1. Total population change 1950-1960, for small places classified by size in 1950, United States.

Size in 1950	Number of places	Per cent change
Under 1000	9714	15
1000-2500	3398	27
2500-10,000	2642	32

and technology. In any event, population growth at a slow rate is no cause for complacency. If growth over a decade is less than natural increase (births minus deaths), then there has been a net migration out of the community. Little research has been done on migration to and from small towns. Work now underway at Wisconsin, however, indicates that of 277 Wisconsin places under 2500 in 1950 which increased between 1950 and 1960, 147 (over one-half) had a net migration loss over the decade.

THE CENTRALIZATION OF ACTIVITIES

To understand the changing status of the small town today, it is necessary to move in for a closer view of its setting. The typical small town in most parts of the country functions as a trade and service center for an agricultural hinterland. The majority of small towns grew up during or shortly after the initial settlement of the open country. Hence their location was strongly influenced by the transportation of an earlier era. Important considerations were location on a railroad and easy access by horse and wagon for farmers being served.

These places are interrelated with larger towns and the open country through trade and service activities. Nearby larger places provide more specialized goods and services and may serve as wholesale centers. This system is sometimes viewed as a heirarchy of places by geographers and sociologists.

Changes in this system of relationships, particularly since about 1920, appear to have inhibited the growth of small places. Trade and service activities have tended to centralize. With improved transportation, rural people have a wider range of choices of places to go for goods and services. At the same time, the demand for goods and services becomes so varied and specialized that their satisfaction is far beyond the scope of an individual small town. So-called "economies of scale" operate to put the small store, creamery, or cheese factory at a competitive disadvantage. The growing complexity of farm machinery means that a store offering complete sales and services must be a relatively large one, drawing on a wide clientele. Hence, one cannot be located in every small town. Technological changes making for fewer but larger farms, then, seem also to encourage fewer but larger establishments to furnish inputs and to serve as markets for farm products. The operation of the same kinds of constraints, moreover, has led to the centralization of professional services (such as private medical practice) and public institutions, such as high schools and hospitals.[1]

In the economic sphere, evidence of centralization was reported as far back as the twenties with studies showing smaller places losing establishments, especially those selling more specialized goods.[2] Recent studies in the Middle West also support the proposition that the market radius of small towns is declining at the expense of larger towns, and that small towns are more and more becoming centers for convenience goods and services in the same way as the corner neighborhood stores perform this function in big cities.[3]

An apparent effect of this centralization trend is shown by all studies of small towns. No matter where they were done, such studies have shown larger places to be more likely to grow, and to grow at a faster rate, than smaller places. This was evident in Table 1 for places under 10,000 between 1950 and 1960. The situation for smaller places in Wisconsin over the 1950-60 decade is given in Table 2. While only one place in five, 1000-2499 in 1950, was losing, almost half of the places under 500 population were losing.[4] These find-

ings are typical of the situation in other parts of the country. From a dynamic point of view, they bring to mind the old saying "growth attracts growth." A town may well obtain new economic or public service activities as it develops more retail establishments and commercial services, builds churches and schools, provides adequate community services, and develops active voluntary organizations—the result of being more attractive than its competitors.

Research also has shown that proximity and size of competing service centers is important in explaining population growth. Small towns in southern Minnesota (under 2000 population) which were near centers slightly larger (2000-5000) were less likely to grow than other small places not so near competing centers.[5] In a more recent study of the Upper Midwest, it was concluded that wherever two centers with similar retail facilities are separated by less than 20 or 25 miles, the smaller center is typically losing an appreciable part of its trade area to the larger. More remote centers, on the other hand, appeared to strengthen their trade areas over time.[6]

In summary, at the local level there is a centralization process going on, with smaller towns in many instances losing out to larger ones nearby. Smaller towns are not growing as rapidly as larger ones as a rule, and neighboring places may often be in competition with each other for trade or public or private institutions.

POPULATION CHANGE IN THE LOCAL AREA

Another important consideration for the small town is the population changes taking place throughout the setting in which it is located. Thus general rural and urban population trends strongly affect the population past and future of these places. The connection is most obvious with respect to the loss of the farm population. If most small towns are service centers for rural America, then the decline of the open country farm population should spell decline for these places as they fight over smaller and smaller numbers of customers. This evidently has happened, but perhaps not to the extent that one might first suppose.

Economists have noted that decline of the farm population is generally accompanied by consolidation of farms into larger units, with attendant added mechanization. Thus, sales of farm inputs may actually increase, and the marketing volume of farm output may also increase as productivity rises with fewer, larger farm units. Consumer goods stores in small

---

[1]For a general discussion of many of these trends see Harlan W. Gilmore, *Transportation and the Growth of Cities* (Glencoe, Illinois: The Free Press, 1953); and John H. Kolb, *Emerging Rural Communities* (Madison: The University of Wisconsin Press, 1959). The economic side is discussed in Philip M. Raup, "Economic Aspects of Population Decline in Rural Communities," *Labor Mobility and Population in Agriculture* (Ames: Iowa State University Press, 1961), pp. 95-106.
[2]For example see C. R. Hoffer, *Changes in Retail and Service Facilities of Rural Trade Centers in Michigan 1900 and 1930*, Michigan Agricultural Experiment Station Special Bulletin 279 (East Lansing: Michigan State University, 1933).
[3]John R. Borchert and Russell B. Adams, *Trade Centers and Trade Areas of the Upper Midwest*, Upper Midwest Economic Study, Urban Report No. 3 (Minneapolis: University of Minnesota, 1963), pp. 21-22; and A. H. Anderson, *The "Expanding" Rural Community*, Agricultural Experiment Station Bulletin SB 464 (Lincoln: University of Nebraska), pp. 19-23.
[4]For a more complete analysis of Wisconsin villages, see Glenn V. Fuguitt, *Growing and Declining Villages in Wisconsin 1950-1960*, Department of Rural Sociology Population Report No. 8 (Madison: University of Wisconsin, 1963).

Table 2. Per cent of places losing, 1950-1960, by size of place in 1950, Wisconsin.

Size of place 1950	Number of places	Per cent places losing 1950-1960
Under 500	177	46
500-1000	135	33
1000-2500	112	20
All places under 2500 in 1950	424	34

---

[5]Edward W. Hassinger, "Trade Center Population Change and Distance From Larger Centers," *Rural Sociology*, XXII (June, 1957), 131-36.
[6]Borchert and Adams, *op. cit.*, p. iii.

Table 3. Per cent of places losing, 1950-1960, by change in non-village population of county, Wisconsin.

County non-village per cent change	Number of places	Per cent places losing 1950-1960
Loss	201	55
Gain 0-19	151	21
Gain 20+	72	1
All places under 2500 in 1950	424	34

Table 4. Per cent of places losing, 1950-1960, by size of largest center within 30 miles, Wisconsin.

Size center within 30 miles	Number of places	Per cent places losing 1950-1960
Under 10,000	145	62
10,000-50,000	188	28
50,000 up	91	4
All places under 2500 in 1950	424	34

towns, however, may experience changes in the blend of farm-family spending. If the remaining fewer farmers gain larger net incomes, there should be less spent overall for groceries, but more for housing, furniture, appliances, and recreation.[7] If this proposition is valid, it should help to explain the expansion of many medium-sized small towns even in areas losing farmers. On the other hand, it holds little comfort for the hamlet unable to offer specialized services.

The total population trends of areas in which small towns are located are closely associated with village growth. A study in progress, for example, considers the United States divided into economic areas as designated by the census. With these units, total population change over the 1950-60 decade is highly correlated with average change of towns 1000 to 10,000 in size.

In Wisconsin, the 72 villages under 2500, located in counties where the non-village population increased more than 20 per cent, grew, with one exception, between 1950 and 1960. On the other hand, of the 201 villages in counties where the non-village population is declining, over half lost population. (See Table 3.) Studies in other states have yielded similar findings. The facts that the farm population continues to decline and that each recent decade has seen more counties experiencing heavy total population loss cannot speak well for the future of small towns in remote rural areas, particularly those of hamlet size.

Small towns of all sizes near large cities, however, have tended to grow. There is evidence that such towns can take on a new function. Many are shifting from strictly agricultural service centers to serving also as commuter towns. In Wisconsin, only 4 out of 91 small towns located within 30 miles of a center of 50,000 or more declined between 1950 and 1960, according to Table 4. In marked contrast, 62 per cent of the small towns located more than 30 miles from a center of 10,000 or more declined. (Here, as before, incorporated places under 2500 population in 1950 are under consideration.)

A number of studies in other areas have shown similar relationships, including work covering Iowa, Southern Minnesota, and the entire Upper Midwest area.[8] In the Upper Midwest area, 85 per cent of isolated towns under 1000 lost population between 1950 and 1960, compared with only 55 per cent of the more accessible places in this size group. The author of the Upper Midwest study concluded that small towns within future commuting ranges (say, 50 miles) of thriving urban centers have good chances for survival and growth.

COMMUNITY ACTION

If the inhabitants of small towns in rural areas view population stability or decline with alarm, what are they to do? If their reason for existence has been to serve a clientele primarily engaged in extractive industries such as farming, forestry, or mining (which is now declining in numbers if not in volume of business) adding new functions would appear to be necessary. For example, the possible transformation to a commuter town, or "dormitory community," has already been discussed. This new role, however, is more likely to be imposed on the town by its location than obtained by activities of its townspeople.

Certainly the most commonly mentioned course of action is to try to obtain new industry. The view of many seems to be that new industry is a panacea for the "ills" of the small town. Some industry is of course moving into rural areas. But it seems unlikely that the magnitude of this shift, now and in the future, will be sufficient to bring added life to some 20,000 odd places. Such prospects run counter to the general trend of industrial centralization in and around large

[7]Arnold Paulsen and Jerry Carlson, "Is Rural Main Street Disappearing?" *Better Farming Methods*, XXXIII (December, 1961), 12-13 ff. See also Dean S. Roussos, "A Study of Changes in Retail Sales Patterns by City Size Classes," in Clyde F. Kohn (ed.), *Urban Responses to Agricultural Change* (Iowa City: State University of Iowa, 1961), pp. 141-49.

[8]John Doerflinger, *Geographic and Residential Distribution of Iowa's Population and Change 1950-1960* (Ames: Iowa State University Department of Economics and Sociology, 1962); Hassinger, *op. cit.*, pp. 131-36; and Russell B Adams, *Population Mobility in the Upper Midwest*, Upper Midwest Economic Study, Urban Report No. 6 (Minneapolis: University of Minnesota, 1964), pp. 43-51.

cities. Among small towns themselves, the larger places have it all over smaller places. If a town has a hospital, a high school, and adequate commercial services, it will be much more attractive to prospective small industry.[9] Again size attracts growth, and the small hamlet is left farther behind.

A third new function for many communities is recreation. Recreational activities are expanding, and many small places have locations which would allow them to move into this field—especially in light of continuing transportation improvements. Beale and Bogue give the interesting example of a remote rural county transformed through the building of a dam. Camden County, Missouri, had a 16 per cent increase in population during the 1950's as the result of business and retirement homes fostered by the Bagnell Dam and its reservoir, the Lake of the Ozarks. Yet the population had been declining in this county for the 50 previous years.[10]

Acting as service centers for persons engaged in recreational activities is no more a panacea for all small towns than is attracting industry. Increased population densities in and around the cities of our nation, however, puts a higher premium on what is in abundance over much of the countryside—land, space, water, and wildlife. Further, the increasing level of living and mobility of urban people certainly suggest a future expansion of recreation in selected rural areas.

Individuals can and do make a difference in any community. Aggressive leadership, the absence of controversies which may divert energy from community goals, a willingness to work, and a program for development could well mean the difference between a stagnant and a thriving small town. But there is dan-

ger that a vicious circle may evolve, with decline leading to pessimism on the part of inhabitants, which may lead to further decline.

Without denying all this, it is striking that recent population trends of villages are closely associated with several factors that are simply beyond the control of the residents of individual villages. In the Wisconsin study, there were 21 villages which had optimum growth potential in terms of the three population variables considered. They were all larger, with populations between 1000 and 2000, in counties with non-village growth of over 20 per cent during the 1950's, and located less than 30 miles from a city of 50,000 or more. All of these 21 places were growing, eight by more than 50 per cent over the decade, and only one by less than 10 per cent. At the other extreme of growth potential, there were 12 places under 500 in size, in counties losing non-village population, and located more than 30 miles from a city of over 10,000. Nine of these places declined in size, and the other three grew less than 10 per cent. This illustrates how growth or decline may be strongly influenced by the town's setting, and by its place in that setting as indicated by its initial size. Villages, then, need to work in close contact with other population groups over a wide area, if they are to solve problems arising through population growth or decline.

CONCLUSION

This review has shown that the future of the small town is tied up with the processes of urbanization and population redistribution taking place in America. If these trends continue as at present, most villages in areas where population is concentrating will grow, and some will even become cities. No doubt many of these will be dormitory communities for families of persons who work in nearby cities, as well as trade and service centers for a growing, open-country, non-farm population. Elsewhere, slow growth or decline may well continue to be the rule for most population segments, including the small town.

[9]Dwight A. Nesmith, "The Small Rural Town," in Alfred Stefferud (ed.), *A Place to Live: The Yearbook of Agriculture 1963* (Washington: U.S. Government Printing Office, 1963), pp. 177-84.

[10]Calvin L. Beale and Donald J. Bogue, *Recent Population Trends in the United States with Emphasis on Rural Areas*, Agriculture Economic Report No. 23 (Washington: United States Department of Agriculture), p. 39.

The land is no escape

JUDY STRASSER

The urge to flee the hassles and headaches of modern urban life overwhelms most of us occasionally. Communities readers include the small vanguard of a back-to-the-land movement. But millions of Americans share the desire to escape the wreckage of the urban environment, the deadly speed-up of urban life, the high cost of city living. Over half of the people surveyed in a Gallup poll several years ago wished they could live in rural areas or in small towns. Two thirds of the Americans in a different survey said they really wanted to live in the country, or in very small cities or towns.

Most people who hanker after a country life continue to live in cities, the only places they can get jobs. But we should not feel too sorry for them, or too smug about our own ability to simplify our lives by moving back to the land. There is no escape from the city in the United States today.

I started thinking about the relationships between cities and countryside one day in Fresno, California, a couple of years ago. My husband and I had just left the urban sprawl of the San Francisco Bay Area for a long van trip through the United States. We had spent three weeks in the mountains, backpacking and car-camping, learning wild-flowers, trees, and rocks, watching animals and birds. We had met very few people. I thought we had at last begun to free ourselves from our overdependence on urban lures and city ways.

We drove down the west side of the Sierra Nevada into the broad, terribly hot flatlands of the Central Valley, arriving in Fresno one early afternoon. We spent only twenty-four hours in town. But by the time we left, we had bought fine tweezers and a sharp-needled flower dissection probe; dried food for our backpacks and canned and fresh food for the van; two pairs of blue jeans; vitamin B1 (against mosquitos) and vitamin C; fishing licenses, two rods and reels, and a splendid assortment of flies. We had eaten dinner at a very good, cheap Mexican restaurant, seen "The Godfather," taken showers, washed our hair, and slept in a motel, and laundered our dirty clothes.

Fresno was just our first lesson in what cities are all about. Whenever we went into a town we spent money. Gradually we realized that permanent residents of rural America shared our dependence on the stores of the closest big city—and that in still other ways they, like we, were snared in an urban trap.

COLONIES IN THE COUNTRY

Cities dominate the American countryside economically, politically, and through insidious cultural controls. Decisions made on the topmost floors of towering marble slabs determine the fates of rural lands and the futures of country people. Urban values become national standards; mass media beam the message from the cities to every hollow and backwater town. Neither communication nor control often flows in the other direction.

This pattern of influence is common and long-established in the United States. It has inspired Americans of widely differing political persuasions, living in quite different times, to compare the cities' omnipresent power with the control great empires wield over their far-flung colonies. A nineteenth-century observer called Chicago's domination of the Mississippi River Valley "urban imperialism." The historian Carl Bridenbaugh used the same phrase to describe the dominance of seventeenth and eighteenth-century American cities over the less settled countryside. A few years ago, a leftist social critic analyzed the effects of "colonialism" on the state of Vermont. The president of the Wyoming Stock Growers Association recently used the vocabulary of imperialism to explain his fears that strip-miners will destroy the Northern Plains. He worried that outsiders would dictate the future use of his region's land. "The power blocks in Washington treat us as colonies," he complained.

I call the domination of American cities over American countryside "domestic imperialism." But whatever it is named, it is especially important that people considering a move back to the land understand this complex relationship which shapes rural reality.

Observant people who drive through the countryside looking for their own piece of rural land immediately confront the effects of domestic imperialism. The high price of land is itself one of the results. The poverty of many rural people, their run-down houses and worn-out farms, are other familiar consequences of urban power and control. Domestic imperialism disrupts rural ecologies as well: strip-mined moun-

□ From Communitas **11**:12-18, Dec. 1974.

tains and clear-cut woods, multi-acre monocultures of agribusiness fields, polluted rivers and acid rains result from the cities' domination over rural land.

People who seek to build community outside the metropolis must learn to recognize the city's shadow as it falls across their homes. More difficult, we must understand the many methods, both subtle and overt, by which cities exert their control. Finally, we must join our country neighbors in working for rural equality, in the long fight for self-determination which every colony desires.

CITIES HAVE ALWAYS BEEN ON TOP

Domestic imperialism appeared at the same time as the first cities in colonial America, commercial centers like Boston and New Amsterdam, Philadelphia and Charles Town, South Carolina. These tiny communities—in terms of area and population, no more than small towns by any modern standards—offer us the key to understanding how cities control the surrounding countryside. Each of these cities housed a merchant class: a small group of people who made a great deal of money by uniquely urban means. These prosperous traders dominated the economic, political, and cultural life of the cities in which they lived. The merchant class also learned to dominate both the people and the use of land far beyond their urban homes.

The earliest colonial merchants made their fortunes as agents of the traditional form of imperialism known as the mercantile system. They shipped valued natural resources from American colonies to European nations: tall trees for British masts and luxurious pelts for wealthy Parisians' coats. But these agents of the British empire soon realized that there also were profits to be made in domestic trade. Frontier settlers needed goods and services only the city merchants could provide. Boston's traders began to develop this hinterland market as early as 1650, and the commercial classes in other colonial cities quickly followed suit. Philadelphia Quakers, for example, imported tools and clothes from Europe and sold them to settlers in Maryland, New Jersey, and western Pennsylvania. The settlers paid for the European goods with cash they received for grain and other agricultural products, bought by the merchants for sale to city people or for export across the Atlantic.

THE CITIES MOVE WEST

British imperial restrictions limited the scope of domestic imperialism before the American Revolution. Merchants had to content themselves with building commercial domains in the rural regions surrounding existing colonial cities. But the Revolution opened broad new vistas for well-to-do urbanites, and

gave new meaning to domestic imperialism. The entire country west of the Appalachian Mountains awaited development and domination. White Americans, guided (they insisted) by a divine mission, a Manifest Destiny to reach the Pacific Ocean, set out to create their own vast continental empire. Visions of brand new towns and cities, surrounded by rich farm markets and untapped reserves of minerals and timber, inspired wealthy men to fast and furious speculations in western land. Within a hundred years, the United States had been stolen or bought "dirt cheap" by capitalists and speculators, railroaders and lumber barons, mining companies and cattle kings.

These men—city people—directed American expansion to the west. The pretty schoolbook pictures of hearty pioneers hundreds of miles from civilization clearing small openings in the dense virgin woods for the little plots of corn illustrate myth more than historic fact. Westward expansion was an urban movement, the extension of the cities' domestic empire across the nation to the Pacific Ocean. In many areas of the country, growth of cities and towns preceeded agricultural settlement. The river ports of Pittsburgh, St. Louis, Louisville, and Cincinnati were established as commercial centers in the late eighteenth century, before farmers tamed the surrounding land. A generation later, the towns built along the Great Lakes attracted pioneers to farm the nearby countrysides. The same process repeated itself through the nineteenth century, in the south and across the frontier west.

Investors from cities on the eastern seaboard and in Europe frequently provided the capital needed for townsite development on the frontier months or years before any pioneers arrived in the region. The success of each fledgling town, like that of any beginning commercial enterprise, depended on the good salesmanship of its boosters and the extent of its backers' influence in the worlds of business and politics. The men in state capitol buildings and in New York and Washington who chose routes for government-subsidized canals and railroads sealed the fate of many a prospective town.

But political influence alone did not ensure a town's success. A city's primary function in the nineteenth century, as in colonial times, was to serve as a commercial center. Speculators and town fathers knew that the prosperity of their new communities (and their own wealth and prominence) depended on the extent to which they developed the market potential of the surrounding countryside. Local merchants, bankers, and real estate salesmen, usually using the money of their cohorts in eastern cities, promoted roads, canals, and railroads to connect people in outlying areas with the new market centers. Urban leaders thus added a new dimension to the traditional commercial relationship between city and countryside. The cities now controlled development of transportation and communication facilities far beyond their borders; indeed, urban Americans directed the pattern of westward expansion across the United States.

INDUSTRIALISM AND THE MODERN METROPOLIS

Industrialization introduced job specialization to American working men and women during the nineteenth century. At the same time, it specialized the functions of the American city and countryside. The farmlands surrounding industrial cities, for example, had to provide food for growing urban populations. The modern economy had no real place for small, subsistence-level, self-sufficient farms which fed and housed families who tilled the land with their own labor. Enormous farms and ranches—heavily mechanized, scientifically managed money-making agricultural factories designed to supply the urban markets and produce substantial profits for their businessman owners—took over the countryside and squeezed out the competition. Owners of small farms sold out, and either rented a little land or worked as hired hands for the successful businessman farmers. Farm children left rural America and sought jobs in factories and city stores.

The business leaders in the major cities which encompassed all modern urban functions (distribution, manufacturing, transportation-communication, and finance) controlled the lives of people living many miles outside of town. The raw material requirements of their industries created jobs and shaped lifestyles in distant rural regions. Their workers' need for food molded agricultural economics. Even people who lived in medium sized cities and towns—people who helped distribute the region's products, or who manufactured certain goods, or who helped run the transportation system—found their activities directed from the major urban centers. Residents of mining towns, forests, farms, suburbs, and small communities surrounding each urban center responded to desires and demands created in the city on which their lifestyle and livelihoods depended. Domestic imperialism thrived as the modern metropolis was born.

DOMESTIC IMPERIALISM TODAY

Since 1900 cities have expanded their control over the American countryside, inspiring people to coin new terms to express the urbanization of the American earth. Journalists and social scientists speak of "Megalopolis" spreading along the Atlantic seaboard from Boston to Washington, D.C. They say that "ur-

ban fields" exist, extending 60 or 100 miles, or two hours driving time from every central city. They say that the problem of urban sprawl is growing rapidly: new development covers over a million acres of open space and natural areas in the United States each year.

These basically geographical effects are among the least important consequences of urbanization. Cities still cover only a tiny percentage of the land area of the United States ($7/10$ of 1% in 1960, according to the Census Bureau). But the few people who hold power within the cities—people with money, bankers and businessmen—now control most of the activity in the huge, open, sparsely peopled regions which cannot be called urban in any geographic sense. Today, domestic imperialism affects virtually the entire nation.

SOCIO-CULTURAL DOMINATION

Cities determine the development of rural values, attitudes and ideas. The process of urban socio-cultural domination of the countryside began on this continent in colonial times, when the active international and intercolonial trade required extensive communication between the merchant classes of various cities. Urban acquaintances transmitted new ideas and cultural values (often imported from European cities) along with business information. By the time of the Revolution, commercial capitalism had created a sophisticated, urbane society in the cities, which set the cultural standards for both the agricultural countryside and the back country wilderness. Political and religious philosophy, new theories of education and science, popular fads and fashions adopted by city-dwellers eventually spread into remote regions, though the process could take years.

The relative abundance of social and cultural (as well as economic) opportunities in the cities had lured millions of American families away from their farms and rural homes in the past one hundred years. The proud people who remain in the countryside resist city notions and deny urban cultural superiority, but they nonetheless continue to absorb urban values, standards, and ideas. Modern mass media, especially television, inundate rural people with messages about a world seen from a peculiarly urban perspective. "They're all rich people, the ones you see on television—rich city people," a poor white Southern farmer notes.

Urban ideas, considered by themselves or in the context of the city, may seem quite sensible. But their imposition in an alien context can create serious conflicts for the country people forced to accept and live with them. Coal miners struck their jobs this fall to protest school curricula and textbooks which, while perhaps suitable for children growing up on the streets of Wheeling or Morgantown, contained information which seemed both irrelevant and heretical to parents in remote West Virginia hollows.

Urban socio-cultural domination is not limited to such obvious and highly sensitive areas as controlling children's education. A resident of Stehekin, Washington told me the following story in a tone of resigned exasperation. Stehekin, a tiny community with a winter population of about four dozen hardy souls, lies in the rugged North Cascades at the far end of fifty mile long Lake Chelan. People get to Stehekin by boat; the ride takes four hours on the Lady of the Lake. You can't drive to the village, but if you pay the boat company to barge your car up the lake, you will find fifteen miles of rutted road, extending from the post office-general store into the deep green woods. City people who own cabins along this road barge their cars "up the lake" at the beginning of each summer and "down lake" when they return to the city in the fall. The year-round residents barge old cars and pick-ups into Stehekin, but it's expensive to barge them out when they finally break down. So the heaps sit in front yards and under trees, providing parts for other cars and trucks which need to be repaired.

At least that's how it was until 1968, when the government created North Cascades National Park with Stehekin at one entrance. The National Park Service began to make rules for the town. Park officials decided the abandoned cars were eyesores—not suitable decoration for the front door of a National Park. A clean up campaign collected dozens of rusting jalopies, and the barge towed them all down lake for decent burial in a proper urban junkyard. The new policy works real hardships on Stehekin residents. These people now must spend considerable time and money to find, and then obtain from distant towns, the parts they need to repair their old Chevrolets and Fords. They have to pay the boat company to barge away cars which no longer run. But the countryside does look nicer to the visiting urban eye.

City-determined aesthetic standards applied to rural places make a good deal of sense from an urban point of view. Visitors to National Parks spend most of their lives in the chaos, confusion, dirt, and junk cluttering the average metropolis. These tourists seek restful scenes and visual harmony when they visit the countryside. But the urban aesthetic conflicts with needs of country people. Abandoned cars, power lines, and rusting John Deere tractors—important components of the working rural scene—intrude on the rustic scenery the urban visitor travels so far to see.

The desire to pretty up the countryside is closely related to the most destructive of all the urban attitudes which dominate rural life: "the notion that rural America is a place to make money, not to live." Rural people, especially the poorest among them, find this notion (as it was recently rephrased by a Montana underground newspaper) absurdly contrary to the facts of their own lives. For them, the country is first of all their home, the place they hope to make enough money to continue to get by. But the attitude—expressed clearly and publicly in every land-sales pitch —guides the economic exploitation of the countryside by the urban powers-that-be. This particular citified attitude is dangerously close to becoming rural reality.

ECONOMIC EXPLOITATION

As industrial capitalism developed, and as the scope of domestic imperialism broadened and increased in complexity, the number of ways in which cities exercised economic power over the countryside also multiplied. Some of the methods of economic control obvious today differ very little from those used by the urban merchants in early colonial times. Boston traders thwarted the development of a local commercial class in New Hampshire in the 1600's. The similarly stunted growth of local entrepreneurial skill is frequently identified as among the chief problems of "underdeveloped" regions in the nation to this day. In Vermont, for example, outsiders—banks, insurance companies, timber, mining, and manufacturing corporations based in Boston, New York, and Philadelphia—own the state's major industries, most of its land, and its natural resources. Local business interests control only low-level, relatively unprofitable economic activities, including some retail and wholesale trade, penny ante land speculation, some services and other small industries. In Appalachia, the coal industry's extremely low wages and its importation of managers from outside the mining region restricted the accumulation of local capital and the creation of local entrepreneurs. Northern capitalists invested their money in Appalachia, and the profits dug by Appalachian miners from the region's land flowed right back into the vaults of northern city banks.

Not only the methods, but many of the specific tools now used to exploit rural economies originated long ago. The deeds which legalized the depradation of the Appalachian land and people bear remarkable similarity to those which will open the Northern Plains states to the strip-miners' earthmoving machines. Nineteenth-century documents reserve mineral rights across most of Montana, Wyoming, and North Dakota for railroads (especially the Northern Pacific) and the federal government. The head of the Wyoming Stock Growers correctly reads these old deeds as tools of modern domestic imperialism. The "power blocks in Washington" who control the land his cattle graze will, he fears, have little sympathy with the opinions or needs of local folk. "They are aliens to our locality and would run us under standards—from a different society."

Thoroughly modern financial schemes and business organization have also been developed in the cities to control the countryside. The most dramatic of these twentieth-century forms of economic control, agribusiness, is especially obvious in a state like California, where the small farm tradition never took firm hold. But this invidious form of economic power is also invading farmland elsewhere in the nation with appalling speed.

Agribusiness corporations, vertically integrated to control crops from the time the seed is selected until the processed food is on the kitchen shelf, invest heavily in agricultural land. These corporate "farmers" meet their smaller competition with financial ground rules firmly biased in their favor. Agribusiness corporations need not show a profit on their actual farming operations; they often find it more profitable to write off farming losses against gains in other aspects of their business. Such unfair competition drives smaller farmers off the land, but this is not the end of agribusiness economic rule. These corporations also control the welfare of non-farm people living in rural regions. A few years ago, for example, the residents of Mendota, California wanted to establish a special taxing district to raise money for a badly needed hospital. Three agribusiness corporations (two based in distant California cities and one in Houston, Texas) owned over half the affected land. These giant absentee landlords, unaffected by local health services and unwilling to pay higher taxes, rallied together to defeat the hospital financing plan.

The modern financial tools of rural economic exploitation which give agribusiness corporations so much power also benefit individuals who make their money from completely urban sources—for instance, city doctors and well-paid professionals. These "tax-loss farmers" speculate in vineyards, cattle raising, and orchard crops: high-risk, potentially high-profit agricultural operations. They may reap windfalls from the "farms" they finance (but do not manage), and they never worry, as small farmers must, about bad weather or possible crop disasters. Their farming losses merely lower their income taxes.

Modern, centralized financial institutions based in the biggest cities plan and control the use of rural American land. Two tendencies in the current banking system remove judgments about rural land use from the people most affected and increase urban control of the countryside. First, rural banks, run by conservative officers interested in preserving the local power structure, often hesitate to invest rural savings in major local projects. Second, branches of urban banks with larger, more diverse assets, step forward boldly to loan money for rural development. These loans encourage land uses which make urban, but not necessarily rural, economic sense. To city bankers, the needs of the rural economy, rural environment, and rural people hold little real relevance.

The drain of rural financial resources into the cities continues today as it did in the 1690's when Marylanders tried to stanch the flow of their money to Quaker merchants in the City of Brotherly Love. Loans made by banks in rural regions (including both independents and branches) do not equal the savings generated and banked in these same rural regions. So the money made in the country finances urban-industrial growth. A recent study demonstrates, for example, that metropolitan development of Minneapolis-St. Paul depends on capital accumulated in rural Minnesota and North Dakota. Another study estimates that in 1967 alone, $109 million flowed city-ward from central Appalachia. Rural economies thus increase urban wealth, which perpetuates economic exploitation of the American countryside.

American concern with the importance of spending leisure time in properly re-creative ways developed at the turn of this century, as masses of people collected in industrial towns. Union agitation shortened factory hours, but laborers still suffered from miserable working conditions. Thoughtful writers suggested that city-dwellers would benefit both their minds and bodies by pursuing healthful exercise and seeking rejuvenating contact with the natural world in their hours away from work. Many people considered being out-of-doors invigorating enough: sitting in the bleachers watching baseball and football grew in popularity along with Scouting, camping out, and vacation drives to scenic rural spots.

Outright salesmanship spread the gospel of leisure time in both rural and urban regions. Investing and then selling people ways to use their free time quickly grew into booming businesses, including tourism and spectator sports. These industries (and their modern descendents), created to induce Americans to spend money on relaxations, help set socio-cultural standards for the use of our spare time. They encourage us to carefully distinguish working time from pleasure; they advocate salable forms of escapism as the fastest routes to fun. The propaganda job has been thorough and remarkably effective. It is almost unpatriotic to deny urban Americans their real need to get away from it all, to refresh their weary souls and bodies at summer spas and winter ski resorts. Country people, struggling to preserve their rural ways of life against the invasion of urban hordes, dare not suggest that city people might find it equally refreshing to spend their vacations in the city, making their own homes enjoyable and relaxing places to live.

Economic exploitation accompanies and reinforces the socio-cultural hype. The second home industry, the recreation vehicle and camping industries, the entire tourist industry—all the businesses developed to fill city-generated "needs"—wreak havoc everywhere outside the city that one may care to look. Chambers of Commerce in rural regions frequently promote tourist development. Yet new motels and marinas, campgrounds, and casinos rarely improve local economies. The jobs tourism creates usually end when the season is over and the urban visitors go home. But the prices of groceries and other goods needed by local people inflate rapidly and then stay high. Recreation opportunities, once free and open to all, are reserved for those who can afford to pay. Relatively wealthy urban visitors benefit from tourist development. So does the tourist industry itself, which is usually city-based. Local store owners may profit from increased tourist trade. But most residents of rural areas—and especially the poor among them—suffer economically, as well as in other ways, when city visitors arrive.

The booming industry in recreation land, closely linked with tourism, also benefits the urban rich at the expense of rural people. Development of a reservoir or other possible recreation resource, either by government agencies or private investors, immediately increases the attractiveness of the surrounding land. All too often, speculators buy this acreage before the impondment or other development exists. The original rural owners profit little from the rising prices of their land. The vacation homes (often sold as havens for future retirement as well) built on the site offer city buyers financial benefits in addition to relaxation and rest. Most second-home salespeople hawk their wares as great bargains for speculation. Some of these sites make only grief for gullible purchasers. But other vacation lands do increase handsomely in value. And even if gambling fails to make the second home buyer a million dollars right away, he still benefits by deducting mortgage interest, finance charges, and property taxes from his income tax return.

Major corporations speculating in recreation land control the economies of many resort areas in much the same way as agribusiness corporations control agricultural regions. A single company, Horizon Corporation, sells $80 million worth of lots each year in New Mexico, Arizona, Texas, and Florida—a small percentage of the total rural land it owns. Boise-Cascade, Weyerhauser, and other lumber companies control the futures of their cut-over timberlands. They sell thousands of acres each year for vacation homes, rather than replant them with new trees. The economic and environmental rape of southern Florida by speculators is virtually complete. Coloradans know that the corporate assault on the Rocky Mountains has only just begun.

The residents of areas ripe for recreation/speculation suffer the fates of people who do not control their own lives. Two thousand farm families go out of business every week. The jobs of farm laborers, miners, woodcutters, and other rural workers may be even less secure. One small country business—a farm supplier or rural store—closes its door for each six farmers forced off the land. Few of these people can afford to wait for urban sprawl to make rich men and women out of owners of country land. Recreation development and speculation force them into the city, seeking new ways to survive.

The rural land suffers, along with the rural people. The terrain begins to resemble the scene in the cities so many people want to escape. Real estate developments, hastily landscaped, replace rolling farmlands and wooded mountain sides. (Authorities at Lake Tahoe, on the California/Nevada line, recently contemplated lining the area's roads, in the midst of a national forest, with plastic shrubs and trees!) Highway departments pave over working farms. Increased population and endless construction pollute lakes and streams. Weekend traffic dims the sky above popular resorts with the same emissions that fill every metropolis. Urban socio-cultural dominance and economic exploitation together threaten the very existence of our rural countryside.

It is time to forget the idea that we can escape disruptions and ugliness simply by moving to some other place. The fragile beauty and illusory peace occasionally found in the countryside may soon shatter and disappear completely, wrecked by the cities' power. There is only one way to counter domestic imperialism: that is, to stand and fight.

People who move back to the land must have stronger reasons than some necessarily futile attempt at escape. The move can be a shift in position, a strategic maneuver in the long-term struggle to build a new society in both cities and countryside. The fight for local self-determination, for local governmental autonomy, for simpler, self-sufficient economies, seems especially urgent outside the cities, in rural communities whose colonial status affects each resident's life, every day. People who move back to the land should carefully consider how they can work with their neighbors to achieve rural equality and rural independence, to resist the cities' destructive exploitation and dominance.

The person who moves back to the land without such a commitment will be no different than the white-putteed British imperialist sipping cold drinks on his Indian verandah—no different than Nelson Rockefeller cooling his heels and refreshing his spirit on the grounds of his four elegant country retreats.

9

The impact of transportation and communication changes on rural people and communities

Illinois cities thrive when near interstate highways

From a small city "dead as a doornail" 15 years ago to "transportation hub of Southern Illinois."

That is how Mt. Vernon business and civic leaders describe how the arrival of the interstate highways rescued their town. The appraisal is justified according to a survey by Lindsay-Schaub newspapers of the economic and social impact of the 1,727-mile network of interstate routes on state communities.

Mt. Vernon is located at the intersection of I-57 and I-64. It also gets the traffic from I-24 which comes up from Tennessee, crosses the Ohio river near Paducah, Ky., and connects with I-57 northwest of Vienna. The I-24 traffic goes past Mt. Vernon on I-57, picking up I-65 at the northwest edge of the city and following it to St. Louis.

"Not many cities in the country are on two interstate routes, and we feel that being on three is most fortunate for us," said Chester B. Lewis, vice president of First Bank & Trust Co. He served as city manager of Mt. Vernon for 12 years.

I-57 is completed from Chicago to near Cairo, I-65 is scheduled for completion in the Mt. Vernon area late next year or early in 1975, I-24 is under contract to the Ohio river and the river bridge has been built.

Other Illinois cities where economic benefits having more than one interstate route are visible include Effingham, Champaign-Urbana, Bloomington and Rock Island–Moline.

Most evident of the new development in these and at other cities served by the interstate, are the two to four-story motels and restaurants, the large gasoline service stations and truck service plazas at the interchanges. Construction is underway near many of the interchanges for new industrial plants.

☐ From Southern Illinoisan, Carbondale, Ill., Feb. 25, 1973.
*Lindsay-Schaub News Service.

Social impact of the interstate routes, while less spectacular than the economic impact, also has been great. On the plus side obviously is the greater ease and convenience of travel and access to cultural and recreational facilities in distant parts of the state. Tourism is growing, as evidenced by the fact that visitation at the state parks and at scenic and historic sites is up every year.

Another and very important social benefit is reduction of deaths and injuries from traffic accidents.

On the minus side, social impact of the interstate roads had brought headaches. Traffic has built up in many of the cities, despite the fact the interstate routes, in bypassing most urban areas, take much truck and other through travel off the city streets. The latter is more than offset by the traffic buildup from population growth of the cities, increased tourism and travel to the cities by employes from surrounding areas who come to work in the new motels, restaurants and other service establishments, and in the new factories being built.

At Mt. Vernon, Mayor Ronald W. Lewis says growing pains include having to enlarge the police force, add classrooms and other facilities at the schools and enlarge the city's sewage treatment plant. Efforts are being made, the mayor said, to get the state to "give us a bypass on U.S. 460 to take through traffic of that heavily traveled route off our streets."

PROPERTY VALUE UP

To help finance the sewage plant expansion, City Manager Raymond P. Botch reports, Mt. Vernon is negotiating for a $4.8 million federal and state grant. Prices of residential property and rents, Botch said, have risen sharply in the last few years. This, he believes, will lead many outsiders who get jobs in Mt. Vernon to continue to live in their home towns.

"Few residential units are available here now, for rent or purchase," he said, "and owners can get almost any price they ask; prices have gone up 20 to 25 per cent in the last three years. Announcement that General Tire & Rubber Co. was coming with a big plant really gave us a bull market.

"The city council in the last six months has approved zoning of subdivisions for 500 lots, and sites for apartment buildings with 3,500 units. Not all these will be built, but the residential building that will take place in the next two years should bring rents and residential prices down."

Rev. Rosemary Harris, associate pastor of First United Methodist church, has an idea of the effect the highways have had on the city.

"Development of the interstate highways is a big factor in all the growth that is taking place here," Mrs. Harris said. "It has created a socially different living pattern, and property values and rents have gone up rapidly. Traffic increase has brought headaches, I have heard much about farms being cut in two, and I'm told some filling stations and fruit stands have closed after traffic they used to get was shifted to the interstate. I am confident, though, that the long run benefits will outweigh the hurts the new highways have caused."

POPULATION GROWTH

"Due largely to the interstate highways," Mayor Lewis said, "our population has grown 1,500 to 2,000 in the last three years (highway signs at the edge of the city say it is now 16,400), and besides the travel service businesses at the I-57 interchange, industries are moving in. Biggest of these is General Tire & Rubber Co., whose $54 million plant they tell us eventually will employ 1,800.

"Holiday Inn, Ramada Inn and Regal 8 have built at the interchange, and Howard Johnson is starting to build a four-story motel and restaurant. Three smaller motels have been built in other parts of town since development of the interstate highways began. Quite a number of traveling salesmen have been moving to Mt. Vernon; cities in their territories will be readily accessible from the interstate roads out of here.

"People are being pushed out of their normal routines by our growth pains, but they seem to enjoy the new activity. This is made easier for all those who remember the dark days that followed closing down of the car shops here in 1955; that industry had a payroll of 1,500, the largest in Southern Illinois."

Banker Lewis, city manager in the late fifties, recalled that Mt. Vernon "long was part of an economically depressed area," and along with numerous towns in the southern part of the state had a struggle to keep from losing population. The car shops made steel cars used by several railroads.

SHOPS DECLINED

"Business at the shops had been in a decline for several years before the industry folded," Lewis said, "and from about 1940 to the late sixties Mt. Vernon had no growth. We started to come out of the long slump in 1968, when changes that would be possible with building the interstate highways became apparent."

Lewis, whose fellow townsmen give credit for having a leading role in getting the city started toward better times even before prospective benefits from building the interstate highways became apparent, listed some other things that are happening or in the planning stage besides the big tire and rubber plant.

About $10 million is to be spent in enlarging and improving the airport. A $41 million regional hospital is in the planning stages; it is to be known as the Southern Illinois Medical Center, will have 500 beds and be a sophisticated medical center on the Mayor concept.

Recent development of the $10 million Rend Lake Junior College on Rend Lake 10 miles south of town has had a beneficial impact on business and employment in the community.

Ambitious plans for a recreational development and convention center to cost an estimated $75 million, have been made for what is called the Gun Creek area between I-57 and Rend Lake. A contract already has been awarded for a 27-hole championship golf course; the convention center building, to be known as McCormick Place South, would seat 5,000 persons.

STATE FINANCING POSSIBLE

Two governors, promoters of the development report, have indicated the state may help finance the convention building. Other forms of recreation to be provided include boating, sailing, water skiing, fishing, swimming and hunting.

Downtown Mt. Vernon has been given an impressive facelifting by construction of new buildings by First Bank & Trust Co., Security Bank & Trust Co., Bank of Illinois, Mt. Vernon Savings & Loan Co., and King City Savings & Loan Co.

The five buildings, first of which was erected in 1968, occupy sites provided by razing 27 old store and office buildings, mostly across the streets that surround the courthouse square. A new Federal Building, to cost about $1 million, is under construction.

Mt. Vernon civic and business leaders all see great future potential for the community in 19,000-acre Rend Lake, second largest in the state. The Army Corps of Engineers, who completed building it in 1971, have forecast an annual visitation of its recreational facilities that will build up to more than 3 million.

City Manager Botch is convinced, he said, that the

lake would not have been built "without good access to the area like that provided by the interstate highways."

Guy Henry, managing editor of the Mt. Vernon Register-News and who has had a good chance to watch Mt. Vernon's comeback from economic distress, points out that its claim to be the transportation hub of Southern Illinois is based in part on its expanding airport and four railroads. They are the Missouri Pacific, Chicago & Eastern Illinois, Louisville & Nashville, and Southern Railway, which provide only freight service.

EFFINGHAM'S EXPERIENCE

Effingham is another city whose slow growth has been put in higher gear by coming of the interstate routes. Effingham is located at the intersection of I-57 and I-70. It has three interchanges, but most of its development has occurred at the interchange with route 33.

The four big motels at the interchanges have 310 sleeping units, and three truck plazas service about 3,000 trucks a day, according to E. B. Zipprodt, executive vice president of the Effingham Chamber of Commerce. Effingham's population has grown by 650 in the last two years, he said, to 11,100.

In addition to recent industrial development discernible from Mattoon's I-57 intersection with four-lane route 16, the city is exploiting its interstate service by development around the I-57 and U.S. 45 interchange about two miles south of the city. This is near Lakeland College. A new Sheraton Inn is being built there.

"Mattoon has annexed a strip of land south that includes the I-57 and U.S. 45 interchange, and a strip along highway 16 that ends at the airport which is north of highway 16," it is explained by Mayor Roger Dettro. "Charleston has strip-annexed along highway 16 to the east edge of the airport, so the two cities abut each other at the airport. A new $11 million hospital is to be built north of the airport."

OTHER CITIES

Champaign and Urbana are served by three interstate routes, I-57, I-74 and I-72. They have brought considerable business and industrial development on the north edge of those cities. Bloomington is on I-55 and I-74, but the routes have generated little noticeable development. Rock Island–Moline are on I-80 and I-74 which are giving much needed transportation service to that industrialized community.

Some Springfield residents complain that, although there has been extensive new commercial development around the five interchanges on I-55, the downtown is hurting.

East St. Louis is served by three interstate routes, I-55, I-70 and I-64. To avoid plowing up too much of the city, I-70 and I-55 have been built to converge at Troy, well outside the city, and go through the city on the same location. I-64 will converge with the other two inside the city and use the same location for several blocks before all three cross Interstate Bridge to St. Louis.

While the interstates are giving improved transportation service to industries in East St. Louis, new industries coming to the area are in many cases preferring to locate in suburban territory traversed by those routes outside the city.

A bad social impact in East St. Louis has been the razing of many residential properties near the center of the city.

Development of Illinois's interstate highways, like the coming of the railroads over a century ago, has had a negative impact on several villages bypassed by the expressways, lacking an interchange for easy access to the new routes.

An example is Alma, a village of 350 persons on Highway 37 about 10 miles north of Salem, I-57, which generally parallels U.S. 45 and Highway 37 from Chicago to near Cairo, bypasses within sight of Alma. But Alma is four miles to the nearest interchange.

Alma has been badly hurt, its residents will tell you. "Since we were bypassed by I-57, three of our four gasoline filling stations have closed and the fourth has less business than he had before, and two fruit markets have suffered heavily," said William Hester, real estate dealer and a member of the village board.

"We have only a third to a fourth the traffic we used to have. A fertilizer firm here that used to do a big business over a considerable area now suffers because its customers can't find their way to a cross off I-57 and then to Highway 37 to bring them in here," he added.

Hester was asked if Alma was going to dry up and blow away as did some towns in the early days missed by the railroads.

"Oh, no, we won't blow away. They resurfaced Highway 37 recently and we have a good road, which is far different from the days when travel was by dirt roads that were made impassable by mud or snow part of the year. But anything is felt in a town this size; we are within noise distance of 57 but no access."

The village of Bonnie, eight miles south of Mt. Vernon on 37, has been similarly affected. Residents have to go to Mt. Vernon or three miles south on 37 to get to an I-57 interchange. Samuel Bennett, village treasurer, reports that the settlement's two service stations have faded out, and farmers from the west who used to do their grocery and furniture shopping in Bonnie, can't get across I-57 to shop there now.

About two dozen villages in the state are on old routes close to interstate roads but lack interchanges to provide access to the interstates, according to Roger F. Musbaum, in charge of engineering and standards for the state Department of Transportation.

"We have been building interchanges where the interstates cross state primary routes, and at some county roads," Musbaum said. "Distance between the interchanges in rural areas varies from three to about 18 miles, depending largely on traffic volume and population to be served. Since they cost an average of $1½ million, we can't justify building one for every village the interstate routes pass."

Besides Alma and Bonnie, the villages that failed to get interchanges include Humboldt and Sigel on U.S. 45, Deere Creek and Congerville on U.S. 150 east of Peoria.

BOON TO COMMUNITY

James F. Newton, highway district engineer for District 9 at Carbondale, reported that residents of West City, on the west edge of Benton, were disturbed when building I-57 plowed up a part of their town, but after the readjustments that followed coming of the interstate now, see it as a boon to their community.

Several Illinois cities 15 to 50 miles or more from any interstate route feel a different kind of injury. Some report industries pass them up to locate along interstate routes. Their city leaders are pushing hard for earliest possible completion of the proposed 1,950 miles of supplemental freeways, which would provide an interstate-type highway for about every city of any importance in the state.

Olney is such a city. Along with Lawrenceville and Flora, Olney felt it was robbed of an interstate when highway 64 was moved from its originally designated location of paralleling U.S. 50, about 30 miles south past Mt. Vernon to where it would better serve Evansville, Ind., a city of 200,000 population that would have been 40 miles from any interstate route.

"Route 50 is being improved, but we see no sign of a divided pavement highway," said Allen Yount, editor of the Olney Daily Mail. "To get on an interstate we have to go 40 miles to I-70 at Greenup or Montrose. We are a pretty prosperous town, but not because we have been treated right by the state government."

ALTON'S PROBLEM

Alton Mayor Paul Lenz believes his city suffers because it is not on an interstate highway. While it is on the Great River Road, a scenic drive between the Mississippi river and its bluffs, Alton is about 20 miles from the nearest interstate, I-55.

"We have lost what I am sure would have been some good industrial and business development," Lenz said. "We had planned a big intercity mall and shopping center, where the large St. Louis department stores planned to locate branches if we could have obtained service of an interstate route. We don't have a beltline, and have bad downtown traffic congestion."

Among cities left considerable distances off the interstate routes are Jacksonville, Quincy, Freeport, Taylorville, Pana, Paris and Dixon.

An interesting reaction from a city 10 miles from an interstate is given by Dean Bunting, editor and publisher of the Journal-Register in Albion—"We are grateful to be within 10 miles of an interstate" (I-64).

Illinois' interstate system as it will look by 1976.

The proposed Northeast-Midwest rail reorganization on rural areas

SUMMARY AND CONCLUSIONS

This is a report on a study undertaken to evaluate the impacts on agriculture and rural development likely to flow from rail service reorganization in the "Midwest-Northeast region." The reorganization is proceeding under terms of the Regional Rail Reorganization Act of 1973.

The study primarily examined potential impacts on established firms using rail service at 100 rural rail stations. All of these stations were considered subject to loss of rail service because of their being on rail lines failing to meet standardized tests for financial viability.

The study shows that the impacts of rail abandonments are likely to affect established agribusiness and nonagricultural industries somewhat differently. Established feed and fertilizer dealers now shipping to or from stations on nonviable lines of bankrupt railroads in the Northeast and fertilizer dealers in comparable circumstances in the Midwest are likely to suffer either direct financial loss or a reduction of their growth potential. Grain dealers in many parts of the Midwest will not suffer significantly because of their use of truck-rail and truck-barge transportation. There were few nonfarm related firms using rail service at the stations studied, except in the forested areas.

Farmers and consumers are not considered likely to suffer overall adverse effects, although some farmers may alter enterprise combinations in response to changing price relationships, and potentially face increased transportation costs.

Many rural lines now serving agribusiness and a few other types of firms in the region are likely to discontinue service within the next two years unless legislative provisions beyond those contained in the 1973 Act are brought into effect. Use of a criterion or criteria of financial viability was recommended by the Department of Transportation (DOT) to the United States Railway Association (USRA) in planning for the provision of local service in the Midwest-Northeast. Several economic viability criteria are in use. Other criteria may also affect the system plans, and some States in the region may decide to recommend some nonviable local-service lines to receive Federal and other rail service continuation subsidies as pro-

☐ Excerpts from USDA-ERS Senate Committee on Agriculture and Forestry, 94th Congress, Washington, D.C., 1974, U.S. Government Printing Office, pp. ix, 34-36.

vided for in the Act. If all of the present system is retained without further subsidy, both DOT and USRA have stated that viability of the reorganized system will be weakened, if not prevented.

Hearings held by the Rail Services Planning Office on the DOT report suggested that principal impacts visualized by representatives of agribusiness firms from loss of service were added costs of trucking, potential loss of income by farmers, and threats to the viability of some farm trading centers. Some agricultural representatives also mentioned road deficiencies and difficulty in finding an adequate supply of trucks.

Expected impacts of rail reorganization

Although testimony at the public hearings concerning agriculture came from all States in the Region, rural agricultural areas in Illinois, Ohio, Pennsylvania, and New York were particularly well represented.

Persons testifying at the RSPO hearings concerning reorganization of the railroads in the Midwest and Northeast indicated that agriculture and agri-business would require considerable readjustment if abandonment of all potentially excess rail lines as identified in the DOT report occurred. Loss of rail service was thought likely to dictate use of other modest and more intermodal shipments, bringing increased cost and added inconvenience to the shipper. Some expected marginal businesses and producers to be forced out by the higher costs. In some cases, it was stated that reorganization or relocation of agricultural service firms would increase cost of agricultural products to consumers. Little change in farm enterprise combinations apparently was expected to occur, perhaps because immobility of land resources limits the possibilities for changes in agricultural production.

New England states. The six New England states are in the affected region, but they are not heavily agricultural. No New England State has as much as one-third of its area in farms. Principal agricultural enterprises are dairy, poultry, and vegetables—all with products that are typically moved by truck to nearby population centers. Bulky farm inputs such as feedgrains and fertilizer are brought into the region by rail.

In Maine, abandonment of the line from South Paris to Gilead over which the Agway Corporation, one of the largest feed, fertilizer, and farmer service companies in the country, imported 15 carloads of feedgrain annually, would, according to Agway's testimony, force people to travel 40 miles to get grain for their livestock.

The Maine Potato Growers Association testified that 10,000 carloads and $7 million in rail revenue had been lost by railroads to motor carriers since 1970 because of poor service, suggesting that rail management rather than low traffic volume was the source of problems of Northeast railroads. The magnitude of current rail movement of potatoes was not stated.

New Hampshire produced $58 million worth of fruits and vegetables in 1973. These products were moved to market largely by truck, but railroads were used to bring in fertilizer. Merrimack Farmers Exchange, Inc., a substantial shipper of agricultural material in New Hampshire, estimated an increased cost of $15.10 per ton if rail services were lost on the Lincoln-Concord line and trucks were used.

In 1960, the Vermont Public Services Commission determined that railroads were vital to the State for movement of many commodities, particularly agricultural products. Thus, the State emphasized the need to maintain all of its rail service. The 5,200 farmers in Vermont were stated to rely on rail delivery of an estimated 500,000 tons per year of feedgrains. Evidence presented indicated that a 3 to 5 percent freight cost increase would occur if rail service were curtailed and competition reduced by eliminating potentially excess lines in Vermont. The Commissioner of Agriculture in Vermont estimated that a 17 percent reduction in labor income would result from a 5 percent increase in the cost of feedgrain, machinery, and fertilizer to farmers. The expected average income loss of Vermont dairy farmers was estimated at about $1,500.

The New York–New England Dairy Cooperative Coordinating Committee, which represents 20,000 dairy farmers, stated that if rail lines designated as potentially excess in the DOT report should be abandoned, the aggregate increase in costs of grain shipments to New York and the New England would range from $18.1 million to $72.6 million annually.

State Representative John Savage of Connecticut testified that the eastern region of Connecticut would be hard hit by changes mandated by loss of service over rail lines declared potentially excess by DOT. He stated that there were 20 agri-businesses, grain dealers, or mills with retail outlets, that import 6,100 carloads per year from Chicago over two lines listed as potentially excess to eastern Connecticut. Grain received by rail was milled and shipped by truck throughout Massachusetts, Connecticut, and Rhode Island. In a poll, Representative Savage found that 11 of the 20 firms felt they could not continue in business with the added cost of $8-$10 per ton expected from discontinuance of existing freight service, and the shift to alternate lines. Feed was expected to be imported by truck from more distant mills in Albany, New York. Such a two-day trip was expected not to be economically feasible for millers or dairymen.

Mid-Atlantic states. The Mid-Atlantic States (New York, Pennsylvania, New Jersey, Maryland, Delaware, Virginia, West Virginia, and the District of Columbia) like the New England States are not primarily agricultural. They are, however, more agriculturally-oriented with about 35 percent of their land in farms. New York and Pennsylvania were among the five largest producers of agricultural products among all States in the Midwest and Northeast, and the third and fourth largest producers respectively of dairy products in the United States. Mid-Atlantic States also depended on other regions for much of their dairy and poultry feed. Fertilizer and other farm inputs were also imported from other regions.

Agway Corporation reported that shipping costs would triple if that cooperative completely converted to trucks. Intermodal transportation, including trucking from the nearest rail point to the distribution point, was estimated to cost $4.05 per ton more than direct rail service which would result in an estimated 10-12 percent increase in farmers' feed costs.

During 1972, 761,000 tons of feed, 126,000 tons of fertilizer and 123,000 tons of lime were said by a farmer from northeastern Pennsylvania to have been delivered to northeastern Pennsylvania, mostly by rail. Trucks were said not to be available to move that volume of material. Truck movements of foodgrains were reportedly attempted after Hurricane Agnes caused damage in the area in 1972, but trucks proved to be inadequate and rail service had to be resumed. Rail service was preferred even though open gondola cars were used and much waste resulted.

According to one witness, the cost of transporting a ton of grain from Buffalo to Scranton by rail was $7.80; truck shipment cost $11. The difference would add $3¼ million to farmers' costs. The net income of Pennsylvania farmers averaged only $3,673 and 20 percent of the area's dairymen were said to have been forced out of business in the past two years (1971-72) by the cost-price squeeze.

According to testimony at the Baltimore hearings, elimination of 28 percent of the rail service and 65 percent of trackage on the Maryland part of the Delmarva Peninsula would have severe economic repercussions. The Penn Central lines on the Peninsula were stated to "... represent the only economic freight carriers for the Peninsula."

A representative of Borden Chemical Division of Borden, Inc., testified on the effect of rail abandonment on manufacturing and marketing of fertilizer, farm chemicals and feed supplements by Borden

Chemicals. His company terminated 720 carloads of freight and generated $415,097 revenues for the railroad in 1973 on lines now designated as potentially excess. According to this witness, use of alternative rail lines to plants on segments of track not listed as potentially excess "would likely triple our transit time and double our rail freight costs." The bulk, volume, and distances involved were stated to preclude use of motor carriers to move raw materials and products. Intermodal transport was expected to add $330,953 to freight costs. The expected effect of rail abandonment on Borden Chemicals was said to be abandonment of a number of their facilities in Maryland.

The entire eastern shore of Maryland was heavily (80 percent) agricultural. A number of food processing plants, poultry operators, and businesses and representatives of civic organizations testified that there would be great hardship in the area if rail service were curtailed. Motor carriers were said not to be available to move the freight and the expected increase in costs would be prohibitive.

Mid-Western states. The four midwestern States included in the region of rail reorganization (Ohio, Illinois, Indiana, and Michigan) were major producers of agricultural commodities, including corn and soybeans as the principal cash crops. Michigan also pro-

duces and processes much fruit and vegetables. The midwest area was the origin of much of the feedgrain for the Northeast. The midwest also shipped such commodities to the South, West, and overseas. Rail, truck-rail, and truck-water modes were used for such long distance moves of dry bulk commodities.

Testimony given at hearings in these States were often from rural businessmen and community leaders who felt that loss of rail service to their area would be an unnecessary hardship to rural people and would eventually bring about the demise of family farms and small, agriculture-oriented towns. Rail transportation was said to be the most economical method of moving grain out and bringing fertilizer and farm supplies to the countryside. Smaller grain handlers would, according to testimony, be forced out of business without rail service and farmers would have to haul their grain farther for sale. Some testimony given indicated that the rural road system was inadequate for increased use by heavy grain trucks.

A frequent criticism of railroads by midwest witnesses concerned the shortage of cars. Many said they would use more cars if they were available when needed. According to the RSPO, typical testimony indicated that four times as many cars were needed as were received.

Caliente

FRED COTTRELL

In 1949 I made a study of a little desert town which I called Caliente at which was located a railroad division point with roundhouse and repair shops. I set out to see what happened there when the diesel locomotive replaced the steam engine. I need not repeat here the entirety of what I wrote in 1949, but the reader who does not wish to go back to that article[1] may be helped by having at least its outline to understand what I am saying here.

Caliente was created to serve the transcontinental railroad that was then being built between Salt Lake City and Los Angeles. Its location was set by the tech-

nological requirements of the steam locomotive, which were such that it had to be serviced at some point in that vicinity—and by local geographic features such as a limited but adequate supply of water, in a canyon which widens at this point as it cuts through the barrier between the Great Basin and the watershed of the Colorado River. From a junction at Caliente a branch line was extended to nearby mining areas that once produced a great deal of wealth but which were, over time, to decline in output. The railroad prolonged the life of these mines by making it cheaper to get the ore to smelters, refineries and markets but it is questionable whether the costs of extending, maintaining and servicing the railroad to Caliente would ever have been met from the income generated by these primary producers. So in a sense Caliente was always dependent for its existence on de-

☐ From Technology, man, and process, Columbus, Ohio, 1972, Charles E. Merrill Publishing Co., pp. 67-86.
[1]Fred Cottrell, "Death by Dieselization: a Case Study in the Reaction to Technological Change," *American Sociological Review*, 16 (June 1951).

cisions of men in places remote from it. The decision to build the railroad was made by investors and speculators who were hardly aware of and cared little for the community that was being created as an adjunct to their enterprise. Caliente had value for them only so long as it was necessary to service locomotives, repair cars, and maintain track and signalling systems there. Then, when technology changed so that the demands for such services were reduced or disappeared, Caliente's claims on the outside world declined accordingly. Thus, when the diesel locomotive was put into operation it altered the significance of the geographic environment. It did not need to be serviced at such short intervals as the steam engine, so trains could be run further before they required attention. The railroad company reduced *its* costs by abandoning Caliente as a division point. This wiped out the value of most of the physical structures it had built there. Jobs were eliminated and those who had held them were forced to discover new ones, off the railroad, in or near Caliente, or move to other places where their seniority would guarantee them a railroad job. One of the primary social consequences of this decision was the separation of Caliente residents into sets of people with different life chances. Those with seniority, like the men who operate the trains, used what power they had to take a job at other points. Those who had no property were free to move without suffering the losses incurred by those who owned property. Most of those who had served the railroad employees—the business and professional men—found themselves with heavy investments which they could liquidate only with catastrophic losses. When the immediate results of the closure were concluded only those with a stake in the community, or who saw few life chances elsewhere, were left. So those who were—by middle class norms—most moral were most heavily penalized. Those who had refused, or had been unable, to attain such status, paid a lower price. I predicted a continuing loss of population for Caliente, and assumed that there would be concomitant social disorganization.

In this study I will have to modify those conclusions somewhat. The changed outlook derives in part from the fact that I did not fully understand what was going on at that time. In part it results from changes that have since taken place that I could not then have foreseen.

There does remain a sub-stratum of geographical, ecological, and technical factors which continue to exert influence on the present and future of this little town. We need here to sort the ones whose influence is direct, and unavoidable, from those whose consequences can be and have been modified by variables intervening between them and the people who live there.

This is barren country. The county in which Caliente is located has an area of 10,649 square miles and there are barely more than 2,500 people living in it. It is wild and beautiful but it is extremely demanding of those who stay there. In all that area there are only a few places where man could permanently live without support from outside, and even there with no great certainty. The streams of water necessary for life are few and short and run only intermittently. Most of the sparse rain that falls and the snow that melts evaporates or sinks almost immediately into the soil. Some of this water flows into subterranean pools from which it can be pumped to supply man's needs. But to lift it out of the ground requires a great deal of energy, energy which only recently has become so cheap that crops irrigated with its help can be sold for enough to support the farmer and pay for the pumping. Apart from a few spots then, man lives here only as he can maintain a connection with people outside the desert which induces them to send him the goods and deliver to him the services he requires. In exchange he must either obtain primary products from the earth, or deliver services that are valuable to the people who furnish him with the means necessary to his survival. In many cases the value they place on his product will have as much as or more to do with what happens to him than do his own efforts. It is these anonymous decision-makers who set a value both on what he has to offer and on what he seeks in return for it. Thus it is they who will in large measure determine how many can stay in the desert and how they will live.

In the first study I concentrated primarily on the city of Caliente itself. This put into bold relief what is, in more complex situations, hidden. In many densely populated areas there are a number of different sources of wealth. It is produced in a system that includes numerous institutions that are necessary to production and to the survival of the society in which it takes place. As a consequence it is difficult to determine how much any person or other factor in production, has contributed to their joint product. But both individuals and institutions exert power to secure for themselves a share which they then claim represents their contribution to production, and in turn they consume or distribute this share as their own value priorities indicate they should.

The only contribution of value which Caliente had to offer when it was built was the delivery of the services necessary to keep the railroad running through Caliente. This was paid for in the form of wages and taxes. The amount paid was the resultant of a complex which was determined by, on the one hand, how much the railroad system was able to charge for its services, and on the other, the outcome of conflict between various sets of people, each trying to maximize what they could get as compensation for cooperating in making the railroad run. Obviously we cannot investigate fully all the elements of the complexes that determined either what the railroad took in or those involved in distributing those earnings. But since Caliente itself was so heavily dependent upon this single source of income it is easier to follow the consequences of its reduction than would be true in an environment less demanding than that of the desert.

WHAT DID HAPPEN AFTER CLOSURE?

In this study I have examined not only the city of Caliente but also other communities immediately associated with it in meeting the immediate ecological and economic demands which must be met by Caliente residents. As we have already noted, there were mines and some stock raising as well as subsistence agriculture in this area before the railroad came. The income from these products was exchanged for some of the goods and services produced by Caliente residents. Early in its history Caliente became a shopping center for miners and stockmen, and its hospital took care of many of the sick and injured. But services to Caliente residents were also delivered under the auspices of the county government. Some of these were performed in neighboring communities. In turn these places depended in part on taxes paid by the people of Caliente. To understand what went on in Caliente city we need to enlarge our focus to a county-wide basis. But this picture is still much easier to deal with than would be that of an area with more diverse resources.

The impact of this geographical and biological environment remains very strong. What has altered since I first looked at Caliente is primarily the economic environment. In place of the very few strands that once connected Caliente with the outside world there is a growing network of relationships that influence both what the Caliente resident is able to do and what he tries to do. It also affects what will be the results of his endeavor.

There is little leeway within which the local community can control how its financial resources will be used. Few individuals living there get large incomes which could be seized for redistribution through taxation or claimed by the family, the church, or other means. There is general agreement that some people have a right to consume without working. The younger child, the very old, and the greatly handicapped deserve to be supported by diverting income from the channels set for it by the market. But the list is short. All other persons must fend for themselves. Even the families expect that the grown child, if he does not have a job or otherwise contribute finan-

cially, will leave the desert and find a way elsewhere to support himself. The effects of these values and attitudes showed up very quickly when the railroad abolished most of the jobs previously located there.

There were no new ones created by the release of job holders into the local economy. It was thus forced to contract. The railroad destroyed or otherwise disposed of most of the physical structures it had built. The residences it had owned were sold off at very low prices to people who expected to remain in the town. This depressed whatever market there might have been for the sale of houses owned by others. Thus much of their value was destroyed even though they remained physically intact. Some of the men who took jobs elsewhere kept their families in Caliente where they could use up the value of their property. They could also keep their children in the schools their taxes were in part paying for. Those who had invested their whole life's earnings in a business which could *not* be moved had to consider how they might survive in Caliente though at a level much lower than that to which they had become accustomed. Those who were unlikely to get a job even if they moved had to estimate what their life chances were to be in a community which was unlikely to justify any great expenditure of local funds in their behalf.

Some of the first effects of the closure were a kind of shocked disbelief. Some people could not really accept the fact that the railroad shops were permanently gone, the jobs eliminated. It was assumed that when management discovered the error of its ways, it would reverse itself. Many railroad families kept their houses with the idea of renting them. This practice was not irrational. The ordinary life of the train and engine men had previously called for them, during the time they were coming up through the ranks, to move away from the place where they owned property. Fluctuations in the demand for railroad service had always resulted in layoffs and furloughs. Shifts in the amount of money spent by the railroad on maintenance of ways and equipment which resulted from managerial decisions based on data totally remote from the ken of most workers, had often occurred, and reorganizations which resulted in shifting the location of various kinds of work were familiar. The worker simply waited for fate to deal a new hand, for the man with more seniority to retire or die, or for new business, generated by war or migration, or shifts in the market, to create the demand for more workers, or for employment resulting from the installation of new equipment or structures to create an opportunity to get back on the railroad which paid most of them far more than they could make in any other occupation. So the psychological results were not immediately what they might have been in a community with a different base. Postponement of purchases of all kinds of durable goods, exhaustion of credit, doubling up of families for the duration, and efforts to create some kind of public works to carry them over a period of unemployment were characteristic ploys. But finally it had to be admitted that Caliente was no longer to be a railroad town. Those left behind as others moved on realized more completely how the survival of each depended on the acts of the others, and values that contributed to the survival of the community began to move up relative to those emphasizing the primacy of private profit.

Even as the economic base of the community shrunk there was active effort to find a new one. There was divided council as to the way resources might be used. Some took a traditional turn. The desert dweller had long depended on local wood for fuel. So a group of townsmen located an area where in the past a forest fire had left the dead trunks of standing pine trees which made excellent firewood. After it was felled and cut they had to bring it down a precipitous canyon, or take a long roundabout, tire and gasoline consuming trip. It was not long before it became clear that, in the absence of the teams of horses that once could be used "free" while they were not needed to till and harvest or to round up cattle, the cost of getting wood for fuel was prohibitive, particularly since few houses were equipped to burn it and the local demand was small. The distance to any market not itself equally able to get firewood nearby made shipping prohibitive. So this form of "regression" to an earlier source proved unsuccessful.

A great many juniper trees grow in the area around Caliente. Many westerners who have camped out are more familiar with the odor and the taste juniper imparts to food cooked over it than they are with the taste and odor of burning hardwood charcoal. Some in Caliente thought that they could develop a market for charcoal chips made from juniper to be used in outdoor cooking. Locally the product sold well. But there was not a large enough base to place and sell this exotic product in the larger cities. Even if demand did increase the crude equipment surviving from early smelting (that first was used to make the charcoal) could not have been cheaply reproduced and those who labored hard and long found that the returns for their work were very low compared with what they had gotten from the railroad, the mines, the highways, and other urban-connected employment. So this venture too failed to create a new base.

But then fate took another turn. The federal government, looking for empty space in which to test and develop atomic devices, found this largely publicly owned and sparsely settled area well suited to their needs. There was no strong resistance to prevent this

use of the land. The empty area where the testing was to go on was to be subjected to all kinds of unknown and unknowable risks. Men, women and children in the area wore devices to record how much radioactivity they had been exposed to. And even the jackrabbits were shot and their carcasses analyzed to discover what nuclear pollution was doing to the country. The most important thing to the desert dweller was that this dangerous experiment provided a lot of high-paying jobs. The sons of miners who had been exposed to silicosis and lead poisoning now offered to dig the shafts and tunnels in which atomic devices could be exploded without harm to others. Some of the younger men from Caliente and nearby mining settlements commuted the 320 mile round trip to get the work while living at home. Some of them just pitched a tent and slept on a bedroll for four nights, then drove home for the long week-end. Some "outsiders" who were attracted to the testing area found cheap houses in Caliente and located their families there while they too worked at the test sites. So a few jobs were created, a few children were kept in school, a few customers were served by the stores and service stations, the hospital and the doctor.

Fate further delayed contraction during the Korean War when the primary source of tungsten used in the United States was cut off. The federal government offered very lucrative contracts to those who would find and deliver it. One of the few places where it could be mined profitably is near Caliente. The government paid for a mill and for some housing near the mine, but many of the families remained to use the conveniences found in Caliente itself. This provided a respite. But over time the tungsten mine was closed, and most of the workers at the nuclear test site moved closer to their work as facilities there were improved. Some quit and tried to find jobs nearer to Caliente.

Two other kinds of adaptation to their environment continue to be tried by the people of Caliente. One emphasizes agriculture, the other recreation.

AGRICULTURE AS A NEW BASE

There are a few areas in the vicinity where cattle can be grown profitably. This is familiar to the Western pioneers. Whenever there is sufficient ground water to grow grass, hay can be put up to provide winter feed for cattle. Then the beasts can be turned loose to graze on the sparse feed provided on the government-owned open range in the spring and early summer. Cattle are moved up to the highlands as the snow recedes and plants spring up. They are moved back down as the fall comes on, and wintered in the lowlands, feeding on hay. Thus, a limited amount of hay land can support a herd much larger than would be possible if the cattle were pastured or fed from it all year, as is necessary in lands more heavily populated. Caliente itself was founded on one such ranch, but the water and land once used for growing hay became much more valuable as a supply for the railroad engines, shops, and for the needs of people. In areas not more than fifty miles or so from Caliente some new ranches are today being developed as a result of the extension of cheap Hoover Dam power which can pump water to create new crop lands. Big owners with capital, able to take losses for tax purposes, are buying out most of what is privately owned or can be secured from the government. There does not seem to be future employment for more than a handful of people from this source. Raising riding horses for sale or show stock provides a variant of this kind of land use with, again, only a very limited employment opportunity. Most of the land that could be farmed or ranched in the old way is already occupied by the descendants of the pioneers who used every resource they knew about to make a future for their children, most of whom have, even so, had to leave the home place as they matured.

TOURISM

The other alternative was to use the country for recreation. Caliente, in common with most western towns, has looked upon tourism as a sort of second class industry. The kind of personality most often developed in a little desert community must be twisted and reshaped before it can fit the servile occupations that deal successfully with the demands of tourists. But there is money in it, and sometimes "beggars can't be choosers." Tourists are attracted actively in a number of ways. Caliente is surrounded by mountains that grow enough browse to feed a fairly large herd of deer. The "crop" can be harvested regularly without damage if hunting is not overdone, for deer are very prolific, but the plants they feed on would quickly be destroyed if the deer were not killed off either by carnivores or guns. Deer season finds Caliente and all the country around it filled with hunters. Many are former residents who come home during the deer season not only to hunt but to renew friendships and family ties. Others are city people who find it invigorating to get into the mountains in the fall, eat and sleep outdoors and throw off some of the effluvia of the city. The deer crop is large enough to keep an increasing number of hunters coming back, but this has necessitated shortening the season, which in turn reduces the income which the businessmen of Caliente can expect to secure from them. So this source too is about as great now as it can be expected to be in the future.

Fishing is another kind of recreation that will attract tourists. In the spring, summer, and early fall, there is fishing in the canyons and the government has increased this by planting fish and putting dams where water can be stored. It is hard to keep these dams from filling with silt, gravel, and stones. Their watersheds support few plants to hold back the water that falls, and erosion is constant. So unless there is recurrent effort to contain the runoff by building upstream dams and dikes to slow it down before it reaches the fishing area, there must be equally constant dredging. Otherwise the dams will fill and their function be destroyed. The cost of this effort is so great that it is highly unlikely that it could be paid for from taxes on the profit the tourists leave with the local residents. If this source is to be maintained, neighboring counties, the state and/or the national government must subsidize these projects for the benefit of fishermen who live elsewhere.

Where the gasoline tax, paid by the tourist, and the state and national government together, pay the cost of building highways, they become net assets to the towns through which they pass. Local businessmen have made considerable efforts to encourage travel on a highway which joins two large national parks and passes through Caliente. One year they sent brochures by first class mail (to prevent their being thrown away unopened!) to a sample of people selected at random from the telephone directory of a large metropolitan area. The results did not encourage further efforts of this kind. A local businessman made motion pictures of the country around Caliente which he showed to service clubs in the cities nearest to it. But the effects did not encourage others to continue in this effort. The highway through Caliente is a main road from parts of Western Canada and the wintering places in Arizona. Caliente has fought to keep this road because some travelers on it stop there and use its motels, hotel, restaurant and filling stations. The old road was put where it would serve early mining and railroad towns. Today road planners are looking for the shortest distance between major cities. The road going through Caliente is not on this shortest route. Towns like Caliente had in the past sufficient representation in the state legislature to exert considerable influence on the road builders. After the United States Supreme Court issued its "one man–one vote" ukase the "cow counties" lost a lot of influence. A new road is to be built which will not go through Caliente.

The federal government is interested in creating opportunities for recreation for the people of the cities and has spent some money to that effect in the Caliente area. It bought a valley long used for pasture and hay production and converted it into a wild life refuge. This however will be on the new road, and its effects will perhaps be to lessen rather than increase economic opportunity in Caliente.

So, in spite of continuous effort to provide a new economic base, the economic picture is bleak. The people of Caliente have continued to believe in the ideas of self-help and enterprise even though this has often meant that they had to turn to the government in their efforts to sustain private business. If we look only at the failure of private enterprises one would expect that contraction would quickly reach the point at which Caliente would no longer be able to keep the minimum number of people to hold a doctor, a hospital, a police department, or perhaps even a school. The decline in population until recently certainly bore out this kind of prediction. Caliente City was incorporated in 1944 with a population just over a thousand. By 1960 it had fallen to 792. But now there are 916 people living there. The population of the 10,649 square mile county has had a parallel history. In 1940, 4,130 people lived there, in 1950, 3,837, in 1960, 2,431, but in 1970 the census showed 2,557.

WHAT ABOUT SOCIAL DISORGANIZATION?

With this kind of economic and demographic contraction one would also expect to find evidence of many kinds of social disorganization, such as divorce, desertion, juvenile delinquency and crime. The facts are, however, that such evidence is hard to discover. Instead we find what is in standard terms a sound community, plagued with fewer problems than most areas where "progress" and affluence are evident. This is so different from the expected that we need perhaps to cite the evidence that it is true before we try to explain why things are the way they are.

There are no empty houses in Caliente, so the familiar use of such places for "immoral" purposes does not exist. There are a half dozen empty stores on the street that fronts the railway rather than the highway. None of their windows are broken, none are boarded up though the shelving and counters and other fixtures are clearly visible within. The street in front of them is as clean and orderly as in front of the stores still in use. There are a half dozen "saloons" in Caliente. In only one or two are there often more than the bartender and a few customers. They are kept open by owners who have nothing else to do and nowhere to go. They manage to pay their taxes and seldom require police attention.

Caliente has little crime, and since the railroad closed up shop the rate has, if anything, fallen. Most of those who commit crimes are outsiders who are clearly visible and likely to be caught and often part of the sentence they get, if convicted, is the provision

that they leave town and stay out. Delinquency is no more prevalent now than in more prosperous times. It fluctuates a little but there is no regular trend. Only one boy has been sent to the state training school since the shops closed. He was so frightened by the hard-core youngsters with whom he was forced to live at the school that he spent most of his time with staff members.

There are a few people receiving local relief. This may result from the fact that the payments made by the town are extremely small and it would be impossible for anybody to survive on them alone. As a result, many of those who might be eligible for welfare payments have had to go elsewhere. The state- and federal-supported Aid to Dependent Children program administered from the county seat has in Caliente about the same proportion of clients as is Caliente's share of the county population. The illegitimacy rate among them is about the same as elsewhere in the state.

So in terms of such indicators as dependency, delinquency or criminality Caliente presents a record far more favorable than do many prosperous and expanding towns.

WHAT ABOUT EDUCATION?

The schools contribute to the paradox. In 1956 Caliente had 174 children in elementary school (the county high school is not in Caliente). In 1960 there were 159, in 1965 enrollment dropped to 148 but by 1969 it was up to 188. Since the rest of the schools in the county have not shrunk much it is evident that Caliente has not been absorbing many students from other closed schools. The explanation for this situation cannot come from traditional ideas about the way economic contraction affects a community.

The traditional position, that economic contraction will be accompanied by increased disorganization, simply does not fit the picture in Caliente. The economic base *has* shrunk but basic institutions still persist and impart traditional values to the children. In part this has come about through upgrading the values that support the family and the school, at the cost of downgrading other values that in more affluent days seemed important. An example is found in the response to the decline in railroad taxes. The railroad tore down, gave away or abandoned much of its fixed structure. In turn it demanded and got a reappraisal that reduced Caliente's tax revenue.

We can get an insight into the values and attitudes of the people by looking at the way they responded to the loss of railroad taxes. They could simply accept the decline in revenue and cut public expenditures accordingly. Or they could maintain tax revenue by changing the tax rate or by altering the tax appraisals. The first of these alternatives was denied them because city governments in this state may not levy more than one and a half dollars per thousand dollars appraised value on real estate and this was already being done before closure. So Caliente was forced to accept a decline in tax revenue or to increase appraised values. It was evident that in market terms Caliente real estate *has* declined in value. There are a good many evidences of this decline. One was the price put on the "company houses" which the railroad had owned. After giving to the town their water supply and fire fighting equipment, and destroying the things like the roundhouse for which they had no further use, the railroad sold the residences that it had previously rented only to its employees to any who would buy. These brought a very low price. The sale not only evidenced the declining value of all residential property, it also further depressed that price. Houses can be bought today at very low cost. Under "normal" circumstances in most places the reduction in price would sooner or later be accompanied by a reduction in the appraised value for tax purposes. This doesn't take place. Although apart from those not subject to local taxation there have been only two buildings erected since the shop closure, Caliente city has continued to receive almost as much money from local real estate as before. Valuation for tax purposes is shown in table 1.

Two things should be noted. The first is that even with the decline in their economic position the people elected to retain the appraisals previously put on their property for tax purposes. They were thus *increasing* their taxes relative to the value of their property. The second factor is the fact of inflation, which has greatly *reduced* tax income relative to the *cost* of government. Tax income from real estate would buy in 1969 only forty percent of what it bought in 1940. So even though local people overtaxed themselves they could not continue the services that they previously enjoyed. If these services were to be maintained the income would have to come from elsewhere.

As we pointed out in the first Caliente study the decline in economic opportunity forced a recognition of

the significance of values which emphasizes the priority of values contributing to the survival of the community over strictly hedonistic indulgence. This has become more apparent over time. The people in Caliente were intent on supporting their community in spite of market imperatives. Collective effort to secure the ends shared by most community members became more significant as the loss of jobs continued, and the sale of primary products declined. And so in spite of their deep-seated belief in rugged individualism, the people turned to government for help.

NEW BASES OF COMMUNITY SUPPORT

At the frontier, particularly in the desert, the location of governmental services has always been looked upon as a very significant factor affecting local prosperity. The county seat was located in a nearby mining town for some time before Caliente was built. So it could not directly benefit from the jobs county government provided. After the New Deal, federal and state money began to flow in increased amounts through the county, so it was to the state that local legislators turned to provide Caliente with new jobs. With the then current overrepresentation of the "cow counties" in the state legislature Caliente was in a good bargaining position. Its representatives succeeded in getting a girls' training center located there. This resource has had a very stabilizing effect on Caliente's economy, as indicated in table 2.

The school pays a fee of 40,000 dollars to the county for the education of the girls who go to the public high school. It also pays 6,000 dollars to a dentist and 4,800 dollars to the local doctor. It pays a flat fee of 2,400 dollars to the hospital for nonsurgical cases. (There being no surgeon in Caliente such cases are taken to hospitals in other cities.)

The budget for 1969-70 was 744,000 dollars of which

Table 1. Valuation of taxable real estate

1940	$794,704
1945	$789,299
1950	$765,057
1955	$829,025
1960	$799,809
1965	$786,818
1968	$786,091

Table 2

Fiscal period	Average girls in residence	Yearly no. staff	Budget	Payroll
62-63	42	28	379,861	169,292
63-64	62	38	491,919	275,741
64-65	59	38	538,854	327,780
65-66	57	38	611,188	315,292
66-67	53	40	614,151	325,541
67-68*	49	41	588,103	314,782
68-69*	56	43	617,293	333,747

*Note: During the fiscal periods of 1967-68 and 1968-69, the girls' training center entered into a contract with the county school district for educational services. This provided an additional academic staffing consisting of a principal, secretary, orientation director and six teachers.

about sixty percent will be paid out in salaries and wages. Annually about 60,000 dollars worth of the supplies used by the school are purchased locally. The local merchants involved make a profit from the sale of these supplies.

The greatest impact of the center came from the new jobs it created. As of 1969 it employed forty-three people. These include professionals who were educated elsewhere, and a larger number of para-professionals—local people who were trained for the jobs they now hold in special classes conducted by the state government and by the center itself—plus skilled and unskilled labor. It is obvious that this center provides a very important part of a new economic base for Caliente even though it produces nothing for sale in the market and the value of the service it performs cannot be measured there.

PENSIONS AND SOCIAL SECURITY

There is another growing source of legitimate income that is increasingly available to people who produce nothing whose worth is measured in the market. These include Social Security payments, veterans' allowances and pensions, railroad retirement annuities, and pensions received by those living in Caliente who receive income from the state retirement system.

For a time it looked as if Caliente was to become a retirement center. Some of the houses which the railroad sold when it closed the shops were bought by people intending to retire there. At first the community welcomed them but enthusiasm waned somewhat as the limited income they brought proved to be low. They were in some cases not able to attain even the spartan level of living the local population had ordained for those not working. Concern over this has diminished since Medicare now prevents the aging from becoming an overwhelming burden on local medical welfare funds. Older people would now be more welcome since Medicare payments help support the doctor and the hospital. But now there are no unoccupied private residences and if vacancies occur they will probably immediately be filled by employees of the center or by people living in nearby ranches who want to move into the town.

In some cases houses are being reclaimed for their own use by railroad men who previously had to leave Caliente in order to get work but now wish to retire in the houses they still own. Their income will in most cases be confined to railroad retirement.

OTHER SOURCES OF INCOME

There are a number of federal agencies represented in Caliente. In addition to the post office there are the Bureau of Land Management and the Soil Conservation Service. Around ninety percent of the land in this state is still owned by the federal government. The government, as owner, is represented by the Bureau of Land Management which has had a great deal to say about how public land will be used. It has encouraged the development of grazing and agriculture, and in lesser degree, recreation. It has built a new building in Caliente and maintains a few employees. The Soil Conservation Service, as its name implies, is concerned with practices that reduce destructive erosion through such things as over-grazing, and tries to prevent the introduction of noxious plants. It also maintains an office and a few employees in Caliente.

Other sources of income include Old Age Survivors and Dependents Insurance, Medicare, and Old Age Assistance, which is administered by the state government. The latter has declined in recent years as more of those reaching retirement age become eligible for support from other programs. A good deal of the income deriving from these sources is spent within Caliente.

Another source of income is derived from the educational system. The public schools employ seventy-five people. They constitute the largest employer in the county. Caliente children go to another community when they reach high school. Caliente families thus receive imputed income from the services their children get from this source. On the other hand part of the taxes that support the high school comes *from* Caliente. But most of the income received by the schools comes from either state or federal funds. In 1969 programs sponsored by the latter brought $101,953 into the county. The state government spent $521,136 on the county school, while a small part of the taxes from which these funds were derived were originally collected in Caliente and the county where it is located. Most of the money came from other sources outside that county. As we indicated above, a very large part of the money spent by the girls' training center came from state or federal government, as did incomes to those who worked on the highways, for the Bureau of Land Management, Soil Erosion Control, the state parks, and Wild Life Refuge.

To summarize, a very small part of Caliente's income is now derived from performing services for those extracting raw material from the earth. The largest part comes through providing services to people in Caliente who do not "earn" their incomes. The remainder comes from delivering services to those who cater to the "dependent" clientele. In Caliente fifty years ago these sets of services would have been important in the reverse order of that which they now occupy. It is in this inversion that we find the reason which permits Caliente to survive.

There are many ghost towns in this region. When they stopped delivering ore to be exported they lost any claim on imports, and they died. Ecology and economy were enough to account for what happened. Apparently there are now means to alter the impact of these factors on communities, else Caliente would have met the decline suffered by many of its erstwhile neighbors. It was expected that the decline would come and would be accompanied by *social* disorganization. We need then to see just why it was thought that social disorganization would accompany economic contraction, if we are to understand why that hasn't happened to Caliente.

Most economists and some sociologists adhere to an exchange theory as the basis for human cooperation and organization. It is assumed that the individual learns by being rewarded when what he does brings satisfaction to others and deprived when he fails to do so. Thus he becomes acculturated or socialized. Those from whom he gets rewards give them only for acts approved in that culture (or in a subculture if he is raised among "deviants"). Somehow a comparison of these inputs and outputs is made by the individual and if this is favorable he continues to act in socially rewarding ways. Some economists use this model particularly in relation to "foreign trade" where boundaries are set so that one can distinguish between those inputs and outputs taking place within the system and those between systems. These economists are often not so much concerned about persistent imbalances within a system as they are about those existing between systems. They account for the value of goods and services exchanged in terms of price, and values that cannot thus be compared are left out of the input-output account. So the market, and price-measured values, are regarded as *the* significant variables to be observed. This model developed for the analysis of foreign trade has frequently come to be used domestically also.

Sociologists, anthropologists, and political scientists have to deal with the whole array of values that humans share if they are to use them in prediction. But many of these factors that affect choice cannot be converted into price-measured quantities. There is endemic conflict over the priority to be given among things that *are not* in the market as well as with those that *are* distributed through price. Nevertheless a good deal of theory rests on the assumption that it is the failure or success of a complex system to deliver *price-measured values* that determines its fate. This is so because values created by older, simpler institutions like the family are not adequate to maintain the elaborate set of relationships which it is necessary to use if one is to make use of complex technology in order to escape the limitations of local ecology. So other values must be subordinated to those that support complex organizations.

In the United States the market and the corporation are presumably thought to be legitimate because they promote and enhance values necessary to technological progress. Many people see these institutions as being less of a threat than government. So in the past if the market ordained that a community be destroyed, that was sufficient reason to wipe it out. On the other hand, the use of the power of the state to preserve a community because it performed other necessary social functions, some of them of a character that the market itself destroys, was thought to be immoral and unnatural.

Under this theory, when Caliente ceased to perform needed functions for the railroad and could not find other means to command goods and services through the market, it should and would die. The reason it did not is of course apparent now. We need to recall that the first response to closure of the shops was selective emigration. We must remember that those left behind as the system contracted were just those most devoted to the preservation of Caliente. They were business and professional men whose life chances could, in their judgment, be better preserved by keeping the town alive than by letting it die. Their way of life depended heavily on such virtues as self-control, delayed gratification, and self-help. They have taught these to their children. They have discouraged the entry of new residents with different ideas. They have prevented the creation of a dependent population and limited the survival of those who were already there through extremely stringent rules pertaining to locally supported welfare. They have in large measure prevented criminal deviation from their norms. They have maintained streets, water and sewer systems, police and fire departments, and partially supported their school system. They do not regard these cooperative efforts as being different from an individual's direct pursuit of his own idiosyncratic ends. These collective efforts are not apart *from* but a part *of* their idea of legitimate activity. A given flow of imports into the community will be and has been used to sustain their whole way of life.

Caliente people assume that, because they are being paid for what they do, it must have economic worth. Not a lot of attention is given to the shift in the structure under which they earn, and within which the value of the kinds of service they perform, is determined. They got money from the railroads for performing acts whose worth they could not judge. It is sufficient for them now that they are paid for performing other services which presumably give satisfaction to others living at a distance from them. They are perhaps more realistic in their assessment of the situation than are those who find it necessary to explain what goes on under a theory that emphasizes reciprocity in exchange.

It is difficult to justify by exchange theory the kind of relationship that keeps Caliente alive today. As we have seen, it still does provide some market-sanctioned services. It houses the traveler, provides a few miners and railroad employees with goods and services and does a few other things that are paid for only because they give satisfaction to those who consume them. But the income of most Caliente people does not come from this kind of activity. Instead it comes from outside sources who pay Caliente people for doing things mostly for each other. They care for the sick. They educate their own children. They work to rehabilitate juvenile girls. They house and provide amenities for older people. They provide parks and other free services for the traveler. They maintain law and order. They keep dependent people from falling below a standard which is set, not in Caliente, but in the state capital or in Washington. So it is only as people elsewhere maintain their own values and the social structure that this requires that Caliente is provided with an income. But with that income it can continue to teach and maintain a set of values that are in many respects contradictory to the values that make the community viable.

We cannot here even suggest how the larger set of priorities is created and maintained. We want only to point out that the system in operation cannot be an "exchange" system unless one arbitrarily decides that nobody contributes anything unless he gets from the source to which he has contributed a *quid pro quo*. Most of those who keep Caliente alive don't even know that it exists, or through what channels their taxes have reached their ultimate destination and been converted into consumption goods and services. They can only receive psychic satisfaction from supporting a total system which they believe will in the long run be, in their judgment, better than one that denies consumption by some people who are not, in the judgment of the market place, entitled to consume. Those who vote for taxes to take care of the old, the young, the sick, the crippled, the disabled, children without adequate parental care, veterans, delinquents, and even criminals certainly consume nothing to which these categories of people have necessarily contributed. It is easier to account for their voting behavior by ascribing it to "ideals" and "ideas" as a source of value judgment than to trace it back to some "consumatory" response: such as is basic to some kinds of psychological theory. To account for their behavior we look at the results of institutional controls that indoctrinate (or "socialize") people so that they feel better when they contribute to the support of the unfortunate among them. Thus the means that Caliente uses to adapt to its ecology run from immediate efforts like digging wells or building dams to the maintenance in other places of religious and moral systems.

Analysis demonstrates that the economic system of the United States is increasingly producing and distributing services (as distinguished from things) as the source of consumer satisfaction. Caliente demonstrates to a perhaps startling degree what can in lesser degree be seen in almost any area of the country. Some of the services the total system provides are distributed by reliance upon values measured in the market place. Increasingly the by-products of the market, such as exhaustion of natural resources, the waste of human beings, pollution, and crime, give rise to group action restraining the unbridled pursuit of profit. People are increasingly becoming aware of the effects that disregard of ecological imperatives can have on the maintenance of a viable society. Those disdvantaged in the market turn to other means to establish new priorities. Caliente reflects these changes. Once it was dependent on decisions made in distant places by railroad stockholders, directors, and managers. Now its fate depends more on the decisions made by voters, many of whom live far away, concerning such things as schools, old age pensions, medical and rehabilitative services. The desert gives it little room in which to maneuver. As a consequence men living there must respond more directly and immediately to the voices of power and influence than do those in most communities. For all the rugged individualism of these men on the frontier, they must listen ever more closely to the beat of a distant drummer to whose cadence they must march.

Tomorrow may provide a different tune. The physical structures that already exist, the schools, hospitals, stores, streets, and residences provide physical assets which can at the moment be combined with the income now being sent into the community through government programs to provide services adequate in the eyes of those who control those programs. As the buildings wear out, as they inevitably must do, a decision will have to be made as to whether there is any reason why these or similar structures should be rebuilt. This will force a kind of quantum jump which may, in the light of then existing social and governmental structure and the values of the people, be too great to be justified. Until then it looks as if Caliente will continue to survive though it produces nothing for export that can be sold in the market place. But when and if that moment does come, the desert will reclaim its own.

The meaning of "rurality" in American society: some implications of alternative definitions

ROBERT C. BEALER, FERN K. WILLITS, and **WILLIAM P. KUVLESKY***

ABSTRACT

A plea is made for the current need to consider carefully exactly what is meant by the term "rural." It is suggested that, while ambiguity in usage prevails, most understandings involve ecological, occupational, or cultural dimensions in some measure. By taking each of these three broad classes of variables separately as the defining characteristic of "rurality", some of the strengths and weaknesses of each in terms of logic, scientific needs, professional precedents, and the demands from the larger society for pragmatic operation in the discipline are set down. While incomplete, the specification and analysis of the alternative lines of meaning are offered as a step in the necessary direction of clarifying the concept "rural".

INTRODUCTION

In the early history of this country, the term "rural" referred to areas of low population density, small absolute size, and relative isolation, where the major economic base was agricultural production and where the way of life of the people was reasonably homogeneous and differentiated from that of other sectors of society, most notably the "city". In other words, there were at least three substantive aspects to the meaning of "rural": (1) ecological, (2) occupational, and (3) sociocultural. It was presumed, and perhaps with some justification, that a high correlation existed among these sets of factors. Thus, in most cases, to know where a person resided was to know what he did for a living, the pattern of his values, and his normal interaction situations. Similarly, one could predict the other components of "rurality" by starting with occupation or, with some reservations, the sociocultural aspect. Because the understanding of "rural" was fairly unambiguous, concern for its meaning was not crucial. This is no longer true.

Time has eroded the simple interconnections among the ecological, occupational, and sociocultural

☐ From Rural Sociology **30**(3):255-266, Sept. 1965.

A revised version of a paper read at the annual meetings of the Rural Sociological Society, Northridge, California, August, 1963. The report stems from project number 1388 of the Pennsylvania Agricultural Experiment Station carried out under supervision of the senior author.
*Robert C. Bealer and Fern K. Willits are Professors of Rural Sociology, Pennsylvania State University, University Park, Pennsylvania; William P. Kuvlesky is Professor of Sociology, Texas A. & M. University, College Station, Texas.

facets of the American "rural" scene. Many residents of the relatively low population density areas are not engaged in either agricultural production or other types of "field activities" and a unique, Gemeinschaft-like culture is not descriptive either of most present-day farmers or of persons residing in areas of low population density.[1]

THE PROBLEM

If we accept as true the fact that currently the above three aspects of "rurality" are not necessarily interrelated, the question arises: To what shall the term "rural" refer in the American context?[2] This question cannot be unequivocally answered and, indeed, if one is willing to accept "rural" as a fuzzy, descriptive designation, the matter becomes relatively unimportant. However, to be a useful analytical tool for empirical research, we must derive an operational form

[1] See, for example, Howard W. Beers' review of the last decade of research centering on community structure: "The Rural Community," in Joseph B. Gittler (ed.), *Review of Sociology: Analysis of a Decade,* New York: John Wiley and Sons, Inc., 1957, pp. 186-220.

[2] The answer to the question has been the concern directly or indirectly of other persons at various times. Thus, in one of the earliest issues of *Rural Sociology*, C. K. Nichols pointed to the vagueness of the terms "rural" and "urban". He suggested that "the pursuit for logically accurate *definitions* of the terms should be abandoned" in favor of the task of seeking "objective *indicators*" of community differences. See "A Suggested Technique for Determining Whether a Community Can be Classified as Rural or Urban," *Rural Sociology,* 5 (December, 1940), pp. 454-460. Lewis Jones observed that: "Sense of the need for refinement and respecification of a concept found to be unwieldy as an analytical tool is not an uncommon experience for the sociologist. The concept 'rural' is one of those whose usefulness would be enhanced by some refinement." See "The Rural Hinterland," *American Sociological Review,* 20 (February, 1955), p. 40. Harold Hoffsommer's presidential address to the Rural Sociological Society in 1959 took as its theme the meaning of the term "rural". His thesis was that: "Rural sociology as a scientific area of study is in need of a formal redefinition of its subject matter scope so that (1) it may be more applicable to present-day social relationships, (2) its content as a scholarly pursuit may be more logically and readily defined, and (3) its significance may be better understood and appreciated by the public." See "Rural Sociological Intradisciplinary Relations Within the Field of Sociology," *Rural Sociology,* 25 (June, 1960), pp. 175-196. The authors have profited from reading his treatment and at times this paper parallels his analysis. However, Hoffsommer appeared to be more concerned with advancing a specific viewpoint than with charting alternatives. As a result, we feel the very necessary discussion among sociologists of the meaning for the term "rural" was unfortunately short-circuited.

of the concept that will measure degrees of "rurality" in the real world. This means that we must either: (1) determine a single specific aspect that can be assessed and take this as the defining criterion of "rural" or (2) specify a composite definition wherein the measurable component parts are explicitly weighted and rationalized. It is the latter alternative which would probably receive the most widespread acceptance within the discipline of rural sociology. But the weighting and detail for a useful definition of this order are currently unspecifiable. Its derivation would require extensive research designed to assess the relative utility of the various components singly and in combination for explaining differences in human action.[3] Such research is sorely needed if an empirically useful meaning is to be developed. However, predictive utility is but one consideration in determining the nature of any definition. In addition to scientific acumen, any choice must also consider what its acceptance would mean in terms of professional precedents, an implied research focus, and the demands for pragmatic operation placed upon sociology because it is an institution accountable to the larger society.[4] While it may be argued that such things are, or ought to be, superfluous, in reality, they are often as important or more important than sheer theoretical sophistication in determining what developments in any field will be. As such, these matters seem worthy of systematic consideration.

The purpose of this paper is to evaluate some of the theoretical and practical consequences of using "rural" to refer to the various substantive components that have historically been subsumed under the term.[5]

To do this, the ecological, occupational, and sociocultural meanings will be dealth with separately and the implications of choosing "rural" to refer to only one of these areas is examined. The discussion, however, should also be relevant to any composite definition of "rurality" utilizing these components. In the latter case the "weighting" of the respective advantages and disadvantages might be expected to follow the weights assigned to the component parts.

SOME CONSEQUENCES OF CHOICE
"Rural" as an occupational construct

"Rural" has been used to refer to people engaged in agricultural production. In these terms, "rural" denotes an employment category, differentiated from most others by a characteristic direct confronting of nature's physical elements and a primary economic conversion function.[6] Acceptance of this definition implies that the task for rural sociology consists of explicating the structure and functioning of an industrial grouping and following its vicissitudes over a period of time. It logically places rural sociology as an area of specialization within what is currently called the sociology of occupations or industrial sociology.

This path seems to be the one suggested, for example, by Walter Slocum when he titled his recent introductory text *Agricultural Sociology*.[7] However, despite the number of rural sociologists in this country and the common use of such variables as size and type of farm, it is widely held that we lack a "sociology of the farmer".[8] The point seems to be not so much that relevant information on farming is lacking, but that it is not organized around this particular focal point. Some such emphasis may be justified.

The changing face of American agriculture has been noted by many writers. The growth of vertical integration of production and the recognition of events implied by the term "agribusiness" point to the need to interpret carefully the place of the farmer in the larger society. But before we can logically and clearly relate agriculture as an industry to other industries, we must know its limits so that points of linkage or sys-

---

[3]Some small beginnings have been made in this direction by the present writers. See Fern K. Willits and Robert C. Bealer, "An Empirical Evaluation of Some Alternative Meanings of Rurality," a paper read at the Rural Sociological Society meetings, Macdonald College, Province of Quebec, Canada, August, 1964; Fern K. Willits, "An Exploratory Analysis of Individual and Social Level Meanings of Rurality," Unpublished Ph.D. dissertation, University Park: Pennsylvania State University, 1964.

[4]For a provocative discussion of this proposition, see Gideon Sjoberg, "Operationalism and Social Research," in Llewellyn Gross (ed.), *Symposium on Sociological Theory*, Evanston, Illinois: Row, Peterson & Company, 1959, pp. 603-627, esp. pp. 612-616. C. Arnold Anderson's account of the institutional structure of rural sociology in the U.S.A., while sometimes out of date, overdrawn, and incorrect, nonetheless documents the point cogently. See his "Trends in Rural Sociology," in Robert K. Merton, Leonard Broom, and Leonard S. Cottrell, Jr. (eds.), *Sociology Today* New York: Basic Books, 1959, pp. 360-375.

[5]In addition to the substantive distinctions made above, there is at least one other line of differentiation within the complex of ideas historically subsumed under the term "rural". The question here is the *type* of empirical referent chosen. "Rural" has been used to refer both to the characteristics of areas and the attributes of individuals in terms of the three components delimited above. Taking an areal unit or the attributes of individuals does not lead to the same designation of empirical events. But, while they may be an important distinction, it will not be directly considered in this essay. For further discussion of this point, see, Willits, *op. cit.*

[6]It might make sense to link farming with such other "field activities" as fishing, mining, and forestry. In this regard note Charles P. Loomis and J. Allan Beegle, *Rural Social Systems*, New York: Prentice-Hall, Inc., 1950, p. 204.

[7]Walter Slocum, *Agricultural Sociology*, New York: Harper and Brothers, 1962.

[8]M. E. John and James H. Copp have stated the matter as follows: "With all the emphasis on the sociology of occupations and professions in general sociology there is not a single contemporary study on farming as an occupation. We know little about current recruitment, career histories, or changes from a farm to a non-farm occupation. Information about the part-time farmer, the suitcase farmer, and the gentleman farmer is practically non-existent." "Rural Sociology in an Industrialized Society," a paper read at the American Sociological Society meetings, Chicago, Illinois, September, 1959, p. 6.

temic connections can be established and studied. We can hardly confront agriculture without raising the question of just who is and who is not a farmer. Thus, explicit attention would be turned to the broad problem of class limits. Moreover, the focusing of rural sociology on agriculture might mean increased efforts toward delimiting types of farmers.[9] On purely logical grounds, such endeavors to increase the homogeneity of classes would likely increase the predictive utility of subsequent analyses.

An occupational definition of "rural" would probably improve our relations with agricultural economists with whom we are so often institutionally tied. They have chided us for not attacking the "most significant" problems of agriculture such as explaining why unsuccessful farmers do not leave their vocation faster than they do.[10] Choice of the occupational meaning for "rural" would tend to channel our efforts toward problem areas held jointly with agricultural economists. It would also make much of our work directly and clearly useful to agricultural extension personnel. While these persons may sometimes serve a wider clientele, the principal focus of their endeavors is still farmers and their families.

The fact that the occupational definition of "rural" is perhaps the most limited in scope may offend the sensibilities of many sociologists. No matter how imprecisely the term has been used historically, there seems to be some tacit agreement that "rural" does not refer simply to a delimited, specific phenomenon. The unpopularity of this position is shown by the fact that even those few persons who have tentatively given an occupational meaning to "rural" do not consistently follow it through. Thus, Slocum, while titling his book *Agricultural Sociology*, finds room to include discussions of religion, delinquency, divorce, and a host of other aspects of man's behavior that are somewhat incongruous with a discipline predicated on an occupational category. He uses the strategy (recently in vogue in industrial sociology) of talking about "industry and community relations", a process of examining the total fabric of society from the special vantage point of economic organization. While this improves on any tendency to give an isolated institutional description of agriculture, it also flirts with economic determinism.

"Rural" as an ecological construct

"Rural" has also been used as an ecological concept to refer to the distribution of people in space. The most common usage of the term here has been to designate as "rural" regions of small population size or low density.[11] This definition conforms to most common sense understandings of the word and hence can facilitate communication between the rural sociologist and the layman. In a pragmatic and problem oriented discipline, such communication with the general public is important.[12] Moreover, a size and density meaning adheres to the criteria utilized by the U.S. Census Bureau whose tabulations have provided prime data for sociology. Acceptance of the population factor as the defining characteristic for "rural" means that these data can be directly applicable to the sociologist's work.[13] "Rural" defined in terms of size is precise, convenient, and easily operationalized.

However, it may not prove to be a meaningful sociological variable. If sociology is to be concerned with the structure and functioning of society, an ecological construct is not relevant *per se*.[14] To be sociologically significant, the distribution of population must have some causal importance for other patterned forms of interaction. If this implied relationship is true, it means that wherever certain population sizes occur there will also be found certain patterns of social action. The correctness of this position has been questioned in a provocative article by Richard Dewey.[15] His major thesis is that while variations in size and density of population induce concomitant variation in (1) anonymity, (2) division of labor, (3) heterogeneity, (4) impersonal and formally prescribed

[9]For some beginnings in this direction see George A. Donahue, "Socio-Economic Characteristics of Part-time and Full-time Farmers in the Twin-Cities Area," *Journal of Farm Economics*, 39 (November, 1957), pp. 984-992; and Glenn V. Fuguitt, "A Typology of the Part-time Farmer," *Rural Sociology*, 26 (March, 1961), pp. 39-48.

[10]See Earl O. Heady and Joseph Ackerman, "Farm Adjustment Problems and Their Importance to Sociologists," *Rural Sociology*, 24 (December, 1959), pp. 315-325.

[11]When the areal unit is constant, small absolute size and low density necessarily show perfect correlation. Hence, for simplicity, we use the terms interchangeably unless otherwise noted.

[12]This also can be a considerable detriment. For a discussion of this idea, see Robert C. Bealer, "Theory-Research: A Suggestion for Implementation from the Work of Florian Znaniecki," *Rural Sociology*, 28 (December, 1963), pp. 342-351.

[13]This does not mean that the sociologist must accept a Census definition of "rural". The Bureau has to balance greatest scientific acumen among other demands in making its choices. However, it seems likely that the sociologist starting with a conception of "rural" in terms of population density could extrapolate from almost any foreseeable Census definition by (if nothing else) obtaining special runs.

[14]Although there is no general consensus concerning the *exact* nature of what sociology ought to be, there is little professional support for making it simply the study of population characteristics. One need only recall the place of human ecology in sociology to be informed on this point. For some insight here, *cf.* O. D. Duncan and Leo F. Schnore, "Cultural, Behavioral and Ecological Perspectives in the Study of Social Organizations," *American Journal of Sociology*, 65 (September, 1959), pp. 132-146; Peter H. Rossi's "Comment," *ibid.*, pp. 146-149; and "Rejoinder," *ibid.*, pp. 149-153.

[15]Richard Dewey, "The Rural-Urban Continuum: Real But Relatively Unimportant," *American Journal of Sociology*, 66 (July, 1960), pp. 60-66.

interaction, and (5) symbols of status which are independent of personal acquaintance, such relationships do not hold for the entire range of interactional forms implied by the common error of equating "the general [ecological] terms 'rural-urban' with such classification as 'sacred-secular', 'Gemeinschaft-Gesellschaft', . . . [and] 'agricultural-nonagricultural'."[16] The linking of only five structural qualities to absolute size and the assumption that sociology ought to study the full range of "cultural facts" leads Dewey to the conclusion, "that if this be all that there is to the rural-urban continuum, it is of minor importance for sociology."[17]

While Dewey regards the five structural aspects, which he asserts are related to population size, as insignificant in number and of limited importance, many sociologists would disagree with him.[18] Although it appears that neither Dewey's reasoning nor his data interpretation is free from flaws,[19] his discussion points to the need to give careful attention to the causal relationships of ecological phenomena to other areas of behavior.

The preceding discussion has defined "rural" in terms of *absolute* qualities. The term could be used instead to refer to areas of *relatively* small size and density. Using "rural" in this way provides flexible and likely changing class limits and hence loses the precise connotation available when the referent is a population aggregate of 2,500 or some equally definite figure. This, in turn, may cause difficulties in generalizing among studies. And, of course, this usage is under the same restrictive doubts in regard to sociological meaningfulness cast by Dewey in regard to absolute size. At the same time, a relative size definition gains the likelihood of immortality. While it is entirely possible that America may some day have no areas of absolutely low population, we shall always be able to distinguish those places which are small relative to others. This use of the term may have some professional appeal, for paradoxically, the discipline of rural sociology in the United States seems to be strongest and research most profuse in precisely those areas in greatest danger of being engulfed by the megalopolis!

In addition to the above stated meanings of "rural", there is another way of viewing the ecological compo-nent. This is the idea of isolation or, conversely, accessibility of one region to others, most particularly to the larger population centers. Historically, "rurality" generally has been taken to refer not only to regions with a small number of inhabitants, but also to isolated settlements with little contact with the more densely populated areas. Absolute isolation for any geographical area currently is rare. However, as long as communication is not instantaneous and transportation does involve costs, there shall be relative isolation and, hence, areas which can be identified as "rural".

As with the previous ecological definitions, this meaning, if it is to be sociologically relevant, must be causally linked with patterned interaction. This has been done, at least implicitly, by the human ecologists through the concept of urban dominance.[20] Others have questioned their analysis[21] and, in doing so, point to the need to carefully address the crucial question of the relationship of this ecological phenomenon to nonecological qualities.

If the ecologists are correct and if isolation is an important sociological variable, there are certain advantages in defining "rural" in this way. It would permit the rural sociologist to utilize and build on much ecological and demographic data that has been compiled already. At the same time it would offer a clear avenue for supplementary study. Most dominance research has been concerned with the patterning of economic functions and related aggregate population characteristics. The place of noneconomic-nondemographic factors in the dominance scheme has received only limited attention, and most of the work that has been done focuses on the central city itself. There is a need to examine the effects of urban accessibility on *all* aspects of society, particularly its influence on the hinterland. Rural sociologists have institutional precedents and contacts that make them particularly well suited to carry out this task.

Defining "rural" in terms of isolation emphasizes

[16]*Ibid.*, p. 63.

[17]*Ibid.*, p. 66.

[18]See, for example, Emile Durkheim, *The Division of Labor*, tr. by George Simpson, Glencoe, Illinois: The Free Press, 1960; and Louis Wirth, "Urbanism as a Way of Life," in Paul K. Hatt and Albert J. Reiss, Jr. (eds.), *Cities and Society*, rev. ed., Glencoe, Illinois: The Free Press, 1957, pp. 46-63.

[19]See Robert C. Bealer, "Some Critical Points in Richard Dewey's Handling of the Rural-Urban Continuum," University Park, Pa.: Pennsylvania State University, Department of Agricultural Economics and Rural Sociology, 1963 (mimeographed).

[20]Thus, it is usually assumed: (1) that urban areas, when defined as those places with large total populations and high density of residence, tend to direct the structural patterning of at least the economic organization of the territorial space surrounding the city (usually termed the hinterland); (2) that the nature of the economic organization vitally affects not only the directly related aggregate population characteristics, but the remaining aspects of social structure as well; and (3) the influence of the city is inversely related to the isolation of any region from it. *Cf.* Amos H. Hawley, *Human Ecology*, New York: Ronald Press, 1950, esp. chapter 12.

[21]See, for example, Walter Firey, "Sentiment and Symbolism as Ecological Variables," *American Sociological Review*, 10 (April, 1945), pp. 140-148; Jerome K. Myers, "Assimilation to the Ecological and Social Systems of a Community," *American Sociological Review*, 15 (June, 1950), pp. 367-372; and A. B. Hollingshead, "A Re-examination of Ecological Theory," *Sociology and Social Research*, 31 (January-February, 1947), pp. 194-204.

the necessity for awareness of what is occurring in the rest of society. The hinterland cannot be distinguished except in relation to other aspects of the larger social structure. This necessity of viewing "rural" in relation to the larger urban structure may correct the characteristic lack of concern by rural sociologists with part-whole relationships. Moreover, it can give balance to the equally popular tendency to see American society as having an undifferentiated, mass quality. All too often we stress the fact that television saturates the countryside, but we forget to note whether it makes any difference that the city dweller has his choice of channels while there may be only a single T.V. station available in the hinterland. To have access to the high school, library, or museum "on foot" is perhaps importantly different from having to commute 20 miles by a once-a-day scheduled school bus or the need for a special 100-mile trip to the city. The definition of "rurality" in terms of relative degree of isolation logically emphasizes these ideas.

While defining "rural" in terms of ecological notions of accessibility provides certain advantages, it also had disadvantages. Most important, it introduces a defining concept that is itself complex and given to ambiguity. For instance, should isolation be construed in terms of physical distance, commuting costs, availability of communication media, some other factors or combination of factors? Which population centers should be taken as points of reference in determining accessibility? Questions such as these need to be addressed if we would define "rural" in terms of isolation.

"Rural" as a sociocultural construct

"Rural" as a sociocultural construct is the least circumspect of the alternative definitions considered in this paper, for it can be used to refer to any and all aspects of society's structure and functioning. Because of its all-inclusiveness, such an understanding appears at first to most nearly tap what many sociologists argue "rural really is". But, also due to its all-inclusiveness, this meaning is not unambiguous. Subsumed under such a sociocultural meaning are two broad substantive components—a social or interactional facet and a cultural dimension. The distinction between these two ideas is frequently taken as important, but often not carefully drawn or followed.[22]

[22]Marion Levy, Jr., penetratingly states the matter this way: "The concept [of culture] is virtually everywhere held to be a different one than that of society, but in few if any cases are the two defined in such a way as to be analytically distinct from one another. In the general literature of social science these terms sometimes seem to be used interchangeably, even though they may have been differently defined, and what is equally confusing, they sometimes are apparently intended to denote different phenomena (or different aspects of phenomena) although just where the difference lies is unclear." *The Structure of Society*, Princeton, New Jersey: Princeton University Press, 1952, pp. 144-145.

Where a differentiation is made, "culture" usually connotes, not action *per se*, but rather the directives for action, the shared *ideals* of behavior, the value configurations by which means and ends *ought* to be selected.[23] Whether actual behavior conforms to values is problematic. Characteristically, the ideal pattern is but approximated by actual behavior, for values are general directives while action situations are specific. Culture in this sense is never a sufficient cause of behavior. Rather, along with genetic and physiological differences in personalities, physical conditions, and such structural conditions as the size of groups, their number and heterogeneity, culture helps to determine individual behavior. Whatever patterning, in fact, occurs in human interaction is taken as representing "society"; *i.e.*, society is a system of action that involves a plurality of interacting individuals whose operation is vitally affected by shared ideals and values but not totally determined by them.

Whether one chooses an interactional or a cultural meaning for "rural", the nature of the problem and the implications of the choice are similar in certain ways and, hence, these two forms can be discussed together.

Throughout the preceding pages our premise is that the meaning of "rurality" should be explored in an analytical rather than a descriptive capacity. In this context, there has always been implied some phenomenon toward which the given definition has some presumed explanatory significance. This dependent variable has been sometimes left unspecified and at other times identified as "patterned interaction", "behavior", or some other similar terminology. Thus, we have assigned the status of dependent variable to the sociocultural facet. As a dependent variable, the term refers to the behavioral characteristics and interaction patterns of persons defined as "rural" by one of the preceding definitions (or some other alternative). In this sense, "rural" loses its unique identifying character. It means simply the culture and or behavior of people defined as "rural" in regard to ecology or occupation rather than some distinctive cultural or interactional form.

But, "rural" as a sociocultural construct can also be used as an independent variable and as a source of explanatory factors. Precedent dictates that the ideas selected here ought to have been included historically in descriptions of "rurality". Thus, for example, "rural" culture has been pictured as traditional, slow to change, provincial, and fatalistic. "Rural" society has been described (among other things) as homogeneous, with little specialization of labor and with predominately primary, face-to-face relationships among

[23]*Ibid.*; and Robin Williams, *American Society*, rev. ed., New York: Alfred A. Knopf, 1960, pp. 37ff.

members.[24] Any sociocultural meaning for "rural" should logically draw its criteria from ideas such as these.

Unfortunately, there has been no great agreement, even at the descriptive level, on the cultural and/or interactional qualities comprising "rurality".[25] This makes the problem of specification of the sociocultural meaning a particularly vexing one. Choosing any single characteristic from an array of traits considerably simplifies problems of operationalization but, lacking initial consensus, undoubtedly would draw more critics than supporters whatever the choice. If more than one criterion were chosen, the problem of selecting the specific components would be compounded by the task of specifying appropriate weights for each.

In either case, there may well be reluctance generally on different grounds to singling out certain aspects of the sociocultural dimension as explanatory factors while utilizing others as dependent variables. Society and culture are characteristically taken as systemic wholes with mutual dependence among the parts. To designate some aspects of the whole as "independent" variables, and hence presumably of causal significance, would seem to violate the very idea of a patterned whole. Yet, the logic of analysis requires at least a provisional assignment of some factors as more critical or important than others. Furthermore, to help guard against *ad hoc* interpretation, designations of the independent variables should occur before investigations are initiated. Thus, the demands of an appropriate analytical use of the sociocultural facet tends to be blunted by the presumed "basic nature" of the dimension.[26]

Let us suppose that these problems can be overcome and a designation of "rural" can be made in terms of a particular cultural form or specific interactional characteristics. This meaning—what we have previously called Gemeinschaft—is distinct from "rural" defined in terms of ecology or occupation and need not covary with them. Selection of such a meaning would imply that rural sociologists would study Gemeinschaft society and/or culture wherever it occurs—in areas of low population density or in cities, in conjunction with agriculture or not. While in principle this is easy, the empirical task of merely locating one's

universe may be extremely difficult, time consuming, and expensive.

There are administrative and professional pressures which make the acceptance of a solely sociocultural definition of "rural" unlikely. It is probable that only a limited number of farmers are best classified as Gemeinschaft and many of those who are "rural" in culture are not commercially oriented.[27] This might create serious problems in obtaining support from traditional sources where interests center on the commercial farmer—the Department of Agriculture, farm organizations, and agricultural industries. In addition, the historical position of rural sociology in the land-grant university could be altered from a relatively independent department in the school of agriculture to a specialty within sociology. This would have further implication for broader academic relationships, training of professionals, and types of problems researched.

SUMMARY

If the term "rural" is to serve as a worthwhile scientific construct, the need for clarification of its meaning is imperative. The primary goal of this article, however, has not been the impossible derivation of a definitive meaning for "rural". Rather, it has attempted to sketch some of the less willingly recognized dimensions of the definition problem. While the assigning of a useful definition is not an arbitrary matter based on whim, neither is it predicated simply on demonstrated empirical utility. The meaning given to "rurality" has practical consequences in regard to the relationship of rural sociology to other disciplines, to its sources of support, and its programs of study. The strategy of this paper, therefore, has been to deal separately with three components of "rural" and to examine some of the logical and practical implications of defining "rural" *only* in terms of the ecological, the occupational, or the sociocultural facet. Such a specification of "rural" as a single dimension, however, would probably not receive widespread acceptance. A composite definition has more overwhelming appeal. However, to be analytically useful, this alternative must have the component parts explicitly rationalized and weighted. This means, among other things, that the nature and empirical utility of the parts must be addressed and the implications of choosing the separate components examined. By briefly considering some of the practical consequences of selecting various alternative meanings for "rural", this paper hopefully has highlighted the importance of the nature of the definition chosen and, above all, demonstrated the need for focusing explicit attention on the matter.

[24]Pitirim A. Sorokin and Carle C. Zimmerman, *Principles of Rural-Urban Sociology*, New York: Henry Holt Company, 1929.

[25]For evidence here see Dewey, *op. cit.*, pp. 60-62.

[26]If one gets enthralled by the idea of system and mutual causal influence of parts then it is easy enough to assume it follows methodologically that one can begin an analysis wherever one wishes, for "all streets lead ultimately to the same end". The door is thus opened for and encouragement given to the conduct of inquiry so nicely bared and criticized by R. K. Merton under the label of *post factum* analysis. See *Social Theory and Social Structure*, rev. ed., Glencoe, Illinois: The Free Press, 1957, pp. 93-95.

[27]See, for example, Frederick C. Fliegel, "Traditionalism in the Farm Family and Technological Change," *Rural Sociology*, 28 (March, 1962), pp. 70-76.

The city and countryside

GLENN V. FUGUITT*

ABSTRACT

Throughout history the city and the countryside have been interdependent, but in the present century the degree of this interdependence has greatly increased in the United States. This transformation is traced in terms of changes in the following: (1) transportation and communication; (2) trade, institutional, and social relationships; (3) occupational structure; and (4) population. Implications of this change for practical affairs in specific settings such as the rural-urban fringe, for the concepts "community" and "rural-urban," and for the future of rural and urban sociology are discussed.

Throughout history the city and the countryside have been interdependent. The city has depended on the country, for example, for agricultural products, raw materials, and people, while the country has depended on the city for protection, for goods, and for economic and social services. The nature and degree of this relationship has no doubt varied considerably between societies and over time. Here in the United States, the nature of the relationship between city and country has been radically transformed in this century. It is this transition with which the present paper is concerned.

Let us begin with a view of the traditional town-country community. All indications are that this form was rather typical in the United States prior to about 1920, especially in the Middle West. Most rural settlement was in the form of scattered farmsteads. Social relationships in many areas centered about the country neighborhood. Within the neighborhood, informal visiting and exchange of work took place. Also, families built and carried on many of their own institutions, such as schools, churches, cemeteries, stores, and creameries. Beyond the country neighborhood was the nearby city or village, which often was the only center to which the rural person turned for other goods and services and to market his farm products.[1]

Thus the traditional rural community, as usually conceived, includes not only the trade center, but the trade center (which may in fact be a city) and the persons living in the open country. The open-country residents may be in or out of neighborhoods which provide limited social and economic services. Such communities were never, of course, completely self-sufficient. The centers themselves were and are interdependent with other centers, so that one can conceive of a hierarchy of cities and their hinterlands oriented about a great metropolis, a region, or a nation.[2]

Nevertheless, for the period prior to 1920, there is reason to believe that most people in the open country lived most of their lives within the confines of their rural community. Such communities and neighborhoods within them were important social entities for most of their members. This is not to say that they were necessarily highly cohesive, or without conflict. It is too easy to idealize older ways of life gone by.

Carl Taylor, a rural sociologist, has described the changes which have taken place in the small Iowa community in which he lived as a boy. Until he was 16 years old, in 1900, he was not out of his local neighborhood from one year's end to the other, except for three or four trips per year to the town seven miles away, and a few special occasions such as the county fair. After he was 16, and before he left home, he went out of his neighborhood perhaps 20 times a year.[3] If such experiences were typical, it is hard to minimize the importance of the local area in the lives of the rural people of those days.

It is trite to say that in the time intervening tremendous changes have taken place in our society. One important aspect is the change in the relationship between the city and the countryside. It is the objective of this paper to review systematically the changing interdependence between city and country,

□ From *Rural Sociology* **28**(3):246-261, Sept. 1963.
*The author is Professor, Department of Rural Sociology, The University of Wisconsin, Madison.

[1]John H. Kolb, *Emerging Rural Communities*, Madison: University of Wisconsin Press, 1959, pp. 1-41; Walter A. Terpenning, *Village and Open-Country Neighborhoods*, New York: The Century Company, 1931, pp. 62-76; and James M. Williams, *Our Rural Heritage*, New York: Alfred A. Knopf, 1925, pp. 19-24.

[2]There is much literature on the metropolitan community. Representative works include R. D. McKenzie, *The Metropolitan Community*, New York: McGraw-Hill Book Company, 1933; Donald J. Bogue, *The Structure of the Metropolitan Community*, Ann Arbor; University of Michigan, Horace H. Rackham School of Graduate Studies, 1949; and Otis Dudley Duncan, Richard Scott, Stanley Lieberson, Beverly Duncan, and Hal H. Winsborough, *Metropolis and Region*, Baltimore; The Johns Hopkins Press, 1960.

[3]Carl C. Taylor, "Changes I Have Seen in the Farming Community." Text of an address given at Eighth Annual Institute on Local History, State Historical Society of Wisconsin, October 19, 1957.

and to trace some of the implications of this change.[4]

In analyzing this transition in the relation between city and the countryside, four interrelated sets of trends will be considered here. These are:

1. Changes in transportation and communication
2. Changes in trade, institutional, and social relationships
3. Rural occupational changes
4. Population changes.

This list is not exhaustive, and certainly other schemes might well be used.[5] Nevertheless, it is possible to order a great deal of work in this area on the basis of these four categories. Each will be taken up in turn.

CHANGES IN TRANSPORTATION AND COMMUNICATION

The availability and wide use of new transportation and communication facilities has erased isolation from the rural scene. The automobile, coming into general use after World War I, and the complementary development of a far-flung system of all-weather hard surface roads made it possible for people in the country to greatly expand their areas of contacts. In both 1921 and 1959 there were approximately 3,000,000 miles of rural roads in the United States. In the former year, however, only 13 percent of this mileage was surfaced, while in the latter year 69 percent was surfaced.[6] The old "team haul" has been replaced by the much larger radius of a comfortable one-day auto trip.[7]

Carl Taylor, comparing his isolation as a youth with the current situation in his Iowa community, noted that today:

All members of their families go to town once or twice a week —to market, to picture shows, and to basketball games. They range quite generally over a radius of 25 to 50 miles from their farm, and make two or three trips to a large city 120 miles away each year. They take summer vacations, ranging

from the Pacific Northwest to the Florida coast. They are not isolated physically, socially, or mentally.[8]

The wider geographic circulation of city newspapers and magazines in rural areas and the diffusion of the newer media, radio and TV, has brought the city world to the country person's mailbox and into his living room.

Recent sample surveys have shown that an increasing proportion of rural people have television, and that the difference in this regard between rural and urban areas is declining. By 1960, 76 percent of rural farm, 88 percent of rural nonfarm, and 89 percent of urban people had television, while in 1955 corresponding figures were 42, 61, and 74 percent, respectively.[9]

A very interesting field survey pertaining to the use of mass media by farm people has been carried out by Bostian and Ross.[10] They interviewed a sample of farmers in six counties in Wisconsin which differed in degree of urbanization. It was found that 96 percent of the respondents owned a radio, and 86 percent owned a television set. Seventy-four percent took a daily paper, and the same proportion took a weekly paper, while 96 percent received a farm magazine.

Each respondent was asked to fill out a diary of time use. It was found that on an average day farm operators spent nine hours working, and had eight and one-half hours free time. Of this free time, farmers spent on an average 38 minutes reading, one hour and 19 minutes listening to the radio, and an hour and 42 minutes watching television. Thus, on an average, 20 percent of the operator's time between 5:00 a.m. and 11:30 p.m., or 40 percent of his free time away from work within these hours, is spent with mass media. Bostian and Ross further point out that a comparison with comparable urban studies reveals little difference between these farm operators and urban males in the use of mass media.

The increase in the availability and use of mass media in rural areas, up to the point reported in this Wisconsin study, certainly suggests that more and more of what people in the country know and believe comes to them from outside their own localities.

CHANGES IN TRADE, INSTITUTIONAL, AND SOCIAL RELATIONSHIPS

With the wider range of movement afforded by the advent of the motor car, people in rural areas are no longer required to trade at neighborhood stores or at the nearest centers. Increased demands for more specialized goods and services means that many travel

[4]For an earlier article surveying rural-urban relations in England, see: W. H. Ashby, "The Effects of Urban Growth on the Countryside," *Sociological Review*, 21 (1939), pp. 345-369. Recent general articles which touch on the work of this paper at several points are: Lowry Nelson, "Rural Life in a Mass-Industrial Society," *Rural Sociology*, 22 (1957), pp. 20-30; Sheldon G. Lowry and Edward O. Moe, "In Transition: The Community," *Adult Leadership*, 11 (1962), pp. 72-74 ff; and Thomas R. Ford and Willis A. Sutton, Jr., "The Impact of Change on Rural Communities and the Fringe: Review of a Decade's Research," a paper presented at the 1961 Meetings of the Rural Sociological Society, Ames, Iowa, August 27-29, 1961.

[5]For example, see Ashby, *loc. cit.*

[6]U.S. Bureau of the Census, *Statistical Abstract of the United States: 1961*, Washington: U.S. Government Printing Office, 1961, p. 546.

[7]Early in this century Warren H. Wilson defined the country community by the "team haul," or the distance from a given center one could conveniently travel with a team of horses in one day. Warren H. Wilson, *The Evolution of the Country Community*, Boston: The Pilgrim Press, 1912, pp. 91-107.

[8]Taylor, *loc. cit.*

[9]U.S. Bureau of the Census, *op. cit.*, p. 516.

[10]Lloyd R. Bostian and John E. Ross, *Mass Media and the Wisconsin Farm Family*, Madison: Wisconsin Agr. Exp. Sta., Bull. 234, 1962.

to more remote but larger centers—particularly to obtain items such as dress clothing and furniture, or specialized medical services, not available nearby. Thus, specialization of centers has developed, and every town cannot try to offer all kinds of services.

Studies of small trade centers over the period 1900-30 in South Dakota, Minnesota, Michigan, Louisiana, and Washington showed that over this period such towns lost many of their functions to larger cities. A number of them lost population, and some passed out of existence.[11] Recent work, based on census data for the entire United States, has indicated that the village is not disappearing from the rural scene, though many, especially smaller ones, are declining in size.[12]

Following the pioneer community study by C. J. Galpin in 1911, two re-studies of Walworth County, Wisconsin, were made. The first was by Kolb and Polson in 1929, and the second by Kolb and Day in 1947. These studies found a trend toward specialization of services and growing interdependence between centers, larger service areas, and more overlapping of areas.[13]

Other recent studies in Wisconsin, North Carolina, Nebraska, and Oklahoma revealed overlapping trade center areas, with rural people going to more than one center, usually including a city of at least moderate size.[14] The 1953 Nebraska study and the Oklahoma

study also found younger rural people were more likely to travel to larger and more distant urban centers. This trend suggests that, with the passage of time, the tendency to go to larger centers will become more prevalent as the older generation is replaced by their children.

In some instances small trade centers were found in these studies to have become like the neighborhood grocery store in large cities. People use them to pick up small items to avoid traveling long distances, but they make major purchases elsewhere.[15]

Institutional changes have also taken place which have implications for rural-urban relationships. Over much of the Middle West the one-room school has been a focal point of activities in the rural neighborhood. These schools are rapidly declining in number. Thus, in 1930 there were more than 148,000 one-teacher schools in the nation. Eighteen years later in 1948, the number had been halved, with approximately 75,000 such schools remaining. Within just the ten years following there was a decline by two-thirds to 26,000.[16]

The expansion of school districts and the decline in their number also is a force tying town and country together. In 1932 there were approximately 127,000 school districts in the United States, and by 1948 the number diminished to about 102,000. Decline was much more rapid after this date, and by 1960 there were approximately 42,000 districts remaining.[17]

Uniform data are not available, but studies in isolated areas have shown that the number of open country churches also is declining.[18] In Walworth County, Wisconsin, it was found that, while the open country church survives, it is no longer exclusively a neighborhood institution.[19]

In discussing trends in the social relationships of country people, the generalization is often made that social groups based on neighborhood and community lines are being partially replaced by formally organized special interest groups. Further, these organi-

[11]Paul H. Landis, *South Dakota Town-Country Trade Relations 1901-1931*, Brookings: South Dakota Agr. Exp. Sta., Bull. 274, 1932; Paul H. Landis, *The Growth and Decline of South Dakota Trade Centers 1901-1933*, Brookings: South Dakota Agr. Exp. Sta., Bull. 279, 1933; C. E. Lively, *Growth and Decline of Farm Trade Centers in Minnesota, 1905-1930*, St. Paul: Minnesota Agr. Exp. Sta., Bull. 287, 1932; C. R. Hoffer, *Changes in Retail and Service Facilities of Rural Trade Centers in Michigan, 1900 and 1930*, East Lansing: Michigan Agr. Exp. Sta., Special Bull. 261, 1935; T. Lynn Smith, *Farm Trade Centers in Louisiana, 1901-1931*, Baton Rouge: Louisiana Agr. Exp. Sta., Bull. 234, 1933; and Paul H. Landis, *Washington Farm Trade Centers 1900-1935*, Pullman: Washington Agr. Exp. Sta., Bull. 360, 1938. See also the more recent work by Chittick, *Growth and Decline of South Dakota Trade Centers 1901-1951*, Brookings: South Dakota Agr. Exp. Sta., Bull. 448, 1955.

[12]Edmund deS. Brunner and T. Lynn Smith, "Village Growth and Decline, 1930-1940," *Rural Sociology*, 9 (1944), pp. 103-115; Edmund deS. Brunner, "Village Growth 1940-1950," *Rural Sociology*, 16 (1951), pp. 111-118; and Edmund deS. Brunner, "The Small Village: 1940-1950," *Rural Sociology*, 17 (1952), pp. 127-131.

[13]Kolb, *op. cit.*, esp. pp. 87-135. The studies first appeared as Wisconsin Agricultural Experiment Station bulletins.

[14]Kolb, *op. cit.*, pp. 111-120; Selz C. Mayo and Robert McD. Bobbitt, *Rural Organization: A Restudy of Locality Groups in Wake County, North Carolina*, Raleigh: North Carolina Agr. Exp. Sta., Tech. Bull. 95, 1951, pp. 19-24; A. H. Anderson and C. J. Miller, *The Changing Role of the Small Town in Farm Areas*, Lincoln: Nebraska Agr. Exp. Sta., Bull. 419, 1953, pp. 21-32; A. H. Anderson, *The "Expanding" Rural Community*, Lincoln: Nebraska Agr. Exp. Sta., Bull. 464, 1961, and John C. Belcher, *Service Relationships of Farmers in Lincoln County, Oklahoma*, Stillwater: Oklahoma Agr. Exp. Sta., Bull. B-383, 1952. For a schematic presentation of former and contemporary trade patterns see Charles R. Hoffer, "The Changing Ecological Pattern in Rural Life," *Rural Sociology*, 13 (1948), pp. 176-180.

[15]For a development of this analogy see Karl A. Fox, "The Study of Interactions Between Agriculture and the Nonfarm Economy: Local, Regional, and National," *Journal of Farm Economics*, 44 (1962), pp. 15-21.

[16]M. C. S. Noble, Jr. and Howard A. Dawson, *Handbook on Rural Education*, Washington, D.C.: Department of Rural Education of the National Education Association of the United States, 1961, p. 64.

[17]*Ibid.*, p. 63.

[18]Edmund deS. Brunner and Irving Lorge, *Rural Trends in the Depression Years*, New York: Columbia University Press, 1937, pp. 299-316; Lawrence M. Hepple and Margaret L. Bright, *Social Change in Shelby County, Missouri*, Columbia: Missouri Agr. Exp. Sta., Research Bull. 456, 1950, pp. 33-35; Indiana Congregational Christian Conference Rural Life Committee, *Hoosier Churches*, Muncie: Indiana Congregational Christian Conference, 1943, p. 17; and Theodore C. Scheifele and William G. Mather, *Closed Rural Pennsylvania Churches*, State College: Pennsylvania Agr. Exp. Sta., Bull. 512, 1949.

[19]Kolb, *op. cit.*, p. 131.

zations often are urban centered and affiliated with some national or state organization. While there is impressionistic evidence to support these contentions, only a little empirical evidence can be found, owing to the paucity of studies of changes in the same areas over time. A New York rural community near Ithaca was studied in 1926 and 1951.[20] The number of voluntary organizations increased during the period, and the researchers observed that this increase has been largely in the number operating as part of county, state, or national organizations. Also, there was increased participation in these organizations by residents over the time period. Similar findings were reported by Buck and Ploch for a small rural community in Pennsylvania.[21]

In a statewide Wisconsin study, Wileden has shown that between about 1935 and 1945 the number of rural organizations increased, with an increasing number of local groups becoming affiliates of larger county and statewide organizations. It was also noted that there was a growing tendency for local groups to work together in councils or federations.[22]

It is not known to what extent these small studies reflect a general trend toward more town-country interrelations through formal voluntary organizations. It is easy, however, to overemphasize the importance of participation in voluntary organizations. A recent sample survey of the entire United States showed that more than forty percent of the adults in each residence group belong to no voluntary organizations.[23]

There is evidence that much informal as well as formal group life is not, today at least, limited to narrow locality boundaries. This is particularly true in areas near cities. For example, a recent sample survey was carried out in the area between Madison and Milwaukee in which farm operators were asked to list three friends, not related to them, with whom they visited. Thirty-six percent of the respondents reported at least one friend who lived in a city of more than 2,500 people, while just 49 percent reported only friends living in the open country within a radius of three miles.[24]

The changes in institutional and social relationships considered here are all reflected in the decline of the open-country neighborhood. Four studies, each a decade apart, were made in Dane County, Wisconsin, by Professor J. H. Kolb. He found that neighborhoods, usually having recognized names and built around trade, religious, and social relationships, ecompassed nearly all the country area in 1920-21. In the last study, carried out in 1950-51, only about one-half of the country area of Dane County was found to be included in neighborhoods.[25] Restudies in other areas also have shown declines in the distinct, locally recognized country neighborhood.[26]

RURAL OCCUPATIONAL CHANGES

Recent years have seen tremendous changes in the nature of agriculture. Under the continuing impact of technological development fewer workers are needed for the production of food and fiber. It is estimated that in 1910 one farm worker supported seven other people. At that time the number of farm workers in the United States was at its peak (14 million). In 1960 one farm worker provided food and fiber for 26 nonfarm people. There were about seven million persons in farming, whereas at 1910 productivity levels 26 million would have been needed to support the 1960 population.[27] This increase in productivity has come about through changes such as the use of improved management techniques, adoption of machinery powered by gasoline and electricity, the introduction of hybrid seed, improved animal breeds, new chemicals, and fertilizer, mostly coming from the nonfarm sector of society.

Thus the typical farm is coming to be a large commercial family enterprise. Farms are getting larger, and the average investment per farm is going up. It is estimated that during the 1950's, the total number of farms declined at a constant annual rate of about $2^{1}/_{3}$ percent. However, large farms with annual sales of $10,000 or more increased at an accelerating rate, while farms with sales of less than $5,000 decreased in number at an accelerating rate. Proportionately, how-

[20]W. A. Anderson, Olaf F. Larson, Fathalla A. S. Halloul, *Social Change in the Slaterville Springs-Brooktondale Area of Tompkins County, New York: 1926-1951*, Ithaca: New York Agr. Exp. Sta., Bull. 920, 1956.

[21]Roy C. Buck and Louis A. Ploch, *Factors Related to Changes in Social Participation in a Pennsylvania Rural Community*, State College: Pennsylvania Agr. Exp. Sta., Bull. 586, 1954.

[22]Arthur F. Wileden, *Trends in Rural Organization in Wisconsin*, Madison: Wisconsin Agr. Ext. Serv., Spec. Ext. Cir., 1951.

[23]Charles R. Wright and Herbert H. Hyman, "Voluntary Association Memberships of American Adults: Evidence from National Sample Surveys," *American Sociological Review*, 23 (1958), pp. 284-294.

[24]Unpublished data from a study carried out by the writer and Ramon E. Henkel. See also Ramon E. Henkel and Glenn V. Fuguitt, "Nonfarm Occupational Role Involvement and the Visiting Relationships of Farmers," *Rural Sociology*, 27 (1962), p. 57.

[25]Kolb, *op. cit.*, p. 54. The neighborhood studies appeared as Wisconsin Agricultural Experiment Station bulletins.

[26]Dwight Sanderson and Warren S. Thompson, *Social Areas of Otsego County*, Ithaca: New York Agr. Exp. Sta., Bull. 422, 1923; and Dwight Sanderson and Harold Dorn, *The Rural Neighborhoods of Otsego County, New York, 1931*, Ithaca: Cornell University, Department of Rural Social Organization, Mimeo Bull. 2, 1934; Carl C. Taylor and Carle C. Zimmerman, *Rural Organization*, Raleigh: North Carolina Agr. Exp. Sta., Bull. 245, 1922; and Mayo and Bobbitt, *loc. cit.*

[27]Earl O. Heady, "The Farm Problem" in *Adjustments in Agriculture—a National Basebook*, edited by Carlton F. Christian, Ames: Iowa State University Press, 1961, pp. 72-73.

ever, the family farm seems to be holding its own against other types of farm enterprises.[28]

With increasing commercialization, farming has more and more become a business rather than a way of life. The farmer strives to make rational decisions to maximize his profit, and is more and more dependent on the urban marketplace, not only to sell his product but also to purchase the tools of production. The extent to which modern agriculture is dependent upon other businesses and services is illustrated by the fact that for every worker engaged directly in agricultural production, there are two workers engaged in providing production inputs and services for farms and in processing and marketing agricultural products after they leave the farm.[29] The present situation is summed up well by the following quotation:

Farmers stand in the *middle* of a *sequence of urban activities* involving those which fabricate and handle necessary inputs and those which handle and process farm outputs.[30]

The successful farmer today must keep abreast of new innovations in his field, taking advantage of mass media, public and private agencies, and other sources of information, rather than depending solely upon his own past experience or the traditions of his locality. He is in a complex business, requiring a high degree of managerial and technical skill, as well as considerable capital.

The decline in the number of farm workers since 1910 has been accompanied by an increase in the number of nonfarm workers living in the country. There have always been nonfarm workers in rural areas in lumbering, mining, retail trade at the crossroads or in small hamlets, and so forth. This recent increase is largely due to the migration of former city people out into areas near cities. Also, more and more farm people stay in rural areas and take nonfarm employment either by commuting to the city or working in rural areas. Thus, a household head may cease to farm and take nonfarm work, or his wife or other family member may get a nonfarm job while he continues to farm.

In addition, there is an increasing tendency for people in the country to combine farm and nonfarm work. This is particularly true in areas near large cities, and areas of low agricultural potential. Some such workers are young people hoping to use this means to build up enough capital to become successful full-time farmers. Others, near cities, have moved out into the country and taken up farming while continuing their nonfarm job. For others "part-time farming" is a long-term career.[31] The proportion of farmers working off their farms 100 days or more has gone up steadily with each successive Census of Agriculture. In 1959 thirty percent of the farm operators of the United States were so classified. A special analysis of 1950 Census figures showed that at that time only 38 percent of farm operator families were wholly dependent on agriculture.[32]

Farming was never synomymous with "rural," but today occupational heterogeneity is found in some areas to a degree formerly thought to be characteristic only of cities. A field survey was carried out recently in Kenosha County, Wisconsin, which revealed a scattered open-country settlement pattern. Yet nonfarm families, dispersed over the entire county, lived in a high proportion of the scattered dwellings, while many members of farm families also held nonfarm jobs.[33]

RURAL POPULATION CHANGES

Now let us turn to the last aspect of change affecting rural-urban relationships. Population trends have led to a transformation of the farm-nonfarm composition and of the distribution of rural people. Trends in the rural farm population, that is, the number of people living on farms, have followed closely trends in the number of people employed in farming. Thus, the farm population reached a peak in 1910 and has declined since then from 32 million to approximately 16 million, or to less than nine percent of the total population. This change, coming despite high fertility and low mortality levels, has come about through a movement out of agriculture. To some extent this shift has come through changing occupation from farm to nonfarm without a residence change, but primarily it is due to actual emigration to urban areas. Between 1920 and 1950 net migration from farms to other areas amounted to about 20 million people. It is estimated that in this thirty-year period about two-thirds of the youth born on American farms were destined to live

[28]H. L. Stewart, "What the New Census Figures Mean to Agriculture." Text of talk given to Newspaper Farm Editors Association, May 15, 1961. Also Radoje Nikolitch, *Family and Larger-than-Family Farms*, Washington, D.C.: U.S. Department of Agriculture, Agr. Econ. Report 4, 1962.

[29]John H. Davis, "Policy Implications of Vertical Integration in U.S. Agriculture," *Journal of Farm Economics*, 39 (1957), p. 301. See also John H. Davis and Ray A. Goldberg, *A Concept of Agribusiness*, Boston: Harvard University, 1957.

[30]Clyde F. Kohn, *Urban Responses to Agricultural Change*, Iowa City: The State University of Iowa, 1961, p. 2.

[31]Glenn V. Fuguitt, "A Typology of the Part-time Farmer," *Rural Sociology*, 26 (1961), pp. 39-48.

[32]Louis J. Ducoff, "Classification of the Agricultural Population in the United States," *Journal of Farm Economics*, 37 (1955), pp. 511-523.

[33]Jon A. Doerflinger, *Kenosha County, Wisconsin Study: An Overview of the Social Effects of Population Change*, Madison: University of Wisconsin, Department of Rural Sociology Bulletin, 1961, pp. 18-19. Also see Walter C. McKain, Jr. and Nathan L. Whetten, *Occupational and Industrial Diversity in Rural Connecticut*, Storrs: Connecticut Agr. Exp. Sta., Bull. 263, 1949.

in urban and rural-nonfarm areas.[34] Much of this migration has, of course, been a movement of young adults to cities, and this is one of the most important ties between the city and the countryside.

During this period the nonfarm population has gained relatively and absolutely. In 1920 the rural nonfarm segment was approximately 40 percent of the rural total, while in 1960 it made up about 70 percent of the rural population. Some of this nonfarm population is no doubt rural only in name, being part of thickly settled areas, outside smaller cities, since such areas are not included in the urban definition of the census.[35] Nevertheless, a preponderance of the nonfarm segment in the rural population is clearly evident.

A great deal of the rural nonfarm growth may be attributed to urban decentralization, the movement of people into the areas peripheral to cities. In most cases areas around large cities are growing more rapidly than the cities themselves.[36] At the same time rural population segments remote from large metropolitan centers have, in general, declined in population in recent years. As a result of these trends the rural population has come to be distributed more like the urban in our country.

SUMMARY AND IMPLICATIONS

Changes affecting the relationship between city and country in the United States have been examined in this paper. This examination has been in terms of four interrelated sets of trends in: (1) transportation and communication; (2) trade, institutional, and social relationships of rural residents; (3) the nature and types of occupations of rural residents; and (4) population size and composition.[37]

The basic conclusion of this analysis is that these

changes have led to an increasing degree of interdependence between the city and the countryside. The old isolation is gone. The occupation of farming has become more closely tied to urban areas. More people with other occupations live in the country, and many of them work in the city. The old rural neighborhoods are dying out. Town-country relationships are becoming more and more complex as many rural people turn to a variety of large and small centers spread over a wide territory.

The implications of this transformation are far-reaching. First of all, adjusting to these changes constitutes an important challenge to individuals and organizations. This is perhaps most obvious in areas where the change is most rapid, that is, the specific setting where city and country come together. This amorphous territory, often called the "rural-urban fringe," is characterized by changes from rural to urban land use, and may be thought of as at the "cutting edge" of urban expansion. Problems of land use, zoning, political and institutional relationships, farming as an occupation, and other social aspects of this transformation, represent important challenges to action agencies.[38]

Rural-urban relations in other settings, of course, also present practical problems which may call for careful planning if desired individual or group goals are to be achieved. This is true not only in growing, rapidly urbanizing areas, but also in more rural declining areas.[39]

This transformation also has important implications for the discipline of sociology. Concepts, to form a fruitful basis for research, or to be meaningful for action programs, must bear a relationship to empirical reality. Thus, the changing degree of interdependence between city and countryside in the United States affects the very core of at least two hallowed sociological concepts: the community, and the distinction between rural and urban. There has never been a high degree of consensus as to the meaning of these terms, yet applying most former definitions to the current situation in the United States leads many persons to ask whether the community, or even for that matter genuinely rural areas, survive today. Are these concepts outmoded for the study of modern Western society? Do we need to ". . . shed the old ideas and images inherited from an education and

[34]C. Horace Hamilton, "The Sociology of a Changing Agriculture," *Social Forces*, 37 (1958), p. 3. On this subject see also Dale E. Hathaway, "Migration from Farms and Its Meaning," *Monthly Labor Review*, 83 (1960), pp. 136-140.

[35]See Vincent Heath Whitney, "Changes in the Rural-nonfarm Population, 1930-1950," *American Sociological Review*, 25 (1960), pp. 363-368.

[36]For an historical review of metropolitan growth and decentralization in this century see Leo F. Schnore, "Metropolitan Growth and Decentralization," *American Journal of Sociology*, 63 (1957), pp. 171-180.

[37]At the outset, it was stated that these factors are interrelated; however, space does not permit the exploration of these relationships. A common hypothesis, for example, is that transportation and communication development are behind changes in trade, social relationships, and population trends, especially urban decentralization. See for example R. D. McKenzie, *op. cit.*, pp. 129-143; Harlan Gilmore, *Transportation and the Growth of Cities*, Glencoe: The Free Press, 1953, pp. 103-120. Nathan L. Whetten, "Suburbanization as a Field for Sociological Research," *Rural Sociology*, 16 (1951), pp. 319-330; and W. A. Anderson, *The Flight to the Fringe*, Ithaca: Cornell University, Department of Rural Sociology, Publication 46, 1956.

[38]For a survey of literature on the rural-urban fringe, see Glenn V. Fuguitt, "The Rural-Urban Fringe," in *Proceedings American Country Life Association, 1962*, 1963, pp. 88-98.

[39]See for example Jean Gottman, *Megalopolis: The Urbanized Northeastern Seaboard of the United States*, New York: The Twentieth Century Fund, 1961; A. H. Anderson, *The "Expanding" Rural Community*; and Douglas G. Marshall and Jon A. Doerflinger, *The Story of Price County, Wisconsin*, Madison: Wisconsin Agr. Exp. Sta., Res. Bull. 220, 1960.

vocabulary that have not kept up with the changes going on around us," as Gottman says in his study of Megalopolis?[40]

For the concept community there has been a varied reaction to this challenge. Clearly the rural community, as outlined at the beginning of this paper, has almost completely vanished from the American scene. Further, it may never have been as typical as was once supposed. Some writers, however, prefer to include in the definition of a community that it be small and noncomplex, and thus by default they concentrate attention on the less urbanized parts of the world.[41] At the other extreme, perhaps, is the operational approach of Jonassen. He rationalizes the use of the county as equivalent to community, by arguing that the student of communities in modern urban societies is faced with problems of delineation and overlapping boundaries of community systems, no matter what type of unit he chooses to call a community for analysis.[42]

Several writers have called for a modification of the concept so that the community may be viewed less as a "closed system." Stewart, for example, makes the following statement:

Most studies, however, have treated the community as if it were a primitive tribe—that is, as if it were a self-contained structural and functional whole which could be understood in terms of itself alone. Scholars are quite aware that any modern community is a functionally dependent part of a much larger whole; but in general they have not yet taken account of this larger frame of reference in community study. Individual communities are often studied as if the larger whole were simply a mosaic of such parts.[43]

The relation of the local community to other systems has received recent attention in a survey article

by Hassinger.[44] This problem constitutes a major frontier in community conceptualization and research, and especially so in the light of trends discussed in the present paper.

Modification of approaches to the distinction between rural and urban also has been demanded by changes in the real world. The difficulty involved in defining rural and urban and making a precise distinction between the two has long been noted.[45] Recent changes outlined in the present paper have compounded this difficulty in the United States. On an operational level this is reflected in efforts of the U.S. Bureau of the Census to keep abreast of the situation by distinguishing between rural farm and rural nonfarm population, and later by modifying the definition of urban so as to include built-up areas around large cities.[46]

On a more abstract level, the existence of a gradation between rural and urban has tended to receive more attention in recent years, and the concept of the rural-urban continuum has been introduced.[47] This scheme postulates that areas or communities may be placed on a continuum from rural to urban. It has been criticized, particularly on its assumption that the set of variables involved fit together as one dimension from rural to urban.[48] But perhaps a more fundamental criticism of both the rural-urban dichotomy and continuum can be made in terms of the growing interdependence between city and country. Even if the rural-urban continuum were valid empirically, it remains basically a scheme for classifying different

[40]Gottman, *op. cit.*, p. 216.

[41]George A. Hillery, Jr., "A Critique of Selected Community Concepts," *Social Forces*, 37 (1957), pp. 237-242; and George P. Murdock, "Feasibility and Implementation of Comparative Community Research," *American Sociological Review*, 15 (1950), pp. 713-720. Also see discussion in Albert J. Reiss, Jr., "Some Logical and Methodological Problems of Community Research," *Social Forces*, 33 (1954), esp. pp. 52-53.

[42]Christian T. Jonassen, "Functional Unities in 88 Community Systems," *American Sociological Review*, 26 (June, 1961), p. 400.

[43]Julian H. Stewart, *Area Research*, New York: Social Science Research Council, Bull. 63, 1950, p. 22. See also Reiss *op. cit.*, pp. 54-55; Albert J. Reiss, Jr., "The Sociological Study of Communities," *Rural Sociology*, 24 (1959), pp. 127-130; Maurice R. Stein, *The Eclipse of Community*, Princeton: Princeton University Press, 1960, pp. 107-113; and Roland L. Warren, "Toward a Reformulation of Community Theory," *Human Organization*, 15 (Summer, 1956), pp. 8-11. In reviewing research dealing with urban and metropolitan communities, Schnore calls for an "open system" conceptualization. See Leo F. Schnore, "Urban Form: The Case of the Metropolitan Community," in Werner Z. Hirsch, editor, *Urban Life and Form*, New York: Holt, Rinehart, and Winston, 1963, pp. 169-197.

[44]Edward Hassinger, "Social Relations between Centralized and Local Social Systems," *Rural Sociology*, 26 (1961), pp. 354-364.

[45]For an early treatment see John M. Gillette, *Constructive Rural Sociology*, New York: Sturgis and Walton Co., 1913; ch. 2. A good recent discussion is in Paul K. Hatt and Albert J. Reiss, Jr., "The Nature of the City," in *Cities and Society*, edited by Paul K. Hatt and Albert J. Reiss, Jr., Glencoe: The Free Press, 1957, pp. 17-21.

[46]See Leon E. Truesdale, "The Development of the Urban-Rural Classification in the United States," *Current Population Reports*, Washington, D.C.: Bureau of the Census, Series P-23, 1949; and Howard G. Brunsman and Charles P. Brinkman, "Problems of Defining the Urban Population of the United States," *International Population Conference, Vienna 1959*, Vienna: The Working Committee of the Conference, 1959, pp. 1-6.

[47]Neal Gross, "Sociological Variation in Contemporary Rural Life," *Rural Sociology*, 13 (1948), pp. 256-273; Alvin Boskoff, "An Ecological Approach to Rural Society," *Rural Sociology*, 14 (1949), pp. 306-316; and Stuart A. Queen and David B. Carpenter, *The American City*, New York: McGraw-Hill Book Co., 1953, p. 38.

[48]Otis Dudley Duncan, "Community Size and the Rural-urban Continuum," in *Cities and Society*, edited by Paul K. Hatt and Albert J. Reiss, Jr., Glencoe: The Free Press, 1957, pp. 35-45; and Charles T. Stewart, Jr., "The Urban-rural Dichotomy: Concepts and Uses," *American Journal of Sociology*, 64 (1958), pp. 152-158. See also Richard Dewey, "The Rural-Urban Continuum: Real but Relatively Unimportant," *American Journal of Sociology*, 66 (1960), pp. 60-66. Evidence supporting the continuum has been presented by Jonassen, *loc. cit.*

communities or areas as "closed systems" with no allowance for relationships between them. To illustrate, consider the problem of placing on any rural-urban continuum an extended fringe area, with low population density, partly agricultural in character, but with a sizable portion of its people recent migrants from an adjacent metropolitan center who continue to work there. This difficulty has been recognized, but it still presents an important challenge in the development of adequate concepts for research.[49]

These conceptual problems raise an even more fundamental issue: What of the future of subdisciplines such as rural and urban sociology? This question has received considerable attention among rural sociologists, and has not been ignored by urban sociologists.[50]

Increasing rural and urban interrelations and the decline of the farm population in Western countries have been a cause of concern to rural sociologists. Supporters of the field have pointed out that rural-urban differences do survive, even in the United States, that rural sociologists do not limit their purview to the study of farmers, and that the world as a whole is mostly rural, so that many opportunities to make a contribution exist in other countries. Fur-

thermore, the demand for work done by rural sociologists, and, hence, for persons to be rural sociologists, continues to increase.[51]

Such statements, however, have failed to distinguish clearly, as do Mannheim and Reiss in their discussions of urban sociology, between sociological research done in a rural setting and rural sociology as a subdiscipline of general sociology. In the former sense the future of rural sociology appears reasonably secure, as persons with responsibilities in rural areas (however these areas are defined) become more and more appreciative of the potential contribution of sociology to their activities. It seems safe to predict that important sociological research will be continued in rural and urban settings, carried out by persons who call themselves rural and urban sociologists, and that this work will contribute to other sociological subfields, such as the study of social change, communication, the sociology of occupations, and formal organizations.

But if rural and urban sociology are to continue as specialized subfields of the parent discipline, distinguished from other subfields on a meaningful conceptual basis, the need for new orientations is evident.[52] As Hoffsomer and Mannheim point out, both rural and urban sociologists have long been concerned with rural-urban relationships. Much of the literature cited in the present paper attests to this fact. Such work should certainly continue by persons who identify themselves with both subdisciplines. The growing interdependence between city and countryside, however, demands that this research be buttressed by more conceptual work on the place of rural and urban sociology as subfields within sociology. This is not to insure their future in Agricultural Experiment Stations or urban research institutes, but to contribute to the ongoing development of sociology itself.

[49]Boskoff, *op. cit.*, pp. 315-316; T. Lynn Smith, "Rural Sociology in the United States and Canada," *Current Sociology*, 6 (1957), p. 5; and Hatt and Reiss, *op. cit.* p. 20.

[50]C. Horace Hamilton, "Some Current Problems in the Development of Rural Sociology," *Rural Sociology*, 15 (1950), pp. 315-321; Charles R. Hoffer, "The Development of Rural Sociology," *Rural Sociology*, 36 (1961), pp. 1-14; Harold C. Hoffsommer, "Rural Sociology Interdisciplinary Relations Within the Field of Sociology," *Rural Sociology*, 25 (1960), pp. 175-196; M. E. John, "Rural Sociology in the Years Ahead," *Rural Sociology*, 27 (1962), pp. 107-115; Olaf F. Larson, "The Role of Rural Sociology in a Changing Society," *Rural Sociology*, 24 (1959), pp. 1-10; Ernest Mannheim, "Theoretical Prospects of Urban Sociology in an Urbanized Society," *American Journal of Sociology*, 66 (1960), pp. 226-229; and Albert J. Reiss, Jr., "The Sociology of Urban Life: 1946-1956," in *Sociology in the United States of America*, edited by Hans L. Zetterburg, Paris: UNESCO, 1956. See also Howard H. Beers, "Rural-urban Differences: Some Evidence from Public Opinion Polls," *Rural Sociology*, 18 (1953), pp. 1-11; Nels Anderson, "Urbanism and Urbanization," *American Journal of Sociology*, 65 (1959), pp. 68-73; and Paul Meadows, "The City—Technology, and History," *Social Forces*, 36 (1957), pp. 141-147.

[51]Hamilton, Hoffer, Hoffsommer, John, and Beers, *loc. cit.*
[52]This point is forcefully made by Hoffsommer, who argues for the unity of rural and urban sociology as a single subdiscipline. (Hoffsommer, *loc. cit.*)

Rural-urban differences in attitudes and behavior in the United States

NORVAL D. GLENN and LESTER HILL, Jr.*

ABSTRACT

Recent American data reveal moderate to substantial farm-nonfarm differences on a few kinds of attitudes and behavior, but since farm people now are only about 4 percent of the population, the farm-nonfarm distinction cannot account for much of the total variation of any kind of attitudes or behavior. The kinds of attitudes and behavior which differ substantially between farm and nonfarm people usually differ monotonically by community size; hence, "ruralism" seems to some extent to characterize residents of the smaller dense settlements and, to a lesser extent, those of intermediate-sized cities. Furthermore, city residents with rural backgrounds tend to retain rural attitudes and behavior characteristics, size of community of origin being a stronger predictor of some attitudes than size of community of current residence. Although the association of community size with a more or less representative list of attitudinal variables is weak, such correlates of community size as age and socioeconomic status do not largely account for the larger associations, which probably reflect a tendency for social and cultural change to occur earlier in the larger communities. The explanatory utility of size of community of origin and of residence seems less than that of age and education but at least as great as that of several other explanatory variables favored by social scientists, such as family income and occupational prestige.

There is considerable disagreement among social scientists concerning the importance of the rural-urban distinction in modern societies. At least three rather distinctive viewpoints have some prominence. The first, exemplified in Louis Wirth's classic essay on "Urbanism as a Way of Life," posits direct, universal effects of population size, density, and heterogeneity on important aspects of social structure, culture, and personality.[1] According to this view, the concentration of people of diverse characteristics and backgrounds into large, dense settlements necessarily produces social isolation, individualism, social disorganization, and a number of other phenomena.

A second major viewpoint, exemplified in the writings of Richard Dewey[2] and Herbert Gans,[3] among others, is that few if any social, cultural, and personality characteristics are necessarily and invariably associated with the size, density, and heterogeneity of settlements. Critics of the Wirth thesis also often point out that population size, density, and heterogeneity are imperfectly correlated with one another and that the effects of each may not be the same as the effects of the other two. According to this view, the correlates of urbanization vary from society to society and from time to time in any one society and are often little more than the results of historical accident. For instance, it is pointed out that many present rural-urban differences in the United States result from inclusion among the later immigrants—who arrived after the closing of the frontier and thus generally settled in the industrial cities—of a relatively large percentage of Catholics, Jews, and persons from southern and eastern Europe. Hence, rural-urban differences tend to reflect religious and ethnic differences.

Related to this second view is the thesis that rural-urban differences, whatever their source, tend to disappear during the advanced stages of urbanization and industrialization.[4] This view, which the senior author has called the "massification thesis,"[5] is that due to such influences as standardized education, improved means of transportation which break down rural isolation, and saturation of small towns and the countryside with stimuli from the mass media, urban culture and lifestyles are diffused to the hinterland—that rural people become almost indistinguishable

☐ Reprinted from volume no. 429 of The Annals of the American Academy of Political Science, Jan. 1977, pp. 36-50.

*Norval D. Glenn is Professor of Sociology at the University of Texas at Austin. Formerly on the faculties of Miami University and the University of Illinois at Urbana, his publications include four books and more than 80 journal articles and book chapters, primarily on social stratification, political sociology, the family, aging and the life cycle, and urban sociology. He is author of a forthcoming monograph on the methodology of cohort analysis.

Lester Hill, Jr., a doctoral candidate in the Department of Sociology at the University of Texas at Austin, is writing a dissertation on the relationship between attitudes and behavior.

[1] Louis Wirth, "Urbanism as a Way of Life," *American Journal of Sociology*, vol. 44 (July 1938), pp. 3-24.

[2] Richard Dewey, "The Rural-Urban Continuum: Real but Relatively Unimportant," *American Journal of Sociology*, vol. 66 (July 1960), pp. 60-6.

[3] Herbert J. Gans, "Urbanism and Suburbanism as Ways of Life: A Re-Evaluation of Definitions," in Arnold M. Rose, ed., *Human Behavior and Social Processes* (Boston: Houghton-Mifflin, 1962), pp. 625-28.

[4] For instance, see Kenneth Boulding, "The Death of the City: A Frightened Look at Post-Civilization," in Oscar Handlin and John Burchard, eds., *The Historian and the City* (Cambridge, Mass.: MIT and Harvard University Press, 1963), p. 143.

[5] Norval D. Glenn, "Massification versus Differentiation: Some Trend Data from National Surveys," *Social Forces*, vol. 46 (December 1967), pp. 172-80.

from their city cousins. So far as we know, no social scientist has denied that considerable urban-to-rural cultural diffusion has occurred in modern societies, but the extent to which this diffusion has obliterated rural-urban differences remains an issue of debate.

An intermediate viewpoint—articulated most completely and clearly in a recent essay by Claude Fischer[6] but presented in at least embryonic form in several earlier publications—is that whereas population size, density, and heterogeneity do not have all of the effects attributed to them by Wirth, they are conducive to innovation and unconventional behavior. According to Fischer, population concentration "produces a diversity of subcultures, strengthens them, and fosters diffusion among them. . . ." Presumably, the concentration of diverse people into dense settlements is conducive to a cross-fertilization of ideas, to an awareness of and tolerance of diverse values and lifestyles, and thus to innovation and unconventionality.

If in each society the cities tend to be the sources of innovation and to be in the vanguard of social and cultural change, appreciable rural-urban differences are likely to exist even if much urban-to-rural diffusion of culture has occurred and is occurring. During the initial phases of any particular process of change, the urban population will tend to change more rapidly, leading to rural-urban divergence. Later, "ceiling effects" will tend to limit the rate of change in the urban population, and urban-to-rural diffusion will lead to more rapid change in the rural population and to rural-urban convergence. Thus, as older rural-urban differences diminish or disappear, new ones will appear. Whereas no particular culture traits, aside from those closely associated with receptivity to change, will invariably be associated with rural or urban communities, important rural-urban differences of some kind will tend to persist even in the most highly urbanized and industrialized societies.

The social scientific literature does not provide the evidence (at least not in a systematic fashion) which would allow a definitive choice among the differing viewpoints. Although the preponderance of evidence seems to suggest that the Wirth thesis is not correct without important qualifications, survey data from virtually all modern societies reveal remaining rural-urban differences in regard to a variety of kinds of attitudes and behavior. There is evidence that in the United States some rural-urban differences have recently increased rather than diminished,[7] but the evidence does not allow any conclusion about the

magnitude or direction of the overall change. The evidence that social and cultural change typically originates in cities and proceeds more rapidly among urban than rural people is convincing but not definitive. It is easy to demonstrate that change often has occurred in this fashion, but we do not know that it has always done so, even in modern societies, or that it usually has done so in most societies.

Even though the Fischer thesis is not undeniably correct, presently available evidence, as we assess it, makes it more credible than any competing theoretical perspective. We suspect that it (or some slight variant) will soon become the most widely accepted view among students of rural-urban differences (if it is not already), and we provisionally accept it. However, even a developing consensus on the basic sources of rural-urban cultural and behavioral differences will not still debate concerning the practical and theoretical importance of these differences in modern societies. For instance, the importance of differences created by any differing receptivity to change depends in large measure on whether the receptivity varies in a more or less linear fashion with community size or whether the main difference is a disjunctive one between the most truly rural people (those who both live and work in the open countryside) and the remainder of the population. If the latter should be correct, the resulting rural-urban differences would be of rapidly diminishing practical importance in most modern societies as the rural-farm population becomes a very small proportion of the total. Furthermore, as Fischer is careful to point out, if his theory is correct, it does not necessarily follow that rural-urban differences are usually large enough to be of much practical importance or that the rural-urban distinction accounts for a large proportion of the variation in attitudes, behavior, and lifestyles in any society. To those who would understand, or who would utilize knowledge of, variations in attitudes and behavior in the United States, an important question remains unanswered: does the rural-urban distinction make enough difference to warrant serious attention? Our purpose here is to provide a provisional answer to that question.

THE MAGNITUDE AND NATURE OF CONTEMPORARY RURAL-URBAN DIFFERENCES

The magnitude of rural-urban differences in attitudes and behavior shown by American national surveys varies according to kind of attitudes and behavior and according to the way the rural-urban distinction is made. Usually, although not always, the largest differences appear when farmers (and their families), or rural-farm people, are compared with the rest of the population. Although students of rural and urban

---

[6]Claude Fischer, "Toward a Subcultural Theory of Urbanism," *American Journal of Sociology*, vol. 80 (May 1975), pp. 1319-41.
[7]Glenn, "Massification versus Differentiation," and Norval D. Glenn, "Recent Trends in Intercategory Differences in Attitudes," *Social Forces*, vol. 52 (March 1974), pp. 395-401.

society and culture do not agree on just how the rural-urban distinction should be made (or whether it should be conceived of as a continuum rather than a dichotomous distinction), there are compelling reasons for considering rural-farm people the most truly rural segment of the population and for considering the farm-nonfarm distinction the most theoretically meaningful of any dichotomous rural-urban distinction. As an aggregate, the farm population differs to an important degree in many demographic characteristics from even the residents of the smaller dense settlements, and farmers are the only major segment of the population for which both place of work and place of residence are usually in the open countryside. Residents of the open countryside who are in nonfarm occupations often (perhaps usu-

ally) both work and maintain most of their social relations in dense settlements of some size. Therefore, it is useful to begin a treatment of rural-urban differences with a farm-nonfarm comparison.

Recent national survey data show that farmers (and their families) do not differ substantially from other occupational categories in a large proportion of the kinds of attitudes and behavior covered by the surveys. However, differences not likely to have resulted from sampling error appear in responses to at least a large minority of the questions. For instance, Norval Glenn and Jon Alston drew on data from 92 questions asked on American opinion polls from 1953 to 1965 and found farmers, as a whole, to be relatively prejudiced, ethnocentric, isolationist, intolerant of deviance, opposed to civil liberties, distrustful of people,

Table 1. Responses (in percent) to selected attitudinal questions asked on American Gallup Polls, by occupation of head of household

	Professional and business	White collar	Farm	Manual
Religious beliefs				
believe in the Devil (1968)	57	56	75	61
believe in life after death (1968)	76	66	86	71
believe in hell (1968)	60	56	86	68
believe in heaven (1968)	77	81	93	89
Issues concerning personal morals and vices				
think that birth control information should be available to anyone who wants it (1968)	86	81	64	76
think use of marijuana should be made legal (1969)	18	22	5	10
would like to see stricter state laws concerning sale of obscene literature on newsstands (1969)	71	69	81	79
would find pictures of nudes in magazines objectionable (1969)	64	64	89	76
have smoked cigarettes in past week (1972)	48	54	29	48
Minority-majority issues				
would vote for a well-qualified Jew for president (1969)	95	92	73	87
would vote for a well-qualified Catholic for president (1969)	95	93	80	91
would vote for a well-qualified Negro for president (1969)	76	74	56	70
would vote for a well-qualified woman for president (1969)	55	58	47	54
think the U.S. would be governed better if women had more say in politics (1969)	21	21	13	25
would vote for a well-qualified woman for Congress (1970)	90	90	71	82
approve of marriage between Catholics and Protestants (1969)	73	67	46	62
approve of marriage between Jews and non-Jews (1968)	71	69	34	59
approve of marriage between whites and nonwhites (1968)	28	24	9	20
Political issues				
consider themselves conservative (1972)	37	34	41	41
favor lowering voting age to 18 (1969)	60	62	72	67
think law enforcement agencies should be tougher in dealing with crime and lawlessness (1972)	80	81	93	84
would favor a law requiring a police permit to buy a gun (1971)	76	69	47	71
think college students should have a greater say in the running of colleges (1969)	29	33	16	27
have favorable view of Red China (1972)	30	20	17	22
have favorable view of Russia (1972)	54	40	35	38

Source: Various issues of the *Gallup Opinion Index*.

traditionally religious, ascetic, work-oriented, Puritanical, uninformed, and favorable to early marriage and high fertility.[8] These differences existed not only in the adult population as a whole but also among young nonsouthern Protestants. Although these differences tend to confirm popular stereotypes of rural-farm people, most of them were fairly small, and in many cases only a small minority of farmers exhibited the characteristics which were more prevalent among farmers than among persons in other occupations.

Rural-farm people have become such a small proportion of the total population that the most recent national surveys do not give reliable estimates of the characteristics of the remaining farmers. For instance, the American Institute of Public Opinion (the American Gallup Poll) stopped reporting separate data for the farm respondents late in 1973. However, data from the late 1960s and early 1970s show that farmers were still the most distinctive (and usually the most conservative) segment of the population in regard to many kinds of attitudes (see table 1). For instance, farmers tended to be more fundamentalist in religious beliefs, Puritanical, prejudiced, and conservative on political issues than persons in any other occupational category. In general, they resembled manual workers more than they resembled persons in higher-status occupations (although Glenn and Alston found farmers' attitudes on labor-management issues to resemble those of business and professional people).

Although a few of the farm-nonfarm differences in table 1 are fairly large, it should be kept in mind that we generally selected for reporting the largest differences we could find; therefore, the reported differences should not be considered representative of farm-nonfarm differences in general. Furthermore, the farm-nonfarm distinction accounted for only a small proportion of the total variation in responses even in the case of the items for which the differences were the largest. Since the rural-nonfarm population was no more than about 5 percent of any of the samples, even categorical differences between farmers and nonfarmers would not have produced substantial variation in the total samples.[9] Thus, in many respects the practical importance of even the largest farm-nonfarm differences is not very great. For instance, farmers do not constitute a "market" distinctive and large enough to be of much concern to most manufacturers

and retailers, except those whose goods are specifically for the agricultural industry. On the other hand, farm-nonfarm differences do have some practical importance, the best example perhaps being in regard to politics. Farmers retain political influence disproportionate to their numbers (for instance, because "agricultural states," such as the Dakotas, with small populations but relatively large numbers of farmers, have two U.S. senators, the same as the populous industrial states), and any small portion of the electorate can be crucial to the outcome of a close election.

The theoretical importance of the farm-nonfarm attitudinal differences depends largely on whether they reflect largely socioeconomic, demographic, and religious-ethnic differences or whether they are in some way causally related to population concentration. Glenn and Alston conclude that most of the differences they found did not reflect differences in age, religious preference, region, income, or education; the differences existed among young nonsouthern Protestants as well as in the total population, and farmers often differed from manual workers, whom they resembled in income and education. Although we have not subjected the data in table 1 to the controls used by Glenn and Alston, we are confident that the controls would not eliminate most of the differences, since the topics are similar to those studied by Glenn and Alston. Furthermore, socioeconomic differences can hardly account for most of the attitudinal differences, in view of the often substantial attitudinal differences between the farm and manual classes.

It is apparent from community-size breakdowns of responses to the items used for table 1 (not shown) and from responses to a number of questions asked on more recent national surveys (table 2) that the farm-nonfarm distinction is not the only rural-urban distinction useful for explaining attitudes and behavior. Again, it must be pointed out that we tended to select for reporting the items showing the greatest variation in responses by our independent variable, and thus the data do not indicate the typical degree of variation in expressed attitudes among communities of different sizes. However, the reported data are very nearly representative of all of the data we examined in one important respect:[10] when there is any appreciable variation in responses by community size, the variation is usually monotonic rather than being a disjunctive difference between the smallest communities and all others. That is, the largest communities usually differ from the medium-sized communities about as much (and in the same direction) as the medium-sized communities differ from the smallest com-

[8] Norval D. Glenn and Jon P. Alston, "Rural-Urban Differences in Reported Attitudes and Behavior," *Southwestern Social Science Quarterly*, vol. 47 (March 1967), pp. 381-400. See, also, Norval D. Glenn and Jon P. Alston, "Cultural Distances among Occupational Categories," *American Sociological Review*, vol. 33 (June 1968), pp. 365-82.

[9] Rural-farm people were about 5 percent of the total U.S. population in 1970 and are now only about 4 percent.

[10] We examined all of the data in recent (since the late 1960s) issues of the *Gallup Opinion Index*.

Table 2. Responses (in percent) to selected attitudinal questions asked on American Gallup Polls, by size of community*

	Under 2,500, rural	2,500-49,999	50,000-499,999	500,000-999,999	1,000,000 and over
Religious beliefs					
believe that religion is old-fashioned and out-of-date (1975)	12	18	20	19	35
have a great deal of confidence in the church or in organized religion (1975)	51	48	41	44	32
are very religious (1975)	30	29	24	27	20
Issues concerning personal morals and vices					
think abortion under any circumstances should be legal (1975)	9	19	23	29	31
would favor anti-abortion constitutional amendment (1975)	53	43	45	38	38
think use of marijuana should be made legal (1974)	21	21	27	33	35
believe it is wrong for people to have sex relations before marriage (1973)	61	50	44	41	34
would find topless nightclub waitresses objectionable (1973)	68	69	58	51	46
Minority-majority issues					
favor Equal Rights Amendment (1975)	53	59	55	65	67
would vote for woman for president (1976)	68	73	73	76	80
consider being married, with children, and no full-time job to be ideal lifestyle (women only, 1976)	53	39	45	38	38
Political issues					
favor registration of all firearms (1975)	50	64	71	77	81
would favor conservative over liberal political party (1975)	42	43	39	44	36
feel that war is outmoded as a way of settling differences between nations (1975)	37	45	48	51	48
are politically liberal (1974)	16	26	28	27	35
favor unconditional amnesty for draft evaders (1974)	29	26	38	39	40
favor reestablishing diplomatic relations with Cuba (1974)	58	62	60	70	71
have a great deal of confidence in labor unions (1973)	11	14	16	15	18

Source: Various issues of the *Gallup Opinion Index*.
*Suburban residents are classified according to the size of their central cities.

munities. This pattern of variation suggests that it is useful to conceive of a rural-urban continuum rather than a dichotomous rural-urban distinction. It also indicates that attitudinal and behavioral variation associated with degree of population concentration will not become unimportant simply because the most truly rural people become a very small proportion of the population. A rather substantial proportion of the population lives, and probably will long continue to live, in intermediate-sized communities;[11] and the differences between these people and the residents of the largest cities (and their suburbs) constitute rural-urban differences in one sense. Furthermore, there is no immediate prospect that rural-nonfarm people (residents of dense settlements of less than 2,500 population and nonfarm residents of the

[11]Thirty-one percent of the respondents to two national surveys conducted in 1974 and 1975 (the General Social Surveys conducted by the National Opinion Research Center) lived in cities with populations of from 2,500 to 249,999.

open countryside) will soon become an insignificant segment of the population.[12]

THE IMPORTANCE OF RURAL BACKGROUND

Even if the only important differences associated with population concentration were between the "truly rural" people and others in the society, "ruralism" would not soon virtually disappear from American society, assuming that early socialization has enduring effects on individuals. Although few Americans are now "truly rural," a substantial proportion of the adults have rural backgrounds (see table 3), varying from around half of the elderly to about a fourth of the young adults.

Rural-urban differences in backgrounds undoubtedly contribute to the attitudinal and behavioral differentiation of the urban population, although apparent-

[12]In 1970, rural-nonfarm people were 21.3 percent of the total U.S. population.

Table 3. Size of community lived in at age 16, U.S. adult population, by age, combined data from surveys conducted in 1972, 1973, 1974, and 1975

	Age							
	18-29	**30-39**	**40-49**	**50-59**	**60-69**	**70-79**	**80 and up**	**Total**
Open countryside	22.3	28.5	30.2	38.9	44.6	46.9	55.6	32.9
Dense settlements with less than 50,000 residents	30.4	30.2	34.1	27.3	29.8	31.4	22.2	30.3
Cities with 50,000 or more population and their suburbs	47.3	41.3	35.7	33.7	25.6	21.6	22.2	36.8
Total	100.0	100.0	100.0	100.0	100.0	100.0	100.0	100.0
N	1,565	1,119	1,027	989	781	462	117	6,060

Source: The General Social Surveys conducted by the National Opinion Research Center (James A. Davis, principal investigator).

Table 4. Relationship of occupational prestige (males) or spouse's occupational prestige (married females) to selected dependent variables, with and without rural-urban background controlled, whites, United States, 1974

	Males		Females	
Dependent variable	**Zero-order correlation**	**Partial beta**	**Zero-order correlation**	**Partial beta**
Frequency of church attendance	.116	.134	.021	.023
Republican party identification	.088	.112	.113	.118
Political conservatism	−.026	−.019	−.043	−.034
Belief that luck is more important than hard work in getting ahead	.017	.018	.038	.032
Frequency of socializing with relatives	−.167	−.155	−.112	−.121
Frequency of socializing with neighbors	−.005	.023	.046	.045
Frequency of socializing with friends who are not neighbors	.023	.006	.211	.191
Frequency of going to bar or tavern	.011	−.014	.067	.056
Expressed ideal family size	.023	.044	−.021	−.005
Permissiveness concerning premarital sex	.135	.095	.111	.089
Permissiveness concerning extramarital sex	.200	.178	.133	.125
Permissiveness concerning homosexual sex	.191	.171	.162	.151
Tolerance of communism	.148	.134	.142	.126
Belief in greater expenditures for education	.015	−.003	.084	.072
Belief in greater expenditures for welfare	−.058	−.042	.017	.007
Belief in greater expenditures for the military	−.249	−.230	−.155	−.142
Willingness to invite a black to dinner	.068	.055	.037	.021
Vocabulary test score	.473	.444	.317	.292
Number of children (persons age 45 and older)	−.181	−.169	−.138	−.127

Source: The 1974 General Social Survey conducted by the National Opinion Research Center (James A. Davis, principal investigator).
Note: Data in this and subsequent tables are limited to whites in order to control race. Truncation is used for control since race interacts with some of the predictor variables. All dependent variables are scored to form ordinal or interval scales with at least three categories.

ly not in quite the way that some social scientists have speculated. For instance, Leo Schnore speculates that class differences in attitudes reflect to a large extent the fact that a larger percentage of the people in the lower than in the higher classes have rural backgrounds.[13] To test this hypothesis, we did a regression

analysis of 19 attitudinal and behavioral variables from the 1974 General Social Survey (see table 4).[14] We first regressed each variable on prestige of occu-

[13]Leo F. Schnore, "The Rural-Urban Variable: An Urbanite's Perspective," *Rural Sociology*, vol. 31 (June 1966), pp. 131-43.

[14]Since we were concerned with representativeness rather than with illustrating extreme cases, we selected the variables before we examined the data in order to avoid biasing the results via the selection process. For discussion of the "no peeking" rule, see Herbert H. Hyman, *Secondary Analysis of Sample Surveys* (New York: John Wiley, 1972).

pation (males) or prestige of spouse's occupation (married females), and then we added size of place of residence at age 16 (rural-urban dichotomy) as a control variable. For most of the dependent variables, adding the control variable did reduce the strength of the association, but in no case was the reduction more than slight (see table 4). For males, the mean correlation coefficient (which is equivalent to the zero-order beta) is .115 and the mean partial beta (standardized regression coefficient) is .107. For females, the values are .104 and .094, respectively. Therefore, at least in regard to the variables included in this analysis (which, of course, are not necessarily representative of all attitudinal and behavioral variables), the higher proportion of low-status than of high-status people who have rural origins does not seem to be an important source of so-called class differences.

However, it is important that, in the case of several of the variables, size of community of residence at age 16 was a better predictor of the responses than size of present (at the time of the survey) community of residence (see table 5).[15] In the case of eight of the 19 variables for males and 14 of the 19 for females, the partial unstandardized regression coefficient is larger for size of community of residence at age 16 than for size of present community of residence. For males, the mean beta is .060 for size of community of residence at age 16 and .059 for size of present community of residence.[16] The corresponding means for females are .075 and .043.

Obviously, neither of the community size variables was an important predictor of most of the dependent variables we selected from the 1974 General Social Survey; most of the associations are neither statistically significant nor large enough to be important, even if they did not result from sampling error. This is true even for several variables which, according to the literature, should bear a rather strong relationship

[15]For this analysis, we used the same three-category community-size breakdown for community of origin and of current residence, namely, (1) open countryside, (2) dense settlements of less than 50,000 residents, and (3) cities of 50,000 or more population and their suburbs.
[16]We disregarded the signs of the betas in computing these means.

Table 5. Relationship (partial) of size of community lived in at age 16 and of size of community of current residence to selected dependent variables, whites, United States, 1974

	Standardized partial regression coefficient (beta)			
	Males		Females	
Dependent variable	Community of origin	Community of residence	Community of origin	Community of residence
Frequencey of church attendance	−.007	−.051	.051	−.103
Republican party identification	−.067	−.038	−.020	−.017
Political conservatism	−.088	−.051	−.115	−.035
Belief that luck is more important than hard work in getting ahead	.062	−.004	.034	−.033
Frequency of socializing with relatives	.009	−.041	.065	−.033
Frequency of socializing with neighbors	−.066	−.022	.093	−.055
Frequency of socializing with friends who are not neighbors	.059	.083	.087	.019
Frequency of going to bar or tavern	.072	.083	.008	−.110
Expressed ideal family size	−.081	.034	−.081	−.001
Permissiveness concerning premarital sex	.074	.039	.050	.128
Permissiveness concerning extramarital sex	.095	.137	.077	−.011
Permissiveness concerning homosexual sex	.075	.146	.050	.027
Tolerance of communism	.084	.015	.055	.019
Belief in greater expenditures for education	−.032	.126	.091	.023
Belief in greater expenditures for welfare	−.028	.010	−.011	.073
Belief in greater expenditures for the military	−.074	−.074	−.074	.014
Willingness to invite a black to dinner	−.014	.096	.033	−.055
Vocabulary test score	.052	.051	.189	−.027
Number of children (persons age 45 and older)	−.096	−.016	−.119	−.043

Source: The 1974 General Social Survey conducted by the National Opinion Research Center (James A. Davis, principal investigator).
Note: Only the two community-size variables are predictor variables in the regression equations.

to community size. For instance, expressions of the ideal number of children for a family were virtually unrelated to size of present community of residence and only weakly related to size of community of origin. Some researchers require that a beta be at least .15 before it is considered worthy of interpretation; by that criterion, only the association among females of size of community of origin with the vocabulary test scores was large enough to be important. However, several other betas do not fall far short of .15 and, thus, probably reflect associations of some importance in the population. For males, these include the associations of size of present community of residence with permissive attitudes toward premarital and homosexual sex and with favorable attitudes toward formal education. For females, these include the associations of size of present community of residence with permissive attitudes toward premarital sex and of size of community of residence at age 16 with number of children and with liberal political orientations.

A MULTIVARIATE ANALYSIS

Of course, even the larger associations may not reflect direct effects of community size but rather may be spurious or reflect indirect effects through variables which intervene between community size and the dependent variables. If so, both the Wirth and the Fischer views of the effects of population concentration would tend to lose their credibility. To test for this possibility, we added nine background and current characteristics, all of which seemed likely to have some effect on some of the dependent variables, to the regression equation as predictors along with the two community-size variables.[17] We then selected each dependent variable with a zero-order correlation of at least .10 with one of the community-size vari-

[17]We also recoded the community-size variables into the maximum number of categories consistent with retaining ordinal scales, which made the two variables incomparable with one another but allowed each to explain the maximum amount of variance in the dependent variables.

Table 6. Zero-order and partial relationships of community-size variables to selected dependent variables, whites, United States, 1974

	Males				Females			
	Community of origin		Community of residence		Community of origin		Community of residence	
Dependent variable	Zero-order correlation	Partial beta	Zero-order correlation	Partial beta	Zero-order correlation	Partial beta	Zero-order correlation	Partial beta
Political conservatism	−.112	−.091	*	*	−.118	−.058	*	*
Frequency of socialization with friends who are not neighbors	.172	.079	.147	.084	.189	.090	*	*
Frequency of going to bar or tavern	.167	.108	.118	.065	.103	.023	*	*
Permissiveness concerning premarital sex	.171	.093	.118	.036	.212	.042	.211	.137
Permissiveness concerning extramarital sex	.162	.073	.204	.152	.101	.045	*	*
Permissiveness concerning homosexual sex	.173	.064	.204	.148	.132	.016	.109	.060
Belief in greater expenditures for education	.086	.028	.114	.090	.137	.085	*	*
Belief in greater expenditures for the military	−.158	−.087	−.110	.048	−.148	−.059	*	*
Vocabulary test score	.225	.077	.184	.053	.333	.215	.127	.005
Number of children (persons age 45 and older)	−.123	−.101	*	*	−.142	−.100	*	*

Source: The 1974 General Social Survey conducted by the National Opinion Research Center (James A. Davis, principal investigator).
Note: For the multiple regression analysis, the independent variables include all of the independent variables listed in table 7.
*Data not reported because zero-order correlation is less than .1.

ables and compared the correlation coefficient (zero-order beta) with the partial beta (see table 6).

Generally, the controls diminished the associations to an important degree, but only in a few cases were the associations reduced to virtually zero. We cannot be sure, of course, that we controlled all antecedent and intervening variables which could account for the remaining associations, as indicated by the betas, but it appears likely that population concentration, or some very close correlates, had rather direct effects on some of the dependent variables, such as vocabulary (females), fertility, attitudes toward family size, attitudes toward communism, and attitudes toward premarital sex. If so, we speculate that, with the probable exception of the effect on vocabulary, the effects were mainly a matter of the people in the smaller communities lagging behind those in the larger communities as attitudes and behavior have changed.

The multivariate analysis also allows tentative conclusions about the relative explanatory power of the community-size variables and the other predictor variables, most of which are often used in social scientific research. The means in table 7 indicate that the explanatory power of age and education exceeded those of both size of community of origin and size of community of current residence by a considerable margin. Even region of residence had slightly better predictive power, on the average, than either of the community-size variables. On the other hand, the community-size variables did not fare badly in competition with some other variables often used as explanatory variables in social scientific research, such as occupational prestige and family income. Of course, the 19 dependent variables used for these comparisons are not necessarily representative, and the relative predictive power of the different independent variables varies a great deal among the 19 dependent variables.[18]

CONCLUSIONS

What, then, is the importance of the rural-urban distinction and of the community-size variable to

[18]For a somewhat similar comparison, see George W. Lowe and Charles W. Peek, "Location and Lifestyle: The Comparative Explanatory Utility of Urbanism and Rurality," *Rural Sociology*, vol. 39 (Fall 1974), pp. 392-419. More recent research by Lowe and Peek, as yet unpublished, reveals that, for a large number of attitudinal variables from the General Social Surveys, a cluster of "status" variables has considerably greater predictive power than a cluster of rural-urban-community-size variables.

Table 7. Mean partial relationship (beta) of two community-size variables and nine other independent variables to 19 selected dependent variables, whites, United States, 1974

Independent variable	Males	Married females
Size of community of origin	.067	.069
Size of community of residence	.059	.040
Region	.084	.076
Region of origin	.047	.071
Age	.159	.131
Family income	.049	.044
Subjective economic standing of family	.068	.071
Subjective economic standing of family at age 16	.041	.058
Occupational prestige (of spouse in case of females)	.055	.040
Father's occupational prestige	.041	.040
Years of school completed	.103	.102

Source: The 1974 General Social Survey conducted by the National Opinion Research Center (James A. Davis, principal investigator). Note: Means are computed without regard to signs of the betas. All 11 of the independent variables are in the regression equations. The 19 dependent variables are those listed in tables 4 and 5.

those who would understand and deal with attitudinal and behavioral variation in the United States? The answer, clearly, is that the importance is more than negligible and that there is little reason to believe that the importance is diminishing or will soon diminish very much. It would certainly be premature to suggest that students of rural-urban differences should find more fruitful topics to study.

On the other hand, the importance of rural-urban differences should not be exaggerated. The rural-urban variable, along with many other explanatory variables long favored by social scientists, is losing much of its apparent importance as researchers increasingly use "proportional-reduction-in-error" measures of association and interpret their findings in terms of proportion of variance explained. For most attitudinal and behavioral variables, the predictive utility of the rural-urban variable is modest at best; "overinterpretation" of rather small differences between percentages has often obscured the fact that on most issues the rural and urban populations each has almost as much internal differentiation in attitudes as does the total population.

10

The impact of changes in urban population distribution and rural economic base on rural people and communities

Population and functional changes of villages in western Pennsylvania

E. WILLARD MILLER*

The village from the earliest period of land occupance has been an important unit in the settlement pattern of western Pennsylvania. The role of the villages has changed from time to time largely depending upon the economic conditions of the area which it serves. It is the purpose of this study to investigate and analyse changes in the population and functions of villages in six west-central Pennsylvania counties— Armstrong, Butler, Venango, Clarion, Jefferson, and Forest. All settlements with a population between 25 and 1000 persons are included. The lower limit was set in order that a definite grouping of houses would occur.[1] There has, thus, been an attempt to eliminate those places where no effective agglomerated settlement exists, such as crossroad hamlets where a single store or filling station and possibly one or two houses are located. The upper limit of 1000 people was selected for it differentiated basically residential and service communities from multifunctional towns and cities where manufacturing plays a significant role.

SOURCES AND METHODOLOGY

The obtaining of precise data on village population is difficult because the United States census is given by political units and all unincorporated villages appear in the total figure of township population. In the

□ From Western Pennsylvania Historical Magazine **43**:59-75, Mar. 1960.
*Dr. Miller is Head and Professor of the Department of Geography at The Pennsylvania State University. He is co-author of *The World's Nations: An Economic and Regional Geography*, editor of *Global Geography*, and author of many articles on Pennsylvania.
[1]Because many of the smaller villages have lost their economic functions in recent years, a compact residential area was used as the criteria for the designation of the village structural form. The residential village with no other functions is a common phenomenon in this region.

six counties selected for this study over 95 per cent of the villages were unincorporated. As a consequence village population can only be estimated.

A number of sources are available that aid in determining the distribution of settlements and their population. The annual Rand McNally Commercial Atlas and Marketing Guide first published in 1876 locates essentially all settlements and presents their approximate population. A number of individual maps are also available, such as those published by the George F. Cram Company that give population data for unincorporated places. These sources, however, rely for population data upon the estimates of local residents. The accuracy of this type data must frequently be questioned. Also, a number of smaller villages are omitted which actually exist, and conversely a number of villages are listed which have no genuine settlement.

There are a number of map sources available that present only the distributional pattern of the villages. The railroad maps published by the Pennsylvania Department of Internal Affairs are one of the most important of these map sources. There are also two important series of highway maps by counties on Pennsylvania. The first are highway maps published by the United States Bureau of Public Roads. The second series are highway maps published by the Pennsylvania Department of Highways and based on the Statewide Highway Planning Survey. These maps were prepared between 1939 and 1941 under the general supervision of the United States Bureau of Public Roads. The maps for the six counties under study are published at a scale 1 inch = 1 mile. A wealth of cultural information includes residences, churches, hotels, schools, businesses, factories and many others. Inset maps of many of the smaller villages present the street patterns, and buildings are identified by type of use. From field study some errors have been found on these maps, but considering that the mapping was done from moving cars by untrained men, and data recorded on blank sheets of paper, the results are good.

Two sets of aerial photographs prepared by the Production and Marketing Administration and the U.S. Geological Survey are available for the entire six counties; one set was made in 1938-39 and the second in 1951-52. They were valuable in securing the location of buildings, for most of the photographs were taken in winter or spring before the leaf cover obscured the pattern. The photographs were of limited value in determining the functional uses of the buildings.

Other sources of information on villages include county histories and atlases. Most of these were published between 1875 and 1900. Five of the six counties have local histories.[2] The Dun and Bradstreet annual Reference Books are valuable sources on the commercial functions of the region. The Pennsylvania Industrial Directory published approximately every three years since 1913 lists every factory, its location and number of employees. The village newspapers, usually published weekly, are important sources of information.[3] There have been more than 24 village papers published since 1860 in the six counties. At present about ten local papers are in existence. The publication of books and pamphlets commemorating special historical events also present information on villages.[4] The libraries in the larger villages and towns

have been found to be a storehouse for local and regional data.

Although library sources were necessary to the development of the present study, field surveys were also fundamental. Because the accuracy of many of the sources could be questioned, only by field survey could data be authenticated. The author also feels that an intimate knowledge of the area extending over several decades was of the utmost importance. During the summer of 1955 the author spent six weeks in the field surveying in detail Turkey City and its environs, in lesser detail twelve other villages, and visiting every village in the six counties to validate its existence and then estimate its population.

EARLY ORIGINS OF THE VILLAGE PATTERN

The first settlers entered this area shortly before 1800, and the initial hamlets appear on maps in the early 1800's. Because the area under study is part of the dissected Allegheny Plateau it was among the last regions of Pennsylvania to be settled, and population grew slowly. By 1850 the total population of the six counties was about 115,000 of which approximately 6 to 8 per cent lived in villages, possibly 10 per cent were in larger towns, and over 80 per cent were rural dwellers. The villages were few in number and widely scattered.[5] The economy of this region until the late 1850's was based predominantly on a self-sufficiency agricultural system. In Clarion County local deposits of bog iron ore provided the raw material for a small iron industry beginning in the 1820's. A few villages such as Monroe Furnace, Black Forest Furnace, Old Forge and Martha Furnace grew around these installations. Since the furnaces were small, they supported only a few people and the village population did not increase greatly. By the late 1850's most of the iron furnaces had disappeared due to competition from the larger blast furnaces in the Pittsburgh area. Consequently, as late as 1860 this isolated region had a pioneer economy which required little in the form of services which would have encouraged the growth of villages.

ESTABLISHMENT OF MODERN VILLAGE PATTERN 1859-1880

After 1859 the local economy expanded rapidly with the increasing importance of agriculture and the exploitation of the region's petroleum, coal and timber resources. The discovery of petroleum at Titusville in 1859 created a new source of wealth that attracted thousands of people to this backwoods country. This was the greatest single impetus to the growth of the local economy. Between 1860 and 1880 scores of

[2]Beach Nichols: *Atlas of Armstrong County, Pennsylvania*, Chicago, 1876, 83 pp. Robert W. Smith: *History of Armstrong County, Pennsylvania*, Chicago, 1883, 624 pp.
Robert C. Brown: *History of Butler County, Pennsylvania*, Chicago, 1895, 1360 pp.
Joseph A. Caldwell: *Caldwell's Illustrated, Historical Combination Atlas of Clarion County, Pennsylvania*, Condit, Ohio, 1877, 230 pp.
A. J. Davis, Editor: *History of Clarion County, Pennsylvania*, Syracuse, 1887, 664 pp.
William J. McKnight: *A Pioneer History of Jefferson County, Pennsylvania*, Philadelphia, 1898, 670 pp.
History of Venango County, Pennsylvania, Chicago, 1890, 1164 pp.
Atlas of Pennsylvania, Bureau of the Census, Washington, D.C., 1900, 56 pp.
History of Venango County, Pennsylvania, Columbus, Ohio; Published by J. A. Caldwell, 1879, 651 pp.
[3]Special issues of newspapers are of particular value such as: Samuel J. M. Eaton: Centennial Discourse: A Sketch of the History of Venango County, Pennsylvania, *Venango Spectator*, Franklin, July 4, 1876; and A Century of Progress, 1840-1940—100th Anniversary Edition. *The Clarion Republican*, Vol. 100 (47), August 22, 1940.
[4]W. T. Bell: *Notes on the Early History of Franklin and Venango County, Pennsylvania*, Old Home Week Historical Committee, Franklin, 1910, 19 pp.; and *The Petroleum Industry 1859-1934*, Diamond Jubilee of the Petroleum Industry, The Oil and Gas Journal and the Oil City Derrick, August 27, 1934, 268 pp.

[5]Data from map by A. W. Harrison: *The Keystone State, Pennsylvania and Her Eminent Men*, Philadelphia, 1847.

towns developed to serve the expanding oil economy (Fig. 1D). Such names as Petroleum Center, Petrolia, Greece City, Shamburg, Oleopolis and Pithole attest to the influence of petroleum in the creation of the village pattern.[6] Many of the oil villages came into existence on the completion of an oil well, grew to modest size, and then declined rapidly on exhaustion of the oil pool. Therefore, at the same time that the village pattern was rapidly evolving, villages were also disappearing. There are several scores of oil "ghost towns" in the area. The unrestricted exploitation of petroleum has frequently created "boom and bust" conditions causing a fluid state in the settlement pattern of a region.

Other local resources of the six counties were also developed after 1859. The demand for lumber in the oil industry provided a large local market. The ex-

[6]Henry F. Walling and O. W. Gray: *New Topographic Atlas of the State of Pennsylvania*, Philadelphia, 1872, p. 53.

ploitation of the mixed deciduous-coniferous forests began on a significant scale in the 1860's. Because the lumbering industry required relatively few workers, and was migratory, only a few villages developed as lumber communities. A number of the smaller villages reflect their role as lumber centers such as Newton Mills, Hickory, and Cooper Tract.

The southern and central portions of these six counties are well endowed with coal resources, and mining became important in the 1860's (Fig. 1C). By 1880, 2100 miners were employed in the coal industry and a number of coal mining settlements had developed. Villages such as Coal Glen, Clarion Mines, Coaltown, Carbon Center, Red Bank and Coal Hill appear on maps of the 1880 period.

Agriculture also experienced a considerable expansion between 1860 and 1880. Not only was a local market for agricultural products created by the influx of population to exploit the region's resources,

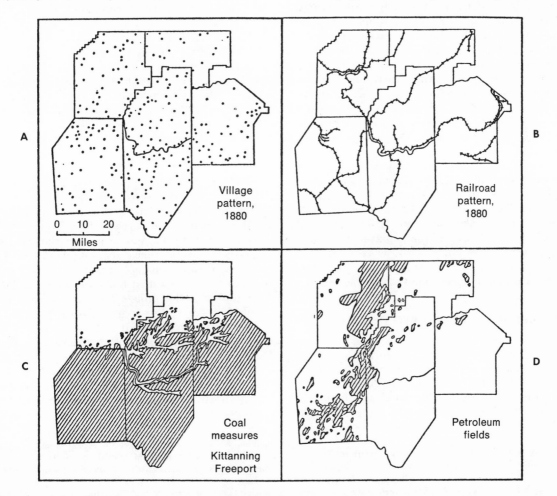

Fig. 1. Distribution of villages in 1880. Notice the relationship between the location of the villages and the railroad pattern, petroleum deposits, and coal deposits.

but the growing railroad system gave an outlet for marketing some agricultural products beyond the immediate area. Self-sufficiency agriculture gradually declined as commercial agriculture replaced it. By 1880 the amount of land in farms reached its all time peak within the six counties of 1,766,000 acres.[7] Many villages such as Rural Valley, West Valley, Knox Dale, Agnews Mills and Cool Springs grew to serve the needs of a prosperous agricultural section.

By 1880 the rural economy was highly developed. Because local service centers were needed, the village population had grown rapidly. Of a total population in the six counties of 216,594, about 41,400, or 19.2 per cent, were located in villages, 50,100, or 23.1 per cent, were in towns and cities, but 125,094, or 57.7 per cent, were still rural dwellers.

At this time there was a total in the six counties of 269 villages (Fig. 1A).[8] The intensity of the development of the local resource base was the major factor in determining the density of the village pattern (Figs. 1C and 1D). Where more than one economic activity existed in an area, such as farming and the petroleum industry in Clarion and Venango Counties, the village pattern became quite dense. By contrast, in Forest and northern Jefferson Counties where forest industries predominated only a few villages developed. The village density pattern also depended upon the size of the area served by larger towns and cities. Because towns and cities were able to service a larger area, the number of villages was notably fewer around these major urban agglomerations. This is particularly noticeable in central Butler County, where Butler, one of the largest cities in the six counties, is located.

In the specific location of villages, accessibility to transportation was the major localizing factor. Of transportation facilities, railroads played the dominant role. Of the 269 villages, 140 were located on railroad routes (Fig. 1B). These villages were also larger in size than villages found along the unpaved roads.

CONTINUED VILLAGE GROWTH 1880 TO THE 1920's

For about 40 years after 1880 the rural economy of the region remained strong with expansion in many of its phases. Although farmland acreage declined slightly after 1880, the value of farmland and buildings rose from $60,460,000 in 1880 to a peak of $93,166,000 in 1920.[9] The coal mining industry also expanded

rapidly after 1880, reaching a peak in employment of over 18,000 workers about 1920. Production of petroleum in the six counties reached its peak in the early 1880's, and although output declined sharply after 1900, employment in the oil industry remained fairly stable until the 1920's.[10] Lumbering remained an important economic activity until about World War I.

As a result of the prosperous rural economy, the village population, as well as the total population, continued to expand. Of a total population in the six counties of 317,751 in 1920, 63,250, or 20.0 per cent, were located in villages,[11] 118,412, or 37.2 per cent, were rural dwellers, and 136,089, or 42.8 per cent, were urban dwellers in towns of over 1000 population. Between 1880 and 1920, although the percentage of people in villages remained essentially stationary, the larger towns and cities were increasing their percentage from 23.0 to 42.8 per cent of the total. At the same time the rural population declined from 57.7 per cent of the total to 37.2 per cent.

The absolute increase in village population between 1880 and 1920 is reflected in both larger villages and greater numbers. The number of villages reached its maximum about 1920 when 322 were found in the region.[12] The same general distribution pattern remained as in 1880. The localizing influence of the railroads persisted with 181 of the 322 villages located on railway routes.

VILLAGE FUNCTIONS 1860-1930

During the period 1860 to the late 1920's when the rural economy of this region was expanding, the village was the economic and cultural center of the small region which it served. The village nodes developed primarily because transportation was slow and difficult, and the local inhabitants needed a service center that was not more than one to two hours distance from their home by horse and buggy.

To illustrate the village functions from 1860 to about 1930, Turkey City in west-central Clarion County has been selected for it is believed to represent typical village development in the region (Fig. 2). This village came into existence during the oil boom of the 1870's and for a few years may have had a population of about 400. By 1880 its population had declined to about 100. In 1930 its population was 129.

[7]Tenth Census of the United States, *Agriculture*, Vol. III, p. 131.

[8]*Cram's Township and Railroad Map of Pennsylvania*, Philadelphia, 1881. Population estimates are given for villages.

[9]*Op. Cit.*, Tenth Census of the United States 1880, p. 131; and Fourteenth Census of the United States 1920, *Agriculture*, Vol. VI, Part I, pp. 262-265.

[10]William S. Lytle: *Crude Oil Reserves of Pennsylvania*, Topographic and Geologic Survey, Bulletin M32, 1950, pp. 56-59.

[11]*Rand McNally Commercial Atlas of America*, Chicago, 1924, pp. 143-163.

[12]*Railroad map of Pennsylvania*, Department of Internal Affairs, Harrisburg, 1920; and Op. Cit., *Rand McNally Commercial Atlas of America*, pp. 141-142.

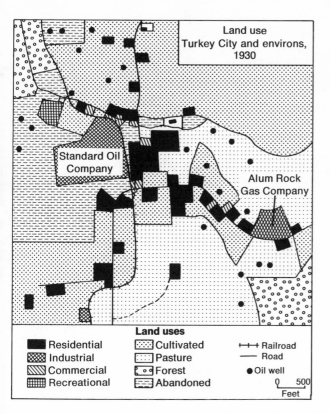

Land use
Turkey City and environs,
1930

Standard Oil
Company

Alum Rock
Gas Company

Land uses

■ Residential	▨ Cultivated	┼┼┼ Railroad
▧ Industrial	⬚ Pasture	— Road
▨ Commercial	⚬ Forest	● Oil well
▤ Recreational	▤ Abandoned	0 500
		Feet

Fig. 2. Land use in Turkey City and environs, 1930.

The economic and cultural functions of the village portray its importance to its immediate area. The commercial services of the village were well developed in 1930. The village contained two general stores, two garages, a meat market, a postoffice, a barber shop, a watch repairman, a boarding house, and a machine shop. Turkey City could provide for most of the basic economic needs of the rural people within several miles of the village.

Turkey City was also a local transportation node. The village was served by four passenger trains daily, two north to Buffalo and two south to Pittsburgh, and two freight trains. A railroad paddy crew operated from headquarters in this village for maintaining the railroad facilities. There was also a road repair crew working from headquarters in this village. Largely because Turkey City occupied a crossroads position, it was a focal center for distributing the farm products and minerals of the local area. A large percentage of the immediate area around the village was in farms specializing in dairying. A milk depot in the village, established by the farmers, served as a collecting point for fluid milk which was marketed in the Pittsburgh area. The natural gas pumping station of the

Alum Rock Gas Company and the petroleum pumping station of the Standard Oil Company provided links in the transportation system of western Pennsylvania to market the petroleum and natural gas resources of the region.

The village was also a cultural and recreational center for the local area. A one room school existed in Turkey City in which the first eight grades were taught. A community church, non-denominational in nature, was the center for many community endeavors such as socials and dinners. The village general stores were major gathering spots for a social evening of card playing and dispersal of local news. There was also a community picnic park with a roller skating rink-dance pavilion.

Of the age structure of the village population in 1930, 72 of the 129 persons were between 20 and 60 years of age, 52 were less than 20 years, and only five were over 60 years old. There were only two retired men in the village, and one widow. At this time there were 38 wage earners in the village. Of the 35 men employed in the community, nine farmers lived in the village, 10 were employed in the oil industry, nine in transportation industries, six in commercial and professional activities, and one was a handy man. Only three men were employed outside the local area, one in St. Petersburg, three miles away, and two in Foxburg, five miles away.

There was no manufacturing in this village in 1930. Manufacturing was noticeably absent in more than 95 per cent of the villages of the six counties. In a survey of manufacturing in the six counties in 1930, of a total of 16,560 employees, 80 per cent were located in the larger towns and cities, 17 per cent in villages and only three per cent in rural areas.[13] Where manufacturing had developed in villages, the refining of petroleum was most important and in a few places the processing of local agricultural products, particularly dairy products, and lumber had developed.

Besides the economic and cultural functions of the village, there was also the residential function. Thirty-two families maintained homes in Turkey City in 1930. All families lived in single houses. Although the houses were sufficiently close to give a sense of compactness there was considerable open space in the village. Most of the residential structures were modest. In Turkey City only four houses could have been considered above average for the village as a whole, and only two were below average. Most of the village dwellers lived on the same economic level. The homes reflected a fairly prosperous middle income economy. The village lot was large so that 30 of the 32 homes

[13]*Seventh Industrial Directory of the Commonwealth of Pennsylvania*, Department of Internal Affairs, 1931.

had a vegetable garden. Many of the village dwellers also raised chickens, pigs, and kept a cow and a calf. Consequently the village dweller occupied a mid-position between the rural dweller and the city dweller in providing his own food supplies.

DECLINE OF THE RURAL ECONOMY SINCE THE LATE 1920's

Beginning in the late 1920's the rural economy began a decline which is still in progress. This decline has been experienced by all phases of the rural economy. The abandonment of farmland and lowering of agricultural productivity is quite striking within the six counties. The amount of farmland has declined from 1,513,000 acres in 1920 to 1,062,000 in 1950.[14] The decrease in value of farmland and buildings from $93,166,000 in 1920 to $54,111,000 by 1940 is even more significant.[15] This reflects decline not only in quantity of farmland but also its quality. A considerable amount of cultivated land reverted first to pasture, which in turn was abandoned.

There has also been a noticeable decline in the mineral output of the region. The number of coal miners has decreased from about 18,000 in 1920 to 4,220 by 1955.[16] Coal mining as a source of livelihood has essentially disappeared from many sections of the six counties where it was once of major importance. The oil industry has declined sharply in the region. Oil output has decreased from 2,693,000 barrels in 1921 to 1,270,000 in 1954.[17] A majority of the full-time oil workers in the region have disappeared, and most of the remaining oil field operators are part-time employees. The virgin forests of the six counties are depleted and there is little second-growth timber to foster a thriving lumber industry.

As a result of the decline of the rural economy, the economic basis which fostered village growth prior to 1920 has greatly deteriorated. A pertinent question now is, how has the village population adjusted to the altered economic conditions? Between 1920 and 1950 the total population of the six counties grew from 317,751 to 335,921, certainly a modest increase. The total village population rose from 63,250 to 66,200.[18] Although village population grew mod-

erately from 1920 to 1950, the town and city population actually declined from 136,089 to 133,486. In contrast the rural population grew from 118,412 to 136,235. This increase is due to the growth of the rural non-farm population reflecting the trend of movement of people from the cities to nearby rural areas. The villages, however, have attracted few people from this migration. If people prefer to live in uncongested areas, then neither the environment of villages nor cities is particularly attractive, and they usually seek the open country. Rural areas are no longer isolated due to the rapid transportation provided by the automobile.

Within the region, the village population reflects some differences in its growth patterns. In the least industrialized counties of Clarion and Forest, the village population has actually declined since 1920. The village population has had its greatest growth in Butler and Armstrong Counties since 1920. The increase in village population in these counties has been in the larger villages near major industrial cities.

The number of villages has decreased from 322 in 1920 to 273 in 1955.[19] With the decline in the importance of the railroad, many of the smaller railroad villages, that were also poorly served by highways, have decreased in population and some have disappeared as agglomerated settlements. Also, some of the smaller villages, particularly those serving the needs of mining areas, have disappeared.

PRESENT DAY VILLAGE FUNCTIONS

As the original economic basis for village existence ebbed, the functions of the villages have been altered since the 1920's. Basically, the commercial and social functions have declined and the residential function has become increasingly important. Turkey City will be used as a typical example to illustrate present day village functions (Fig. 3). In 1955 the population of this village was 123, just slightly below its population of 1930. However, its economic and cultural functions have changed remarkably. Of its commercial functions only two general stores remained in 1955, one of which was open only part of the time. The decline of commercial service is primarily due to two factors. The local economy has declined and with it the local market. Possibly more important, the local inhabitants are now able to shop, due to the automobile, in the larger towns where there is not only a greater choice of goods, but also lower prices due to chain stores.

The transportation function has also deteriorated. Passenger train service was discontinued in the early

[14]*Op. Cit.*, Fourteenth Census of the United States 1920, pp. 262-265; and Sixteenth Census of the United States 1950, *Agriculture*, Vol. 1, Part II.

[15]Fifteenth Census of the United States 1940, *Agriculture*, Vol. I, Part I, pp. 354-359.

[16]*Report of the Department of Mines of Pennsylvania*, Part II—Bituminous, 1919-1920, pp. 44-47; and *Annual Report*, Bituminous Division, Department of Mines, Pennsylvania, 1955, pp. 26-27.

[17]John J. Schanz, Jr.: *Historical Statistics of Pennsylvania's Mineral Industries 1759-1955*, Mineral Conservation Series, Paper I, University Park, Pennsylvania, pp. 32-35.

[18]*Rand McNally Commercial Atlas and Marketing Guide*, Chicago, 1951, pp. 377-387.

[19]*Rand McNally Commercial Atlas and Marketing Guide*, Chicago, 1956, pp. 372-373. Personal survey ascertained present village distribution.

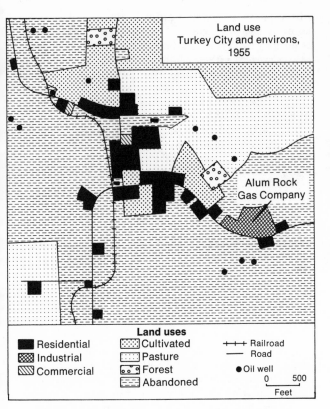

Land use
Turkey City and environs,
1955

Alum Rock
Gas Company

Land uses

■ Residential	░ Cultivated	+++ Railroad
▨ Industrial	░ Pasture	— Road
▧ Commercial	◦ Forest	● Oil well
	▤ Abandoned	0 500
		Feet

Fig. 3. Land use in Turkey City and environs, 1955.

1930's and freight service in 1937. With the abandonment of farm land, and decrease in agricultural output, the milk depot was closed in 1935. With the decline of local oil supplies, for the last well was drilled in 1926, and the development of more powerful oil pumping stations elsewhere, the oil pumping station was abandoned in 1933. The gas pumping station remains, but it is now a booster station receiving its gas from outside the state.

No manufacturing industries developed in Turkey City between 1930 and 1955. Of a total employment of 29,114 in manufacturing in 1955 within the six counties, 23,455, or 80.5 per cent, were located in cities, 3,365 in villages, or 11.5 per cent, and 2,294, or 7.8 per cent, in rural areas.[20] As a percentage of total employment in manufacturing the villages declined 5.5 per cent since 1930; at the same time the rural areas increased 4.8 per cent. The percentage of manufacturing employment in towns and cities remained stable.

A number of cultural functions have likewise declined. The building of a consolidated school in St.

[20]*Industrial Directory of the Commonwealth of Pennsylvania,* Fourteenth Edition, Department of Internal Affairs, 1956.

Petersburg, three miles away, resulted in the closing of the local school in 1931. The ball park has been abandoned, and the roller rink-dance pavilion was destroyed by fire in 1934 and not rebuilt. The picnic park has also been abandoned. The custom of visiting when purchasing supplies at the local stores, has declined with the importance of the local stores. However, one new church has been added to the community since 1930, and regular services are held in the two existing churches. In the past 25 years, there has been little or no decline of the religious functions of the villages in the six counties.

Of the age structure of the village population in 1955, 61 of the 123 persons were between 20 and 60 years of age, 38 were less than 20 years, and 24 were over 60. There were six retired men in the village and five widows. The average of the village population was considerably older than in 1930. In 1955, 38 wage earners maintained a home in Turkey City, the same number as in 1930. Of these 38 only five were employed locally, and of these five, two were in business, and one each in farming, the gas industry, and transportation. The other 33 wage earners were employed from three to 114 miles away. The importance of trades learned locally appears in the type of employment of many of the commuting workers at the present time: ten are engaged in the oil industry, six in construction, eight are factory employees, three are in transportation, and one each in coal mining, teaching and accounting. Three women were employed outside the village in secretarial work.

Although the economic and social functions of the village have declined greatly, the residential function has correspondingly grown in importance. This function, now the basic motive for village existence, has remained for a number of reasons. With the excellent paved road system and the rapid transportation of the automobile, a wage earner is no longer limited to local job opportunities. Commuting 60 to 100 miles a day is common in this six county area.

Commuting is practical because of certain economic and intrinsic values which the villages possess. In the larger towns and cities, housing is frequently scarce and if available costly. The village homes are fairly old and demand for housing is limited, so that if a house owner were to sell his home he could not purchase a comparable house in the larger urban centers. Besides this factor, cost of living in villages is lower than in cities due to such factors as lower taxes, and fewer expenses such as for water, sewage disposal, and police protection.

There is also the consideration that many people prefer the village environment in which to live. This may be due to family attractions, lack of congestion, or to the friendliness of the village group. Although many of the younger people are migrating from the villages because of lack of economic opportunity, others remain simply because it is home. There is considerable evidence that village life is becoming more urbanized. In 1955 only about one-half of the village dwellers had gardens, and only a few raised pigs and chickens for home consumption.

CONCLUSIONS

The village is today in a period of transition. The maintenance of the village form of settlement appears to depend on the availability of economic opportunity in the larger towns and cities in the region, and the continuance of a type of life within the villages that is desired by certain individuals. In conclusion, most of the present villages will persist, but in the role of residential dormitory centers serving as dispersed suburbs of larger towns and cities.

ACKNOWLEDGMENTS

The writer wishes to express his appreciation for aid granted by the College of Mineral Industries of the Pennsylvania State University for field work and for valuable cartographic assistance from Reed J. Dunn, Jr., research graduate assistant.

Why city workers live in agricultural villages

P. D. CONVERSE and RAMONA J. RUSSELL *

Agricultural villages came into existence as supply, shipping, and service stations for farmers. Farm population has been declining for some forty years. Paved roads and automobiles enable the farmers to by-pass the villages and transact some of their business in larger towns. This has meant a declining business for the villages, which has led to a surplus of workers or a surplus of houses. Some men who could no longer find employment in the villages found jobs in larger towns and continued to live in their former homes, driving back and forth to work. Some workers in larger towns secured houses and moved into these villages.

The study reported here was undertaken to ascertain to what extent the agricultural villages in East Central Illinois have become residential suburbs of the larger towns; why workers in large towns live in villages; how they like village life; and how the place of employment affects their shopping habits.

It was found that 23 percent of heads of village households work out of town; 48 percent work in their home villages or in villages or on farms near by; and 29 percent are retired. Omitting households of retired persons, one-third of the employed persons in these villages work out of town. In villages situated within 12 miles of a large town (over 10,000 population), 55 percent of the employed heads of households work out of town, principally in the nearest large town. This percentage drops to 29 for villages 12 to 25 miles from large towns, and to 15 for villages 25 miles or more from the large towns. Out-of-town workers from the last group work in widely scattered places. This fact indicates that workers do not like to drive 25 miles to work.

Most villages within 12 miles of large towns have become residential suburbs of the larger towns, whereas villages situated more than 25 miles from a large town have not. Those situated 12 to 25 miles from large towns might be called quasi-suburbs.

The principal reasons why workers from larger towns move to villages have been their inability to find houses in the larger towns; lower rents and other living costs in the villages; the fact that people in the villages are friendlier than those in large towns; and their feeling that the villages are good places in which to live and to raise their children. Most of those working out of town are satisfied with life in the villages, although a considerable portion would move to the larger towns to get closer to their work if they could find houses there.

Before taking up the detailed findings of this survey, let us take a look at the history of the problem.

HISTORICAL BACKGROUND

The Mississippi Valley was settled under a railroad-and-horse geography. The railroads placed their stations four to six miles apart and around these grew up villages which served as supply depots for surrounding farms, as shipping points for farm products, and as service stations (schools, churches, doctors,

☐ From Current Economic Comment **12**:37-46, Aug. 1950.
*P. D. Converse is Professor of Marketing at the University of Illinois. Ramona J. Russell is Junior Statistician at the University of Illinois.

banks, repair shops) for the population. County seats were established every twenty to thirty miles. Most of them grew into larger trading centers with more stores and stores carrying wider assortments of goods than were available in the small villages. Many of the county seats developed into *primary* trading centers. This system developed with the railroads in the 1850-1890 period in Illinois and continued until the coming of the automobile in the 1920's. Although the automobile came into considerable use in the 1910's, it was not until the 1920's, with the coming of improved roads and more widespread ownership, that it materially changed our rural economy.

A general statement has been made that people do not want to spend more than an hour going to market except on unusual shopping trips. With villages four to six miles apart, most farmers were within four miles of a village trading center and could reach it in an hour with a team and wagon (except at times when the roads were so deep in mud that they were well-nigh impassable). With the coming of the automobile the farmer could travel ten, twenty, thirty, or forty miles in an hour, depending upon conditions of the road and car and parking difficulties. Thus in the early 1920's many students of marketing were saying that the small agricultural villages were doomed; that they were no longer needed. Some village residents disputed this statement and contended that their villages still served a useful purpose.

INTRODUCTION

In 1926, the senior writer became interested in this situation and started to gather information on it. This resulted in a bulletin published by the Bureau of Business Research of the University of Illinois in 1928, *The Automobile and the Village Merchant.* That study found that rural population was declining as a result of larger farms and smaller families; and that the sales of village merchants were declining but at a much slower rate than was generally supposed. A second study on this subject, by Robert V. Mitchell, was published by the Bureau in 1939, *Trends in Rural Retailing in Illinois, 1926 to 1938.* This study showed a continued although slow decline in the sales of village stores. A third study of the subject is planned by the Bureau of Economic and Business Research (the name was changed in 1942).

The first study pointed out that traffic could move in both directions on a highway and that the village merchants might be able to pull trade from the larger towns by their lower prices. In the 1938 survey it was found that very few village merchants, except filling stations and restaurants, had been successful in attracting much trade from residents of larger towns. However, although the villages might not attract cus-

tomers to their stores from the larger towns, they could and did attract workers in these towns as residents.

In the first study (1926-27), it was found that some families from larger towns were living in near-by villages, attracted by lower rents; and some workmen from these villages were working in the larger towns but continuing to live in their home towns. With the decline of sales in village stores and of services demanded by a smaller rural population (e.g., doctors, bankers, teachers) fewer houses were needed by local workers. Were these houses to be left empty and allowed to fall to ruin? In a few cases that happened. However, one observes in driving through these villages that most of the houses are occupied. Conversation with residents of these villages and with employers in larger towns revealed that many people live in the agricultural villages and work in larger towns. In 1938 businessmen in some villages said that villages near larger towns could survive as residential suburbs, but that those at a distance would have to develop local industries or gradually "dry up." Is this true? Just how far will people drive to work?

The area selected for study lies between Kankakee on the north and Mattoon on the south; and between Bloomington and Decatur on the west and the Indiana state line on the east. This area is approximately 75 × 110 miles and is thought to be representative of much of Illinois.

In many parts of the nation, large numbers of industrial workers have moved to the country and live along the highways. Some of these have gardens or "subsistence" farms. Others do not and apparently moved to the country because of lower-priced land, to erect their own houses free from building restrictions, or because they like the "fresh air and openness" of the country. If our observations are correct there has been less of this in East Central Illinois than in some other regions. Instead there is considerable use of houses in the agricultural villages by people working in the larger towns; in this area the principal larger places are Kankakee, Chanute Field (at Rantoul), Champaign-Urbana, Danville, Bloomington, Decatur, and Mattoon.

THE SURVEY

The territory contains 118 villages which had 1940 populations of between 200 and 2,500. Of these villages, 29 were selected for the sample by giving each a number and selecting numbers at random. This sample was modified in a few instances by omitting a few villages located at considerable distances from other selected villages and substituting villages of similar size located at similar distances from larger towns. This was done to reduce travel distances for the interviewers. Within the villages, interviewers were instructed to call on every second, third, fourth, or fifth household. In case this proportion would not cover the entire village, interviewers were instructed to select territories in different parts of the village. Thus a modified random sample was used.

A somewhat larger proportion of the households were interviewed in the small than in the large villages. If conditions were different in villages of different sizes, this might distort the results, and so some of the questions were weighted by village populations. Results were changed so little that most of the figures presented here are unweighted by village size.

The 29 villages chosen were divided into three area groups according to their distances from a large town. Area 1 includes 9 villages within twelve miles of a large town. Area 2 includes 13 villages between twelve and twenty-five miles from a large town. Area 3 includes 7 villages twenty-five miles or more from a large town. In all, 940 interviews were made, distributed as follows: Area 1, 244 interviews; Area 2, 432 interviews; and Area 3, 264 interviews.

The survey covered households and not individuals. The word "household" instead of "family" is used in order to follow the changed nomenclature of the Bureau of the Census. As used in this study it is synonymous with the former "family," including one-person families.

The survey was a joint study by the advanced marketing research class of the University of Illinois and the Bureau of Economic and Business Research. The interviewing was done by students working under the immediate supervision of staff members who acted as crew leaders or foremen.

DISTRIBUTION OF INCOMES

The percentages of households in each income group for the three groups of households—heads employed out of town, heads employed in town, and heads retired—are shown in Table 1.

It will be noted that those working out of town tend

Table 1. Percentage distribution of households by income groups

Income group (yearly basis)	Head of household		
	Working out of town	Working in town	Retired
A—$7,200 or more	3	6	3
B—$4,200-$7,199	22	23	5
C—$2,500-$4,199	57	42	12
D—$1,300-$2,499	15	24	25
E—less than $1,300	3	5	55

to concentrate somewhat more in the middle or C income group than do those working in town or near by. Somewhat larger proportions of households with heads working in town are found in the A, D, and E income groups. Retired families are mostly in the D and E groups, although 8 percent are in the A and B groups.

Rents paid. Seventy-nine percent of the village households own their homes and 21 percent rent the dwellings they occupy. Ninety-two percent of the retired group, 77 percent of those employed locally, and 67 percent of those employed out of town own their homes.

The average monthly rental paid by respondents giving the information was $31.42. The most common figure was $40 a month, with $30 next. Other typical figures were: $15, $25, $35, and $50. Eighty-two percent of those reporting paid from $15 to $50 a month. Twelve percent paid less than $15 and 6 percent paid more than $50.

WHERE VILLAGE RESIDENTS WORK

Twenty-three percent of the heads of village households work out of town; 48 percent work in town, or at a nearby village or farm; and 29 percent are retired, pensioned, on relief, unemployed, or odd-job workers. Those in the third group will hereafter be referred to as retired.

The proportion of people working out of town varies greatly with the distance from a larger town. In Area 1, 42 percent of household heads work out of town; in Area 2 this percentage drops to 20; and in Area 3 to 10. The following tabulation summarizes, in percentages, the information as to where heads of households work.

	Area			
	1	2	3	Average
Works out of town	42	20	10	23
Works in home town or near by	34	50	59	48
Retired	24	30	31	29

Omitting the retired group, and considering only those households where the heads are employed, it is found that almost one-third of these employed persons work out of town and two-thirds in their home towns or near by. In Area 1, 55 percent of employed heads of households work out of town; in Area 2, 29 percent; and in Area 3, 14 percent. The sample in Area 3 included 7 villages. Three of these had 1940 populations between 1,000 and 2,500, and 4 had populations of less than 1,000. In the 3 larger villages 13 percent of the employed heads of households, and in the 4 smaller villages 18 percent, worked out of town.

In Area 1, most of the out-of-town workers (92 percent) work in the nearest large town. In Area 2, this percentage drops to 50; and in Area 3 to 17. Some out-of-town workers work in other states and even in foreign countries, but the majority of those who do not work in the nearest large town work in smaller towns closer to their homes.

These figures refer only to heads of households. Eleven percent of the households whose heads are employed out of town reported other members of the household also working out of town. Additional members of 10 percent of the households whose head is employed locally work out of town. In 6 percent of the households where the head is not employed other members work out of town. As the total number of employed persons in these households is not known, no definite figure can be given as to the total proportion of employed persons working out of town. However, it may be somwhat more than one-third. In villages within 12 miles of a primary trading-industrial center, probably three-fifths of the employed persons work out of town.

It appears that villages within 12 miles of industrial-trading centers are primarily suburbs of the larger towns. The proportion of people working out of town decreases beyond 12 miles, and there appears to be a strong resistance to driving 25 or more miles to work.

KIND OF WORK DONE BY PERSONS EMPLOYED OUT OF TOWN

Most of the persons employed out of town are skilled workers, unskilled workers, and business and professional men. Skilled workers easily lead in number. Skilled and unskilled workers constitute 63 percent of out-of-town workers. Business and professional men make up 15 percent of the total. The other 22 percent are engaged in a great variety of occupations. These proportions do not vary greatly among the 3 areas, with the exception that most of the military employees at Chanute Field interviewed lived within 12 miles of the Field. The following tabulation presents the percentage distribution of out-of-town workers by type of work.

Type of work	Percentage of workers
Skilled	41
Unskilled	22
Business and professional	15
Truck and bus drivers	6
Army	6
Clerical	4
Salesmen	4
Government	2

RETIRED FAMILIES

It is well known that a considerable number of people living in the small towns and villages are retired. In the households surveyed, 29 percent are in this group. Many of these are one-person households. Of the total in this group 72 percent reported the head of the household as "retired," 23 percent as pensioned, 4 percent as doing odd jobs, and 1 percent as on relief. Probably many of those classifying themselves as "retired" are on relief. There is very little variation in the proportions of households in these classifications for the three areas.

WHY OUT-OF-TOWN WORKERS LIVE IN VILLAGES

The second object of the survey was to learn why persons working in other towns live in the villages. They may be people who had lived in these villages and who, when they were unable to find work or to find jobs at satisfactory wages there, obtained jobs elsewhere and continued to live in their established homes. On the other hand, they may be persons who work in larger towns and live in smaller towns either because they are unable to find houses in the towns where they work or because they prefer living in a smaller town. People may prefer to live in villages for several reasons: rents may be lower; other living costs may be lower; they may think the environment is better for raising children; people may be friendlier; there may be more room for a garden, chickens, or pets; and possibly other reasons. One man said he preferred to live in a village because the summer nights were cooler.

The reasons out-of-town workers gave for living in these villages are summarized as follows:

Reason given	Percentage of households
Have always lived here, this is my home, etc.	34
Own property here	4
Relatives live here	3
Like it here	5
Quieter here	3
People are friendlier	5
Better place to raise children	6
Couldn't get house in town where I work	17
Cheaper to live here	10
Rent lower	3
Convenient to work	5
Miscellaneous reasons	5

One-third of the out-of-town workers are obviously old residents who have obtained work out of town either because there is no local work available or because they can get higher pay elsewhere. If with these are included those who own property and those who have relatives in the villages, the conclusion is that two-fifths are old residents who now work out of town.

One-sixth of the out-of-town workers live in the villages because they could not find places to live in the towns where they work. Most of these apparently moved to the villages since the housing shortage developed, probably since 1943. It may be that the majority of those who say they live in the village because living costs or rents are lower are also relative newcomers.

The length of time workers have lived in their present towns will throw some light on the question.

	Percentage of household heads	
Years of residence	**Working out of town**	**Working in town**
Less than 1	14	6
1 or 2	13	9
3 or 4	18	14
5 or 6	9	6
7 or 8	7	7
9 or 10	4	7
More than 10	35	51

It will be observed that 27 percent of the out-of-town workers have lived in the villages two years or less and 54 percent have lived there six years or less. It seems safe to assume that the great majority of these families are not natives of these villages but moved there to find a place to live or because they like village life. Thirty-five percent of the households of out-of-town workers have lived in the villages more than 10 years. Most of these are probably old residents who have found work in other towns and continue to live in their village homes. Considering all the evidence, we may conclude that one-half or more of the out-of-town workers are relative newcomers in their villages and moved there because of ability to find a house, because rents are lower, because other living costs are lower, or because they like village life. This would indicate that 10 to 15 percent of all village households are those of workers in other towns who are relative newcomers in the villages. The percentage is higher in Area 1 and lower in Area 3.

HOW VILLAGE RESIDENTS LIKE VILLAGE LIFE

In order to ascertain how the respondents like life in the villages, they were asked: "Would you move to another town if you could find a place to live there?" The following tabulation shows a percentage distribution of the replies.

Reply	**Working out of town**	**Working in town**	**Retired**
Yes	31	16	10
No	60	81	83
Don't know	9	3	7

Thus, less than one-third of those working out of town say that they would move if they could find a place to live in another town.

Those who answered "yes" were asked: "Why do you want to move?" The percentages of those who gave various reasons are shown, by employment location:

Reason given	**Working out of town**	**Working in town**	**Retired**
Like larger town	12	25	11
To get closer to work	62	8*	11*
To get closer to friends or relatives		2	26
To get better jobs	7	43	19
Other reasons	19	22	33

*Other members of household

The main reason why those working out of town would like to move is to be closer to work, whereas those working in town would like to get better jobs. They are satisfied to live where they are but would be willing to move if they could secure higher-paying employment.

Those who answered "no" were asked, "Why don't you want to move?" A percentage distribution of their reasons for not wishing to move is as follows:

Reason given	**Working out of town**	**Working in town**	**Retired**
Like it here	32	19	21
This is home	13	13	23
Like small town	7	5	
Own home	21	13	21
Friends or relatives here	8	5	12
Cheaper here	5		1
Too old to move	3	2	14
Work here	3*	34	4*
Other reasons	8	9	4

*Other members of household

When those who said they did not want to move were asked whether they had ever considered moving,

84 percent of the retired households, 79 percent of those who work in their home towns, and 58 percent of the out-of-town workers said they had not done so. Thirty-eight percent of the out-of-town workers who reported that they had considered moving said that they had not done so because they couldn't find places to live; 15 percent because they like it "here"; 8 percent because they couldn't afford higher rent in larger towns; 7 percent because they own their homes; and 7 percent additional who own their homes, because they couldn't sell them; 2 percent because living costs are lower; and the others gave a variety of reasons.

These answers indicate that some of the respondents live in the villages only because they were able to find houses there, and that they would really prefer to live elsewhere. However, the great majority of village residents are satisfied with living conditions. The answers to these questions throw considerable light on the advantages of village life. A friendlier, quieter, better place to raise children, and lower living costs are very definite and often valuable reasons. It may be pointed out in passing that village life is not the drab, isolated existence which was so often pictured in the decades prior to the automobile, moving pictures, and radio. Village residents not only have the home entertainment of papers, magazines, and television and radio but community entertainment through school, church, and other local organizations. The automobile brings them close to the amusement, recreational, and cultural facilities of the larger towns. A resident of a small village put it this way: "I live 24 miles from a city of 50,000. In 30 minutes I can be at any of the city stores, movies, lectures, athletic contests, entertainments, or cultural events. As for drive-in movies or roadside tea rooms near the city, I can get there as quickly as most of the city residents."

GETTING TO WORK

Seventy-five percent of those who work out of town travel to work in their own cars, 9 percent in friends' cars, and 8 percent in car pools. Thus 92 percent travel by car. The others travel by bus, employers' truck, interurban, airplane, ship, and railroad. The three last-named types of transportation are used by those working long distances from their homes. The great majority (97 percent) said that they were satisfied with their transportation.

The majority of out-of-town workers have apparently given little thought to the cost of transportation. Less than half would attempt to estimate the cost. Of those who did make estimates, one-half thought it was less than 60 cents a day, and one-third, more than $1 a day.

HOW PLACE OF EMPLOYMENT AFFECTS PLACE OF SHOPPING
Shopping goods

Do persons who work out of town do more shopping out of town than persons who work in the town where they live? In order to answer this question, the respondents were asked, "Where did your family last purchase woman's coat, woman's good dress, man's suit, man's shoes, groceries, and drugs?" Four of these articles are shopping items and two are convenience goods. Based on past experiences in trade area surveys, it was felt that these items are typical of the two classifications and would provide a reasonably accurate answer. This question was asked only of households that had lived in a village for two or more years. People who move to a different town bring shopping goods with them and do some of their shopping in their former homes until they become familiar with the stores in the new area. Two years was thought long enough for households to wear out most of the clothing brought along when they moved and to adjust their shopping habits to their new residences.

It was found that the households of persons who work in town, as well as those of persons who work out of town, buy most of their clothing out of town. These villages for the most part do not have stores carrying satisfactory assortments of shopping goods. Households of locally employed persons, however, do buy somewhat more of their clothing locally and somewhat less in the nearest large shopping center than do those of persons who work out of town. The following tabulation shows percentage distributions of places where clothing is purchased, classified by employment location of household head.

Place of clothing purchases	Working out of town	Working in town
Nearest large trading center	69	58
Home town	2	8
Chicago	3	5
By mail	3	3
Other towns	23	26

Distance is a factor in deciding where people trade. Households in Area 1 buy a larger portion of their clothing in the nearest trading center than those in Area 2, and those in Area 2 buy more of their clothing in the nearest trading center than do those in Area 3. This is true both of households whose heads are employed out of town and of those whose heads are employed in town. This finding is in line with the law which says that the drawing power of a trading center decreases with distance. The households in Area 3 make only about one-third of their purchases of the apparel articles listed in the nearest shopping center. Several of the villages in Area 3 are approximately equidistant from two or more large shopping centers, and some are much closer to smaller shopping centers (towns between 5,000 and 10,000 population). Since a larger trading center has more gravitational pull or attraction than a smaller one, the nearest trading center not necessarily the dominant one. The finding here agrees with those of trade area studies in that towns at some distance from primary trading centers divide their trade among more towns than do those close to a large trading center.

One other question arises: What effect does size of village have on the proportion of shopping done out of town? It happened that three of the seven villages in Area 3 had more than 1,000 population. It is to be expected that the stores in the larger villages carry larger assortments of apparel than do the stores in the small villages. Therefore separate tabulations were made for households with employed heads in the villages having populations between 1,000 and 2,500 and in those of less than 1,000. It was found that in the three larger villages 25 percent of the apparel articles listed were purchased in home-town stores, as compared with one percent for the four smaller villages.

Convenience goods

Most groceries and drugs are bought locally both by households with heads employed out of town and by those with heads working in town. However, the former buy more of their convenience goods out of town than the latter do. The place of employment seems to have more influence on the places where convenience goods are purchased than on those where shopping goods are purchased. It appears that many persons employed in trading center towns buy many of their groceries and drugs there and bring them home as they return from work. Percentages for the two groups, shown in the following tabulation, support these conclusions.

Place of convenience goods purchases	Working out of town	Working in town
Nearest trading center	32	16
Home town	54	74
Near-by small town	6	8
Other towns	8	2

As the distance from the trading center increases, fewer groceries are purchased in the trading center and more are purchased in the home town. This is true both of those who work in town and of the out-of-town workers.

Socio-economic characteristics of part-time and full-time farmers in the twin-cities area

GEORGE A. DONOHUE*

The downward trend in the percent of population engaged in farming over the years is more striking when the increasing percentage of farm operators working off their farms is taken into consideration. Approximately one fourth of the nation's farm operators engage in such a practice. In some states the trend has been not only to have more of the farm population engaged in off-farm work, but those who work off the farm to do so for longer periods of time.[1]

The extent to which farm operators are dependent on nonfarm sources of income is considered as contributing to increased heterogeneity and instability in the rural social structure.[2] Current sociological analysis holds that the distinctly rural society is characterized by a relatively high degree of homogeneity with respect to social values and behavior patterns, and that the urban or rural-urban fringe is characterized by heterogeneity with respect to occupation, social values, personal behavior and interest groups. The general hypothesis is that variations in social and economic factors contribute to behavior variations along the continuum from one extreme to the other.

The present paper bears upon this general hypothesis in analyzing the socio-economic and attitudinal differences between part-time and full-time operators. Part-time farmers are defined as those working 100

☐ From *Journal of Farm Economics* **39**(4):984-992, 1957.
*Professor of Rural Sociology, University of Minnesota.
[1]A. F. Raper, *Rural Trends*, U.S.D.A., Washington, D.C., 1952, p. 8.

[2]Cf. Lowry Nelson, *Rural Sociology*, New York: American Book Company, 1948, pp. 8-11; C. P. Loomis and J. A. Beegle, *Rural Social Systems*, New York: Prentice Hall, Inc., 1950, Appendix A; S. A. Queen and D. B. Carpenter, *The American City*, New York: McGraw Hill Book Co., 1953, pp. 19-27.

days or more off farm in the calendar year or with income from nonfarm sources exceeding the value of farm products sold. Full-time farmers are those with less than 100 days work off farm and value of farm products sold exceeding that from off-farm sources.

SOURCE OF DATA

The sample design was basically areal in nature. Initially a purposive selection of census tracts was made so as to exclude from the sample the immediate environs of the City of Minneapolis. The square-mile sections of land in these tracts were numbered to exclude from the sample any incorporated area. Then the selection was made by use of a table of random numbers. In view of the limitation on sample size the procedure of interviewing every part-time farmer in each area and every other full-time farmer was followed, to obtain an approximately equal split between full-time and part-time farmers for comparative purposes. Thus, the universe consideration consists of farmers residing outside of urban or incorporated areas in six purposively selected representative census tracts in Hennepin County, Minnesota.

The data were gathered by the technique of personal interview with 167 farm operators (census definition) during the later part of 1954 and the spring of 1955. The attitude data were gathered by field administration of a modified form of the Rundquist-Sletto Scale which included ten items from each of five of the original scales, only four of which are used in this analysis.[3]

METHOD OF ANALYSIS

The analysis is divided into two parts. In the first part the dependent variables under consideration are marital status, religion, socio-economic status (Sewell Scale),[4] farm organization membership, family size, visiting pattern, father's occupation, church attendance, income, size of farm.

The second part consists of an analysis of the factors associated with attitude scores of operators of a modified version of the Rundquist-Sletto Scale in the areas of family, law, education, and economic conservatism. The major independent variable is the type-of-farming operation. This is measured by the extent of off-farm work engaged in by the operator. The criterion of 100-or-more days of off-farm work segregated full from part-time farmers.[5]

---

[3]For an analysis of the scale construction and establishment of norms see E. A. Rundquist and R. F. Sletto, *Personality in the Depression*, Minneapolis: University of Minnesota Press, 1936. The scores on the modified form using ten items correlated .89 or higher on all four scales with the total scores on all the items. The items in the Rundquist-Sletto Scales consist of declarative statements with which the individual may indicate whether or not he agrees or disagrees and the intensity with which he agrees or disagrees on a five-point scale. The declarative statements are constructed on the basis of values and patterns considered to be generally accepted institutional patterns. For example, the family scale includes items such as "A man should be willing to sacrifice everything for his family;" "In making plans for the future, parents should be given first consideration." In the law scale are such items as "A man should obey the law no matter how much they interfere with his personal ambitions;" "Laws are so often made for the benefit of small selfish groups that a man cannot respect the law." In the education scale such items as "A man can learn more by working four years than by going to high school;" "An educated man can advance more rapidly in business and industry" are included. In the economic conservatism scale such items as "The government should take over all large-scale industry;" "Private ownership of property is necessary for economic progress" are included. In these scales values were assigned to the responses in such a way that a low total score indicated favorable attitudes toward existing family patterns, respect for existing law practices, economic conservatism and a high regard for the value of education. The items were arranged in random order.

Thus, when one refers to a favorable attitude towards law it indicates that the individual has respect for existing practices in the area of law, and an unfavorable attitude would be indicative of a desire to see changes in the basic value orientation of our legal institutions. The favorable attitude toward the economic institution would be one that reflects a general agreement on the part of the respondent with the values of a laissez faire model such as lack of government intervention, private property, profit maximization and individual initiative. A favorable attitude toward the family institution would indicate a desire to maintain a strong family bond with primary obedience and obligation to the parents. The favorable attitude towards education would be one that supported a value of compulsory public education and viewed education as both an end in itself and as a valuable aid to social and economic adjustment. Unfavorable attitudes in all cases would be ones that reflect the desire for social change in the basic institutional patterns of our culture.

[4]This scale contains 14 items relating to material possessions, cultural possessions, and social participation and has been found to be a valid and reliable indicator of socio-economic status among farm families in several states. The scale includes such items as type of house construction, presence or absence of lighting facilities, piped water, refrigeration, radio, telephone, automobile, power washer, room-person ratio, subscription to daily newspaper, education of wife and husband, and church participation. These items are scored so that the presence or absence of these characteristics within a family unit will indicate the relative socio-economic status of the farm families contained in the study. For a complete analysis of the scale construction and items, see, "A Short Form of the Farm Family Socio-Economic Status Scale," *Rural Sociology*, Vol. 8:2, June, 1943, pp. 161-170.

[5]A further sub-classification of part-time farmers was made on the basis of their long-term interest in carrying on the practice, and the economic relationship of their off-farm work to their farming operations. These divisions consisted of: (1) "Expanding Farmers," made up of individuals who engaged in off-farm work as a means of building up their farm with the intention of going into full-time farming in the future; (2) "Farming-Working," made up of individuals who considered it as a "Way of Life" with both the farm and nonfarm work necessary to their economic livelihood; and (3) "Hobby Farmers," consisting of persons of moderate and relatively high economic means, who engaged in the practice primarily as an avocation and were primarily dependent upon their nonfarm source of income. An analysis of differences in attitude orientation among these three groups was also carried out.

In analyzing the results of the attitude scales the independent variables used were (1) religion, (2) education, (3) age, (4) socio-economic status, (5) political affiliation, (6) union membership (for part-time farmers only), and (7) farm organization membership.

The Chi-square technique was used to test significance of differences and where the values were significant to the .05 level, corrected contingency coefficients were computed. Both total and partial association techniques were used in the analysis of attitude scales.

FINDINGS

Social differences. The part-time and full-time operators did not differ significantly on the following factors: (1) religious preference, (2) citizenship, (3) nationality, (4) church attendance and (5) motion picture attendance. Both groups were largely German-Catholics and German-Lutherans with church attendance averaging three times a month. Motion picture attendance averaged slightly more than once a year for both groups with the advent of television the reason most frequently given for the low rate.

While the full-time operators were traditionally Republican in their affiliation (53 per cent), part-time farmers differed by affiliating more frequently with the Democratic party (37 per cent) and Independent (33 per cent) than with the Republican (30 per cent).[6] The influence of the off-farm work situation, especially where union membership was required, appeared to have considerable effect on political affiliation among the part-time group.

Membership in farm organizations was significantly greater among full-time operators (35.4 per cent) than part-time operators (17.9 per cent). However, both groups were vocal about the lack of interest in the small farmer which they felt characterized the large farm organizations. The lack of membership by the part-time operator might be construed as a lack of identification with the full-time farmer and his problems. Such an interpretation might be warranted except for the relatively low membership and nominal participation of full-time operators in such organizations. Tradition rather than specific benefits was the reason most frequently given by those having active membership.[7]

Although 70 per cent of the part-time operators were born on a farm, the part-time farmer is more apt to have been born in a town (15 per cent) or city (15 per cent) than the full-time farmer. Only 9 per cent of

the full-time operators had nonfarm birth places.[8] When father's occupations of both the operator and his wife are considered, 46 per cent of part-time families have a history of farming as compared to 78 per cent of the full-time families. Neither the operator's father nor the wife's father engaged in farming among 19 per cent of the part-time farmers and 2 per cent of the full-time farmers.[9]

The visiting pattern of the part-time farmer differed significantly from that of the full-time farmer. The part-time farmer less often restricted himself to visiting only fellow farmers and visited much more frequently (28 per cent) with persons employed in other occupations than did the full-time farmer (9 per cent). Fellow workers in the nonfarm work situation appeared to be the major source of nonfarm friendships among part-time operators. The differential association of the part-time farmer in social visiting would be an additional source of nonfarm attitudes, interests, and problems.[10]

All of the part-time farmers in the sample were married while 7.1 per cent of the full-time farmers were single.[11] The single full-time operators were those who had taken over their parents' farm while the father went into semi-retirement, and in most cases still retained part or full ownership. Although part-time farmers were more frequently married, they tended to have a smaller family than the full-time operators,[12] as 62 per cent of the part-time farmers had 3-or-less children compared with 44 per cent of the full-time operators. The older age of full-time operators may account for more completed families and a higher average number of children.

The conception of the part-time operator as the marginal individual in the farm population, which largely resulted from the series of studies in the 1930's, is not supported by the data on socio-economic status of part-time and full-time farmers in the Twin Cities area. Among the part-time farmers 26.9 per cent rated high, 53.7 per cent medium and 19.4 per cent low on the Sewell scale, while the percentages for the full-time operators were 10.3, 64.9, and 24.7 respectively. Several of the part-time farmers with high socio-economic ratings were professional and businessmen who operated "hobby farms." Even if this group is excluded from consideration the part-time operator rates higher on socio-economic status than the full-time operator.[13]

Economic differences. The type of farming practiced by the part-time farmer does not differ from that

---

[6]p < .02, c = .34. In this notation p indicates the level of significance and c is the degree of association based on the corrected value of the contingency coefficient which approximates r.

[7]p < .02, c = .27

[8]p < .01, c = .40

[9]p < .01, c = .42

[10]p < .001, c = .43

[11]p < .01, c = .32

[12]p < .01, c = .36

[13]p < .05, c = .31

of the major type of farming practiced in the area. The dominant factors in determining the type of farming practiced appear to be the allied manufacturing, processing and commercial facilities, and the farming background of the part-time operators, most of whom are native to the area, rather than the nature and requirements of the off-farm job.

The average size of the part-time farm was 72 acres, 45 of which were under cultivation compared with an average size of 110 acres and 72 under cultivation for the full-time operator. The majority (51 per cent) of the part-time farmers had between 40 and 120 acres. Only 12 per cent had more than 120 acres compared with 37 per cent having more than 120 acres among the full-time farmers.[14] Gross farm income averaged $2,960 for the part-time group and $7,430 for the full-time operator. Although the discrepancy is rather large the economic picture for the part-time operator brightens when the average off-farm cash income of $3,678 is added to the farm income. Slightly more than one fourth (26 per cent) of the part-time farmers earned in excess of $5,000 at their nonfarm jobs.

In addition, 51 per cent of the part-time farm families reported other members besides the operator were working at nonfarm jobs as compared with 17 per cent of the full-time operators.[15]

The difference between full-time and part-time farmers was not only in of terms of the number of days worked off the farm but also in the type of off-farm work. The part-time operator was found largely in the skilled (46 per cent) and semi-skilled (28 per cent) areas while the full-time operator worked at clerical (16 per cent), unskilled (18 per cent), and custom agricultural work (45 per cent).[16]

The part-time operators also had a higher rate of farm ownership than the full-time operator, 88 per cent and 81 per cent respectively.[17]

There were no significant differences in the attitudes of part-time farmers and full-time farmers towards the type of government support program preferred. Slightly more than a third of each group preferred rigid supports, approximately a third flexible supports and a fourth of each group would like to see supports dropped completely. Both groups were practically unanimous in support of the thesis that agriculture is the backbone of the economy.

Differences in attitudes towards basic social institutions. Both total and partial association techniques were used in the analysis of the Rundquist-Sletto Scale scores on the family, law, education, and busi-

ness. Eight independent variables, (1) type-of-farming operation (part-time, full-time), (2) religion, (3) education, (4) age, (5) socio-economic status, (6) political affiliation, (7) union membership (part-time farmers only), and (8) farm organization membership were analyzed to determine their relationship to attitudes in each of the four areas. The results of this analysis are summarized below.

TOTAL ASSOCIATION

Attitudes towards family institution. No significant relationships were found between any of the independent variables and attitudes towards the family. The percentages of favorable and unfavorable responses among the independent variables were rather constant, with some variation with age. The younger and old-age groups expressed somewhat less favorable attitudes towards the family than did the middle-age group. Also the proportion of favorable responses towards the family increased with educational attainment. However, these differences were not statistically significant at the .05 level.

Attitudes towards law. Two variables, education[18] and type-of-farming operation (part-time, full-time)[19] showed a significant association with attitudes towards the law while the remaining seven did not. The more highly educated group had a much greater percentage of favorable responses than did either the medium- or low-education groupings. The part-time farming group, also, showed more favorable attitudes towards law than did the full-time farming group.

Attitudes towards economic institution. The factors age[20] and education[21] showed a significant association with attitudes towards the economic institution. Among the age groupings, the difference existed largely between the younger age grouping with 95 per cent favorable and the older age groups having only 78 per cent favorable. Among the education groups, the high group had 97 per cent responding favorably, the medium group, 81 per cent, and the low group, 70 per cent. The only other variable of the remaining seven to approach significance at the .05 level was the factor of political affiliation, the Republican and Independent had a more favorable attitude toward the economic institution than did the Democrats.

Attitudes towards education institution. Among the eight variables considered in the total association analysis with attitudes towards education, only type of *part-time* farming[22] and educational attainment[23] were significantly associated with the dependent var-

[14]p < .01, c = .24
[15]p < .01, c = .51
[16]p < .01, c = .74
[17]p < .02, c = .34

[18]p < .02, c = .33
[19]p < .05, c = .24
[20]p < .05, c = .29
[21]p < .02, c = .32
[22]p < .05, c = .47
[23]p < .01, c = .35

iable. The percentage of favorable responses towards education increased from the low (0-7 years) group to the medium group (8-10 years) to the high group (11 years and over). Among the part-time farmers, the "hobby" group, who rely primarily upon their non-farm employment, were the most favorable, and the "expanding farming" group, those who intend to go into full-time farming in the long run, and hence, may not value education so highly, tend to be the least favorable. The only other factor to approach statistical significance at the .05 level is that of socio-economic status with the high group somewhat more favorable in their attitudes towards education.

PARTIAL ASSOCIATION

Where an independent variable showed a significant relationship on the basis of total association a mechanical partialing was carried out to determine the extent to which the relationship held when the influence of other variables was controlled. The sample size prevented controlling more than one variable at a time. The degree of partial association was measured by computing the Chi-square value for the two-fold tables in the subsamples and where significant differences were found c was computed.

In the total association analysis two variables, education and type-of-farming operation showed a significant relationship with attitudes towards law. For purposes of partial analysis education was dichotomized into high (above 8th grade) and low (8th grade and below) and controlled, while type-of-farming operation was allowed to vary. Under these conditions, type-of-farming operation showed no significant relationship to the dependent variable of attitudes towards law. This indicates that the variation in attitude from part-time to full-time farmers in the zero-order analysis was a function of the variation in education rather than in type of farming.

In the partial analysis of attitudes towards education with education controlled and part-time farming, categorized into "hobby," "farming-working," and "expanding," permitted to vary, there was no statistically significant association between type of part-time farming and attitudes towards education as was the case in total association analysis, indicating that variation in attitude towards education was largely a function of education attainment. However, the relationship of education attainment[24] with favorable attitudes towards law when controlled on the basis of type-of-farming operation (full-time, part-time), is significantly associated only in the full-time farming subsample.

The variables of education and age showed a significant relationship to attitudes towards the economic institutions in the zero-order analysis. However, controlling on education (high, above 8th grade;

low, 8th grade and below) and permitting age (20-49, 50-over) to vary results in no statistically significant differences in the subsamples indicating that the variation in attitude is also largely a function of education rather than age. Controlling on age (20-49; 50-over) and permitting education to vary (high; low) a significant relationship is found in only the age group 20-49[25] with the high-education group being very favorable in their attitudes as contrasted with the low-education group.

Only the variable of education remains significantly related to the dependent variables under conditions of partial association and only within two of the subsamples, full-time farmers attitudes towards law and the 20-49 years-of-age group's attitudes toward the economic institution. In both samples the higher education group has more favorable attitudes.

SUMMARY

The part-time farmer differs significantly from the full-time farmer on a number of objective characteristics such as age, education, socioeconomic status, farm ownership, type of off-farm work, marital status and family size. Even though these differences exist they do not appear to have an appreciable effect in creating different attitude patterns among part-time and full-time farmers.

On the basis of the absence of significant differences among part-time and full-time farmers with respect to social attitudes, the thesis that the part-time farmer is a cultural hybrid and contributes to instability in the rural structure appears questionable. A fruitful avenue for further research might be to determine the degree to which the part-time farmers' urban participation tends to be nominal or passive, and thus results in little influence on his attitudes and behaviors outside of the immediate work situation. His reference group appears to be mainly that of the full-time operator.

A factor that may account for lack of significant differences is the extent to which part-time farmers are recruited from the full-time farm population, either as sons of farmers economically unable to engage in full-time farming, or as farmers on the brink of retirement, who have reduced their scale of operations and who engaged in off-farm work in order to supplement their small farm incomes. The individual of urban background without farming experience engaging in part-time farming was an extremely rare occurrence.

Plausibly, persons engaging in part-time farming (e.g., "hobby" farmers) may have, in addition to economic motivation, a personal value orientation in accord with the value orientation of full-time farmers and the rural social structure, thus contributing to homogeneity rather than heterogeneity.

[24] $p < .05$, $c = .32$

[25] $p < .02$, $c = .40$

Land disputes at the urban-rural border

PAUL RELIS*

Physically incoherent, socially disparate, [these new metropolitan districts] are at best statistical collections. Here and there in the mass one may partly trace the outline of a city: but the mass itself is not a city, in a functional sense, any more than the immediate countryside that surrounds it is a rural area.

LEWIS MUMFORD
The Culture of Cities

Over the past five years a land-use struggle has emerged in America that promises to be profoundly important to the future viability of our cities and our agricultural communities. This struggle has pitted our country's land speculation and development interests, as well as its banking institutions against a powerful grass-roots political movement whose aim is to contain urban sprawl at the existing urban-rural border.[1]

While the struggle is still being fiercely contested there are now many hopeful signs that suggest that containment of such sprawl may be achieved within the decade. Certain local and state governments have already implemented policies that have greatly curtailed the uncontrolled spread of urban development, and many more will no doubt follow their example in the very near future.

Five years ago no one would have predicted when or how urban sprawl could be controlled. It had such tremendous economic and political momentum that its spread seemed inexorable. Yet the past three years have seen the birth of an environmental revolution in our country. Americans have awakened to the fact that their resources are finite and that personal action is necessary to effect policies that will carefully conserve and distribute those resources that remain. In the process of their awakening, large segments of the public have come to identify sprawl as a major culprit in the deterioration of their environment and the decline of the quality of their lives.

This chapter discusses briefly some of the major problems created by urban sprawl into rural areas and some of the difficulties and successes citizen groups and governments have had in trying to contain it. I will be drawing heavily on examples from

California—since it is an area of our nation where the problem has been very acute and the public response most dramatic.

CALIFORNIA: A GOLDEN STATE TURNING GRAY

Nowhere in history have a people consumed natural resources as voraciously and rapidly as they have in the state of California. In barely one hundred years much of this fabled "golden state," noted for its rich and broad valleys, its vast timber resources, and seemingly endless coastline has been transformed into a depleted gray wasteland of spent opportunities.[2]

Already the landscape between the Mexican border and northern Los Angeles County (an area of about 700 square miles)—once an abundant stretch of agricultural lands, small towns, and metropolises—has disappeared under a wave of suburbs and shopping centers.

This tendency to expand the metropolis into the country has brought about a general surrender of human values and an undermining of the genuine values of the metropolis itself. The loss of any inner cohesion has left California cities, and indeed most other American cities, without the means to draw to themselves the rich and varied resources of their surrounding regions.

Consider the fate of the Los Angeles-Orange County area of southern California. As late as the postwar 1940s the city of Los Angeles was surrounded by prime agricultural lands. Within a radius of fifty miles from the civic center was enough agricultural productivity to satisfy most of the city's produce, dairy, and poultry needs and enough citrus to supply most of the nation. This fertile agricultural environment was the site of many small towns (generally with populations of less than 10,000) that provided goods and services for the farms and orchards of the region and acted as the supply, packaging, and shipping centers for the foodstuffs destined for Los Angeles and elsewhere in the nation.

Yet in the span of less than fifteen years this reciprocity between urban and rural functions was lost under a flood tide of urban expansion. Only a few scattered fields of croplands and orchards remained—more museum pieces than functional components of a once-healthy urban-rural economy.

*Paul Relis is director of the Community Environmental Council in Santa Barbara, California.

This change in the landscape of southern California was so alarming to many northern California residents that they began to suggest that California be divided into two separate states. But it wasn't long before the same forces that had virtually destroyed southern California were at work on the rich lands surrounding San Francisco and other communities on the coast and interior.

To the south of San Francisco lay the Santa Clara Valley, otherwise known as the "Valley of the Heart's Delight." Back in 1940 this valley was a fine example

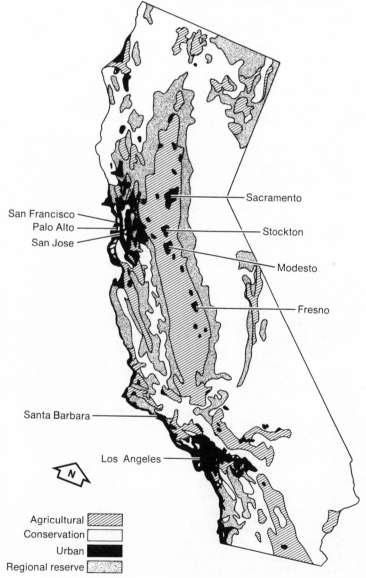

San Francisco
Palo Alto
San Jose

Sacramento

Stockton

Modesto

Fresno

Santa Barbara

Los Angeles

N

Agricultural
Conservation
Urban
Regional reserve

Fig. 1. The four state zones of California, showing the major urban areas described in text.

of a fully integrated agricultural community. The cities were functionally related to the entire agricultural matrix. San Jose, with a population of about 50,000, was the county seat and the center of a food processing industry. Six other towns with about 5,000 persons each were distributed around the valley, each performing specialized but interrelated agricultural functions.

These towns were the service centers for roughly 100,000 acres of orchards and 8,000 acres of vegetable crops, situated on two alluvial fans. The topsoil was a fine loam, thirty to forty feet deep in places, and underlaid by a tremendous underground water storage basin with a capacity of roughly one million acre-feet.[3] But within twenty years this California treasure, like its counterpart in the southern half of the state, became a victim of uncontrolled and unplanned urban expansion.

The stories of Santa Clara Valley and Los Angeles are only part of the continuing tragedy of California's (and the nation's) settlement pattern. For example, current estimates by the U.S. Soil Conservation Service, with respect to California, indicate that:

A total of 1,173,656 acres are expected to be urbanized and a total of 808,871 acres are expected to be devoted to recreation subdivision between 1967 and 1980 for a gross of 1,982,527 acres. This calculates out to be an average of 388 acres per day that will be converted during this period (1967-1980).

Approximately 25 percent of the total acreage that is expected to be converted is prime agricultural land (land capability classes I and II). This amounts to 528,600 acres which is 7.5 percent of the total 7.2 million acres of prime land available for agriculture in California.

It is largely on these prime lands that the specialty crops are produced that make a substantial contribution to the total agricultural economy of California and the nation.[4]

If this rate is allowed to continue it has been projected that within thirty years the remaining three-fourths of California's existing farmland will be gone.[5]

Most of these changes are destined to take place around California's major metropolitan areas. Already the amenities that originally brought people out of the cities have vanished. Even within the suburbs there is precious little open space or wild area for recreation; there are no effective public transit systems to link suburbanites to the cultural benefits of the cities (the car is rapidly becoming too expensive to operate on a day-to-day basis), and the congestion and polluted air make a second migration from the metropolitan areas almost a certainty.

Even in areas that are currently committed to California's multibillion-dollar agricultural industry, the same suburbanization is becoming a threat. Agriculturally oriented cities like Fresno, Modesto, and Sacramento are now large metropolises, swelling and spilling over into the heart of the prime farmlands that surround them (see Figure 1).

THE TAX RELIEF STRATEGY
FOR FARMLANDS

Conservationists battling sprawl have historically embraced the arguments put forth by farmers that new housing developments drive the farmland taxes so high that the farmers are forced to sell out. Farmers have pointed out that since developers prefer the flat lands of prime agricultural areas, there is a real danger of much of the country's food supply being paved over. In unison farmers and conservationists have pleaded that the only way of preserving agricultural land and open space at the edge of the cities is to lower the taxes on farmlands.

Partially in response to this combined plea for agricultural land preservation by farmers and conservationists, the state of Maryland enacted a tax relief law to farmers in 1956. Since then some twenty-seven states, including California, have adopted similar measures of their own.

Dr. Thomas Hady of the USDA's Economic Research Service has divided these tax relief laws into three categories: "preferential assessment" for farmland, which is pure tax relief with no strings; "deferred taxation," under which varying percentages of back taxes come due when the farmland is developed; and "restrictive agreements," under which the landowner agrees to certain restrictions in return for tax relief.

But none of these programs which have aimed at preserving farm lands and open space near the city has really been effective. Maryland's "preferential assessment" legislation has had no apparent effect on slowing down the exodus of farmers from the land or encouraging the "development" of open space. A 1962 study of six Maryland counties showed that 71 percent of rural land buyers were not farming, and 79 percent had not previously farmed. More important, the study indicated that these buyers paid much higher prices for the land than their "farmable" value would justify. All of which suggests that Maryland's "preferential assessment" legislation has become more of a tool for land speculation than land preservation.

California's "restrictive agreement" has fared no better. Known both as the "Land Conservation" or "Williamson" Act, it requires farmers, in return for tax relief, to sign contracts to keep their land undeveloped for at least ten years, though a landowner desirous of developing his property earlier can usually abdicate the agreement by paying a substantial penalty. Land under contract is taxed in proportion to its agricultural productivity rather than its potentially higher real estate value.

By 1972, some 9,562,706 acres of California lands had come under Williamson Act contracts: almost one-tenth of California's privately owned land, 25 percent of private farmland, and 50 to 75 percent of the land in some counties. But a 1970 survey revealed that less than 20 percent of the land then under this act was "prime agricultural land"; that only 1.33 percent of it was within a mile of any city, and less than 5 percent was within three miles of any city.[6]

The fact is that the Williamson Act has failed to preserve agricultural lands adjacent to the cities. In addition, it has cost California's local governments a staggering $40 million a year because of the tax breaks it provides.[7] Among the largest benefactors of these reduced taxes are gigantic landholders whose properties are under little threat of urban encroachment (see Chapter 3).

Preservation of farmland and open space against urban sprawl has not been accomplished by the Williamson Act or any other state farm tax relief program because the legislations misinterpret the fundamental reasons for urban sprawl and because they are so full of tax loopholes that developers are able to manipulate them to their own advantages.

Consider the Williamson Act in California. The act was conceived on the premise that prime agricultural lands around cities should be preserved because they are vital to the maintenance of our nation's food supply. Yet the fact is that neither California nor the United States is currently short of agricultural land, nor do they expect to be in the future. For, despite the U.S. Soil Conservation District's alarming figures, which indicate rapid depletion of California's existing farmlands,[8] the state continues to increase its total farm acreage. With the aid of enormously costly water aqueducts like the California Water Project and the massive energy support systems consisting of farm machinery, chemical fertilizers, and pesticides, thousands of new acres—mostly in marginal areas—have been added to California's farmlands. For example, when metropolitan development in Los Angeles moved into orchard lands, the oranges and lemons that succumbed to the bulldozers moved up to the southeast San Joaquin Valley and over to Arizona. And when the fruit orchards of the Santa Clara Valley likewise fell before the bulldozers, the orchards were similarly relocated.

Thus the argument for urban containment in prime agricultural areas is not justifiable in terms of simply preserving our food production potential. A stronger argument would be made if the act had stressed the importance of the location value of prime soils near the cities. Maintenance of farm production adjacent to the cities ensures a food supply that is not dependent on the high-energy support system required to make marginal lands fertile. The precariousness of this dependence becomes apparent once the energy system underlying it begins to falter—as our petroleum economy is now doing. When that happens, the real costs of removing agriculture from the urban periphery to marginal areas begin to surface, in the form of greater production and distribution changes and increased ecological damage.

Paul Shepard, Dartmouth professor of environmental perception, has powerfully described these costs.

Unless our course is altered, the years from 1970 until the end of the century will see the construction of huge pipelines running thousands of miles into the interior of all the continents. Besides being irrigated by reactor-operated desalination processes, soils will be fumigated. The night sky will be illuminated; gigantic electric-generating plants will empower fertilizer factories so that several multi-crops will be grown per year. On the surface this seems to be the epitome of progress and human betterment. However factory mono-culture—the dream of engineers and politicians—is a dependent enterprise, requiring heavy industrial support for sifting the planet for materials and energy. . . . The economic and social superiority of modern farming as a way of life is a fiction; as technology it is destructive; as a Green Revolution, hopeless.[9]

The Williamson Act and the other state farm tax relief programs have only remotely touched on this scenario raised by Professor Shepard, which is shared by others in this book, yet it may be the strongest argument conservationists and planners have in favor of preserving agriculture at the urban-rural border.

Another strong argument in support of saving prime agricultural lands near the city is that although 25 percent of the nation's land is capable of sustaining agriculture, only 0.5 percent is capable of producing specialty crops. The problems of agricultural overproduction (which has already been cited as an argument used against prime land preservation near cities) is irrelevant to the question of prime land, since much overproduction is limited primarily to grain crops, which do not require prime land. If future generations are to have available a wide variety of produce at reasonable prices, then prime lands adjacent to cities must be preserved. According to Robert Goodier, chief of the California Division of Soil Conservation, destruction of the prime agricultural land adjacent to one southern California city will force transfer of production to poorer lands that require an additional $1,500 per acre of capital investment to bring under production. Finally, it is worth mentioning that the mounting problems of organic waste disposal in the cities will sooner or later have to be alleviated through a massive program of recycling into rural

areas. The advantages of having farmlands near the cities under these circumstances is obvious.

Other examples of misinterpretation in most state farm tax relief programs include: (1) the erroneous assumption that open space can best be achieved through the preservation of prime agricultural lands and (2) the belief that farmers want tax relief because they want to remain farmers.

One of the major motivations behind measures such as the Williamson Act is that preservation of agricultural land around the city will serve as badly needed open space. This is the planners' old greenbelt idea of ensuring at least a ring of open land between urban settlements.[10] The concept, of course, is a good one provided that one doesn't confuse the purposes of agriculture and that of open space; which is apparently what most farm tax relief programs have done. While it is true that the farmer is our greatest land resource custodian it does not follow that farmland is, in the public sense, "open space." Unfortunately, prime agricultural land does not resemble the urban bucolic idea of a recreational retreat. The working farm of today means toxic fertilizers and pesticides, noisy farm machinery, foul smells, and contaminated runoff water from fields and feed lots (which incidentally suggests that nonchemical or "organically" oriented farming is a more desirable form of agriculture around urban areas).

And as for the Williamson Act's implied assumption that farmers want to remain farmers if given a tax break, a few brief remarks need only be made to dispel this illusion. Conservationists and legislators have overly sentimentalized the farmer as the committed steward of civilization's soil. Given a tax break it is assumed that he will stand fast in pursuit of his ancient art. But this is the exception rather than the rule. Today's farmer is basically a businessman and, therefore, is often satisfied to abandon his fields for a good price. And farm tax relief measures like the Williamson Act help him to get that good price. They provide him the tax relief that enables him to keep farming until urban pressures force the land values to a lucrative point. This real estate option, inherent in all farmland tax relief programs, helps to explain why so few acres of agricultural land have been preserved near our cities.

The only effective way to ease the urban growth pressures on farm and open-space lands near the cities is to attack the economic incentives that make farmers want to sell and speculators want to buy. These incentives, which include tax and service subsidies, are the real loopholes that cause sprawl to continue in spite of land conservation measures.

The fact is that federal, state, and local taxpayers have massively subsidized urban sprawl. A number of tax policies have made it profitable for speculators to hold land that should be developed, forcing other developers to leap-frog over these holdings to cheaper land farther from town. This has resulted in the familiar pattern of larger and looser urban masses thinly spread across vast expanses of otherwise scenic and ecologically important land.

While the list of land income shelters that promote sprawl run into the dozens, there are a few that are particularly abused. Probably the most familiar is the federal capital gains tax that allows a "person" to make an investment in land and be taxed at the capital gains rate of only 25 percent when the land is sold. An individual or a corporation in a high income tax bracket finds the capital gains tax on land investments particularly lucrative. Instead of having his investment in a savings account taxed at a rate of 50 percent or more annually, he puts his investment in land and has the investment taxed at 35 percent or less. Moreover, until he actually sells the land he pays no income tax at all, although he can borrow against the land's appreciated value and deduct the interest payments to boot. Farmers are also permitted to deduct against their income improvements to land, such as planting an orchard or building up a herd of cattle. Deduction of this sort enables persons and corporations in high income tax brackets to operate orchards or breed herds at an economic loss, while at the same time making a handsome profit on saved taxes.[11]

On top of income tax loopholes are local property tax assessors who tend to assess raw land at a smaller fraction of market value than developed land.

Farmland tax break laws legitimize and greatly extend this practice. The resulting undertaxation makes it even cheaper to hold land out of development, increasing still further the value of land to the speculator.

While vacant land is undertaxed, buildings are often overtaxed, particularly in slum areas. Sources of slum overtaxation include: lagging reassessment as the buildings decline in value, numerous tax breaks for homeowners which do not apply to the rental units typical of slums, and political gerrymandering that leaves the areas most in need of services with the poorest property tax base. Any tax on buildings, as opposed to the land under them, penalizes the owner who develops and maintains his property. But the slum landlord faces a disproportionately whopping tax increase should he try to renew his buildings or construct new housing. . . . As a result, the development that might have occurred in the rundown areas instead sprawls onto new land.[12]

Compounding the problems caused by tax loopholes are federal, state, city, and county boons to sprawl that come in the form of subsidies for services such as streets, sewers, and utilities. Roads, for example, are frequently built in undeveloped subdivisions at public cost. The highway lobby made this possible through highway trust funds, which earmark gas tax money for new highway construction. Because of this policy, developers have been able to rely on state and local governments to run roads to their subdivisions.

Complementing this form of subsidy has been the prevailing policy among growing communities that they should provide services such as sewers and water to peripheral or leap-frogged subdivisions at low prices to encourage further development and thus expand the "heralded community tax base." Proponents of this form of subsidy have been the community chambers of commerce, realtors' associations, banks, and lending institutions. They have been campaigning for decades on the platform that new housing and commercial development would expand the tax base and thus freeze or drive down individual property taxes. But recent studies by several planning consulting firms and city and county planning agencies have proved these beliefs to be misleading. Among the most widely proclaimed of these studies was the Foothills Environmental Design Study for the city of Palo Alto[13]—a suburban community on the San Francisco Bay Peninsula. The report's economic analysis revealed that it would actually be cheaper for the city to buy the foothills and conserve them for open space than it would be to permit them to be developed.

Studies such as Palo Alto's, together with a growing concern over the *total* costs of suburban life have given opponents of sprawl strong political ammunition. Conservationists in particular have seized upon the information provided by these studies and used it as the basis for successful land reform campaigns across the country. Open space or antidevelopment measures spearheaded by conservationists won voter support in the fall of 1972 in New York, Florida, Washington, and California and brought into office a wave of new environmentally oriented politicians.

In some cases the political fledglings of land reform have embarked on bold efforts to create land use policies and plans that would help to reestablish the role of agriculture at the city's edge. Employing such tactics as down-zoning, land acquisition bonds, and land trusts, these policy makers have begun to contain the ominous urban flood.

But the strength of this embryonic land reform movement remains to be seen. Containment and slowdown measures may prove short-lived unless their advocates address the root causes of sprawl. People who can afford it will continue to buy land and thus inflate rural space in order to pursue life-styles no longer possible in urban settings as they now exist. And why not? For the prosperous American who feels crowded or rootless, tradition suggests that what he needs is land of his own. Thus he buys ten acres of farmland in Maine, or ranchland in California, retreats to it for three weeks a year, and thereby perpetuates the sprawl syndrome.

SANTA BARBARA: A COMMUNITY STRUGGLES FOR LAND REFORM

Because of an absence of effective federal and state land settlement policies, cities and counties seeking to contain sprawl have had to develop their own regulatory measures. Borrowing from the containment experiments of one another, a handful of communities have already managed to successfully implement no-sprawl policies.

One such community is Santa Barbara, California. Better known for its infamous oil disaster of January 1969, Santa Barbara has been engaged in a fierce political struggle to contain sprawl for the past five years.

In the mid 1950s, this sedate coastal community began to experience intense growth. While farmworkers quietly went about tending to the truck crops and the bountiful lemon, avocado, and walnut orchards, land speculators visited the homes of their employers offering them tempting prices for their land.

These speculators had advance knowledge that the quiet little agricultural community of Goleta, just north of Santa Barbara, was on the verge of a development boom. They had learned that the University of California was about to expand greatly its campus just a few miles from the town of Goleta, and that a number of large research and development industries were interested in locating branches near a growing campus. Correctly viewing the university as the magnet that would attract development and create an accompanying need for housing and services, speculators from all over the country began buying up Goleta Valley lands as fast as they could. At the same time they also began demanding protective zoning ordinances to secure or increase the value of the lands they had purchased.[14]

With the Chamber of Commerce fanning the flames of anticipation and excitement, land values soared, and finally, when supplemental water was brought to the valley, a building frenzy began.

Confronted with unprecedented pressure for development, the local government faced the unenviable task of determining the future shape of the Santa Barbara area landscape. How was growth to be accommodated? What was to become of agriculture, which was then the area's primary economic base? These were hard questions demanding immediate answers. Two opposing viewpoints soon emerged.

On one side people argued that new development should be guided into the foothills behind the valley, thereby sparing the prized agricultural lands. Opposed to this view was a large and powerful force of speculators and builders who argued that the valley floor was the place for development and that agriculture should make way for housing and commercial sites. The county's planning director, siding with speculator and developer interests, suggested that the entire valley be zoned for urban purposes and that agriculture should retreat into the foothill canyons.

But by early 1970 there were some indications of opposition to this position. Santa Barbara's oil blowout in January 1969, which had precipitated a feeling of fear and outrage through the community, had the secondary effect of awakening otherwise complacent people to the plight that was affecting their local government, land as well as sea.

Subdivisions were going up at a phenomenal rate (Santa Barbara County was then the second fastest developing county in the nation); the newspapers were filled with announcements of subdivision openings; and the agenda of local agencies were glutted with requests for more building permits.

Alarmed by the speed of the transformation of the valley floor, citizens began to organize and seek out courses of action to curb the urban onslaught. Their only apparent handle on the situation appeared to exist in the Santa Barbara County General Plan. It prescribed a boundary beyond which urban development was not to spread and established planning goals such as "protecting the fertile lands of the Valley for the growing of crops" and "providing for the sound growth of cities through careful balancing of and proper relationship between residential, commercial, industrial, and open uses." Though the plan itself was not legally binding in its prescriptions for land use, and did in fact recommend the urbanization of the entire valley floor, it did give citizens a reference point from which to base their goals and actions.

The importance of having such a document surfaced when a major Los Angeles developer announced plans to develop some 3,638 acres of virgin Santa Barbara coastland. The proposed development would have extended upper-class suburbia into the middle of agricultural and grazing lands about eight miles beyond the county's General Plan boundary, and opened the intervening area to rapid development. Citizen opposition to the proposal was unprecedented, but the combined campaigning by the Santa Barbara Building and Trades Council, the Chamber of Commerce, the Board of Realtors, and the local television station made it relatively easy for the county administrators to nod their approval of the scheme.

Infuriated by what seemed to be a flagrant act of ignoring the popular sentiments of the community, the citizen opposition united under the auspices of "Citizens for the General Plan" and initiated referendum action. The struggle that followed was one of California's first and certainly most bitter efforts to subdue urban sprawl. A classic land use battle—"El Capitan," as it was known—pitted citizen suburbanites against the unified forces of the banking and lending institutions, the Building and Trades Council, a highly successful developer, the Chamber of Commerce, and the county government.

But all the publicity tactics they could muster failed to stimulate voter support for the project. When the votes finally were counted, "El Capitan" went down to a smashing defeat—marking one of California's first successful attacks against urban sprawl.

Inspired by the decisiveness of the vote and the political awakening which "El Capitan" had stimulated, participants of Citizens for the General Plan began to direct their actions toward a more extensive land control campaign. This program took the form of educational forums in land-use planning plus political campaigns for local government offices.

Through a series of planning forums sponsored by Santa Barbara's continuing education division of the city college, entitled "Last Call for Santa Barbara," citizens learned of the fallacies inherent in the argument that urban sprawl is good for the tax base and for taxpayers. A panel of lay planners exposed their fellow citizens to the wide array of subsidies that were available to the speculator and showed them a blueprint of what the future of the valley would be if these subsidies continued to be provided by their county government.

The citizen panel suggested that a new plan for the valley be developed that would preserve open space and agricultural lands at the peripheries of suburbia and would direct all future development to select areas that had been skipped over in the sprawl process.

The panel suggested that the county employ such controversial land use measures as down-zoning and open-space bonds and that it develop a land bank as a way of realizing the objectives of the new plan.

Concurrent with this educational program were a series of "minor" political campaigns over control of the valley's water and sanitation districts. Armed with the information developed in the "lay planning forum," a coalition of land reformers challenged and defeated a series of pro-sprawl incumbents who had reigned over the water district for more than a decade. The new water board immediately initiated policies prohibiting the extension of water services beyond the General Plan's prescribed urban boundary, and also banned future water service to areas not already supplied with a water meter. In addition, it authorized a research program designed to explore alternatives to importation of supplemental water from the California Water Project.

Following the election of the water board coalition a political campaign was mounted to elect land reform candidates to the board of supervisors, the most powerful political body of county government. Once again citizens faced the combined forces of the Chamber of Commerce, the banking and lending institutions, and the Building and Trades Council. After another bitter campaign the land reformists scored another decisive victory.

At the time of this writing it appears that Santa Barbara is well on its way to ending further urban encroachments into the countryside. It has initiated severe water conservation policies that all but preclude further urban development. It has also initiated downzoning policies, and has started a comprehensive land use review for the entire county.

Hopefully, Santa Barbara's present policies will mature and bear fruit in the form of a community that blends the values of agriculture with urbanity. Perhaps its experiences will serve as a small example for other cities and communities of the country who seek to integrate in a more positive way the values and economies of a rural society with those of the city.

Certainly the climate in America is ripe for embarking on land settlement programs that redirect our energies away from the social, economic, and environmental ravages of sprawl. The urban crises of our time compel us to seek and realize a more symbiotic relationship between the city and the rural lands that surround it.

NOTES

1. Mason Gaffney, "Containment Policies for Urban Sprawl," Univ. Kansas Publ., Gov. Research Series #27, Lawrence, Kansas.
2. Raymond Dasmann, *Destruction of California* (New York: Macmillan Co., 1965); Robert C. Fellmeth, ed., "Power and Land in California," in *Ralph Nader Task Force on Land Use in the State of California*, vol. 1 (Washington, D.C.: Center for the Study of Responsive Law, 1971).
3. Jay Thorwaldson, "The Palo Alto Experience," *Cry California* (681 Market St., San Francisco), Spring 1973, pp. 4-17.
4. U.S. Dept. of Agriculture, U.S. Soil Conservation Service, California Soil and Water Conservation Need Inventory, California Conservation Needs Committee, 1970.
5. Dean Eckbo, Austin & Williams, "State Open Space and Resource Conservation Program for California," prepared for California Legislature, Joint Committee on Open Space Lands, April 1972 (from Library and Courts Building, Room 509, Sacramento, California).
6. Polly Roberts, "Farmland Tax Breaks: How Not to Stop Sprawl" (unpublished manuscript), Berkeley, California, 1972.
7. Don Demain, "Tax Shelter Costing Millions," *Oakland Tribune*, 2 January 1973.
8. Eckbo et al., "State Open Space Program."
9. Paul Shepard, *The Tender Carnivore and the Sacred Game* (New York: Charles Scribner's Sons, 1973).
10. F. J. Osborn, *Green Belt Cities* (New York: Schocken Books, 1969); Ebenezer Howard, *Garden Cities of Tomorrow*, ed. F. J. Osborn (Cambridge, Mass.: M.I.T. Press, 1965).
11. Fellmeth, "Power and Land."
12. Roberts, "Farmland Tax Breaks."
13. Livingston and Blaney, Foothills Environmental Design Study for the City of Palo Alto, Land Use Study, Department of Planning, City of Palo Alto, California, 1971.
14. Paul Relis, "Contemporary Planning: Evolution or Repression?," Part 2, "The Search for an Alternative," *Survival Times* 2, no. 6 (1972): 19-23, Santa Barbara Community Council, Santa Barbara, California.

Appalachia

JAMES BRANSCOME*

No one has done more to hold Appalachian life up for national ridicule than the producers of the "Beverly Hillbillies," "Green Acres" and "Hee Haw." It is no surprise, therefore, to find this brochure being handed out to tourists flocking into the Great Smokies through Asheville, North Carolina, airport:

"Hello! I'm Eddie Albert . . . and I want to personally invite you to see my new film about the 'un-City'. . . . Connestee Falls. As you may know, I have been involved in the fight for the preservation of our environment for many years. I am proud to be associated with Realtec Incorporated, the developers of Connestee Falls, because here in the Blue Ridge Mountains of North Carolina, Realtec is creating an Un-City: uncrowded, unhurried, unpolluted.

"I sincerely want you to see my film about this remarkable environmental achievement.
    Signed: Eddie Albert
    Star of 'Green Acres.' "

Connestee Falls, and dozens of new developments like it in the North Carolina Blue Ridge, may be an eerie "Un-City" to Eddie Albert, but to the farmers of the mountains, it is an intrusion, the kind of intrusion that has driven the price of marginal farm and timber land from $100 an acre to a whopping $1,000 an acre in a half decade. So high has the price and taxation on mountain land become in the last few years that the dream of a mountain farmer to have at least one son stay home to till the soil has changed to the nightmare that he may not even be able to maintain the farm for his own retirement.

Sons and daughters of small, subsistence farmers along the Blue Ridge Parkway in Carroll County, Virginia, have been returning home lately to learn that the Groundhog Mountain Developers Corporation, a firm that sells lots to professional people from North Carolina cities, has used high-pressure tactics to force their parents to sell their land to them. According to Larry Bowman, a law student at Wake Forest and a native of the area, "These old folks—many of whom can't read or write—believe that they are only leasing, not selling, their land to these corporations. Oth-

ers are so poor that the promise of a new roof or some worthless gratuity is traded for a small-print contract that in effect amounts to the theft of the land."

Only a few miles further down the Blue Ridge Parkway in Carroll County—the county that Mike Seeger says "has best preserved all those things that make up the Appalachian culture"—another firm is building a ski resort. The headline in the *Carroll News* on December 8, 1972, proclaimed, "Cascade Mountain—New Way of Life," and continued, "First there was Beech, then Sugar, and now Cascade. Yes, Cascade Mountain Resort will have one of the finest ski slopes in southwestern Virginia." As one of its many features the ski resort will have an "Olympic Village" with a lodge and motel named "Liebenschuen." And, of course, there will also be a country store. Carroll County needs a ski resort like San Francisco needs skyscrapers.

Thanks to these kinds of developments, the price of farmland is far beyond the means of farmers to buy it. An eighty-acre farm in Carroll, for example, was recently offered for public auction—something that mountaineers have traditionally done when there are several heirs to a farm and the community is in need of a social event. The hope has always been that one of the family or a close neighbor would "buy the old homeplace." This farm was privately offered by the heirs to a local man for $7,500, a figure that he considered excessive and rejected. At the public auction, flooded by land speculators and professionals from North Carolina in search of a "second home," the farm brought $20,000. A few weeks later one half of it was subdivided and sold for $40,000—$40,000 for a hillside that once grossed only a crop of wheat sufficient for the family's bread, pasture for four cows for the family's milk and a few cord of pulpwood to be sold to "put the kids in school" for the winter.

Carl Salmons, a small dairy farmer whose farm borders on the one mentioned above, says, "These people from North Carolina now own land on all four sides of me. I guess I'm next." The Salmons family is one of four families in the same hollow who have not sold out. Land speculation, urban affluence and overcrowding and the decline of small farmers has led to a situation where the right to be a hollow dweller—as most mountaineers have been for centuries and want to be now—carries with it the attendant obligation to

☐ From the Mountain Eagle, Whitesburg, Ky. Reprinted from Barnes, Peter, editor: The people's land, Emmaus, Pa., 1975, Rodale Press.
*James Branscome is a native of the region who writes for the Mountain Eagle.

be rich, an obligation that few mountaineers can meet.

Hundreds of proposals have been put forward in the past few years to revitalize the rural economy. Cooperatives, rural loan banks and other kinds of palliatives have been advocated. All have failed to halt the stream of migration north. If Appalachia as a rural area is to survive, then more dramatic steps such as the following have to be taken:

1. Corporate farming nationally must be stopped. It is a monopoly which allows high prices to be charged for inferior food.
2. A regional producing and marketing system must be adopted which would forbid importing any food to Appalachia that could be grown locally by mountain farmers. This would entail the creation of a kind of Appalachian state, similar to a country of the European Common Market, which would protect mountain farmers at the expense of corporate farmers in Idaho and Colorado. Without doubt, the food produced under such a system would be cheaper, of higher quality and result in a rejuvenation of the region's economy.
3. Land reform must be instituted. The giant holdings of corporations in Appalachia should be federalized and homesteaded the way the U.S. government seized and homesteaded the West. If we can do this to the poor Indians, there is no reason why we cannot do it to the rich corporations. This would simply be returning to the mountaineers the timber and land that they were swindled out of at the turn of the century. With this land, small family farms could again flourish in the mountains. Each homesteader would be required to sign a pledge that he would preserve his land for the next generation, and not allow it to be stripped or destroyed.
4. Resort complexes that serve only middle-class skiers and other kinds of intruders should be prohibited. They bring only high land prices and disrespect for mountaineers. Either mountaineers stop this trend of exploitation, or there will be no native mountaineers left in a few years. Folks migrating to Northern cities know that mountaineers are not welcome in the rich suburbs, so there is no reason for us to make the suburbanites welcome in the mountains. There should be a regional law or gentlemen's understanding that mountaineers sell their land to each other, preserve it for their children, and never sell it to outsiders except when no other buyer can be found.

New England

GEOFFREY FAUX*

Almost 200 years ago the people of northern New England revolted against an absentee landowner, George III. We have all been taught that that particular land reform was successful. But look hard and you will see that after 200 years we have simply traded one set of absentee owners for another. The new aristocrats have names like International Paper, Scott Paper, IT&T, Gulf and Western, Chase Manhattan, Merrill Lynch, Pierce, Fenner and Smith.

☐ From a statement to the First National Conference on Land Reform, San Francisco, 1973. Reprinted from Barnes, Peter, editor: The people's land, Emmaus, Pa., 1975, Rodale Press.
*Faux is a former director of economic development programs at the Office of Economic Opportunity. He now works with the Exploratory Project for Economic Alternatives and lives on a 60-acre blueberry farm in Whitefield, Maine.

They don't tell us very much about their holdings, but what we do know gives a hint of how much of a colony northern New England is. In Vermont 19 out of the 22 firms employing more than 500 people are headquartered out of state. In New Hampshire 16 out of 20 are headquartered out of state. In Maine 32 of 43, almost 75 percent of all firms employing more than 500, are headquartered out of state.

These are low estimates. Many firms headquartered in these states are owned by outsiders, including the power companies, railroads and financial institutions.

And of course there is the land. Recent estimates put the percentage of absentee ownership as high as 80 percent of the state of Maine. A dozen pulp and timber companies own 52 percent of the state. They buy and sell whole townships like kids playing monopoly. Among the losers are the men who cut pulp in the woods; the price the monopolists pay for wood pulp is about the same that it was twenty years ago.

And things are getting worse. The demand for recreation land has spurred developers to overrun Vermont, New Hampshire and Maine. Along the coast, large energy companies are moving in on natural deep water harbors to build their refineries. The economic development that the corporations boast of provides few jobs for local people. For example, it takes only a handful of people to run an oil refinery. But one oil spill can completely destroy the clam, lobster, and fishing beds from which thousands of New Englanders make their living.

As in most places, the family farm in our region is rapidly becoming a curiosity. New England is not generally good farming country, but even in the crops we can grow to advantage, like potatoes, and blueberries and in the fishing industry, the corporations are taking over.

In recent years northern New England has become a tourist and retirement mecca. People from the cities of the Northeast corridor have flocked to Maine, Vermont and New Hampshire to escape congestion, overcrowding and pollution. Between 1964 and 1969 spending by tourists almost doubled and it has continued to rise since. Tourism is now the number one industry in the area, and prices have skyrocketed as a result. Land that sold for $20 an acre in 1961 cannot be had for less than $200 today. Stories abound of how land speculators and wealthy people from Boston and New York bought land dirt cheap from poor farmers a few years ago and have made fortunes on the increase in value.

The effect of this on the poor is profound. Where previously people could pretty much get by with a garden, by hunting and fishing and by digging clams, the rise in taxes, rents and the general cost of living is squeezing them mercilessly. And the land itself, which used to be open for hunting and fishing, is now being fenced off for the pleasure of outsiders. Out of 1800 miles of coastline in Maine, only thirteen are open to the public.

Gradually the poor rural New Englander is being driven out of his community, forced into Boston, Hartford, Providence, or the sparsely settled backwoods areas, where opportunities are practically nil. It reminds one of the cycle of uprooting and resettlement that destroyed the native American Indian during the 19th Century.

The tragedy is that tourism and recreation is the most important force to hit northern New England in a century. It could open up all kinds of opportunities for the underemployed, especially now that recreation has become a four-season activity. But the poor can't get a handle on these opportunities because they are controlled by out-of-staters in the context of rampant disregard for the indigenous population.

It's not that we in New England have not been trying to change the situation. We have tried all the conventional solutions—land use regulation, planning, zoning and other controls. But none of these work very well. The lure of profits from land speculation and the weight of corporate power have defeated all our reasonable, liberal efforts.

Some efforts, like zoning which consistently benefits the large landowner with capital and political power, have made things worse. We also are beginning to tax farmland at present, rather than highest use. But that seems to be doing more for the speculators than for the farmers.

If land use planning, regulation, zoning and lower tax assessments are not the answer, what is? I don't have a magic formula. But I do have some general notions on land reform that I would like to share with you.

For openers, it is clear that we have to stop encouraging absentee land ownership and speculation by closing the tax loopholes that subsidize this kind of non-productive activity.

Second, we have to actively discourage large landholdings through tax policies that work against size perhaps, for example, through progressive property taxes with exemptions for homesteads and small land holdings.

Third, we should levy heavy if not confiscatory taxes on large capital gains arising from land speculation. It makes no economic sense to permit huge profits from the ownership of land the value of which rises through no effort on the part of the owner.

Fourth, we should stop thinking only in terms of controls and start examining what is really meant by private land ownership.

My point is reflected in the story of the hobo who was found sleeping on a rich man's lawn one morning. "See here," shouted the rich man out of his window. "You will have to get out of here. This is my land."

"Oh, where did you get it?" asked the hobo.

"My father gave it to me," replied the rich man.

"And where did he get it?" asked the hobo.

"From his father," said the rich man.

"And where did his father get it?" asked the hobo.

"Why, he fought the Indians for it," said the rich man proudly.

"O.K." said the hobo. "Come on down here and I'll fight you for it right now."

We in New England are beginning to fight. Maine saw its first state-wide land reform conference in 1973. Represented were farmers, woodcutters, fishermen, environmentalists and a variety of Maine people.

Up in Aroostook County, where we grow rocks and potatoes—in that order—a large out-of-state corporation recently bought up a number of small potato processing plants. Its first acts were to lay off some workers and to cut the price it offered farmers for potatoes. The workers struck the plant and the farmers organized a boycott. Workers and farmers have not had much of an alliance in the past, but now for perhaps the first time they are seeing a common enemy and they have begun to talk to each other.

It's only a beginning, but we feel good about it.

The loss of agricultural land

ROGER BLOBAUM

INTRODUCTION
Where we stand today

American agriculture is one of this Nation's strongest assets. We enjoy an envied role as a leader in world food production, and the benefits this abundance brings to most of our citizens contribute in great measure to our high standard of living and well-being.

It is unfortunately true that until recently, agriculture's significant contribution to our society has for the most part been taken for granted. The terms "urban," "suburban," and "rural" seemed to denote separate worlds where dependence upon each other was obviously acknowledged but not consciously intertwined. This perception of the separateness of American agriculture has been held not only by its practitioners, who traditionally have guarded their independence, but also by most people in cities and suburbs, who were not overly interested in the details of food production beyond the availability of items appearing on supermarket shelves.

These perceptions are neither realistic nor sufficient for us any longer. We cannot afford to sustain them. The reason why we all must begin to share our views and work out our life styles together is that we face an increasing problem that threatens us all. The United States is continuing to lose its agricultural land to development. The net loss of this agricultural land, which has been going up in recent years, now runs around 1.4 million acres a year.

The issues involved here are multi-faceted. They include the availability and price of food to consumers, the role of the United States as a major exporter of agricultural products, the building of new homes to accommodate our growing population, the use by agriculture of increasing amounts of our current energy supply, and the effect on agricultural lands of the search for new energy sources. In sum, agricultural concerns are really broader concerns, many of which have environmental overtones. Thus, they must be absolutely essential ingredients in any local, State, or Federal land-use policy.

This report presents the results of a special study requested by the Citizen's Advisory Committee on Environmental Quality to examine the insidious loss of our agricultural land.

Basically, the study indicates that the problem is underestimated by Federal officials and by most State governments, although there is evidence of rapidly increasing attention by additional States and by some local governments.

Good agricultural land, like other natural resources, is finite. We do not have a limitless amount available, and thus we cannot afford its loss. Urban development, for one, is increasing at a rapid rate, leading to predictions that it will consume the equivalent of the total areas of New Hampshire, Vermont, Massachusetts, and Rhode Island over the next 25 years. Additional agricultural land is being consumed by strip mining, reservoirs, highways, and other development.

Because we in the United States have not formulated policies, agricultural land decisions are being left to speculators, developers, some local groups, and others who view land as a commodity. Little thought is given to finding ways to alleviate factors that force agricultural land conversion or to placing a high priority on preserving land for agricultural production.

This situation cannot continue. Recent events have shown us that to do nothing is in fact to do something—to increase the loss of an irretrievably precious

□ A study report to the Citizens' Advisory Committee on Environmental Quality, Washington, D.C., 1974.

resource upon which this country and the world strongly depend.

Changing views about agricultural land

The United States began the 1970's with an apparent abundance of good agricultural land, controls on crop production, a declining birth rate, and a desire to sell more of its farm output in world markets.

Surpluses of major commodities had piled up during the 1960's, and as many as 60 million acres were held out of production in a single year. This led to an assumption that the Nation's supply of crop land and capacity to produce were virtually unlimited and that there was no pressing need to prevent conversion of agricultural land to other uses.

Although warnings about possible world food shortages had been sounded in the mid-1960's, they were dismissed for the most part. The resulting complacency was reinforced by reports concluding that increasing production efficiency, declining population growth, and plenty of water and good land ensured the Nation's food needs over the next 25 years with enough left over for exports and other purposes.

A series of dramatic and unexpected events that began unfolding in 1972, however, raised questions about the validity of these conclusions. Large foreign grain sales, representing a sizeable boost over 1971 and a 37 percent increase over the 1968-1971 average, were made, including massive sales over a period of several weeks in late summer that virtually depleted the Nation's reserves.

Strong foreign demand continued in 1973, making it clear the situation was changing. Acreage controls were eased in an attempt to increase production, and nearly all the land idled under Federal programs was brought back into production. These changing conditions were reflected in the 1973 Agricultural Act, which gave the Secretary of Agriculture greater flexibility in determining whether the land-withholding program was needed and established target price guarantees designed to stimulate all-out wheat and feed grain production.

As these events took shape, the Nation was jolted by an energy crisis that convinced the public that petroleum had critical uses extending far beyond the corner service station. One was a food production system with a growing appetite for energy—an appetite that included gasoline and other petroleum products needed to power and lubricate tractors, harvesters, and other farm machinery; natural gas used to manufacture fertilizer; propane used to dry grain; and electricity to operate milking machines and other equipment.

Competing for public attention was a deteriorating international situation. The balance of payments problem was still critical after two devaluations of the dollar, and an even higher level of farm exports was called for to help pay for imported oil that had quadrupled in price.

The Nation also continued to receive grim news regarding hundreds of millions of hungry people in poor and drought-stricken areas of a world that is expected to double in population over the next 25 years. The Agriculture Committee of the House of Representatives reported that the world demand for cereals was expanding by 30 million tons per year by 1970—the equivalent of the annual wheat crops of Canada, Australia, and Argentina. The hope of reaching a world food production growth rate of 4 percent a year, a United Nations target, will be difficult to attain in view of rising oil prices, bad weather, fertilizer shortages, and other unexpected problems.

The World Hunger Action Coalition, organized in 1974 by a number of nongovernment organizations working in the relief and development fields, reported that the Sahara Desert is moving south at the rate of 30 miles a year, that global grain reserves are nearly depleted, and that the world is entering a period of food scarcity of immense proportions and indefinite duration.

A rapid rise in food prices at home during this period has probably done the most to help stimulate public awareness of how important agriculture is in a nation that has taken food abundance for granted. The most serious question to be raised is whether enough land and other resources are available to meet all these requirements that events have thrust upon us.

OUR AGRICULTURAL LAND BASE

Although the United States has more than 2.2 billion acres of land, only about 1.4 billion is non-Federal land available for agricultural use. Nearly half of this non-Federal land is considered marginal or worse because it is too steep, has soil that is too wet or shallow, has a short growing season, is too susceptible to erosion, or has other serious cropping limitations.

Because of individual landowner decisions, most but not all of the good agricultural land is utilized for crop production; and most but not all of the crop production is on the good agricultural land that is available.

To understand the status of our Nation's agricultural land base, we must look at two factors: the capability of the land itself and the use to which the land is put. For this information we have turned primarily to the National Inventory of Soil and Water Conservation Needs, developed by the U.S. Department of Agriculture (USDA) and issued in 1967 by its Soil Conservation Service (SCS).[1]

Agricultural land capability

The *land capability classification* is a reliable indicator because it is based on the type of soil involved, its hazards and limitations when put to various uses, and its response to treatment. The capability groupings range from Class I, which has few limitations and a low risk of erosion or other damage, to Class VIII, which is suitable only for recreation and wildlife.

On the basis of capability, the Inventory shows only 631 million acres in Classes I-III, which are those suitable for regular cultivation. Another 180 million acres of land are in Class IV, which is considered unsuitable for regular cultivation, although it could be used to produce certain crops if absolutely necessary. Even with extensive land treatment and careful management, it would not return high yields. Several acres of this land class would be required to produce the crops that can be grown on one acre of Class I land.

The remaining 627 million acres are in Classes V-VIII and are considered extremely marginal for crop production. This land is suitable for range, pasture, forest, and wildlife areas.

Of the 631 million acres suitable for regular cultivation, only 47 million acres are left in the Class I category—land with nearly level fields and soils that are deep, well-drained, resistant to erosion, and easily worked. This "prime" agricultural land is highly productive, suitable for intensive cropping, and irreplaceable. It also is the type sought out for urban expansion because it offers few, if any, constraints on developers.

Agricultural land use

The *use patterns category* is nothing more than a report of what owners were doing with their land in 1967 when the SCS Inventory was completed. It shows that 438 million acres were in crop land, 482 million acres in pasture, and 462 million acres in forest. The 438 million acres in crop land included 365 million acres suitable for regular cultivation, 50 million acres suitable for limited cultivation, and 23 million acres considered extremely marginal cultivation but utilized to some degree.

What this Inventory points out is that it is not possible to make a direct correlation in all cases between land in a certain class and its use. Primarily because of landowner preferences, some land highly suitable for cropping is not being farmed, while some land unsuitable for cultivation is being cropped. Some good land not being farmed is in small parcels cut off by a river or other barrier or in hilly areas where it is part of a larger pasture or forest unit. Some of the 23 million acres of unsuitable land is worked by individuals who have only a small amount of land and till what they have. Other land considered unsuitable for culti-

vation is used for fruit and nut crop production, which in many instances is within its capability.

A more recent report on crop land use, prepared in 1973 from USDA and Bureau of the Census information, shows that 318 million acres produced crops that were actually harvested.[2] Another five million acres were in crops that failed because of drought or other hazards, 31 million acres were in cultivated summer fallow, and 28 million acres were idled or in soil improvement crops. The balance of land in the crop land category that year was used for pasture.

Severe erosion problems and land abandonment

Less than half the Nation's 631 million acres of good land in Classes I-III is well cared for. The balance has serious production limitations due to lack of treatment needed to protect it from erosion and other damage. Badly needed are terracing, establishment of grassed waterways, contouring, and other soil-conserving practices.

The Soil Conservation Service estimates that more than 3.5 billion tons of soil are lost each year through erosion on privately owned land. However, it reports that the amount of land in the adequately treated category has risen from 35 percent in 1965 to nearly 50 percent now.

The Department of Agriculture also is attempting to shift several million acres of badly eroded cultivated land in the Great Plains into permanent grass land. So far, about 2 million acres have been converted, and data gathered in 1967 showed another 6 million should be put back to grass.

Continued irrigation of farm land in areas without adequate drainage to flush irrigation water below the root systems of crops also is producing serious salinity buildups that can make soil sterile.[3] Deep tile systems help keep the salinity problem under control in areas where there is sufficient water to flush the salts.

These situations warrant additional Federal action in two areas: increased public support for the improvement of conservation practices and increased data collection on soils. USDA for many years has shared with landowners the cost of terracing and other permanent soil conservation practices. These were justified on the grounds that the public benefits of soil and water management on farms often outweigh those received by the landowner. Recent surveys, however, show that a substantial portion of the Nation's best crop land still needs extensive treatment to control soil loss.

Implementation of an agricultural land preservation effort requires basic natural resources data from the National Cooperative Soil Survey, which the Soil Conservation Service is carrying out in all the States. The funding level for fiscal year 1975 is $25 million.

At this rate, however, it will be sometime in the 1980's before the Survey is completed. Concern about the need to accelerate completion of this Survey was also expressed by USDA's Public Advisory Committee on Soil and Water Conservation in its annual meeting in November 1974.

Finally, a substantial amount of agricultural land, much of it used in the past for cotton, has been abandoned or converted to grass or trees in the southeastern part of the Nation. Most of this land is no longer farmed because it is low in fertility, is too hilly, or is in fields too small for modern machinery.

Helping to offset these losses are about a million acres a year of new land being brought into production. Most of it is the result of drainage/irrigation projects in Florida; drainage and clearing in the Delta; expanded irrigation in California, Washington, and the Texas High Plains; and clearing, leveling, and drainage in the Corn Belt.

BUILDING A SECOND AMERICA

If the current estimates prove correct, we are going to build in the United States as much in the next 25 years of this century as we have in the Nation's entire history. Before the year 2000, according to material developed by the Senate Committee on Interior and Insular Affairs, urban development will consume additional lands equal to the total areas of New Hampshire, Vermont, Massachusetts, and Rhode Island.[4] Each decade, it is estimated, this growth will take an area greater than the State of New Jersey.

The Urban Land Institute has reported similar findings, estimating that the land area of designated urban regions will increase from 196,958 square miles in 1960 to 486,902 square miles by the year 2000, or from 6.6 percent of the total land area of the United States (excluding Alaska and Hawaii) to 16.4 percent.[5]

These figures have tremendous significance for crop production if we continue to rely heavily upon agricultural land as one of the bases for this growth. As previously mentioned, the net loss of agricultural land, which has been going up in recent years, now runs around 1.4 million acres a year. One study of this problem concluded that land in urbanized areas alone increased from 27.2 million acres in 1960 to 34.2 million in 1970, with about half of this representing conversion of crop land.[6] During the first four years of the 1970's, the loss rate has been even higher.

State studies of land loss

The most illustrative of the trends toward increasing agricultural land loss are to be found in studies made in States, mainly in the Northeast and on the West Coast, where major concern over the loss of such land has led to attempts to preserve what is left.

A study prepared in 1972 for the California Legislature showed that the State was losing agricultural land at the rate of 134,000 acres a year in 1972, up from an average annual conversion of less than 100,000 acres 10 years earlier.[7] The State Environmental Council estimated in 1972 that if agricultural land conversion continues to increase at this rate, over three fourths of California's agricultural land will be gone within 30 years.

A 1973 Vermont study shows that active farms now occupy less than one third of the State's land area, down from two thirds in 1945.[8] Harvested crop land dropped from 15 percent of the State's land area in 1949 to 9 percent by 1969. A study of dairy farm purchases in Vermont in 1970-1971 shows that only 76 of the buyers in 350 farm sales continued these farms as operating units.

Other New England States have experienced the same trends. Between 1959 and 1972 Connecticut lost half of its farms, and the actual farm acreage is continuing to decline yearly. A recent report on the Connecticut situation commented that "When a farm goes out of business, the land goes out of production. Much of that which goes out of production goes under concrete." In announcing the establishment in 1973 of an Emergency Commission on Food, the Governor of Massachusetts said the State must reverse a 30-year trend which had resulted in virtual disappearance of its food production capability.[9]

The Blueprint Commission on the Future of New Jersey Agriculture in 1973 proposed a plan to retain 70 percent of the 1.5 million acres of crop land still remaining for agricultural use.[10] At the time the plan was announced, it was reported that urban development was consuming another farm every other day.

Finally, a report from the State of Michigan in 1973 shows that the State had lost more than one third of its original base of 18 million acres of agricultural land over the last 30 years.[11] Each year roughly 35,000 acres of prime farm land and another 50,000 acres of open and rural land are converted to a more intensive and usually urban-associated use. If this trend continues, the report concluded, Michigan will have only 2.5 million acres of agricultural land left by the year 2000.

Urban growth momentum

A significant amount of agricultural land is a prime target for urbanization. It is estimated that about 17.2 percent of all U.S. farms are within the 242 Standard Metropolitan Statistical Areas (SMSA's), putting them directly in the path of this urban expansion.

These units produce about 21 percent of the value of all agricultural products sold and about one fifth of the Nation's food.[12]

As land values rise because of growing development potential, the burden of higher property taxes increases the pressure on owners to convert this good agricultural land to urban uses. It should come as no surprise that this land is in demand. The land consumed by urban development in most areas normally is level, well-drained soil that becomes available on a square mile grid pattern. An examination of air-photo index sheets used by the Soil Conservation Service shows clearly how residential subdivisions utilize roads and highways in existence and spread over well-defined land areas that formerly were fields or entire farming units.

One study of urbanization of land in eight Western States specifically showed that a high proportion of the land urbanized was previously used for crop production—usually high-value, irrigated crops.[13] It showed 464,000 acres consumed in 48 selected counties in an average span of 11 years, with crop land making up 361,980 acres of the total. It also showed that the land was consumed for these purposes: 328,845 acres for dense residential; 62,115 for open residential; 26,190 for industrial; 17,160 for institutional; 16,235 for commercial; 10,770 for recreation; and 3,565 for airports.

Most land converted to urban uses is in huge metropolitan corridors where most of the Nation's population growth has taken place the last 20 years. The outlook is for increasing pressure on available land there because these areas have strong, built-in growth momentum.

A major urban conversion indicator is the number of counties added to the Nation's SMSA's. A county is added to this category when a city within its boundaries grows to 50,000 or more. It is estimated that these urbanized counties added another 7 million acres to SMSA's in the 10-year period ending in 1970. It is also estimated that about one third of an acre is urbanized per capita population increase in these areas, with about half of this area classified as crop land.

These trends are significant because more than two thirds of the Nation's people are concentrated in these areas now, and an even greater proportion of the 80 million population increase expected by 2000 will live there. The result is increasing urban pressure on agricultural land that, as pointed out, produces about one fifth of the Nation's food.

Recreation home land boom

A tremendous amount of agricultural land also is involved in the activities of land developers who have been subdividing and selling staggering amounts of raw, rural acreage. In New Mexico, for example, the Environmental Improvement Agency estimated in 1971 that well over 1 million acres had been staked out for "homesites." This would be enough to house up to 8 million people, the agency said, several times more than the projected 1,336,000 expected to live in the State 30 years from now.[14] Movement of top soil for roads and other development involved has destroyed thousands of acres or prime New Mexico land.

It is estimated that subdivided lots in California, located both on urban fringes and far out in the country, would support housing for growth anticipated in that State for as long as 300 years. This uncontrolled subdividing wastes vast amounts of land and stimulates urban conversion.

Nationally, the number of lots in registered recreation home land projects alone was estimated at more than 15 million in 1974 by the Office of Interstate Land Sales Registration of the Department of Housing and Urban Development.[15] With unregistered subdivisions added, real estate brokers and government officials say the total may exceed 25 million. It is significant that the demand for recreation home land has declined since the energy crisis dramatized fuel shortages, and it is likely that sales peaked late in 1973, at least for the present time.

Although USDA has a report showing that about 2 million second homes had been constructed by 1965, the Department has no good figures on the impact on this trend on agricultural land.[16] However, it is clear that recreation home land sales have been up sharply in rural areas adjacent to most large population centers, creating "exurbs" that often are converted from weekend to permanent retirement residences.

A report by the American Society of Planning Officials concludes that recreation land development invariably stimulates urbanization of the countryside, raises property taxes, leads to demands for new public services, and undermines the agricultural economy in areas where farming exists.[17]

Land consumed by highways and other public services

What about the highway network needed to tie all these urban areas together? Streets and alleys at one time took about one third of the area in towns and cities. It is likely that they take an even greater percentage now, with service roads and wide streets that handle traffic from the expressways that encircle and criss-cross most metropolitan areas.

The Economic Research Service of USDA reports that rural highways and roads cover about 21 million acres of land, including about 1 million consumed so far in building the interstate highway system, which is virtually completed. The construction of freeways, expressways, and highway relocations continue to take about 100,000 acres of agricultural land each year.[18]

The figures probably underestimate the total impact of the interstate highway system on agricultural land. Diagonal stretches of interstate across farm areas have unnecessarily ruined thousands of acres of prime farm land. These diagonal routings, all too common in rural areas, cut across farms and leave hundreds of small, odd-shaped fields too small or irregular to work efficiently. One way to deal with this is Federal legislation to deny construction funds for State road construction projects that use diagonal routings for highways across agricultural land when other less damaging routing is a reasonable alternative. Highway planners should avoid unnecessary routings over land which is needed for agricultural purposes.

The beltline systems that ring most of the Nation's metropolitan areas expand boundaries of metropolitan growth, attracting strip development and helping commuters reach subdivisions even further out in the country. Areas between these highways and built-up city areas immediately become attractive for urban development.

In spite of the energy situation, demands for land to accommodate the automobile unfortunately may continue to increase. The Department of Transportation has projected a 50 percent increase in motor vehicle registrations in the 1970-1990 period and a 100 percent increase in miles traveled in urban areas.[19] The agency also has estimated a need for approximately 18,000 miles of additional freeways and expressways within the boundaries of urbanized areas, compared with about 8,000 in 1968.

It is estimated that about 35,000 acres of agricultural land are taken annually by airport construction in rural areas. These large complexes, usually built out in the open country to take advantage of lower priced land and avoid city congestion, are almost always overtaken by urbanization. It is estimated that airports serving the Nation's cities now cover about 1.8 million acres of land.

Another use of land is about 14,000 disposal areas spread across the Nation to handle about three fourths of the residential, industrial, and institutional waste. These areas average 34 acres in size and occupy about 476,000 acres, about half in areas of active agriculture. At the present rate of filling, it is estimated about 500 new disposal sites a year are required.

Substantial land also is flooded permanently each year by man-made impoundments. The total estimated by USDA at about 300,000 acres a year does not include deterioration of other crop land in nearby areas caused by recreation traffic connected with multiple-use projects.

It is estimated that large reservoirs now take up an area of well over 10 million acres, including much river bottom land that was excellent for crop production. There also are about 2 million farm ponds that occupy several million acres of land formerly used for crops or pasture.

ENERGY-RELATED LAND DEMANDS
Strip mining

Coal has now become the resource which many people look to for a way out of our energy difficulties. However, coal often lies underneath agricultural land, and the effects of strip mining can be devastating.

The Economic Research Service, in a report issued in May 1974, said that about 4 million acres of rural land has been stripped so far, mainly in Illinois and Appalachia.[20] In another 25 years, it reported, the total may add up to an area the size of Maryland.

Involved is land taken for excavations or pits, for waste or spoil disposal, and for mine access roads and exploration activities. In addition to ruining the land for agriculture in most instances, strip mining rips up ground aquifers and releases acids that pollute streams over a much wider area.

A big increase in strip mining would have a devastating land use impact. According to the Preliminary Report of the Ford Foundation Energy Policy Project, *Exploring Energy Choices*, "there is much more coal ultimately available by deep mining than by stripping, about 12 times as much."[21] Deep mining is decreasing, however, because of lower costs associated with stripping operations.

In 1950, only about one fifth of the Nation's coal came from stripping operations. Since then, this kind of mining has climbed steadily, according to a report prepared for the Council on Environmental Quality in 1972, and is now approaching 50 percent.[22] This type of mining also is moving west, with the Illinois Basin now the leading area for stripped coal.

About three fourths of the Nation's economically strippable coal reserves lie in 13 States west of the Mississippi, including a substantial amount under agricultural States like Iowa and North Dakota. Much of this is low-sulfur coal, which is in great demand by utilities pressed by Federal pollution standards.

Western energy development

Much of the land involved in energy projects in the West is public domain, administered by the Bureau of Land Management, and has limited value for crops. But much of it provides grazing for an important cattle and sheep industry that also utilizes privately owned grasslands and irrigated hayfields, all of which would be damaged by strip mining. Stripping also threatens to destroy agriculture in many rich river valleys in the West that are covered with highly productive irrigated farms.

It is clear that greatly accelerated energy-related activity will consume large amounts of agricultural land over the next 30 years and create unprecedented demands for scarce water resources in States west of the Mississippi. This is sure to slow irrigation development and may even produce shortages of water for land already being irrigated, putting more pressure on land in the Midwest and elsewhere that has regular rainfall. These energy-related land losses must be considered as a major factor in dealing with the growing problem of agricultural land losses.

One blueprint for Western coal development is the North Central Power Study, issued by a group representing the U.S. Bureau of Reclamation and 35 major private and public electric power suppliers.[23] It calls for development of coal and water resources in Wyoming, Montana, and the Dakotas for generation of vast amounts of electric power.

An analysis of the plan prepared for the Environmental Defense Fund showed that the 210 million tons of coal needed per year for the 50,000-megawatt level proposed for 1980 would require the companies to strip 10 to 30 square miles a year. At the 200,000-megawatt level, planned for the year 2000, land subjected to strip mining would be several times greater. This has serious implications for food production because reclamation of stripped areas in semiarid regions of the West appears economically infeasible with present technology.

These staggering land losses do not include areas needed for sites proposed in the North Central plan for coal gasification plants, for 42 huge generating plants throughout the region, or for the housing and other facilities for hundreds of thousands of new residents that mining and power development will attract. Nor do they include land needed for about 40 new hydro-electric installations of 100 megawatts or more and about 50 new pumped storage hydroelectric installations that the Federal Power Commission reports may be needed.

They also do not include requirements for the development of two new energy sources proposed for the West—geothermal and oil shale. This development, however, will be mainly on public land unsuitable for most agricultural purposes. Nor do they include land requirements for large numbers of breeder-type nuclear power plants the Atomic Energy Commission estimates may be operating by 2000.

The figures also fail to consider the impact on irrigation of the transfer of tremendous amounts of scarce water now used by or committed to agriculture from this purpose to mining, power plant cooling, coal gasification, slurrying of coal for movement through pipelines, shale oil development, and other power-related uses.

The problem of generating plants, it should be pointed out, is not limited to the West. In 1970 the Office of Science and Technology projected a need for 1,000 new electric generating plants across the Nation by 1990, with cooling ponds of an acre or more per megawatt or banks of cooling towers needed for each one.[24] One example of such a plant is a 2,800-megawatt coal-burning plant being built by the Kansas Power & Light Company on 13,500 acres of agricultural land in northeast Kansas. Included in the plan is a 3,000-acre reservoir and a 560-acre ash storage land fill.

TO THE YEAR 2000 AND BEYOND

If the Nation continues to allow urban and other development to consume its agricultural land over a long period, it appears inevitable that food and fiber shortages will develop.

Too many agricultural authorities, however, seem unconcerned about the possibility of major land losses. Recent studies indicate they are convinced that the Nation's requirements can be met by continuing technological advances and productivity increases and that the number of acres of land available is not that important.

Our Land and Water Resources, a major report issued in May 1974 by USDA's Economic Research Service, is probably the most important of these studies.[25] It was issued in response to a March 1974 memorandum from the Secretary of Agriculture and includes a number of basic assumptions regarding population, exports, water, and other variables. Its projections go as high as 309 million acres of land needed for crops in the year 2000, well within the present inventory of good crop land available now to produce crops on a regular basis.

The report concludes that increasingly efficient production methods, a declining population growth rate, and abundant water and land with agricultural potential should ensure domestic food and fiber needs to the year 2000 and leave enough left over for exports and non-agricultural purposes.

An examination of these assumptions suggests they are subject to serious challenge in view of emerging energy, land use, and world developments. These emerging developments could upset the conclusions of that report in terms of pressure likely to build over the next 25 years on available agricultural land.

The following are some examples of important assumptions made by USDA and others in projecting future production requirements, along with an overview of important developments that may dictate a much different set of conditions regarding land use and allocation in the 1970's and beyond.

Fertilizer use

USDA puts heavy emphasis on increased use of inorganic fertilizers, even though prices increased 81 percent during the year ending September 15, 1974, and critical shortages are predicted for natural gas, a home-heating fuel that is also used in making nitrogen fertilizer. Scientists have concluded that increased fertilizer use over the past 40 years has raised yields enough to allow an actual decrease in cultivated crops of about 50 million acres.

A National Academy of Sciences report issued in 1974 said that fertilizer applications predicted for 1980 range from a low of 23.1 million tons to a high of 30.9 million tons of nitrogen, phosphates, and potash, compared with about 16 million tons applied in 1970.[26] The report said these projections assumed fertilizer prices would continue to decline and production capacity would be more than adequate to satisfy demand.

The sharp rise in fertilizer prices already has invalidated one of these assumptions, and predictions that domestic natural gas reserves may not last beyond the 1980's threatens the other. Low natural gas supplies have forced production cutbacks already.

This has had a disproportionate impact on the price of anhydrous ammonia, a nitrogen source derived from natural gas. In another report, the Department of Agriculture reported this source had gone up in price to $229 a ton on September 15, 1974, compared to $92.50 a ton a year earlier. Nitrogen fertilizer production depends on ammonia, and ammonia production is dependent in the United States on natural gas as a feed stock to supply hydrogen. It normally takes from 36,000 to 40,000 cubic feet of gas to produce a ton of ammonia.

Demands for more cutbacks in the manufacture of nitrogen fertilizer, which accounts for nearly 60 percent of all fertilizer used, may occur when reserves begin running low. This already has brought some problems for natural gas customers with low-priority ratings and "interruptible" service. Increasing public awareness of the competition between such uses as home heating and fertilizer manufacturing might result in future fertilizer constraints and demands that manure and other types of natural fertilizer be substituted.

Studies at the University of Illinois concluded that the amount of corn that could be grown on 100 acres using 120 pounds of nitrogen per acre would require up to 300 acres with less or no fertilizer. The implications of a drastic cutback in the use of nitrogen fertilizer on crop land acreage, under present agricultural practices at least, would appear to be enormous.

Farm exports

The USDA study projects only moderately increasing exports over the next 30 years despite the fact that farm exports jumped from a $12.9 billion level to $21.3 billion in the year that ended June 30, 1974. Yet, foreign sales are being pushed even higher in response to a deteriorating balance of payments situation caused by quadrupled crude oil import prices, and world food shortages caused by drought and unprecedented population growth are growing worse.

Huge foreign sales of grain in 1972 wiped out the Nation's reserves and required production from 85 million acres, compared to acreage equivalents of 54 million in 1968, 61 million in 1969, 72 million in 1970, and 62 million in 1971. Demand since has brought 44 million additional acres of crop land back into production and resulted in termination of production controls.

There is every reason to believe that foreign demand for U.S. grain will continue. A recent House Agriculture Committee report concludes that most of the world's good crop land is already under cultivation and that the estimated cost of reclaiming substantial new land would be phenomenal.

The highest export levels projected by the USDA study are up only 25 percent in 1980 and 75 percent in 2000 when another 3.5 billion people are expected to double the world's population.[27] The study estimates that 6 to 7 million acres of crop land are required for each $1 billion increase in farm exports. Thus, even if these projections are understated by only $5 billion, certainly not a big difference in today's world market, another 30 to 35 million acres of crop land would be required.

It is likely that this additional land would have to come from acreage outside the present inventory of crop land acres. The amount needed would be considerably higher than the estimate of 30 million acres or more if water, fertilizer, and other technological inputs are limited and this additional production has to come from marginal land with limited productivity.

Continued conversion of agricultural land to other uses would appear to be most unwise in view of these possibilities. As a report prepared by the Western Agricultural Research Council points out, the comparative advantage that American agriculture enjoys in world trade is due in large part to the large areas of high-quality soils in the Midwest and to intensive irrigated agriculture in the West. It would seem to be in the public interest, the report suggests, to preserve the best of these agricultural lands for crop production.

Marginal land

Most of the studies that suggest the United States has plenty of land for future needs put considerable emphasis on a reserve of 266 million acres of trees and grass that presumably are available for cultivation. This land, however, has severe cropping limitations and would require costly clearing, draining, or other treatment if it were converted to crop land.

The SCS Inventory, referred to earlier, reports that part of this marginal land is in areas where the growing season is too short to produce the high-value crops needed to render an adequate economic return for developing it. It also points out that some of this land would require extremely expensive treatment. That cost would have to be covered either through government cost-sharing with the producers involved or higher commodity prices that sould create the incentive necessary. Even with treatment and good management, most of it would still have serious cropping limitations due to erosion hazards and rocky or shallow soils.

It also is strongly suggested that these fragile lands should be kept in forest and grass because they are highly vulnerable to erosion and the topsoil could be lost with present farming methods. In addition, the SCS Inventory suggests some marginal land now used for crops should be converted back to trees and grass.

It seems obvious that the continuing loss of good crop land to development will eventually force the Nation to use more of this type of fragile land for crop production. It also seems clear that it will take two acres and probably more of this marginal land to produce the equivalent of one acre of good land and that this production will involve increased management and energy requirements, costs that will undoubtedly be reflected in food prices. In addition, there would be some effects from taking this marginal land away from such competing uses as pasture for livestock, wildlife habitat, and recreation.

Water availability

USDA places increasing reliance on irrigation, even though large amounts of water in the West that normally would go to agriculture may, under various plans proposed, be committed to strip mining, oil shale, and other energy-related development.

Furthermore, dropping water levels in parts of Texas and several other States signal substantial cutbacks in deep-well irrigation. A paper presented at a 1968 symposium sponsored by USDA reported that 5 million of the 8 million acres cropped in the Texas High Plains are irrigated from ground water.[28] It also suggested that depletion of this water could force the area to go to dry land farming in the early 1980's, resulting in drastic yield reductions. The area now produces about one sixth of the Nation's cotton and one third of its grain sorghum.

Agricultural pumping accounts for about 60 percent of all ground water pumped in the United States. Agriculture also accounts for at least half, and in many cases nearly all, of the water consumed in 13 of the 18 water resource regions of the lower 48 States.

The U.S. Water Resources Council has predicted that water use for irrigation will increase by 40 percent to 90 billion gallons a day over the next 35 years.[29] It is not clear, in view of recent energy and other developments, where all this water will be obtained.

A National Academy of Sciences study of Western coal development concluded that water in the Colorado Basin has been appropriated many times over and that energy companies eventually will drain off Missouri Basin water faster than it can be replaced.[30] A Northern Plains Resource Council study of the Yellowstone Basin in 1973 concluded that energy-related diversions threaten present irrigation needs and will eliminate further development of irrigable lands in that area.[31]

In view of this rapidly developing situation, it is difficult to see how the net increase in irrigated acreage of 5 million acres by 1980 and 7 million by 2000 projected by the USDA can be reached. If irrigation expansion is slowed or stopped, as appears likely now, it becomes even more important to preserve agricultural land in areas where rainfall is dependable and adequate. As a clear indication of this concern, the State of Montana has imposed a three-year halt to use of its water from the Yellowstone River Basin for energy projects pending further study.

Technological inputs

The USDA report puts heavy emphasis on sustained productivity increases over the next 30 years, even though an energy shortage is raising prices and threatening supplies of gasoline, propane, farm chemicals, and other petroleum-based inputs.

American agriculture has increasingly substituted technology for both land and labor, relying on relatively cheap petroleum and electricity in mechanizing most farm operations. It also has ended up with a type of agriculture that permits maximum use of machinery but requires increasing amounts of farm chemicals to deal with insect and weed infestations. This technology has been a major factor in a 50 percent increase in output per crop acre over the last 20 years. The study's assumption that technology will continue to increase yields so that more can be produced on less acreage appears to be questionable in light of the energy shortage, growing environmental concerns, and indications of difficulty in sustaining steady increases in crop yields.

A more realistic position may be the one taken by

the State of Michigan's Department of Agriculture in a 1973 report projecting that State's agricultural land needs over the next 25 years.[32] It concluded that society will continue to impose restrictions, such as bans on certain farm chemicals, that will limit per acre yields to what are essentially today's levels. It is unreasonable to project big productivity increases, the report said, not because the technology will not be discovered, but rather because society will show an increasing disposition to assert constraints. In addition to farm chemicals, these constraints may also include restrictions on use of drug and other additives to animal feed.

The implications of continued loss of agricultural land are suggested in a Western Agricultural Research Council report which notes that current projections to the mid-1980's are based on continued yield increases due largely to improved technology.[33] Any reversal in technology expectations, it states, could raise the question of whether measures should be taken not only to conserve but even to develop additional crop land.

Some observers suggest that many indicators of increasing yields are no longer rising as rapidly as they once were, even with ideal conditions of the last few years. Corn yields no longer are rising rapidly in response to increased use of fertilizer. Yields of wheat, rice, peanuts, cotton, and sugar beets seem to be leveling off. There also has been little increase in soybean yields.

Weather

The Department of Agriculture projections assume normal weather conditions for the next 25 years—even though serious droughts and other violent weather can occur in most areas of the country, and crop failures in the last 20 years have wiped out the production of as much as 22 million acres in a single season.

Crop failure averaged a modest 5.3 million acres in the first four years of the 1970's. But figures compiled by the Statistical Research Service in USDA show the average was 13.5 million acres in the 1950's and much higher than that in the early 1930's, when a large area of the Nation was turned into a dust bowl. Severe drought hit many areas of the country again in 1974. Projections made October 1, 1974, by the Department of Agriculture showed that corn production was expected to be down 16 percent compared to a year earlier despite many more acres planted in 1974 and soybean production to be down 24 percent.

A factor to consider regarding weather is the tendency of adverse climatic cycles to appear with some regularity. An article by Lester Brown of the Overseas Development Council notes there is considerable evidence that North America has been subject to recurrent clusters of drought years roughly every 20 years.[34] He stated that the cyclical drought phenomenon has now been established as far back as the Civil War, when data were first collected on rainfall.

The director of the University of Wisconsin's Institute for Environmental Studies told a Congressional committee recently that the outlook is for poorer growing years in the next couple of decades because the earth is cooling as it did in the 16th and 17th centuries.[35] The American Association for the Advancement of Science reports that the cooling trend in the Northern Hemisphere amounts to a drop of approximately three degrees Fahrenheit since 1945.[36] It said that climatologists now fear the good crop years since World War II may have been deceptive ones and that the world now faces the strong possibility of less hospitable climate, posing a serious threat to a food supply that is already strained.

Specialty crops

Another implication of agricultural land conversion is loss of areas producing specialty crops that do well only in certain areas and have a low tolerance for different soils and climates. These crops usually are produced where weather is tempered by large bodies of water. It is often these same areas that are sought after for subdivisions, recreation, and second-home development.

A USDA official, quoted in 1971 in *The Wall Street Journal*, conceded that specialty crops grown only in limited areas could disappear under the pressures of urbanization. One of the most striking examples is the increasing impact of second-home development on red tart cherries, an important crop that thrives on soil and weather conditions in several counties along Lake Michigan in northwest Michigan.

Elsewhere, it is reported that avocados, Brussels sprouts, and artichokes are in danger of disappearing in California. These areas, like those producing Michigan's cherries, have come under heavy development pressure that could eventually crowd them out of areas suited to their soil or climatic requirements unless protective action is taken.

The pattern of agricultural land conversion makes it increasingly difficult to produce fresh vegetables and fruits near metropolitan areas, where truck farms and orchards traditionally have operated. The Economic Research Service reports that 60 percent of all vegetables sold in 1969 came from urban areas (SMSA's), as did 43 percent of the fruits and nuts.[37]

ECONOMIC IMPLICATIONS

As pointed out earlier, 17 percent of all U.S. farms are within designated metropolitan areas and thus generally are in the path of urban expansion. The economic impact of these units is even greater, since they produce about 21 percent of the value of all agricultural products sold.

In addition to the impact of a steady decline in farm income on the economy, a major implication of continuing conversion of agricultural land is its effect on the viability of agriculture as an economic venture. A certain amount of productive land is needed to provide an economic base for cooperatives, implement dealers, veterinarians, and the many other small businesses that serve farmers.

Involved is an agricultural complex that includes both suppliers of feed, seed, and other purchased farm inputs, and the processors and other buyers who handle the production when it leaves the farm.

A study prepared for the New Jersey Department of Agriculture calculated the estimated requirements for certain agriculture-based enterprises.[38] It found, for example, that the minimum requirement necessary to support dairying was at least 90,000 acres of crop land and pasture and 26,000 cows within a radius of 30 to 50 miles. These requirements ranged down to 10,000 acres in a 10-mile radius for vegetable and potato operations.

Related to this is the tendency of farmers near large cities to avoid long-term investments, deferring costly improvements because they have little value when land is subdivided. Only when farmers are secure for a long period of time are they free to make long-term investments that can be economically justified. This includes houses, barns, fences, and other improvements as well as soil conservation investments such as terraces and grass waterways. Young people often hesitate to start farming in these areas because they do not want to make heavy investments in machinery and livestock when they know they face rising taxes, increased regulation, and other pressures associated with urbanization and may eventually be forced to sell out.

Part of this problem stems from the capital gains provisions of Federal tax policies. Huge profits can be made buying and selling land, with speculators using tax provisions that make this activity an unusually attractive investment opportunity. Land held by speculators is estimated to be about 6 million acres at any one time.

Impact on farm economy

The economic impact of continued conversion of agricultural land can be seen in a State like California, which has nearly 20 million acres of land suitable for cultivation and sells more than $4 billion worth of agricultural products annually. It also is a State that was losing agricultural land at the rate of 134,000

acres a year in 1972, up from an earlier annual conversion of less than 100,000 acres 10 years earlier.

As noted earlier, the State Environmental Quality Council estimated in 1972 that if agricultural land conversion continues to increase at this rate, over three fourths of California's agricultural land will be gone within 30 years. The Soil Conservation Service reports that roughly one fourth of the land now being converted in the State is prime agricultural land.

This is a serious matter for California, which has a climate edge over most areas of the country and is able to double-crop most of its lands. The $4 billion-plus figure does not include economic activity generated by businesses that supply materials to farm operators, processing and shipping of fresh produce, or economic activity from moving cotton and grain through the State's ocean ports.

Another economic consequence of crop land conversion is the higher prices that result when a region has to bring large quantities of food in from other parts of the country or to import it from abroad. These higher prices include costs of transportation and handling by several middlemen. The best example is New England, where agriculture as an industry has almost disappeared. As a region, New England was 100 percent self-sufficient during the late 1800's, and 50 percent self-sufficient during World War II. Now, a recent report shows, it has to import almost 98 percent of its food from outside the region.

Another economic implication of agricultural land losses is the growing likelihood of temporary shortages of basic farm commodities that are in demand for both export and domestic uses. An example is soybeans, the source of oil for margarine and other shortening products and of protein meal for livestock.

When soybean prices soar to more than $12 a bushel, as they did before export controls were imposed in 1972, prices of soybean oil products and meal shoot up. Corn and other competitive vegetable oil products do likewise. Since export commitments are difficult to cut back or cancel, even under political pressure, the possibility of shortages and skyrocketing consumer prices becomes much more likely as land is consumed by urbanization.

Impact on public service costs

In addition to consuming good land unnecessarily, the type of sprawl that results from leap-frogging or development spreading out from built-up areas along major highway routes is usually accompanied by costly development inefficiencies. Providing public facilities is much more costly when roads, sewer and water lines, and other facilities have to be extended over longer distances and in uneconomical patterns.

Unnecessary branches or stubs of main trunk lines

for sewer and water may have to be provided, for example, and inability to anticipate demand may require replacement later of those that were too small. Mass transportation systems have difficulty serving these areas, and accessibility to schools and shopping is often hampered. The public pays for all this, of course, both in higher taxes and inconvenience.

Most governmental units make charges or assessments against farm land for the costs of construction or installation of certain public facilities such as sanitary sewer lines extended into a rural area. These charges are often made on the basis of amount of acreage owned or on foot frontage of the property. In most instances, these facilities speed the process of urbanization and are of little or no direct benefit to the farm operator.

SELECTED EFFORTS TO PRESERVE AGRICULTURAL LAND

Most of the effort to preserve agricultural land or to protect it from premature or haphazard urban conversion now occurs at the State and local level. The amount of interest in a given State appears to be roughly proportionate to the rate and extent of the loss of good agricultural land and the impact of this loss on the State's economy.

In the past, most States have attempted to deal with urban growth by empowering local units of government to control it through zoning, subdivision regulations, sanitary codes, and official mapping. These procedures are generally viewed as inadequate, however, in areas where urban expansion has strong momentum and the need to control land conversion is greatest.

Although several innovative approaches are being tried throughout the country, there is neither clear-cut evidence nor consensus as to which works best. Either careful studies have not been conducted, or the approaches have not been applied broadly enough for a long period of time to permit valid conclusions.

The most widely applied approach is preferential taxation of agricultural land, which permits assessment of land on the basis of its actual use rather than its development potential. In highly urbanized areas—such as Long Island, New York, for example—the development potential portion of total value is as much as 80 percent.

More than 30 States have adopted preferential taxation of agricultural land, and the trend is likely to continue as urban expansion continues. This does not mean that these States have the solution to halting agricultural land conversion, but it does mean they consider it a serious problem and are trying to control it. Indeed, preferential tax treatment provisions are viewed by many as weak holding actions at best.

Rather than assuring that land will be preserved for agricultural use, they often encourage speculation buying by "pseudo-farmers" who hold land for 15 years or more at low taxes and then sell to a developer at a big profit.

Some that have tried preferential taxation of agricultural land have found it does little more than slow land losses near cities and are striking out in new directions. They appear to be headed toward the use of some kind of purchase agreement, such as buying development rights to provide permanent protection for agricultural land.

Attempts also are being made to control urbanization from another angle—using local control of the life line of roads, water and sewer lines, and other facilities to make development less wasteful in terms of agricultural land consumed and of public investment in services.

Here are selected examples of innovative programs around the Nation that offer possible solutions for others as well:

Purchase of development rights

The cost of purchasing endangered agricultural land in an attempt to preserve it would be staggering. It also is unnecessary because the same objective can be accomplished by purchasing the development rights—paying owners for the portion of the land value that represents developmental potential. This reduces both uncertainty and the tax burden for farmers and makes it possible for them to retain all other ownership rights, to make long-term investments in their farming operations, and to pass the land intact on to the next generation.

The Legislature of Suffolk County, at the eastern end of Long Island, has committed $60 million to be used over the next four years in buying development rights on agricultural land.[39]

Suffolk's population was 600,000 in 1960, had grown to 1.26 million by 1973, and is expected to reach 2 million by 1985. During this same period, its land in farms dropped from 89,700 to 57,000 acres, and its ability to support an agricultural economy that included such specialties as cauliflower and ducks, was threatened. Farmers selling rights to develop their land get a substantial property tax cut because they are assessed only on that portion of the land that represents its value for agricultural use. In Suffolk County, it is estimated that agricultural use represents about 20 percent of the value and development rights the other 80 percent.

Once purchased by the county, the rights become capital assets and cannot be sold or transferred without voter approval in a referendum. This first-in-the-Nation plan was shaped by County Executive John V.

Klein, who hopes it will rescue at least 12,000 acres of prime agricultural land from developers.

Under the Suffolk County law, farmers may negotiate the sale to the county of development rights on their land. The county may not force the farmer to sell his rights as long as the land remains in agricultural use. If, however, the farmer decides to convert the land from agriculture, the county has the right to acquire the land through eminent domain.

One of the arguments raised against this proposal is that it too would be prohibitively expensive and funds for it difficult to raise. In Connecticut, a governor's task force on agricultural preservation recently recommended that this type of purchase plan be adopted, with financing of acquisition to come from a $500 million State bond issue. The bonds would be repaid by a 19 percent conveyance tax on the sale of all real estate. Projections indicate that about $30 million would be available annually for such acquisition.

Another suggestion for financing the development rights purchase proposal is through a Federal/State matching grants program. Matching grants from the Land and Water Conservation Fund are available for the purchase of land for recreation and open space purposes. Other than this, there are presently no significant grants available for other categories of open space, such as scenic easements in highway corridors, less-than-fee rights in agricultural lands, or acquisition of flood plains.

Agricultural districts

More than 1.75 million acres of land have been put in agricultural districts under a 1971 State law aimed at keeping New York's agriculture viable in the face of growing urban pressure and speculation.[40] Land put in districts includes such unique and irreplaceable areas as the entire grape belt in western New York, the mucklands in Orange County and southeastern New York, and tree fruit areas along Lake Ontario.

The statewide program, proposed by the State Commission on Preservation of Agricultural land, provides these special features: (1) Local ordinances cannot restrict structures and activities normal to farmers; (2) public agencies cannot take farm land by eminent domain without special justification; (3) sewer and water taxes cannot be levied on farm land, beyond a house and lot, once a district has been formed; and (4) property tax assessments may be based on agricultural instead of market value.

The tax assessment feature includes a rollback requiring an owner selling for development land that has been assessed at its agricultural value to pay the difference between taxes paid on the agricultural assessment and the tax he would have paid without the lower assessment for the previous five years.

Coastal zone management

California's Coastal Zone Conservation Commission is coming out strongly for preservation of agricultural land under its power to regulate all construction within 1,000 yards of the State's 1,170-mile coastline.[41] The Commission was set up under provisions of a coastline protection proposal approved in a 1972 statewide referendum.

In preparing a Coastal Zone plan to be submitted to the Legislature in 1976, the Commission appears determined to keep all agricultural lands and all land suitable for coastal-related crops out of the hands of developers. It has determined that much of this area is prime land and that other land with lower quality soil also is valuable for producing avocados, broccoli, artichokes, and other crops with special climate requirements. Included are extensive coastal farm lands in Santa Cruz, Monterey, and Mendocino counties.

Development controls

The Town of Ramapo, New York, is controlling development with a regulation tying it to the availability of existing public services or to their planned expansion.[42] This is significant because it provides a way to deal with the prevailing pattern in most urban areas of sprawl: leap-frog development and waste of land and resources.

A State court has approved the Town's ordinance keying development permission to availability of public services. It has the effect of deferring housing development in some instances for as long as 18 years. The ordinance, tied to an 18-year plan and a capital budget, also provides property tax relief to owners of land where development is delayed.

Future needs projections

In February 1973 the Michigan Department of Agriculture estimated that 8 million acres of productive agricultural land would be needed to serve the population projected for the State in the year 2000.

The estimate was included in a future needs policy statement that reported 6 million acres had been lost since 1945 from an agricultural land base of about 18 million.[43] If nothing is done, it concluded, the only agricultural land left by 2000 will be small islands surrounded by vast urban areas in the southern half of the State.

Included in the statement was a proposal to preserve the 8 million acres by creating agricultural districts, acquiring development rights to agricultural land, and taxing agricultural land at its current use value. It proposed using bonds backed by tax revenues to provide funds for purchasing the rights.

Most significant, however, is the fact that the State took an inventory to see where it stood and to try to determine whether it could meet its responsibilities to the number of people expected in the year 2000. This inventory helped focus public attention on the issue of loss of agricultural land and the possible ways this loss could be slowed or avoided.

CONCLUSIONS

From the foregoing, it is clear that action taken thus far to control urbanization of agricultural land and to prevent mining companies and others from consuming it is far short of what is needed. Too much of the Nation's agricultural land is being wasted, and the time has come to permanently dedicate what is left to food production.

Zoning, subdivision regulations, and other local controls clearly are inadequate to withstand the growing pressures of urbanization. Interim controls, such as moratoria on development, have only a temporary impact, and preferential tax treatment provisions adopted by many States are weak holding actions at best.

The cost of purchasing endangered agricultural land in an attempt to preserve it would be staggering. It is also unnecessary because the same objective can be accomplished by purchasing the development rights and paying owners for the land value that represents development potential. That reduces both uncertainty and the tax burden for farmers and makes it possible for them to retain all other ownership rights, to make long-term investments in their farming operations, and to pass the land on to the next generation.

Rapid loss of agricultural land in States like California and New Jersey, the expected consumption of millions of acres of land by strip mining and other energy-related development, the strong momentum of urban growth in huge metropolitan corridors and elsewhere, and the lack of land capability information all point to the critical need for a nationwide land use planning effort. The fact that land is both a finite resource and the basic resource for the Nation's food production capability make the need even more pressing.

FOOTNOTES

1. National inventory of soil and water conservation needs, 1967. Soil Conservation Service. Statistical Bulletin No. 461.
2. Our land and water resources, current and prospective supplies and uses. Economic Research Service. Publication No. 1290. May, 1974.
3. Agriculture in the environment. Economic Research Service. Bulletin No. 481. July, 1971.
4. National land use policy. Background papers on past and pending legislation. Senate Interior Committee. April, 1972.
5. A state research report: agricultural land in the richmond region. Richmond Regional Planning District Commission. July 1974.
6. National land use policy. Proceedings of a special conference sponsored by the Soil Conservation Society of America. Ankeny, Iowa. 1973.

7. State open space and resource conservation program for California. Prepared for California Legislature Joint Committee on Open Space Lands. April, 1972.
8. The Vermont farm and a land reform program. State Planning Office. Montpelier. June, 1973.
9. "Some Eastern states focus on protecting farmlands." Christian Science Monitor. November 2, 1973.
10. Report of the Blueprint Commission on the future of New Jersey agriculture. Trenton. April, 1973.
11. Agricultural land requirements: a projection to 2000 A.D. Prepared by Michigan Department of Agriculture. February, 1973.
12. Farming in the city's shadow. U.S Department of Agriculture. Agricultural Economics Report No. 250. February, 1974.
13. Urbanization of land in the Western states. Economic Research Service. Report No. 428. January, 1970.
14. "What should be done to improve consumer protection in land sales?" Urban Land. July-August, 1974.
15. *Ibid.*
16. Our land and water resources, *op. cit.*, p. 47.
17. *Ibid.*, p. 11.
18. *Ibid.*
19. The use of land. Report of the Task Force on Land Use and Urban Growth. New York. 1973.
20. Agriculture in the environment, *op. cit.*, p. 7.
21. Exploring energy choices. Energy Policy Project. Ford Foundation. 1974.
22. Third annual report. Council on Environmental Quality. Washington, D.C. 1972.
23. Josephy, Alvin M., Jr. "Agony of the Northern Plains." Audubon. July, 1973.
24. Electric power and the environment. Energy policy staff, Office of Science and Technology. Washington, D.C. 1970.
25. Our land and water resources, *op. cit.*
26. Productive agriculture and a quality environment. National Academy of Sciences. Washington, D.C. 1974.
27. Our land and water resources, *op. cit.*, p. vi.
28. Secondary impacts of public investment in natural resources. Proceedings of a symposium. Economic Research Service. Publication No. 1177.
29. The nation's water resources. U.S. Water Resources Council. Summary report. Washington, D.C. 1968.
30. *Ibid.*
31. McCaull, Julian. "Wringing out the environment," Environment. Vol. 16, No. 7. p. 16.
32. Agricultural land requirements, *op. cit.*
33. Land use planning and control requirements. Statement prepared by a committee of the Western Agricultural Research Council for the Western Governors Conference. March, 1974.
34. Brown, Lester R. "Global food insecurity." The Futurist. April, 1974. p. 63.
35. Bryson, Dr. Reid A. "Testimony presented to Senate Agriculture and Forestry Subcommittee." October 17, 1973.
36. "Climate vs. food: some ominous signs." Omaha World-Herald. July 14, 1974.
37. Farming in the city's shadow, *op. cit.*
38. Issues in agricultural land use management in New Jersey. Special Report No. 17. Rutgers University. February, 1973.
39. Environment. New York State Department of Environmental Conservation. Albany. December, 1974.
40. Toward an effective land use policy for Michigan. Conference proceedings. Michigan State University. Lansing. pp. 46-52.
41. "Public hearing notice." California Coastal Zone Conservation Commission. August 21, 1974.
42. Measures to preserve agricultural and undeveloped lands. Prepared for Wisconsin Legislative Council. State Planning Office, Madison, August, 1974.
43. Agricultural land requirements, *op. cit.*

Appalachia

HARRY CAUDILL*

Appalachia's history has bequeathed to us two very severe difficulties respecting land ownership. They combine to doom the vast region to continuing exploitation and poverty.

After the Civil War industrialists were able to glimpse the outlines of the nation's coming growth and they foresaw the indispensability of Appalachian coal. Agents of coal and iron companies and ambitious speculators moved in to corner title to the mineral deposits the geologists had located. These mineral buyers soon learned two things about Appalachia: the mineral wealth was vast, varied and of high quality; and the mountaineers were so poor and undiscerning that they would sell cheaply.

Some genius produced a printed deed form with appropriate blank spaces for names, dates and boundary descriptions, and purchasing got underway. Prices ranged from as little as a dime to as much as five or six dollars per acre, and the "northern" or "broad-form" deed was recorded thousands of times in hundreds of deed books. These documents transferred to absentee steel and coal corporations and to huge holding companies ownership of "all coal, oil and gas, all salt and salt water, all stone, slate and shale, all mineral and metallic substances, and all combinations of the same lying upon or within" the lands. The deeds conveyed, also, sweeping privileges to operate mines and wells, to store wastes and residues, to pollute and divert surface and underground waters, and to do any and all things deemed "necessary or convenient" in order to get out the minerals and send them to market.

The sellers, for themselves and their successors, waived all claims and demands for damages resulting from mining, drilling, the laying of pipelines and so on. They preserved for themselves and all other mountaineers who might claim the land in coming centuries only "the surface of the land, together with the right to use same for such agricultural purposes as are not inconsistent with" the rights of the mineral owners. Thus the majority of land-owning mountaineers became by contract and law little more than tenants by sufferance in their own hills.

☐ From a statement to the First National Conference on Land Reform, San Francisco, 1973. Reprinted from Barnes, Peter, editor: *The people's land*, Emmaus, Pa., 1975, Rodale Press.
*Harry Caudill is an attorney in Whitesburg, Ky. and the author of *My Land Is Dying* and other books about Appalachia.

The arrogance of Appalachia's new corporate landlords knew—and knows—no bounds. State mining laws were weak and weakly enforced. Immense slate dumps piled up near hundreds of tipples and sent palls of black, sulfurous smoke down into towns and across farms. The tipples rained clouds of dust and grit onto the same communities. The trees were cut down for lumber and mine props and flood waters roared down the denuded slopes to drown and sicken. The companies sliced off mountain tops to get the upper coal seams and "contour-stripped" and augered at lower levels, choking rivers with mud, filling lakes with silt, and emptying entire valleys. Underground mines became the deadliest on earth, killing men at four or five times the rate experienced in the pits of Holland, Germany and England.

Coal trains, lumber trains, barges, trucks and pipelines have carried half a trillion dollars worth of raw materials out of Appalachia in the last 140 years. Scores of counties have been systematically plundered for wood, limestone, talc, marble, clays, copper, iron ore, coal and gas. As the much touted "energy crisis" deepens the exploitation will steadily worsen unless the region's minerals—particularly its coal—are put to work in new and rejuvenative ways.

The people of Appalachia can bring their counties to economic health and social well-being by an enlargement of a device pioneered in the state of Washington —the public utility district. This tool has been thoroughly tested in that state and would involve little pioneering in Appalachia.

Forty years ago much of the state of Washington was cut-over timber land and semi-desert. After the lumber companies had logged the forests, fire swept through the wood residues leaving the earth blackened and naked. Erosion did immeasurable harm, but slowly the land healed itself with thickets as nature struggled to restore her forests. Thousands of people moved away and some of the counties were threatened with extinction. The people who remained came to the desperate realization that they, too, must abandon the territory or rebuild their economy along new and diverse lines. And for the task they could rely only on themselves.

They stumbled upon a novel, practical and democratic concept. The legislature authorized the formation of public utility districts having the right to own land and to exercise eminent domain. The PUDs were authorized to sell revenue bonds, generate and sell electricity and devote the proceeds of such sales to public purposes. A PUD could consist of a part of a county or of a number of counties.

In 1960 Chelan County, Washington, contained some 40,000 inhabitants. Since the Chelan County Public Utility District was established thirty-five years ago, it has sold more than $400 million worth of bonds and invested the money in hydro-electric dams and generators. It now owes $352 million, having retired the balance through its sinking fund. Total power sales amount to $30 million per year. More than a million dollars out of such income is contributed annually to finance schools, hospitals, libraries, land reclamation, reforestation and other essential public facilities and services. Abundant cheap power has attracted new industry. Good schools, a growing economy and a pleasant environment are drawing people into a county once threatened with wholesale abandonment. A "depressed area" has become a land of opportunity and growth.

A similar transformation has occurred in neighboring Grant County. That county had 42,000 inhabitants in 1960 and its income from electric power sales exceeded $20 million last year. The Grant County PUD is investing impressive sums in the development of plant sites and other facilities designed to spawn new economic muscle.

Appalachian states should emulate Washington by enacting similar enabling laws and organizing PUDs with boards appointed by the appropriate governor or elected by local inhabitants. Since a single county in Washington has sold $400 million worth of tax free debentures, a huge territory in Appalachia ought to be able to raise by the same method three or four billion dollars for regional rehabilitation.

An Appalachian PUD would formulate an over-all development plan—a program involving land, water, scenery, minerals, timber and people. It would build huge dams at strategic locations and create a vast complex of lakes. The lakes would generate hydro-electric power and provide cooling water for thermal generators. Most of the power would be fed into the growing national electric power grid for transmission to urban load centers. A part of the profits from power sales would be used for bond retirement and the balance would finance long-deferred public facilities and services, including schools, colleges, hospitals, health centers, libraries, land reclamation and sewage plants.

The local PUDs would purchase (by condemnation if necessary) the holdings of many of the absentee corporations. These minerals would be leased for mining, with guarantees written into the contracts for protection of the land and streams. Strip-mining would be prohibited except in those limited areas where total restoration of the land could be assured. Royalties would go into the treasury and substantial sums would be invested in watershed development, riding trails, camp sites and other facilities designed to convert the land into a recreation area.

The concept could be expanded beyond anything contemplated thus far. The idea of interstate compacts is an intriguing one. Such compacts have met with varying degrees of success and have often been stymied by ultra-conservative policies in the state houses. But the states are close to the people and, when wisely led, can act more effectively and precisely than the federal government.

The people of western Maryland, West Virginia, eastern Tennessee, eastern Kentucky, northern Alabama, western Virginia and western Pennsylvania share many similar problems and afflictions. All suffer in varying degrees from worn-out lands, dwindling populations and absentee ownership. All are mountainous and all have important mineral deposits. By compact the states could create an Appalachian Mountain Authority to accomplish on an interstate basis the things I have outlined for local PUDs.

The territory of the Appalachian Mountain Authority would be as big as that of the TVA. Its power to raise money would be vast. Its opportunities for service to the nation would be immeasurable.

Such an interstate authority could return the mineral wealth to the people without doing an injustice to the present owners. It could put the immense profits now flowing out of the region to work within the mountains. It could educate the highland people to a level equal to that enjoyed by America's most fortunate communities.

And it could demonstrate to the ranchers and Indians of the coal-rich Western states that if their lands are to be ransacked for fuel, the profits don't necessarily have to go to Wall Street. There are alternatives, and the profits could flow into Western improvements and Western pockets.

Copper firm says mine may help clean river

LADYSMITH, Wis.—Can the quality of water in a major river be improved by the presence of a copper mine nearby?

The Kennecott Copper Corp. believes so.

In a four volume environmental impact report it has filed with the Department of Natural Resources, Kennecott's Bear Creek Mining Co. subsidiary said its proposed Flambeau Copper Mine near here would extract ore that may be responsible for an already high copper content in the Flambeau River. According to Kennecott's report, the Flambeau River now has a copper content twice the maximum levels permitted by the US Environmental Protection Agency.

The mining company believes that by extracting the copper-bearing ore lode, which is close to the river, it would remove the major source of natural copper pollution.

The DNR is assessing Kennecott's impact report and will submit written remarks to the company by early September. It then will be six to eight months before a public hearing will be held on the company's report.

Kennecott hopes to have its open pit copper mine in operation here in the Town of Grant, one and one-half miles south of Ladysmith, by late 1976 or early 1977.

It will be the state's first copper mine. Inland Steel Co. has been producing taconite pellets from its Jackson County Iron Mine for three years and International Minerals Corp. (IMC) of Libertyville, Ill., is exploring for vanadium, a steel hardening mineral, 50 miles north of here beneath the Tiger Cat Flowage.

Kennecott plans an open pit mine and intends to use about 300 of the 3,000 acres for an ore concentration mill and pond into which it will dump ore tailings (waste). Powdered ore will be shipped by rail to Kennecott smelters in Utah or Nevada.

The report says the lode contains 4% copper, much higher than the average mine. It also contains .1% of known US copper reserves.

Two primary concerns outlined in Kennecott's impact statement are the mill's effect on the river and the open pit rehabilitation plan.

It will take an estimated 11 years of open pit mining to remove a substantial portion of the ore. However,

□ From Milwaukee Journal, Milwaukee, Wis., July 30, 1974.

the company said it might embark on another 11 year underground mine operation if it is profitable.

"No (adverse) impact on the Flambeau River water quality is anticipated. . . ." the report states.

Kennecott retained A. J. Hopwood of the University of Minnesota to study the pit rehabilitation as a lake. He said the bottom 190 feet of the 240 foot deep lake would be laden with toxic sulfide salts.

He said oxygen would not be present below the 130 foot level.

At a mining conference at St. Menario College here two weeks ago Brent McCown of the University of Wisconsin's Institute for Environmental Studies suggested the lake might be of little value after mining ceases except that "it might be a nice thing to look at."

He believes it would not support fish or plant life and that it would be too small for boating. McCown suggested the lake might be useful for "depositing contaminants or other noncyclable materials."

Because of the presence of copper ores on the stepped sides, the company said it would seed the lake with lime at 10 or 15 year intervals to eliminate what could be a "significant danger" of copper concentration.

WATER NEEDED

It will take an estimated 2 billion gallons of water to fill the 2,200 by 735 foot pit when mining ceases. Kennecott is asking permission from the DNR to siphon 500 million gallons of water from its 186 acre pond and from the Flambeau River at the rate of 5,950 gallons of water a minute for 108 days. A company hydrologist said this would be 0.7 of the average river flow.

The company said the scenic value of the river banks would not be compromised.

The company also anticipates "displacement or loss" of 1,000 to 3,000 mouse sized animals, which could create a difficult situation for predators, and displacement of 30 chipmunks, 20 red squirrels and 10 gray squirrels.

The impact of blasting ore rock with dynamite may be of considerable magnitude, but the importance "will depend on proclivities of the observer," according to the company report. Blasting will be once weekly in summer and once daily in winter; traffic will be stopped on Highway 27 for five minutes during blasting.

Swamp men oppose mining

OSCEOLA NATIONAL FOREST, Fla.—The two of them ignored the stranger for at least five minutes while they puttered with the engine of the son's pickup truck.

Then the father lifted his eyes for the first time and said, "You from the Internal Revenue?"

The stranger said no, but he knew his answer made no difference. He was being judged on some scale that did not depend on words.

LEASES SOUGHT

The decision finally fell in his favor, and an hour later the father and son told him that if his intentions were serious he should get his feet wet, brave the cottonmouth moccasins and see for himself what strip mining would do to the Osceola National Forest. The son would take him to Big Gum Swamp.

Four large corporations have asked the Interior Department for phosphate leases on about one-third of the Osceola forest, which lies just east of the Suwanee River and just south of Georgia's Okefenokee Swamp. The top elected officials of Florida are fighting the mining proposal.

The government's environmental impact statement tells in scientific detail what would happen if phosphate mining were permitted here. It warns that stripping away a large part of the forest's surface would, among many other consequences, diminish the habitat of several rare and endangered species, including the black bear, the Florida panther, the bald eagle, the red cockaded woodpecker and the alligator.

Oddly, the statement, which is six inches thick and fills three volumes, says nothing about Bob and Oedis Blanks and the remaining few thousands like them who live in the shrinking woods of the South and who, as a species, are as surely threatened as the Florida panther.

CAN'T TOLERATE CITY

It is not just that they get their living from the forest. The Blanks men sell lumber from dead cypress trees that the US Forest Service allows them to salvage. Others of the same cut make their living hauling the forest's pine for lumber and pulpwood.

More than that, however, men like Bob and Oedis Blanks live in and around the forests because they seem unable to tolerate cities. As a young man Bob

Blanks lived in the vast and unpeopled Okefenokee Swamp. He caught alligators for a living. He passed that skill on to his son, along with many others that could not be used in an urban world even if the son consented to live there.

Men like these are probably a little more violent than city people, by some standards. They seem to require more space. The impact statement compiled by the Interior Department on the proposed mining says of the black bear: "It, like the panther, requires a large home range with minimal human disturbance." So does Oedis Blanks.

"I don't know what Watergate is," he said, "and don't give a damn." But he can estimate the diameter of a tree within a tolerance of one inch by sighting across his splayed hands. He knows how to break a saw palmetto bush to get its inner bud, which is good to eat. He knows that it is pointless to worry about cottonmouth moccasins, even though they are almost certainly swimming in the tannic darkened swamp water just ahead of and just behind the splashing of a man's boots.

Oedis has no more use for ecologists, whom he blames for the ban, than he has for the Monsanto Corp., the Kerr-McGee Corp., the Pittsburgh and Midway Co. and the Global Exploration and Development Corp., the four companies that want to strip the phosphate from under the forest and convert it to fertilizer for the purpose, they say, of heading off a worldwide food shortage.

Strip mining boom jars Plains States

PAUL RECER

The economics of coal have changed. It's suddenly profitable to mine the rich beds just below the prairie in Montana, Wyoming and North Dakota. The boom is bringing prosperity and frenetic growth to small, rural towns—and fear the northern Great Plains might become another Appalachia.

COLSTRIP, Mont. (AP)—Rancher Wally McRae calls Colstrip his hometown, but he's a stranger here now. The production of energy has made this lonesome corner of "the Big Sky Country" an industrial outpost.

Colstrip, a nearly abandoned railroad town only a few months ago, throbs and rumbles today with the pulsating symphony of industrial man.

Hundreds of construction workers are building a huge power plant to plug distant cities into untapped arteries of coal under the vast plains. The 700-megawatt plant will produce enough electricity for a city of 200,000 people.

Remote valleys echo the thunder of massive machines brought here to savage virgin land for a bonanza of coal.

A picturesque highway winding leisurely through the open hills is jammed with big trucks growling under heavy loads. Wild animals flee. Clean air is suddenly filled with the reek of burning diesel.

The character of Montana, Wyoming and North Dakota, where the coal treasure is buried just below the prairie, has changed for the 1.6 million people who lived here three years ago, when the boom began.

"The isolation and solitude, the open spaces, the community of neighbors—I can see all that going out the window," says Wally McRae. "It's something I had hoped to save for my children. It's important and precious."

McRae operates a 30,000-acre ranch, part of a family empire started when his grandfather bought 160 acres from a fur trapper in 1886. His cousin, Evan McRae, owns 34,000 acres. The coal is less than 200 feet below the rolling grasslands of the two spreads.

Three generations of the family have built a life rooted in respect for this awesome, open prairie; an endless land that makes a man think even God would be lonely here.

That's how McRae and his neighbors feel. Not so the 40,000 or more industrial workers, miners, engineers

and others—no one knows exactly how many—who have come to the three states to mine the coal and turn it into energy. In Colstrip, there were 200 people in 1972, and now there are 3,000, mining and building the power plant.

The construction workers cluster in metal ghettos scattered around Colstrip and other boom towns. They overwhelm the schools, crowd the highways and walk upon private land as if it was public sidewalk.

"I guess it's a small thing, but it used to be when you passed someone on the road, you would both wave," says McRae, who is 38. "People were friendly like that around here. But you drive by Colstrip now and nobody waves.

"I went to grade school in Colstrip, but now I don't even feel welcome in my hometown any more. The town is so unsettled, nobody knows anybody.

"There's a lot of wander-on trespassing. They see an empty piece of land and think it's not owned. I've seen thirsty cattle and horses waiting for people to leave a pond so they can get water . . . And there's a lot of poaching. I have less antelope and deer now."

There are hundreds of Wally McRaes in Montana and Wyoming where the incipient Great Plains coal boom has had its greatest impact so far. They are banding together in associations to protect this land. McRae is a founding member of the Rosebud Protective Association. The members give each other moral support in their battle against the mining boom. And the association has a platform to protect the Colstrip area from a list of ills: ecological damage to the land from strip mining, higher school taxes, destruction of game, even damage to Montana's two-lane macadam highways from heavy coal trucks.

The three states have an estimated coal reserve of 260 billion tons. That's enough to generate all the electricity America currently consumes for 300 years. It's the nation's largest single reserve of coal reachable by strip mining. And it's a big percentage of the three trillion tons which the U.S. Bureau of Mines lists as America's total coal reserve.

Coal production in Montana, Wyoming and North Dakota was under 20 million tons in 1972 and it jumped to 40 million in 1973, almost all of it so far in Wyoming and Montana. The U.S. Bureau of Mines says this will increase to 600 million tons by 1985, if plans now proposed by energy companies are carried

□ From the State Journal, Lansing, Mich. Oct. 28, 1974. Reprinted by permission of The Associated Press.

out. Total U.S. production last year was 600 million tons.

About half of the coal reserve is on federal land controlled by the U.S. Department of Interior. The federal government had leased only small parcels when the state governments, especially Montana, began to resist. Now the federal government has agreed not to lease any more land for mining until it completes an environmental impact study early next year.

"Up to now we're definitely in control," said one state official. But Wally McRae isn't sure. "Anytime the federal government decides cowboys are expendable, they'll move in," he says. "There's just not much you can do."

Much of the strip mining started since 1972 is on railroad company land leased now to mining companies. There had been mining on a small scale for decades, mostly to fuel trains passing through the states.

Only a few ranchers have leased or sold to the coal companies. Evan McRae is one. He sold 3,200 acres to the Peabody Coal Co. just before the boom started, and used the money to buy twice that many acres of other grassland.

America's post-war industrial boom bypassed Montana, Wyoming and North Dakota. While the rest of the country—fueled by cheap energy from oil—went on a binge of construction and economic growth, the northern Great Plains experienced little industrial progress.

The three states were too far from major markets for factories or trade centers. Their economies remained, basically, agricultural. The coal just under the plains was easy to mine, but the cost of shipping it hundreds of miles to industrial centers was too great.

Population in the area declined. University students graduated and moved elsewhere to find jobs.

The vast plains and mountains remained lonely. And most people here liked it that way.

Then the energy crisis changed the economics of northern Great Plains coal.

They call themselves "boomers" and they're proud of it. They are the skilled construction workers who bring muscle and know-how to the boom, men who wander the country building power plants, bridges, reservoirs, mines and refineries. They have come here with wives and children to live in hardship among natives who often don't want them.

"You've got to go where the money is," said Rod Savage, a 35-year-old pipefitter from Lewistown, Mont., earning $450 a week in the coal boom.

"At home, I'd be lucky to earn $300 a month. What's the sense of living in a crackerbox house and driving an old car. Here I've got a new car, a new house and money in the bank."

The Savages and their 4-year-old son live in a mobile home that is wedged like a metal sardine among scores of others on a flat plain of sand and sage five unpaved miles from Rock Springs, Wyo.

There's no lawn, trees or park nearby. Dust rises at the faintest breath, coating cars, houses and people and filtering into every room.

Savage is helping build the Jim Bridger electric power plant, an $800 million, 2,000-megawatt complex that will burn Wyoming coal, enough for a city of half-a-million, like Seattle. To reach the plant, he must commute 80 miles a day.

Boomers in Colstrip feel even more isolated. The nearest doctor or supermarket or department store or movie is 40 miles away. Children often play on a gravel-topped road, dodging 10-ton trucks.

"You have to draw on inner resources to endure here," said Mrs. Clarence McMurtrey, the 29-year-old wife of a pipefitter from California. Her husband is helping build the Colstrip Power Plant. They live in a 22-foot motor home with their three children.

Gillette, Wyo., is another of the five Great Plains towns caught in the coal boom so far. But the boom there is in its second decade. Oil discoveries in the 1960s started it and now coal mining continues it. Gillette had 3,000 people in 1960 and is well over 20,000 today.

"This has got to be one of the most exciting places in the world right now," says Mike Enzi, 30, a shoe store owner, recently arrived in Gillette and recently elected mayor. Several stripping operations are planned for the area, and a coal gasification plant.

During the earlier oil boom, Gillette residents watched instant mobile home ghettos appear on the frozen plains. In the spring thaw they sank into the mud.

Schools were packed. Pupils spilled into temporary buildings, including an old wooden church.

This time Gillette is preparing. A $4 million junior high school has just opened. Mobile home parks are strictly regulated. The police force is beefed up. Educated by one boom, Gillette is prepared for the second.

But Rock Springs isn't. Besides the Bridger power plant, strip mines are planned, a refinery and a $75 million trona plant. The population has jumped from 25,000 to 45,000 since 1972. The new construction will add $40 million a year to the school tax rolls, town officials say.

"The town will be on easy street after the building is over," said a company executive. "But until then, it's gonna be tough."

Gillette is the town where the "Gillette syndrome" was first identified and described. A psychologist gave that name to the effect of boom town life on the boomers. It's a syndrome born of the boredom that infects families of itinerant construction workers.

Boomers laugh when the term is mentioned, but their wives nod their heads.

"It's true," said Mrs. McMurtrey in Colstrip. "Most of the women around here are bored. When their husbands come home, they expect him to entertain them and the children. He comes in tired and the next thing you know there's trouble."

Bars in and near the boom towns do a thriving business with the men. But dust and the empty plains around many mobile home camps keep most of the construction workers' wives inside their metal houses.

"My wife spends all day working puzzles," said one man. "We must have a hundred of them."

"It's crummy here," says Mrs. Jewen Sullivan, wife of a welder at the Bridger plant in Rock Springs. "There's nothing to do. The townspeople are unfriendly. It's so dry you can't grow flowers."

Mrs. Savage listened to her neighbor speak and offered: "We watch a lot of television, and thank God for the soap operas."

The turnover is great at many construction jobs. Workers often quit without explanation.

"I suspect a lot of it's domestic problems," said one company official. "Sometimes the wives will just pack up and leave. The guy'll find an empty house when he goes home. The truck rental places always do a heavy business in the spring."

The economics of coal is such that it's often more expensive to ship than to mine. As a result, industry, until recently, had little interest in going West to tap coal deposits, no matter how rich.

Eastern and Appalachian deposits were more than ample for the early American industrial machine and interest in even that waned in the postwar era when cheap oil and gas became the fuel of convenience.

Environmental concern and the energy shortage changed the picture.

Montana, Wyoming and North Dakota have 23 billion tons of low-sulphur coal. It can be burned so cleanly that utility companies using it can easily meet clean air standards effective next July.

There's enough of the low-sulphur fuel in the three states to generate all the nation's current electricity consumption for 30 years. And strip mining is so easy the coal can be shipped 1,000 miles and still be cheaper than deep-mined Eastern coal, whose cost is rising.

The Northern Great Plains coal rush began with energy companies acquiring the coal properties of the railroads. Then other leasing began, and by this fall there were hundreds of proposals for coal development.

Wyoming has seven mines operating now, producing 18.6 million tons a year. Six Montana mines produced about 40 million tons last year. North Dakota has four strip mines, and output is small. A number of proposals have been made to start major production in that state.

Coal economics make it most attractive of all to burn the fuel near the mine. As a result, $2 billion now is being invested in plants, machinery and facilities. Energy from the coal will be exported by wire, as electricity, and by pipeline, as synthetic gas.

The massive Bridger plant and mine near Rock Springs, costing $800 million alone, "will have four units of 500 megawatts each," says Ken Worrell of Pacific Power & Light, the plant's owner. "One unit would be enough to serve all of Wyoming."

And there's more to come.

A company called Energy Transportation System, Inc., has proposed a coal slurry pipeline. The system would pipe ground coal mixed with water from Wyoming to Arkansas.

Burlington Northern Railroad Co. has proposed construction of 135 miles of new tracks from Gillette southward. The track, the most constructed in 30 years in this country, would be to haul coal.

There are rumors each day of other new projects. "The real boom hasn't hit yet," said one company official.

The massive, sharp-toothed bucket sliced into the rich fuel and in one bite scooped up enough coal to heat a home for a winter.

Around the 120-foot-deep pit are huge mounds of loose dirt, the soil that once covered the coal. When the area is mined out, more than 12,000 acres will be torn up near this Colstrip mine alone.

Bringing jobs to people: does it pay?

GENE F. SUMMERS and JEAN M. LANG

Over the last twenty-five years manufacturing industries have been moving out of the city and into the countryside at an ever increasing rate. Between 1960 and 1970 manufacturing employment in nonmetropolitan areas grew by 22 percent while manufacturing jobs in metropolitan areas grew only four percent.

Industries have had their own reasons for expanding into rural areas: lower local taxes, cheaper land and water costs, and a good supply of laborers, presumably steeped in the American work ethic.

Industry's interest in rural factory sites has been strongly encouraged by the eager solicitations of potential host communities and by federal policy. For example, nonmetropolitan location of industry has been an explicit goal of recent federal anti-poverty legislation including the Economic Opportunity Act of 1964, the Public Works Act of 1965, the Appalachian Regional Act of 1965, and the Rural Development Act of 1972.

The apparent logic behind this interventionist strategy is fairly simple. Both rural poverty and urban socioeconomic problems are seen as products of a geographic mismatch of labor supply and demand. The mismatch has been caused by a decline in economic opportunities in rural areas and an increase of the same opportunities in urban areas. One means of correcting this imbalance is to stimulate the rural economy, thereby increasing job opportunities and halting the exodus of rural labor to the city.

An industry, particularly a manufacturing plant that generates a direct flow of money to the local community, is considered an ideal stimulus for the rural economy. Industry's presence is expected to spark

This article was prepared by Gene F. Summers, Professor of Rural Sociology, University of Wisconsin-Madison, and Jean M. Lang, Editor and Science Writer, Institute for Environmental Studies, University of Wisconsin-Madison. It is based upon material in Gene F. Summers, Sharon Evans, Frank Clemente, Elwood M. Beck, Jr. and Jon Minkoff, *Industrial Invasion of Nonmetropolitan America;* Praeger, 1976.

The University of Wisconsin Department of Rural Sociology issues a semi-annual list of "Publications in Print." Many of these deal with applied programs in Wisconsin, others with specific studies in community development and rural industrialization related to problems discussed in this article. For a copy of the publications list, write Gene Summers at the Department of Rural Sociology, 603 WARF Building, University of Wisconsin, Madison, Wisconsin, 53706.

income growth, population redistribution, housing improvements, better community services, and other amenities. It is exactly these presumed benefits that make large industry so attractive to the small community. But are these benefits being delivered? Do rural communities really profit from industry's arrival, or are there undesirable side effects?

In a study sponsored by the Economic Development Administration, U.S. Department of Commerce, a team of sociologists attempted to answer these questions.[1]

Our group reviewed almost 100 case studies of the impacts of industrial location on nonmetropolitan communities. The case studies encompassed more than 700 manufacturing plants in 245 locations and 34 states. The predominant industries were ·metals production and fabrication, chemicals manufacture and wearing apparel assembly. The factories ranged in size from those with less than ten workers to plants with over 4,000 employees. The majority of factories were located in the Midwest and the South.

Although the studies included a great diversity of industries and locations, they did not constitute a representative sample and should be judged accordingly.

EMPLOYMENT—DIRECT HIRING

There is no question that industry brings new jobs to a community. Some of the jobs come from direct hiring of plant personnel, and others follow indirectly as the new industry stimulates growth in existing sectors of the local economy. The important question is who gets the new jobs.

Our study revealed that new factories generally *did not* hire the local unemployed. In the majority of cases only a small portion of the jobs were filled by local disadvantaged or unemployed persons (Table 1). There was also considerable evidence that nonwhites were underrepresented in rural factories.

There appeared to be two primary reasons why local poor, minorities and disadvantaged were infrequently hired:

First, the labor pool for a rural industry extends well beyond the area of the host community. Long distance commuters are not uncommon, and the new factory generates considerable in-migration and settlement of workers from the surrounding area (Table 2). From

Table 1. Percentage of new plant workers previously unemployed

Study site	Industry	No. of jobs	% of jobs filled by previously unemployed
Linton, Ind.	Aluminum chairs	100	25.0%
Wynne, Ark.	Apparel; copper tubing	1,900	11.2
Rochester, Minn.	Business machines	1,862	14.0
Ravenswood, W. Va.	Aluminum	894	11.0
E. Oklahoma Comm.	12 plants (mixed)	554	7.7
A.R.A. Area survey	33 plants (mixed)	1,262	43.0
Mt. Airy, N.C.	Appliances	435	8.0
Jefferson, Ia.	Stamping, athletic equipment	369	3.0
Orange City, Ia.	10 plants (mixed)	364	19.0
Creston, Ia.	Appliance, chemicals, oil filters	424	1.0
Grinnell, Ia.	Farm machinery, stadium bleachers, plastics	200	7.0
Decorah, Ia.	Screws; undetermined	212	8.0
Star City, Ark.	Apparel (shirts)	336	9.5

Table 2. Proportion of plant workers migrating to take new employment

Census region	No. of studies	Average percent
North Central	6	32
South	4	32
West	1	18
All regions	11	30

this widespread labor force, industry selects the better educated, more highly skilled worker with the "right" racial heritage. The local unskilled resident often has little hope of qualifying.

Second, many jobs are taken by newcomers to the labor force, primarily women. Many rural industries, particularly textiles and electronics assembly, prefer female labor. Thus previously nonworking women fill the factory jobs. This increases the number of people in the labor force but does not decrease the number of unemployed workers in the community.

Ironically, it is possible for new industry to reduce unemployment and poverty in a community without providing a single job to the disadvantaged who live

Table 3. Unemployment rates before and after industrial development

Study sites	Dates		Rates (%)		Change
	Before	After	Before	After	
Jackson Co., Ia.	1950	1960	1.8	3.7	+1.9
Cross Co., Ark.	1960	1970	5.2	4.6	−0.6
Washington Co., Miss.	1950	1963	10.1	4.2	−5.9
Box Elder Co., Utah	1955	1965	6.7	7.0	+0.3
Putnam, LaSalle and Bureau Co., Ill.	1966	1973	3.6	5.0	+1.4
Adair Co., Okla.	1960	1970	16.4	17.5	+1.1
Cherokee Co., Okla.	1960	1970	16.2	10.0	−6.2
Muskogee Co., Okla.	1960	1970	8.9	7.4	−1.5
Hot Springs Co., Ark.	1958	1970	11.9	7.0	−4.9
Baxter Co., Ark.	1964	1970	8.2	4.7	−3.5
Howard Co., Ark.	1960	1970	4.3	3.9	−0.4
Logan Co., Ark.	1958	1970	15.6	6.8	−8.8
Randolph Co., Ark.	1964	1970	9.4	9.3	−0.1
Benton Co., Ark.	1960	1970	5.5	4.5	−1.0
White Co., Ark.	1960	1970	12.1	12.1	0.0
Laurel Co., Ky.	1960	1963	12.6	7.1	−5.5
Lamar Co., Texas	1952	1962	6.0	5.2	−0.8

there. Although the labor force may expand faster than the ranks of the unemployed, the absolute number of persons in economic distress may be unchanged or slightly increased (Table 3). In general, the case studies showed that the operations of the local labor market often work against the needs of the people for whom rural industrial development has been allegedly promoted.

EMPLOYMENT—MULTIPLIER EFFECT

Besides hiring local workers for its factory, new industry is expected to generate secondary jobs in the retail, wholesale and service trades of the host community. This indirect effect on employment is called a "multiplier." A multiplier of 1.0 means the industry brings no new jobs except those by direct hiring. A multiplier of 1.65 means that for every new job in the factory, another .65 job is created within the community.

A significant finding of the case study review was that the majority of industries in the rural community had a multiplier effect of *less than 1.2.* Several reasons were given for these low multipliers:

First, the less diversified the existing manufacturing, commercial and service industries are, the less impact the new industry will have on local economy.

Second, commuters, who generally make up a substantial part of the rural factory work force, often spend their

Table 4. Employment multipliers

Study site	Unit of analysis	Research time period	Industrial product	Direct employment	Employment multiplier
1. Linton, Ind.	City	1964	Aluminum chairs	119	1.02
2. Gassville, Ark.	8-County Area	1960-63	Shirt plant	750	1.11
3. Summerville, S.C.	4-County Area	1963	Brick factory	25	1.36
4. Pickens, Miss.	4-County Area	1964-65	Tissue paper mill	57	1.14
5. Braxton Co., W. Va.	County	1963	Particle board plant	77	1.50
6. Hart Co., Ky.	County	1963	Bedding plant	111	1.06
7. Fleming Co., Ky.	County	1958-63	Auto & appliance trim, shoes	328	1.11
8. Laurel Co., Ky.	County	1958-63	Yarn	107	1.18
9. Lincoln Co., Ky.	County	1958-63	Apparel	380	1.00
10. Marion Co., Ky.	County	1958-63	Barrels, communications equipment, apparel	496	1.11
11. Russell Co., Ky.	County	1958-63	Apparel	206	1.03
12. Howard Co., Ind.	County	1949-60	All manufacturing	4,006	1.44
13. Box Elder Co., Utah	County	1955-61	Chemicals	5,688	1.34
14. Lawrence Co., Tenn.	County	1954-63	Bicycles	2,270	1.36
15. Select U.S. Counties	11 Counties	1950-60	All manufacturing	17,116	1.65
16. Select U.S. Counties	10 Counties	1960-70	All manufacturing	25,677	1.68
17. Leflore Co., Miss.	County	1959-64	All manufacturing	1,430	1.59
18. White Co., Ark.	County	1951-59	All manufacturing	590	1.71

salary in their place of residence rather than their place of work. Much of the factory income "leaks out" of the host community.

Third, many small towns already have excess under-utilized business capacity. As a result, the firm can handle industry-induced increases in sales without hiring additional workers or enlarging their capital stock.

Fourth, many industries are linked by a national network to outside suppliers and processors and have no need to draw upon local services or products.

At worst, the local community may become little more than a labor source for the factory with virtually no indirect or induced employment.

Four often cited studies (nos. 15, 16, 17, and 18 in Table 4) that depict nonmetropolitan industry with a multiplier of 1.5 or more were closely examined by the review team. In each of the studies it was found that only those rural counties had been selected that had relatively large manufacturing sectors (more than 15 percent of total employment) and were undergoing rapid and substantial economic growth. According to these criteria, only 30 counties in the entire U.S. qualified in 1970.

INCOME

Industrialization of the rural area does bring an increase in average income over a period of time. The case studies showed that average increases in individual income varied from 5.3 to 183.0 percent, and average family income increases ranged from 25.6 to 178.4

percent. However, in most cases both family and individual income increases were less than 50 percent.

Three factors were largely responsible for the frequent cases of relatively small income growth:
- Small income increases were usually associated with lower wage industries such as wood, textiles and apparel.
- Industries importing raw materials into the area and exporting products out of the area created smaller secondary income effects as discussed above.
- A substantial amount of commuting by nonresidents into an area for work, and by residents out of an area to shop, reduced the size of income growth.

Significantly, of the numerous case studies on industry's impact, very few had considered how income growth is distributed throughout the population. Of those studies which did examine this factor, all suggested that certain sectors of the population receive no benefits from industrial development. Indeed, for groups such as the elderly and blacks, industrialization often has negative effects. As the community's standard of living rises, prices go up and the purchasing power of these disadvantaged groups decreases.

In addition, several of the impact studies showed that the greatest gain in benefits went to newcomers in the community rather than to the original residents. This suggests that the people who bear the cost of the development (by increased taxes for land development, for example) may not be the *same* people who will capture the benefits and in fact they may find themselves in a *worse* relative position after development than before.

The question arises as to whether industrial development is a desirable community goal simply because it may marginally increase *average* income. The basic issue boils down to whether growth in "community" well-being should be purchased at the expense of the disadvantaged.

POPULATION CHANGES

Does industrial development halt population decline in small towns or rural communities? The answer is unequivocally, yes.

All case studies dealing with industry's impact on rural population showed that the rate of population decline had been slowed, halted, or—as in the majority of cases—reversed after industry's arrival. However, the studies also made it clear that most population growth was based on an increased migration of workers into the area.

In eleven case studies, an average 30 percent of factory workers had moved into the host communities to take their jobs. The majority of these workers had originally commuted to the factory from neighboring areas within a radius of 50 miles. Eventually, however, as the workers became more settled and secure in their jobs, most of them moved into the host community or nearby towns. Exceptions to this trend occurred when a county had well-developed transportation and educational systems, as well as a surplus of labor. In such instances, employees preferred to commute rather than move to town.

The population growth that accompanied industrialization was found to be centered in the factory town rather than being spread throughout the country. In almost all cases, the population in the host town increased while the rural and farm population of the surrounding area decreased. Thus, industrialization frequently caused more of the county population to become "urbanized" or "suburbanized" without causing any overall increase in county population.

Industrial location is often promoted as a technique for achieving urban-rural population balance. Our findings, however, suggest that what industry does achieve is a redistribution of the local rural population rather than a movement of people into the area from distant metropolitan areas.

In a number of case studies, the age composition of the population also showed slight change with the arrival of industry. The changes were primarily due to migration in one form or another. In some instances, age declined due to in-migration of young workers with young families.

A close look at twelve case studies revealed that most industries preferred to hire young adults who could handle physically hard work. Yet, surprisingly, industrial development failed to stem the flow of young people migrating out of rural communities. This is noteworthy in light of the popular notion that attracting more industry to the small town will eliminate the need for the young to leave home in search of work.

BENEFITS TO THE PUBLIC SECTOR

Industry is actively sought by small communities in the hopes of enlarging the community's tax base. An enlarged tax base means an increase in public income and the expansion of community services. In general, industry's contributions to the public income can be divided into two categories: direct payments and induced (or indirect) payments.

Direct payments

Property tax. The actual size of industry's property tax bill is largely determined by local and state tax structures and by negotiated agreements between local government officials, development representatives and industrial management. Case studies show that frequently local government is willing to grant "tax holidays" exempting industrial property from taxation for 5, 10, or 15 years. This is a form of subsidization for industrial development and as such is a *cost* to local government.

Fees and service charges. Communities with municipally owned utilities can expect direct payments from industry for services rendered. These utility fees should at least equal the cost of extending service to the plant. The evidence suggests that in many communities costs are, in fact, all that is recovered from fees and there are no net gains from utility payments.

The few studies which focused on industry's direct payments to local government suggest that most of the potential for income gain by the host community is bargained away. Many local leaders are willing to trade direct revenues from new industry for indirect funds on the apparent assumption that the latter will outweigh the former.

Indirect payments

Indirect payments by industry to the public sector are more diverse and are based on industry's ability to boost local average income and subsequently increase the value—and tax assessments—of local properties and businesses.

Wages and salaries paid by the new industry are a stimulus to growth and add to local income only to the extent that the plant's payroll is spent in the host community. However, one case study revealed that through leakage of income to nonlocal recipients, an

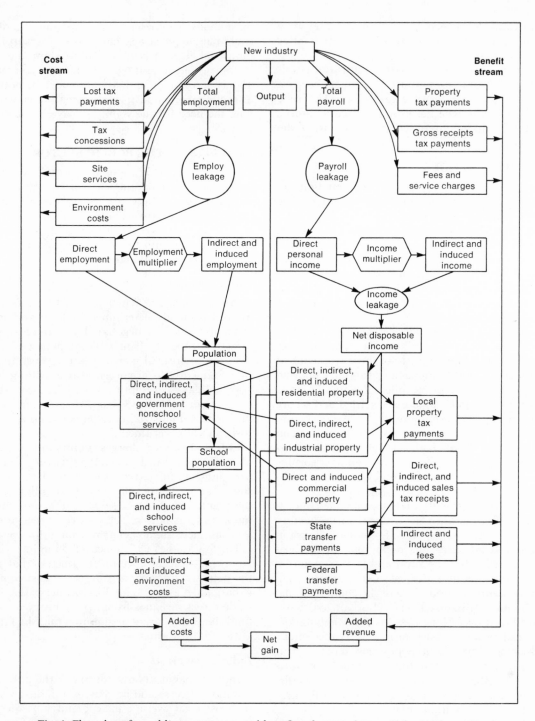

Fig. 1. Flow chart for public sector costs and benefits of new industry. (Adapted from Hirsch, 1961.)

average weekly plant payroll of $6,000 shrunk to $4,779. The "leaked" money was spent primarily on food, services and investments in neighboring communities; was put into savings; and was used to pay off old debts. In rural communities, gains in aggregate disposable income may be more apparent than real for the local market.

Increases in local public revenues result from industrial development only when growth in the private sector is converted into public monies. These monies include increased property taxes from the expansion or construction of new homes and businesses, increased retail sales and sales tax, increased utility fees and an increase in the transfer of state and federal revenues to the local community.

Residential and commercial property tax. New manufacturing jobs in a community generally mean that more income will flow into home construction and improvements. This in turn means an increase in property values and proportionately, property taxes. Likewise, as residents spend more disposable income and as industry draws upon the services of local businesses, existing commercial establishments will expand. In fact, all the case studies showed that industrial development did bring increases in assessed valuation of property and subsequent increases in local property tax revenues.

However, the case studies also revealed that increases in housing construction or business expansion cannot be predicted with certainty. Many small towns have both underutilized housing and excess business capacity. This slack means that the town can accommodate a certain amount of growth without ever increasing its commercial or residential tax base.

Retail sales. Case studies showed that retail sales in industrially developing communities increased substantially from preindustry levels. In those communities which have a local sales tax, or which receive a transfer of state sales tax receipts, this growth in sales can mean increased revenues.

Fees for services. User fees and charges such as licenses, building permits and rental fees on publicly owned land generally increased as a result of increases in disposable income or a change in the consumption pattern of residents.

Public utility income was seen to rise in a number of case studies.

Intergovernmental transfer of payments. Because of legislative constraints placed upon their taxing authority, many municipalities appeal to state and federal governments for a transfer of funds back to the local level. The case studies indicate that as industrial development increases the local average income and as industry's output grows, the volume of these transfer payments also increases. Larger amounts of the taxes on personal income (gasoline, sales, and income tax are typical) find their way back to the local community. Similarly, a greater proportion of corporate income taxes or gross receipt taxes on industrial output are turned back to the host community rather than being added to the state's general fund.

The case studies suggest, however, that industrialized communities may come to depend on state and federal payments for a larger share of their total receipts. Frequently, this dependence on transfer payments is only temporary and declines after a period of adjustment. For example, since the gasoline tax is more immediately responsive to growth in economic activity than is assessed valuation of property, local officials may temporarily rely on gasoline tax transfer payments rather than on property tax to meet immediate costs.

The case studies are very consistent in reporting increases in local revenue following industrial location. The assessed valuation of property clearly is expanded and property tax receipts increased in every community. Retail sales consistently increased resulting in added revenue from sales tax. Intergovernmental transfer payments increased in absolute dollar amounts and communities appeared to shift the tax burden from local toward nonlocal revenue sources. The sum in the benefit column can add up to a substantial amount.

COST TO THE PUBLIC SECTOR

If one considers only the benefit stream, the conclusion must be that new industry produces added revenue for the local public sector. But an often overlooked fact is that the added revenue brought to the community by industry may be equalled or even exceeded by added and often unexpected costs. For this reason it is extremely important to consider how new industry contributes to the costs of the public sector.

Attracting new industry. The initial costs of new industry arise when a community attempts to attract a plant to its area. The most frequently incurred costs in the wooing of industry are as follows:
• land acquisition costs,
• site preparation (including extension and improvement of access roads and preliminary landscaping),
• loss of previously collectable property taxes in instances where new industry is given a tax "holiday" or reduced rate,
• increased police and fire protection,
• provision of water and sewerage, electricity and/or gas, often for fees that are less than cost.

As an example of the large investments that some communities have in their efforts to attract industry, consider the city in Kentucky that issued $250,000 worth of industrial revenue bonds to finance land acquisition and building construction for a shoe factory. Since the land and building were city-owned, they were exempt from real property tax. In addition, the city granted the company a five-year exemption from personal property taxes.

In another case, a Kentucky city issued a $650,000 revenue bond and held title to the land, building and part of the equipment of the plant making them nontaxable. The city also extended a water line to the plant at a cost of $10,000 to the city.

All these development efforts by the local community are forms of subsidy and must be regarded as costs to the community. In some instances, part of the subsidy cost is recovered, but in other instances only a partial recovery is achieved. Often local public officials underestimate a new industry's requirements for community services above and beyond the initial commitment to land, building and equipment. These additional costs of government services, plus costs of school expansion and environmental degradation, also must be recovered by the public sector if it is to realize a net gain from new industry.

Accommodating growth. Besides the costs of attracting industry, the host community must also accommodate the costs of a growing population. As mentioned above, industry frequently brings an influx of new workers who are primarily young adults with families. These in-migrants place increased demands on the community for schools, health care, and recreational and general services.

Growth in the number of residential and business properties also places greater demands on local government to provide improved police and fire protection, road maintenance and water and sewerage services. Eleven out of twelve case studies showed substantial increases in costs of community services to residents with the arrival of industry. Water and sewerage services, particularly, were important sources of increased cost. Rockdale, Texas, for example, was forced to drill a new city well and to issue a bond for sewerage line extension as a result of industrial development.

The case studies suggest that while public officials often overestimate their communities' growth capacities, they underestimate the capacity of existing utilities and services to accommodate development. The result is a major outlay of public funds that increase the per capita cost of public services.

Expanding school services. The case studies provided consistent evidence that new industry increases the population of school-age children. It is also clear that increased enrollment resulted in increased operating budgets for schools and sometimes in high capital outlay to accommodate new students.

While some of these additional costs are recovered through increased taxes and intergovernmental transfer payments, part of the burden must be carried by the host community.

Environmental degradation. Industry brings long-term alterations of the environment: loss of open space and agricultural land, increased man-land density and changes in land use patterns. In addition, industry frequently brings problems of air, noise and water pollution. At the time most of the case studies were made, the environment was not a major concern and one observer made this comment:

The most striking social cost to the town imposed by industry is water pollution, which in most of the towns studied has reached serious proportions. The concern for this problem shown by town governments is after the fact. Since industry is primarily responsible, the weak position taken by local government suggests that the absence of water pollution control is one form of industrial incentive.[2]

NET GAINS

The net gain of new industry to the local public sector is the difference between its direct and indirect cost and its direct and indirect benefits. While most case studies have stressed the benefits side of the ledger, a few have also looked at the cost side and found some interesting facts. In one study five Kentucky towns with eight new plants were examined. It was found that only two of the plants produced revenues in excess of that yielded by the property prior to the plant location. Analysis of secondary impacts, where one might expect net benefits due to operation of the multiplier effect, corroborated the negative impact of new industry.

Other studies which compared estimated net gains of the private sector with net gains by the public sector also showed some sharp contrasts. One estimate, which closely approximated actual conditions in twelve communities, showed the private sector averaging a net gain of $152,981. The public sector averaged only $521 and the school district $401. This kind of evidence challenges the belief that new industry will substantially improve the fiscal burden of many nonmetropolitan communities. The evidence also suggest that were local government more assertive in channeling private sector gains into the public sector, industrial location could contribute more positively to a community's fiscal well-being.

In summary, industrial location in the rural community can bring employment, population growth and economic prosperity to the area; but as the studies have shown, these benefits do not come automatically nor do they apply in all cases. In some instances the structure of the community and the character of the particular industry merge to the benefit of both parties. More often the industry clearly gains while having a negligible or even negative effect on the host community over the long run.

[1] Gene F. Summers, Sharon Evans, Jon Minkoff, Frank Clemente, and Elwood M. Beck, Jr., *Industrial Invasion of Nonmetropolitan America*, New York: Praeger Publishers, 1976.

[2] Abt Associates, Inc., "The Industrialization of Southern Rural Areas: A Study of Industry and Federal Assistance in Small Towns with Recommendations for Future Policy," Washington, D.C.: U.S. Dept. of Commerce, Economic Development Administration, Office of Economic Research, December, 1968.

Alternative responses to changes in farm technology, structural characteristics, and rural communities

Jim Converse, Isao Fujimoto, and Richard D. Rodefeld

Section five contains thirty-one items, about equally drawn from newspaper articles and series, popular magazines, and academic or agency publications and reports. Much of the information is either direct reporting by or about people affected by the changes chronicled in the previous sections of this collection. Immediately apparent are the many groups that assume they have some right to pontificate about the desired state of affairs in rural America and the many that assume that things as they are currently going do not contain even small germs of possible solutions.

A point underlying many of the suggestions is the tension over establishing policies. Some suggest the continued domination by whichever groups get control of the policymaking apparatus (Paarlberg, Federation of Southern Cooperatives, Pierce). Others point to the need for intervention around specific problems (Perry, Browne, Livmere, Swann, Henkes). Others point to the need for more comprehensive changes, often with a heavy role for outside agencies or forces that are seen as capable of rising above the fray of local battles (Belden and Forte; Bible, Chapter 6; Barnes, Chapter 5; Breimyer and Flinchbaugh, 1973). Of a more far-reaching nature are proposals involving either radical restructuring of society, with a diminished role for capitalistic-competitive values or moving more toward locally autonomous, small-scale units (Stoltzfus; Cox; Blobaum; Todd, Chapter 4).

In many of the selections writers propose alternatives that would open some doors to new farmers or increase the survival capacity of small and family farms. Some people merely want to stay in operation at some level above poverty (Searle, Pierce). Others want to get into farming as an alternative to other jobs or to become less dependent on full-time employment (Penta, Associated Press, Hanson, Pfefferkorn). Alternative ways to increase earnings include cooperative marketing (Federation of Southern Cooperatives), diversification (Pierce), local marketing (Houriet, Myers, 1976), and part-time work off the farm (Donohue, Chapter 10).

Included are proposals for and actual experiences in gaining greater access to land (Limvere; Swann; Berry, Chapter 3), adapting technology so it is less expensive (Stoltzfus), less depleting of natural and human resources (Nelson; Merrill, Chapter 7), and more easily accessible across the spectrum of farm types (Todd, Chapter 4; Guither, Krause, and Bottom, 1972). The idea of efficiency growing out of economies of scale is viewed by some writers more as unequal access to cost-reducing subsidies than as any inherent advantage to large size (Bulbulian). Such subsidies are political in origin; leaving them in effect or removing them is also a matter of politics. That their existence changes the nature of competition is a matter of considerable importance for small farmers, who either do not have access to them (Pierce) or find the ways they operate inappropriate (Belden and Forte). We suggest that there are appropriate policies for small farmers, as well as appropriate technologies. If subsidies were equalized across farm types, or simply eliminated for larger-than-family farm operations, it would do much to permit many of the overlooked strong points of small and family farms to emerge.

The question of whether we can turn back the technological clock is raised in some readings (Kendall) and answered indirectly in others (Nelson, Searle). Some writers express the need for the question to be addressed to a broad segment of American citizenry, which needs to include more than the commercial farmers and the technobureaucracy surrounding them (Hightower, Chapter 7; Berry, Chapter 3; Todd, Chapter 4). Organizational efforts to obtain redress both in the past and present are reviewed (Taylor). Excerpts from testimony before Congress suggest that the traditional avenue of mobility of hired laborer to tenant to small holder to family-size farmer is no longer possible (Bulbulian, Leon). Farmers seldom have hired laborers. This tendency has been replaced by vertical integration.* "Marrying the farmer's daughter" now means becoming a stockholder in a family corporation. For rural young people born in poverty, and for an increasing number of middle-income-level people, the bottom rung on the new agricultural ladder is simply beyond reach.

Changes in values with regards to technology

Some of the articles propose changing the nature of technology utilized on the farms. Others suggest that technology created the problem, and more or different technology will only further exacerbate the probelm. Of special interest is the growing debate over appropriate technology, with the government taking a standard approach: fund some centers on a small scale and expand its role. Presumably this will result in multiple proposals for future funds and deflect attention to how well some centers do things, rather than focusing on the needs for concerted actions reflecting structural roots to problems.

Probably the idea of appropriate technology has been around since someone decided square wheels could give smoother rides by cutting off the corners to make eight-sided wheels (we obviously imply that further improvements are possible). It has gained much recent support through the writings of Schumacher, Illich, and others. Much research in the rural sociological field has viewed technology as a given and constantly increasing force in rural areas. Social and cultural patterns get bent, spindled, and otherwise mutilated in the ongoing rush of technical change. Those who refuse to use it at all are deemed antichange, fatalistic, and all the other opprobriums social scientists can heap on their heads. Only recently have such terms as violent technology (that which causes strain in the social fabric or damages the environment in other ways) come into common usage among analysts of the current scene. That certain aspects of our common existence transcend the "need" to produce more (and presumably better) crops, cars, and a variety of throw-away items has not yet been universally accepted, but serves at least to calm somewhat the voices clamoring for "progress" as opposed to permanence (Fujimoto, 1977).

Schumacher (1973) suggests that the idea that problems all have technological solutions is based on an illusion created by past "breakthroughs." Such new "discoveries" often involve different ways to replace labor with fossil fuels or use their derivatives in more intensive ways. Little thought is given to ways to better use simpler and renewable forms of energy. Current economics treats both fossil fuels and the cleanliness and viability of the ecosystem as things that can be infinitely maintained or replaced, rather than as things that are gone forever, once used. Both Marxian and capitalist economic theory miss the point of "found" resources being part of the capital stock of society that must be maintained if production is to continue. In lauding the "made" components of the productive process (science and technology), both theoretical systems contribute to humankind's alienation by treating as valueless things that are not created by people. By overspecializing in research

---

*Needs for additional labor are met usually by mechanization. The farmer through contracting to deliver crops or livestock is often assuming a role similar to a hired worker who furnishes labor and land to off-farm companies engaged in processing or resale.

applied to very large scale systems of production, the scientific establishment has failed to generate humble models that work in microenvironments, where the goal is to keep things in self-supportive relationship rather than to control out all possible factors (Todd, Chapter 4).

Such a view of appropriate technology considers also the need for tools to become again an expression of the creativity of the toolmaker and tool user. While modern agricultural machinery has done much to reduce the drudgery in farmwork, all too often it has also resulted in dependence on mechanics, parts suppliers, and other off-the-farm institutions. The machines often replace the farmer's work with capital expenditures that drain the capital from the operation. The result is an increase in the volume of production and cash flow through the farm enterprise, but also, in many cases, the replacement of labor by machinery (Table 1, Chapter 1). In that machinery is often cheaper on a per unit of production basis for larger farms, the labor of the smaller farmer is valued at a lower level than would be the case in a nonmechanized context.

11 Alternative responses to changes in farm technology and structural characteristics

One alternative to the current situation is to allow existing mechanisms to operate, assuming they will affect whatever changes are needed. Another is to do nothing and allow past changes to continue. A variant of this is to speed up the rate of such changes. All of these imply an acceptance of the situation as it exists.

Paarlberg suggests that the trend toward industrialized agriculture will not result in the demise of family farms. He sees a mix of the two as the probable end result, admitting that currently existing political mechanisms can best translate the desires of the public into whatever legislative or other action is needed. He notes that not all people agree on the present form of agricultural organization, but feels those who disagree, if a minority, can only hope to change the situation when it becomes of sufficient importance for larger segments of the population to lend their support. Kendall (summarizing a paper by a USDA researcher) suggests that the desire to return to simpler forms of agricultural production is unrealistic, as is, by implication, the future survival of whatever remains of such forms. An estimate is reported of the large amount of land that would have to be diverted from production of food for people to production of feed for animals (mainly horses) if we were to return to animal power as a major source of energy. Posing the issue in this way misses the point behind extensive machine use. Other writings (especially Perelman, Chapter 2) suggest that the currently high levels of machine use and chemical control of pests—both of which are major factors in the high profitability of large farms—are the result of public underwriting of the cost of the development of these technologies. Also important is the continued subsidy through underpricing petroleum products for agriculture, whether through tax mechanisms, volume purchase discounts, or permitting the externalization of the cost of waste disposal (absence of runoff or other environmental degradation controls). These factors are not considered. The concern over the possibility of a food shortage overlooks the prospect of getting more total energy from grain by eating foods lower down the food chain and consuming less grain indirectly as animal protein.

An article from the *NFO Reporter* (Chapter 6) suggests that to allow such trends to continue is to side in favor of the destruction of rural communities and family farms. It criticizes U.S. Chamber of Commerce opposition to legislation to slow the spread of corporations into agriculture and points out that corporate farms bypass local communities in their purchases and pass their profits on to absentee stockholders, rather than leaving them available to local area banks or investing them in local institutions, such as schools, churches, and businesses. Seckler (Chapter 6) is more optimistic about corporations in agriculture. He sees them as channeling additional capital into rural areas where high-cost farming technology, especially irrigation equipment, may be above the financial capacity of local farmers. He also sees employment on corporate farms as a higher-paying prospect for local people who have no hope of buying their own farms. Such people, usually descendents of hired workers (who often had only meager wages and few prospects for advancement into ownership of land) are of different origin than the local landowning classes. As such, Seckler sees them as representing "seeds of profound social change."

In the face of contradictory evidence about the impact of corporation farming, Bible (Chapter 6) suggests that the trend needs to be slowed until more evidence is in. To allow the trend to pick up speed will predetermine much of the future direction of U.S. agriculture, ruling out other options that, at present, are still open.

Allowing past trends to continue, but attempting to reassess the viability of small farms is another alternative. Such efforts also look to the "pre–intensive-chemical" past, as a way to get out of the cost-price squeeze, the environmental deterioration trend, and other negative side effects of chemical-intensive agriculture.

Nelson reviews the problems larger farms run into in the cost-price squeeze and suggest that profits can be made through cost reduction. While nonchemical methods to increase productivity or protect crops are not developed to such a point as to make it possible to maintain overall production at the same level as with chemically dependent production techniques, the price reduction in changing to lower levels of chemical inputs is greater than the income reduction resulting from smaller overall yields. This happens even in the absence of costs assigned to environmental degradation (or conversely, assigning positive values to nonpolluting production methods). Should such costs also be included, the difference would be even more marked. The recent rapid rise in both price and level of application of chemical inputs (Table 1, Chapter 1) has paved the way for increasing profits through producing less rather than more (a goal never reached by major withholding actions). As suggested by other writings (Perelman, Chapter 2, Clark, Chapter 5; Pimentel and others, 1973), the already high level of chemical fertilization is of major importance because it has pushed application rates to such a high level that very little additional return comes from unit increases. The same logic works going back the other way on the curve. A slight reduction in yield means a (proportionally) large reduction in cost. That consumers are often willing to pay a premium for foods without chemical residues is an additional source of earnings.

Blobaum describes how such logic works in China. The use of organic methods has permitted continuous cultivation over centuries, supporting a population four times that of the United States on approximately the same acreage. Also, the absence of soil or environmental degradation resulting from recycling all available wastes is a benefit of the Chinese methods of production. A major factor is the use of night soil in fertilizing fields. Decentralized settlement patterns facilitate such practices (Todd, Chapter 4). Relis (Chapter 10) noted that such a practice, if and when it becomes accepted and used in the United States, could be greatly facilitated if farmland close to major urban centers were still available. He suggested that keeping highly productive land in production is much easier and cheaper (especially if large amounts of organic waste are available) than bringing marginal land back into production, often at a cost of $1500 per acre. Since the main cost in recovery is fertilizer, he sees a major energy impact of continued land diversion. Organic agriculture near cities could also do much to restore the green-belt concept. Chemical agriculture, on the other hand, results in usage of high levels of pesticide, large machinery, and other factors that make the romantic notion of intermingling farms with residential settlements untenable.

A further aspect of organic agriculture that assumes added importance in an economy increasingly unable to provide employment of any sort, much less meaningful jobs, is that it uses more labor and less capital. Blobaum noted that in China, this has resulted in a system that more closely approximates gardening than industrial agriculture as practiced in the United States. Of interest is the policy of incorporating scientists into the ongoing life and work of the communes on a regular basis (Stavis, 1974). The major result of this is close contact with the realities to which their research results will be applied. This form of structuring the science-extension linkage makes questions of accountability meaningless. One could ask whether Dow Chemical Company chemists would modify their positions on reentry to sprayed fields if they were the ones reaping the harvest.

Searle suggests that many advantages accrue from production on diversified small farms that get overlooked in a system that is locked into a "bigger is better" psychology (or psychosis, as some would view it). Economic advantages included diversified production, a crop mix that can be more easily altered to accommodate changes in preferences and prices, higher levels of employment at acceptable wage levels that results from larger farms with hired labor, and possibly the most important (at least for *Successful Farming* editors) a return on capital that is often as high as that of larger (and higher-cost) operations. Admittedly, most of the farmers interviewed said they could not make a go of it if they did not own their farms. They also pointed to their high vulnerability. Crises often mean going out of business.

Penta suggests that the pressures toward industrialized agriculture have been held in abeyance in the Northwest by irregular terrain and climatic factors. The concomitant pressure toward higher living standards for the farm population has resulted in exodus of many farm families from small holdings in the area. Given the limited profitability of such holdings and the consequent brake on land consolidation or speculation, such farms are fairly available to people wanting to acquire small holdings and engage in production on a subsistence level. Penta also suggests that such production permits a life-style less dependent on full-time employment than is the case for families who must meet all their food (and shelter) needs in a market context.

Cox further elaborates such ideas by suggesting that reduced levels of purchased inputs in agriculture will reduce the profits of petrochemical and other input suppliers. Such reduction will translate directly into reduced action of these firms and their lobbyists, as well as reduced pressure on land-grant institutions to follow energy-intensive research and extension activities. That politicians directly tied to these sectors will also be less subject to legislative pressures may do much to open the agenda for other types of changes. Such an event will not be automatic, since no group willingly acquiesces to a decrease in its power. The awareness of new groups to the need for change must translate itself into pressures on such groups to help effect the needed change. To quote the American Civil Liberties Union, "the price of liberty is eternal vigilance."

The articles mentioned share an implicit assumption that runs counter to many previous analyses of technological change in American agriculture, namely, that those who do not incorporate all the latest and most expensive inventions may in fact behave in a rational and profit-maximizing fashion. Stoltzfus takes the discussion a step further, showing how one group, the Amish, who are currently considered by most rural analysts as backward looking, tradition bound, and hostile to change, often do in fact have a rationale for their decisions. He shows how historically this group produced some of the early profit-increasing inventions in agriculture. He shows how the effort to keep religious and social traditions intact has isolated Amish families from the pressure to acquire and consume items pushed by the larger society as the symbols of a successful life. The capital thus retained within the family and larger Amish community is available for investment. This permits ongoing expansion of the basis-of-production operations, even with limited earnings from a level of sales that is low compared to farms that use more inputs, especially machinery, to obtain a higher level of production. Of equal importance is the pattern of expenditure that normally means that more is spent for land acquisition in comparison with the levels of machinery, fertilizer, and other chemical purchases on non-Amish farms. The large families provide a labor pool that makes lower machine use possible, as well as necessitate continued acquisition of new lands. Levels of indebtedness are high for Amish families, showing a willingness to utilize societal institutions when necessary.

Biohazards, chemicals in agriculture, and other energy issues. With regard to low-energy agriculture, the Small Farm Energy Project Newsletter (1976a) reports that biological control research has come up with various nonpoisoning (to the actual crops or the surrounding environment) methods of control. The need for biological controls is highlighted in reports that over two hundred arthopod species have developed chemical resistance. In efforts to eradicate these pests, heavier doses of traditional pesticides, and use of stronger pesticides have had a variety of consequences. Buildup of residues on foods and in human cell tissue is perhaps the most obvious threat (Wellford, Chapter 2). Possibly of greater economic importance is the destruction of natural predators because this causes even greater dependency on nonnatural controls.

The alternatives to high levels of chemical control are both more obvious and less costly than chemical companies suggest in their scare tactics about humans being in a war with pests for foods. Todd (Chapter 4) describes an integrated production system that utilizes nutrient-rich water from fish ponds to fertilize crops. Soybeans, the plant many view as a major future source of protein (already being used by many people as a meat substitute), can sustain the loss of 40% of the leaf area without yield loss, according to research from the University of Mississippi (Small Farm Energy Project Newsletter, 1976a). Slight damage from pests that affects only the cosmetic aspects of plants is probably preferable, from a medical standpoint, to residues of pesticides. This becomes an even more important issue when fruits or vegetables are machine processed, and cosmetic aspects drop out. Also, in machine harvesting slight damage to the fruit or vegetable often occurs making it more difficult to remove pesticides. (Grapes often turn to a juicy mass when machine harvested, making it impossible to remove anything from the skins.)

A problematical issue is the high level of funding for promotion of chemical usage compared to resources for both control of chemical use and education about alternatives. Farm relations persons from chemical companies outnumber cooperative extension agents in most parts of the country. Large-scale food and wine producers have incorporated "educational campaigns" about the need for fertilizer into their advertisements. Chemical industry public relations efforts often directly enlist the support of researchers and extensionists at various policy levels. Paradoxically, the major challenges to the chemical industry may come from within the land-grant colleges also, although such challenges are at times long in coming. The difficulties of Michigan dairy farmer Rick Halbert in tracking down PBB poisoning of his herd, and later getting the U.S. Department of Agriculture to help come up with a solution are a case in point (Chen, 1977). The high level of toxicity made even a "slight" mistake spread very rapidly both to herds and consumers. That the same company that makes the fire-retardant chemical also makes the cattle feed supplement supplement (Nutrimaster) he thought was in the feed is further testimony to the problems that come when too many things get hooked together. The same food-research-enforcement complex that dragged its feet in diagnosing the problem later refused to permit rapid disposal of the poisoned animals. Thus Halbert bankrupted his farm feeding animals he could not sell, but was not allowed to destroy. The Battle Creek Farm Bureau, which mixed with their feed the Firemaster that came in mislabeled bags, and Michigan Chemical Corporation, the distributor, paid heavily for damages. The ulcers and chemical accumulation in consumer bodies were not cured by out-of-court cash settlements. Probably the Farm Bureau passed the settlement costs on to farmers in higher feed prices.

With regard to heating and other energy needs, results of research in Minnesota suggest that wood chips, when gassified, can do much to meet rural energy needs. Green Mountain, Vermont, runs a 50 megawatt wood-fueled generator on lower operating costs than coal, and spent an equivalent amount in construction (Small Farm Energy Project Newsletter, 1976b). Short rotation of forests can increase yields of wood for energy. By cutting every 3 to 5 years, the same roots can grow new trees. Such operations would have additional benefits on a continuous harvest, rotational method when incorporated into windbreaks on semiarid lands. The roots would hold more water, and the growth left standing would reduce wind evaporation of surface waters. (Often the electricity used in these areas goes in large part to water pumping, to replace water lost when trees were removed to make larger "more profitable"— that is, more amenable to overly large machines—fields.)

Efforts to increase earnings: marketing, off-farm jobs, cooperatives, and crop or produce shifts. Not all farmers have reacted to declining profits by leaving farming— to be replaced by larger farmers—nor have many attempted to reduce their costs through organic farming. Group actions have been most common in periods of downward price spirals. Among farmers with very limited resources group actions often are the only way to survive in a competitive market (Breimyer and Flinchbaugh, 1973). Taylor summarizes the many different large organizations created, which in their totality constitute a social movement, not isolated events of minor importance. He sees the farmer's movement as consistently arguing, and often taking direct action, to further its case and seek out better prices, market conditions, and credit in times of market lags or outright depressions. From the founding of the country, the actions were strong in the commercially oriented agricultural regions and spread to other regions as market ties grew stronger. There was never anything in American agriculture approaching total subsistence, thus throwing all farmers into the pool of potential recruits in the struggle for redress of their economic grievances.

Taylor outlines the nature of change in a static society, where accumulated grievances only find outlet in revolution, and in dynamic societies, where pressures for change result eventually in new legislation. With such legislation comes a dissipation of energy and a shift to other issues until the next depression or recession accentuates once again the weak position of farming groups vis à vis the rest of the society. In a more detailed analysis of agricultural movements, Paige (1975) shows how different ways of transferring the costs to workers or small producers causes different types of social movements. Changes in the role of large organizations of farmers since the time Taylor wrote have seen the Farm Bureau further consolidate its power and take a more active lobbying stance, opposing laws that would benefit farm workers and smaller farmers, such as raising the cost of labor to larger-than-family farmers (Berger, 1971). The cooperatives that grew out of the earlier efforts have in many cases grown powerful and, in some cases, approximate regional oligopolies (Berger, 1971). Newer forms of cooperatives and groups working with small farmers and landless laborers have arisen, such as farm-worker unions and federations of small cooperatives.

The National Farmers' Organization (NFO) has also come into existence, voicing earlier complaints about lack of control by the farmer over the prices received and proposing collective bargaining as a tool for getting higher prices. Thousands of cans of milk being dumped, young chickens being killed, hogs being shot, and other headline-catching events have given the NFO an image reminiscent of the more militant historical farmer organizations.

The Federation of Southern Cooperatives (FSC) has pursued a less militant stance. It has combined the traditional cooperative role of bulk purchase of inputs and sale of production with additional functions. It finances small rural enterprises and gives technical assistance to aspiring rural entrepreneurs. It also finances the expansion of existing minority businesses—in one case helping the women workers assume ownership when a garment factory threatened to close. The Federation's close contact with member cooperatives has added numerical strength to newly enacted voter-rights laws in a way that would have been impossible if rural communities had to deal individually with southern politicians. In this regard, it is acting in accord with

Paarlberg's suggestion that existing political mechanisms are an efficient avenue for redress of complaints, adding perhaps the dimension of an organization to stimulate concerted action.

Berger (1971) points out the similar role cooperative extension played in helping create and give policy guidance to local advisory boards, which in many cases either were the precursors to local Farm Bureau chapters, or were closely allied thereto. That the FSC has had very little federal extension assistance suggests, however, the constraints on such a role imposed by politics of agriculture in the southern part of the country. Also of limited assistance is the Farmers' Cooperative Service, which has "grown and prospered" with the farmer members it serves. Along the way, it has picked up the "bigger is better" philosophy that results in pronouncements of nonviability rather than assistance to small cooperatives with limited-resource members.

Pierce uses four case studies to show how groups of small- and medium-scale farm operations have survived in spite of institutional neglect. He indicates that smaller farms are even put at a disadvantage by government policies of helping the rich and powerful. This selective help gives them an artificial appearance of efficiency. In Georgia, black-owned cotton farms with allotments under one acre struggle to make ends meet on meagre earnings, while larger white-owned farms get a variety of subsidies and new technologies. This is especially problematical for smaller farmers who either do not get, or cannot use them. The cotton harvester lowers the labor cost to larger farmers, usually resulting in decreasing the amount of labor hired into the operation. Providing this labor input as a part-time hired worker has often been the income source of smaller producers that has let them stretch their earnings enough to get by. War on Poverty and National Sharecropper Federation (NSF) funds let the members of this cooperative diversify into vegetable production, at a considerable increase in earnings. Applying their surplus labor to their own farms through intensified cropping gave a higher return than performing off-farm labor.

In a similar situation in Virginia (Halifax County), tobacco producers were able to raise their incomes from $343 to $1285 as a result of a farm-management program paired with diversification into organic farming. This change required more labor. Since it was their own or family labor, these farmers were more competitively endowed than larger farmers in that they did not have to pay supervisors, and they usually worked harder on their own farms. They also needed additional funds, which the Office of Equal Opportunity and the NSF made available. Previous funding requests had been denied because they were "too small" to be good risks. The verdict of "too small" simply meant they were trying to compete in areas where too many other props under large operations gave the larger farms an advantage (Pierce; Hightower, Chapter 7).

A cooperative of former Kansas wheat farmers diversified into fruit production on part of its acreage. While the farms were too small to provide adequate incomes when totally in wheat, they were too large to convert entirely to fruit production. Also, the start-up time was long for tree fruits, meaning cash crops (strawberries) had to be used to provide income while trees were maturing. Income from one acre of strawberries equalled that from 100 acres of wheat. Obviously, warehousing, marketing, and acquiring credit to buy the plants and other inputs were needed to permit this (Pierce). A similar attempt by Cooperativa Campesina encountered more difficulty. It too was trying to break into strawberry production, but in this case there were already large and powerful producers as competitors. Under pressure from the bigger growers, local banks denied them financing. Only after substantial effort was it possible to get financing, once again with no assistance from the Farmers' Cooperative Service at the outset. While not directly espousing governmental support of farm-cooperative or collective-bargaining organizations, Bible (Chapter 6) did recommend that obstruction of such efforts be prohibited. He also recommended more research funds be directed toward structural aspects of agriculture to generate information for regulatory and educational purposes.

An interesting point raised by Pierce and others, is that small farmers cannot defend themselves. They need the assistance of food-quality–conscious consumers (Goldstein, 1976). The government agencies are so closely aligned with larger producers and so dedicated to large-scale agriculture that Pierce considers them more as opposition than as allies to small farmers. He thus sees the solution in the same terms as Paarlberg: in the operation of political forces as they decide to exert themselves. Possibly the resulting coalition is different from the one Paarlberg envisioned, and the mix of farm firms envisions a less dominant role for larger-than-family farms, but the mechanism is similar. One difference lies in painting an alternate future possibility and correcting some of the myths about the supposed efficiency of large farms. Another difference in this strategy (detailed by Myers, 1976) is the democratization of the marketplace, as well as the election system, by hooking cooperative producers with large urban buying groups.

Houriet focuses attention on the desirability of locally produced food as a matter overriding food cost. He views locally grown food sold through local (farmers') markets as paying for itself in a variety of ways. While food produced on distant, large-scale farms may be cheaper, it also drains money from the community and undermines local food-producing capacity. In the case of Vermont, this means 80% of the food is shipped in, with a large part of the food dollar going to pay energy costs for packaging, storing, shipping, final sale, storage at home (often in a freezer), and final preparation. All this has happened in a state that used to be dotted with creameries, canneries, mills, and general stores. From 1880 to 1900 New England was largely self-sufficient in food production. By the middle of World War II it still produced about half of its food needs locally. By the early 1970's, nearly 98% of its food came from outside (Blobaum, Chapter 10). While rural Vermont boys were off defending democracy in various wars, agribusiness was shortening the leash on the in-state food-producing capability. Each war saw a shift toward more machines to meet the rural labor shortage. When the war was over, machines never went back into their boxes to return the tasks to humanpower. Price structures giving benefits to those (large) producers who could guarantee supply of critical materials were not repealed and had already translated themselves into permanent or long-term advantages for certain producer groups and certain geographical regions.

Cheap transportation meant altering even further the structure of competition that already worked against cooler regions. Continued failure to tax large profits (even when made by supplying goods for the war effort) resulted in the very rapid capital accumulation by farm and nonfarm corporations, which expanded their control into other sectors of agriculture and food processing and marketing.

Such areas as New England thus found themselves in a continuously eroding position vis à vis food production. Already high food production costs were added on top of the reduced participation of the regions in the cost-cutting and profit-hoarding operations just mentioned. The small scale of most New England farms usually left them on the sidelines of such activities. The shift south and west meant that New England dollars spent for food added to the rapid increase in profits of the same industries against which New England farmers found themselves expected to compete. Bible (Chapter 6) proposes prohibiting chain stores and other food processors and distributors from engaging in production operations. Relis (Chapter 10) notes that the food supply system of even southwestern states (especially California near Los Angeles) was being undermined. While he points specifically to land conversion for residential and industrial purposes, part of the shift is the result of what land remains in agriculture being used to provide vegetables for much of the eastern part of the country, as well as California.

Houriet does not intend to attack all these forces. He simply points out that buying from local producers, even if at slightly higher prices, is one way out of the dilemma. It will take time to get the reversal process started. Local farms will need to expand local sales to get capital to finance expansion of their production base and to diversify into other crops. From an energy standpoint, the cost of fertilizer to upgrade local production capacity should be weighed against the many costs cited previously, most of which already are artificially low, as a result of volume discounts, tax shelters, and other subsidies. Such investment in the local area could restore depleted soil to bring it back into production. Use of solar energy could also lengthen the growing season. Vail (ruralamerica, 1977b) points to diversification into seedlings in the spring and root crops, dried herbs, baked goods, and other simple-to-preserve products as ways to extend production for sale beyond the low level that currently characterizes most of the Maine farmers he studied.

Another example of a way to supplement farm income, or gain some return on equipment already owned if forced to leave dairying, is to convert to fish farming (Associated Press). Many Wisconsin farmers have succumbed to the aggressive expansion of the larger dairy farms, but have tried to stay on their farms while taking up other jobs. From 1964 to 1975 dairy farms dropped in number from 83,700 to 52,600, a drop paralleled by (though not necessarily directly related to) a 50% decline in Great Lakes fish yield. The plumbing already in the barns, and the concrete walls of the basements make conversion to fish tanks fairly economical. The income earned thereby usually is not sufficient to replace dairying as an income source but may provide some return at a level that makes it possible to work only part time, rather than full time off the farm. It may also be sufficient to supplement other income, such as from rental of the land to larger farms, retirement income, or other sources. It also means greater food self-sufficiency for the Midwestern region. Todd (Chapter 4) summarized a system in New England that uses a plastic dome to create tropical conditions for summer fish production and changes to other fish in the winter, for a year-round production operation.

Alternative policies to simplify acquisition, facilitate transfer, and permit capital accumulation by small farms. The cost of going out of business is very high, especially in terms of buildings and equipment, which often do not fit into the larger-scale operation of neighboring farms that are the major buyers of farms that close down. A major cause of a farm folding is the death of the owner. High taxes often make it necessary to sell part of the land or machines so the heirs can pay the inheritance taxes. Such transitional expenses are not equally distributed, for incorporated farms and nonagricultural corporations with farming subsidiaries do not pay these taxes. In the 1950's and 1960's about 1 million farms were forced out of business each decade (Perry). Many of these farms got into debt in some way (either to pay inheritance taxes, to buy machinery, or from other costs) and never got out again. The rapid increase in land values made both local and estate taxes increase rapidly. The $60,000 exemption from estate taxes has lost any correspondence with reality; Senator Bayh and Representative Myers (both from Indiana) introduced legislation to raise the ceiling to $200,000 for family-type farms. Other proposals to reduce costs of both land taxes and estate taxes include selling the development rights to the county, imposing development controls, creating tax districts (Blobaum, Chapter 10), and putting the land into trusts (Swann). The latter often is a form of protecting the land from speculation and ensuring its future availability to the community or region.

In the South, the problem is both one of retaining small plots for those that have them and gaining access to land for others. The severity of the problem among black landowners is evidenced by the 54% drop in black-owned land from 1950 to 1969 (Browne). The postwar adjustments discussed previously fed into the rapid black exodus in the 1950's. In the 1960's the push was accelerated by rapid mechanization, aided by cotton subsidy payments to white growers that sped the process of mechanization (Vandiver, Chapter 7). The same voter registration that the FSC saw as strengthening black community power also added to white nervousness. White politicians were active in support of policies to reduce the black population in the rural south by blocking other programs that would have permitted the adjustment of black families to the changes that were occurring. When black families left, service adequacy for poor whites deteriorated also, as community stores adjusted to reduced sales. Loftsgard and Voelker (Chapter 3) analyze similar trends in the Plains States.

Browne suggests that since it costs to live anywhere, rent paid for a place to live could more justifiably go to a black community-oriented land purchase institution than to (white) urban slumlords. He sees the major problem of "low income lifestyle" as capital scarcity. The way to deal with it is to create structures that permit the retention of capital and convert it into productive resources. Using public housing still transfers income from lower-middle–and middle-class taxpayers to upper-income groups, whether through purchase of the land, payment for construction, or salaries for the bureaucrats who make their livings "helping" the residents "adjust" to the new housing and living situation. Browne places any realistic treatment of urban poverty in the north squarely on the elimination of what T. Lynn Smith (1974) termed the "great rural taprots of poverty" in the South. The legacy of dependence of poor blacks on federal dole rather than "the massah" provides no basis for development.

Limvere notes that the country is undergoing a land-tenure crisis. He suggests that as a nation Americans have forgotten the historical role of access to land by family farms as the most important ingredient of a viable rural economy. Current farm-support programs are not even doing a very good job of helping family farms stay in existence. They do nothing to help meet the high entry cost brought about by competition for land from speculators and by industrialized agricultural activity of large corporations. Limvere fears a future dominated by a landed gentry or corporate agriculture, if present trends continue. Even survival of currently existing farms depends on measures to discourage corporate farms.

To establish a land base for new farmers is almost out of the question with current policies and high land prices. Most young farmers have scaled down their aspirations to building up only some limited equity in the land they farm. Top-heavy mortgages and rental agreements drain most of the capital from the farm, leaving little for machinery and other improvements that could raise the profitability to a point where later purchases might become possible. Off-farm jobs to meet capital scarcity have created a situation in which "the farmer is supporting the farm, rather than the farm supporting the farmer."

To develop what Limvere calls a "family sustaining agriculture system," the North Dakota Farmers Union proposed a state Trust Lands Division, to which a landowner could sell land. The seller could designate who would have lease or purchase rights. Lease periods would be 5 years with the option to renew or purchase the land at that time. As the Trust Lands Division would pay for the land, a retiring farmer would have money in an estate for heirs, one or some of whom might wish to lease or buy back the farm. This removes the burden of having to buy out shares from other heirs, a major problem with current transfers. A direct benefit to society might be lower food costs, since each generation would not have to recapitalize land cost at ever higher levels.

With regard to further access to land, Swann notes that land trusts enlist support of a variety of groups. He suggests that distribution via land reform probably is too divisive an issue to gain the support needed in a democratic context. Barnes (Chapter 5) shows that democracy had very little to do with the creation of the current pattern of land ownership. For young farmers trying to get started and for poor farmers trying to stay in business, trusts can do much to reduce both start-up and operating costs. They also permit access to enough land to utilize drudgery-reducing machinery. Swann notes that most small farmers and farm workers do not share the romanticist notion of the value of hard work. They do expect some return on their labor and fear being made obsolete, but this does not make stoop labor any more attractive than it ever was. What they most want is participation in the benefits accruing to them as part owners, at least of the crops that absorb their labor, if not of the land and machinery (Swann). As one farmworker states: "We have felt despair and frustration because we were so aware that the farmer inside the house enjoying the warmth of his living room could have been us" (Leon). In testifying about the exclusion from state and federally mandated protection, Leon notes that neither he nor his people are asking for anything to which they do not have a legal right. He notes that it is the sea of brown-faced people, his people, that do the work when the white and black people will not do it. He felt that with even a little land, his people could also realize their dreams.

That the government could take a different role is one possibility. Smaller farms could benefit from lease-back operations on currently government owned land (Spitze and Christiansen, 1973). Such practices are less drastic than they appear on the surface. Large grazing and timber acreage units are now leased. If anything, the level of government activity is too little, not too much, as far as land regulation is concerned (Coughlin, 1977). This is especially problematical for smaller farms who are denied access to lands by farmers in California who hold over the amount for which they are entitled to receive federally provided water. (This is 160 acres per family member working on the farm, up to 640 acres total.) While not directly affecting land access, most crops grown are affected by government programs of some sort (Sundquist and Guither, 1973). Those programs involving acreage diversion or price supports benefit farmers directly in proportion to the size of their production. Ceilings on such payments will reduce this effect, especially for very large farms, but smaller farms will continue to receive smaller shares of benefits than the middle size farms still getting unreduced payments.

Also in the legislative realm and dealing with attempts to protect the earning potential of family farms are a series of laws attempting to regulate entry of nonfarm corporations into agricultural operations. Especially problematical are corporations and wealthy investors who seek tax shelters, and do not need to realize a profit every year. In such cases simply being more efficient will not help the family farmer, who has to make money *from the farm operation* and does not have the capital to get volume purchase benefits (Sundquist and Guither, 1973). In that such volume purchases are usually from nonlocal sources, the local economy also loses. Often the outside supply source is a branch operation of the same corporation, thus enabling it to shift costs internally in a way that independent suppliers cannot do (Bible, Chapter 6). The profits thus generated are sufficient to hire the kind of help that will in fact "sit up with the corporate sow" (Henkes). The hope of outlasting "them" through dedication to one's operation is ill founded. Family farmers simply do not have the capital or scale (Breimyer and Barr, 1972).

The Saint Paul Pioneer Press article also suggests that if subsidies have any role at all, it is in guaranteeing the survival of small farms. They provide employment, a satisfactory life-style, and a means of subsistence to the family at a cost much below what society would pay to relocate and support the same worker and family in an urban area. If the subsidy to a larger-than-family farm or an economically successful family farm erodes the position of the small farm, the cost of the relocation and re-integration into the urban economy needs to be charged against the presumed benefits of large-scale agriculture. Bible (Chapter 6) suggests that parity price and income protection legislation is needed, but should be restricted to family farms.

Bulbulian puts the matter very simply in stating that the only efficiency of agribusiness firms is in mining the government. He cites the successful history of his immigrant father, but says inflated land values and the other high costs of farming have closed this door to new would-be farmers. He cites the preferential treatment given to larger-than-160-acre farms via cheap water and suggests new farmers deserve a similar break. He also points to technical assistance programs for small farmers in the rest of the world that his own neighbors are denied by employees of their own (our own) government. The absentee owners and large farmers, whose major source of earnings is rapid rise in land value, make no contribution to society that justifies this rapid wealth accrual. Labor of the workers is taxed much more heavily (and paid by the workers) than capital gains paid by owners. Bible (Chapter 6) proposes that government land up for sale go only to family or small (noncorporate) farms, that the farm credit system be expanded, and county boards be established to regulate land transfers and prevent land use patterns contrary to prevalent patterns in the county. Spitze and Christiansen (1973) also suggest that a larger role for the government in enforcing wage laws for farm workers could benefit family farms by eliminating cheap labor for overly large farm units. Such a procedure is not uncommon in most other countries at similar levels of development or in other sectors of the U.S. economy.

Another way to raise incomes of farm families is through off-farm work. For small farmers (farm sales from $2599 to $4999) this comprised 73% of their total income (Sundquist and Guither, 1973). Donohue (Chapter 10) noted that farmers with off-farm jobs generally had higher levels of living and total income than those working only on the farm. While there are many issues involved, such as whether farm income should be raised to permit earning enough solely from farm work, Donohue simply notes that such work does permit many to stay in farming who would not otherwise be able to do so, even on a part-time basis. Other aspects of this are treated elsewhere in this chapter.

Restructuring the nature and operations of technical assistance agencies. In addition to the tax laws, land laws, private banks, and nonresponsive federal agencies, Belden and Forte add the land-grant colleges to the list of institutions whose existence and operations do more to limit than expand the options of small farmers. Guither, Krause, and Bottum (1972) suggest that without public institutions, private schools and research agencies would probably be more restrictive than the land-grant colleges. Belden and Forte question how federal cooperative extension funds could increase from $38 to $332 million in the post-war period, as the number of farms declined from 6 million to 2.9 million. At the same time, over half of extension funds and time went to farmers who sell over $10,000 in production. The summary picture is one of increasingly technical advice to a progressively smaller and more affluent group of farmers. The smaller farmers underwrite this situation, both through taxes that they pay at a much higher rate, and through underutilization of services to which they should have access but do not receive. When they do receive "technical assistance," often the recommendation is that they go out of business (Hightower and Demarco, Chapter 7).

If the large farmers are doing so well, ask Belden and Forte, why do they need so many free (to them) inputs? Alternatively, if the research results are so good, why do people have to be paid to disseminate them? To suggest that they do not understand the recommendations is less convincing than it was at the founding of the extension service, when the client group was somewhat different. Research carried out in Africa (Leonard, 1975) may offer a simple answer. If extensionists bypass the farm of the headman to help smaller neighbors, the headman tells the extension agent's boss. If the extensionist cites national policy of helping small producers, the boss says "you do not understand." If the extensionist persists, a more "understanding" extensionist is found.

Rural sociology probably has done more than most other professions to contribute to this phenomenon by enshrining (as innovators) bigger and wealthier farmers who protect their positions by getting the jump on their neighbors through using new technology when it is still profitable (rather than having to adopt it to avoid a loss, as is the case with the smaller farmer down the road, who the extensionist assumes would not listen and would only adopt it after seeing a more affluent neighbor pull in the windfall profits).

Spitze and Christiansen (1973) acknowledge the important role played by research and extension in developing technology that favors one type or size farm operation more than another. Such a policy, if made explicit, could be used to strengthen the role of any sector. They admit that a more aggressive role for the government would weaken the position currently enjoyed by agribusiness firms.

Belden and Forte state directly that public funds should be used to assist those farms that cannot underwrite the cost of new technology generation and dissemination directly out of their earnings. Where special technologies or adaptations are needed for large farms, their presumed efficiency of operation should generate sufficient income to underwrite these costs without public assistance. They cite work in Missouri with small farmers using paraprofessional outreach people with fairly good results.

Another U.S. Department of Agriculture program that could be reoriented to support small-farm expansion or survival is procurement for school lunches, which currently is mainly relief for agribusiness. Of thirty-five commodities made available to schools, all but two are in processed form. The two fresh products make a meager impact on raising the quality of school lunches. Federal support to local producers of fresh fruits and vegetables would do much to make school lunches more nutritious, attractive, and affordable. The impact of additional capital made available to smaller farmers through a market mechanism to produce food that is actually eaten and enjoyed, rather than processed and then dressed up to look palatable, would do much to redress past imbalances.

Creation of marketing boards could establish mechanisms to both stimulate production through assuring access by small growers to markets and restrict domination by large farms and corporate conglomerates (Spitze and Christiansen, 1973). Vertical integration has already produced a level of concentration in the vegetable industry that gives farms with sales over $40,000 a high (85%) share of the market. For poultry, the figure for 1969 was 84.6%, with a trend for more complete consolidation since then (Sundquist and Guither, 1973). While the nature of those helped by redirecting marketing actions may differ, this is not a departure from U.S. Department of Agriculture policy, as stated. They say the purpose of food programs is to improve farm income, and that feeding people is for the Department of Health, Education, and Welfare to worry about (Hightower, 1975). The issue needs to be addressed in terms of *whose* farm income is being raised. Also, the quality of the food produced and purchased and the energy utilized are matters within the domain of the Department of Agriculture. Possibly a method to stimulate more action would be to delineate what portion of funding goes to each activity. If the agency in question denies responsibility for such a program, or does not have a mechanism to deliver the needed service to specified target groups, interagency service arrangements, or direct transfer of funds could be effected. Operation Hitchhike was one such experiment, in which the Department of Labor contracted with a variety of public and private agencies to determine how best to deliver services in areas beyond the urban labor markets that previously received the major part of Department of Labor attention. Possibly if such a criterion were applied, the real beneficiaries of Department of Agriculture feeding programs would be shown to be neither large nor small farmers, but the intermediaries, who do all the buying and processing and can move additional commodities through the market channels at the taxpayers' expense.

Belden and Forte see local banks as adding to family-farm operational difficulties. For recommendation regarding credit for purchase of inputs, they normally follow cooperative extension guidelines, which in only a few states have provisions for organic fertilizers and biological controls. Farmers are thus pushed into higher usage of chemical fertilizers or have to finance the entire cost themselves. The cost of processing loans is also a factor in shaping banklending policy. Large loans to agribusiness usually involve a few phone calls to professionally trained farm managers for the farm firms involved on farms where credit is not automatically provided by the home office (often out of excess profits in other parts of the company, to avoid taxes).

For small farms, there is need of more information, endless forms, and often difficulty on the part of the banker in determining how the farm in fact operates and how the loan will be used. A larger time input is required for a smaller loan. Thus diversified farms are at a disadvantage. Gilles (1977) cites how bankers discourage Montana farmers from raising cattle and pressure them to tear down fences, enlarge fields, and plant cash grains.

Size of farm loans has increased from about $4000 shortly after the depression to an average of over $100,000. The very high cost of interest is directly tied to rapid rise in land cost, as investors have to decide how to invest at the most profitable rate of return. Merrill, Lynch, Pierce, Fenner, & Smith, Inc. is now developing a program whereby Continental Bank of Chicago will buy large amounts of land to be leased back to farmers. A reduced level of rent will be charged, since a major factor in the earnings will be the appreciation of the land value. This is happening at the same time that banks deny loans for land acquisition to small farmers. By not owning the land, farm renters lose the value from rising land costs, a major source of earnings. Should such a program be legalized, it will usher in a new generation of farm tenants, in the view of *ruralameriea* writers (1977a). Bible (Chapter 6) recommends a graduated land tax and prohibition of offsetting gains in one part of a corporation with losses in another part as ways to discourage large nonagricultural investments in farmland. He further recommends a maximum number of stockholders in *any* corporation involved in purchase of farmland.

These pressures on land resources result in rapid conversion to nonagricultural uses, at about 1.4 million acres per year according to Blobaum (Chapter 10). This is from a total of 631 million acres suitable for regular cultivation. (Of the 2.2 billion acres in the country, only about 1.4 billion is nonfederal land available for agricultural use. Of this land 627 million acres are extremely marginal.) Prime farmland is also the type most desired by developers. Blobaum estimates that over half of this land is not well cared for, with wind and water erosion and salinization through continued irrigation the major threats.

The pressure of growing cities will remove each decade an area greater than the size of New Jersey, with about one-third of an acre per capita of population increase for urbanized areas. If the back-to-the-land movement gains steam, probably more, rather than less, land will be converted to residential use for the simple reason that those who move further out often have as the major attraction cheaper land that permits larger lots. With about 15 million recreation home lots registered, and another 10 million unregistered, there is an additional threat to usable land. While the energy crisis has slowed the rate of growth, and while available figures indicate "only" 2 million homes built thus far on these lots, the impact is still substantial, though unknown in specific acreage terms. While U.S. Department of Agriculture projections of land use and needs until the year 2000 do not indicate a shortage, Blobaum (Chapter 10) and Belden and Forte point to various factors that are overlooked. High fertilizer prices are producing a shift to more extensive production patterns (more land with lower levels of fertilization). Grass-fed cattle are picking up a share of the market lost to feedlots as grain prices stay high. Exports are becoming a more important feature, since food is continuing to be in short supply in much of the world. (Also the lagging performance of the U.S. industrial sector has resulted in balance-of-payments deficits on the industrial side that require agricultural exports to at least diminish the deficit.) High reliance on irrigation may be approaching an upper limit, for reuse of water is resulting in both higher levels of mineral buildup in the water itself and in the land (through salinization). Climatic variability is also putting a strain on available water reserves. These factors have resulted in a lessening of the productivity increases that have up until now been built into the system. Continued decrease in available land may no longer be as easily offset by higher yields per unit. Increasing consumer awareness of pesticide threats and growth-stimulating feed additives coming under question together may limit the potential use of new technologies.

12 Alternative responses to rural community decline and change

The cobwebs in the window of the little brown church may give rise to nostalgic pangs among those who return to visit. To the local people they only show that small villages, like other outdated things, are headed for oblivion, says Carlyle. He further adds that this is all to the good—without saying whose good. As a major contributor to the demise, the finger points first to the storekeeper who refuses to stock what the pretty girls want to buy with their maple sugar money, so they will look as nice as the girls in the next town. When the storekeeper refuses, business is lost to a competitor in the nearby town. That transportation has broken the local monopoly is a point not lost on customers.

Other towns do survive when the storekeeper takes the new tastes of the "more interesting housewife of today" into consideration. Rising incomes among farm people mean that even with fewer people, a business can survive, if it is attuned to new tastes and the items that are purchased close to home on a regular basis. While farm population declined by 4.25 million in the 20 years preceding the writing of the article, gross cash income of the farm population stayed at slightly over $10 billion. A needed revision to this position of the early 1930's has been suggested by Bible (Chapter 6), who suggests that for every six farms that go out of operation, one local business is dragged down with them. A probable factor bringing about this decline in business is the fact that many farms now are bought up by absentee individuals, corporations, or very large family-type farms that often bypass local businesses. In the 1930's, smaller farms that folded were bought most often by only slightly larger neighboring farms that were not that different in their buying patterns.

Closing roads and relocating dwellings where necessary are part of cost-reducing adjustments to the antiquated living patterns that Clawson sees as placing an unfair burden on other taxpayers. He proposes planning in terms of a future dominated by progressively larger farms (1200 acres, 1- by 2- mile blocks) that will need fewer roads, both for internal access to parts of the farm and for commerce with towns and cities. Changes in farm technology have made distance between points less a factor than such matters as loading and unloading, volume buying at a discount from more distant supply points, and related changes.

Raising the level of adequacy of services means, to Clawson, increasing the size of—and therefore the distance between—service centers. Farm people increasingly expect the same quality food products (which they buy rather than produce in ever increasing proportions) and services from government and private agencies that town people receive. Getting closer to town means greater access to the services. Reducing the number and expanding the size of the towns means better-quality services, by Clawson's logic.

Present settlement patterns deeply rooted both in sentiment and in actual investment in physical structures are the major barriers to change. That changes are made incrementally (pave a few miles of road, put a new roof on a house or church) rather than in their totality (build a whole road, or close it; design a new town with all needed buildings, evacuating the old one) means a gradual process that determines the entire structure.

That Clawson's article predated the "small is beautiful" thesis does not detract from the power his arguments hold among many policy makers. That it comes from the opposite direction of Paarlberg's suggestion that people will decide what is best for them is also of interest. That public-service employment makes many jobs available opens a new prospect. Paraprofessional outreach people, mobile-service units, and other ways to extend the service area of existing agencies are overlooked. The higher level of education of houseparents makes decentralized education with a larger role for inhouse learning aspects a possibility. Home-school aides fill this function in schools in poverty areas. Greater cultural stimulation within rural areas can come from community theater and youth groups doing various homemade cultural and artistic events. That urban centers experience the same cultural voids and launch "neighborhood" art fairs stands as a further caveat to the "metropollyana" nature of Clawson's proposals. (Metropollyana is the myth that sooner or later everybody will go to the big city and live happily ever after; the term was coined at the First National Conference on Rural America in 1975.)

While attempting to create communications alternatives to continued decline in rural towns, Goldmark also sides with the "victim blamers" who see the causes of decline of rural towns and villages as lying within these areas. He points to limited employment expansion possibilities, overlooking the void of support structure for either small farms or labor-intensive agricultural production practices. He points to inadequate health care, with not a thought to ways to restructure health care delivery toward preventive care, turning responsibility for wellbeing back to people. He proposes instead ways to get overly specialized and culturally hostile (to local culture and values) medical professionals into media contact with the center institutions, which are those of the larger society that define how things will be done (Tudiver, 1972).

He points to inadequate education and ways to get more people into college-oriented curricula, so they also can make hostile pronouncements about working people. Learning community-based job skills through local people could result from deprofessionalizing the career tracks in high schools. Tracks are making us a nation of college people who cannot nail soles on our own shoes, get our cars to start, or plane doors so they do not bind.

With regard to cultural events, the suggestion that some communities could broadcast their events to other communities raises the prospect of greater local pride in cultural expression. Whether piped-in culture (even if generated in a nearby small town rather than a large urban center) surpasses live performances is not addressed. Possibly a community bus that could haul the performers and their props would generate more cultural dissemination at lower cost.

It stops going when it is all gone: the end of rural population decline. Many small towns and rural areas may be in less drastic shape than these writers think. Recent survey results point to nearly 80% of the population preferring life in rural areas, especially if within 30 miles of cities of 50,000 or more. While Fuguitt and Zuiches show that living in remote areas is less preferred than in places closer to cities, even the remote areas outrank major cities. Most people felt the advantages of rural living could be had fairly close to metropolitan areas, without sacrificing the recreational and cultural amenities and the diversity of people present in the larger towns and cities. As their major points of attraction, rural areas are seen as offering better air and water, a better place for children, and lower crime rates. That this is not simply nostalgia is shown by the predominance of current place of residence over place of birth as a predictor of preferences.

Expansion of economic activity, often resulting from aggressive efforts to attract industry, has resulted in a larger job base in many small towns. Paired with desires to escape urban congestion, high-pressure jobs, high crime rates, and the realization that higher wages in urban areas often do not translate into an acceptable life-style, this economic expansion has both attracted disenchanted urbanites and helped retain locals who previously would have had to leave if they wanted a decent job. Hanson cites various small towns that have turned around and reports on the enthusiasm many new inhabitants show for their new jobs and locations.

Beale comments on the surprisingly low level of recent rural out-migration, which averaged 1 million annually from 1940 to 1960, and only came to public view following the focus of attention on urban protests and uprisings following the assassination of Martin Luther King, Jr. That many of the riot participants were urban born does not detract from his point about public neglect of the extent of the exodus or the forces behind it.

Beale asks why a population trend as important as the reversal in rural population decline went unpredicted and unnoticed. He suggests that rapid out-migration resulted in decline of agriculture as a mainstay of the economy in two harbinger regions. Once the forces feeding into the decline were depleted, the prospect of turn-around and eventual growth was less difficult. Thus, the actions immediately preceding the turnaround (such as building a factory, a road, or a medical center) may be of less importance than the fact that all who were there to be pushed out had already gone. An oval area between St. Louis and Dallas and another bounded by Memphis, Atlanta, Louisville, and Birmingham both benefitted from industrial decentralization already underway in the early 1960's. This move from the Northeast and Midwest accelerated with the events of the middle and late 1960's.

The extent of the change nationwide became apparent from 1970 to 1973, with a 4.2% population growth rate for nonmetropolitan counties (with no city of 50,000), while metropolitan counties grew at a rate of 2.9%. While the rate for counties adjacent to a city (4.7%) was somewhat higher than nonadjacent rates, the latter (3.7%) also was higher than the metropolitan rate. This change holds for all but three states (two with military bases to offset the change): Alaska, Connecticut, and New Jersey. The number of counties declining fell from 1300 in the 1960's to 600 in the early 1970's.

Industrial growth produced only 18% of the total job growth for the period, down from 50% for the 1962 to 1969 period. Counties with high percentages of net immigration of retirement-age people showed the highest growth rates, with those having senior colleges also high. In both cases the kinds of institutions and the types of communities created to meet the needs of these people also attracts others who may not be attracted by industry, for some left their previous areas to get away from industry.

Heavily agricultural counties (with 40% or more of the population in farming) continued to drop a little, but at a low rate. They now comprise less than 1% (400,000 people) of the nonmetropolitan population, and it could be said that they have already given most of what they have to give. The young people left some time ago, and the ones remaining no longer are having children at such high rates. That they are still declining suggests that the changing structure of agriculture is still important, but on a lower order of magnitude with regard to out-migration.

A similar picture obtains with predominantly black nonmetropolitan counties. Of the 98 remaining, only one has over 35% of the workers in farming (bearing out Browne's contention). These areas contain 1.75 million people, and have not yet shifted to growth, although the rate of decline has slowed.

Beale concludes that we are not on the verge of dismantling our cities, but all major metropolitan areas except Boston have experienced slowdowns in growth. The eight major metropolitan regions that hold over a fourth of the nation's population exceeded the national growth rate in the 1960's. In the early part of the 1970's, they fell below the national rate. Once again, the notion of an urban solution to rural problems is shown to rest on shaky ground.

They are bringing it with them: new people, new priorities. What happens when all these former urbanites come to the country? As Parren Mitchell phrased it, "I don't know what they are running away from, but it looks like they are bringing it with them" (Rural America Conference, 1975). Diversion of agricultural land from production has been reviewed (Blobaum, Chapter 10) earlier. Higher taxes in many rural areas are the result of the desire for better services that Clawson saw as the major deficit in rural areas. Preinvasion ruralites often see their own future placed in jeopardy, as fixed or declining incomes must bear the further strain of creating structures without which they have thus far survived. The carving up of farmland, often under pressure of high taxes and the onslaught of what one observer termed "the five acre liberals" has given rise to other pressures for tax relief, especially for farmland near cities.

Blobaum (Chapter 10) criticizes such actions as growing out of an increasing tendency to view land as a commodity, rather than as a capital good, the source of future production. Even for local governments, who view land as a source of tax revenue, there is an expectation of increased earnings from land as values rise. Preferential taxation costs California local governments $40 million each year, according to Relis (Chapter 10). In addition to reducing current earnings, such measures also reduce the capacity of local governments to obtain financing for longer-term expenditures, since the future earning base no longer can be expected to grow at the same rate. Relis notes that preferential taxing of farmland did not slow urban growth, and merely increased profits of speculators. The Williamson law in California covers 10% of all privately owned land. Giving tax relief in exchange for 10 years of no development has simply meant that when the 10 years ends, the land will be worth all that much more. That such land is taxed at a low rate makes it all that much easier for speculators. They can borrow against the appreciated value to purchase additional land.

That some of this land is held by tax-exempt bodies creates an additional problem for local governments. In a tongue-in-cheek attempt to cash in on tax exemption, 213 Hardenburgh, New York, residents became ordained in the Universal Life Church. Since much of the land surrounding this community in the Catskills is already in the hands of tax-exempt groups, ranging from the Boy Scouts to Tibetan Monks; local taxpayers, tired of underwriting the service costs for all these freeloaders, hoped to attract the Governor's attention (Potter, 1977). The result of their actions was to totally eliminate the tax base of the community. The future remains unclear, but taxing the locals to support outsiders has been temporarily stopped.

Billed as a compromise, Honey Creek was to blend the desire for rural living with joint use of space in productive and ecologically harmonious use (Pfefferkorn). The "whole earth condominium" had a farm manager budgeted to help determine what to grow for internal food needs, as well as how much additional could be marketed. Control through a homeowners' association was also envisioned. Such a concept has difficulty translating itself into reality. Many who share the basic premise go one step further and place their land into a trust. Those who do not go quite as far as the concept envisions are dubious about not having ownership rights to the shared area. The poor financial performance of urban condominium apartments compared to single-family dwellings has further slowed acceptance of such an idea. As with all compromises, it includes a little of the undesirable as well as the desirable aspects of the alternatives.

If attempts to blend new people a few at a time are not always well received, attempts to incorporate one of the world's largest multinational mineral companies are even more difficult. While none of the northern Wisconsin people drew the analogy in these terms, it was not unlike when the city mouse brought his elephant friend home for the weekend, and he refused to go back to the zoo. What began as exploration rights on land that all "knew" was not worth much, ended up meaning many later had to sell at previously established prices (Dorgan). These prices were both substantially below the inflated values produced by the copper boom, and more problematical, below the cost of somewhere else to live. When a social system undergoes an experience that leaves it less well-adapted to its environment than it previously was, some writers refer to it as underdevelopment.

To extend the analogy, after the elephant put the whole filet mignon on his plate and ate it, he then told those present that he could not help pay for the groceries, since his presence alone would bring them ample benefit. Tax receipts both to the state and to the community impacted are well below even conservative estimates of the cost of reparation on a long-term basis. The state legislature was caught unprepared, with all the information needed to make a determination of the impact in the hands of Kennecott and its competitors. The obvious point is to do like the Boy Scouts and be prepared for any eventuality. The difficulty comes in the underfinancing of the relevant agencies (both federal and state) and the pervasive myth that any industry is better than no industry (Summers and Lang, Chapter 10).

New defenders recreate old problems: the limits of "rural development." Almost two decades of farm consolidation and farmer out-migration were taken as part of needed adjustments to "misallocated" people by U.S. Department of Agriculture policies, according to Heady. Aggregate growth at the societal level was seen as the major mechanism to employ such people, in what Heady refers to as urban fundamentalism among land-grant college agricultural economists. (It is interesting to recall the opprobriums heaped on rural sociologists for trying to "save the family farm." The implication was that economics, the devoid-of-sentimentality, tell-it-like-it-is, dismal science, had the inside road on truth.) Such policies furthered the growth of large farms, while depleting rural communities of the people who lost their farms or jobs on farms. Probably the trend was accelerated above what would have otherwise happened as a direct result of federal policies.

The foundations were pulled from under rural economic activity in medium and small towns as declining employment levels were not offset by the stepped-up level of buying and selling by the larger farms. That progressively more of this economic activity was through regional and national suppliers was well-known by small-town implement and fertilizer dealers. As they were forced to reduce inventories of parts, even their regular customers (smaller local farmers) were forced to seek more distant and regular sources for spare parts or cheaper inputs. Banking operations are also affected by changes caused by corporate and industrial-type farms. Large firms usually get the major part of their credit from banks in their home cities, and in turn, deposit earnings from local production activity in outside banks. These earnings not circulating through local financial institutions thus reduces their volume of business. Smaller farms operated by local families, on the other hand, either brought in credit (through the Farmer's Home Administration), which they spent locally, or obtained local bank credit, when possible (Bible, Chapter 6).

Legislators and urban political leaders are adding to the clamor for rural community development, often in hopes of relieving the pressures on the cities. Nonfarm rural groups continue to have little input into the process. Designing programs to decentralize industry or expand employment in some growth centers probably will continue to erode the economic base of smaller and more remote communities. These areas will continue as dispersed slums of low visibility. Programs to clean up lakes and rivers or to protect mountain retreats will do little to improve services to rural poor people, who often also are elderly. Such programs may further exacerbate the problem, for they serve as testimony to urbanites (who come by freeway or airplanes) that things are being done to "help rural America," thus reducing the pressure for other policies to increase incomes and improve services in the remote areas.

Rural industrialization stands about the same chance of helping as did the programs that sped the spread of commercial and industrialized agriculture (Heady). Those areas in a position to attract industry will continue to grow, probably draining people and resources from surrounding towns.

Efforts to arrest corporate farms are missing the brunt of the problem, in Heady's view. He sees the expansion of already large family farms as the major pressure on smaller farms. He fails to take his analysis the next logical step and suggest that the policy props to expansion of already large farms be removed and scaled down to slow the erosion of the position of the smaller farms.

Remedial actions relevant to these problems are proposed (Bible, Chapter 6). Setting a maximum size for farms would prevent their growth to points where large-scale purchase from distant sources becomes cheaper. Tighter antitrust laws would prevent the same firm from producing, processing, and selling farm products. Additional funds for research and required disclosure of size and ownership data would allow researchers to assess the effects based on more detailed information. Heady merely suggests instead the need for imaginative programs as innovative as the past policies that facilitated the occupation of most of the Midwest (the rectangular land survey, for example).

Heady points also to the diversity of rural communities and the lack of information about the priorities of the various groups in these localities. Is there a range of diversity, or are there common things they want for their towns? Many, if they were in charge of their own policies or policies affecting their surrounding areas, would probably choose policies resulting in a larger number of farmers on a small or medium scale. Spitze and Christiansen (1973) point out that governmental action to boost the earnings of these groups could do much to increase the economic base of rural communities. They doubt this will happen on any large scale, since direct governmental assistance to rural communities will probably occur outside the farming system.

Such a policy (pouring in additional funds) seems to have only limited prospect of success in those communities where the erosion of the resource base is tied to growing size and change in type of farm operations. As long as such trends continue, capital outflows of at least as large an amount will put federal funds into a holding action at best. As Clawson points out, the past is one indication of a possible desired future state. As the present authors have suggested, turning back is not impossible, nor is it necessarily undesirable.

If current trends are toward a less viable future situation, and the viable aspects of the past can be strengthened or at least allowed to survive, possibly this is an option needing more attention. That policy makers have sided with an influential minority and succeeded in convincing the majority that their own demise is in their best interest is perhaps one of the wonders of American society and all it has stood for. That most people refuse to keep being fooled all the time is probably an even greater (though less heralded) wonder.

Conclusion

Possibly one of the major functions of alternatives is to make the present more bearable. Knowing it is possible to organize one's life in a different way and that many others are already doing it may help one accept the rut of daily existence as only one of several ways to live. Only when there is no alternative does the current situation weigh more heavily, to the point of making change more drastic when it does in fact come. To this extent, the present exercise may in fact add strength to a status quo badly in need of alteration. Fuguitt and Zuiches note that people have continued to live in other places than they would choose to live. This is part of the problem of not coming to grips with any issues of any one locality. If things get too bad, you leave. If we take seriously the idea of a finite world, however, we are faced with the fact that there is no place else to go, or that if we go there, we will encounter the same problems. (Many of these problems come with the others who went there previously to get away, to paraphrase Parren Mitchell.) As Kenneth Boulding says, the garbage can be pushed "over there" (he says into New Jersey) but cannot ever be thrown away. In a closed system, there isn't any away.

REFERENCES

Berger, Samuel A.: Dollar harvest: the story of the Farm Bureau, Lexington, Mass., 1971, D.C. Heath & Co.

Berry, Wendell: Where cities and farms come together. In Merrill, Richards, editor: Radical Agriculture, New York, 1976, Harper and Row Publishers, pp. 12-25.

Boulding, Kenneth E.: The economics of the coming spaceship Earth. In Jarret, Henry, editor: Environmental quality in a growing economy: essays from the Sixth Resources for the Future Forum, Baltimore, 1966, Johns Hopkins University Press.

Breimyer, Harold F., and Barr, Wallace: Issues in concentration versus dispersion. In Guither, Harold D., editor: Who will control U.S. agriculture? North Central Regional Publication 32, Urbana, Ill., 1973, University of Illinois.

Breimyer, Harold F., and Flinchbaugh, Barry L.: A dispersed, open market. In Guither, Harold D., editor: Who will control U.S. agriculture? A series of six leaflets, North Central Regional Extension Publication 32-2, Urbana, Ill., 1973, University of Illinois.

Chen, Edwin: Michigan: if something happens . . . Atlantic **240**(2):12-20, Aug. 1977.

Commoner, Barry: The poverty of power: energy and the economic crisis, New York, 1976, Bantam Books, Inc.

Coughlin, Ken: The 160-acre backlash: long dormant measure rouses East and West, ruralamerica **2**:12, Nov. 1977.

Fujimoto, Isao: The values of appropriate technology and visions for a saner world, National Center for Appropriate Technology, Butte, Mont., 1977.

Gilles, Jere Lee: Big sky agriculture, Unpublished Ph.D. dissertation, Ithaca, N.Y., 1977, Cornell University.

Goldstein, Jerome: Organic force. In Merrill, Richard, editor: Radical agriculture, New York, 1976, Harper and Row, Publishers, pp. 212-223.

Goodwin, Mary T.: Improving your school lunch program. In Lerza, Catherine, and Jacobson, Michael, editors: Food for people not for profit, New York, 1975, Ballantine Books, Inc., pp. 319-326.

Guither, Harold D., Krause, Kenneth R., and Bottum, J. Carroll: Effects of access to technical knowledge and commercial inputs. In Guither, Harold, D., editor: Who will control U.S. agriculture? North Central Regional Publication 32, Urbana, Ill., 1972, University of Illinois.

Hardin, Garrett: The tragedy of the commons, Science **162**:1243-1248, Dec. 1968.

Hightower, Jim: Government: a helping hand. In Hightower, Jim: Eat your heart out: How food profiteers victimize the consumer, New York, 1975, Vintage Books, pp. 218-255.

Knutson, Ronald, and Black, William E.: A cooperative agriculture. In Guither, Harold D., editor: Who will control U.S. agriculture? A series of six leaflets, North Central Regional Extension Publication 32-2, Urbana, Ill., 1973, University of Illinois.

Leonard, David: Why does Kenya's Extension Service only work with large farmers, Center for International Studies, Rural Development Committee, Cornell University, 1975.

McLeod, Darryl: Urban-rural food alliances: a perspective on recent community food organizing. In Merrill, Richard, editor: Radical agriculture, New York, 1976, Harper and Row, Publishers, pp. 188-211.

Merrill, Richard, editor: Radical agriculture, New York, 1976, Harper and Row, Publishers.

Myers, Robin: The national sharecroppers fund and the farm co-op movement in the South. In Merrill, Richard, editor: Radical agriculture, New York, 1976, Harper and Row, Publishers, pp. 129-142.

Paige, Jeffrey: Agrarian revolution: social movements and export agriculture in the underdeveloped world, New York, 1975, The Free Press.

Pimentel, David, and others: The food production and the energy crisis, Science **182**(4111):443-449, Nov. 1973.

Potter, Joan: Assessor's nightmare: Catskills farmers get religion, ruralamerica **2**:12, Nov. 1977.

ruralamerica: Corporate land grab draws criticism, and What is ag land fund 1? ruralamerica, **2**:1, Mar. 1977a.

ruralamerica: Farmers markets in Maine get mixed reviews, ruralamerica **2**(12):10, Nov. 1977b.

Salamon, Lester M.: Black-owned land: profile of a disappearing equity base. Report to the Office of Minority Business Enterprise, Washington, D.C., 1974, U.S. Department of Commerce.

Schumacher, E. F.: Small is beautiful: economics as if people mattered, New York, 1973, Harper and Row, Publishers.

Simple Living Collective, American Friends Service Committee: Taking charge, New York, 1977, Bantam Books, Inc.

Small Farm Energy Project Newsletter: Biological agriculture: pesticides losing out, Issue 1, May 1976a.

Small Farm Energy Project Newsletter: Wood fuel, Issue 3, Nov. 1976b.

Smith, T. Lynn: Studies of the great rural taproots of urban poverty in the United States, New York, 1974, Carlton Press.

Spitze, Robert G. F., and Christiansen, Martin: A government-administered agriculture. In Guither, Harold D., editor: Who will control U.S. agriculture? A series of six leaflets, North Central Regional Extension Publication 32-5, Urbana, Ill., 1973, University of Illinois.

Staley, Oren Lee: The National Farmers' Organization. In Heady, Earl O., editor: Farm goals in conflict, Ames, Iowa, 1963, The Iowa State University Press.

Stavis, Benedict: The role of agricultural science and scientists, Making green revolution: the politics of agricultural development in China, Ithaca, New York, 1974, Cornell University Press.

Sundquist, W. B., and Guither, H. D.: The current situation and the issues. In Guither, Harold D., editor: Who will control U.S. agriculture? A series of six leaflets, North Central Regional Extension Publication 32-1, Urbana, Ill., 1973, University of Illinois.

11

Alternative responses to changes in farm technology and structural characteristics

---

What form of agriculture? A social-political-economic issue

DON PAARLBERG*

With a representative government, the people can have any kind of agriculture they want. And I think they will insist on having what they want.

Suppose for a moment that the large-scale farming units are more efficient than family farms. People are asking whether, in as affluent a country as the United States, efficiency should be the sole criterion for the form of agriculture we are to have. We now supply ourselves with food—the best diet ever, anywhere—with about 16 percent of our income. If we stay with the family farm and improve its efficiency, the percentage of income spent for food will go still lower. Should we adopt a new and greatly different system so as to drive food costs down even faster? Should we sacrifice a form of agricultural production that has served us well, better than any other country has ever been served?

This is a fair question. The answer to it is properly social and political as well as economic. I believe this to be a major farm policy issue of the decade ahead.

□ From *Agricultural Science Review* 11(1): 29, 1973.
*Director, Agricultural Economics, U.S. Department of Agriculture, from his comments before the 1973 Outlook Conference, Washington, D.C.

And I do not think our agriculture need be or will become monolithic, relying on one managerial concept only. We are a pluralistic country socially, politically, and economically. The fact that the trend has been in the direction of large-scale units does not mean that this trend must be extended until it embraces all of agriculture. Nor does it mean that large-scale farming units should be abolished. I see no good reason to prevent us from having a farming system that is partly large-scale and partly family farms. Those who believe in market competition should also believe in the appropriateness of competing institutional forms.

For most American agriculture, the family farm can continue to be the major organizational form:

If it is permitted the flexibility that will allow the efficient use of modern technology and management.

If it is provided with good research, education, and credit.

If it makes wise use of the principles of cooperation.

If it has access to the market.

If it continues to enjoy the good will of the public.

As I judge the mood of the American public, this is the wish and the intent.

Back-to-farm idea impractical dream

DON KENDALL

WASHINGTON (AP)—However romantic it may be to think about using horses to save fuel on U.S. farms and put food production on an organic fertilizer footing, their heyday is long past and is not likely to return, says an Agriculture Department specialist.

Here are some of the drawbacks of shifting from tractors and other fuel-guzzling machines to hay-burning horsepower, as listed by Earle E. Gavett of USDA's Economic Research Service:

- Based on the farm use of 26.7 million horses and mules in 1918, it would require about 61 million of them today to sustain current farm production. Only about three million such work animals exist now.
- About 31 million farm workers, including farmers themselves and hired laborers, would be needed. Last year, an average of fewer than 4.4 million persons worked on farms.

Gavett, whose views are in a current issue of Farm Index published by the research service, said some critics of modern farming see the use of horses as "the solution to many problems that have plagued America recently" such as the energy shortage, pollution and unemployment.

The article, based on a recent speech by Gavett, said "it is biologically impossible" to breed 61 million horses and mules from the three million now on hand before 1992 or 1993, even assuming ideal reproduction.

Further, such a large herd of work animals would require feed from "some 180 million acres of prime farmland," which would mean taking huge acreages from crops currently needed for food and fiber.

"Although there is no shortage of people to work on farms, a movement of 26 million workers (in addition to the 4.4 million already on them) from city to farm would provide mind-boggling problems," the report said.

☐ From The State Journal, Lansing, Mich., Oct. 24, 1975. Reprinted by permission of the Associated Press.

For many of the nation's 8.5 million unemployed, opportunities for farm jobs would be welcome, Gavett said. "But the remaining 18 million farm workers needed would have to come from the industrial labor force, thus creating massive labor shortages."

Another hurdle in the shift of millions from town jobs to farms would be the relatively low pay for agricultural workers, which currently is less than one-half that of factory workers.

"In fact, nonfarm workers on unemployment insurance earn more than many farm workers if the value of food stamps is included." Gavett said. "Of course, this is somewhat offset by the fact that some farm workers also receive food stamps and, in some cases, free housing."

But to lure 26 million or more laborers out of cities for non-mechanized farming, the agricultural industry would have to provide far more than free housing and food stamps, he said. Wage increases to $6 or $7 per hour would be needed.

"The impact of such wage hikes would be painful to the American consumer, who would pay much greater prices to absorb the wage increases," Gavett said.

Farmers sometimes are blamed for using excessive amounts of energy in their mechanized programs to produce food, Gavett said. Some critics "erroneously contend" that it takes five calories of energy input to produce one calorie of food value in U.S. agriculture, he said.

"In reality, the U.S. farmer produces about three calories of food for every calorie invested," Gavett said. "Yet, by the time the food is packaged and it reaches the consumer, five calories are invested for each calorie of food value."

Gavett's report said that although American agriculture can stand improvement, "such theoretical panaceas as demechanized farming and a return to nonchemical techniques appear impractical" unless major obstacles are overcome.

Big farms try kicking the chemical habit

BRYCE NELSON*

"Our land smells sweet again, like it did 30 years ago," said farmer Kenneth Livermore. "It don't have that sour smell anymore like when we were using chemicals. Our farm smelled dead then."

"It looks a lot better," he said. "We have life cn our farm again—worms, birds, pheasants. The seagulls fly over the other farms and stop to eat here.

"I'm so happy about how things are going that I'm glad to take time out from my chores to talk to you or anyone else about it. I've got soybeans this year that stand almost to my shoulder—50 bushels to the acre. I've never seen anything like it in my life. And my neighbors are afraid to even grow soybeans."

Livermore, a Nebraskan, is one of the small but growing number of full-time farmers and livestock raisers who have stopped using chemicals—synthetic fertilizers, herbicides and insecticides—and have switched to organic farming in the last few years. They use a variety of alternatives for chemical fertilizer, including manure, fish oil, crop rotation and "green manure"—plowing under a cover crop. To control pests they rely on other insects—and the "natural balance" of their fields.

There are about a dozen such farmers around Greeley, a town of 180 in Eastern Iowa, 40 miles west of Dubuque.

Ralph Engelken has been farming organically here for 13 years. He now farms 700 acres and says he gets yields and quality that are considerably higher than those of "my chemical neighbors."

Many of Engelken's neighbors laughed at him or were hostile to the change when he began farming without chemicals.

"The whole mood has changed now," he said. "Three years ago the press wouldn't print nothing bad about these sprays. Now, some farmers are learning more about what the sprays have done and want to know what I'm doing." . . .

"The question that's always been asked is whether you can have an organic operation and keep your yields and profits. Engelken and others have proved that you can," said Roger Blobaum, a Creston, Iowa, agricultural consultant. Blobaum said that he had been skeptical about whether organic farming could

be profitable on a large scale until he visited the farms of Engelken and other Midwestern organic farmers.

"A lot more farmers are getting into manure this year with the chemical fertilizer shortage," said Frank Ford, who has farmed 1,800 acres of wheat organically in Deaf Smith County in the western Texas Panhandle for 13 years. Ford said his yields were about the same as those of his chemical-using neighbors and his quality was higher. "I don't need any insecticides; I have a good supply of ladybugs to control the green bugs for me."

If there is a significant movement toward more organic farming in American agriculture, it is at its earliest stages among large-scale commercial farmers.

A number of farmers, however, are becoming more concerned about the amount of chemicals they have used in the last few decades. Robert E. Hall, agricultural agent of Delaware County here, is a strong advocate of "proper use of chemicals in farming" and is not regarded as an ally by the county's organic farmers. However, he said that he and many farmers had changed their "philosophy in the last half dozen years on the indiscriminate use of chemicals."

"Farmers have used chemicals whether they needed it or not; farmers have put on fertilizers just to be putting it on. Farmers have brought on this problem themselves," Hall said. "There have been many tons of pesticides put on acres, not because the pest was there, but because he might come along.

"The philosophy is now coming to the forefront among farmers to restore the balance of nature. Farmers are more careful about what they're doing."

But Hall thinks that the yield of corn in this county would fall to 75 bushels an acre (from about 90 to 95 bushels this year) if all farmers here adopted organic methods. "Organic gardening is practical, but not organic farming," he said.

Engelken, who farms in a difficult hilly area, said he averaged 125 bushels of corn an acre and got 185 bushels an acre on his best land.

Like other organic farmers Engelken says that his costs of production are significantly less because he does not use pesticides and because his fertilizer costs are much less.

Organic farmers say also that their crops are more "stress resistant" to plant diseases, to insects and to severe weather.

They emphasize the quality of their crops and livestock, saying the protein content of their crops is considerably higher than other farmers' and that their cattle need less feed and gain more on what they receive. Engelken says that his animals also are healthier.

"Our veterinary bill has been nil since we stopped using chemicals," Engelken said.

Engelken sells about 70 percent of his meat on the open market and about 30 percent directly to buyers who travel to Greeley to buy organically raised animals. Several of his customers are packinghouse workers who claim some of the animals they slaughter are diseased, he said.

What Engelken, his wife, Rita, and their 11 children value most is their conviction that their own health has improved markedly since they began to farm organically.

"I always broke out when I handled chemical fertilizer," Engelken said. The family went from doctor to doctor trying to find out what was wrong. "There was no choice for us; it was give up chemicals or get out of farming," Engelken said.

The rashes disappeared within a few years after they gave up chemical farming, the Engelkens said, although, they said, a child will occasionally get a rash when spray drifts over from a neighbor's farm.

The man who led the Engelkens and others here into organic farming is a 73-year-old Roman Catholic priest, Louis White. Father White has raised a two-acre organic garden each year since 1946, much of it in strawberries, and some of his parishioners began to follow his example after they tasted the produce.

"We had to go through hard times," Father White said. "The press made fun of the organic farmer, agribusiness made fun of him, but now he's in the driver's seat. His costs are lower. The organic farmers are the only farmers in my parish who are making money."

A couple of farmers here, however, have been heretics to Father White's faith in organic farming. Jim Funke and his brother Francis farmed organically for about five years but have gone back to chemicals.

"Organic fertilizer is too time-consuming," Funke said. "It's harder to get it here and it's harder to put it on."

Funke does say that "my ground is plowing hard" since he started using chemicals again.

Farmers in other parts of the Midwest have switched to organic farming for several reasons. Bob Steffen, manager of the 1,000-acre farm at Father Flanagan's Boys Town west of Omaha, Neb., refuses to use chemicals.

"I once watched heifers die after an application of nitrogen and I decided—never again," he said.

In addition to getting yields equal to or better than they were getting when using chemicals, the organic farmers interviewed said they were getting more cash for their farm products, including several cents a pound more for the meat they raised.

If organic farmers have been successful, why don't more farmers try these methods? The organic farmers argue that it is difficult for the average farmer to get much information about organic farming—his county agricultural extension agent, farm organization and a state university often aren't very helpful . . .

Livermore said that farmers in the valley area 30 miles west of Omaha were farming so much acreage that "they're afraid to quit using chemicals for a year. They're afraid they couldn't put in the time to keep the weeds from taking over if they got a lot of rain."

Organic farmers believe that many "chemical farmers" do not understand the relationship of the life under the soil—the earthworms, the insects, the bacteria.

"They're so busy making money that they don't take the time to study it out," Livermore said.

Engelken urges farmers to take a couple of years to switch from chemical to organic methods. "The farmer shouldn't get discouraged. The chemicals have killed off the live bacteria in the soil; it takes time to build them back . . . If you work with your bacteria, with your bugs, with your earthworms, they'll work for you. They'll balance it out."

But farmers like Engelken and Akerlund are satisfied to have "kicked the chemical habit" even if they are unable to persuade their neighbors to do the same. For Akerlund, it is a matter of trust—of giving the farm he inherited from his father in good condition to the next generation:

Why should we be so selfish? Why should we have to go whole hog making money in our lifetime? Why should we pass on these problems to the next generation? We owe the next generation a decent life; we owe them decent land. That's why we decided to change the way we've farmed.

How China uses organic farming methods

ROGER BLOBAUM

A trip to China is a fascinating experience for anyone interested in organic agriculture and its ability to keep soil fertile through centuries of extensive and continuous cropping.

Most of the sights in the rural areas suggest a highly productive agriculture. The visitor sees electric irrigation pumps, leveled land stretching far into the distance, sizable hog and poultry layouts, and third-crop stubble standing in fields where only two crops grew in the past.

Visitors to rural areas from Shanghai to Peking in late winter also see thousands of groups of bundled-up men and women using shovels and baskets to level land, build dikes and terraces, dig mud from canals, and prepare the fields for spring planting.

The combination of hard physical labor and modern agricultural methods enables the Chinese to produce food for 800 to 900 million, roughly a fourth of the world's people. They do it with few tractors or other technological inputs on approximately the same amount of cropland utilized in the United States.

Growing enough food to keep pace with population growth is an enormous undertaking anywhere in Asia. But even the Department of Agriculture concedes that China is getting impressive results. A recent USDA report shows Chinese peasants are producing as much grain as highly-mechanized farmers in the United States, and have three times as many hogs and sheep.

China is developing its own brand of Green Revolution. Technology is adopted selectively, wastes are recycled into agriculture, diversified farming is promoted. Yields are raised without paying a high ecological price.

These choices are possible because China's agriculture is labor intensive. Stress is placed on increasing productivity of the land rather than minimizing use of labor. The result is much less emphasis on mechanization and energy-expensive technology.

Emphasized in this kind of farming is the recycling of a tremendous amount of human, animal and plant waste. Chinese agriculture offers significant lessons to farmers elsewhere on effective use of organic materials.

An important winter job, for example, is scraping silt and other material from the bottoms of canals and fish ponds and, where possible, the rivers themselves. In that mud is organic material from algae and other water plants, the waste from both millions of ducks and the fish that are harvested annually, and rich soil that erodes during the monsoon rains and needs to be reclaimed.

Sometimes this mud is transported by boat to sandy fields that are short of organic material, making it possible to develop new land and build up poor soils considered unsuitable for cropping.

The most common source of fertilizer in China is "night soil," the human waste that has been gathered, composted and applied through the centuries in Asian countries. Using human waste was not viewed with enthusiasm by American farm visitors. But night soil is an important source of plant nutrients in China. In fact, were it not used on the land, China would have vast water pollution problems.

Another organic material is garbage collected in the cities and hauled daily into the countryside in the thousands of concrete boats that ply China's vast network of canals. It is unloaded at the water's edge on commune fields and composted there.

Compost is an important source of fertilizer at Lou-Tang People's Commune in a rural county near Shanghai, which has a population of more than 10 million and is one of the world's largest cities. Lou-Tang is one of more than 109 communes that use garbage from Shanghai and, in turn, raise enough vegetables to supply the city's needs.

"City garbage is brought out here by boats, is piled in the fields, and then has silt from the canal spread on it before it begins to ferment," it was explained. "Then it can be used for fertilizer."

Some of this rich, brown, composted material had been applied a few days earlier, and an occasional piece of broken glass or bowl was the only reminder of its city origin. Picked up during spring planting, the material is used to stabilize canal banks.

Similar garbage recycling situations were seen at Soochow, a provincial city of 520,000 people, and at the Red Star Commune on the outskirts of Peking to the north.

"Garbage from Soochow is brought by boat and composted by the brigades (peasants at the village

☐ From *Organic Gardening and Farming* **22**(7): 45-49, July 1975.

level)," Sun Ping-Shing of the Evergreen People's Commune explained. "However, it is a small percentage of the natural fertilizer used on the land here."

Some of the garbage is kept by city people for feeding chickens. It is not unusual to see laying hens in the streets of large cities, or to be awakened at a hotel by roosters announcing a new day. Garbage is a scarce commodity in rural areas, too, because table wastes are fed to the millions of pigs Chinese peasants raise on their private plots.

Production of hogs is an important link in the recycling process, with larger feedlots located where food-processing wastes are available. Hogs consume these by-products, making it unnecessary to build sewage treatment plants as we do, and provide a lot of valuable fertilizers as well.

One example of these hog-feeding units was seen at Lou-Tang Commune, where hogs were fed by-products of a nearby plant that made huge quantities of sweet potato starch noodles. The manager said this ration was supplemented with some bran, corn and vegetables.

Another was at Red Star Commune, where hogs consume the by-products of a dairy plant drying the milk from more than 2,000 Holsteins, plus wastes from a sizable grain-processing operation. A commune manager said it was unnecessary to include grain in the ration for the 1,600 pigs in this confined feeding setup.

Pig manure is highly prized. Because it is so valuable, it was explained a decision has been made to step up hog production in the communes to a level of about three pigs per acre. With millions of pigs in private plots already working as household garbage disposals, the priority these animals have in agricultural recycling in China is clearly shown.

Straw, fodder and thatch also become fertilizer when they are worked into the fields, the visitors were told. Bacteria is added to the soil in most cases to speed decomposition and make the nutrients available.

The Chinese apparently have also developed an advanced technological process for handling industrial waste water in large cities. They reported that water from industrial plants goes through a process that reclaims gold, silver, mercury and similar metals. This also has the effect of eliminating the possibility of heavy metals problems in municipal wastes that are composted and put on the land. In developing heavy industry virtually from scratch, one Chinese spokesman pointed out, his country has had an advantage in being able to avoid many of the mistakes made by other industrialized nations.

Prompt and careful recycling of wastes help solve another important problem—control of flies and ro-

dents. Scientists at the Agricultural Research Institute at Changchou reported that insecticides made from herbs have been effective in controlling flies. The combination of high sanitation standards and herbal insecticides, they said, has virtually eliminated flies in China.

The visit to the provincial institute was a high point of the trip, providing an inside look at efforts to develop pesticides and fertilizers less harmful than the agricultural chemicals usually pushed in developing countries.

"We are making progress with new kinds of insecticides that are less poisonous, that still retain the ability to kill pests, and that have no aftereffects," Chairman Yang Jian Ming explained. "We stress that pesticides not only eliminate the harmful pests, but also that they are selective and protect our beneficial insects."

The Changchou facility appeared to be the kind of institution organic enthusiasts in this country are looking for. There is none of the resistance to organic methods so common in land grant universities.

It's quite an experience to hear a country's leading agricultural scientist stress that good crop rotation is the best way to control weeds, that composting of agricultural wastes is an essential practice, that green manure crops are needed to maintain soil fertility, that beneficial insects should be propagated and released in large numbers, that biological controls get top priority, and that everything possible must be done to eliminate use of chemicals in the food chain.

The Chinese peasant may look backward to the casual observer—particularly when he is seen guiding a plow behind a slow-moving water buffalo—but he actually is involved in a highly organized program of agricultural education that results in rapid adoption of new farming techniques.

Most of the research projects carried on by the Changchou institute are in the communes where peasants propose many of the projects and witness the results first hand. Seventeen "problem research centers" are scattered across the province, and more than 100 areas are set aside for crop experimentation.

"We combine experiments, popularization, and demonstration in providing direct services to the people," the institute chairman emphasized, "with both professors and technical people going out into the rural areas to carry out this objective."

The institute's "open door" policy puts its staff on a 3-year rotation. They spend one year doing research at the institute, another working on research projects while living and working with peasants, and the third year touring the province to examine problems to be researched and conducting adult education classes to explain research findings.

The Chinese have not given up farm chemicals. They have used dangerous pesticides in the past, they concede, but intend to phase these out and are doing everything possible to develop substitutes.

Chemical fertilizer use is headed up, though. Because of the shift from double-cropping to triple-cropping in many areas, policy makers in China apparently have concluded that organic fertilizer sources will fall short of meeting needs in future years. Steps have been taken to develop a fertilizer industry that will be manufacturing substantial amounts by 1980.

The American group, the first group of farmers to visit since the country "opened up," was told that organic fertilizers now provide somewhere between 70 and 80 percent of the requirements. The remainder is chemical fertilizer, most of it imported and distributed where the need is greatest.

Small farms: overlooked and underestimated

LEE SEARLE*

"You can make a darn good living on 160 acres if you own the ground," says Darrah Roberts, Iowa Falls, Iowa. He farms 186 acres, and raises 150 hogs a year. "I think we live pretty well," his wife says. She doesn't mention it, but it's easy to tell she's proud of their big white house and park-like farmyard. "I've had every opportunity to get bigger," says Roberts. "It hasn't been one of my goals. But I'm not jealous of anyone who does." Even though *Successful Farming* has been a proponent of expansion, we believe Roberts is right. If your goal is a good income, not spectacular growth, one family can make a good living on a quarter section.

"I'd sure like to convince some farmers they don't need to farm 1,000 acres to make a good living."

Attribute that quote to Bob Bernhardt. He's the Extension director in Wright County, Iowa. His opinions were molded by a farm record-keeping project he and area Extension economist Vince Harrell head up for local farmers.

When Bernhardt starts talking about small farm success stories, his first case-in-point is Jim Arndorfer. Arndorfer lives near Clarion in north-central Iowa. By local standards he is a small farmer. Arndorfer owns 160 acres. He rents another 80. Besides corn and soybeans Arndorfer raises hogs. Normal output is about 400 a year, farrow to finish. The impressive statistics on Arndorfer's farm are his management returns. His returns consistently meet and beat those on some much bigger farms.

Shiny new machinery, fancy confinement buildings or a radically different management philosophy aren't the reason. Arndorfer knows he can't afford

*Farm management editor.

to operate with new iron. His main tractor is 15 years old, his combine is about the same age. His finishing building is a self-remodeled two-story chicken house. Low machinery investment doesn't handicap yields. His 240-acre average is usually 150-bu. corn and 40- to 45-bu. beans. This combination of high yields and low cost is what makes him look good on the bottom line at year end, says Bernhardt.

Economics on a quarter-section farm. A big reason some small farms like Arndorfer's and Robert's make money is they operate with few borrowed assets. In other words, they own land, own machinery and pay cash.

A 1974 corn growing budget from the University of Illinois helps make the point. The budget estimated a $218 cost of growing corn in that state last year. But only $78 of that total was seed, fertilizer, fuel and repairs. Big costs were a $58 per acre interest charge on land and another $21 interest charge for other expenses. That $79 stays in your pocket if it's not borrowed at the bank, Bernhardt points out.

Bernhardt's point about small farms: If your goal is a good income, with acceptable financial growth, income might be better on a small farm you own than it will be if you borrow money and double farm size.

High-profit small farms are the exception. It takes higher management to get top profit on smaller farms.

Under average management, medium and large farms make much higher returns to total assets than do average small farms. That's what a careful analysis of state farm records in Michigan showed. The records show return on total assets to farms under 400 acres was only 6.1% in '73. On 400- to 800-acre farms the figure more than doubled—14.3%.

A big reason for low returns on small farms was poor management. Michigan records show crop yields are 12-15% lower, on the average, for farms under 200 acres. Livestock productivity was low too. Small farms average only 60% calf crops when 90% is possible. Swine litter averages were lower and milk production was down 1,000 lbs. per cow from the average for bigger farms.

Another reason for lower profit is higher costs on small farms. Machinery costs, for instance, averaged $22 per acre higher.

How to keep costs down. Almost without exception the small farms that make money have found ways to beat the built-in cost inefficiencies that most small farms bear. One of the first is to trim machinery budget to bare bones.

• *Trade labor for machinery.* That's a management technique Virgil Knight, Sheridan, Illinois uses. Knight owns 120 acres. But he plants his 90 acres of corn with an 8-row planter, harvests it with a big combine. The machinery belongs to two of Knight's neighbors. Both are big farmers. Knight trades labor to them during busy periods in exchange for the use of their machinery.

• *Buy used machinery.* New paint doesn't necessarily mean higher yields, believes Darrah Roberts, Iowa Falls, Iowa. He farms 186 acres. "A small farmer can usually be timely with a piece of machinery a bigger farmer has outgrown. If that's the case, it's pretty hard to justify new stuff."

• *Own it together.* "I'll admit I haven't seen it done much, but I'd like to see a group of two or three farmers buy machinery together," says Ohio Extension ag economist John Moore. "It would work especially well with hay equipment, for instance."

Do something better than average. "Unless you have other income it's pretty hard to be average and make a living on a small farm," says Michigan State economist Ralph Hepp. "You can starve to death out breathing that clean country air."

"The successful small farmer is the one who works for the top profit per hour," says Del Wilken, farm management specialist at the University of Illinois. The best mix usually works out to be some combination of corn, soybeans and hogs.

High yields always seem to have a direct correlation to high profits, says Bernhardt. "Arndorfer's 150-bu. corn yields are the reason he's able to compete with bigger farms with lower yield averages."

Hogs are winners on small farms. The Michigan survey points out hogs as the best livestock enterprise for most small farmers. "I don't see how small dairy farms can survive unless they're subsidized," says economist Leonard Kyle. He's also discouraging beef cattle as an alternative for the small farm unless there are no other enterprises available.

Technology is expensive. One of the biggest problems ahead for small farms is the high price of modern technology.

"It comes in costly lumps," says Illinois' Del Wilken. "It becomes more difficult to fit these lumps into small business."

Roberts is one farmer who has been able to adapt new technology to the small farm. His narrow-row soybean system is an example. His 12-in skip-row planter and cultivator cost him under $500. With the system he hopes to raise yields up to a 50-bu. average from his present 40.

But sometimes there are no low-cost alternatives. That's what Virgil Knight found. When we first talked to him a year ago he was farming 120 acres, growing all the corn he could and putting every kernel of it through 600-700 head of hogs he farrowed and fed.

"But I had some bad luck since then," says Knight. "High winds totally demolished most of my hog facilities. I had insurance but when I figured the cost of rebuilding I decided the cost of getting back into the hog business was just too high. I'd have had to expand numbers more than I wanted to make the investment pay."

As an alternative, Knight took an off-farm job. He still farms the cropland but only on a part-time basis.

Knight's point is a good one to remember: It's hard to be in debt and still make a living on a small farm.

Subsistence farming on the North Pacific Coast

AL PENTA

The North Pacific Coast is a rather unique farming area in that the main products grown there are the trees (i.e. forestry for lumber); yet it also provides good opportunities for the family or communal farmers. The region includes coastal Oregon, Washington west of the Cascade Mountains, and southwest British Columbia, including Vancouver Island.

The climate is fine, but takes some getting used to. There are essentially two seasons: a long, mild, rainy winter and a short, cool, dry summer. From October to April there is almost daily rainfall and an average temperature of perhaps 40°. In December and January there is some snow as well as rain and an average temperature of about 30°. By the first of April the frost is usually gone and gardening begins. Spring is mixed rain and sunshine, but by May the sunny weather prevails. The average temperature from April to October is perhaps 60°, with a few days near 80° in midsummer.

Forestry is the main economy of the region and the land is heavily covered with evergreen trees. Because there are no vast stretches of cleared land, agribusiness and the corporations leave the coastal farmers pretty much to themselves. There are, however, many large successful spreads of 50 to 250 acres which are used for dairy or beef cattle or fruit production. More important to our discussion are innumerable smaller places of 10 to 25 acres which are easily available and used for growing and cash crops, particularly plums, apples, and raspberries. It should be noted though that very, very few of these smaller places are entirely self-sufficient and that outside income is necessary or, at the very least, desirable.

There are many of these small sites of 10-25 acres for sale cheaply, or for rent. Many were former homesteads and usually have a few cleared acres and the rest forested. We rent a log cabin, 10 acres and a creek

☐ From WIN **8**(12):31, July 1972.

for $60 a month in western Washington, but about $100 a month would be average. The region as a whole is beset with the twin problems of increasing property taxes and very high unemployment. Still, it is a good region in which to survive. For those not quite ready for a complete rural plunge there are three large cities within the region: Portland, Seattle, and Vancouver.

Back to the land. The soil is acidic, but usually needs no additive other than good organic manure. Steer, horse, goat, or chicken shit is usually available cheaply or free for the hauling. Wood shavings are free from the lumber mills to mix in and aerate the earth. Better yet, get some chickens, fill their coops with the free shavings and clean out in the spring and fall for the garden (chicken eggs are also a good cash crop or item for trade). Of course dig a compost heap for garbage. Get a pair of ducks (they require no feed) to eat the slugs (large shell-less snails) which may eat your lettuce and other greens.

As early as March, potatoes, radishes, beets, and peas may be planted. Most other crops can be put in after the last frost. Insects and plant diseases are not severe, although most local people use pesticides. Because of the long frost-free period many people make a final planting in September or October and dig out of the soggy soil carrots, beets, turnips, etc. all winter long as they are needed. Dig it. Happy gardening.

One more thing: fuel. Almost everyone burns wood which is available free, if not in your backyard, then along county roads where trees are cut down as they encroach the road.

Before the white man came, the Indians of the North Pacific Coast were not big on farming. Still they had one of the highest standards of living in aboriginal North America because of fish (salmon and trout) and wild plant foods which are still in abundance. These two food sources coupled with small scale farming can make subsistence possible. Can maybe make a lot of things possible.

The political implications of organic farming

JEFF COX

Giffen, Inc., of Fresno County, California, grows cotton, fruit, sugar and cattle on a 100,000-acre farm. In 1970, despite a Congressional law limiting farm subsidies to $55,000 per crop, Giffen, Inc., collected $4 million in U.S. Department of Agriculture subsidies. It turned the trick by leasing most of its cotton acreage allotment out to smaller growers. That way Giffen was eligible for subsidies of 15¢ a pound on cotton grown on those acres as well as collecting $762,000 in lease fees and maybe more from farmers willing to pay to farm the land. So Giffen collected while its tenant farmers—they used to call them serfs—did the work.

Giffen is a GOP supporter and contributor. He was in prominent attendance at the Salute to Agriculture Day festivities hosted by President Nixon in May of 1971.

Some of the other big winners in the milk-the-taxpayer sweepstakes include giant agribusiness conglomerates like J. G. Boswell Co., Bangor Punta, and Tenneco (all million-dollar plus winners), and individuals like John Wayne and associates ($218,000) and Sen. James Eastland of Mississippi ($160,000).

Serfs of a similar kind have developed in the chicken business. Have you noticed the low price of poultry lately? Overproduction is killing every poultryman, just about, except the large operators in thrall to agribusiness integrators like Ralston-Purina (which is moving out of this aspect of farming, having milked the best of the profits from the industry). Harrison Wellford in his excellent book, *Sowing the Wind*, written for the Nader organization, shows how one Southern poultryman ended up making a personal wage of a penny a day. When agribusiness moves in, they first control the chick farms. Then they force the local poultrymen to do things their way or refuse to sell them chicks. "Their way" often means that the poultryman must use his profits to buy expensive equipment from agribusiness subsidiaries.

And by the way, getting back to Bangor Punta which received $1.8 million in farm subsidies in 1970 (third highest in the nation) . . . did you know its public securities division, Smith & Wesson, makes police revolvers, mace, pepper fog, plastic helmets, gas masks, sirens, handcuffs, radar systems and suspect identification systems for police?

Our so-called agricultural colleges get most of their research funds from the chemical fertilizer, insecticide and herbicide people—the same people in some instances that manufacture explosives for bombs. In most of these schools there is an official line on farming: you do it with chemicals or everybody will starve. As for organic farming, they don't want to hear it. At one school in North Carolina; years of research has paid off in a mechanical tobacco harvester capable of putting thousands and thousands of black field hands out of work. Not that there's anything wrong with replacing such menial tasks with machines . . . it's just that nobody thought about what the field hands will do when they're automated out of the field. They'll move to the city, of course, where subsidiaries of conglomerates in the supermarket industry can sell them the crappy food raised on chemical farms at "stabilized" prices they can hardly afford, and which will make them so sick they'll have to use the medicines manufactured by other subsidiaries. Sounds paranoid? Yeah. And cynical too.

But it's ever true that the desire to be master of one's own ship burns brightly in the human heart—and nowhere can a man or woman master his ship more personally than on a farm.

Against the take-over of American agriculture by the vertical monopolies we call corporate conglomerates, with all their ties to the government, we find the growing organic movement. Some characteristics of the organic farm movement are:

- It lends itself to smaller farms.
- It's basically decentralist in nature.
- It avoids monocropping, which is the planting of a jillion acres in one crop.
- It avoids the use of chemicals to do the job that soil bacteria do better. (And you can't package and sell the soil bacteria. They come free.)
- The food produced by the organic farm is nutrition and quality-oriented, rather than profit and quantity-oriented. In other words, its humanistic.
- The organic farm, it goes without saying, is enjoying the free flow of all nature's life forces within its system. The chemical farm, on the other hand, uses man's analogs, artificial and commercially produced substitutes, for nature's ways. Man's analogs

☐ From WIN **8**(12): 34-35, July 1972.

have a way of disrupting the natural order. But you can control, package and sell man's analogs.

What if America were to kick the chemical habit and go back to organic farming? It looks more and more as if there's no "what if" to it—the real question is when it will happen. When our soil fertility is finally gone, ruined by chemicals, our vitality as a people will be gone. That day seems close. When the pilgrims arrived there was an average of a few feet of rich topsoil on the continent. Today there's an average of seven inches, sinking fast. Earthworms die in wholesale slaughter as chemicals infiltrate soil. Nitrate buildups from agricultural chemicals change healthy red blood to a sickening chocolate brown unable to carry oxygen to tissues. Loss of humus from the soil by chemical practices causes erosion and washouts and water loss. Soil is caking up, used only to prop up plants rather than impart life. The fire in the soil is going out.

Sen. Gaylord Nelson sees what's happening. His Family Farm Act of 1972 is as radical a piece of legislation as has been proposed in Congress since Jefferson and other rabble-rousers of his time made the recommendation that no farm be over 160 acres. The Nelson act calls for a similar limit. As a matter of fact, when this country was founded, the original land grant acts firmly specified that nobody was allowed more than 160 acres. But land cheats soon had rolled up farms of hundreds of thousands of acres out west, where no one could check, using influence and salt money to do it. We live with the legacy of those illegal farms today—the big California farms owned by one family stem from that time. Someone recently suggested we enforce our laws and break up these huge holdings, but people seem to have gotten used to the idea of Hoss Cartwright and his family empire as a fine thing.

Nelson's bill stands a snowballs' chance. The real agricultural power in Congress is held by people like Jamie Whitten of Mississippi who runs the Department of Agriculture from behind the scenes. Books have been written detailing the horrible misuse of the public trust by this man, but he goes blithely on. When Jamie wants to know something, he calls his friends in the FBI and gets a little checking done. When poverty programs were scheduled for his state, Jamie killed them. Other power-holders are men like Dr. Earl Butz, who left a lucrative job with Ralston-Purina to head the Department of Agriculture. The man he replaced went to Ralston-Purina. Funny.

Back to the question: What if everyone went organic? Well, the more people who do, the fewer agricultural chemicals will be used. So expect the chemical companies and their friends to try to discredit everything about the family farm movement and the organic method. You can expect them to say that there is no way to feed our people by organic methods. Bullshit. Don't you believe it. Organic farms consistently outproduce chemical farms. It's just harder to run an organic operation of more than 160 acres.

The political implications of organic farming are immense. It will mean a transfer of power from the large conglomerates back into the hands of the people. It will mean land for people and people on the land. Instead of fewer, larger farms and more crowding in the cities, it means that the traditional way of making a living, the stewardship of a piece of dirt, will be given to the disenfranchised and poor. Blacks are forming organic growing cooperatives in the South now and the trend will continue.

It will mean local growers supplying local folks. An end to plastic supermarkets. It will mean building up the fertility of the soil as a national policy instead of subsidizing those who can rip off the most land.

It will mean, in other words; a complete breakdown in the way we now do things. And it can be done. Chemical companies can get into the business of recycling organic waste (that's turned into humus by composting) back to the land . . . or the thousands of other things organic farmers will need. Getting back to the land in 1972 means having enough technological help to free oneself from being a sway-backed peasant. Peasants, yes; swaybacks, no. Tillers are wonderful inventions. So are tractors. So are harvesters.

Growth hormones, insecticides, and the rest of the chemical armanentarium are not.

The organic movement is more than a populist movement, for it includes the whole web of life, not just people. It's a return to the Jeffersonian ideal of the yeoman farmer. Now some say that the idea of the yeoman farmer—the rugged individualist living life on his own land on his own terms—was always a myth, and existed more as a romantic ideal than a national reality. Maybe so. But ideals give us direction.

Our current politics have become the servant, not of the people, but of the corporation comprised of a miniscule number of wealthy people. As such it reduces the individual to second class status. Property rights have taken precedence over human rights for so long that it seems the natural order of things. But human rights, although important, cannot take precedence over, say, pig rights. Or insect rights. In other words, human rights only take their proper place and assume their proper perspective when all other living things and the land itself are accorded their rights. The organic farmer, with his orientation toward feeding the life in the soil, respects the rights of the other biotic communities on his spread. What profits a human to have a TV and dishwasher if he lose his earthworms?

As the number of organic farmer increases, the number of organic consumers will increase. These people, simply by being aware of the ecological relationships under which their food was grown, will be more sensitive to the environment in other areas. It has to be. Emphasis subtly shifts from quantity to quality. The institutionalization of schlock—like MacDonalds—will lose force and cheap hamburgers and thick shakes will lose appeal.

With more people back on the land, improving it and learning once again about the harmonies that actually can exist for a human being if he cares to still his cravings and listen, consumption of "luxury items" will fall. I realize all this is wild speculation, but it seems to follow logically from a return to the land. People will again take on some of the life support functions they now buy from corporations. Thus those institutional giants will lose their viability as the determiners of life quality, and as intermediaries between us and raw life experience.

Organic farming is basically family farming. Thus if the trend continues toward organic farming, the family farm will necessarily make a reappearance. It also means that families may again become self-sufficient and able to turn away from the dog-eat dog competitiveness of the marketplace for the cooperation of the community. This will make for a diversity of life that's been lacking in our lifetimes. Where life is most diverse it is most colorful and rich. Where external sameness prevails, the spirit sickens.

Organic farming will arrive when we cease to call it organic. When it becomes just farming. Until then it is a reaction to devastatingly corrupt ways of producing our food. Whatever evils characterize America in this decade characterize its agriculture. Whatever rational and human solutions transform our society in the years ahead, must include organic farming, for organic farming is nothing more than farming in obedience to laws we cannot break . . . the higher laws of nature.

Amish agriculture: adaptive strategies for economic survival of community life

VICTOR STOLTZFUS*

THE PROBLEM

For the sociologist, adaptation refers to "those aspects of a *culture*, the culture traits and complexes, that represent a society's adjustment to its physical environment and enable it to survive" (Theodorson and Theodorson, 1969:96). This paper is intended to present research findings among farm operators of the Amish religious community in Coles, Douglas, and Moultrie counties of east central Illinois regarding the group's adaptive responses to socio-economic trends of the larger society. The approach of the discussion is to view Amish farm management strategy as an adaptive device in relation to the ongoing problem of social and economic viability. I shall be occupied largely with the facts of Amish adaptation as a particular and

exotic group, but I want also to remember the possible relevance of their adaptive strategies for a larger grouping of persons in contemporary America—the concerned environmentalist.

THE SOCIO-ECONOMIC CONTEXT OF AMISH AGRICULTURE

One of the most striking indicators of change in America is the drop in the proportion of the nation's workers engaged in agriculture. In the first census in 1790 the figure was 95 percent. It dropped to 72 percent by 1820, then to 53 percent at the end of the Civil War, 27 percent by the end of World War I, and 14 percent at the end of World War II (Miller, 1957:341). A preliminary estimate for the 1971 farm population was 4.4 percent of the total (*St. Louis Post Dispatch*, 1972).

Another measure of change is the number of persons supplied with farm products by 1 U.S. farm worker. In 1820 this was 4.1, in 1945 it had grown to 14.6, and the

☐ From Rural Sociology **38**(2):196-205, Summer 1973. Funding for this research was provided by the Center for the Biology of Natural Systems, Washington University, St. Louis, Mo.
*Department of Sociology, Eastern Illinois University, Charleston, Ill.

1969 estimate was 45.3 (Handbook of Agricultural Charts, 1970).

An important factor in these changes has been the use of new energy sources such as gasoline, diesel fuel, and electricity to replace or supplement human and animal energy. In addition, new scientific advances in cropping, animal science, marketing, and processing have been translated into powerful technologies forming large agribusiness structures.

The power of the federal government is directly involved in today's agriculture with programs of research, price supports, commodity storage, and indirect incentives to reduce the acreage of crops which are in oversupply.

Another significant change area is managerial forms. Don Paarlberg, Director of Agricultural Economics for the U.S.D.A., points out (1972:235) that the successful farm before the agricultural scientific revolution was based on a combination of capital, manual skill, and managerial ability vested in one man.

But with the advance of agricultural science, the burden of management has become intense. The technical knowledge which an up-to-date farmer must master is much broader than is required of most businessmen with equal investment. The capital needed to operate a modern farm is beyond the reach of most farm boys. Rarely do we find combined in one man, the financial resources, the technical knowledge and the managerial ability to operate a modern farm . . .

Therefore managerial innovators developed a far-reaching technique. Instead of simply accepting what the economists call "the factors of production" . . . as they happened to be combined in one man, the family farm operator, the new concept is to split up the factors of production and recombine them in optimum form.

Such "rational management" makes possible much larger units for using highly trained managers. It attracts larger capital investments; it can make more economical use of the expensive mechanization through economies of scale; and it can respond to the demands for quality and timing of the large buyers. For example, the poultry industry, through rational management and production systems, reduced costs by about one-fourth in the last 15 years while the population's consumption of chicken almost trebled. Paarlberg goes on to argue that the new management concepts need not be the death of the family farm. They can be incorporated into some existing family farms. His view of the future is for large-scale, corporation units to be operating along with the family farm as the major organizational form.

TRADITIONAL AMISH AGRICULTURE

The religious controversy which led to the split in late 17th Century Europe between the Mennonites and the Amish had nothing to do with agricultural issues. The intense persecution which both groups received forced them to find new farming methods suitable to the inhospitable soils and climates in which they were forced to live. In the 18th and 19th centuries in America the Amish, along with other Swiss-German immigrants, were noted for their agricultural innovations. They were among the first to practice:

the stall-feeding of cattle, rotation of crops, meadow irrigation, and to use natural fertilizers and clover and alfalfa pasture as a means of restoring fertility to the soil (Kollmorgen in Nagata, 1968).

They avoided the practice of "mining the soil," depleting a succession of farms, and moving as fertility declined.

It is only in recent years with the intense mechanization of American farming via tractor introduction, trucks, and rural electrification that the Amish became a visible minority along the lines of new farm practices (Nagata, 1968:81).

From interviews with older members of the community, Nagata lists some of the reasons for Amish resistance to many technological innovations of the past 50 years. The tractor was resisted to keep labor opportunities for young people. According to a study in Oklahoma, each tractor added to a farm was associated with a loss of 3 or 4 persons (Cavin, 1969:47). A second reason was the Amish preference for land purchase as an alternative use for scarce funds. The high rate of reproduction, 7.01 per family, made land purchase a high priority choice. Tractors are now permitted on Amish farms but their use is limited to work around the buildings as a source of power for grinding, threshing, and loading manure. An exception is made for Amish renters on "English" farms where full utilization of tractor power is permitted. Variation also occurs today on tractor usage among the various Amish communities in other regions of the country.

In brief, the Amish did not regard technological innovation as an end in itself. Their core culture of religiously reinforced family and community values was safeguarded against the social costs of changes which in their estimation did more harm than good to the community as a whole.

The typical Amish farm of past decades retained a balance between livestock operations and field crops. Traditionally, it had a variety of farm animals, often hogs, cows, horses, and chickens. The typical field crops provided hay and pasture for the cattle and horses, oats for the horses, and corn for the hogs. The diversity of livestock enterprises gave some economic hedge against price fluctuations and disease losses. The diversity of field crops provided for crop rotation and the attendant soil improvement properties of legumes.

Labor was frequently shared along kinship lines and neighborhood harvest rings for haying, threshing, and silo filling. Much of the capital was generated out of a very small initial investment and the slow build-up of profit and reinvestment. Other capital needs were frequently supplied by kinship resources.

A simple life style has been a traditional Amish value with direct linkage to core religious values. The horse and buggy transportation and severely modest, homemade clothes are visually distinctive and attract immediate tourist attention. But their economic significance to the family farm enterprise is also substantial if not as obvious. Socialization to the high level of material consumption that characterizes the larger society would make the necessary profitability in the first years of farming impossible.

The economic implications of Amish culture for the care of the aged are also important for an understanding of farm management alternatives. In the majority culture, it is a highly desired goal to secure an income that will permit payments into various types of retirement plans and insurance policies that cushion the individual from the shocks of prolonged illness, mental disorder, unemployment, and other disabilities. These are often assumed fringe benefits of employment in public and private bureaucracies. The self-employed farmer, however, must generate substantial profits to buy his protection from the unwelcome contingencies of old age. Since care of the aged is an important kinship and community value within Amish life, the Amish farmer does not have the economic burden of diverting a substantial amount of his profit from the farm to such purposes. He even has the additional benefit that comes from being cared for in his years of dependency from kinfolk and community neighbors rather than by the hired services of strangers in an unfamiliar setting.

In summary, traditional Amish agriculture has been the expression of a core culture where a harmonious balance among God, nature, family, and community was the goal. The outlines of such harmony were understood to be given in the Bible as interpreted through their folk tradition. The ideology of Western civilization that directs man to energetically transform the resources of nature into economic products which, in turn, are processed into status enhancement has had little appeal to the Amish. Their notion of selfhood through reciprocated services in the community has been in contrast to the majority culture's idea of selfhood through autonomy. Continuity and slow change are preferred to rapid change.

When Amish agricultural practices are placed in that culture's values, their farm management de-

cisions become rational choices rather than eccentric choices in light of the majority culture.

CURRENT AMISH ADAPTATION TO NATIONAL SOCIO-ECONOMIC TRENDS IN FARMING

Preliminary analysis of our data shows a pronounced trend toward specialization in contrast to the traditional diversification in Amish farming.[1] The trend is not as fully developed as in the surrounding farms but it is clearly in evidence and growing. The study area specializes in cash grain farming. The Amish are specializing in their livestock operations rather than field cropping, which remains diversified. They are adapting in other words to the economic necessities of modern agriculture but have managed to retain elements of their own cultural style.

Several economic pressures from the larger economy favor such a trend. Capital investment in improved technology, for example, demands greater production volume if costs per unit are to be kept low. I observed Amish dairymen using drylot feeding methods, bulk milk tanks, and increased herd sizes. These are all recent innovations for the Amish of Illinois. Other economic prods toward specialization include higher management skills needed for the new technologies, less hazard from disease losses with modern methods, government regulation of market prices to prevent extremely sharp declines, and the marketing requirements for volume production (Wilcox and Cochrane, 1960:26).

The cultural significance of this trend is important. Specialization makes the Amish farm more vulnerable to fluctuations in the larger economy. Capital requirements expose the Amish farmer to the risks of com-

---

[1] This investigation was conducted among 4 of the 12 geographical Amish church districts in Illinois. As of August, 1971, an estimated 1,790 people were in this Old Order Amish community. The total 1961 Amish population in the United States was estimated at 49,371 persons. (The first estime is that of a businessman in Arthur, Illinois, who is writing a doctoral dissertation on the economics of Amish life. He requested anonymity. The U.S. figure is from Hostetler, 1963:80.)

One of the districts was used largely to establish rapport and to determine what research information could be gained from a tightly-knit community which has erected linguistic, religious, and social barriers between itself and the larger society. The remaining 3 districts were chosen to include the main variability of the total community in kinds of farm enterprises, degree of conservatism in ministerial leadership, and population density. A 50 percent random sample was selected from each district. Permission to interview was initially sought from the bishop of each church district and then appointment times were arranged with the individual farmers. The interviews contained 54 questions and took from 2.5 to 4 hours. For the most part there was excellent cooperation. Only a few refused to be interviewed. As a general rule, the farm operators consulted income tax records and farm record books in order to give accurate answers.

mercial credit and make his community less self-sufficient. But it is an apparent economic necessity for survival. Profits are needed to finance some of the highest-priced land in the nation (about $1,000 an acre) and increasingly high real estate taxes (from $10 to $20 an acre).

Intensification of livestock enterprises is the favored Amish adaptive device. When asked about the means they would choose to increase their income, most respondents indicated they would expand their livestock operations rather than add more acres for increased crop production. Preference for the livestock alternative is rational given the inefficiencies of horse farming, the relatively low profitability of field crops, and the high costs of land, seeds, fertility maintenance, and taxes. Livestock production is also more labor intensive. It requires daily, rather than seasonal, labor inputs. It permits several production cycles per year rather than one. This enables more efficient use of family labor resources which are typically plentiful due to the cultural norm of large families in Amish society.

The increased labor requirements of today's livestock operations, however, have accelerated the Amish life pace and put strain on the symbolic uses of farming for community solidarity. The cooperative aspects of labor sharing are most heavily concentrated on field cropping activities. Harvest rings for threshing, haying, and silo filling offer pleasurable expressions for community solidarity. My data show that the Amish farmer spends as many as 30 days a year in labor exchanges. If the trend of livestock specialization continues, the amount of time necessary to be at home caring for animals will increase and the significance of shared labor in the fields may diminish.

There is another side to the disparity in acculturation between the livestock enterprises and field crops. Modern hog farrowing equipment and especially dairy equipment contrast sharply with the Amish, horse-drawn grain binders and threshing rigs. There also seems to be no hesitation to draw on the services of veterinary medicine. My data show the Amish expending upwards of $200 per year for the veterinarian on many livestock farms. Artificial insemination is frequently utilized for dairy herds and sometimes for swine. The mixer-grinder unit for livestock feed processing is usually the single most expensive piece of equipment on the Amish farm. Tractors are permitted in limited ways to assist in the livestock enterprise with belt power, manure forklift, and as power units for feed griding. They are not permitted as a general rule in the field.

If the observation that a more rapid rate of acculturation to conventional agriculture on the part of livestock enterprises is correct, it is useful to speculate why. General economic pressure is only part of the answer. Alternative responses to economic pressures in the past have included migration. It would seem that livestock enterprise innovations are less likely to run afoul of morally sanctified past agricultural precedents. Cage layer operations and specialized calf raising are relatively new in conventional agriculture. There is therefore less of a past Amish heritage that change would "violate."

In 1970, the most important single innovation in livestock technology was the experimental adoption of bulk milk tanks. The "experiment" was made to satisfy both secular and sacred authorities. The Illinois state health department had to be satisfied that a bulk milk tank could function correctly without electrical power or controls. Amish adaptive skills were equal to the task of using diesel cooling power and an air motor for agitation to the bulk units to satisfy the state. The church issue was more complicated since neither the church members nor the bishops were unified in their understanding on the effects of this innovation on community life. After the year's experimental period elapsed in January, 1972, an informal agreement emerged among the bishops not to formally oppose or endorse the bulk tank innovation. In the absence of a specific prohibition, Amish dairymen are now installing bulk tanks.

Another adaptive device is the increasing use of commercial credit among Amish farmers for purchasing buildings, land, farm equipment, and livestock. One bank in the area had $1,300,000 in loans to Old Order Amish customers. This was distributed among 135 borrowing customers and represented 14 percent of the bank's total loan volume as of August, 1971. The high land prices and the shift to more capital intensive livestock operations make it impossible for the Amish community to generate sufficient capital from within community resources alone. There has been a strong tradition of kinship and community loans with low rates of interest. This still plays a significant role. But with debt reaching as high as $50,000 on some Amish farms, the necessity for commercial help is apparent. The Amish are proud that the bank has never written off one of their loans as a loss. If an individual falters, kin and community resources have come to the rescue. Another reason for the greater use of commercial credit today is the increasing cost of starting a farm operation. When farmers of more than 10 years experience were asked about their starting costs, exclusive of land, the answers ranged from $700 to a few thousand. A typical response for start up costs now is $8,000 to $10,000.

The use of outside capital has produced no startling observable changes in the short run. Indeed, it has operated to extend farming as an occupational alternative to young Amishmen who might otherwise be forced off the land. Moreover, farming in the matrix of a strong, sacred tradition can suppress certain economic questions from even surfacing to consciousness. For example, when one farmer was asked if horse farming was economic for field work in contrast to tractor farming, he replied that he had never thought much about it but supposed that horse farming was cheaper. When I asked if he had considered the additional profits from dairy herd expansion that eliminating 8 horses would provide, he said that if you figured it that way, maybe horse farming was not cheaper. He also noted that with tractor farming, "we would not be the community that we are now." His observation is apt.

With the emphasis on record keeping, calculation of profits specific to various farm enterprises, and the need to meet a fixed repayment schedule it seems inevitable that the long-run, social effect of extensive bank credit use will be to make the Amish farmer more responsive to external management advice and external market trends. However, the present high morale and strength of Amish community life seems strong enough to buffer much of the cultural effects of such dependence for the current generation.

Tourism is another force in the larger economic world to which Amish life is subject. So far it has not impinged greatly on their economic structure. One former Amish person has opened a tourist-oriented farm called Rockhome Gardens. It offers horse and buggy rides, a tour of a furnished Amish house and seasonal displays of horse farming operations and equipment. The hundreds of thousands of people who annually come to Rockhome Gardens are able to glimpse family operated businesses: harness shops, a sorghum mill, a cider mill, a lamp shop, a bakery, a carpet weaving business, a grocery store, a butcher shop, and buggy shops. One of the buggy shops caters to antique restorations of old cars and carriages. A farmer's market enjoys gross sales of $25,000 and a substantial fraction of this is tourist trade. Produce from gardens is often offered for sale in season at various Amish farmsteads to the tourists who wish to drive there. With the exception of 1 family who deliberately planned a part of its farm enterprise to meet the fresh vegetable trade, the sales of fresh garden items were economically trivial.

Currently the vast majority of tourist dollars end up in non-Amish bank accounts. This is likely one source of the resentment some Amish people feel toward Rockhome Gardens. There is also a feeling that it is improper for someone to commercialize the faith of his fathers.

However, an economic symbiosis between tourism and the general Amish community could develop. The Amish, who have not used any commercial fertilizer, have some of the most extensive tracts of land that would be regarded as "clean" by the organic purist. An entrepreneur who would provide marketing and transportation connections between Amish producers and "health food" consumers could open up a significant new enterprise. It is an adaptive economic possibility for the future. At present, a small goat milk operation oriented to the "organic" market for goat milk cheese is going.

An indirect effect of the tourist industry on Amish community life is also present. Leaders who represent economic, educational, and political power outside the Amish community are aware that it is the uniqueness of Amish life that draws tourists and tourist dollars to their community. This likely operates as a socio-economic force toward cooperation with the Amish in maintaining their lifeways.

Another area of Amish adaptation represents no new development in relation to current economic pressures but is an important coping device within Amish tradition. I refer to the substantial savings in family living costs which are due to the industry and frugality of the Amish housewife. Even with the trend toward specialization in farming already discussed, it is still customary to have enough of a variety of livestock and garden crops to feed the family. Even with large families, Amish housewives reported out-of-pocket grocery bills for food and non-food items in the range of $10 to $15 per week. Much of the clothing is homemade and used until there is patch upon patch of the farmer's denim trousers. The Amish home is furnished simply with sturdy, often hand-crafted furniture built to serve more than one generation.

In recent times, propane gas refrigerators and stoves have become commonplace and some battery powered mixers can be found in Amish kitchens. One Amish farmer piped compressed air into the house basement to operate his home laundry with an air motor. Horse and buggy transportation is expensive at approximately $1400 for a new rig and horse but even with the costs of horseshoeing, grain and hay for several horses, car rental for longer public trips, it is clear that the Amish family economizes on transportation. The slow moving vehicles are a dangerous form of economy, however.

The most difficult area for Amish economy is the cost of medicine. A plan is now in operation to help with very large medical bills when people request some help through the church. But since church limits on education at the eighth grade prevents the training of Amish doctors, they are forced to purchase all such services outside of their own kinship structure. Medical bills are often a larger than expected proportion of total living expenses. Still, the cost of living is low. A comparatively well to do older farmer with 14 children, of which 12 were at home reported an out-of-pocket living expense of only $4,700 for the year. Such a modest scale of consumption is clearly related to Amish ability to retain their agricultural base.

AMISH ADAPTATION AS A PROTOTYPE

The Amish life style is one model of human community that has appealing features from the viewpoint of environmental concern. The use of windmills, human and animal energy supplemented by modest amounts of fossil fuels, and no electrical consumption is in sharp contrast to the larger society. The balance between livestock and field cropping prevents the extremes of huge livestock concentrations in confined feedlots with the attendant pollution problems of animal waste, on the one hand, and large land tracts forced to receive inorganic chemicals rather than manure for fertility maintenance on the other.

The modest scale of consumption is also appealing to those who wish to preserve natural resources and the energy required to produce and distribute a vast industrial product.

My investigation also supports the claim that Amish family and community are resilient institutions that have endured far more hostile economic circumstances than the difficulties of the present decade. Bank data comparing 88 Amish accounts between 1964 and 1971 showed they increased in net worth from $2,379,000 to $4,045,000 (local informant).

The economic foundations of their unique social and cultural lifeways are under strain, but by no means do they appear in danger of collapse in the near future. Amish capacity to innovate, even within a tradition that values continuity rather than change, has served them well.

It is a difficult task to assess the significance of their management strategies for environmentalists. One cannot pick and choose a few items from a total cultural configuration that excite admiration and then tack it on to the larger culture, even when a society is as syncretistic and pluralistic as our own. Furthermore not all Amish lifeways are environmentally admirable, e.g., the high birth rate.

There are, however, several ways in which Amish culture has something to offer the concerned environmentalist. First, the Amish necessity to cope with energy needs apart from electricity makes them inventive in ways that may be useful on a technological level if ever the inefficiencies of burning fossil fuels to generate electrical power necessitate a new policy on this matter. For example, an Amish poultry house with propane gas for lights and cooling and a building design which makes maximum use of air currents in-

stead of electrical fans is now operating with about a one-third cost savings compared with an all electric cage layer operation. The Illinois Amish can now support full-time metal workers, woodworkers, and motor repair men. Their technological adaptations deserve closer attention.

There is also a benefit to be gained from some sustained exposure to Amish culture in the most general sense. It is a truism that to learn another language is to really learn one's mother tongue. Learning about Amish cultural preferences makes an observer more conscious of the unconscious choices that are the patterned responses of our own culture. The sociologist Phillip Slater (1970:45) has a pertinent observation about conventional attitudes toward technology in our society:

. . . when evaluating its effects we always adopt the basic assumptions and perspective of technology itself, and never examine it in terms of the totality of human experience. We say this or that invention is valuable because it generates other inventions—because it is a means to some other means —not because it achieves a human end. We play down the "side effects" that so often become the main effects and completely negate any alleged benefits.

The Amish experience is valuable as a historical benchmark, as an exposure to a life style that draws the human technological balance at a conspicuously different point. It is not likely that the Amish model will be directly imitated by many people in the near future but it can aid us in more critically and consciously evaluating our own man-machine equilibrium in light of our own professed humane values.

A third value that acquaintance with Amish experience can contribute is a clue to the important question of motivation for ecological concerns. The larger society not only faces alternative allocation of scarce energy resources but also the difficult cultural question of how to generate substitute human gratifications for consumption patterns that now go beyond the satisfaction of elementary needs for shelter, food, and clothing. Our consumption patterns are linked to ideologically tinged economic and political systems which are no longer simply an arrangement of skills and power to make things happen. They have taken on emotionally charged meanings as important aspects of the national culture. At the social psychological level, the work tools and consumption habits characteristic of high energy society have vitally entered into our self conceptions. Sherif and Sherif (1956:689) say:

. . . objects and influences from material culture which people grow up with, which they face and use daily in vital activities, acquire considerable personal and motivational significance. . . . The farmer can scarcely conceive of himself without his plow and tractor. Reduced to a hand plow, he would be in a state of personal misery. The traveling salesman's car becomes almost as much a part of himself as his own face. The grounded pilot has an empty existence until he sits at the controls of his plane once again.

Should ecological considerations make it prudent for our society to change some of its lifeways, we would be faced with the problem of alternate engineering technologies and alternate social and personal satisfactions.

The Amish alternative to ego-involvement in complex technology and high material consumption is an elaborate ego-involvement in family and community. My data show that the family is a major source of gratification to the Amish individual. Even their attachment to farming, which is sometimes cited as a major gratification in and of itself, is frequently referred to as a means of being with the family. Amish concern for clean land and streams is vitally related to a religious sense of duty and to a real feeling of pleasure an Amishman gets in the success of his children and grandchildren.

If persons in the larger society are to be motivated to sacrifice technological "advantage" and convenience and personal pleasure in high energy life styles, some substitute social and personal gratifications must be found. This is especially true if Professor Amitai Etzioni's claim (1972:6) is correct, that:

. . . a central feature shared by the rising postmodern subcultures . . . is the promotion of hedonism . . . achieve and produce in order to enjoy.

It is doubtful that arguments for change to ecologically sound lifeways based on appeals to individual self-interest in the context of mass society will be motivationally compelling. A one generation definition of self puts the long-range appeal for new ecological strategies into somewhat the same motivational framework as an appeal to the combat soldier not to smoke cigarettes for health reasons. Only a minority of citizens in our pluralistic society would likely find old or new forms of family life an attractive source of substitute gratification for the "losses" of some aspects of changed technology. But whatever the direction of search in a free society, the Amish experience is a living, more-than-hypothetical alternative to the pattern of conventional gratifications. Folk cultures of other traditions may also be helpful to the search for answers in this area not merely because they lack high energy technology but because of their positive capacity to generate cultural motivation for simplicity of consumption and respect for nature.

REFERENCES

Cavin, Ruth S.
   1969 The American Family. New York: Crowell Co.
Conversation with member of business community of Arthur, Ill.
   1972 This individual requested anonymity as he was writing a doctoral dissertation on the economics of Amish life.
Etzioni, Amitai
   1972 "The search for political meaning." The Center Magazine 5 (March-April):6.
Handbook of Agricultural Charts
   1970 Washington, D.C.: USDA. No. 397.
Hostetler, John A.
   1963 Amish Society. Baltimore: Johns Hopkins Press.
Miller, Delbert C.
   1957 "Impact of technology on agriculture." Pp. 324-351 in Francis R. Allen *et al.*, Technology and Social Change. New York: Appleton Century Crofts.
Nagata, Judith
   1968 "Continuity and change among the old order Amish of Illinois, 1968." Urbana: University of Illinois, unpublished Ph.D. dissertation.
Paarlberg, Don
   1972 Vital Speeches 38 (February):235.
Theodorson, George A., and Achilles G. Theodorson
   1969 Modern Dictionary of Sociology. New York: T. Y. Crowell Co.
Sherif, Muzafer, and Carolyn W. Sherif
   1956 An Outline of Social Psychology. New York: Harper and Row.
Slater, Phillip E.
   1970 The Pursuit of Loneliness. Boston: Beacon Press.
St. Louis Post Dispatch
   1972 (January 15).
Wilcox, Walter W., and Willard W. Cochrane
   1960 Economics of American Agriculture. Englewood Cliffs, New Jersey: Prentice-Hall.

The farmers' movement and large farmers' organizations

CARL C. TAYLOR

WHAT THE FARMERS' MOVEMENT IS

The farmers' movement, like the labor movement, is based on demands for relief from maladjustments. The need for "farm relief" is as old as commercialized agriculture in the United States and is definitely related to the problems of prices, markets, credits, and taxes. Appearing first among the cash-crop tobacco farmers of Virginia and Maryland in the middle of the seventeenth century, the demand rose to one of its highest tides in Shays' Rebellion, which took place in the latter part of the eighteenth century. And is has continued to exist from those days to the present.

Farmers' revolts have not all been marked by the violence of the tobacco insurgents or of the participants in Shays' Rebellion; more often they have been marked by demands for legislative action on the part of the Federal Congress and state legislatures or by attempts at co-operative buying and selling; a number of times they have taken the form of direct political action. They are, and have been since 1870, best and most truly represented by the programs of such general farmers' organizations as the Grange, the Farmers' Alliance, the American Society of Equity, the Farmers' Union, and the Farm Bureau. Actually, only the high tides in farmer discontent have been marked by revolts and rebellion, and direct action farmers' groups have constituted only the left wing of a more stable and consistent farmers' movement which over the years has more or less persistently attempted to make necessary adjustments to a price and market economy into which American farming has gradually entered.

So long as American agriculture was largely a self-sufficient family economic enterprise and was largely represented by home-owning farmers, there was little occasion for a farmers' movement beyond general farmer protests against the quit-rents imposed by England in colonial days. Theoretically the self-sufficient farmer had no market or price problems. His sole task was to produce year after year the products for his own food, clothing, and shelter, while he went without those things that he could not produce and, so to speak, let the world go by. But American agriculture never was fully self-sufficient; even in earliest

colonial times wheat, livestock, maize, and other products were grown for sale, and almost from the beginning of American settlement tobacco was a cash crop. Indeed, certain areas in Maryland and Virginia, at the very outset of their settlement, were converted into commercialized agriculture, and interestingly enough the first farmers' revolt, as well as later ones, arose in highly commercialized agricultural areas.

The Farmers' movement has seldom if ever been recognized in terms other than those of open rebellion and demands for relief legislation. It has never been thought of as a significant historic movement growing out of deep and persistent maladjustments between the economic enterprise of agriculture and the social status of rural people on one hand, and the economic enterprises and social status of people in other fields of endeavor. People are surprised and shocked when they read accounts of roads to markets blocked and picketed, of thousands of gallons of milk meant for delivery to city consumers dumped on the highways, of crowds of farmers stopping mortgage foreclosure sales, of sheriffs locked up or spirited away, and of interference with courts. Then the public becomes more or less convinced that otherwise conservative, isolated farmers must be in deep distress to band together in crowds and mobs and be so easily led by revolutionary reformers. But when one realizes that similar incidents have occurred a great many times in American history, and that the farmers' protests have always been against the same things, it is only reasonable to describe the total process and the whole sequence of events as a Farmers' Movement.

In 1620 Virginia planters protested against the tobacco monopoly granted by King James I. They were so persistent and so vocal in their protests that in 1621 the King withdrew the monopoly charter. Then, because prices for tobacco fell rapidly between 1620 and 1640, a demand was made for control of the industry, first by price-fixing and next by control of production. In fact, conditions got so bad and farmers were so deeply in debt in 1639 that the Virginia Assembly declared that all debts could be legally cancelled upon payment of 40 per cent in terms of tobacco, the price of which was already fixed by law above the level that would have been ordained by supply and demand. The point to be made is that the earliest farmers' movement in the United States arose

☐ From Taylor, Carl, and others: *Rural Life in the United States,* New York, 1949, Alfred A. Khopf, pp. 510-521.

in the agricultural area of the colonies that were the first to be highly commercialized. And the significance of the point is that the American farmers' movement has, from this first farmer protest in the 1620's to the farmer protests of today, revolved about price and market problems. Prices, credits, and markets are the common thread that has run through the farmers' movement just as persistently as the common thread of hours, wages, and working conditions has run through the labor movement. By following this common thread through one farmer protest or revolt after another we come to recognize an American farmers' movement.

A movement may be defined as an attempt by a large segment of some specific society to accomplish an adjustment of factors and conditions that are, or are believed to be, in maladjustment. In a static society and under a highly autocratic government, social and economic change must often be accomplished by revolution. In a dynamic society and under a democratic government, revolts and revolution are often forestalled by meeting the demands of a persistent movement. The study of a movement thus leads to an analysis of class consciousness, group conflict, class prejudices, crowd behavior, publics, and a number of other psychological phenomena and group techniques, as well as to an analysis of the economic and social conditions that give rise and persistent impetus to the movement.

The periods of uprisings by farmers are but the ebb and flow of an historic movement that deserves careful consideration not only because of its militant demands but also because of its many accomplishments, and because of the nature of the adjustments that it has sought to effect. An index to some of these adjustments is supplied by the protests that farmers have made. For the most part these protests have been against low prices or inadequate credit. In many instances, economic demands have sooner or later become political demands, so that farmer protests have evolved self-conscious farmer publics. The high tides in the farmers' movement in the United States have almost universally come during periods when farmers found themselves at a comparative disadvantage in relation to prices, markets, or credits—that is, during periods of agricultural depressions. If a curve were drawn to represent the high and low tides of the farmers' movement, the crests of this curve would quite regularly coincide with the troughs of a curve representing farmer commodity prices. It is significant, too, that large farmers' organizations came into existence, one after another, during periods of depression. Ever since 1870 there has continuously been at least one general farmers' organization in the nation. These organizations publish economic, social,

and political programs; hold national, state, and local conventions; issue house organs; and maintain national and state legislative representatives. The farmers' movement was in existence long before any of the presently existing general farmers' organizations were founded, but since the organization of the Grange in the late 1860's, large farmers' organizations have carried the torch for the movement.

LARGE FARMERS' ORGANIZATIONS AN INDEX TO THE FARMERS' MOVEMENT

A real understanding of the purpose, scope, and accomplishments of this country's large farmers' organizations cannot be secured merely by discussing the trials, errors, and success of a single such organization, for all of them, past and present, were and are part of the farmers' movement. The Farmers' Alliance, the largest farmers' organization ever to appear in the United States and probably the largest to appear in the whole world, is no longer in existence. The Grange waxed, waned, and then became great again. The Farmers' Union has lost nationally but it is gaining steadily in a few states. The American Society of Equity split into two organizations, one of which is still strong, the other, extinct. The Non-Partisan League is practically dead as an organization, but its influence is still definitely felt in certain areas. Other interesting fluctuations have occurred in other organizations, but only a very general description of these can be offered here.

The Patrons of Husbandry (the Grange) was organized in 1867 as a purely fraternal organization. During the early 1870's it rushed headlong into economic and political activities, and as a result its expansion was phenomenal. In 1868 there were in existence only four subordinate Granges, which were located in three states and had very few members; but by 1875 there were 21,697 subordinate Granges in thirty-three states, and they had an estimated total membership of 858,050. The Grange finally entered every state in the Union except Rhode Island. At its height the Grange was running stores, maintaining state purchasing agents, selling raw farm commodities cooperatively, and operating buying clubs, some manufacturing plants, and even a bank. In a few states the Grangers elected legislators, governors, and other officers, and in half a dozen states they were the dominant influence in as many independent parties. In all of these activities they were striking directly or indirectly at price, market, and credit adjustments. When the Farmers' Alliance was at its height around 1890, the Grange fell to its lowest ebb, but afterwards it recovered and has grown steadily ever since.

The subordinate Grange is a local community fraternal organization whose programs cover everything that concerns farming and rural life. Any three subordinate Granges may unite to form a Pomona Grange, which is generally a county Grange. A state Grange may be organized in any state in which there are fifteen subordinate Granges, and the Masters of the state Granges and their wives are always official delegates to the national Grange. As a whole the organization constitutes a national farm fraternity with seven degrees, the first four being given in the subordinate, the fifth in the Pomona, the sixth in the state, and the seventh in the national Grange. It is an impressive fact that, as a mouthpiece of the farmers' movement, the Grange has been constantly operative for eighty years.

The Southern Farmers' Alliance was organized in 1878, but its roots can be traced back, in some places, to a still earlier period. In 1882 the Grand Alliance was reported to have 120 locals in Texas. By 1887 it claimed 2,800 sub-Alliances and a total membership of 35,000. It combined with the Louisiana Farmers' Union in 1887 and 1888 with the Agricultural Wheel, which had previously absorbed a farmer-labor organization called the Brothers of Freedom. In 1889 the total membership of all these organizations was claimed to be between one and two millions, and as a consolidation of these groups the Farmers' Alliance became the largest single farmer organization ever to exist in the United States.

The Southern Farmers' Alliance, although fraternal, was also avowedly an economic organization. It established an elaborate plan for both buying and selling, began a number of manufacturing enterprises, attacked the credit problem by means of a definite organization, and claimed to have done millions of dollars' worth of business through its various economic projects. During the 1880's it took up the political cudgels that the Grange had dropped and in the sections where it was active exercised almost as great an influence as the Grange had during the previous decade. It finally drifted into the Populist Party, which comprised the greatest political farmer uprising in our history.

The Agricultural Wheel was organized in Arkansas in 1882, and by 1887 it claimed 500,000 members. After absorbing the Brothers of Freedom in 1885, it was united in 1888 with the Farmers' Alliance. *The Louisiana Farmers' Union,* organized in Louisiana in 1880, was reorganized in 1885, and in 1887 also united with the Farmers' Alliance. Its membership at that time is apparently not known.

The Colored Farmers' Alliance and Cooperative Union was organized in 1886. By 1890 it claimed a membership of 1,200,000, and had state organizations in Texas, Louisiana, Mississippi, Alabama, Florida, Georgia, South Carolina, North Carolina, Virginia,

and Tennessee. At that time it was an amalgamation of the colored Wheels and Alliances. But in 1889 and 1890 it held its national meeting concurrently with the Farmers' Southern Alliance meeting and joined with this organization.

The (Northern) National Alliance was the largest of the northern farmers' organizations during the 1880's and 1890's. It was organized in 1880 and although it spread chiefly in Iowa, Nebraska, and Minnesota, it had thousands of members in other neighboring states, and by 1889 was said to have had 400,000 members. During that year an attempt was made to combine it with the Southern Alliance. This attempt was unsuccessful, although a number of members of the Northern Alliance joined the other organization and in 1890 some of its state organizations sent delegates to the national meeting of the Southern Farmers' Alliance.

The Farmers' Mutual Benefit Association was organized in southern Illinois in 1882 and was incorporated in 1887. At that time it claimed to have 15,000 members; by 1890 it had 1,000 "branches" (locals) in Illinois, and claimed a membership of 200,000. Although it sent representatives to the meetings of the Southern Farmers' Alliance in 1888, 1889, and 1890, it apparently never considered forming any organic union with that organization.

The Ancient Order of Gleaners, organized in Michigan in 1894, is primarily a fraternal association with locals which are called "arbors." At one time it claimed 80,000 members, but it now claims about 45,000, which are in Michigan, Iowa, Illinois, and Ohio. Its chief economic activities are buying and selling, and providing a farm market information service; it also conducts a substantial insurance business, publishes a paper (the *Gleaner Forum*), and owns its own central building in Detroit (the *Gleaners' Temple*), while its local and county organizations operate grain elevators and livestock shipping associations.

The Farmers' Educational and Cooperative Union was organized in Texas in 1902. It grew very rapidly, and by the end of 1903 had spread into Arkansas, Georgia, Louisiana, and Oklahoma; by 1905 it had organizations in eleven states and by 1910, in twenty-seven. It reached its maximum membership in 1918 or 1919 when it had twenty-six state organizations as well as locals in five other states.

Organized as a fraternal and educational association, the Farmers' Union quickly engaged, however, in elaborate economic activities, operating grain elevators, mines, cotton and tobacco warehouses, cotton gins, livestock yards, packing houses, creameries, and cheese factories. It also organized fire, hail, and life insurance companies. Like all the other farm organizations that have been discussed, it declared itself nonpartisan. But it has exercised considerable political influence, and, as a matter of fact, in a few states political issues and activities have at times been its chief concern. It is today a militant economic and political organization, although in the areas where it is strongest it is still a fraternal and local community association.

The American Society of Equity was organized in Indiana in 1902, after its principles were announced previously in some local farmers' clubs in southern Illinois. By 1906 it had spread into thirteen states, chiefly those north and west of Indiana, although it was also active in Kentucky, New York, and Oklahoma. The Equity differed slightly from other farmer organizations in that it laid greater emphasis on buying than on selling activities. Moreover, it was not a fraternal society, but was, rather, a purely business organization, and it has never been involved in politics. In 1908 it split, and the *Farmers' Society of Equity* was organized. After that, the original Society of Equity drifted more toward co-operative marketing activities. At one time or another it had organizations in thirty states as it devoted itself to the various phases of the farmers' economic problems in the different sections of the country—to tobacco marketing in Kentucky and Wisconsin, grain marketing in the Northwest, and livestock shipping in the Middle West. In 1908 it organized the *Equity Cooperative Exchange* (which until 1915 was located at St. Paul, Minnesota) for the purpose of securing profitable prices, distributing products, operating a crop-reporting service and storage plants, and offering protection against false grading; and ever since 1915 this Exchange has been the heart of the Society, which since 1926, has been taken over almost completely by the Farmers' Union.

The Farmers' Equity Union was organized in 1910, and is, like the Society of Equity, purely a business organization. It has no state or county organizations, and all of its local or centralized organizations are business units which carry on marketing activities for their members. There are 156 local Equity Union exchanges located in ten different states, with Ohio, which has 47, leading. These exchanges both buy and sell for their members, but their chief concern is the operation of grain elevators, stores, and produce concerns. The national association, with headquarters at Greenville, Illinois, is the organizing and educational agency of the Union. Membership in the national organization is purely voluntary while in the locals it is limited to the farmers who buy stock in the local Equity business enterprises. The purpose of the Equity Union is to eliminate marketing machinery as much as possible, returning to its members the savings thus effected. It usually pays a dividend of only 3 to 5 per cent on the capital stock subscribed by its members, since it prefers that they receive their greater gain from patronage dividends.

The American Farm Bureau Federation was organized in 1920 as a federation of state Farm Bureaus. The first local Bureau was organized in Broome County, New York, in 1911, and the first state Bureau, in West Virginia in 1915. An organization similar to that in Broome County was started in Pettis County, Missouri at about the same time, and both were sponsored by city chambers of commerce. The Farm Bureau had its real beginning, however, in 1913 when at a county-wide mass meeting the farmers of Broome County took over the existing organization. Also in that year, West Virginia required farmers to join the Farm Bureau and pay a membership fee of $1.00 before they could be supplied with a county agent. New York State made the same provision the following year.

The Farm Bureau is a local association of rural people, with the family the unit of membership. It attempts to include within the scope of its activities every phase of agriculture and of rural life. In some states—for example, Iowa—there are local neighborhood clubs and also township, county, and state organizations, the latter being a member of the American Farm Bureau Federation. The full scheme of organization and operation, worked out in detail, is as follows: The local community or township Farm Bureau, which has its own officers, committees, and projects, often serves as a community social club in addition to its role as an agricultural production and economic organization. The county Farm Bureau is both a "mass meeting" and a "delegate" organization, for its executive committee may be composed of the chairmen of the township locals, but there is at least one general mass meeting each year which is open to all the members. The state Farm Bureau is composed of delegates from the county Bureaus. It usually provides a number of specialized services through the county Bureaus, and also holds an annual meeting in which anything connected with agriculture may be discussed. In addition, it has a home and community committee which is in reality the women's division of the organization.

The Nonpartisan League, one of the most militant farmers' organizations in recent times, began in North Dakota in 1915 and six months later had 20,000 members in that state. It eventually spread into twelve other states and gained a membership of 234,659, all of whom were farmers. While its purposes were purely political, it arose as a result of economic conditions, primarily as the farmers' protest against bad marketing conditions. It gained control of the state government in North Dakota by persuading the farmers there to vote on a nonpartisan basis for the candidates who pledged their loyalty and support to the issues in which the farmers were interested. As a result of its activities, the legislature of that state in 1917 passed twelve laws that struck directly and drastically at conditions and agencies that the farmers intended to reform, and seventeen other similar laws were passed in 1919. The League's success in North Dakota accounts for its spread into twelve other states, chiefly those in the Northwest. But it has now been practically eliminated as an organization because of the failure of some of its business projects, its seeming alliance with radical labor elements, and a concrete and well-organized fight that has been made against it.

The Farmers' Holiday Association arose at the beginning of the 1929 depression. It developed into one of the most violent farmers' uprisings since Shays' Rebellion. It operated chiefly in the Middlewest and remained in existence for only a few years.

Today the Grange has more members than it has had at any time in its eighty years of continued existence, and it is the largest farmers' organization in the United States, while the Farmers' Alliance and its associated organizations are no longer in existence. During the past twenty-five years the Farmers' Union has lost many members in the South, but it is quite active in Iowa, Nebraska, Oklahoma, and Colorado, and very strong in the Dakotas and the Northwest. It is of real service to farmers both in the purchasing of consumption goods and operating products for its thousands of members and in the successful marketing of agricultural produce in such central outlets as Omaha, St. Joseph, Sioux City, and Chicago. The American Society of Equity has followed several different courses. In Iowa, by mutual agreement on the part of the state officers of the two organizations, it joined the Farmers' Union in 1924. Since 1926 the Equities in Minnesota, Wisconsin, the Dakotas, and the Northwest have been doing likewise, and the Farmers' Society of Equity is no longer in existence as a national organization. The Farmers' Equity Union, which is making steady progress, has kept to one line of endeavor, namely, operating locals and such centralized exchanges as are essential to the locals. The Farm Bureau, which was organized to facilitate demonstrations of improved production methods, has claimed from the very first that its primary purpose was to promote every aspect of rural life, social welfare, agricultural production, and economic organization and efficiency. As soon as it became state- and nation-wide, however, it began to exert an influence in economic and political fields. Locally it has consistently emphasized production and, in some states, a well-rounded community; but

nationally it has chiefly emphasized great economic issues and projects. The Nonpartisan League and all the other farmer organizations whose aims have been avowedly political have more or less disintegrated. On the whole, however, their members or former members are making their demands quite clearly known with some effectiveness. The Farmer-Labor Party, the Farmer-Labor Union, the remnants of the Nonpartisan League, the Western Progressive Farmers, and the Farmers' Union undoubtedly made up a large proportion of the farmers who voted for the La Follette electors in the presidential campaign of 1924.

Regardless of its purpose or creed, each farmer organization has sooner or later become concerned with the price, market, and credit problems and adjustments that confront farming today. The expansion and growing membership of these organizations have been based on faith that the modes of attack proposed by them will bring some solution to these problems.

Every farmer organization discussed in this chapter has established agricultural co-operative marketing associations. During the early days of the Grange, the Alliance, the Farmers' Union, and the Equity, co-operative buying was emphasized more than co-operative selling, and considerable, if sporadic, progress was made in establishing co-operative stores and making purchasing arrangements. As each organization gained strength, however, it was the co-operative marketing of farm products that became its most important project. Today the Grange, the Farm Bureau, and the Farmers' Union are this country's most outstanding and militant supporters of the agricultural co-operative movement. In 1876 the Grange actually exported wheat, and in the 1880's the Farmers' Alliance exported cotton and operated tobacco warehouses. The co-operative association for the sale of grain organized by the American Society of Equity was, prior to 1920, the largest in the country. This Society was also especially prominent in the early movement concerning livestock shipping and, with the Farmers' Union, sponsored the earliest attempts at the co-operative marketing of tobacco. The Farmers' Union, which not only operated many cotton yards but also exported cotton, is now very successfully operating livestock commission agencies in our great central markets. The Farmers' Equity Union has been successful in marketing wheat and eggs; the Gleaners provided a rather extensive market information service during its early history; the Nonpartisan League owned and operated both local and terminal grain elevators; and the American Farm Bureau has sponsored some of our great wheat, livestock, dairy, fruit, and vegetable co-operatives. In addition to the support given these activities by the national organizations, a number of state and local branches have sponsored local, county, and state marketing and shipping organizations.

These general farm organizations, with their educational and promotional programs, have played a large part in the development of co-operative attitudes throughout the world. It is probably true that although these organizations cannot claim the sole honor of having developed co-operative marketing, and although they have not confined their activities exclusively to fostering this form of marketing, they have during the past fifty years accomplished to some degree the major objective of their common purpose—a partial adjustment to the market and price system.

The co-operatives are today a quiet element in the farmers' movement, and they increase their volume of business without much vocalizing. If and when farmers' interests are threatened, however, they join with other organizations to wield political influence. Their achievements represent the consistent long-time accomplishments of the farmers' movement.

THE FARMERS' MOVEMENT AND THE PUBLIC

A movement is a specific type of social phenomenon, for as we have said, it is a steady attempt on the part of a large group in a given society to effect a harmony of maladjusted economic or social factors or conditions. A movement is likely to attack commonly accepted economic, social, or political arrangements as well as the accepted ways of thinking about them. The great majority of economic and social maladjustments are remedied in piecemeal fashion, if at all. If they affect only scattered individuals, they may be—and often are—disregarded; if they affect only a few, highly localized people, they are remedied by local community action. If they affect a relatively small but widespread section of the population, or if they are of long standing, these inequities are most often considered natural or inevitable. But when they are persistent and affect a large section of the population, then they are usually attacked. In a dynamic and fairly democratic society they must be attacked; even if the society is not democratic some effort is generally made toward correcting them.

The farmer movement took root early in this country because agriculture became commercial at an early time, but the agricultural revolution did not appear here in all of its phases until the 1850's, and it was after the Civil War that it came with a rush. The Granger movement followed closely upon the postwar deflation of agricultural prices, and it constituted the farmers' first well-organized attack upon the problem of prices and markets. Since then one farmer's organization after another has arisen.

Psychologically, a movement usually takes a long time to develop and gathers momentum slowly, but at its high tide it rushes with headlong fervor, sometimes with mob fury. The Grange, for example, moved slowly for four years and then suddenly seemed to catch fire. At the end of 1871, after two years of incubation and another two of actual propagation, it had 161 subordinate Granges, or community locals; in 1872 it added 1,105; in 1873 it increased by 8,568 and during the first three months in 1874 it gained over 2,000 a month. The Alliance developed similarly, as did the Farmers' Union, the Nonpartisan League, the Farm Bureau, and several large cooperative marketing organizations.

The causes of the origin, growth, and decline of a specific part of any movement are illuminated if one correlates the cycle of that part of the movement with other cultural trends, such as those taking place in the geographic, economic, political, religious and, possibly, the ethnic factors. Since their common object is the correction of what are generally considered widespread economic and social maladjustments, there is both similarity and difference between movements, revolutions, and revolts. There is a difference between the peasant revolts of ancient and medieval times and the modern farmer movements—a difference that can probably be explained in terms of their different cultural *milieux*. In a dynamic or so-called democratic society improvements can be effected that could be gained only by revolt in a static or so-called autocratic and feudal society. Except for the night riders among the Kentucky and other tobacco growers, American farmers have attempted to correct their maladjustments peaceably and through organizations; it is the combined history of these organizational activities that we have called the farmers' movement.

The advent of commercial agriculture and the forcing of the market and price regime upon practically every farmer have given homogeneity and unity to the farm people of the United States. Thus something approaching the technique of a public has developed among farmers, and the farmers' movement has thereby developed and expanded. It probably will continue to do so until the maladjustments in the market and price system, in the standard of living, and in social status are remedied.

As a matter of fact, farmers have always constituted a power public in American life. The first great spokesman for agrarianism was Jefferson and Andrew Jackson's election constituted a revolt of frontiersmen against the industrial East. Although there has never been what could be called an agrarian party in the United States, there have been "third parties" whose chief adherents were farmers and there have been periods when the problems of farmers have been the dominant national political issues. It was in the 17th Century that the Virginia and Maryland tobacco growers revolted against the market economy, and Shays' Rebellion was a farmer revolt against debts. But it was not until after the Civil War that farmer organizations became strong enough to exercise powerful political influence. It is true that thousands of the farmers who participated in the so-called Granger Revolt in the 1870's were not members of the Grange, but the Grange was, in a way, the mouthpiece of that revolt. The upheaval carried over into the Greenback party and into almost a dozen "Antimonopoly," "Independent," and "Reform" parties, which elected state officials and congressmen. The greatest upheaval came in the late 1880's and early 1890's with the development of the Populist Party, which was a direct outgrowth of the powerful Farmers' Alliance. In fact, the "Populist Revolt" ranks among the great political episodes in American history.

All during the 1920's and early 1930's the fight for Equality for Agriculture was a major national economic and political issue, and it was the occasion for the organization of the "Agricultural Bloc," which not only operated with precision and power in both houses of Congress but also mobilized a farmers' public including as adherents thousands of influential persons who were not themselves farmers. Farmers' publics have always been developed according to a pattern that can be generalized, so that although the specific events that constitute their mobilization have varied, the pattern of events that took place in the fight for Equality for Agriculture will serve to illustrate the ways in which publics rise to power and decline. First, a need was felt for adjustments of some kind, and there was a period of about three years during which numerous trial and error attempts were made by farmers' groups, the press, the President, and Congress to define the issues. During this period, too, the older farm organizations were repeating their already announced stands on agricultural questions, politicians were offering old patented remedies, and college men and Department of Agriculture officials were trying to channel and guide the militant farmers. Next came a clear formulation of the issue in terms of a slogan, "Equality for Agriculture," which was sufficiently broad to encompass nearly all the demands of all groups, but at the same time sufficiently concrete to be formulated into a legislative proposal. This step was followed by a series of trades and compromises in terms of amendments until the legislative proposal was satisfactory to most of the farming areas of the nation. The fourth phase saw the defeat of the legislative proposal. But the absence of

alternative proposals that would be acceptable led to an intensification and spread of public support for the amended bill. Then came success whereby the bill was passed as a result of the widespread and effective political pressure that was exercised by farmers and their numerous friends. Finally there was a shift in public issues which forestalled a test of strength in which a political election would have hinged on the old issue, so that as a consequence, the public focus turned from farm relief and the farmer public was for the moment dissipated.

During the periods of their greatest unity as a public, the farmers operate in accordance with the typical techniques displayed by all publics. They move upon a minimum of analysis and a maximum of slogans and shibboleths. Songs, poems, symbols, trade marks, slogans, shibboleths, and trite sayings are techniques of publics in general, and they have played their part in the operation of farmer publics. Many people of today remember the phrase and even the song itself that was current during the Populist period: "The farmer is the man who feeds them all"; and everyone is familiar with the slogan that was popular from 1921 to 1930: "Equality for Agriculture." The same motif, weaving together the ideas of these two slogans, has run through the farmers' movement from the Granger era of the 1870's to the present. Such techniques are especially valuable as a means of creating class consciousness and morale; but they have an even greater value as a means of interpreting the issues to the masses, who are abolutely essential to the movement's successful development and continuance.

At its points of highest fervor or during its periods of greatest integration and homogeneity, the farmers' movement is quite definitely a public in action—a public created by the common thinking that results from some degree of identity in occupational techniques and common problems. Therefore the farmers' movement, as an aspect of American history, has actually been composed of a chain of farmers' "action publics" with each succeeding public linked, most often unconsciously, with similar action publics of the past. Each has arisen because farmers felt that in some, if not in many, ways they were not living on a parity with certain other segments of American society. Although the movement has experienced high and low tides, it has been in continuous existence almost from the beginning of American agriculture. It will probably continue in existence even though farmers become a decreasing proportion of the national population, for how they live is naturally important to them and what they produce is of great importance to others.

Annual report 1973-74: background, present programs and developmental thrust of the Federation of Southern Cooperatives

Over the past seven years, since 1967, the Federation of Southern Cooperatives has created and served a constituency of 30,000 low income, rural families, in the South. Welded together at the community level out of the necessity of economic survival, the cooperative movement has grown steadily in loyal supporters dedicated with its ideals. Having this solid base in many rural communities, the Federation seeks to take steps toward more sophisticated development of member cooperatives, credit unions, and minority small businesses, through vertical economic integration of our productive, marketing, and consumptive powers.

The Federation has over 130 affiliated member cooperatives, operating in over one hundred counties across the rural South. Member cooperatives and credit unions are generally non-profit corporations, organized to fulfil multi-purpose functions of economic development, for low income people in the rural communities and counties they are serving. Among the major activities engaged in by our members are: agricultural production; consumer and retail service, fishing, handicraft production, commercial contract sewing, and a variety of other small business pursuits. The Federation is a service, resource, and advocacy association for this constituency of community development enterprises.

Ten thousand (10,000) small farmers are organized in the over thirty (30) agricultural cooperatives in our membership. These Black farmers own and operate over a million acres of land in counties across the South. Members cultivate: 10-50,000 acres of fresh market and processed vegetables, 200,000 acres of soybeans and feed grain, 25,000 acres of cotton, and 100,000 acres or more in improved pastures for livestock. The remaining land is: in timber, reserved for recreational use, or idle awaiting agricultural development. The Federation has succeeded in organizing these farmers into joint marketing and purchasing associations, as an initial step in maximizing the collective productive wealth of this community resource.

The Federation's twenty (20) or more member community credit unions have over $1 million in assets for use in making personal and business loans. More

☐ Excerpts from the annual report of the Federation of Southern Cooperatives, Epes, Alabama, pp. 1-6.

than a million in credit has been extended by these community based financial institutions. Many of the borrowers were poor people, who otherwise would not have had access to needed credit.

The Federation's handicraft cooperatives had combined sales of close to one-quarter million dollars in 1973-74. Many of these sales were generated through publicity and exposure given the co-ops by the Federation in catalogs, exhibits, and gift shows. One cooperatively owned cut and sew garment factory in our membership was able to employ twenty-five (25) people year round, at wages five times their previous earnings. Many of the member consumer cooperatives, while experiencing difficulty in wholesale volume purchasing, were able to generate surplus earnings for expansion and patronage refund.

The FSC/National Business Development Network compiled an outstanding record of reaching rural people and especially rural small businessmen. Over 1,000 minority small businesses, with a combined networth of $25 million have been assisted in some way by the Federation's business development component, which is sponsored on a contract with the Office of Minority Business Enterprise (OMBE-U.S. Department of Commerce). During our initial contract year, we were able to secure over $10 million in new financing to start and expand 114 minority businesses.

In response to the activities and needs of the membership, the Federation has developed a regional approach to assist and serve our Southwide network of cooperatives, and small businessmen. In each state or area, the cooperatives are organized together into a "state association of co-operatives" to deal with local problems, to secure local resources, and coordinate local concerns. Each state association selects a person, to represent the cooperatives in its state, on the overall Board of Directors of the Federation of Southern Cooperatives. This gives all members and member cooperatives a voice in the overall direction of the Federation.

We feel this regional approach to the community economic development of the rural South, is the soundest way to share resources—informational, technical and financial—among our network of cooperatives, and small businesses. This approach allows us to share, circulate and replicate successful ideas and experiences among the cooperatives, businesses, and community development enterprises. Our regional scope allows for the formulation of integrated marketing, purchasing and development plans, which can have a greater impact on scattered and isolated rural communities. The synergistic effect of many small units working together cooperatively across the region has already proved its value in moving the Federation to this critical point in its history.

The present components of the Federation's regional approach include:

1. an expanding and productively engaged membership in hundreds of rural communities, possessing many untapped resources;
2. an open democratic leadership structure, which allows the grassroots membership to fully express its interests and desires;
3. a responsive, hard-working, dedicated staff at co-op, state association and central organization level, to serve the membership;
4. a Rural Training, Research, and Demonstration Farming Center on 1,325 acres of land, near Epes, Alabama, which serves as the headquarters of the movement, sending out information and technical resources and gathering-in members for training and exposure to ideas and demonstration projects;
5. a series of outreach offices in the several states, providing loan packaging, management and technical services, and training to individual minority entrepreneurs, community enterprises, and cooperatives, this program is supported on a contractual basis by the Office of Minority Business Enterprises;
6. a regional housing, health care, education and social services program, promoted by the Federation for its members;
7. a thrust to insure the involvement of community people and groups in the benefits of the Tennessee-Tombigbee Waterway and other major government and private attempts to develop the rural South, through infrastructure improvement and its consequent industrialization.

We recognize that there are dynamic currents and changes taking place in our environment, in the rural South, which we must be aware of and make best advantage of for poor and Black people. These changes are creating greater opportunities for economic growth of the region. We realize that for minority people to gain full participation and equality in sharing these benefits, we must be aware, organized, and ready to act.

The South, and the rural Southeast, in particular is now the fastest growing area of our nation. The South remains a "new and open frontier" for economic and industrial development. To aid this development, large public and private investments in infra-

structure improvements are being made. Highways, nuclear power plants, transportation and port facilities are being built and expanded throughout the South. The clearest and closest example of this is the construction of the Tennessee-Tombigbee Waterway —a major public works project to open a new inland water route connecting the mid-West and Appalachia with the Port of Mobile.

These infrastructure developments create jobs and income both in their construction phase and in the economic development spinoffs that follow. We are closely monitoring the development of the Tennessee-Tombigbee Waterway to secure maximum involvement and benefits of this project for poor and minority people.

As a basically rural and agrarian area, the South has benefited from the recent renaissance in the agricultural sector of the total economy. Most farm prices and incomes have risen to record levels. Idle lands are being reclaimed and pressed into agricultural production. Domestic and international "food shortages" as well as expanding exports of food, fiber, and fertilizer production, indicate intensification of the importance of agricultural production, and land ownership in the South.

We look to these trends in the continued importance of agriculture in the region, as a reason for FSC's significant programmatic involvement in assisting small Black farmers and agricultural workers. We see in these trends an opportunity to develop more integration of our production through common processing and marketing. We hope to develop a series of agri-industrial projects: feed mills, greenhouse complexes, processing plants, a marketing corporation and other similar enterprises, for purpose of income generation both for our members and the Federation.

There are political changes as well, which interact with the economic, to focus greater emphasis on development of the rural South. New General Revenue Sharing and special revenue sharing programs, like those in manpower, give State and local governments more funds and authority to engage in community and economic development activities.

The intent and provisions of the Rural Development Act, focus national attention on the importance of promoting a policy of balanced rural and urban growth. The Rural Development Act provides loans and some grant funds for development in rural areas.

The Federation's network of cooperatives and small businesses has already begun to tap these resources and guarantees to promote our program.

The emergence of Black voting strength and political sophistication has enhanced the leverage of all community economic development organizations in the rural South. Governors, Senators, Congressmen, state politicians, and others cannot afford to ignore Black people and Black concerns. Our political strengths allow us to gain more economic rights and privileges.

Realizing the importance of these trends, and the growing maturity of our membership and organization to deal with them, we have formulated the Federation's developmental thrust for the future.

The elements of this new thrust are:

- development of our present FSC Rural Training and Research Center, into a Two-Year, Degree Granting, Technical College;
- expanding capability of our Research-Resource Team, with increased staff, library materials, and a computer center to do the feasibility studies and implementation planning necessary to carry forth our program;
- increased State Association development, to relate to State and local resources, e.g., Revenue Sharing; Rural Development Act, Industrial Bond issues, State planning commission and economic development districts; Concentrated Employment and Training Act (CETA) manpower training programs, and others;
- development of increased income generation for the Federation—from our farm operations, agri-busi-

ness enterprises, collective marketing and purchasing efforts; direct mail advertising; and capitalization of the "Forty Acres and A Mule Endowment Fund";

- supporting programs of the "Minority Peoples Council on the Tennessee-Tombigbee Waterway," and other activities accentuating development in relation to the Waterway;
- intensifying efforts toward protection and retention of Black land resources, as a productive and equity base;
- greater development of housing, health care, and education programs for our membership;
- strengthening our minority business development program to make it more efficient and effective in assisting in reaching our regional economic development objectives;

The remainder of the report discusses in detail the accomplishments of the present programs and the specific ground-work steps that are underway to achieve success with these elements of our new development thrust. The Federation has always viewed the problems and inadequacies of our people in their environment, as opportunities around which to formulate a program for their amelioration. We still see these opportunities, in our programs, for the present and the future.

A farmworker speaks

MANUEL LEON*

Many words have been written and many promises have been made to my people. According to the promises, I was to be fully educated, employed in a job that was paying a better than average salary, have all of the benefits and protections enjoyed by the accepted citizen, and be in a position to borrow whatever money I might need to start a business of my own.

We are not jealous of the millions of dollars that are

□ Statement before U.S. Senate Subcommittee on Migratory Labor, *Farmworkers in rural America*, 1971-1972, Part 3B, U.S. Committee on Labor and Public Welfare, 92nd Congress, Washington, D.C., 1972, U.S. Government Printing Office, pp. 1326-1329.
*Manuel Leon is one of the founders of a small grape growing co-op in Ripon, California. Leon testified in Spanish at the Senate Migratory Labor Subcommittee hearings in Fresno. Here are his words, translated into English.

granted to rich farmers to hold back production, nor the millions given to railroads and aircraft companies to cover up thefts and bad management. Even the billions spent on trips to the moon, Mars and the space shuttle do not upset us because that is beyond our comprehension. We think only in terms of the thousands of dollars that we hope will be invested in human lives and not in cold machines.

There is so very little that we ask for. The great majority of our people do not want things given to us free. We prefer to work for what we get. As it is, a day does not pass that a charity worker or a neighbor does not press us to apply for free assistance, food stamps or free medical care from the authorities. We do not desire this. We desire to make it on our own either through employment or through self-employment.

It is a matter of record that many of us have all but managed the ranches at which we have been employed. In most cases we have been given the job of preparing the soil for planting; have been left to determine the amount of nutrients needed to bring the soil to a productive level; and, finally, have had to apply the nutrients. The jobs of planting, irrigating, pruning, thinning, spraying, fertilizing and nurturing the soil have not been done by the average big farmer. Outside of an occasional visit by the owner, the entire operation in most ranches is left to the trained *campesino*. Late at night, while we are struggling to keep a secondhand tractor, a dull disc harrow or a dilapidated plow in workable condition in some windswept barn under a dim light, we feel despair and frustration because we are so aware that the farmer inside the house enjoying the warmth of his living room could have been us.

To put it in simple words, we, the *campesinos*, have been for years the backbone of agriculture. How many times have I seen only a sea of brown faces pruning, thinning or picking, and how many times have I heard the farmer sigh a sigh of relief when we showed up?

The irony is that as a reward we are being cursed as revolutionaries, are being sprayed with sulfur because we demand better wages and working conditions, and, finally are being denied the basic rights of health insurance, unemployment insurance, and the right of all rights, the opportunity to put together a business of our own.

Gentlemen, I want to be very frank with you. This is a very difficult thing for me to say because I am not accustomed to making demands. My trust has always been in God and I have always left all things to Him. But now, deep in my heart, I feel that He is pressing me to ask for this one thing. Please, gentlemen, make it possible for my people to buy their own land and to care for it with hands that are full of love for the soil. As a simple man I do not know how this can be done. But if it is, we will be able to build a life for ourselves that will make this country more fruitful and more aware that, unlike others, we have never resorted to violence to bring about change.

Thank you for allowing me to reveal the depths of my heart.

The small farmer's struggle to survive

JAMES M. PIERCE

The public has become increasingly aware in the past year that something ominous is happening down on the farm. The invasion of agriculture by giant business conglomerates with unlimited economic and political power threatens to drive out all but the largest independent farmers and to transform rural America into a vast zone of poverty and unemployment. Corporate domination brings rising prices, declining food quality, and greater ecological hazards. Rural poverty proliferates as the government, which had paved the way for the corporate invasion, continues to give massive subsidies to the rich and powerful, letting small farmers and farm workers fend for themselves.

The rural poor wage a determined struggle to survive. The United Farm Workers Organizing Committee has made significant gains, but it faces mounting attacks on its boycott weapon which is so essential to

☐ From WIN **8**(12):28-30, July 1972.

farm union organizing. Cooperatives of all kinds keep sprouting up as rural residents, who would otherwise be forced to flee to city slums, seek to maintain their roots in the countryside. Whether or not these efforts of the poor themselves will succeed depends on a radical reordering of policies, programs and priorities.

The dismal story that more than 100,000 farmers are being forced off the land every year has become as familiar as its corollary—the mass unplanned migration which has poured millions of rural refugees into our cities since World War II. Not so well know, for they are neither so dramatic nor so devastating, are the small success stories of farmers once marked for failure who are sticking with the land, and how the experience of a few thousand is frought with hope for many.

As long ago as 1966, a Tennessee Pilot Farm Management Project (through a training project sponsored by the National Sharecroppers Fund) showed that poor farmers could raise their incomes in one year from an average of $343 to an average of $1,285; not much, but the change meant hope. Asked if he would take a job in town, each program graduate said no. Instruction was provided for them in literacy, bookkeeping, soil testing, crop diversification, and livestock raising. Those who received small loans for capital improvements (i.e., $2,500 for a cooler and slaughterhouse) did better. NSF files are full of protracted struggles in the early years of the anti-poverty program to gain the loans, individual by individual, that saved small farms and farm families. Not infrequently, it took years of struggle with bureaucracy to get one loan.

Cooperatives offer greater hope because of greater essential strength: more people and more land to work with; more efficient use of technical assistance; more opportunity for people to help themselves—yet greater difficulty because of the need for larger investment and credit. In the past decade, thousands of poor people across the rural South have come together in more than a hundred cooperatives: farming, quilt-making, housing, crafts. The story of two in the South and another two further West reveals the potential.

Just as the great city-ward migration of the fifties and sixties was caused in part by mechanization and consolidation of land which drove sharecroppers, tenants and farmhands from cotton plantations, everyone connected with agriculture knows that for the same reasons the next group to be driven from the land will be the tobacco farmers. No advance planning helped the hundreds of thousands of refugees from cotton who piled into the cities unprepared, unskilled, and unhappy. Little is now being done to avoid similar suffering and exodus from the tobacco fields. Mechanization of tobacco is behind schedule only because larger and corporate farmers have hesitated to make the necessary land and machinery investments in view of the medical attack on tobacco—not because the Department of Agriculture and the universities have lagged in research and prototype machinery.

In 1967 a local effort was initiated with NSF's help in Halifax County, which ranks second among Virginia counties in production of flue-cured tobacco. The average allotment for poverty-level Halifax farm families was less than one acre of tobacco, but it was their only cash crop and they clung to it. Median family income in Halifax County is lower than in 86% of all U.S. counties. Three-quarters of the housing is substandard. One-quarter of the people have fourth grade or less education. This is the familiar pattern of those rural counties that have sent their poor to the cities by the thousand.

When the farmers turned to NSF's Rural Advancement Fund, it provided technical assistance and helped them get an OEO grant for administrative pur-

poses as they set up a co-op, the Southern Agricultural Association of Virginia. But success didn't come easy. In the first years the farmers proved that they could grow sweet potatoes, but they lost out in the cutthroat complexities of marketing. By fall of 1969 the co-op faced failure.

A new idea—organic farming—and $100,000 from funds unexpectedly secured by NSF gave the co-op a new lease on life. The practicality of organic farming was assured by a growing specialized market to solve the hardest problem. An unexpected bonus was that, despite a drought, the forty acres cultivated organically outproduced the others, and the vegetables were superior. Crop choices are limited to those suited to the rather poor land available and to poor farmers with little equipment. Cucumbers, squash, and peppers were first, with turnips for a winter crop. Now the organic acres will be expanded to 100, and crops including field tomatoes, carrots, beets, early peas, string beans, sweet corn, and white and sweet potatoes are planned.

The $100,000 went to buy both land and tools: four new and used tractors; a small irrigation pump, pipe and sprinklers; a planter, cultivator, and other farm equipment. It also paid for experts in organic farming and the fertilizer they recommended. There is now a warehouse and loading shed to which brokers and supermarkets send refrigerator trucks, reversing the traditional process through which individual farmers took crops to brokers with no bargaining status whatsoever.

The Wilkins family are strong cooperators. With a tobacco allotment of 1.55 acres, they had lived through years of mounting debt . . . "So I was with the co-op idea from the start," Mr. Wilkins reflects. "What other hope could I see? All the white farmers, they laughed at it. Said you couldn't raise vegetables, couldn't sell 'em if you did . . .

"Anyway, that first year I raised sweet potatoes. Crop was good but we lost every cent through people runnin' a game on us. Last year, drought took most of my cucumbers at the peak. It started to look like things never would get turned around. But the co-op board got that good NSF money and we saw a way out. One big thing needed was more acreage so you could guarantee production to those market men. So I agreed to go from three acres of cucumbers last year to thirty."

That act of faith paid off, for when drought again threatened, NSF brought in irrigation equipment and saved the harvest. Mrs. Wilkins sees change ahead, though they still live in a dilapidated home without running water or other conveniences. "Before," she says, "from the time we would harvest tobacco and pay off debts there wouldn't be any money until the next harvest. Then you'd see it for a week or two, pay off and start borrowin' all over again. Now I see a little cash ahead. And if the co-op keeps goin' good, Mr. Wilkins, he can take a chance and plant more. Then maybe we can do some things . . . you know, just get some nice things like other people have."

There are 300 members in the co-op, and their meager income is now starting to go up. Three hundred families on the land will stay because it will now give them a living. Indirect byproducts of the farm co-op are a credit union, a meeting place for community activities, and a newly organized community family health council. With wages from picking, neighborhood young people are even making it to a nearby community college. SAAV hasn't gone far yet, but it has a road and a direction, and the city slums have dropped from view.

NSF's decision to concentrate available funds on two needy co-ops saved the one in Halifax County. Its second major investment was in an even poorer area —Burke County, Georgia. Average black income there was less than $1,000 a year. Small farmers still tried to make a living from meager cotton allotments without the help from the Department of Agriculture that had enabled their white neighbors to diversify, expand, and prosper. NSF's Southern Rural Project had helped them to organize the Eastern Georgia Farmers Cooperative in 1968 and Newburke Housing Corporation in 1969. Despite difficulties, the co-op idea had really taken hold. There was a small sewing co-op. A modest contribution was used to start a co-op gas station. But the going was rough until NSF put in the same investment it had advanced in Virginia.

The 170-odd farmers, working from half an acre to eighty acres, are now raising cucumbers, squash, and peas sold under guaranteed contract to a local canner. Costs are cut by purchasing fertilizer cooperatively, and seed is supplied on credit. The members have elected a Farm Management Committee which runs an experimental co-op farm. It makes a small profit but needs five times its present 160 acres for good year-round production. Capital and credit are still stumbling blocks.

The NSF money provided 25 acres of land, a well, a 2½-ton truck, a large tractor fully equipped, a pickup truck, a home-crafted cucumber picker, and an $18,500 pea picker and tote-lift box, a $7,500 steel warehouse and, best of all, a $35,000 irrigation system. "Folks who have been blindfolded for 100 years, you can't expect to get their eyes open with just promises," the co-op board chairman says. "They been down that road. But now we show them we can irrigate, we show them savings on fertilizer and at the co-op food store . . . We show them that big old Ford harvester ready if they plant enough acres with the

Management Committee staggering the planting cycle so that the harvester don't have to be six places at once . . ."

". . . and the biggest savin' of all," says another founding member, "was savin' the farm."

There are plans far beyond their budget for both the Eastern Georgia Farmers Co-op and Newburke Housing Corporation: housing, if they can get loans; 271 acres of land available for purchase if funds or credit can be found; small industries that can be developed and locally controlled. Yet the articulation of these needs shows that 170 more farm families are on their way. But why should it be so hard when there are government millions for subsidies and other agricultural expenditures?

In Southeastern Kansas, small farmers (white this time, but just as squeezed by the agribusiness threat) have joined in the Farm Products Management Co-op with an eight-acre plan to save their farms. Horticulturalist Earl Shell, who devised it, says that the plan is built around the fact that you can make more money with an acre of strawberries than with 100 acres of wheat. The plan is for one acre of strawberries, with an estimated net return of $1,200; two acres of blackberries and raspberries which should return a minimum $500 an acre; and five acres of apples or peaches that will bear from the fifth year on with a minimum net of $1,500. The secret is an almost limitless market for fruit, plus the ability of family and local labor to handle an income-giving crop without either land or machinery investment that is too burdensome for debt-driven farmers. And it could be modified to suit almost any part of the country.

The co-op made the difference by hiring a marketing specialist, making it possible to sell the fruit by the truckload, and guaranteeing a market for everything raised. Starting with 21 growers, FPM expects to have 250 by the end of the year, and each will put in $200. There is a potential of 10,000 members. But to reach and service them FPM needs some really large loans. It wants to branch out with a network of climate-controlled warehouses, its own refrigerated trucks, and, hopefully, a plan to control the middle process where money disappears between producer and consumer. Will it get the help that will revive a whole rural area?

Strawberries are also a key crop for Cooperativa Campesina near Watsonville, California. Formed about two years ago by four Mexican-American families, it grew to 25 within a year and is still going. The co-op has leased 140 acres of which 80 are now in strawberries and all soon will be. California yield or prices must be better than Kansas, for these farmers figure on 3,000 trays of strawberries to an acre, selling at $3 for a gross of $9,000 and a net of half that.

Getting started was the worst hurdle. The original

members scraped up $500 each, but the Farmers Home Administration turned down their loan application. So did local banks under pressure from large growers. Finally, Wells Fargo advanced a $150,000 crop loan to be paid after the first harvest this year; then $100,000 came through on OEO consulting firm, repayable in three years; hard terms, both. The money bought tractors, root stock, and chemicals, and put the Cooperativa Campesina label on the market. Optimism is boundless, as is hospitality to new co-op members.

The strawberry co-op's problems with OEO and FHA—and even with the Farmers Cooperative Service which believes that "bigness" is the order of the day— are not unique. When Father A. J. McKnight of Louisiana asked FCS for management training assistance for a federation of a hundred low-income co-ops in Southern states, he was advised to ask private foundations for help. He points out that while the co-ops are turning to labor intensive crops like okra, tomatoes, sweet potatoes, and cucumbers to improve the incomes of poor farmers, the Department of Agriculture continues to finance research to develop strains of these vegetables that can be harvested mechanically. It is doing the same for strawberries.

So, despite the "inevitability" of agribusiness, small farmers need not accept defeat. But they must have help, not hindrance, from government agencies. Cooperation, technical assistance including knowledge of specialty markets, credit. Beyond this, a growing interest among consumers in quality food, not mass-produced pap.

But do these consumers, and other Americans concerned about urban problems and the quality of life as well as of food, realize how urgent it is to help people who love the land remain there—to till it with personal care that is better than bigness?

For too long, Giantism has been an American disease. Social policies, especially government policies, have been directed to maximize size in production, in machines, in farms, in profit. Bigger seemed to mean better. And, of course, such concentration built pressure on government by the giants to increase the favoritism in a spiral.

Small farmers can survive and prosper with help. Their survival will help all of us. But they can't do it on pilot projects alone or on the limited resources of the National Sharecroppers Fund. The need is for far more help like that provided by NSF and for an overall shift in direction—in legislation, in the Department of Agriculture, in consumer expectations. Farm pressure alone won't do it. There aren't enough farmers left now. Every one who cares must help.

Farmers' market: toward independence

ROBERT HOURIET*

A farmers market is an important first step to meeting the food needs of Vermont and the food crisis in the world.

It is based on the understanding that most of the food that we eat must be grown and distributed by ourselves—across the shortest possible distance.

By localizing production, we can insure ourselves a supply of fresh, nutritious food at good prices. While those prices may not be a whole lot lower than the supermarkets', it makes sound economic sense to buy locally-grown. The food dollar which goes through a farmers' market is recycled by small farmers, home gardeners, crafts people, and home-makers back into

our local economy through businesses, stores and services. Otherwise, spent at a chain supermarket, our money is siphoned out-of-state to corporations.

At present, Vermont imports over 80 percent of its food products. It is trucked and air-freighted from as far away as California and Mexico. In a sense, this means we're eating mostly oil. With the high cost of fuel, and the threat of starvation elsewhere in the world, we should not, cannot, permit the continuance of such a wasteful system.

It takes natural gas to make chemical fertilizer; gas and oil to irrigate land and run huge, highly-specialized machinery; petroleum by-products to make insecticides, pesticides, herbicides and preservatives; and more gas and oil to ship the food across a continent. Every step along the way, brokers, wholesalers,

☐ From *Environment Action Bulletin* 5(27):7, Aug. 24, 1974.
*Natural Organic Farmers' Association.

truckers and retailers add their shares of the cost.

If energy stays at its present price, and food corporations exact more profit, Vermonters may be faced with the highest food prices in the country.

The irony is that we are considered a "farm state."

Many people can still recall when Vermont did grow most of its own food. Before World War II, around every town, there were creameries, canneries, grain mills and many small stores which carried everything from locally grown beans to beef.

Since the end of World War II, this local economy has been undermined and nearly replaced by a national food system controlled by a group of multi-million dollar corporations known as "agribusiness."

Using huge amounts of technology, capital and mass advertising, by exploiting migrant workers, the land and non-renewable resources, agribusiness has been able to produce low-cost, low-quality food. But the hidden price to our health, environment and our economy has been nearly deadly.

In Vermont, these same forces of agribusiness, allied with a bigger-is-better economic policy, has forced thousands of dairymen each year to sell their farms. We find ourselves in the predicament of "consumers who cannot afford to eat and farmers who cannot afford to grow."

We can do something about this crisis, not only to help ourselves, but the rest of the world to survive. Despite the statements of the U.S. Department of Agriculture (which is on the payroll of agribusiness) and the state extension service (on the payroll of the USDA). Despite what the bureaucracy says about the shortness of our growing season and "other economic factors," the fact is we *can* grow more of the food we eat—right here in Vermont. The beauty of it is that we can do it without any government help. This is because a farmers' market answers basic needs: it brings together producers who need an income and consumers who want better food for their dollar.

This first year, there may not be enough quantity and variety of locally-grown produce to satisfy demand. But once established, the market will induce more growers to plant more acreage. Marginal dairy farmers will be shown that there is some alternative to the auctioneer's gavel.

By growing more for ourselves we will take less from the total supply of American food reserves desperately needed by other countries whose agricultural production has fallen behind their population growth.

Of course, to become food sufficient in Vermont, we will need more than the farmers' markets. Beyond this first step, we will need warehouses, canning centers, root cellars, mills and intensive consumer re-education.

We do not have the capital to do all of this. But we have one renewable resource—the power of the people. This is our only strength: to work cooperatively for ourselves, the land and the life-survival of future generations.

Dairy barn to fish farm

MADISON, Wis.—The familiar moo from the farmer's barn soon may be replaced by the soft sound of bubbles floating up through fish tanks.

It all depends on the success of University of Wisconsin researchers who are working on a project to show how farmers can convert their vacant dairy barns into fish factories.

They say the fish farms will produce yellow perch and walleye pike, native species that are among the favorite fare at fish fries.

"They're crying for the fish," said Harold Calbert, a university food scientists coordinating the project. "We're not going to solve the world's food shortage; what we're trying to do is fill a demand that is here and now."

DAIRY FARMS DECLINE

The number of dairy farms in Wisconsin, nicknamed "American's Dairyland," dropped from about 83,700 in 1964 to about 52,600 at present, according to Herbert M. Walters, chief statistician with the state Department of Agriculture.

An Agriculture Department spokesman said most dairymen closed down because of economic reasons. "The cost-price squeeze was too much for many of them," the spokesman said.

During the same period, researchers say, the demand for perch and walleye increased by 15 percent, while commercial fishing in the Great Lakes dropped

☐ From Christian Science Monitor, Feb. 7, 1975. Reprinted by permission of the Associated Press.

by 50 percent. They say fish farms could help fill the demand.

"There's a lot of dairy barns standing around empty that could be used for something like this," Mr. Walters said.

SUITABILITY FOUND

Mr. Calbert said dairy barns are well-suited to fish farming because they already have adequate plumbing, water supplies, and drainage.

Researchers working on the project, funded by grants from government and industry, have been growing fish in similar tanks since late in 1972. They estimate that a fish farm could produce one-half pound of fish per gallon of water each growing season, he said.

Mr. Calbert said both perch and walleye pike provide high protein food and have excellent flavor.

He compared the project to catfish farming operations in the Southern states and salmon and trout farming in the West.

Fish farming could provide a supplemental income for someone living on a farm but working in the city, Mr. Calbert said, but it might also turn into a full-time operation. "It looks like it's going to be economical for them without too much investment," he said.

Bayh, Myers seek to save family farms

WAYNE PERRY*

The family farm may be a dying institution in the opinion of many people, but two local legislators are attempting to save family owned and operated farms in America.

Both Sen. Birch Bayh (D-Indiana) and Rep. John Myers (R-Seventh District) have introduced legislation designed to ease inheritance taxes that frequently force the sale of all or part of a family farm.

Oftentimes, the legislators note, the children of a family who have labored on a farm for years with their parents suddenly find themselves saddled with an enormous tax when the owner passes away.

The solution to paying those taxes often means selling off a parcel of the land, taking out a mortgage on the farm, or selling needed equipment.

Both Bayh and Myers have introduced bills that would provide for the exclusion of the first $200,000 in the value of a family farm from the taxable estate of those farmers who have managed their own farms and have willed those farms to relatives who will continue to carry out farm operations.

The bills would not apply to corporate farming interests or to so-called "hobby farmers" who are urban residents seeking a tax shelter.

All family farms benefitting from the provisions of the bill must be actively used to raise agricultural crops or livestock for profit rather than as a hobby or part-time effort.

In order to qualify for the exemption, the decedent must have owned the farm for at least five years and have exercised substantial management and control over the farm before he died.

Those who inherit must not only continue to exercise substantial management and control over the farm, but also must maintain ownership and live on the farm for at least five years.

In the event that a farm is willed to several children, all inheritors are covered by the bills if one of them meets the residency and management qualifications set forth.

Local farmers agree that the inheritance tax is a problem—a problem that is too often ignored.

Wayne Livengood, RR 52, who farms 180 acres in northeastern Vigo County, comments, "It is something that you don't talk about too much, but it is a real problem."

He notes that with current inflation, the present inheritance tax exclusion on the first $60,000 in the value of a farm is not sufficient.

"I don't think that the $200,000 exemption is out of line at all," Livengood adds.

The local farmer notes that the inheritance tax problem has been a subject of discussion at County Extension Office meetings and at other gatherings of farmers.

☐ From The Terre Haute Tribune-Star, Terre-Haute, Ind., Mar. 23, 1975.
*Tribune staff writer.

"I would agree that an increase in the exemption is needed—very much so," Livengood concludes.

William L. Miller, RR 25, who farms 360 acres near Riley notes, "Sure this is a problem—and a bigger problem now than it was before.

"It is something that probably isn't discussed as much as it should be—the cost can be astronomical when the taxes are settled after an inheritance," he points out.

"New legislation would be a good thing and should be of some benefit—it is good to keep the farm operating as a family unit," Miller adds.

As stated, family farmers often have to sell part of their land to raise enough money to pay estate taxes.

The result has been the increased ownership of land by corporations.

With the rise of corporate farming, the individual farm owner has been having a progressively harder time making ends meet.

Bayh first introduced an inheritance tax revision measure last year to protect the family farm.

During the last session of Congress, the bill passed the Senate, but was not acted upon by the House.

In January this year, Bayh re-introduced the measure.

Myers introduced his similar version in the House on March 17.

He noted that in Indiana alone, the number of farms has declined from 134,000 to 1960 to only 106,000 now.

"If something is not done, the traditional family farm we have known and cherished in this country will be a thing of the past," he said.

Myers explained the rationale for his bill, "One of the major reasons for the decline in the number of family farms is the burden of the high estate taxes. Presently, the tax exclusion is limited to the first $60,000 in the value of the farm. With the higher costs of machinery and good farm land selling in excess of $1,000 an acre, this figure is no longer reasonable.

"I believe it is in the best interests of our nation that we keep our American farm families in sound operation. They have been the backbone of the success story in this country. I hope the House Ways and Means Committee will consider this proposal in the near future."

Figures show that 50 years ago there were about 32 million Americans—more than 30 per cent of the population—living on farms. Today, there are only about 9 million Americans—about four per cent of the population—still on the farm, and this number is decreasing steadily.

"It is the small farmer who is forced off the farm into our already overcrowded cities. Every week hundreds of family farms have to be abandoned because they are no longer viable," Myers argues.

"Cumulatively, a million family-sized farms were consolidated out of existence in the 1950's and another million in the 1960's," the congressman concludes.

The South

ROBERT S. BROWNE*

For blacks in the South, the problem of land acquisition has been second only to the problem of land retention.

In the years following the Emancipation Proclamation, black people received title to a not insignificant portion of land in the South as bequests from former slave-masters or as inheritances via illegitimate unions which were for one reason or another publicly

☐ From the Center for Community Economic Development, Cambridge, Mass. Reprinted in Barnes, Peter, editor: The people's land, Emmaus, Pa., 1975, Rodale Press.
*Director of the Black Economic Research Center.

admitted to. These black landowners tended to be uneducated and totally ignorant of the legal intricacies involved in property ownership. Given the growing hostility toward blacks in the South from 1877 onward, it is not surprising that these simple black folk had great difficulty holding on to whatever land they had. There were no black lawyers or black real estate agents to protect their interests, and for the civil authorities to connive with their white compatriots at the expense of blacks was the rule rather than the exception.

In 1910, blacks were operating 890,000 farms in the South. Of these, 218,000 were fully or partially owned, while the rest were operated by tenants. In all, blacks managed to become full or part owners of 15 million acres of Southern land by 1910 without benefit of the Homestead Act and in the face of great hostility and violence.

But that was the peak. By 1950, black land ownership had declined to 12 million acres, and in 1969 it was down to 5.5 million acres, a drop of 54 percent in twenty years. It is probably accurate to say that white people own more of North America today than at any time in history, and this percentage continues to rise. Meanwhile, black Americans, whose stake in the United States is tenuous at best, are rapidly losing title to what little land they do have.

The blacks' loss of land in the South has coincided with the steady Northward migration. Unfortunately, the decision to migrate has not always proved to be a route to a better life. Whereas the migration of blacks to the urban North during World War II was largely inspired by the availability of well-paying jobs, the migration of the Fifties and Sixties derived primarily from the mechanization of Southern agriculture, especially the machine harvesting of cotton and corn. This time the Northern economies were unable to absorb the flood of unskilled immigrants, largely because the demand for unskilled industrial labor was being reduced by automation in industry. The result was a rapid growth of slums and the emergence of what is euphemistically termed "the urban crisis."

Any effective attack on the urban problem cannot ignore the roots of that problem, which is to say, it must attempt to deal with the poverty of black people in the rural South. There are a number of fronts upon which this poverty must be attacked. One is that of assuring that existing governmental programs are genuinely placed at the disposition of black people. Bitter experience has demonstrated how difficult it is to achieve this in the Southern states. Racial discrimination is merely a major but by no means the sole problem. Another is that many of the programs—for example, the Bank for Cooperatives and its sister institutions—are designed to help the solvent farmer. They cannot deal meaningfully with the problems of the very poor, be they black or white. These very poor people have no credit standing, no assets, often very little in the way of skills. Thus, they usually fail to meet the minimum qualification for participation in existing programs.

What the area urgently requires is an institution, or series of institutions which would have as an objective the creating of economically viable family units whose labor power, however unskilled, would be building equity for them. It is of the utmost importance that the descendants of slaves, these families which have never owned anything of substance since their arrival

in North America, be afforded a means to acquire some minimal amount of wealth and to enjoy a modest degree of security. A legacy of dependence, whether on plantation masters or on federal doles, is not a sound basis for self-respect.

Specifically, what is needed is a new institution dedicated to the goals of: (a) transfering land to poor, especially black, rural people; (b) facilitating the improvement of this land through the provision of housing, water, and the like; and (c) developing profitable employment opportunities on this land. Without specifying what the final design of such an institution might be, the following broad outline may be suggestive.

One possible approach is an institution which would collectively own land on behalf of those who live on it. The community institution in which title was vested would lease land on a long-term basis to those who lived on it. Improvements could be made by both the community and the individual; in the latter case, title to the improvement would rest in the dweller and could be sold by him to the community should he move off the land.

Collective ownership is, of course, not a *sine qua non* for a large-scale transference of land to poor black folk. It can be done on a straight private ownership basis, but with some "title protection" built in. Presumably, plots would be contiguous so that opportunities for cooperative efforts would be available.

At least two types of financial provisions would be required to realize such a land reform effort: a mortgage plan and an equity plan. Some governmental agency would need to guarantee the mortgage on the land. It would also have to provide the equity portion of the transaction, in the form of a long-term or deferred payment, interest-free second mortgage loan. Additionally, it would have to subsidize the interest rate on the first mortgage.

Families on welfare should not be excluded from the program. Rather, inasmuch as their meager stipends must cover a rental payment to someone, how much better to permit this payment to be used to purchase some equity in a piece of real property!

An alternative approach would be to revive the concept of the Homestead Act, from which black people obtained so little benefit. Many blacks feel that the government should give them land just as it gave land to white settlers. There are, of course, limitations to such a proposal, since most of the remaining public land is not suitable for human habitation, or is located where black people do not live. Nevertheless, there are publicly owned parcels scattered throughout the South which would be suited for homesteading. The Departments of Defense and Interior are both large title-holders to such land, as are other departments to a lesser degree.

In addition to transferring land, the new institution should help develop income-producing programs which would enable new landowners to sustain economically viable family units. In some cases this will mean truck farming; sometimes it may mean large-scale cultivation on a cooperative basis; elsewhere it can mean that processing facilities, or perhaps some

industrial opportunity, will be developed, perhaps with a government subsidy during an initial period. Since such a subsidy would be largely in lieu of a welfare payment, it might very well be an economical way of dealing with rural poverty. It is certainly likely to be cheaper than continued out-migration with its incalculable costs in terms of urban and human deterioration.

An alternative to meet the land-tenure crisis

KARL LIMVERE*

While there are many ways to describe the situation in rural America today, perhaps an appropriate description would be that rural America is in a land tenure crisis.

In the latest quarter of American history, land tenure policies for the most part have been overlooked as an essential key to the future of family-farm agriculture.

In its early history (outside of the southern plantation system), this nation recognized that the most important ingredient of a viable farm economy was the opportunity to secure a land base.

The Homestead Act, the Land Grant College system are examples of programs instituted during the first three-quarters of American history that were geared to providing this opportunity for a secure land base.

Today, agriculture has moved steadily towards a factory system of production. At the same time because of national inflation the ownership of land has become more profitable than the production of food from that land. Land is becoming a commodity to be bought and sold as a hedge against inflation and as a capital-gains investment.

We have moved from a labor-intensive agriculture system with easy access to land, to a capital-intensive and energy-intensive system with extremely limited access to land.

The ever-increasing capitalization requirements for starting new farm units is limiting the "land opportunity" that has been the basis of American agriculture.

☐ From an unpublished paper.
*Director, Department of Communications and Research, North Dakota Farmers Union, Jamestown, North Dakota.

The continuing trend towards a capital and energy intensive agriculture system predicts that entry into agriculture will be limited to those that can assemble the necessary financial resources. In other words it will be limited to a landed gentry or a corporate agriculture.

As a society, we have not addressed ourselves to this land-tenure crisis. Instead we have placed our reliance on programs that are peripheral to the land tenure question. While these programs are essential for the family-farm system, they do not come to grips with the land question.

For example, at the present time the federal government is in the process of revamping the nation's agricultural programs. While the farm program is essential for stability in farm market prices and consumer food costs, the farm program does not provide the opportunity for new farm units. It presently only provides a weak guarantee that a farmer will be able to continue to farm once the farm unit is established.

Even if payment limitations and other incentives for small producers and discouragements for large producers were incorporated into the farm program, realistically it could only serve to preserve the status quo in our agricultural system.

Because of the increasing amount of capitalization required to establish even small farm units, the various farm credit systems that have been established can also only serve to preserve the status quo.

Even if farm credit programs could be further improved and interest rates fully subsidized, they could not significantly improve the opportunity for young farmers. This is unfortunately true because the pressures on land produced by increased population, energy and resource shortages in the world, and the present American life-style will continue to escalate the speculative value of farmland. Ironically, the farm credit program, as evidenced by the recent livestock emergency program, tends to subsidize the bankers more than they assist the farmer in gaining financial stability.

The one area of land tenure that has received increasing attention is the unfair competitive advantages built into our economic and political system and enjoyed by large corporations. While this attention is long overdue, the establishment of anticorporation farming laws such as the one in North Dakota, Family-Farm Acts, and revisions in state and federal taxation loopholes that permit tax-loss farming can only be considered holding actions or maintenance functions.

Such laws might significantly reduce the corporate influence in our agricultural system, but they would not prevent the establishment of a new landed gentry, which would be inevitable unless land opportunities are provided to new farmers. The same is true of estate and probate law revisions at both the state and federal levels.

By themselves or even in combination these absolutely necessary public policy decisions cannot generate the direction that is needed in opening up new "land opportunities." There needs to be another ingredient—the opportunity for new farmers to establish secure land bases. Increasingly, today's new farmers have no security with their land bases. Rental agreements, top-heavy mortgages, and similar conditions are at the best very tenuous arrangements. Many young farmers are entering agriculture without the hope of ever owning the land they farm. They state they will feel successful if they are able to acquire even a limited equity in their land. They will then pass this equity and the accompanying mortgages to their children.

Often the mortgage holders are the same financial structures that are competing with the family farms in corporate farm endeavors and are enterprises that exist on land and energy speculation.

Farming in many parts of this country is becoming a secondary occupation, with farmers working in factories and other vocations and farming after the 40-hour work week. In other words we have moved into a situation where the farmer is supporting the farm, rather than the farm supporting the farmer.

We are now in a period of decision critical to the future of family-farm agriculture. The causes of the lack of opportunity and results of this inability to enter farming are combining into a social and economic design that is similar in its compounding cycles to Barry Commoner's concept of a closing circle. That circle must be broken, and the only viable means of changing this course in agriculture is through public policy decisions that deal directly with the problem.

Some have suggested that what is needed is a new Homestead Act. But it must be remembered that the Homestead Act is the prologue to our present situation. The Homestead Act as a means of distributing opportunity was only good for the first generations on the land. No, what is needed is something beyond a one-time distribution or redistribution of opportunity. What is needed is a system that transcends generations and facilitates the transfer of opportunity from one generation to the next.

We must move to a new system of agriculture and change our concept of what constitutes a family farm unit. We must move to a system comprised of small diversified and intensive farm units capable of providing a livable income to farm families and the rural life-style that the majority of people in this nation want to recapture for themselves. This is not only essential in terms of economic policy to provide a stable food supply at stable prices, but in a real sense it is also essential as a social policy to provide stability to population distribution and opportunity. It is also essential as political policy to provide stability to the political processes of the society as envisioned in the Jeffersonian concepts of agrarian democracy.

We need to combine social and economic public policy decisions to develop what might be termed a "family-sustaining agriculture system." A fundamental and essential ingredient of this family-sustaining system is a new land tenure process.

What is needed is the innovative and experimental concepts that the Farm Security Administration attempted to implement during the Depression when we as a nation experienced our last land tenure crisis. Some of FSA experiments are still operating successfully in serving small ranchholders. Such is the case of the grazing associations in existence in North Dakota.

This FSA concept has been expanded into a new land-transfer system in the provinces of Saskatchewan and Manitoba. These two Canadian provinces are now providing the leadership in the Western world in developing an alternate system of distributing opportunity to new farmers. Basically, the Saskatchewan Land Bank program, and a similar one in Manitoba, involves the provincial governments purchasing land from retiring farmers and distributing this land to new small farmers through secure leasing arrangements. Using these provincial programs as a basis, North Dakota Farmers Union members have adapted their concepts with the FSA grazing association mechanics to develop a similar program adapted to the social and economic climate of the northern plains states.

Under the program that NDFU members submitted to the legislature, a trust-lands division would be established in the state department of agriculture. It would be the responsibility of this division to facilitate the transfer of family-size farm units from one generation to the next and assist new farmers in establishing secure land bases.

Under this land-transfer program, any farmer, landowner, estate, or other who wished to transfer agricultural land may sell the land at its appraised value to the Trusts Lands Division, with the agreement that the seller of the land would have the right to designate who would have the first option to lease and subsequently purchase the land from the Trust Lands Division. For example, the seller could designate a son, daughter, son-in-law, nephew, other relative, neighbor, or some other potential young farmer in the community. The seller could be provided a variety of contractual arrangements for the sale and payment of the land, depending on the needs of the seller. Financing for the operation of the land-transfer system would be provided through the Bank of North Dakota at the direction of the Trust Lands Division.

If the seller of the farmland or farm unit designated in the sale contract an individual to have first option on that land, the Trust Lands Division would offer the designated individual the opportunity to lease that land. If no one were designated to receive the first option to lease the land, the Trust Lands Division would make the farmland available to other capable young farmers. If two or more starting farmers want to lease the same land from the Trust Lands Division, a point system could be used to determine the lessee. Such a point system would consider the farm plans of the applicants, the needs of the farmland, and the needs of the starting farmer. The lease would be for 5-year intervals. The lease rental would be not less than 5% of the appraised agricultural value of the land, nor more than 1% above the cost of the Trust Lands Division of procuring money through the Bank of North Dakota.

The right of the leasing farmer to either renew the lease or purchase the land would provide the starting farmer a secure land base. The lease would be renewable at the option of the lessee on a noncompetitive basis at the end of each 5-year lease period. At the end of any 5-year lease, the lessee would have the right to purchase the land at its current appraised value.

Without the heavy burdens of land payments and mortgage interest, the leasing farmer would be able to concentrate his investments in machinery, livestock, buildings, equipment, and so forth, which would allow the new farmer to intensify the production from the farm unit. Thus the new farmer would be placing investments in those areas that would provide the greatest economic returns and subsequently make it easier for the farmer to eventually purchase the land.

The leasing farmer would have full authority to determine the crops produced on leased lands, crop rotation, and other practices in accordance with normal land management.

Because this land-transfer program is both a social and economic program designed to help new farmers establish new, small, intensive farm units, certain lease conditions would be necessary to protect the interests of the state and the public in the program and to ensure that it continues to provide opportunities to new farmers beyond this or the next generation:

> While any size farm unit could be sold to the Trust Lands Division, no farmer leasing land from the Division could operate a farm unit larger than the average size of farm units of comparable land productivity in the county.

> The leasing farmer would have to be a resident of the farming community in which the leased land is located.

> No lessee could sublease or otherwise rent the leased land to any other individual. However, the lessee could operate the leased land with another individual through a partnership, cooperative farm corporation, or cooperative grazing association.

> To avoid any tax loss to local governmental units, the leasing farmer would be required to pay taxes on the leased land.

The beauty of this type of program is that it can be easily integrated into the present economic structures of rural America without disrupting the present situation, but at the same time providing a new direction and an alternate system. It can be implemented at the same pace as the normal transfer of land from one generation to the next would occur.

It may be a revolutionary concept, but it will not cause the social and economic disruptions normally associated with "revolutionary" programs. It would not be limited to a one-generation redistribution of opportunity, but instead would provide an ongoing process of distributing opportunity. This type of land-transfer program is essential if we are to move to a "family-sustaining agriculture system."

It has other advantages as well. It would promote intensified agriculture production on a scale in which land management is better served through ecological processes than extensive outside production inputs. It also would encourage utilization of farm equipment of a size better suited for the conservation of land resources and, therefore, would be less energy intensive.

The new farmer would not be what USDA has curiously termed "underemployed"; therefore, there would be less incentive for the continual expansion of farm size and equipment that has become a basic tenet of USDA and its Extension Service philosophy. We would begin to move away from the bigness syndrome to a family-sustaining agriculture.

The effect of this movement on rural institutions is self-evident. Small rural businesses and social structures would become more viable. Obviously the more people there are on the land, making a living from the land, the greater their need for rural institutions and services. This translates into more job opportunities and greater economic activity in both rural and urban America.

But such a movement to a self-sustaining family agriculture system has other national and international implications. The establishment of such a land-transfer system would generate a process of regearing agricultural credit programs, national food policies, and other institutions to again serve the needs of the small farm unit.

Since the program would not require that each generation recapitalize land costs at ever-increasing levels, the land-capitalization cost factor in food would be substantially stabilized, if not reduced. This would mean that consumers could enjoy stabilized food prices and, just as important, more healthful, more natural, and more edible food.

Removing the recapitalization of land each generation would further enhance the ability of this nation to effectively compete in world food markets in producing food at a lower cost. More importantly, the intensification and diversification that would result from such a land-transfer system would allow the world to more effectively compete against the food and hunger crises.

Land distribution remains the key to releasing human potential, achieving social stability, and economic justice. It may be a dream and just a vision of a potential future, but the land tenure crisis demands a new beginning, and we believe that this new beginning is in the implementation of a new process of land transfer that continually provides a secure land base to new farmers.

The community land trust

ROBERT SWANN*

The community land trust is a legal entity, a quasi-public body, chartered to hold land in a stewardship for all mankind present and future while protecting the legitimate use-rights of its residents.

The community land trust is not primarily concerned with common ownership. Rather, its concern is for ownership for the common good, which may or may not be combined with common ownership. The word "trust" is used more to connote the idea of trusteeship or stewardship than to define the legal form. Most often the land trust will be a non-profit corporation rather than a legal trust.

The following key features differentiate the community land trust from the ordinary real estate trust or conservation trust, and enable it to achieve its goal of "ownership for the common good":

1. The trust holds land only.

☐ From paper presented at The First National Conference on Land Reform. Reprinted from Barnes, Peter, editor: The people's land, Emmaus, Pa., 1975, Rodale Press.
*Director of the International Independence Institute.

2. The land *user* is protected by his long-term lease —99 years and renewable.
3. The *land* itself is protected by the charter of the trust.
4. The trustees do not "control" the users of the land; they implement the trust charter and ensure that the provisions of the charter and of the lease contract are fulfilled.

There are several reasons why land trusts are advantageous in a strategy of regional decentralization. First, trusts can be established immediately. They do not require any legislation for implementation. Land trusteeship utilizes the legal principle of the leasehold, but in perpetuity (99 years and renewable). Such long-term leasehold systems are being utilized increasingly in urban areas (in New York City most skyscrapers are on leased ground) and even in new towns (Irvine, California, for instance), but generally for maximizing profit. In the concept of trusteeship, all profits return to the trust, which in turn can donate them to the community via special agreements.

Second, trusteeship and stewardship can be built on a long tradition in many societies: Indians of North and South America, the *ejidos* of Mexico, the tribes of Africa, the "commons" in England and New England, the Crofters system in Scotland, the Eskimos of Alaska, and in recent history the Gramdan movement in India and the Jewish National Fund in Israel.

A third advantage of the land trust is that it bypasses one of the problems traditionally associated with land reform, *i.e.*, forcible expropriation. Many homeowners are afraid of the term "land reform" because they fear (irrationally) loss of their homes. Such fear is not associated with the words "trust" or "trusteeship," nor is expropriation advocated under the land trust concept. In fact, since trusteeship implies and includes a concern for the land itself in a conservation or ecological sense, new allies can be found in the environmental movement. This creates a basis for a broader political coalition than land redistribution, *per se*.

At the same time, it should be pointed out that under traditional land redistribution, land typically reverts to its former absentee landlords (or new ones) in about twenty years, partly because other factors or forces in the economy (control of money, etc.) are not changed. Under land trusteeship, on the other hand, land is taken out of private ownership voluntarily and placed in trusteeship in perpetuity.

Fourth, a trust can be used as a holding mechanism for all sizes and tracts of land. Some of these tracts may be large enough to build entire new towns, or simply used as farms or conservation tracts. This flexibility permits both short and long range strategies which can include small farms, large farms, or combinations of both. In this way, the modern technology of the large scale farm can be utilized while, at the same time, the trust can encourage and promote new ecological farming systems to avoid the dangers of monoculture and pesticides.

Another aspect of this same issue which must be considered is the assumption that farmworkers and agriculturalists want small farms. I doubt this is true in most cases if it means giving up labor-saving technology. Farm workers want real participation in the ownership of their production, but not at the expense of more stoop labor. In our planning sessions for New Communities, Inc., in southwest Georgia, we ran into this issue any number of times. Farmers did not want to divide the farm (about 6,000 acres) into small individual tracts because it would make the use of machinery more difficult. Cucumbers, which meant a great deal of stoop labor, were voted out as a cash crop even though they bring good prices.

To those who are concerned about chemical fertilizers and pesticides, as well as those who believe in the small farm system, this attitude presents a problem and a challenge. I suggest that a land trust which helps remove the burden of land payments from the back of the farmworker is the best approach to this problem. Since so-called organic farming generally costs more in terms of labor, the farmer is often forced to use pesticides and chemicals on his fields in order to meet his mortgage obligations. In our planning at New Communities we decided to combine large-scale farming with small plots for home gardens and animals. This planning permits families to live reasonably close together in villages where other needs such as schooling, recreation, buying clubs and marketing co-ops can be provided.

In Israel, over two-thirds of the best land is held in trust by the Jewish National Fund. There, everything from small farms, *kibbutzim*, *moshavim* and whole new towns are planned and established on trust land.

In short, the trusteeship concept is an activist approach to the problem of redistribution of resources, and while it is initially aimed at the land, as it grows and develops as a movement it can begin to reach out into other areas of resource management.

Legislating protection for the family farm

ROLLIE HENKES

In an effort to preserve the institution of the family farm, more and more states are passing laws that forbid certain corporations to farm.
☐ From the Furrow **81**(1):3-4, Jan.-Feb. 1976.

This legislative activity is concentrated in the central areas of the U.S. and Canada, traditional strongholds of the owner-operator farm that uses little, if any, hired labor.

One ban against farm corporations, North Dakota's, goes back to the 1930s. A new wave of legislation has come in the 1970s; Oklahoma passed a law in 1971; Kansas, Minnesota, and Wisconsin in 1973; South Dakota and Saskatchewan in 1974; Missouri in 1975. Bills have been introduced in the Nebraska and Iowa legislatures.

The laws reflect mounting concern that agriculture is shifting from a dispersed system of many small, independent producers to a centralized system dominated by large corporations.

Centralization has occurred elsewhere in the economy, but some economists say it would be a bad thing for North America if it were allowed to go too far in agriculture. The family farm, big enough to be efficient yet small enough to preserve competition, has served society well, they say. But they warn of forces at work that are steadily eroding away the entrepreneurial position of the family farmer. Among those forces:

Integration. Some economists predict that as agri-industrial firms become more conglomerate in nature, there will be more pressure for them to gain control over agricultural production. Either through contracting or ownership, integration allows them to strengthen their marketing positions.

The outside investor. The world food shortage, inflation, and tax laws have made agriculture a hot investment since the early 1970s. This has attracted large amounts of capital from off-farm interests, and in the process these interests have acquired more control over some of agriculture's assets. The actual extent of this control is not known. Some believe it is not significant. Others disagree. Whatever the extent, non-farmers have at times found investments in land, cattle, and other farm assets to be a good way to shelter nonfarm income from high taxes while possibly reaping capital gains. This type of investment helped fuel the growth of the custom feedlot, and contributed to the over-expansion of cattle feeding. It's estimated that 25 to 30 percent of all U.S. cattle fed in 1973 were owned by outside investors.

The ability to be big. High-capacity field machinery, automation . . . these and other technologies make it possible to farm ever-larger units. Despite the celebrated failures of some large corporation farms, others are showing that with good salaries and other benefits someone can indeed be induced to sit up with the corporate sow.

According to one scenario, these and other forces could combine to divest many family farmers of entrepreneurial control, leaving them on the land but perhaps as little more than hired managers or laborers. Should this come to pass, important decisions would be made in executive suites outside of the community. Many local dealers and other agribusinessmen would be bypassed, helping to gut the economies of small towns.

It's also argued that consumers would pay higher prices if the food supply were to come under the control of powerful firms likely to become rigid, bureaucratic, and unresponsive to changes in demand.

Can the family farm resist these forces? Simply being more efficient won't save the family farm, according to Harold F. Breimyer, agricultural economist at the University of Missouri. He contends that large firms have tax advantages; they have better access to capital, and they have better access to marketing channels.

"I'm willing to let farmers compete with those who receive all or most of their income from farming," says Douglass Bereuter, a Nebraska state senator who has sponsored a bill limiting corporation farming. "But no matter how efficient they are, farmers cannot compete with companies and individuals who for tax reasons or other incentives funnel off-farm income into farming operations that they can afford to operate at a loss over the short term."

THE LAWS

The so-called "family farm" laws attempt to even the odds by barring large investor-type corporations from certain farming activities, while permitting smaller enterprises to enjoy the advantages of incorporating.

In Minnesota, South Dakota, and Missouri, the only corporations that are not subject to restrictions are "family farm corporations" or "authorized farm corporations." Family farm corporations may have any number of stockholders, but the majority must be related and at least one must reside on or actively operate the farm. In an authorized farm corporation, stockholders need not be related; however, there is a limit on the number of stockholders—five in Minnesota, 10 in South Dakota. Missouri sets no limit, but there an authorized corporation must receive at least two-thirds of its total net income from farming. In Wisconsin, family-type corporations or corporations with 15 or fewer stockholders are not subject to restrictions.

Corporations still enjoy considerable freedom to operate under some of the laws. Oklahoma's law allows any food-processing corporation to own land for growing its own crops. The law also has no restrictions on corporations engaged in feeding livestock, and the same is true of the Kansas and South Dakota laws.

The law in Saskatchewan forbids corporations from owning more than 160 acres for farming, except "agricultural corporations" in which at least 60 percent of the stockholders are farmers living in the province.

The North Dakota law bans all corporations from farming except "cooperative corporations" in which 75 percent of the members are farmers.

The main targets of the laws are corporate conglomerates that might want to set up farming divisions. However, the laws do not keep out big operations per se. Some of the largest farms in the U.S. and Canada are partnerships or individual proprietorships that would be legal under any of the "family farm" laws.

The laws also do not prevent outside investors, operating as individuals or partnerships, from buying up big chunks of farmland. Saskatchewan might be the exception. There, nonresidents are limited to owning land up to $15,000 in taxed-assessed value. That amounts to about 480 acres of prime farmland.

Finally, the laws do not affect corporations that acquire control of production by contracting with farmers.

Some policy experts say the most significant thing about the laws is not their content, but the precedent they set. The laws represent a consensus by the body politic that the family farm is being threatened and that it is worth saving for both economic and social reasons. The laws are seen as springboards for additional policies to help protect the family farm.

PROBLEMS

Others, however, see the laws as setting harmful, rather than hopeful, precedents. They claim the laws will not prevent a drift to a centralized, corporate agriculture—if indeed that is actually happening. What's worse, they fear the laws could actually hurt family farming.

"We just don't know if anyone is smart enough to write a law that will keep out the big boys while not making it harder for the family farmer to compete," says Paul Johnston, executive secretary of the Nebraska Livestock Feeders Association.

Critics say some of the laws might prevent a family corporation from renting land. The residency requirements for stockholders could be another hangup. So far, however, there's no evidence that the laws have actually hampered the organization or operation of a family farm corporation.

"The Minnesota law doesn't affect our operation right now," says Keith Langmo, Litchfield, Minn. "But I worry that our legislators might slap on amendments that would eventually restrict the size of family farm corporations. I think the law has an inherent bias against bigness of any sort."

And Langmo Farms is big—25 farms, a million-bird turkey operation, plus cattle and hog enterprises. Langmo and his brother, Jim, didn't swoop in from Wall Street, however. They are local agribusinessmen who built up their operation over the years.

Some professional farm managers express fears that the laws could open the door to statutes that would restrict their stock-in-trade, the absentee landowner.

"Absentee ownership provides a ready supply of rentable land, allowing local farmers to expand their operations without tying up a lot of capital in real estate," says Glenn H. LeDioyt, President of LeDioyt Land Company, Omaha, Nebr. "Many of our clients are individuals who inherited farms or who once lived in the area. They are as concerned about conservation and good farming practices as any resident."

Delbert Wells of the Missouri Chamber of Commerce says that antitrust laws are a better way to prevent corporate farms from exerting too much power. Wells, who does not see efficient family farmers as an endangered species, says there should be complete freedom of entry into agriculture to ensure a mix of enterprises.

FILLING A VOID

Bigness doesn't always cause apprehension. For instance, North Carolina has generally welcomed the efforts of First Colony farms, a gargantuan corporate farm covering 375,000 acres, most of it unfarmable scrub timber and swamp. The firm is draining and clearing the land for cultivation, and eventually may have $200 million invested in the development.

Large-scale corporate farming also does not evoke the alarm in the U.S. West and Southwest that it does in the Midwest. Though many of California's some 63,000 farms are large and use large amounts of hired labor, the vast majority are still family-owned and managed, according to Hoy Carman, agricultural economist at the University of California.

CAUTION

"When setting up legislative fences to preserve family farming, we have to be careful that we don't keep out things that farmers need to survive," says Neil Harl, agricultural economist at Iowa State University. "If farmers are to obtain the massive amounts of capital required today, and in the future, they will have to stay linked to the rest of the economy."

Harl asserts that the family farmer has considerable room to expand and remain competitive without losing his owner-operator identity . . . so long as he has access to capital, technology, and modern management knowledge.

This trend toward expansion of family farms has led Harl and some others to conclude that the main threat to the smaller family farmer is not the large outside corporation, but his innovative, aggressive neighbor who is expanding at every opportunity.

It is hard to find conclusive statistical proof that the family farm is or isn't in trouble. The 1969 census shows that farm corporations with more than 10 shareholders accounted for only 2.8 percent of total farm marketings. But some claim these data are outdated and misleading. A somewhat different picture comes from a study by Donn Reimund, a USDA economist. His research turned up 410 large "multiestablishment" corporations involved in farming. Reimund determined that the gross agricultural sales of these large firms were about $3.3 billion in 1969, or 7 percent of farm marketings.

More data are on the way. Research economists are digging into the issue more than ever. A new Iowa law requires an annual report from farming corporations, and also from limited partnerships and nonresident landowners. Perhaps this and other information will shed new light on who does and who will control agriculture.

Marginal farm is threatened

One of the problems with the Nixon Administration's plan to phase out some major farm subsidies is that it does not give sufficient consideration to the differences that exist on American farms.

Basically there are three kinds of farms now drawing subsidies: large corporation farms, economically successful family farms and marginal family farms. Obviously the corporation farms should not be entitled to subsidies which were designed originally to help the family farmer. Many successful family farms are sufficiently solvent to remain profitable in the event subsidy programs are reduced. It is the marginal family farm that stands to be hurt by the phaseout.

A study by Dr. Walter Wilcox, a veteran Library of Congress farm economist, prepared for the Senate Agriculture Committee, substantiates the Nixon program's threat to the small family farm. The question Congress must ask as it seeks to write a farm bill in 1973 is whether the small, marginal family farm is worth fighting the White House to preserve.

☐ From the St. Paul Sunday Pioneer Press, St. Paul, Minn., Mar. 4, 1973.

It is really a social rather than an agricultural problem. If the small farms that cannot survive without a subsidy program are cut off from government funds, the people living there will have no choice but to sell out and find other employment. Most often this means moving to the city and looking for work in an already crowded labor market. It means a new and often unsatisfactory life style for the farmer and his family. All too frequently it means an addition to the welfare rolls.

Depending upon the complications that arise from displacement, it may be cheaper to subsidize the small farmer than to uproot him. Certainly he and his family will be happier if they can stay on the farm.

What is needed is a farm program that takes these differences into consideration. The same set of regulations that works for the corporate farm won't be exactly right for the thriving family farm and certainly won't apply to the small, marginal family operation. The present subsidy program, devised during an agricultural crisis, and patched and jury-rigged ever since, needs an overhaul. But Congress and the Administration should be careful not to kill the patients with the cure.

Statement before the Subcommittee on Migratory Labor

BERGE BULBULIAN*

Mr. Bulbulian: Thank you, Senator.

I could very briefly say, "Hear, hear" to what you said, but I will go ahead.

I am speaking today as a private citizen and also on behalf of the National Coalition for Land Reform. This is a new organization we have just started here in the West. We hope it will grow over the next few years to include forward-looking citizens in the South, the East, and the Midwest. We hope that among those who will join the coalition are small farmers, farm workers, city workers, minority groups, young people, persons concerned about the environment, and all citizens who believe that America must be something more than a happy hunting ground for giant corporations.

Our coalition hopes through educational, legal, and political action to preserve and strengthen the voice of the independent citizen in America, to ease poverty in both rural areas and in the cities, to encourage population dispersal in such a way that more people can live decently off the land without destroying it and to redirect Government policies so that they help workers of the land rather than absentee owners.

Our family has been farming since 1929 and my father, who is 79 years old, and I farm 150 acres of wine and raisin grapes in Fresno County. In spite of his advanced age my father still is actively involved in the day-to-day operation of our farm. Together we do all the work we can and hire only that which we cannot do ourselves. He came to this country from Armenia in 1920 after the massacres by the Turks and did various forms of labor, including farm labor, until he was able to save enough money to make a down payment on 20 acres of vineyard. He has had a total of 4 years of schooling and my mother, who is deceased, was illiterate. In spite of my parents' lack of education, we were able to progress in the business of farming and today we earn a very satisfactory living. We have been able to progress from illiteracy to a university degree in one generation. Two of my children are now in college and the third will be in the fall.

The point I am trying to make is that it has been

☐ From statement before the Subcommittee on Migratory Labor, Farm workers in rural America, 1971-1972, Part 3A, U.S. Senate Committee on Labor and Public Welfare, 92nd Congress, Washington, D.C., 1972, U.S. Government Printing Office, pp. 668-674.
*Farmer, Sanger, Calif.

possible for a man with a meager education, at best, to become self-sufficient and attain a measure of success. Today, his accomplishment, however modest, can be attained with difficulty, if at all. The family farm is disappearing from the agricultural scene and being replaced by corporate conglomerates who have no particular love for the land but are involved for investment purposes. Obviously, no semiliterate farmworker would, in his wildest dreams, dream of owning a major land holding. This is not surprising, nor is it particularly a problem. What is a problem is that he cannot even dream of owning a small piece of land. A 40-acre vineyard sells for approximately $80,000 in my area, with about $24,000 needed for a down payment plus the cash or credit to farm and live through one crop year, at least. On such a farm one can expect to earn a meager living at best if he has to pay interest and principal but can survive if he owns the farm outright. It would take at least 80 acres of grapes to farm with some degree of efficiency to earn a satisfactory living. In short, the ambitions of people like my father were often realized in the 1920's and 1930's, but today no young man who is not a part of a farm family dreams of owning a piece of land, big or small. It is simply an unrealistic dream.

If America is to survive and prosper, this situation must be remedied. The flow of people from the farm to the city must be stemmed and, indeed, reversed. There is no longer either room nor need for more people in our cities. Much of our pollution problem is caused by concentration of people and every effort must be expended to deconcentrate populations. This can be done only by upgrading conditions on the farm and making it possible for the millions still employed there to remain on the farm and live a life of dignity. Farm people, whether they are employees or employers, must be able to remain on the farm out of choice and not necessity. Impossible? No. Difficult? Yes. But aren't most of the problems we face today?

Probably the biggest obstacle we face in our struggle to save the family farm is the attitude of many Americans, including some farm people, that the family farm is obsolete, it is inefficient, and, therefore, unable to compete with the efficient and well-financed conglomerates. Well financed they are, but efficient they are not. I challenge any giant agribusiness corporation to match my efficiency. There is no way a large concern with various levels of bureaucracy and managed by absentee owners can compete in terms of true efficiency with a small, owner-operated concern. I cannot hire anyone to perform with the level of competence and efficiency that I perform. I seldom do one job at a time, but often two and three jobs simultaneously. While driving the tractor I watch for other things that need to be done. I watch for pests, for nutrient or water deficiency and generally consider management problems while doing a purely physical job. I work long hours each day and seldom have even a Sunday completely without work.

I am the manager, personnel director, equipment operator, maintenance man, bookkeeper, laborer, welder, and so on. When I do hire labor, I usually work with them. I can afford to buy any equipment ever built, which will lower my cost of operation. I have never failed to secure the capital needed to make purchases of land or equipment.

With 150 acres of vineyard, I believe that we are at or near the optimum level of operation for our type of farming. No, I can't sell for a loss and make it up in taxes, nor can I lose on the farming end of the business and make it up at another level as a vertically integrated operation can, and I happen to market many of my crops, too, through a cooperative, so to some extent I have attempted to cash in on integration, but certainly not to the extent giant farmers do.

I have no political clout and lobbying to me means writing a letter to my Congressman or Senator. But that is not what efficiency is all about.

Efficiency has to do with the relation between input and output. No, the big agri-business firms are not efficient except in farming the government, and, even if they were, do you think that this efficiency will be translated into lower prices to the consumer when and if a small handful of agri-business giants control agriculture? And if they do give you food for a lower price, what about the social costs involved in the out-migration of people from the rural farms and towns? There are many costs that must be considered and most of them will not be paid at the corner supermarket.

While there are no panaceas, there are solutions to the problem. I propose that we pursue a plan of land reform, yes, land reform. We have preached its efficacy for other countries, in Latin America, in Southeast Asia, et cetera, but for our own country it has been viewed with alarm. The cry for land reform dates back to ancient times and is not even a new concept in our own country.

We have on the legislative books an excellent piece of legislation which I believe was meant by its framers as a vehicle for land reform, but it has been any-

thing but that. I am referring to the Reclamation Act, the so-called 160-acre limitation.

The Reclamation Act provides that no one will receive more water than is required to irrigate 160 acres from any federally financed irrigation project. A couple can farm 320 acres under this law and irrigate it with subsidized water, substantially more land than it takes our two families to earn a good living. Any land in excess of the 160 acres per person must be sold within 10 years for the price of land, not to include the value of the subsidized water.

Unfortunately, the law has been enforced with less than complete devotion to law and order. Vast acreages in the State portion of the combined State-Federal water project in the west side of the San Joaquin Valley are or will be irrigated with no limitation in force, a situation which three other farmers and I are trying to remedy with a suit against the State and Federal Governments.

In the Federal portion of this project contracts are being signed with the Department of Interior which provide for the eventual sale of the excess land, but in many cases the land is being assessed at too high a price. First these giants of agriculture—and there is not much sweat-of-the-brow type of land acquisition there—used their political muscle to get the best terms they could in terms of repayment, then they delayed the signing of contracts as long as they could on technical grounds, and then they received land assessments too high to conform to the spirit of the law, and then they will continue to farm the land for an indefinite period of time, in many cases not just 10 years, for there will be few, if any, buyers in parcels which will conform to the law, less than 160 acres per person.

I propose that the Federal Government acquire this land at realistic prices which conform to the law and sell it to qualified buyers with long-term, no-interest loans. Yes, no-interest, not low interest, for the present landowners are being provided with water with similar terms. The buyers may be farmworkers who want to have the pride of owning the land they work. They could be city people who are tired of the compression chamber that is the modern city. The parcels may be privately owned and operated by individuals; they may be larger units farmed cooperatively. It may even be necessary to provide these new landowners with technical assistance through a program similar to VISTA and the Peace Corps. We have provided technical assistance to much of the world; it should not be too much of a strain to provide it for our own people.

I propose a major overhaul of our tax structure which is now supporting and encouraging the conglomerates to invade the field of agriculture. Under present laws, they need not make money in farming and, indeed, can afford to lose large sums of money in farming and still profit on their overall operation. Professional people are encouraged to buy land not for farming but for speculation. They make no contribution to the land or society, but they do profit. We put a greater value on the income from money than we do the income from labor, for we tax labor at a higher rate than we do the gain on the purchase and sale of property. We must change the law so that each business is taxed separately so that farm losses cannot be offset by profits in other businesses. We must do away with the capital gains tax. Put the giant corporate farms on the same level we family farms operate and we will see who is efficient and who is not.

In any event, efficiency is not the problem. American agriculture has been all too efficient already.

I propose a thorough investigation of all corporate conglomerates in agriculture and other giant farming and processing firms to determine if their operations are legal within the framework of antitrust laws.

In our own area an investigation of Tenneco and the Gallo Wine Co. are certainly in order. Many wine grape growers who have been traditional Gallo suppliers were unable to sell their crops this year in spite of ever-increasing demands for wine. Rumors were rampant in the field that there was some kind of agreement between Tenneco and Gallo that caused these problems. These rumors may well be unfounded, but certainly grape growers in the San Joaquin Valley who are alarmed by the heavy planting of grapes by conglomerates and other investors are entitled to know the facts as uncovered by objective investigators. Similar conditions probably exist in other commodity areas.

Karl Marx wrote of a class-structured society in which the classes would eventually conflict. Here in America we have felt that this situation would not prevail. We are now rapidly moving toward a socioeconomic milieu with an elite propertied class, a professional class, and a class of uneducated, unemployed or underemployed hard-core poor which is ever increasing in numbers. The free enterprise system is probably even now more of a "closed enterprise system," in Ralph Nader's words. Must we continue to work to make Marx' prophecies come true, or will we strive to solve our problems with at least as much respect for people as we have shown for money and property?

To me the choice is clear. Let us solve the problems in rural America, difficult though they may be, before they spawn even more difficult problems else-

where. If we don't solve these problems, perhaps we should change the inscription on the Statue of Liberty from the now-present, "Give me your tired, your poor," and so on, to something like this, "Keep out, enterprise closed."

Senator Stevenson: When did your father buy land after coming to these shores from Armenia?

Mr. Bulbulian: He came in 1920 and bought the farm in 1929, the first 20 acres.

Senator Stevenson: Where was that, in the San Joaquin Valley?

Mr. Bulbulian: Yes. Near the small town of Del Rey in Fresno County.

Senator Stevenson: He bought 20 acres, you say. Could he support himself on 20 acres?

Mr. Bulbulian: Not with just 20, no. He did farm labor even then.

Senator Stevenson: How much did the 20 acres cost?

Mr. Bulbulian: As I recall, about $5,000.

Senator Stevenson: And you testified that the price of similar land would now be roughly $2,000 per acre?

Mr. Bulbulian: In our area, yes, and more.

Senator Stevenson: If he arrived on these shores today, penniless, a farmer, could he get started, could he buy land to support himself?

Mr. Bulbulian: No. We have great difficulty ever saving enough money to make a downpayment, even considering how conservative my father was with money then and even now.

Senator Stevenson: It is hard to get started in farming?

Mr. Bulbulian: It is impossible to get started, not hard.

Senator Stevenson: Once started, whether through inheritance or however it is you come by the land, it is hard to stay in farming, too, isn't it?

For example, you said the small farmer is more efficient than the large farmer. If that is so, if he can produce more efficiently than the corporation, then why can't he survive in our free enterprise system?

Mr. Bulbulian: There are a number of market problems and, of course, the problems I cited here, the tax problems which make it difficult for him to compete with a situation that is not really fair competition. I think he could compete very, very easily if everybody in agriculture were in it for a profit, but many people aren't.

Certainly, I am not saying a 20-acre farmer of 1929 or 1930 period could make it today. Even then, he couldn't make it on that small an acreage.

Senator Stevenson: One of the points you are making is that the family farmer now has to compete with corporate farmers who don't have to make a profit in order to survive, that is what you call tax-loss farming?

Mr. Bulbulian: That situation prevails now.

It does take a little more land, but certainly not the thousands of acres the conglomerates want.

Senator Stevenson: It takes more land and it takes more equipment.

Mr. Bulbulian: Indeed.

Senator Stevenson: And it takes more credit to acquire the equipment as well as the land. Is that one of the problems?

Mr. Bulbulian: Yes. You very often have to live through perhaps 2 crop years before you get your return, especially if you are marketing through a co-op as we do. I still am not paid off on the 1969 crop of raisins and we probably won't be for several more months. So we are talking about at least a 2-year investment in the crop.

Senator Stevenson: I don't suppose the large corporations have much difficulty obtaining the necessary credit at a reasonable rate. You say the cost of credit is lower for the larger corporation than it is for the family farmer?

Mr. Bulbulian: Indeed. The price of interest is higher for the smaller borrowers.

Senator Stevenson: Continuing on the assumption that the little fellow, the family farmer, is a more efficient producer, he can produce at a lower cost than the large fellow, are there other policies of the Government or activities of governmental agencies which discriminate against him to the advantage of the large corporation? The Labor Department's Farm Labor Service, for example? Do they help the little fellow as much as the large corporation?

Mr. Bulbulian: I can answer from personal experience to the latter part of that question. Rarely, if ever, am I able to get any help from the Farm Labor Service except when I don't need it.

Senator Stevenson: Except when you don't need it?

Mr. Bulbulian: Right. When I do need it, they don't have any labor. So I don't even bother in most cases,

except to kid myself I have done something to try to find some labor. As far as I am personally concerned, and this would probably be true of a number of other farmers in my area, they could probably close up the Farm Labor Service and we wouldn't miss it.

In addition to the first part of your question, I think much of the research of the University of California is aimed at the large farm. I think they have already sold out to the idea that the small farmer is down the drain, so they had better think of research for the large landowner.

An example, there will be an implement show in Tulare next month and one of the topics that will be discussed, along with the showing of the implements, if I remember the exact terms, "Substitution of Capital for Labor." Much of the machinery that will be shown at this show, some of which was developed by university research, is aimed at extremely large operations and certainly not the small, efficient, family sized operation.

Senator Stevenson: You mentioned university research. Do you have any opinions about the activities of Land Grant Colleges and whom those activities primarily benefit?

Mr. Bulbulian: On this short notice, no specific opinion, unfortunately.

Another point I would like to make, Senator, is that I think the free enterprise system does not imply merely the right to get bigger; it should imply the right to get started. I think that situation no longer prevails in agriculture.

Senator Stevenson: You made that point very eloquently, Mr. Bulbulian, in your statement. And I think it is a most significant aspect of our subcommittee investigation. You have pinpointed many issues that I am hopeful will be discussed by other persons as we proceed. I appreciate your help.

Thank you very much for appearing here this morning.

A new direction II: rejuvenating the small family farm

JOE BELDEN and GREGG FORTE

THE FAMILY FARM AND AGRICULTURAL RESEARCH

The small farmer has been hurt by one Federal program which was designed over one-hundred years ago to assist him. That is the American land grant college complex, which today consists of 69 schools, 1.5 million students and an annual government outlay of over half a billion dollars. There is at least one agricultural college in each of the fifty states, Puerto Rico and the District of Columbia. In addition there are 14 schools which were created as separate black institutions under the Morrill Act of 1890. As might be expected they are located in the southern and border states. Teaching, research, and extension are the basic goals of the land grant system. These aims find their legislative foundation in the Morrill Act of 1862, the Hatch Act of 1887, and the Smith-Lever Act of 1914.[1]

The problem with the contemporary land grant colleges is that they have become the handmaidens of agribusiness, to the detriment of consumers and small agricultural producers. The Agribusiness Accountability Project has calculated that in fiscal 1969 state agricultural experiment stations (part of the land grant college apparatus) devoted less than 5 percent of their expenditure of scientific person years to "people oriented" research. The schools direct considerable research efforts toward increased mechanization of agriculture, which primarily helps the big grower and the bigger middleperson. The Agribusiness Accountability Project turned up research into mechanized harvests of a total of 25 different crops, most of them foods. *Hard Tomatoes, Hard Times*, the title of the AAP book on the land grant college complex,

is drawn from the circular logic of a system of research which first created a machine to harvest tomatoes and then needed to create a tomato tough enough to be grasped by the machine.[2]

In theory, the Extension Service is the land grant system's means of reaching rural people. In truth, the Extension Service has a weak record on race, does little for the non-urban poor, and devotes most of its efforts to greater output and efficiency. Those goals parallel the efforts of the research and teaching portions of the land grant complex. The Extension Service spends over half its time and money on the one-fourth of farmers who sell over $10,000 each year.[3] While the number of farms in the United States fell from 6 to 2.9 million between 1945 and 1971, the annual appropriation for extension work was increasing from $38 million to $332 million.[4] Obviously it was not the small farmers, the ones going out of business in that quarter century, who saw much of that $300 million passing them in the opposite direction.

The General Accounting Office, after conducting a review of the relationship of small farmers and agricultural research, reached conclusions of some similarity to the Agribusiness Project's.

New and improved agricultural technology and farm management techniques developed through publicly supported research projects have greatly increased the production capabilities of farmers over the years and have helped keep prices for farm commodities from increasing more rapidly than they might have because of rising demand. Such research has also contributed to some loss of income and relatively lower standards of living for many small-farm operators who did not or could not effectively use the research findings.

Although USDA and the land-grand colleges have made some limited efforts to extend training and technical assistance to small-farm operators and have done some research applicable to the problems of small-farm operators, such efforts could be greatly intensified with the objective of creating a better life for many small-farm operators and increasing productivity of the land under their management.[5]

Jim Hightower describes what the official research complex has actually done:

The new food economy, and even the new food, has been designed with the full advice and consent of government of-

□ Excerpts from Toward a national food policy, Exploratory project for Economic Alternatives, Washington, D.C., pp. 103-119.
In the first part of this article the authors argue that the role of small and medium-sized family farms in U.S. agriculture should be expanded. Numerous reasons are given for this recommendation, including the detrimental effects of large, corporate or industrial-type farms on rural communities. A good deal of evidence is presented showing the decline of smaller, family-type farms in recent years and the growth of larger, nonfamily farm types. This and other evidence is reviewed in the Rodefeld article in Chapter 5. The reduced independence and decision-making power of farm operators and the growing power of other sectors, particularly large agribusiness corporations is also discussed.

ficials, and the economists and scientists of government have worked side by side with their corporate peers. Much of that consultation has been by researchers at state colleges of agriculture and by researchers attached to the Department of Agriculture. There are thousands of these, and they spend more than half a billion tax dollars a year in their work. . . .

This is work that ought to be done by the corporations themselves, if it should be done at all. Not only is it a waste of taxpayer's money, but it is an unforgivable diversion of publicly employed expertise. These researchers could be at work on the needs of family farmers, rather than enhancing the power of oligopsonies; they could be working to improve job conditions and developing the productive capacity of workers, rather than eliminating them; they could be considering means to improve the competitive position of small businesses, rather than servicing the giants; and they could be working directly with consumers, rather than tinkering around with nature to meet the marketing specifications of oligopolies.[6]

This apparatus must be made to serve the interests of a broader public. Rising food costs may help forge the alliance that is necessary for change. Hightower and Susan DeMarco of the Agribusiness Project put it this way:

Except for agribusiness, land grant colleges research has been no bargain. Hard tomatoes and hard times are too much to pay. . . .
Change will come only if those interests now being abused by land grant research begin to make organized demands on the system. If independent family farmers, consumers, small town businessmen, farm workers, environmentalists, farmer cooperatives, small town mayors, taxpayers' organizations, labor unions, big city mayors, rural poverty organizations and other "outsiders" will go to the colleges and to the legislatures, changes can occur.[7]

An example of what research and extension might do is found in the Missouri Extension Service's Small Farm Program. The University of Missouri started this program in 1971 as a pilot effort ". . . to increase the opportunities and quality of living for families on small farms."[8] By 1976 almost 900 farm families had participated in the program. It involves assistance primarily to farmers with annual sales of less than $10,000. Help is provided mainly by education assistants, who are local farmers hired by the Extension Service as paraprofessional teachers. Program participants have generally made more progress than non-participants. Participants have achieved

higher farm sales, higher net farm income, larger enterprises, more livestock assets, slightly more efficient resource utilization, more professional assistance and information, more changes in housing and more stability in level of production.[9]

STRUCTURAL AID TO FAMILY FARMING

Small and medium-sized growers could be helped by the federal government's multi-billion dollar pur-

chases of food for the school lunch and breakfast programs and for surplus commodity distributions. Instead this buying benefits largely the middleperson processing giants. Almost all government food procurement is of the processed variety. In fiscal 1971 over $296 million was spent on USDA procurement of a total of 35 separate categories of surplus commodities. Only two categories were fresh: apples and onions. And there were additional processed apples bought in juice and sauce forms. Fourteen canned items were bought, and other commodities were processed to a greater or lesser degree.[10]

Martha M. Hamilton, in another study by the Agribusiness Accountability Project, has discussed the plight of small farmers and consumers in an agribusiness world:

For years now, the Agriculture Department has maintained that it serves the farmer. If hungry people don't like the Department's food distribution programs, they should keep in mind that they were designed to improve farm income, not to feed people, USDA says. If consumers don't like food prices or quality, the [USDA] tells them high food prices mean high farm income and low quality means low farm costs. If taxpayers balk at the tremendous outlay of funds of the Department of Agriculture, USDA says it goes for a worthy cause—improving farm income.
The butt of the joke is the farmer, who often benefits not at all from the Department of Agriculture's programs and promises. The real beneficiary of the Agriculture Department's time and attention is the middleman, the agribusinessman who takes his off the top. . . .
There are reasons for keeping the farmer who wants to stay on the farm on the job. He is a careful tender of the earth, a man who must consider the land's long-term ability to produce as well as short-term profits. He is the backbone of the rural economy. When he is not under the domination of the food processors, he represents a healthy element where there is competition in the food chain. And he is the representative of an alternative type of life that we may want to preserve.[11]

Many if not most small and medium-sized farmers are increasingly unable to compete in modern agriculture. One alternative is being attempted by the National Sharecroppers' Fund, which has begun the Frank P. Graham Experimental Farm and Training Center, on 500 acres near Wadesboro, North Carolina. Farm workers and small farmers are taught labor-intensive, efficient and environmentally sound growing, as well as agricultural marketing, cooperative management, and rural vocational skills such as welding and carpentry.[12]

The National Sharecroppers' Fund, among others, has also suggested land grant system reform and a number of other steps to aid small producers: (1) provide price supports only to small farmers; (2) ban farming by large non-agricultural corporations; (3) ban corporate and urban investors' use of tax loss farming as write-offs against nonfarm income; (4) enforce the residence and acreage limitation requirements in the federal land reclamation laws; (5) provide federal workman's compensation and unemployment compensation for farm workers; and (6) fully fund and implement the Rural Development Act.[13]

One way in which small farmers in the U.S. should be encouraged and supported is through enforcement of already existing laws. The excess land statute, administered by the Interior Department's Bureau of Reclamation, is such a law. It states that a farmer who owns over 160 acres may not receive irrigation aid from a federally supported water project. The farmer also must live on the land or in the area to be eligible for water. This acreage limit has been ignored in the western part of the rich central valley of California for years. Huge holdings have been amassed, helped by inexpensive water. For example, in California's Westlands Water District, the largest federal water contractor in the reclamation program, farms receiving irrigation support in 1975 averaged not 160 but 2,800 acres.[14]

In June 1975 there was a rare indictment—against a developer—for violation of the excess ownership law. The first prosecution in 20 years under the Bureau of Reclamation Statute grew out of California land sales to the developer by Russell Giffen. Giffen was one of those who had long ago become rich through nonenforcement of the statute, accumulating over 100,000 acres in the western central valley until selling much of it recently. On November 15, 1973, Giffen sold 12 parcels making up a total of 1,754 acres. The plots 160 acres or less, a size meeting the requirements of the law, were sold less than two weeks later by the 12 buyers to 12 new buyers, all of whom were connected in one way or another to the defendant real estate developer. The government contends that the 12 original buyers were sham purchasers, and that they were paid by the defendants for their signatures. David Weiman of the National Farmers' Union has called such landowners "paper farmers." Government lawyers could recall only one other prosecution—about twenty years ago—under the excess land law, even though the statute dates from 1902.[15]

Giffen himself was not indicted, but this case is only the tip of the iceberg concerning his land. When he began selling his huge holdings, many people hoped to buy small portions. Of course they would need enforcement of the 160 acre limit. It seemed that small farmers were getting the Giffen land in lots under 160 acres. But in actuality complicated systems of transfers and facades were operating. One of them was the alleged conspiracy cited above. In another a Japanese company was the true buyer. The Bureau of Reclamation approved these transfers with apparent knowledge of the true facts.

Small farmers and farm workers in the western valley area of California are trying to get land, but are faced with such problems as the Giffen deals. Since 1973 the West Side Planning Group, a local development organization, has helped groups of workers get into independent farming, growing mainly vegetables. Their operations, small and labor-intensive, are much more efficient than the huge agribusinesses. Yet because of manipulations such as the Giffen sales, the small holders have great difficulty in putting together farms. The Land Dynamics indictment is a step in a long-neglected right direction.[16]

A straightforward way of helping small farmers acquire land and compete is simply to prohibit big corporate agriculture. Senators Gaylord Nelson (D.-Wis.) and James Abourezk (D.-S.D.) have sponsored an amendment to the Clayton Anti-trust Act that would ban from agriculture those with over $3 million in assets and/or those not directly engaged in farming.* In big corporate agriculture, declares Abourezk, the "very quality, taste and texture of food—to say nothing of the price—can be subordinated to profit-making efficiency."[17] A number of states already have such provisions for the protection of the family farm. Minnesota has one of the best versions. It bans non-family corporations from entry into farming, restricts expansion of existing non-family agricultural corporations into new farm ventures, and requires annual reports on farming corporations.

REFORMING AGRICULTURAL FINANCE

Farm producers also need some aid in their enslavement to financial indebtedness. The total farm debt between 1960 and 1975 has risen from $23.6 billion to a preliminary figure of $93.1 billion, a fourfold increase.[18] Interest charges on mortgaged real estate have also shot up in the last few years, from 106.7 cents per acre in 1965 to 204.5 cents in 1972. Between 1950 and 1964 interest went up from 24.6 to 94.3 cents per acre. Total real estate interest charges for farmland were $264 million in 1950 and $3 billion in 1974.[19] Total interest charged on farmers' non-real property debt was $169 million in 1945, $1.1 billion in 1965, and $3.3 billion in 1974.[20]

Producers who are willing to farm organically have had difficulties in getting loans and credit. For example, the Farmers' Home Administration, in granting agricultural loans, controls what and how much is planted, and is reluctant to support organic methods. Chemical farming is the FHA's preferred modus operandi and most other lenders usually follow the

---

*This bill has had only one hearing since its introduction four years ago and has otherwise been given short shrift.

same line. Well over half of the 1972 farm mortgage debt of $31.4 billion was controlled by the FHA, banks, and life insurance companies. About $13 billion was held by individuals and other non-reporting lenders.[21]

One observer of the farm financial situation has summed it up in this fashion:

... due to a monopoly structure in rural banking, an agricultural credit system which has helped induce a labor saving agricultural technology, and private and public flow of funds ... impediments to rural development and incentives for rural out-migration have been created.[22]

The large banks, the agribusinesses and many government policy makers seek a more capital intensive farming sector, with little consideration of what the effects of such a development will be for small farmers and the agricultural system generally. Barry Commoner observes that the banks and the petrochemical industry

pretty well dictate, between them ... how crops are raised. [In Nebraska the] banks are called the "fence pullers." When you go for a loan they make you pull up your fences and raise corn because that's a more secure return on their loan. That's a condition on the loan. You can get a quicker return on the loan if you slop fertilizer on the soil. I imagine it would be very difficult to get a loan in order to spend five years building up the organic content of the soil, and get away from fertilizers.[23]

Two USDA economists have suggested that renewal of the family farm and consequent greater public financing are the least likely developments of the future. Trends are rather in favor of fewer and larger farming units and more corporate farm ownership. These writers believe that, among other factors,

... increasing capital requirements ... run counter to the predominance of the family farm. This does not mean the family farm is going to disappear. For it to continue predominant, however, we feel some policy action will probably be necessary.[24]

After the Second World War private banks making agricultural loans began to seek more of a voice in decisions on principles of agricultural management. Bank loans are based in large part on a farm's productivity, and in contemporary agriculture this has usually meant that farmers are expected to use chemical fertilizers. More than two decades ago, a Texas bank president spoke of the growing role of bankers in farming decisions:

Every banker has ... specific roles to follow in aiding our farmers. One is indirect. Through the support of scientific institutions ... we can make certain that the farmer has the very best information to guide him in obtaining ... agricultural know-how which will enable him to get the maximum dollar yields per acre.[25]

The American Bankers Association has advised its members to stay informed of the latest technological improvements in agriculture. The aim of such watchfulness is that the banker should be able to insist on the latest mechanical advances.[26]

The Agricultural Committee of the Bankers Association also recommends a very detailed loan application form for members to use in processing farm requests. Under operating expenses spaces for listing estimated costs of "feed, seed, fertilizers, pesticides, and fuel and oil" are listed prominently—and in that order. On a separate form a bank officer subjectively evaluates a loan applicant, including decisions on "strong or weak factors" and "borrower's management ability."[27]

A survey by the ABA showed that in 1967 bankers viewed the "inefficiency of small farm operators" as a major problem of farm credit. That "problem" was second only to the cost-price squeeze as an area of concern. Of larger banks—with over $10 million in deposits—9.7 percent saw this supposed small farm inefficiency as the biggest problem.[28]

Land and capitalization costs are a major plague of the contemporary small farmer. Forty years ago the average annual farm operating loan was $4,000. Today it is over $100,000. Don Paarlberg, USDA's Director of Economic Research, says that costs are so high that land and labor may have to be supplied by two different entities—a tame way of describing vertical integration and the end of the independent farmer. Farm land costs are rising rapidly. A 600 acre farm and its buildings in central Iowa were worth a minimum of $480,000 in 1975, an increase of 30 percent in two years and 100 percent in ten years. Seventy thousand dollars more would be needed for machinery.[29]

Solutions to the debt problem have been attempted in Canada. The province of Saskatchewan in 1972 established the Saskatchewan Land Bank Commission to buy farms from owners wanting to sell and lease them to qualified persons wanting to start farming or increase their holdings. Leases are for ten years at 5¾ percent of the land's market value. Lessees pay the property taxes and may if they wish buy the land when five years of a lease has elapsed. In 1972-73 the Land Bank bought 168,481 acres and leased 425 parcels of an average size of 404 acres each. This system avoids the burden of a large down payment. Preference in leasing is given to full-time farmers with a net worth of less than $60,000 and an average net income of under $10,000 for the three years prior to application.[30]

A forerunner to the Saskatchewan Land Bank is the Prince Edward Island Development Corporation, established in 1969. Both have basically the same goals and methods. Farms on P.E.I. are purchased by the Corporation and resold or leased for five year periods to new and small farmers. From 1970 to 1974 purchases were made of about 80,000 acres, more than 10 percent of the agricultural land of the province. Over that period, the Corporation put 9,000 idle acres back into production.[31] The Saskatchewan plan has been the model for proposals of similar leasing programs in parts of the U.S. The National Farmer's Union in Minnesota and North Dakota is pushing the idea, and in Minnesota a bill on the subject was recently enacted.

PRESERVING FARM LAND

The rapid buildup of farm land values is a symptom of the development pressures that are helping destroy a net of 1.4 to 1.7 million acres of U.S. farm land per year.[32]

As we saw in Chapter 2, the USDA's Soil Conservation Service estimate of land not now cropped that is potentially convertible to productive farming dropped from 266 million acres in 1967 to 111 million in 1976. (Four hundred million acres were farmed in 1975.) Also in those intervening years, the SCS study showed that the amount of Class I (highest quality) farmland in production dropped from 47 million to 33 million acres.[33]

A 1974 USDA report, *Our Land and Water Resources*, projected that the U.S. would have more than enough land in farming in the year 2000 to meet domestic and export needs. The projection relied, however, on the dubious assumptions of steadily rising use of inorganic fertilizers (despite skyrocketing prices), moderate export increases (despite high world demand growth), rising reliance on irrigation (despite scarce Western water and competing energy demands), steady growth in productivity (despite a leveling off since the 1960s), and continued favorable weather (despite widely expected disruptions).[34]

Zoning regulations to preserve farm land long ago succumbed to more powerful urbanization pressures. The second line of defense became preferential tax assessments, under which a farmer's land was taxed *as if* it were to be used only for open space or farming.[35]

The farm-preservation powers of preferential taxation, however, have proved to be as vulnerable to development profits as zoning. As the Citizens' Advisory Committee on Environmental Quality (CACEQ) put it in 1974

So far . . . preferential assessment has done little more than delay some losses in the direct path of urban growth. Preferential assessment does not take away the farmer's development rights—it just taxes him as though it did. The hard fact is that the profits to be made by development are far

greater than the savings to be had by farming, and far greater than any roll-back tax payment required [i.e., the requirement that several years' worth of tax discounts be refunded if the farm is sold for development].[36]

The fundamental need is for localities to develop farm land preservation tools that fit within an overall long-range land use plan. Such local plans (and the ability to guide development on the basis of them), if they are to be successful, must in turn be the basis of similarly long-range national land use planning. Localities often cannot withstand wider regional pressures not encompassed by a local plan.[37] Calls for such a national effort were heard from many quarters, including the CACEQ 1974 *Report:*

In the light of the . . . dramatic changes in the food suuply picture [since 1970], it is now clear that the preservation of an adequate supply of agricultural land is essential to the welfare and security of the Nation and should be a major objective of [national] land use planning legislation.[38]

While there has been no national land use legislation, many localities have gone far beyond preferential taxation in the struggle to protect farm land from development.

The town of Ramapo, New York, pioneered the use of timed, or phased, development planning in 1969. Under Ramapo's ordinance, commercial, industrial, and residential development takes place according to a preset plan for the construction of public facilities to service the growth. Proposed developments that would "leapfrog" ahead of the 18-year public-facilities development plan legally can be prohibited by the town.[39] Ramapo's approach is significant for its ability to prevent the carving-up of rural land and the waste of resources through scattershot development.

Another important basis of any local preservation effort could be a long-range assessment of need for farm land, an estimate that the Michigan Department of Agriculture made in 1973. The state estimated that it had lost one-third of its farm land to development since 1945, and land being farmed in 1973 would be all but lost to agriculture under current trends by 2000. Included in the department's recommendations was the creation of agricultural districts and the purchase of development rights to farm land.

The agricultural district approach was adopted by New York State in 1971 to preserve 1.75 million acres, including the grape belt in Western New York, mucklands in the southeast and fruit trees along Lake Ontario. The district approach prohibits local restrictions on normal farming activities, requires special justification for taking farm land through eminent domain, prohibits imposing additional water and sewer taxes once the district is formed, and lowers property taxes subject to a roll-back agreement.[40]

Long Island's Suffolk County has pioneered in the purchase of development rights. After being unexpectedly stalled when the county legislature tabled the bill in May 1976, the measure was finally enacted in September 1976, after four years' development. It provides up to $80 million to be raised through bonds to purchase the development rights to about 15,000 acres. Taxes on the land would then be lowered. The county cannot resell the rights without approval from a voter referendum.[41] (See also pp. 160-167 [original text].)

REFORM OF AGRICULTURAL COOPERATIVES

Another way in which small producers could be aided is through reform of the system of agricultural cooperatives, which have begun to favor big business techniques and interests and neglect the small farmer. Linda Kravitz, in *Who's Minding the Coop?*, writes that

Cooperatives . . . are intended to be more than simply another "American business group". They are intended to be a unique form of business, owned and controlled by the farmers who are members and patrons of the coop. It is their difference that counts. But the difference is being obscured, and they are becoming just another agribusiness.[42]

As a democratic organization with more than simply profit motives, cooperatives are somewhat unique and deserve preservation.

Agricultural cooperatives began in the United States as early as 1810 with interaction among dairy producers in Connecticut. A California fruit marketing association of the late nineteenth century became one of the successful farm coops. This beginning was the stimulus behind the formation of Sunkist in 1905. Sunkist today markets 85 percent of the fresh lemons sold in the U.S. and 45 percent of the fresh oranges. The Sunkist cooperative example was tried in other areas of the country in the early 1920s but was largely a failure. The Capper-Volstead Act was passed in 1922 and gave considerable anti-trust exemption to cooperatives.[43] The government, however, has put very little money into coops: only $2.2 million was authorized for USDA's Farmer Cooperative Service in fiscal 1974, a miniscule .024 percent of the Department's budget.[44]

Farm coops did not fade away. There were about 7,800 of them in the United States in 1970, marketing one-quarter of the farm product. But the largest 100 cooperatives in 1972 had 47 percent of the business volume and half or more of total assets, borrowed capital, and net savings and losses. Among the 500 largest corporations in the country in 1972 were six coops, led by Associated Milk Producers, Inc., with over $1 billion in sales. In structure local groups and federated coops with authority at the local level have been giving way over the past 20 years to centralized associations with little member control.[45]

Kravitz and the Agribusiness Accountability Project have recommended a number of steps for improvement of the coop network: (1) federated structures; (2) more membership voting on issues and election of directors; (3) no office-holding by management; (4) more open membership to smaller farmers; (5) use of machinery pools; (6) farmers only on the board of directors; (7) greater member control of management; (8) increased federal funding and promotion of better farmer-consumer programs through the Department of Agriculture; (9) better Extension Service and agricultural college support of cooperatives; and (10) retention of the Capper-Volstead exemption.[46] The Consumer Federation of America suggests that

. . . immunity from the antitrust laws conferred upon farmers by the Capper-Volstead Act was intended and should be limited to those activities which do not violate the antitrust laws. Congress should reexamine the adequacy of the Capper-Volstead Act to protect and regulate against marketing cooperatives to determine what changes, if any, may be required to achieve the basic objectives of fair prices for food to consumers and a fair return to farmers and ranchers for their capital, labor, and management.[47]

Nearly everyone agrees that family farmers are the most efficient producers of food and fiber, and that their predominance results in social and economic benefits to rural society and to the nation as a whole. Yet the best evidence indicates that the family producer is in decline. A new direction for agricultural policy must seek to reverse this trend.

FOOTNOTES

1. Jim Hightower and Susan DeMarco, *Hard Tomatoes, Hard Times* (Cambridge, Massachusetts: Schenkman, 1973), pp. 9-15, 152-55.
2. *Ibid.*, pp. 26, 29-30.
3. *Ibid.*, pp. 118-120.
4. Statistics of Bureau of the Census and USDA, quoted in *ibid.*, p. 120.
5. U.S. General Accounting Office, *Some Problems Impeding Economic Improvement of Small-Farm Operations: What the Department of Agriculture Could Do*, 15 August 1975, p. 23.
6. Hightower, *Eat Your Heart Out*, pp. 188, 190.
7. Hightower and DeMarco, *Hard Tomatoes, Hard Times*, p. 64.
8. University of Missouri-Columbia Extension Division, *Missouri Small Farm Program: Report*, March 1976, p. 4.
9. University of Missouri-Columbia Extension Division, *Missouri Small Farm Program: An Evaluation With a Control Group*, October 1975, p. 25.
10. Martha M. Hamilton, *The Great American Grain Robbery and Other Stories* (Washington: Agribusiness Accountability Project, 1972), pp. 101-116.
11. *Ibid.*, pp. i, 8.
12. "R.A.F. At Work," pamphlet of the Rural Advancement Fund of the National Sharecroppers' Fund, Inc.
13. James M. Pierce, *The Condition of Farm Workers and Small Farm-*

ers, 1975 Report to the National Board of the National Sharecroppers Fund and Rural Advancement Fund.

14. U.S. Senate, Select Committee on Small Business and Committee on Interior and Insular Affairs, Joint Hearings on *Will the Family Farm Survive in America?*, 22 July 1975, p. 120.

15. 16 USC 201 ff.; *Washington Post*, 8 June 1975.

16. "Agriculture: Giffen Land Deal," *Elements*, June 1975.

17. S. 1458, 94th Congress, 1st Session; "News from Jim Abourezk" (press release), 30 January 1975.

18. USDA, ERS, *Economic Tables*, June 1975, p. 28.

19. USDA, ERS, *Agricultural Finance Statistics*, June 1974, p. 17; USDA, ERS, *Farm Income Statistics*, July 1975, p. 50.

20. *Ibid.*, p. 49.

21. "Why Some Organic Farmers Can't Make It," *Organic Gardening and Farming*, November 1973, p. 45; USDA, *Agricultural Finance Statistics*, p. 2.

22. Mathew Shane, *Financial Restraint, Banking and Rural Development*, Staff Paper P74-1, Department of Agricultural and Applied Economics, University of Minnesota, January 1974, pp. 1-2.

23. Barry Commoner, Interview in *Ruralamerica;* reprinted in *Congressional Record*, 24 September 1976, p. S16608.

24. Allen G. Smith and Kenneth R. Krause, "Financing Future Farm Production: A Look at Three Scenarios," *Agricultural Finance Review*, USDA, ERS, October 1974, p. 13.

25. Ben H. Wooten, "Texas Bankers Help Region Convert to a Modern System of Agriculture," *Texas Bankers Record*, January 1952.

26. American Bankers Association, *Better Agricultural Banking* (New York: American Bankers Association, 1963), p. 10.

27. *Ibid.*, pp. 34, 37.

28. American Bankers Association, *Agricultural Banking Developments, 1962-1967* (New York: American Bankers Association, 1967), p. 28.

29. *Washington Post*, 11 May 1975; *New York Times*, 9 June 1974.

30. John McClaughry, "Rural Land Banking: The Canadian Experience," *North Carolina Central Law Journal*, Fall 1975, pp. 82-84.

31. *Ibid.*, pp. 77-81.

32. USDA, *Potential Cropland Study*, News release #1832-76, 29 June 1976; Citizens' Advisory Committee on Environmental Quality

(CACEQ), *Report to the President and to the Council on Environmental Quality*, December 1974, p. 24; Beman, "A New Case . . .," *Fortune*, April 1976.

33. Roger Blobaum, *The Loss of Agricultural Land*, A Study Report to the Citizens' Advisory Committee on Environmental Quality, 1974, p. 4, for the 1967 figure; and USDA, *Potential Cropland Study*, Table 1 (National), for the latest estimate.

34. Blobaum, *The Loss of Agricultural Land*, pp. 14-19.

35. Harris Wagenseil, "Property Taxation of Agricultural and Open Space Land," *Harvard Journal on Legislation*, v. 8, 1970-71; *Washington Post*, 14 June 1975.

36. CACEQ, *Report*, p. 25.

37. See Randall W. Scott et al., eds., *Management and Control of Growth* (Washington: Urban Land Institute, 1975), Vol. III, Chapter 16, for a selection of articles.

38. *Ibid.*, p. 30.

39. For an important analysis of the rationale for timed development, see Henry Fagin, "Land Planning in a Democracy," *Law and Contemporary Problems*, Spring 1955, reprinted in Scott, *Management and Control of Growth*, Vol. I, p. 296. For review of the Ramapo plan, see Scott, *Management and Control of Growth*, Vol. II, Chapter 8, especially pp. 62-77.

40. *Consolidated Laws of New York*, Vol. 2B, Sec. 300, 303-305.

41. These and other local measures are discussed in Blobaum, *The Loss of Agricultural Land*, and CACEQ, *Report; New York Times*, 12-13 May 1976.

42. Linda Kravitz, *Who's Minding the Coop?* (Washington: Agribusiness Accountability Project, 1974), p. 110.

43. Luther Tweeten, *Foundations of Farm Policy* (Lincoln, Nebraska: University of Nebraska Press, 1970), pp. 73-75.

44. Kravitz, *Who's Minding the Co op?*, p. 91.

45. *Ibid.*, pp. 8-9, 11-12. See also, National Consumers Congress, *Consumer Action for Improved Milk Marketing*, Report #3.

46. Kravitz, *Who's Minding the Co op?*, pp. 112-116.

47. Carol Foreman, Statement of the CFA, in U.S. Senate, Committee on Agriculture and Forestry, *Farm and Food Policy 1977*, 15 September 1976, p. 100.

12

Alternative responses to rural community decline and change

Villages are dying—and who cares?

JOHN CARLYLE

America's hamlets seem to be fading out. They are following into oblivion the high-wheeled buggy, the little red schoolhouse and the quaint custom of bobbing for apples. Not long ago the State of Illinois sold a perfectly good village as abandoned property. All it lacked was people.

Figures from the eight states that ring the 1920 center of population near the Illinois and Indiana line show that 60 per cent of the small towns counted have lost population. A few villages showed increases which were less than what should have been the normal boost through the beneficent processes of nature. The wayside inn is giving way to the road house and the hot-dog stand. The country doctor is practicing in the city, and likes it better. There are cobwebs on the windows of the little brown church at the crossroads. General stores in the hamlets are dealing in gasoline and canned cakes.

All of this seems very sad indeed.

SMALLER HAMLETS

I am a confirmed but theoretic lover of the good old days. For a very little I would burst into tears.

For all that—so it seems to me—we will be better off without the hamlets.

However, the promise that we will be without them is not definite as yet. The preliminary figures of the census carry no guarantee. They seem to show that:

The small town, the hamlet, the unincorporated village, ranging in population from practically nothing to about 1,500, is decreasing in habitants.

The somewhat larger towns are increasing in population. The compilers have not ceased compiling, but the indications are that the larger and more comfortable the town the greater its rate of increase.

☐ From *Nation's Business*, Jan. 1931, pp. 23-26.

The agricultural population is diminishing in numbers but growing in *per capita* dollars and appetites.

That seems to be all to the good. But what is the reason for the shrinkage in small towns?

One reason seems to be the general storekeeper.

The general storekeeper will now rise and call me names. Of course he has a defense. He is often old and there are too many of him and his farmer clients have been used to his ways and he did not realize that they were dying off and the younger ones wanted other things. There are plenty of things to be said for him. But listen to this:

Down on the Mexican border is a general storekeeper who may be introduced as *Señor* Bill. Up north we would call him a good old guy. He has an ivory-handled six shooter under the counter, a book filled with bad debts and an unconquerable optimism. Every Mexican for 60 miles around has been *Señor* Bill's customer, because he likes them and trusts them. The other day he shook his head at Dolores:

"Listen, kid," said he. "You don't want those silk stockings. They won't wear, *niña*. Here's what you're looking for."

He threw out a pair of rugged cotton stockings, reinforced toe and heel. Dolores looked at them. A slender Dolores, with neat ankles and a straight back and the sorrow of the world in her big, black eyes:

"*Gracias, Señor* Beel," whispered Dolores, "*Muchas gracias.*" Then she walked out on him.

THEY BUY WHAT THEY WANT

Señor Bill said he did not know what has been getting into the Mexican girls. They will not wear shawls as their mothers do. They call for high-heeled shoes and fancy hats and little silk frocks like the girls wear in Dallas. He said that we all know that ain't right.

"What's happened to your trade, *Señor* Bill?"

"Shot," said Bill.

Not only his trade is shot, his hamlet is shot. If he will not sell his customers what they want they will get it somewhere else. The cautious reader may say this is an isolated incident.

But the same thing is going on all over the land in big and little villages.

A Department of Commerce investigator told me another sock story to illustrate the backwardness of the village merchant. One of the chain stores had been featuring a chilled steel sock for 29 cents a pair. It would never wear out. The *Señor* Bills operating the village stores cried bitterly about it:

"We cannot compete against prices like that," they said.

Thereupon a wholesaler determined to help his storekeeping friends fight the chain. Incidentally, he would help himself, of course. He had made the super-stock of Christendom. It could not be marred by an emery wheel and its brilliance was that of a wolf's eye in the underbrush.

"Sell that at a quarter," he said to his village store-keeping clients. "You'll not make much money, but you will drive that 29-cent sock off the field. Advertise it. That is the most superb bargain ever woven."

Every village storekeeper—every one of them, mind —put that sock on sale for from half a dollar to six bits.

"It's the first chance we ever had to get a little gravy," they said.

Of course the 29-cent sock went on getting the business and the hamlet storekeepers and their hamlets lost.

Here is another illustration of that same stubbornness among hamlet merchants. In a small town in Vermont is a general store run by a nice old man. It has always been a good general store. It has brought trade to his little town. Farmers come to buy from him, because they know he will have whatever it is they want. They buy something of some other local merchant before they get out of town.

That is the way cities and businesses are built up. It is not too much to say that the small towns are built around their stores. Churches, schoolhouses, scandals, sewers and bond issues come later.

When the girls began to hike their dresses up to their knees and wear silk stockings the storekeeper's better nature revolted:

REVOLT AGAINST MODERNIZING

"I won't sell 'em," he said. "They gotta go some-where else for those contraptions."

They did go somewhere else. The little town felt their going tremendously. Imagine a countryside filled with good-looking girls, each determined to spend the maple-sugar money on new clothes, and all diverted to the town's nearest rival! This is not a fable or any exaggeration. The thing actually happened. Good roads lead almost everywhere nowadays except to the door of the stick-in-the-mud storekeeper.

There was a time when we lived in a horse and rail-road geography. When we had only a few miles to go a horse dragged us through the dust or mud. When we went a more considerable distance we got cinders in our eyes and made it a state occasion. Maybe mother went down to see us off and we carried fried chicken in a basket.

Under such conditions a hamlet with a general store was a necessity every five or six miles. If the store-keeper carried nothing but red underwear the whole population flamed at dawn and eve. They had no op-tion.

Now we live in a concrete and rubber geography. We drive long distances like the Old Harry. Dr. C. J. Galpin, the principal agricultural economist of the Department of Agriculture, told an illuminative story. He was visiting a farmer friend in New York State, in the at-one-time isolated community where as a young man he taught school. After they had wandered about the farm and listened to the rich chuckles of the fat pigs the farmer said:

"Let's go to the Syracuse Fair."

"But that's 60 miles," said Galpin.

"What of it?" asked the farmer.

The city man could not believe it. He had not yet adjusted himself to the livelier agricultural age, al-though he is the principal agricultural economist.

They climbed into the farmer's automobile and drove to Syracuse in an hour and a half. They dined at the hotel that night and until ten o'clock talked over a new food ration with an expert and were in bed by midnight.

The farmer thought nothing of it. It was the city man who goggled.

I am honest in my conviction that incalculable harm has been done the hamlets by merchants who have not gotten out of the mud. When the villagers and those who live nearby begin to drive 20 miles to shop the hamlet is ruined. It may not know it, but it is. That is precisely what has happened to hundreds of townlets.

But the right sort of storekeeper can keep a village propped on its tottering legs. He can even make it sound again.

ROADS RUN TO THE VILLAGES

George L. Coyle, the alert head of a large depart-ment store in Charleston, W. Va., listened to me sound off what seemed an undebatable platitude:

"Good roads draw the country people into the city."

"Good roads run both ways," said Mr. Coyle.

He told of a country storekeeper, located in a hamlet beset by good roads. The other storekeepers note gloomily that the good roads are sapping their trade. They sit behind the dinky windows of dark stores. Women who come in to shop are made welcome to the kitchen chairs which hem in the barrel stove, if any are not occupied by ancients engaged in mastication. Usually the storekeeper tries to sell the feminine shopper a dress.

"Women do not go to a village store to buy party dresses," observed Mr. Coyle. "They know better. They window shop in the larger towns for a time. When they know what they want they buy."

The storekeeper admired by Coyle is doing a nice business and has been doing it for years and it is getting better annually. He has a clean, bright store and up-to-date goods. When a housewife wants a paper of pins or a yard and a half of blue ribbon she knows that she can get it. He knows his customers do not come to him for Paris gowns. If he has not precisely kept his hamlet alive he has at least arrested the processes of decay.

"Farmer folk do not want to drive into the city for every little purchase," said Coyle. "A store equipped with the conveniences will hold their trade except for the luxury lines. And the good roads take city people into the country for some part of their shopping. They like to ride in the fresh air and buy vegetables and eggs at the farm stands. The little stores can—if their keepers know how to do it—work up a nice business in ice creams and soft drinks and the lesser marketing. Just as the country people wish to avoid the congested city streets, the city people like to get out on the open country roads."

These conclusions are supported by certain facts.

The Canner reports that a daily average of $100 was taken in on the sale of home-made jellies and jams by 12 wayside stands on farms in two midwest states.

The University of Illinois found that a majority of the small-town storekeepers who are offering their customers what they want are holding or increasing their trade.

Economist Galpin maintains that the farmer, far more than the city man, enjoys a personal relationship with his storekeeper and editor and banker. He will remain loyal to them, says Galpin, if they deliver the goods.

But they must deliver.

A survey made for the Retailers National Council notes that the stores of certain towns have been losing business to other towns because they did not give service. They were dark and poorly arranged. There is no excuse nowadays for a storekeeper remaining ignorant of the more effective ways of mapping his store.

FARMERS WANT BETTER MARKETS

Women shoppers were not offered pleasant rest rooms. Underpaid and immature clerks gave the impression of snootiness. Buyers nowadays know too much to be fooled often. They take their eggs to better markets.

This survey stressed the fact that the towns were losing ground because of the faults of the storekeepers. Opinion seems to be fairly general that appeals to local patriotism stir no red corpuscles in the buyer's veins. He does not care particularly whether this town or that grows or diminishes. He would not stir a hand to help either process. What he wants to know is how much money he can get for his eggs.

The farm population has been decreasing for 20 years. It has been on the down grade in some parts for 50 years. Better machines and methods have enabled fewer men in the fields to feed an increasing number of people in the cities. That down-turn in agricultural population is proof of the farmer's efficiency.

The farmer's wife is a more interesting woman than she was two decades ago. She has the magazines and newspapers and radio and telephone and she drives her own car.

The hamlet has no attraction for her. She whizzes on to the nearest larger town, where she can have her hair bobbed and go to a movie and pick up the latest novel at the library. Here is a conclusion worth noting:

The University of Texas has worked out what it calls a "definite law of retail gravitation."

Briefly stated it is that towns and cities draw from smaller intermediate towns and hamlets in direct proportion to some power of the population of the larger cities.

Folks move from the hamlets to the villages and then to the towns and then to the smaller cities and then to the larger cities.

With apologies to Dean Swift, the law laid down in his couplet must be reversed. Nowadays:

"The smaller fleas have larger fleas to bite 'em."

If there are fewer men and women on the farms, they have more money *per capita* to spend in the "farmers' towns" than they had 20 years ago. Nowadays the "farmer's town" is in the 5,000 to 10,000 classification instead of the 200 to 1,000 of a few years ago. Dr. Galpin holds that the farm population has decreased four and one-quarter million persons in 20 years. But he also declares that the gross cash income of the American farmer has been steadily maintained at slightly more than ten billion dollars annually. If there are four and a quarter million fewer persons to spend that ten billion, then the relative prosperity of the "farmer's town" is accounted for. And the "farmer's town"—as distinguished from the hamlet—is prosperous.

The American Press Association gets out an annual book in which advertisers are told of the trade outlets in the smaller towns. Many of the counties in which these small towns are found have no daily newspapers. The weekly paper brings the home news to the farmers and is read from Friday to Friday while a metropolitan daily covers the comics and fashions and the state of crime in Chicago. In a hasty glance through the A. P. A. book one fact leaped to the eye.

THE MODERN FARMERS' TOWN

There are almost as many plumbing-supply stores as there are stores in which radios are sold. There is a noticeable frequency of stores which sell music, apart from the dealers in radios and phonographs. There are tea shops and haberdasheries. The consolidated schools which were originally set on country roads in the presumable center of a farming district are being placed with increasing frequency in the "farmer's town." The farmer's wife can do her shopping and be beautified when she brings the kids to school. When the farmer retires he moves into his town for the sake of the church and the school and the library. Sometimes he moves in before he has retired and drives out to do his farming. Is it any wonder that the hamlet is declining?

Suppose the habitant of a hamlet district gets sick.

I know a doctor in a New England hamlet. He is a lively, wide-awake young man who is so competent that he has several times been asked to go to Boston at a guaranteed income which seems a fortune by the side of his meager intake. In the summer he covers a wide district by automobile. In winter he turns his car into a snow caterpillar and eventually hitches Old Dobbin to the sleigh and when the drifts are toprail deep he visits by snowshoe. He was born and brought up among his people and he will not leave. No doctor would come to fill his place. He is a hero. He will continue to be a hero until his wife's sane representations finally wear him down. But—

He is out of step with the times.

THERE ARE FEWER COUNTRY DOCTORS

A hard thing to say. But the fact is that the larger medical colleges are turning out specialists. A medical education costs so much in time and money that the fledglings sensibly decide to locate in cities where the potential rewards are higher. These young men will not go to the hamlets. Nor will the graduates from the less costly colleges go to the hamlets. But the towns of 5,000 to 10,000 are equipping hospitals and offering a present certainty and a future competence to them. Those who have not been able to pursue the long and expensive studies which precede specialization in medicine are being attracted.

This is tough for the hamlet. But in the process of evolution the first monkey to lose his tail probably suffered terribly.

The character of the rural population is changing. When I was a youngster I was mildly acquainted with a farming county in Ohio. The farmers were prosperous, Republican and Methodist. If one of them put a mortgage on his farm, he and his wife and his manservant and his maidservant and his children worked day and night and fudged a little on Sunday until it was paid off.

A HISTORIC FURNACE

That county has the fattest cattle and the biggest horses and the most persistent odor of lantern wick at four o'clock in the morning that I have ever known. The first doubt I ever felt of its orthodoxy was when one of its most eminent citizens put a hot-air furnace in his house. It had been the custom to sit about the kitchen stove until bed time came.

One of the farm boys in that county recently dedicated what has been a pasture to polo and is making a reasonably good thing of it. The farmers' boys who not many years ago would have walked to town on Saturday night rather than drive a horse which had pulled a plough all week are now making polo ponies out of western cayuses.

The old-time farmer believed in hard work and saving. When he had a little money he made the first payment on another farm. Driven by his fear of debt, he slaved until he owned it. Then he bought another. He grew rich but he did not live. These toads that hop occasionally out of Texas boulders have been positively dissolute by comparison. When his arteries finally cracked he died surrounded by assets and greed. To escape the farm his daughters had married streetcar conductors. His sons argued in the hall over the division of the gray mule as their father took his last whistling breath.

The new-style farmer is becoming more and more a business man.

He has no superstitious fear of a banker. He may owe plenty of money. So does the merchant with whom he trades. He has learned the uses of the credit system. He manages to have a fairly good time as he goes along. His first easy steps toward a realization that this is essentially a good world may have been taken when he joined a farmers' club. He began to discover wants he had never known and new ways of farming by which he could get the money to satisfy them. His wife ceased to be a drudge and learned how to handle the wind-blown bob.

EVERYBODY BENEFITED

He discovered that the storekeepers of the "farmers' towns" are friendly to his club. His shrewdness told him that the reason was that the retailers knew that the farther his horizon expanded the more goods they would sell. He liked that. Both sides profited by it. Twenty years ago the Saturday night tub was a fix-

ture. Now farming communities are putting in swimming pools and using them.

"I know a pair of farmers on the Pacific Coast," said Bohannon, of the Bureau of the Census. "Just farmers, farming in partnership 900 miles away from San Francisco. What do you think they did?"

No one can answer a question like that.

"They bought an airplane," said Bohannon, "and they fly it into the big town on alternate Friday nights for the week-end and take their families along. You can't beat that."

What good would a hamlet be to farmers like that?

Factors and forces affecting the optimum future rural settlement pattern in the United States

MARION CLAWSON*

Many factors and forces will affect the optimum future rural settlement pattern in the United States. The *optimum* pattern will be strongly affected by the present pattern, because present capital improvements and existing social arrangements have great value which can be realized only by their continued use. The *probable* pattern will be dominated, to a still greater extent, by the presently existing pattern, because resistances to change are numerous and powerful. But what would be the optimum form of future rural settlement patterns, if somehow the slate could be wiped clean, and a new settlement pattern emerged which was optimum for technological, economic, social, and political conditions of the future? Such a hypothetical settlement pattern, to the extent we can visualize it, will reveal the ultimate effects of forces now operative or likely to become so. To the extent that public leaders and administrators wish to facilitate adjustments to operative social forces, some concepts of an ultimate or future pattern will provide opportunities for ongoing adjustments.

There has been much concern in the literature of several professional groups about the location and form of cities but the optimum pattern of rural settlement has had relatively little attention; apparently it has been taken for granted or considered not worth

study. While people live in rural areas in the United States for many reasons, we shall consider only the farm population and its immediate urban service population—as a practical matter, towns and cities of less than 5000, for the most part. Such towns are not likely to have much industrial or other employment unrelated to agriculture, nor much tributary open-country nonfarm population. We are thinking of the more purely agricultural areas of the Great Plains, Corn Belt, and other farming regions.

By "optimum," we mean a settlement pattern which will offer maximum satisfactions to all the people involved, and at the least cost for the satisfactions obtained. Satisfactions are of several kinds, as we shall note; interests of various individuals are likely to diverge to some extent, necessitating difficult interpersonal comparisons; satisfactions of one kind may be obtainable only at the cost of satisfactions of other kinds; and, to the extent that greater satisfactions mean greater costs, difficult cost-value comparisons will necessarily be involved. Nevertheless, it is believed that practically useful comparisons of satisfactions and costs can be made for different settlement patterns. A more or less explicit assumption is that such enormous gains are possible, comparing various alternatives to the present patterns, that one need not be required to measure the merits of possible future alternatives precisely.

By "settlement pattern," we mean the pattern of where people live in relation to their work, their

☐ From Economic Geography **42**(4):283-293, Oct. 1966.
*Dr. Clawson is Director, Land Use and Management Program, Resources for the Future, Inc.

schools, their places of play, and the like; and in relation to where other people live. While a farmer has some concern with distant markets, recreation places, shopping centers, and seats of government, our concern is with the local or primary ones—where the vast majority of all personal contacts by farmers are centered.

It should be obvious—or, at least, it is to this writer —that the present pattern of rural settlement in the United States is not optimum to meet present conditions, much less those of the future. Farm size, farmstead location, road network, local schools, location and functions of local service towns, county government, and many other aspects of rural settlement were established long ago, in an age of animal power and before the presently dominant factors in modern life were known. Even if one concedes that rural settlement pattern was perfect to meet those conditions, it can scarcely be argued that it has adjusted fully to the changing technological, economic, social, and political changes of the intervening years. It is not difficult to show how horse and buggy settlement patterns are unsuitable in a jet or rocket age. But what patterns would be optimum? How does one go about constructing a model of what is optimum? What alternatives exist? What are the forces for and against change? By why processes might future adjustments, to future forces, be facilitated? This article deals with only some of these questions; construction and testing of specific alternative models of future settlement patterns is a further research project.

What are the forces and factors one should consider, in trying to construct an optimum model?

INTRA-FARM FACTORS

One set of factors or forces involves the travel a farmer must make from where he lives to the fields where he grows crops and to the land where his livestock graze or are fed. This in turn depends on the kinds of crops grown and on the soil cultivation requirements. If the land must be plowed, how many days are likely to be spent annually in plowing? The same question can be asked for other cultural operations, but the kinds of cultural operations will depend on the climate, the soil, the crops and the customary methods of crop production. The time spent at each will depend upon the capacity of machinery. Today, with a tractor a man can plow, seed, cultivate, and harvest many times as many acres as his father or grandfather could with animal-drawn machines. Hence, numbers of trips from home to fields is enormously reduced for a given acreage of farm land. Likewise, today the farmer can move from home to field by pickup truck or by auto, in a small fraction of the time that horses or mules would require to travel the

same distances. Today, the tractor can be left in the field until the job is done, and then quickly moved to the next field and job; formerly, work animals were usually returned to the farmstead every night.

Farm size in the United States today is double what it was 30 years ago—approximately 300 acres compared with approximately 150 acres. Moreover, part-ownership of farms has risen greatly. That is, many men today farm some land they own and farm additional land they rent. Farms today are less likely to be contiguous blocks of land, than they once were. When I went to agricultural college in the early 1920's, it was not difficult to show that travel time from home to fields could be minimized by location of farmsteads in the center of the farm; but, even then, most farmers preferred location along the roads, to facilitate social intercourse if for no other reason. Today, there is comparatively less advantage to having the farmstead near the center of a farm, or even on the farm at all. Travel time is much less than formerly, and scattered location of farm tracts may make central location of the home difficult in any case.

Farm size is likely to quadruple by 2000, to perhaps 1100 to 1200 acres on the average, and the tendency toward farming several geographically separated tracts of land to rise still further. This would further weaken the importance of a home location central to the farm land.

Many of the foregoing comments about crops apply to livestock also, depending in part upon the kind of livestock. The frequency with which livestock must be attended and the time required directly affect the best place for keeping them, in relation to where the owner lives. Dairy cows and poultry should ordinarily not be too far away; beef cattle and sheep can graze further away, with less frequent attendance. Farm-grown feeds may be stored in the fields and fed there later— as has often been true with hay in the past. More often, especially with grain and silage, they will be hauled from field to farmstead, stored, and fed later. But, with modern farm hauling equipment, the major costs are in loading and unloading; distance traveled is today far less a factor than formerly.

All of this is to argue in a general way that the intra-farm locational forces are vastly weaker than they once were. The relative costs in money, time, and bother of different home locations with respect to fields, and of livestock with respect to both, will vary from one specific situation to another, but are measurable.

MARKETING OF FARM OUTPUT

The cost and time involved in moving marketable farm output from the farm to the nearest local market depends upon many factors: the volume of output; the perishability of the product, hence the frequency of movement, the special conditions for its protection, and thus the special costs involved; the distance from farm to market and the kind of road; and others. Wool can be moved when convenient, but whole milk must be picked up daily and refrigerated, for instance. When wheat is harvested by combine, it is ordinarily vastly more economical to move it in bulk by truck to the nearest elevator than by any other method. This requires transport closely geared to harvest rate. Livestock can be moved by special trucks from feedlot or pasture to nearest central market.

While farmers can and sometimes do provide their own transport, often it is much cheaper to employ specialized truckers. Their ability to provide adequate equipment to do the job, when needed, may be even more important than cost savings. In either case, loading and unloading costs and time are likely to be relatively more important than costs related to distance traveled. Moreover, trucks or other equipment which pick up farm products at the farm are increasingly more economical as means of moving those same products to a more or less central market, than once was the case. Trucks and trailers are likely to move cattle and hogs direct from farm to slaughtering plant, with no rail shipment. Grain may move to elevators located on railroads, but the differences in cost between additional truck mileage and rail haul may not be large enough to prevent grain movement beyond the nearest elevator, if there are other advantages in doing so. Market milk moves increasingly longer distances by tank truck.

All of this is to argue that costs of marketing farm products are relatively less a locational factor for either farm or first market point than they once were. When a farmer hauled any product to market by horse-drawn wagon, he was anxious to have that market point nearby. Hence small hamlets often existed at rail-sidings. Today, the truck may take the same product 25, 50, 100, 200, or more miles to a more nearly central market, either eliminating rail haul completely or continuing it only from a larger town. There is less need, or no need at all, for formerly intermediate market points.

PURCHASE OF FARM INPUTS AND OF HOME SUPPLIES FOR CONSUMPTION ON THE FARM

A considerably different situation exists for farm inputs and home supplies purchased at some market center and brought to the farm and home for consumption. The volume and kind of purchased farm inputs, and hence the cost of their transport, depends upon the kind of farming following. Feed for dairy cows, poultry, and other livestock, fertilizer, and many other inputs may be purchased. Often they are

delivered to the farm by the seller, but sometimes the farmer hauls them. In either case, there are often considerable advantages of buying in moderately large towns; we shall discuss some of these later. While there are many economies in modern transport, and hence distance from market is less of a locational factor than it once was, yet farmers today purchase a substantially larger proportion of total inputs than they did 30 years or longer ago. Since crops inputs must be used on the land, economies of scale in location affect location of the service town, rather than location of farm headquarters. Location near the land permits reductions in transport costs, but larger towns have their own advantages. Inputs into livestock enterprises, like feed, depend on where the livestock are kept; and this might be on the land where crops are grown, or in more centralized locations. Here, economies of other kinds would also enter. The balance of these forces would depend upon the facts in a particular situation.

The modern farm family is almost as dependent upon frequent access to the supermarket and drugstore as the suburban family. Whereas the farm family once drank milk from its family cow, ate vegetables out of its own garden or went without, ate its own smoked or fresh meat, depending on the season, etc., today the farm family buys all of these in town food stores. Farms may have more frozen food storage and more fresh refrigeration than do city homes, but they are still highly dependent upon frequent access to city food stores. Moreover, farm people today increasingly demand the same freshness and quality in foods that city people demand.

All of this is greatly to *increase* the cost of bringing farm and home inputs from town to farm. If cost were the only factor, this would argue for location of towns close to farms. But quality of services requires larger markets, hence larger towns. The latter means more pressure for moving farm homes into or nearer the large local town or small city, away from the farm itself.

In considering purchased inputs for farm and farm home, one must not overlook mail service, electricity, telephone, and domestic water supply. All of these are essential for modern farm living; each costs someone something, even if the farmer gets free rural delivery. All of these costs, and quality of service considerations, argue for farmsteads nearer the small urban centers.

FARM AND FAMILY SERVICES NORMALLY CONSUMED IN TOWN

The modern farm and its family require a number of services which normally are available only in towns —services which must be bought in town but consumed on the farm. One major farm service which falls in this category is automobile and farm equipment repair. While the farmer can often do the smaller repair jobs on the farm, the larger ones can be done far better and cheaper in town. It would be uneconomic to have the necessary repair and service equipment on the farm, even if the farmer possessed the necessary knowledge and skill. Modern motors and transmissions, to name but two parts, require highly competent workers and often require specialized machinery for their repair. These jobs can thus best be done in town.

Farm children must go to school—high school as well as grade school, and increasingly college as well. The overwhelming evidence is that schools below some minimum size are both costly and poor in quality. To attain even the smallest effective size schools in purely rural territory, children must be transported by bus for considerable distances, if the farm family lives on the land it crops. This is costly in money to the whole community; to the children involved it is also costly in time and often lowers their opportunity to participate in rewarding extracurricular activities.

Farm families need or want church, hospital, library, movie, and other types of services which today can only be available in towns and for considerable numbers of people. Effective services of these kinds are simply impossible in open country locations or in very small towns. The drive-in movie may indeed be in the country at the edge of a town, but this is basically a town location for our present purpose. While the auto and the modern road have enormously lifted the horizons of farm families as far as these services are concerned, yet costs in time and in money are still involved in travel. As a result, most farm families consume less of these services than they would if they lived in town and had the same income.

A special type of town-based services are those involving governmental services of all kinds. The modern farm is much more dependent on governmental services for agriculture than was its predecessor of a generation ago. Federal and state agencies of various kinds will have their offices in rural towns, often in the county-seat town. The farmer will have occasion to visit such offices as part of his farm business operations; to a lesser extent, the farm family will visit them for various aspects of family living.

The types of services discussed in this section must be in town; for reasons to be discussed below, there are important advantages in having them in moderately large rural towns—towns of over 2500 and preferably in towns of 5000, and larger, rather than in the small country towns of 500 to 1500 which were quite important in the days of animal transportation. Because these services must be in town, they will op-

erate powerfully to draw farm people into or toward the towns. In this regard, their effect will be similar to, but perhaps stronger than, the town-drawing power of the goods and services which can be bought in town but taken to the farm for consumption.

ECONOMIES OF SCALE IN GROUP SERVICES

Passing reference has been made to the advantages of larger rather than smaller rural towns, but now those advantages may be considered more explicitly. The costs of virtually all group services probably exhibit a U-shape, with regard to scale of operation. That is, a very small grocery store has a very high costs per unit of sales; costs per unit fall steadily and sometimes sharply as volume increases, up to some point where further increases in volume mean only small reductions in cost per unit; then, often for a considerable range in volume, costs per unit are more or less constant; finally, costs per unit begin to rise as inefficiencies due to increased size begin to be serious and as further economies are small or negligible. This U-shaped curve is nearly ubiquitous. It almost surely applies to clothing, drug, hardware, auto, farm equipment, and other retail stores as well as to groceries. It applies to services, as schools, hospitals, libraries, etc. It also applies to governmental activities, especially to county government.

The pertinent practical questions about these U-shaped cost-volume curves are: how steeply dished are they? at what volume do they begin to flatten out? how wide is the size range of the trough, where costs per unit are nearly constant, regardless of volume? at what volume do costs per unit begin to rise significantly again? how important in absolute dollar terms, are potentially realizable economies, to the average consumer or user? The answers to these questions will vary from product to product, or service to service, and will depend on various specific factors in each situation. But these questions are quantitatively answerable. We may, at this point, hazard the judgment that most farm, rural, and small town areas are in the steeply-falling phase of the U-curve for most goods and services, rarely will scale be at near minimum unit costs and never, we think, in the rising cost phase.

But efficiency in cost of services is only part, and perhaps a small part, of the scale-of-operations problem. Quality and variety of services will almost surely rise as volume increases. A small grocery store at a cross-roads hamlet cannot begin to have the variety and freshness of goods that a modest supermarket in a small city of 5000 population could have. The same is true for other stores and for services—more marked for some than for others. Farm people are increasingly unwilling to accept inferior services; they demand the same goods and services as do urban people with similar incomes. A frequently critical element in attaining reasonably good services is competition among suppliers. It is not eough to have one grocery store of adequate volume; there must often be two, three, or even more. And similarly with other providers of goods and services. Hospitals, schools, libraries, government offices of all kinds, and some other services will be monopolies, but it is highly probable that quality of service will be higher, as well as costs lower, in large towns or small cities than in small towns.

The better quality and lower costs of goods and services in larger than in smaller towns do provide strong drawing power to farmers. If the latter live on the land they farm, they incur larger costs in traveling further to the larger towns, rather than shopping in the small towns. But the sad state of most small rural towns is dramatic evidence that most farmers find the drawing power of the larger towns relatively very powerful. Many farmers drive past the small towns in order to shop in the larger ones. The same drawing power will surely operate also to persuade some farm families to live in towns and commute to work on their farms.

ROADS AND ROAD-RELATED SERVICES

One major element of cost in rural areas is the construction and maintenance of roads, and the provision of some services, such as school bussing, associated with roads. To the farmer of 50 years and more ago, passable all-weather roads were an aspiration of great importance. Roads were typically on every mile-apart section line, as farms were typically quarter-section (160 acre) in size. Over the years, rural road mileage has changed relatively little, but road quality has risen enormously. Many purely farm roads today are paved and most of the rest are gravelled; except in time of deep snow or severe flood, all are readily traveled at all times. Road travel per farm has enormously increased; total travel per capita of the whole national population has risen from about 500 miles before World War I to over 6000 miles today. Although specific data are lacking, it seems highly probable that farmer travel has increased proportionately or more. Good rural roads, therefore, are as important today as they ever were.

But the number of farmsteads per mile of rural road has fallen about in half in the past 30 years; in the next generation, it may well decline to only one-fourth of the present level. On some rural roads, nonfarm population has risen, but on others it has not.

Question may well be raised: is not much of rural America "over-roaded" today? That is, might not major savings be realized by closing extensive road mileages, while maintaining the remaining roads in as good or better shape as at present? Savings would accrue to the whole tax-paying public—the county, in large part, for most of the roads that might be closed are county roads. Farmers would often be inconvenienced, or worse, by road closings. Presumably no section of a road could be closed if a farmer lived along it. If, however, the savings in cost from road closings were sufficiently great, the county could pay the farmer the cost of moving his farmstead to another road, or to town, and still achieve a net saving. If other forces were tending in any case to pull the farm family to another residence location, then such financial help might well be decisive. Savings in school bus operation and in other road-related services might be large if total road mileage were sharply reduced.

MEASURING OPTIMUM RURAL SETTLEMENT PATTERN

The combined effect of all the forces discussed above and possibly of others, could be used to design an optimum rural settlement pattern. Various alternative patterns could be designed and tested. Total costs, and their incidence upon various groups, could be estimated for each alternative pattern. Some costs and some advantages would be hard to measure in monetary terms—the desirability of variety and competition in goods and services or the attractiveness to school children of extracurricular school activities possible only if the family lives in town, etc. While the number of possible models is very large, possibly infinite, as a practical matter models should probably move by rather large discrete steps rather than incrementally. Roads could be 1, 2, or more miles apart, but hardly 1.1 or 1.86 miles apart; farmers could live on their own land or in town or in some clustered fashion with other farmers, but hardly at intermediate points; and so on.

Although the essence of an inquiry into optimum settlement patterns is the consideration and the synthesizing of all relevant factors, yet one has to start somehwere, taking up each factor in turn, and interrelating the others to it, and summarizing the whole into some form of balance sheet, monetary and otherwise. The following seem some of the more important variables and questions:

1. How closely spaced should roads be placed in purely rural areas? At intervals of 1, 2, 3, or more miles? At one set of intervals in one direction, at a much larger set in the right-angle direction?
2. Where should farm families live? On the land they farm, in nucleated clusters along the more widely spaced roads, or in larger towns? If in clusters, how large? How far are farmers willing to commute, from home to land?
3. Where will farmers keep their livestock and store

their crops? On the crop and pasture land, or at the farmstead—assuming these may be widely separated?

4. How many rural service towns, in what locations and of what size can best serve the farm population and its necessary service population? If towns of different sizes and functions are needed, what is the best pattern among them?

5. What units of local government (counties, school districts, etc.) would best serve farm and associated service population, at least cost? How large a territory should be included in each, what should be its functions, and where should its central and branch offices be located?

Each of these factors could vary independently, and a variety of arrangements as to the other factors measured against each. However, attention could well be focused on 3 to 5 major contrasting patterns. Within each pattern, the various variables should be coordinated or harmonized. Thus, one might set up one model with many roads, farmers living on their land, many relatively small towns, relatively small units of local government; another contrasting model might have roads rather widely spaced, many farmers living in town, relatively large towns, relatively large units of local government, etc.

ONE POSSIBLE PATTERN

The foregoing rather general ideas can perhaps be made to seem more realistic by taking a hypothetical example. Let us assume a general farming area, where farms once averaged 150 acres each but now average 300 acres; where roads typically follow section lines and almost every section line has a road, though perhaps only a dirt one; where farmers live on their land; where small towns of 500 to 1000 population are 10 to 12 miles apart, and larger ones less frequently, each with retail and other services typical of such towns; and where counties typically are about 30 miles square. While this is a hypothetical example, several of its factors correspond rather closely to national averages.

Suppose we assume now that in 30 years farms will average 1200 acres in size. Suppose the road network were modified so that roads were 2 miles apart on an east-west axis and 4 miles apart on a north-south axis (or the reverse), to form "super blocks" of 2 by 4 miles. The average farm, if all in one piece, would have 1 mile of road frontage and 2 miles of depth, or 2 miles of frontage and 1 mile of depth. All public roads now within these blocks would be closed and abolished, when this could conveniently be done, and all farmsteads within each block moved, to its periphery or further. There would be no public roads, and few if any permanent private roads, within each block. Each

farmer would travel over his own land in pickup, jeep, or tractor to its more remote parts.

Suppose further that towns were located at intervals of 50 miles apart, on north-south and east-west axes from one another. Those who lived along connecting roads between towns would not have to travel more than 25 miles to the nearest town; those living internally in the major blocks between towns, traveling along roads running in cardinal directions, would never have to travel more than 50 miles to the nearest town. This probably would mean a maximum travel time of one hour—though roads would not be superhighways, they would not be crowded. Some farmers might be willing to travel further to a town they liked better, rather than go to the nearest one. But if every farmer shopped in the town nearest his land, each town would have 1250 farms, or approximately 5000 farm people, as its trade base. If there were an equal population of service people, the town would have a total of 10,000 total customers—a size adequate to provide many services on a minimum adequate scale.

Farmers could live on their land, or at crossroads where the major roads intersect, or in the town. Not all farmers would have to live in the same pattern. Many might live in town. Crop farmers, particularly, who would not have to work on the land every day, might well live in town, and commute when necessary. Or some farmers might have the family home in town, with a mobile home to provide temporary living quarters nearer the seasonal job. Some livestock farmers would live on the land, but others would haul feed to small towns where they lived and had their livestock.

Suppose further that at intervals of 75 miles there were established county seats. Each would have 8 tributary towns, as well as itself performing the local town function for nearby farmers. Each larger town would thus have a total tributary population of 90,000 or more—perhaps not ideal or adequate for some urban functions, but large enough to provide many services that would be uneconomic in the smaller towns. No farmer would be more than 150 miles—3 hours—from his county seat; most would be within 2 hours, and many with 1 hour. Large economies in local government would be possible, with counties of this size and population.

Obviously, every one of the factors in this model could be different: between-road blocks could be 1 × 2, or 2 × 2, or 2 × 4, or 3 × 6, or 4 × 8, or some other number of miles per side; primary towns could be 15, 25, 40, 50, 75, or even 100 miles apart; each could be a county seat, or the latter might include 4, 8, 15, or some other number of tributary towns; one might have small service towns with relatively large central towns at longer intervals, or one might have larger service towns with no ordered ranking of larger towns, and so on. The possibilities are numerous; each could be tested, in more or less quantitative terms, monetary and otherwise, and a "budget" of total living compared for each.

FORCES FOR AND AGAINST CHANGE

What economic and social forces favor, and which oppose, change in the rural settlement pattern?

Among the opposing forces, perhaps the most powerful is the existence of the present settlement pattern. Many people on farms and in small towns have strong sentimental attachments to their present locations which would tend to hold them there even if better housing were available elsewhere. Many in fact have comfortable homes. Schools are often strongly supported, as are other community institutions. There is a strong local political hierarchy in most counties that strongly resists any change that may affect them. Farmers have accustomed ways of doing things, including living-working travel patterns. In a score or more of ways, resistance will arise to *any* change in rural settlement pattern, but especially to planned change of the magnitude we have suggested.

A further factor impeding planned reorganization of rural settlement is the fact that most improvements, replacements, or additions which do occur are incremental in character. That is, the county road department decides to surface or resurface a particular stretch of road, but never is forced to decide on rebuilding the whole road network of the county at one time. Or the school district decides on repairs or additions to present buildings, but does not explicitly reconsider the whole school organization for the county. Or a farmer decides whether to build a new home, or modernize the old one, or move to town, without having at the same time a proposal for a complete remodelling of the local road network and of small town location and functioning. There is almost no mechanism which now brings the whole of the settlement pattern up for scrutiny and review at one time. People make incremental decisions without realization that the whole structure is thereby determined.

On the other hand, there are other powerful forces pushing for change. The highly probable massive reduction in farm numbers over the next generation will force many changes. Many present farm homes will stand idle and ultimately disappear; so will many rural schoolhouses; the small rural town is rapidly disappearing too. Many farm and town homes will be built, or rebuilt, or remodelled; so will many business properties, and governmental structures. Major economic, social, and political changes are under way in the rural countryside, and presumably they might be directed toward a planned goal.

A closely allied force is the fact that present rural and small town settlement pattern often does not provide satisfactory service. Schools are often poor, stores small with poor choices available to consumers, and small units of local government incompetent. Some farm people are fully aware that many rural services are poor, and they are unwilling to accept them. The old distinctions between farm and town have gone, or are going fast; rural people in the future are increasingly going to demand better social, economic and governmental services. Unless they get such better services, they will increasingly leave rural areas and small towns, for larger towns and cities. The dissatisfactions may not be with the settlement pattern as such, but with the kind of life it almost invariably leads to.

Another aspect of this force for change is the fact that economic, social, and governmental services are needlessly costly under the existing pattern of rural settlement, and are likely to grow more so. It seems fairly clear that substantial economies could be achieved by carefully planned changes in settlement pattern. If this tentative conclusion were widely accepted by farm and small town people, considerable pressure for change might be built up.

In any event, actual settlement pattern will always lag behind optimum pattern. Changes will almost surely always be under way; the processes of change are perhaps as important as the goals of change. However, without a goal, change can become mere wandering.

Finally, one major point of this article has been that meaningful research on future rural land settlement pattern is both possible and desirable.

The need for a new rural society

PETER C. GOLDMARK*

The energy crisis, which evolved in part from the great migration from rural America to urban concentrations, has heightened the urgency to solve the nation's population imbalance between the large cities and our vast rural areas. Consequently, society is being threatened by the closely linked urban, rural and energy crises.

Ever since World War II there has been an unprecedented flow of people from the country to the city. This continued migration has created today's huge urban complexes with their unmanageable problems of crime, drugs, pollution, transportation and, now, energy. Conversely, rural communities offer few employment opportunities, inadequate health care and education with no entertainment and cultural activities to reverse the migration of people to the cities. As a result, more than three-quarters of our population concentration is urban and suburban, yet 95 percent of our land is essentially rural.

We have not planned for our future very wisely, and we are on a dangerous trend. A quick glance at history bears this out. During the past 10,000 years little has changed in the physiological, mental and behavioral characteristics of man. Yet, in the last 200 years, science and technology have radically changed our living pattern. If these developments were combined in a single graph and plotted on the scale of man's history, the curve would remain constant for 10,000 years, but shoot up almost vertically during the past 200 years. This upturn would reflect the sudden changes in all aspects of our lives and the rapid rate at which we are depleting our resources.

There is mounting evidence that sociological and environmental problems increase with higher population concentrations. This evidence also shows that man is physiologically and psychologically unprepared for the resultant stresses and strains. For example, four times more crimes per unit population are committed in a city of one-million, compared to

□ From Michigan business review **26**(3):5-9, May 1974.
*Peter C. Goldmark, now deceased, was President and Director of Research of Goldmark Communications Corporation, a subsidiary of Warner Communications Inc. He served as President of CBS Laboratories for 36 years and was world-renowned for his scientific contributions. He held more than 160 patents and was the inventor of the long-playing phonograph record, the first practical television broadcasting system and the electronic video cassette player.

a town of ten thousand. The concentration of pollutants is roughly the same ratio.

Is there a way out of this? I believe there is. One meaningful approach to the problem is the concept of the New Rural Society (NRS), a national pilot study now in its second year and funded by the U.S. Department of Housing and Urban Development through a grant to Fairfield University.

TELECOMMUNICATIONS TECHNOLOGY

The objective of the NRS is to provide some 80-million families with a choice by 1994 of living and working in an attractive rural or urban environment. Basic to the concept of the New Rural Society is the thesis that existing communications technology can be applied imaginatively to business and government operations so that their components can be decentralized to rural areas and continue to operate effectively. Telecommunications techniques will also be adapted to educational needs, health care, cultural and recreational pursuits to upgrade the quality of life in rural areas.

It is essential to the implementation of the NRS plan that a voluntary population redistribution involve the majority of our many thousands of small communities ranging in size from 2,500 to 150,000 people. Appropriate state-wide and community planning will be essential to assure that the growth rate of the individual community be tailored to suit its long-term local objectives. Our studies have shown that such a plan would fully preserve existing land resources, because the growth of the individual communities can take place within their geographical boundaries.

The basic steps in accomplishing the NRS goal were established during our initial studies. These steps are directed toward combining three key ingredients—Places, Jobs and People—under properly planned conditions.

Initial "quality of life" studies by the New Rural Society task force revealed that there are more than 4,000 existing communities in this country with populations ranging from 2,500 to 150,000 which have the potential of becoming viable growth centers with proper planning.

In order to develop workable methods of applying telecommunications technology to rural communities, the Windham Regional Planning Area in northeastern Connecticut was selected with the cooperation of the Governor as a model for study and demonstration purposes. This area is economically undeveloped, and its ten townships are typical of rural Connecticut. It is located approximately 30 miles from Hartford, the state's capitol.

Baseline analyses of the region's living conditions and the expressed attitudes of the residents have been carried out in cooperation with the Windham Regional Planning Agency. Among these analyses was the important consideration of where people prefer to work. Most residents who work in the area want to continue to do so. Those who commute to their jobs in nearby cities, such as Hartford, would rather work where they live if employment opportunities suitable to their individual skills were available. As a corollary, a recent Gallup Poll reported that approximately one-half of all the urban population of the United States would like to live and work in a rural community, beyond the suburbs.

BUSINESS COMMUNICATIONS

The New Rural Society project has placed special emphasis on the uses of telecommunications techniques in order to assure business and government operations that the location of individual units in small communities permits the same continuity of contact with internal and external operations as they do in urban areas. Among the various communications audits undertaken was the important matter of business meetings on an informal or scheduled basis. Back-to-back laboratory studio experiments using a variety of telecommunications methods were conducted during these audits, followed by actual electronic teleconferencing field tests with Connecticut business organizations and government agencies.

Because organizations have found that business conferences can be conducted efficiently with telecommunications as a substitute for face-to-face meetings, the system has drawn considerable attention since the emergence of the national energy shortage. A large Connecticut financial institution, the Union Trust Company, has been working with the NRS team to hold regularly scheduled intercity executive committee meetings for several months using an electronic communications system designed by the NRS team. Union Trust maintains headquarter offices in Stamford and New Haven, located 40 miles apart. In the past, executives from the two locations have had to travel from one city to the other to conduct their business in joint sessions.

The NRS teleconferencing program has not only saved gasoline and travel time for Union Trust officials, but it has actually shortened the duration of each meeting. Participants tend to be more inclined to adhere to the prepared agenda and to confine themselves to relevant discussion.

The system uses special acoustical technology to create individual sound images of the participants. Leased telephone lines link the two communications terminals and specially connected microphones are provided for each participant in the teleconference. As a participant talks, his associates at the other location are able to identify him through the permanent location of his sound. Documents, reports and other graphic materials can be transmitted back and forth during meetings by facsimile equipment for review by the participants.

The comprehensive NRS field tests using various methods of electronic teleconferencing have shown that a two-way, point-to-point video link is, in most cases, economically prohibitive. The tests also demonstrated that the new audio system can equal or surpass the performance of a video system at a fraction of the initial capital and operating costs. The practicality of audio teleconferencing is a major step in the over-all objective of the New Rural Society to provide business and government with the tools to operate effectively regardless of a community's location or size.

This application of telecommunications to major problem areas providing employment opportunities for rural communities exemplifies the philosophy upon which the New Rural Society concept is based.

APPLICATION IN HEALTH CARE

Another pressing problem for most rural areas is the lack of trained personnel for primary health care. Our studies have revealed that in the Windham Region the ratio of primary care physicians to the population is half that of the national average—roughly one-quarter doctor per 1,000 people.

With the assistance of the New Rural Society team, primary care physicians of the Windham Region have organized to seek methods of alleviating the situation. This calls for the training and use of paramedical personnel supported by telecommunications facilities. The goal is to optimize utilization of the area's hospital and physician resources and to take advantage of the diversified services available at large medical care complexes in nearby larger cities.

One approach by the NRS study team is training paramedical personnel to provide preventive, curative and rehabilitative services at low cost with existing telecommunications technology and systems.

To improve medical service to rural areas covered by the few and often overburdened rural physicians, a team approach to health delivery is contemplated. In this approach, the physician remains the central person, assisted by a nurse and by a paramedic driving a small mobile health bus equipped with emergency and diagnostic equipment. The physician or nurse will be able to communicate with the "medibus" from his office over a two-way FM radio link capable of carrying simultaneously voice, facsimile and diagnostic data. Calls from patients would be handled by the nurse and referred to the paramedic or, when necessary, to the doctor. Another communication link will connect the physician's office with the nearest hospital for certain emergencies.

In addition, the physician assistant would also be responsible for doing periodic screening of teachers and students in nearby rural schools for early detection and treatment of illness.

Adequate health care is essential to businesses when considering relocation to know that their personnel will be provided with sufficient and efficient medical services when they are needed.

Along with assurance of proper health care, people who are considering a community as a place in which to live are equally concerned with the quality of educational facilities for their children.

Electronic teaching aids can bridge much of the gap between big-city and small-town educational resources. A number of rural schools can pool closed-circuit television, for example, and reap the benefit of pre-programmed learning material, prepared by outstanding educators.

Telecampuses can be established to bring higher education to small communities. Audio/video telecommunications can make it possible for people to listen to lectures and participate in classroom discussions.

The continuing output by a small community of its youth educated to their fullest capacities is an incentive to a business organization to consider location in a town where manpower needs are likely to be available.

When a community can provide employment, effective health care, broad educational facilities, what else does it need to make it an attractive place in which to work and live? It needs facilities to provide its people with recreation and entertainment, and opportunities for cultural pursuits of individual appeal. It needs all the advantages, including public services, which people can find in urban areas.

As a focal point of these needed facilities, the New Rural Society team has proposed a Community Communications Center where the local citizenry can find under one roof a multitude of services provided by electronic communications, both for intracommunity contact and for contact with other communities and cities.

ENTERTAINMENT SATELLITES

Complementing the concept of the Center is a proposed ENT/SAT (Entertainment Satellite) system. Use of FCC-approved domestic satellite television channels would enable the transmission live, as they occur, of theater and concert performances, of major sports events, of all important happenings to a nation-wide chain of Community Communications Centers. Receiving and transmitting equipment would be standard Center facilities.

A major feature of the Community Communications Center would be a multi-purpose theater or auditorium, equipped for television reception and transmission as well as for conventional conference usage. It would contain a large-image television projector to enable video presentation of the wealth of material brought in from outside by the ENT/SAT system and other sources, as well as offering programs by local remote pick-up and from a library of video recordings.

The auditorium stage would be large enough to serve as a meeting area for the community's social and service groups. The use of the stage as a meeting area would permit the broadcasting of proceedings to home receivers and to other community centers. The theater's technological equipment would make it possible to televise and record or transmit any activity from the stage—locally produced plays, musical performances and so on.

A speaker from anywhere in the world, live or on tape, could address a community audience assembled in the theater. In these days of drastic shortages, state and federal elected officials, without consuming precious fuel for travel, could meet electronically with their local constituents to discuss important issues at hand.

Electronic mail service would be maintained in the Community Communications Center. Copying and printing services could be provided for businesses not regularly using facsimile.

The Community Communications Center could establish a shared computer service for local business. Remote access terminals would be provided on a time charge basis and connected to commercial interactive computer systems. For more extensive computer needs, standard peripheral devices, such as card readers, punches and high speed printers, could be operated locally by linkage with remote computer systems.

NRS AND ENERGY

These are examples of how a New Rural Society can be achieved to benefit the large city and the rural town in America; but this process will also permit us to preserve our energy resources. Stopgap measures to save fuel will not accomplish lasting results.

The huge consumption of oil by our urban centers can be eased only to a limited degree by use-restrictions.

We have plenty of coal, but if we return to this source of energy for our large cities, the concentration of pollution in the air becomes prohibitive.

If people could live again in a decentralized fashion, power generation could also be dispersed and the resultant pollution can become tolerable.

Fuel for transportation uses up one-quarter of the country's entire energy demands. Automobiles consume about half of this amount of which one-half is used by automobiles for daily commuting to and from work.

The New Rural Society plan envisions people living and working in the same rural community. With proper local planning, the growth of these communities could ensure that new businesses, homes, shopping centers and other community services would be located to encourage walking or bicycling. Under such conditions, significant amounts of fuel could be saved.

As we have discovered in our NRS studies, many people, given the option, would prefer to live and work in the same small town. Lack of planning is responsible for much of our complex situation today.

The tremendous geographical imbalance of our population distribution, brought about largely by business concentration in urban centers, has been the major factor in the current economic and social decline and the depletion of our natural resources. We must have the courage and the wisdom to realize that our present course is leading to the decline of society, as we know it.

It has been proposed that new towns be built to accommodate more people. A few have been built. The truth is that a new town would have to be completed every second day from now to 1994 to accommodate the population which may choose to live in rural areas.

In rural America, thousands of small, potentially viable towns already exist. On this foundation can be built a New Rural Society to provide jobs and services for those already living in these towns and for those who will want to move into them from the large cities.

Residential preferences and population distribution

GLENN V. FUGUITT and JAMES J. ZUICHES*

ABSTRACT

Public opinion research has revealed decided preferences for living in rural areas and small towns, and proponents of population deconcentration have interpreted this as support for their policies. This study, based on a national sample, yielded similar results, but when we introduced the additional possibility of a preference for proximity to a larger city, then the rural areas preferred were found, for most respondents, to be those within the commuting range of a metropolitan central city. Although persons wishing to live near large cities were found to be looking for the same qualities of living sought by those who prefer a more remote location, these findings are not, in general, consistent with the argument that public preferences support strategies of population dispersal into nonmetropolitan areas. Instead they indicate that most of those who wish to live in a different location favor the peripheral metropolitan ring areas that have, in fact, been growing rapidly by in-migration.

☐ From Demography **12**(3):491-504, Aug. 1975.

*Glenn V. Fuguitt is in the Department of Rural Sociology, University of Wisconsin, Madison, Wisconsin 53706. James J. Zuiches is in the Department of Sociology, Michigan State University, East Lansing, Michigan 48824.

INTRODUCTION

Recent social trends relating to the decline of central cities, urban sprawl, rural depopulation, and disparities among communities have served to focus attention on the need for population distribution policies in the United States (see, for example, Ad Hoc Subcommittee on Urban Growth, 1969; Advisory Commission on Intergovernmental Relations, 1968; Beale, 1972; Commission on Population Growth and the American Future, 1972; Fuguitt, 1971; Hansen, 1970; Morrison, 1970; National Goals Research Staff, 1970; President's National Advisory Commission on Rural Poverty, 1967). Specific recommendations have included proposals to develop depressed rural areas, to encourage migration to middle-sized cities, and to plan for more orderly urban expansion. Various strategies also have been suggested to redistribute the population away from metropolitan areas and to retain population in nonmetropolitan areas.

An important element figuring in this discussion is concern about public preferences and attitudes on desirable places to live. A policy that provides community and housing options compatible with preferences should have a greater chance of success and could be expected to lessen any discrepancy between the actual and ideal distribution of the population. That such a discrepancy exists is one argument used by proponents of population deconcentration. For more than a decade, national public opinion surveys have found a decided preference for living in small towns and rural areas as contrasted to larger cities. Thus the coincidence of public interest and private preference is pointed to as a positive reason for a population dispersal policy since, "except for the economic pressures, many city dwellers would eagerly move to the country" (National Goals Research Staff, 1970, p. 54).

Despite this stated dissatisfaction with large cities, there has been no major exodus to medium-sized

cities, small towns and rural areas of nonmetropolitan counties. In fact, during the 1950's over 1,400 nonmetropolitan counties experienced such heavy out-migration that they declined in population, and about 1,300 nonmetropolitan counties declined in the 1960's. Since 1960 a number of formerly declining nonmetropolitan areas have begun to grow (see Hansen, 1973; Beale, 1974), and since 1970 a net migration gain has been reported for the nonmetropolitan sector as a whole. Nevertheless, Current Population Survey results (U.S. Bureau of the Census, 1974) indicate that between 1970 and 1973 the rate of net migration gain for metropolitan areas outside central cities was three times the rate for the nonmetropolitan United States.

In this paper, we offer evidence that this paradox between expressed public opinion and actual migration can be explained at least in part by the way residential preference questions have been asked in earlier surveys. Whereas previous studies have generally considered only the *size* of place in which respondents prefer to reside, we have further distinguished places according to *proximity* to large cities. Our initial work

Table 1. A comparison of surveys of residential preferences in the United States from 1948 to 1972

Preferred residence	Roper (1948)	Gallup 1966	Gallup 1968	Gallup 1970	Gallup 1972	National Wildlife Federation (1969)	Harris (1970)	Population Commission (1971)	Zuiches-Fuguitt (Wisconsin) (1971) Total	Within 30 miles	Beyond 30 miles
Cities	15%	22%	18%	18%	13%	6%	21%	17%[d]	10%[e]		
Suburbs	20	28	25	26	31	18	27	18[d]	11		
Small towns	41[a]	31	29	31	32	25	31	30[d]	44[e]	28%[e]	16%[e]
Rural areas	24	18[b]	27[b]	24[b]	23[b]	54[c]	16[b]	34[d]	35	21	14
No opinion, other	0	1	1	1	1	1	5	1	0		
Total	100	100	100	100	100	104	100	100	100		

[a]Includes respondents preferring small cities and small towns. The Roper question was: "If you had a choice, where would you like to live—in the country, a small town, a small city, a suburb, a large city?"

[b]Farm used instead of rural area in the Gallup question, which was: "If you could live anywhere in the U.S. that you wanted to, would you prefer a city, suburban area, small town or farm?" Similarly, Harris question was: "If you could find just what you wanted in the way of a place to live and didn't have to worry about where you worked, would you want to live in a city, suburb, a small town away from a city, on a farm, or where?"

[c]Includes respondents preferring rural areas (30 percent), mountains (15 percent) and seashore (9 percent). The National Wildlife Federation Survey permitted multiple responses and had six possible choices.

[d]"Large and medium" cities combined; suburbs of "large" and "medium" cities combined; small cities and small towns combined; and farm and open country combined in this table. The Population Commission question was: "Where would you prefer to live? On a farm, open country (not on a farm), in a small town, in a small city, in a medium size city, in a large city, in a suburb of a medium size city, in a suburb of a large city?"

[e]Medium-sized city and small city or town combined. Question was: "If you could live in any size community you wanted to, would you prefer to live in a large city of 50,000 or over, in a suburb next to a large city, in a medium-sized city, in a small city or town, or in a rural area." For those giving one of the last three options, this was followed by: "Would you prefer to live within commuting distance—say within 30 miles—of a large city, or be farther away from a large city?"

Sources: 1948 Roper study cited in Lee et al., 1971, p. 33; Gallup results in American Institute of Public Opinion, 1970, and National Area Development Institute, 1973; National Wildlife Federation survey reported in National Wildlife Federation, 1969; Harris survey in Louis Harris and Associates, Inc., 1970; Population Commission results from internal memorandum of The Population Commission, 1971; Zuiches-Fuguitt from Zuiches and Fuguitt, 1972.

(Zuiches and Fuguitt, 1972) was based on a survey of Wisconsin residents. This paper reports the results of a nationwide sample survey which allow us to draw conclusions relating to preferences by city size and proximity to a metropolitan center for the adult population of the continental United States.

PREVIOUS RESEARCH ON RESIDENTIAL PREFERENCES

Some previous results on preferences by size of community are reported and cited in Table 1. Because of differences in the questions asked, these distributions are not precisely comparable; yet the findings are broadly similar, showing that (1) most respondents would like to live in small towns and rural areas and (2) the proportion having this preference exceeds that currently residing there. All of these studies, however, have a common limitation: they fail to distinguish certain key relational characteristics of places people claim to prefer. Among these, nearness to a large city may be of paramount importance. Failure to distinguish proximity differences could well mix, on the one hand, the respondent who prefers the small town or country milieu of, say, Philadelphia's suburban Main Line with, on the other hand, the respondent who has a small town in central Nebraska in mind. The same "small town" descriptor on the survey can have quite different meanings to different respondents.

This potentially misleading effect was first examined in our statewide survey of Wisconsin in 1971. After an initial size-of-place question, we asked respondents not preferring a large city whether or not they would prefer to live within 30 miles of a large city. Judging from the initial question, our results broadly agreed with those of Gallup, the Population Commission, and others. The distance-qualifying question, however, showed that well over one-half of the 79 percent preferring to live in small towns and rural areas stated that they would like their residence to be within 30 miles of a city over 50,000 in size (compare last two columns of Table 1). This finding shed considerable light on the paradox noted above: the realization of these preferences would result in a net movement out of central cities and nonmetropolitan areas and into metropolitan rings, which is consistent with the overall trends that prevailed in Wisconsin at least through 1970 (Zuiches and Fuguitt, 1972).

A study by Dillman and Dobash (1972) done at about the same time in Washington State also casts doubt on the interpretation of earlier surveys that a high proportion of citizens would prefer to live in small towns and rural areas away from large cities.

Since their questions were worded quite differently, the results are not shown in Table 1.

QUESTIONS AND SAMPLE

The data reported here are from a nationwide study building on our earlier work for Wisconsin. Basic questions very similar to those included in the Wisconsin 1971 survey were included in NORC's Amalgam Survey of the total noninstitutional U.S. population 18 and over conducted in November 1972. The questions were worded as follows:

"First, we are interested in the kind of community you would prefer to live in now, if you had your choice.

1. In terms of size, if you could live in any size community you wanted, which one of these would you like best?

    A large metropolitan city (over 500,000 in population)

    A medium-sized city (50,000 to 500,000 in population)

    A smaller city (10,000 to 50,000 in population) (ASK A)

    A town or village (under 10,000 in population) (ASK A)

    In the country, outside of any city or village (ASK A)

    Don't know

A. If smaller than medium-sized city:

    In terms of *location*, would you like that place to be within 30 miles of a large or medium-sized city, or would you rather be farther away from such a city?

    Within 30 miles

    Farther away

    Don't know/doesn't matter"

Similar questions yielded classifications with the same categories for present residence and residence at time of birth. In addition we obtained information on the respondent's view of specific aspects of communities as related to his preferences and a ranking of preferred locations. These were analyzed giving particular attention to the relation between actual and preferred residence.

Those interviewed appeared to have little difficulty responding to specific questions on distance from a large city and size of place. To get an impression of how accurately respondents could determine whether or not they live within 30 miles of a city over 50,000, the sample segments, usually census tracts, were classified by distance edge-to-edge to places of that size. We found that 64 respondents who were in PSU's more than 40 miles from a large city reported being within 30 miles of such a place, and 23 respondents who were in PSU's less than 20 miles from a large city reported living more than 30 miles away. These 87 were less than 6 percent of the total number interviewed, so we concluded that estimating distance is not a serious problem. Similarly, we compared reported present location with a classification of PSU's by size of place and found only 14 percent of the respondents differed by more than one class interval. Moreover, inspection shows that most of these deviant responses were plausible as, for example, some who reported being in large cities appeared to be in rural territory adjacent to a large city according to the PSU designation based on the 1970 census.

The NORC sample is a multi-stage area probability sample down to the block level, where quota sampling is used. The primary sampling units are SMSA's and nonmetropolitan counties. Because of the quota feature, tests of significance are not appropriate. For details of the sampling procedure, see King and Richards (1972).

RESIDENCE AND PREFERENCES

In Table 2 actual residence is compared with preferred residence according to both size of place and proximity to a large city. Almost one-half of the re-

Table 2. Actual and preferred residence of respondents by size of place and location with respect to a large city, United States, 1972

Type of location	Current residence	Preferred residence[a]
City over 500,000	20%	9%
City 50,000-500,000	24	16
Subtotal	44	25
Within 30 miles of city over 50,000		
City 10,000-50,000	13	16
Places under 10,000	10	15
Rural area	11	24
Subtotal	34	55
More than 30 miles from city over 50,000		
City 10,000-50,000	6	6
Places under 10,000	6	4
Rural area	9	9
Subtotal	21	19
Not ascertained	1	1
Total	100	100
Number of cases	1,481	1,481

[a]Forty-eight persons who responded "don't know" or "doesn't matter" to living within 30 miles of a city were given a distance classification consistent with their current residence in this and succeeding tables.

Source: National Opinion Research Center Amalgam Survey conducted in November, 1972.

spondents in this nationwide survey reported living in cities of over 50,000 population, one-third within 30 miles of a city of 50,000 or more, and 20 percent in more distant locations. If everyone were to live in the location that he preferred, however, the distribution of population would look somewhat different. Under those conditions only one-quarter would live in large cities, and over one-half would be in easy commuting distance of such places. The proportion living more distant, however, would remain almost the same. The largest drop in percentage, were such a shift to come about, would be for cities over 500,000, and the largest gain would be for rural areas near large cities.

Our results accord well with previous survey findings (shown in Table 1) if proximity to a large city is ignored. The Gallup and Harris surveys of 1970 and 1972, for example, show 55 and 47 percent, respectively, wanting to live in small towns or on farms. The Population Commission study and both our Wisconsin and U.S. surveys show almost two-thirds to three-fourths of the respondents preferring small cities and towns or rural areas.

Our data, however, reveal a key *relational* prerequisite for desiring to live in small towns and rural areas: Table 2 shows that only nine percent of all respondents in the nationwide survey would prefer to live in rural areas, and another ten percent in small and medium-sized towns, if these locales were more than 30 miles from a large city. (Comparable percentages for Wisconsin are 14 and 16.) Many people respond positively to the idea of rural living, but not where it would entail disengagement from the metropolitan complex. This suggests a clear desire to have the best of both environments—which may include proximity to metropolitan employment, services, schools and facilities, along with the advantages of the smaller local-residential community for familial and neighborhood activities.

A complete cross-classification of respondents by their reported current and preferred residence is given in Table 3. The percentages in the principal diagonal represent those respondents whose actual and preferred types of residence coincide. This group includes 42 percent of the persons interviewed; the other 58 percent preferred a setting that differs from their current location. In only two residence categories (places under 10,000 within 30 miles and rural areas within 30 miles) do current and preferred residences coincide for more than one-half the respondents. For communities within the 30-mile zone, there is also a systematic inverse relationship between size of residence and preference for this residence. Only 36 percent of the residents in cities over 500,000 se-

Table 3. Preferred residence by current residence, United States, 1972[a]

	Preferred residence										
			With 30 miles of city over 50,000			More than 30 miles from city over 50,000					
Current residence	City over 500,000	City 50,000-500,000	City 10,000-50,000	Place under 10,000	Rural area	City 10,000-50,000	Place under 10,000	Rural area	Not ascertained	Total	Number
City over 500,000	36%	15%	14%	12%	11%	3%	4%	5%	0%	100%	291
City 50,000-500,000	4	41	17	8	20	6	2	2	0	100	353
Within 30 miles of city over 50,000											
City 10,000-50,000	3	7	43	13	14	7	3	8	2	100	194
Places under 10,000	2	4	10	51	23	1	6	3	0	100	151
Rural area	1	3	7	4	67	1	2	14	1	100	159
More than 30 miles from city over 50,000											
City 10,000-50,000	5	16	15	3	11	35	7	8	0	100	88
Places under 10,000	0	7	4	27	21	6	21	14	0	100	94
Rural area	2	1	1	9	37	1	2	45	2	100	126

[a]This table excludes 25 respondents who did not answer the question on current residence.
Source: National Opinion Research Center Amalgam Survey conducted in November, 1972.

lected this type as their preferred location, but 67 percent of near (less than 30 miles) rural residents selected near rural areas as preferred. The least "popular" locations, as measured here, are large cities and medium and small towns away from a large center. Diagonal values for these residence types are 36, 35 and 21, respectively. This is true also for the Wisconsin study, with diagonal values, respectively, of 28, 22, and 33.

Most of the differences between actual residence and preferences indicate a desire for smaller and/or more remote locations. About 40 percent of the responses are above and to the right of the diagonal, and only 17 percent below and to the left. Overall, however, the data show the predominance of suburban and fringe-type locations in residential preferences. These are the categories with the highest agreement between residence and preferences and the categories most preferred by people currently living elsewhere.

This generalization is shown clearly by combining the categories of residence and preference into three groups: cities over 50,000; smaller places and rural areas near large cities; and smaller places and rural areas away from large cities. Of people currently living in cities over 50,000, 52 percent would prefer smaller places. Conversely, of people not currently living in large cities, only eight percent would prefer to do so. More than three-fourths of those now living in smaller places near large cities would prefer this type of location, as would 42 percent of those not now living there. Of those more than 30 miles from a large city, over one-half preferred living nearer. But only 13 percent of the people living near or in a large city chose a more remote location. Table 4 is the cross-classification of current and preferred residences using this trichotomy of residence types. The remainder of the analysis is based on data grouped in this way, with the three categories referred to as "big city," "near" and "away," for convenience. (Whether a city of 50,000 is indeed big depends, of course, on one's viewpoint.)

ORIGINS AND RESIDENTIAL PREFERENCES

Is a respondent's residential preference related to where he grew up or formerly lived? Table 5 shows the relationships between the size and location of birthplaces (as reported by respondents) and preferred residence and current residence for the three location types. Comparison of origin with current residence indicates the movement from more remote areas into big cities and their peripheries which has taken place over the last generation. If the preferred residences were realized, however, there would be a reverse shift out of cities, so that the proportion of residents in large cities and in rural areas would be less than the proportion born there; whereas the periphery of large cities would again capture an increasing proportionate share.

Table 4. Preferred residence by current residence trichotomized, United States, 1972[a]

| Current residence | Number | Preferred residence | | | |
		City over 50,000	Other, less than 30 miles from city	Other, more than 30 miles from city	Total
City over 50,000	641	48%	41%	11%	100
Other, less than 30 miles from city	500	7	78	15	100
Other, more than 30 miles from city	306	9	44	47	100
Total	1,447	25	55	20	100

[a]Thirty-four cases were dropped due to "don't know" or "no response" to the preference or the residence question.
Source: National Opinion Research Center Amalgam Survey conducted in November, 1972.

Table 5. Proportion of respondents born in, living in, and preferring a residence type[a]

	City over 50,000	Other, less than 30 miles from city	Other, more than 30 miles from city	Total
Residence of parents when born	30%	30%	40%	100%
Current residence	44	35	21	100
Preferred residence	25	55	20	100

[a]N = 1,380 respondents who answered these three questions.
Source: National Opinion Research Center Amalgam Survey conducted in November, 1972.

Next we considered the association of place of origin as well as current residence with the preferences given for each of the three general residence types. Each cell of Table 6 gives the percent of people in the current residence and origin indicated by the row, who prefer the residence type indicated by the column heading. By comparing the first two rows, and the third and fourth rows, one can see the effect of origin separately for the two current residence possibilities. These differences are all consistent in direction and similar in size. The next to the last line of the table gives the average origin difference over the two current residence groupings, values ranging from 7 to 12 percentage points. The last line gives corresponding average differences between groups similar in

Table 6. Percent of respondents preferring a type of residence by current residence and residence of birth, United States, 1972 (value in each cell is percent of respondents preferring this residence type)

| Current residence and residence of birth | Type of residence | | |
	Big city	Near	Away
Current residence in area indicated			
Origin			
In area	57%	84%	49%
Not in area	40	74	41
Current residence not in area indicated			
Origin			
In area	14	53	16
Not in area	6	39	11
Average differences			
Origin effect	12	12	7
Current residence effect	39	33	31

Source: National Opinion Research Center Amalgam Survey conducted in November, 1972.

origin but different in current residence (line 1 compared with 3, and 2 compared with 4). These values are also consistent, and about three times the size of the average origin differences. Thus current residence has an important effect in that people who live in an area are more likely to prefer it than people who do not, regardless of origin. But place of origin, representing an influence which may be more remote in time, also has a smaller but consistent effect on people's preferences for those preferring to live in a big city, near a big city, or farther away. Mazie and Rawlings (1972) reported similar results with their residence categories.

REASONS FOR PREFERENCES

After stating their preference for a community size and location, respondents were read a list of reasons people might have for preferring to live in one kind of community or another and asked whether or not each was one of their reasons. The percent of people reporting each reason was tabulated by the three location types and graphed in Figure 1. In order to clarify the distinction between locations, the reasons were ordered by the percent of people who preferred to live away from a big city reporting them. These ranged from 13 percent for higher wages to 89 percent for less crime and danger.

This ordering gives a clear discrimination between big city and other preferences. Those preferring small towns and rural areas near big cities have almost the same pattern of response as persons preferring more remote locations. People who want to live near big cities, then, seek the same qualities as those preferring to live farther away; but both groups differ markedly from those who prefer large cities. This latter group differentially seeks higher wages or salaries, better job opportunities, the possibility of contacts with a variety of people, better schools, nearness to family or friends, and recreation or cultural facilities.

Almost all those preferring more rural locations mentioned quality of life factors often associated with the country: less crime, quality air and water, better place for children. On the other hand, only about 20 percent favored more rural locations because of better job opportunities or higher wages there. These five reasons showed the maximum differences between the urban and rural preference groups.

The analysis of reasons was extended by controlling for present location. Present location made little difference, however, in comparison to the differences between preferences for big cities and more rural areas. The people wanting to live in a different area thus respond in terms of the same qualities as those already there who wish to remain.

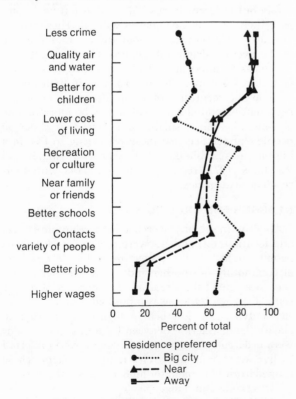

Fig. 1. Proportion of respondents stating a reason is important in their residential preference by type of preference. Reasons have been ranked according to proportion of mention by respondents who prefer an "away" location.

Tables of reasons also were constructed separately by categories of age, income, and sex, but differences were small and not systematic. Perhaps people are simply responding to generally recognized stereotypes concerning the types of residences they prefer. The fact that over 40 percent of those preferring big cities gave reasons of less crime and danger there, and better quality of air and water, suggests that many respondents were simply assenting to factors desirable in any community. Nevertheless, systematic differences did emerge between those preferring big cities and those preferring other locations. A thorough analysis of possible reasons would require considerably more interview time than was available to us for detailed questions tailored to specific preferences.

THE RANKING OF PREFERENCES

An unanswered question is whether the basic preference pattern described in our data is for the metropolitan area itself (with the smaller city or open country therein viewed as a more pleasant living alternative); or whether basic preference is really for small towns or rural areas themselves (with proximity to a big city representing a kind of cost paid for urban advantage). In an effort to ferret out this subtle distinction, we asked respondents to rank in order of preference three types of location: a city over 50,000, a smaller city or rural area within 30 miles of a city over 50,000, and a smaller city or rural area more than 30 miles from a city over 50,000. The results are given in Table 7 for persons classified by current residence. The first-rank choices to these questions show a somewhat lower proportion preferring large cities (19 versus 25 percent) and a somewhat higher proportion preferring remote rural areas (26 versus 20 percent) than the trichotomous classification of responses

Table 7. Preference ranking of residence types by current residence, United States, 1972

Preference ranking by respondent			Current residence			
Big city	**Near**	**Away**	**Big city**	**Near**	**Away**	**Total**
First	Second	Third	33%	4%	3%	17%
First	Third	Second	4	1	—	2
Second	First	Third	17	9	5	12
Third	First	Second	32	60	42	43
Second	Third	First	1	1	0	1
Third	Second	First	13	25	50	25
Total			100	100	100	100
Number			637	500	302	1,439

Source: National Opinion Research Center Amalgam Survey conducted in November, 1972.

based on the two initial residential preference questions. Such response differences are to be expected in survey research, and the general conclusions of the study are the same with either preference measure.

The pattern of first and second choices is of interest here. Whereas 43 percent of the respondents ranked a near location first and a more rural location second, only 12 percent ranked a near location first and a big city second (compare line 4 and line 3). In all only 32 percent ranked the big city either first or second, whereas 71 percent ranked an away location either first or second, and 97 percent ranked the near location first or second. Such results indicate that the desire for a small town or rural setting is extremely pervasive and that most respondents view the advantages of living in such a setting even at some distance from a large city as preferable to living in a large city.

DISCUSSION AND SUMMARY

Antiurbanism in America appears to be qualified: although many people do not prefer to live in big cities, few want to live far from one. Previous survey data on residential preferences considerably overestimated the popularity of nonmetropolitan rural environments by failing to define them precisely in people's minds. When respondents are allowed to express a preference for the degree of proximity to a large city of over 50,000 population, they favor the peripheral metropolitan ring areas that have, in fact, been gaining rapidly in population.

These findings have a direct meaning for policy, since they call into question arguments for population dispersal into nonmetropolitan areas based on public preferences alone. Other worthy objectives may be served by such a national goal, but the proportion of people eager to move to a remote nonmetropolitan setting appears to be small and balanced by an equal number already in nonmetropolitan areas who want to move closer to a big city.

The findings illuminate an issue of population distribution policy which, like the controversy about whether or not voluntary family planning can suffice to achieve lowered growth rates, hinges on the matter of what voluntarism would produce. Our research suggests that, if people were to sort themselves out into the kinds of residential environments they claim to prefer, there would be no massive exodus to remote areas. Americans' residential preferences, when properly interpreted, lend no credence to the view that measures aiding dispersal to nonmetropolitan areas would simply be satisfying a large unmet public need, although such measures may be justified on other grounds.

Despite the massive movements into metropolitan areas during this century, we found little evidence of a desire by migrants to return to their place of rural origin. We found that origins influence preferences but that present location is considerably more important. Furthermore, this small origin effect prevailed for those born in all three types of location considered, not just in rural areas. As Mazie and Rawlings (1972) point out, the place-of-origin effect may move aggregate preferences toward big cities for later generations having higher proportions born there.

These conclusions should not minimize the favorable orientation to rural and small town life expressed by the respondents on this as well as previous surveys. The reasons given here for preferences show that the monly held advantages of rural life are believed to be present even within proximity of a large city. The ranking question showed that four out of five of the respondents who preferred to live near large cities as a first choice gave rural areas away from large cities as a second choice, rather than the large city itself. Among all respondents two-thirds ranked the large city least desirable of the three options.

The discrepancy between preference and current residence which we found is consistent with trends in U.S. population redistribution over the past several decades. But as yet there is little direct evidence concerning the interrelations between residential preferences and migration behavior or between both of these and other attitudinal variables such as community satisfaction. Such knowledge would increase our understanding of population movements and is needed by those interested in formulating and attempting to implement population distribution policies on a national or local level.

ACKNOWLEDGMENTS

This work was supported by the College of Agricultural and Life Sciences, University of Wisconsin, Madison, through a cooperative agreement with the Economic Development Division, U.S. Department of Agriculture; by the Graduate School Research Committee, University of Wisconsin; by the Agricultural Experiment Station (Article No. 6605), the College of Social Science, Michigan State University; and by the Center for the Study of Metropolitan Problems, NIMH (MH23489-01). Our questions were included on the November 1972 Amalgam Survey of the National Opinion Research Center, Chicago, Illinois. Analysis was done on the computer of the Center for Demography and Ecology, University of Wisconsin, provided through a grant from the Center for Population Research of the National Institute of Child Health and Human Development. We are grateful to Calvin L. Beale, David R. Brown, Philip Groth, Gordon DeJong, and especially two anonymous reviewers, who made helpful comments on earlier drafts of this paper.

REFERENCES

Ad Hoc Subcommittee on Urban Growth. 1969. Population Trends. Hearings for use of the Committee on Banking and Currency, House of Representatives. Washington, D.C.: U.S. Government Printing Office.

Advisory Commission on Intergovernmental Relations. 1968. Urban and Rural America: Policies for Future Growth. Report A-32. Washington, D.C.: U.S. Government Printing Office.

American Institute of Public Opinion. 1970. Gallup Opinion Index, Report No. 57. Princeton: The Gallup Organization, Inc.

Beale, Calvin L. 1972. Rural and Nonmetropolitan Population Trends of Significance to National Population Policy. Pp. 665-677 in Sara Mills Mazie (ed.), Commission on Population Growth and the American Future, Vol. V, Population, Distribution and Policy. Washington, D.C.: U.S. Government Printing Office.

————. 1974. Rural Development: Population and Settlement Prospects. Journal of Soil and Water Conservation 29:23-27.

Commission on Population Growth and the American Future. 1972. Population and the American Future. Washington, D.C.: U.S. Government Printing Office.

Dillman, Don A., and Russell P. Dobash. 1972. Preferences for Community Living and Their Implications for Population Redistribution. Washington Agricultural Experiment Station, Bulletin 764. Pullman: Washington State University.

Fuguitt, Glenn V. 1971. The Places Left Behind: Population Trends and Policy for Rural America. Rural Sociology 36:449-470.

Hansen, Niles M. 1970. Rural Poverty and the Urban Crisis: A Strategy for Regional Development. Bloomington: Indiana University Press.

————. 1973. The Future of Nonmetropolitan America: Studies in the Reversal of Rural and Small Town Population Decline. Lexington: Lexington Books.

Louis Harris and Associates, Inc. 1970. A Survey of Public Attitudes towards Urban Problems and toward the Impact of Scientific and Technical Developments. Study No. 2040. New York: Louis Harris and Associates, Inc.

King, Benjamin F., and Carol Richards. 1972. The 1972 NORC Probability Sample. Unpublished preliminary draft. Chicago: National Opinion Research Center.

Lee, Everett S., J. C. Bresee, K. P. Nelson, and D. A. Patterson. 1971. An Introduction to Urban Decentralization Research. Department of Housing and Urban Development ORNL-HUD-3. Oak Ridge: Oak Ridge National Laboratory.

Mazie, Sara Mills, and Steve Rawlings. 1972. Public Attitude towards Population Distribution Issues. Pp. 599-615 in Sara Mills Mazie (ed.), Commission on Population Growth and the American Future, Vol. 5, Population, Distribution, and Policy. Washington, D.C.: U.S. Government Printing Office.

Morrison, Peter A. 1970. The Rationale for a Policy on Population Distribution. Santa Monica: The RAND Corporation.

National Area Development Institute. 1973. Public Opinion Favors Nonmetro Areas. Area Development Interchange 3:1, ff.

National Goals Research Staff. 1970. Toward Balanced Growth: Quantity with Quality. Washington, D.C.: U.S. Government Printing Office.

National Wildlife Federation. 1969. The U.S. Public Considers Its Environment. A National Opinion Trends Report. Princeton: The Gallup Organization, Inc.

President's National Advisory Commission on Rural Poverty. 1967. People Left Behind. Washington, D.C.: U.S. Government Printing Office.

U.S. Bureau of the Census. 1974. Mobility of the Population of the United States: March 1970 to March 1973. Current Population Reports, Series P-20, No. 262. Washington, D.C.: U.S. Government Printing Office.

Zuiches, James J., and Glenn V. Fuguitt. 1972. Residential Preferences: Implications for Population Redistribution in Nonmetropolitan Areas. Pp. 617-630 in Sara Mills Mazie (ed.), Commission on Population Growth and the American Future, Vol. V, Population, Distribution, and Policy. Washington, D.C.: U.S. Government Printing Office.

RUNNING FROM RAW LIFE IN CITIES

Migration grows to rural areas

GORDON HANSON

IOWA FALLS, Iowa (AP)—Rubbed raw by city living, thousands of Americans are migrating to small towns and rural areas.

U.S. Census Bureau figures show that the population declines of the 1960s have been halted or reversed in a dozen or more rural states.

Some who have moved from urban areas say they are seeking a life with less violence, less pressure, less pollution. Others say they're going back to childhood homes. The majority say they are migrating to states like Iowa because jobs are available now in small towns.

Iowa (population 2.9 million) lost 183,500 people in the decade of the '60s, the Census Bureau says, but the net in-migration from 1970 to 1973 was 34,000. A similar population trend has appeared in other farm states in the American heartland—Wisconsin, Minnesota, South Dakota, Nebraska, Kansas and Oklahoma. These six states lost 309,000 people from 1960 to 1970, but their combined population increased by 113,000 from '70 to '73, according the latest Census Bureau figures.

□ From The State Journal, Lansing, Mich., Feb. 23, 1975. Reprinted by permission of the Associated Press.

Nationwide, the population in nonmetropolitan areas increased by 2.3 million people, or 4 per cent, in the first quarter of the decade. The fifteen largest metropolitan areas, on the other hand, gained only 65,000 residents from '70 to '73, about 0.1 per cent, the Census Bureau says. The slight increase was due only to the fact that births exceeded deaths. More people moved out than moved in.

"There's a mixture of reasons for the migration reversal," says Calvin Beale, head of population studies for the U.S. Agriculture Department. "There is an improved economy in rural areas, which provides more jobs. There is the changed attitude of people who, if they've got children, are afraid of the cities. And there are the younger persons who want to live in harmony with a natural environment.

". . . The biggest improvement in retaining people is in small towns or open country. The trend is to small towns of less than 10,000 people and to rural living, and it's continuing."

Carlisle Bean, a 30-year-old architect who had gone to college in Iowa, is one of the converts. He gave up his job in Washington, D.C., last year and moved his family to Iowa Falls, population 6,700 and growing at a rate of 3 per cent annually.

"It's working out beyond our wildest expectations," says Bean, who is now chief designer for a modular home manufacturing company here. "The tranquility of a small town, which had to be a big bore, suddenly became a nice place to live."

Charles Bursik, 62, was marketing director for a New York publishing company. He's now among the 1,356 people of Ravenna, Neb., a state whose net loss was 73,000 people in the '60s, but the population grew by 29,000 from 1970 to 1973. It's now more than 1.5 million.

"The doctors told me to get out of the pressure cooker in New York City," Bursik says. Ravenna was chosen four years ago because Bursik was born there and his two daughters wanted to seek their origins "where grandma and grandpa came from."

In the rich oil and cattle country around Duncan, Okla., a retired Air Force officer, Leon Hooten, 48, his Italian-born wife, Lucia, 47, and their seven children seem ecstatic.

"I've come home," whoops the gregarious Hooten, who is managing editor of the Duncan Daily Banner, and whose career has taken him around the world. In 1970, he lost a job as an electronics engineer in El Paso, Texas, and decided to return to his native Oklahoma.

"My parents are up in years. I felt an obligation to come back to them," he says. His wife has opened an Italian restaurant in Duncan and the five Hooten girls pitch in as waitresses.

Oklahoma added 13,000 people to its population

from 1960 to 1970, when the population reached 2.5 million. In the next three years, the flow of new people grew to 48,000.

"We have had quite a bit of growth in rural communities, especially in the eastern part of the state where there are many lodges and lakes," says W. J. Bowman, of the Oklahoma Employment Security Commission. "Employment in manufacturing in Oklahoma has increased substantially in the last few years, and a lot of it has occurred in the smaller cities, and to a great extent in rural areas."

Bowman and state officials interviewed in Iowa, Nebraska and Kansas say population has increased mainly because of concerted efforts to attract new industry and new jobs to small towns.

Aurora, Neb., is described as typical. An 80-acre industrial park opened there eight years ago. Nine new industries, including a pickle plant and a mobile home manufacturer, have located at the park, with 300 jobs.

"We were dormant for 40 years," says Ken Wortman, 56, a car dealer. "But now we've had a complete turnabout. We've gone from 2,500 to 3,500 population in five years. We're building 50 new homes a year."

Other states that lost population in the '60s and reversed the trend in this decade, in some cases by increasing urban populations, include Montana, Idaho, Wyoming, New Mexico, Utah, Nevada, North Dakota, Arkansas, Maine, Indiana, Illinois, Ohio and Tennessee.

Here in Iowa Falls, where land for an industrial park was acquired two years ago, Bean said he and his wife, Denise, 27, left Arlington, Va., a suburb of Washington, because "we wanted to strike out on our own for ecological and economic reasons."

Bean was employed almost immediately in one of the new light industries that have located here. Mrs. Bean says their second child, Jessica, was born at the Town's municipal hospital and the treatment "was so nice and Carlisle even got to be in the delivery room."

The Ted Wells family recently moved to Staplehurst, Neb. Wells is a former marketing development manager for the Rock Island Railroad in Chicago.

"I was so determined I was going to change my lifestyle that I just plain resigned without having anywhere else to go," Wells said. New he's president of the fledgling Great Plains Railway, trying to make a profitable venture out of an abandoned branch line.

At nearby Ravenna, Bursik, back in his boyhood town, said that many others who left realize that those who stayed "have been living a pretty darned good life. They missed a lot of the pressures, the difficulties, the competition for everything.

"We spent our careers to get back out of the cities. Some, like myself, were fortunate enough to be forced out."

The revival of population growth in nonmetropolitan America

CALVIN L. BEALE*

The vast rural-to-urban migration of people that was the common pattern of U.S. population movement in the decades after World War II has been halted and, on balance, even reversed. During 1970-73, nonmetropolitan areas gained 4.2 percent in population compared to only 2.9 percent for metro areas. In the eyes of many Americans, the appeal of major urban areas has diminished and the attractiveness of rural and small town communities has increased, economically and otherwise. The result is a new trend that is already having an impact, one that modifies much we have taken for granted about population distribution.

THE OLD TREND

In the 1960's, the United States passed through a period of acute consciousness of the movement of people from rural and small town areas into the metropolitan cities. This awareness was greatly heightened by the urban disorders that began in Los Angeles and Detroit and culminated in massive riots following the 1968 murder of Martin Luther King, Jr. There was thus a racial context to concern about rural-to-urban migration, although suppositions about the rural origin of rioters proved largely incorrect. The racial aspect in turn was part of a larger national focus on the extent and nature of urban poverty, and of a growing sense of increasing urban problems of pollution, crime, congestion, social alienation, and other real or suspected effects of large-scale massing of people.

Although there is usually some lag in public awareness of social and demographic movements, it is still rather remarkable that it took so long for concern to develop over rural-to-urban migration and the extensive impact this movement had on the Nation's major urban areas.

Rapid rural outmovement had been occurring since 1940, with the beginning of the U.S. defense effort. It continued apace in the 1950's as farms consolidated and as the worker-short cities welcomed rural manpower. From 1940 to 1960, a net average of more than 1 million people left the farms annually (although not

□ From Economic Research Service, U.S. Department of Agriculture, No. 605, Washington, D.C., 1975, U.S. Government Printing Office.
*Economic Development Division Economic Research Service; leader, Population Studies.

all moved to metro cities) and a majority of nonmetro counties declined in population despite high birth rates.

By the mid-1960's, this massive movement had drained off so much population previously dependent on agriculture and other extractive industries that the peak of potential migration was reached and passed. Yet, the impact of the movement had not been well recognized by cities or reflected in public policy. By the time that alarm over rural-to-urban migration arose around 1965, the economy of the nonmetro areas, as well as the social outlook and affluence of netro residents, were already changing in ways that would lead to a halt in the net outflow. Since 1970, changes in rural and urban population flows have occurred so rapidly that nonmetro areas are not only retaining people but are receiving an actual net inmigration as well—an event not anticipated in the literature of the day.

THE RURAL EXODUS

In the 1950's, a net of 5 million people left nonmetro areas. In the South, farm population dropped by 40 percent in the decade, especially as a result of the mechanization of cotton harvesting and rapid abandonment of the cropper system of farming. By the mid-1950's, the Department of Agriculture began its advocacy of general rural development, urging communities to attract alternative types of employment. The emerging Interstate Highway Program began to shorten road travel times between places or entire regions. But only here and there in that decade were there actual population reversals from loss to gain in nonmetro areas—the beginnings of revival in the Colorado slopes; the start of recreation and retirement in the Ozarks; oil related development in south Louisiana; and the sprawling influence of Atlanta, Kansas City, or Minneapolis-St. Paul on accessible nonmetro counties.

In the 1960's, people continued to leave many of the areas of chronic rural exodus, such as the Great Plains (both north and south), the western Corn Belt, the southern coal fields, and the cotton, tobacco, and peanut producing southern Coastal Plain, especially the Delta. However, closer examination of these losses reveals that, in a majority of cases, rates of net outmigration or decline had diminished compared with the

1950's. Indeed, about 250 nonmetro counties in the South had net outmigration only in the black population, with the white population undergoing net inmigration into the same counties.

HARBINGERS OF CHANGE

A clear-cut and major reversal of nonmetro decline occurred in two large upland areas of the South in the 1960's. One area stretched in an oval shape from St. Louis to Dallas, encompassing the Ozarks, the lower Arkansas Valley, the Ouachita Mountains, and northeast Texas. The other, of somewhat less dramatic size and reversal, was bounded by Memphis, Louisville, Atlanta, and Birmingham. Both areas were comprised heavily of districts with low previous income, low educational attainment, and low external prestige. Their reversal illustrated clearly the potential for rural turnaround in almost any part of the eastern half of the country once reliance on agriculture had been minimized. By 1960, only a sixth of the labor force in these two areas was in farming, after a rapid decline in the 1950's. They were major beneficiaries of the decentralization trend of manufacturing that gathered speed in the mid-1960's. The Ozark-Ouachita area also had extensive development of reservoir-centered recreation and retirement districts.

The great majority of nonmetro counties had greater retention of population in the 1960's than they had during the 1950's. Nonmetro counties of that day lost only 2.2 million people by outmovement during the 1960's, a reduction of 60 percent from the prior decade. Population decline was more common than gain in most counties where a third or more of the employed labor force worked in any combination of agriculture, mining, and railroad work at the beginning of the decade. In such cases, only a very rapid increase in other sources of work could fully offset continued displacement from extractive industry. But, because of this displacement, we entered the 1970's with far fewer counties depending primarily on the extractive sector of the economy. Thus, many more counties were in position in 1970 to see future gains in manufacturing, trade, services, or other activity flow through to net job growth and population gain, without being offset by declines in traditional industries.

Our best single source of population data for the 1970's is the Bureau of the Census county estimates series published annually. Accurate local population estimates are not easy to make. In some counties it is difficult to be fully certain even of the direction of change, much less the amount. Nevertheless, the estimates of the Bureau for 1966 (the only county series in the 1960's) caught clearly the turnarounds of that period in the Ozarks, Tennessee Valley, Texas hill country, and Upper Great Lakes cutover lands, although mistaking the direction of trend in the Mississippi Delta. The subsequent improvement of techniques, the strength of the demographic changes now occurring, and the support of independent data series on employment bolster confidence in the current series, although no one would prudently interpret small changes for small counties literally.[1]

___

[1]The 1973 estimates used in this paper are being revised by the Bureau of Census to reflect additional data that have become available. But the revisions will not change conclusions reached here. They will show less increase in nonmetro population retention in the western Corn Belt and the Wheat Belt than is implied in the data used here, but more such retention in a number of Southern States and scattered other areas of predominantly nonmetro character.

Table 1. U.S. population change by residence, 1970 and 1973

Residence	Population			Net migration		
	1973	1970	Increase 1970-73	1970-73	1960-70	
	Thou.	*Thou.*	*Pct.*	*Thou.*	*Thou.*	
Total	209,851	203,301	3.2	1,632	3,001	
Metro[1]	153,252	149,002	2.9	486	5,997	
Nonmetro	56,599	54,299	4.2	1,146	−2,996	
Nonmetro						
Adjacent counties[2]	29,165	27,846	4.7	722	−724	
Nonadjacent counties	27,434	26,452	3.7	424	−2,273	

[1]Metro status as of 1974.
[2]Nonmetro counties adjacent to Standard Metropolitan Statistical Areas.
Source: Current Population Records, U.S. Bureau of the Census.

THE REVERSAL

The remarkable recent reversal of long-term population trends is demonstrated by growth in nonmetro counties of 4.2 percent between April 1970 and July 1973, compared with 2.9 percent in metro counties (see table 1 which sums counties by current metro-nonmetro status).[2] This is the first period in this century in which nonmetro areas have grown at a faster rate than metro areas. Even during the 1930's Depression, there was some net movement to the cities. As late as the 1960's, metro growth was double the rate in nonmetro areas.

Curiously, both metro and nonmetro classes had some net improvement of people from 1970 to 1973. This is possible because the total population grew, partly by immigration from abroad.

During the 1960's, nonmetro counties of today were averaging a 300,000 loss per year from outmigration. Thus far in this decade, they have averaged a 353,000 inmovement per year while metro areas, in sharp contrast, have dropped from 600,000 net inmigrants annually to 150,000.

A common first reaction to these data and the basic change they indicate is to ask whether the higher nonmetro growth might not just be increased spillover from the metro areas into adjacent nonmetro counties. To examine this logical question, nonmetro counties were classed by whether or not they are adjacent to a metro area. As might be expected, adjacent counties have had the higher population growth since 1970 (4.7 percent) and have acquired about five-eighths of the total net in movement into all nonmetro counties. However, the more significant point is that nonadjacent counties have also increased more rapidly than metro counties (3.7 percent vs. 2.9 percent). Thus, the decentralization trend is not confined to metro sprawl. It affects nonmetro counties well removed from metro influence. Indeed, the trend can be said especially to affect them. Their net migration pattern has shifted more than that of the adjacent counties, going from a loss of 227,000 annually in the 1960's to an annual gain of 130,000, a shift in the annual average of 357,000 persons. On a slightly larger base, adjacent counties have shifted from an average annual loss of 72,000 persons in the 1960's to an average gain of 222,000 from 1970 to 1973, an annual shift of 294,000 persons.

Increased retention of population in nonmetro areas is characteristic of almost every part of the United States. As measured by migration trends, all States

[2] In general, Standard Metropolitan Statistical Areas—here called metro areas—are designated by the Government wherever there is an urban center of 50,000 or more people. Neighboring commuter counties of metro character are also included in these areas. All other counties are nonmetro.

but three (Alaska, Connecticut, and New Jersey) show it, and two of the three exceptions are controlled by events in military-base counties. Nonadjacent counties have had some net inmigration in every major geographic division.

There were still nearly 600 nonmetro counties declining in population during 1970-73, but this was less than half as many as the nearly 1,300 declining in the 1960's. The largest remaining block of such counties is in the Great Plains, both north and south. Former large groups of declining counties in the Old South and the southern Appalachian coal fields have been broken up except in the Mississippi Delta.

FACTORS AFFECTING GROWTH

Major centers of nonmetro population are found in counties with cities of 25,000-49,999 people. These counties contain a little more than a sixth of the total nonmetro population. Their growth rate for 1970-73 was 4.2 percent, identical with that in all other nonmetro counties. Thus, recent nonmetro population growth has not gone disproportionately into counties with the largest nonmetro employment centers. Since these counties have a favorable age structure for childbearing, their rate of natural increase was higher than that of the rest of nonmetro counties, but the rate of inmigration was lower.

At the other residential extreme are the completely rural nonmetro counties that are not adjacent to a metro area and have no town of even 2,500 inhabitants. Such counties have been subject to population decline in the past. In the 1960's they had considerable outmigration and declined by 4.5 percent in the decade. However, from 1970 to 1973 their population grew by 4.2 percent. This reflects a definite reversal of the previous trend. Natural increase of population in the completely rural counties has been very low since 1970, because of the comparative shortage of adults of childbearing age (resulting from past outmigration), and the growth of older populations of higher mortality as retirement settlement spreads. The growth in these counties has come principally from inmigration, with a rate nearly double that of counties with cities of 25,000 or more people.

The decentralization trend in U.S. manufacturing has been a major factor in transforming the rural and smalltown economy, especially in the upland parts of the South. From 1962 through 1969, half of all U.S. nonmetro job growth was in manufacturing. However, population growth has not been high since 1970 in areas with heavy concentration of manufacturing activity. Counties with 40 percent or more of their 1970 employment in this sector contained about 16 percent of the total nonmetro population and grew by 3.3 percent between 1970 and 1973. This increase re-

Table 2. Nonmetropolitan population change by selected county characteristics[1]

Characteristic in 1970	Number of counties	Population					Net migration			
		Number			Percentage change		1970-73		1960-70	
		1973	1970	1960	1970-73	1960-70	Number	Rate[2]	Number	Rate[2]
		Thou.	*Thou.*	*Thou.*	*Pct.*	*Pct.*	*Thou.*	*Pct.*	*Thou.*	*Pct.*
Counties with city of 25,000 or more	138	10,351	9,936	8,916	4.2	11.4	148	1.5	−74	−0.8
Counties with no city of 25,000	2,356	46,248	44,363	43,850	4.2	1.2	998	2.2	−2,922	−6.7
Entirely rural nonadjacent counties[3]	620	4,441	4,264	4,474	4.2	−4.7	123	2.9	−551	−12.3
Counties with 10 percent or more net inmigration at retirement ages[4]	377	8,672	7,887	6,655	10.0	18.5	646	8.2	619	9.3
15 percent or more	214	5,310	4,728	3,764	12.3	25.6	509	10.8	642	17.1
10.0 to 14.9 percent	163	3,362	3,159	2,891	6.4	9.3	137	4.3	−23	−.8
Counties with a senior State college	187	8,852	8,369	7,419	5.8	12.8	265	3.2	78	1.1
Counties with 40 percent or more employed in manufacturing	263	8,936	8,647	8,057	3.3	7.3	73	.8	−294	−3.7
Counties with 35 percent or more employed in agriculture	193	916	919	1,039	−.4	−11.5	−12	−1.3	−201	−19.4
40 percent or more	104	398	402	463	−.9	−13.3	−8	−1.9	−100	−21.5
35.0 to 39.9 percent	89	518	518	576	(5)	−10.1	−5	−.9	−102	−17.6
Counties with 50 percent or more black population	98	1,750	1,763	1,947	−.7	−9.5	−67	−3.8	−459	−23.6
Counties with 10 percent or more military population	29	1,172	1,177	955	−.4	23.2	−66	−5.6	21	2.2

[1]Metro status as of April 1974.
[2]Net migration expressed as a percentage of the population at beginning of period.
[3]Nonmetro counties not adjacent to Standard Metropolitan Statistical Areas.
[4]Counties with specified 1960-70 net inmigration rate for white persons 60 years old and over, 1970.
[5]Less than .05 percent.
Source: U.S. Census of Population 1970 and Current Population Reports. U.S. Bureau of the Census.

quired some net inmigration and was slightly above the total U.S. growth rate, but was well below the increase of 4.2 percent for all nonmetro counties. Thus, although growth of manufacturing has been a centerpiece of the revival of nonmetro population retention, the recent reversal of population trends has not been focused in areas already heavily dependent on manufacturing. Growth of jobs in trade and other nongoods producing sectors has now come to the fore. From 1969 to 1973, manufacturing jobs comprised just 18 percent of all nonmetro job growth, compared with 50 percent from 1962 to 1969.

A second and increasingly important factor in nonmetro development has been the growth of recreation and retirement activities, often occurring together in the same localities. Recreational employment is not easily assessed, but by means of net migration estimates by age, it is possible to identify counties receiving significant numbers of retired people. Using unpublished estimates prepared by Gladys Bowles of the Economic Research Service in joint work with Everett Lee at the University of Georgia, counties were identified in which there was a net inmigration of 15 percent or more from 1960 to 1970 of white residents who were age 60 and over in 1970. Migration patterns at other ages were disregarded and may have been either positive or negative. These counties, which had already become a source of nonmetro population growth in the 1960's, are by far the most rapidly growing class of nonmetro counties in the 1970's.

Although a number of the retirement counties are in the traditional Florida and southwestern belts, it is the spread of retirement settlement to other regions that is a key characteristic of recent years. Clusters of nonmetro retirement counties are found in the old cutover region of the Upper Great Lakes (especially in Michigan), the Ozarks, the hill country of central Texas, the Sierra Nevada foothills in California, and the east Texas coastal plain. In general, coasts, lakes, reservoirs, and hills are favorite locations.

"Retirement counties" is probably too narrow a label for a number of the counties described. In about five-eighths of the cases, inmigration rates were highest at retirement age and lower (or at times negative) at younger ages. But in the other three-eighths of the "retirement counties," inmigration was higher at some age under age 60 than it was above that point. These areas often attract younger families because of climate, or amenities, or because manufacturing or other employment may have begun to flourish as well. Indeed the very influx of people into attractive areas for noneconomic reasons can stimulate follow-on types of job development—a case of supply creating demand. Further, it should be noted that, for many people today, "retirement" may at first mean simply an optional departure from a career job and pension system at a comparatively unadvanced age; for example, most Federal Government workers can retire at age 55. Increasingly large numbers of such people then move to a different place where they may or may not reenter the labor force.

The nonmetro counties with net inmigration of 15.0 percent or more of whites at age 60 and over grew by an average of one-fourth in total population in the 1960's. The pace of their growth has risen further, with a 12.3 percent population increase from 1970 to 1973.

The very rapid growth of these counties suggested a look at counties with a more modest level of inmovement of older people. Counties of 10.0 to 14.9 percent retirement-age migration rates in the 1960's were examined and proved to have grown in population by 6.4 percent from 1970 to 1973. This is a little more than half the total growth rate for counties with higher retirement rates in the 1960's. However, the counties with modest retirement rates in the 1960's have had a relatively more rapid buildup in their total growth trend since 1970. During the 1960's, their overall growth of 9.3 percent was well below the national average, but their growth since 1970 is well above the national average. The two classes of retirement counties have between them 8.7 million people in 377 counties, and make up an increasingly significant part of the total nonmetro population.

An equal number of nonmetro people live in counties having senior State colleges and universities.[3] The expansion of these schools has been substantial since the end of World War II. Many have evolved from teachers colleges into major institutions. Some observers tend to denigrate the importance of non-metro population growth stemming from college growth, as if it were somehow less real or permanent in its consequences than other growth. But the rise of nonmetro State schools has greatly increased availability and quality of higher education in nonmetro areas and has also made the affected towns more attractive for other development. In fact, many new metro areas over the last two decades have come from the ranks of college towns. From 1970 to 1973, nonmetro counties containing senior State colleges and universities grew in population by 5.8 percent, well above the nonmetro average, despite the slight national downturn in college enrollment rates that began at this time.[4]

Eventually, these counties should experience a drop in students as the decline in the birthrate since 1960 affects enrollment. But towns and counties containing State colleges are unlikely to return to their earlier size or status. Perhaps equally important to nonmetro areas has been the founding of numerous community junior colleges and technical education centers. These institutions typically do not have residential facilities and thus do not swell the local population with students, but they have made it much more feasible for nonmetro residents to obtain post-high school education, and they are often able to cooperate with business firms in providing specific skills needed for new or expanded plants. More than 150 nonmetro counties acquired public community colleges or college-accredited technical education centers during the 1960's.

Tabulations were also made for two types of counties known to have been highly susceptible to loss in the 1960's. Heavily agricultural counties, with 40 percent or more of their employment in farming, were the most vulnerable to population decline and outmigration in the 1960's, losing jobs faster in the course of farm adjustments than other sources of work could be found. From 1970 to 1973, such counties declined by 0.9 percent in population, contrary to the general trend of nonmetro population. But the more crucial statistic about these counties is that they have only 400,000 people, which is less than 1 percent of the nonmetro population. Their trends now have little weight in shaping the national nonmetro trend. Counties where 35.0 to 39.9 percent of all workers are in agriculture contained a half million people and were stationary in population from 1970 to 1973. Heavily agricultural counties clearly are still different in population retention from the mass of nonmetro coun-

[3]The lists of retirement counties and college counties are almost mutually exclusive. Only 19 counties are in both categories.

[4]Private colleges are omitted from this discussion because they are considerably smaller than State schools on the average and have had much less growth than have State schools. Some private schools do, of course, exercise an effect on the nonmetro population.

ties, and are not absorbing the equivalent of their natural population increase (their combined outmigration amounted to 12,000 people). Even so, they have been affected by the recent trend, for these same counties declined by 11.5 percent in the 1960's with a decade outmovement of 200,000 people.

Among the most uniformly heavy losers of population in prior decades were the nonmetro counties of predominantly black population. They were once disproportionately agricultural and they received less industrialization than the rest of the South. Further, their black residents had an impetus toward city migration that transcended what might have been expected from the dependence on farming or the slower pace of other job development. By 1970, 98 predominantly black nonmetro counties remained, although only one of them still had 35 percent or more workers in farming. These counties contained 1.75 million total population. From 1970 to 1973, they decreased by 13,000, or -.7 percent. Thus, predominantly black areas of the South have not yet shifted to growth. However, net outmigration has been reduced from an average of 46,000 people annually in the 1960's to 20,000 in the early 1970's. Some increased retention is evident.

Several other less numerous and less populated types of counties that had increased population retention can be identified, although no data are shown here for them. These include mining counties, counties with major prisons or long-stay hospitals, those containing State capitals, and counties with Indian majorities.

Increased retention is so pervasive that only one type of county could be found with diminished population retention. This type was military base counties—defined as those where 10 percent or more of the total 1970 population consisted of military personnel. Military work was a major rural growth industry in the post World War II decades. Military bases were disproportionately located in nonmetro areas, and they employed many civilians as well as armed forces. However, since 1970, domestic military personnel has declined by about a fifth. Nonmetro counties with 10 percent or more of military personnel among their residents declined slightly in total population (-.4 percent), with a net outmigration of 66,000 people. By contrast, these counties grew very rapidly during the 1960's (23.2 percent).

In summarizing categories of counties for which trends have been computed, highest rates of nonmetro growth are found among retirement counties, counties adjacent to metro areas, and counties with senior State colleges.

Geographically, several commonly recognized subregions have had rapid growth. In the 3¼ years after the 1970 Census, the Ozark-Ouachita area increased by 9.4 percent, the Upper Great Lakes cutover area by 8.0 percent, the Rocky Mountains by 7.1 percent, and the Southern Appalachian coal fields by 6.3 percent. The latter is a remarkable turnaround from a loss of over 15 percent in the coal fields in the 1960's. Each of the four areas cited is comparatively remote from metro centers.

RESIDENTIAL PREFERENCES

A change in attitudes may be of equal importance to economic factors in producing the recent reversal in migration. In the middle 1960's, we became aware of the great disparity between the actual distribution of the U.S. population by size of place and the expressed preferences of people. Millions of people presumed heretofore to be happily content in their big city and suburban homes said—in response to opinion polls—they would prefer to live in a rural area or small town.

When Zuiches and Fuguitt subsequently reported from a Wisconsin survey that a majority of such dissidents in that State preferred their ideal rural or small town residence to be within 30 miles of a city of at least 50,000 people,[5] there was noticeable discounting by urban-oriented interests of the message of previous polls. It appeared that basic trends were not being altered. Rather, only additional sprawl within the metro areas was implied. The validity of the point established by Zuiches and Fuguitt was indisputable, especially when confirmed in a later national survey by the same researchers. However, in the opinion of this writer, a second finding in the national survey greatly modified the significance of the preference for a close-in rural or small town location, although it received little notice. By a very wide margin (65 percent to 35 percent), the big city people who preferred a nearby rural or small town residence ranked a more remote rural or small town place as their second choice, and thus as preferable to the big city.[6] Therefore, most of this group were positively oriented toward nonmetro locations compared with their current metro urban residence regardless of whether an opportunity arose to relocate within 30 miles of the city.

A second statistic foreshadowing the 1970-73 trends reported here appeared in another national survey done for the Commission on Population Growth and

[5]James J. Zuiches and Glenn V. Fuguitt, "Residential Preferences: Implications for Population Redistribution in Nonmetropolitan Areas," *Population Distribution and Policy*, Vol. 5 of research reports of the U.S. Commission on Population Growth and the American Future, 1972, pp. 617-630.
[6]Glenn V. Fuguitt and James J. Zuiches, "Residential Preferences and Population Distribution," *Demography*, Vol. 12, No. 3, August 1975.

the American Future. This figure dealt with the likelihood that persons dissatisfied with their size of community would actually move to the type that they preferred.[7]

The Commission found that three-eighths of the people expressing a desire to shift to a different type of residence declared that they were "very likely" to make such a move within the "next few years." An additional fourth thought they would eventually make such a move at a later time. The "very likely" group would have translated into a potential of about 14 million people of all ages moving from metro cities and suburbs to smaller places and rural areas. The expectation of making a move was highest among comparatively young and well educated persons (where migration rates in general are highest), and thus was not primarily a nostalgic hope of older people of rural origin.

I suggest the pattern of population movement since 1970 reflects to a considerable extent many people implementing a preference for a rural or small town residence over that of the metro city, quite apart from the fact that improved economic conditions in nonmetro areas make such moves feasible.

Aside from demographic and opinion survey data, a variety of corroborative local information on the noneconomic aspects of current population distribution trends is now available in the form of newspaper and magazine stories and correspondence. The environmental-ecological movement, the youth revolution with its somewhat antimaterialistic and antisuburban component, and the narrowing of traditional urban-rural gaps in conditions of life all seem to have contributed to the movement to nonmetro areas.

EFFECT OF THE DECLINING BIRTHRATE

An additional factor contributing to higher nonmetro population growth during a period of slower national and metro growth has been the course of the birthrate. The decline of the birthrate since 1970 has basically occurred in the most metropolitan parts of the country. In the 3¼ years after April 1970, for which most of the population figures in this paper are quoted, births numbered 5.2 percent less than for the previous 3¼ years in the Northeast (including Delaware, Maryland, and the District of Columbia), the North Central, and the Pacific States. On the other hand, in the South and the Mountain division of the West, they actually increased by 3.5 percent in the post-1970 period over the prior period. Although nonmetro residents are a minority in both of these two

[7]Sara Mills Mazie and Steve Rawlings, "Public Attitude Towards Population Distribution Issue," *Population, Distribution, and Policy, op. cit.*, pp. 599-616.

super regions, they comprise twice the proportion in the South and Mountain West than they do in the North and Pacific West (40 percent vs. 20 percent). It is highly unlikely that this contrasting pattern in number of births could occur without being substantially associated with the large difference in proportion of nonmetro population. It appears that the difference between average levels of metro and nonmetro fertility rates has somewhat widened since 1970, after three decades of convergence.

The 1970-1973 population trends do not reflect effects of the more recent large increase in the price of oil and gas products. Inasmuch as rural people travel a greater average distance to work or for goods and services than do urban residents, and do not usually have public transportation alternatives, the higher costs of personal transportation could have a depressing effect on the future trend of population dispersal. It is too early as yet to tell. However, the same shortage and higher price of fuels and energy-producing minerals has caused renewed mining activity for oil, gas, coal, and uranium, thus stimulating the economy of a number of nonmetro counties, especially in the West. In a directly related manner, the agricultural economy is being operated in a greatly expanded way, primarily to serve export markets and balance of payment needs. This, too, generates some additional rural employment.

FUTURE IMPACT

How long will the 1970-73 trend persist and what is its larger meaning? One doubts that we are dismantling our system of cities. However, except for Boston, all of the largest U.S. metro areas have had major slowdowns in growth. The largest eight areas—which contain a fourth of the total U.S. population—grew by less than one-third the national growth rate from 1970 to 1973, whereas they were exceeding the national growth in the 1960's. Small and medium sized metro areas have had increased growth and net inmovement of people since 1970, and thus are behaving demographically more like the nonmetro areas than like the larger metro places. The trend that produced the turnaround in nonmetro population is primarily a sharply diminished attraction to the more massive metro areas, and a shift down the scale of settlement—both to smaller metro areas and small towns and rural areas.

Much is said in the literature of demography about the modern demographic transition. The process whereby nations go from high fertility and mortality through a period of rapid total growth as mortality drops, to a subsequent condition of low growth as fertility also falls, is seen to be accompanied by rapid urbanization. But in a nation where this process is essentially completed, another aspect of demographic transition may emerge, in which the distribution of population is no longer controlled by an unbridled impetus to urbanization. General affluence, low total population growth, easy transportation and communication, modernization of rural life, and urban population massings so large that they diminish the advantages of urban life—these factors may make a downward shift to smaller communities seem both feasible and desirable.

The trend in the United States since 1970 was not foreseen in the literature of scientific and public discussion of even 3 or 4 years ago. Its rapid emergence is basically the result of innumerable private decisions—both personal and commercial—which collectively and subtly have created a pattern of population movement significantly different from what went before. Long-held social truths—such as the view that the basic movement of population is out of nonmetro areas and into metro areas—are not easily cast off. But this one seems to have reached the end of its unchallenged validity. Much new thought is needed on the probable course of future population distribution in the United States, uncolored either by value-laden residential fundamentalism or by outmoded analytical premises.

Honey Creek: a compromise

ROBERT PFEFFERKORN*

SAUK CITY—There's a 360-acre farm 4 miles west of here where wooded bluffs sweep down to fertile bottom land bordering on 2 miles of Honey Creek as it winds its way to the Wisconsin River.

It's for sale for $15,000.

Any real estate people, any farmer, or any country-hungry city dweller with a hankering for sunlit greenery and quiet sounds knows there must be more to that price that meets the eye.

And there is.

For one thing, the project is an experiment in creating a new land ethic that will be shared by 25 families—at $15,000 each—in a community to be known as the Honey Creek Settlement.

A compromise between reality and idealism, the idea of real estate broker Martha B. Smith is to bring the seemingly insatiable demand for country seclusion into harmony with productive land use and Aldo Leopold's respect for the sand country ecology.

For another thing, prospective buyers, according to Ms. Smith, will have the rare opportunity to examine a "memorandum of intent" which discloses the details, including the financing, of the planning that went into the project.

The basic plan is to divide the 360 acres into 120 acres of wooded bluffs, ridges, and stream banks as wild life refuge; 120 acres as an experimental organic farm operated as a cooperative, and 120 acres divided into 1½- to 3-acre residential plots with common recreational areas.

Each of the settlers will own his own home site. The farm and commons areas, all under restrictions to preserve the rustic, natural environment and property values, will be owned jointly.

While $15,000 sound like a lot of money for 2 or 3 acres of woods and farm land, Ms. Smith thinks and talks of Honey Creek Settlement as sort of whole earth condominium.

Like the condominium concept, Honey Creek is designed to give each individual owner advantages in joint ownership. In this case, each owner is to share a working farm and a stewardship over a nature preserve.

Describing plans to encourage reliance on alternate sources of energy, Ms. Smith said, "One of the primary goals is to create a nearly autonomous community, producing its own food and energy. The idea is to become as nearly self-sustaining as possible without poisoning the air or water or raping the land."

The homesites lie in a hidden valley nestled at the foot of wooded hills. An access road will circle the 25-acre floor of the valley which will be made into a park with picnic areas, athletic fields, tot lot, and skating pond (and whatever else the settlers may decide).

The sites are restricted in many ways—no property line devices such as fences, only 10,000 square feet (about the size of a city lot) may be disturbed in any

□ From The Wisconsin State Journal, Madison, Wis., July 28, 1974.
*Of The State Journal staff.

way, and only indigenous plants may be used in land-scaping.

The settlers will be the first market both for the labor and the produce from the farm. They may help work the fields in exchange for work credits, which may be used later to pay for fresh food.

A professional farm manager is budgeted for two years in the development plans. While settlers may purchase produce at cost, the farm will be expected to be selfsustaining financially.

Philosophically, Ms. Smith is trying to avoid the major objections that have been raised by the exodus of city people into western Dane County—haphazard development, ecological disruption, wasted farm land, and the frustration of the individual owner who cannot afford enough land to preserve the pastoral environment that attracted them to the countryside in the first place.

She understands the last point well: She plans to live at the Honey Creek Settlement.

"The only true way to preserve something, someplace, is to have complete control over it," she explained, adding that she never would be able to afford 360 acres of farm land herself.

A homeowners association will provide that control. Ms. Smith said, "We're trying to show that, if people band together and exercise careful planning, they can do something."

Massive copper hunt catches state off guard

MIKE DORGAN*

A smooth and sophisticated billion dollar industry has slipped into the state and caught the natives napping.

At least that is the feeling of some experts who believe that the "Great Wisconsin Copper Rush" now underway in the north woods may result in one of the biggest rip-offs in the history of the state.

The discovery in recent years that upper state Pre-Cambrian rock may contain vast amounts of precious base metals, particularly copper, has lured at least 35 major mining corporations to northern Wisconsin.

For the nation's largest copper mining company, Kennecott Copper Corporation, the search has already paid off. Kennecott has announced plans to exploit an ore deposit in Rusk County.

Located just south of Ladysmith in the Town of Grant, the Rusk County deposit is rich but small by industry standards. Kennecott, through its fully-owned subsidiary, Flambeau Mining Corporation, plans to mine the ore through an open pit covering 55 surface acres and descending to a depth of 285 feet.

The life expectancy of the operation is 11 years. If the deposit proves large enough, however, the company will continue mining through underground methods for another 11-year period.

☐ From The Capital Times, Madison, Wis., July 29, 1974.
*Of The Capital Times staff.

The yield from the possible underground operation is uncertain, but from the open pit mining Kennecott expects to extract 300,000 tons of ore each year. The ore is assessed at four per cent copper, as opposed to the one-half per cent common to ores mined in Western states. It is also laced with significant amounts of gold and silver.

A concentrate mill to be constructed on the site will upgrade the ore before it is shipped to Arizona for smelting and refining. Waste from the operation, estimated by the company to be 4,000 tons per day, will be dumped into a 186-acre tailings pond located about 1½ miles south of the mine and within the 2,603-acre tract held by Kennecott.

Kennecott's announcement has intensified the search by other companies, which are secretively yet feverishly searching for minerals at an estimated cost of $30 million per year.

They are gobbling up thousands of acres of land through exploration leases for which the companies often pay $5 per acre per year. Then, if copper is discovered, the company has the option of buying the land.

If the Rusk County find is followed by others, as seems likely, the economic and environmental implications for the state will be enormous. Yet, an investigation shows that almost every level of government within the state is ill prepared to deal with the exploitation of Wisconsin's non-renewable resources.

A frantic effort to obtain the information and develop the expertise necessary in negotiating with huge corporations over irreplaceable resources is now being made by some officials. But many fear that the information and expertise may come too late.

They view the proposed Rusk County operation as a case in point.

Copper bonanza was given away as Kennecott wrote its own ticket

MIKE DORGAN*

LADYSMITH—"All income," says Werner Doering of the State Department of Revenue, "comes from earnings, findings or stealings."

Future students of the Kennecott Copper Corporation's venture in Rusk County may conclude that the company first found the rich mineral deposit near Ladysmith and then stole it.

Neither conclusion would be true.

The first samples of copper bearing ore were picked up in Ladysmith by the State Geological Survey in 1905, although the size of the deposit was not learned until much later, according to State Geologist Meredith Ostrom.

And if Kennecott makes out like a bandit on the Ladysmith mine, it will not be because the company stole the ore. It will be because it was given away.

Assembly Bill 1511. Even the number of the bill sounds suspicious to Rep. Midge Miller (D-Madison), a member of the Assembly Taxation Committee.

"Nobody would think a bill with that high a number would pass," she said in a recent interview. "At first I didn't worry about it because bills entered that late (in the session) just don't pass."

But 1511, the state's first copper tax law, did pass. Through the combined efforts of Rep. Joseph Sweda (D-Lublin), Sen. Clifford Krueger (R-Merrill) and Kennecott Copper, the bill swept past both houses in a period of less than two weeks between first consideration and final vote.

Assembly records show that the proposal was submitted to the Assembly Taxation Committee for examination on March 18. By March 20, recalls Miller, she and Committee Chairman Harvey Dueholm (D-Luck) were beginning to develop doubts about certain aspects of the bill.

☐ From the Capital Times, Madison, Wis., July 29, 1974.
*Of The Capital Times staff.

"We kept asking questions," she said, "and we weren't getting good answers."

The very next day Sweda, whose name was on the bill, grew angry with the delay and had the bill pulled from the taxation committee through a motion on the floor and referred to the Joint Survey Committee on Tax Exemption, of which he is a member.

The committee finished with the bill on March 26, and on March 27, after less than 10 days consideration, the bill was brought to a vote and passed on an 81 to 18 margin.

The bill was sent to the Senate on March 28 and was referred to the Senate Natural Resources Committee the same day. The very next day it was released by the committee, called to a vote and passed 29 to 2.

In its whirlwind trip through the Legislature, the bill was tagged with only two amendments. Both introduced by Miller, one amendment raised the tax levy on the market value of the minerals taken from the mine by four-tenths of one per cent, from 1.1 per cent to 1.5 per cent.

The other amendment called for study committee to be established to review the tax and determine if the Legislature had made a big mistake.

Miller attributed the swift passage of the bill to the reports circulating the capitol that if the Legislature did not act quickly, it would be killing a chance of employment for job-hungry Rusk County residents.

She said she is still uncertain as to whether the tax is adequate, but has serious suspicions that it is not. Rep. Dueholm chairman of the Assembly Taxation Committee, also has his doubts.

"I felt there was something wrong about it," says Dueholm, "but we didn't have time to really look at it. It was so complicated and all so fast. And Kennecott said that if we didn't come up with something, they wouldn't come in."

"My complaint," adds Miller, "is that there was not time to find out all we should have known about it. It was so complicated that I don't believe there was the expertise in the state, and not just in the Legislature, to deal with it."

She noted that economists for the University of Wisconsin's Institute for Environmental Studies were doing research on mining taxation, but said that when the bill came through their information was not yet in a "digestible form."

Much of the expertise involved in writing the tax bill came from Kennecott itself. In fact, it was a bill written by Kennecott which, after some modification, became the copper tax law of Wisconsin.

According to Edwarde May, a Kennecott geologist who has been nursing the proposed project in Ladysmith for the past five years, the behind-the-scenes development of the bill was as follows:

On April 10, 1973, Kennecott representatives went to the State Department of Revenue, announced that they wanted to exploit an ore deposit in Ladysmith and asked what the copper taxes were in Wisconsin.

Revenue informed Kennecott that Wisconsin did not have a specific tax for Copper—it had never previously been mined in the state—and suggested that Kennecott "submit a proposal."

Kennecott did, of course, and delivered it to Revenue in August, 1973. Revenue made certain modifications, says May, and then showed it to Kennecott for review in November.

"When we read it," recalled May, "we said we liked it."

Not without reason. Institute for Environmental Studies economist William Bateson, who has done extensive research into the proposed project, states flatly that if Kennecott were to mine an ore body in Arizona identical to the one in Ladysmith, it would pay "three times the taxes."

Bateson estimates that when the Rusk County mine swings into full operation in 1977, it will begin providing Kennecott with $20 million worth of copper and $5 million worth of gold and silver each year. The copper, gold and silver will all be taxed at the same rate, which is 1.5 per cent of their market value.

Simple arithmetic shows that on each $25,000,000 worth of minerals taken from the mine Kennecott will pay $375,000 to the state under the new production tax.

Ten per cent of the revenues raised through the tax will go to the state general fund, 86 per cent to the state shared tax account, 2.75 per cent to the municipality in which the mine operates and 1.25 per cent to the county in which it operates.

So for the estimated $25 million worth of minerals taken from its bedrock each year, Rusk County will

receive $4,688 and the Town of Grant will get $10,312. The state general fund will get $37,500 and the remaining $322,500 will go to the shared tax account.

In addition to the production tax, within the state Kennecott will pay local property taxes and a corporate income tax which will range between 2.3 and 7.9 per cent (minus deductions) of profits.

Included in the production tax bill, however, was an order that the "value of the mineral content" on the land being mined be excluded from the property tax assessment.

IES economists estimate that the value of the deposit at Ladysmith, as it now sits, is between $40 million and $70 million. Those figures represent the amount Kennecott could probably get for the deposit if it were to sell it to another mining corporation.

But because of the production tax bill, Kennecott will pay absolutely no property taxes on the value of the deposit itself. The company's property taxes will be based solely on the regular surface land values and the improvements it makes in the form of buildings, roads, and the like.

Werner Doering, the Department of Revenue representative who worked closest with Kennecott in designing the bill, said in a recent interview that a property tax on the ore deposit was considered during talks with the company, but was rejected because the value of the ore would be "very difficult" to assess.

"We have no mining expert on the staff," said Doering, head of the department's utility tax division, "and assessing a tax on the deposit is very difficult."

Doering noted, however, that in the past the department has taxed high-grade iron ore deposits, and conceded that "ideally it's the best way to do it."

"But Kennecott was not enthused about it," he added.

Another feature of the production tax bill was that it defined copper mining as a manufacturing activity. The definition was significant in that all machinery and equipment used by Kennecott at the Ladysmith mine will be exempt from property taxation.

In addition, recent legislation provided that all manufacturer's materials and finished products will be fully exempt from property taxation by 1978.

According to IES economist Monroe Rosner, this exemption alone will save Kennecott about $12,500 per year. "Assuming once-weekly shipments from the mine site to the smelter," he wrote recently for a study paper, "average value inventories would be about $500,000. At a mill rate of .025 this would produce $12,500 in property taxes."

In 1973, on Rusk County land holdings valued at $1,061,000, Kennecott paid $24,000 in property taxes. The total property taxes the company will pay once it has constructed the concentrate mill and made other land "improvements" is difficult to estimate, but by Rosner's calculations they will probably not exceed $80,000 per year.

Kennecott spokesmen refuse to discuss the profits the company expects to make off the Ladysmith operation. When pressed on the issue at a recent symposium at Ladysmith's Mt. Scenario College, May said he is not permitted to disclose the figure.

"I can't discuss profits," he said.

The question about expected profits was then put to Norman R. Lutz, president of the Flambeau Mining Company. Lutz said that yes, of course he knew what his company (which is Kennecott's company) expects to make on the deal. But he added: "I'm not saying."

IES economist Bateson, however, says a "conservative figure for the company's pre-federal tax profits is $8 million to $10 million per year."

Bateson said the amount of federal income taxes Kennecott will pay on the venture cannot now be determined because the corporation may be allowed to write off its Ladysmith assessment against credits on foreign operations.

He said, though, that a "very conservative estimate" of Kennecott's profits from the Rusk County mine after all taxes are paid is $5 million per year.

Even at that "very conservative" estimate of return, he noted, Kennecott could pay off its total capital investment in the project—about $15 million—within three years.

Among legislators, Miller and Dueholm are particularly anxious to get another shot at the copper tax bill. "Next time," said Dueholm, "we want to be damn sure we know what we're doing." Miller suggested that an entirely new approach to the taxation of non-renewable resources might have to be developed.

When Gov. Patrick Lucey signed Assembly Bill 1511, he also expressed concern and instructed the study committee, which has not yet begun its task, to carefully examine the issue.

But most observers would agree that, at least as of now, one bill in the hands of Kennecott is worth two in the bushes of possible future legislation.

BIG HOPES FOR JOBS HAVEN'T MUCH BASIS

Copper: fool's gold for Ladysmith?

MIKE DORGAN*

LADYSMITH—"The people up here basically agree that this will be a good thing for them, said Rep. Joseph Sweda (D-Lublin) about the proposed Kennecott copper mine in Rusk County.

"The only people objecting to it are a few outside agitators—these environmentalists from outside," he said. "I've not gotten a single letter from anybody in the area objecting to the operation. If they had any concerns, I would have heard about it."

Perhaps Sweda was not listening when Mr. and Mrs. Michael Jansen told him straight to his face that they had concerns, very serious concerns, about what the effects of the operation might be.

"All we have up here is milk, timber and kids," said Jansen a teacher and 10-year resident of Rusk County. "We need the mining, but it has to be done right. That mining company should have to leave more money lying on the table of this community.

☐ From The Capital Times, Madison Wis., July 30, 1974.
*Of The Capital Times staff.

"Kennecott's going to come in here, take out millions of dollars and then leave. They get the minerals; we get the hole in the ground and unemployment.

"Copper isn't like trees or cows," he continued. "Once it's gone, it's gone forever. We should get a hell of lot more than 4 per cent of that lousy 1.5 per cent."

The "lousy 1.5 per cent" was a reference to the production tax rate the state will charge Kennecott on the market value of the minerals taken from the mine. Rusk County and the Town of Grant, in which the deposit is located, will together receive 4 per cent of the revenues collected on the 1.5 per cent tax.

That means for each $10 million worth of minerals taken from the mine, Rusk County will directly receive $1,875 from the production tax and the Town of Grant will get $4,125.

The town and county will also receive a fraction of the tax revenues from the mine through the state's municipal and county shared tax account, into which

86 per cent of the money raised by the production tax will go.

That fraction, however, will be small. Under the present distribution formula Rusk County is eligible for eight-tenths of 1 per cent of shared tax account revenues.

Sweda, whose name appeared at the top of the original proposal which asked for only a 1.1 per cent production tax, defends the final bill and takes personal credit for winning town and county residents additional revenues by fighting to keep Kennecott property on the local tax roles.

But the land was already on the local property tax rolls when it was purchased by Kennecott, and because the bill exempted the ore deposit itself from property taxes the only additional property tax revenues for the community will come from surface "improvements" Kennecott makes on the site.

There are economic considerations other than taxes. The one most often mentioned in Rusk County is jobs. With an average annual unemployment rate of 8.9 per cent and a median family income of about $6,700, the residents of Rusk County are job hungry.

"Up in this country we need employment," said Rusk County Board supervisor Carroll Graves in a recent interview with The Capital Times. "You people down there holler more about taxes (on the mining operation) than we do."

Asked how many jobs the mining operation is expected to create, Graves said: "I don't know." Asked if he had any idea how much money the operation is likely to bring to the community, he said: "No."

County Board Chairman Marvin Hanson also said he believes the mining proposal, in its present form, is "good for the community." "There's lots of unemployment here," he said. "We need the jobs."

He added, however, that he also is not sure how many jobs the mine will create because he was "out of town" when the recent symposium on the matter was held in Ladysmith and was "out of town" when Sweda held his only meeting on the mine with county board members.

That meeting, according to Graves, was not held with the entire 21 members of the board but with six supervisors who happened to be assembled for a Welfare Board meeting when Sweda came to town.

"Sweda explained what he had in mind," said Graves, "and it sounded pretty good."

Asked if he is satisfied with the amount of taxes Rusk County will receive from the mine, board chairman Hanson said: "Yes, I think the county will get enough taxes."

He mentioned again, however, that he was out of town when the symposium was held and admitted that he wasn't really sure about the tax structure. "The way I understand it," he said, "there really isn't a set rate, we get some kind of royalties."

Hanson mistakenly said he was under the impression the "land is now being taxed like it had ore on it."

Hanson said no countywide public meetings have been held on the issue.

No public meetings on the proposed mine have been held in the Town of Grant, either, according to town chairman Peter Koska. Koska said the only official meeting he attended on the matter was the Welfare Board meeting where Sweda met with the six supervisors.

Asked what the mine will mean to the Town of Grant, Koska said: "I don't think it will hurt the town any. It should help some."

He added, though, that he hasn't yet "gotten down to brass tacks" on the matter. "I won't worry about it until it (the mine) starts up," he said. "Hell, they haven't even started the mine yet."

Kennecott hopes to begin construction on the mine next year. During the estimated 18-month construction period, approximately 91 persons will be employed at the mine site. But since construction will require mostly employes with specialized skills, the company estimates that only 15 per cent of the jobs —13 or 14 of them—will go to residents of the community.

Once in operation, the open pit mine is expected to employ 78 persons: 28 at salaried positions at about $18,000 per year, and 50 at wage labor positions at about $10,000 per year.

Salaried positions will include engineers and skilled technicians, all of whom Kennecott expects to bring in from outside the county. When the operation is over, it is expected the skilled workers will leave.

Kennecott spokesmen said they expect that "most" of the 50 wage positions, particularly truck driving and heavy equipment operating, will go to local residents.

The company estimates that it will pay $1,020,000 in wages and salaries each year of the 11-year open pit mining operation.

Where that money will be spent is another important consideration for the community, but one which is difficult to calculate. Kennecott assumes that most of it will be spent within the community and thereby "stimulate" about 66 other jobs in the "service sector," meaning restaurants, shops, hotels and the like.

Institute of Environmental Studies economist William Bateson, however, maintains that a "surplus capacity" exists in the service sector of Rusk County. He said a more likely figure for indirect employment from the mine is 15 to 40 jobs at an average income level of $6,500 to $7,500 per year.

So the total number of jobs this multi-million dollar open pit operation will probably create is 50 at most, while "stimulating" somewhere between 15 and 66 other jobs.

Bateson also said it is likely that much of the new income to Rusk County will be spent in "regional trade centers" such as nearby Eau Claire and Minneapolis.

Even Englishman Edwarde May, Kennecott's promotion man at Ladysmith, said Bateson, "has to go to Eau Claire to get a cup of tea."

Another economic repercussion from the proposed mine is the dramatic increase in land prices throughout the county.

Most of the land which comprises Kennecott's 2,603-acre mine site was picked up by the company five or six years ago through exploration leases, according to Rusk County Register of Deeds James Arts.

The typical lease, said Arts, was one in which Kennecott would pay the landowner $5 per acre per year for a period of five years for exploration rights. Contained within the lease would be an option for Kennecott to buy the land at the end of the five-year period for a predetermined amount.

"Most people around here optioned their land because they never thought Kennecott would buy it," Arts said. "They didn't think there was any copper here and they figured it was a good deal—they'd get $5 per acre per year for five years and then Kennecott would leave.

"And they figured that even if they were forced to sell at the end of five years they would do all right, since the price Kennecott offered was a lot higher than they could get anywhere else," he said.

Arts said his aunt sold a 76-acre farm to Kennecott three years ago for $84,000. At that time, he said, the normal market price for the farm was $25,000.

The dilemma many residents face, according to Arts and others, is that the pre-set sale prices which seemed so enticing five years ago when the leases were signed are now often insufficient to even replace the lost property. Copper speculation has made land values soar.

Merlin Holman and his partners in H & H Haulers, a milk transporting business presently located at the very edge of the proposed mine pit, signed a lease six years ago giving Kennecott exploration rights to the 37 acres surrounding their shop.

Holman would not say just how much Kennecott paid for the land when it exercised its option to buy last year. But he said if he and his partners had gotten "twice the price," they would have "come out all right on the deal."

Luckily, Holman said, he and his partners have found an old building in Ladysmith which will serve as a repair shop. Considering skyrocketing land and construction costs, they would have taken an economic beating had they been forced to build a new shop, he said.

"If people around here would have known five years ago when they signed the leases what the economy would be like now, they never would have signed," Holman added.

Holman professed he held no bitterness against Kennecott. "A deal's a deal; we signed the contract," he said. But he commented that the people of Rusk County are "confused". . . .

One of Holman's partners wouldn't do it again, at least not on the same terms. In addition to the land he optioned to Kennecott as a partner in H & H Haulers, Ed Thummel optioned his home and the 10 acres on which it stands. Last year Kennecott exercised the option and forced Thummel to look for a new home.

He said he could not replace the home and land on the sale price that was determined six years ago. As an indication of soaring land prices, he said the property taxes on his previous home and land tripled the last year he owned them. "Nobody could have predicted what would happen," he said.

Jansen, who lives on 160 acres eight miles south of the proposed mine site, said his property taxes "doubled last year," and blamed the rising taxes on "land speculation."

"Just in this township (Willard), there were more than 40 land transactions last year," he reported. "That's unheard of in this area."

Jansen said he has personally been contacted by at least eight mining corporations which want his land. Besides Kennecott, he said the companies that have approached him included Anaconda, Cerro, Exxon, Gulf Oil and Superior Oil.

As the rich companies compete for land, the prices are driven beyond the reach of farmers and other residents. He said Anaconda recently offered a farmer $6,500 per acre for his 180-acre farm. That comes to $1,170,000.

For those farmers who cling to their land, Jansen said, taxes keep rising. "There are farms here that have been in families for more than 100 years, and now the families are having to sell part of their farm just to pay taxes," he said.

"They are a nice bunch of people up here who work damn hard and get very little," Jansen continued. "But a lot of people here still don't realize the impact of this thing. They just haven't been educated as to what the impact of this will be."

MANY FARMERS COULD LOSE THEIR LANDS

Only copper firms know what's there

MIKE DORGAN*

Will Kennecott Copper Corporation's venture in Ladysmith be repeated throughout the northern counties of Wisconsin? Will the intense exploration now being conducted by numerous mining companies lead to new copper discoveries, new mining proposals and economic and environmental consequences almost too vast to contemplate?

State Geologist Meredith Ostrom says that at the present time there is no way of knowing.

The amount and location of copper that was sealed into the bedrock of Wisconsin when the volcanic eruptions ended and the lava cooled more than 800 million years ago has remained one of nature's closely guarded secrets.

Ostrom says the exact amount will probably never be known. In most areas of the state the Pre-Cambrian rock which may contain copper rests deep beneath the surface of the land, buried by deposits from ancient glaciers.

In northern counties, however, millions of years of erosion have cleared the glacial debris and brought the Pre-Cambrian formations again close to the surface. And scientists have in recent years discovered that those formations bear a strong resemblance to formations in Canada which contain large amounts of precious minerals.

But even in those counties, says Ostrom, head of State Geological Survey, "we have no way of knowing how much copper there is."

Part of the job of the Geological Survey is to "survey and assess the state's mineral resources." For that task the Survey is budgeted $30,000 per year.

On that amount of money, explains Ostrom, the Survey is barely able to continue its geological mapping program (less than 10 per cent of the state's surface is now mapped to geological specifications). Ostrom says his office can't even afford to dream of employing the manpower and sophisticated equipment necessary to make a close estimate of the state's mineral resources.

"We just can't do it," he says. "it's up to private capital."

Ostrom estimates there are 35 to 50 mining corporations presently involved in mineral exploration within the state, with 12 to 15 of those companies in "intensive" exploration programs.

He said a "ballpark" estimate of the amount of money the companies are spending each year in their search for minerals in Wisconsin is "$30 million."

For the most part, mining corporations do not talk about what they learn in their expensive explorations. Fear that other companies will move in on their findings and worry that land speculation may drive acquisition costs sky high, as well as to other concerns, create a shroud of secrecy around their operations.

Nonetheless, the feverish exploration, coupled with Kennecott's plans in Rusk County, has forced the state to hurriedly develop a copper mining policy.

Three major mining bills were passed in the last session of the Legislature: a copper tax-law (discussed earlier in this series), a land reclamation act and a bill requiring registration of mineral rights.

The land reclamation act establishes a Mine Reclamation Council and demands that companies post bonds to assure that they make reasonable repairs on the environmental damage caused by prospecting and mining operations.

"The purpose of this act," reads Senate Bill 39, Chapter 318, "Is to provide that air, lands, waters, plants, fish and wildlife affected by prospecting and mining in this state will receive the greatest practicable degree of protection and reclamation."

The strength of the bill has not yet been tested. But Brent McCown, an assistant professor of horticulture at the University of Wisconsin-Madison, maintains that the bill speaks timidly to immediate rehabilitation and does not at all address long-term maintenance of a site once it is deserted by the mining company.

McCown, who has done research on the proposed Rusk County mine for the UW's Institute for Environmental Studies, uses that mine proposal as an example.

When the mine is of no more use to Kennecott, the company plans to let the 55-acre hole fill with water, and even help it fill by pumping in water from the nearby Flambeau River.

But as water pours into the 285-foot hole, a festering solution of sulfuric acid and toxic metal particles

---

☐ From The Capital Times, Madison, Wis., July 31, 1974.
* Of The Capital Times Staff.

will be created by contact with the open veins of sulfide on the walls of the pit.

Added to this alchemist's pot will be the sediment and poisonous byproducts of the concentrate mill, which will be drained from the dumping pond to the "lake."

According to Kennecott officials, who maintain that the pit lake will have "recreational potential," the sinister brew will only fill the first 240 feet of the pit. The 40 feet of water closest to the surface, they maintain, will be relatively pure and separated from the acid, suspended gases and poisonous particles by a "thermal bar."

This imaginary bar of geophysic principle is the level at which the colder and heavier particle-filled solution will supposedly separate from the warmer, lighter and purer water which is expected to occupy the surface area of the lake.

Kennecott geologist Edwarde May promised those attending a recent symposium on the mine that the company would cover the sulfide veins close to the surface of the pit with rock or some other material to prevent contamination of the upper water levels.

And May assured the audience that the Wisconsin winds are not sufficiently strong to "turn the lake over," exposing the poisons to the surface. "It's very unlikely," he said.

But McCown cautioned the same audience that the pit, at least in the lower layers, would "remain toxic for the life of the lake." The poisons would remain a threat, he said, for "many hundreds of years."

McCown seriously questioned the "recreational potential" of the pit lake. He said that no fish or any other known form of plant or animal life could exist in the lake's lower waters, and he speculated that even the lake's upper waters may prove too contaminated and sparse in nutrition to support life.

That, of course, would eliminate fishing. And McCown said the surface area of the lake would be too small for most kinds of boating. One would also expect that there would be signs prohibiting deep skin diving.

Kennecott's reclamation proposals, which are now under consideration by the Department of Natural Resources, also include plans to cover the 186-acre tailings pond with 18 inches of topsoil to prevent runoff of the remaining poisonous materials after the liquid from the pond has been drained into the mine pit.

In an interview with The Capital Times, McCown questioned who would be responsible for remedying the hazards which may develop after the immediate rehabilitation has been completed and Kennecott has been returned its bond.

If drought or heavy rains break up the topsoil cov-

ering the pond and expose the poisons, which would then probably run off into the Flambeau River, who is financially responsible for repairing the damage? he asked.

Or, he asked, "what happens if the pit does not become a stable, layered lake?" If the lake "turns over," or if the sulfide veins prove to be rich at the upper levels of the lake, McCown said the entire pit would be transformed into a vat of acid which would require massive treatments with lime to reduce acid levels.

"The reclamation bill does not address the continual maintenance that a mine like this requires," complained McCown. He said responsibility for long-term maintenance would probably fall upon the county in which the mine is located.

DNR attorney James Kurtz maintains that the reclamation bill does indeed address long term maintenance of a mine site. "Kennecott will be responsible for any damage that occurs there," he said in an interview.

But he added that once the bond is refunded, the state might have a very hard time collecting any money from the company to cover environmental repairs. "It depends a lot on whether the company keeps the land or sells it after it's done mining," he said. "The owner of the land is often liable in these cases."

Collection of damage money is also difficult, he said, when a major corporation (like Kennecott) sets up a "shell corporation" (like Flambeau Mining) to run a particular operation.

When the operation is finished," he noted, "the shell corporation folds up and it is hard to legally determine who is liable.

"It depends a lot on each individual case," Kurtz continued. "There's a lot of questions yet to be cleared up by the Legislature."

If the land reclamation bill can be considered "too little," the mineral rights registration law can certainly be considered "too late."

The law requires that—for the first time in Wisconsin history—mineral rights which have been separated from surface land rights must be registered with the state.

Presently, there is no unit of government within the state which keeps records of severed mineral rights. "It's a real mess," says Ostrom. "Nobody knows who owns what where."

According to Ostrom, years ago mineral rights were particularly popular as currency in poker games. How many mineral rights were won and lost or bought and sold over the years is anyone's guess, he said, but he added that the number is probably large.

And he further added, ominously, that often the

separation of mineral rights has gone unrecorded even on the property deed.

So it is possible, continued Ostrom, that unsuspecting land owner John Q. Public could be approached by a company with mineral rights to his land and told that his farm will be the site of a mining operation.

"When mineral rights are separated, the separation implies the right to mine and to utilize as much of the surface as is necessary to conduct the mining operation," wrote geologist G. Hanson in a study paper on the issue.

"In the case of sinking a shaft this might be a small fraction of the surface, but in the case of an open pit mine this could constitute the entire surface.

"It would appear," continued Hanson, "that the surface owner could not prohibit mining, but it also would seem that the surface owner would have to be compensated for any damage done to surface property."

Hanson concluded that unless the "document separating the mineral rights specifies the respective rights of both owners . . . it might be extremely difficult to reconcile the rights of the respective owners and the compensation due."

The law gives persons or corporations who now claim separated mineral rights until December, 1977, to register their holdings. Failure to register severed mineral rights within three years will result in the reversion of the rights to the surface land owner.

As the disclosure deadline approaches, a large number of Wisconsin land owners may meet with the unwelcome surprise of learning that they do not own what they think they own. Major court battles likely loom on the horizon.

Also on the horizon lies the larger question of whether state and local officials can manage Wisconsin's non-renewable resources in the best interest of the people they represent.

"We ought to wake up," says an economist who has been closely following developments in the state's copper policy. "We're getting plucked like a banana republic when we could be acting like an oil sheikdom.

"Not that we should act like an oil sheikdom," he added, "but we should start discussing what this means for the state—what stands to be gained; what stands to be lost."

Rural development and rural communities of the future

EARL O. HEADY*

Widespread national concern and social plight of rural communities is a phenomenon of the relatively recent past. True, an attempt was made, aside from specific distressed area programs, to crank up some rather small rural development programs beginning in the 1950s. However, these were modest and philosophically oriented mainly to solving the farm component of rural problems in isolation from the rest of the community. It was expected that some rural industries could go part way in absorbing labor replaced from agriculture as a result of the ongoing rush of capital technology. But even then, aside from concepts of shortrun solutions through various supply

☐ From Rural industrialization: problems and potentials, North Central Regional Center for Rural Development, Ames, Iowa, 1974, Iowa State University Press.
*Earl O. Heady is Distinguished Professor of Agriculture, Professor of Economics and Director, North Central Regional Center for Rural Development, Iowa State University.

control and price support programs, the concentration was on longer-run solutions of the farm problem through aggregate national economic growth regardless of its location–and usually not at the local rural level. A few economists even did a considerable amount of arithmetic to calculate the rate of national growth necessary (gross national product [GNP] being the overall indicator) to absorb all the farm workers expected to be displaced over the next two decades and to get them out of the rural community more quickly. Don Paarlberg, director of Agricultural Economics, U.S. Department of Agriculture, has stated that economists in land-grant universities were serving more nearly as urban fundamentalists than as rural fundamentalists during this period.

THE NATIONAL GAME

Of course, the national economic and employment policy for more than two decades after World War

II was almost a pure strategy of national growth without regard to its distribution. This nearly single-valued objective of "just national economic growth" dominated for two reasons: (1) We still remembered the depression just prior to the war, and even those depressions which had gone before. Thus national growth without regard to its geographic distribution was pursued as the major means to maintain full employment. (2) Also, economic growth in North America and the OECD (Organization for Economic Cooperation and Development) countries was taken as a necessity in the Cold War competition which prevailed so intensely in the 1950s and 1960s.

The rural community, aside from programs for commercial farmers, drew little attention from national society during the 1950s and early 1960s. This was true even though rapid economic decay was beginning in the nonfarm sector of rural communities and some agricultural economists emphasized the need for a general economic and social policy for rural areas. It was simply assumed that the problems of the nonfarm rural economy would be automatically solved by programs which maintained a sufficient rate of national economic growth or through higher support prices and payments to commercial farmers. Neither of these policy orientations, as we now know, was a solution to the developing problems of the nonfarm, rural community sector. More nearly, these two sets of national policies hurried the economic and social decay of rural communities. The force of farm programs during the 1960s and 1970s, when the public was more active in farm policies than in the 1950s, was toward a further decline of employment and economic opportunity in towns of rural communities because they accentuated the trend to fewer and larger farms and a diminished work force in agriculture. The reasons are somewhat obvious and include a payment distribution favoring large farms, the capitalization of benefits into land values with the results that small operators could best gain through capital gains in land sold to more highly capitalized larger operators in a position to realize scale economics, and the existence of niggardly absolute benefits on small farms with highly underemployed labor. To the extent that the configuration of farm programs over the last two decades has hurried the decline in farm numbers and a reduced agricultural work force, it also has pulled this foundation out from under the rural community economy. A much larger volume of capital inputs which substitutes for farm labor and encourages larger units does flow through the rural community business sector. Yet it does not offset in employment opportunity the labor released from farms and its consumption expenditures among rural

businesses. As in the case of farms, the distribution of capital inputs to agriculture also is by highly capitalized methods which can realize scale economies best as the number of firms and the labor employed in them are decreased.

Our postwar obsession with growth in GNP without regard to its distribution also had little, or even negative, economic impact in typical rural communities. Largely, it maintained the momentum of growth and employment in population and industrial centers which already had these endowments. And because it caused a rapid growth in per capita incomes and employment, with particular growth in demand for personal services, it more rapidly drew population out of rural towns where economic opportunity was either stagnant or declining—the majority of rural communities. The rush of unskilled migrants, especially from the rural South to the urban North, was encouraged accordingly.

Then the cities erupted, and we began to concentrate national policies on their employment, housing, and social problems. We now had major national policies for larger commercial farms and the rest of the rural community. Farmers realized large capital gains as land values rose with farm program payments. In contrast, the value of capital assets in other sectors of rural communities diminished more rapidly and to a larger extent than the central city sector which also was faced with low incomes, underemployment, and a dearth of social services.

THE CONCERN FOR RURAL COMMUNITIES

Now, almost as a second and reluctant thought, we have wide public and national concern over the economic plight of rural communities. From the pronouncements of the last year and legislature proposals now in prospect, it appears at times that every candidate for national office rest his hope for election on the best things he can say for rural community development. Urban leaders are adding weight to these needs, perhaps with thoughts of rural economic development not as an objective for nonmetropolitan areas but as a means for attaining the objectives of cities (restrain population concentration, environmental degradation, violence, etc.). The voice and political power of the nonfarm rural community have always been small and loosely woven in comparison with the systematic organization of commercial farm groups and city groups. These voices from the "outside" may turn the tide and bring about standardized economic relief to rural communities, even if those from country towns are still too weak and unorganized to be heard.

PROSPECTS OF PROPOSED ACTION PROGRAMS

But how will economic relief be brought, and can the methods be standardized? Can a national policy of population redistribution with a scattering of new cities and growth centers do it? Is it as simple as revenue sharing by the federal government? Can more funds for the Soil Conservation Service (SCS) to clean up the environment, or more funds for the Farmers Home Administration (FHA) to improve sewers and water systems of country towns, do it? Can the relocation of plants in rural areas, to avoid the congestion, environmental problems, and higher labor costs of cities, bring economic salvation to the majority of rural communities? None of these are promising major programs for solving the basic economic and developmental needs of the majority of rural communities, although they might complement other programs and policies that are more central and effective for the problems involved. However, as near as one can interpret the rash of interest at the national level, these would appear to be the major program elements for solving employment, income, and welfare problems throughout the nonfarm rural community.

It is not clear how or if these programs can add much industrial and other economic activity to generate income and employment opportunities in typical rural communities. A new cities program to redistribute the national population is not yet near implementation and when initiated may require two decades for successful execution. Even then, the economic basis upon which all of these new population centers can be launched and become commercially and market perpetuated in areas of greatest need in rural communities is not readily apparent. Some large-scale public investments, continuous tax, and other subsidies may be required to initiate them and keep them ongoing. Brought to this stage, they could add employment in the rural states and eliminate the need for migration of rural persons to urban centers of other states in the quest of economic opportunity. They could help the development commissions of states to easier attain their goal of "more development and tax base for the state." While these could be salutary attainments of a national policy of population redistribution and new cities, they will not themselves solve all problems of typical rural communities. They can, in fact, catalyze the long-run depopulation of rural communities in their hinterlands. Country towns within commuting distance can, of course, become "dormitory settlements" for families who wish to live nearer nature and in smaller settlements or recipients of leakages from the larger towns that might otherwise hope to gain all the

growth. But towns at greater distances will experience a more rapid and vigorous draw down on their work force and population. A program of new cities and growth centers that is large enough to stem soon the net migration from rural to urban centers would certainly require national funds and resources on a scale precluding much further help for those smaller towns and settlements of nonmetropolitan areas.

Large increments of funds to the SCS and the FHA to retard runoff of pollutants, reclaim streams, improve town water systems and sewers, and increase the supply of improved low-cost housing in rural areas can improve the milieu and quality of living in these areas. They can provide a more favorable environment for plants which firms wish to transfer from the congested population and environments of cities. Given the relative concentration of aged and low-income persons, substandard housing, and a dearth of health and recreational services in nonmetropolitan areas, these are laudatory programs for people and can increase the "utility readings" for a segment of the rural population whose life and outlook are rather dismal. As a social investment to increase the enjoyment of life for an immobile and low-income segment of the rural and national population, this set might command higher priority than large public outlays for vast development of natural resources of site-specific locations. The latter better supplies recreational services to the middle- and higher-income classes of distant locations who are not entirely lacking in recreational and housing services in their home locations. They own the automobiles, boats, mobile homes, and camping and other equipment to travel and fully exhaust the recreational opportunities of developed natural resources. I am not arguing against development of natural resources for recreation. In a wealthy high-income society these are the services that have high-income elasticities of demand and, at a national level, rightfully become an orientation for development and increased welfare of the national society. I only emphasize that over some range, improving the milieu of services and amenities to low-income, immobile people in many rural areas stands to increase national welfare or utility more than enhancing the off-flow of recreational services from natural resources for middle- and high-income families. The physical concentration of environmental degradation in large water bodies and central cities provides visual evidence. It gives rise to a large public voice to "do something about it." The development of slums and the degradation of the human environment are even greater in the sum of the nation's rural areas. The country slums are only so dispersed, in the inadequate human-oriented services of small towns and the crumbling buildings of abandoned farms and villages, that their sum is not apparent to the large body of the public now traveling down the interstates or flying from urban concentrations to natural recreation centers or from one urban concentration to another.

While more of our population is in cities, has higher income, owns cars, and travels the country's turnpikes more than ever before, it now sees and knows less about the depreciation and problems of rural areas than ever before.

Improving the natural environment, upgrading sanitation facilities, and extending the supply of more adequate, low-cost housing in rural areas can improve the welfare of many people in rural communities. Yet it is not a means for successful long-run alleviation of their income and employment problems. Outside of some meager initial effects, it will not create new employment opportunities or per se serve as the basis for location of many new plants. Upcoming generations will move on, as they have been doing, to other locations where jobs prevail—along with housing, sewer, water, and recreational supplies which already (and still will) exceed the quantity and quality of those generated through modest SCS and FHA inputs of developing programs.

Rural industrialization is a big hope for those communities which have the characteristics favoring it. We can find many outstanding examples where the initiation of a new plant by an outside firm caused a turnaround in the employment and income decline of a rural community. To an extent, national leaders equate rural development with rural industrialization. The thrust is to spread plants over the country and disperse economic activity, employment, and the population. It would be fine if all rural communities faced with economic decline could have industrialization to serve these needs—if they want it. However, there are many more communities seeking location of a plant in their town than there are plants available for relocation, and the minority of typical rural communities have the conditions and endowment which mesh with requirements for these locations. Thus industrialization through entrance of an outside firm is the answer for some communities; for more, it is not. I previously mentioned that our earlier hopes were wrong; namely, that commercial farm programs and emphasis on growth at the national level did not revitalize the typical rural community but hurried its demise as people were squeezed from rural areas through larger farms and were pulled from them by national growth which took place mainly at urban locations. We could be just as wrong on programs of a few new cities and industrialization to solve the problem of all rural communities. This remedy also stands to make some communities better

off but to hurry the decline of those in their hinterlands. In the short run, some of the surrounding villages may become dormitory towns with increased incomes as present residents commute to the newly industrialized center. But it is almost certain, unless the inputs of SCS and FHA can really explode in their efforts, that the next generation will move nearer the central place or near enough to be "pioneers" in its developing suburbs.

Finally, revenue sharing as it is now proposed promises no more, and perhaps less, for rural towns than for metropolitan areas of the states. Just as industry now selects larger towns with concentrated labor supplies, adequate public facilities, and adequate transportation over the smaller dispersed country towns, it will still do so for any "flat" tax relief which applies equally among communities and human settlements within states. Further, revenue-sharing programs and tax adjustments proposed thereunder still emphasize metropolitan rather than rural communities.

CORE PROBLEMS

Obviously, I believe that the "core employment problems" of typical rural communities will not be solved over the long run through the major rural development action programs that have first prospect for initiation, namely, new cities for population redistribution, environmental improvement through SCS activities, improved human sanitation, and services through FHA and federal revenue sharing. These programs can improve the quality of life of the occupationally fixed, immobile older persons and highly underemployed females and others of rural areas, but job opportunities and per unit costs of local services will continue their existing trends as large family farms continue to absorb neighboring units, to become super family farms. It is not corporation farms which threaten rural communities over the vast range of the nation's farming space. Instead, the major reduction in numbers of farms and the increase in scale of farms have come as family operating units have increased their holdings. Hence, some of the pending bills to restrain corporation farming, as a savior of economic opportunities in rural communities, stand at about the same level as improved sewers in a town of 800 population to attract new industry.

The economic problems of many rural communities will be best solved with programs that deal head-on with possibilities in employment and industry. But the problems of all rural communities cannot be solved in this manner. To concentrate all resources on rural industrialization as it is encouraged by existing economic structure and forces mainly will extend opportunities and welfare for those larger towns which already are favorably endowed by location, public investments, transportation facilities, and existing industry which serve as a magnet for raw material, labor, and financial services and supplies. As mentioned previously, rural community development and industrialization are used widely as synonyms. Yet not every small country town has opportunities in industrialization and we will mislead them unless we tell them so. The majority of typical rural communities will continue to serve as a "shadow economy," shifting some with the "outside economy" but more particularly with the structure of agriculture about it. We must come up with some real imagination for these communities if the quality of life, the unit cost of human services, and employment opportunities for youth and females are to approach those in larger towns of rural areas and metropolitan centers. Action programs which break from past thought and ongoing precedents with respect to transportation facilities, public services, and human settlements generally must be developed and initiated. In the initial settlement of the majority of the Midwest, an active and somewhat revolutionary plan of human settlement and economic activity was drawn up and implemented. Relative to the times and stage of economic development, we currently have no such "revolutionary" plan on the drawing boards or in public dialogue. The rectangular land survey with legal restraints on settlement, the distribution of land resources through the public rather than the private sector, the retention of a portion of the land supply as public property (e.g., for roads) with implied transportation and marketing facilities (i.e., land grants to railroads), the specification of the spatial properties and extent of townships and counties as civil units— these and other elements did represent a very specific and well-implemented human settlement program and, in a planning sense, were revolutionary in comparison with other precedents of moderately large societies. How, now, would one draw up a settlement pattern for nonmetropolitan space if it were made to conform with modern technology and social organization? And how would we get from the prevailing pattern of property rights, public investments, and existing capital facilities to this optimum settlement pattern? Proposals have been made of commuting fields and functional economic areas as a broad outline, if supplemented by consolidation of counties and public service units.

These are considerations and problems to be faced eventually. We need to be drawing up models and blueprints which recognize them accordingly. Small increments in public programs and investments then can be made consistent with the longer-run needs and prospects. Yet, to my knowledge, we have no

major effort devoted to the modeling of alternative future settlement patterns for rural space. Some might consider the agitation for land use planning as a forerunner of this activity. Land use planning should not be accepted as a substitute for or equivalent of the restructuring of human settlements, regionalization of economic and public services, and other facets of optimization in terms of people and their welfare. It is no more than one of many needed elements, just as the rectangular survey was a single physical element of the initial human settlement plan.

We do need to be imaginative in looking to the future for the best salvage of rural communities and a better use of our rural space. I am not sure we are as imaginative as we were 150 years ago when it comes to planning our rural space to meet the needs of people. The rectangular survey, for example, was a revolutionary concept and detoured entirely from land settlements of the past. It was a physical plan to which other social and economic dimensions of human settlements were oriented. Now, with today's technology, what would be a counterpart plan as revolutionary as the rectangular survey in its day? Perhaps such a plan would do away with the majority of country roads, letting farm producers invest in their own helicopters or in the use of helicopters. Certainly, the cost of farming would increase, but if the supply function of food declined accordingly, revenue from farming would even increase because of the extremely low demand elasticities for food. A whole new pattern of capital values would emerge, but this also was true of initial public land settlement patterns.

INDUSTRIALIZATION AND RESTRUCTURING

So, just as industrialization can be the answer for communities endowed appropriately, a long-term restructuring of settlement, economic, and administrative patterns (along with equal claim with other settlement centers on public investment in environmental and social services) must be the answer for a large number of typical rural communities. While industrialization is the important opportunity and prospect for some rural communities, it is not the opportunity for all. Hence, a single-dimensional rural development program resting only on industrialization would largely bring gain to those larger nonmetropolitan or rural area towns which tend to "already have something going for them." It would add employment and income, especially for those towns which are experiencing growth, and draw more people out of the surrounding communities. Admittedly, it is difficult to bring gains to some communities without dumping costs and sacrifices on others through specific types of programs.

Industrialization itself provides different types of opportunities for towns with alternative endowments and suggests the needs for different types of activities on the part of professionals serving the public if benefits of rural industrialization are to be spread broadly. Those state developmental efforts which focus mainly on travel to distant firm headquarters and attempt to convince them to locate in "our state" tend to benefit those communities which already have the "show on the road." This is true since the goal mainly is just to get a new plant in the state and not to bring economic renaissance to a decayed rural community with pressing problems.

STRATIFICATION BY OBJECTIVES AND PROSPECTS IN DEVELOPMENT

It is not certain, of course, that all rural communities desire industrialization. Certainly a growing number of them do not want just any industry, as reflected by the number of Midwest communities that have taken legal or other action to prevent location of large-scale chemical and cattle-feeding plants. It is possible that industrialization is lower in priority for the majority of truly rural communities, especially those without the characteristics and endowments sought by firms considering a plant relocation, than simply maintaining the level of economic activity and employment that they already have. A very large number of rural groups are highly concerned about the decay of their communities. But I interpret this concern as much one of how to arrest the decay as one of how to add some large plant and industry. Rural communities are far from a homogeneous lot. Their needs, interests, and objectives certainly range as broadly as those of the various farm organizations and commodity groups which try to speak, often through conflicting philosophies and proposals of competitive means as well as ends, on behalf of the farm sector. Perhaps the range is even broader and the homogeneity of interest is even weaker, since there is not a major special interest or pressure group to speak systematically on behalf of any strata of rural communities. States—yes, there is a consistency of interest among them—all want more industry and imported recreational participants (at least until the recent past when Oregon and Colorado groups reacted contrarily). But we cannot be sure that this interest encompasses the goals of the majority of rural communities. As a step underlying our efforts to bring industrialization to more rural communities, I propose that we need to know much more about goals and attitudes of rural communities toward developmental ends generally and industrial growth specifically. We know very little about the desires, values, and goals of individual community groups

in these respects. The interest of the community in itself can be quite different from (1) the expanding firm seeking low-cost raw materials and labor, (2) the state development commission charged with the responsibility per se of bringing more industry to the state, (3) the national leader serving as the proponent of a massive but clearly undefined and currently unidentifiable rural development program, and (4) similar thrusts. It is entirely probable, and certainly likely, that a number of communities might select farm policies that encourage smaller farms and a larger farm population over industrialization. Some may want to slow down or restrain the rate of community economic retrogression to a level where it can be absorbed and maintain some value of "in place" people and capital. Surveys and studies to identify goals, values, and attitudes of different communities and groups within them toward development are necessary for intelligent university programs. From the standpoint of state extension services, this knowledge would tell us how to direct our very scarce resources among communities which desire industrialization and those which desire other economic and social programs.

A stratification of communities by their objectives in rural development is one need in programming aid and help. A parallel and equal need is the stratification of communities according to their resource base and linkage with other economic systems, to be able to match the desire for industrialization with types of economic activity which guarantees some prospect of success. A concurrent need in stratification is the characterization of industries by their requirements in community resource structure, location, and economic linkage with outside sectors. This was the set of measurements most emphasized at our conference. But equally, communities need to know what various industries can offer them—the street is not just one way, with industrial firms looking for communities which can offer them an industrial park, a sufficient sewer and water system, a node in an adequate transportation network, and a proximity where their senior management can live in the country and readily slip in to the cultural activities of the nearby city. We need to know "the content of development" from the standpoint of a range of communities, as well as from the standpoint of firms with a plant to locate. Computer assignment models then might be used to match communities with goals of industrialization and firms seeking plant locations and public bodies contemplating new institutional investments and installations. "Assignments" also would consider equity aspects of development and would emphasize the distribution of industrial opportunities to communities which have had little previously. Obviously, some communities and industries would fall entirely outside these potentially quantifiable sets.

Groups of communities

Rural communities can be aggregated under numerous groupings. Three of relevance in problems of industrialization are these:

1. *Endowed communities* which possess the characteristics of location, leaders who can generate local support for an industrial park, improved water and sewer facilities, transportation facilities, transportation facilities, closeness to larger urban centers of greater cultural scope, and similar items. These communities, while there are more of them than potential plants to be located, do have hope through industrialization by an outside firm and capital inflow. Our university extension programs typically have been focused on these communities, rather than those below.

2. *Bootstrap communities* which possess none of the above characteristics and will never see the advance team of the foreign firm scouting them for a plant location. There are many more bootstrap than endowed communities. Also, their problems are more complex and they are harder to help through a rural development program. So far, regardless of their intense needs, the concept of rural development has been much less about them and more about the endowed communities. If they get industrialization, it will be because of the imagination or luck of a local individual or small group that strikes upon a successful product and can amass the capital to start up. He probably will do so regardless of the town's lack in water and sewer facilities, the "not perfect" transportation system, and the distance of the locality from a city where management can "duck in" occasionally for "extended cultural participation." This set of circumstances—the person, town, and capital—is much harder to identify and help than are the endowed communities. If these communities "make it," it generally will be "on their own" rather than through a foreign firm which exports management and capital to them by means of a plant relocation.

3. *Purely agricultural communities* which lack endowments as above and are never blessed with the "local free-lancer" who starts up on his own. This group includes the majority of typical rural communities. Income of their citizens will be increased more through a restructuring of farms into more efficient units and the training and transfer of workers for employment elsewhere. Their welfare also can be increased through reor-

ganization of public administrative units and services to provide better products at lower cost, through publicly or privately initiated delivery systems which improve the quality of services and similar reorganizations. Largely, their long-run answer is in restructuring the community to a declining resource base rather than restructuring to meet industrial growth. Their salvation is in intervention of outside governmental entities, as state or federal, rather than through intervention of a foreign firm which brings in capital and management to generate local employment.

Rural colonialism

In a sense, the setting of these groups of rural communities is not unlike the categories of underdeveloped countries over the world. Some have endowments which draw foreign firms to them in order that their resources might be exploited in terms of the goals of the foreign entity. In this sense, do we also have a kind of colonialism for rural communities? While the activity generates employment and has some multiplier effects in community economic activity, the surplus or profits go back to the home headquarters. In several of our discussions, it has been emphasized that the properly endowed community is mainly a fabricating or manufacturing plant which uses, for example, unemployed wives of employed males in the community and which brings in mainly supervisory personnel from other locations. It has been suggested in the discussions that a nonmetropolitan community is not a candidate for a management firm or even the location for the management division of a manufacturing firm because these personnel are better inspired in a large population center. Further, it has been suggested by the experts on plant location that the favored rural community must not be too far from a sizable metropolitan center so that the wives who move out to the community with the management will have frequent access to the markets and cultural opportunities of the city.

This is a somewhat bleak set of suppositions for the rural community which aspires to be more than "just a plant earning its bread and butter." It is not unlike the old days of colonialism when the urge was to "go out and make the fortune, then bring it home." It is an aspect of rural development that needs intensive thought in the long-run planning and efficient use of rural space. Does it mean, for example, that society in general should finance regional cultural centers and even the staging of events in them? This would widen the number of "fully endowed" rural communities and give the permanent residents of them as much access to a higher quality of life and cultural advantage as the "outside colonists" who come to spend a short time as a foreign firm's employees in a rural community. These possibilities seem realistic in providing all people with equity in environment as well as economic opportunity.

Not only are communities heterogeneous with respect to their resources and goals in development but also the programs needed to aid them are varied and diverse. This is particularly true with respect to the equity basis for rural community development programs. I identify the upsurge in concern for rural community development to have its basis in equity. The nonfarm rural community sector has long gone unaided and has, along with small farmers gaining little from commercial farm programs, borne the brunt of the revolution in agricultural technology and the spatial reconfiguration of economic opportunity through growth at the national level over the last three decades. Farm programs have fairly well compensated commercial farms for sacrifices they might otherwise have made under a regime of inelastic demands, resource immobility, and rapid technical advance. They have brought continuous capital gains to the farm sector with capitalization of payments into land prices. In contrast, nonfarm people in smaller towns have experienced a collapse not only in employment opportunities but also in capital values as larger farms and a smaller rural population have caused the boarding up of country businesses and abandonment of dwellings in country towns. In the last three decades, our public investments and the configuration of ongoing national growth have generally been in the favor of larger urban or megalopolis centers. The public attack on slums has been focused on the central cities, although the relative concentration of slum conditions is greatest in rural areas (as measured by income levels, housing conditions, human services, etc.) Even concern over decentralization of population and economic activity has first emphasis on cities.

RURAL COMMUNITY DEVELOPMENT AND EQUITY

The crux of the rural community development problem is one of inequity in the distribution of gains and costs of technological and economic development at state and national levels. The challenging task in rural community development is to identify the nature, location, and extent of inequities falling on rural communities and various population strata of them, then to evaluate and provide alternative means of alleviating or redressing them. In favored locations, an important extent of these inequities can be erased through industrialization. In a greater number,

however, the inequities can be removed only through entirely different means and programs.

Inequitable distributions of the gains and costs of development among communities and between metropolitan and nonmetropolitan areas are the foundation upon which broader public concerns over rural area development are coming to rest.

But just as unrestrained and heavily promoted aggregate growth at the national level spews a complex distribution of costs and benefits among regions and communities, a single goal of development at state levels also can bring an inequitable distribution among metropolitan and nonmetropolitan areas or among rural communities. If we seek development without regard to its distribution effects, the programs and processes have almost a single dimension. The process of rural development then is almost entirely industrialization (or an equivalent such as recreational development, tourism, etc.). We will work to add industries where they have the most obvious advantage and where the thrust typically is already in this direction because of endowments such as financial resources, location, existing transportation networks, and large public installations already in place. We will neglect all other communities which are in the process of decline. There is the chance that to those who have gains, we will bring more; to those experiencing social and economic costs as the labor force and population are drawn away to growth centers, we will speed the burden.

IMAGINATION AND PLANS FOR THE TIME

Industrialization as a means of rural development does involve complex considerations and processes. However, communities falling outside the category of industrialization are faced with much more complex group decision processes. As national growth and per capita incomes increase further and as the average plane of living increases, the latter communities can only begin to stay abreast through a rather complete restructuring of economic and service-supplying sectors of their spatial entity. Over the long run, it appears that a whole new settlement pattern will be necessary. As the chapters in this book have emphasized, it will involve fewer major towns or commercial centers and facilities generally. These consolidations will require "writing off" the capital values of many private and public installations. It is likely that transition to the new patterns will require public or group subsidies and financing, as much as does industrial development at other rural locations. Certainly it will require state and federal legislation to enable and facilitate the new patterns and to create needed institutions.

Unfortunately, we still lack analysis to suggest the

optimal structure of a rural community for which industrialization is not a major prospect. We have little analysis to indicate optimal regional or state networks for supplying services to this set of communities. Yes, the task of initiating and implementing rural industrialization where more of it is wanted and is adapted involves phenomena to which it is somewhat difficult to attach handles. The task of creating viable communities and service-supplying sectors for those that do not fall in the industrialization category is even more difficult. But certainly we have the spirit, knowledge, and ability to do it—at least on a par with those original planners who knew little economics or other science, had only the primitive computers of pencils and paper, and no formal planning models or econometric devices. Their accomplishments were superb, given the knowledge and tools of the time, in planning the initial settlements of the Midwest. The resources of land and space with which they had to work are still there. Added has been an immense accumulation of physical capital and knowledge. Many decades back and under much more difficult circumstances, the public decided to and did come up with a resource development and settlement plan for the benefit of the people. They did so successfully for the time. Certainly we can be as imaginative now.

Index